2000
Third Edition

America's Top-Rated Smaller Cities

A Statistical Profile

Grey House Publishing

LAKEVILLE, CT 06039

PUBLISHER: Leslie Mackenzie
EDITOR: David Garoogian
EDITORIAL DIRECTOR: Laura Mars
CONTRIBUTING WRITERS: John Townes, Elaine Alibrandi
MARKET RESEARCH: Jessica Moody
GRAPHIC DESIGN: Deb Fletcher

Grey House Publishing, Inc.
Pocket Knife Square
Lakeville, CT 06039
860.435.0868
FAX 860.435.6613
www.greyhouse.com
www.citystats.com
e-mail: books@greyhouse.com

While every effort has been made to ensure the reliability of the information presented in this publication, Grey House Publishing neither guarantees the accuracy of the data contained herein nor assumes any responsibility for errors, omissions or discrepancies. Grey House accepts no payment for listing; inclusion in the publication of any organization, agency, institution, publication, service or individual does not imply endorsement of the editors or publisher.

Errors brought to the attention of the publisher and verified to the satisfaction of the publisher will be corrected in future editions.

First edition published 1995
Third edition published 2000

Printed in the USA

Library of Congress Cataloging in Publication Data available

ISBN 1-891482-65-3   softcover
ISBN 1-891482-66-1   hardcover

Introduction

This third edition of *America's Top-Rated Smaller Cities (ATRSC)* is designed to provide a current and concise statistical profile of 60 top U.S. cities with populations between 25,000 and 100,000. Previously published by Universal Reference Publications, *ATRSC* selects cities based on their rankings for Business and Living in various national magazine surveys (*Places Rated Almanac, Forbes, Fortune, Money, Entrepreneur, Outdoor Explorer, Ladies Home Journal, Travel & Leisure, Condé Nast Travel*) and other public and private sources.

This year, we have reviewed many sources to come up with the final list of cities. We have replaced from the last edition 31 cities in 21 states:

Albany, NY	Chapel Hill, NC	Melbourne, FL
Asheville, NC	Charleston, SC	Missoula, MT
Augusta, GA	Charleston, WV	Napa, CA
Bangor, ME	Davenport, IA	Ogden, UT
Bellevue, WA	Harrisburg, PA	Portland, ME
Biloxi, MS	Hattiesburg, MS	Saginaw, MI
Bloomington, IL	Hickory, NC	Santa Fe, NM
Burlington, VT	Huntington, WV	Scranton, PA
Canton, OH	Iowa City, IA	South Bend, IN
Champaign, IL	Lancaster, PA	Trenton, NJ
		Youngstown, OH

ATRSC is arranged alphabetically by city and includes such Business Environment topics as finances, population, income, employment, taxes, and transportation, and such Living Environment topics as cost of living, housing, health care, education, public safety, and climate. You'll find hotels and convention centers, in-demand occupations, profiles of radio and television stations, and many more area characteristics.

Each chapter has charts and tables in over 50 categories. New data this year include Number of Households, Ancestry of Population, and Water System Violations. Most charts have been updated with 1999 figures, and some include projections to 2004. Each city begins with a detailed overview, an updated economic report and, new this year, a General Rankings and Evaluative Comments section.

Government sources used for this book include the *U.S. Bureau of the Census, U.S. Department of Commerce, Bureau of Labor Statistics,* and *FBI Uniform Crime Reports.* Some private sources we gathered information from are *Claritas, Economic Research Institute, Moody's* and *Standard Rate and Data Service.* In addition, many organizations were consulted, including the *Federation of Tax Administrators, National Association of Realtors,* and *National Association of Home Builders.*

America's Top-Rated Smaller Cities includes three appendices:

Appendix A – Metropolitan Statistical Areas (MSA): Includes the counties that combine to form each city's MSA – an official designation used to define the area.

Appendix B – Chambers of Commerce and Economic Development Organizations: Includes address, phone and fax numbers, and web sites of these additional resources.

Appendix C – State Departments of Labor and Employment: Source for specific economic and employment data for each city, with address and phone numbers for easy access.

America's Top-Rated Smaller Cities is designed for a wide range of readers, as are the other titles in this series: *America's Top-Rated Cities; Crime in America's Top-Rated Cities*; and *Health and Environment in America's Top-Rated Cities*. Their audience includes private individuals considering relocating a residence or business, professionals considering expanding their business or changing careers, corporations considering relocation, additional offices or new divisions, government agencies, general and market researchers, real estate consultants, human resource personnel, urban planners, investors, and urban government students.

Grey House Publishing wishes to thank all who responded to our requests for information, especially Chambers of Commerce, Economic Development Corporations, and State Departments of Labor and Employment.

Thanks also goes to John Townes, who wrote backgrounds for the cities new to this edition, and to researchers Rosemary Jette and Eileen Gloster.

Grey House Publishing
Statistical & Demographic Reference Books

America's Top-Rated Cities, 2000

America's Top-Rated Cities provides current, comprehensive statistical information in one easy-to-use source on 76 cities which have been cited as the best for business and living in the U.S. Previously published by Universal Reference, this four-volume set offers a concise social, business, economic, demographic and environmental profile of each city, including brief evaluative comments. Comparisons with MSA and U.S. figures are shown and a special section with comparative statistics is also included. Each of the four volumes covers a specific region of the country: Southern, Western, Central and Eastern. This outstanding source of information will be widely used in any reference collection.

4 Volume Set	ISBN 1-891482-50-5	1,528 pages	softcover	$195.00
Vol. 1: Southern	ISBN 1-891482-51-3	387 pages	softcover	$59.95
Vol. 2: Western	ISBN 1-891482-52-1	383 pages	softcover	$59.95
Vol. 3: Central	ISBN 1-891482-53-X	375 pages	softcover	$59.95
Vol. 4: Eastern	ISBN 1-891482-54-8	383 pages	softcover	$59.95

Crime in America's Top-Rated Cities, 2000

This brand new volume includes over 20 years of crime statistics in all major crime categories: violent crimes, property crimes and total crime. *Crime in America's Top-Rated Cities* is arranged alphabetically by city and covers the 76 cities listed in *America's Top-Rated Cities, 2000*. It offers details that compare the number of crimes and crime rates for the city, suburbs and metro area and national crime trends for violent, property and total crimes. This handbook contains important statistics on Anti-Crime Programs, Crime Risk, Crime Statistics, Hate Crimes, Illegal Drugs, Law Enforcement, Correctional Facilities and much more. Designed for people who are relocating, business professionals, general researchers, the press, law enforcement officials and students of criminal justice, this would be a well-used addition to the reference collection of public, academic or special libraries.

ISBN 1-891482-84-X	841 pages	softcover	$155.00
ISBN 1-891482-85-8	841 pages	hardcover	$180.00

Health & Environment in America's Top-Rated Cities, 2001

This comprehensive publication provides critical health and environmental statistics for the 76 top-rated cities listed in *America's Top-Rated Cities*. Diverse topics are covered for each city, such as children's well being, infant mortality, air pollutants and death rates. From health and environmental protection agencies to school classrooms and libraries, this fact-filled handbook continues to educate the public through providing the most accurate and current statistics for 76 top-rated cities.

ISBN 1-891482-92-0	800 pages	softcover	$155.00
ISBN 1-891482-93-9	800 pages	hardcover	$180.00

Weather America, 2001

This valuable resource provides extensive climatological data for over 4,000 places throughout the United States – states, counties, cities and towns. Last published in 1996 by Toucan Valley Publications, *Weather America* represents a different approach in the way weather data is compiled, and a step forward in the way it is presented. Organized into 50 state sections, each section begins with a narrative description of climatic conditions, followed by maps and data tables that provide information about maximum and minimum temperatures, precipitation, snowfall, local weather stations and much more. Also, each state section contains a Rankings Table for Temperature, Precipitation and Snowfall with the 25 highest and lowest places listed in each state.

A *Library Journal* Best Reference Book.

ISBN 1-891482-29-7	1,500 pages	hardcover	$175.00

Working Americans, 1880-1999 Volume I: The Working Class

This brand new reference work focuses on the lifestyles and economic life of the American working class from 1880 to 1999. Family Profiles include real data on Income & Job Descriptions, Selected Prices of the Times, Annual Income, Annual Budget of Individuals, Family Finances & Budget, Life at Work, Life at Home, Life in the Community, Working Conditions, Cost of Living, Amusements and much more. You'll also find Economic Profiles with Average Wages of other Professions, a selection of Typical Pricing, Key Events and Inventions, Historical Snapshots, News Profiles, Articles from Local Media and Illustrations. This volume contains 72 Family Profiles that cover 34 occupations, and more than 25 ethnic groups. Geographically, the text travels the entire country, from the East Coast to Hawaii, to provide comprehensive coverage of the social and economic life of working class families available nowhere else. This interesting and useful compilation of portraits of the working class during the last 120 years will be an important addition to any high school, public or academic library reference collection.

ISBN 1-891482-81-5　　　*558 pages*　　　*hardcover*　　　*$125.00*

The Value of a Dollar – Millennium Edition

A guide to practical economy, *The Value of a Dollar* records the actual prices of thousands of items that consumers purchased from the Civil War to the present, along with facts about investment options and income opportunities. The first edition, published by Gale Research in 1994, covered the period of 1860 to 1989. This second edition has been completely redesigned and revised and now contains two new chapters, 1990-1994 and 1995-1999. Each 5-year chapter includes a Historical Snapshot, Consumer Expenditures, Investments, Selected Income, Income/Standard Jobs, Food Basket, Standard Prices and Miscellany. This interesting and useful publication will be widely used in any reference collection.

ISBN 1-891482-49-1　　　*660 pages*　　　*hardcover*　　　*$125.00*

The Comparative Guide to Elementary & Secondary Schools, 1998

This comprehensive volume offers a snapshot profile of each public school district in the United States that serves 2,500 or more students (approximately 80% of all schools). You'll find important contact information for each school district (name, address, phone number and web site) plus Grades Served, the Numbers of Students and Teachers and the Number of Regular, Special Education, Alternative and Vocational Schools in the district. Also, *The Comparative Guide to Elementary & Secondary Schools* provides statistics to help evaluate educational programs, including Student/Classroom Teacher Ratios, Number of Librarians, Number of Guidance Counselors, District Expenditures per student and a National Socioeconomic Indicator for the district.

ISBN 1-884925-63-4　　　*774 pages*　　　*softcover*　　　*$85.00*

The Comparative Guide to American Suburbs, 1997

This unique reference focuses on the individual and suburban communities within each of the 50 largest metro areas. You'll find profiles of over 1,800 suburban communities with a 10,000+ population, a selection of Statistics on Population, Geography, the Economy, Safety, Housing and Education, plus details on Local Newspapers, Chambers of Commerce, School Districts and Place Name Origins. For each metro area, a Ranking Table is included that compares the suburbs in six critical indicators: Per Capita Income, Unemployment Rate, New Housing Permits, Median Home Prices and Crime Rates for Violent and Property Crimes. *The Comparative Guide to American Suburbs* is conveniently arranged by metro area. For anyone looking to relocate, as well as those doing preliminary market research, this volume is a must-have reference.

ISBN 1-884925-61-8　　　*816 pages*　　　*softcover*　　　*$85.00*

To preview any of our Directories for 30 days, please call toll-free (800) 562-2139 or fax to (860) 435-3004

Table of Contents

Albany, New York

Appleton, Wisconsin

Asheville, North Carolina

Augusta, Georgia

Bangor, Maine

Bellevue, Washington

Bellingham, Washington

Biloxi, Mississippi

Bloomington, Illinois

Boulder, Colorado

Table of Contents

Bryan, Texas

Burlington, Vermont

Canton, Ohio

Champaign, Illinois

Chapel Hill, North Carolina

Charleston, South Carolina

Charleston, West Virginia

Charlottesville, Virginia

Columbia, Missouri

Davenport, Iowa

Daytona Beach, Florida

Duluth, Minnesota

Eau Claire, Wisconsin

Fargo, North Dakota

Fayetteville, Arkansas

Fort Myers, Florida

Gainesville, Florida

Greenville, South Carolina

Harrisburg, Pennsylvania

Hattiesburg, Mississippi

Hickory, North Carolina

Huntington, West Virginia

Iowa City, Iowa

Johnson City, Tennessee

Kalamazoo, Michigan

La Crosse, Wisconsin

Lafayette, Indiana

Lancaster, Pennsylvania

Melbourne, Florida

Missoula, Montana

Napa, California

Ogden, Utah

Portland, Maine

Provo, Utah

Roanoke, Virginia

Rochester, Minnesota

Saginaw, Michigan

Saint Cloud, Minnesota

San Luis Obispo, California

Santa Barbara, California

Santa Fe, New Mexico

Sarasota, Florida

Scranton, Pennsylvania

South Bend, Indiana

Trenton, New Jersey

West Palm Beach, Florida

Wilmington, Delaware

Youngstown, Ohio

Albany, New York

Background

Albany, New York is the state capital. The city is situated on a hillside on the western bank of the Hudson River, about 150 miles north of New York City and 30 miles from Massachusetts and Vermont. It is the county seat of Albany County, located in the upper Hudson River Valley. The region's terrain includes the Taconic ridge to the east, the steep Helderbergs to the west and the Catskills to the southwest.

Albany is part of the larger Capital District metropolitan area, which includes the neighboring cities of Troy and Schenectady and numerous other communities. This is a primary commercial and services center for eastern upstate New York and nearby sections of Massachusetts, Vermont and Connecticut. Throughout its history the Albany area has also been a transportation hub, where primary east-to-west and north-to-south land and water routes intersect. It is an inland port on the Hudson River, which extends south to New York and the Atlantic Ocean. The Albany area is also a connecting point for highways and railroads, and home to Albany International Airport.

Incorporated as a city in 1686, Albany is among the oldest communities in the United States. It is a mix of newer development and traditional characteristics, including architecture reflecting its Dutch origins. Two of the city's most distinctive physical features are the ornate State Capitol building, completed in 1899, and the Empire State Plaza, a modern multi-purpose state government complex, completed in 1978, with tall towers rising from a large open courtyard.

The area was occupied originally by Mahicans and other Native American tribes. In 1609, Henry Hudson explored the river for Dutch commercial interests, who later established forts and fur-trading outposts. In 1664 the British took over the area, and the settlement at the site of Albany was renamed for the Duke of York and Albany. However, the Dutch remained influential. Albany became the state capital in 1797.

The area prospered. The nearby confluence of the Hudson and Mohawk Rivers, and the opening of the Erie Canal in 1824, provided a waterway from New York City to the Great Lakes and the west, while the Champlain Canal was a route to Lake Champlain to the north. Manufacturing industries grew, which attracted immigrants from Ireland, Scotland, Germany and other nations. However, the region's manufacturing base declined in the 20th Century, which caused economic problems. After the 1980s, the Capital District experienced some economic renewal, including new technology and service industries, although economic challenges continued to exist.

Albany's modern economy is based on public and private-sector services, education and manufacturing. Government is one of the largest employers. The Capital District has over 20 public and private schools of higher education. These include The University at Albany of the State University of New York, Albany Medical College and the College of St. Rose in Albany, among others.

The area has the diverse cultural and recreational activities of a large metropolitan area. Among the venues for the arts, entertainment and sporting events is the Pepsi Arena downtown. The Empire State Plaza includes "The Egg," a theatre named for its unusual shape. Performing arts organizations include the Albany Symphony and the Albany-Berkshire Ballet, among others. Local attractions include the New York State Museum, the Albany Institute of History and Art and the Henry Hudson Planetarium. Albany is also near several resort and recreation regions, including the Adirondacks, the Catskills and Berkshire County.

Albany was named an "All America City" in 1991 by the National League of Cities. The U.S. Conference of Mayors named it the "Most Livable City in the U.S." in 1998.

Albany is governed by an elected Mayor and City Council.

General Rankings and Evaluative Comments

■ Albany was ranked #78 out of 354 metropolitan areas in *Places Rated Almanac*. Criteria: cost of living, climate, crime, transportation, job outlook, education, the arts, health care, and recreation. *Places Rated Almanac, Millennium Edition, 2000*

■ Zero Population Growth ranked 229 cities in terms of children's health, safety, and economic well-being. Albany was ranked #56 out of 112 independent cities (cities with populations greater than 100,000 which were neither Major Cities nor Suburbs/Outer Cities) and was given a grade of C. Criteria: total population and population change, percent of population under 18 years of age, household language, percent of births to teens, infant mortality rate, percent of low birth weights, dropout rate, enrollment in preprimary school, violent and property crime rates, unemployment rate, percent of children in poverty, percent of owner occupied units, number of bad air days, percent of public transportation commuters, and average travel time to work. *Zero Population Growth, Children's Environmental Index, Fall 1999*

■ Cognetics studied 273 metro areas in the United States, ranking them by entrepreneurial activity. Albany was ranked #50 out of the 50 largest metro areas. Criteria: Significant Starts (firms started in the last 10 years that still employ at least 5 people) and Young Growers (percent of firms 10 years old or less that grew significantly during the last 4 years). *Cognetics, "Entrepreneurial Hot Spots: The Best Places in America to Start and Grow a Company," 1999*

■ Reliastar Financial Corporation ranked the 125 largest metropolitan areas according to the general financial security of residents. Albany was ranked #71 out of 125 with a score of 2.2 (the percentage a metropolitan area is above or below the metropolitan norm; a metro area with a score of 10.6 is 10.6% above the metro average). Criteria: Earnings and Wealth Potential (household income, education, net assets, cost of living); Safety Net (health insurance, retirement savings, life insurance, income support programs); Personal Threats (unemployment rate, low-income households, crime rate); Community Economic Vitality (cost of community services, job quality, job creation, housing costs). *Reliastar Financial Corporation, "The Best Cities to Earn and Save Money: A Ranking of the Largest 125 U.S. Cities," 2000 Edition*

■ Albany was given an Outstanding Achievement Award for its Lead-Based Paint Hazard Control Program by the U.S Conference of Mayors and Waste Management as part of their 1999 City Livability Awards Program. The program honors mayors and their city governments for developing programs that enhance the quality of life in urban areas. The awards are given annually to ten mayors and their cities—a first-place award and four Outstanding Achievement Awards for cities under 100,000 population, and a first-place and four Outstanding Achievement Awards for cities of 100,000 or more inhabitants.

Business Environment

STATE ECONOMY

State Economic Profile

"New York is starting to decelerate from its strongest performance in over a decade. Manufacturing employment continues to contract, particularly in upstate. Since most of its growth downstate is driven by Wall Street, New York's job outlook remains vulnerable to swings in the stock market. Population declines will continue to be one of New York's primary problems.

Almost all of 1998's job gains were in the New York City-Long Island area. New York state added some 140,800 jobs in 1998, 134,300 of those in NYC/Long Island. The bulk of these were concentrated in the services sector, particularly business and financial services. The raging bull market has done wonders for NYC and the surrounding suburbs. Since we do not expect a downturn in the stock market in the near future, job growth in New York will continue, albeit at a slower rate.

While NYC has been on a roll, upstate is only seeing some modest easing in its stagnant economy. Buffalo witnessed an increase of 0.2% job growth in 1998. Similar weak growth (0.3%) occurred in Rochester. Job cuts by Kodak and Xerox only added to the troubled upstate economy. Increased state tax revenues, largely from Wall Street, have allowed some government employment gains in Albany.

New York's primary constraint is its continued loss of residents, particularly among younger households. Although home sales rose 6% in 1998, appreciation has only been modest in the NYC area and weak upstate. Rising construction payrolls were largely concentrated in the NYC commercial market, with only an 8% increase in residential permits. As a result of declining population, New York is likely to lose two congressional seats in the post-2000 redistricting, pushing the decline of its political capital and accompanying federal dollars." *National Association of Realtors, Economic Profiles: The Fifty States and the District of Columbia, http://nar.realtor.com/databank/profiles.htm*

EXPORTS

Total Export Sales

Area	1995 ($000)	1996 ($000)	1997 ($000)	1998 ($000)	% Chg. 1995-98	% Chg. 1997-98
MSA[1]	1,061,194	1,101,029	1,666,230	1,613,036	52.0	-3.2
U.S.	583,030,524	622,827,063	687,597,999	680,474,251	16.7	-1.0

Note: (1) Metropolitan Statistical Area - see Appendix A for areas included
Source: U.S. Department of Commerce, International Trade Association, Metropolitan Area Exports: An Export Performance Report on Over 250 U.S. Cities, November 10, 1999

CITY FINANCES

City Government Finances

Component	1995 ($million)	1995 (per capita $)
Revenue	100.3	956
Expenditure	111.1	1,060
Debt Outstanding	246.3	2,349

Source: 1999 County and City Extra, Annual Metro, City, and County Data Book

City Government Revenue by Source

Source	1995 ($million)	1995 (per capita $)
Intergovernmental	39.3	374
Taxes	37.4	357
Property	32.8	313
Sales and Gross Receipts	2.4	23

Source: 1999 County and City Extra, Annual Metro, City, and County Data Book

City Government Expenditures by Function

Function	1995 ($million)	1995 (per capita $)	1995 (%)
Public Welfare	0.0	0	0.0
Highways	7.9	76	7.2
Parking Facilities	0.0	0	0.0
Education	0.0	0	0.0
Health and Hospitals	0.1	1	0.1
Police Protection	24.6	235	22.2
Sewerage and Sanitation	7.4	71	6.7
Parks and Recreation	7.4	71	6.7
Housing and Community Development	0.0	0	0.0
Interest on Debt	16.4	156	14.8

Source: 1999 County and City Extra, Annual Metro, City, and County Data Book

Municipal Bond Ratings

Area	Moody's
City	A3

Source: Mergent Bond Record, 2/2000

POPULATION

Population Growth

Area	1980 Census	1990 Census	1999 Estimate	2004 Projection	Population Growth (%) 1990-1999	Population Growth (%) 1999-2004
City	101,727	101,082	103,849	104,698	2.7	0.8
MSA[1]	835,880	874,304	870,412	870,033	-0.4	0.0
U.S.	226,545,805	248,765,170	272,212,864	283,625,312	9.4	4.2

Note: (1) Metropolitan Statistical Area - see Appendix A for areas included
Source: 1990 Census of Population and Housing, Summary Tape File 3C; Claritas, Inc.

Number of Households and Average Household Size

Area	1980 Census	1990 Census	1999 Estimate	2004 Projection	1999 Average Household Size
City	40,760	42,034	44,432	45,371	2.34
MSA[1]	296,948	335,818	340,815	345,150	2.55
U.S.	80,389,592	91,993,582	102,048,200	107,302,392	2.67

Note: (1) Metropolitan Statistical Area - see Appendix A for areas included
Source: 1990 Census of Population and Housing, Summary Tape File 3C; Claritas, Inc.

Race/Ethnicity of City Population

Race/Ethnicity	1990 Census Population	1990 Census %	1999 Estimate Population	1999 Estimate %	% Change 1990-1999
White, Non-Hispanic	74,500	73.7	72,881	70.2	-2.2
Black, Non-Hispanic	20,526	20.3	22,772	21.9	10.9
Asian, Non-Hispanic	2,272	2.2	3,330	3.2	46.6
Other, Non-Hispanic	559	0.6	570	0.5	2.0
Hispanic	3,225	3.2	4,296	4.1	33.2

Source: 1990 Census of Population and Housing, Summary Tape File 3C; Claritas, Inc.

Race/Ethnicity of Metropolitan Statistical Area Population

Race/Ethnicity	1990 Census		1999 Estimate		% Change 1990-1999
	Population	%	Population	%	
White, Non-Hispanic	805,161	92.1	790,007	90.8	-1.9
Black, Non-Hispanic	40,117	4.6	42,503	4.9	5.9
Asian, Non-Hispanic	10,682	1.2	15,574	1.8	45.8
Other, Non-Hispanic	2,654	0.3	2,651	0.3	-0.1
Hispanic	15,690	1.8	19,677	2.3	25.4

Note: See Appendix A for areas included in the Metropolitan Statistical Area
Source: 1990 Census of Population and Housing, Summary Tape File 3C; Claritas, Inc.

Ancestry

Area	German	Irish	English	Italian	U.S.	French	Polish	Dutch
City	17.2	23.0	8.2	15.1	1.5	4.9	6.5	3.2
MSA[1]	23.0	26.0	14.8	17.4	2.5	10.1	8.8	5.8
U.S.	23.3	15.6	13.1	5.9	5.3	4.2	3.8	2.5

Note: Figures are percentages and include persons that reported multiple ancestry (eg. if a person reported being Irish and Italian, they were included in both columns); (1) Metropolitan Statistical Area - see Appendix A for areas included
Source: 1990 Census of Population and Housing, Summary Tape File 3C

Median Age

Area	1990 Census	1999 Estimate
City	30.7	34.8
MSA[1]	33.9	36.9
U.S.	32.9	35.7

Note: (1) Metropolitan Statistical Area - see Appendix A for areas included
Source: 1990 Census of Population and Housing, Summary Tape File 3C; Claritas, Inc.

Male/Female Population

Area	Number of Males		Number of Females		Males per 100 Females	
	1990	1999	1990	1999	1990	1999
City	47,041	48,612	54,041	55,237	87.0	88.0
MSA[1]	422,710	420,460	451,594	449,952	93.6	93.4
U.S.	121,172,379	132,803,736	127,537,494	139,409,136	95.0	95.3

Note: (1) Metropolitan Statistical Area - see Appendix A for areas included
Source: 1990 Census of Population, General Population Characteristics; Claritas, Inc.

INCOME

Per Capita/Median/Average Income

Area	Per Capita ($)			Median Household ($)			Average Household ($)		
	1989	1999	% Chg.	1989	1999	% Chg.	1989	1999	% Chg.
City	13,742	18,918	37.7	25,152	31,780	26.4	32,059	43,062	34.3
MSA[1]	15,167	21,095	39.1	32,416	41,373	27.6	38,932	53,105	36.4
U.S.	14,420	21,350	48.1	30,056	40,525	34.8	38,453	56,184	46.1

Note: (1) Metropolitan Statistical Area - see Appendix A for areas included; 1989 data is from the 1990 Census; 1999 data is estimated by Claritas, Inc.
Source: 1990 Census of Population, General Population Characteristics; Claritas, Inc.

Household Income Distribution

Area	Percent of Households Earning								
	Under $5,000	$5,000 -14,999	$15,000 -24,999	$25,000 -34,999	$35,000 -49,999	$50,000 -74,999	$75,000 -99,000	$100,000 -149,999	$150,000 and up
City	4.9	18.3	16.6	13.8	16.1	16.9	7.4	4.1	2.0
MSA[1]	2.7	12.6	13.6	13.0	17.5	21.5	10.1	5.9	3.1
U.S.	3.9	13.3	13.8	12.6	16.2	19.4	9.7	6.6	4.6

Note: Data as of 1999; (1) Metropolitan Statistical Area - see Appendix A for areas included
Source: Claritas, Inc.

Effective Buying Income

Area	Per Capita ($)	Median Household ($)	Average Household ($)
City	15,392	28,120	36,531
MSA[1]	17,108	37,063	44,193
U.S.	17,496	36,603	47,036

Note: Data as of 1/1/2000; (1) Metropolitan Statistical Area - see Appendix A for areas included
Source: Standard Rate & Data Service, Newspaper Advertising Source, March 2000

Effective Household Buying Income Distribution

Area	% of Households Earning						
	$10,000 -$19,999	$20,000 -$34,999	$35,000 -$49,999	$50,000 -$74,999	$75,000 -$99,000	$100,000 -$124,999	$125,000 and up
City	19.5	24.6	16.8	15.2	5.1	1.6	1.3
MSA[1]	14.9	22.9	19.3	21.3	7.8	2.4	2.0
U.S.	15.0	21.6	17.6	19.6	8.4	3.0	3.3

Note: Data as of 1/1/2000; (1) Metropolitan Statistical Area - see Appendix A for areas included
Source: Standard Rate & Data Service, Newspaper Advertising Source, March 2000

Poverty Rates by Age

Area	People of All Ages	People Under 18 Years Old	Related Children Age 5-17 in Families in Poverty
City	18.3	n/a	n/a
County	10.2	15.9	14.1
U.S.	13.8	20.8	18.7

Note: Figures show the percent of people living below the poverty line in 1995. The average poverty threshold was $15,569 for a family of four in 1995; n/a not available
Source: Bureau of the Census, Small Area Income and Poverty Estimates Program; U.S. Department of Housing and Urban Development

EMPLOYMENT

Labor Force and Employment

Area	Civilian Labor Force			Workers Employed		
	Dec. 1998	Dec. 1999	% Chg.	Dec. 1998	Dec. 1999	% Chg.
City	52,633	52,509	-0.2	50,885	50,478	-0.8
MSA[1]	451,476	449,308	-0.5	437,594	434,095	-0.8
U.S.	138,297,000	139,941,000	1.2	132,732,000	134,696,000	1.5

Note: Data is not seasonally adjusted and covers workers 16 years of age and older;
(1) Metropolitan Statistical Area - see Appendix A for areas included
Source: Bureau of Labor Statistics, http://stats.bls.gov

Unemployment Rate

Area	1999											
	Jan.	Feb.	Mar.	Apr.	May	Jun.	Jul.	Aug.	Sep.	Oct.	Nov.	Dec.
City	4.2	4.3	4.2	3.7	3.9	3.8	4.0	3.7	4.5	4.1	3.9	3.9
MSA[1]	4.0	4.1	4.0	3.3	3.4	3.2	3.3	3.0	3.5	3.3	3.2	3.4
U.S.	4.8	4.7	4.4	4.1	4.0	4.5	4.5	4.2	4.1	3.8	3.8	3.7

Note: Data is not seasonally adjusted and covers workers 16 years of age and older; all figures are percentages; (1) Metropolitan Statistical Area - see Appendix A for areas included
Source: Bureau of Labor Statistics, http://stats.bls.gov

Employment by Industry

Sector	MSA[1]		U.S.
	Number of Employees	Percent of Total	Percent of Total
Services	147,500	32.1	30.2
Retail Trade	77,800	16.9	18.1
Government	112,200	24.4	15.8
Manufacturing	38,500	8.4	14.1
Finance/Insurance/Real Estate	26,400	5.7	5.9
Wholesale Trade	20,700	4.5	5.4
Transportation/Public Utilities	18,100	3.9	5.3
Construction	17,600	3.8	4.8
Mining	500	0.1	0.4

Note: Figures cover non-farm employment as of 12/99 and are not seasonally adjusted;
(1) Metropolitan Statistical Area - see Appendix A for areas included
Source: Bureau of Labor Statistics, http://stats.bls.gov

Employment by Occupation

Occupation Category	City (%)	MSA[1] (%)	U.S. (%)
White Collar	70.5	65.2	58.1
Executive/Admin./Management	14.4	13.5	12.3
Professional	18.1	16.2	14.1
Technical & Related Support	5.4	4.3	3.7
Sales	9.3	11.0	11.8
Administrative Support/Clerical	23.2	20.3	16.3
Blue Collar	12.9	20.8	26.2
Precision Production/Craft/Repair	5.0	9.5	11.3
Machine Operators/Assem./Insp.	2.7	4.3	6.8
Transportation/Material Movers	2.6	3.8	4.1
Cleaners/Helpers/Laborers	2.6	3.2	3.9
Services	15.9	12.7	13.2
Farming/Forestry/Fishing	0.7	1.2	2.5

Note: Figures cover workers 16 years of age and older;
(1) Metropolitan Statistical Area - see Appendix A for areas included
Source: 1990 Census of Population and Housing, Summary Tape File 3C

Occupational Employment Projections: 1996 - 2006

Occupations Expected to Have the Largest Job Growth (ranked by numerical growth)	Fast-Growing Occupations[1] (ranked by percent growth)
1. Salespersons, retail	1. Computer scientists
2. Home health aides	2. Systems analysts
3. Cashiers	3. Computer engineers
4. Teachers, secondary school	4. Computer support specialists
5. Systems analysts	5. Data processing equipment repairers
6. Teachers, special education	6. Database administrators
7. Personal and home care aides	7. Electronic pagination systems workers
8. Maintenance repairers, general utility	8. Teachers, special education
9. Guards	9. Medical assistants
10. Stock clerks, stockroom or warehouse	10. Physical therapy assistants and aides

Note: Projections cover New York State; (1) Excludes occupations with total job growth less than 1,000
Source: New York State Department of Labor, Occupational Outlook, Employment & Openings by Occupation, 1996-2006

Average Wages

Occupation	$/Hr.	Occupation	$/Hr.
Accountants and Auditors	19.83	Maids and Housekeepers	7.24
Assemblers and Fabricators	9.96	Maintenance Repairers	11.63
Automotive Mechanics	12.48	Marketing/Advertising/PR Managers	26.84
Bookkeepers	11.86	Nurses, Licensed Practical	12.50
Carpenters	14.99	Nurses, Registered	18.17
Cashiers	7.00	Nursing Aides/Orderlies/Attendants	9.40
Clerks, General Office	10.72	Physicians and Surgeons	45.40
Clerks, Shipping/Receiving/Traffic	11.75	Receptionists/Information Clerks	9.35
Computer Programmers	23.92	Sales Reps., Exc. Scientific/Retail	19.20
Computer Support Specialists	18.54	Sales Reps., Scientific, Exc. Retail	21.60
Cooks, Restaurant	8.02	Salespersons, Retail	8.70
Electricians	17.16	Secretaries, Except Legal/Medical	12.32
Financial Managers	28.06	Stock Clerks, Sales Floor	7.66
First-Line Supervisors/Mgrs., Sales	16.38	Systems Analysts	24.55
Food Preparation Workers	7.05	Teacher Aides	9.24
General Managers/Top Executives	30.20	Teachers, Elementary School	20.17
Guards	8.96	Teachers, Secondary School	22.50
Hand Packers	8.14	Telemarketers	9.09
Janitors and Cleaners	8.80	Truck Drivers, Heavy/Tractor-Trailer	14.23
Laborers, Landscaping	10.02	Truck Drivers, Light	10.52
Lawyers	27.75	Waiters and Waitresses	6.08

Note: Wage data is for 1998 and covers the Metropolitan Statistical Area (see Appendix A for areas included). Hourly wages for elementary and secondary school teachers were calculated by the editors from annual wage data assuming a 40 hour work week; Dashes indicate that data was not available.
Source: Bureau of Labor Statistics, 1998 Metropolitan Area Occupational Employment and Wage Estimates

TAXES

Major State and Local Tax Rates

State Corporate Income (%)	State Personal Income (%)	Residential Property (%)	Sales & Use		State Gasoline (cents/ gallon)	State Cigarette (cents/ pack)
			State (%)	Local (%)		
8.5[a]	4.0 - 6.85	2.18	4.0	4.0	8.0[b]	56.0[c]

Note: Personal/corporate income, sales, gasoline and cigarette tax rates as of January 2000. Property tax rates as of April 2000; (a) Or 1.78 (0.1 for banks) mills per dollar of capital (up to $350,000; or 3.0% of the minimum taxable income; or a minimum of $100 to $1,500 depending on payroll size ($250 plus 2.5% surtax for banks); if any of these is greater than the tax computed on net income, the higher figure is used. An additional tax of 0.9 mills per dollar of subsidiary capital is imposed on corporations. Small corporations with income under $200,000 pay a 7.5% tax on all income.; (b) Carriers pay an additional surcharge of 22.21 cents. Sales tax applicable; (c) Tax rate is projected to increase to $1.11 per pack on March 1, 2000
Source: Federation of Tax Administrators, www.taxadmin.org; ERI's Relocation Assessor software database, quarterly effective date 4/1/2000

Total Taxes Per Capita and as a Percent of Income

Area	Per Capita Income ($)	Per Capita Taxes ($)			Percent of Income (%)		
		Total	Federal	State/Local	Total	Federal	State/Local
New York	34,730	13,414	8,506	4,909	38.6	24.5	14.1
U.S.	28,878	10,298	7,026	3,273	35.7	24.3	11.3

Note: Figures are for 1999
Source: Tax Foundation, www.taxfoundation.org

COMMERCIAL UTILITIES

Typical Monthly Electric Bills

Area	Commercial Service ($/month)		Industrial Service ($/month)	
	12 kW demand 1,500 kWh	100 kW demand 30,000 kWh	1,000 kW demand 400,000 kWh	20,000 kW demand 10,000,000 kWh
City	253	3,812	39,781	459,926
U.S.	150	2,174	23,995	508,569

Note: Based on rates in effect January 1, 1999
Source: Edison Electric Institute, Typical Residential, Commercial and Industrial Bills, Winter 1999

TRANSPORTATION

Transportation Statistics

Average minutes to work (1990)	17.2
Interstate highways	I-87; I-90; I-787; US-4; US-9; US-20
Bus lines	
In-city (1998)	Capital District Transportation Authority, 183 buses
Inter-city (1999)	9
Passenger air service	
Airport	Albany International
Airlines (1999)	6
Enplaned passengers (1998)	1,089,109
Amtrak service	Yes
Motor freight carriers (1999)	120
Major waterways/ports	Hudson River

Source: FAA DOT/TSC CY1998 ACAIS Database; National Transit Database, 1998; Editor & Publisher Market Guide, 2000; Amtrak National Time Table, Fall 1999/Winter 2000; 1990 Census of Population and Housing, STF 3C; Jane's Urban Transport Systems 1999-2000

Means of Transportation to Work

Area	Car/Truck/Van		Public Transportation			Bicycle	Walked	Other Means	Worked at Home
	Drove Alone	Car-pooled	Bus	Subway	Railroad				
City	56.4	11.8	14.5	0.0	0.0	0.4	13.6	1.3	1.9
MSA[1]	74.6	12.8	4.0	0.0	0.0	0.2	5.0	0.9	2.4
U.S.	73.2	13.4	3.0	1.5	0.5	0.4	3.9	1.2	3.0

Note: Figures shown are percentages and only include workers 16 years of age and older;
(1) Metropolitan Statistical Area - see Appendix A for areas included
Source: 1990 Census of Population and Housing, Summary Tape File 3C

BUSINESSES

Major Business Headquarters

Company Name	1999 Rankings	
	Fortune 500	Forbes 500
No companies listed	-	-

Note: Companies listed are located in the city; dashes indicate no ranking
Fortune 500: Companies that produce a 10-K are ranked 1 to 500 based on 1999 revenue
Forbes 500: Private companies are ranked 1 to 500 based on 1998 revenue
Source: Forbes, December 13, 1999; Fortune, April 17, 2000

HOTELS & MOTELS

Hotels/Motels

Area	Hotels/ Motels	Rooms	Luxury-Level Hotels/Motels		Average Minimum Rates ($)		
			♦♦♦♦	♦♦♦♦♦	♦♦	♦♦♦	♦♦♦♦
City	15	1,531	0	0	n/a	n/a	n/a
Airport	22	3,100	0	0	n/a	n/a	n/a
Suburbs	17	1,498	0	0	n/a	n/a	n/a
Total	54	6,129	0	0	n/a	n/a	n/a

Note: n/a not available; classifications range from one diamond (budget properties with basic amenities) to five diamond (luxury properties).
Source: OAG Business Travel Planner, Winter 1999-2000

Estimated Daily Food and Lodging Costs

Area	Food/Other ($/day)	Average Hotel Cost ($/day)
City	42	74
U.S.	30	55

Source: ERI's Relocation Assessor software database, quarterly effective date 4/1/2000

CONVENTION CENTERS

Convention Centers and Event Sites

Name	Guest Rooms	Meeting Space (sq. ft.)	Capacity (Theatre Style)
Albany Marriott	359	16,000	1,400
Best Western Albany Airport Inn	153	n/a	0
Crowne Plaza Albany Hotel	386	21,000	1,200
Empire State Plaza Convention Center	n/a	n/a	2,500
Knickerbocker Arena	n/a	n/a	17,500

Note: n/a not available
Source: EventSource.com, 3/15/2000

Living Environment

COST OF LIVING

Cost of Living: Homeowner

Cost Element	U.S. ($)	City ($)	Differential ($)	Percent of U.S. Average
Consumables	14,516	16,014	1,498	110.3
Transportation	5,957	6,324	367	106.2
Health Services	2,012	2,085	73	103.6
Housing/Utilities/Prop. Tax	16,337	20,080	3,743	122.9
Income+Payroll Taxes	12,615	12,734	119	100.9
Miscellaneous	8,563	8,563	0	100.0
Total Cost of Living	60,000	65,800	5,800	109.7

Note: Figures are based on a single income, four person family with gross annual earnings of $60,000, owning an 1,800 square-foot home, and driving two automobiles worth $22,000 30,000 miles per year.
Source: ERI's Relocation Assessor software database, quarterly effective date 4/1/2000

Cost of Living: Renter

Cost Element	U.S. ($)	City ($)	Differential ($)	Percent of U.S. Average
Consumables	10,486	11,628	1,142	110.9
Transportation	2,107	2,248	141	106.7
Health Services	1,632	1,701	69	104.2
Rent/Utilities/Insurance	9,299	12,314	3,015	132.4
Income+Payroll Taxes	8,607	8,895	288	103.3
Miscellaneous	7,869	7,869	0	100.0
Total Cost of Living	40,000	44,655	4,655	111.6

Note: Figures are based on a single income, three person family with gross annual earnings of $40,000, renting a 1,000 square-foot home, and driving one automobile worth $8,000 12,000 miles per year.
Source: ERI's Relocation Assessor software database, quarterly effective date 4/1/2000

HOUSING

Median Home Prices and Housing Affordability

Area	Median Price[2] 4th Qtr. 1999 ($)	HOI[3] 4th Qtr. 1999	Affordability Rank[4]
MSA[1]	107,000	73.9	71
U.S.	139,000	63.8	–

Note: (1) Metropolitan Statistical Area - see Appendix A for areas included; (2) U.S. figures calculated from the sales of 687,516 new and existing homes in 192 markets; (3) Housing Opportunity Index - percent of homes sold that were within the reach of the median income household at the prevailing mortgage interest rate; (4) Rank is from 1-192 with 1 being most affordable
Source: National Association of Home Builders, Housing Opportunity Index, 4th Quarter 1999

Estimated Home Price

Area	Price ($)
City	147,392
U.S.	135,855

Note: Figures are based on an 1,800 square-foot home
Source: ERI's Relocation Assessor software database, quarterly effective date 4/1/2000

Estimated Rent

Area	Rent ($/month)
City	875
U.S.	651

Note: Figures are based on a 1,000 square-foot home
Source: ERI's Relocation Assessor software database, quarterly effective date 4/1/2000

Median Home Price Projection

It is projected that the median home price in the metropolitan area will increase from $107,147 in 1999 to $156,637 in 2010, an increase of 46.2%
Kiplinger's Personal Finance Magazine, January 2000

RESIDENTIAL UTILITIES

Average Residential Utility Costs

Area	All Electric ($/mth)	Part Electric ($/mth)	Other Energy ($/mth)	Phone ($/mth)
City	n/a	n/a	n/a	n/a
U.S.	99.25	55.47	43.48	20.29

Note: n/a not available
Source: ACCRA, Cost of Living Index, 3rd Quarter 1999

HEALTH CARE

Average Health Care Costs

Area	Hospital ($/day)	Doctor ($/visit)	Dentist ($/visit)
City	n/a	n/a	n/a
U.S.	440.96	53.83	68.42

Note: n/a not available
Source: ACCRA, Cost of Living Index, 3rd Quarter 1999

Distribution of Office-Based Physicians

| Area | Family/Gen. Practitioners | Specialists | | |
		Medical	Surgical	Other
MSA[1]	185	615	466	475

Note: Data as of 12/31/97; (1) Metropolitan Statistical Area - see Appendix A for areas included
Source: American Medical Assn., Physician Characteristics & Distribution in the U.S., 1999

Hospitals

Albany has 4 general medical and surgical hospitals, 1 psychiatric, 1 eye, ear, nose and throat.
AHA Guide to the Healthcare Field, 1999-2000

According to *U.S. News and World Report,* Albany has one of the best hospitals in the U.S.: **Albany Medical Center Hospital**, noted for urology.
U.S. News Online, "America's Best Hospitals," July 19, 1999

EDUCATION

Public School District Statistics

District Name	Num. Sch.	Enroll.	Classroom Teachers	Pupils per Teacher	Minority Pupils (%)	Current Exp.[1] ($/pupil)
Albany City SD	18	10,250	662	15.5	n/a	n/a
Menands Union Free SD	1	240	21	11.4	n/a	n/a
South Colonie Central SD	8	5,682	370	15.4	n/a	n/a

Note: Data covers the 1997-1998 school year unless otherwise noted; (1) Data covers fiscal year 1996; SD = School District; ISD = Independent School District; n/a not available
Source: National Center for Education Statistics, Common Core of Data Public Education Agency Universe 1997-98; National Center for Education Statistics, Characteristics of the 100 Largest Public Elementary and Secondary School Districts in the United States: 1997-98, July 1999

Educational Quality

School District	Education Quotient[1]	Graduate Outcome[2]	Community Index[3]	Resource Index[4]
Albany City School Dist.	105	86	82	148

Note: Over 1,000 secondary school districts were rated in terms of educational quality. The scores range from a low of 50 to a high of 150; (1) Combination of the Graduate Outcome, Community and Resource indexes weighted to reflect the greater importance of the Graduate Outcome and Resource Index; (2) Based on graduation rates and college board scores (SAT/ACT); (3) Based on the surrounding community's level of affluence and adult education; (4) Based on teacher salaries, per-pupil expenditures and student-teacher ratios.
Source: Expansion Management, Ratings Issue, 1999

Educational Attainment by Race

Area	High School Graduate (%)					Bachelor's Degree (%)				
	Total	White	Black	Other	Hisp.[2]	Total	White	Black	Other	Hisp.[2]
City	77.7	79.7	67.7	82.8	76.5	29.5	32.5	12.4	47.0	29.5
MSA[1]	79.7	80.2	68.1	77.0	69.1	23.4	23.4	14.0	43.3	22.8
U.S.	75.2	77.9	63.1	60.4	49.8	20.3	21.5	11.4	19.4	9.2

Note: Figures shown cover persons 25 years old and over; (1) Metropolitan Statistical Area - see Appendix A for areas included; (2) people of Hispanic origin can be of any race
Source: 1990 Census of Population and Housing, Summary Tape File 3C

School Enrollment by Type

Area	Preprimary				Elementary/High School			
	Public		Private		Public		Private	
	Enrollment	%	Enrollment	%	Enrollment	%	Enrollment	%
City	798	48.2	856	51.8	8,556	73.9	3,016	26.1
MSA[1]	10,316	56.7	7,875	43.3	120,363	89.5	14,047	10.5
U.S.	2,679,029	59.5	1,824,256	40.5	38,379,689	90.2	4,187,099	9.8

Note: Figures shown cover persons 3 years old and over;
(1) Metropolitan Statistical Area - see Appendix A for areas included
Source: 1990 Census of Population and Housing, Summary Tape File 3C

School Enrollment by Race

Area	Preprimary (%)				Elementary/High School (%)			
	White	Black	Other	Hisp.[1]	White	Black	Other	Hisp.[1]
City	66.7	30.1	3.1	2.1	55.9	39.6	4.5	4.6
MSA[2]	92.4	4.8	2.8	2.1	90.3	6.9	2.8	2.4
U.S.	80.4	12.5	7.1	7.8	74.1	15.6	10.3	12.5

Note: Figures shown cover persons 3 years old and over; (1) people of Hispanic origin can be of any race; (2) Metropolitan Statistical Area - see Appendix A for areas included
Source: 1990 Census of Population and Housing, Summary Tape File 3C

Higher Education

Two-Year Colleges		Four-Year Colleges		Medical Schools	Law Schools	Voc/ Tech
Public	Private	Public	Private			
0	3	1	2	1	1	7

Source: College Blue Book, Occupational Education, 1999; Medical School Admission Requirements, 1999-2000; Peterson's Guide to Two-Year Colleges, 2000; Peterson's Guide to Four-Year Colleges, 1999; Barron's Guide to Law Schools, 1999

MAJOR EMPLOYERS

Major Employers

Albany Medical Center	Albany Medical College
Empire Blue Cross & Blue Shield	Goldstein Enterprises (automobiles)
Memorial Hospital of Albany	Mercycare Corp.
NYS Thruway Authority	Niagara Mohawk Power Corp.
St. Peter's Hospital	TransWorld Entertainment Corp.

Note: Companies listed are located in the city
Source: D&B Business Rankings, 1999; Ward's Business Directory, 1999; America's Corporate Families, 1999

PUBLIC SAFETY

Crime Rate

Area	All Crimes	Violent Crimes				Property Crimes		
		Murder	Forcible Rape	Robbery	Aggrav. Assault	Burglary	Larceny -Theft	Motor Vehicle Theft
City	7,165.2	1.9	71.7	375.1	523.4	1,749.6	4,014.9	428.4
Suburbs[1]	n/a	n/a	n/a	n/a	n/a	n/a	n/a	n/a
MSA[2]	n/a	n/a	n/a	n/a	n/a	n/a	n/a	n/a
U.S.	4,615.5	6.3	34.4	165.2	360.5	862.0	2,728.1	459.0

Note: Crime rate is the number of crimes per 100,000 population; (1) Defined as all areas within the Metropolitan Statistical Area but located outside the central city; (2) Metropolitan Statistical Area - see Appendix A for areas included; n/a not available
Source: FBI Uniform Crime Reports, 1998

RECREATION

Culture and Recreation

Museums	Symphony Orchestras	Opera Companies	Dance Companies	Professional Theatres	Zoos	Pro Sports Teams
6	1	0	1	2	0	0

Source: Musical America, International Directory of the Performing Arts, 1999; Official Museum Directory, 2000; Stern's Performing Arts Directory, 1997; USA Today Four Sport Stadium Guide, 1997; Career Opportunities in Theatre and the Performing Arts, 1999

Library System

The Albany Public Library has four branches and holdings of 375,514 volumes.
American Library Directory, 1999-2000

MEDIA

Newspapers

Name	Type	Freq.	Distribution	Circulation
The Jewish World	Religious	1x/wk	Local	5,000
The Legislative Gazette	General	1x/wk	Area	19,100
The Source	General	1x/wk	Local	16,000
Times Union	General	7x/wk	Area	106,000

Note: Includes newspapers with circulations of 200 or more located in the city;
Source: Burrelle's Media Directory, 1999 Edition

Television Stations

Name	Ch.	Affiliation	Type	Owner
WTEN	10	ABCT	Commercial	Young Broadcasting Inc.
WNYT	13	NBCT	Commercial	Hubbard Broadcasting Inc.
WXXA	23	FBC	Commercial	Clear Channel Broadcasting Inc.
WYPX	55	PAXTV	Commercial	Paxson Communications Corporation

Note: Stations included broadcast in the Albany metro area; n/a not available
Source: Burrelle's Media Directory, 1999 Edition

AM Radio Stations

Call Letters	Freq. (kHz)	Target Audience	Station Format	Music Format
WROW	590	General	N/T	n/a
WGY	810	General	N/T	n/a
WTRY	980	General	M	Oldies
WTMM	1300	General	N/S/T	n/a
WHAZ	1330	Religious	M/N/T	Christian
WABY	1400	General	M/N	Adult Standards/Big Band/MOR
WGNA	1460	General	M/N	Country
WDCD	1540	G/R	M/T	Christian

Note: Stations included broadcast in the Albany metro area; n/a not available
Target Audience: A=Asian; B=Black; C=Christian; E=Ethnic; F=French; G=General; H=Hispanic;
M=Men; N=Native American; R=Religious; S=Senior Citizen; W=Women; Y=Young Adult; Z=Children
Station Format: E=Educational; M=Music; N=News; S=Sports; T=Talk
Music Format: AOR=Album Oriented Rock; MOR=Middle-of-the-Road
Source: Burrelle's Media Directory, 1999 Edition

FM Radio Stations

Call Letters	Freq. (mHz)	Target Audience	Station Format	Music Format
WVCR	88.3	General	M	Alternative/AOR/Urban Contemporary
WAMC	90.3	General	M/N/S	Classical/Jazz
WCDB	90.9	General	E/M/N/S/T	n/a
WRPI	91.5	General	E/M/N/S/T	Alternative/Blues/Classic Rock/Country/Jazz/Latin/ Modern Rock/Oldies/ Reggae/Urban Contemporary/World Music
WOSR	91.7	General	M/N	Classical/Jazz
WCEL	91.9	General	M/T	Classical/Jazz
WFLY	92.3	General	M	n/a
WCAN	93.3	General	E/M/N/T	Classical/Jazz
WYJB	95.5	General	M	Adult Contemporary
WAJZ	96.3	General	M/N/S	Rhythm & Blues/Urban Contemporary
WDCD	96.7	General	M/T	Christian
WMYY	97.3	Religious	M/N/T	Christian
WTRY	98.3	General	M	Oldies
WRVE	99.5	General	M	Adult Contemporary/Classic Rock
WKLI	100.9	General	M/N/S	Adult Top 40
WJIV	101.9	General	E/M/N	Christian
WXCR	102.3	General	M	Classic Rock
WHRL	103.1	General	M/N/S	Jazz
WANC	103.9	General	M/N/S	Classical/Jazz
WQBK	103.9	Young Adult	M/N/T	Alternative
WABT	104.5	General	M/N	Oldies
WZMR	104.9	General	M/N/S	Modern Rock
WAMQ	105.1	General	E/M/N	Classical/Jazz
WPYX	106.5	General	M	AOR
WGNA	107.7	General	M	Country

Note: Stations included broadcast in the Albany metro area; n/a not available
Station Format: E=Educational; M=Music; N=News; S=Sports; T=Talk
Target Audience: A=Asian; B=Black; C=Christian; E=Ethnic; F=French; G=General; H=Hispanic;
M=Men; N=Native American; R=Religious; S=Senior Citizen; W=Women; Y=Young Adult; Z=Children
Music Format: AOR=Album Oriented Rock; MOR=Middle-of-the-Road
Source: Burrelle's Media Directory, 1999 Edition

WEATHER

Temperature/Precipitation/Humidity

	Jan	Feb	Mar	Apr	May	Jun	Jul	Aug	Sep	Oct	Nov	Dec	Yr.
Max. High Temp. (°F)	64	67	86	92	94	99	100	99	100	89	82	71	100
Avg. High Temp. (°F)	31	33	43	58	69	78	83	81	73	62	48	35	58
Avg. Temp. (°F)	22	24	34	47	58	67	72	70	61	51	40	27	48
Avg. Low Temp. (°F)	13	14	25	36	46	55	60	58	50	39	31	19	37
Min. Low Temp. (°F)	-28	-21	-21	10	26	36	40	34	24	16	5	-22	-28
Avg. Precip. (in.)	2.4	2.3	2.8	2.9	3.6	3.4	3.1	3.3	3.1	2.9	3.1	2.9	35.8
Avg. Snowfall (in.)	16	14	11	3	Tr	0	0	0	0	Tr	4	14	63
Avg. Rel. Hum. 7am (%)	77	77	76	72	74	77	80	85	88	86	82	80	79
Avg. Rel. Hum. 4pm (%)	64	60	54	49	51	53	53	55	57	56	64	67	57

Note: Tr = Trace amounts (less than 0.05 inches of rain or less than 0.5 inches of snow)
Source: National Climatic Data Center, International Station Meteorological Climate Summary, 3/95

Weather Conditions

Temperature			Precipitation		
5°F & below	32°F & below	90°F & above	0.01 inch or more precip.	1.5 inch or more snow/ice	Thunderstorms
22	147	11	133	13	24

Note: Figures are average number of days per year
Source: National Climatic Data Center, International Station Meteorological Climate Summary, 3/95

AIR & WATER QUALITY

Maximum Pollutant Concentrations

	Particulate Matter (ug/m^3)	Carbon Monoxide (ppm)	Sulfur Dioxide (ppm)	Nitrogen Dioxide (ppm)	Ozone (ppm)	Lead (ug/m^3)
MSA[1] Level	45	5	0.020	0.014	0.10	0.03
NAAQS[2]	150	9	0.140	0.053	0.12	1.50
Met NAAQS	Yes	Yes	Yes	Yes	Yes	Yes

Note: (1) Metropolitan Statistical Area - see Appendix A for areas included; (2) National Ambient Air Quality Standards; ppm = parts per million; ug/m^3 = micrograms per cubic meter; n/a not available
Source: EPA, National Air Quality and Emissions Trends Report, 1997

Pollutant Standards Index

In the Albany MSA (see Appendix A for areas included), the Pollutant Standards Index (PSI) exceeded 100 on 3 days in 1997. A PSI value greater than 100 indicates that air quality would have been in the unhealthful range on that day.
EPA, National Air Quality and Emissions Trends Report, 1997

Drinking Water

Water System Name	Pop. Served	Primary Water Source Type	Number of Violations in 1998-99	Type of Violation/ Contaminants
Albany City	101,082	Surface	None	None

Note: Data as of January 19, 2000
Source: EPA, Office of Ground Water and Drinking Water, Safe Drinking Water Information System

Albany tap water is alkaline, very soft, and not fluoridated.
Editor & Publisher Market Guide, 2000

Appleton, Wisconsin

Background

Appleton, Wisconsin is situated in the east-central section of the state on the Fox River. The site was first settled in 1833 by fur-traders dealing with the Fox River Valley Indians. Incorporated as a village in 1853, it became a city in 1857.

From Appleton's beginnings, education formed the foundation on which the community was built. In 1847, with the financial backing of Amos Lawrence, the Lawrence Institute was chartered. When Samuel Appleton, Lawrence's father-in-law contributed $10,000 to the college library, the community was named in honor of him. Education continues to be a prominent focus of the city. Lawrence University rests on 84 acres on which 32 buildings accommodate 1,200 students and 114 faculty. The campus provides a source of culture and sports to the community. In addition to the university, Fox Valley Technical College has contributed to vocational education since 1965. Supporting the schools is the Appleton Public Library, which numbers among the nation's 50 outstanding libraries and offers a 240,000-volume book collection as well as audiovisual and software rentals.

Its population of 69,103 enjoys economic prosperity from industries such as paper processing, wood products and retail trade.

Appleton's innovation and progressive character has made it a place of many "firsts." The nation's first hydroelectric center began operations in 1882. In 1886, the country's first electric streetcar company was established. Electric street lights were installed in 1912, replacing the gas lamps in the city's downtown retail center.

The Outagamie County Historical Society is responsible for preserving Appleton's proud heritage. Its museum is home to, among other exhibits, artifacts chronicling the life of one of the city's most famous natives, escape artist Harry Houdini.

General Rankings and Evaluative Comments

- Appleton was ranked #98 out of 354 metropolitan areas in *Places Rated Almanac*. Criteria: cost of living, climate, crime, transportation, job outlook, education, the arts, health care, and recreation. *Places Rated Almanac, Millennium Edition, 2000*

- Cognetics studied 273 metro areas in the United States, ranking them by entrepreneurial activity. Appleton was ranked #12 out of 134 smaller metro areas. Criteria: Significant Starts (firms started in the last 10 years that still employ at least 5 people) and Young Growers (percent of firms 10 years old or less that grew significantly during the last 4 years). *Cognetics, "Entrepreneurial Hot Spots: The Best Places in America to Start and Grow a Company," 1999*

Business Environment

STATE ECONOMY

State Economic Profile

"Wisconsin's expansion has begun to slow. For the first time in some years, 1998 saw Wisconsin grow at a rate below the national. Wisconsin's manufacturing sector remains stagnant and its farm sector struggling. Wisconsin's tight labor market will help to absorb some of these declines. An unsustainable increase in construction has driven job growth. Wisconsin's economy should trail the nation for some years before rebounding in 2001.

Wisconsin's construction industry remains a lone bright spot. Several commercial projects are under way in Milwaukee, such as the new convention center and baseball park. In addition, industrial and office construction is picking up in the suburbs. Public construction is also set to rise as the new federal transportation regulation raised Wisconsin's federal transportation funding by 48% to $520 million.

Wisconsin's residential market remains healthy with residential permits growing at a torrid pace in 1998. Existing home sales along with house prices are rising. Despite recent price appreciation, affordability still exceeds the national average. In the long run, however, the fast pace of construction will slow as residential construction is outpacing household formation in the state.

Wisconsin exports a large share of its manufacturing and agricultural output. Weak export demand is resulting in cutbacks to its papermaking, pulp, and equipment manufacturing industries. Farm income also dropped by over 90% in 1998 as commodity prices tumbled and export demand shrank. Commodity prices will remain weak, leaving little promise of a resurgence in Wisconsin's farm sector (outside of dairy, which is performing well). Slowing population growth, especially among younger households, will slow long-run growth. Wisconsin's high exposure to manufacturing and agriculture will continue to create downside risks for the state. Wisconsin will moderately underperform the nation in the near term."
National Association of Realtors, Economic Profiles: The Fifty States and the District of Columbia, http://nar.realtor.com/databank/profiles.htm

EXPORTS

Total Export Sales

Area	1995 ($000)	1996 ($000)	1997 ($000)	1998 ($000)	% Chg. 1995-98	% Chg. 1997-98
MSA[1]	593,726	608,521	647,857	658,018	10.8	1.6
U.S.	583,030,524	622,827,063	687,597,999	680,474,251	16.7	-1.0

Note: (1) Metropolitan Statistical Area - see Appendix A for areas included
Source: U.S. Department of Commerce, International Trade Association, Metropolitan Area Exports: An Export Performance Report on Over 250 U.S. Cities, November 10, 1999

CITY FINANCES

City Government Finances

Component	1995 ($million)	1995 (per capita $)
Revenue	63.6	913
Expenditure	71.5	1,027
Debt Outstanding	117.1	1,683

Source: 1999 County and City Extra, Annual Metro, City, and County Data Book

City Government Revenue by Source

Source	1995 ($million)	1995 (per capita $)
Intergovernmental	18.6	267
Taxes	24.8	356
Property	23.3	336
Sales and Gross Receipts	0.0	0

Source: 1999 County and City Extra, Annual Metro, City, and County Data Book

City Government Expenditures by Function

Function	1995 ($million)	1995 (per capita $)	1995 (%)
Public Welfare	0.0	0	0.0
Highways	11.0	158	15.4
Parking Facilities	3.5	50	4.9
Education	0.0	0	0.0
Health and Hospitals	0.8	12	1.2
Police Protection	7.9	114	11.1
Sewerage and Sanitation	13.8	199	19.4
Parks and Recreation	4.5	64	6.3
Housing and Community Development	1.6	23	2.3
Interest on Debt	4.5	65	6.4

Source: 1999 County and City Extra, Annual Metro, City, and County Data Book

Municipal Bond Ratings

Area	Moody's
City	Aa1

Source: Mergent Bond Record, 2/2000

POPULATION

Population Growth

Area	1980 Census	1990 Census	1999 Estimate	2004 Projection	Population Growth (%) 1990-1999	Population Growth (%) 1999-2004
City	59,040	65,651	64,615	64,496	-1.6	-0.2
MSA[1]	291,369	315,121	346,380	357,718	9.9	3.3
U.S.	226,545,805	248,765,170	272,212,864	283,625,312	9.4	4.2

Note: (1) Metropolitan Statistical Area - see Appendix A for areas included
Source: 1990 Census of Population and Housing, Summary Tape File 3C; Claritas, Inc.

Number of Households and Average Household Size

Area	1980 Census	1990 Census	1999 Estimate	2004 Projection	1999 Average Household Size
City	21,174	24,915	25,705	26,315	2.51
MSA[1]	99,334	115,895	132,516	139,716	2.61
U.S.	80,389,592	91,993,582	102,048,200	107,302,392	2.67

Note: (1) Metropolitan Statistical Area - see Appendix A for areas included
Source: 1990 Census of Population and Housing, Summary Tape File 3C; Claritas, Inc.

Race/Ethnicity of City Population

Race/Ethnicity	1990 Census Population	1990 Census %	1999 Estimate Population	1999 Estimate %	% Change 1990-1999
White, Non-Hispanic	63,213	96.3	60,599	93.8	-4.1
Black, Non-Hispanic	210	0.3	215	0.3	2.4
Asian, Non-Hispanic	1,472	2.2	2,561	4.0	74.0
Other, Non-Hispanic	237	0.4	301	0.5	27.0
Hispanic	519	0.8	939	1.5	80.9

Source: 1990 Census of Population and Housing, Summary Tape File 3C; Claritas, Inc.

Race/Ethnicity of Metropolitan Statistical Area Population

Race/Ethnicity	1990 Census		1999 Estimate		% Change 1990-1999
	Population	%	Population	%	
White, Non-Hispanic	305,585	97.0	332,022	95.9	8.7
Black, Non-Hispanic	853	0.3	963	0.3	12.9
Asian, Non-Hispanic	3,559	1.1	5,986	1.7	68.2
Other, Non-Hispanic	2,877	0.9	3,528	1.0	22.6
Hispanic	2,247	0.7	3,881	1.1	72.7

Note: See Appendix A for areas included in the Metropolitan Statistical Area
Source: 1990 Census of Population and Housing, Summary Tape File 3C; Claritas, Inc.

Ancestry

Area	German	Irish	English	Italian	U.S.	French	Polish	Dutch
City	66.7	13.5	8.1	1.9	1.5	6.9	5.8	9.7
MSA[1]	67.8	12.1	6.9	1.6	1.5	5.9	7.0	10.6
U.S.	23.3	15.6	13.1	5.9	5.3	4.2	3.8	2.5

Note: Figures are percentages and include persons that reported multiple ancestry (eg. if a person reported being Irish and Italian, they were included in both columns); (1) Metropolitan Statistical Area - see Appendix A for areas included
Source: 1990 Census of Population and Housing, Summary Tape File 3C

Median Age

Area	1990 Census	1999 Estimate
City	31.6	35.2
MSA[1]	31.8	35.1
U.S.	32.9	35.7

Note: (1) Metropolitan Statistical Area - see Appendix A for areas included
Source: 1990 Census of Population and Housing, Summary Tape File 3C; Claritas, Inc.

Male/Female Population

Area	Number of Males		Number of Females		Males per 100 Females	
	1990	1999	1990	1999	1990	1999
City	31,638	31,134	34,013	33,481	93.0	93.0
MSA[1]	155,100	170,337	160,021	176,043	96.9	96.8
U.S.	121,172,379	132,803,736	127,537,494	139,409,136	95.0	95.3

Note: (1) Metropolitan Statistical Area - see Appendix A for areas included
Source: 1990 Census of Population, General Population Characteristics; Claritas, Inc.

INCOME

Per Capita/Median/Average Income

Area	Per Capita ($)			Median Household ($)			Average Household ($)		
	1989	1999	% Chg.	1989	1999	% Chg.	1989	1999	% Chg.
City	14,735	24,202	64.2	33,006	48,057	45.6	38,409	59,332	54.5
MSA[1]	13,698	22,393	63.5	31,954	47,274	47.9	36,852	57,589	56.3
U.S.	14,420	21,350	48.1	30,056	40,525	34.8	38,453	56,184	46.1

Note: (1) Metropolitan Statistical Area - see Appendix A for areas included; 1989 data is from the 1990 Census; 1999 data is estimated by Claritas, Inc.
Source: 1990 Census of Population, General Population Characteristics; Claritas, Inc.

Household Income Distribution

Area	Percent of Households Earning								
	Under $5,000	$5,000 -14,999	$15,000 -24,999	$25,000 -34,999	$35,000 -49,999	$50,000 -74,999	$75,000 -99,000	$100,000 -149,999	$150,000 and up
City	1.7	9.5	12.0	11.8	17.2	25.7	11.1	6.9	4.1
MSA[1]	1.5	9.7	12.2	12.3	17.2	25.8	11.4	6.5	3.3
U.S.	3.9	13.3	13.8	12.6	16.2	19.4	9.7	6.6	4.6

Note: Data as of 1999; (1) Metropolitan Statistical Area - see Appendix A for areas included
Source: Claritas, Inc.

Effective Buying Income

Area	Per Capita ($)	Median Household ($)	Average Household ($)
City	18,519	41,870	48,134
MSA[1]	18,089	42,031	48,479
U.S.	17,496	36,603	47,036

Note: Data as of 1/1/2000; (1) Metropolitan Statistical Area - see Appendix A for areas included
Source: Standard Rate & Data Service, Newspaper Advertising Source, March 2000

Effective Household Buying Income Distribution

Area	% of Households Earning						
	$10,000 -$19,999	$20,000 -$34,999	$35,000 -$49,999	$50,000 -$74,999	$75,000 -$99,000	$100,000 -$124,999	$125,000 and up
City	12.8	20.7	21.9	24.1	9.1	2.4	2.7
MSA[1]	12.9	21.1	21.0	24.8	9.1	2.7	2.3
U.S.	15.0	21.6	17.6	19.6	8.4	3.0	3.3

Note: Data as of 1/1/2000; (1) Metropolitan Statistical Area - see Appendix A for areas included
Source: Standard Rate & Data Service, Newspaper Advertising Source, March 2000

Poverty Rates by Age

Area	People of All Ages	People Under 18 Years Old	Related Children Age 5-17 in Families in Poverty
City	5.7	n/a	n/a
County	4.9	7.0	6.2
U.S.	13.8	20.8	18.7

Note: Figures show the percent of people living below the poverty line in 1995. The average poverty threshold was $15,569 for a family of four in 1995; n/a not available
Source: Bureau of the Census, Small Area Income and Poverty Estimates Program; U.S. Department of Housing and Urban Development

EMPLOYMENT

Labor Force and Employment

Area	Civilian Labor Force			Workers Employed		
	Dec. 1998	Dec. 1999	% Chg.	Dec. 1998	Dec. 1999	% Chg.
City	43,719	44,224	1.2	42,658	43,224	1.3
MSA[1]	223,579	225,519	0.9	218,498	221,400	1.3
U.S.	138,297,000	139,941,000	1.2	132,732,000	134,696,000	1.5

Note: Data is not seasonally adjusted and covers workers 16 years of age and older;
(1) Metropolitan Statistical Area - see Appendix A for areas included
Source: Bureau of Labor Statistics, http://stats.bls.gov

Unemployment Rate

Area	1999											
	Jan.	Feb.	Mar.	Apr.	May	Jun.	Jul.	Aug.	Sep.	Oct.	Nov.	Dec.
City	3.4	3.7	3.5	3.0	3.0	3.3	3.0	2.7	2.2	2.3	2.3	2.3
MSA[1]	3.1	3.2	3.0	2.5	2.4	2.6	2.2	2.0	1.6	1.8	1.9	1.8
U.S.	4.8	4.7	4.4	4.1	4.0	4.5	4.5	4.2	4.1	3.8	3.8	3.7

Note: Data is not seasonally adjusted and covers workers 16 years of age and older; all figures are percentages; (1) Metropolitan Statistical Area - see Appendix A for areas included
Source: Bureau of Labor Statistics, http://stats.bls.gov

Employment by Industry

Sector	MSA[1]		U.S.
	Number of Employees	Percent of Total	Percent of Total
Services	48,200	23.2	30.2
Retail Trade	35,700	17.2	18.1
Government	23,500	11.3	15.8
Manufacturing	60,600	29.1	14.1
Finance/Insurance/Real Estate	9,600	4.6	5.9
Wholesale Trade	9,000	4.3	5.4
Transportation/Public Utilities	9,000	4.3	5.3
Construction	n/a	n/a	4.8
Mining	n/a	n/a	0.4

Note: Figures cover non-farm employment as of 12/99 and are not seasonally adjusted;
(1) Metropolitan Statistical Area - see Appendix A for areas included; n/a not available
Source: Bureau of Labor Statistics, http://stats.bls.gov

Employment by Occupation

Occupation Category	City (%)	MSA[1] (%)	U.S. (%)
White Collar	60.7	51.4	58.1
Executive/Admin./Management	12.8	9.9	12.3
Professional	15.8	12.0	14.1
Technical & Related Support	3.9	3.5	3.7
Sales	12.7	10.8	11.8
Administrative Support/Clerical	15.5	15.2	16.3
Blue Collar	26.7	32.8	26.2
Precision Production/Craft/Repair	10.1	11.9	11.3
Machine Operators/Assem./Insp.	9.5	12.2	6.8
Transportation/Material Movers	2.9	4.0	4.1
Cleaners/Helpers/Laborers	4.2	4.7	3.9
Services	12.1	12.8	13.2
Farming/Forestry/Fishing	0.5	3.0	2.5

Note: Figures cover workers 16 years of age and older;
(1) Metropolitan Statistical Area - see Appendix A for areas included
Source: 1990 Census of Population and Housing, Summary Tape File 3C

Occupational Employment Projections: 1996 - 2006

Occupations Expected to Have the Largest Job Growth (ranked by numerical growth)	Fast-Growing Occupations[1] (ranked by percent growth)
1. Janitors/cleaners/maids, ex. priv. hshld.	1. Systems analysts
2. General managers & top executives	2. Desktop publishers
3. Cashiers	3. Personal and home care aides
4. Truck drivers, light	4. Database administrators
5. Salespersons, retail	5. Paralegals
6. Systems analysts	6. Securities, financial services sales
7. Home health aides	7. Occupational therapists
8. Teachers aides, clerical & paraprofess.	8. Home health aides
9. Registered nurses	9. Teachers, special education
10. Waiters & waitresses	10. Medical assistants

Note: Projections cover Wisconsin; (1) Excludes occupations with total job growth less than 300
Source: U.S. Department of Labor, Employment and Training Administration, America's Labor Market Information System (ALMIS)

Average Wages

Occupation	$/Hr.	Occupation	$/Hr.
Accountants and Auditors	17.41	Maids and Housekeepers	7.05
Assemblers and Fabricators	9.86	Maintenance Repairers	12.65
Automotive Mechanics	12.17	Marketing/Advertising/PR Managers	25.06
Bookkeepers	10.58	Nurses, Licensed Practical	12.55
Carpenters	15.04	Nurses, Registered	18.42
Cashiers	7.51	Nursing Aides/Orderlies/Attendants	9.49
Clerks, General Office	9.66	Physicians and Surgeons	51.51
Clerks, Shipping/Receiving/Traffic	10.77	Receptionists/Information Clerks	8.49
Computer Programmers	21.15	Sales Reps., Exc. Scientific/Retail	22.66
Computer Support Specialists	17.17	Sales Reps., Scientific, Exc. Retail	25.09
Cooks, Restaurant	8.14	Salespersons, Retail	9.13
Electricians	17.83	Secretaries, Except Legal/Medical	10.82
Financial Managers	24.44	Stock Clerks, Sales Floor	7.72
First-Line Supervisors/Mgrs., Sales	16.51	Systems Analysts	22.69
Food Preparation Workers	6.81	Teacher Aides	8.25
General Managers/Top Executives	27.02	Teachers, Elementary School	20.17
Guards	7.88	Teachers, Secondary School	19.26
Hand Packers	9.49	Telemarketers	10.61
Janitors and Cleaners	8.21	Truck Drivers, Heavy/Tractor-Trailer	14.89
Laborers, Landscaping	10.23	Truck Drivers, Light	8.57
Lawyers	31.74	Waiters and Waitresses	6.03

Note: Wage data is for 1998 and covers the Metropolitan Statistical Area (see Appendix A for areas included). Hourly wages for elementary and secondary school teachers were calculated by the editors from annual wage data assuming a 40 hour work week; Dashes indicate that data was not available.
Source: Bureau of Labor Statistics, 1998 Metropolitan Area Occupational Employment and Wage Estimates

TAXES

Major State and Local Tax Rates

State Corporate Income (%)	State Personal Income (%)	Residential Property (%)	Sales & Use		State Gasoline (cents/ gallon)	State Cigarette (cents/ pack)
			State (%)	Local (%)		
7.9	4.73 - 6.75[a]	2.44	5.0	None	25.8[b]	59.0

Note: Personal/corporate income, sales, gasoline and cigarette tax rates as of January 2000. Property tax rates as of April 2000; (a) Tax rates scheduled to decrease for tax years 2001 and beyond (ranging from 4.6% to 6.75%). Personal exemption amounts scheduled to increase to $700 for tax year 2001; (b) Portion of the rate is adjustable based on maintenance costs, sales volume, or cost of fuel to state government
Source: Federation of Tax Administrators, www.taxadmin.org; ERI's Relocation Assessor software database, quarterly effective date 4/1/2000

Total Taxes Per Capita and as a Percent of Income

Area	Per Capita Income ($)	Per Capita Taxes ($)			Percent of Income (%)		
		Total	Federal	State/Local	Total	Federal	State/Local
Wisconsin	27,342	10,308	6,546	3,761	37.7	23.9	13.8
U.S.	28,878	10,298	7,026	3,273	35.7	24.3	11.3

Note: Figures are for 1999
Source: Tax Foundation, www.taxfoundation.org

COMMERCIAL UTILITIES

Typical Monthly Electric Bills

Area	Commercial Service ($/month)		Industrial Service ($/month)	
	12 kW demand 1,500 kWh	100 kW demand 30,000 kWh	1,000 kW demand 400,000 kWh	20,000 kW demand 10,000,000 kWh
City	113	1,949	19,554	330,406
U.S.	150	2,174	23,995	508,569

Note: Based on rates in effect January 1, 1999
Source: Edison Electric Institute, Typical Residential, Commercial and Industrial Bills, Winter 1999

TRANSPORTATION

Transportation Statistics

Average minutes to work (1990)	15.5
Interstate highways	US-41; US-10
Bus lines	
In-city (1998)	Valley Transit, 31 buses
Inter-city (1999)	3
Passenger air service	
Airport	Outagamie County Regional
Airlines (1999)	7
Enplaned passengers (1998)	266,132
Amtrak service	Bus Connection
Motor freight carriers (1999)	8
Major waterways/ports	None

Source: FAA DOT/TSC CY1998 ACAIS Database; National Transit Database, 1998; Editor & Publisher Market Guide, 2000; Amtrak National Time Table, Fall 1999/Winter 2000; 1990 Census of Population and Housing, STF 3C; Jane's Urban Transport Systems 1999-2000

Means of Transportation to Work

Area	Car/Truck/Van		Public Transportation			Bicycle	Walked	Other Means	Worked at Home
	Drove Alone	Car-pooled	Bus	Subway	Railroad				
City	81.8	7.9	1.8	0.0	0.0	0.6	5.4	0.4	2.0
MSA[1]	79.9	8.9	1.0	0.0	0.0	0.5	5.3	0.6	3.8
U.S.	73.2	13.4	3.0	1.5	0.5	0.4	3.9	1.2	3.0

Note: Figures shown are percentages and only include workers 16 years of age and older;
(1) Metropolitan Statistical Area - see Appendix A for areas included
Source: 1990 Census of Population and Housing, Summary Tape File 3C

BUSINESSES

Major Business Headquarters

Company Name	1999 Rankings	
	Fortune 500	Forbes 500
Aid Association for Lutherans	457	-

Note: Companies listed are located in the city; dashes indicate no ranking
Fortune 500: Companies that produce a 10-K are ranked 1 to 500 based on 1999 revenue
Forbes 500: Private companies are ranked 1 to 500 based on 1998 revenue
Source: Forbes, December 13, 1999; Fortune, April 17, 2000

HOTELS & MOTELS

Hotels/Motels

Area	Hotels/ Motels	Rooms	Luxury-Level Hotels/Motels		Average Minimum Rates ($)		
			♦♦♦♦	♦♦♦♦♦	♦♦	♦♦♦	♦♦♦♦
City	10	1,168	0	0	n/a	n/a	n/a
Airport	8	799	0	0	n/a	n/a	n/a
Total	18	1,967	0	0	n/a	n/a	n/a

Note: n/a not available; classifications range from one diamond (budget properties with basic amenities) to five diamond (luxury properties).
Source: OAG Business Travel Planner, Winter 1999-2000

Estimated Daily Food and Lodging Costs

Area	Food/Other ($/day)	Average Hotel Cost ($/day)
City	30	55
U.S.	30	55

Source: ERI's Relocation Assessor software database, quarterly effective date 4/1/2000

CONVENTION CENTERS

Convention Centers and Event Sites

Name	Guest Rooms	Meeting Space (sq. ft.)	Capacity (Theatre Style)

None listed in city
Source: EventSource.com, 3/15/2000

Living Environment

COST OF LIVING

Cost of Living: Homeowner

Cost Element	U.S. ($)	City ($)	Differential ($)	Percent of U.S. Average
Consumables	14,516	13,368	-1,148	92.1
Transportation	5,957	5,751	-206	96.5
Health Services	2,012	1,925	-87	95.7
Housing/Utilities/Prop. Tax	16,337	20,907	4,570	128.0
Income+Payroll Taxes	12,615	13,158	543	104.3
Miscellaneous	8,563	8,563	0	100.0
Total Cost of Living	60,000	63,672	3,672	106.1

Note: Figures are based on a single income, four person family with gross annual earnings of $60,000, owning an 1,800 square-foot home, and driving two automobiles worth $22,000 30,000 miles per year.
Source: ERI's Relocation Assessor software database, quarterly effective date 4/1/2000

Cost of Living: Renter

Cost Element	U.S. ($)	City ($)	Differential ($)	Percent of U.S. Average
Consumables	10,486	9,668	-818	92.2
Transportation	2,107	2,036	-71	96.6
Health Services	1,632	1,564	-68	95.8
Rent/Utilities/Insurance	9,299	9,186	-113	98.8
Income+Payroll Taxes	8,607	9,663	1,056	112.3
Miscellaneous	7,869	7,869	0	100.0
Total Cost of Living	40,000	39,986	-14	100.0

Note: Figures are based on a single income, three person family with gross annual earnings of $40,000, renting a 1,000 square-foot home, and driving one automobile worth $8,000 12,000 miles per year.
Source: ERI's Relocation Assessor software database, quarterly effective date 4/1/2000

HOUSING

Median Home Prices and Housing Affordability

Area	Median Price[2] 4th Qtr. 1999 ($)	HOI[3] 4th Qtr. 1999	Affordability Rank[4]
MSA[1]	n/a	n/a	n/a
U.S.	139,000	63.8	–

Note: (1) Metropolitan Statistical Area - see Appendix A for areas included; (2) U.S. figures calculated from the sales of 687,516 new and existing homes in 192 markets; (3) Housing Opportunity Index - percent of homes sold that were within the reach of the median income household at the prevailing mortgage interest rate; (4) Rank is from 1-192 with 1 being most affordable; n/a not available
Source: National Association of Home Builders, Housing Opportunity Index, 4th Quarter 1999

Estimated Home Price

Area	Price ($)
City	160,791
U.S.	135,855

Note: Figures are based on an 1,800 square-foot home
Source: ERI's Relocation Assessor software database, quarterly effective date 4/1/2000

Estimated Rent

Area	Rent ($/month)
City	649
U.S.	651

Note: Figures are based on a 1,000 square-foot home
Source: ERI's Relocation Assessor software database, quarterly effective date 4/1/2000

Median Home Price Projection

It is projected that the median home price in the metropolitan area will increase from $93,971 in 1999 to $131,971 in 2010, an increase of 40.4%
Kiplinger's Personal Finance Magazine, January 2000

RESIDENTIAL UTILITIES

Average Residential Utility Costs

Area	All Electric ($/mth)	Part Electric ($/mth)	Other Energy ($/mth)	Phone ($/mth)
City	–	47.01	42.56	16.90
U.S.	99.25	55.47	43.48	20.29

Source: ACCRA, Cost of Living Index, 3rd Quarter 1999

HEALTH CARE

Average Health Care Costs

Area	Hospital ($/day)	Doctor ($/visit)	Dentist ($/visit)
City	291.00	61.10	63.80
U.S.	440.96	53.83	68.42

Note: Hospital—based on a semi-private room; Doctor—based on a general practitioner's routine exam of an established patient; Dentist—based on adult teeth cleaning and periodic oral exam.
Source: ACCRA, Cost of Living Index, 3rd Quarter 1999

Distribution of Office-Based Physicians

Area	Family/Gen. Practitioners	Specialists		
		Medical	Surgical	Other
MSA[1]	104	147	141	147

Note: Data as of 12/31/97; (1) Metropolitan Statistical Area - see Appendix A for areas included
Source: American Medical Assn., Physician Characteristics & Distribution in the U.S., 1999

Hospitals

Appleton has 2 general medical and surgical hospitals.
AHA Guide to the Healthcare Field, 1999-2000

EDUCATION

Public School District Statistics

District Name	Num. Sch.	Enroll.	Classroom Teachers	Pupils per Teacher	Minority Pupils (%)	Current Exp.[1] ($/pupil)
Appleton Area Sch Dist	25	14,483	823	17.6	n/a	n/a

Note: Data covers the 1997-1998 school year unless otherwise noted; (1) Data covers fiscal year 1996; SD = School District; ISD = Independent School District; n/a not available
Source: National Center for Education Statistics, Common Core of Data Public Education Agency Universe 1997-98; National Center for Education Statistics, Characteristics of the 100 Largest Public Elementary and Secondary School Districts in the United States: 1997-98, July 1999

Educational Quality

School District	Education Quotient[1]	Graduate Outcome[2]	Community Index[3]	Resource Index[4]
Appleton Are School Dist.	135	145	122	117

Note: Over 1,000 secondary school districts were rated in terms of educational quality. The scores range from a low of 50 to a high of 150; (1) Combination of the Graduate Outcome, Community and Resource indexes weighted to reflect the greater importance of the Graduate Outcome and Resource Index; (2) Based on graduation rates and college board scores (SAT/ACT); (3) Based on the surrounding community's level of affluence and adult education; (4) Based on teacher salaries, per-pupil expenditures and student-teacher ratios.
Source: Expansion Management, Ratings Issue, 1999

Educational Attainment by Race

Area	High School Graduate (%)					Bachelor's Degree (%)				
	Total	White	Black	Other	Hisp.[2]	Total	White	Black	Other	Hisp.[2]
City	85.3	85.8	88.9	54.4	72.8	23.7	23.9	31.7	12.9	30.8
MSA[1]	80.9	81.2	71.4	64.4	58.9	17.0	17.0	16.5	17.1	12.1
U.S.	75.2	77.9	63.1	60.4	49.8	20.3	21.5	11.4	19.4	9.2

Note: Figures shown cover persons 25 years old and over; (1) Metropolitan Statistical Area - see Appendix A for areas included; (2) people of Hispanic origin can be of any race
Source: 1990 Census of Population and Housing, Summary Tape File 3C

School Enrollment by Type

Area	Preprimary				Elementary/High School			
	Public		Private		Public		Private	
	Enrollment	%	Enrollment	%	Enrollment	%	Enrollment	%
City	995	60.1	660	39.9	9,922	87.2	1,461	12.8
MSA[1]	4,525	62.4	2,731	37.6	46,429	85.0	8,182	15.0
U.S.	2,679,029	59.5	1,824,256	40.5	38,379,689	90.2	4,187,099	9.8

Note: Figures shown cover persons 3 years old and over;
(1) Metropolitan Statistical Area - see Appendix A for areas included
Source: 1990 Census of Population and Housing, Summary Tape File 3C

School Enrollment by Race

Area	Preprimary (%)				Elementary/High School (%)			
	White	Black	Other	Hisp.[1]	White	Black	Other	Hisp.[1]
City	97.3	0.3	2.4	1.3	93.6	0.7	5.7	1.4
MSA[2]	96.2	0.3	3.5	0.8	96.3	0.3	3.4	1.2
U.S.	80.4	12.5	7.1	7.8	74.1	15.6	10.3	12.5

Note: Figures shown cover persons 3 years old and over; (1) people of Hispanic origin can be of any race; (2) Metropolitan Statistical Area - see Appendix A for areas included
Source: 1990 Census of Population and Housing, Summary Tape File 3C

Higher Education

Two-Year Colleges		Four-Year Colleges		Medical Schools	Law Schools	Voc/ Tech
Public	Private	Public	Private			
1	0	0	1	0	0	5

Source: College Blue Book, Occupational Education, 1999; Medical School Admission Requirements, 1999-2000; Peterson's Guide to Two-Year Colleges, 2000; Peterson's Guide to Four-Year Colleges, 1999; Barron's Guide to Law Schools, 1999

MAJOR EMPLOYERS

Major Employers

Aid Association for Lutherans	Anchor Food Products
Appleton Medical Center	Fox Valley Corp. (paper mills)
Great Northern Corp. (boxes)	Miller Electric Manufacturing
Pierce Manufacturing	Riverside Paper Corp. (paper mills)
St. Elizabeth Hospital	

Note: Companies listed are located in the city
Source: D&B Business Rankings, 1999; Ward's Business Directory, 1999; America's Corporate Families, 1999

PUBLIC SAFETY

Crime Rate

Area	All Crimes	Violent Crimes				Property Crimes		
		Murder	Forcible Rape	Robbery	Aggrav. Assault	Burglary	Larceny -Theft	Motor Vehicle Theft
City	2,987.4	0.0	16.9	24.0	56.5	404.0	2,344.7	141.2
Suburbs[1]	2,723.2	0.7	14.8	7.0	74.7	371.1	2,135.1	119.8
MSA[2]	2,778.0	0.6	15.2	10.5	70.9	377.9	2,178.6	124.2
U.S.	4,930.0	6.8	35.9	186.3	382.3	919.4	2,893.4	506.0

Note: Crime rate is the number of crimes per 100,000 population; (1) Defined as all areas within the Metropolitan Statistical Area but located outside the central city; (2) Metropolitan Statistical Area - see Appendix A for areas included
Source: FBI Uniform Crime Reports, 1997

RECREATION

Culture and Recreation

Museums	Symphony Orchestras	Opera Companies	Dance Companies	Professional Theatres	Zoos	Pro Sports Teams
2	1	0	0	1	0	0

Source: Musical America, International Directory of the Performing Arts, 1999; Official Museum Directory, 2000; Stern's Performing Arts Directory, 1997; USA Today Four Sport Stadium Guide, 1997; Career Opportunities in Theatre and the Performing Arts, 1999

Library System

The Appleton Public Library has no branches, holdings of 253,645 volumes, and a budget of $2,730,340 (1997-1998).
American Library Directory, 1999-2000

MEDIA

Newspapers

Name	Type	Freq.	Distribution	Circulation
Packerland Trader	General	1x/wk	Area	30,000
The Post-Crescent	General	7x/wk	Area	58,200

Note: Includes newspapers with circulations of 200 or more located in the city;
Source: Burrelle's Media Directory, 1999 Edition

Television Stations

Name	Ch.	Affiliation	Type	Owner

No stations listed.
Note: Stations included broadcast in the Appleton metro area; n/a not available
Source: Burrelle's Media Directory, 1999 Edition

AM Radio Stations

Call Letters	Freq. (kHz)	Target Audience	Station Format	Music Format
WJOK	1050	General	S	n/a
WHBY	1150	General	T	n/a

Note: Stations included broadcast in the Appleton metro area; n/a not available
Target Audience: A=Asian; B=Black; C=Christian; E=Ethnic; F=French; G=General; H=Hispanic; M=Men; N=Native American; R=Religious; S=Senior Citizen; W=Women; Y=Young Adult; Z=Children
Station Format: E=Educational; M=Music; N=News; S=Sports; T=Talk
Source: Burrelle's Media Directory, 1999 Edition

FM Radio Stations

Call Letters	Freq. (mHz)	Target Audience	Station Format	Music Format
WLFM	91.1	General	M	n/a
WEMY	91.5	Religious	M/N/S/T	Christian
WEMI	91.9	Religious	M/N/S/T	Christian
WOZZ	93.5	General	M/N/T	Classic Rock
WNCY	100.3	General	M	Country
WEXT	104.7	General	n/a	n/a
WAPL	105.7	General	M	AOR/Top 40

Note: Stations included broadcast in the Appleton metro area; n/a not available
Station Format: E=Educational; M=Music; N=News; S=Sports; T=Talk
Target Audience: A=Asian; B=Black; C=Christian; E=Ethnic; F=French; G=General; H=Hispanic; M=Men; N=Native American; R=Religious; S=Senior Citizen; W=Women; Y=Young Adult; Z=Children
Music Format: AOR=Album Oriented Rock; MOR=Middle-of-the-Road
Source: Burrelle's Media Directory, 1999 Edition

WEATHER

Temperature/Precipitation/Humidity

	Jan	Feb	Mar	Apr	May	Jun	Jul	Aug	Sep	Oct	Nov	Dec	Yr.
Max. High Temp. (°F)	57	62	83	86	104	102	107	102	99	89	78	60	107
Avg. High Temp. (°F)	27	29	38	55	68	78	84	82	73	61	43	30	56
Avg. Temp. (°F)	18	20	29	44	57	67	72	71	62	51	35	22	46
Avg. Low Temp. (°F)	10	11	21	34	46	57	61	60	51	41	27	15	36
Min. Low Temp. (°F)	-32	-34	-18	5	23	30	41	32	25	8	-8	-26	-34
Avg. Precip. (in.)	1.3	1.2	1.7	2.7	3.3	4.0	3.3	3.0	3.3	2.1	1.9	1.3	29.1
Avg. Snowfall (in.)	7.6	8.8	8.5	2.1	0.3	0	0	0	0	0.1	4.2	7.9	39.5
Avg. Rel. Hum. (%)	75	76	74	69	68	72	73	76	75	75	75	78	74

Source: National Climatic Data Center, International Station Meteorological Climate Summary, 3/95

Weather Conditions

Temperature			Precipitation		
0°F & below	32°F & below	90°F & above	0.1 inch or more precip.	1.5 inch or more snow/ice	Thunder-storms
25	164	9	57	9	37

Note: Figures are average number of days per year
Source: National Climatic Data Center, International Station Meteorological Climate Summary, 3/95

AIR & WATER QUALITY

Maximum Pollutant Concentrations

	Particulate Matter (ug/m³)	Carbon Monoxide (ppm)	Sulfur Dioxide (ppm)	Nitrogen Dioxide (ppm)	Ozone (ppm)	Lead (ug/m³)
MSA[1] Level	n/a	n/a	n/a	n/a	0.09	n/a
NAAQS[2]	150	9	0.140	0.053	0.12	1.50
Met NAAQS	n/a	n/a	n/a	n/a	Yes	n/a

Note: (1) Metropolitan Statistical Area - see Appendix A for areas included; (2) National Ambient Air Quality Standards; ppm = parts per million; ug/m³ = micrograms per cubic meter; n/a not available
Source: EPA, National Air Quality and Emissions Trends Report, 1997

Pollutant Standards Index

Data not available.
EPA, National Air Quality and Emissions Trends Report, 1997

Drinking Water

Water System Name	Pop. Served	Primary Water Source Type	Number of Violations in 1998-99	Type of Violation/ Contaminants
Appleton Waterworks	70,001	Surface	None	None

Note: Data as of January 19, 2000
Source: EPA, Office of Ground Water and Drinking Water, Safe Drinking Water Information System

Appleton tap water is neutral, soft, and fluoridated.
Editor & Publisher Market Guide, 2000

Asheville, North Carolina

Background

Asheville, North Carolina is located in western North Carolina about 120 miles west of Charlotte and 115 miles southeast of Knoxville, Tennessee. The city is situated in a mountainous region of the state on a plateau approximately 2,200 feet above sea level. It is on the French Broad and Swannanoa rivers, and close to the Great Smoky Mountain National Park, the Blue Ridge Parkway and several other national forests and parks.

Asheville is the county seat of Buncombe County and a regional commercial and services center for the western section of North Carolina. With its scenic location, diverse culture and other amenities, Asheville is a popular resort area and has gained high rankings for its quality of life. Asheville and Buncombe County are among the most rapidly growing regions in North Carolina.

The mountains of western North Carolina were occupied by numerous Native American peoples prior to European colonization. Cherokees were among the dominant tribes at the time of white settlement. Buncombe County was established in 1791. Asheville is named for Samuel Ashe, North Carolina's governor from 1796-1798. The site developed from a small settlement in the 18th and early 19th Centuries to a regional transportation and commerce center due to western migration.

The region's economy was based on a mix of tobacco and foods, forest products and manufacturing. Asheville was incorporated as a city in 1883 and experienced significant growth in the latter 19th Century, following the creation, in 1880, of a railroad stop in the city. The Asheville area also gained prominence for resorts and health facilities. The Depression of the 1930s brought economic decline, but the economy improved in the latter 20th Century, and the city benefited from the national migration to the Sunbelt.

Manufacturing and health care are leading contemporary economic sectors, along with retail, construction and services. In addition to traditional industries, Asheville has attracted new technology-based operations, for products such as plastics and electronics. Tourism is also an important contributor to the region's economy.

The amenities and lifestyle of the city and surrounding area have also helped attract new residents and industries. Asheville is near large wilderness and recreational areas. Among the area's venues for concerts and events is the Asheville Civic Center and the Asheville Community Theater for smaller events. One regional theme of cultural activity is preservation of traditional arts and crafts of the southern Appalachian mountains. Asheville supports contemporary and classical arts and music, as well as an alternative community. Revitalization of the downtown and historic neighborhoods were a priority in the 1980s and 1990s. Asheville and nearby areas feature numerous distinctive buildings and properties. The skyline of downtown Asheville is noted for several Art Deco buildings designed by Douglas Ellington, including the 1928 City Hall.

One of the area's most famous nearby landmarks is the 255-room Biltmore Estate, a mansion built by George Vandervilt on sprawling property. Biltmore's mansion was completed in 1895 and is now a museum. Asheville was the hometown of the early 20th Century novelist Thomas Wolfe. His works, such as Look Homeward Angel, include fictionalized but autobiographical depictions of his memories of his boyhood home and Asheville of that era. His family home is now a museum.

Institutions of higher education in or near the city include the Asheville campus of the University of North Carolina, Asheville Buncombe Technical Community College and Warren Wilson College, among others.

Asheville has an elected Mayor and six-member City Council.

General Rankings and Evaluative Comments

- Asheville was ranked #113 out of 354 metropolitan areas in *Places Rated Almanac*. Criteria: cost of living, climate, crime, transportation, job outlook, education, the arts, health care, and recreation. *Places Rated Almanac, Millennium Edition, 2000*

- Asheville was selected as one of North America's "Best Small Metro Areas" (population under 250,000). The area ranked #8 out of 20. Criteria: cost of living, climate, crime, transportation, job outlook, education, the arts, health care, and recreation. *Places Rated Almanac, Millennium Edition, 2000*

- Asheville was selected as one of America's best places to retire. Criteria: safety, climate, housing, culture and recreation, social compatibility, affordability, medical care, transportation, and jobs and/or volunteer opportunities. *Where to Retire: America's Best and Most Affordable Places, 1998*

- Asheville was selected as one of the best places to retire by *Retirement Places Rated*. Criteria: cost of living, climate, crime, services, working, and leisure living. The city was ranked #35 out of 187. *Retirement Places Rated, 1999*

- Asheville was selected as one of "America's Best Towns to Raise an Outdoor Family" by *Outdoor Explorer* magazine. Criteria: easy access to the outdoors, quality education and health care, affordable housing, favorable employment opportunities, and low crime rates. The city was ranked #14 out of 25. *Outdoor Explorer, Summer 1999*

- Cognetics studied 273 metro areas in the United States, ranking them by entrepreneurial activity. Asheville was ranked #73 out of 134 smaller metro areas. Criteria: Significant Starts (firms started in the last 10 years that still employ at least 5 people) and Young Growers (percent of firms 10 years old or less that grew significantly during the last 4 years). *Cognetics, "Entrepreneurial Hot Spots: The Best Places in America to Start and Grow a Company," 1999*

- Asheville was selected as one of the "hottest cities" for expanding or relocating companies. The city ranked #43 out of 50. Criteria: business climate, work force quality, operating costs, incentive programs, and ease of working with local officials. *Expansion Management, January 2000*

- Asheville was selected as one of "The 50 Most Alive Places to Live" in the U.S. Criteria: ethnic diversity, recreational options, cultural vitality, low crime rate, opportunities for lifelong learning, good hospitals and restaurants, public transportation, walking accessibility, civic activities, and the kitsch factor. The area was ranked #1 out of 10 in the "Small Towns" category. *Modern Maturity, May-June 2000*

Business Environment

STATE ECONOMY

State Economic Profile

"In spite of declines in textiles and apparels, North Carolina has seen impressive job growth in the last few years. As North Carolina continues to diversify its economy away from its traditional manufacturing base and toward its newer high-tech and financial services sectors, job growth will outpace the nation for a number of years to come, albeit at a slightly slower rate than those seen in 1997 and 1998.

Raleigh-Durham has been and will continue to be one of North Carolina's growth engines. High-tech firms in the Research Triangle Park have expanded employment considerably. Cisco Systems, for one, is planning to expand its operations, adding as many as 4,000 jobs over the next three years. Raleigh's housing market has more than doubled in size during the 1990s. Price appreciation has been strong, although homes still remain affordable.

North Carolina's other hot spot has been Charlotte. While many parts of the country have been hurt by consolidation in the financial services industry, many of these jobs have made their way to Charlotte. As this wave of consolidation has slowed, so has job growth in Charlotte, reflected in its 0.6% job growth rate in 1998, far below that of previous years. Continued restructuring in North Carolina's textiles, apparel and furniture industries will slow job growth in the Charlotte area.

The outlook for North Carolina, while a slowdown from its recent pace, is still one of impressive job growth, far outpacing the nation. With its business friendly atmosphere and the decision of Federal Express to locate its Mid-Atlantic hub here, North Carolina will likely attract more corporate relocations. Its affordable housing markets and overall high quality of life will also attract residents, helping fuel job growth." *National Association of Realtors, Economic Profiles: The Fifty States and the District of Columbia, http://nar.realtor.com/databank/profiles.htm*

EXPORTS

Total Export Sales

Area	1995 ($000)	1996 ($000)	1997 ($000)	1998 ($000)	% Chg. 1995-98	% Chg. 1997-98
MSA[1]	185,185	236,684	294,162	232,955	25.8	-20.8
U.S.	583,030,524	622,827,063	687,597,999	680,474,251	16.7	-1.0

Note: (1) Metropolitan Statistical Area - see Appendix A for areas included
Source: U.S. Department of Commerce, International Trade Association, Metropolitan Area Exports: An Export Performance Report on Over 250 U.S. Cities, November 10, 1999

CITY FINANCES

City Government Finances

Component	1995 ($million)	1995 (per capita $)
Revenue	61.8	960
Expenditure	57.9	900
Debt Outstanding	65.0	1,011

Source: 1999 County and City Extra, Annual Metro, City, and County Data Book

City Government Revenue by Source

Source	1995 ($million)	1995 (per capita $)
Intergovernmental	21.2	329
Taxes	22.7	354
Property	19.9	310
Sales and Gross Receipts	0.4	7

Source: 1999 County and City Extra, Annual Metro, City, and County Data Book

City Government Expenditures by Function

Function	1995 ($million)	1995 (per capita $)	1995 (%)
Public Welfare	<0.1	<1	0.1
Highways	8.1	126	14.1
Parking Facilities	0.7	11	1.3
Education	0.0	0	0.0
Health and Hospitals	<0.1	<1	0.1
Police Protection	9.6	149	16.6
Sewerage and Sanitation	10.2	159	17.7
Parks and Recreation	6.7	105	11.7
Housing and Community Development	2.5	39	4.4
Interest on Debt	1.3	21	2.4

Source: 1999 County and City Extra, Annual Metro, City, and County Data Book

Municipal Bond Ratings

Area	Moody's
City	Aaa

Source: Mergent Bond Record, 2/2000

POPULATION

Population Growth

Area	1980 Census	1990 Census	1999 Estimate	2004 Projection	Population Growth (%) 1990-1999	Population Growth (%) 1999-2004
City	53,583	61,654	61,411	61,982	-0.4	0.9
MSA[1]	177,761	174,821	215,427	228,130	23.2	5.9
U.S.	226,545,805	248,765,170	272,212,864	283,625,312	9.4	4.2

Note: (1) Metropolitan Statistical Area - see Appendix A for areas included
Source: 1990 Census of Population and Housing, Summary Tape File 3C; Claritas, Inc.

Number of Households and Average Household Size

Area	1980 Census	1990 Census	1999 Estimate	2004 Projection	1999 Average Household Size
City	24,828	26,890	26,989	27,396	2.28
MSA[1]	66,117	70,755	87,142	92,712	2.47
U.S.	80,389,592	91,993,582	102,048,200	107,302,392	2.67

Note: (1) Metropolitan Statistical Area - see Appendix A for areas included
Source: 1990 Census of Population and Housing, Summary Tape File 3C; Claritas, Inc.

Race/Ethnicity of City Population

Race/Ethnicity	1990 Census Population	1990 Census %	1999 Estimate Population	1999 Estimate %	% Change 1990-1999
White, Non-Hispanic	48,447	78.6	45,963	74.8	-5.1
Black, Non-Hispanic	12,144	19.7	13,426	21.9	10.6
Asian, Non-Hispanic	365	0.6	609	1.0	66.8
Other, Non-Hispanic	170	0.3	203	0.3	19.4
Hispanic	528	0.9	1,210	2.0	129.2

Source: 1990 Census of Population and Housing, Summary Tape File 3C; Claritas, Inc.

Race/Ethnicity of Metropolitan Statistical Area Population

Race/Ethnicity	1990 Census		1999 Estimate		% Change 1990-1999
	Population	%	Population	%	
White, Non-Hispanic	158,154	90.5	193,867	90.0	22.6
Black, Non-Hispanic	14,027	8.0	16,458	7.6	17.3
Asian, Non-Hispanic	917	0.5	1,365	0.6	48.9
Other, Non-Hispanic	562	0.3	744	0.3	32.4
Hispanic	1,161	0.7	2,993	1.4	157.8

Note: See Appendix A for areas included in the Metropolitan Statistical Area
Source: 1990 Census of Population and Housing, Summary Tape File 3C; Claritas, Inc.

Ancestry

Area	German	Irish	English	Italian	U.S.	French	Polish	Dutch
City	16.8	16.1	17.6	1.9	6.7	3.2	1.0	3.1
MSA[1]	18.1	18.0	19.3	1.8	10.5	3.1	0.9	3.7
U.S.	23.3	15.6	13.1	5.9	5.3	4.2	3.8	2.5

Note: Figures are percentages and include persons that reported multiple ancestry (eg. if a person reported being Irish and Italian, they were included in both columns); (1) Metropolitan Statistical Area - see Appendix A for areas included
Source: 1990 Census of Population and Housing, Summary Tape File 3C

Median Age

Area	1990 Census	1999 Estimate
City	37.9	40.1
MSA[1]	36.7	39.5
U.S.	32.9	35.7

Note: (1) Metropolitan Statistical Area - see Appendix A for areas included
Source: 1990 Census of Population and Housing, Summary Tape File 3C; Claritas, Inc.

Male/Female Population

Area	Number of Males		Number of Females		Males per 100 Females	
	1990	1999	1990	1999	1990	1999
City	27,905	28,093	33,749	33,318	82.7	84.3
MSA[1]	82,894	102,682	91,927	112,745	90.2	91.1
U.S.	121,172,379	132,803,736	127,537,494	139,409,136	95.0	95.3

Note: (1) Metropolitan Statistical Area - see Appendix A for areas included
Source: 1990 Census of Population, General Population Characteristics; Claritas, Inc.

INCOME

Per Capita/Median/Average Income

Area	Per Capita ($)			Median Household ($)			Average Household ($)		
	1989	1999	% Chg.	1989	1999	% Chg.	1989	1999	% Chg.
City	13,079	19,970	52.7	22,267	30,848	38.5	29,067	43,105	48.3
MSA[1]	13,211	19,915	50.7	25,847	35,787	38.5	32,131	48,105	49.7
U.S.	14,420	21,350	48.1	30,056	40,525	34.8	38,453	56,184	46.1

Note: (1) Metropolitan Statistical Area - see Appendix A for areas included; 1989 data is from the 1990 Census; 1999 data is estimated by Claritas, Inc.
Source: 1990 Census of Population, General Population Characteristics; Claritas, Inc.

Household Income Distribution

Area	Percent of Households Earning								
	Under $5,000	$5,000 -14,999	$15,000 -24,999	$25,000 -34,999	$35,000 -49,999	$50,000 -74,999	$75,000 -99,000	$100,000 -149,999	$150,000 and up
City	5.4	18.4	17.8	13.8	16.8	15.9	6.0	3.6	2.3
MSA[1]	4.2	14.9	15.7	14.1	18.2	18.7	7.3	4.3	2.6
U.S.	3.9	13.3	13.8	12.6	16.2	19.4	9.7	6.6	4.6

Note: Data as of 1999; (1) Metropolitan Statistical Area - see Appendix A for areas included
Source: Claritas, Inc.

Effective Buying Income

Area	Per Capita ($)	Median Household ($)	Average Household ($)
City	16,013	27,593	36,114
MSA[1]	16,409	31,670	39,817
U.S.	17,496	36,603	47,036

Note: Data as of 1/1/2000; (1) Metropolitan Statistical Area - see Appendix A for areas included
Source: Standard Rate & Data Service, Newspaper Advertising Source, March 2000

Effective Household Buying Income Distribution

Area	% of Households Earning						
	$10,000 -$19,999	$20,000 -$34,999	$35,000 -$49,999	$50,000 -$74,999	$75,000 -$99,000	$100,000 -$124,999	$125,000 and up
City	20.4	24.4	17.6	13.7	4.4	1.4	1.8
MSA[1]	17.5	24.8	19.2	16.8	5.4	1.7	1.8
U.S.	15.0	21.6	17.6	19.6	8.4	3.0	3.3

Note: Data as of 1/1/2000; (1) Metropolitan Statistical Area - see Appendix A for areas included
Source: Standard Rate & Data Service, Newspaper Advertising Source, March 2000

Poverty Rates by Age

Area	People of All Ages	People Under 18 Years Old	Related Children Age 5-17 in Families in Poverty
City	17.5	n/a	n/a
County	12.2	18.9	16.6
U.S.	13.8	20.8	18.7

Note: Figures show the percent of people living below the poverty line in 1995. The average poverty threshold was $15,569 for a family of four in 1995; n/a not available
Source: Bureau of the Census, Small Area Income and Poverty Estimates Program; U.S. Department of Housing and Urban Development

EMPLOYMENT

Labor Force and Employment

Area	Civilian Labor Force			Workers Employed		
	Dec. 1998	Dec. 1999	% Chg.	Dec. 1998	Dec. 1999	% Chg.
City	34,193	34,379	0.5	33,329	33,583	0.8
MSA[1]	111,383	112,141	0.7	109,275	110,105	0.8
U.S.	138,297,000	139,941,000	1.2	132,732,000	134,696,000	1.5

Note: Data is not seasonally adjusted and covers workers 16 years of age and older;
(1) Metropolitan Statistical Area - see Appendix A for areas included
Source: Bureau of Labor Statistics, http://stats.bls.gov

Unemployment Rate

Area	1999											
	Jan.	Feb.	Mar.	Apr.	May	Jun.	Jul.	Aug.	Sep.	Oct.	Nov.	Dec.
City	3.8	3.8	3.1	2.5	2.8	2.7	2.9	2.8	2.3	2.4	2.5	2.3
MSA[1]	2.9	2.9	2.4	1.9	2.1	2.0	2.2	2.1	1.7	1.8	1.9	1.8
U.S.	4.8	4.7	4.4	4.1	4.0	4.5	4.5	4.2	4.1	3.8	3.8	3.7

Note: Data is not seasonally adjusted and covers workers 16 years of age and older; all figures are percentages; (1) Metropolitan Statistical Area - see Appendix A for areas included
Source: Bureau of Labor Statistics, http://stats.bls.gov

Employment by Industry

Sector	MSA[1]		U.S.
	Number of Employees	Percent of Total	Percent of Total
Services	35,000	30.8	30.2
Retail Trade	22,500	19.8	18.1
Government	16,500	14.5	15.8
Manufacturing	18,300	16.1	14.1
Finance/Insurance/Real Estate	4,100	3.6	5.9
Wholesale Trade	4,900	4.3	5.4
Transportation/Public Utilities	5,300	4.7	5.3
Construction	n/a	n/a	4.8
Mining	n/a	n/a	0.4

Note: Figures cover non-farm employment as of 12/99 and are not seasonally adjusted; (1) Metropolitan Statistical Area - see Appendix A for areas included; n/a not available
Source: Bureau of Labor Statistics, http://stats.bls.gov

Employment by Occupation

Occupation Category	City (%)	MSA[1] (%)	U.S. (%)
White Collar	58.8	54.1	58.1
Executive/Admin./Management	11.7	11.1	12.3
Professional	15.9	13.3	14.1
Technical & Related Support	3.5	3.6	3.7
Sales	14.1	12.6	11.8
Administrative Support/Clerical	13.5	13.5	16.3
Blue Collar	24.0	30.8	26.2
Precision Production/Craft/Repair	8.7	13.1	11.3
Machine Operators/Assem./Insp.	8.2	9.8	6.8
Transportation/Material Movers	3.2	4.1	4.1
Cleaners/Helpers/Laborers	3.8	3.8	3.9
Services	16.1	13.2	13.2
Farming/Forestry/Fishing	1.1	1.9	2.5

Note: Figures cover workers 16 years of age and older; (1) Metropolitan Statistical Area - see Appendix A for areas included
Source: 1990 Census of Population and Housing, Summary Tape File 3C

Occupational Employment Projections: 1996 - 2006

Occupations Expected to Have the Largest Job Growth (ranked by numerical growth)	Fast-Growing Occupations[1] (ranked by percent growth)
1. Cashiers	1. Occupational therapy assistants
2. Registered nurses	2. Computer engineers
3. General managers & top executives	3. Database administrators
4. Nursing aides/orderlies/attendants	4. Systems analysts
5. Salespersons, retail	5. Physical therapy assistants and aides
6. Child care workers, private household	6. Physical therapists
7. Food service workers	7. Occupational therapists
8. Marketing & sales, supervisors	8. Home health aides
9. Janitors/cleaners/maids, ex. priv. hshld.	9. Desktop publishers
10. Truck drivers, light	10. Respiratory therapists

Note: Projections cover North Carolina; (1) Excludes occupations with total job growth less than 300
Source: U.S. Department of Labor, Employment and Training Administration, America's Labor Market Information System (ALMIS)

Average Wages

Occupation	$/Hr.	Occupation	$/Hr.
Accountants and Auditors	18.29	Maids and Housekeepers	7.00
Assemblers and Fabricators	9.82	Maintenance Repairers	11.41
Automotive Mechanics	11.09	Marketing/Advertising/PR Managers	23.83
Bookkeepers	10.27	Nurses, Licensed Practical	12.75
Carpenters	10.85	Nurses, Registered	-
Cashiers	6.94	Nursing Aides/Orderlies/Attendants	7.86
Clerks, General Office	9.11	Physicians and Surgeons	41.45
Clerks, Shipping/Receiving/Traffic	10.63	Receptionists/Information Clerks	8.47
Computer Programmers	20.03	Sales Reps., Exc. Scientific/Retail	14.49
Computer Support Specialists	16.20	Sales Reps., Scientific, Exc. Retail	17.62
Cooks, Restaurant	7.69	Salespersons, Retail	8.58
Electricians	13.27	Secretaries, Except Legal/Medical	10.05
Financial Managers	25.82	Stock Clerks, Sales Floor	8.03
First-Line Supervisors/Mgrs., Sales	14.28	Systems Analysts	23.39
Food Preparation Workers	6.67	Teacher Aides	7.24
General Managers/Top Executives	27.55	Teachers, Elementary School	15.27
Guards	7.31	Teachers, Secondary School	15.37
Hand Packers	8.60	Telemarketers	-
Janitors and Cleaners	7.84	Truck Drivers, Heavy/Tractor-Trailer	15.43
Laborers, Landscaping	8.71	Truck Drivers, Light	10.03
Lawyers	27.93	Waiters and Waitresses	5.66

Note: Wage data is for 1998 and covers the Metropolitan Statistical Area (see Appendix A for areas included). Hourly wages for elementary and secondary school teachers were calculated by the editors from annual wage data assuming a 40 hour work week; Dashes indicate that data was not available.
Source: Bureau of Labor Statistics, 1998 Metropolitan Area Occupational Employment and Wage Estimates

TAXES

Major State and Local Tax Rates

State Corporate Income (%)	State Personal Income (%)	Residential Property (%)	Sales & Use		State Gasoline (cents/ gallon)	State Cigarette (cents/ pack)
			State (%)	Local (%)		
6.9[a]	6.0 - 7.75	1.51	4.0	2.0	22.25[b]	5.0

Note: Personal/corporate income, sales, gasoline and cigarette tax rates as of January 2000.
Property tax rates as of April 2000; (a) Financial institutions are also subject to a tax equal to $30 per one million in assets; (b) Rate is comprised of 22 cents excise and 0.25 cents motor carrier tax
Source: Federation of Tax Administrators, www.taxadmin.org; ERI's Relocation Assessor software database, quarterly effective date 4/1/2000

Total Taxes Per Capita and as a Percent of Income

Area	Per Capita Income ($)	Per Capita Taxes ($)			Percent of Income (%)		
		Total	Federal	State/Local	Total	Federal	State/Local
North Carolina	26,549	8,937	6,132	2,805	33.7	23.1	10.6
U.S.	28,878	10,298	7,026	3,273	35.7	24.3	11.3

Note: Figures are for 1999
Source: Tax Foundation, www.taxfoundation.org

COMMERCIAL UTILITIES

Typical Monthly Electric Bills

Area	Commercial Service ($/month)		Industrial Service ($/month)	
	12 kW demand 1,500 kWh	100 kW demand 30,000 kWh	1,000 kW demand 400,000 kWh	20,000 kW demand 10,000,000 kWh
City	128	1,667	24,794	421,160
U.S.	150	2,174	23,995	508,569

Note: Based on rates in effect January 1, 1999
Source: Edison Electric Institute, Typical Residential, Commercial and Industrial Bills, Winter 1999

TRANSPORTATION

Transportation Statistics

Average minutes to work (1990)	15.9
Interstate highways	I-26; I-40; I-240; US-19; US-23; US-25; US-70; US-74
Bus lines	
In-city (1998)	Asheville Transit Authority, 12 buses
Inter-city (1999)	1
Passenger air service	
Airport	Asheville Regional
Airlines (1999)	4
Enplaned passengers (1998)	284,239
Amtrak service	No
Motor freight carriers (1999)	40+
Major waterways/ports	None

Source: FAA DOT/TSC CY1998 ACAIS Database; National Transit Database, 1998; Editor & Publisher Market Guide, 2000; Amtrak National Time Table, Fall 1999/Winter 2000; 1990 Census of Population and Housing, STF 3C; Jane's Urban Transport Systems 1999-2000

Means of Transportation to Work

Area	Car/Truck/Van		Public Transportation			Bicycle	Walked	Other Means	Worked at Home
	Drove Alone	Car-pooled	Bus	Subway	Railroad				
City	79.4	11.9	2.6	0.0	0.0	0.2	3.0	1.0	1.9
MSA[1]	80.2	12.9	1.0	0.0	0.0	0.1	2.3	0.8	2.7
U.S.	73.2	13.4	3.0	1.5	0.5	0.4	3.9	1.2	3.0

Note: Figures shown are percentages and only include workers 16 years of age and older;
(1) Metropolitan Statistical Area - see Appendix A for areas included
Source: 1990 Census of Population and Housing, Summary Tape File 3C

BUSINESSES

Major Business Headquarters

Company Name	1999 Rankings	
	Fortune 500	Forbes 500
No companies listed	-	-

Note: Companies listed are located in the city; dashes indicate no ranking
Fortune 500: Companies that produce a 10-K are ranked 1 to 500 based on 1999 revenue
Forbes 500: Private companies are ranked 1 to 500 based on 1998 revenue
Source: Forbes, December 13, 1999; Fortune, April 17, 2000

HOTELS & MOTELS

Hotels/Motels

Area	Hotels/ Motels	Rooms	Luxury-Level Hotels/Motels		Average Minimum Rates ($)		
			♦♦♦♦	♦♦♦♦♦	♦♦	♦♦♦	♦♦♦♦
City	41	3,852	0	0	55	97	n/a
Airport	2	210	0	0	n/a	n/a	n/a
Suburbs	1	125	0	0	n/a	n/a	n/a
Total	44	4,187	0	0	n/a	n/a	n/a

Note: n/a not available; classifications range from one diamond (budget properties with basic amenities) to five diamond (luxury properties).
Source: OAG Business Travel Planner, Winter 1999-2000

Estimated Daily Food and Lodging Costs

Area	Food/Other ($/day)	Average Hotel Cost ($/day)
City	30	55
U.S.	30	55

Source: ERI's Relocation Assessor software database, quarterly effective date 4/1/2000

CONVENTION CENTERS

Convention Centers and Event Sites

Name	Guest Rooms	Meeting Space (sq. ft.)	Capacity (Theatre Style)
Asheville Civic Center	n/a	n/a	7,654
Great Smokies Holiday Inn Resort Sunspree	276	n/a	1,000
Great Smokies Holiday Inn SunSpree	280	10,000	800
Grove Park Inn Resort	510	51,200	2,000
Haywood Park Hotel	33	n/a	150
Holiday Inn Asheville	131	n/a	180
Holiday Inn Asheville Airport	150	n/a	400
Holiday Inn East	111	n/a	200
Holiday Inn West	225	n/a	260
Quality Inn Biltmore	160	n/a	140
Radisson Hotel Asheville	156	n/a	320

Note: n/a not available
Source: EventSource.com, 3/15/2000

Living Environment

COST OF LIVING

Cost of Living: Homeowner

Cost Element	U.S. ($)	City ($)	Differential ($)	Percent of U.S. Average
Consumables	14,516	14,085	-431	97.0
Transportation	5,957	5,930	-27	99.5
Health Services	2,012	1,918	-94	95.3
Housing/Utilities/Prop. Tax	16,337	22,789	6,452	139.5
Income+Payroll Taxes	12,615	12,486	-129	99.0
Miscellaneous	8,563	8,563	0	100.0
Total Cost of Living	60,000	65,771	5,771	109.6

Note: Figures are based on a single income, four person family with gross annual earnings of $60,000, owning an 1,800 square-foot home, and driving two automobiles worth $22,000 30,000 miles per year.
Source: ERI's Relocation Assessor software database, quarterly effective date 4/1/2000

Cost of Living: Renter

Cost Element	U.S. ($)	City ($)	Differential ($)	Percent of U.S. Average
Consumables	10,486	10,221	-265	97.5
Transportation	2,107	2,107	0	100.0
Health Services	1,632	1,563	-69	95.8
Rent/Utilities/Insurance	9,299	9,866	567	106.1
Income+Payroll Taxes	8,607	9,217	610	107.1
Miscellaneous	7,869	7,869	0	100.0
Total Cost of Living	40,000	40,843	843	102.1

Note: Figures are based on a single income, three person family with gross annual earnings of $40,000, renting a 1,000 square-foot home, and driving one automobile worth $8,000 12,000 miles per year.
Source: ERI's Relocation Assessor software database, quarterly effective date 4/1/2000

HOUSING

Median Home Prices and Housing Affordability

Area	Median Price[2] 4th Qtr. 1999 ($)	HOI[3] 4th Qtr. 1999	Affordability Rank[4]
MSA[1]	127,000	56.3	145
U.S.	139,000	63.8	–

Note: (1) Metropolitan Statistical Area - see Appendix A for areas included; (2) U.S. figures calculated from the sales of 687,516 new and existing homes in 192 markets; (3) Housing Opportunity Index - percent of homes sold that were within the reach of the median income household at the prevailing mortgage interest rate; (4) Rank is from 1-192 with 1 being most affordable
Source: National Association of Home Builders, Housing Opportunity Index, 4th Quarter 1999

Estimated Home Price

Area	Price ($)
City	198,803
U.S.	135,855

Note: Figures are based on an 1,800 square-foot home
Source: ERI's Relocation Assessor software database, quarterly effective date 4/1/2000

Estimated Rent

Area	Rent ($/month)
City	693
U.S.	651

Note: Figures are based on a 1,000 square-foot home
Source: ERI's Relocation Assessor software database, quarterly effective date 4/1/2000

Median Home Price Projection

It is projected that the median home price in the metropolitan area will increase from $128,952 in 1999 to $194,987 in 2010, an increase of 51.2%
Kiplinger's Personal Finance Magazine, January 2000

RESIDENTIAL UTILITIES

Average Residential Utility Costs

Area	All Electric ($/mth)	Part Electric ($/mth)	Other Energy ($/mth)	Phone ($/mth)
City	97.36	–	–	16.56
U.S.	99.25	55.47	43.48	20.29

Source: ACCRA, Cost of Living Index, 3rd Quarter 1999

HEALTH CARE

Average Health Care Costs

Area	Hospital ($/day)	Doctor ($/visit)	Dentist ($/visit)
City	283.00	54.75	62.25
U.S.	440.96	53.83	68.42

Note: Hospital—based on a semi-private room; Doctor—based on a general practitioner's routine exam of an established patient; Dentist—based on adult teeth cleaning and periodic oral exam.
Source: ACCRA, Cost of Living Index, 3rd Quarter 1999

Distribution of Office-Based Physicians

Area	Family/Gen. Practitioners	Specialists		
		Medical	Surgical	Other
MSA[1]	74	158	139	119

Note: Data as of 12/31/97; (1) Metropolitan Statistical Area - see Appendix A for areas included
Source: American Medical Assn., Physician Characteristics & Distribution in the U.S., 1999

Hospitals

Asheville has 2 general medical and surgical hospitals, 1 psychiatric, 1 rehabilitation.
AHA Guide to the Healthcare Field, 1999-2000

EDUCATION

Public School District Statistics

District Name	Num. Sch.	Enroll.	Classroom Teachers	Pupils per Teacher	Minority Pupils (%)	Current Exp.[1] ($/pupil)
Asheville City Schools	9	4,310	347	12.4	n/a	n/a
Buncombe County Schools	36	24,814	1,600	15.5	8.8	4,931

Note: Data covers the 1997-1998 school year unless otherwise noted; (1) Data covers fiscal year 1996; SD = School District; ISD = Independent School District; n/a not available
Source: National Center for Education Statistics, Common Core of Data Public Education Agency Universe 1997-98; National Center for Education Statistics, Characteristics of the 100 Largest Public Elementary and Secondary School Districts in the United States: 1997-98, July 1999

Educational Quality

School District	Education Quotient[1]	Graduate Outcome[2]	Community Index[3]	Resource Index[4]
Asheville City Schools	80	81	74	78

Note: Over 1,000 secondary school districts were rated in terms of educational quality. The scores range from a low of 50 to a high of 150; (1) Combination of the Graduate Outcome, Community and Resource indexes weighted to reflect the greater importance of the Graduate Outcome and Resource Index; (2) Based on graduation rates and college board scores (SAT/ACT); (3) Based on the surrounding community's level of affluence and adult education; (4) Based on teacher salaries, per-pupil expenditures and student-teacher ratios.
Source: Expansion Management, Ratings Issue, 1999

Educational Attainment by Race

Area	High School Graduate (%)					Bachelor's Degree (%)				
	Total	White	Black	Other	Hisp.[2]	Total	White	Black	Other	Hisp.[2]
City	75.1	78.3	59.7	75.9	75.7	23.0	25.8	9.3	29.1	15.4
MSA[1]	74.5	75.5	61.3	77.4	79.3	19.1	19.8	9.3	22.6	15.4
U.S.	75.2	77.9	63.1	60.4	49.8	20.3	21.5	11.4	19.4	9.2

Note: Figures shown cover persons 25 years old and over; (1) Metropolitan Statistical Area -
see Appendix A for areas included; (2) people of Hispanic origin can be of any race
Source: 1990 Census of Population and Housing, Summary Tape File 3C

School Enrollment by Type

Area	Preprimary				Elementary/High School			
	Public		Private		Public		Private	
	Enrollment	%	Enrollment	%	Enrollment	%	Enrollment	%
City	597	59.1	413	40.9	7,677	93.2	559	6.8
MSA[1]	1,430	57.8	1,043	42.2	23,968	91.9	2,106	8.1
U.S.	2,679,029	59.5	1,824,256	40.5	38,379,689	90.2	4,187,099	9.8

Note: Figures shown cover persons 3 years old and over;
(1) Metropolitan Statistical Area - see Appendix A for areas included
Source: 1990 Census of Population and Housing, Summary Tape File 3C

School Enrollment by Race

Area	Preprimary (%)				Elementary/High School (%)			
	White	Black	Other	Hisp.[1]	White	Black	Other	Hisp.[1]
City	68.5	30.7	0.8	0.8	69.0	29.8	1.2	1.1
MSA[2]	85.7	13.6	0.7	0.8	88.0	10.7	1.3	0.8
U.S.	80.4	12.5	7.1	7.8	74.1	15.6	10.3	12.5

Note: Figures shown cover persons 3 years old and over; (1) people of Hispanic origin can be of any
race; (2) Metropolitan Statistical Area - see Appendix A for areas included
Source: 1990 Census of Population and Housing, Summary Tape File 3C

Higher Education

Two-Year Colleges		Four-Year Colleges		Medical Schools	Law Schools	Voc/ Tech
Public	Private	Public	Private			
1	2	1	1	0	0	0

Source: College Blue Book, Occupational Education, 1999; Medical School Admission Requirements,
1999-2000; Peterson's Guide to Two-Year Colleges, 2000; Peterson's Guide to Four-Year Colleges,
1999; Barron's Guide to Law Schools, 1999

MAJOR EMPLOYERS

Major Employers

Biltmore Co. (amusements)	Grove Park Inn Resort
Hydrologic Inc. (testing labs)	Ingles Markets Inc. (grocery stores)
Memorial Mission Hospital	Mills Manufacturing
Peppertree Resorts	St. Joseph's Hospital
Zemex Corp. (metal products)	

Note: Companies listed are located in the city
Source: D&B Business Rankings, 1999; Ward's Business Directory, 1999; America's Corporate
Families, 1999

PUBLIC SAFETY

Crime Rate

Area	All Crimes	Violent Crimes				Property Crimes		
		Murder	Forcible Rape	Robbery	Aggrav. Assault	Burglary	Larceny -Theft	Motor Vehicle Theft
City	7,627.6	3.0	33.5	260.6	682.7	1,339.6	4,738.1	570.0
Suburbs[1]	2,425.1	4.0	11.4	28.8	181.1	735.0	1,307.1	157.6
MSA[2]	4,014.9	3.7	18.2	99.7	334.4	919.8	2,355.5	283.6
U.S.	4,615.5	6.3	34.4	165.2	360.5	862.0	2,728.1	459.0

Note: Crime rate is the number of crimes per 100,000 population; (1) Defined as all areas within the Metropolitan Statistical Area but located outside the central city; (2) Metropolitan Statistical Area - see Appendix A for areas included
Source: FBI Uniform Crime Reports, 1998

RECREATION

Culture and Recreation

Museums	Symphony Orchestras	Opera Companies	Dance Companies	Professional Theatres	Zoos	Pro Sports Teams
9	1	0	0	0	1	0

Source: Musical America, International Directory of the Performing Arts, 1999; Official Museum Directory, 2000; Stern's Performing Arts Directory, 1997; USA Today Four Sport Stadium Guide, 1997; Career Opportunities in Theatre and the Performing Arts, 1999

Library System

The Asheville-Buncombe Library System has nine branches, holdings of 383,769 volumes, and a budget of $3,037,501 (1997-1998).
American Library Directory, 1999-2000

MEDIA

Newspapers

Name	Type	Freq.	Distribution	Circulation
The Asheville Citizen-Times	General	7x/wk	Local	67,311

Note: Includes newspapers with circulations of 200 or more located in the city;
Source: Burrelle's Media Directory, 1999 Edition

Television Stations

Name	Ch.	Affiliation	Type	Owner
WLOS	13	ABCT	Commercial	Sinclair Communications Inc.

Note: Stations included broadcast in the Asheville metro area; n/a not available
Source: Burrelle's Media Directory, 1999 Edition

AM Radio Stations

Call Letters	Freq. (kHz)	Target Audience	Station Format	Music Format
WWNC	570	General	M/N/S	Country
WFGW	1010	Religious	E/M/N/S	Gospel
WSKY	1230	General	M/T	Christian
WISE	1310	General	M/N/S	Adult Standards
WKJV	1380	G/R	E/M/N/T	Christian
WTZQ	1600	General	M/N/S	Adult Standards

Note: Stations included broadcast in the Asheville metro area
Target Audience: A=Asian; B=Black; C=Christian; E=Ethnic; F=French; G=General; H=Hispanic; M=Men; N=Native American; R=Religious; S=Senior Citizen; W=Women; Y=Young Adult; Z=Children
Station Format: E=Educational; M=Music; N=News; S=Sports; T=Talk
Source: Burrelle's Media Directory, 1999 Edition

FM Radio Stations

Call Letters	Freq. (mHz)	Target Audience	Station Format	Music Format
WCQS	88.1	General	E/M/N/T	Classical/Jazz
WZLS	96.5	General	M	AOR/Classic Rock
WKSF	99.9	General	M	Country
WMXF	104.3	General	E/M/N/S/T	Adult Contemporary/Adult Top 40/Top 40
WMIT	106.9	Religious	E/M/N/T	Christian

Note: Stations included broadcast in the Asheville metro area
Station Format: E=Educational; M=Music; N=News; S=Sports; T=Talk
Target Audience: A=Asian; B=Black; C=Christian; E=Ethnic; F=French; G=General; H=Hispanic; M=Men; N=Native American; R=Religious; S=Senior Citizen; W=Women; Y=Young Adult; Z=Children
Music Format: AOR=Album Oriented Rock; MOR=Middle-of-the-Road
Source: Burrelle's Media Directory, 1999 Edition

WEATHER

Temperature/Precipitation/Humidity

	Jan	Feb	Mar	Apr	May	Jun	Jul	Aug	Sep	Oct	Nov	Dec	Yr.
Max. High Temp. (°F)	78	79	83	89	93	99	101	100	96	88	81	81	101
Avg. High Temp. (°F)	47	51	58	68	76	82	84	83	77	69	58	50	67
Avg. Temp. (°F)	37	40	47	56	63	70	74	73	67	56	47	40	56
Avg. Low Temp. (°F)	26	28	35	43	51	58	63	62	55	44	35	28	44
Min. Low Temp. (°F)	-16	-3	5	22	28	35	44	42	30	16	-2	-7	-16
Avg. Precip. (in.)	3.1	3.6	4.6	3.4	4.0	3.8	4.2	4.5	3.6	3.3	3.3	3.4	44.8
Avg. Snowfall (in.)	4	4	3	1	0	0	0	0	0	Tr	1	2	14
Avg. Rel. Hum. 7am (%)	84	83	84	83	89	92	94	96	96	93	87	85	89
Avg. Rel. Hum. 4pm (%)	56	53	50	47	56	59	63	64	62	55	54	56	56

Note: Tr = Trace amounts (less than 0.05 inches of rain or less than 0.5 inches of snow)
Source: National Climatic Data Center, International Station Meteorological Climate Summary, 3/95

Weather Conditions

Temperature			Precipitation		
32°F & below	45°F & below	90°F & above	0.01 inch or more precip.	1.5 inch or more snow/ice	Thunder-storms
99	186	11	125	3	45

Note: Figures are average number of days per year
Source: National Climatic Data Center, International Station Meteorological Climate Summary, 3/95

AIR & WATER QUALITY

Maximum Pollutant Concentrations

	Particulate Matter (ug/m³)	Carbon Monoxide (ppm)	Sulfur Dioxide (ppm)	Nitrogen Dioxide (ppm)	Ozone (ppm)	Lead (ug/m³)
MSA[1] Level	48	n/a	n/a	n/a	0.09	n/a
NAAQS[2]	150	9	0.140	0.053	0.12	1.50
Met NAAQS	Yes	n/a	n/a	n/a	Yes	n/a

Note: (1) Metropolitan Statistical Area - see Appendix A for areas included; (2) National Ambient Air Quality Standards; ppm = parts per million; ug/m³ = micrograms per cubic meter; n/a not available
Source: EPA, National Air Quality and Emissions Trends Report, 1997

Pollutant Standards Index

Data not available.
EPA, National Air Quality and Emissions Trends Report, 1997

Drinking Water

Water System Name	Pop. Served	Primary Water Source Type	Number of Violations in 1998-99	Type of Violation/ Contaminants
Asheville-Buncombe WA	125,000	Surface	None	None

Note: Data as of January 19, 2000
Source: EPA, Office of Ground Water and Drinking Water, Safe Drinking Water Information System

Asheville tap water is acid, very soft, and fluoridated.
Editor & Publisher Market Guide, 2000

Augusta, Georgia

Background

Augusta, Georgia is located in the eastern section of the state, approximately 125 miles northwest of Savannah and 140 miles east of Atlanta. It is on the Savannah River, across from South Carolina. The area's terrain includes both level land and higher sites.

Augusta, nicknamed "The Garden City," is part of the primary metropolitan area for the central Savannah River region. The metropolitan area includes neighboring communities in Georgia and across the river in South Carolina, including North Augusta and Aiken. Augusta is the traditional county seat of Richmond County. In 1996, the governments of Augusta and Richmond County were consolidated.

The U.S. Army's Fort Gordon, established in 1942, is a major facet of the Augusta economy. Another primary sector is medical services, research and education, including a large complex at the state Medical College of Georgia and at other area hospitals and health-care providers and companies. Other significant activities include manufacturing of various products, business and professional services, education, retail and wholesale trades, and construction. Augusta has been a resort area since the early 20th Century, with attractions that include the annual Masters Golf Tournament, held since 1934 at the Augusta National Country Club.

Cherokee were among the Native Americans who originally occupied the region. In 1736, Georgia's founder, General James Edward Oglethorpe, initiated settlement of Fort Augusta, named for a British princess. In the late 1700s Augusta served as the capital of Georgia. The city was chartered in 1798. Augusta grew as a trading, agricultural and manufacturing city. Among other activities, it was a major center for the cotton trade. Industry also developed based on resources such as clay and kaolin. The Augusta Canal provided hydro-power and stimulated the economy after 1845. During the Civil War, Augusta manufactured gunpowder for the Confederacy.

In the early 20th Century, a levee was constructed to deal with serious floods that periodically occurred. In 1916, a fire caused extensive damage to central Augusta. In the late 1940s, construction was undertaken on Clark Hill Dam, which created a large man-made lake that provides power to support economic development, and which became a popular recreation area. In the 1950s the Savannah River Site, a nuclear facility in South Carolina, stimulated the region's growth. Augusta experienced heightened racial tensions during the civil-rights movement of the 1960s.

In the early 20th Century, population and business growth began to shift from Augusta's city center to the outlying suburban areas. In recent years, numerous efforts to revitalize central Augusta have been undertaken, including redevelopment initiatives for neighborhoods and historic districts such as Broad St. In the 1980s redevelopment was undertaken on Riverwalk, a riverside path that serves as a focal point for shops and other community activities. Among Augusta's numerous historic attractions is the restored Cotton Exchange visitor center.

Schools of higher education include Medical College of Georgia, Augusta State University, Paine College and Augusta Technical Institute. The area also has a significant number of private elementary and secondary schools. The National Science Center at Fort Discovery, near Riverwalk, is a collaboration between the Army and the non-profit NSC Discovery Center, Inc. to develop innovative educational activities for math, science and technology, both on-site and in schools.

Golf and water-based activities are popular recreational pastimes. There are numerous parks and recreation facilities in the area. The Augusta Green Jackets baseball team is an affiliate of the Pittsburgh Pirates. Cultural offerings include programs at area colleges, as well as the Augusta Symphony, Augusta Ballet, the Morris Museum of Art, Augusta Players, and others. The Augusta-Richmond County Civic Center Complex is a downtown multi-use facility.

General Rankings and Evaluative Comments

- Augusta was ranked #111 out of 354 metropolitan areas in *Places Rated Almanac*. Criteria: cost of living, climate, crime, transportation, job outlook, education, the arts, health care, and recreation. *Places Rated Almanac, Millennium Edition, 2000*

- Cognetics studied 273 metro areas in the United States, ranking them by entrepreneurial activity. Augusta was ranked #63 out of 134 smaller metro areas. Criteria: Significant Starts (firms started in the last 10 years that still employ at least 5 people) and Young Growers (percent of firms 10 years old or less that grew significantly during the last 4 years). *Cognetics, "Entrepreneurial Hot Spots: The Best Places in America to Start and Grow a Company," 1999*

- Reliastar Financial Corporation ranked the 125 largest metropolitan areas according to the general financial security of residents. Augusta was ranked #94 out of 125 with a score of -3.1 (the percentage a metropolitan area is above or below the metropolitan norm; a metro area with a score of 10.6 is 10.6% above the metro average). Criteria: Earnings and Wealth Potential (household income, education, net assets, cost of living); Safety Net (health insurance, retirement savings, life insurance, income support programs); Personal Threats (unemployment rate, low-income households, crime rate); Community Economic Vitality (cost of community services, job quality, job creation, housing costs). *Reliastar Financial Corporation, "The Best Cities to Earn and Save Money: A Ranking of the Largest 125 U.S. Cities," 2000 Edition*

Business Environment

STATE ECONOMY

State Economic Profile

"Georgia came out of the 1991-92 recession with a bang and has been on a roll ever since. By almost any measure of strength, Georgia has outpaced the nation by a considerable degree. Such a rate of growth is not sustainable for too much longer. Growth in employment and Gross State Product (GSP), while still expected to outpace the nation, will likely slow in the years ahead.

The Georgia economy can be called the Atlanta economy. More than 80% of GSP growth is occurring within the Atlanta metro area. Atlanta is also the magnet for the vast majority of migrates to Georgia, which account for 60% of the state's population growth. To some extent Atlanta's gains have been at the expense of the rest of Georgia. Educated workers in the rest of the state have been, on net, moving to Atlanta, leaving a shortage of skilled labor in the rest of Georgia.

For most of the 1990s, Georgia's growth in per capita income outpaced the nation. In recent years, while still strong, per capita income growth has lagged the nation. This trend should continue as much of Georgia's job growth is taking place in lower paying service sector jobs, particularly temporary help services. Wage growth in the smaller metros continues to lag Atlanta by a considerable amount.

Atlanta's housing boom seems to be never-ending. 1998 witnessed a 19% increase in single-family permits and a 15% increase in multifamily permits. In spite of a large amount of construction in the pipeline, home price appreciation in 1998 exceeded the nation's and should continue to do so. Current efforts at controlling growth, such as building moratoria, and a lack of infrastructure in some areas make it likely that price appreciation will remain robust in the inner suburbs, although construction will continue at the fringe." *National Association of Realtors, Economic Profiles: The Fifty States and the District of Columbia, http://nar.realtor.com/databank/profiles.htm*

EXPORTS

Total Export Sales

Area	1995 ($000)	1996 ($000)	1997 ($000)	1998 ($000)	% Chg. 1995-98	% Chg. 1997-98
MSA[1]	405,183	443,888	433,793	519,588	28.2	19.8
U.S.	583,030,524	622,827,063	687,597,999	680,474,251	16.7	-1.0

Note: (1) Metropolitan Statistical Area - see Appendix A for areas included
Source: U.S. Department of Commerce, International Trade Association, Metropolitan Area Exports: An Export Performance Report on Over 250 U.S. Cities, November 10, 1999

CITY FINANCES

City Government Finances

Component	1995 ($million)	1995 (per capita $)
Revenue	48.8	1,122
Expenditure	58.4	1,343
Debt Outstanding	36.4	838

Source: 1999 County and City Extra, Annual Metro, City, and County Data Book

City Government Revenue by Source

Source	1995 ($million)	1995 (per capita $)
Intergovernmental	11.0	253
Taxes	17.0	391
Property	5.6	131
Sales and Gross Receipts	10.0	231

Source: 1999 County and City Extra, Annual Metro, City, and County Data Book

City Government Expenditures by Function

Function	1995 ($million)	1995 (per capita $)	1995 (%)
Public Welfare	0.0	0	0.0
Highways	5.7	133	9.9
Parking Facilities	0.1	4	0.3
Education	0.0	0	0.0
Health and Hospitals	0.0	0	0.0
Police Protection	6.4	149	11.1
Sewerage and Sanitation	8.9	205	15.3
Parks and Recreation	4.2	96	7.2
Housing and Community Development	2.5	59	4.4
Interest on Debt	1.3	30	2.3

Source: 1999 County and City Extra, Annual Metro, City, and County Data Book

Municipal Bond Ratings

Area	Moody's
City	A2

Source: Mergent Bond Record, 2/2000

POPULATION

Population Growth

Area	1980 Census	1990 Census	1999 Estimate	2004 Projection	Population Growth (%) 1990-1999	Population Growth (%) 1999-2004
City	47,532	44,639	39,067	37,665	-12.5	-3.6
MSA[1]	363,446	396,809	460,338	484,730	16.0	5.3
U.S.	226,545,805	248,765,170	272,212,864	283,625,312	9.4	4.2

Note: (1) Metropolitan Statistical Area - see Appendix A for areas included
Source: 1990 Census of Population and Housing, Summary Tape File 3C; Claritas, Inc.

Number of Households and Average Household Size

Area	1980 Census	1990 Census	1999 Estimate	2004 Projection	1999 Average Household Size
City	20,401	18,795	16,809	16,397	2.32
MSA[1]	120,598	142,723	167,928	178,475	2.74
U.S.	80,389,592	91,993,582	102,048,200	107,302,392	2.67

Note: (1) Metropolitan Statistical Area - see Appendix A for areas included
Source: 1990 Census of Population and Housing, Summary Tape File 3C; Claritas, Inc.

Race/Ethnicity of City Population

Race/Ethnicity	1990 Census Population	1990 Census %	1999 Estimate Population	1999 Estimate %	% Change 1990-1999
White, Non-Hispanic	18,730	42.0	14,073	36.0	-24.9
Black, Non-Hispanic	24,949	55.9	23,963	61.3	-4.0
Asian, Non-Hispanic	299	0.7	396	1.0	32.4
Other, Non-Hispanic	193	0.4	92	0.2	-52.3
Hispanic	468	1.0	543	1.4	16.0

Source: 1990 Census of Population and Housing, Summary Tape File 3C; Claritas, Inc.

Race/Ethnicity of Metropolitan Statistical Area Population

Race/Ethnicity	1990 Census Population	%	1999 Estimate Population	%	% Change 1990-1999
White, Non-Hispanic	261,950	66.0	285,995	62.1	9.2
Black, Non-Hispanic	122,845	31.0	151,903	33.0	23.7
Asian, Non-Hispanic	5,387	1.4	9,641	2.1	79.0
Other, Non-Hispanic	1,156	0.3	1,330	0.3	15.1
Hispanic	5,471	1.4	11,469	2.5	109.6

Note: See Appendix A for areas included in the Metropolitan Statistical Area
Source: 1990 Census of Population and Housing, Summary Tape File 3C; Claritas, Inc.

Ancestry

Area	German	Irish	English	Italian	U.S.	French	Polish	Dutch
City	7.4	8.3	10.0	1.1	9.3	1.5	0.5	0.7
MSA[1]	14.0	13.8	12.0	1.7	12.2	2.6	1.1	1.6
U.S.	23.3	15.6	13.1	5.9	5.3	4.2	3.8	2.5

Note: Figures are percentages and include persons that reported multiple ancestry (eg. if a person reported being Irish and Italian, they were included in both columns); (1) Metropolitan Statistical Area - see Appendix A for areas included
Source: 1990 Census of Population and Housing, Summary Tape File 3C

Median Age

Area	1990 Census	1999 Estimate
City	33.7	35.0
MSA[1]	31.2	33.9
U.S.	32.9	35.7

Note: (1) Metropolitan Statistical Area - see Appendix A for areas included
Source: 1990 Census of Population and Housing, Summary Tape File 3C; Claritas, Inc.

Male/Female Population

Area	Number of Males 1990	1999	Number of Females 1990	1999	Males per 100 Females 1990	1999
City	19,917	17,976	24,722	21,091	80.6	85.2
MSA[1]	192,709	224,809	204,100	235,529	94.4	95.4
U.S.	121,172,379	132,803,736	127,537,494	139,409,136	95.0	95.3

Note: (1) Metropolitan Statistical Area - see Appendix A for areas included
Source: 1990 Census of Population, General Population Characteristics; Claritas, Inc.

INCOME

Per Capita/Median/Average Income

Area	Per Capita ($) 1989	1999	% Chg.	Median Household ($) 1989	1999	% Chg.	Average Household ($) 1989	1999	% Chg.
City	10,367	15,246	47.1	15,315	20,055	31.0	23,956	33,919	41.6
MSA[1]	12,721	17,396	36.8	28,490	35,659	25.2	34,684	46,545	34.2
U.S.	14,420	21,350	48.1	30,056	40,525	34.8	38,453	56,184	46.1

Note: (1) Metropolitan Statistical Area - see Appendix A for areas included; 1989 data is from the 1990 Census; 1999 data is estimated by Claritas, Inc.
Source: 1990 Census of Population, General Population Characteristics; Claritas, Inc.

Household Income Distribution

Area	Percent of Households Earning								
	Under $5,000	$5,000 -14,999	$15,000 -24,999	$25,000 -34,999	$35,000 -49,999	$50,000 -74,999	$75,000 -99,000	$100,000 -149,999	$150,000 and up
City	14.9	25.5	17.4	12.3	12.2	8.9	4.3	2.4	2.2
MSA[1]	6.1	14.7	14.7	13.5	17.5	19.2	7.9	4.3	2.1
U.S.	3.9	13.3	13.8	12.6	16.2	19.4	9.7	6.6	4.6

Note: Data as of 1999; (1) Metropolitan Statistical Area - see Appendix A for areas included
Source: Claritas, Inc.

Effective Buying Income

Area	Per Capita ($)	Median Household ($)	Average Household ($)
City	11,360	17,307	26,462
MSA[1]	14,038	31,418	38,444
U.S.	17,496	36,603	47,036

Note: Data as of 1/1/2000; (1) Metropolitan Statistical Area - see Appendix A for areas included
Source: Standard Rate & Data Service, Newspaper Advertising Source, March 2000

Effective Household Buying Income Distribution

Area	% of Households Earning						
	$10,000 -$19,999	$20,000 -$34,999	$35,000 -$49,999	$50,000 -$74,999	$75,000 -$99,000	$100,000 -$124,999	$125,000 and up
City	22.5	21.7	9.9	8.0	2.4	1.1	1.5
MSA[1]	16.4	23.9	18.8	17.5	5.4	1.7	1.4
U.S.	15.0	21.6	17.6	19.6	8.4	3.0	3.3

Note: Data as of 1/1/2000; (1) Metropolitan Statistical Area - see Appendix A for areas included
Source: Standard Rate & Data Service, Newspaper Advertising Source, March 2000

Poverty Rates by Age

Area	People of All Ages	People Under 18 Years Old	Related Children Age 5-17 in Families in Poverty
City	42.7	n/a	n/a
County	21.4	32.6	33.3
U.S.	13.8	20.8	18.7

Note: Figures show the percent of people living below the poverty line in 1995. The
average poverty threshold was $15,569 for a family of four in 1995; n/a not available
Source: Bureau of the Census, Small Area Income and Poverty Estimates Program;
U.S. Department of Housing and Urban Development

EMPLOYMENT

Labor Force and Employment

Area	Civilian Labor Force			Workers Employed		
	Dec. 1998	Dec. 1999	% Chg.	Dec. 1998	Dec. 1999	% Chg.
City	78,755	76,321	-3.1	74,324	72,161	-2.9
MSA[1]	201,157	197,170	-2.0	192,398	188,456	-2.0
U.S.	138,297,000	139,941,000	1.2	132,732,000	134,696,000	1.5

Note: Data is not seasonally adjusted and covers workers 16 years of age and older;
(1) Metropolitan Statistical Area - see Appendix A for areas included
Source: Bureau of Labor Statistics, http://stats.bls.gov

Unemployment Rate

Area	1999											
	Jan.	Feb.	Mar.	Apr.	May	Jun.	Jul.	Aug.	Sep.	Oct.	Nov.	Dec.
City	5.6	6.1	6.1	5.3	5.2	7.1	7.2	6.9	6.7	5.9	5.5	5.5
MSA[1]	4.5	5.0	4.8	4.4	4.6	5.7	5.6	5.3	5.3	5.1	4.8	4.4
U.S.	4.8	4.7	4.4	4.1	4.0	4.5	4.5	4.2	4.1	3.8	3.8	3.7

Note: Data is not seasonally adjusted and covers workers 16 years of age and older; all figures are percentages; (1) Metropolitan Statistical Area - see Appendix A for areas included
Source: Bureau of Labor Statistics, http://stats.bls.gov

Employment by Industry

Sector	MSA[1]		U.S.
	Number of Employees	Percent of Total	Percent of Total
Services	51,900	25.2	30.2
Retail Trade	39,900	19.4	18.1
Government	41,100	20.0	15.8
Manufacturing	29,300	14.3	14.1
Finance/Insurance/Real Estate	6,000	2.9	5.9
Wholesale Trade	4,800	2.3	5.4
Transportation/Public Utilities	18,700	9.1	5.3
Construction	13,600	6.6	4.8
Mining	300	0.1	0.4

Note: Figures cover non-farm employment as of 12/99 and are not seasonally adjusted;
(1) Metropolitan Statistical Area - see Appendix A for areas included
Source: Bureau of Labor Statistics, http://stats.bls.gov

Employment by Occupation

Occupation Category	City (%)	MSA[1] (%)	U.S. (%)
White Collar	50.2	55.1	58.1
Executive/Admin./Management	8.2	10.7	12.3
Professional	15.2	15.2	14.1
Technical & Related Support	4.1	4.1	3.7
Sales	10.3	10.9	11.8
Administrative Support/Clerical	12.4	14.3	16.3
Blue Collar	25.1	29.7	26.2
Precision Production/Craft/Repair	9.7	13.9	11.3
Machine Operators/Assem./Insp.	7.1	8.1	6.8
Transportation/Material Movers	3.4	3.8	4.1
Cleaners/Helpers/Laborers	4.9	4.0	3.9
Services	23.3	13.9	13.2
Farming/Forestry/Fishing	1.4	1.4	2.5

Note: Figures cover workers 16 years of age and older;
(1) Metropolitan Statistical Area - see Appendix A for areas included
Source: 1990 Census of Population and Housing, Summary Tape File 3C

Occupational Employment Projections: 1996 - 2006

Occupations Expected to Have the Largest Job Growth (ranked by numerical growth)	Fast-Growing Occupations[1] (ranked by percent growth)
1. General managers & top executives	1. Medical assistants
2. Cashiers	2. Physical therapy assistants and aides
3. Salespersons, retail	3. Occupational therapists
4. Child care workers, private household	4. Home health aides
5. Truck drivers, light	5. Occupational therapy assistants
6. General office clerks	6. Personal and home care aides
7. Systems analysts	7. Paralegals
8. Registered nurses	8. Respiratory therapists
9. Marketing & sales, supervisors	9. Customer service representatives
10. Receptionists and information clerks	10. Child care workers, private household

Note: Projections cover Georgia; (1) Excludes occupations with total job growth less than 300
Source: U.S. Department of Labor, Employment and Training Administration, America's Labor Market Information System (ALMIS)

Average Wages

Occupation	$/Hr.	Occupation	$/Hr.
Accountants and Auditors	18.54	Maids and Housekeepers	6.55
Assemblers and Fabricators	10.15	Maintenance Repairers	13.18
Automotive Mechanics	12.58	Marketing/Advertising/PR Managers	23.28
Bookkeepers	10.28	Nurses, Licensed Practical	11.82
Carpenters	12.17	Nurses, Registered	18.55
Cashiers	6.44	Nursing Aides/Orderlies/Attendants	7.78
Clerks, General Office	9.30	Physicians and Surgeons	40.51
Clerks, Shipping/Receiving/Traffic	10.97	Receptionists/Information Clerks	8.24
Computer Programmers	22.04	Sales Reps., Exc. Scientific/Retail	16.78
Computer Support Specialists	16.35	Sales Reps., Scientific, Exc. Retail	18.96
Cooks, Restaurant	7.61	Salespersons, Retail	8.76
Electricians	15.07	Secretaries, Except Legal/Medical	10.39
Financial Managers	24.49	Stock Clerks, Sales Floor	7.42
First-Line Supervisors/Mgrs., Sales	14.25	Systems Analysts	23.31
Food Preparation Workers	6.84	Teacher Aides	6.42
General Managers/Top Executives	25.57	Teachers, Elementary School	18.88
Guards	9.40	Teachers, Secondary School	-
Hand Packers	7.35	Telemarketers	-
Janitors and Cleaners	6.88	Truck Drivers, Heavy/Tractor-Trailer	12.87
Laborers, Landscaping	7.31	Truck Drivers, Light	9.96
Lawyers	28.71	Waiters and Waitresses	6.17

Note: Wage data is for 1998 and covers the Metropolitan Statistical Area (see Appendix A for areas included). Hourly wages for elementary and secondary school teachers were calculated by the editors from annual wage data assuming a 40 hour work week; Dashes indicate that data was not available.
Source: Bureau of Labor Statistics, 1998 Metropolitan Area Occupational Employment and Wage Estimates

TAXES

Major State and Local Tax Rates

State Corporate Income (%)	State Personal Income (%)	Residential Property (%)	Sales & Use		State Gasoline (cents/ gallon)	State Cigarette (cents/ pack)
			State (%)	Local (%)		
6.0	1.0 - 6.0	1.48	4.0	3.0	7.5[a]	12.0

Note: Personal/corporate income, sales, gasoline and cigarette tax rates as of January 2000.
Property tax rates as of April 2000; (a) 3% sales tax applicable
Source: Federation of Tax Administrators, www.taxadmin.org; ERI's Relocation Assessor software database, quarterly effective date 4/1/2000

Total Taxes Per Capita and as a Percent of Income

Area	Per Capita Income ($)	Per Capita Taxes ($)			Percent of Income (%)		
		Total	Federal	State/Local	Total	Federal	State/Local
Georgia	27,410	9,509	6,574	2,935	34.7	24.0	10.7
U.S.	28,878	10,298	7,026	3,273	35.7	24.3	11.3

Note: Figures are for 1999
Source: Tax Foundation, www.taxfoundation.org

COMMERCIAL UTILITIES

Typical Monthly Electric Bills

Area	Commercial Service ($/month)		Industrial Service ($/month)	
	12 kW demand 1,500 kWh	100 kW demand 30,000 kWh	1,000 kW demand 400,000 kWh	20,000 kW demand 10,000,000 kWh
City	175	2,152	23,993	358,567
U.S.	150	2,174	23,995	508,569

Note: Based on rates in effect January 1, 1999
Source: Edison Electric Institute, Typical Residential, Commercial and Industrial Bills, Winter 1999

TRANSPORTATION

Transportation Statistics

Average minutes to work (1990)	18.0
Interstate highways	I-20; I-520; US-1; US-25; US-78; US 278
Bus lines	
In-city (1998)	Augusta-Richmond County Public Transit, 18 buses
Inter-city (1999)	8
Passenger air service	
Airport	Augusta Regional at Bush Field
Airlines (1999)	3
Enplaned passengers (1998)	220,876
Amtrak service	No
Motor freight carriers (1999)	15
Major waterways/ports	Savanah River

Source: FAA DOT/TSC CY1998 ACAIS Database; National Transit Database, 1998; Editor & Publisher Market Guide, 2000; Amtrak National Time Table, Fall 1999/Winter 2000; 1990 Census of Population and Housing, STF 3C; Jane's Urban Transport Systems 1999-2000

Means of Transportation to Work

Area	Car/Truck/Van		Public Transportation			Bicycle	Walked	Other Means	Worked at Home
	Drove Alone	Car-pooled	Bus	Subway	Railroad				
City	67.4	18.0	3.8	0.0	0.0	0.7	6.0	2.1	2.0
MSA[1]	76.0	16.6	1.0	0.0	0.0	0.2	3.6	1.2	1.5
U.S.	73.2	13.4	3.0	1.5	0.5	0.4	3.9	1.2	3.0

Note: Figures shown are percentages and only include workers 16 years of age and older;
(1) Metropolitan Statistical Area - see Appendix A for areas included
Source: 1990 Census of Population and Housing, Summary Tape File 3C

BUSINESSES

Major Business Headquarters

Company Name	1999 Rankings	
	Fortune 500	Forbes 500
Morris Communications	-	452

Note: Companies listed are located in the city; dashes indicate no ranking
Fortune 500: Companies that produce a 10-K are ranked 1 to 500 based on 1999 revenue
Forbes 500: Private companies are ranked 1 to 500 based on 1998 revenue
Source: Forbes, December 13, 1999; Fortune, April 17, 2000

HOTELS & MOTELS

Hotels/Motels

Area	Hotels/ Motels	Rooms	Luxury-Level Hotels/Motels		Average Minimum Rates ($)		
			◆◆◆◆	◆◆◆◆◆	◆◆	◆◆◆	◆◆◆◆
City	21	2,114	0	0	56	74	n/a
Airport	1	161	0	0	n/a	n/a	n/a
Suburbs	3	463	0	0	n/a	n/a	n/a
Total	25	2,738	0	0	n/a	n/a	n/a

Note: n/a not available; classifications range from one diamond (budget properties with basic amenities) to five diamond (luxury properties).
Source: OAG Business Travel Planner, Winter 1999-2000

Estimated Daily Food and Lodging Costs

Area	Food/Other ($/day)	Average Hotel Cost ($/day)
City	30	55
U.S.	30	55

Source: ERI's Relocation Assessor software database, quarterly effective date 4/1/2000

CONVENTION CENTERS

Convention Centers and Event Sites

Name	Guest Rooms	Meeting Space (sq. ft.)	Capacity (Theatre Style)
Augusta-Richmond County Civic Center Complex	n/a	n/a	9,000
Radisson Riverfront Hotel Augusta	237	26,000	1,400
Radisson Suites Inn Augusta	176	3,540	150
Sheraton Augusta Hotel	179	9,000	900

Note: n/a not available
Source: EventSource.com, 3/15/2000

Living Environment

COST OF LIVING

Cost of Living: Homeowner

Cost Element	U.S. ($)	City ($)	Differential ($)	Percent of U.S. Average
Consumables	14,516	13,943	-573	96.1
Transportation	5,957	5,799	-158	97.3
Health Services	2,012	1,927	-85	95.8
Housing/Utilities/Prop. Tax	16,337	17,001	664	104.1
Income+Payroll Taxes	12,615	12,403	-212	98.3
Miscellaneous	8,563	8,563	0	100.0
Total Cost of Living	60,000	59,636	-364	99.4

Note: Figures are based on a single income, four person family with gross annual earnings of $60,000, owning an 1,800 square-foot home, and driving two automobiles worth $22,000 30,000 miles per year.
Source: ERI's Relocation Assessor software database, quarterly effective date 4/1/2000

Cost of Living: Renter

Cost Element	U.S. ($)	City ($)	Differential ($)	Percent of U.S. Average
Consumables	10,486	10,099	-387	96.3
Transportation	2,107	2,057	-50	97.6
Health Services	1,632	1,568	-64	96.1
Rent/Utilities/Insurance	9,299	9,508	209	102.2
Income+Payroll Taxes	8,607	8,407	-200	97.7
Miscellaneous	7,869	7,869	0	100.0
Total Cost of Living	40,000	39,508	-492	98.8

Note: Figures are based on a single income, three person family with gross annual earnings of $40,000, renting a 1,000 square-foot home, and driving one automobile worth $8,000 12,000 miles per year.
Source: ERI's Relocation Assessor software database, quarterly effective date 4/1/2000

HOUSING

Median Home Prices and Housing Affordability

Area	Median Price[2] 4th Qtr. 1999 ($)	HOI[3] 4th Qtr. 1999	Affordability Rank[4]
MSA[1]	n/a	n/a	n/a
U.S.	139,000	63.8	–

Note: (1) Metropolitan Statistical Area - see Appendix A for areas included; (2) U.S. figures calculated from the sales of 687,516 new and existing homes in 192 markets; (3) Housing Opportunity Index - percent of homes sold that were within the reach of the median income household at the prevailing mortgage interest rate; (4) Rank is from 1-192 with 1 being most affordable; n/a not available
Source: National Association of Home Builders, Housing Opportunity Index, 4th Quarter 1999

Estimated Home Price

Area	Price ($)
City	136,951
U.S.	135,855

Note: Figures are based on an 1,800 square-foot home
Source: ERI's Relocation Assessor software database, quarterly effective date 4/1/2000

Estimated Rent

Area	Rent ($/month)
City	663
U.S.	651

Note: Figures are based on a 1,000 square-foot home
Source: ERI's Relocation Assessor software database, quarterly effective date 4/1/2000

Median Home Price Projection

It is projected that the median home price in the metropolitan area will increase from $116,395 in 1999 to $117,792 in 2010, an increase of 1.2%
Kiplinger's Personal Finance Magazine, January 2000

RESIDENTIAL UTILITIES

Average Residential Utility Costs

Area	All Electric ($/mth)	Part Electric ($/mth)	Other Energy ($/mth)	Phone ($/mth)
MSA[1]	–	54.91	51.79	21.98
U.S.	99.25	55.47	43.48	20.29

Note: (1) Metropolitan Statistical Area - see Appendix A for areas included
Source: ACCRA, Cost of Living Index, 3rd Quarter 1999

HEALTH CARE

Average Health Care Costs

Area	Hospital ($/day)	Doctor ($/visit)	Dentist ($/visit)
MSA[1]	348.40	59.57	60.80
U.S.	440.96	53.83	68.42

Note: Hospital—based on a semi-private room; Doctor—based on a general practitioner's routine exam of an established patient; Dentist—based on adult teeth cleaning and periodic oral exam; (1) Metropolitan Statistical Area - see Appendix A for areas included
Source: ACCRA, Cost of Living Index, 3rd Quarter 1999

Distribution of Office-Based Physicians

Area	Family/Gen. Practitioners	Specialists		
		Medical	Surgical	Other
MSA[1]	66	305	229	229

Note: Data as of 12/31/97; (1) Metropolitan Statistical Area - see Appendix A for areas included
Source: American Medical Assn., Physician Characteristics & Distribution in the U.S., 1999

Hospitals

Augusta has 5 general medical and surgical hospitals, 1 psychiatric, 1 rehabilitation.
AHA Guide to the Healthcare Field, 1999-2000

EDUCATION

Public School District Statistics

District Name	Num. Sch.	Enroll.	Classroom Teachers	Pupils per Teacher	Minority Pupils (%)	Current Exp.[1] ($/pupil)
Richmond County School Dist	57	36,780	2,336	15.7	69.2	4,780

Note: Data covers the 1997-1998 school year unless otherwise noted; (1) Data covers fiscal year 1996; SD = School District; ISD = Independent School District; n/a not available
Source: National Center for Education Statistics, Common Core of Data Public Education Agency Universe 1997-98; National Center for Education Statistics, Characteristics of the 100 Largest Public Elementary and Secondary School Districts in the United States: 1997-98, July 1999

Educational Quality

School District	Education Quotient[1]	Graduate Outcome[2]	Community Index[3]	Resource Index[4]
Richmond Co. School Dist.	66	64	77	67

Note: Over 1,000 secondary school districts were rated in terms of educational quality. The scores range from a low of 50 to a high of 150; (1) Combination of the Graduate Outcome, Community and Resource indexes weighted to reflect the greater importance of the Graduate Outcome and Resource Index; (2) Based on graduation rates and college board scores (SAT/ACT); (3) Based on the surrounding community's level of affluence and adult education; (4) Based on teacher salaries, per-pupil expenditures and student-teacher ratios.
Source: Expansion Management, Ratings Issue, 1999

Educational Attainment by Race

Area	High School Graduate (%)					Bachelor's Degree (%)				
	Total	White	Black	Other	Hisp.[2]	Total	White	Black	Other	Hisp.[2]
City	57.2	71.9	42.2	81.1	86.5	17.4	28.6	6.0	37.9	42.6
MSA[1]	71.8	77.3	57.3	78.3	82.3	18.0	21.2	9.1	26.8	24.3
U.S.	75.2	77.9	63.1	60.4	49.8	20.3	21.5	11.4	19.4	9.2

Note: Figures shown cover persons 25 years old and over; (1) Metropolitan Statistical Area - see Appendix A for areas included; (2) people of Hispanic origin can be of any race
Source: 1990 Census of Population and Housing, Summary Tape File 3C

School Enrollment by Type

Area	Preprimary				Elementary/High School			
	Public		Private		Public		Private	
	Enrollment	%	Enrollment	%	Enrollment	%	Enrollment	%
City	332	58.2	238	41.8	6,333	92.6	506	7.4
MSA[1]	3,664	53.1	3,235	46.9	68,864	92.0	5,953	8.0
U.S.	2,679,029	59.5	1,824,256	40.5	38,379,689	90.2	4,187,099	9.8

Note: Figures shown cover persons 3 years old and over;
(1) Metropolitan Statistical Area - see Appendix A for areas included
Source: 1990 Census of Population and Housing, Summary Tape File 3C

School Enrollment by Race

Area	Preprimary (%)				Elementary/High School (%)			
	White	Black	Other	Hisp.[1]	White	Black	Other	Hisp.[1]
City	37.2	58.4	4.4	3.5	23.7	75.2	1.1	1.5
MSA[2]	67.4	30.1	2.4	1.6	58.8	38.7	2.5	1.7
U.S.	80.4	12.5	7.1	7.8	74.1	15.6	10.3	12.5

Note: Figures shown cover persons 3 years old and over; (1) people of Hispanic origin can be of any race; (2) Metropolitan Statistical Area - see Appendix A for areas included
Source: 1990 Census of Population and Housing, Summary Tape File 3C

Higher Education

Two-Year Colleges		Four-Year Colleges		Medical Schools	Law Schools	Voc/Tech
Public	Private	Public	Private			
1	1	1	0	1	0	3

Source: College Blue Book, Occupational Education, 1999; Medical School Admission Requirements, 1999-2000; Peterson's Guide to Two-Year Colleges, 2000; Peterson's Guide to Four-Year Colleges, 1999; Barron's Guide to Law Schools, 1999

MAJOR EMPLOYERS

Major Employers

Club Car Inc. (transportation)	Columbia Augusta Medical Center
Doctors Hospital of Augusta	Morris Communications Corp.
Shivers Trading & Operating (newspapers)	Sizemore Security International
Southeastern Newspaper Group	St. Joseph Hospital

Note: Companies listed are located in the city
Source: D&B Business Rankings, 1999; Ward's Business Directory, 1999; America's Corporate Families, 1999

PUBLIC SAFETY

Crime Rate

Area	All Crimes	Violent Crimes				Property Crimes		
		Murder	Forcible Rape	Robbery	Aggrav. Assault	Burglary	Larceny -Theft	Motor Vehicle Theft
County[3]	7,581.1	11.9	72.9	285.4	116.8	1,334.3	4,952.4	807.5
Suburbs[1]	3,929.4	7.7	23.1	85.6	309.3	768.2	2,424.4	311.1
MSA[2]	5,443.1	9.4	43.7	168.4	229.5	1,002.9	3,472.3	516.9
U.S.	4,615.5	6.3	34.4	165.2	360.5	862.0	2,728.1	459.0

Note: Crime rate is the number of crimes per 100,000 population; (1) Defined as all areas within the Metropolitan Statistical Area but located outside the central city; (2) Metropolitan Statistical Area - see Appendix A for areas included; (3) Figures are for Richmond County.
Source: FBI Uniform Crime Reports, 1998

RECREATION

Culture and Recreation

Museums	Symphony Orchestras	Opera Companies	Dance Companies	Professional Theatres	Zoos	Pro Sports Teams
3	1	1	1	0	0	0

Source: Musical America, International Directory of the Performing Arts, 1999; Official Museum Directory, 2000; Stern's Performing Arts Directory, 1997; USA Today Four Sport Stadium Guide, 1997; Career Opportunities in Theatre and the Performing Arts, 1999

Library System

The East Central Georgia Regional Library has 12 branches, holdings of 482,856 volumes, and a budget of $2,900,568 (1997-1998).
American Library Directory, 1999-2000

MEDIA

Newspapers

Name	Type	Freq.	Distribution	Circulation
The Augusta Chronicle	General	7x/wk	Local	78,000
Augusta Focus	Black	1x/wk	Local	23,000
Metro Courier	Black	1x/wk	Local	23,660

Note: Includes newspapers with circulations of 200 or more located in the city;
Source: Burrelle's Media Directory, 1999 Edition

Television Stations

Name	Ch.	Affiliation	Type	Owner
WJBF	n/a	ABCT	Commercial	Spartanburg Radiocasting Company
WAGT	26	NBCT	Commercial	Schurz Communications Inc.
WFXG	54	FBC	Commercial	Fisher Broadcasting Inc.

Note: Stations included broadcast in the Augusta metro area; n/a not available
Source: Burrelle's Media Directory, 1999 Edition

AM Radio Stations

Call Letters	Freq. (kHz)	Target Audience	Station Format	Music Format
WGAC	580	General	N/S/T	n/a
WFAM	1050	Religious	E/M/N/S/T	Christian
WKZK	1600	Black	M/N/S	Christian

Note: Stations included broadcast in the Augusta metro area; n/a not available
Target Audience: A=Asian; B=Black; C=Christian; E=Ethnic; F=French; G=General; H=Hispanic; M=Men; N=Native American; R=Religious; S=Senior Citizen; W=Women; Y=Young Adult; Z=Children
Station Format: E=Educational; M=Music; N=News; S=Sports; T=Talk
Source: Burrelle's Media Directory, 1999 Edition

FM Radio Stations

Call Letters	Freq. (mHz)	Target Audience	Station Format	Music Format
WACG	90.7	General	M/N	Classical/Jazz/World Music
WLPE	91.7	General	E/M	Christian
WGOR	93.9	General	M/N/S	Oldies
WAAW	94.7	General	M/N	Oldies
WCHZ	95.1	General	M/N/S	Classic Rock/Oldies
WAKB	96.9	Black	M/N/S	Urban Contemporary
WLGP	100.3	Religious	E/M/N/S/T	Christian

Note: Stations included broadcast in the Augusta metro area
Station Format: E=Educational; M=Music; N=News; S=Sports; T=Talk
Target Audience: A=Asian; B=Black; C=Christian; E=Ethnic; F=French; G=General; H=Hispanic;
M=Men; N=Native American; R=Religious; S=Senior Citizen; W=Women; Y=Young Adult; Z=Children
Source: Burrelle's Media Directory, 1999 Edition

WEATHER

Temperature/Precipitation/Humidity

	Jan	Feb	Mar	Apr	May	Jun	Jul	Aug	Sep	Oct	Nov	Dec	Yr.
Max. High Temp. (°F)	80	86	88	96	99	105	107	108	101	97	90	82	108
Avg. High Temp. (°F)	57	61	68	77	84	90	92	91	86	77	68	59	76
Avg. Temp. (°F)	45	48	55	63	71	78	81	80	75	64	55	47	64
Avg. Low Temp. (°F)	33	36	42	49	58	66	70	69	63	51	41	35	51
Min. Low Temp. (°F)	-1	9	12	26	35	47	55	54	36	22	11	5	-1
Avg. Precip. (in.)	3.8	4.1	4.5	3.3	3.7	3.8	4.4	4.2	3.2	2.6	2.3	3.3	43.2
Avg. Snowfall (in.)	Tr	1	Tr	0	0	0	0	0	0	0	Tr	Tr	1
Avg. Rel. Hum. 7am (%)	84	82	83	84	86	86	88	91	91	90	88	85	86
Avg. Rel. Hum. 4pm (%)	51	47	45	43	47	51	55	55	54	48	47	51	50

Note: Tr = Trace amounts (less than 0.05 inches of rain or less than 0.5 inches of snow)
Source: National Climatic Data Center, International Station Meteorological Climate Summary, 3/95

Weather Conditions

Temperature			Precipitation		
10°F & below	32°F & below	90°F & above	0.01 inch or more precip.	1.5 inch or more snow/ice	Thunder-storms
< 0.5	55	76	106	1	56

Note: Figures are average number of days per year
Source: National Climatic Data Center, International Station Meteorological Climate Summary, 3/95

AIR & WATER QUALITY

Maximum Pollutant Concentrations

	Particulate Matter (ug/m³)	Carbon Monoxide (ppm)	Sulfur Dioxide (ppm)	Nitrogen Dioxide (ppm)	Ozone (ppm)	Lead (ug/m³)
MSA[1] Level	54	n/a	0.013	n/a	0.12	0.01
NAAQS[2]	150	9	0.140	0.053	0.12	1.50
Met NAAQS	Yes	n/a	Yes	n/a	Yes	Yes

Note: (1) Metropolitan Statistical Area - see Appendix A for areas included; (2) National Ambient Air Quality Standards; ppm = parts per million; ug/m³ = micrograms per cubic meter; n/a not available
Source: EPA, National Air Quality and Emissions Trends Report, 1997

Pollutant Standards Index

Data not available.
EPA, National Air Quality and Emissions Trends Report, 1997

Drinking Water

Water System Name	Pop. Served	Primary Water Source Type	Number of Violations in 1998-99	Type of Violation/ Contaminants
Augusta-Richmond Co. WS	160,000	Surface	None	None

Note: Data as of January 19, 2000
Source: EPA, Office of Ground Water and Drinking Water, Safe Drinking Water Information System

Augusta tap water is neutral, very soft, and fluoridated.
Editor & Publisher Market Guide, 2000

Bangor, Maine

Background

Bangor, Maine is 130 miles northeast of Portland and about 30 miles inland from the Atlantic coastline, at the intersection of Kenduskeag Stream and the Penobscot River. Bangor is the county seat of Penobscot County, and it is the largest city in upper Maine. The city's heritage reflects its 19th Century identity as the "Lumber Capital of the World."

Bangor is a metropolitan center for commercial activity and other services for a large area that includes interior northern Maine and the "Down East" coast. Bangor's primary economic market encompasses 28 communities within a 20-mile radius and a secondary market that includes six Maine counties, according to the Bangor Area Chamber of Commerce. Bangor also has economic and other ties with Quebec and Canada's maritime provinces.

The first European to visit the site of Bangor is believed to be Estevan Gomez, a Portuguese explorer sailing for Spain in 1525. French explorer Samuel de Champlain sailed up the Penobscott in 1604. A small settlement was later established, and the community was legally incorporated as Bangor in 1834. Bangor's name is from an old hymn.

In the mid-19th Century, Bangor experienced rapid growth as an international center for logging and wood products. The city has a harbor on the Penobscot River, which flows into Penobscot Bay and the Atlantic Ocean. Logs from Maine's forests were floated down the river to Bangor where they were processed for transport. Shipbuilding and papermaking also developed in the region. During this era, Bangor was very prosperous. Wealthy businessmen built mansions and they supported civic and cultural activities. Bangor claims to be the hometown of the legendary lumberjack Paul Bunyon, and there is a statue of him on the city's Main Street. Bangor's role in the lumber industry declined in the latter 19th Century due to increased logging activity in the western United States.

While lumber and paper products remain important to the Bangor area, its economy became more diversified in the 20th Century. Manufacturing industries have included electronics, shoes, automotive and machine parts, among other products. Regional financial, government and other services are based in Bangor. Retailing is another important sector of the economy, including the Bangor Mall. Bangor is a regional transportation gateway and distribution center. Bangor International Airport is an air-traffic hub. The city is located on Interstate 95, the east coast's primary north/south highway. The Bangor area also has a tourism economy, based on its local attractions and its proximity to parks and other vacation destinations in coastal and interior Maine.

Recreational and cultural amenities in Bangor include the multi-purpose Bass Park complex, with indoor and outdoor facilities for concerts and conventions, harness racing and the annual Bangor State Fair. The Bangor Symphony Orchestra, founded in 1896, is the oldest continuously operating community orchestra in the United States. The Bangor Public Library is known for its extensive collection. The Penobscot Theatre is a regional live theater in Bangor and, in the summer, sponsors the Maine Shakespeare Festival.

Orono, about ten miles north of Bangor, is home of the University of Maine. Institutions of higher education within Bangor include University College of Bangor (a campus of the University of Maine at Augusta), Bangor Theological Seminary, Husson College, Eastern Maine Technical College and Beal College.

Today, Bangor is characterized by a mix of historic Victorian mansions, other traditional structures and newer buildings. The "Great Fire of 1911" destroyed many original structures in Bangor, and prompted a major reconstruction drive. In recent decades an emphasis has been placed on preserving the surviving historic buildings and neighborhoods.

One of Bangor's most prominent contemporary residents is author Stephen King, who lives in one of the city's mansions.

General Rankings and Evaluative Comments

■ Bangor was ranked #142 out of 354 metropolitan areas in *Places Rated Almanac*. Criteria: cost of living, climate, crime, transportation, job outlook, education, the arts, health care, and recreation. *Places Rated Almanac, Millennium Edition, 2000*

■ Bangor was selected as one of North America's "Best Small Metro Areas" (population under 250,000). The area ranked #13 out of 20. Criteria: cost of living, climate, crime, transportation, job outlook, education, the arts, health care, and recreation. *Places Rated Almanac, Millennium Edition, 2000*

Business Environment

STATE ECONOMY

State Economic Profile

"Maine continues to grow along its traditional stable, yet slow, growth path. Job losses in Maine's resources and manufacturing sectors have been more than balanced by job growth in the services sector, particularly telemarketing. Weak demographics, specifically low in-migration and the loss of younger households, will constrain Maine's housing and construction markets to slow growth.

Maine's service's sector added jobs at 4.0% during 1998, twice the overall rate of state job growth. MBNA, which expanded its telemarketing call centers in the state, plans to add more jobs in the near future. Several other telemarketers, such as ICT Telemarketing, are also planning to expand operations in Maine. A boom in tourism has also added to Maine's services and retails sectors.

Manufacturing employment continued its long-term decline, shedding over 2,000 jobs in 1998. Maine's textile and paper products industries have been hurt by both weak foreign demand and strong foreign competition. Maine's cost structure in these industries makes it uncompetitive with textile and paper products produced elsewhere in the US, not to mention lower-cost overseas producers. Manufacturing employment should continue to contract in the near term.

Construction employment provided a much needed boost in 1998, providing almost 1 in 5 new non-farm jobs created. Although home sales were at record levels in 1998, the state's weak demographics and current level of construction, indicate a contraction in construction activity. These same factors will moderate the unusually high level of home price appreciation witnessed in 1998." *National Association of Realtors, Economic Profiles: The Fifty States and the District of Columbia, http://nar.realtor.com/databank/profiles.htm*

EXPORTS

Total Export Sales

Area	1995 ($000)	1996 ($000)	1997 ($000)	1998 ($000)	% Chg. 1995-98	% Chg. 1997-98
MSA[1]	n/a	n/a	n/a	n/a	n/a	n/a
U.S.	583,030,524	622,827,063	687,597,999	680,474,251	16.7	-1.0

Note: (1) Metropolitan Statistical Area - see Appendix A for areas included
Source: U.S. Department of Commerce, International Trade Association, Metropolitan Area Exports: An Export Performance Report on Over 250 U.S. Cities, November 10, 1999

CITY FINANCES

City Government Finances

Component	1995 ($million)	1995 (per capita $)
Revenue	90.3	2,821
Expenditure	87.1	2,721
Debt Outstanding	57.7	1,803

Source: 1999 County and City Extra, Annual Metro, City, and County Data Book

City Government Revenue by Source

Source	1995 ($million)	1995 (per capita $)
Intergovernmental	29.1	909
Taxes	32.0	999
Property	31.7	991
Sales and Gross Receipts	0.0	0

Source: 1999 County and City Extra, Annual Metro, City, and County Data Book

City Government Expenditures by Function

Function	1995 ($million)	1995 (per capita $)	1995 (%)
Public Welfare	2.7	84	3.1
Highways	5.0	157	5.8
Parking Facilities	0.4	13	0.5
Education	23.6	737	27.1
Health and Hospitals	2.4	76	2.8
Police Protection	4.1	130	4.8
Sewerage and Sanitation	5.0	157	5.8
Parks and Recreation	4.1	130	4.8
Housing and Community Development	1.8	57	2.1
Interest on Debt	2.7	87	3.2

Source: 1999 County and City Extra, Annual Metro, City, and County Data Book

Municipal Bond Ratings

Area	Moody's
City	Aa3

Source: Mergent Bond Record, 2/2000

POPULATION

Population Growth

Area	1980 Census	1990 Census	1999 Estimate	2004 Projection	Population Growth (%) 1990-1999	Population Growth (%) 1999-2004
City	31,643	33,181	30,138	28,867	-9.2	-4.2
MSA[1]	86,079	88,704	87,936	86,151	-0.9	-2.0
U.S.	226,545,805	248,765,170	272,212,864	283,625,312	9.4	4.2

Note: (1) Metropolitan Statistical Area - see Appendix A for areas included
Source: 1990 Census of Population and Housing, Summary Tape File 3C; Claritas, Inc.

Number of Households and Average Household Size

Area	1980 Census	1990 Census	1999 Estimate	2004 Projection	1999 Average Household Size
City	11,772	13,373	13,008	12,724	2.32
MSA[1]	29,712	32,901	34,814	34,817	2.53
U.S.	80,389,592	91,993,582	102,048,200	107,302,392	2.67

Note: (1) Metropolitan Statistical Area - see Appendix A for areas included
Source: 1990 Census of Population and Housing, Summary Tape File 3C; Claritas, Inc.

Race/Ethnicity of City Population

Race/Ethnicity	1990 Census Population	1990 Census %	1999 Estimate Population	1999 Estimate %	% Change 1990-1999
White, Non-Hispanic	32,009	96.5	28,950	96.1	-9.6
Black, Non-Hispanic	385	1.2	340	1.1	-11.7
Asian, Non-Hispanic	266	0.8	390	1.3	46.6
Other, Non-Hispanic	245	0.7	219	0.7	-10.6
Hispanic	276	0.8	239	0.8	-13.4

Source: 1990 Census of Population and Housing, Summary Tape File 3C; Claritas, Inc.

Race/Ethnicity of Metropolitan Statistical Area Population

Race/Ethnicity	1990 Census		1999 Estimate		% Change 1990-1999
	Population	%	Population	%	
White, Non-Hispanic	85,833	96.8	84,870	96.5	-1.1
Black, Non-Hispanic	533	0.6	508	0.6	-4.7
Asian, Non-Hispanic	759	0.9	978	1.1	28.9
Other, Non-Hispanic	997	1.1	949	1.1	-4.8
Hispanic	582	0.7	631	0.7	8.4

Note: See Appendix A for areas included in the Metropolitan Statistical Area
Source: 1990 Census of Population and Housing, Summary Tape File 3C; Claritas, Inc.

Ancestry

Area	German	Irish	English	Italian	U.S.	French	Polish	Dutch
City	9.1	22.9	26.1	4.5	6.1	14.5	2.0	1.4
MSA[1]	9.0	21.1	28.2	3.7	7.9	16.0	1.8	1.4
U.S.	23.3	15.6	13.1	5.9	5.3	4.2	3.8	2.5

Note: Figures are percentages and include persons that reported multiple ancestry (eg. if a person reported being Irish and Italian, they were included in both columns); (1) Metropolitan Statistical Area - see Appendix A for areas included
Source: 1990 Census of Population and Housing, Summary Tape File 3C

Median Age

Area	1990 Census	1999 Estimate
City	32.1	35.7
MSA[1]	31.6	35.5
U.S.	32.9	35.7

Note: (1) Metropolitan Statistical Area - see Appendix A for areas included
Source: 1990 Census of Population and Housing, Summary Tape File 3C; Claritas, Inc.

Male/Female Population

Area	Number of Males		Number of Females		Males per 100 Females	
	1990	1999	1990	1999	1990	1999
City	15,554	14,238	17,627	15,900	88.2	89.5
MSA[1]	42,860	42,611	45,844	45,325	93.5	94.0
U.S.	121,172,379	132,803,736	127,537,494	139,409,136	95.0	95.3

Note: (1) Metropolitan Statistical Area - see Appendix A for areas included
Source: 1990 Census of Population, General Population Characteristics; Claritas, Inc.

INCOME

Per Capita/Median/Average Income

Area	Per Capita ($)			Median Household ($)			Average Household ($)		
	1989	1999	% Chg.	1989	1999	% Chg.	1989	1999	% Chg.
City	13,418	18,509	37.9	24,674	30,355	23.0	32,299	41,576	28.7
MSA[1]	13,024	17,832	36.9	27,473	33,107	20.5	34,045	43,668	28.3
U.S.	14,420	21,350	48.1	30,056	40,525	34.8	38,453	56,184	46.1

Note: (1) Metropolitan Statistical Area - see Appendix A for areas included; 1989 data is from the 1990 Census; 1999 data is estimated by Claritas, Inc.
Source: 1990 Census of Population, General Population Characteristics; Claritas, Inc.

Household Income Distribution

Area	Percent of Households Earning								
	Under $5,000	$5,000 -14,999	$15,000 -24,999	$25,000 -34,999	$35,000 -49,999	$50,000 -74,999	$75,000 -99,000	$100,000 -149,999	$150,000 and up
City	4.5	18.1	17.9	15.8	17.7	15.3	5.4	2.7	2.6
MSA[1]	3.6	16.3	16.9	15.4	18.2	18.1	6.2	3.0	2.2
U.S.	3.9	13.3	13.8	12.6	16.2	19.4	9.7	6.6	4.6

Note: Data as of 1999; (1) Metropolitan Statistical Area - see Appendix A for areas included
Source: Claritas, Inc.

Effective Buying Income

Area	Per Capita ($)	Median Household ($)	Average Household ($)
City	15,396	27,864	36,974
MSA[1]	14,383	30,407	37,746
U.S.	17,496	36,603	47,036

Note: Data as of 1/1/2000; (1) Metropolitan Statistical Area - see Appendix A for areas included
Source: Standard Rate & Data Service, Newspaper Advertising Source, March 2000

Effective Household Buying Income Distribution

Area	% of Households Earning						
	$10,000 -$19,999	$20,000 -$34,999	$35,000 -$49,999	$50,000 -$74,999	$75,000 -$99,000	$100,000 -$124,999	$125,000 and up
City	19.3	26.6	18.6	13.3	3.7	1.7	2.2
MSA[1]	18.5	25.7	19.4	16.9	4.1	1.2	1.5
U.S.	15.0	21.6	17.6	19.6	8.4	3.0	3.3

Note: Data as of 1/1/2000; (1) Metropolitan Statistical Area - see Appendix A for areas included
Source: Standard Rate & Data Service, Newspaper Advertising Source, March 2000

Poverty Rates by Age

Area	People of All Ages	People Under 18 Years Old	Related Children Age 5-17 in Families in Poverty
City	17.4	n/a	n/a
County	14.7	19.1	16.7
U.S.	13.8	20.8	18.7

Note: Figures show the percent of people living below the poverty line in 1995. The
average poverty threshold was $15,569 for a family of four in 1995; n/a not available
Source: Bureau of the Census, Small Area Income and Poverty Estimates Program;
U.S. Department of Housing and Urban Development

EMPLOYMENT

Labor Force and Employment

Area	Civilian Labor Force			Workers Employed		
	Dec. 1998	Dec. 1999	% Chg.	Dec. 1998	Dec. 1999	% Chg.
City	18,212	19,040	4.5	17,702	18,502	4.5
MSA[1]	51,580	53,848	4.4	50,294	52,565	4.5
U.S.	138,297,000	139,941,000	1.2	132,732,000	134,696,000	1.5

Note: Data is not seasonally adjusted and covers workers 16 years of age and older;
(1) Metropolitan Statistical Area - see Appendix A for areas included
Source: Bureau of Labor Statistics, http://stats.bls.gov

Unemployment Rate

Area	1999											
	Jan.	Feb.	Mar.	Apr.	May	Jun.	Jul.	Aug.	Sep.	Oct.	Nov.	Dec.
City	3.5	3.3	3.1	2.9	2.8	2.6	2.4	2.5	2.3	2.5	2.5	2.8
MSA[1]	3.3	3.1	3.0	2.5	2.4	2.6	2.2	2.3	2.0	2.2	2.4	2.4
U.S.	4.8	4.7	4.4	4.1	4.0	4.5	4.5	4.2	4.1	3.8	3.8	3.7

Note: Data is not seasonally adjusted and covers workers 16 years of age and older; all figures are percentages; (1) Metropolitan Statistical Area - see Appendix A for areas included
Source: Bureau of Labor Statistics, http://stats.bls.gov

Employment by Industry

Sector	MSA[1]		U.S.
	Number of Employees	Percent of Total	Percent of Total
Services	n/a	n/a	30.2
Retail Trade	n/a	n/a	18.1
Government	n/a	n/a	15.8
Manufacturing	n/a	n/a	14.1
Finance/Insurance/Real Estate	n/a	n/a	5.9
Wholesale Trade	n/a	n/a	5.4
Transportation/Public Utilities	n/a	n/a	5.3
Construction	n/a	n/a	4.8
Mining	n/a	n/a	0.4

Note: Figures cover non-farm employment as of 12/99 and are not seasonally adjusted;
(1) Metropolitan Statistical Area - see Appendix A for areas included; n/a not available
Source: Bureau of Labor Statistics, http://stats.bls.gov

Employment by Occupation

Occupation Category	City (%)	MSA[1] (%)	U.S. (%)
White Collar	62.9	61.6	58.1
Executive/Admin./Management	12.3	11.8	12.3
Professional	18.5	17.4	14.1
Technical & Related Support	4.3	4.1	3.7
Sales	12.9	12.8	11.8
Administrative Support/Clerical	14.9	15.6	16.3
Blue Collar	18.6	21.1	26.2
Precision Production/Craft/Repair	9.0	10.5	11.3
Machine Operators/Assem./Insp.	3.4	3.9	6.8
Transportation/Material Movers	3.2	3.4	4.1
Cleaners/Helpers/Laborers	3.0	3.3	3.9
Services	17.8	16.2	13.2
Farming/Forestry/Fishing	0.7	1.0	2.5

Note: Figures cover workers 16 years of age and older;
(1) Metropolitan Statistical Area - see Appendix A for areas included
Source: 1990 Census of Population and Housing, Summary Tape File 3C

Occupational Employment Projections: 1996 - 2006

Occupations Expected to Have the Largest Job Growth (ranked by numerical growth)	Fast-Growing Occupations[1] (ranked by percent growth)
1. Home health aides	1. Database administrators
2. Registered nurses	2. Adjustment clerks
3. Nursing aides/orderlies/attendants	3. Personal and home care aides
4. General managers & top executives	4. Physical therapists
5. Truck drivers, light	5. Medical assistants
6. Cashiers	6. Home health aides
7. Salespersons, retail	7. Systems analysts
8. Child care workers, private household	8. Human services workers
9. Marketing & sales, supervisors	9. Bill and account collectors
10. Food service workers	10. Dental hygienists

Note: Projections cover Maine; (1) Excludes occupations with total job growth less than 300
Source: U.S. Department of Labor, Employment and Training Administration, America's Labor Market Information System (ALMIS)

Average Wages

Occupation	$/Hr.	Occupation	$/Hr.
Accountants and Auditors	16.03	Maids and Housekeepers	6.47
Assemblers and Fabricators	9.97	Maintenance Repairers	10.02
Automotive Mechanics	11.64	Marketing/Advertising/PR Managers	20.46
Bookkeepers	10.12	Nurses, Licensed Practical	12.15
Carpenters	11.10	Nurses, Registered	-
Cashiers	6.87	Nursing Aides/Orderlies/Attendants	8.09
Clerks, General Office	9.08	Physicians and Surgeons	49.91
Clerks, Shipping/Receiving/Traffic	9.01	Receptionists/Information Clerks	7.88
Computer Programmers	20.01	Sales Reps., Exc. Scientific/Retail	16.10
Computer Support Specialists	15.54	Sales Reps., Scientific, Exc. Retail	22.58
Cooks, Restaurant	7.64	Salespersons, Retail	8.36
Electricians	16.87	Secretaries, Except Legal/Medical	9.90
Financial Managers	23.27	Stock Clerks, Sales Floor	8.67
First-Line Supervisors/Mgrs., Sales	14.97	Systems Analysts	20.58
Food Preparation Workers	6.84	Teacher Aides	9.25
General Managers/Top Executives	25.88	Teachers, Elementary School	15.31
Guards	7.95	Teachers, Secondary School	16.45
Hand Packers	6.83	Telemarketers	-
Janitors and Cleaners	8.15	Truck Drivers, Heavy/Tractor-Trailer	12.70
Laborers, Landscaping	7.80	Truck Drivers, Light	12.51
Lawyers	28.08	Waiters and Waitresses	6.11

Note: Wage data is for 1998 and covers the Metropolitan Statistical Area (see Appendix A for areas included). Hourly wages for elementary and secondary school teachers were calculated by the editors from annual wage data assuming a 40 hour work week; Dashes indicate that data was not available.
Source: Bureau of Labor Statistics, 1998 Metropolitan Area Occupational Employment and Wage Estimates

TAXES

Major State and Local Tax Rates

State Corporate Income (%)	State Personal Income (%)	Residential Property (%)	Sales & Use		State Gasoline (cents/ gallon)	State Cigarette (cents/ pack)
			State (%)	Local (%)		
3.5 - 8.93[a]	2.0 - 8.5	2.24	5.5	0.5	22.0	74.0

Note: Personal/corporate income, sales, gasoline and cigarette tax rates as of January 2000.
Property tax rates as of April 2000; (a) Or a 27% tax on Federal Alternative Minimum Taxable Income
Source: Federation of Tax Administrators, www.taxadmin.org; ERI's Relocation Assessor software database, quarterly effective date 4/1/2000

Total Taxes Per Capita and as a Percent of Income

Area	Per Capita Income ($)	Per Capita Taxes ($)			Percent of Income (%)		
		Total	Federal	State/Local	Total	Federal	State/Local
Maine	24,930	9,048	5,602	3,446	36.3	22.5	13.8
U.S.	28,878	10,298	7,026	3,273	35.7	24.3	11.3

Note: Figures are for 1999
Source: Tax Foundation, www.taxfoundation.org

COMMERCIAL UTILITIES

Typical Monthly Electric Bills

Area	Commercial Service ($/month)		Industrial Service ($/month)	
	12 kW demand 1,500 kWh	100 kW demand 30,000 kWh	1,000 kW demand 400,000 kWh	20,000 kW demand 10,000,000 kWh
City	194	3,663	43,882	718,982
U.S.	150	2,174	23,995	508,569

Note: Based on rates in effect January 1, 1999
Source: Edison Electric Institute, Typical Residential, Commercial and Industrial Bills, Winter 1999

TRANSPORTATION

Transportation Statistics

Average minutes to work (1990)	14.0
Interstate highways	I-95; I-395; US-2; US-202; US-ALT 1
Bus lines	
In-city (1998)	City of Bangor, 10 buses
Inter-city (1999)	5
Passenger air service	
Airport	Bangor International
Airlines (1999)	4
Enplaned passengers (1998)	417,236
Amtrak service	No
Motor freight carriers (1999)	28
Major waterways/ports	Penobscot River

Source: FAA DOT/TSC CY1998 ACAIS Database; National Transit Database, 1998; Editor & Publisher Market Guide, 2000; Amtrak National Time Table, Fall 1999/Winter 2000; 1990 Census of Population and Housing, STF 3C; Jane's Urban Transport Systems 1999-2000

Means of Transportation to Work

Area	Car/Truck/Van		Public Transportation			Bicycle	Walked	Other Means	Worked at Home
	Drove Alone	Car-pooled	Bus	Subway	Railroad				
City	75.9	12.4	1.4	0.0	0.0	0.4	4.9	1.9	3.0
MSA[1]	75.5	12.3	0.9	0.0	0.0	0.5	6.4	1.1	3.3
U.S.	73.2	13.4	3.0	1.5	0.5	0.4	3.9	1.2	3.0

Note: Figures shown are percentages and only include workers 16 years of age and older;
(1) Metropolitan Statistical Area - see Appendix A for areas included
Source: 1990 Census of Population and Housing, Summary Tape File 3C

BUSINESSES

Major Business Headquarters

Company Name	1999 Rankings	
	Fortune 500	Forbes 500
No companies listed	-	-

Note: Companies listed are located in the city; dashes indicate no ranking
Fortune 500: Companies that produce a 10-K are ranked 1 to 500 based on 1999 revenue
Forbes 500: Private companies are ranked 1 to 500 based on 1998 revenue
Source: Forbes, December 13, 1999; Fortune, April 17, 2000

HOTELS & MOTELS

Hotels/Motels

Area	Hotels/ Motels	Rooms	Luxury-Level Hotels/Motels		Average Minimum Rates ($)		
			♦♦♦♦	♦♦♦♦♦	♦♦	♦♦♦	♦♦♦♦
City	10	985	0	0	55	89	n/a
Airport	5	543	0	0	n/a	n/a	n/a
Suburbs	1	98	0	0	n/a	n/a	n/a
Total	16	1,626	0	0	n/a	n/a	n/a

Note: n/a not available; classifications range from one diamond (budget properties with basic amenities) to five diamond (luxury properties).
Source: OAG Business Travel Planner, Winter 1999-2000

Estimated Daily Food and Lodging Costs

Area	Food/Other ($/day)	Average Hotel Cost ($/day)
City	30	56
U.S.	30	55

Source: ERI's Relocation Assessor software database, quarterly effective date 4/1/2000

CONVENTION CENTERS

Convention Centers and Event Sites

Name	Guest Rooms	Meeting Space (sq. ft.)	Capacity (Theatre Style)
Bangor Auditorium and Civic Center	n/a	n/a	6,000
Four Points Hotel Bangor Airport	n/a	n/a	0
Holiday Inn Bangor - Civic Center	122	n/a	200

Note: n/a not available
Source: EventSource.com, 3/15/2000

Living Environment

COST OF LIVING

Cost of Living: Homeowner

Cost Element	U.S. ($)	City ($)	Differential ($)	Percent of U.S. Average
Consumables	14,516	17,126	2,610	118.0
Transportation	5,957	7,495	1,538	125.8
Health Services	2,012	2,338	326	116.2
Housing/Utilities/Prop. Tax	16,337	22,319	5,982	136.6
Income+Payroll Taxes	12,615	12,540	-75	99.4
Miscellaneous	8,563	8,563	0	100.0
Total Cost of Living	60,000	70,381	10,381	117.3

Note: Figures are based on a single income, four person family with gross annual earnings of $60,000, owning an 1,800 square-foot home, and driving two automobiles worth $22,000 30,000 miles per year.
Source: ERI's Relocation Assessor software database, quarterly effective date 4/1/2000

Cost of Living: Renter

Cost Element	U.S. ($)	City ($)	Differential ($)	Percent of U.S. Average
Consumables	10,486	12,434	1,948	118.6
Transportation	2,107	2,696	589	128.0
Health Services	1,632	1,906	274	116.8
Rent/Utilities/Insurance	9,299	13,059	3,760	140.4
Income+Payroll Taxes	8,607	8,847	240	102.8
Miscellaneous	7,869	7,869	0	100.0
Total Cost of Living	40,000	46,811	6,811	117.0

Note: Figures are based on a single income, three person family with gross annual earnings of $40,000, renting a 1,000 square-foot home, and driving one automobile worth $8,000 12,000 miles per year.
Source: ERI's Relocation Assessor software database, quarterly effective date 4/1/2000

HOUSING

Median Home Prices and Housing Affordability

Area	Median Price[2] 4th Qtr. 1999 ($)	HOI[3] 4th Qtr. 1999	Affordability Rank[4]
MSA[1]	n/a	n/a	n/a
U.S.	139,000	63.8	–

Note: (1) Metropolitan Statistical Area - see Appendix A for areas included; (2) U.S. figures calculated from the sales of 687,516 new and existing homes in 192 markets; (3) Housing Opportunity Index - percent of homes sold that were within the reach of the median income household at the prevailing mortgage interest rate; (4) Rank is from 1-192 with 1 being most affordable; n/a not available
Source: National Association of Home Builders, Housing Opportunity Index, 4th Quarter 1999

Estimated Home Price

Area	Price ($)
City	155,853
U.S.	135,855

Note: Figures are based on an 1,800 square-foot home
Source: ERI's Relocation Assessor software database, quarterly effective date 4/1/2000

Estimated Rent

Area	Rent ($/month)
City	915
U.S.	651

Note: Figures are based on a 1,000 square-foot home
Source: ERI's Relocation Assessor software database, quarterly effective date 4/1/2000

Median Home Price Projection

It is projected that the median home price in the metropolitan area will increase from $99,239 in 1999 to $147,046 in 2010, an increase of 48.2%
Kiplinger's Personal Finance Magazine, January 2000

RESIDENTIAL UTILITIES

Average Residential Utility Costs

Area	All Electric ($/mth)	Part Electric ($/mth)	Other Energy ($/mth)	Phone ($/mth)
City	n/a	n/a	n/a	n/a
U.S.	99.25	55.47	43.48	20.29

Note: n/a not available
Source: ACCRA, Cost of Living Index, 3rd Quarter 1999

HEALTH CARE

Average Health Care Costs

Area	Hospital ($/day)	Doctor ($/visit)	Dentist ($/visit)
City	n/a	n/a	n/a
U.S.	440.96	53.83	68.42

Note: n/a not available
Source: ACCRA, Cost of Living Index, 3rd Quarter 1999

Distribution of Office-Based Physicians

Area	Family/Gen. Practitioners	Specialists		
		Medical	Surgical	Other
MSA[1]	33	80	70	82

Note: Data as of 12/31/97; (1) Metropolitan Statistical Area - see Appendix A for areas included
Source: American Medical Assn., Physician Characteristics & Distribution in the U.S., 1999

Hospitals

Bangor has 2 general medical and surgical hospitals, 2 rehabilitation.
AHA Guide to the Healthcare Field, 1999-2000

EDUCATION

Public School District Statistics

District Name	Num. Sch.	Enroll.	Classroom Teachers	Pupils per Teacher	Minority Pupils (%)	Current Exp.[1] ($/pupil)
Bangor	10	4,431	294	15.1	n/a	n/a
Glenburn	1	523	35	14.9	n/a	n/a
Hermon	3	1,076	65	16.6	n/a	n/a

Note: Data covers the 1997-1998 school year unless otherwise noted; (1) Data covers fiscal year 1996; SD = School District; ISD = Independent School District; n/a not available
Source: National Center for Education Statistics, Common Core of Data Public Education Agency Universe 1997-98; National Center for Education Statistics, Characteristics of the 100 Largest Public Elementary and Secondary School Districts in the United States: 1997-98, July 1999

Educational Quality

School District	Education Quotient[1]	Graduate Outcome[2]	Community Index[3]	Resource Index[4]
Bangor	118	124	107	107

Note: Over 1,000 secondary school districts were rated in terms of educational quality. The scores range from a low of 50 to a high of 150; (1) Combination of the Graduate Outcome, Community and Resource indexes weighted to reflect the greater importance of the Graduate Outcome and Resource Index; (2) Based on graduation rates and college board scores (SAT/ACT); (3) Based on the surrounding community's level of affluence and adult education; (4) Based on teacher salaries, per-pupil expenditures and student-teacher ratios.
Source: Expansion Management, Ratings Issue, 1999

Educational Attainment by Race

Area	High School Graduate (%)					Bachelor's Degree (%)				
	Total	White	Black	Other	Hisp.[2]	Total	White	Black	Other	Hisp.[2]
City	83.5	83.4	93.5	85.2	83.3	24.4	24.6	21.1	17.4	17.5
MSA[1]	82.7	82.6	93.8	81.7	92.2	23.7	23.6	26.6	33.0	33.2
U.S.	75.2	77.9	63.1	60.4	49.8	20.3	21.5	11.4	19.4	9.2

Note: Figures shown cover persons 25 years old and over; (1) Metropolitan Statistical Area - see Appendix A for areas included; (2) people of Hispanic origin can be of any race
Source: 1990 Census of Population and Housing, Summary Tape File 3C

School Enrollment by Type

Area	Preprimary				Elementary/High School			
	Public		Private		Public		Private	
	Enrollment	%	Enrollment	%	Enrollment	%	Enrollment	%
City	416	53.6	360	46.4	4,117	92.6	329	7.4
MSA[1]	1,126	62.3	681	37.7	12,233	94.2	754	5.8
U.S.	2,679,029	59.5	1,824,256	40.5	38,379,689	90.2	4,187,099	9.8

Note: Figures shown cover persons 3 years old and over;
(1) Metropolitan Statistical Area - see Appendix A for areas included
Source: 1990 Census of Population and Housing, Summary Tape File 3C

School Enrollment by Race

Area	Preprimary (%)				Elementary/High School (%)			
	White	Black	Other	Hisp.[1]	White	Black	Other	Hisp.[1]
City	97.3	0.9	1.8	2.2	96.9	0.9	2.2	0.6
MSA[2]	96.5	0.7	2.8	1.1	96.7	0.4	2.9	0.6
U.S.	80.4	12.5	7.1	7.8	74.1	15.6	10.3	12.5

Note: Figures shown cover persons 3 years old and over; (1) people of Hispanic origin can be of any race; (2) Metropolitan Statistical Area - see Appendix A for areas included
Source: 1990 Census of Population and Housing, Summary Tape File 3C

Higher Education

Two-Year Colleges		Four-Year Colleges		Medical Schools	Law Schools	Voc/Tech
Public	Private	Public	Private			
1	3	1	0	0	0	2

Source: College Blue Book, Occupational Education, 1999; Medical School Admission Requirements, 1999-2000; Peterson's Guide to Two-Year Colleges, 2000; Peterson's Guide to Four-Year Colleges, 1999; Barron's Guide to Law Schools, 1999

MAJOR EMPLOYERS

Major Employers

Acadia Hospital
Bangor Hydro-Electric Co.
Eastern Main Medical Center
Hall Security Services
Webber Oil Co.

Affiliated Healthcare Systems
Bangor Publishing
Erin Inc. (motels)
St. Joseph Hospital

Note: Companies listed are located in the city
Source: D&B Business Rankings, 1999; Ward's Business Directory, 1999; America's Corporate Families, 1999

PUBLIC SAFETY

Crime Rate

Area	All Crimes	Violent Crimes				Property Crimes		
		Murder	Forcible Rape	Robbery	Aggrav. Assault	Burglary	Larceny -Theft	Motor Vehicle Theft
City	6,775.6	0.0	50.7	79.2	66.5	902.8	5,391.4	285.1
Suburbs[1]	2,537.4	0.0	9.0	17.9	26.9	364.2	1,970.2	149.3
MSA[2]	4,593.7	0.0	29.2	47.6	46.1	625.5	3,630.0	215.2
U.S.	4,615.5	6.3	34.4	165.2	360.5	862.0	2,728.1	459.0

Note: Crime rate is the number of crimes per 100,000 population; (1) Defined as all areas within the Metropolitan Statistical Area but located outside the central city; (2) Metropolitan Statistical Area - see Appendix A for areas included
Source: FBI Uniform Crime Reports, 1998

RECREATION

Culture and Recreation

Museums	Symphony Orchestras	Opera Companies	Dance Companies	Professional Theatres	Zoos	Pro Sports Teams
2	1	0	0	1	0	0

Source: Musical America, International Directory of the Performing Arts, 1999; Official Museum Directory, 2000; Stern's Performing Arts Directory, 1997; USA Today Four Sport Stadium Guide, 1997; Career Opportunities in Theatre and the Performing Arts, 1999

Library System

The Bangor Public Library has no branches, holdings of 430,576 volumes, and a budget of $1,464,791 (1997-1998).
American Library Directory, 1999-2000

MEDIA

Newspapers

Name	Type	Freq.	Distribution	Circulation
Bangor Daily News	General	6x/wk	U.S./Can.	78,000

Note: Includes newspapers with circulations of 200 or more located in the city;
Source: Burrelle's Media Directory, 1999 Edition

Television Stations

Name	Ch.	Affiliation	Type	Owner
WLBZ	n/a	NBCT	Commercial	Gannett Broadcasting
WABI	n/a	CBST	Commercial	Community Broadcasting Inc.
WVII	n/a	ABCT	Commercial	Roclfleet Broadcasting Inc.
WCBB	10	PBS	Public	Maine Public Broadcasting Corporation
WMEB	12	PBS	Public	Maine Public Broadcasting Corporation

Note: Stations included broadcast in the Bangor metro area; n/a not available
Source: Burrelle's Media Directory, 1999 Edition

AM Radio Stations

Call Letters	Freq. (kHz)	Target Audience	Station Format	Music Format
WZON	620	General	S	n/a
WABI	910	General	M	Big Band
WSYY	1240	General	M/N/S	Oldies

Note: Stations included broadcast in the Bangor metro area; n/a not available
Target Audience: A=Asian; B=Black; C=Christian; E=Ethnic; F=French; G=General; H=Hispanic; M=Men; N=Native American; R=Religious; S=Senior Citizen; W=Women; Y=Young Adult; Z=Children
Station Format: E=Educational; M=Music; N=News; S=Sports; T=Talk
Source: Burrelle's Media Directory, 1999 Edition

FM Radio Stations

Call Letters	Freq. (mHz)	Target Audience	Station Format	Music Format
WHCF	88.5	Religious	M/N/S	Christian
WHSN	89.3	General	M/N/S	Alternative/AOR
WMED	89.7	General	M/N	Classical/Jazz
WMEA	90.1	General	M/N	Classical/Jazz
WMEH	90.9	General	M/T	Classical/Jazz
WMEW	91.3	General	M/N	Classical/Jazz
WMEB	91.9	General	M/N/S	Alternative
WEZQ	92.9	General	M	Adult Contemporary
WSYY	94.9	General	M/N/S	Country
WWMJ	95.7	General	M/N	Oldies
WWBX	97.1	General	M	Top 40
WKIT	100.3	General	M	AOR/Classic Rock
WGUY	102.1	General	M/N/S	Oldies
WVOM	103.9	General	N/T	n/a
WBFB	104.7	General	M/N	Country
WQCB	106.5	General	M/N	Country
WBZN	107.3	General	M/N	n/a

Note: Stations included broadcast in the Bangor metro area; n/a not available
Station Format: E=Educational; M=Music; N=News; S=Sports; T=Talk
Target Audience: A=Asian; B=Black; C=Christian; E=Ethnic; F=French; G=General; H=Hispanic; M=Men; N=Native American; R=Religious; S=Senior Citizen; W=Women; Y=Young Adult; Z=Children
Music Format: AOR=Album Oriented Rock; MOR=Middle-of-the-Road
Source: Burrelle's Media Directory, 1999 Edition

WEATHER

Temperature/Precipitation/Humidity

	Jan	Feb	Mar	Apr	May	Jun	Jul	Aug	Sep	Oct	Nov	Dec	Yr.
Max. High Temp. (°F)	56	56	72	80	91	95	99	98	91	84	70	61	99
Avg. High Temp. (°F)	28	32	38	52	65	74	80	78	69	58	45	32	54
Avg. Temp. (°F)	17	20	28	41	52	61	67	65	57	46	36	22	43
Avg. Low Temp. (°F)	7	9	18	31	40	49	55	52	45	35	28	13	32
Min. Low Temp. (°F)	-30	-33	-16	-1	22	31	41	35	23	16	-1	-29	-33
Avg. Precip. (in.)	3.6	3.8	3.3	3.5	3.2	3.2	2.9	3.2	3.4	4.0	4.8	4.4	43.2
Avg. Snowfall (in.)	18.6	23.2	15.8	1.5	0.2	0	0	0	0	0.4	4.1	14.6	78.4
Avg. Rel. Hum. (%)	75	73	70	71	69	73	74	76	79	78	79	77	75

Source: National Climatic Data Center, International Station Meteorological Climate Summary, 3/95

Weather Conditions

Temperature			Precipitation		
0°F & below	32°F & below	90°F & above	0.1 inch or more precip.	1.5 inch or more snow/ice	Thunder-storms
27	180	5	86	15	16

Note: Figures are average number of days per year
Source: National Climatic Data Center, International Station Meteorological Climate Summary, 3/95

AIR & WATER QUALITY

Maximum Pollutant Concentrations

	Particulate Matter (ug/m³)	Carbon Monoxide (ppm)	Sulfur Dioxide (ppm)	Nitrogen Dioxide (ppm)	Ozone (ppm)	Lead (ug/m³)
MSA[1] Level	52	n/a	n/a	n/a	0.09	n/a
NAAQS[2]	150	9	0.140	0.053	0.12	1.50
Met NAAQS	Yes	n/a	n/a	n/a	Yes	n/a

Note: (1) Metropolitan Statistical Area - see Appendix A for areas included; (2) National Ambient Air Quality Standards; ppm = parts per million; ug/m³ = micrograms per cubic meter; n/a not available
Source: EPA, National Air Quality and Emissions Trends Report, 1997

Pollutant Standards Index

Data not available.
EPA, National Air Quality and Emissions Trends Report, 1997

Drinking Water

Water System Name	Pop. Served	Primary Water Source Type	Number of Violations in 1998-99	Type of Violation/ Contaminants
Bangor Water District	24,908	Surface	None	None

Note: Data as of January 19, 2000
Source: EPA, Office of Ground Water and Drinking Water, Safe Drinking Water Information System

Bangor tap water is alkaline, very soft, and fluoridated.
Editor & Publisher Market Guide, 2000

Bellevue, Washington

Background

Bellevue, Washington is located in the metropolitan corridor that includes Seattle and other communities near Puget Sound in western Washington state. Bellevue is both a suburb of neighboring Seattle, and a rapidly-growing city in its own right.

The lowlands and hills around Puget Sound are situated between two high mountain chains, the Olympics to the west and the Cascades to the east. Bellevue is located in an area of King County known as the Eastside, which includes suburbs and outlying rural communities extending east from Seattle and Lake Washington toward the Cascade Mountains. The city borders the eastern shoreline of Lake Washington, directly across the lake from Seattle, and covers 31 square miles.

Bellevue (French for "beautiful view") was founded in 1869 by William Meydenbauer. Bellevue was a small community until the mid-1940s, when the first of two floating bridges were constructed across Lake Washington. This made the drive between Seattle and Bellevue only a few minutes, which stimulated commuter-oriented residential and retail development in Bellevue. The city was incorporated in 1953. Today, Bellevue's land-use patterns and building styles are predominantly contemporary and suburban.

The Puget Sound economy was traditionally based on logging, shipping, seafood and the aircraft manufacturer Boeing Corp. The region began to experience increasing growth in the 1970s. This was prompted by increased trade with the Pacific Rim and the emergence of the computer and high-tech industries. The population grew also from an influx of residents from other parts of the country, attracted by Bellevue's mix of urban activities, scenic environment and outdoor recreation.

Bellevue is among the more affluent communities in the region. In addition to residents who work in Seattle and other nearby communities, Bellevue's own economy has grown and diversified significantly since the 1970s. The Eastside is a center for the region's computer and technology industry, including biotechnology, aerospace and software. Microsoft Corporation is headquartered in Redmond, a community adjacent to Bellevue. Bellevue's economy also includes manufacturing, retailing, and professional and services sectors.

While economic and population growth has brought prosperity and major development to the region, there is concern over such issues as pollution, sprawl, traffic, high costs of living, etc. Since significant growth is expected to continue in Bellevue, planning policies have been established to balance development with preservation of land and quality of life. The city has preserved approximately 1,700 acres of open space, including 56 parks and nearly 40 miles of trails. In recent years, municipal planning policies have also tried to steer growth into Bellevue's 443-acre downtown area by encouraging high-rise structures and mixed-use development. The intent is to foster an active and diverse urban center while reducing development pressure in other sections of the city.

Bellevue residents have access to numerous recreational activities in the area. National parks and forests are within a short drive from the city, and many local parks are on the water. Water activities play a major role in Bellevue's recreational offerings, as the city has easy access to Puget Sound, Lake Washington and many other lakes and channels.

Cultural facilities within Bellevue include the Bellevue Art Museum and the Meydenbauer Convention Center and Theater for the Performing Arts. The Rosalie Whyel Museum of Doll Art features over 1,200 dolls. Performing arts organizations include the Bellevue Philharmonic and the Bellevue Chamber Chorus, among others.

Bellevue has one institution of higher education, Bellevue Community College, with many other colleges and universities in the surrounding area.

Bellevue has a Council-Manager form of government. The Council elects a Mayor and appoints the City Manager.

General Rankings and Evaluative Comments

- Bellevue was ranked #3 out of 354 metropolitan areas in *Places Rated Almanac*. Criteria: cost of living, climate, crime, transportation, job outlook, education, the arts, health care, and recreation. *Places Rated Almanac, Millennium Edition, 2000*

- Bellevue was selected by *Yahoo! Internet Life* as one of "America's Most Wired Cities & Towns." The city ranked #3 out of 50. Criteria: home and work net use, domain density, hosts per capita, directory density, and content quality. *Yahoo! Internet Life, March 1999*

- Cognetics studied 273 metro areas in the United States, ranking them by entrepreneurial activity. Bellevue was ranked #40 out of the 50 largest metro areas. Criteria: Significant Starts (firms started in the last 10 years that still employ at least 5 people) and Young Growers (percent of firms 10 years old or less that grew significantly during the last 4 years). *Cognetics, "Entrepreneurial Hot Spots: The Best Places in America to Start and Grow a Company," 1999*

- Bellevue was included among *Entrepreneur* magazine's listing of the "20 Best Cities for Small Business." It was ranked #20 among large metro areas and #2 among western metro areas. Criteria: entrepreneurial activity, small-business growth, economic growth, and risk of failure. *Entrepreneur, October 1999*

- Reliastar Financial Corporation ranked the 125 largest metropolitan areas according to the general financial security of residents. Bellevue was ranked #5 out of 125 with a score of 15.8 (the percentage a metropolitan area is above or below the metropolitan norm; a metro area with a score of 10.6 is 10.6% above the metro average). Criteria: Earnings and Wealth Potential (household income, education, net assets, cost of living); Safety Net (health insurance, retirement savings, life insurance, income support programs); Personal Threats (unemployment rate, low-income households, crime rate); Community Economic Vitality (cost of community services, job quality, job creation, housing costs). *Reliastar Financial Corporation, "The Best Cities to Earn and Save Money: A Ranking of the Largest 125 U.S. Cities," 2000 Edition*

Business Environment

STATE ECONOMY

State Economic Profile

"After some recent years of very strong growth, the Washington economy is quickly losing steam. Washington's manufacturing employment shrank in 1998, mostly as the result of continued layoffs by Boeing.

Further layoffs and a slowing US economy will dampen the Washington economy. Strong migration and a young, educated workforce will lead to strong long-term growth for Washington after its current problems have run their course.

Spokane's employment base shrank by almost 2% in 1998, shedding some 3,700 jobs on net. The bulk of these were in manufacturing, where employment declined by 13.7%, losing 3,100 jobs on net. Construction employment also declined by 11.2%, even as multifamily housing permits increased by 69% and single family permits by 19%. Given its current economic contract, both Spokane' residential and commercial properties markets are facing increasing inventories and rising vacancies. While the rest of the nation enjoyed a booming housing market, home price appreciation in Spokane was negative in 1998. The housing market should stabilize, but remain weak in the near future.

The Puget Sound economy fared well in 1998 in light of the expected Boeing cutbacks. The employment base expanded by 2.7% in 1998, even as manufacturing declined by 0.6%. An increase of 3.4% in services and 6.6% in construction helped to offset losses in manufacturing. With the manufacturing sector declining even further, the current level of construction is not sustainable, and construction employment should contract in 2000. Home price appreciation in Seattle was weak in 1998 at around 2%, and both volume and prices in Seattle should decline in 2000.

Washington's economy is headed for a substantial turbulence in the near term. Fortunately, the economy is mostly in good shape, which will help with the absorption of workers leaving Boeing. Long term, stabilization at Boeing, the ongoing expansion of the software industry, and a rebound in migration will lead to above-average growth." *National Association of Realtors, Economic Profiles: The Fifty States and the District of Columbia, http://nar.realtor.com/databank/profiles.htm*

EXPORTS

Total Export Sales

Area	1995 ($000)	1996 ($000)	1997 ($000)	1998 ($000)	% Chg. 1995-98	% Chg. 1997-98
MSA[1]	17,815,388	21,391,133	27,005,836	34,003,330	90.9	25.9
U.S.	583,030,524	622,827,063	687,597,999	680,474,251	16.7	-1.0

Note: (1) Metropolitan Statistical Area - see Appendix A for areas included
Source: U.S. Department of Commerce, International Trade Association, Metropolitan Area Exports: An Export Performance Report on Over 250 U.S. Cities, November 10, 1999

CITY FINANCES

City Government Finances

Component	1995 ($million)	1995 (per capita $)
Revenue	138.2	1,640
Expenditure	114.9	1,364
Debt Outstanding	130.6	1,550

Source: 1999 County and City Extra, Annual Metro, City, and County Data Book

City Government Revenue by Source

Source	1995 ($million)	1995 (per capita $)
Intergovernmental	16.9	200
Taxes	86.4	1,025
Property	22.6	269
Sales and Gross Receipts	44.9	534

Source: 1999 County and City Extra, Annual Metro, City, and County Data Book

City Government Expenditures by Function

Function	1995 ($million)	1995 (per capita $)	1995 (%)
Public Welfare	0.2	2	0.2
Highways	16.8	200	14.7
Parking Facilities	0.0	0	0.0
Education	0.0	0	0.0
Health and Hospitals	0.9	10	0.8
Police Protection	13.7	163	12.0
Sewerage and Sanitation	13.5	160	11.8
Parks and Recreation	15.8	188	13.8
Housing and Community Development	3.4	40	3.0
Interest on Debt	4.3	51	3.8

Source: 1999 County and City Extra, Annual Metro, City, and County Data Book

Municipal Bond Ratings

Area	Moody's
City	Aaa

Source: Mergent Bond Record, 2/2000

POPULATION

Population Growth

Area	1980 Census	1990 Census	1999 Estimate	2004 Projection	Population Growth (%) 1990-1999	Population Growth (%) 1999-2004
City	73,883	86,878	107,061	116,213	23.2	8.5
MSA[1]	1,607,469	1,972,961	2,330,597	2,480,525	18.1	6.4
U.S.	226,545,805	248,765,170	272,212,864	283,625,312	9.4	4.2

Note: (1) Metropolitan Statistical Area - see Appendix A for areas included
Source: 1990 Census of Population and Housing, Summary Tape File 3C; Claritas, Inc.

Number of Households and Average Household Size

Area	1980 Census	1990 Census	1999 Estimate	2004 Projection	1999 Average Household Size
City	28,355	35,786	45,562	50,137	2.35
MSA[1]	633,816	788,542	942,435	1,011,384	2.47
U.S.	80,389,592	91,993,582	102,048,200	107,302,392	2.67

Note: (1) Metropolitan Statistical Area - see Appendix A for areas included
Source: 1990 Census of Population and Housing, Summary Tape File 3C; Claritas, Inc.

Race/Ethnicity of City Population

Race/Ethnicity	1990 Census Population	1990 Census %	1999 Estimate Population	1999 Estimate %	% Change 1990-1999
White, Non-Hispanic	74,065	85.3	84,096	78.5	13.5
Black, Non-Hispanic	1,779	2.0	3,229	3.0	81.5
Asian, Non-Hispanic	8,603	9.9	15,120	14.1	75.8
Other, Non-Hispanic	392	0.5	443	0.4	13.0
Hispanic	2,039	2.3	4,173	3.9	104.7

Source: 1990 Census of Population and Housing, Summary Tape File 3C; Claritas, Inc.

Race/Ethnicity of Metropolitan Statistical Area Population

Race/Ethnicity	1990 Census		1999 Estimate		% Change 1990-1999
	Population	%	Population	%	
White, Non-Hispanic	1,686,640	85.5	1,899,004	81.5	12.6
Black, Non-Hispanic	77,777	3.9	105,770	4.5	36.0
Asian, Non-Hispanic	132,478	6.7	201,316	8.6	52.0
Other, Non-Hispanic	24,442	1.2	26,688	1.1	9.2
Hispanic	51,624	2.6	97,819	4.2	89.5

Note: See Appendix A for areas included in the Metropolitan Statistical Area
Source: 1990 Census of Population and Housing, Summary Tape File 3C; Claritas, Inc.

Ancestry

Area	German	Irish	English	Italian	U.S.	French	Polish	Dutch
City	26.1	14.4	21.7	3.6	2.0	5.2	2.4	2.4
MSA[1]	27.1	15.6	18.6	3.7	2.7	5.4	2.2	3.2
U.S.	23.3	15.6	13.1	5.9	5.3	4.2	3.8	2.5

Note: Figures are percentages and include persons that reported multiple ancestry (eg. if a person reported being Irish and Italian, they were included in both columns); (1) Metropolitan Statistical Area - see Appendix A for areas included
Source: 1990 Census of Population and Housing, Summary Tape File 3C

Median Age

Area	1990 Census	1999 Estimate
City	35.6	38.7
MSA[1]	33.3	36.4
U.S.	32.9	35.7

Note: (1) Metropolitan Statistical Area - see Appendix A for areas included
Source: 1990 Census of Population and Housing, Summary Tape File 3C; Claritas, Inc.

Male/Female Population

Area	Number of Males		Number of Females		Males per 100 Females	
	1990	1999	1990	1999	1990	1999
City	42,528	52,143	44,350	54,918	95.9	94.9
MSA[1]	973,534	1,149,979	999,427	1,180,618	97.4	97.4
U.S.	121,172,379	132,803,736	127,537,494	139,409,136	95.0	95.3

Note: (1) Metropolitan Statistical Area - see Appendix A for areas included
Source: 1990 Census of Population, General Population Characteristics; Claritas, Inc.

INCOME

Per Capita/Median/Average Income

Area	Per Capita ($)			Median Household ($)			Average Household ($)		
	1989	1999	% Chg.	1989	1999	% Chg.	1989	1999	% Chg.
City	23,816	40,499	70.0	43,800	67,065	53.1	57,587	94,751	64.5
MSA[1]	17,921	29,094	62.3	36,338	54,743	50.6	44,337	70,969	60.1
U.S.	14,420	21,350	48.1	30,056	40,525	34.8	38,453	56,184	46.1

Note: (1) Metropolitan Statistical Area - see Appendix A for areas included; 1989 data is from the 1990 Census; 1999 data is estimated by Claritas, Inc.
Source: 1990 Census of Population, General Population Characteristics; Claritas, Inc.

Household Income Distribution

Area	Percent of Households Earning								
	Under $5,000	$5,000 -14,999	$15,000 -24,999	$25,000 -34,999	$35,000 -49,999	$50,000 -74,999	$75,000 -99,000	$100,000 -149,999	$150,000 and up
City	1.3	5.5	7.1	9.8	12.6	19.5	13.4	13.5	17.3
MSA[1]	1.9	7.7	9.6	10.3	15.1	23.1	14.0	10.4	7.9
U.S.	3.9	13.3	13.8	12.6	16.2	19.4	9.7	6.6	4.6

Note: Data as of 1999; (1) Metropolitan Statistical Area - see Appendix A for areas included
Source: Claritas, Inc.

Effective Buying Income

Area	Per Capita ($)	Median Household ($)	Average Household ($)
City	31,612	61,227	76,515
MSA[1]	25,065	51,050	62,844
U.S.	17,496	36,603	47,036

Note: Data as of 1/1/2000; (1) Metropolitan Statistical Area - see Appendix A for areas included
Source: Standard Rate & Data Service, Newspaper Advertising Source, March 2000

Effective Household Buying Income Distribution

Area	% of Households Earning						
	$10,000 -$19,999	$20,000 -$34,999	$35,000 -$49,999	$50,000 -$74,999	$75,000 -$99,000	$100,000 -$124,999	$125,000 and up
City	6.9	15.0	14.4	20.9	16.4	9.6	13.1
MSA[1]	9.5	16.9	16.7	24.0	13.9	6.4	6.9
U.S.	15.0	21.6	17.6	19.6	8.4	3.0	3.3

Note: Data as of 1/1/2000; (1) Metropolitan Statistical Area - see Appendix A for areas included
Source: Standard Rate & Data Service, Newspaper Advertising Source, March 2000

Poverty Rates by Age

Area	People of All Ages	People Under 18 Years Old	Related Children Age 5-17 in Families in Poverty
City	6.2	n/a	n/a
County	8.6	12.3	10.4
U.S.	13.8	20.8	18.7

Note: Figures show the percent of people living below the poverty line in 1995. The average poverty threshold was $15,569 for a family of four in 1995; n/a not available
Source: Bureau of the Census, Small Area Income and Poverty Estimates Program; U.S. Department of Housing and Urban Development

EMPLOYMENT

Labor Force and Employment

Area	Civilian Labor Force			Workers Employed		
	Dec. 1998	Dec. 1999	% Chg.	Dec. 1998	Dec. 1999	% Chg.
City	63,236	63,951	1.1	61,881	62,697	1.3
MSA[1]	1,414,106	1,431,642	1.2	1,371,151	1,389,230	1.3
U.S.	138,297,000	139,941,000	1.2	132,732,000	134,696,000	1.5

Note: Data is not seasonally adjusted and covers workers 16 years of age and older;
(1) Metropolitan Statistical Area - see Appendix A for areas included
Source: Bureau of Labor Statistics, http://stats.bls.gov

Unemployment Rate

Area	1999											
	Jan.	Feb.	Mar.	Apr.	May	Jun.	Jul.	Aug.	Sep.	Oct.	Nov.	Dec.
City	2.4	2.5	2.3	2.2	2.2	2.3	2.4	2.3	2.4	2.5	2.0	2.0
MSA[1]	3.4	3.6	3.4	3.1	3.2	3.4	3.5	3.3	3.6	3.7	3.0	3.0
U.S.	4.8	4.7	4.4	4.1	4.0	4.5	4.5	4.2	4.1	3.8	3.8	3.7

Note: Data is not seasonally adjusted and covers workers 16 years of age and older; all figures are percentages; (1) Metropolitan Statistical Area - see Appendix A for areas included
Source: Bureau of Labor Statistics, http://stats.bls.gov

Employment by Industry

Sector	MSA[1]		U.S.
	Number of Employees	Percent of Total	Percent of Total
Services	418,500	29.8	30.2
Retail Trade	245,200	17.4	18.1
Government	190,300	13.5	15.8
Manufacturing	206,900	14.7	14.1
Finance/Insurance/Real Estate	85,800	6.1	5.9
Wholesale Trade	93,000	6.6	5.4
Transportation/Public Utilities	86,900	6.2	5.3
Construction	79,400	5.6	4.8
Mining	700	<0.1	0.4

Note: Figures cover non-farm employment as of 12/99 and are not seasonally adjusted;
(1) Metropolitan Statistical Area - see Appendix A for areas included
Source: Bureau of Labor Statistics, http://stats.bls.gov

Employment by Occupation

Occupation Category	City (%)	MSA[1] (%)	U.S. (%)
White Collar	77.5	65.2	58.1
Executive/Admin./Management	20.2	14.7	12.3
Professional	19.6	16.8	14.1
Technical & Related Support	4.5	4.4	3.7
Sales	17.1	12.7	11.8
Administrative Support/Clerical	16.1	16.6	16.3
Blue Collar	12.2	22.2	26.2
Precision Production/Craft/Repair	6.2	11.1	11.3
Machine Operators/Assem./Insp.	2.9	4.7	6.8
Transportation/Material Movers	1.5	3.3	4.1
Cleaners/Helpers/Laborers	1.7	3.1	3.9
Services	9.3	11.2	13.2
Farming/Forestry/Fishing	1.0	1.4	2.5

Note: Figures cover workers 16 years of age and older;
(1) Metropolitan Statistical Area - see Appendix A for areas included
Source: 1990 Census of Population and Housing, Summary Tape File 3C

Occupational Employment Projections: 1996 - 2006

Occupations Expected to Have the Largest Job Growth (ranked by numerical growth)	Fast-Growing Occupations[1] (ranked by percent growth)
1. Salespersons, retail	1. Personal and home care aides
2. Cashiers	2. Systems analysts
3. Child care workers, private household	3. Paralegals
4. General managers & top executives	4. Electronic semiconductor processors
5. Computer engineers	5. Directors, religious activities & educ.
6. Systems analysts	6. Physical therapy assistants and aides
7. Database administrators	7. Respiratory therapists
8. Food service workers	8. Human services workers
9. Truck drivers, light	9. Medical assistants
10. Janitors/cleaners/maids, ex. priv. hshld.	10. Medical records technicians

Note: Projections cover Washington; (1) Excludes occupations with total job growth less than 300
Source: U.S. Department of Labor, Employment and Training Administration, America's Labor Market Information System (ALMIS)

Average Wages

Occupation	$/Hr.	Occupation	$/Hr.
Accountants and Auditors	21.72	Maids and Housekeepers	8.14
Assemblers and Fabricators	11.08	Maintenance Repairers	13.76
Automotive Mechanics	14.86	Marketing/Advertising/PR Managers	28.44
Bookkeepers	13.19	Nurses, Licensed Practical	14.94
Carpenters	19.13	Nurses, Registered	24.42
Cashiers	9.24	Nursing Aides/Orderlies/Attendants	9.61
Clerks, General Office	11.69	Physicians and Surgeons	42.25
Clerks, Shipping/Receiving/Traffic	12.78	Receptionists/Information Clerks	10.13
Computer Programmers	25.00	Sales Reps., Exc. Scientific/Retail	20.96
Computer Support Specialists	18.25	Sales Reps., Scientific, Exc. Retail	24.24
Cooks, Restaurant	9.44	Salespersons, Retail	10.65
Electricians	21.44	Secretaries, Except Legal/Medical	13.42
Financial Managers	28.59	Stock Clerks, Sales Floor	9.31
First-Line Supervisors/Mgrs., Sales	18.72	Systems Analysts	-
Food Preparation Workers	7.86	Teacher Aides	10.48
General Managers/Top Executives	32.24	Teachers, Elementary School	19.50
Guards	9.71	Teachers, Secondary School	19.64
Hand Packers	7.97	Telemarketers	9.46
Janitors and Cleaners	9.54	Truck Drivers, Heavy/Tractor-Trailer	16.69
Laborers, Landscaping	10.97	Truck Drivers, Light	11.15
Lawyers	38.74	Waiters and Waitresses	6.38

Note: Wage data is for 1998 and covers the Metropolitan Statistical Area (see Appendix A for areas included). Hourly wages for elementary and secondary school teachers were calculated by the editors from annual wage data assuming a 40 hour work week; Dashes indicate that data was not available.
Source: Bureau of Labor Statistics, 1998 Metropolitan Area Occupational Employment and Wage Estimates

TAXES

Major State and Local Tax Rates

State Corporate Income (%)	State Personal Income (%)	Residential Property (%)	Sales & Use		State Gasoline (cents/ gallon)	State Cigarette (cents/ pack)
			State (%)	Local (%)		
None	None	1.17	6.5	2.1	23.0	82.5

Note: Personal/corporate income, sales, gasoline and cigarette tax rates as of January 2000. Property tax rates as of April 2000.
Source: Federation of Tax Administrators, www.taxadmin.org; ERI's Relocation Assessor software database, quarterly effective date 4/1/2000

Total Taxes Per Capita and as a Percent of Income

Area	Per Capita Income ($)	Per Capita Taxes ($)			Percent of Income (%)		
		Total	Federal	State/Local	Total	Federal	State/Local
Washington	30,430	11,355	7,688	3,667	37.3	25.3	12.0
U.S.	28,878	10,298	7,026	3,273	35.7	24.3	11.3

Note: Figures are for 1999
Source: Tax Foundation, www.taxfoundation.org

COMMERCIAL UTILITIES

Typical Monthly Electric Bills

Area	Commercial Service ($/month)		Industrial Service ($/month)	
	12 kW demand 1,500 kWh	100 kW demand 30,000 kWh	1,000 kW demand 400,000 kWh	20,000 kW demand 10,000,000 kWh
City	114	2,013	23,085	328,663
U.S.	150	2,174	23,995	508,569

Note: Based on rates in effect January 1, 1999
Source: Edison Electric Institute, Typical Residential, Commercial and Industrial Bills, Winter 1999

TRANSPORTATION

Transportation Statistics

Average minutes to work (1990)	21.4
Interstate highways	I-90; I-405
Bus lines	
In-city (1998)	King County Dept. of Transportation (Seattle area), 932 buses
Inter-city (1999)	2
Passenger air service	
Airport	Seattle-Tacoma International
Airlines (1999)	13
Enplaned passengers (1998)	12,671,843
Amtrak service	No
Motor freight carriers (1999)	2
Major waterways/ports	Lake Washington; Near Puget Sound

Source: FAA DOT/TSC CY1998 ACAIS Database; National Transit Database, 1998; Editor & Publisher Market Guide, 2000; Amtrak National Time Table, Fall 1999/Winter 2000; 1990 Census of Population and Housing, STF 3C; Jane's Urban Transport Systems 1999-2000

Means of Transportation to Work

Area	Car/Truck/Van		Public Transportation			Bicycle	Walked	Other Means	Worked at Home
	Drove Alone	Car-pooled	Bus	Subway	Railroad				
City	77.2	9.2	6.4	0.0	0.0	0.2	2.1	1.0	3.9
MSA[1]	72.8	11.6	7.2	0.0	0.0	0.6	3.3	1.1	3.4
U.S.	73.2	13.4	3.0	1.5	0.5	0.4	3.9	1.2	3.0

Note: Figures shown are percentages and only include workers 16 years of age and older;
(1) Metropolitan Statistical Area - see Appendix A for areas included
Source: 1990 Census of Population and Housing, Summary Tape File 3C

BUSINESSES

Major Business Headquarters

Company Name	1999 Rankings	
	Fortune 500	Forbes 500
Paccar	189	-

Note: Companies listed are located in the city; dashes indicate no ranking
Fortune 500: Companies that produce a 10-K are ranked 1 to 500 based on 1999 revenue
Forbes 500: Private companies are ranked 1 to 500 based on 1998 revenue
Source: Forbes, December 13, 1999; Fortune, April 17, 2000

HOTELS & MOTELS

Hotels/Motels

Area	Hotels/ Motels	Rooms	Luxury-Level Hotels/Motels		Average Minimum Rates ($)		
			♦♦♦♦	♦♦♦♦♦	♦♦	♦♦♦	♦♦♦♦
City	17	2,284	0	0	n/a	n/a	n/a
Airport	1	181	0	0	n/a	n/a	n/a
Suburbs	1	152	0	0	n/a	n/a	n/a
Total	19	2,617	0	0	n/a	n/a	n/a

Note: n/a not available; classifications range from one diamond (budget properties with basic amenities) to five diamond (luxury properties).
Source: OAG Business Travel Planner, Winter 1999-2000

Estimated Daily Food and Lodging Costs

Area	Food/Other ($/day)	Average Hotel Cost ($/day)
City	30	55
U.S.	30	55

Source: ERI's Relocation Assessor software database, quarterly effective date 4/1/2000

CONVENTION CENTERS

Convention Centers and Event Sites

Name	Guest Rooms	Meeting Space (sq. ft.)	Capacity (Theatre Style)
Bellevue Club Hotel	67	n/a	375
Bellevue Conference Center	n/a	n/a	0
Bellevue Hilton	180	8,000	250
Best Western Bellevue Inn	181	n/a	0
Courtyard by Marriott	152	n/a	0
Days Inn Bellevue	110	560	0
Doubletree Hotel Bellevue	353	17,355	1,200
Doubletree Hotel Bellevue Center	208	3,294	120
Embassy Suites Bellevue	240	5,316	500
Hyatt Regency Bellevue	382	5,850	815
Meydenbauer Center	n/a	n/a	3,500
WestCoast Bellevue Hotel	176	6,426	300

Note: n/a not available
Source: EventSource.com, 3/15/2000

Living Environment

COST OF LIVING

Cost of Living: Homeowner

Cost Element	U.S. ($)	City ($)	Differential ($)	Percent of U.S. Average
Consumables	14,516	16,537	2,021	113.9
Transportation	5,957	6,539	582	109.8
Health Services	2,012	2,513	501	124.9
Housing/Utilities/Prop. Tax	16,337	37,397	21,060	228.9
Income+Payroll Taxes	12,615	8,434	-4,181	66.9
Miscellaneous	8,563	8,563	0	100.0
Total Cost of Living	60,000	79,983	19,983	133.3

Note: Figures are based on a single income, four person family with gross annual earnings of $60,000, owning an 1,800 square-foot home, and driving two automobiles worth $22,000 30,000 miles per year.
Source: ERI's Relocation Assessor software database, quarterly effective date 4/1/2000

Cost of Living: Renter

Cost Element	U.S. ($)	City ($)	Differential ($)	Percent of U.S. Average
Consumables	10,486	11,881	1,395	113.3
Transportation	2,107	2,300	193	109.2
Health Services	1,632	2,028	396	124.3
Rent/Utilities/Insurance	9,299	15,203	5,904	163.5
Income+Payroll Taxes	8,607	7,183	-1,424	83.5
Miscellaneous	7,869	7,869	0	100.0
Total Cost of Living	40,000	46,464	6,464	116.2

Note: Figures are based on a single income, three person family with gross annual earnings of $40,000, renting a 1,000 square-foot home, and driving one automobile worth $8,000 12,000 miles per year.
Source: ERI's Relocation Assessor software database, quarterly effective date 4/1/2000

HOUSING

Median Home Prices and Housing Affordability

Area	Median Price[2] 4th Qtr. 1999 ($)	HOI[3] 4th Qtr. 1999	Affordability Rank[4]
MSA[1]	205,000	48.6	165
U.S.	139,000	63.8	–

Note: (1) Metropolitan Statistical Area - see Appendix A for areas included; (2) U.S. figures calculated from the sales of 687,516 new and existing homes in 192 markets; (3) Housing Opportunity Index - percent of homes sold that were within the reach of the median income household at the prevailing mortgage interest rate; (4) Rank is from 1-192 with 1 being most affordable
Source: National Association of Home Builders, Housing Opportunity Index, 4th Quarter 1999

Estimated Home Price

Area	Price ($)
City	366,317
U.S.	135,855

Note: Figures are based on an 1,800 square-foot home
Source: ERI's Relocation Assessor software database, quarterly effective date 4/1/2000

Estimated Rent

Area	Rent ($/month)
City	1,179
U.S.	651

Note: Figures are based on a 1,000 square-foot home
Source: ERI's Relocation Assessor software database, quarterly effective date 4/1/2000

Median Home Price Projection

It is projected that the median home price in the metropolitan area will increase from $216,846 in 1999 to $338,737 in 2010, an increase of 56.2%
Kiplinger's Personal Finance Magazine, January 2000

RESIDENTIAL UTILITIES

Average Residential Utility Costs

Area	All Electric ($/mth)	Part Electric ($/mth)	Other Energy ($/mth)	Phone ($/mth)
City	n/a	n/a	n/a	n/a
U.S.	99.25	55.47	43.48	20.29

Note: n/a not available
Source: ACCRA, Cost of Living Index, 3rd Quarter 1999

HEALTH CARE

Average Health Care Costs

Area	Hospital ($/day)	Doctor ($/visit)	Dentist ($/visit)
City	n/a	n/a	n/a
U.S.	440.96	53.83	68.42

Note: n/a not available
Source: ACCRA, Cost of Living Index, 3rd Quarter 1999

Distribution of Office-Based Physicians

Area	Family/Gen. Practitioners	Specialists		
		Medical	Surgical	Other
MSA[1]	867	1,480	1,177	1,490

Note: Data as of 12/31/97; (1) Metropolitan Statistical Area - see Appendix A for areas included
Source: American Medical Assn., Physician Characteristics & Distribution in the U.S., 1999

Hospitals

Bellevue has 1 general medical and surgical hospital.
AHA Guide to the Healthcare Field, 1999-2000

EDUCATION

Public School District Statistics

District Name	Num. Sch.	Enroll.	Classroom Teachers	Pupils per Teacher	Minority Pupils (%)	Current Exp.[1] ($/pupil)
Bellevue	32	15,442	784	19.7	29.9	5,893

Note: Data covers the 1997-1998 school year unless otherwise noted; (1) Data covers fiscal year 1996; SD = School District; ISD = Independent School District; n/a not available
Source: National Center for Education Statistics, Common Core of Data Public Education Agency Universe 1997-98; National Center for Education Statistics, Characteristics of the 100 Largest Public Elementary and Secondary School Districts in the United States: 1997-98, July 1999

Educational Quality

School District	Education Quotient[1]	Graduate Outcome[2]	Community Index[3]	Resource Index[4]
Bellevue	121	124	149	108

Note: Over 1,000 secondary school districts were rated in terms of educational quality. The scores range from a low of 50 to a high of 150; (1) Combination of the Graduate Outcome, Community and Resource indexes weighted to reflect the greater importance of the Graduate Outcome and Resource Index; (2) Based on graduation rates and college board scores (SAT/ACT); (3) Based on the surrounding community's level of affluence and adult education; (4) Based on teacher salaries, per-pupil expenditures and student-teacher ratios.
Source: Expansion Management, Ratings Issue, 1999

Educational Attainment by Race

Area	High School Graduate (%)					Bachelor's Degree (%)				
	Total	White	Black	Other	Hisp.[2]	Total	White	Black	Other	Hisp.[2]
City	94.2	95.1	93.8	85.7	83.9	45.7	45.1	31.2	52.6	28.5
MSA[1]	87.7	88.8	79.5	78.1	79.0	29.8	30.3	16.4	30.0	20.3
U.S.	75.2	77.9	63.1	60.4	49.8	20.3	21.5	11.4	19.4	9.2

Note: Figures shown cover persons 25 years old and over; (1) Metropolitan Statistical Area - see Appendix A for areas included; (2) people of Hispanic origin can be of any race
Source: 1990 Census of Population and Housing, Summary Tape File 3C

School Enrollment by Type

Area	Preprimary				Elementary/High School			
	Public		Private		Public		Private	
	Enrollment	%	Enrollment	%	Enrollment	%	Enrollment	%
City	790	43.6	1,021	56.4	10,973	88.5	1,420	11.5
MSA[1]	22,997	51.8	21,435	48.2	264,909	90.2	28,825	9.8
U.S.	2,679,029	59.5	1,824,256	40.5	38,379,689	90.2	4,187,099	9.8

Note: Figures shown cover persons 3 years old and over;
(1) Metropolitan Statistical Area - see Appendix A for areas included
Source: 1990 Census of Population and Housing, Summary Tape File 3C

School Enrollment by Race

Area	Preprimary (%)				Elementary/High School (%)			
	White	Black	Other	Hisp.[1]	White	Black	Other	Hisp.[1]
City	87.9	2.3	9.8	1.2	78.7	3.3	18.0	3.2
MSA[2]	86.9	4.4	8.7	3.0	82.4	5.6	12.0	3.7
U.S.	80.4	12.5	7.1	7.8	74.1	15.6	10.3	12.5

Note: Figures shown cover persons 3 years old and over; (1) people of Hispanic origin can be of any race; (2) Metropolitan Statistical Area - see Appendix A for areas included
Source: 1990 Census of Population and Housing, Summary Tape File 3C

Higher Education

Two-Year Colleges		Four-Year Colleges		Medical Schools	Law Schools	Voc/ Tech
Public	Private	Public	Private			
1	0	0	0	0	0	12

Source: College Blue Book, Occupational Education, 1999; Medical School Admission Requirements, 1999-2000; Peterson's Guide to Two-Year Colleges, 2000; Peterson's Guide to Four-Year Colleges, 1999; Barron's Guide to Law Schools, 1999

MAJOR EMPLOYERS

Major Employers

Attachmate Corp. (computer design)
Data Dimensions (computer consulting)
Overlake Hospital Medical Center
Pacific Recreation Associates
Unigard Indemnity

CoinStar
Optiva Corp. (dental equipment)
Paccar Inc. (automotive stores)
Pugent Sound Energy
Unigard Insurance

Note: Companies listed are located in the city
Source: D&B Business Rankings, 1999; Ward's Business Directory, 1999; America's Corporate Families, 1999

PUBLIC SAFETY

Crime Rate

Area	All Crimes	Violent Crimes				Property Crimes		
		Murder	Forcible Rape	Robbery	Aggrav. Assault	Burglary	Larceny -Theft	Motor Vehicle Theft
City	4,826.4	1.1	31.7	67.6	70.8	517.5	3,761.8	376.0
Suburbs[1]	6,267.8	4.3	51.6	150.9	241.1	965.5	3,969.2	885.2
MSA[2]	6,208.4	4.2	50.8	147.5	234.1	947.1	3,960.7	864.2
U.S.	4,615.5	6.3	34.4	165.2	360.5	862.0	2,728.1	459.0

Note: Crime rate is the number of crimes per 100,000 population; (1) Defined as all areas within the Metropolitan Statistical Area but located outside the central city; (2) Metropolitan Statistical Area - see Appendix A for areas included
Source: FBI Uniform Crime Reports, 1998

RECREATION

Culture and Recreation

Museums	Symphony Orchestras	Opera Companies	Dance Companies	Professional Theatres	Zoos	Pro Sports Teams
2	1	0	0	0	0	0

Source: Musical America, International Directory of the Performing Arts, 1999; Official Museum Directory, 2000; Stern's Performing Arts Directory, 1997; USA Today Four Sport Stadium Guide, 1997; Career Opportunities in Theatre and the Performing Arts, 1999

Library System

The King County Library System has 40 branches, holdings of 3,139,812 volumes, and a budget of $46,334,052 (1997-1998).
American Library Directory, 1999-2000

MEDIA

Newspapers

Name	Type	Freq.	Distribution	Circulation
Eastside Journal	General	7x/wk	Local	32,000

Note: Includes newspapers with circulations of 200 or more located in the city;
Source: Burrelle's Media Directory, 1999 Edition

Television Stations

Name	Ch.	Affiliation	Type	Owner
KOMO	n/a	ABCT	Commercial	Fisher Broadcasting Inc.
KING	n/a	NBCT	Commercial	A.H. Belo Corporation
KIRO	n/a	CBST	Commercial	A.H. Belo Corporation
KCTS	n/a	n/a	Public	KCTS
KCPQ	13	FBC	Commercial	Kelly Television Company
KONG	16	n/a	Commercial	n/a
KTZZ	22	WB	Commercial	Dudley Broadcast Management
KWPX	33	n/a	Commercial	Paxson Communications Corporation

Note: Stations included broadcast in the Bellevue metro area; n/a not available
Source: Burrelle's Media Directory, 1999 Edition

AM Radio Stations

Call Letters	Freq. (kHz)	Target Audience	Station Format	Music Format
KVI	570	General	N/T	n/a
KCIS	630	Religious	M/N/S/T	Christian
KIRO	710	General	N/S/T	n/a
KNWX	770	General	N/T	n/a
KGNW	820	Religious	E/T	n/a
KIXI	880	General	M	Oldies
KJR	950	General	S	n/a
KOMO	1000	General	N/T	n/a
KBLE	1050	General	M/T	Christian
KRPM	1090	General	M/N/S	Country
KSRB	1150	General	M	Oldies/Rhythm & Blues
KBSG	1210	General	E/M/N	Oldies
KKDZ	1250	General	M	n/a
KKOL	1300	n/a	T	n/a
KRIZ	1420	General	M/N/T	Rhythm & Blues/Urban Contemporary
KARR	1460	General	M	Christian
KBLV	1540	General	M/N/S	Country
KXPA	1540	General	n/a	n/a
KZIZ	1560	General	M/N/T	Christian/Rhythm & Blues/Urban Contemporary
KLFE	1590	n/a	M	Classical/Easy Listening/Gospel
KYIZ	1620	General	M	Urban Contemporary
KAZJ	1680	n/a	M	Classical/Easy Listening/Gospel

Note: Stations included broadcast in the Bellevue metro area; n/a not available
Target Audience: A=Asian; B=Black; C=Christian; E=Ethnic; F=French; G=General; H=Hispanic;
M=Men; N=Native American; R=Religious; S=Senior Citizen; W=Women; Y=Young Adult; Z=Children
Station Format: E=Educational; M=Music; N=News; S=Sports; T=Talk
Source: Burrelle's Media Directory, 1999 Edition

FM Radio Stations

Call Letters	Freq. (mHz)	Target Audience	Station Format	Music Format
KASB	89.3	General	M/N/S	Alternative
KNHC	89.5	General	M/N	Adult Top 40
KGRG	89.9	General	M/N/S	Alternative
KCMU	90.3	General	M	Reggae/Rhythm & Blues/World Music
KBCS	91.3	General	E/M	Blues/Jazz/Rhythm & Blues/World Music
KLSY	92.5	General	M	Adult Contemporary
KUBE	93.3	General	M	Urban Contemporary
KMPS	94.1	General	M	Country
KUOW	94.9	General	E/M/N/T	Big Band
KJR	95.7	General	M	Adult Contemporary
KYCW	96.5	General	M	Country
KBSG	97.3	General	E/M/N	Oldies
KING	98.1	General	M	Classical
KISW	99.9	General	M	AOR
KIRO	100.7	General	T	n/a
KPLZ	101.5	General	M/N/S	Adult Contemporary
KZOK	102.5	General	M/N	Classic Rock
KMTT	103.7	General	M	Alternative
KMIH	104.5	G/W	E/M	Top 40
KCMS	105.3	General	M	Adult Contemporary/Christian
KBKS	106.1	General	M	Classic Rock
KRWM	106.9	General	M	Adult Contemporary
KNDD	107.7	General	M	Alternative

Note: Stations included broadcast in the Bellevue metro area; n/a not available
Station Format: E=Educational; M=Music; N=News; S=Sports; T=Talk
Target Audience: A=Asian; B=Black; C=Christian; E=Ethnic; F=French; G=General; H=Hispanic;
M=Men; N=Native American; R=Religious; S=Senior Citizen; W=Women; Y=Young Adult; Z=Children
Music Format: AOR=Album Oriented Rock; MOR=Middle-of-the-Road
Source: Burrelle's Media Directory, 1999 Edition

WEATHER

Temperature/Precipitation/Humidity

	Jan	Feb	Mar	Apr	May	Jun	Jul	Aug	Sep	Oct	Nov	Dec	Yr.
Max. High Temp. (°F)	64	70	75	85	93	96	98	99	98	89	74	63	99
Avg. High Temp. (°F)	44	48	52	57	64	69	75	74	69	59	50	45	59
Avg. Temp. (°F)	39	43	45	49	55	61	65	65	60	52	45	41	52
Avg. Low Temp. (°F)	34	36	38	41	46	51	54	55	51	45	39	36	44
Min. Low Temp. (°F)	0	1	11	29	28	38	43	44	35	28	6	6	0
Avg. Precip. (in.)	5.7	4.2	3.7	2.4	1.7	1.4	0.8	1.1	1.9	3.5	5.9	5.9	38.4
Avg. Snowfall (in.)	5	2	1	Tr	Tr	0	0	0	0	Tr	1	3	13
Avg. Rel. Hum. 7am (%)	83	83	84	83	80	79	79	84	87	88	85	85	83
Avg. Rel. Hum. 4pm (%)	76	69	63	57	54	54	49	51	57	68	76	79	63

Note: Tr = Trace amounts (less than 0.05 inches of rain or less than 0.5 inches of snow)
Source: National Climatic Data Center, International Station Meteorological Climate Summary, 3/95

Weather Conditions

Temperature			Precipitation		
5°F & below	32°F & below	90°F & above	0.01 inch or more precip.	1.5 inch or more snow/ice	Thunder-storms
< 0.5	38	3	157	3	8

Note: Figures are average number of days per year
Source: National Climatic Data Center, International Station Meteorological Climate Summary, 3/95

AIR & WATER QUALITY

Maximum Pollutant Concentrations

	Particulate Matter (ug/m³)	Carbon Monoxide (ppm)	Sulfur Dioxide (ppm)	Nitrogen Dioxide (ppm)	Ozone (ppm)	Lead (ug/m³)
MSA[1] Level	115	7	0.012	0.019	0.10	0.87
NAAQS[2]	150	9	0.140	0.053	0.12	1.50
Met NAAQS	Yes	Yes	Yes	Yes	Yes	Yes

Note: (1) Metropolitan Statistical Area - see Appendix A for areas included; (2) National Ambient Air Quality Standards; ppm = parts per million; ug/m³ = micrograms per cubic meter; n/a not available
Source: EPA, National Air Quality and Emissions Trends Report, 1997

Pollutant Standards Index

In the Bellevue MSA (see Appendix A for areas included), the Pollutant Standards Index (PSI) exceeded 100 on 1 day in 1997. A PSI value greater than 100 indicates that air quality would have been in the unhealthful range on that day.
EPA, National Air Quality and Emissions Trends Report, 1997

Drinking Water

Water System Name	Pop. Served	Primary Water Source Type	Number of Violations in 1998-99	Type of Violation/ Contaminants
City of Bellevue	114,000	Purchased surface	None	None

Note: Data as of January 19, 2000
Source: EPA, Office of Ground Water and Drinking Water, Safe Drinking Water Information System

Bellevue tap water is soft.
Editor & Publisher Market Guide, 2000

Bellingham, Washington

Background

Bellingham, Washington is situated on the northern edge of Puget Sound in northwestern Washington, about 60 miles from Vancouver and 90 miles from Seattle. It is the last major city on the Washington coast before the Canadian border.

Bellingham's bustling waterfront supports fishing, cold storage, boat building, shipping, and paper processing. Washington, which has no state income tax, is an attractive lure for people looking to fill the 3,500 jobs that have been created since 1990.

By the 1850s, the local Lummi, Semiahmoo, and Nooksack Indians had lived in the region for thousands of years, utilizing its natural resources to support their needs and culture. Their population probably numbered about 3,000. In 1852, two California miners, Henry Roeder and Russell Peabody, built a lumber mill on this site with the help of the Lummi Indians. This became the first permanent settlement on Bellingham Bay. Coal was discovered that same year, and by the 1880s, the demand for West Coast resources promoted the area's industry and expanded its population.

By 1900, lumber mills, salmon canneries, can-making companies and shipyards developed around Bellingham Bay. Pacific American Fisheries became the largest salmon canning company in the world, and Whatcom County lumber was exported throughout the Pacific. Bellingham emerged as the consolidation of four small towns - Fairhaven, Sehome, Whatcom, and Bellingham.

An abundance of outdoor recreational activities enhance the quality of life in the region and include whale watches, tours to Victoria on Vancouver Island, and cruises to the San Juan Islands. Sailing thrives with 1,900 boats moored on Squalicum Harbor, the second largest harbor in Puget Sound. Visitors heading for Alaska depart from Bellingham Cruise Terminal.

In the Mount Baker area, hikers can enjoy extensive and scenic trails, while skiers partake of the longest ski season in the state, with the world's highest measurable snowfall record at 1,140 inches in one season. Snoqualmie National Forest is nearby, as is the Lummi Indian reservation five miles northwest of the city. The area is also a Mecca for golfers.

Bellingham has an average annual rainfall of 35 inches, with only 6 days below freezing.

Western Washington University is located atop Sehome Hill, which provides a panoramic view of the harbor and the San Juan Islands. In the downtown area, restaurants, art galleries and specialty shops abound, including the Whatcom Museum of History and Art, originally built in 1892 as the city hall, and the Fairhaven District with a Victorian-era building that houses shops, restaurants, and galleries.

General Rankings and Evaluative Comments

- Bellingham was ranked #168 out of 354 metropolitan areas in *Places Rated Almanac*. Criteria: cost of living, climate, crime, transportation, job outlook, education, the arts, health care, and recreation. *Places Rated Almanac, Millennium Edition, 2000*

- Bellingham was selected as one of America's best small art towns. The city was ranked #43 out of 100. Criteria: easy and affordable access to the visual arts, performing arts and music, strong sense of community, low crime rate, and full-time population less than 65,000. *The 100 Best Small Art Towns in America: Discover Creative Communities, Fresh Air, and Affordable Living, 1998*

- Bellingham was selected as one of America's best places to retire. Criteria: safety, climate, housing, culture and recreation, social compatibility, affordability, medical care, transportation, and jobs and/or volunteer opportunities. *Where to Retire: America's Best and Most Affordable Places, 1998*

- Bellingham was selected as one of the best places to retire by *Retirement Places Rated*. Criteria: cost of living, climate, crime, services, working, and leisure living. The city was ranked #27 out of 187. *Retirement Places Rated, 1999*

- Bellingham was selected as one of "America's Best Towns to Raise an Outdoor Family" by *Outdoor Explorer* magazine. Criteria: easy access to the outdoors, quality education and health care, affordable housing, favorable employment opportunities, and low crime rates. The city was ranked #21 out of 25. *Outdoor Explorer, Summer 1999*

- Bellingham was selected as one of "The 50 Most Alive Places to Live" in the U.S. Criteria: ethnic diversity, recreational options, cultural vitality, low crime rate, opportunities for lifelong learning, good hospitals and restaurants, public transportation, walking accessibility, civic activities, and the kitsch factor. The area was ranked #4 out of 10 in the "Green & Clean" category. *Modern Maturity, May-June 2000*

Business Environment

STATE ECONOMY

State Economic Profile

"After some recent years of very strong growth, the Washington economy is quickly losing steam. Washington's manufacturing employment shrank in 1998, mostly as the result of continued layoffs by Boeing.

Further layoffs and a slowing US economy will dampen the Washington economy. Strong migration and a young, educated workforce will lead to strong long-term growth for Washington after its current problems have run their course.

Spokane's employment base shrank by almost 2% in 1998, shedding some 3,700 jobs on net. The bulk of these were in manufacturing, where employment declined by 13.7%, losing 3,100 jobs on net. Construction employment also declined by 11.2%, even as multifamily housing permits increased by 69% and single family permits by 19%. Given its current economic contract, both Spokane' residential and commercial properties markets are facing increasing inventories and rising vacancies. While the rest of the nation enjoyed a booming housing market, home price appreciation in Spokane was negative in 1998. The housing market should stabilize, but remain weak in the near future.

The Puget Sound economy fared well in 1998 in light of the expected Boeing cutbacks. The employment base expanded by 2.7% in 1998, even as manufacturing declined by 0.6%. An increase of 3.4% in services and 6.6% in construction helped to offset losses in manufacturing. With the manufacturing sector declining even further, the current level of construction is not sustainable, and construction employment should contract in 2000. Home price appreciation in Seattle was weak in 1998 at around 2%, and both volume and prices in Seattle should decline in 2000.

Washington's economy is headed for a substantial turbulence in the near term. Fortunately, the economy is mostly in good shape, which will help with the absorption of workers leaving Boeing. Long term, stabilization at Boeing, the ongoing expansion of the software industry, and a rebound in migration will lead to above-average growth." *National Association of Realtors, Economic Profiles: The Fifty States and the District of Columbia, http://nar.realtor.com/databank/profiles.htm*

EXPORTS

Total Export Sales

Area	1995 ($000)	1996 ($000)	1997 ($000)	1998 ($000)	% Chg. 1995-98	% Chg. 1997-98
MSA[1]	253,540	275,374	316,687	256,449	1.1	-19.0
U.S.	583,030,524	622,827,063	687,597,999	680,474,251	16.7	-1.0

Note: (1) Metropolitan Statistical Area - see Appendix A for areas included
Source: U.S. Department of Commerce, International Trade Association, Metropolitan Area Exports: An Export Performance Report on Over 250 U.S. Cities, November 10, 1999

CITY FINANCES

City Government Finances

Component	1995 ($million)	1995 (per capita $)
Revenue	67.1	1,174
Expenditure	60.0	1,050
Debt Outstanding	54.5	954

Source: 1999 County and City Extra, Annual Metro, City, and County Data Book

City Government Revenue by Source

Source	1995 ($million)	1995 (per capita $)
Intergovernmental	9.2	161
Taxes	33.7	590
Property	9.0	159
Sales and Gross Receipts	17.0	298

Source: 1999 County and City Extra, Annual Metro, City, and County Data Book

City Government Expenditures by Function

Function	1995 ($million)	1995 (per capita $)	1995 (%)
Public Welfare	0.0	0	0.0
Highways	9.8	172	16.4
Parking Facilities	0.4	7	0.7
Education	0.0	0	0.0
Health and Hospitals	0.7	13	1.3
Police Protection	6.9	121	11.6
Sewerage and Sanitation	5.7	100	9.6
Parks and Recreation	7.8	137	13.1
Housing and Community Development	1.4	25	2.4
Interest on Debt	3.0	52	5.0

Source: 1999 County and City Extra, Annual Metro, City, and County Data Book

Municipal Bond Ratings

Area	Moody's
City	A1

Source: Mergent Bond Record, 2/2000

POPULATION

Population Growth

Area	1980 Census	1990 Census	1999 Estimate	2004 Projection	Population Growth (%) 1990-1999	Population Growth (%) 1999-2004
City	45,805	52,278	61,781	65,068	18.2	5.3
MSA[1]	106,701	127,780	159,493	170,561	24.8	6.9
U.S.	226,545,805	248,765,170	272,212,864	283,625,312	9.4	4.2

Note: (1) Metropolitan Statistical Area - see Appendix A for areas included
Source: 1990 Census of Population and Housing, Summary Tape File 3C; Claritas, Inc.

Number of Households and Average Household Size

Area	1980 Census	1990 Census	1999 Estimate	2004 Projection	1999 Average Household Size
City	18,398	21,277	25,696	27,284	2.40
MSA[1]	39,630	48,645	61,464	66,103	2.59
U.S.	80,389,592	91,993,582	102,048,200	107,302,392	2.67

Note: (1) Metropolitan Statistical Area - see Appendix A for areas included
Source: 1990 Census of Population and Housing, Summary Tape File 3C; Claritas, Inc.

Race/Ethnicity of City Population

Race/Ethnicity	1990 Census Population	1990 Census %	1999 Estimate Population	1999 Estimate %	% Change 1990-1999
White, Non-Hispanic	48,249	92.3	55,699	90.2	15.4
Black, Non-Hispanic	399	0.8	583	0.9	46.1
Asian, Non-Hispanic	1,521	2.9	2,265	3.7	48.9
Other, Non-Hispanic	899	1.7	997	1.6	10.9
Hispanic	1,210	2.3	2,237	3.6	84.9

Source: 1990 Census of Population and Housing, Summary Tape File 3C; Claritas, Inc.

Race/Ethnicity of Metropolitan Statistical Area Population

Race/Ethnicity	1990 Census		1999 Estimate		% Change 1990-1999
	Population	%	Population	%	
White, Non-Hispanic	117,593	92.0	142,797	89.5	21.4
Black, Non-Hispanic	618	0.5	887	0.6	43.5
Asian, Non-Hispanic	2,397	1.9	3,815	2.4	59.2
Other, Non-Hispanic	3,926	3.1	4,793	3.0	22.1
Hispanic	3,246	2.5	7,201	4.5	121.8

Note: See Appendix A for areas included in the Metropolitan Statistical Area
Source: 1990 Census of Population and Housing, Summary Tape File 3C; Claritas, Inc.

Ancestry

Area	German	Irish	English	Italian	U.S.	French	Polish	Dutch
City	27.5	14.7	20.2	2.9	2.8	4.9	2.2	5.6
MSA[1]	26.7	13.3	18.9	2.5	3.5	4.6	1.9	11.2
U.S.	23.3	15.6	13.1	5.9	5.3	4.2	3.8	2.5

Note: Figures are percentages and include persons that reported multiple ancestry (eg. if a person reported being Irish and Italian, they were included in both columns); (1) Metropolitan Statistical Area - see Appendix A for areas included
Source: 1990 Census of Population and Housing, Summary Tape File 3C

Median Age

Area	1990 Census	1999 Estimate
City	30.9	34.6
MSA[1]	32.7	35.4
U.S.	32.9	35.7

Note: (1) Metropolitan Statistical Area - see Appendix A for areas included
Source: 1990 Census of Population and Housing, Summary Tape File 3C; Claritas, Inc.

Male/Female Population

Area	Number of Males		Number of Females		Males per 100 Females	
	1990	1999	1990	1999	1990	1999
City	25,049	29,538	27,229	32,243	92.0	91.6
MSA[1]	63,196	78,181	64,584	81,312	97.9	96.1
U.S.	121,172,379	132,803,736	127,537,494	139,409,136	95.0	95.3

Note: (1) Metropolitan Statistical Area - see Appendix A for areas included
Source: 1990 Census of Population, General Population Characteristics; Claritas, Inc.

INCOME

Per Capita/Median/Average Income

Area	Per Capita ($)			Median Household ($)			Average Household ($)		
	1989	1999	% Chg.	1989	1999	% Chg.	1989	1999	% Chg.
City	13,698	19,977	45.8	24,714	32,942	33.3	32,500	46,677	43.6
MSA[1]	13,753	20,410	48.4	28,367	39,068	37.7	35,506	52,254	47.2
U.S.	14,420	21,350	48.1	30,056	40,525	34.8	38,453	56,184	46.1

Note: (1) Metropolitan Statistical Area - see Appendix A for areas included; 1989 data is from the 1990 Census; 1999 data is estimated by Claritas, Inc.
Source: 1990 Census of Population, General Population Characteristics; Claritas, Inc.

Household Income Distribution

Area	Percent of Households Earning								
	Under $5,000	$5,000 -14,999	$15,000 -24,999	$25,000 -34,999	$35,000 -49,999	$50,000 -74,999	$75,000 -99,000	$100,000 -149,999	$150,000 and up
City	4.1	15.7	17.3	15.3	16.9	15.9	7.3	4.6	3.1
MSA[1]	3.1	12.5	14.8	14.1	18.1	19.8	8.9	5.4	3.4
U.S.	3.9	13.3	13.8	12.6	16.2	19.4	9.7	6.6	4.6

Note: Data as of 1999; (1) Metropolitan Statistical Area - see Appendix A for areas included
Source: Claritas, Inc.

Effective Buying Income

Area	Per Capita ($)	Median Household ($)	Average Household ($)
City	17,564	31,740	43,195
MSA[1]	18,439	37,845	48,518
U.S.	17,496	36,603	47,036

Note: Data as of 1/1/2000; (1) Metropolitan Statistical Area - see Appendix A for areas included
Source: Standard Rate & Data Service, Newspaper Advertising Source, March 2000

Effective Household Buying Income Distribution

Area	% of Households Earning						
	$10,000 -$19,999	$20,000 -$34,999	$35,000 -$49,999	$50,000 -$74,999	$75,000 -$99,000	$100,000 -$124,999	$125,000 and up
City	17.6	25.2	16.5	16.2	6.9	2.2	3.1
MSA[1]	14.5	22.6	17.9	20.4	8.8	3.0	3.7
U.S.	15.0	21.6	17.6	19.6	8.4	3.0	3.3

Note: Data as of 1/1/2000; (1) Metropolitan Statistical Area - see Appendix A for areas included
Source: Standard Rate & Data Service, Newspaper Advertising Source, March 2000

Poverty Rates by Age

Area	People of All Ages	People Under 18 Years Old	Related Children Age 5-17 in Families in Poverty
City	15.4	n/a	n/a
County	11.6	14.5	11.8
U.S.	13.8	20.8	18.7

Note: Figures show the percent of people living below the poverty line in 1995. The average poverty threshold was $15,569 for a family of four in 1995; n/a not available
Source: Bureau of the Census, Small Area Income and Poverty Estimates Program; U.S. Department of Housing and Urban Development

EMPLOYMENT

Labor Force and Employment

Area	Civilian Labor Force			Workers Employed		
	Dec. 1998	Dec. 1999	% Chg.	Dec. 1998	Dec. 1999	% Chg.
City	34,598	33,629	-2.8	32,652	32,019	-1.9
MSA[1]	80,833	78,558	-2.8	76,212	74,735	-1.9
U.S.	138,297,000	139,941,000	1.2	132,732,000	134,696,000	1.5

Note: Data is not seasonally adjusted and covers workers 16 years of age and older;
(1) Metropolitan Statistical Area - see Appendix A for areas included
Source: Bureau of Labor Statistics, http://stats.bls.gov

Unemployment Rate

Area	1999											
	Jan.	Feb.	Mar.	Apr.	May	Jun.	Jul.	Aug.	Sep.	Oct.	Nov.	Dec.
City	6.4	7.0	5.6	4.8	4.7	4.6	5.0	4.7	4.8	4.8	4.5	4.8
MSA[1]	6.5	7.1	5.7	4.9	4.8	4.7	5.1	4.8	4.9	4.9	4.5	4.9
U.S.	4.8	4.7	4.4	4.1	4.0	4.5	4.5	4.2	4.1	3.8	3.8	3.7

Note: Data is not seasonally adjusted and covers workers 16 years of age and older; all figures are percentages; (1) Metropolitan Statistical Area - see Appendix A for areas included
Source: Bureau of Labor Statistics, http://stats.bls.gov

Employment by Industry

Sector	MSA[1]		U.S.
	Number of Employees	Percent of Total	Percent of Total
Services	n/a	n/a	30.2
Retail Trade	n/a	n/a	18.1
Government	n/a	n/a	15.8
Manufacturing	n/a	n/a	14.1
Finance/Insurance/Real Estate	n/a	n/a	5.9
Wholesale Trade	n/a	n/a	5.4
Transportation/Public Utilities	n/a	n/a	5.3
Construction	n/a	n/a	4.8
Mining	n/a	n/a	0.4

Note: Figures cover non-farm employment as of 12/99 and are not seasonally adjusted;
(1) Metropolitan Statistical Area - see Appendix A for areas included; n/a not available
Source: Bureau of Labor Statistics, http://stats.bls.gov

Employment by Occupation

Occupation Category	City (%)	MSA[1] (%)	U.S. (%)
White Collar	58.8	53.4	58.1
Executive/Admin./Management	11.2	10.9	12.3
Professional	15.9	12.7	14.1
Technical & Related Support	2.8	2.7	3.7
Sales	14.1	12.8	11.8
Administrative Support/Clerical	14.8	14.2	16.3
Blue Collar	22.5	26.6	26.2
Precision Production/Craft/Repair	10.4	13.0	11.3
Machine Operators/Assem./Insp.	4.6	4.9	6.8
Transportation/Material Movers	3.2	4.2	4.1
Cleaners/Helpers/Laborers	4.2	4.5	3.9
Services	16.7	14.9	13.2
Farming/Forestry/Fishing	2.0	5.1	2.5

Note: Figures cover workers 16 years of age and older;
(1) Metropolitan Statistical Area - see Appendix A for areas included
Source: 1990 Census of Population and Housing, Summary Tape File 3C

Occupational Employment Projections: 1996 - 2006

Occupations Expected to Have the Largest Job Growth (ranked by numerical growth)	Fast-Growing Occupations[1] (ranked by percent growth)
1. Salespersons, retail	1. Personal and home care aides
2. Cashiers	2. Systems analysts
3. Child care workers, private household	3. Paralegals
4. General managers & top executives	4. Electronic semiconductor processors
5. Computer engineers	5. Directors, religious activities & educ.
6. Systems analysts	6. Physical therapy assistants and aides
7. Database administrators	7. Respiratory therapists
8. Food service workers	8. Human services workers
9. Truck drivers, light	9. Medical assistants
10. Janitors/cleaners/maids, ex. priv. hshld.	10. Medical records technicians

Note: Projections cover Washington; (1) Excludes occupations with total job growth less than 300
Source: U.S. Department of Labor, Employment and Training Administration, America's Labor Market Information System (ALMIS)

Average Wages

Occupation	$/Hr.	Occupation	$/Hr.
Accountants and Auditors	17.67	Maids and Housekeepers	7.34
Assemblers and Fabricators	10.20	Maintenance Repairers	14.94
Automotive Mechanics	14.21	Marketing/Advertising/PR Managers	27.31
Bookkeepers	11.44	Nurses, Licensed Practical	12.39
Carpenters	18.42	Nurses, Registered	19.92
Cashiers	9.40	Nursing Aides/Orderlies/Attendants	7.78
Clerks, General Office	10.13	Physicians and Surgeons	45.68
Clerks, Shipping/Receiving/Traffic	11.61	Receptionists/Information Clerks	9.58
Computer Programmers	23.73	Sales Reps., Exc. Scientific/Retail	18.33
Computer Support Specialists	16.05	Sales Reps., Scientific, Exc. Retail	21.38
Cooks, Restaurant	8.54	Salespersons, Retail	9.63
Electricians	21.30	Secretaries, Except Legal/Medical	11.70
Financial Managers	25.50	Stock Clerks, Sales Floor	9.09
First-Line Supervisors/Mgrs., Sales	15.80	Systems Analysts	32.40
Food Preparation Workers	7.15	Teacher Aides	9.12
General Managers/Top Executives	25.62	Teachers, Elementary School	19.99
Guards	9.72	Teachers, Secondary School	20.50
Hand Packers	7.68	Telemarketers	8.95
Janitors and Cleaners	9.16	Truck Drivers, Heavy/Tractor-Trailer	15.52
Laborers, Landscaping	9.87	Truck Drivers, Light	9.79
Lawyers	31.67	Waiters and Waitresses	5.84

Note: Wage data is for 1998 and covers the Metropolitan Statistical Area (see Appendix A for areas included). Hourly wages for elementary and secondary school teachers were calculated by the editors from annual wage data assuming a 40 hour work week; Dashes indicate that data was not available.
Source: Bureau of Labor Statistics, 1998 Metropolitan Area Occupational Employment and Wage Estimates

TAXES

Major State and Local Tax Rates

State Corporate Income (%)	State Personal Income (%)	Residential Property (%)	Sales & Use		State Gasoline (cents/ gallon)	State Cigarette (cents/ pack)
			State (%)	Local (%)		
None	None	1.04	6.5	1.4	23.0	82.5

Note: Personal/corporate income, sales, gasoline and cigarette tax rates as of January 2000. Property tax rates as of April 2000.
Source: Federation of Tax Administrators, www.taxadmin.org; ERI's Relocation Assessor software database, quarterly effective date 4/1/2000

Total Taxes Per Capita and as a Percent of Income

Area	Per Capita Income ($)	Per Capita Taxes ($)			Percent of Income (%)		
		Total	Federal	State/ Local	Total	Federal	State/ Local
Washington	30,430	11,355	7,688	3,667	37.3	25.3	12.0
U.S.	28,878	10,298	7,026	3,273	35.7	24.3	11.3

Note: Figures are for 1999
Source: Tax Foundation, www.taxfoundation.org

COMMERCIAL UTILITIES

Typical Monthly Electric Bills

Area	Commercial Service ($/month)		Industrial Service ($/month)	
	12 kW demand 1,500 kWh	100 kW demand 30,000 kWh	1,000 kW demand 400,000 kWh	20,000 kW demand 10,000,000 kWh
City	114	2,013	23,085	328,663
U.S.	150	2,174	23,995	508,569

Note: Based on rates in effect January 1, 1999
Source: Edison Electric Institute, Typical Residential, Commercial and Industrial Bills, Winter 1999

TRANSPORTATION

Transportation Statistics

Average minutes to work (1990)	15.3
Interstate highways	I-5
Bus lines	
In-city (1998)	Whatcom Transportation Authority, 29 buses
Inter-city (1999)	1
Passenger air service	
Airport	Bellingham International
Airlines (1999)	2
Enplaned passengers (1998)	89,876
Amtrak service	Yes
Motor freight carriers (1999)	19
Major waterways/ports	Georgia Straight; Bellingham Bay

Source: FAA DOT/TSC CY1998 ACAIS Database; National Transit Database, 1998; Editor & Publisher Market Guide, 2000; Amtrak National Time Table, Fall 1999/Winter 2000; 1990 Census of Population and Housing, STF 3C; Jane's Urban Transport Systems 1999-2000

Means of Transportation to Work

Area	Car/Truck/Van		Public Transportation			Bicycle	Walked	Other Means	Worked at Home
	Drove Alone	Car- pooled	Bus	Subway	Railroad				
City	72.6	11.1	2.9	0.0	0.0	2.1	7.4	1.3	2.7
MSA[1]	75.2	11.2	1.4	0.0	0.0	1.1	5.1	1.1	4.8
U.S.	73.2	13.4	3.0	1.5	0.5	0.4	3.9	1.2	3.0

Note: Figures shown are percentages and only include workers 16 years of age and older;
(1) Metropolitan Statistical Area - see Appendix A for areas included
Source: 1990 Census of Population and Housing, Summary Tape File 3C

BUSINESSES

Major Business Headquarters

Company Name	1999 Rankings	
	Fortune 500	Forbes 500
Haggen	-	479

Note: Companies listed are located in the city; dashes indicate no ranking
Fortune 500: Companies that produce a 10-K are ranked 1 to 500 based on 1999 revenue
Forbes 500: Private companies are ranked 1 to 500 based on 1998 revenue
Source: Forbes, December 13, 1999; Fortune, April 17, 2000

HOTELS & MOTELS

Hotels/Motels

Area	Hotels/ Motels	Rooms	Luxury-Level Hotels/Motels		Average Minimum Rates ($)		
			♦♦♦♦	♦♦♦♦♦	♦♦	♦♦♦	♦♦♦♦
City	14	1,068	0	0	57	73	n/a
Airport	2	207	0	0	n/a	n/a	n/a
Total	16	1,275	0	0	n/a	n/a	n/a

Note: n/a not available; classifications range from one diamond (budget properties with basic amenities) to five diamond (luxury properties).
Source: OAG Business Travel Planner, Winter 1999-2000

Estimated Daily Food and Lodging Costs

Area	Food/Other ($/day)	Average Hotel Cost ($/day)
City	34	50
U.S.	30	55

Source: ERI's Relocation Assessor software database, quarterly effective date 4/1/2000

CONVENTION CENTERS

Convention Centers and Event Sites

Name	Guest Rooms	Meeting Space (sq. ft.)	Capacity (Theatre Style)
Best Western Lakeway Inn	132	10,000	700

Source: EventSource.com, 3/15/2000

Living Environment

COST OF LIVING

Cost of Living: Homeowner

Cost Element	U.S. ($)	City ($)	Differential ($)	Percent of U.S. Average
Consumables	14,516	15,149	633	104.4
Transportation	5,957	6,094	137	102.3
Health Services	2,012	2,427	415	120.6
Housing/Utilities/Prop. Tax	16,337	23,500	7,163	143.8
Income+Payroll Taxes	12,615	9,872	-2,743	78.3
Miscellaneous	8,563	8,563	0	100.0
Total Cost of Living	60,000	65,605	5,605	109.3

Note: Figures are based on a single income, four person family with gross annual earnings of $60,000, owning an 1,800 square-foot home, and driving two automobiles worth $22,000 30,000 miles per year.
Source: ERI's Relocation Assessor software database, quarterly effective date 4/1/2000

Cost of Living: Renter

Cost Element	U.S. ($)	City ($)	Differential ($)	Percent of U.S. Average
Consumables	10,486	10,884	398	103.8
Transportation	2,107	2,144	37	101.8
Health Services	1,632	1,959	327	120.0
Rent/Utilities/Insurance	9,299	13,467	4,168	144.8
Income+Payroll Taxes	8,607	7,183	-1,424	83.5
Miscellaneous	7,869	7,869	0	100.0
Total Cost of Living	40,000	43,506	3,506	108.8

Note: Figures are based on a single income, three person family with gross annual earnings of $40,000, renting a 1,000 square-foot home, and driving one automobile worth $8,000 12,000 miles per year.
Source: ERI's Relocation Assessor software database, quarterly effective date 4/1/2000

HOUSING

Median Home Prices and Housing Affordability

Area	Median Price[2] 4th Qtr. 1999 ($)	HOI[3] 4th Qtr. 1999	Affordability Rank[4]
MSA[1]	n/a	n/a	n/a
U.S.	139,000	63.8	–

Note: (1) Metropolitan Statistical Area - see Appendix A for areas included; (2) U.S. figures calculated from the sales of 687,516 new and existing homes in 192 markets; (3) Housing Opportunity Index - percent of homes sold that were within the reach of the median income household at the prevailing mortgage interest rate; (4) Rank is from 1-192 with 1 being most affordable; n/a not available
Source: National Association of Home Builders, Housing Opportunity Index, 4th Quarter 1999

Estimated Home Price

Area	Price ($)
City	224,543
U.S.	135,855

Note: Figures are based on an 1,800 square-foot home
Source: ERI's Relocation Assessor software database, quarterly effective date 4/1/2000

Estimated Rent

Area	Rent ($/month)
City	1,042
U.S.	651

Note: Figures are based on a 1,000 square-foot home
Source: ERI's Relocation Assessor software database, quarterly effective date 4/1/2000

Median Home Price Projection

It is projected that the median home price in the metropolitan area will increase from $145,169 in 1999 to $211,879 in 2010, an increase of 46.0%
Kiplinger's Personal Finance Magazine, January 2000

RESIDENTIAL UTILITIES

Average Residential Utility Costs

Area	All Electric ($/mth)	Part Electric ($/mth)	Other Energy ($/mth)	Phone ($/mth)
City	–	35.84	43.02	19.77
U.S.	99.25	55.47	43.48	20.29

Source: ACCRA, Cost of Living Index, 3rd Quarter 1999

HEALTH CARE

Average Health Care Costs

Area	Hospital ($/day)	Doctor ($/visit)	Dentist ($/visit)
City	465.00	57.80	99.80
U.S.	440.96	53.83	68.42

Note: Hospital—based on a semi-private room; Doctor—based on a general practitioner's routine exam of an established patient; Dentist—based on adult teeth cleaning and periodic oral exam.
Source: ACCRA, Cost of Living Index, 3rd Quarter 1999

Distribution of Office-Based Physicians

Area	Family/Gen. Practitioners	Specialists Medical	Specialists Surgical	Specialists Other
MSA[1]	66	62	58	64

Note: Data as of 12/31/97; (1) Metropolitan Statistical Area - see Appendix A for areas included
Source: American Medical Assn., Physician Characteristics & Distribution in the U.S., 1999

Hospitals

Bellingham has 1 general medical and surgical hospital.
AHA Guide to the Healthcare Field, 1999-2000

EDUCATION

Public School District Statistics

District Name	Num. Sch.	Enroll.	Classroom Teachers	Pupils per Teacher	Minority Pupils (%)	Current Exp.[1] ($/pupil)
Bellingham	26	10,388	490	21.2	n/a	n/a
Meridian	5	1,475	74	19.9	n/a	n/a

Note: Data covers the 1997-1998 school year unless otherwise noted; (1) Data covers fiscal year 1996; SD = School District; ISD = Independent School District; n/a not available
Source: National Center for Education Statistics, Common Core of Data Public Education Agency Universe 1997-98; National Center for Education Statistics, Characteristics of the 100 Largest Public Elementary and Secondary School Districts in the United States: 1997-98, July 1999

Educational Quality

School District	Education Quotient[1]	Graduate Outcome[2]	Community Index[3]	Resource Index[4]
Bellingham	125	134	113	108

Note: Over 1,000 secondary school districts were rated in terms of educational quality. The scores range from a low of 50 to a high of 150; (1) Combination of the Graduate Outcome, Community and Resource indexes weighted to reflect the greater importance of the Graduate Outcome and Resource Index; (2) Based on graduation rates and college board scores (SAT/ACT); (3) Based on the surrounding community's level of affluence and adult education; (4) Based on teacher salaries, per-pupil expenditures and student-teacher ratios.
Source: Expansion Management, Ratings Issue, 1999

Educational Attainment by Race

Area	High School Graduate (%)					Bachelor's Degree (%)				
	Total	White	Black	Other	Hisp.[2]	Total	White	Black	Other	Hisp.[2]
City	85.2	86.0	88.9	65.1	76.0	28.2	28.5	17.9	20.3	19.6
MSA[1]	83.2	84.1	85.9	65.0	58.8	22.0	22.4	20.1	13.5	10.4
U.S.	75.2	77.9	63.1	60.4	49.8	20.3	21.5	11.4	19.4	9.2

Note: Figures shown cover persons 25 years old and over; (1) Metropolitan Statistical Area - see Appendix A for areas included; (2) people of Hispanic origin can be of any race
Source: 1990 Census of Population and Housing, Summary Tape File 3C

School Enrollment by Type

Area	Preprimary				Elementary/High School			
	Public		Private		Public		Private	
	Enrollment	%	Enrollment	%	Enrollment	%	Enrollment	%
City	393	50.9	379	49.1	6,128	92.8	475	7.2
MSA[1]	1,339	58.8	938	41.2	18,997	89.7	2,177	10.3
U.S.	2,679,029	59.5	1,824,256	40.5	38,379,689	90.2	4,187,099	9.8

Note: Figures shown cover persons 3 years old and over;
(1) Metropolitan Statistical Area - see Appendix A for areas included
Source: 1990 Census of Population and Housing, Summary Tape File 3C

School Enrollment by Race

Area	Preprimary (%)				Elementary/High School (%)			
	White	Black	Other	Hisp.[1]	White	Black	Other	Hisp.[1]
City	94.2	2.1	3.8	1.7	88.6	1.3	10.2	3.6
MSA[2]	90.9	0.9	8.3	2.5	89.7	0.7	9.6	4.0
U.S.	80.4	12.5	7.1	7.8	74.1	15.6	10.3	12.5

Note: Figures shown cover persons 3 years old and over; (1) people of Hispanic origin can be of any race; (2) Metropolitan Statistical Area - see Appendix A for areas included
Source: 1990 Census of Population and Housing, Summary Tape File 3C

Higher Education

Two-Year Colleges		Four-Year Colleges		Medical Schools	Law Schools	Voc/ Tech
Public	Private	Public	Private			
2	0	1	0	0	0	5

Source: College Blue Book, Occupational Education, 1999; Medical School Admission Requirements, 1999-2000; Peterson's Guide to Two-Year Colleges, 2000; Peterson's Guide to Four-Year Colleges, 1999; Barron's Guide to Law Schools, 1999

MAJOR EMPLOYERS

Major Employers

Allsop Inc. (audio equipment)
Georgia-Pacific Corp.
Trillium Corp. (timber)
Veco Engineering

Alpha Technologies (management consulting)
Seafood Producers Cooperative
U.S. Savings Bank of Washington
Visiting Nurse Personal Services

Note: Companies listed are located in the city
Source: D&B Business Rankings, 1999; Ward's Business Directory, 1999; America's Corporate Families, 1999

PUBLIC SAFETY

Crime Rate

Area	All Crimes	Violent Crimes				Property Crimes		
		Murder	Forcible Rape	Robbery	Aggrav. Assault	Burglary	Larceny -Theft	Motor Vehicle Theft
City	7,549.9	3.2	51.0	116.4	145.1	954.9	5,909.5	369.8
Suburbs[1]	4,237.3	2.1	70.4	19.2	193.2	1,250.9	2,463.4	238.0
MSA[2]	5,565.7	2.6	62.7	58.2	173.9	1,132.2	3,845.4	290.9
U.S.	4,615.5	6.3	34.4	165.2	360.5	862.0	2,728.1	459.0

Note: Crime rate is the number of crimes per 100,000 population; (1) Defined as all areas within the Metropolitan Statistical Area but located outside the central city; (2) Metropolitan Statistical Area - see Appendix A for areas included
Source: FBI Uniform Crime Reports, 1998

RECREATION

Culture and Recreation

Museums	Symphony Orchestras	Opera Companies	Dance Companies	Professional Theatres	Zoos	Pro Sports Teams
2	1	0	2	1	1	0

Source: Musical America, International Directory of the Performing Arts, 1999; Official Museum Directory, 2000; Stern's Performing Arts Directory, 1997; USA Today Four Sport Stadium Guide, 1997; Career Opportunities in Theatre and the Performing Arts, 1999

Library System

The Bellingham Public Library has one branch, holdings of 273,947 volumes, and a budget of $2,370,315 (1997-1998).
American Library Directory, 1999-2000

MEDIA

Newspapers

Name	Type	Freq.	Distribution	Circulation
The Bellingham Herald	General	7x/wk	Local	27,700

Note: Includes newspapers with circulations of 200 or more located in the city;
Source: Burrelle's Media Directory, 1999 Edition

Television Stations

Name	Ch.	Affiliation	Type	Owner
KVOS	12	n/a	Commercial	Ackerley Communications Inc.
KBCB	24	n/a	Commercial	World Television of Washington

Note: Stations included broadcast in the Bellingham metro area; n/a not available
Source: Burrelle's Media Directory, 1999 Edition

AM Radio Stations

Call Letters	Freq. (kHz)	Target Audience	Station Format	Music Format
KARI	550	Religious	N/S/T	n/a
KGMI	790	General	N/S/T	n/a
KIXT	930	General	M/N/S	Country
KPUG	1170	General	N/S/T	n/a
KNTR	1550	Religious	M/N/T	Christian

Note: Stations included broadcast in the Bellingham metro area; n/a not available
Target Audience: A=Asian; B=Black; C=Christian; E=Ethnic; F=French; G=General; H=Hispanic; M=Men; N=Native American; R=Religious; S=Senior Citizen; W=Women; Y=Young Adult; Z=Children
Station Format: E=Educational; M=Music; N=News; S=Sports; T=Talk
Source: Burrelle's Media Directory, 1999 Edition

FM Radio Stations

Call Letters	Freq. (mHz)	Target Audience	Station Format	Music Format
KUGS	89.3	G/H	E/M/N/T	Alternative/Jazz/Latin
KZAZ	91.7	General	M/N	Classical
KISM	92.9	General	M	Classic Rock
KAFE	104.3	General	M/N/S	Adult Contemporary
KWPZ	106.5	Religious	M/T	Christian

Note: Stations included broadcast in the Bellingham metro area
Station Format: E=Educational; M=Music; N=News; S=Sports; T=Talk
Target Audience: A=Asian; B=Black; C=Christian; E=Ethnic; F=French; G=General; H=Hispanic; M=Men; N=Native American; R=Religious; S=Senior Citizen; W=Women; Y=Young Adult; Z=Children
Source: Burrelle's Media Directory, 1999 Edition

WEATHER

Temperature/Precipitation/Humidity

	Jan	Feb	Mar	Apr	May	Jun	Jul	Aug	Sep	Oct	Nov	Dec	Yr.
Max. High Temp. (°F)	59	65	65	73	87	93	92	94	89	76	68	61	94
Avg. High Temp. (°F)	41	46	50	57	63	67	72	71	68	58	50	45	57
Avg. Temp. (°F)	35	39	42	47	53	58	62	61	57	49	42	39	49
Avg. Low Temp. (°F)	29	32	34	38	44	50	52	52	47	41	35	33	41
Min. Low Temp. (°F)	-2	-2	10	24	25	37	40	40	32	25	3	9	-2
Avg. Precip. (in.)	4.5	3.8	3.3	2.3	2.0	1.6	0.8	1.1	1.9	4.1	4.8	4.6	34.8
Avg. Snowfall (in.)	5.9	1.8	4.1	0	0	0	0	0	0	0	0.3	2.3	14.4
Avg. Rel. Hum. (%)	75	77	75	73	75	76	75	79	79	83	82	81	78

Source: National Climatic Data Center, International Station Meteorological Climate Summary, 3/95

Weather Conditions

Temperature			Precipitation		
0°F & below	32°F & below	90°F & above	0.1 inch or more precip.	1.5 inch or more snow/ice	Thunder-storms
0	75	1	95	4	3

Note: Figures are average number of days per year
Source: National Climatic Data Center, International Station Meteorological Climate Summary, 3/95

AIR & WATER QUALITY

Maximum Pollutant Concentrations

	Particulate Matter (ug/m³)	Carbon Monoxide (ppm)	Sulfur Dioxide (ppm)	Nitrogen Dioxide (ppm)	Ozone (ppm)	Lead (ug/m³)
MSA[1] Level	48	n/a	n/a	n/a	0.07	n/a
NAAQS[2]	150	9	0.140	0.053	0.12	1.50
Met NAAQS	Yes	n/a	n/a	n/a	Yes	n/a

Note: (1) Metropolitan Statistical Area - see Appendix A for areas included; (2) National Ambient Air Quality Standards; ppm = parts per million; ug/m³ = micrograms per cubic meter; n/a not available
Source: EPA, National Air Quality and Emissions Trends Report, 1997

Pollutant Standards Index

Data not available.
EPA, National Air Quality and Emissions Trends Report, 1997

Drinking Water

Water System Name	Pop. Served	Primary Water Source Type	Number of Violations in 1998-99	Type of Violation/ Contaminants
City of Bellingham Water Div.	66,644	Surface	None	None

Note: Data as of January 19, 2000
Source: EPA, Office of Ground Water and Drinking Water, Safe Drinking Water Information System

Bellingham tap water is neutral, soft, filtered, and chlorinated.
Editor & Publisher Market Guide, 2000

Biloxi, Mississippi

Background

Biloxi, Mississippi is the state's second-largest city located on the Gulf of Mexico, at the eastern end of a narrow peninsula between Biloxi Bay and Mississippi Sound. The culture and economy of Biloxi reflect its coastal location. The city's primary industries include tourism, gaming, seafood processing, military facilities and government services.

The city of Biloxi is one of the two county seats of Harrison County, and part of a larger population center along the Mississippi Gulf Coast that includes neighboring Gulfport, D'Iberville, Long Beach, Pass Christian and other communities. This region, called "Playground of the South," has experienced rapid growth since the introduction of casino gaming in the early 1990s.

In 1969 Biloxi suffered significant damage from Hurricane Camille, which required a major recovery and rebuilding effort, and resulted in an effort by regional and local officials to capitalize on the growth of Gulf Coast tourism and the appeal of the area's lifestyle to stimulate economic development and diversification.

In the early 1990s, the tourism industry was bolstered by the legalization of dockside casino gaming. In Biloxi, gaming was introduced in 1992 with the Isle of Caprice casino resort, which opened with 370 rooms. Within seven years, Biloxi had nine major waterfront resorts with adjacent gaming casinos on the water. Beau Rivage, built in 1999, can accommodate almost 2,000 guests. These gaming resorts stimulated additional tourism activity, including employment, real estate, construction and retailing. Gaming tax revenue has helped to fund significant public works projects and services. Harrison County has several industrial parks and a Foreign Trade Zone. Biloxi has undertaken annexation of unincorporated areas nearby to upgrade its infrastructure and manage growth.

Biloxi is among the oldest communities in the United States. In 1699 Pierre Le Moyne Sieur d'Iberville, while exploring and claiming the lower Mississippi River regions for France, established a colonial settlement there. He named the area Biloxi, after the Indians who lived there. The early French settlers relied on agriculture and fishing, and making tar and pitch. From 1720 to 1723, Biloxi was the capital of France's Louisiana territory. It was included in lands France turned over to England in 1763. In 1779 Biloxi became a Spanish colonial holding. In 1817, after several years as a territory of the United States, Mississippi gained statehood. Biloxi was legally incorporated in 1838. During the Civil War, Biloxi was part of the Confederacy, but it was occupied by invading Union forces.

After 1880, Biloxi became an international center for the seafood industry, which included fishing, shellfish harvesting, canneries and other processing and support operations. The seafood and maritime industries brought many immigrants to the area, and continue to be important in Biloxi's economy.

In 1940 the U.S. Army established an air-corps training base in Biloxi. In 1947 the facility became Keesler Air Force Base, which currently operates as an electronics-training center. Keesler and other government facilities, including naval operations and a NASA Space Center, are significant contributors to the area's civilian economy.

In the 19th Century, the Biloxi area of the Gulf Coast became a popular resort region for residents of New Orleans and other southerners who were attracted by its beaches and moderate climate. Among the estates built along Beach Boulevard by wealthy southerners is Beauvoir, the retirement home of Jefferson Davis, president of the Confederacy, which is now a museum.

Biloxi's recreational amenities include a 26-mile man made white sand beach, over 20 golf courses, 28 parks, deep-sea fishing and other aquatic activities. The area has an 11,500-seat coliseum for sporting events and concerts. Cultural activities include six performing arts theaters and almost 50 annual festivals. Other attractions include the Mardi Gras Museum in the historic Magnolia Hotel, the George E. Ohr Arts and Cultural Center, the Saenger Theater, the J.L. Scott Marine Education Center and Aquarium, and the 1848 Biloxi Lighthouse, among others.

Biloxi is governed by a Mayor and City Council.

General Rankings and Evaluative Comments

- Biloxi was ranked #147 out of 354 metropolitan areas in *Places Rated Almanac*. Criteria: cost of living, climate, crime, transportation, job outlook, education, the arts, health care, and recreation. *Places Rated Almanac, Millennium Edition, 2000*

- Biloxi was selected as one of America's best places to retire. Criteria: safety, climate, housing, culture and recreation, social compatibility, affordability, medical care, transportation, and jobs and/or volunteer opportunities. *Where to Retire: America's Best and Most Affordable Places, 1998*

- Cognetics studied 273 metro areas in the United States, ranking them by entrepreneurial activity. Biloxi was ranked #103 out of 134 smaller metro areas. Criteria: Significant Starts (firms started in the last 10 years that still employ at least 5 people) and Young Growers (percent of firms 10 years old or less that grew significantly during the last 4 years). *Cognetics, "Entrepreneurial Hot Spots: The Best Places in America to Start and Grow a Company," 1999*

- Biloxi was selected as a first-round winner in the small city category for its "Housing in High Gear" program by the U.S Conference of Mayors and Waste Management as part of their 2000 City Livability Awards Program. The program honors mayors and their city governments for developing programs that enhance the quality of life in urban areas. The awards are given annually to ten mayors and their cities—a first-place award and four Outstanding Achievement Awards for cities under 100,000 population, and a first-place and four Outstanding Achievement Awards for cities of 100,000 or more inhabitants.

- The Biloxi/Gulfport area was selected as one of "The 50 Most Alive Places to Live" in the U.S. Criteria: ethnic diversity, recreational options, cultural vitality, low crime rate, opportunities for lifelong learning, good hospitals and restaurants, public transportation, walking accessibility, civic activities, and the kitsch factor. The area was ranked #6 out of 10 in the "Small Towns" category. *Modern Maturity, May-June 2000*

Business Environment

STATE ECONOMY

State Economic Profile

"Mississippi's economy continues to lag the nation and is projected to slow further in 2000. Mississippi's manufacturing sector continues to shed jobs, which are not being offset by the slow growth in the services sector. Mississippi's healthiest sectors remain gaming and construction, neither of which is expected to provide significant long-term job growth.

The textiles and apparel industries have lost 35% of their employment base in the last five years. Falling trade barriers have allowed much of low-skilled manufacturing to shift offshore. The weakness in Asian currencies has made Mississippi much less cost effective.

The damage inflicted by Hurricane George and the expansion of the gaming industry have resulted in a significant increase in construction activity. Construction employment increased almost 10% in 1998. Residential permits were up 28%, driven by a boom in multifamily construction activity. In addition highway projects in Tunica County and along the Gulf have added to construction employment. Most of this activity should taper off in 2000.

Mississippi's growth engine has been the gaming industry. The $650 million Beau Rivage Resort recently opened in Biloxi. With its 1,780 hotel rooms and 25,000 sq. ft. retail complex, the development will boost tax revenues, employment and tourism dollars. Gaming, however, is very sensitive to the business cycle. A weakening US economy in 2000 will dampen gaming revenues.

Mississippi's dependence on gaming and construction does not leave it well positioned to weather the next downturn. Mississippi's outlook for the near future is one of slowing economic growth and housing markets." *National Association of Realtors, Economic Profiles: The Fifty States and the District of Columbia, http://nar.realtor.com/databank/profiles.htm*

EXPORTS

Total Export Sales

Area	1995 ($000)	1996 ($000)	1997 ($000)	1998 ($000)	% Chg. 1995-98	% Chg. 1997-98
MSA[1]	281,040	119,916	76,868	117,892	-58.1	53.4
U.S.	583,030,524	622,827,063	687,597,999	680,474,251	16.7	-1.0

Note: (1) Metropolitan Statistical Area - see Appendix A for areas included
Source: U.S. Department of Commerce, International Trade Association, Metropolitan Area Exports: An Export Performance Report on Over 250 U.S. Cities, November 10, 1999

CITY FINANCES

City Government Finances

Component	1995 ($million)	1995 (per capita $)
Revenue	38.9	815
Expenditure	31.5	660
Debt Outstanding	0.0	0

Source: 1999 County and City Extra, Annual Metro, City, and County Data Book

City Government Revenue by Source

Source	1995 ($million)	1995 (per capita $)
Intergovernmental	10.9	228
Taxes	23.0	482
Property	11.0	232
Sales and Gross Receipts	9.1	192

Source: 1999 County and City Extra, Annual Metro, City, and County Data Book

City Government Expenditures by Function

Function	1995 ($million)	1995 (per capita $)	1995 (%)
Public Welfare	0.0	0	0.0
Highways	6.5	136	20.7
Parking Facilities	0.0	0	0.0
Education	0.0	0	0.0
Health and Hospitals	0.0	0	0.0
Police Protection	6.3	132	20.1
Sewerage and Sanitation	3.5	73	11.2
Parks and Recreation	1.6	34	5.2
Housing and Community Development	0.3	6	1.0
Interest on Debt	1.4	31	4.7

Source: 1999 County and City Extra, Annual Metro, City, and County Data Book

Municipal Bond Ratings

Area	Moody's
City	Baa1

Source: Mergent Bond Record, 2/2000

POPULATION

Population Growth

Area	1980 Census	1990 Census	1999 Estimate	2004 Projection	Population Growth (%) 1990-1999	Population Growth (%) 1999-2004
City	49,311	46,319	47,821	48,103	3.2	0.6
MSA[1]	300,217	197,125	352,155	364,232	78.6	3.4
U.S.	226,545,805	248,765,170	272,212,864	283,625,312	9.4	4.2

Note: (1) Metropolitan Statistical Area - see Appendix A for areas included
Source: 1990 Census of Population and Housing, Summary Tape File 3C; Claritas, Inc.

Number of Households and Average Household Size

Area	1980 Census	1990 Census	1999 Estimate	2004 Projection	1999 Average Household Size
City	16,088	16,697	18,265	18,696	2.62
MSA[1]	97,972	71,307	131,191	138,152	2.68
U.S.	80,389,592	91,993,582	102,048,200	107,302,392	2.67

Note: (1) Metropolitan Statistical Area - see Appendix A for areas included
Source: 1990 Census of Population and Housing, Summary Tape File 3C; Claritas, Inc.

Race/Ethnicity of City Population

Race/Ethnicity	1990 Census Population	1990 Census %	1999 Estimate Population	1999 Estimate %	% Change 1990-1999
White, Non-Hispanic	33,765	72.9	32,310	67.6	-4.3
Black, Non-Hispanic	8,545	18.4	9,700	20.3	13.5
Asian, Non-Hispanic	2,661	5.7	3,710	7.8	39.4
Other, Non-Hispanic	125	0.3	191	0.4	52.8
Hispanic	1,223	2.6	1,910	4.0	56.2

Source: 1990 Census of Population and Housing, Summary Tape File 3C; Claritas, Inc.

Race/Ethnicity of Metropolitan Statistical Area Population

Race/Ethnicity	1990 Census		1999 Estimate		% Change 1990-1999
	Population	%	Population	%	
White, Non-Hispanic	153,408	77.8	264,589	75.1	72.5
Black, Non-Hispanic	35,189	17.9	70,667	20.1	100.8
Asian, Non-Hispanic	4,220	2.1	8,390	2.4	98.8
Other, Non-Hispanic	679	0.3	1,203	0.3	77.2
Hispanic	3,629	1.8	7,306	2.1	101.3

Note: See Appendix A for areas included in the Metropolitan Statistical Area
Source: 1990 Census of Population and Housing, Summary Tape File 3C; Claritas, Inc.

Ancestry

Area	German	Irish	English	Italian	U.S.	French	Polish	Dutch
City	18.0	15.0	12.4	4.1	5.5	10.5	1.6	1.7
MSA[1]	16.9	16.4	12.1	4.4	10.1	13.4	1.3	1.6
U.S.	23.3	15.6	13.1	5.9	5.3	4.2	3.8	2.5

Note: Figures are percentages and include persons that reported multiple ancestry (eg. if a person
reported being Irish and Italian, they were included in both columns); (1) Metropolitan Statistical Area -
see Appendix A for areas included
Source: 1990 Census of Population and Housing, Summary Tape File 3C

Median Age

Area	1990 Census	1999 Estimate
City	28.4	31.4
MSA[1]	31.1	34.2
U.S.	32.9	35.7

Note: (1) Metropolitan Statistical Area - see Appendix A for areas included
Source: 1990 Census of Population and Housing, Summary Tape File 3C; Claritas, Inc.

Male/Female Population

Area	Number of Males		Number of Females		Males per 100 Females	
	1990	1999	1990	1999	1990	1999
City	24,010	24,352	22,309	23,469	107.6	103.8
MSA[1]	98,416	173,826	98,709	178,329	99.7	97.5
U.S.	121,172,379	132,803,736	127,537,494	139,409,136	95.0	95.3

Note: (1) Metropolitan Statistical Area - see Appendix A for areas included
Source: 1990 Census of Population, General Population Characteristics; Claritas, Inc.

INCOME

Per Capita/Median/Average Income

Area	Per Capita ($)			Median Household ($)			Average Household ($)		
	1989	1999	% Chg.	1989	1999	% Chg.	1989	1999	% Chg.
City	10,036	17,846	77.8	19,824	30,886	55.8	25,457	43,976	72.7
MSA[1]	10,393	17,649	69.8	21,977	34,596	57.4	27,824	46,339	66.5
U.S.	14,420	21,350	48.1	30,056	40,525	34.8	38,453	56,184	46.1

Note: (1) Metropolitan Statistical Area - see Appendix A for areas included; 1989 data is
from the 1990 Census; 1999 data is estimated by Claritas, Inc.
Source: 1990 Census of Population, General Population Characteristics; Claritas, Inc.

Household Income Distribution

Area	Percent of Households Earning								
	Under $5,000	$5,000 -14,999	$15,000 -24,999	$25,000 -34,999	$35,000 -49,999	$50,000 -74,999	$75,000 -99,000	$100,000 -149,999	$150,000 and up
City	5.9	16.0	18.0	15.4	15.3	15.5	6.7	4.5	2.8
MSA[1]	5.6	15.3	16.1	13.4	17.0	18.3	7.7	4.4	2.3
U.S.	3.9	13.3	13.8	12.6	16.2	19.4	9.7	6.6	4.6

Note: Data as of 1999; (1) Metropolitan Statistical Area - see Appendix A for areas included
Source: Claritas, Inc.

Effective Buying Income

Area	Per Capita ($)	Median Household ($)	Average Household ($)
City	13,947	27,567	38,184
MSA[1]	15,082	32,268	40,970
U.S.	17,496	36,603	47,036

Note: Data as of 1/1/2000; (1) Metropolitan Statistical Area - see Appendix A for areas included
Source: Standard Rate & Data Service, Newspaper Advertising Source, March 2000

Effective Household Buying Income Distribution

Area	% of Households Earning						
	$10,000 -$19,999	$20,000 -$34,999	$35,000 -$49,999	$50,000 -$74,999	$75,000 -$99,000	$100,000 -$124,999	$125,000 and up
City	19.3	27.0	16.4	13.0	5.5	1.6	1.5
MSA[1]	17.0	22.9	17.6	17.4	7.1	2.2	1.9
U.S.	15.0	21.6	17.6	19.6	8.4	3.0	3.3

Note: Data as of 1/1/2000; (1) Metropolitan Statistical Area - see Appendix A for areas included
Source: Standard Rate & Data Service, Newspaper Advertising Source, March 2000

Poverty Rates by Age

Area	People of All Ages	People Under 18 Years Old	Related Children Age 5-17 in Families in Poverty
City	18.0	n/a	n/a
County	16.8	26.0	23.6
U.S.	13.8	20.8	18.7

Note: Figures show the percent of people living below the poverty line in 1995. The average poverty threshold was $15,569 for a family of four in 1995; n/a not available
Source: Bureau of the Census, Small Area Income and Poverty Estimates Program; U.S. Department of Housing and Urban Development

EMPLOYMENT

Labor Force and Employment

Area	Civilian Labor Force			Workers Employed		
	Dec. 1998	Dec. 1999	% Chg.	Dec. 1998	Dec. 1999	% Chg.
City	19,664	20,174	2.6	18,986	19,413	2.2
MSA[1]	170,822	175,913	3.0	165,887	169,622	2.3
U.S.	138,297,000	139,941,000	1.2	132,732,000	134,696,000	1.5

Note: Data is not seasonally adjusted and covers workers 16 years of age and older;
(1) Metropolitan Statistical Area - see Appendix A for areas included
Source: Bureau of Labor Statistics, http://stats.bls.gov

Unemployment Rate

Area	1999											
	Jan.	Feb.	Mar.	Apr.	May	Jun.	Jul.	Aug.	Sep.	Oct.	Nov.	Dec.
City	4.6	3.6	4.4	3.7	3.9	4.3	3.8	3.8	4.4	5.8	3.5	3.8
MSA[1]	3.7	2.7	3.2	2.8	3.4	3.7	3.3	3.5	4.0	4.1	3.3	3.6
U.S.	4.8	4.7	4.4	4.1	4.0	4.5	4.5	4.2	4.1	3.8	3.8	3.7

Note: Data is not seasonally adjusted and covers workers 16 years of age and older; all figures are percentages; (1) Metropolitan Statistical Area - see Appendix A for areas included
Source: Bureau of Labor Statistics, http://stats.bls.gov

Employment by Industry

Sector	MSA[1]		U.S.
	Number of Employees	Percent of Total	Percent of Total
Services	n/a	n/a	30.2
Retail Trade	n/a	n/a	18.1
Government	n/a	n/a	15.8
Manufacturing	n/a	n/a	14.1
Finance/Insurance/Real Estate	n/a	n/a	5.9
Wholesale Trade	n/a	n/a	5.4
Transportation/Public Utilities	n/a	n/a	5.3
Construction	n/a	n/a	4.8
Mining	n/a	n/a	0.4

Note: Figures cover non-farm employment as of 12/99 and are not seasonally adjusted;
(1) Metropolitan Statistical Area - see Appendix A for areas included; n/a not available
Source: Bureau of Labor Statistics, http://stats.bls.gov

Employment by Occupation

Occupation Category	City (%)	MSA[1] (%)	U.S. (%)
White Collar	58.8	55.3	58.1
Executive/Admin./Management	11.5	10.4	12.3
Professional	17.0	14.7	14.1
Technical & Related Support	4.8	4.1	3.7
Sales	12.1	12.6	11.8
Administrative Support/Clerical	13.4	13.6	16.3
Blue Collar	19.9	27.3	26.2
Precision Production/Craft/Repair	9.7	12.5	11.3
Machine Operators/Assem./Insp.	3.6	5.8	6.8
Transportation/Material Movers	3.3	4.9	4.1
Cleaners/Helpers/Laborers	3.4	4.1	3.9
Services	18.9	15.7	13.2
Farming/Forestry/Fishing	2.4	1.7	2.5

Note: Figures cover workers 16 years of age and older;
(1) Metropolitan Statistical Area - see Appendix A for areas included
Source: 1990 Census of Population and Housing, Summary Tape File 3C

Occupational Employment Projections: 1996 - 2006

Occupations Expected to Have the Largest Job Growth (ranked by numerical growth)	Fast-Growing Occupations[1] (ranked by percent growth)
1. Salespersons, retail	1. Database administrators
2. Cashiers	2. Paralegals
3. General managers & top executives	3. Systems analysts
4. Truck drivers, light	4. Home health aides
5. Teachers aides, clerical & paraprofess.	5. Physical therapy assistants and aides
6. Marketing & sales, supervisors	6. Medical assistants
7. Nursing aides/orderlies/attendants	7. Physical therapists
8. Registered nurses	8. Emergency medical technicians
9. Maintenance repairers, general utility	9. Teachers, special education
10. Home health aides	10. Medical records technicians

Note: Projections cover Mississippi; (1) Excludes occupations with total job growth less than 300
Source: U.S. Department of Labor, Employment and Training Administration, America's Labor Market Information System (ALMIS)

Average Wages

Occupation	$/Hr.	Occupation	$/Hr.
Accountants and Auditors	19.05	Maids and Housekeepers	6.50
Assemblers and Fabricators	9.04	Maintenance Repairers	10.41
Automotive Mechanics	12.14	Marketing/Advertising/PR Managers	23.66
Bookkeepers	10.40	Nurses, Licensed Practical	10.90
Carpenters	12.77	Nurses, Registered	18.57
Cashiers	6.79	Nursing Aides/Orderlies/Attendants	7.28
Clerks, General Office	8.36	Physicians and Surgeons	52.29
Clerks, Shipping/Receiving/Traffic	11.39	Receptionists/Information Clerks	7.95
Computer Programmers	19.40	Sales Reps., Exc. Scientific/Retail	15.34
Computer Support Specialists	16.80	Sales Reps., Scientific, Exc. Retail	18.74
Cooks, Restaurant	8.06	Salespersons, Retail	7.99
Electricians	14.79	Secretaries, Except Legal/Medical	9.52
Financial Managers	22.18	Stock Clerks, Sales Floor	7.02
First-Line Supervisors/Mgrs., Sales	13.62	Systems Analysts	22.53
Food Preparation Workers	6.25	Teacher Aides	5.72
General Managers/Top Executives	23.39	Teachers, Elementary School	14.96
Guards	8.04	Teachers, Secondary School	15.49
Hand Packers	6.14	Telemarketers	7.21
Janitors and Cleaners	7.10	Truck Drivers, Heavy/Tractor-Trailer	11.93
Laborers, Landscaping	7.30	Truck Drivers, Light	9.88
Lawyers	32.79	Waiters and Waitresses	5.60

Note: Wage data is for 1998 and covers the Metropolitan Statistical Area (see Appendix A for areas included). Hourly wages for elementary and secondary school teachers were calculated by the editors from annual wage data assuming a 40 hour work week; Dashes indicate that data was not available.
Source: Bureau of Labor Statistics, 1998 Metropolitan Area Occupational Employment and Wage Estimates

TAXES

Major State and Local Tax Rates

State Corporate Income (%)	State Personal Income (%)	Residential Property (%)	Sales & Use		State Gasoline (cents/ gallon)	State Cigarette (cents/ pack)
			State (%)	Local (%)		
3.0 - 5.0	3.0 - 5.0	1.04	7.0	None	18.4[a]	18.0

Note: Personal/corporate income, sales, gasoline and cigarette tax rates as of January 2000. Property tax rates as of April 2000; (a) Rate is comprised of 18 cents excise and 0.4 cents motor carrier tax
Source: Federation of Tax Administrators, www.taxadmin.org; ERI's Relocation Assessor software database, quarterly effective date 4/1/2000

Total Taxes Per Capita and as a Percent of Income

Area	Per Capita Income ($)	Per Capita Taxes ($)			Percent of Income (%)		
		Total	Federal	State/Local	Total	Federal	State/Local
Mississippi	20,422	6,923	4,567	2,356	33.9	22.4	11.5
U.S.	28,878	10,298	7,026	3,273	35.7	24.3	11.3

Note: Figures are for 1999
Source: Tax Foundation, www.taxfoundation.org

COMMERCIAL UTILITIES

Typical Monthly Electric Bills

Area	Commercial Service ($/month)		Industrial Service ($/month)	
	12 kW demand 1,500 kWh	100 kW demand 30,000 kWh	1,000 kW demand 400,000 kWh	20,000 kW demand 10,000,000 kWh
City	n/a	n/a	n/a	n/a
U.S.	150	2,174	23,995	508,569

Note: Based on rates in effect January 1, 1999; n/a not available
Source: Edison Electric Institute, Typical Residential, Commercial and Industrial Bills, Winter 1999

TRANSPORTATION

Transportation Statistics

Average minutes to work (1990)	16.5
Interstate highways	I-10; I-110; US-90
Bus lines	
In-city (1998)	Mississippi Coast Transportation Authority, 18 buses
Inter-city (1999)	2
Passenger air service	
Airport	Gulfport-Biloxi Regional
Airlines (1999)	5
Enplaned passengers (1998)	237,684
Amtrak service	Yes
Motor freight carriers (1999)	35
Major waterways/ports	Biloxi Bay; Gulf of Mexico

Source: FAA DOT/TSC CY1998 ACAIS Database; National Transit Database, 1998; Editor & Publisher Market Guide, 2000; Amtrak National Time Table, Fall 1999/Winter 2000; 1990 Census of Population and Housing, STF 3C; Jane's Urban Transport Systems 1999-2000

Means of Transportation to Work

Area	Car/Truck/Van		Public Transportation			Bicycle	Walked	Other Means	Worked at Home
	Drove Alone	Car-pooled	Bus	Subway	Railroad				
City	68.4	12.6	0.5	0.0	0.0	0.9	14.6	2.2	0.9
MSA[1]	75.9	14.1	0.4	0.0	0.0	0.6	5.4	1.8	1.7
U.S.	73.2	13.4	3.0	1.5	0.5	0.4	3.9	1.2	3.0

Note: Figures shown are percentages and only include workers 16 years of age and older;
(1) Metropolitan Statistical Area - see Appendix A for areas included
Source: 1990 Census of Population and Housing, Summary Tape File 3C

BUSINESSES

Major Business Headquarters

Company Name	1999 Rankings	
	Fortune 500	Forbes 500
No companies listed	-	-

Note: Companies listed are located in the city; dashes indicate no ranking
Fortune 500: Companies that produce a 10-K are ranked 1 to 500 based on 1999 revenue
Forbes 500: Private companies are ranked 1 to 500 based on 1998 revenue
Source: Forbes, December 13, 1999; Fortune, April 17, 2000

HOTELS & MOTELS

Hotels/Motels

Area	Hotels/ Motels	Rooms	Luxury-Level Hotels/Motels		Average Minimum Rates ($)		
			◆◆◆◆	◆◆◆◆◆	◆◆	◆◆◆	◆◆◆◆
City	30	7,123	0	0	n/a	n/a	n/a

Note: n/a not available; classifications range from one diamond (budget properties with basic amenities) to five diamond (luxury properties).
Source: OAG Business Travel Planner, Winter 1999-2000

Estimated Daily Food and Lodging Costs

Area	Food/Other ($/day)	Average Hotel Cost ($/day)
City	38	72
U.S.	30	55

Source: ERI's Relocation Assessor software database, quarterly effective date 4/1/2000

CONVENTION CENTERS

Convention Centers and Event Sites

Name	Guest Rooms	Meeting Space (sq. ft.)	Capacity (Theatre Style)
Beau Rivage	1,780	n/a	0
Biloxi Beach Resort Inn	186	n/a	300
Biloxi Travelodge	70	n/a	75
Diamondhead Days Inn	152	n/a	400
Grand Casino Hotel-Biloxi	500	n/a	850
Holiday Inn Biloxi Beachfront Coliseum	286	n/a	420
Holiday Inn Express Biloxi	148	n/a	350
Imperial Palace Hotel & Casino	1,000	n/a	0
Mississippi Coast Coliseum & Conv. Ctr.	n/a	n/a	15,000
President Casino Broadwater Beach	850	50,000	1,100
Quality Inn Emerald Beach	62	n/a	125
Travel Lodge Gulf Beach	226	n/a	150
Treasure Bay Resort Hotel & Casino	260	n/a	700

Note: n/a not available
Source: EventSource.com, 3/15/2000

Living Environment

COST OF LIVING

Cost of Living: Homeowner

Cost Element	U.S. ($)	City ($)	Differential ($)	Percent of U.S. Average
Consumables	14,516	14,470	-46	99.7
Transportation	5,957	5,744	-213	96.4
Health Services	2,012	1,941	-71	96.5
Housing/Utilities/Prop. Tax	16,337	16,732	395	102.4
Income+Payroll Taxes	12,615	12,936	321	102.5
Miscellaneous	8,563	8,563	0	100.0
Total Cost of Living	60,000	60,386	386	100.6

Note: Figures are based on a single income, four person family with gross annual earnings of $60,000, owning an 1,800 square-foot home, and driving two automobiles worth $22,000 30,000 miles per year.
Source: ERI's Relocation Assessor software database, quarterly effective date 4/1/2000

Cost of Living: Renter

Cost Element	U.S. ($)	City ($)	Differential ($)	Percent of U.S. Average
Consumables	10,486	10,439	-47	99.6
Transportation	2,107	2,029	-78	96.3
Health Services	1,632	1,573	-59	96.4
Rent/Utilities/Insurance	9,299	9,140	-159	98.3
Income+Payroll Taxes	8,607	8,871	264	103.1
Miscellaneous	7,869	7,869	0	100.0
Total Cost of Living	40,000	39,921	-79	99.8

Note: Figures are based on a single income, three person family with gross annual earnings of $40,000, renting a 1,000 square-foot home, and driving one automobile worth $8,000 12,000 miles per year.
Source: ERI's Relocation Assessor software database, quarterly effective date 4/1/2000

HOUSING

Median Home Prices and Housing Affordability

Area	Median Price[2] 4th Qtr. 1999 ($)	HOI[3] 4th Qtr. 1999	Affordability Rank[4]
MSA[1]	90,000	68.5	104
U.S.	139,000	63.8	–

Note: (1) Metropolitan Statistical Area - see Appendix A for areas included; (2) U.S. figures calculated from the sales of 687,516 new and existing homes in 192 markets; (3) Housing Opportunity Index - percent of homes sold that were within the reach of the median income household at the prevailing mortgage interest rate; (4) Rank is from 1-192 with 1 being most affordable
Source: National Association of Home Builders, Housing Opportunity Index, 4th Quarter 1999

Estimated Home Price

Area	Price ($)
City	134,399
U.S.	135,855

Note: Figures are based on an 1,800 square-foot home
Source: ERI's Relocation Assessor software database, quarterly effective date 4/1/2000

Estimated Rent

Area	Rent ($/month)
City	623
U.S.	651

Note: Figures are based on a 1,000 square-foot home
Source: ERI's Relocation Assessor software database, quarterly effective date 4/1/2000

Median Home Price Projection

It is projected that the median home price in the metropolitan area will increase from $92,196 in 1999 to $138,474 in 2010, an increase of 50.2%
Kiplinger's Personal Finance Magazine, January 2000

RESIDENTIAL UTILITIES

Average Residential Utility Costs

Area	All Electric ($/mth)	Part Electric ($/mth)	Other Energy ($/mth)	Phone ($/mth)
City	n/a	n/a	n/a	n/a
U.S.	99.25	55.47	43.48	20.29

Note: n/a not available
Source: ACCRA, Cost of Living Index, 3rd Quarter 1999

HEALTH CARE

Average Health Care Costs

Area	Hospital ($/day)	Doctor ($/visit)	Dentist ($/visit)
City	n/a	n/a	n/a
U.S.	440.96	53.83	68.42

Note: n/a not available
Source: ACCRA, Cost of Living Index, 3rd Quarter 1999

Distribution of Office-Based Physicians

Area	Family/Gen. Practitioners	Specialists		
		Medical	Surgical	Other
MSA[1]	57	163	162	148

Note: Data as of 12/31/97; (1) Metropolitan Statistical Area - see Appendix A for areas included
Source: American Medical Assn., Physician Characteristics & Distribution in the U.S., 1999

Hospitals

Biloxi has 3 general medical and surgical hospitals.
AHA Guide to the Healthcare Field, 1999-2000

EDUCATION

Public School District Statistics

District Name	Num. Sch.	Enroll.	Classroom Teachers	Pupils per Teacher	Minority Pupils (%)	Current Exp.[1] ($/pupil)
Biloxi Public School Dist	12	6,223	387	16.1	n/a	n/a

Note: Data covers the 1997-1998 school year unless otherwise noted; (1) Data covers fiscal year 1996; SD = School District; ISD = Independent School District; n/a not available
Source: National Center for Education Statistics, Common Core of Data Public Education Agency Universe 1997-98; National Center for Education Statistics, Characteristics of the 100 Largest Public Elementary and Secondary School Districts in the United States: 1997-98, July 1999

Educational Quality

School District	Education Quotient[1]	Graduate Outcome[2]	Community Index[3]	Resource Index[4]
Biloxi Public School Dist.	103	115	93	82

Note: Over 1,000 secondary school districts were rated in terms of educational quality. The scores range from a low of 50 to a high of 150; (1) Combination of the Graduate Outcome, Community and Resource indexes weighted to reflect the greater importance of the Graduate Outcome and Resource Index; (2) Based on graduation rates and college board scores (SAT/ACT); (3) Based on the surrounding community's level of affluence and adult education; (4) Based on teacher salaries, per-pupil expenditures and student-teacher ratios.
Source: Expansion Management, Ratings Issue, 1999

Educational Attainment by Race

Area	High School Graduate (%)					Bachelor's Degree (%)				
	Total	White	Black	Other	Hisp.[2]	Total	White	Black	Other	Hisp.[2]
City	75.2	79.5	65.2	38.9	73.2	18.0	20.4	9.8	5.8	15.7
MSA[1]	73.6	76.5	61.4	50.1	74.4	16.0	17.4	9.2	9.9	17.3
U.S.	75.2	77.9	63.1	60.4	49.8	20.3	21.5	11.4	19.4	9.2

Note: Figures shown cover persons 25 years old and over; (1) Metropolitan Statistical Area - see Appendix A for areas included; (2) people of Hispanic origin can be of any race
Source: 1990 Census of Population and Housing, Summary Tape File 3C

School Enrollment by Type

Area	Preprimary				Elementary/High School			
	Public		Private		Public		Private	
	Enrollment	%	Enrollment	%	Enrollment	%	Enrollment	%
City	450	54.1	382	45.9	6,701	91.7	604	8.3
MSA[1]	2,088	57.9	1,516	42.1	32,596	89.6	3,769	10.4
U.S.	2,679,029	59.5	1,824,256	40.5	38,379,689	90.2	4,187,099	9.8

Note: Figures shown cover persons 3 years old and over;
(1) Metropolitan Statistical Area - see Appendix A for areas included
Source: 1990 Census of Population and Housing, Summary Tape File 3C

School Enrollment by Race

Area	Preprimary (%)				Elementary/High School (%)			
	White	Black	Other	Hisp.[1]	White	Black	Other	Hisp.[1]
City	75.5	13.6	10.9	1.9	61.2	26.4	12.4	2.3
MSA[2]	79.2	17.5	3.2	0.9	71.2	24.8	4.1	2.1
U.S.	80.4	12.5	7.1	7.8	74.1	15.6	10.3	12.5

Note: Figures shown cover persons 3 years old and over; (1) people of Hispanic origin can be of any race; (2) Metropolitan Statistical Area - see Appendix A for areas included
Source: 1990 Census of Population and Housing, Summary Tape File 3C

Higher Education

Two-Year Colleges		Four-Year Colleges		Medical Schools	Law Schools	Voc/ Tech
Public	Private	Public	Private			
0	0	0	0	0	0	0

Source: College Blue Book, Occupational Education, 1999; Medical School Admission Requirements, 1999-2000; Peterson's Guide to Two-Year Colleges, 2000; Peterson's Guide to Four-Year Colleges, 1999; Barron's Guide to Law Schools, 1999

MAJOR EMPLOYERS

Major Employers

Biloxi Casino Corp.	Grand Casinos of Mississippi
Gulf Coast Community Hospital	Imperial Palace of Mississippi
Mississippi Gaming	New Palace Casino
President Riverboat Casino	Treasure Bay Corp.

Note: Companies listed are located in the city
Source: D&B Business Rankings, 1999; Ward's Business Directory, 1999; America's Corporate Families, 1999

PUBLIC SAFETY

Crime Rate

Area	All Crimes	Violent Crimes				Property Crimes		
		Murder	Forcible Rape	Robbery	Aggrav. Assault	Burglary	Larceny -Theft	Motor Vehicle Theft
City	9,667.0	14.3	53.1	285.8	394.0	1,643.5	6,667.9	608.4
Suburbs[1]	n/a	n/a	n/a	n/a	n/a	n/a	n/a	n/a
MSA[2]	n/a	n/a	n/a	n/a	n/a	n/a	n/a	n/a
U.S.	4,615.5	6.3	34.4	165.2	360.5	862.0	2,728.1	459.0

Note: Crime rate is the number of crimes per 100,000 population; (1) Defined as all areas within the Metropolitan Statistical Area but located outside the central city; (2) Metropolitan Statistical Area - see Appendix A for areas included; n/a not available
Source: FBI Uniform Crime Reports, 1998

RECREATION

Culture and Recreation

Museums	Symphony Orchestras	Opera Companies	Dance Companies	Professional Theatres	Zoos	Pro Sports Teams
5	1	1	0	0	0	0

Source: Musical America, International Directory of the Performing Arts, 1999; Official Museum Directory, 2000; Stern's Performing Arts Directory, 1997; USA Today Four Sport Stadium Guide, 1997; Career Opportunities in Theatre and the Performing Arts, 1999

Library System

The Biloxi Public Library has three branches and holdings of 83,998 volumes.
American Library Directory, 1999-2000

MEDIA

Newspapers

Name	Type	Freq.	Distribution	Circulation
Biloxi D'Iberville Press	General	1x/wk	Local	6,000
Gulf Pine Catholic	Religious	1x/wk	Area	4,600

Note: Includes newspapers with circulations of 200 or more located in the city;
Source: Burrelle's Media Directory, 1999 Edition

Television Stations

Name	Ch.	Affiliation	Type	Owner
WLOX	13	ABCT	Commercial	Cosmos Broadcasting Corporation
WXXV	25	FBC	Commercial	Morris Communications Corporation

Note: Stations included broadcast in the Biloxi metro area; n/a not available
Source: Burrelle's Media Directory, 1999 Edition

AM Radio Stations

Call Letters	Freq. (kHz)	Target Audience	Station Format	Music Format
WVMI	570	General	N/T	n/a
WQFX	1130	n/a	M/N	Gospel
WGCM	1240	General	M/N/S	Country
WROA	1390	General	M	Easy Listening
WXBD	1490	General	M/N/S	Big Band

Note: Stations included broadcast in the Biloxi metro area; n/a not available
Target Audience: A=Asian; B=Black; C=Christian; E=Ethnic; F=French; G=General; H=Hispanic; M=Men; N=Native American; R=Religious; S=Senior Citizen; W=Women; Y=Young Adult; Z=Children
Station Format: E=Educational; M=Music; N=News; S=Sports; T=Talk
Source: Burrelle's Media Directory, 1999 Edition

FM Radio Stations

Call Letters	Freq. (mHz)	Target Audience	Station Format	Music Format
WQYZ	92.5	General	M	Adult Contemporary
WMJY	93.7	General	M/N	Adult Contemporary
WLNF	95.3	Young Adult	M/N/T	Alternative/Top 40
WKNN	99.1	General	M/N	Country
WGCM	102.3	General	M	Oldies
WXRG	105.9	General	M/N/S	Classic Rock
WXLS	107.1	General	M/N/T	Adult Contemporary/Christian
WXYK	107.1	General	M/N	Oldies
WZKX	107.9	General	M	Country

Note: Stations included broadcast in the Biloxi metro area
Station Format: E=Educational; M=Music; N=News; S=Sports; T=Talk
Target Audience: A=Asian; B=Black; C=Christian; E=Ethnic; F=French; G=General; H=Hispanic;
M=Men; N=Native American; R=Religious; S=Senior Citizen; W=Women; Y=Young Adult; Z=Children
Source: Burrelle's Media Directory, 1999 Edition

WEATHER

Temperature/Precipitation/Humidity

	Jan	Feb	Mar	Apr	May	Jun	Jul	Aug	Sep	Oct	Nov	Dec	Yr.
Max. High Temp. (°F)	81	80	90	93	97	101	101	104	98	93	86	81	104
Avg. High Temp. (°F)	60	62	68	76	83	88	89	89	86	78	69	62	76
Avg. Temp. (°F)	52	54	60	68	75	81	82	82	78	69	60	54	68
Avg. Low Temp. (°F)	44	47	53	61	68	74	76	75	71	61	52	47	61
Min. Low Temp. (°F)	10	15	24	36	48	57	60	62	45	36	25	12	10
Avg. Precip. (in.)	5.0	4.9	6.2	4.7	4.5	5.3	6.8	6.5	6.3	2.5	4.0	4.8	62.3
Avg. Snowfall (in.)	0	.1	Tr	0	0	0	0	0	0	0	0	.2	.3
Avg. Rel. Hum. 7am (%)	80	84	84	80	81	82	83	83	82	80	81	80	82
Avg. Rel. Hum. 1pm (%)	63	67	65	62	66	67	66	66	63	58	63	65	64

Note: Tr = Trace amounts (less than 0.05 inches of rain or less than 0.5 inches of snow)
Source: National Climatic Data Center, International Station Meteorological Climate Summary, 3/95

Weather Conditions

Temperature			Precipitation		
20°F & below	33°F & below	90°F & above	0.01 inch or more precip.	1.5 inch or more snow/ice	Thunder-storms
2	11	48	109	0	74

Note: Figures are average number of days per year
Source: National Climatic Data Center, International Station Meteorological Climate Summary, 3/95

AIR & WATER QUALITY

Maximum Pollutant Concentrations

	Particulate Matter (ug/m³)	Carbon Monoxide (ppm)	Sulfur Dioxide (ppm)	Nitrogen Dioxide (ppm)	Ozone (ppm)	Lead (ug/m³)
MSA[1] Level	57	n/a	0.025	n/a	0.11	n/a
NAAQS[2]	150	9	0.140	0.053	0.12	1.50
Met NAAQS	Yes	n/a	Yes	n/a	Yes	n/a

Note: (1) Metropolitan Statistical Area - see Appendix A for areas included; (2) National Ambient Air
Quality Standards; ppm = parts per million; ug/m³ = micrograms per cubic meter; n/a not available
Source: EPA, National Air Quality and Emissions Trends Report, 1997

Pollutant Standards Index

Data not available.
EPA, National Air Quality and Emissions Trends Report, 1997

Drinking Water

Water System Name	Pop. Served	Primary Water Source Type	Number of Violations in 1998-99	Type of Violation/ Contaminants
City of Biloxi	41,906	Ground	None	None

Note: Data as of January 19, 2000
Source: EPA, Office of Ground Water and Drinking Water, Safe Drinking Water Information System

Biloxi tap water is slightly acid, very soft, and fluoridated.
Editor & Publisher Market Guide, 2000

Bloomington, Illinois

Background

Bloomington Illinois is located in the central part of the state, approximately 135 miles southwest of Chicago, 65 miles northeast of Springfield, and 160 miles northeast of St. Louis, Missouri. Bloomington is the county seat of McLean County. The city is located on the plains of Illinois, with primarily level terrain.

Bloomington and neighboring Normal are often considered as a single community, sometimes referred to as the "Twin Cities," although they are separate municipalities. The Bloomington and Normal metropolitan area is the commercial center for McLean County and other areas of central Illinois. It is also a transportation hub, with several interstate highways converging there, including I-55, I-39 and I-74. The area has a diverse economy with insurance and financial services and manufacturing. It is among the fastest growing areas in Illinois. The non-urbanized areas in the region are agricultural, producing corn, soy, livestock and other farm products.

Blooomington and Normal also comprise an educational center, with two large universities serving as major employers and important influences in the community. Illinois Weslyan University (founded in 1850) is in Bloomington, and Illinois State University (founded in 1857) is in Normal. Other schools include Heartland Community College in Bloomington and a campus of Lincoln College in Normal.

The area was originally occupied by Kickapoos and other Native American groups. Around 1820 a community known as Blooming Grove developed. The town of Bloomington was established in 1832 as the county seat of McLean County, and it became a city in 1850. Early activities centered on agriculture, and the town grew as a trading center. During his legal and early political career, Abraham Lincoln spent much time in Bloomington, and local residents were instrumental in his campaign for President. Normal was established following an agreement to establish a junction of the Illinois Central and Chicago & Alton railroads. The Bloomington and Normal economies diversified with the establishment of the colleges, and the development of other industries in the latter 19th Century. However, Bloomington suffered extensive damage in a 1900 fire.

The economy continued to diversify in the 20th Century. In 1922, retired farmer George J. Mecherle established State Farm Insurance in Bloomington, which has grown to become the area's largest single employer. Other insurance and financial services corporations, including Country Companies, operate in the area. Beer Nuts was established in Bloomington in 1937, and continues to be based there. Mitsubishi Motor Manufacturing of America, Inc. operates an automotive manufacturing plant. The headquarters of the Eureka Company, which manufactures vacuum cleaners, is based in Bloomington. Other companies make various products including foods, mechanical equipment and other goods. Important economic sectors also include services, agricultural activities, health-care, retail and wholesale trades, transportation, and construction.

Bloomington and Normal contain close to 50 public parks and recreation facilities. The Miller Park Zoo is a popular attraction. Constitution Trail is a multi-use pathway. Approximately ten golf courses are in the area. The Upper Limits is one of the world's tallest indoor climbing facilities.

The Franklin Park Historic District in Bloomington is an area where historic properties (including the family home of former U.N. Ambassador Adlai Stevenson II) are clustered. The McLean County Museum of History is located in the former county courthouse. The Prarie Aviation Museum is located at Central Illinois Regional Airport. The Children's Discovery Museum is in Bloomington.

The universities provide numerous cultural activities and facilities. Local cultural organizations include the annual Illinois Shakespeare Festival at Ewing Manor, the Illinois Symphony, the McLean County Arts Center, Twin Cities Ballet, the Community Players Theater and the Heartland Theater, among others.

Bloomington is governed by a Mayor and City Council and administered by a City Manager.

General Rankings and Evaluative Comments

- Bloomington was ranked #174 out of 354 metropolitan areas in *Places Rated Almanac*. Criteria: cost of living, climate, crime, transportation, job outlook, education, the arts, health care, and recreation. *Places Rated Almanac, Millennium Edition, 2000*

- Cognetics studied 273 metro areas in the United States, ranking them by entrepreneurial activity. Bloomington was ranked #97 out of 134 smaller metro areas. Criteria: Significant Starts (firms started in the last 10 years that still employ at least 5 people) and Young Growers (percent of firms 10 years old or less that grew significantly during the last 4 years). *Cognetics, "Entrepreneurial Hot Spots: The Best Places in America to Start and Grow a Company," 1999*

Business Environment

STATE ECONOMY

State Economic Profile

"Illinois' economy has lagged the nation as it continues to shift from a manufacturing to service-based economy. Its low unemployment rate and rising per capita income mask a major restructuring occurring within its economy. Growth will be weak over the next two years but start to show some rebounding in 2001 as important structural changes now underway take affect.

Over half of the new jobs created in 1998 were in the services sector, and the bulk of those are located in Chicago. Job gains will come from the high-tech and financial services sectors. Manufacturing concerns continued to shed jobs as the state lost some 8,300 manufacturing jobs in 1998. More manufacturing job losses are likely in the short term. Both Mitsubishi and Goodyear are in the process of either laying off workers or planning to do so.

Illinois' farm sector has also been hit particularly hard by low commodity prices and weak foreign demand. Farm income was down more than 20% in 1998. Soybean and corn producers will continue to see their financial health erode. Although foreign demand is expected to pick up, oversupply will guarantee weak prices for bulk commodities.

Although the volume of home sales in 1998 was the highest level in over a decade, price appreciation has continued to lag the nation. Stagnant population growth continues to plague the housing market. Illinois lost over 20,000 residents on net in 1998, many of these are in the "typical buyer" age group of 25 to 44. Unsurprisingly, housing starts have been at their lowest levels in years, rising only 2% in 1998, with most of these taking place in the Chicago area."
National Association of Realtors, Economic Profiles: The Fifty States and the District of Columbia, http://nar.realtor.com/databank/profiles.htm

EXPORTS

Total Export Sales

Area	1995 ($000)	1996 ($000)	1997 ($000)	1998 ($000)	% Chg. 1995-98	% Chg. 1997-98
MSA[1]	n/a	n/a	n/a	n/a	n/a	n/a
U.S.	583,030,524	622,827,063	687,597,999	680,474,251	16.7	-1.0

Note: (1) Metropolitan Statistical Area - see Appendix A for areas included
Source: U.S. Department of Commerce, International Trade Association, Metropolitan Area Exports: An Export Performance Report on Over 250 U.S. Cities, November 10, 1999

CITY FINANCES

City Government Finances

Component	1995 ($million)	1995 (per capita $)
Revenue	37.5	675
Expenditure	46.3	834
Debt Outstanding	45.4	818

Source: 1999 County and City Extra, Annual Metro, City, and County Data Book

City Government Revenue by Source

Source	1995 ($million)	1995 (per capita $)
Intergovernmental	11.2	201
Taxes	19.2	345
Property	8.3	151
Sales and Gross Receipts	9.8	177

Source: 1999 County and City Extra, Annual Metro, City, and County Data Book

City Government Expenditures by Function

Function	1995 ($million)	1995 (per capita $)	1995 (%)
Public Welfare	0.0	0	0.0
Highways	4.6	84	10.1
Parking Facilities	0.6	10	1.3
Education	0.0	0	0.0
Health and Hospitals	0.1	2	0.3
Police Protection	5.0	90	10.8
Sewerage and Sanitation	4.7	85	10.2
Parks and Recreation	3.7	67	8.1
Housing and Community Development	1.1	20	2.4
Interest on Debt	2.4	43	5.2

Source: 1999 County and City Extra, Annual Metro, City, and County Data Book

Municipal Bond Ratings

Area	Moody's
City	Aa1

Source: Mergent Bond Record, 2/2000

POPULATION

Population Growth

Area	1980 Census	1990 Census	1999 Estimate	2004 Projection	Population Growth (%) 1990-1999	Population Growth (%) 1999-2004
City	44,189	51,972	59,903	61,960	15.3	3.4
MSA[1]	119,149	129,180	143,758	147,223	11.3	2.4
U.S.	226,545,805	248,765,170	272,212,864	283,625,312	9.4	4.2

Note: (1) Metropolitan Statistical Area - see Appendix A for areas included
Source: 1990 Census of Population and Housing, Summary Tape File 3C; Claritas, Inc.

Number of Households and Average Household Size

Area	1980 Census	1990 Census	1999 Estimate	2004 Projection	1999 Average Household Size
City	19,183	21,628	24,542	25,296	2.44
MSA[1]	41,702	46,896	52,595	53,899	2.73
U.S.	80,389,592	91,993,582	102,048,200	107,302,392	2.67

Note: (1) Metropolitan Statistical Area - see Appendix A for areas included
Source: 1990 Census of Population and Housing, Summary Tape File 3C; Claritas, Inc.

Race/Ethnicity of City Population

Race/Ethnicity	1990 Census Population	1990 Census %	1999 Estimate Population	1999 Estimate %	% Change 1990-1999
White, Non-Hispanic	46,855	90.2	52,874	88.3	12.8
Black, Non-Hispanic	3,378	6.5	4,354	7.3	28.9
Asian, Non-Hispanic	849	1.6	1,155	1.9	36.0
Other, Non-Hispanic	155	0.3	148	0.2	-4.5
Hispanic	735	1.4	1,372	2.3	86.7

Source: 1990 Census of Population and Housing, Summary Tape File 3C; Claritas, Inc.

Race/Ethnicity of Metropolitan Statistical Area Population

Race/Ethnicity	1990 Census		1999 Estimate		% Change 1990-1999
	Population	%	Population	%	
White, Non-Hispanic	120,427	93.2	131,595	91.5	9.3
Black, Non-Hispanic	5,417	4.2	6,735	4.7	24.3
Asian, Non-Hispanic	1,774	1.4	2,346	1.6	32.2
Other, Non-Hispanic	265	0.2	369	0.3	39.2
Hispanic	1,297	1.0	2,713	1.9	109.2

Note: See Appendix A for areas included in the Metropolitan Statistical Area
Source: 1990 Census of Population and Housing, Summary Tape File 3C; Claritas, Inc.

Ancestry

Area	German	Irish	English	Italian	U.S.	French	Polish	Dutch
City	43.2	21.0	16.4	3.1	3.8	3.9	2.5	3.4
MSA[1]	45.5	19.8	16.1	3.9	4.5	4.1	2.8	3.3
U.S.	23.3	15.6	13.1	5.9	5.3	4.2	3.8	2.5

Note: Figures are percentages and include persons that reported multiple ancestry (eg. if a person reported being Irish and Italian, they were included in both columns); (1) Metropolitan Statistical Area - see Appendix A for areas included
Source: 1990 Census of Population and Housing, Summary Tape File 3C

Median Age

Area	1990 Census	1999 Estimate
City	31.0	34.8
MSA[1]	28.8	32.2
U.S.	32.9	35.7

Note: (1) Metropolitan Statistical Area - see Appendix A for areas included
Source: 1990 Census of Population and Housing, Summary Tape File 3C; Claritas, Inc.

Male/Female Population

Area	Number of Males		Number of Females		Males per 100 Females	
	1990	1999	1990	1999	1990	1999
City	24,324	28,451	27,648	31,452	88.0	90.5
MSA[1]	61,587	68,905	67,593	74,853	91.1	92.1
U.S.	121,172,379	132,803,736	127,537,494	139,409,136	95.0	95.3

Note: (1) Metropolitan Statistical Area - see Appendix A for areas included
Source: 1990 Census of Population, General Population Characteristics; Claritas, Inc.

INCOME

Per Capita/Median/Average Income

Area	Per Capita ($)			Median Household ($)			Average Household ($)		
	1989	1999	% Chg.	1989	1999	% Chg.	1989	1999	% Chg.
City	15,667	25,871	65.1	29,354	46,575	58.7	37,085	62,616	68.8
MSA[1]	14,138	22,947	62.3	31,366	48,132	53.5	37,954	61,780	62.8
U.S.	14,420	21,350	48.1	30,056	40,525	34.8	38,453	56,184	46.1

Note: (1) Metropolitan Statistical Area - see Appendix A for areas included; 1989 data is from the 1990 Census; 1999 data is estimated by Claritas, Inc.
Source: 1990 Census of Population, General Population Characteristics; Claritas, Inc.

Household Income Distribution

Area	Percent of Households Earning								
	Under $5,000	$5,000 -14,999	$15,000 -24,999	$25,000 -34,999	$35,000 -49,999	$50,000 -74,999	$75,000 -99,000	$100,000 -149,999	$150,000 and up
City	2.7	10.3	12.3	11.9	15.8	20.5	11.5	8.6	6.4
MSA[1]	2.4	10.2	12.0	11.3	15.6	22.3	12.4	8.6	5.2
U.S.	3.9	13.3	13.8	12.6	16.2	19.4	9.7	6.6	4.6

Note: Data as of 1999; (1) Metropolitan Statistical Area - see Appendix A for areas included
Source: Claritas, Inc.

Effective Buying Income

Area	Per Capita ($)	Median Household ($)	Average Household ($)
City	21,218	40,312	50,061
MSA[1]	20,071	43,909	54,218
U.S.	17,496	36,603	47,036

Note: Data as of 1/1/2000; (1) Metropolitan Statistical Area - see Appendix A for areas included
Source: Standard Rate & Data Service, Newspaper Advertising Source, March 2000

Effective Household Buying Income Distribution

Area	% of Households Earning						
	$10,000 -$19,999	$20,000 -$34,999	$35,000 -$49,999	$50,000 -$74,999	$75,000 -$99,000	$100,000 -$124,999	$125,000 and up
City	13.5	21.3	16.7	20.5	10.5	4.3	4.4
MSA[1]	12.7	19.4	16.8	22.8	12.0	4.7	4.0
U.S.	15.0	21.6	17.6	19.6	8.4	3.0	3.3

Note: Data as of 1/1/2000; (1) Metropolitan Statistical Area - see Appendix A for areas included
Source: Standard Rate & Data Service, Newspaper Advertising Source, March 2000

Poverty Rates by Age

Area	People of All Ages	People Under 18 Years Old	Related Children Age 5-17 in Families in Poverty
City	6.8	n/a	n/a
County	7.9	10.5	9.1
U.S.	13.8	20.8	18.7

Note: Figures show the percent of people living below the poverty line in 1995. The
average poverty threshold was $15,569 for a family of four in 1995; n/a not available
Source: Bureau of the Census, Small Area Income and Poverty Estimates Program;
U.S. Department of Housing and Urban Development

EMPLOYMENT

Labor Force and Employment

Area	Civilian Labor Force			Workers Employed		
	Dec. 1998	Dec. 1999	% Chg.	Dec. 1998	Dec. 1999	% Chg.
City	36,910	37,710	2.2	36,065	36,609	1.5
MSA[1]	86,853	88,687	2.1	85,237	86,521	1.5
U.S.	138,297,000	139,941,000	1.2	132,732,000	134,696,000	1.5

Note: Data is not seasonally adjusted and covers workers 16 years of age and older;
(1) Metropolitan Statistical Area - see Appendix A for areas included
Source: Bureau of Labor Statistics, http://stats.bls.gov

Unemployment Rate

Area	1999											
	Jan.	Feb.	Mar.	Apr.	May	Jun.	Jul.	Aug.	Sep.	Oct.	Nov.	Dec.
City	3.1	2.7	2.4	2.1	2.5	2.8	2.5	2.5	2.0	2.1	2.3	2.9
MSA[1]	2.6	2.4	2.1	1.9	2.2	2.6	2.5	2.4	2.0	2.1	2.1	2.4
U.S.	4.8	4.7	4.4	4.1	4.0	4.5	4.5	4.2	4.1	3.8	3.8	3.7

Note: Data is not seasonally adjusted and covers workers 16 years of age and older; all figures are percentages; (1) Metropolitan Statistical Area - see Appendix A for areas included
Source: Bureau of Labor Statistics, http://stats.bls.gov

Employment by Industry

Sector	MSA[1]		U.S.
	Number of Employees	Percent of Total	Percent of Total
Services	22,500	24.8	30.2
Retail Trade	15,900	17.5	18.1
Government	15,900	17.5	15.8
Manufacturing	8,900	9.8	14.1
Finance/Insurance/Real Estate	18,500	20.4	5.9
Wholesale Trade	2,800	3.1	5.4
Transportation/Public Utilities	3,000	3.3	5.3
Construction	n/a	n/a	4.8
Mining	n/a	n/a	0.4

Note: Figures cover non-farm employment as of 12/99 and are not seasonally adjusted; (1) Metropolitan Statistical Area - see Appendix A for areas included; n/a not available
Source: Bureau of Labor Statistics, http://stats.bls.gov

Employment by Occupation

Occupation Category	City (%)	MSA[1] (%)	U.S. (%)
White Collar	65.7	61.9	58.1
Executive/Admin./Management	12.3	11.0	12.3
Professional	15.0	15.0	14.1
Technical & Related Support	4.5	3.6	3.7
Sales	13.6	12.8	11.8
Administrative Support/Clerical	20.3	19.6	16.3
Blue Collar	19.7	20.4	26.2
Precision Production/Craft/Repair	8.1	8.4	11.3
Machine Operators/Assem./Insp.	4.8	4.8	6.8
Transportation/Material Movers	3.2	3.7	4.1
Cleaners/Helpers/Laborers	3.5	3.5	3.9
Services	14.0	15.3	13.2
Farming/Forestry/Fishing	0.7	2.4	2.5

Note: Figures cover workers 16 years of age and older; (1) Metropolitan Statistical Area - see Appendix A for areas included
Source: 1990 Census of Population and Housing, Summary Tape File 3C

Occupational Employment Projections: 1996 - 2006

Occupations Expected to Have the Largest Job Growth (ranked by numerical growth)	Fast-Growing Occupations[1] (ranked by percent growth)
1. General managers & top executives	1. Personal and home care aides
2. Cashiers	2. Desktop publishers
3. Salespersons, retail	3. Home health aides
4. Systems analysts	4. Physical therapy assistants and aides
5. Truck drivers, light	5. Medical assistants
6. Registered nurses	6. Physical therapists
7. Food service workers	7. Data processing equipment repairers
8. Hand packers & packagers	8. Occupational therapy assistants
9. Guards	9. Occupational therapists
10. Receptionists and information clerks	10. Human services workers

Note: Projections cover Illinois; (1) Excludes occupations with total job growth less than 300
Source: U.S. Department of Labor, Employment and Training Administration, America's Labor Market Information System (ALMIS)

Average Wages

Occupation	$/Hr.	Occupation	$/Hr.
Accountants and Auditors	20.42	Maids and Housekeepers	6.77
Assemblers and Fabricators	9.42	Maintenance Repairers	12.68
Automotive Mechanics	13.56	Marketing/Advertising/PR Managers	26.16
Bookkeepers	11.45	Nurses, Licensed Practical	12.28
Carpenters	18.87	Nurses, Registered	17.80
Cashiers	6.94	Nursing Aides/Orderlies/Attendants	7.49
Clerks, General Office	9.81	Physicians and Surgeons	-
Clerks, Shipping/Receiving/Traffic	12.50	Receptionists/Information Clerks	8.78
Computer Programmers	21.64	Sales Reps., Exc. Scientific/Retail	18.59
Computer Support Specialists	-	Sales Reps., Scientific, Exc. Retail	26.50
Cooks, Restaurant	8.68	Salespersons, Retail	8.86
Electricians	20.11	Secretaries, Except Legal/Medical	10.50
Financial Managers	30.57	Stock Clerks, Sales Floor	6.79
First-Line Supervisors/Mgrs., Sales	18.73	Systems Analysts	-
Food Preparation Workers	6.52	Teacher Aides	9.63
General Managers/Top Executives	27.06	Teachers, Elementary School	18.82
Guards	-	Teachers, Secondary School	17.62
Hand Packers	6.95	Telemarketers	-
Janitors and Cleaners	8.24	Truck Drivers, Heavy/Tractor-Trailer	15.44
Laborers, Landscaping	11.92	Truck Drivers, Light	9.43
Lawyers	36.66	Waiters and Waitresses	5.89

Note: Wage data is for 1998 and covers the Metropolitan Statistical Area (see Appendix A for areas included). Hourly wages for elementary and secondary school teachers were calculated by the editors from annual wage data assuming a 40 hour work week; Dashes indicate that data was not available.
Source: Bureau of Labor Statistics, 1998 Metropolitan Area Occupational Employment and Wage Estimates

TAXES

Major State and Local Tax Rates

State Corporate Income (%)	State Personal Income (%)	Residential Property (%)	Sales & Use		State Gasoline (cents/ gallon)	State Cigarette (cents/ pack)
			State (%)	Local (%)		
7.3[a]	3.0	2.01	6.25	1.0	19.3[b]	58.0[c]

Note: Personal/corporate income, sales, gasoline and cigarette tax rates as of January 2000. Property tax rates as of April 2000; (a) Includes a 2.5% personal property replacement tax; (b) Rate is comprised of 19 cents excise and 0.3 cent motor carrier tax. Carriers pay an additional surcharge of 6.3 cents. Rate does not include a 5 cent local option tax in Chicago.; (c) Counties and cities may impose an additional tax of 10 - 15 cents per pack
Source: Federation of Tax Administrators, www.taxadmin.org; ERI's Relocation Assessor software database, quarterly effective date 4/1/2000

Total Taxes Per Capita and as a Percent of Income

Area	Per Capita Income ($)	Per Capita Taxes ($)			Percent of Income (%)		
		Total	Federal	State/Local	Total	Federal	State/Local
Illinois	32,087	11,634	8,093	3,541	36.3	25.2	11.0
U.S.	28,878	10,298	7,026	3,273	35.7	24.3	11.3

Note: Figures are for 1999
Source: Tax Foundation, www.taxfoundation.org

COMMERCIAL UTILITIES

Typical Monthly Electric Bills

Area	Commercial Service ($/month)		Industrial Service ($/month)	
	12 kW demand 1,500 kWh	100 kW demand 30,000 kWh	1,000 kW demand 400,000 kWh	20,000 kW demand 10,000,000 kWh
City	n/a	n/a	n/a	n/a
U.S.	150	2,174	23,995	508,569

Note: Based on rates in effect January 1, 1999; n/a not available
Source: Edison Electric Institute, Typical Residential, Commercial and Industrial Bills, Winter 1999

TRANSPORTATION

Transportation Statistics

Average minutes to work (1990)	14.4
Interstate highways	I-39; I-55; I-74; US-51; US-150
Bus lines	
In-city (1998)	Bloomington-Normal Public Transit System, 14 buses
Inter-city (1999)	3
Passenger air service	
Airport	Bloomington-Normal International
Airlines (1999)	3
Enplaned passengers (1998)	190,201
Amtrak service	Yes
Motor freight carriers (1999)	38
Major waterways/ports	None

Source: FAA DOT/TSC CY1998 ACAIS Database; National Transit Database, 1998; Editor & Publisher Market Guide, 2000; Amtrak National Time Table, Fall 1999/Winter 2000; 1990 Census of Population and Housing, STF 3C; Jane's Urban Transport Systems 1999-2000

Means of Transportation to Work

Area	Car/Truck/Van		Public Transportation			Bicycle	Walked	Other Means	Worked at Home
	Drove Alone	Car-pooled	Bus	Subway	Railroad				
City	76.6	13.0	1.2	0.0	0.0	0.4	5.5	0.7	2.6
MSA[1]	72.9	12.6	0.8	0.0	0.0	0.4	9.2	0.6	3.4
U.S.	73.2	13.4	3.0	1.5	0.5	0.4	3.9	1.2	3.0

Note: Figures shown are percentages and only include workers 16 years of age and older;
(1) Metropolitan Statistical Area - see Appendix A for areas included
Source: 1990 Census of Population and Housing, Summary Tape File 3C

BUSINESSES

Major Business Headquarters

Company Name	1999 Rankings	
	Fortune 500	Forbes 500
State Farm Insurance Cos.	15	-

Note: Companies listed are located in the city; dashes indicate no ranking
Fortune 500: Companies that produce a 10-K are ranked 1 to 500 based on 1999 revenue
Forbes 500: Private companies are ranked 1 to 500 based on 1998 revenue
Source: Forbes, December 13, 1999; Fortune, April 17, 2000

HOTELS & MOTELS

Hotels/Motels

Area	Hotels/ Motels	Rooms	Luxury-Level Hotels/Motels		Average Minimum Rates ($)		
			♦♦♦♦	♦♦♦♦♦	♦♦	♦♦♦	♦♦♦♦
City	11	992	0	0	n/a	n/a	n/a
Airport	3	410	0	0	n/a	n/a	n/a
Total	14	1,402	0	0	n/a	n/a	n/a

Note: n/a not available; classifications range from one diamond (budget properties with basic amenities) to five diamond (luxury properties).
Source: OAG Business Travel Planner, Winter 1999-2000

Estimated Daily Food and Lodging Costs

Area	Food/Other ($/day)	Average Hotel Cost ($/day)
City	30	55
U.S.	30	55

Source: ERI's Relocation Assessor software database, quarterly effective date 4/1/2000

CONVENTION CENTERS

Convention Centers and Event Sites

Name	Guest Rooms	Meeting Space (sq. ft.)	Capacity (Theatre Style)
Radisson Hotel and Conference Center	149	5,700	400

Source: EventSource.com, 3/15/2000

Living Environment

COST OF LIVING

Cost of Living: Homeowner

Cost Element	U.S. ($)	City ($)	Differential ($)	Percent of U.S. Average
Consumables	14,516	15,266	750	105.2
Transportation	5,957	5,687	-270	95.5
Health Services	2,012	2,058	46	102.3
Housing/Utilities/Prop. Tax	16,337	20,392	4,055	124.8
Income+Payroll Taxes	12,615	11,456	-1,159	90.8
Miscellaneous	8,563	8,563	0	100.0
Total Cost of Living	60,000	63,422	3,422	105.7

Note: Figures are based on a single income, four person family with gross annual earnings of $60,000, owning an 1,800 square-foot home, and driving two automobiles worth $22,000 30,000 miles per year.
Source: ERI's Relocation Assessor software database, quarterly effective date 4/1/2000

Cost of Living: Renter

Cost Element	U.S. ($)	City ($)	Differential ($)	Percent of U.S. Average
Consumables	10,486	10,978	492	104.7
Transportation	2,107	2,003	-104	95.1
Health Services	1,632	1,662	30	101.8
Rent/Utilities/Insurance	9,299	7,833	-1,466	84.2
Income+Payroll Taxes	8,607	8,303	-304	96.5
Miscellaneous	7,869	7,869	0	100.0
Total Cost of Living	40,000	38,648	-1,352	96.6

Note: Figures are based on a single income, three person family with gross annual earnings of $40,000, renting a 1,000 square-foot home, and driving one automobile worth $8,000 12,000 miles per year.
Source: ERI's Relocation Assessor software database, quarterly effective date 4/1/2000

HOUSING

Median Home Prices and Housing Affordability

Area	Median Price[2] 4th Qtr. 1999 ($)	HOI[3] 4th Qtr. 1999	Affordability Rank[4]
MSA[1]	n/a	n/a	n/a
U.S.	139,000	63.8	–

Note: (1) Metropolitan Statistical Area - see Appendix A for areas included; (2) U.S. figures calculated from the sales of 687,516 new and existing homes in 192 markets; (3) Housing Opportunity Index - percent of homes sold that were within the reach of the median income household at the prevailing mortgage interest rate; (4) Rank is from 1-192 with 1 being most affordable; n/a not available
Source: National Association of Home Builders, Housing Opportunity Index, 4th Quarter 1999

Estimated Home Price

Area	Price ($)
City	170,184
U.S.	135,855

Note: Figures are based on an 1,800 square-foot home
Source: ERI's Relocation Assessor software database, quarterly effective date 4/1/2000

Estimated Rent

Area	Rent ($/month)
City	547
U.S.	651

Note: Figures are based on a 1,000 square-foot home
Source: ERI's Relocation Assessor software database, quarterly effective date 4/1/2000

Median Home Price Projection

It is projected that the median home price in the metropolitan area will increase from $139,838 in 1999 to $195,520 in 2010, an increase of 39.8%
Kiplinger's Personal Finance Magazine, January 2000

RESIDENTIAL UTILITIES

Average Residential Utility Costs

Area	All Electric ($/mth)	Part Electric ($/mth)	Other Energy ($/mth)	Phone ($/mth)
City	–	59.23	36.25	22.29
U.S.	99.25	55.47	43.48	20.29

Source: ACCRA, Cost of Living Index, 3rd Quarter 1999

HEALTH CARE

Average Health Care Costs

Area	Hospital ($/day)	Doctor ($/visit)	Dentist ($/visit)
City	392.45	58.60	71.60
U.S.	440.96	53.83	68.42

Note: Hospital—based on a semi-private room; Doctor—based on a general practitioner's routine exam of an established patient; Dentist—based on adult teeth cleaning and periodic oral exam.
Source: ACCRA, Cost of Living Index, 3rd Quarter 1999

Distribution of Office-Based Physicians

Area	Family/Gen. Practitioners	Specialists Medical	Specialists Surgical	Specialists Other
MSA[1]	28	69	54	59

Note: Data as of 12/31/97; (1) Metropolitan Statistical Area - see Appendix A for areas included
Source: American Medical Assn., Physician Characteristics & Distribution in the U.S., 1999

Hospitals

Bloomington has 1 general medical and surgical hospital.
AHA Guide to the Healthcare Field, 1999-2000

EDUCATION

Public School District Statistics

District Name	Num. Sch.	Enroll.	Classroom Teachers	Pupils per Teacher	Minority Pupils (%)	Current Exp.[1] ($/pupil)
Bloomington Area Voc Ctr	1	619	11	56.3	n/a	n/a
Bloomington Sch Dist 87	9	6,592	338	19.5	n/a	n/a

Note: Data covers the 1997-1998 school year unless otherwise noted; (1) Data covers fiscal year 1996; SD = School District; ISD = Independent School District; n/a not available
Source: National Center for Education Statistics, Common Core of Data Public Education Agency Universe 1997-98; National Center for Education Statistics, Characteristics of the 100 Largest Public Elementary and Secondary School Districts in the United States: 1997-98, July 1999

Educational Quality

School District	Education Quotient[1]	Graduate Outcome[2]	Community Index[3]	Resource Index[4]
Bloomington School Dist. 87	124	137	117	98

Note: Over 1,000 secondary school districts were rated in terms of educational quality. The scores range from a low of 50 to a high of 150; (1) Combination of the Graduate Outcome, Community and Resource indexes weighted to reflect the greater importance of the Graduate Outcome and Resource Index; (2) Based on graduation rates and college board scores (SAT/ACT); (3) Based on the surrounding community's level of affluence and adult education; (4) Based on teacher salaries, per-pupil expenditures and student-teacher ratios.
Source: Expansion Management, Ratings Issue, 1999

Educational Attainment by Race

Area	High School Graduate (%)					Bachelor's Degree (%)				
	Total	White	Black	Other	Hisp.[2]	Total	White	Black	Other	Hisp.[2]
City	83.9	84.7	73.2	78.4	53.2	31.7	32.1	22.8	37.2	7.8
MSA[1]	84.7	84.9	78.6	82.9	58.9	29.0	28.7	26.8	50.9	9.5
U.S.	75.2	77.9	63.1	60.4	49.8	20.3	21.5	11.4	19.4	9.2

Note: Figures shown cover persons 25 years old and over; (1) Metropolitan Statistical Area - see Appendix A for areas included; (2) people of Hispanic origin can be of any race
Source: 1990 Census of Population and Housing, Summary Tape File 3C

School Enrollment by Type

Area	Preprimary				Elementary/High School			
	Public		Private		Public		Private	
	Enrollment	%	Enrollment	%	Enrollment	%	Enrollment	%
City	691	59.5	471	40.5	6,823	89.1	838	10.9
MSA[1]	1,566	61.8	970	38.2	17,890	92.5	1,452	7.5
U.S.	2,679,029	59.5	1,824,256	40.5	38,379,689	90.2	4,187,099	9.8

Note: Figures shown cover persons 3 years old and over;
(1) Metropolitan Statistical Area - see Appendix A for areas included
Source: 1990 Census of Population and Housing, Summary Tape File 3C

School Enrollment by Race

Area	Preprimary (%)				Elementary/High School (%)			
	White	Black	Other	Hisp.[1]	White	Black	Other	Hisp.[1]
City	90.6	7.1	2.2	1.4	84.1	11.7	4.2	2.7
MSA[2]	93.7	3.8	2.5	1.2	91.3	6.2	2.4	1.5
U.S.	80.4	12.5	7.1	7.8	74.1	15.6	10.3	12.5

Note: Figures shown cover persons 3 years old and over; (1) people of Hispanic origin can be of any race; (2) Metropolitan Statistical Area - see Appendix A for areas included
Source: 1990 Census of Population and Housing, Summary Tape File 3C

Higher Education

Two-Year Colleges		Four-Year Colleges		Medical Schools	Law Schools	Voc/ Tech
Public	Private	Public	Private			
1	0	0	1	0	0	1

Source: College Blue Book, Occupational Education, 1999; Medical School Admission Requirements, 1999-2000; Peterson's Guide to Two-Year Colleges, 2000; Peterson's Guide to Four-Year Colleges, 1999; Barron's Guide to Law Schools, 1999

MAJOR EMPLOYERS

Major Employers

Bloomington Broadcasting Corp.	Carpet Weavers
Country Mutual Insurance	Glass Specialty Co. (automotive glass)
Growmark Inc. (fertilizer materials)	Heritage Enterprises (nursing care)
Illinois Agriculture Association	State Farm Mutual Auto Insurance

Note: Companies listed are located in the city
Source: D&B Business Rankings, 1999; Ward's Business Directory, 1999; America's Corporate Families, 1999

PUBLIC SAFETY

Crime Rate

Area	All Crimes	Violent Crimes				Property Crimes		
		Murder	Forcible Rape	Robbery	Aggrav. Assault	Burglary	Larceny -Theft	Motor Vehicle Theft
City	n/a	n/a	n/a	n/a	n/a	n/a	n/a	n/a
Suburbs[1]	n/a	n/a	n/a	n/a	n/a	n/a	n/a	n/a
MSA[2]	n/a	n/a	n/a	n/a	n/a	n/a	n/a	n/a
U.S.	4,615.5	6.3	34.4	165.2	360.5	862.0	2,728.1	459.0

Note: Crime rate is the number of crimes per 100,000 population; (1) Defined as all areas within the Metropolitan Statistical Area but located outside the central city; (2) Metropolitan Statistical Area - see Appendix A for areas included; n/a not available
Source: FBI Uniform Crime Reports, 1998

RECREATION

Culture and Recreation

Museums	Symphony Orchestras	Opera Companies	Dance Companies	Professional Theatres	Zoos	Pro Sports Teams
2	0	0	0	0	1	0

Source: Musical America, International Directory of the Performing Arts, 1999; Official Museum Directory, 2000; Stern's Performing Arts Directory, 1997; USA Today Four Sport Stadium Guide, 1997; Career Opportunities in Theatre and the Performing Arts, 1999

Library System

The Bloomington Public Library has no branches and holdings of 167,000 volumes.
American Library Directory, 1999-2000

MEDIA

Newspapers

Name	Type	Freq.	Distribution	Circulation
The Pantagraph	General	7x/wk	Area	50,305

Note: Includes newspapers with circulations of 200 or more located in the city;
Source: Burrelle's Media Directory, 1999 Edition

Television Stations

Name	Ch.	Affiliation	Type	Owner
WYZZ	43	FBC	Commercial	Sinclair Communications Inc.

Note: Stations included broadcast in the Bloomington metro area; n/a not available
Source: Burrelle's Media Directory, 1999 Edition

AM Radio Stations

Call Letters	Freq. (kHz)	Target Audience	Station Format	Music Format
WMCL	1060	General	M/N	Country
WJBC	1230	General	T	n/a

Note: Stations included broadcast in the Bloomington metro area; n/a not available
Target Audience: A=Asian; B=Black; C=Christian; E=Ethnic; F=French; G=General; H=Hispanic; M=Men; N=Native American; R=Religious; S=Senior Citizen; W=Women; Y=Young Adult; Z=Children
Station Format: E=Educational; M=Music; N=News; S=Sports; T=Talk
Source: Burrelle's Media Directory, 1999 Edition

FM Radio Stations

Call Letters	Freq. (mHz)	Target Audience	Station Format	Music Format
WESN	88.1	General	E/M/N/T	Alternative/Classic Rock
WGLT	89.1	General	M/N	Jazz
WIHN	96.7	General	M	Alternative/Oldies
WBNQ	101.5	General	M/N/T	Adult Top 40

Note: Stations included broadcast in the Bloomington metro area
Station Format: E=Educational; M=Music; N=News; S=Sports; T=Talk
Target Audience: A=Asian; B=Black; C=Christian; E=Ethnic; F=French; G=General; H=Hispanic; M=Men; N=Native American; R=Religious; S=Senior Citizen; W=Women; Y=Young Adult; Z=Children
Source: Burrelle's Media Directory, 1999 Edition

WEATHER

Temperature/Precipitation/Humidity

	Jan	Feb	Mar	Apr	May	Jun	Jul	Aug	Sep	Oct	Nov	Dec	Yr.
Max. High Temp. (°F)	69	71	88	95	103	106	114	105	103	93	82	68	114
Avg. High Temp. (°F)	35	38	50	63	75	84	89	87	80	68	51	38	63
Avg. Temp. (°F)	26	29	40	51	63	72	76	74	67	56	41	30	52
Avg. Low Temp. (°F)	18	21	30	40	51	60	64	62	55	44	32	22	42
Min. Low Temp. (°F)	-24	-24	-15	14	26	31	41	37	22	9	-7	-20	-24
Avg. Precip. (in.)	2.1	1.8	3.0	3.9	4.1	4.2	3.3	3.3	3.6	2.5	2.6	2.1	36.4
Avg. Snowfall (in.)	6.1	5.4	4.7	1.0	0	0	0	0	0	0.2	1.6	4.9	23.9
Avg. Rel. Hum. (%)	77	76	71	66	64	67	69	71	67	67	71	77	70

Source: National Climatic Data Center, International Station Meteorological Climate Summary, 3/95

Weather Conditions

Temperature			Precipitation		
0°F & below	32°F & below	90°F & above	0.1 inch or more precip.	1.5 inch or more snow/ice	Thunder-storms
8	123	37	67	5	47

Note: Figures are average number of days per year
Source: National Climatic Data Center, International Station Meteorological Climate Summary, 3/95

AIR & WATER QUALITY

Maximum Pollutant Concentrations

	Particulate Matter (ug/m³)	Carbon Monoxide (ppm)	Sulfur Dioxide (ppm)	Nitrogen Dioxide (ppm)	Ozone (ppm)	Lead (ug/m³)
MSA[1] Level	n/a	n/a	n/a	n/a	n/a	n/a
NAAQS[2]	150	9	0.140	0.053	0.12	1.50
Met NAAQS	n/a	n/a	n/a	n/a	n/a	n/a

Note: (1) Metropolitan Statistical Area - see Appendix A for areas included; (2) National Ambient Air Quality Standards; ppm = parts per million; ug/m³ = micrograms per cubic meter; n/a not available
Source: EPA, National Air Quality and Emissions Trends Report, 1997

Pollutant Standards Index

Data not available. *EPA, National Air Quality and Emissions Trends Report, 1997*

Drinking Water

Water System Name	Pop. Served	Primary Water Source Type	Number of Violations in 1998-99	Type of Violation/ Contaminants
Bloomington	58,500	Surface	None	None

Note: Data as of January 19, 2000
Source: EPA, Office of Ground Water and Drinking Water, Safe Drinking Water Information System

Bloomington tap water is alkaline, soft, and fluoridated.
Editor & Publisher Market Guide, 2000

Boulder, Colorado

Background

Boulder, Colorado, lies at the foot of the Rocky Mountains in Boulder County. It is the eighth largest city in Colorado, with 27.8 square miles.

Tourism is a major industry in Boulder, which offers spectacular views from its elevation of 5,430 feet, and many outdoor recreation opportunities in over 31,000 acres of open space. In addition to tourism, the city's economy depends on manufacturing of defense systems and mechanical equipment, and the business services, retail, transportation, aerospace and computer industries.

Boulder Valley originally was home to the Southern Arapahoe tribe. The first white settlement was established by gold miners in 1858 near the entrance to Boulder Canyon at Red Rocks. In 1859, the Boulder City Town Company was formed. The town's first schoolhouse was built in 1860, and in 1874, the University of Colorado opened. Boulder was incorporated as a town in 1871, and as a city in 1882.

By 1890, the railroad provided service from Boulder to Golden, Denver, and the western mining camps. In 1905, amidst a weakening economy, Boulder began promoting tourism to boost its finances. The city raised money to construct a first-class hotel, which was completed in 1908 and named Hotel Boulderado.

Although tourism remained strong until the late 1930s, it had begun to decline by World War II. However, the U.S. Navy's Japanese language school, housed at the University of Colorado, proved to be an impressive introduction to the area, and many people later returned to Boulder as students, professionals, and veterans attending the university on the GI Bill. Consequently, Boulder's population grew from 12,958 in 1940 to 20,000 in 1950. To accommodate this huge increase, new public buildings, highways, residential areas, and shopping centers developed, spurring further economic expansion.

Boulder is home to the University of Colorado, which houses a 143-acre research park. Cultural venues in the city include the Boulder Dushanbe Teahouse, a gift to the city from its sister city of Dushanbe in Tajikistan. The Pearl Street Mall, an open-air walkway that was the city's original downtown, is rich with restaurants, cafs, bookstores and street entertainers. Boulder offers many scenic opportunities for outdoor activities, with its parks, recreation areas and hiking trails.

Annual attractions include the Creek Festival in May, Art Fair in July, Fall Festival, and Lights of December Parade. Each Memorial Day, over 40,000 runners participate in the "Bolder Boulder," a popular race that lures 80,000 spectators.

General Rankings and Evaluative Comments

- Boulder was selected as a "Small City Runner Up" in Money magazine's most recent survey of the best places to live. Criteria: 300 metropolitan areas in the U.S. were ranked on 46 quality-of-life factors including the economy, education, culture, recreation, safety, and clean air and water. *Money, "The Best Places to Live 2000"*

- Boulder was ranked #164 out of 354 metropolitan areas in *Places Rated Almanac*. Criteria: cost of living, climate, crime, transportation, job outlook, education, the arts, health care, and recreation. *Places Rated Almanac, Millennium Edition, 2000*

- Boulder was selected as one of America's best places to retire. Criteria: safety, climate, housing, culture and recreation, social compatibility, affordability, medical care, transportation, and jobs and/or volunteer opportunities. *Where to Retire: America's Best and Most Affordable Places, 1998*

- Boulder was selected as one of "America's Best Towns to Raise an Outdoor Family" by *Outdoor Explorer* magazine. Criteria: easy access to the outdoors, quality education and health care, affordable housing, favorable employment opportunities, and low crime rates. The city was ranked #17 out of 25. *Outdoor Explorer, Summer 1999*

- Cognetics studied 273 metro areas in the United States, ranking them by entrepreneurial activity. Boulder was ranked #11 out of the 50 largest metro areas. Criteria: Significant Starts (firms started in the last 10 years that still employ at least 5 people) and Young Growers (percent of firms 10 years old or less that grew significantly during the last 4 years). *Cognetics, "Entrepreneurial Hot Spots: The Best Places in America to Start and Grow a Company," 1999*

- Boulder appeared on *Sales & Marketing Management's* list of the "20 Hottest Cities for Selling." The city ranked #9,999 out of 20. *S&MM* editors looked at Metropolitan Statistical Areas with populations of more than 150,000. The areas were ranked based on population increases, retail sales increases, effective buying income, increase in both residential and commercial building permits issued, unemployment rates, job growth, mix of industries, tax rates, number of corporate relocations, and the number of new corporations. *Sales & Marketing Management, April 1999*

- Reliastar Financial Corporation ranked the 125 largest metropolitan areas according to the general financial security of residents. Boulder was ranked #18 out of 125 with a score of 10.7 (the percentage a metropolitan area is above or below the metropolitan norm; a metro area with a score of 10.6 is 10.6% above the metro average). Criteria: Earnings and Wealth Potential (household income, education, net assets, cost of living); Safety Net (health insurance, retirement savings, life insurance, income support programs); Personal Threats (unemployment rate, low-income households, crime rate); Community Economic Vitality (cost of community services, job quality, job creation, housing costs). *Reliastar Financial Corporation, "The Best Cities to Earn and Save Money: A Ranking of the Largest 125 U.S. Cities," 2000 Edition*

- Boulder was selected as one of "The 50 Most Alive Places to Live" in the U.S. Criteria: ethnic diversity, recreational options, cultural vitality, low crime rate, opportunities for lifelong learning, good hospitals and restaurants, public transportation, walking accessibility, civic activities, and the kitsch factor. The area was ranked #1 out of 10 in the "Green & Clean" category. *Modern Maturity, May-June 2000*

Business Environment

STATE ECONOMY

State Economic Profile

"Colorado has been and is poised to remain one of the fastest growing states in the nation. By almost every positive measure, Colorado has outpaced the nation in recent years. Unemployment is low, job growth has been amazing, and the housing market has been booming. With such a stellar performance in recent years, projected growth will continue to be strong but at a slower rate.

Colorado, like Nevada, Utah and Arizona, benefited from California's slowdown and unfriendly business environment during the early and middle 1990s. California's rebound will likely slow its neighbor's economies. Colorado's diversified economy and high quality of life will allow it to continue to attract residents and fuel its strong economy.

Employment gains in communications, services and retail have more than balanced the slow growth in manufacturing. Telecommunications should add thousands of jobs as Colorado becomes a regional hub on the information highway.

Commercial and residential construction has contributed significantly to Colorado's growth. Both hotel and office construction in Colorado's major metro areas has been strong and should remain so, albiet at a slightly lower rate. Additionally many materials suppliers, such as Dakota Craft, are expanding their Colorado operations, adding both employment and a steady supply of building materials.

A strong economy, amazing income growth and low interest rates have driven Colorado's housing market to record levels. Sales and prices continue to reach new highs. Possible growth controls may dampen supply, but will only add to price appreciation in the years ahead." *National Association of Realtors, Economic Profiles: The Fifty States and the District of Columbia, http://nar.realtor.com/databank/profiles.htm*

EXPORTS

Total Export Sales

Area	1995 ($000)	1996 ($000)	1997 ($000)	1998 ($000)	% Chg. 1995-98	% Chg. 1997-98
MSA[1]	n/a	n/a	n/a	n/a	n/a	n/a
U.S.	583,030,524	622,827,063	687,597,999	680,474,251	16.7	-1.0

Note: (1) Metropolitan Statistical Area - see Appendix A for areas included
Source: U.S. Department of Commerce, International Trade Association, Metropolitan Area Exports: An Export Performance Report on Over 250 U.S. Cities, November 10, 1999

CITY FINANCES

City Government Finances

Component	1995 ($million)	1995 (per capita $)
Revenue	107.2	1,251
Expenditure	91.3	1,066
Debt Outstanding	106.1	1,239

Source: 1999 County and City Extra, Annual Metro, City, and County Data Book

City Government Revenue by Source

Source	1995 ($million)	1995 (per capita $)
Intergovernmental	11.2	130
Taxes	73.6	860
Property	14.5	170
Sales and Gross Receipts	54.3	634

Source: 1999 County and City Extra, Annual Metro, City, and County Data Book

City Government Expenditures by Function

Function	1995 ($million)	1995 (per capita $)	1995 (%)
Public Welfare	0.0	0	0.0
Highways	12.5	147	13.8
Parking Facilities	1.1	13	1.3
Education	0.0	0	0.0
Health and Hospitals	0.0	0	0.0
Police Protection	12.0	140	13.2
Sewerage and Sanitation	8.7	102	9.6
Parks and Recreation	13.2	154	14.5
Housing and Community Development	7.2	84	7.9
Interest on Debt	7.9	92	8.7

Source: 1999 County and City Extra, Annual Metro, City, and County Data Book

Municipal Bond Ratings

Area	Moody's
City	Aaa

Source: Mergent Bond Record, 2/2000

POPULATION

Population Growth

Area	1980 Census	1990 Census	1999 Estimate	2004 Projection	Population Growth (%) 1990-1999	Population Growth (%) 1999-2004
City	76,685	83,312	89,252	91,934	7.1	3.0
MSA[1]	189,625	225,339	270,841	289,637	20.2	6.9
U.S.	226,545,805	248,765,170	272,212,864	283,625,312	9.4	4.2

Note: (1) Metropolitan Statistical Area - see Appendix A for areas included
Source: 1990 Census of Population and Housing, Summary Tape File 3C; Claritas, Inc.

Number of Households and Average Household Size

Area	1980 Census	1990 Census	1999 Estimate	2004 Projection	1999 Average Household Size
City	29,384	34,649	39,210	41,270	2.28
MSA[1]	68,964	88,570	110,124	119,679	2.46
U.S.	80,389,592	91,993,582	102,048,200	107,302,392	2.67

Note: (1) Metropolitan Statistical Area - see Appendix A for areas included
Source: 1990 Census of Population and Housing, Summary Tape File 3C; Claritas, Inc.

Race/Ethnicity of City Population

Race/Ethnicity	1990 Census Population	1990 Census %	1999 Estimate Population	1999 Estimate %	% Change 1990-1999
White, Non-Hispanic	74,704	89.7	77,683	87.0	4.0
Black, Non-Hispanic	847	1.0	1,249	1.4	47.5
Asian, Non-Hispanic	3,125	3.8	4,384	4.9	40.3
Other, Non-Hispanic	495	0.6	417	0.5	-15.8
Hispanic	4,141	5.0	5,519	6.2	33.3

Source: 1990 Census of Population and Housing, Summary Tape File 3C; Claritas, Inc.

Race/Ethnicity of Metropolitan Statistical Area Population

Race/Ethnicity	1990 Census		1999 Estimate		% Change 1990-1999
	Population	%	Population	%	
White, Non-Hispanic	201,860	89.6	236,646	87.4	17.2
Black, Non-Hispanic	1,512	0.7	2,468	0.9	63.2
Asian, Non-Hispanic	5,506	2.4	8,164	3.0	48.3
Other, Non-Hispanic	1,364	0.6	1,483	0.5	8.7
Hispanic	15,097	6.7	22,080	8.2	46.3

Note: See Appendix A for areas included in the Metropolitan Statistical Area
Source: 1990 Census of Population and Housing, Summary Tape File 3C; Claritas, Inc.

Ancestry

Area	German	Irish	English	Italian	U.S.	French	Polish	Dutch
City	30.2	16.9	20.8	4.9	2.3	5.0	4.3	2.6
MSA[1]	34.3	17.1	20.9	5.1	2.5	5.0	3.6	3.1
U.S.	23.3	15.6	13.1	5.9	5.3	4.2	3.8	2.5

Note: Figures are percentages and include persons that reported multiple ancestry (eg. if a person reported being Irish and Italian, they were included in both columns); (1) Metropolitan Statistical Area - see Appendix A for areas included
Source: 1990 Census of Population and Housing, Summary Tape File 3C

Median Age

Area	1990 Census	1999 Estimate
City	28.9	33.3
MSA[1]	31.6	35.0
U.S.	32.9	35.7

Note: (1) Metropolitan Statistical Area - see Appendix A for areas included
Source: 1990 Census of Population and Housing, Summary Tape File 3C; Claritas, Inc.

Male/Female Population

Area	Number of Males		Number of Females		Males per 100 Females	
	1990	1999	1990	1999	1990	1999
City	42,096	45,064	41,216	44,188	102.1	102.0
MSA[1]	113,096	135,419	112,243	135,422	100.8	100.0
U.S.	121,172,379	132,803,736	127,537,494	139,409,136	95.0	95.3

Note: (1) Metropolitan Statistical Area - see Appendix A for areas included
Source: 1990 Census of Population, General Population Characteristics; Claritas, Inc.

INCOME

Per Capita/Median/Average Income

Area	Per Capita ($)			Median Household ($)			Average Household ($)		
	1989	1999	% Chg.	1989	1999	% Chg.	1989	1999	% Chg.
City	17,268	29,881	73.0	29,407	44,037	49.8	40,325	66,192	64.1
MSA[1]	17,359	29,488	69.9	35,322	54,719	54.9	43,609	71,570	64.1
U.S.	14,420	21,350	48.1	30,056	40,525	34.8	38,453	56,184	46.1

Note: (1) Metropolitan Statistical Area - see Appendix A for areas included; 1989 data is from the 1990 Census; 1999 data is estimated by Claritas, Inc.
Source: 1990 Census of Population, General Population Characteristics; Claritas, Inc.

Household Income Distribution

Area	Percent of Households Earning								
	Under $5,000	$5,000 -14,999	$15,000 -24,999	$25,000 -34,999	$35,000 -49,999	$50,000 -74,999	$75,000 -99,000	$100,000 -149,999	$150,000 and up
City	3.9	12.0	13.1	11.4	13.7	15.6	11.2	9.4	9.7
MSA[1]	2.4	8.6	10.2	10.2	14.2	20.4	14.3	11.0	8.8
U.S.	3.9	13.3	13.8	12.6	16.2	19.4	9.7	6.6	4.6

Note: Data as of 1999; (1) Metropolitan Statistical Area - see Appendix A for areas included
Source: Claritas, Inc.

Effective Buying Income

Area	Per Capita ($)	Median Household ($)	Average Household ($)
City	21,197	36,947	49,979
MSA[1]	22,432	44,824	55,326
U.S.	17,496	36,603	47,036

Note: Data as of 1/1/2000; (1) Metropolitan Statistical Area - see Appendix A for areas included
Source: Standard Rate & Data Service, Newspaper Advertising Source, March 2000

Effective Household Buying Income Distribution

Area	% of Households Earning						
	$10,000 -$19,999	$20,000 -$34,999	$35,000 -$49,999	$50,000 -$74,999	$75,000 -$99,000	$100,000 -$124,999	$125,000 and up
City	15.5	21.0	14.0	18.0	10.7	4.7	4.6
MSA[1]	11.9	19.2	16.6	22.9	12.0	4.9	4.7
U.S.	15.0	21.6	17.6	19.6	8.4	3.0	3.3

Note: Data as of 1/1/2000; (1) Metropolitan Statistical Area - see Appendix A for areas included
Source: Standard Rate & Data Service, Newspaper Advertising Source, March 2000

Poverty Rates by Age

Area	People of All Ages	People Under 18 Years Old	Related Children Age 5-17 in Families in Poverty
City	13.5	n/a	n/a
County	8.0	9.3	7.6
U.S.	13.8	20.8	18.7

Note: Figures show the percent of people living below the poverty line in 1995. The
average poverty threshold was $15,569 for a family of four in 1995; n/a not available
Source: Bureau of the Census, Small Area Income and Poverty Estimates Program;
U.S. Department of Housing and Urban Development

EMPLOYMENT

Labor Force and Employment

Area	Civilian Labor Force			Workers Employed		
	Dec. 1998	Dec. 1999	% Chg.	Dec. 1998	Dec. 1999	% Chg.
City	66,915	68,021	1.7	65,094	66,366	2.0
MSA[1]	174,330	177,249	1.7	169,933	173,253	2.0
U.S.	138,297,000	139,941,000	1.2	132,732,000	134,696,000	1.5

Note: Data is not seasonally adjusted and covers workers 16 years of age and older;
(1) Metropolitan Statistical Area - see Appendix A for areas included
Source: Bureau of Labor Statistics, http://stats.bls.gov

Unemployment Rate

Area	1999											
	Jan.	Feb.	Mar.	Apr.	May	Jun.	Jul.	Aug.	Sep.	Oct.	Nov.	Dec.
City	3.1	2.6	2.6	2.6	2.8	3.7	3.2	3.0	2.9	2.9	2.6	2.4
MSA[1]	2.8	2.4	2.4	2.4	2.6	3.5	3.0	2.7	2.7	2.7	2.4	2.3
U.S.	4.8	4.7	4.4	4.1	4.0	4.5	4.5	4.2	4.1	3.8	3.8	3.7

Note: Data is not seasonally adjusted and covers workers 16 years of age and older; all figures are percentages; (1) Metropolitan Statistical Area - see Appendix A for areas included
Source: Bureau of Labor Statistics, http://stats.bls.gov

Employment by Industry

Sector	MSA[1]		U.S.
	Number of Employees	Percent of Total	Percent of Total
Services	57,700	33.0	30.2
Retail Trade	30,400	17.4	18.1
Government	27,700	15.8	15.8
Manufacturing	32,700	18.7	14.1
Finance/Insurance/Real Estate	6,800	3.9	5.9
Wholesale Trade	5,900	3.4	5.4
Transportation/Public Utilities	5,400	3.1	5.3
Construction	n/a	n/a	4.8
Mining	n/a	n/a	0.4

Note: Figures cover non-farm employment as of 12/99 and are not seasonally adjusted;
(1) Metropolitan Statistical Area - see Appendix A for areas included; n/a not available
Source: Bureau of Labor Statistics, http://stats.bls.gov

Employment by Occupation

Occupation Category	City (%)	MSA[1] (%)	U.S. (%)
White Collar	77.5	71.5	58.1
Executive/Admin./Management	15.5	15.6	12.3
Professional	28.4	22.6	14.1
Technical & Related Support	7.1	6.8	3.7
Sales	12.2	11.6	11.8
Administrative Support/Clerical	14.3	14.8	16.3
Blue Collar	9.5	16.8	26.2
Precision Production/Craft/Repair	4.2	8.1	11.3
Machine Operators/Assem./Insp.	2.2	4.4	6.8
Transportation/Material Movers	1.4	2.1	4.1
Cleaners/Helpers/Laborers	1.7	2.2	3.9
Services	12.4	10.7	13.2
Farming/Forestry/Fishing	0.7	1.1	2.5

Note: Figures cover workers 16 years of age and older;
(1) Metropolitan Statistical Area - see Appendix A for areas included
Source: 1990 Census of Population and Housing, Summary Tape File 3C

Occupational Employment Projections: 1996 - 2006

Occupations Expected to Have the Largest Job Growth (ranked by numerical growth)	Fast-Growing Occupations[1] (ranked by percent growth)
1. Salespersons, retail	1. Personal and home care aides
2. General managers & top executives	2. Human services workers
3. Truck drivers, light	3. Instructors/coaches, sports/phys. train.
4. Marketing & sales, supervisors	4. Engineering/science/computer sys. mgrs.
5. Cashiers	5. Physical therapists
6. Janitors/cleaners/maids, ex. priv. hshld.	6. Customer service representatives
7. Systems analysts	7. Directors, religious activities & educ.
8. Waiters & waitresses	8. Adjustment clerks
9. Food service workers	9. Emergency medical technicians
10. General office clerks	10. Child care workers, private household

Note: Projections cover Colorado; (1) Excludes occupations with total job growth less than 300
Source: U.S. Department of Labor, Employment and Training Administration, America's Labor Market Information System (ALMIS)

Average Wages

Occupation	$/Hr.	Occupation	$/Hr.
Accountants and Auditors	19.71	Maids and Housekeepers	7.06
Assemblers and Fabricators	9.09	Maintenance Repairers	11.91
Automotive Mechanics	16.09	Marketing/Advertising/PR Managers	29.29
Bookkeepers	12.75	Nurses, Licensed Practical	13.80
Carpenters	14.05	Nurses, Registered	19.19
Cashiers	8.72	Nursing Aides/Orderlies/Attendants	8.57
Clerks, General Office	10.49	Physicians and Surgeons	52.50
Clerks, Shipping/Receiving/Traffic	11.22	Receptionists/Information Clerks	9.84
Computer Programmers	25.77	Sales Reps., Exc. Scientific/Retail	25.84
Computer Support Specialists	19.55	Sales Reps., Scientific, Exc. Retail	25.25
Cooks, Restaurant	8.15	Salespersons, Retail	9.54
Electricians	14.98	Secretaries, Except Legal/Medical	13.06
Financial Managers	27.41	Stock Clerks, Sales Floor	10.07
First-Line Supervisors/Mgrs., Sales	17.77	Systems Analysts	26.86
Food Preparation Workers	7.12	Teacher Aides	8.66
General Managers/Top Executives	36.12	Teachers, Elementary School	15.65
Guards	8.74	Teachers, Secondary School	-
Hand Packers	7.37	Telemarketers	10.95
Janitors and Cleaners	8.15	Truck Drivers, Heavy/Tractor-Trailer	13.34
Laborers, Landscaping	9.28	Truck Drivers, Light	9.43
Lawyers	33.95	Waiters and Waitresses	6.12

Note: Wage data is for 1998 and covers the Metropolitan Statistical Area (see Appendix A for areas included). Hourly wages for elementary and secondary school teachers were calculated by the editors from annual wage data assuming a 40 hour work week; Dashes indicate that data was not available.
Source: Bureau of Labor Statistics, 1998 Metropolitan Area Occupational Employment and Wage Estimates

TAXES

Major State and Local Tax Rates

State Corporate Income (%)	State Personal Income (%)	Residential Property (%)	Sales & Use		State Gasoline (cents/ gallon)	State Cigarette (cents/ pack)
			State (%)	Local (%)		
4.75	4.75	0.84	3.0	4.46	22.0	20.0

Note: Personal/corporate income, sales, gasoline and cigarette tax rates as of January 2000. Property tax rates as of April 2000.
Source: Federation of Tax Administrators, www.taxadmin.org; ERI's Relocation Assessor software database, quarterly effective date 4/1/2000

Total Taxes Per Capita and as a Percent of Income

Area	Per Capita Income ($)	Per Capita Taxes ($)			Percent of Income (%)		
		Total	Federal	State/Local	Total	Federal	State/Local
Colorado	30,764	10,410	7,446	2,964	33.8	24.2	9.6
U.S.	28,878	10,298	7,026	3,273	35.7	24.3	11.3

Note: Figures are for 1999
Source: Tax Foundation, www.taxfoundation.org

COMMERCIAL UTILITIES

Typical Monthly Electric Bills

Area	Commercial Service ($/month)		Industrial Service ($/month)	
	12 kW demand 1,500 kWh	100 kW demand 30,000 kWh	1,000 kW demand 400,000 kWh	20,000 kW demand 10,000,000 kWh
City	n/a	n/a	n/a	n/a
U.S.	150	2,174	23,995	508,569

Note: Based on rates in effect January 1, 1999; n/a not available
Source: Edison Electric Institute, Typical Residential, Commercial and Industrial Bills, Winter 1999

TRANSPORTATION

Transportation Statistics

Average minutes to work (1990)	17.9
Interstate highways	US-36
Bus lines	
In-city (1998)	Regional Transportation District, 615 buses, 16 light rail cars
Inter-city (1999)	1
Passenger air service	
Airport	Boulder Municipal Airport; Denver Int'l. Airport; (30 miles)
Airlines (1999)	15
Enplaned passengers (1998)	n/a
Amtrak service	Bus Connection
Motor freight carriers (1999)	2
Major waterways/ports	None

Source: FAA DOT/TSC CY1998 ACAIS Database; National Transit Database, 1998; Editor & Publisher Market Guide, 2000; Amtrak National Time Table, Fall 1999/Winter 2000; 1990 Census of Population and Housing, STF 3C; Jane's Urban Transport Systems 1999-2000

Means of Transportation to Work

Area	Car/Truck/Van		Public Transportation			Bicycle	Walked	Other Means	Worked at Home
	Drove Alone	Car-pooled	Bus	Subway	Railroad				
City	61.3	9.5	5.3	0.0	0.0	7.0	10.7	1.1	5.1
MSA[1]	70.9	11.5	3.3	0.0	0.0	2.9	5.5	1.0	4.8
U.S.	73.2	13.4	3.0	1.5	0.5	0.4	3.9	1.2	3.0

Note: Figures shown are percentages and only include workers 16 years of age and older;
(1) Metropolitan Statistical Area - see Appendix A for areas included
Source: 1990 Census of Population and Housing, Summary Tape File 3C

BUSINESSES

Major Business Headquarters

Company Name	1999 Rankings	
	Fortune 500	Forbes 500
No companies listed	-	-

Note: Companies listed are located in the city; dashes indicate no ranking
Fortune 500: Companies that produce a 10-K are ranked 1 to 500 based on 1999 revenue
Forbes 500: Private companies are ranked 1 to 500 based on 1998 revenue
Source: Forbes, December 13, 1999; Fortune, April 17, 2000

HOTELS & MOTELS

Hotels/Motels

Area	Hotels/ Motels	Rooms	Luxury-Level Hotels/Motels		Average Minimum Rates ($)		
			♦♦♦♦	♦♦♦♦♦	♦♦	♦♦♦	♦♦♦♦
City	18	1,218	0	0	n/a	n/a	n/a
Suburbs	6	700	0	0	n/a	n/a	n/a
Total	24	1,918	0	0	n/a	n/a	n/a

Note: n/a not available; classifications range from one diamond (budget properties with basic amenities) to five diamond (luxury properties).
Source: OAG Business Travel Planner, Winter 1999-2000

Estimated Daily Food and Lodging Costs

Area	Food/Other ($/day)	Average Hotel Cost ($/day)
City	42	90
U.S.	30	55

Source: ERI's Relocation Assessor software database, quarterly effective date 4/1/2000

CONVENTION CENTERS

Convention Centers and Event Sites

Name	Guest Rooms	Meeting Space (sq. ft.)	Capacity (Theatre Style)
Best Western Boulder Inn	95	n/a	60
Best Western Golden Bluff Lodge	112	1,400	50
Boulder Marriott in the Village	155	3,588	0
C.U. Coors Events/Conference Center	n/a	n/a	12,000
Coburn Hotel	12	2,843	60
Courtyard by Marriott	149	648	0
Holiday Inn Boulder	165	5,802	140
Homewood Suites Hotel	112	400	25
Hotel Boulderado	160	5,000	350
Macky Auditorium Concert Hall	n/a	n/a	0
Regal Harvest House	269	18,000	700
Residence Inn by Marriott	128	648	0
The Alps Boulder Canyon Inn	12	1,967	0
The Broker Inn	116	4,926	350

Note: n/a not available
Source: EventSource.com, 3/15/2000

Living Environment

COST OF LIVING

Cost of Living: Homeowner

Cost Element	U.S. ($)	City ($)	Differential ($)	Percent of U.S. Average
Consumables	14,516	15,907	1,391	109.6
Transportation	5,957	6,315	358	106.0
Health Services	2,012	2,100	88	104.4
Housing/Utilities/Prop. Tax	16,337	32,143	15,806	196.7
Income+Payroll Taxes	12,615	10,620	-1,995	84.2
Miscellaneous	8,563	8,563	0	100.0
Total Cost of Living	60,000	75,648	15,648	126.1

Note: Figures are based on a single income, four person family with gross annual earnings of $60,000, owning an 1,800 square-foot home, and driving two automobiles worth $22,000 30,000 miles per year.
Source: ERI's Relocation Assessor software database, quarterly effective date 4/1/2000

Cost of Living: Renter

Cost Element	U.S. ($)	City ($)	Differential ($)	Percent of U.S. Average
Consumables	10,486	11,455	969	109.2
Transportation	2,107	2,227	120	105.7
Health Services	1,632	1,699	67	104.1
Rent/Utilities/Insurance	9,299	17,056	7,757	183.4
Income+Payroll Taxes	8,607	8,735	128	101.5
Miscellaneous	7,869	7,869	0	100.0
Total Cost of Living	40,000	49,041	9,041	122.6

Note: Figures are based on a single income, three person family with gross annual earnings of $40,000, renting a 1,000 square-foot home, and driving one automobile worth $8,000 12,000 miles per year.
Source: ERI's Relocation Assessor software database, quarterly effective date 4/1/2000

HOUSING

Median Home Prices and Housing Affordability

Area	Median Price[2] 4th Qtr. 1999 ($)	HOI[3] 4th Qtr. 1999	Affordability Rank[4]
MSA[1]	210,000	50.8	161
U.S.	139,000	63.8	–

Note: (1) Metropolitan Statistical Area - see Appendix A for areas included; (2) U.S. figures calculated from the sales of 687,516 new and existing homes in 192 markets; (3) Housing Opportunity Index - percent of homes sold that were within the reach of the median income household at the prevailing mortgage interest rate; (4) Rank is from 1-192 with 1 being most affordable
Source: National Association of Home Builders, Housing Opportunity Index, 4th Quarter 1999

Estimated Home Price

Area	Price ($)
City	305,122
U.S.	135,855

Note: Figures are based on an 1,800 square-foot home
Source: ERI's Relocation Assessor software database, quarterly effective date 4/1/2000

Estimated Rent

Area	Rent ($/month)
City	1,313
U.S.	651

Note: Figures are based on a 1,000 square-foot home
Source: ERI's Relocation Assessor software database, quarterly effective date 4/1/2000

Median Home Price Projection

It is projected that the median home price in the metropolitan area will increase from $210,789 in 1999 to $337,657 in 2010, an increase of 60.2%
Kiplinger's Personal Finance Magazine, January 2000

RESIDENTIAL UTILITIES

Average Residential Utility Costs

Area	All Electric ($/mth)	Part Electric ($/mth)	Other Energy ($/mth)	Phone ($/mth)
City	–	41.54	40.51	20.89
U.S.	99.25	55.47	43.48	20.29

Source: ACCRA, Cost of Living Index, 3rd Quarter 1999

HEALTH CARE

Average Health Care Costs

Area	Hospital ($/day)	Doctor ($/visit)	Dentist ($/visit)
City	400.00	67.25	66.50
U.S.	440.96	53.83	68.42

Note: Hospital—based on a semi-private room; Doctor—based on a general practitioner's routine exam of an established patient; Dentist—based on adult teeth cleaning and periodic oral exam.
Source: ACCRA, Cost of Living Index, 3rd Quarter 1999

Distribution of Office-Based Physicians

Area	Family/Gen. Practitioners	Specialists Medical	Specialists Surgical	Specialists Other
MSA[1]	130	150	107	190

Note: Data as of 12/31/97; (1) Metropolitan Statistical Area - see Appendix A for areas included
Source: American Medical Assn., Physician Characteristics & Distribution in the U.S., 1999

Hospitals

Boulder has 1 general medical and surgical hospital.
AHA Guide to the Healthcare Field, 1999-2000

EDUCATION

Public School District Statistics

District Name	Num. Sch.	Enroll.	Classroom Teachers	Pupils per Teacher	Minority Pupils (%)	Current Exp.[1] ($/pupil)
Boulder Valley RE 2	53	26,192	1,431	18.3	17.3	4,883

Note: Data covers the 1997-1998 school year unless otherwise noted; (1) Data covers fiscal year 1996; SD = School District; ISD = Independent School District; n/a not available
Source: National Center for Education Statistics, Common Core of Data Public Education Agency Universe 1997-98; National Center for Education Statistics, Characteristics of the 100 Largest Public Elementary and Secondary School Districts in the United States: 1997-98, July 1999

Educational Quality

School District	Education Quotient[1]	Graduate Outcome[2]	Community Index[3]	Resource Index[4]
Boulder Valley RE 2	123	138	134	90

Note: Over 1,000 secondary school districts were rated in terms of educational quality. The scores range from a low of 50 to a high of 150; (1) Combination of the Graduate Outcome, Community and Resource indexes weighted to reflect the greater importance of the Graduate Outcome and Resource Index; (2) Based on graduation rates and college board scores (SAT/ACT); (3) Based on the surrounding community's level of affluence and adult education; (4) Based on teacher salaries, per-pupil expenditures and student-teacher ratios.
Source: Expansion Management, Ratings Issue, 1999

Educational Attainment by Race

Area	High School Graduate (%)					Bachelor's Degree (%)				
	Total	White	Black	Other	Hisp.[2]	Total	White	Black	Other	Hisp.[2]
City	94.9	95.5	94.9	84.4	73.0	58.9	59.2	37.7	56.2	39.2
MSA[1]	91.3	92.2	95.3	72.0	61.9	42.1	42.6	38.2	34.1	18.2
U.S.	75.2	77.9	63.1	60.4	49.8	20.3	21.5	11.4	19.4	9.2

*Note: Figures shown cover persons 25 years old and over; (1) Metropolitan Statistical Area -
see Appendix A for areas included; (2) people of Hispanic origin can be of any race
Source: 1990 Census of Population and Housing, Summary Tape File 3C*

School Enrollment by Type

Area	Preprimary				Elementary/High School			
	Public		Private		Public		Private	
	Enrollment	%	Enrollment	%	Enrollment	%	Enrollment	%
City	832	49.6	847	50.4	7,182	92.6	576	7.4
MSA[1]	2,650	54.1	2,245	45.9	31,151	94.1	1,959	5.9
U.S.	2,679,029	59.5	1,824,256	40.5	38,379,689	90.2	4,187,099	9.8

*Note: Figures shown cover persons 3 years old and over;
(1) Metropolitan Statistical Area - see Appendix A for areas included
Source: 1990 Census of Population and Housing, Summary Tape File 3C*

School Enrollment by Race

Area	Preprimary (%)				Elementary/High School (%)			
	White	Black	Other	Hisp.[1]	White	Black	Other	Hisp.[1]
City	94.6	0.7	4.7	4.3	90.0	1.0	8.9	10.3
MSA[2]	94.7	0.3	5.0	7.6	91.1	0.7	8.3	11.2
U.S.	80.4	12.5	7.1	7.8	74.1	15.6	10.3	12.5

*Note: Figures shown cover persons 3 years old and over; (1) people of Hispanic origin can be of any
race; (2) Metropolitan Statistical Area - see Appendix A for areas included
Source: 1990 Census of Population and Housing, Summary Tape File 3C*

Higher Education

Two-Year Colleges		Four-Year Colleges		Medical Schools	Law Schools	Voc/ Tech
Public	Private	Public	Private			
0	0	1	1	0	1	4

*Source: College Blue Book, Occupational Education, 1999; Medical School Admission Requirements,
1999-2000; Peterson's Guide to Two-Year Colleges, 2000; Peterson's Guide to Four-Year Colleges,
1999; Barron's Guide to Law Schools, 1999*

MAJOR EMPLOYERS

Major Employers

American Coin Merchandising	Community Hospital Association
MicroMotion	Phycor of Boulder
Pro-Dex Corp. (dental material)	Rock Bottom Restaurants
University Corp. for Atmospheric Research	University of Colorado

*Note: Companies listed are located in the city
Source: D&B Business Rankings, 1999; Ward's Business Directory, 1999; America's Corporate
Families, 1999*

PUBLIC SAFETY

Crime Rate

Area	All Crimes	Violent Crimes				Property Crimes		
		Murder	Forcible Rape	Robbery	Aggrav. Assault	Burglary	Larceny -Theft	Motor Vehicle Theft
City	5,200.0	1.1	43.5	42.5	132.7	864.0	3,863.6	252.6
Suburbs[1]	4,373.0	1.7	56.8	36.5	223.6	764.6	3,027.9	261.8
MSA[2]	4,665.0	1.5	52.1	38.6	191.5	799.7	3,323.0	258.6
U.S.	4,615.5	6.3	34.4	165.2	360.5	862.0	2,728.1	459.0

Note: Crime rate is the number of crimes per 100,000 population; (1) Defined as all areas within the Metropolitan Statistical Area but located outside the central city; (2) Metropolitan Statistical Area - see Appendix A for areas included
Source: FBI Uniform Crime Reports, 1998

RECREATION

Culture and Recreation

Museums	Symphony Orchestras	Opera Companies	Dance Companies	Professional Theatres	Zoos	Pro Sports Teams
7	2	0	2	1	0	0

Source: Musical America, International Directory of the Performing Arts, 1999; Official Museum Directory, 2000; Stern's Performing Arts Directory, 1997; USA Today Four Sport Stadium Guide, 1997; Career Opportunities in Theatre and the Performing Arts, 1999

Library System

The Boulder Public Library has three branches, holdings of 428,447 volumes, and a budget of $4,950,163 (1997-1998).
American Library Directory, 1999-2000

MEDIA

Newspapers

Name	Type	Freq.	Distribution	Circulation
Daily Camera	General	7x/wk	Local	35,000

Note: Includes newspapers with circulations of 200 or more located in the city;
Source: Burrelle's Media Directory, 1999 Edition

Television Stations

Name	Ch.	Affiliation	Type	Owner
No stations listed.				

Note: Stations included broadcast in the Boulder metro area; n/a not available
Source: Burrelle's Media Directory, 1999 Edition

AM Radio Stations

Call Letters	Freq. (kHz)	Target Audience	Station Format	Music Format
KLMO	1060	B/G	M/N/S	Big Band/Country
KVCU	1190	General	M/N/S	Alternative/Big Band/Jazz
KWAB	1490	General	E/M/N/T	AOR/Blues/Classic Rock/Reggae/Rhythm & Blues/World Music

Note: Stations included broadcast in the Boulder metro area
Target Audience: A=Asian; B=Black; C=Christian; E=Ethnic; F=French; G=General; H=Hispanic; M=Men; N=Native American; R=Religious; S=Senior Citizen; W=Women; Y=Young Adult; Z=Children
Station Format: E=Educational; M=Music; N=News; S=Sports; T=Talk
Music Format: AOR=Album Oriented Rock; MOR=Middle-of-the-Road
Source: Burrelle's Media Directory, 1999 Edition

FM Radio Stations

Call Letters	Freq. (mHz)	Target Audience	Station Format	Music Format
KGNU	88.5	General	M/N/T	Adult Contemporary/Adult Standards/Alternative/AOR/Big Band/Christian/Classic Rock/Classical/Country/Easy Listening
KCDC	90.7	General	E/M/N/S	Adult Contemporary/AOR
KBCO	97.3	General	M	Alternative/Classic Rock

Note: Stations included broadcast in the Boulder metro area
Station Format: E=Educational; M=Music; N=News; S=Sports; T=Talk
Music Format: AOR=Album Oriented Rock; MOR=Middle-of-the-Road
Source: Burrelle's Media Directory, 1999 Edition

WEATHER

Temperature/Precipitation/Humidity

	Jan	Feb	Mar	Apr	May	Jun	Jul	Aug	Sep	Oct	Nov	Dec	Yr.
Max. High Temp. (°F)	74	79	86	85	93	104	104	102	97	90	79	74	104
Avg. High Temp. (°F)	45	46	52	61	69	80	85	84	77	66	54	46	64
Avg. Temp. (°F)	33	34	39	48	56	66	72	71	63	52	41	34	51
Avg. Low Temp. (°F)	21	22	27	36	44	53	59	58	50	39	29	22	38
Min. Low Temp. (°F)	-33	-28	-13	4	20	30	40	36	23	-2	-12	-20	-33
Avg. Precip. (in.)	0.5	0.8	1.6	2.7	3.1	1.7	1.8	1.6	1.4	1.5	0.9	0.8	18.3
Avg. Snowfall (in.)	8.2	10.2	15.3	11.9	2.8	0	0	0	0.6	4.8	9.6	9.8	73.2
Avg. Rel. Hum. (%)	56	57	55	52	54	47	47	48	47	48	55	56	52

Source: National Climatic Data Center, International Station Meteorological Climate Summary, 3/95

Weather Conditions

Temperature			Precipitation		
0°F & below	32°F & below	90°F & above	0.1 inch or more precip.	1.5 inch or more snow/ice	Thunder-storms
6	130	45	41	15	36

Note: Figures are average number of days per year
Source: National Climatic Data Center, International Station Meteorological Climate Summary, 3/95

AIR & WATER QUALITY

Maximum Pollutant Concentrations

	Particulate Matter (ug/m³)	Carbon Monoxide (ppm)	Sulfur Dioxide (ppm)	Nitrogen Dioxide (ppm)	Ozone (ppm)	Lead (ug/m³)
MSA[1] Level	42	5	n/a	n/a	0.09	n/a
NAAQS[2]	150	9	0.140	0.053	0.12	1.50
Met NAAQS	Yes	Yes	n/a	n/a	Yes	n/a

Note: (1) Metropolitan Statistical Area - see Appendix A for areas included; (2) National Ambient Air Quality Standards; ppm = parts per million; ug/m³ = micrograms per cubic meter; n/a not available
Source: EPA, National Air Quality and Emissions Trends Report, 1997

Pollutant Standards Index

Data not available. *EPA, National Air Quality and Emissions Trends Report, 1997*

Drinking Water

Water System Name	Pop. Served	Primary Water Source Type	Number of Violations in 1998-99	Type of Violation/ Contaminants
City of Boulder	105,740	Surface	None	None

Note: Data as of January 19, 2000
Source: EPA, Office of Ground Water and Drinking Water, Safe Drinking Water Information System

Boulder tap water is neutral, very soft, and fluoridated.
Editor & Publisher Market Guide, 2000

Bryan, Texas

Background

Bryan, Texas is located in Brazos County in east-central Texas, 99 miles northwest of Houston. The city is the namesake of William Joel Bryan, whose uncle, Stephen F. Austin, along with 300 other pioneer families, was one of the founders of Texas.

Bryan's diverse and thriving business community is responsible for approximately 80 percent of gross sales in Brazos County. The city's schools are among the best in the state with special programs to assist students at every level. Bryan's Park and Recreation system, as well as its beautiful weather, regularly attracts many tournaments and events.

The area was first settled in 1859 on 640 acres. In 1860, William Bryan sold a single square-mile tract of land for $3,200 to the Houston and Texas Central Railroads, whose directors developed a town on the site and named it Bryan. Along with the railroads, the area's rich agricultural resources brought rapid growth to the town of Bryan, which was incorporated in 1871.

In 1876, the Agricultural and Mechanical College of Texas, just five miles south of Bryan in College Station, opened to 48 students in its first semester. Texas A&M, now with an enrollment of 44,000 students, is among the 10 largest universities in the country and is one of the world's leading teaching and research institutes.

With its abundance of agricultural farmlands, cotton, cattle, oil and the railroad, the city of Bryan flourished in the early 1900s, withstanding the Great Depression and continuing to grow through the post-WWII era.

In the late 1960s, industrial development was in full swing. Brazos County Industrial Park and Bryan Business Park were created, and in 1992, Bryan developed the Main Street Project, which has revitalized its downtown historic districts, attracting visitors and businesses and improving property values both in the city itself and in the surrounding areas.

Downtown restaurants and commercial establishments cater to every taste with offerings from the city's many different cultures. Victorian-era brick structures have been preserved throughout the downtown area and beyond, providing a vibrant, attractive blend of past and present.

College Station, Bryan's nearby sister city, is home to the George Bush Presidential Library and Museum, which houses one million photographs documenting Bush's public career, a section dedicated to Barbara Bush, and 70,000 museum objects.

General Rankings and Evaluative Comments

■ Bryan was ranked #185 out of 354 metropolitan areas in *Places Rated Almanac*. Criteria: cost of living, climate, crime, transportation, job outlook, education, the arts, health care, and recreation. *Places Rated Almanac, Millennium Edition, 2000*

Business Environment

STATE ECONOMY

State Economic Profile

"Economic growth in Texas has slowed as both its new and old economies are under pressure. Weak commodity prices and over-capacity have hurt Texas' old economic powers, agriculture and oil. Soft global demand has slowed Texas' new economic powers, semiconductors and computer sales. A slowing US economy will also place a drag on Texas' biotech and software companies. Despite the current slowdown, Texas' long-term outlook is extremely bright, and its current problems will last no more than two years.

Weak commodity prices, over-capacity and soft foreign demand have all coincided to undermine Texas' oil and farm sector. Despite OPEC cutbacks, the Texas oil industry remains vulnerable because of its high costs, high inventories and high capacity. Texas' farm sector is similarly positioned; commodity prices are expected to continue their long-term downward trend.

The Texas economy is more diversified today than ever before. Growth in services and hi-tech employment have more than offset declines in Texas' resource economy. Services employment in 1998 grew at 3.8%, adding some 93,000 jobs, while construction employment grew 4.9%, adding 22,700 jobs. Construction employment, along with home sales and starts, should contract in 2000. Texas' demographic situation is positive; the state continues to attract educated, young households. However, the current weakness in the state's semiconductor and computer industry has slowed job growth from its previous feverish pace. In the near-term, Texas' growth should slow along with the US economy. Its long-term prospects are bright given its business friendly atmosphere and central location." *National Association of Realtors, Economic Profiles: The Fifty States and the District of Columbia, http://nar.realtor.com/databank/profiles.htm*

EXPORTS

Total Export Sales

Area	1995 ($000)	1996 ($000)	1997 ($000)	1998 ($000)	% Chg. 1995-98	% Chg. 1997-98
MSA[1]	n/a	n/a	n/a	n/a	n/a	n/a
U.S.	583,030,524	622,827,063	687,597,999	680,474,251	16.7	-1.0

Note: (1) Metropolitan Statistical Area - see Appendix A for areas included
Source: U.S. Department of Commerce, International Trade Association, Metropolitan Area Exports: An Export Performance Report on Over 250 U.S. Cities, November 10, 1999

CITY FINANCES

City Government Finances

Component	1995 ($million)	1995 (per capita $)
Revenue	37.9	623
Expenditure	36.3	597
Debt Outstanding	68.1	1,121

Source: 1999 County and City Extra, Annual Metro, City, and County Data Book

City Government Revenue by Source

Source	1995 ($million)	1995 (per capita $)
Intergovernmental	3.5	57
Taxes	16.0	264
Property	7.9	131
Sales and Gross Receipts	7.7	128

Source: 1999 County and City Extra, Annual Metro, City, and County Data Book

City Government Expenditures by Function

Function	1995 ($million)	1995 (per capita $)	1995 (%)
Public Welfare	0.0	0	0.0
Highways	2.5	41	7.0
Parking Facilities	0.0	0	0.0
Education	0.0	0	0.0
Health and Hospitals	0.0	0	0.0
Police Protection	5.5	90	15.2
Sewerage and Sanitation	6.7	110	18.5
Parks and Recreation	1.8	29	5.0
Housing and Community Development	2.2	37	6.2
Interest on Debt	1.5	25	4.2

Source: 1999 County and City Extra, Annual Metro, City, and County Data Book

Municipal Bond Ratings

Area	Moody's
City	Aaa

Source: Mergent Bond Record, 2/2000

POPULATION

Population Growth

Area	1980 Census	1990 Census	1999 Estimate	2004 Projection	Population Growth (%) 1990-1999	Population Growth (%) 1999-2004
City	44,337	55,002	57,027	59,305	3.7	4.0
MSA[1]	93,588	121,862	134,242	142,411	10.2	6.1
U.S.	226,545,805	248,765,170	272,212,864	283,625,312	9.4	4.2

Note: (1) Metropolitan Statistical Area - see Appendix A for areas included
Source: 1990 Census of Population and Housing, Summary Tape File 3C; Claritas, Inc.

Number of Households and Average Household Size

Area	1980 Census	1990 Census	1999 Estimate	2004 Projection	1999 Average Household Size
City	17,522	20,811	21,974	23,120	2.60
MSA[1]	32,488	43,904	49,747	53,666	2.70
U.S.	80,389,592	91,993,582	102,048,200	107,302,392	2.67

Note: (1) Metropolitan Statistical Area - see Appendix A for areas included
Source: 1990 Census of Population and Housing, Summary Tape File 3C; Claritas, Inc.

Race/Ethnicity of City Population

Race/Ethnicity	1990 Census Population	1990 Census %	1999 Estimate Population	1999 Estimate %	% Change 1990-1999
White, Non-Hispanic	33,882	61.6	30,639	53.7	-9.6
Black, Non-Hispanic	9,436	17.2	9,950	17.4	5.4
Asian, Non-Hispanic	871	1.6	1,388	2.4	59.4
Other, Non-Hispanic	122	0.2	191	0.3	56.6
Hispanic	10,691	19.4	14,859	26.1	39.0

Source: 1990 Census of Population and Housing, Summary Tape File 3C; Claritas, Inc.

Race/Ethnicity of Metropolitan Statistical Area Population

Race/Ethnicity	1990 Census		1999 Estimate		% Change 1990-1999
	Population	%	Population	%	
White, Non-Hispanic	87,286	71.6	87,277	65.0	0.0
Black, Non-Hispanic	13,573	11.1	15,737	11.7	15.9
Asian, Non-Hispanic	4,425	3.6	6,432	4.8	45.4
Other, Non-Hispanic	373	0.3	428	0.3	14.7
Hispanic	16,205	13.3	24,368	18.2	50.4

Note: See Appendix A for areas included in the Metropolitan Statistical Area
Source: 1990 Census of Population and Housing, Summary Tape File 3C; Claritas, Inc.

Ancestry

Area	German	Irish	English	Italian	U.S.	French	Polish	Dutch
City	18.5	14.0	12.2	3.7	4.4	3.4	2.1	1.6
MSA[1]	23.9	14.9	13.1	3.4	4.2	3.7	2.4	1.6
U.S.	23.3	15.6	13.1	5.9	5.3	4.2	3.8	2.5

Note: Figures are percentages and include persons that reported multiple ancestry (eg. if a person reported being Irish and Italian, they were included in both columns); (1) Metropolitan Statistical Area - see Appendix A for areas included
Source: 1990 Census of Population and Housing, Summary Tape File 3C

Median Age

Area	1990 Census	1999 Estimate
City	27.9	30.6
MSA[1]	23.7	25.7
U.S.	32.9	35.7

Note: (1) Metropolitan Statistical Area - see Appendix A for areas included
Source: 1990 Census of Population and Housing, Summary Tape File 3C; Claritas, Inc.

Male/Female Population

Area	Number of Males		Number of Females		Males per 100 Females	
	1990	1999	1990	1999	1990	1999
City	27,560	28,280	27,442	28,747	100.4	98.4
MSA[1]	63,036	68,821	58,826	65,421	107.2	105.2
U.S.	121,172,379	132,803,736	127,537,494	139,409,136	95.0	95.3

Note: (1) Metropolitan Statistical Area - see Appendix A for areas included
Source: 1990 Census of Population, General Population Characteristics; Claritas, Inc.

INCOME

Per Capita/Median/Average Income

Area	Per Capita ($)			Median Household ($)			Average Household ($)		
	1989	1999	% Chg.	1989	1999	% Chg.	1989	1999	% Chg.
City	11,691	17,943	53.5	22,577	31,456	39.3	30,847	46,058	49.3
MSA[1]	10,987	17,179	56.4	20,411	27,953	37.0	29,764	45,236	52.0
U.S.	14,420	21,350	48.1	30,056	40,525	34.8	38,453	56,184	46.1

Note: (1) Metropolitan Statistical Area - see Appendix A for areas included; 1989 data is from the 1990 Census; 1999 data is estimated by Claritas, Inc.
Source: 1990 Census of Population, General Population Characteristics; Claritas, Inc.

Household Income Distribution

Area	Percent of Households Earning								
	Under $5,000	$5,000 -14,999	$15,000 -24,999	$25,000 -34,999	$35,000 -49,999	$50,000 -74,999	$75,000 -99,000	$100,000 -149,999	$150,000 and up
City	6.7	17.4	16.9	13.3	15.7	16.2	6.7	4.8	2.2
MSA[1]	8.2	20.1	17.6	11.7	13.7	14.2	6.6	5.0	2.9
U.S.	3.9	13.3	13.8	12.6	16.2	19.4	9.7	6.6	4.6

Note: Data as of 1999; (1) Metropolitan Statistical Area - see Appendix A for areas included
Source: Claritas, Inc.

Effective Buying Income

Area	Per Capita ($)	Median Household ($)	Average Household ($)
City	15,408	29,979	40,737
MSA[1]	15,364	27,876	42,267
U.S.	17,496	36,603	47,036

Note: Data as of 1/1/2000; (1) Metropolitan Statistical Area - see Appendix A for areas included
Source: Standard Rate & Data Service, Newspaper Advertising Source, March 2000

Effective Household Buying Income Distribution

Area	% of Households Earning						
	$10,000 -$19,999	$20,000 -$34,999	$35,000 -$49,999	$50,000 -$74,999	$75,000 -$99,000	$100,000 -$124,999	$125,000 and up
City	17.7	22.4	15.8	16.0	6.4	2.6	2.3
MSA[1]	18.6	19.6	13.8	14.7	6.9	3.2	3.1
U.S.	15.0	21.6	17.6	19.6	8.4	3.0	3.3

Note: Data as of 1/1/2000; (1) Metropolitan Statistical Area - see Appendix A for areas included
Source: Standard Rate & Data Service, Newspaper Advertising Source, March 2000

Poverty Rates by Age

Area	People of All Ages	People Under 18 Years Old	Related Children Age 5-17 in Families in Poverty
City	17.6	n/a	n/a
County	19.3	23.3	22.0
U.S.	13.8	20.8	18.7

Note: Figures show the percent of people living below the poverty line in 1995. The
average poverty threshold was $15,569 for a family of four in 1995; n/a not available
Source: Bureau of the Census, Small Area Income and Poverty Estimates Program;
U.S. Department of Housing and Urban Development

EMPLOYMENT

Labor Force and Employment

Area	Civilian Labor Force			Workers Employed		
	Dec. 1998	Dec. 1999	% Chg.	Dec. 1998	Dec. 1999	% Chg.
City	36,567	37,709	3.1	36,006	37,129	3.1
MSA[1]	77,040	79,446	3.1	75,875	78,242	3.1
U.S.	138,297,000	139,941,000	1.2	132,732,000	134,696,000	1.5

Note: Data is not seasonally adjusted and covers workers 16 years of age and older;
(1) Metropolitan Statistical Area - see Appendix A for areas included
Source: Bureau of Labor Statistics, http://stats.bls.gov

Unemployment Rate

Area	1999											
	Jan.	Feb.	Mar.	Apr.	May	Jun.	Jul.	Aug.	Sep.	Oct.	Nov.	Dec.
City	1.8	1.8	1.5	1.5	1.8	2.4	2.1	1.9	1.7	1.6	1.6	1.5
MSA[1]	1.8	1.7	1.5	1.5	1.8	2.3	2.1	1.9	1.7	1.5	1.5	1.5
U.S.	4.8	4.7	4.4	4.1	4.0	4.5	4.5	4.2	4.1	3.8	3.8	3.7

Note: Data is not seasonally adjusted and covers workers 16 years of age and older; all figures are percentages; (1) Metropolitan Statistical Area - see Appendix A for areas included
Source: Bureau of Labor Statistics, http://stats.bls.gov

Employment by Industry

Sector	MSA[1]		U.S.
	Number of Employees	Percent of Total	Percent of Total
Services	16,600	21.5	30.2
Retail Trade	14,200	18.4	18.1
Government	31,300	40.5	15.8
Manufacturing	5,300	6.9	14.1
Finance/Insurance/Real Estate	2,700	3.5	5.9
Wholesale Trade	1,500	1.9	5.4
Transportation/Public Utilities	1,600	2.1	5.3
Construction	3,300	4.3	4.8
Mining	700	0.9	0.4

Note: Figures cover non-farm employment as of 12/99 and are not seasonally adjusted;
(1) Metropolitan Statistical Area - see Appendix A for areas included
Source: Bureau of Labor Statistics, http://stats.bls.gov

Employment by Occupation

Occupation Category	City (%)	MSA[1] (%)	U.S. (%)
White Collar	59.3	65.1	58.1
Executive/Admin./Management	10.5	10.3	12.3
Professional	17.7	21.3	14.1
Technical & Related Support	5.7	7.3	3.7
Sales	10.1	10.6	11.8
Administrative Support/Clerical	15.4	15.5	16.3
Blue Collar	23.0	18.5	26.2
Precision Production/Craft/Repair	10.1	8.2	11.3
Machine Operators/Assem./Insp.	4.9	3.6	6.8
Transportation/Material Movers	3.9	3.4	4.1
Cleaners/Helpers/Laborers	4.0	3.4	3.9
Services	16.0	14.0	13.2
Farming/Forestry/Fishing	1.7	2.4	2.5

Note: Figures cover workers 16 years of age and older;
(1) Metropolitan Statistical Area - see Appendix A for areas included
Source: 1990 Census of Population and Housing, Summary Tape File 3C

Occupational Employment Projections: 1996 - 2006

Occupations Expected to Have the Largest Job Growth (ranked by numerical growth)	Fast-Growing Occupations[1] (ranked by percent growth)
1. Cashiers	1. Desktop publishers
2. Salespersons, retail	2. Systems analysts
3. General managers & top executives	3. Customer service representatives
4. Truck drivers, light	4. Physical therapy assistants and aides
5. Child care workers, private household	5. Computer engineers
6. General office clerks	6. Emergency medical technicians
7. Systems analysts	7. Medical assistants
8. Food preparation workers	8. Respiratory therapists
9. Food service workers	9. Telephone & cable TV line install & repair
10. Registered nurses	10. Physical therapists

Note: Projections cover Texas; (1) Excludes occupations with total job growth less than 300
Source: U.S. Department of Labor, Employment and Training Administration, America's Labor Market Information System (ALMIS)

Average Wages

Occupation	$/Hr.	Occupation	$/Hr.
Accountants and Auditors	16.45	Maids and Housekeepers	6.02
Assemblers and Fabricators	8.38	Maintenance Repairers	8.65
Automotive Mechanics	11.81	Marketing/Advertising/PR Managers	23.85
Bookkeepers	9.54	Nurses, Licensed Practical	12.44
Carpenters	11.28	Nurses, Registered	19.71
Cashiers	6.84	Nursing Aides/Orderlies/Attendants	6.63
Clerks, General Office	8.13	Physicians and Surgeons	51.20
Clerks, Shipping/Receiving/Traffic	10.17	Receptionists/Information Clerks	7.90
Computer Programmers	20.40	Sales Reps., Exc. Scientific/Retail	15.33
Computer Support Specialists	16.88	Sales Reps., Scientific, Exc. Retail	19.71
Cooks, Restaurant	7.08	Salespersons, Retail	7.52
Electricians	15.10	Secretaries, Except Legal/Medical	9.24
Financial Managers	24.12	Stock Clerks, Sales Floor	7.77
First-Line Supervisors/Mgrs., Sales	13.79	Systems Analysts	-
Food Preparation Workers	5.98	Teacher Aides	-
General Managers/Top Executives	25.23	Teachers, Elementary School	15.33
Guards	7.64	Teachers, Secondary School	15.55
Hand Packers	6.40	Telemarketers	-
Janitors and Cleaners	6.47	Truck Drivers, Heavy/Tractor-Trailer	12.35
Laborers, Landscaping	7.18	Truck Drivers, Light	9.66
Lawyers	28.36	Waiters and Waitresses	5.85

Note: Wage data is for 1998 and covers the Metropolitan Statistical Area (see Appendix A for areas included). Hourly wages for elementary and secondary school teachers were calculated by the editors from annual wage data assuming a 40 hour work week; Dashes indicate that data was not available.
Source: Bureau of Labor Statistics, 1998 Metropolitan Area Occupational Employment and Wage Estimates

TAXES

Major State and Local Tax Rates

State Corporate Income (%)	State Personal Income (%)	Residential Property (%)	Sales & Use		State Gasoline (cents/ gallon)	State Cigarette (cents/ pack)
			State (%)	Local (%)		
None[a]	None	2.66	6.25	2.0	20.0	41.0

Note: Personal/corporate income, sales, gasoline and cigarette tax rates as of January 2000. Property tax rates as of April 2000; (a) Texas imposes a franchise tax of 4.5% of earned surplus
Source: Federation of Tax Administrators, www.taxadmin.org; ERI's Relocation Assessor software database, quarterly effective date 4/1/2000

Total Taxes Per Capita and as a Percent of Income

Area	Per Capita Income ($)	Per Capita Taxes ($)			Percent of Income (%)		
		Total	Federal	State/Local	Total	Federal	State/Local
Texas	27,531	9,335	6,510	2,825	33.9	23.6	10.3
U.S.	28,878	10,298	7,026	3,273	35.7	24.3	11.3

Note: Figures are for 1999
Source: Tax Foundation, www.taxfoundation.org

COMMERCIAL UTILITIES

Typical Monthly Electric Bills

Area	Commercial Service ($/month)		Industrial Service ($/month)	
	12 kW demand 1,500 kWh	100 kW demand 30,000 kWh	1,000 kW demand 400,000 kWh	20,000 kW demand 10,000,000 kWh
City	n/a	n/a	n/a	n/a
U.S.	150	2,174	23,995	508,569

Note: Based on rates in effect January 1, 1999; n/a not available
Source: Edison Electric Institute, Typical Residential, Commercial and Industrial Bills, Winter 1999

TRANSPORTATION

Transportation Statistics

Average minutes to work (1990)	15.2
Interstate highways	US-190
Bus lines	
In-city (1998)	Brazos Transit System, 8 buses
Inter-city (1999)	1
Passenger air service	
Airport	Easterwood Airport
Airlines (1999)	2
Enplaned passengers (1998)	n/a
Amtrak service	No
Motor freight carriers (1999)	6
Major waterways/ports	None

Source: FAA DOT/TSC CY1998 ACAIS Database; National Transit Database, 1998; Editor & Publisher Market Guide, 2000; Amtrak National Time Table, Fall 1999/Winter 2000; 1990 Census of Population and Housing, STF 3C; Jane's Urban Transport Systems 1999-2000

Means of Transportation to Work

Area	Car/Truck/Van		Public Transportation			Bicycle	Walked	Other Means	Worked at Home
	Drove Alone	Car-pooled	Bus	Subway	Railroad				
City	73.5	16.5	0.8	0.0	0.0	1.9	2.8	2.4	2.1
MSA[1]	71.0	14.0	1.9	0.0	0.0	2.9	5.3	2.1	2.8
U.S.	73.2	13.4	3.0	1.5	0.5	0.4	3.9	1.2	3.0

Note: Figures shown are percentages and only include workers 16 years of age and older;
(1) Metropolitan Statistical Area - see Appendix A for areas included
Source: 1990 Census of Population and Housing, Summary Tape File 3C

BUSINESSES

Major Business Headquarters

Company Name	1999 Rankings	
	Fortune 500	Forbes 500
No companies listed	-	-

Note: Companies listed are located in the city; dashes indicate no ranking
Fortune 500: Companies that produce a 10-K are ranked 1 to 500 based on 1999 revenue
Forbes 500: Private companies are ranked 1 to 500 based on 1998 revenue
Source: Forbes, December 13, 1999; Fortune, April 17, 2000

HOTELS & MOTELS

Hotels/Motels

Area	Hotels/ Motels	Rooms	Luxury-Level Hotels/Motels		Average Minimum Rates ($)		
------	------	------	◆◆◆◆	◆◆◆◆◆	◆◆	◆◆◆	◆◆◆◆
City	2	154	0	0	n/a	n/a	n/a
Suburbs	1	115	0	0	n/a	n/a	n/a
Total	3	269	0	0	n/a	n/a	n/a

Note: n/a not available; classifications range from one diamond (budget properties with basic amenities) to five diamond (luxury properties).
Source: OAG Business Travel Planner, Winter 1999-2000

Estimated Daily Food and Lodging Costs

Area	Food/Other ($/day)	Average Hotel Cost ($/day)
City	30	58
U.S.	30	55

Source: ERI's Relocation Assessor software database, quarterly effective date 4/1/2000

CONVENTION CENTERS

Convention Centers and Event Sites

Name	Guest Rooms	Meeting Space (sq. ft.)	Capacity (Theatre Style)
Brazos County Events Facilities	n/a	n/a	4,850
Brazos County Events Facilities	n/a	n/a	3,200

Note: n/a not available
Source: EventSource.com, 3/15/2000

Living Environment

COST OF LIVING

Cost of Living: Homeowner

Cost Element	U.S. ($)	City ($)	Differential ($)	Percent of U.S. Average
Consumables	14,516	14,172	-344	97.6
Transportation	5,957	6,708	751	112.6
Health Services	2,012	2,166	154	107.7
Housing/Utilities/Prop. Tax	16,337	16,210	-127	99.2
Income+Payroll Taxes	12,615	10,708	-1,907	84.9
Miscellaneous	8,563	8,563	0	100.0
Total Cost of Living	60,000	58,527	-1,473	97.5

Note: Figures are based on a single income, four person family with gross annual earnings of $60,000, owning an 1,800 square-foot home, and driving two automobiles worth $22,000 30,000 miles per year.
Source: ERI's Relocation Assessor software database, quarterly effective date 4/1/2000

Cost of Living: Renter

Cost Element	U.S. ($)	City ($)	Differential ($)	Percent of U.S. Average
Consumables	10,486	10,182	-304	97.1
Transportation	2,107	2,360	253	112.0
Health Services	1,632	1,748	116	107.1
Rent/Utilities/Insurance	9,299	7,632	-1,667	82.1
Income+Payroll Taxes	8,607	7,183	-1,424	83.5
Miscellaneous	7,869	7,869	0	100.0
Total Cost of Living	40,000	36,974	-3,026	92.4

Note: Figures are based on a single income, three person family with gross annual earnings of $40,000, renting a 1,000 square-foot home, and driving one automobile worth $8,000 12,000 miles per year.
Source: ERI's Relocation Assessor software database, quarterly effective date 4/1/2000

HOUSING

Median Home Prices and Housing Affordability

Area	Median Price[2] 4th Qtr. 1999 ($)	HOI[3] 4th Qtr. 1999	Affordability Rank[4]
MSA[1]	n/a	n/a	n/a
U.S.	139,000	63.8	–

Note: (1) Metropolitan Statistical Area - see Appendix A for areas included; (2) U.S. figures calculated from the sales of 687,516 new and existing homes in 192 markets; (3) Housing Opportunity Index - percent of homes sold that were within the reach of the median income household at the prevailing mortgage interest rate; (4) Rank is from 1-192 with 1 being most affordable; n/a not available
Source: National Association of Home Builders, Housing Opportunity Index, 4th Quarter 1999

Estimated Home Price

Area	Price ($)
City	114,813
U.S.	135,855

Note: Figures are based on an 1,800 square-foot home
Source: ERI's Relocation Assessor software database, quarterly effective date 4/1/2000

Estimated Rent

Area	Rent ($/month)
City	513
U.S.	651

Note: Figures are based on a 1,000 square-foot home
Source: ERI's Relocation Assessor software database, quarterly effective date 4/1/2000

Median Home Price Projection

It is projected that the median home price in the metropolitan area will increase from $94,592 in 1999 to $150,322 in 2010, an increase of 58.9%
Kiplinger's Personal Finance Magazine, January 2000

RESIDENTIAL UTILITIES

Average Residential Utility Costs

Area	All Electric ($/mth)	Part Electric ($/mth)	Other Energy ($/mth)	Phone ($/mth)
City	–	54.85	25.78	16.13
U.S.	99.25	55.47	43.48	20.29

Source: ACCRA, Cost of Living Index, 3rd Quarter 1999

HEALTH CARE

Average Health Care Costs

Area	Hospital ($/day)	Doctor ($/visit)	Dentist ($/visit)
City	410.00	48.00	53.60
U.S.	440.96	53.83	68.42

Note: Hospital—based on a semi-private room; Doctor—based on a general practitioner's routine exam of an established patient; Dentist—based on adult teeth cleaning and periodic oral exam.
Source: ACCRA, Cost of Living Index, 3rd Quarter 1999

Distribution of Office-Based Physicians

Area	Family/Gen. Practitioners	Specialists		
		Medical	Surgical	Other
MSA[1]	49	67	58	52

Note: Data as of 12/31/97; (1) Metropolitan Statistical Area - see Appendix A for areas included
Source: American Medical Assn., Physician Characteristics & Distribution in the U.S., 1999

Hospitals

Bryan has 1 general medical and surgical hospital.
AHA Guide to the Healthcare Field, 1999-2000

EDUCATION

Public School District Statistics

District Name	Num. Sch.	Enroll.	Classroom Teachers	Pupils per Teacher	Minority Pupils (%)	Current Exp.[1] ($/pupil)
Bryan ISD	21	13,561	929	14.6	n/a	n/a

Note: Data covers the 1997-1998 school year unless otherwise noted; (1) Data covers fiscal year 1996; SD = School District; ISD = Independent School District; n/a not available
Source: National Center for Education Statistics, Common Core of Data Public Education Agency Universe 1997-98; National Center for Education Statistics, Characteristics of the 100 Largest Public Elementary and Secondary School Districts in the United States: 1997-98, July 1999

Educational Quality

School District	Education Quotient[1]	Graduate Outcome[2]	Community Index[3]	Resource Index[4]
Bryan Ind. School Dist.	91	99	78	78

Note: Over 1,000 secondary school districts were rated in terms of educational quality. The scores range from a low of 50 to a high of 150; (1) Combination of the Graduate Outcome, Community and Resource indexes weighted to reflect the greater importance of the Graduate Outcome and Resource Index; (2) Based on graduation rates and college board scores (SAT/ACT); (3) Based on the surrounding community's level of affluence and adult education; (4) Based on teacher salaries, per-pupil expenditures and student-teacher ratios.
Source: Expansion Management, Ratings Issue, 1999

Educational Attainment by Race

Area	High School Graduate (%)					Bachelor's Degree (%)				
	Total	White	Black	Other	Hisp.[2]	Total	White	Black	Other	Hisp.[2]
City	73.7	81.4	57.3	45.4	40.4	26.9	32.6	6.8	16.2	9.3
MSA[1]	79.8	85.1	59.6	63.5	48.2	35.8	39.1	10.8	39.0	15.2
U.S.	75.2	77.9	63.1	60.4	49.8	20.3	21.5	11.4	19.4	9.2

Note: Figures shown cover persons 25 years old and over; (1) Metropolitan Statistical Area - see Appendix A for areas included; (2) people of Hispanic origin can be of any race
Source: 1990 Census of Population and Housing, Summary Tape File 3C

School Enrollment by Type

Area	Preprimary				Elementary/High School			
	Public		Private		Public		Private	
	Enrollment	%	Enrollment	%	Enrollment	%	Enrollment	%
City	692	60.9	444	39.1	8,893	93.6	606	6.4
MSA[1]	1,151	55.1	938	44.9	15,497	92.8	1,201	7.2
U.S.	2,679,029	59.5	1,824,256	40.5	38,379,689	90.2	4,187,099	9.8

Note: Figures shown cover persons 3 years old and over;
(1) Metropolitan Statistical Area - see Appendix A for areas included
Source: 1990 Census of Population and Housing, Summary Tape File 3C

School Enrollment by Race

Area	Preprimary (%)				Elementary/High School (%)			
	White	Black	Other	Hisp.[1]	White	Black	Other	Hisp.[1]
City	77.5	15.2	7.3	13.6	56.9	25.3	17.8	29.3
MSA[2]	78.9	11.7	9.3	10.8	67.8	18.9	13.3	20.5
U.S.	80.4	12.5	7.1	7.8	74.1	15.6	10.3	12.5

Note: Figures shown cover persons 3 years old and over; (1) people of Hispanic origin can be of any race; (2) Metropolitan Statistical Area - see Appendix A for areas included
Source: 1990 Census of Population and Housing, Summary Tape File 3C

Higher Education

Two-Year Colleges		Four-Year Colleges		Medical Schools	Law Schools	Voc/ Tech
Public	Private	Public	Private			
0	0	0	0	0	0	1

Source: College Blue Book, Occupational Education, 1999; Medical School Admission Requirements, 1999-2000; Peterson's Guide to Two-Year Colleges, 2000; Peterson's Guide to Four-Year Colleges, 1999; Barron's Guide to Law Schools, 1999

MAJOR EMPLOYERS

Major Employers

Airfoil Impellers Corp.	AmWest Savings Association
Elite Software Development	First National Bank
Gooseneck Trailer Manufacturing	Learning Technology Systems
National Feeds	Supreme Well Services

Note: Companies listed are located in the city
Source: D&B Business Rankings, 1999; Ward's Business Directory, 1999; America's Corporate Families, 1999

PUBLIC SAFETY

Crime Rate

Area	All Crimes	Violent Crimes				Property Crimes		
		Murder	Forcible Rape	Robbery	Aggrav. Assault	Burglary	Larceny -Theft	Motor Vehicle Theft
City	6,772.4	5.0	85.2	86.8	459.2	1,486.1	4,364.7	285.5
Suburbs[1]	4,853.0	0.0	58.4	42.5	98.3	803.3	3,753.6	96.9
MSA[2]	5,703.2	2.2	70.3	62.1	258.1	1,105.7	4,024.3	180.5
U.S.	4,615.5	6.3	34.4	165.2	360.5	862.0	2,728.1	459.0

Note: Crime rate is the number of crimes per 100,000 population; (1) Defined as all areas within the Metropolitan Statistical Area but located outside the central city; (2) Metropolitan Statistical Area - see Appendix A for areas included
Source: FBI Uniform Crime Reports, 1998

RECREATION

Culture and Recreation

Museums	Symphony Orchestras	Opera Companies	Dance Companies	Professional Theatres	Zoos	Pro Sports Teams
1	0	0	0	1	0	0

Source: Musical America, International Directory of the Performing Arts, 1999; Official Museum Directory, 2000; Stern's Performing Arts Directory, 1997; USA Today Four Sport Stadium Guide, 1997; Career Opportunities in Theatre and the Performing Arts, 1999

Library System

The Bryan & College Station Public Library System has one branch and a budget of $1,530,000 (1997-1998).
American Library Directory, 1999-2000

MEDIA

Newspapers

Name	Type	Freq.	Distribution	Circulation
Bryan-College Station Eagle	General	7x/wk	Area	28,000

Note: Includes newspapers with circulations of 200 or more located in the city;
Source: Burrelle's Media Directory, 1999 Edition

Television Stations

Name	Ch.	Affiliation	Type	Owner
KBTX	n/a	CBST	Commercial	Brazos Broadcasting Corporation
KAMU	15	PBS	Public	Texas A & M University
KYLE	28	FBC	Commercial	Communications Corporation Inc.

Note: Stations included broadcast in the Bryan metro area; n/a not available
Source: Burrelle's Media Directory, 1999 Edition

AM Radio Stations

Call Letters	Freq. (kHz)	Target Audience	Station Format	Music Format
WTAW	1150	General	N/S/T	n/a
KTAM	1240	General	M/N/S/T	Adult Standards/MOR/Oldies
KAGC	1510	Religious	M/N/T	Christian

Note: Stations included broadcast in the Bryan metro area; n/a not available
Target Audience: A=Asian; B=Black; C=Christian; E=Ethnic; F=French; G=General; H=Hispanic; M=Men; N=Native American; R=Religious; S=Senior Citizen; W=Women; Y=Young Adult; Z=Children
Station Format: E=Educational; M=Music; N=News; S=Sports; T=Talk
Music Format: AOR=Album Oriented Rock; MOR=Middle-of-the-Road
Source: Burrelle's Media Directory, 1999 Edition

FM Radio Stations

Call Letters	Freq. (mHz)	Target Audience	Station Format	Music Format
KEOS	89.1	General	E/M/N/T	Alternative
KAMU	90.9	General	E/M/N/T	Big Band/Classical/Jazz/Rhythm & Blues
KTSR	92.1	General	M	AOR
KAGG	96.1	General	M	Country
KORA	98.3	General	M/N/S	Country
KVJM	103.1	General	M	Urban Contemporary
KHLR	103.9	General	M	Alternative
KKYS	104.7	General	M/N/S/T	Adult Contemporary
KTTX	106.1	General	M/N/S	Country

Note: Stations included broadcast in the Bryan metro area
Station Format: E=Educational; M=Music; N=News; S=Sports; T=Talk
Target Audience: A=Asian; B=Black; C=Christian; E=Ethnic; F=French; G=General; H=Hispanic; M=Men; N=Native American; R=Religious; S=Senior Citizen; W=Women; Y=Young Adult; Z=Children
Music Format: AOR=Album Oriented Rock; MOR=Middle-of-the-Road
Source: Burrelle's Media Directory, 1999 Edition

WEATHER

Temperature/Precipitation/Humidity

	Jan	Feb	Mar	Apr	May	Jun	Jul	Aug	Sep	Oct	Nov	Dec	Yr.
Max. High Temp. (°F)	81	88	89	91	98	102	109	108	105	98	89	85	109
Avg. High Temp. (°F)	62	65	71	79	86	94	97	97	92	82	69	63	80
Avg. Temp. (°F)	52	54	59	68	75	82	85	85	80	70	58	52	68
Avg. Low Temp. (°F)	42	44	48	57	65	71	73	73	68	58	47	42	57
Min. Low Temp. (°F)	15	22	25	37	42	56	68	64	53	32	24	19	15
Avg. Precip. (in.)	3.2	2.9	2.9	3.7	4.8	3.1	2.5	2.3	2.7	2.9	3.4	3.8	38.1
Avg. Snowfall (in.)	0.2	0	0	0	0	0	0	0	0	0	0	0	0.2
Avg. Rel. Hum. (%)	75	69	70	75	75	73	73	69	68	67	72	72	72

Source: National Climatic Data Center, International Station Meteorological Climate Summary, 3/95

Weather Conditions

Temperature			Precipitation		
0°F & below	32°F & below	90°F & above	0.1 inch or more precip.	1.5 inch or more snow/ice	Thunder-storms
0	13	0	70	0	49

Note: Figures are average number of days per year
Source: National Climatic Data Center, International Station Meteorological Climate Summary, 3/95

AIR & WATER QUALITY

Maximum Pollutant Concentrations

	Particulate Matter (ug/m³)	Carbon Monoxide (ppm)	Sulfur Dioxide (ppm)	Nitrogen Dioxide (ppm)	Ozone (ppm)	Lead (ug/m³)
MSA[1] Level	n/a	n/a	n/a	n/a	n/a	n/a
NAAQS[2]	150	9	0.140	0.053	0.12	1.50
Met NAAQS	n/a	n/a	n/a	n/a	n/a	n/a

Note: (1) Metropolitan Statistical Area - see Appendix A for areas included; (2) National Ambient Air Quality Standards; ppm = parts per million; ug/m³ = micrograms per cubic meter; n/a not available
Source: EPA, National Air Quality and Emissions Trends Report, 1997

Pollutant Standards Index

Data not available.
EPA, National Air Quality and Emissions Trends Report, 1997

Drinking Water

Water System Name	Pop. Served	Primary Water Source Type	Number of Violations in 1998-99	Type of Violation/ Contaminants
City of Bryan	55,502	Ground	None	None

Note: Data as of January 19, 2000
Source: EPA, Office of Ground Water and Drinking Water, Safe Drinking Water Information System

Bryan tap water is very soft.
Editor & Publisher Market Guide, 2000

Burlington, Vermont

Background

Burlington, Vermont is located in the northwest section of the state, about 155 miles northwest of Brattleboro and and 100 miles south of Montreal. The city is situated in the Lake Champlain Valley, on the east shore of Lake Champlain, across from New York state.

Burlington, the seat of Chittenden County, is the largest city in Vermont. It is part of a regional economic center that includes Winooski, South Burlington, Essex Junction, Essex and Shelburne. Contemporary economic activities include business, professional and government services, manufacturing, retail and wholesale trade, health care and tourism. Burlington is an educational center, home to the University of Vermont, Champlain College, Burlington College, Trinity College of Vermont, Community College of Vermont and Saint Michael's College.

The city gets consistently high ratings for quality of life due to its combination of urban amenities and scenic, rural surroundings. The community is characterized as a mix of Yankee pragmatism, political independence and receptiveness to diverse viewpoints. In the 1980s, Burlington elected a political progressive, Bernie Sanders, to four terms as mayor.

Among the Native Americans who originally occupied the region were the Algonquin Abenaki and the Iroquois. In 1609 Samuel de Champlain explored the lake and claimed the surrounding area for France. Initial settlement occurred slowly in Vermont, due to the mountains and the French and Indian Wars. Britain gained the territory through a 1763 treaty. Burlington was established in 1773, and named after an early pioneer family.

The colonies of New York and New Hampshire both claimed Vermont. Ethan Allen and his family, who were active in the development of Burlington and Vermont, were leaders of the Green Mountain Boys, a militia which formed around 1770 to gain Vermont's independence. Although members of the Vermont rebellion joined the American Revolution, Vermont remained an independent republic until 1791, when it became the 14th state.

In the 19th and 20th Centuries, Burlington became a transportation hub for northern Vermont on the 120-mile long Lake Champlain, which is part of the network of waterways connecting New York, Canada and western shipping routes. Burlington's economy reflects regional industries including forestry and wood products, agriculture, maple syrup and the mining of marble and other minerals. The manufacture of mechanical, electric and electronic equipment is also an important sector of local industry.

In the latter 20th Century, Burlington experienced economic decline related to recessions and other trends, but recent diversification into high-technology and other industries has helped the city's contemporary economy. In an attempt to encourage sustainable development Burlington initiated in 1999, The Legacy Project, a community effort to develop a 30-year set of goals.

One of the city's well-known features is its redeveloped historic downtown district, including the Church St. Marketplace, as a pedestrian retail center and community gathering place.

Burlington is accessible to recreational water activities on Lake Champlain and to hiking, skiing and other outdoor activities in rural Vermont and New York's Adirondack region. Cultural venues include the Robert Hull Fleming Museum, Vermont Symphony, Flynn Theater for Performing Arts, the Lyric Theater Company and Burlington City Arts. Area museums include Ethan Allen's home near Burlington and the nearby Shelburne Museum, a collection of structures and historical exhibits.

Burlington is governed by an elected Mayor and City Council. The more traditional Town Meeting also plays a role in the city's governance.

General Rankings and Evaluative Comments

- Burlington was ranked #129 out of 354 metropolitan areas in *Places Rated Almanac*. Criteria: cost of living, climate, crime, transportation, job outlook, education, the arts, health care, and recreation. Places Rated Almanac, Millennium Edition, 2000

- Burlington was selected as one of America's best small art towns. The city was ranked #6 out of 100. Criteria: easy and affordable access to the visual arts, performing arts and music, strong sense of community, low crime rate, and full-time population less than 65,000. *The 100 Best Small Art Towns in America: Discover Creative Communities, Fresh Air, and Affordable Living, 1998*

- *Ladies Home Journal* ranked America's 200 largest cities based on the qualities women care about most. Burlington ranked #10 out of 200. Criteria: low crime rate, well-paying jobs, quality health and child care, good public schools, the presence of women in government, size of the gender wage gap, number of sexual-harassment and discrimination complaints filed, unemployment and divorce rates, commute times, population density, number of houses of worship, parks and cultural offerings, number of women's health specialists, how well women cared for themselves, complexion kindness index based on UV radiation levels, odds of finding affordable fashions, rental rates for romance movies, champagne sales, and other matters of the heart. *Ladies Home Journal, November 1998*

- Zero Population Growth ranked 229 cities in terms of children's health, safety, and economic well-being. Burlington was ranked #15 out of 112 independent cities (cities with populations greater than 100,000 which were neither Major Cities nor Suburbs/Outer Cities) and was given a grade of B+. Criteria: total population and population change, percent of population under 18 years of age, household language, percent of births to teens, infant mortality rate, percent of low birth weights, dropout rate, enrollment in preprimary school, violent and property crime rates, unemployment rate, percent of children in poverty, percent of owner occupied units, number of bad air days, percent of public transportation commuters, and average travel time to work. *Zero Population Growth, Children's Environmental Index, Fall 1999*

- Burlington was selected as one of "America's Best Towns to Raise an Outdoor Family" by *Outdoor Explorer* magazine. Criteria: easy access to the outdoors, quality education and health care, affordable housing, favorable employment opportunities, and low crime rates. The city was ranked #1 out of 25. *Outdoor Explorer, Summer 1999*

- Cognetics studied 273 metro areas in the United States, ranking them by entrepreneurial activity. Burlington was ranked #52 out of 134 smaller metro areas. Criteria: Significant Starts (firms started in the last 10 years that still employ at least 5 people) and Young Growers (percent of firms 10 years old or less that grew significantly during the last 4 years). *Cognetics, "Entrepreneurial Hot Spots: The Best Places in America to Start and Grow a Company," 1999*

- Burlington was selected as one of "The 50 Most Alive Places to Live" in the U.S. Criteria: ethnic diversity, recreational options, cultural vitality, low crime rate, opportunities for lifelong learning, good hospitals and restaurants, public transportation, walking accessibility, civic activities, and the kitsch factor. The area was ranked #9 out of 10 in the "Green & Clean" category. *Modern Maturity, May-June 2000*

Business Environment

STATE ECONOMY

State Economic Profile

"Vermont's economy continues to lag the nation and will slip further as the US economy slows in 2000. Vermont's population growth has been weak and Vermont continues to lose younger households. A weak Canadian economy has stunted Vermont's export sector. On the bright side, Vermont's tourism industry has benefited from the current US expansion and New England recovery. Vermont's households have also gained disproportionately from the strong US stock market.

Nearly a fifth of Vermont's household income come from dividend and interest income. Vermont's older, wealthier household structure has benefited consumer spending in the state as the strong stock market has helped drive Vermont households' incomes. While a major correction in the stock market is not likely in 2000, a slowdown in the rate of recent gains, coupled with increased volatility, could dampen consumer spending in Vermont.

Tourism in Vermont is currently benefiting from the strong US economy. Recent favorable ski conditions helped to raise occupancy rates and Vermont hotels. Low vacancy rates have also attracted tourism-related construction spending in the form of new hotels, restaurants and retail establishments. While total Vermont non-farm employment rose only 1.4% in 1998, construction employment grew 2.3%. A softer US economy in 2000 will likely dampen Vermont tourism. Hence, hotel occupancy rates should be lower, and retail sales should slow in 2000 after a strong 1999 summer.

Vermont's economy is becoming potentially more cyclical as its economy depends on tourism, and state consumer spending becomes more dependent upon the stock market. The near-term outlook for Vermont is moderate growth at a rate slightly below that of the nation."
National Association of Realtors, Economic Profiles: The Fifty States and the District of Columbia, http://nar.realtor.com/databank/profiles.htm

EXPORTS

Total Export Sales

Area	1995 ($000)	1996 ($000)	1997 ($000)	1998 ($000)	% Chg. 1995-98	% Chg. 1997-98
MSA[1]	n/a	n/a	n/a	n/a	n/a	n/a
U.S.	583,030,524	622,827,063	687,597,999	680,474,251	16.7	-1.0

Note: (1) Metropolitan Statistical Area - see Appendix A for areas included
Source: U.S. Department of Commerce, International Trade Association, Metropolitan Area Exports: An Export Performance Report on Over 250 U.S. Cities, November 10, 1999

CITY FINANCES

City Government Finances

Component	1995 ($million)	1995 (per capita $)
Revenue	37.7	984
Expenditure	33.6	877
Debt Outstanding	178.6	4,663

Source: 1999 County and City Extra, Annual Metro, City, and County Data Book

City Government Revenue by Source

Source	1995 ($million)	1995 (per capita $)
Intergovernmental	2.4	62
Taxes	16.4	428
Property	13.5	354
Sales and Gross Receipts	2.1	55

Source: 1999 County and City Extra, Annual Metro, City, and County Data Book

City Government Expenditures by Function

Function	1995 ($million)	1995 (per capita $)	1995 (%)
Public Welfare	0.0	0	0.0
Highways	2.8	75	8.6
Parking Facilities	0.9	24	2.8
Education	0.0	0	0.0
Health and Hospitals	<0.1	1	0.2
Police Protection	5.9	154	17.6
Sewerage and Sanitation	4.9	128	14.7
Parks and Recreation	2.2	59	6.8
Housing and Community Development	1.3	35	4.0
Interest on Debt	2.0	52	6.0

Source: 1999 County and City Extra, Annual Metro, City, and County Data Book

Municipal Bond Ratings

Area	Moody's
City	Aaa

Source: Mergent Bond Record, 2/2000

POPULATION

Population Growth

Area	1980 Census	1990 Census	1999 Estimate	2004 Projection	Population Growth (%) 1990-1999	Population Growth (%) 1999-2004
City	37,712	39,127	38,792	38,483	-0.9	-0.8
MSA[1]	133,117	131,441	168,896	174,043	28.5	3.0
U.S.	226,545,805	248,765,170	272,212,864	283,625,312	9.4	4.2

Note: (1) Metropolitan Statistical Area - see Appendix A for areas included
Source: 1990 Census of Population and Housing, Summary Tape File 3C; Claritas, Inc.

Number of Households and Average Household Size

Area	1980 Census	1990 Census	1999 Estimate	2004 Projection	1999 Average Household Size
City	13,107	14,758	15,345	15,564	2.53
MSA[1]	45,239	48,293	65,416	68,997	2.58
U.S.	80,389,592	91,993,582	102,048,200	107,302,392	2.67

Note: (1) Metropolitan Statistical Area - see Appendix A for areas included
Source: 1990 Census of Population and Housing, Summary Tape File 3C; Claritas, Inc.

Race/Ethnicity of City Population

Race/Ethnicity	1990 Census Population	1990 Census %	1999 Estimate Population	1999 Estimate %	% Change 1990-1999
White, Non-Hispanic	37,296	95.3	36,359	93.7	-2.5
Black, Non-Hispanic	571	1.5	651	1.7	14.0
Asian, Non-Hispanic	507	1.3	888	2.3	75.1
Other, Non-Hispanic	193	0.5	141	0.4	-26.9
Hispanic	560	1.4	753	1.9	34.5

Source: 1990 Census of Population and Housing, Summary Tape File 3C; Claritas, Inc.

Race/Ethnicity of Metropolitan Statistical Area Population

Race/Ethnicity	1990 Census		1999 Estimate		% Change 1990-1999
	Population	%	Population	%	
White, Non-Hispanic	127,382	96.9	162,172	96.0	27.3
Black, Non-Hispanic	1,012	0.8	1,489	0.9	47.1
Asian, Non-Hispanic	1,358	1.0	2,511	1.5	84.9
Other, Non-Hispanic	392	0.3	718	0.4	83.2
Hispanic	1,297	1.0	2,006	1.2	54.7

Note: See Appendix A for areas included in the Metropolitan Statistical Area
Source: 1990 Census of Population and Housing, Summary Tape File 3C; Claritas, Inc.

Ancestry

Area	German	Irish	English	Italian	U.S.	French	Polish	Dutch
City	13.1	20.9	19.2	6.7	3.4	20.1	3.1	1.1
MSA[1]	12.9	19.6	21.9	6.2	3.4	25.9	3.1	1.7
U.S.	23.3	15.6	13.1	5.9	5.3	4.2	3.8	2.5

Note: Figures are percentages and include persons that reported multiple ancestry (eg. if a person reported being Irish and Italian, they were included in both columns); (1) Metropolitan Statistical Area - see Appendix A for areas included
Source: 1990 Census of Population and Housing, Summary Tape File 3C

Median Age

Area	1990 Census	1999 Estimate
City	26.5	29.8
MSA[1]	30.3	33.9
U.S.	32.9	35.7

Note: (1) Metropolitan Statistical Area - see Appendix A for areas included
Source: 1990 Census of Population and Housing, Summary Tape File 3C; Claritas, Inc.

Male/Female Population

Area	Number of Males		Number of Females		Males per 100 Females	
	1990	1999	1990	1999	1990	1999
City	18,161	18,165	20,966	20,627	86.6	88.1
MSA[1]	63,679	82,152	67,762	86,744	94.0	94.7
U.S.	121,172,379	132,803,736	127,537,494	139,409,136	95.0	95.3

Note: (1) Metropolitan Statistical Area - see Appendix A for areas included
Source: 1990 Census of Population, General Population Characteristics; Claritas, Inc.

INCOME

Per Capita/Median/Average Income

Area	Per Capita ($)			Median Household ($)			Average Household ($)		
	1989	1999	% Chg.	1989	1999	% Chg.	1989	1999	% Chg.
City	13,918	20,058	44.1	25,523	32,045	25.6	35,026	46,350	32.3
MSA[1]	16,037	22,620	41.0	36,691	46,009	25.4	42,730	56,439	32.1
U.S.	14,420	21,350	48.1	30,056	40,525	34.8	38,453	56,184	46.1

Note: (1) Metropolitan Statistical Area - see Appendix A for areas included; 1989 data is from the 1990 Census; 1999 data is estimated by Claritas, Inc.
Source: 1990 Census of Population, General Population Characteristics; Claritas, Inc.

Household Income Distribution

Area	Percent of Households Earning								
	Under $5,000	$5,000 -14,999	$15,000 -24,999	$25,000 -34,999	$35,000 -49,999	$50,000 -74,999	$75,000 -99,000	$100,000 -149,999	$150,000 and up
City	3.0	19.1	17.4	13.6	14.5	17.5	7.1	4.3	3.4
MSA[1]	1.8	11.6	11.7	12.2	16.5	23.9	11.4	7.3	3.6
U.S.	3.9	13.3	13.8	12.6	16.2	19.4	9.7	6.6	4.6

Note: Data as of 1999; (1) Metropolitan Statistical Area - see Appendix A for areas included
Source: Claritas, Inc.

Effective Buying Income

Area	Per Capita ($)	Median Household ($)	Average Household ($)
City	16,570	29,866	42,514
MSA[1]	18,247	40,868	48,118
U.S.	17,496	36,603	47,036

Note: Data as of 1/1/2000; (1) Metropolitan Statistical Area - see Appendix A for areas included
Source: Standard Rate & Data Service, Newspaper Advertising Source, March 2000

Effective Household Buying Income Distribution

Area	% of Households Earning						
	$10,000 -$19,999	$20,000 -$34,999	$35,000 -$49,999	$50,000 -$74,999	$75,000 -$99,000	$100,000 -$124,999	$125,000 and up
City	19.8	24.2	16.1	16.3	5.8	1.9	3.1
MSA[1]	13.2	21.3	19.1	23.4	9.4	3.0	2.5
U.S.	15.0	21.6	17.6	19.6	8.4	3.0	3.3

Note: Data as of 1/1/2000; (1) Metropolitan Statistical Area - see Appendix A for areas included
Source: Standard Rate & Data Service, Newspaper Advertising Source, March 2000

Poverty Rates by Age

Area	People of All Ages	People Under 18 Years Old	Related Children Age 5-17 in Families in Poverty
City	17.6	n/a	n/a
County	8.1	9.4	7.4
U.S.	13.8	20.8	18.7

Note: Figures show the percent of people living below the poverty line in 1995. The average poverty threshold was $15,569 for a family of four in 1995; n/a not available
Source: Bureau of the Census, Small Area Income and Poverty Estimates Program; U.S. Department of Housing and Urban Development

EMPLOYMENT

Labor Force and Employment

Area	Civilian Labor Force			Workers Employed		
	Dec. 1998	Dec. 1999	% Chg.	Dec. 1998	Dec. 1999	% Chg.
City	24,314	24,326	0.0	23,756	23,910	0.6
MSA[1]	102,129	102,541	0.4	100,181	100,833	0.7
U.S.	138,297,000	139,941,000	1.2	132,732,000	134,696,000	1.5

Note: Data is not seasonally adjusted and covers workers 16 years of age and older;
(1) Metropolitan Statistical Area - see Appendix A for areas included
Source: Bureau of Labor Statistics, http://stats.bls.gov

Unemployment Rate

Area	1999											
	Jan.	Feb.	Mar.	Apr.	May	Jun.	Jul.	Aug.	Sep.	Oct.	Nov.	Dec.
City	3.0	2.9	2.3	1.9	2.0	2.3	2.4	2.1	2.3	2.0	1.7	1.7
MSA[1]	2.7	2.8	2.2	1.7	1.6	1.8	2.0	1.8	1.9	1.8	1.6	1.7
U.S.	4.8	4.7	4.4	4.1	4.0	4.5	4.5	4.2	4.1	3.8	3.8	3.7

Note: Data is not seasonally adjusted and covers workers 16 years of age and older; all figures are percentages; (1) Metropolitan Statistical Area - see Appendix A for areas included
Source: Bureau of Labor Statistics, http://stats.bls.gov

Employment by Industry

Sector	MSA[1]		U.S.
	Number of Employees	Percent of Total	Percent of Total
Services	31,300	29.1	30.2
Retail Trade	18,800	17.5	18.1
Government	17,000	15.8	15.8
Manufacturing	19,500	18.2	14.1
Finance/Insurance/Real Estate	5,400	5.0	5.9
Wholesale Trade	4,600	4.3	5.4
Transportation/Public Utilities	4,800	4.5	5.3
Construction	n/a	n/a	4.8
Mining	n/a	n/a	0.4

Note: Figures cover non-farm employment as of 12/99 and are not seasonally adjusted; (1) Metropolitan Statistical Area - see Appendix A for areas included; n/a not available
Source: Bureau of Labor Statistics, http://stats.bls.gov

Employment by Occupation

Occupation Category	City (%)	MSA[1] (%)	U.S. (%)
White Collar	66.2	67.0	58.1
Executive/Admin./Management	12.5	14.9	12.3
Professional	18.8	18.6	14.1
Technical & Related Support	4.9	5.5	3.7
Sales	14.0	12.8	11.8
Administrative Support/Clerical	16.0	15.3	16.3
Blue Collar	15.7	18.8	26.2
Precision Production/Craft/Repair	7.8	9.4	11.3
Machine Operators/Assem./Insp.	4.0	4.7	6.8
Transportation/Material Movers	1.5	2.3	4.1
Cleaners/Helpers/Laborers	2.3	2.4	3.9
Services	17.1	12.5	13.2
Farming/Forestry/Fishing	1.0	1.6	2.5

Note: Figures cover workers 16 years of age and older; (1) Metropolitan Statistical Area - see Appendix A for areas included
Source: 1990 Census of Population and Housing, Summary Tape File 3C

Occupational Employment Projections: 1996 - 2006

Occupations Expected to Have the Largest Job Growth (ranked by numerical growth)	Fast-Growing Occupations[1] (ranked by percent growth)
1. Truck drivers, light	1. Systems analysts
2. Marketing & sales, supervisors	2. Database administrators
3. Salespersons, retail	3. Human services workers
4. Cashiers	4. Bus drivers, school
5. Registered nurses	5. Hotel desk clerks
6. Janitors/cleaners/maids, ex. priv. hshld.	6. Instructors/coaches, sports/phys. train.
7. General managers & top executives	7. Packaging machine operators
8. Food preparation workers	8. Counter & rental clerks
9. Waiters & waitresses	9. Child care workers, private household
10. Food service workers	10. Writers and editors

Note: Projections cover Vermont; (1) Excludes occupations with total job growth less than 300
Source: U.S. Department of Labor, Employment and Training Administration, America's Labor Market Information System (ALMIS)

Average Wages

Occupation	$/Hr.	Occupation	$/Hr.
Accountants and Auditors	19.85	Maids and Housekeepers	7.29
Assemblers and Fabricators	10.09	Maintenance Repairers	11.54
Automotive Mechanics	12.76	Marketing/Advertising/PR Managers	31.58
Bookkeepers	11.69	Nurses, Licensed Practical	13.61
Carpenters	12.50	Nurses, Registered	20.16
Cashiers	7.08	Nursing Aides/Orderlies/Attendants	8.47
Clerks, General Office	9.54	Physicians and Surgeons	40.40
Clerks, Shipping/Receiving/Traffic	10.12	Receptionists/Information Clerks	9.78
Computer Programmers	23.64	Sales Reps., Exc. Scientific/Retail	18.46
Computer Support Specialists	-	Sales Reps., Scientific, Exc. Retail	23.98
Cooks, Restaurant	8.98	Salespersons, Retail	9.03
Electricians	14.95	Secretaries, Except Legal/Medical	11.36
Financial Managers	28.18	Stock Clerks, Sales Floor	7.51
First-Line Supervisors/Mgrs., Sales	18.66	Systems Analysts	27.40
Food Preparation Workers	7.11	Teacher Aides	7.96
General Managers/Top Executives	32.86	Teachers, Elementary School	21.66
Guards	8.35	Teachers, Secondary School	22.23
Hand Packers	7.88	Telemarketers	9.40
Janitors and Cleaners	8.53	Truck Drivers, Heavy/Tractor-Trailer	13.53
Laborers, Landscaping	8.14	Truck Drivers, Light	9.40
Lawyers	27.78	Waiters and Waitresses	6.35

Note: Wage data is for 1998 and covers the Metropolitan Statistical Area (see Appendix A for areas included). Hourly wages for elementary and secondary school teachers were calculated by the editors from annual wage data assuming a 40 hour work week; Dashes indicate that data was not available.
Source: Bureau of Labor Statistics, 1998 Metropolitan Area Occupational Employment and Wage Estimates

TAXES

Major State and Local Tax Rates

State Corporate Income (%)	State Personal Income (%)	Residential Property (%)	Sales & Use		State Gasoline (cents/ gallon)	State Cigarette (cents/ pack)
			State (%)	Local (%)		
7.0 - 9.75[a]	24.0[b]	1.86	5.0	None	20.0[c]	44.0

Note: Personal/corporate income, sales, gasoline and cigarette tax rates as of January 2000. Property tax rates as of April 2000; (b) 24.0% of federal tax liability. If Vermont tax liability for any taxable year exceeds the tax liability determinable under federal law in effect on December 31, 1998, the taxpayer will be entitled to a credit of 106% of the excess tax; (a) Minimum tax is $250; (c) Large trucks pay a higher tax of 25 cents per gallon
Source: Federation of Tax Administrators, www.taxadmin.org; ERI's Relocation Assessor software database, quarterly effective date 4/1/2000

Total Taxes Per Capita and as a Percent of Income

Area	Per Capita Income ($)	Per Capita Taxes ($)			Percent of Income (%)		
		Total	Federal	State/Local	Total	Federal	State/Local
Vermont	25,500	9,189	6,064	3,125	36.0	23.8	12.3
U.S.	28,878	10,298	7,026	3,273	35.7	24.3	11.3

Note: Figures are for 1999
Source: Tax Foundation, www.taxfoundation.org

COMMERCIAL UTILITIES

Typical Monthly Electric Bills

Area	Commercial Service ($/month)		Industrial Service ($/month)	
	12 kW demand 1,500 kWh	100 kW demand 30,000 kWh	1,000 kW demand 400,000 kWh	20,000 kW demand 10,000,000 kWh
City	200	3,821	42,119	711,103
U.S.	150	2,174	23,995	508,569

Note: Based on rates in effect January 1, 1999
Source: Edison Electric Institute, Typical Residential, Commercial and Industrial Bills, Winter 1999

TRANSPORTATION

Transportation Statistics

Average minutes to work (1990)	15.5
Interstate highways	I-89; I-189; US-2; US-7
Bus lines	
In-city (1998)	Chittenden County Transportation Authority, 29 buses
Inter-city (1999)	2
Passenger air service	
Airport	Burlington International
Airlines (1999)	1
Enplaned passengers (1998)	435,799
Amtrak service	Yes
Motor freight carriers (1999)	6
Major waterways/ports	Lake Champlain

Source: FAA DOT/TSC CY1998 ACAIS Database; National Transit Database, 1998; Editor & Publisher Market Guide, 2000; Amtrak National Time Table, Fall 1999/Winter 2000; 1990 Census of Population and Housing, STF 3C; Jane's Urban Transport Systems 1999-2000

Means of Transportation to Work

Area	Car/Truck/Van		Public Transportation			Bicycle	Walked	Other Means	Worked at Home
	Drove Alone	Car-pooled	Bus	Subway	Railroad				
City	59.6	13.9	3.1	0.1	0.0	1.9	17.3	1.0	3.1
MSA[1]	73.2	12.5	1.4	0.0	0.0	0.8	7.1	0.8	4.2
U.S.	73.2	13.4	3.0	1.5	0.5	0.4	3.9	1.2	3.0

Note: Figures shown are percentages and only include workers 16 years of age and older;
(1) Metropolitan Statistical Area - see Appendix A for areas included
Source: 1990 Census of Population and Housing, Summary Tape File 3C

BUSINESSES

Major Business Headquarters

Company Name	1999 Rankings	
	Fortune 500	Forbes 500
No companies listed	-	-

Note: Companies listed are located in the city; dashes indicate no ranking
Fortune 500: Companies that produce a 10-K are ranked 1 to 500 based on 1999 revenue
Forbes 500: Private companies are ranked 1 to 500 based on 1998 revenue
Source: Forbes, December 13, 1999; Fortune, April 17, 2000

HOTELS & MOTELS

Hotels/Motels

Area	Hotels/ Motels	Rooms	Luxury-Level Hotels/Motels		Average Minimum Rates ($)		
			♦♦♦♦	♦♦♦♦♦	♦♦	♦♦♦	♦♦♦♦
City	10	882	0	0	n/a	n/a	n/a
Airport	10	1,411	0	0	n/a	n/a	n/a
Suburbs	1	73	0	0	n/a	n/a	n/a
Total	21	2,366	0	0	n/a	n/a	n/a

Note: n/a not available; classifications range from one diamond (budget properties with basic amenities) to five diamond (luxury properties).
Source: OAG Business Travel Planner, Winter 1999-2000

Estimated Daily Food and Lodging Costs

Area	Food/Other ($/day)	Average Hotel Cost ($/day)
City	38	82
U.S.	30	55

Source: ERI's Relocation Assessor software database, quarterly effective date 4/1/2000

CONVENTION CENTERS

Convention Centers and Event Sites

Name	Guest Rooms	Meeting Space (sq. ft.)	Capacity (Theatre Style)
Radisson Hotel Burlington	256	16,000	680
Sheraton Burlington Hotel & Conference Ctr.	309	30,000	1,300
The Civic Center of Vermont	n/a	n/a	2,600

Note: n/a not available
Source: EventSource.com, 3/15/2000

Living Environment

COST OF LIVING

Cost of Living: Homeowner

Cost Element	U.S. ($)	City ($)	Differential ($)	Percent of U.S. Average
Consumables	14,516	15,924	1,408	109.7
Transportation	5,957	6,178	221	103.7
Health Services	2,012	2,276	264	113.1
Housing/Utilities/Prop. Tax	16,337	22,500	6,163	137.7
Income+Payroll Taxes	12,615	11,704	-911	92.8
Miscellaneous	8,563	8,563	0	100.0
Total Cost of Living	60,000	67,145	7,145	111.9

Note: Figures are based on a single income, four person family with gross annual earnings of $60,000, owning an 1,800 square-foot home, and driving two automobiles worth $22,000 30,000 miles per year.
Source: ERI's Relocation Assessor software database, quarterly effective date 4/1/2000

Cost of Living: Renter

Cost Element	U.S. ($)	City ($)	Differential ($)	Percent of U.S. Average
Consumables	10,486	11,566	1,080	110.3
Transportation	2,107	2,198	91	104.3
Health Services	1,632	1,856	224	113.7
Rent/Utilities/Insurance	9,299	11,109	1,810	119.5
Income+Payroll Taxes	8,607	8,175	-432	95.0
Miscellaneous	7,869	7,869	0	100.0
Total Cost of Living	40,000	42,773	2,773	106.9

Note: Figures are based on a single income, three person family with gross annual earnings of $40,000, renting a 1,000 square-foot home, and driving one automobile worth $8,000 12,000 miles per year.
Source: ERI's Relocation Assessor software database, quarterly effective date 4/1/2000

HOUSING

Median Home Prices and Housing Affordability

Area	Median Price[2] 4th Qtr. 1999 ($)	HOI[3] 4th Qtr. 1999	Affordability Rank[4]
MSA[1]	125,000	68.1	107
U.S.	139,000	63.8	–

Note: (1) Metropolitan Statistical Area - see Appendix A for areas included; (2) U.S. figures calculated from the sales of 687,516 new and existing homes in 192 markets; (3) Housing Opportunity Index - percent of homes sold that were within the reach of the median income household at the prevailing mortgage interest rate; (4) Rank is from 1-192 with 1 being most affordable
Source: National Association of Home Builders, Housing Opportunity Index, 4th Quarter 1999

Estimated Home Price

Area	Price ($)
City	170,144
U.S.	135,855

Note: Figures are based on an 1,800 square-foot home
Source: ERI's Relocation Assessor software database, quarterly effective date 4/1/2000

Estimated Rent

Area	Rent ($/month)
City	768
U.S.	651

Note: Figures are based on a 1,000 square-foot home
Source: ERI's Relocation Assessor software database, quarterly effective date 4/1/2000

Median Home Price Projection

It is projected that the median home price in the metropolitan area will increase from $136,040 in 1999 to $202,761 in 2010, an increase of 49.0%
Kiplinger's Personal Finance Magazine, January 2000

RESIDENTIAL UTILITIES

Average Residential Utility Costs

Area	All Electric ($/mth)	Part Electric ($/mth)	Other Energy ($/mth)	Phone ($/mth)
City	–	74.51	69.54	25.33
U.S.	99.25	55.47	43.48	20.29

Source: ACCRA, Cost of Living Index, 3rd Quarter 1999

HEALTH CARE

Average Health Care Costs

Area	Hospital ($/day)	Doctor ($/visit)	Dentist ($/visit)
City	587.00	63.00	72.34
U.S.	440.96	53.83	68.42

Note: Hospital—based on a semi-private room; Doctor—based on a general practitioner's routine exam of an established patient; Dentist—based on adult teeth cleaning and periodic oral exam.
Source: ACCRA, Cost of Living Index, 3rd Quarter 1999

Distribution of Office-Based Physicians

Area	Family/Gen. Practitioners	Specialists Medical	Surgical	Other
MSA[1]	63	174	111	150

Note: Data as of 12/31/97; (1) Metropolitan Statistical Area - see Appendix A for areas included
Source: American Medical Assn., Physician Characteristics & Distribution in the U.S., 1999

Hospitals

Burlington has 1 general medical and surgical hospital.
AHA Guide to the Healthcare Field, 1999-2000

EDUCATION

Public School District Statistics

District Name	Num. Sch.	Enroll.	Classroom Teachers	Pupils per Teacher	Minority Pupils (%)	Current Exp.[1] ($/pupil)
Burlington School District	12	3,751	n/a	n/a	n/a	n/a

Note: Data covers the 1997-1998 school year unless otherwise noted; (1) Data covers fiscal year 1996; SD = School District; ISD = Independent School District; n/a not available
Source: National Center for Education Statistics, Common Core of Data Public Education Agency Universe 1997-98; National Center for Education Statistics, Characteristics of the 100 Largest Public Elementary and Secondary School Districts in the United States: 1997-98, July 1999

Educational Quality

School District	Education Quotient[1]	Graduate Outcome[2]	Community Index[3]	Resource Index[4]
Town of Burlington	83	67	116	109

Note: Over 1,000 secondary school districts were rated in terms of educational quality. The scores range from a low of 50 to a high of 150; (1) Combination of the Graduate Outcome, Community and Resource indexes weighted to reflect the greater importance of the Graduate Outcome and Resource Index; (2) Based on graduation rates and college board scores (SAT/ACT); (3) Based on the surrounding community's level of affluence and adult education; (4) Based on teacher salaries, per-pupil expenditures and student-teacher ratios.
Source: Expansion Management, Ratings Issue, 1999

Educational Attainment by Race

Area	High School Graduate (%)					Bachelor's Degree (%)				
	Total	White	Black	Other	Hisp.[2]	Total	White	Black	Other	Hisp.[2]
City	82.4	82.3	93.2	76.7	86.8	34.8	34.7	18.4	51.1	44.7
MSA[1]	86.6	86.6	87.2	83.9	85.9	33.2	33.0	26.0	50.6	42.8
U.S.	75.2	77.9	63.1	60.4	49.8	20.3	21.5	11.4	19.4	9.2

Note: Figures shown cover persons 25 years old and over; (1) Metropolitan Statistical Area - see Appendix A for areas included; (2) people of Hispanic origin can be of any race
Source: 1990 Census of Population and Housing, Summary Tape File 3C

School Enrollment by Type

Area	Preprimary				Elementary/High School			
	Public		Private		Public		Private	
	Enrollment	%	Enrollment	%	Enrollment	%	Enrollment	%
City	219	48.7	231	51.3	3,330	84.8	599	15.2
MSA[1]	1,367	53.4	1,192	46.6	18,277	91.8	1,630	8.2
U.S.	2,679,029	59.5	1,824,256	40.5	38,379,689	90.2	4,187,099	9.8

Note: Figures shown cover persons 3 years old and over;
(1) Metropolitan Statistical Area - see Appendix A for areas included
Source: 1990 Census of Population and Housing, Summary Tape File 3C

School Enrollment by Race

Area	Preprimary (%)				Elementary/High School (%)			
	White	Black	Other	Hisp.[1]	White	Black	Other	Hisp.[1]
City	95.6	3.6	0.9	0.9	92.5	3.6	3.9	2.5
MSA[2]	96.1	1.7	2.2	1.0	96.7	1.3	2.0	1.4
U.S.	80.4	12.5	7.1	7.8	74.1	15.6	10.3	12.5

Note: Figures shown cover persons 3 years old and over; (1) people of Hispanic origin can be of any race; (2) Metropolitan Statistical Area - see Appendix A for areas included
Source: 1990 Census of Population and Housing, Summary Tape File 3C

Higher Education

Two-Year Colleges		Four-Year Colleges		Medical Schools	Law Schools	Voc/ Tech
Public	Private	Public	Private			
0	1	1	3	1	0	4

Source: College Blue Book, Occupational Education, 1999; Medical School Admission Requirements, 1999-2000; Peterson's Guide to Two-Year Colleges, 2000; Peterson's Guide to Four-Year Colleges, 1999; Barron's Guide to Law Schools, 1999

MAJOR EMPLOYERS

Major Employers

Blodgett Corp. (machinery)
Chittenden Trust Co.
General Dynamics Ordinance Systems
McClure Newspapers

Burton Corp. (sporting goods)
Fletcher Allen Health Care
Lane Press
Merchants Bancshares

Note: Companies listed are located in the city
Source: D&B Business Rankings, 1999; Ward's Business Directory, 1999; America's Corporate Families, 1999

PUBLIC SAFETY

Crime Rate

Area	All Crimes	Violent Crimes				Property Crimes		
		Murder	Forcible Rape	Robbery	Aggrav. Assault	Burglary	Larceny -Theft	Motor Vehicle Theft
City	6,345.1	0.0	50.7	58.3	139.3	1,324.8	4,407.4	364.8
Suburbs[1]	4,099.3	0.9	22.1	4.6	75.5	766.8	3,058.1	171.2
MSA[2]	4,698.0	0.7	29.7	18.9	92.5	915.6	3,417.8	222.8
U.S.	4,615.5	6.3	34.4	165.2	360.5	862.0	2,728.1	459.0

Note: Crime rate is the number of crimes per 100,000 population; (1) Defined as all areas within the Metropolitan Statistical Area but located outside the central city; (2) Metropolitan Statistical Area - see Appendix A for areas included
Source: FBI Uniform Crime Reports, 1998

RECREATION

Culture and Recreation

Museums	Symphony Orchestras	Opera Companies	Dance Companies	Professional Theatres	Zoos	Pro Sports Teams
1	1	0	1	0	0	0

Source: Musical America, International Directory of the Performing Arts, 1999; Official Museum Directory, 2000; Stern's Performing Arts Directory, 1997; USA Today Four Sport Stadium Guide, 1997; Career Opportunities in Theatre and the Performing Arts, 1999

Library System

The Fletcher Free Library has no branches, holdings of 130,215 volumes, and a budget of $868,910 (1997-1998).
American Library Directory, 1999-2000

MEDIA

Newspapers

Name	Type	Freq.	Distribution	Circulation
The Burlington Free Press	General	7x/wk	Area	55,000
The Other Paper	n/a	2x/mo	Local	7,000

Note: Includes newspapers with circulations of 200 or more located in the city; n/a not available
Source: Burrelle's Media Directory, 1999 Edition

Television Stations

Name	Ch.	Affiliation	Type	Owner
WCAX	n/a	CBST	Commercial	Mount Mansfield Television Inc.
WVTB	20	n/a	Public	Vermont ETV Inc.
WVNY	22	ABCT	Commercial	Straight Line Communications Inc.
WVER	28	n/a	Public	Vermont ETV Inc.
WETK	33	PBS	Public	Vermont ETV Inc.
WVTA	41	n/a	Public	Vermont ETV Inc.
WFFF	44	FBC	Commercial	Champlain Valley Telecasting Inc.

Note: Stations included broadcast in the Burlington metro area; n/a not available
Source: Burrelle's Media Directory, 1999 Edition

AM Radio Stations

Call Letters	Freq. (kHz)	Target Audience	Station Format	Music Format
WVMT	620	General	N/S/T	n/a
WEAV	960	General	M/T	Adult Contemporary
WJOY	1230	General	M/N/S	MOR
WKDR	1390	General	N/S/T	n/a

Note: Stations included broadcast in the Burlington metro area; n/a not available
Target Audience: A=Asian; B=Black; C=Christian; E=Ethnic; F=French; G=General; H=Hispanic;
M=Men; N=Native American; R=Religious; S=Senior Citizen; W=Women; Y=Young Adult; Z=Children
Station Format: E=Educational; M=Music; N=News; S=Sports; T=Talk
Music Format: AOR=Album Oriented Rock; MOR=Middle-of-the-Road
Source: Burrelle's Media Directory, 1999 Edition

FM Radio Stations

Call Letters	Freq. (mHz)	Target Audience	Station Format	Music Format
WWPV	88.7	General	M/N/S	Alternative/AOR/Christian/Classic Rock/Country/ Jazz/Latin/Rhythm & Blues/Urban Contemporary
WRVT	88.7	General	M/N/T	Classical/Jazz
WVPR	89.5	General	E/M/N/T	Classical/Jazz
WCMD	89.9	Religious	M/N/S	Christian
WRUV	90.1	General	E/M/N/S	Alternative/Jazz/Modern Rock/Oldies/Rhythm & Blues/Urban Contemporary
WCMK	91.7	Religious	M/N/S	Christian
WEZF	92.9	General	M	Adult Contemporary
WXXX	95.5	General	M	n/a
WOKO	98.9	General	M	Country
WGLY	103.3	General	M/N/S	Adult Contemporary/Christian
WKOL	105.1	General	M/N/S	Oldies
WIZN	106.7	General	M	AOR
WVPS	107.9	General	M/N/T	Classical/Jazz

Note: Stations included broadcast in the Burlington metro area; n/a not available
Station Format: E=Educational; M=Music; N=News; S=Sports; T=Talk
Target Audience: A=Asian; B=Black; C=Christian; E=Ethnic; F=French; G=General; H=Hispanic;
M=Men; N=Native American; R=Religious; S=Senior Citizen; W=Women; Y=Young Adult; Z=Children
Music Format: AOR=Album Oriented Rock; MOR=Middle-of-the-Road
Source: Burrelle's Media Directory, 1999 Edition

WEATHER

Temperature/Precipitation/Humidity

	Jan	Feb	Mar	Apr	May	Jun	Jul	Aug	Sep	Oct	Nov	Dec	Yr.
Max. High Temp. (°F)	63	62	80	91	93	97	99	99	92	85	75	65	99
Avg. High Temp. (°F)	26	28	38	53	67	76	81	78	69	57	44	31	54
Avg. Temp. (°F)	18	19	30	43	56	65	70	68	59	48	37	24	45
Avg. Low Temp. (°F)	8	10	21	33	44	54	59	57	49	39	30	16	35
Min. Low Temp. (°F)	-30	-30	-20	2	24	33	39	35	25	15	-2	-26	-30
Avg. Precip. (in.)	1.8	1.8	2.2	2.7	3.0	3.5	3.5	4.0	3.2	2.9	3.1	2.4	34.1
Avg. Snowfall (in.)	19	16	13	4	Tr	0	0	0	Tr	Tr	7	19	78
Avg. Rel. Hum. 7am (%)	73	73	74	74	74	76	78	82	85	82	78	76	77
Avg. Rel. Hum. 4pm (%)	65	61	58	52	51	54	53	56	61	61	68	69	59

Note: Tr = Trace amounts (less than 0.05 inches of rain or less than 0.5 inches of snow)
Source: National Climatic Data Center, International Station Meteorological Climate Summary, 3/95

Weather Conditions

Temperature			Precipitation		
10°F & below	32°F & below	90°F & above	0.01 inch or more precip.	1.5 inch or more snow/ice	Thunder-storms
49	157	6	155	17	22

Note: Figures are average number of days per year
Source: National Climatic Data Center, International Station Meteorological Climate Summary, 3/95

AIR & WATER QUALITY

Maximum Pollutant Concentrations

	Particulate Matter (ug/m³)	Carbon Monoxide (ppm)	Sulfur Dioxide (ppm)	Nitrogen Dioxide (ppm)	Ozone (ppm)	Lead (ug/m³)
MSA[1] Level	42	2	0.012	0.017	n/a	n/a
NAAQS[2]	150	9	0.140	0.053	0.12	1.50
Met NAAQS	Yes	Yes	Yes	Yes	n/a	n/a

Note: (1) Metropolitan Statistical Area - see Appendix A for areas included; (2) National Ambient Air Quality Standards; ppm = parts per million; ug/m³ = micrograms per cubic meter; n/a not available
Source: EPA, National Air Quality and Emissions Trends Report, 1997

Pollutant Standards Index

Data not available.
EPA, National Air Quality and Emissions Trends Report, 1997

Drinking Water

Water System Name	Pop. Served	Primary Water Source Type	Number of Violations in 1998-99	Type of Violation/ Contaminants
Burlington Water Res	47,600	Surface	None	None

Note: Data as of January 19, 2000
Source: EPA, Office of Ground Water and Drinking Water, Safe Drinking Water Information System

Burlington tap water is neutral, soft, and fluoridated.
Editor & Publisher Market Guide, 2000

Canton, Ohio

Background

Canton, Ohio is located in the northeastern section of the state, 60 miles south of Cleveland and 95 miles west of Pittsburg, Pennsylvania. It is the county seat of Stark County. The surrounding region is rolling and hilly countryside. The Canton metropolitan area includes North Canton, Massilon and other nearby communities. Canton has ties with Akron, 20 miles to the north, including the Akron-Canton Regional Airport.

The city was incorporated in 1854, resulting from the natural resources and extensive water and land transportation system that was developed in eastern Ohio. Canton has also served traditionally as a processing and transport center for the area's agricultural economy.

Various Native American tribes originally inhabited the region. Early settlement was hampered by hostilities with Native Americans, and territorial conflicts among European powers. After the American Revolution, Canton was within the territories in Ohio that the U.S. Congress made available to encourage western migration and development. The site of Canton was subdivided in 1805 by Bezaleel Wells, who named the community in honor of a ship captain he knew who had sailed to Canton in China. The settlement was incorporated as a village in 1815. The Canton area became an industrial and commercial center for iron and steel and the manufacture of machinery and other products. The area is also rich in mineral deposits, including bituminous coal, shale, limestone, clay, sand and gravel, which stimulated mining.

In the latter 20th Century, regional and national trends led to a decline in Canton's traditional industrial economy. After 1950, Canton also lost population and businesses to outlying suburban development. The city has undertaken economic redevelopment programs, including cooperative initiatives with other regions, such as the Akron-Canton Foreign Trade Zone.

Manufacturing remains an important segment of the Canton area's economy, and the city government estimates that over 1,500 products are manufactured there. Canton also continues to serve the region's agriculture and food processing economy, which includes dairy products, poultry, vegetables and other food crops. However, there has been a shift towards service industries and to smaller companies. Other major economic sectors include construction, retailing and wholesaling.

In the 1990s extensive redevelopment in the downtown business district took place. While the Canton area has experienced significant contemporary urban and suburban development, many of the city's older buildings and neighborhoods remain, including designated historic districts and sites.

The National Football League was founded in Canton in 1920. In 1962 Canton became the site of the Pro Football Hall of Fame. The McKinley Museum and National Memorial, which honors President William McKinley, who lived in Canton, includes exhibits about the region and the era in which McKinley lived, as well as general exhibits about science, history and a planetarium. The family home of President McKinley's wife Ida, where the couple lived, is a historic museum and the National First Ladies' Library.

The Canton Park Commission operates approximately 60 city parks and recreational facilities. Stark County also operates parks in the area, including a portion of the Ohio and Erie Canal corridor in nearby Massillon. Venues for concerts and other events include the Canton Memorial Civic Center and the Palace Theater, a restored former vaudeville theater now used for films and live events. Performing arts organizations include the Canton Symphony Orchestra and Canton Civic Opera, among others.

Among the institutes of higher education in the Canton area are Malone College, Kent State University's Stark Campus, Walsh University in North Canton and Stark State College.

Canton has a city government with a Mayor and City Council.

General Rankings and Evaluative Comments

■ Canton was ranked #195 out of 354 metropolitan areas in *Places Rated Almanac*. Criteria: cost of living, climate, crime, transportation, job outlook, education, the arts, health care, and recreation. *Places Rated Almanac, Millennium Edition, 2000*

■ Cognetics studied 273 metro areas in the United States, ranking them by entrepreneurial activity. Canton was ranked #67 out of 134 smaller metro areas. Criteria: Significant Starts (firms started in the last 10 years that still employ at least 5 people) and Young Growers (percent of firms 10 years old or less that grew significantly during the last 4 years). *Cognetics, "Entrepreneurial Hot Spots: The Best Places in America to Start and Grow a Company," 1999*

■ Reliastar Financial Corporation ranked the 125 largest metropolitan areas according to the general financial security of residents. Canton was ranked #50 out of 125 with a score of 4.7 (the percentage a metropolitan area is above or below the metropolitan norm; a metro area with a score of 10.6 is 10.6% above the metro average). Criteria: Earnings and Wealth Potential (household income, education, net assets, cost of living); Safety Net (health insurance, retirement savings, life insurance, income support programs); Personal Threats (unemployment rate, low-income households, crime rate); Community Economic Vitality (cost of community services, job quality, job creation, housing costs). Reliastar Financial Corporation, "The Best Cities to Earn and Save Money: A Ranking of the Largest 125 U.S. Cities," 2000 Edition

Business Environment

STATE ECONOMY

State Economic Profile

"Ohio's expansion has started to decelerate. Ohio is expected to lag the nation in growth for some time. The slowdown in employment growth is concentrated in the manufacturing sector and outside of Ohio's larger metro areas. Ohio's weak demographic trends will constrain job growth and the housing market.

Ohio manufacturing shed about 7,000 jobs in 1998. A large share of these losses were in the Cleveland and Columbus areas, while Cincinnati managed to add a small number of manufacturing jobs. Job growth in the services sectors, particularly business, financial and health services, has helped to offset a slowdown in manufacturing in these urban areas. Bank merger and acquisition activity has resulted in jobs being shifted from rural and smaller areas to the larger metropolitan areas.

While Ohio's rural areas have suffered from a declining employment base, economic activity has also been shifting from the northern part of the state toward the middle and south. Last year's employment growth for Cincinnati was 2.5%, compared to only 1.6% for Columbus and 1.6% for Cleveland. Population growth has followed a similar pattern, although the state as a whole is among one of the weakest in the nation, losing a considerable number of younger households.

Ohio's housing market had a strong 1998, with sales up 8.6% and single family permits up 3.2%. Price appreciation was just below the nation and will likely remain modest given the increase in construction. Both construction and sales should contract in 2000. Prices are likely to rise the most in Cincinnati, where construction has been modest and job growth strongest." National Association of Realtors, Economic Profiles: The Fifty States and the District of Columbia, http://nar.realtor.com/databank/profiles.htm

EXPORTS

Total Export Sales

Area	1995 ($000)	1996 ($000)	1997 ($000)	1998 ($000)	% Chg. 1995-98	% Chg. 1997-98
MSA[1]	377,170	405,985	421,568	359,544	-4.7	-14.7
U.S.	583,030,524	622,827,063	687,597,999	680,474,251	16.7	-1.0

Note: (1) Metropolitan Statistical Area - see Appendix A for areas included
Source: U.S. Department of Commerce, International Trade Association, Metropolitan Area Exports: An Export Performance Report on Over 250 U.S. Cities, November 10, 1999

CITY FINANCES

City Government Finances

Component	1995 ($million)	1995 (per capita $)
Revenue	58.8	698
Expenditure	57.9	688
Debt Outstanding	41.4	492

Source: 1999 County and City Extra, Annual Metro, City, and County Data Book

City Government Revenue by Source

Source	1995 ($million)	1995 (per capita $)
Intergovernmental	7.6	90
Taxes	42.9	510
Property	41.3	491
Sales and Gross Receipts	0.0	0

Source: 1999 County and City Extra, Annual Metro, City, and County Data Book

City Government Expenditures by Function

Function	1995 ($million)	1995 (per capita $)	1995 (%)
Public Welfare	0.0	0	0.0
Highways	7.4	88	12.8
Parking Facilities	0.0	0	0.0
Education	0.0	0	0.0
Health and Hospitals	2.8	33	4.9
Police Protection	24.5	291	42.4
Sewerage and Sanitation	0.0	0	0.0
Parks and Recreation	1.9	23	3.4
Housing and Community Development	4.9	58	8.5
Interest on Debt	0.8	9	1.4

Source: 1999 County and City Extra, Annual Metro, City, and County Data Book

Municipal Bond Ratings

Area	Moody's
City	Baa1

Source: Mergent Bond Record, 2/2000

POPULATION

Population Growth

Area	1980 Census	1990 Census	1999 Estimate	2004 Projection	Population Growth (%) 1990-1999	Population Growth (%) 1999-2004
City	94,730	84,161	78,138	75,909	-7.2	-2.9
MSA[1]	404,421	394,106	402,104	406,185	2.0	1.0
U.S.	226,545,805	248,765,170	272,212,864	283,625,312	9.4	4.2

Note: (1) Metropolitan Statistical Area - see Appendix A for areas included
Source: 1990 Census of Population and Housing, Summary Tape File 3C; Claritas, Inc.

Number of Households and Average Household Size

Area	1980 Census	1990 Census	1999 Estimate	2004 Projection	1999 Average Household Size
City	35,739	33,489	32,061	31,638	2.44
MSA[1]	142,715	148,995	157,309	161,447	2.56
U.S.	80,389,592	91,993,582	102,048,200	107,302,392	2.67

Note: (1) Metropolitan Statistical Area - see Appendix A for areas included
Source: 1990 Census of Population and Housing, Summary Tape File 3C; Claritas, Inc.

Race/Ethnicity of City Population

Race/Ethnicity	1990 Census Population	1990 Census %	1999 Estimate Population	1999 Estimate %	% Change 1990-1999
White, Non-Hispanic	67,129	79.8	59,846	76.6	-10.8
Black, Non-Hispanic	15,145	18.0	16,418	21.0	8.4
Asian, Non-Hispanic	367	0.4	288	0.4	-21.5
Other, Non-Hispanic	664	0.8	543	0.7	-18.2
Hispanic	856	1.0	1,043	1.3	21.8

Source: 1990 Census of Population and Housing, Summary Tape File 3C; Claritas, Inc.

Race/Ethnicity of Metropolitan Statistical Area Population

Race/Ethnicity	1990 Census		1999 Estimate		% Change 1990-1999
	Population	%	Population	%	
White, Non-Hispanic	363,976	92.4	365,951	91.0	0.5
Black, Non-Hispanic	24,626	6.2	28,736	7.1	16.7
Asian, Non-Hispanic	1,680	0.4	2,052	0.5	22.1
Other, Non-Hispanic	1,271	0.3	1,537	0.4	20.9
Hispanic	2,553	0.6	3,828	1.0	49.9

Note: See Appendix A for areas included in the Metropolitan Statistical Area
Source: 1990 Census of Population and Housing, Summary Tape File 3C; Claritas, Inc.

Ancestry

Area	German	Irish	English	Italian	U.S.	French	Polish	Dutch
City	34.2	17.3	10.0	8.8	5.1	3.8	2.0	2.4
MSA[1]	44.0	18.4	13.5	8.9	4.1	5.0	2.5	3.3
U.S.	23.3	15.6	13.1	5.9	5.3	4.2	3.8	2.5

Note: Figures are percentages and include persons that reported multiple ancestry (eg. if a person reported being Irish and Italian, they were included in both columns); (1) Metropolitan Statistical Area - see Appendix A for areas included
Source: 1990 Census of Population and Housing, Summary Tape File 3C

Median Age

Area	1990 Census	1999 Estimate
City	33.3	35.5
MSA[1]	34.9	37.7
U.S.	32.9	35.7

Note: (1) Metropolitan Statistical Area - see Appendix A for areas included
Source: 1990 Census of Population and Housing, Summary Tape File 3C; Claritas, Inc.

Male/Female Population

Area	Number of Males		Number of Females		Males per 100 Females	
	1990	1999	1990	1999	1990	1999
City	38,891	36,350	45,270	41,788	85.9	87.0
MSA[1]	189,036	192,753	205,070	209,351	92.2	92.1
U.S.	121,172,379	132,803,736	127,537,494	139,409,136	95.0	95.3

Note: (1) Metropolitan Statistical Area - see Appendix A for areas included
Source: 1990 Census of Population, General Population Characteristics; Claritas, Inc.

INCOME

Per Capita/Median/Average Income

Area	Per Capita ($)			Median Household ($)			Average Household ($)		
	1989	1999	% Chg.	1989	1999	% Chg.	1989	1999	% Chg.
City	10,133	14,950	47.5	19,807	26,133	31.9	25,013	35,193	40.7
MSA[1]	12,848	19,389	50.9	27,685	37,438	35.2	33,677	48,836	45.0
U.S.	14,420	21,350	48.1	30,056	40,525	34.8	38,453	56,184	46.1

Note: (1) Metropolitan Statistical Area - see Appendix A for areas included; 1989 data is from the 1990 Census; 1999 data is estimated by Claritas, Inc.
Source: 1990 Census of Population, General Population Characteristics; Claritas, Inc.

Household Income Distribution

Area	Percent of Households Earning								
	Under $5,000	$5,000 -14,999	$15,000 -24,999	$25,000 -34,999	$35,000 -49,999	$50,000 -74,999	$75,000 -99,000	$100,000 -149,999	$150,000 and up
City	7.3	22.0	18.7	14.4	17.2	13.4	4.3	1.9	0.9
MSA[1]	3.8	14.0	14.9	13.7	19.0	20.1	7.9	4.3	2.1
U.S.	3.9	13.3	13.8	12.6	16.2	19.4	9.7	6.6	4.6

Note: Data as of 1999; (1) Metropolitan Statistical Area - see Appendix A for areas included
Source: Claritas, Inc.

Effective Buying Income

Area	Per Capita ($)	Median Household ($)	Average Household ($)
City	12,550	24,311	31,003
MSA[1]	16,185	34,403	41,888
U.S.	17,496	36,603	47,036

Note: Data as of 1/1/2000; (1) Metropolitan Statistical Area - see Appendix A for areas included
Source: Standard Rate & Data Service, Newspaper Advertising Source, March 2000

Effective Household Buying Income Distribution

Area	% of Households Earning						
	$10,000 -$19,999	$20,000 -$34,999	$35,000 -$49,999	$50,000 -$74,999	$75,000 -$99,000	$100,000 -$124,999	$125,000 and up
City	22.3	25.2	16.4	11.9	3.0	0.7	0.8
MSA[1]	15.8	23.9	20.1	19.1	6.4	1.7	1.8
U.S.	15.0	21.6	17.6	19.6	8.4	3.0	3.3

Note: Data as of 1/1/2000; (1) Metropolitan Statistical Area - see Appendix A for areas included
Source: Standard Rate & Data Service, Newspaper Advertising Source, March 2000

Poverty Rates by Age

Area	People of All Ages	People Under 18 Years Old	Related Children Age 5-17 in Families in Poverty
City	22.3	n/a	n/a
County	10.8	17.5	14.7
U.S.	13.8	20.8	18.7

Note: Figures show the percent of people living below the poverty line in 1995. The average poverty threshold was $15,569 for a family of four in 1995; n/a not available
Source: Bureau of the Census, Small Area Income and Poverty Estimates Program; U.S. Department of Housing and Urban Development

EMPLOYMENT

Labor Force and Employment

Area	Civilian Labor Force			Workers Employed		
	Dec. 1998	Dec. 1999	% Chg.	Dec. 1998	Dec. 1999	% Chg.
City	38,638	39,243	1.6	36,365	36,802	1.2
MSA[1]	205,783	208,650	1.4	198,080	200,456	1.2
U.S.	138,297,000	139,941,000	1.2	132,732,000	134,696,000	1.5

Note: Data is not seasonally adjusted and covers workers 16 years of age and older; (1) Metropolitan Statistical Area - see Appendix A for areas included
Source: Bureau of Labor Statistics, http://stats.bls.gov

Unemployment Rate

Area	1999											
	Jan.	Feb.	Mar.	Apr.	May	Jun.	Jul.	Aug.	Sep.	Oct.	Nov.	Dec.
City	8.1	7.8	7.4	6.7	6.2	7.7	6.9	6.7	6.7	6.3	6.3	6.2
MSA[1]	5.2	5.0	4.8	4.3	4.0	4.9	4.4	4.2	4.2	3.9	3.9	3.9
U.S.	4.8	4.7	4.4	4.1	4.0	4.5	4.5	4.2	4.1	3.8	3.8	3.7

Note: Data is not seasonally adjusted and covers workers 16 years of age and older; all figures are percentages; (1) Metropolitan Statistical Area - see Appendix A for areas included
Source: Bureau of Labor Statistics, http://stats.bls.gov

Employment by Industry

Sector	MSA[1]		U.S.
	Number of Employees	Percent of Total	Percent of Total
Services	51,500	27.3	30.2
Retail Trade	37,200	19.7	18.1
Government	21,200	11.2	15.8
Manufacturing	46,900	24.8	14.1
Finance/Insurance/Real Estate	6,600	3.5	5.9
Wholesale Trade	10,200	5.4	5.4
Transportation/Public Utilities	5,300	2.8	5.3
Construction	9,400	5.0	4.8
Mining	500	0.3	0.4

Note: Figures cover non-farm employment as of 12/99 and are not seasonally adjusted;
(1) Metropolitan Statistical Area - see Appendix A for areas included
Source: Bureau of Labor Statistics, http://stats.bls.gov

Employment by Occupation

Occupation Category	City (%)	MSA[1] (%)	U.S. (%)
White Collar	49.2	53.6	58.1
Executive/Admin./Management	8.6	10.6	12.3
Professional	10.3	12.1	14.1
Technical & Related Support	3.3	3.7	3.7
Sales	12.3	12.1	11.8
Administrative Support/Clerical	14.7	15.1	16.3
Blue Collar	31.8	31.4	26.2
Precision Production/Craft/Repair	9.6	11.4	11.3
Machine Operators/Assem./Insp.	12.0	10.2	6.8
Transportation/Material Movers	4.5	5.2	4.1
Cleaners/Helpers/Laborers	5.6	4.7	3.9
Services	18.3	13.7	13.2
Farming/Forestry/Fishing	0.7	1.3	2.5

Note: Figures cover workers 16 years of age and older;
(1) Metropolitan Statistical Area - see Appendix A for areas included
Source: 1990 Census of Population and Housing, Summary Tape File 3C

Occupational Employment Projections: 1996 - 2006

Occupations Expected to Have the Largest Job Growth (ranked by numerical growth)	Fast-Growing Occupations[1] (ranked by percent growth)
1. Cashiers	1. Systems analysts
2. Salespersons, retail	2. Occupational therapy assistants
3. Systems analysts	3. Desktop publishers
4. General managers & top executives	4. Paralegals
5. Truck drivers, light	5. Physical therapy assistants and aides
6. Registered nurses	6. Medical assistants
7. Food preparation workers	7. Personal and home care aides
8. Nursing aides/orderlies/attendants	8. Home health aides
9. Home health aides	9. Physical therapists
10. Marketing & sales, supervisors	10. Occupational therapists

Note: Projections cover Ohio; (1) Excludes occupations with total job growth less than 300
Source: U.S. Department of Labor, Employment and Training Administration, America's Labor Market Information System (ALMIS)

Average Wages

Occupation	$/Hr.	Occupation	$/Hr.
Accountants and Auditors	18.14	Maids and Housekeepers	6.88
Assemblers and Fabricators	8.95	Maintenance Repairers	11.65
Automotive Mechanics	11.79	Marketing/Advertising/PR Managers	23.03
Bookkeepers	10.10	Nurses, Licensed Practical	12.73
Carpenters	15.39	Nurses, Registered	18.11
Cashiers	6.72	Nursing Aides/Orderlies/Attendants	8.26
Clerks, General Office	8.89	Physicians and Surgeons	53.89
Clerks, Shipping/Receiving/Traffic	10.79	Receptionists/Information Clerks	8.37
Computer Programmers	19.79	Sales Reps., Exc. Scientific/Retail	19.68
Computer Support Specialists	16.54	Sales Reps., Scientific, Exc. Retail	19.60
Cooks, Restaurant	7.00	Salespersons, Retail	8.44
Electricians	19.66	Secretaries, Except Legal/Medical	9.85
Financial Managers	22.17	Stock Clerks, Sales Floor	7.12
First-Line Supervisors/Mgrs., Sales	15.38	Systems Analysts	24.55
Food Preparation Workers	6.31	Teacher Aides	8.02
General Managers/Top Executives	26.93	Teachers, Elementary School	17.28
Guards	7.61	Teachers, Secondary School	19.42
Hand Packers	7.07	Telemarketers	8.64
Janitors and Cleaners	8.15	Truck Drivers, Heavy/Tractor-Trailer	12.99
Laborers, Landscaping	7.86	Truck Drivers, Light	9.09
Lawyers	28.32	Waiters and Waitresses	5.77

Note: Wage data is for 1998 and covers the Metropolitan Statistical Area (see Appendix A for areas included). Hourly wages for elementary and secondary school teachers were calculated by the editors from annual wage data assuming a 40 hour work week; Dashes indicate that data was not available.
Source: Bureau of Labor Statistics, 1998 Metropolitan Area Occupational Employment and Wage Estimates

TAXES

Major State and Local Tax Rates

State Corporate Income (%)	State Personal Income (%)	Residential Property (%)	Sales & Use		State Gasoline (cents/ gallon)	State Cigarette (cents/ pack)
			State (%)	Local (%)		
5.1 - 8.5[a]	0.716 - 7.228[b]	1.70	5.0	None	22.0[c]	24.0

Note: Personal/corporate income, sales, gasoline and cigarette tax rates as of January 2000. Property tax rates as of April 2000; (b) Plus and additional $20 per exemption tax credit; (a) Or 4.0 mils times the value of the taxpayer's issued and outstanding share of stock ($150K max). An additional litter tax is imposed equal to 0.11% on the first $50,000 of taxable income, 0.22% on income over $50,000; or 0.14 mills on net worth; (c) Plus 3 cents commercial tax
Source: Federation of Tax Administrators, www.taxadmin.org; ERI's Relocation Assessor software database, quarterly effective date 4/1/2000

Total Taxes Per Capita and as a Percent of Income

Area	Per Capita Income ($)	Per Capita Taxes ($)			Percent of Income (%)		
		Total	Federal	State/Local	Total	Federal	State/Local
Ohio	27,439	9,709	6,544	3,165	35.4	23.8	11.5
U.S.	28,878	10,298	7,026	3,273	35.7	24.3	11.3

Note: Figures are for 1999
Source: Tax Foundation, www.taxfoundation.org

COMMERCIAL UTILITIES

Typical Monthly Electric Bills

Area	Commercial Service ($/month)		Industrial Service ($/month)	
	12 kW demand 1,500 kWh	100 kW demand 30,000 kWh	1,000 kW demand 400,000 kWh	20,000 kW demand 10,000,000 kWh
City	130	1,659	19,238	299,345
U.S.	150	2,174	23,995	508,569

Note: Based on rates in effect January 1, 1999
Source: Edison Electric Institute, Typical Residential, Commercial and Industrial Bills, Winter 1999

TRANSPORTATION

Transportation Statistics

Average minutes to work (1990)	16.7
Interstate highways	I-77; US-30; US-62
Bus lines	
In-city (1998)	Stark Area Regional Transit Authority, 55 buses
Inter-city (1999)	2
Passenger air service	
Airport	Akron-Canton Regional
Airlines (1999)	7
Enplaned passengers (1998)	344,219
Amtrak service	No
Motor freight carriers (1999)	90
Major waterways/ports	None

Source: FAA DOT/TSC CY1998 ACAIS Database; National Transit Database, 1998; Editor & Publisher Market Guide, 2000; Amtrak National Time Table, Fall 1999/Winter 2000; 1990 Census of Population and Housing, STF 3C; Jane's Urban Transport Systems 1999-2000

Means of Transportation to Work

Area	Car/Truck/Van		Public Transportation			Bicycle	Walked	Other Means	Worked at Home
	Drove Alone	Car-pooled	Bus	Subway	Railroad				
City	80.0	10.6	2.3	0.0	0.0	0.3	4.4	1.0	1.4
MSA[1]	84.7	9.0	0.6	0.0	0.0	0.1	2.8	0.6	2.1
U.S.	73.2	13.4	3.0	1.5	0.5	0.4	3.9	1.2	3.0

Note: Figures shown are percentages and only include workers 16 years of age and older;
(1) Metropolitan Statistical Area - see Appendix A for areas included
Source: 1990 Census of Population and Housing, Summary Tape File 3C

BUSINESSES

Major Business Headquarters

Company Name	1999 Rankings	
	Fortune 500	Forbes 500
No companies listed	-	-

Note: Companies listed are located in the city; dashes indicate no ranking
Fortune 500: Companies that produce a 10-K are ranked 1 to 500 based on 1999 revenue
Forbes 500: Private companies are ranked 1 to 500 based on 1998 revenue
Source: Forbes, December 13, 1999; Fortune, April 17, 2000

HOTELS & MOTELS

Hotels/Motels

Area	Hotels/ Motels	Rooms	Luxury-Level Hotels/Motels		Average Minimum Rates ($)		
			◆◆◆◆	◆◆◆◆◆	◆◆	◆◆◆	◆◆◆◆
City	6	681	0	0	n/a	n/a	n/a

Note: n/a not available; classifications range from one diamond (budget properties with basic amenities) to five diamond (luxury properties).
Source: OAG Business Travel Planner, Winter 1999-2000

Estimated Daily Food and Lodging Costs

Area	Food/Other ($/day)	Average Hotel Cost ($/day)
City	30	55
U.S.	30	55

Source: ERI's Relocation Assessor software database, quarterly effective date 4/1/2000

CONVENTION CENTERS

Convention Centers and Event Sites

Name	Guest Rooms	Meeting Space (sq. ft.)	Capacity (Theatre Style)
Canton Hilton	170	10,576	850
Canton Memorial Civic Center	n/a	n/a	4,500
Hilton Canton	170	10,000	850
Sheraton Inn Canton	152	6,000	300
Four Points Hotel	152	n/a	0

Note: n/a not available
Source: EventSource.com, 3/15/2000

Living Environment

COST OF LIVING

Cost of Living: Homeowner

Cost Element	U.S. ($)	City ($)	Differential ($)	Percent of U.S. Average
Consumables	14,516	14,113	-403	97.2
Transportation	5,957	5,951	-6	99.9
Health Services	2,012	1,919	-93	95.4
Housing/Utilities/Prop. Tax	16,337	18,898	2,561	115.7
Income+Payroll Taxes	12,615	12,622	7	100.1
Miscellaneous	8,563	8,563	0	100.0
Total Cost of Living	60,000	62,066	2,066	103.4

Note: Figures are based on a single income, four person family with gross annual earnings of $60,000, owning an 1,800 square-foot home, and driving two automobiles worth $22,000 30,000 miles per year.
Source: ERI's Relocation Assessor software database, quarterly effective date 4/1/2000

Cost of Living: Renter

Cost Element	U.S. ($)	City ($)	Differential ($)	Percent of U.S. Average
Consumables	10,486	10,308	-178	98.3
Transportation	2,107	2,130	23	101.1
Health Services	1,632	1,574	-58	96.4
Rent/Utilities/Insurance	9,299	9,271	-28	99.7
Income+Payroll Taxes	8,607	8,575	-32	99.6
Miscellaneous	7,869	7,869	0	100.0
Total Cost of Living	40,000	39,727	-273	99.3

Note: Figures are based on a single income, three person family with gross annual earnings of $40,000, renting a 1,000 square-foot home, and driving one automobile worth $8,000 12,000 miles per year.
Source: ERI's Relocation Assessor software database, quarterly effective date 4/1/2000

HOUSING

Median Home Prices and Housing Affordability

Area	Median Price[2] 4th Qtr. 1999 ($)	HOI[3] 4th Qtr. 1999	Affordability Rank[4]
MSA[1]	90,000	80.5	22
U.S.	139,000	63.8	–

Note: (1) Metropolitan Statistical Area - see Appendix A for areas included; (2) U.S. figures calculated from the sales of 687,516 new and existing homes in 192 markets; (3) Housing Opportunity Index - percent of homes sold that were within the reach of the median income household at the prevailing mortgage interest rate; (4) Rank is from 1-192 with 1 being most affordable
Source: National Association of Home Builders, Housing Opportunity Index, 4th Quarter 1999

Estimated Home Price

Area	Price ($)
City	153,736
U.S.	135,855

Note: Figures are based on an 1,800 square-foot home
Source: ERI's Relocation Assessor software database, quarterly effective date 4/1/2000

Estimated Rent

Area	Rent ($/month)
City	638
U.S.	651

Note: Figures are based on a 1,000 square-foot home
Source: ERI's Relocation Assessor software database, quarterly effective date 4/1/2000

Median Home Price Projection

It is projected that the median home price in the metropolitan area will increase from $103,949 in 1999 to $133,709 in 2010, an increase of 28.6%
Kiplinger's Personal Finance Magazine, January 2000

RESIDENTIAL UTILITIES

Average Residential Utility Costs

Area	All Electric ($/mth)	Part Electric ($/mth)	Other Energy ($/mth)	Phone ($/mth)
City	n/a	n/a	n/a	n/a
U.S.	99.25	55.47	43.48	20.29

Note: n/a not available
Source: ACCRA, Cost of Living Index, 3rd Quarter 1999

HEALTH CARE

Average Health Care Costs

Area	Hospital ($/day)	Doctor ($/visit)	Dentist ($/visit)
City	n/a	n/a	n/a
U.S.	440.96	53.83	68.42

Note: n/a not available
Source: ACCRA, Cost of Living Index, 3rd Quarter 1999

Distribution of Office-Based Physicians

Area	Family/Gen. Practitioners	Specialists		
		Medical	Surgical	Other
MSA[1]	84	194	147	139

Note: Data as of 12/31/97; (1) Metropolitan Statistical Area - see Appendix A for areas included
Source: American Medical Assn., Physician Characteristics & Distribution in the U.S., 1999

Hospitals

Canton has 2 general medical and surgical hospitals.
AHA Guide to the Healthcare Field, 1999-2000

EDUCATION

Public School District Statistics

District Name	Num. Sch.	Enroll.	Classroom Teachers	Pupils per Teacher	Minority Pupils (%)	Current Exp.[1] ($/pupil)
Canton City SD	28	13,414	858	15.6	n/a	n/a
Canton Local SD	5	2,581	139	18.6	n/a	n/a
Plain Local SD	10	6,324	380	16.6	n/a	n/a
Stark County Bd Ed Data Proc	n/a	n/a	n/a	n/a	n/a	n/a

Note: Data covers the 1997-1998 school year unless otherwise noted; (1) Data covers fiscal year 1996; SD = School District; ISD = Independent School District; n/a not available
Source: National Center for Education Statistics, Common Core of Data Public Education Agency Universe 1997-98; National Center for Education Statistics, Characteristics of the 100 Largest Public Elementary and Secondary School Districts in the United States: 1997-98, July 1999

Educational Quality

School District	Education Quotient[1]	Graduate Outcome[2]	Community Index[3]	Resource Index[4]
Canton City School Dist.	91	86	59	107

Note: Over 1,000 secondary school districts were rated in terms of educational quality. The scores range from a low of 50 to a high of 150; (1) Combination of the Graduate Outcome, Community and Resource indexes weighted to reflect the greater importance of the Graduate Outcome and Resource Index; (2) Based on graduation rates and college board scores (SAT/ACT); (3) Based on the surrounding community's level of affluence and adult education; (4) Based on teacher salaries, per-pupil expenditures and student-teacher ratios.
Source: Expansion Management, Ratings Issue, 1999

Educational Attainment by Race

Area	High School Graduate (%)					Bachelor's Degree (%)				
	Total	White	Black	Other	Hisp.[2]	Total	White	Black	Other	Hisp.[2]
City	67.0	68.5	59.6	57.0	72.0	9.7	10.6	4.5	8.8	11.6
MSA[1]	75.7	76.5	62.3	69.4	76.1	13.9	14.2	5.4	29.1	17.7
U.S.	75.2	77.9	63.1	60.4	49.8	20.3	21.5	11.4	19.4	9.2

Note: Figures shown cover persons 25 years old and over; (1) Metropolitan Statistical Area -
see Appendix A for areas included; (2) people of Hispanic origin can be of any race
Source: 1990 Census of Population and Housing, Summary Tape File 3C

School Enrollment by Type

Area	Preprimary				Elementary/High School			
	Public		Private		Public		Private	
	Enrollment	%	Enrollment	%	Enrollment	%	Enrollment	%
City	1,089	66.7	543	33.3	13,262	91.9	1,163	8.1
MSA[1]	4,169	58.0	3,016	42.0	62,027	90.7	6,323	9.3
U.S.	2,679,029	59.5	1,824,256	40.5	38,379,689	90.2	4,187,099	9.8

Note: Figures shown cover persons 3 years old and over;
(1) Metropolitan Statistical Area - see Appendix A for areas included
Source: 1990 Census of Population and Housing, Summary Tape File 3C

School Enrollment by Race

Area	Preprimary (%)				Elementary/High School (%)			
	White	Black	Other	Hisp.[1]	White	Black	Other	Hisp.[1]
City	77.3	21.0	1.7	1.8	71.7	26.5	1.8	1.0
MSA[2]	91.7	7.3	1.0	1.1	89.9	9.1	1.1	0.7
U.S.	80.4	12.5	7.1	7.8	74.1	15.6	10.3	12.5

Note: Figures shown cover persons 3 years old and over; (1) people of Hispanic origin can be of any
race; (2) Metropolitan Statistical Area - see Appendix A for areas included
Source: 1990 Census of Population and Housing, Summary Tape File 3C

Higher Education

Two-Year Colleges		Four-Year Colleges		Medical Schools	Law Schools	Voc/ Tech
Public	Private	Public	Private			
1	0	1	1	0	0	5

Source: College Blue Book, Occupational Education, 1999; Medical School Admission Requirements,
1999-2000; Peterson's Guide to Two-Year Colleges, 2000; Peterson's Guide to Four-Year Colleges,
1999; Barron's Guide to Law Schools, 1999

MAJOR EMPLOYERS

Major Employers

Aultman Hospital	Camelot Music
Diebold	Fresh Mark (meat products)
Graphic Enterprises of Ohio	Hoover Co.
Ohio Power	Timken Co. (roller bearings)
United States Postal Service	Waterlink Inc.

Note: Companies listed are located in the city
Source: D&B Business Rankings, 1999; Ward's Business Directory, 1999; America's Corporate
Families, 1999

PUBLIC SAFETY

Crime Rate

Area	All Crimes	Violent Crimes				Property Crimes		
		Murder	Forcible Rape	Robbery	Aggrav. Assault	Burglary	Larceny -Theft	Motor Vehicle Theft
City	7,988.3	11.1	125.7	401.8	1,036.4	1,560.2	4,180.2	672.9
Suburbs[1]	n/a	n/a	n/a	n/a	n/a	n/a	n/a	n/a
MSA[2]	n/a	n/a	n/a	n/a	n/a	n/a	n/a	n/a
U.S.	4,615.5	6.3	34.4	165.2	360.5	862.0	2,728.1	459.0

Note: Crime rate is the number of crimes per 100,000 population; (1) Defined as all areas within the Metropolitan Statistical Area but located outside the central city; (2) Metropolitan Statistical Area - see Appendix A for areas included; n/a not available
Source: FBI Uniform Crime Reports, 1998

RECREATION

Culture and Recreation

Museums	Symphony Orchestras	Opera Companies	Dance Companies	Professional Theatres	Zoos	Pro Sports Teams
4	1	0	1	0	0	0

Source: Musical America, International Directory of the Performing Arts, 1999; Official Museum Directory, 2000; Stern's Performing Arts Directory, 1997; USA Today Four Sport Stadium Guide, 1997; Career Opportunities in Theatre and the Performing Arts, 1999

Library System

The Stark County District Library has nine branches and holdings of 809,651 volumes.
American Library Directory, 1999-2000

MEDIA

Newspapers

Name	Type	Freq.	Distribution	Circulation
Jackson Journal	General	1x/wk	Local	7,500
The Repository	General	7x/wk	Local	62,000
The Sun Journal	General	1x/wk	Local	10,000

Note: Includes newspapers with circulations of 200 or more located in the city;
Source: Burrelle's Media Directory, 1999 Edition

Television Stations

Name	Ch.	Affiliation	Type	Owner
WDLI	17	n/a	Commercial	Trinity Broadcasting Network

Note: Stations included broadcast in the Canton metro area; n/a not available
Source: Burrelle's Media Directory, 1999 Edition

AM Radio Stations

Call Letters	Freq. (kHz)	Target Audience	Station Format	Music Format
WTIG	990	General	S	n/a
WRCW	1060	General	M/N/T	Adult Contemporary
WDPN	1310	General	M	MOR
WHBC	1480	General	M/N/S	Adult Standards
WINW	1520	General	M/N/S	Christian

Note: Stations included broadcast in the Canton metro area; n/a not available
Target Audience: A=Asian; B=Black; C=Christian; E=Ethnic; F=French; G=General; H=Hispanic; M=Men; N=Native American; R=Religious; S=Senior Citizen; W=Women; Y=Young Adult; Z=Children
Station Format: E=Educational; M=Music; N=News; S=Sports; T=Talk
Music Format: AOR=Album Oriented Rock; MOR=Middle-of-the-Road
Source: Burrelle's Media Directory, 1999 Edition

FM Radio Stations

Call Letters	Freq. (mHz)	Target Audience	Station Format	Music Format
WRMU	91.1	General	E/M/N/S	AOR/Blues/Classical/Gospel/Jazz/Modern Rock/Rhythm & Blues/Urban Contemporary
WZKL	92.5	General	M	Oldies
WHBC	94.1	General	M	Adult Contemporary
WNPQ	95.9	Religious	M	Christian
WRQK	106.9	General	M/N/S	AOR

Note: Stations included broadcast in the Canton metro area
Station Format: E=Educational; M=Music; N=News; S=Sports; T=Talk
Target Audience: A=Asian; B=Black; C=Christian; E=Ethnic; F=French; G=General; H=Hispanic;
M=Men; N=Native American; R=Religious; S=Senior Citizen; W=Women; Y=Young Adult; Z=Children
Music Format: AOR=Album Oriented Rock; MOR=Middle-of-the-Road
Source: Burrelle's Media Directory, 1999 Edition

WEATHER

Temperature/Precipitation/Humidity

	Jan	Feb	Mar	Apr	May	Jun	Jul	Aug	Sep	Oct	Nov	Dec	Yr.
Max. High Temp. (°F)	70	68	81	88	92	100	101	98	99	86	80	76	101
Avg. High Temp. (°F)	33	36	46	59	70	79	82	81	74	62	49	37	59
Avg. Temp. (°F)	26	28	37	49	59	68	72	71	64	53	42	31	50
Avg. Low Temp. (°F)	18	20	28	38	48	57	61	60	53	43	33	23	40
Min. Low Temp. (°F)	-24	-13	-3	10	24	32	43	41	32	20	-1	-16	-24
Avg. Precip. (in.)	2.6	2.3	3.2	3.3	3.7	3.4	4.0	3.2	3.1	2.3	2.8	2.8	36.7
Avg. Snowfall (in.)	11	9	9	3	Tr	0	0	0	0	1	5	10	47
Avg. Rel. Hum. 7am (%)	80	80	79	77	77	80	83	87	87	84	80	80	81
Avg. Rel. Hum. 4pm (%)	68	65	59	53	53	54	54	55	56	56	64	70	59

Note: Tr = Trace amounts (less than 0.05 inches of rain or less than 0.5 inches of snow)
Source: National Climatic Data Center, International Station Meteorological Climate Summary, 3/95

Weather Conditions

Temperature			Precipitation		
5°F & below	32°F & below	90°F & above	0.01 inch or more precip.	1.5 inch or more snow/ice	Thunder-storms
12	129	8	153	10	38

Note: Figures are average number of days per year
Source: National Climatic Data Center, International Station Meteorological Climate Summary, 3/95

AIR & WATER QUALITY

Maximum Pollutant Concentrations

	Particulate Matter (ug/m³)	Carbon Monoxide (ppm)	Sulfur Dioxide (ppm)	Nitrogen Dioxide (ppm)	Ozone (ppm)	Lead (ug/m³)
MSA[1] Level	58	3	0.025	n/a	0.10	n/a
NAAQS[2]	150	9	0.140	0.053	0.12	1.50
Met NAAQS	Yes	Yes	Yes	n/a	Yes	n/a

Note: (1) Metropolitan Statistical Area - see Appendix A for areas included; (2) National Ambient Air Quality Standards; ppm = parts per million; ug/m³ = micrograms per cubic meter; n/a not available
Source: EPA, National Air Quality and Emissions Trends Report, 1997

Pollutant Standards Index

Data not available.
EPA, National Air Quality and Emissions Trends Report, 1997

Drinking Water

Water System Name	Pop. Served	Primary Water Source Type	Number of Violations in 1998-99	Type of Violation/ Contaminants
Canton Water Dept.-Northeast	40,000	Ground	None	None
Canton Water Dept.-Northwest	30,000	Ground	None	None
Canton Water Dept.-Sugarcreek	70,000	Ground	None	None

Note: Data as of January 19, 2000
Source: EPA, Office of Ground Water and Drinking Water, Safe Drinking Water Information System

Canton tap water is alkaline, very hard, and fluoridated.
Editor & Publisher Market Guide, 2000

Champaign, Illinois

Background

Champaign, Illinois is 135 miles south of Chicago and 120 miles west of Indianapolis, Indiana. It is on the Kaskaskia River in Champaign County, near the intersection of interstate highways I-57 and I-74. The terrain is predominantly level. Outside of the urban and suburban centers, Champaign County is a rural, agricultural region, producing corn and other foods.

Champaign and the adjacent city of Urbana are often characterized as one community, although they are separate municipalities. The two cities, and other nearby communities, comprise the commercial and services center for Champaign County, which has a diverse economy. The University of Illinois, a large, multi-faceted institution located in both Champaign and Urbana, is a major employer in the community and active in economic development.

The University is the site of The National Center for Supercomputing Applications, which is engaged in advanced research in computing. The basic technology for Internet browsers was developed there. These activities prompted the emergence of a growing cluster of high-tech enterprises in Champaign and Urbana, including many networking systems. In 1998, the two cities were jointly named among the top 10 "Hot New High-Tech Cities" by Newsweek magazine.

Various Native American groups originally occupied the region, and it remained largely unoccupied by whites during the colonial era. Around 1820 an increasing number of farms and small settlements were established. Champaign County was created in 1833, named for a community in Ohio. The arrival of the Illinois Central Railroad and opening of a railroad depot in nearby Urbana in 1853 prompted the subsequent development of Champaign, which was incorporated in 1860. The University of Illinois was chartered in 1867 as the state-supported Illinois Industrial University, and it acquired its present name in 1885.

In the 19th and 20th Centuries, Champaign and Urbana grew as a transport and commercial center for the region, with mills and other industries serving the region's agricultural economy. A manufacturing economy for other products also developed. In 1917, the Army established a pilot-training facility in nearby Rantoul, which became Chanute Air Force Base until it closed in 1993. That site is being redeveloped for multiple uses.

In addition to technology, the contemporary economy of Champaign and Urbana is based on the manufacture of a variety of goods, including foods, plastics products, apparel and hobby supplies. Other primary economic sectors include regional agriculture, health services, wholesale and retail trades, and business, government and professional services. Parkland College, a two-year professional and technical school is also located in Champaign.

The University of Illinois offers numerous cultural activities, including the Krannert Center for the Performing Arts and the Krannert Art Museum. Community venues include the domed Assembly Hall for sporting events, concerts and other activities, the historic Virginia Theater, Station Theater and the Springer Cultural Center. Museums include the Orpheum Children's Science Museum, William M. Staerkel Planetarium and the Champaign County Historic Museum, among others.

The Champaign Park District has received the National Gold Medal Award of the National Recreation and Park Association three times since 1979. There are a variety of parks and recreational facilities in Champaign, including Kaufman Lake and Sholem Farm, a traditional farming park. The Champaign County Forest Preserve District maintains facilities in outlying areas, including the Lake of the Woods, Salt Fork River Forest and Middlefork River preserve.

Champaign is governed by a Council-Manager form of government with a nine-member City Council that includes the Mayor. A City Manager serves as a City Executive.

General Rankings and Evaluative Comments

- Champaign was ranked #156 out of 354 metropolitan areas in *Places Rated Almanac*. Criteria: cost of living, climate, crime, transportation, job outlook, education, the arts, health care, and recreation. *Places Rated Almanac, Millennium Edition, 2000*

- Champaign was selected as one of North America's "Best Small Metro Areas" (population under 250,000). The area ranked #20 out of 20. Criteria: cost of living, climate, crime, transportation, job outlook, education, the arts, health care, and recreation. *Places Rated Almanac, Millennium Edition, 2000*

- Cognetics studied 273 metro areas in the United States, ranking them by entrepreneurial activity. Champaign was ranked #97 out of 134 smaller metro areas. Criteria: Significant Starts (firms started in the last 10 years that still employ at least 5 people) and Young Growers (percent of firms 10 years old or less that grew significantly during the last 4 years). *Cognetics, "Entrepreneurial Hot Spots: The Best Places in America to Start and Grow a Company," 1999*

Business Environment

STATE ECONOMY

State Economic Profile

"Illinois' economy has lagged the nation as it continues to shift from a manufacturing to service-based economy. Its low unemployment rate and rising per capita income mask a major restructuring occurring within its economy. Growth will be weak over the next two years but start to show some rebounding in 2001 as important structural changes now underway take affect.

Over half of the new jobs created in 1998 were in the services sector, and the bulk of those are located in Chicago. Job gains will come from the high-tech and financial services sectors. Manufacturing concerns continued to shed jobs as the state lost some 8,300 manufacturing jobs in 1998. More manufacturing job losses are likely in the short term. Both Mitsubishi and Goodyear are in the process of either laying off workers or planning to do so.

Illinois' farm sector has also been hit particularly hard by low commodity prices and weak foreign demand. Farm income was down more than 20% in 1998. Soybean and corn producers will continue to see their financial health erode. Although foreign demand is expected to pick up, oversupply will guarantee weak prices for bulk commodities.

Although the volume of home sales in 1998 was the highest level in over a decade, price appreciation has continued to lag the nation. Stagnant population growth continues to plague the housing market. Illinois lost over 20,000 residents on net in 1998, many of these are in the "typical buyer" age group of 25 to 44. Unsurprisingly, housing starts have been at their lowest levels in years, rising only 2% in 1998, with most of these taking place in the Chicago area." *National Association of Realtors, Economic Profiles: The Fifty States and the District of Columbia, http://nar.realtor.com/databank/profiles.htm*

EXPORTS

Total Export Sales

Area	1995 ($000)	1996 ($000)	1997 ($000)	1998 ($000)	% Chg. 1995-98	% Chg. 1997-98
MSA[1]	103,421	214,409	423,556	393,951	280.9	-7.0
U.S.	583,030,524	622,827,063	687,597,999	680,474,251	16.7	-1.0

Note: (1) Metropolitan Statistical Area - see Appendix A for areas included
Source: U.S. Department of Commerce, International Trade Association, Metropolitan Area Exports: An Export Performance Report on Over 250 U.S. Cities, November 10, 1999

CITY FINANCES

City Government Finances

Component	1995 ($million)	1995 (per capita $)
Revenue	50.2	750
Expenditure	43.0	644
Debt Outstanding	6.7	100

Source: 1999 County and City Extra, Annual Metro, City, and County Data Book

City Government Revenue by Source

Source	1995 ($million)	1995 (per capita $)
Intergovernmental	23.3	348
Taxes	17.7	265
Property	12.1	181
Sales and Gross Receipts	4.0	61

Source: 1999 County and City Extra, Annual Metro, City, and County Data Book

City Government Expenditures by Function

Function	1995 ($million)	1995 (per capita $)	1995 (%)
Public Welfare	0.0	0	0.0
Highways	4.1	62	9.7
Parking Facilities	2.0	30	4.7
Education	0.0	0	0.0
Health and Hospitals	<0.1	1	0.2
Police Protection	6.5	97	15.2
Sewerage and Sanitation	4.8	72	11.3
Parks and Recreation	3.6	55	8.6
Housing and Community Development	1.9	28	4.5
Interest on Debt	0.4	6	1.0

Source: 1999 County and City Extra, Annual Metro, City, and County Data Book

Municipal Bond Ratings

Area	Moody's
City	Aa2

Source: Mergent Bond Record, 2/2000

POPULATION

Population Growth

Area	1980 Census	1990 Census	1999 Estimate	2004 Projection	Population Growth (%) 1990-1999	Population Growth (%) 1999-2004
City	58,133	63,502	64,284	65,581	1.2	2.0
MSA[1]	168,392	173,025	167,570	169,271	-3.2	1.0
U.S.	226,545,805	248,765,170	272,212,864	283,625,312	9.4	4.2

Note: (1) Metropolitan Statistical Area - see Appendix A for areas included
Source: 1990 Census of Population and Housing, Summary Tape File 3C; Claritas, Inc.

Number of Households and Average Household Size

Area	1980 Census	1990 Census	1999 Estimate	2004 Projection	1999 Average Household Size
City	21,574	24,234	24,774	25,344	2.59
MSA[1]	58,405	63,993	63,023	63,736	2.66
U.S.	80,389,592	91,993,582	102,048,200	107,302,392	2.67

Note: (1) Metropolitan Statistical Area - see Appendix A for areas included
Source: 1990 Census of Population and Housing, Summary Tape File 3C; Claritas, Inc.

Race/Ethnicity of City Population

Race/Ethnicity	1990 Census Population	1990 Census %	1999 Estimate Population	1999 Estimate %	% Change 1990-1999
White, Non-Hispanic	50,782	80.0	48,311	75.2	-4.9
Black, Non-Hispanic	8,981	14.1	10,307	16.0	14.8
Asian, Non-Hispanic	2,497	3.9	3,767	5.9	50.9
Other, Non-Hispanic	162	0.3	185	0.3	14.2
Hispanic	1,080	1.7	1,714	2.7	58.7

Source: 1990 Census of Population and Housing, Summary Tape File 3C; Claritas, Inc.

Race/Ethnicity of Metropolitan Statistical Area Population

Race/Ethnicity	1990 Census		1999 Estimate		% Change 1990-1999
	Population	%	Population	%	
White, Non-Hispanic	144,824	83.7	135,058	80.6	-6.7
Black, Non-Hispanic	16,534	9.6	18,113	10.8	9.6
Asian, Non-Hispanic	7,819	4.5	9,940	5.9	27.1
Other, Non-Hispanic	559	0.3	503	0.3	-10.0
Hispanic	3,289	1.9	3,956	2.4	20.3

Note: See Appendix A for areas included in the Metropolitan Statistical Area
Source: 1990 Census of Population and Housing, Summary Tape File 3C; Claritas, Inc.

Ancestry

Area	German	Irish	English	Italian	U.S.	French	Polish	Dutch
City	33.4	17.3	16.1	3.6	3.0	3.4	4.7	2.8
MSA[1]	35.9	17.1	16.2	3.3	4.4	3.9	3.5	2.9
U.S.	23.3	15.6	13.1	5.9	5.3	4.2	3.8	2.5

Note: Figures are percentages and include persons that reported multiple ancestry (eg. if a person reported being Irish and Italian, they were included in both columns); (1) Metropolitan Statistical Area - see Appendix A for areas included
Source: 1990 Census of Population and Housing, Summary Tape File 3C

Median Age

Area	1990 Census	1999 Estimate
City	25.1	28.1
MSA[1]	27.7	30.9
U.S.	32.9	35.7

Note: (1) Metropolitan Statistical Area - see Appendix A for areas included
Source: 1990 Census of Population and Housing, Summary Tape File 3C; Claritas, Inc.

Male/Female Population

Area	Number of Males		Number of Females		Males per 100 Females	
	1990	1999	1990	1999	1990	1999
City	32,802	33,459	30,700	30,825	106.8	108.5
MSA[1]	87,279	84,381	85,746	83,189	101.8	101.4
U.S.	121,172,379	132,803,736	127,537,494	139,409,136	95.0	95.3

Note: (1) Metropolitan Statistical Area - see Appendix A for areas included
Source: 1990 Census of Population, General Population Characteristics; Claritas, Inc.

INCOME

Per Capita/Median/Average Income

Area	Per Capita ($)			Median Household ($)			Average Household ($)		
	1989	1999	% Chg.	1989	1999	% Chg.	1989	1999	% Chg.
City	13,025	19,529	49.9	22,967	31,711	38.1	32,400	48,259	48.9
MSA[1]	13,130	20,090	53.0	26,541	37,483	41.2	33,832	51,448	52.1
U.S.	14,420	21,350	48.1	30,056	40,525	34.8	38,453	56,184	46.1

Note: (1) Metropolitan Statistical Area - see Appendix A for areas included; 1989 data is from the 1990 Census; 1999 data is estimated by Claritas, Inc.
Source: 1990 Census of Population, General Population Characteristics; Claritas, Inc.

Household Income Distribution

Area	Percent of Households Earning								
	Under $5,000	$5,000 -14,999	$15,000 -24,999	$25,000 -34,999	$35,000 -49,999	$50,000 -74,999	$75,000 -99,000	$100,000 -149,999	$150,000 and up
City	5.7	18.8	16.7	12.3	13.0	17.3	7.8	4.9	3.5
MSA[1]	3.9	13.7	15.7	13.4	15.5	20.0	9.0	5.4	3.4
U.S.	3.9	13.3	13.8	12.6	16.2	19.4	9.7	6.6	4.6

Note: Data as of 1999; (1) Metropolitan Statistical Area - see Appendix A for areas included
Source: Claritas, Inc.

Effective Buying Income .

Area	Per Capita ($)	Median Household ($)	Average Household ($)
City	16,769	30,209	43,292
MSA[1]	17,471	35,043	46,838
U.S.	17,496	36,603	47,036

Note: Data as of 1/1/2000; (1) Metropolitan Statistical Area - see Appendix A for areas included
Source: Standard Rate & Data Service, Newspaper Advertising Source, March 2000

Effective Household Buying Income Distribution

Area	% of Households Earning						
	$10,000 -$19,999	$20,000 -$34,999	$35,000 -$49,999	$50,000 -$74,999	$75,000 -$99,000	$100,000 -$124,999	$125,000 and up
City	19.6	20.3	14.7	17.5	6.5	2.3	3.3
MSA[1]	16.5	22.1	16.8	19.8	7.9	2.6	3.0
U.S.	15.0	21.6	17.6	19.6	8.4	3.0	3.3

Note: Data as of 1/1/2000; (1) Metropolitan Statistical Area - see Appendix A for areas included
Source: Standard Rate & Data Service, Newspaper Advertising Source, March 2000

Poverty Rates by Age

Area	People of All Ages	People Under 18 Years Old	Related Children Age 5-17 in Families in Poverty
City	15.9	n/a	n/a
County	11.6	15.6	13.8
U.S.	13.8	20.8	18.7

Note: Figures show the percent of people living below the poverty line in 1995. The
average poverty threshold was $15,569 for a family of four in 1995; n/a not available
Source: Bureau of the Census, Small Area Income and Poverty Estimates Program;
U.S. Department of Housing and Urban Development

EMPLOYMENT

Labor Force and Employment

Area	Civilian Labor Force			Workers Employed		
	Dec. 1998	Dec. 1999	% Chg.	Dec. 1998	Dec. 1999	% Chg.
City	37,087	37,833	2.0	36,109	37,054	2.6
MSA[1]	94,635	96,920	2.4	92,336	94,754	2.6
U.S.	138,297,000	139,941,000	1.2	132,732,000	134,696,000	1.5

Note: Data is not seasonally adjusted and covers workers 16 years of age and older;
(1) Metropolitan Statistical Area - see Appendix A for areas included
Source: Bureau of Labor Statistics, http://stats.bls.gov

Unemployment Rate

Area	1999											
	Jan.	Feb.	Mar.	Apr.	May	Jun.	Jul.	Aug.	Sep.	Oct.	Nov.	Dec.
City	3.0	2.8	2.4	2.2	2.4	3.2	2.9	2.8	2.2	2.1	2.0	2.1
MSA[1]	3.1	2.9	2.5	2.2	2.4	3.2	3.1	2.9	2.4	2.1	2.1	2.2
U.S.	4.8	4.7	4.4	4.1	4.0	4.5	4.5	4.2	4.1	3.8	3.8	3.7

Note: Data is not seasonally adjusted and covers workers 16 years of age and older; all figures are percentages; (1) Metropolitan Statistical Area - see Appendix A for areas included
Source: Bureau of Labor Statistics, http://stats.bls.gov

Employment by Industry

Sector	MSA[1]		U.S.
	Number of Employees	Percent of Total	Percent of Total
Services	22,200	21.2	30.2
Retail Trade	19,900	19.0	18.1
Government	35,900	34.4	15.8
Manufacturing	12,100	11.6	14.1
Finance/Insurance/Real Estate	3,900	3.7	5.9
Wholesale Trade	3,300	3.2	5.4
Transportation/Public Utilities	3,500	3.3	5.3
Construction	n/a	n/a	4.8
Mining	n/a	n/a	0.4

Note: Figures cover non-farm employment as of 12/99 and are not seasonally adjusted; (1) Metropolitan Statistical Area - see Appendix A for areas included; n/a not available
Source: Bureau of Labor Statistics, http://stats.bls.gov

Employment by Occupation

Occupation Category	City (%)	MSA[1] (%)	U.S. (%)
White Collar	69.7	65.4	58.1
Executive/Admin./Management	12.0	11.3	12.3
Professional	24.3	22.2	14.1
Technical & Related Support	5.5	5.5	3.7
Sales	10.6	10.2	11.8
Administrative Support/Clerical	17.3	16.3	16.3
Blue Collar	14.8	18.4	26.2
Precision Production/Craft/Repair	5.5	7.4	11.3
Machine Operators/Assem./Insp.	3.3	4.1	6.8
Transportation/Material Movers	3.0	3.4	4.1
Cleaners/Helpers/Laborers	3.0	3.4	3.9
Services	14.5	14.0	13.2
Farming/Forestry/Fishing	1.0	2.1	2.5

Note: Figures cover workers 16 years of age and older; (1) Metropolitan Statistical Area - see Appendix A for areas included
Source: 1990 Census of Population and Housing, Summary Tape File 3C

Occupational Employment Projections: 1996 - 2006

Occupations Expected to Have the Largest Job Growth (ranked by numerical growth)	Fast-Growing Occupations[1] (ranked by percent growth)
1. General managers & top executives	1. Personal and home care aides
2. Cashiers	2. Desktop publishers
3. Salespersons, retail	3. Home health aides
4. Systems analysts	4. Physical therapy assistants and aides
5. Truck drivers, light	5. Medical assistants
6. Registered nurses	6. Physical therapists
7. Food service workers	7. Data processing equipment repairers
8. Hand packers & packagers	8. Occupational therapy assistants
9. Guards	9. Occupational therapists
10. Receptionists and information clerks	10. Human services workers

Note: Projections cover Illinois; (1) Excludes occupations with total job growth less than 300
Source: U.S. Department of Labor, Employment and Training Administration, America's Labor Market Information System (ALMIS)

Average Wages

Occupation	$/Hr.	Occupation	$/Hr.
Accountants and Auditors	18.71	Maids and Housekeepers	6.95
Assemblers and Fabricators	9.08	Maintenance Repairers	10.95
Automotive Mechanics	15.12	Marketing/Advertising/PR Managers	20.18
Bookkeepers	10.56	Nurses, Licensed Practical	11.71
Carpenters	18.85	Nurses, Registered	17.80
Cashiers	6.86	Nursing Aides/Orderlies/Attendants	7.60
Clerks, General Office	9.27	Physicians and Surgeons	55.69
Clerks, Shipping/Receiving/Traffic	12.16	Receptionists/Information Clerks	8.49
Computer Programmers	17.83	Sales Reps., Exc. Scientific/Retail	15.52
Computer Support Specialists	18.34	Sales Reps., Scientific, Exc. Retail	18.22
Cooks, Restaurant	7.54	Salespersons, Retail	8.26
Electricians	21.10	Secretaries, Except Legal/Medical	10.55
Financial Managers	24.44	Stock Clerks, Sales Floor	6.91
First-Line Supervisors/Mgrs., Sales	15.24	Systems Analysts	23.11
Food Preparation Workers	6.98	Teacher Aides	10.05
General Managers/Top Executives	24.25	Teachers, Elementary School	16.23
Guards	9.27	Teachers, Secondary School	18.80
Hand Packers	7.93	Telemarketers	8.77
Janitors and Cleaners	9.80	Truck Drivers, Heavy/Tractor-Trailer	15.21
Laborers, Landscaping	9.68	Truck Drivers, Light	10.11
Lawyers	33.19	Waiters and Waitresses	6.00

Note: Wage data is for 1998 and covers the Metropolitan Statistical Area (see Appendix A for areas included). Hourly wages for elementary and secondary school teachers were calculated by the editors from annual wage data assuming a 40 hour work week; Dashes indicate that data was not available.
Source: Bureau of Labor Statistics, 1998 Metropolitan Area Occupational Employment and Wage Estimates

TAXES

Major State and Local Tax Rates

State Corporate Income (%)	State Personal Income (%)	Residential Property (%)	Sales & Use		State Gasoline (cents/ gallon)	State Cigarette (cents/ pack)
			State (%)	Local (%)		
7.3[a]	3.0	2.60	6.25	1.0	19.3[b]	58.0[c]

Note: Personal/corporate income, sales, gasoline and cigarette tax rates as of January 2000.
Property tax rates as of April 2000; (a) Includes a 2.5% personal property replacement tax; (b) Rate is comprised of 19 cents excise and 0.3 cent motor carrier tax. Carriers pay an additional surcharge of 6.3 cents. Rate does not include a 5 cent local option tax in Chicago.; (c) Counties and cities may impose an additional tax of 10 - 15 cents per pack
Source: Federation of Tax Administrators, www.taxadmin.org; ERI's Relocation Assessor software database, quarterly effective date 4/1/2000

Total Taxes Per Capita and as a Percent of Income

Area	Per Capita Income ($)	Per Capita Taxes ($)			Percent of Income (%)		
		Total	Federal	State/Local	Total	Federal	State/Local
Illinois	32,087	11,634	8,093	3,541	36.3	25.2	11.0
U.S.	28,878	10,298	7,026	3,273	35.7	24.3	11.3

Note: Figures are for 1999
Source: Tax Foundation, www.taxfoundation.org

COMMERCIAL UTILITIES

Typical Monthly Electric Bills

Area	Commercial Service ($/month)		Industrial Service ($/month)	
	12 kW demand 1,500 kWh	100 kW demand 30,000 kWh	1,000 kW demand 400,000 kWh	20,000 kW demand 10,000,000 kWh
City	n/a	n/a	n/a	n/a
U.S.	150	2,174	23,995	508,569

Note: Based on rates in effect January 1, 1999; n/a not available
Source: Edison Electric Institute, Typical Residential, Commercial and Industrial Bills, Winter 1999

TRANSPORTATION

Transportation Statistics

Average minutes to work (1990)	13.8
Interstate highways	I-57; I-72; I-74; US-45; US-150
Bus lines	
In-city (1998)	Champaign-Urbana Mass Transit District, 68 buses
Inter-city (1999)	3
Passenger air service	
Airport	Willard Airport
Airlines (1999)	4
Enplaned passengers (1998)	139,862
Amtrak service	Yes
Motor freight carriers (1999)	37
Major waterways/ports	None

Source: FAA DOT/TSC CY1998 ACAIS Database; National Transit Database, 1998; Editor & Publisher Market Guide, 2000; Amtrak National Time Table, Fall 1999/Winter 2000; 1990 Census of Population and Housing, STF 3C; Jane's Urban Transport Systems 1999-2000

Means of Transportation to Work

Area	Car/Truck/Van		Public Transportation			Bicycle	Walked	Other Means	Worked at Home
	Drove Alone	Car-pooled	Bus	Subway	Railroad				
City	62.5	10.2	6.1	0.0	0.0	2.1	15.2	0.7	3.1
MSA[1]	66.4	11.7	4.4	0.0	0.0	1.8	11.4	0.8	3.4
U.S.	73.2	13.4	3.0	1.5	0.5	0.4	3.9	1.2	3.0

Note: Figures shown are percentages and only include workers 16 years of age and older;
(1) Metropolitan Statistical Area - see Appendix A for areas included
Source: 1990 Census of Population and Housing, Summary Tape File 3C

BUSINESSES

Major Business Headquarters

Company Name	1999 Rankings	
	Fortune 500	Forbes 500
No companies listed	-	-

Note: Companies listed are located in the city; dashes indicate no ranking
Fortune 500: Companies that produce a 10-K are ranked 1 to 500 based on 1999 revenue
Forbes 500: Private companies are ranked 1 to 500 based on 1998 revenue
Source: Forbes, December 13, 1999; Fortune, April 17, 2000

HOTELS & MOTELS

Hotels/Motels

Area	Hotels/ Motels	Rooms	Luxury-Level Hotels/Motels		Average Minimum Rates ($)		
			♦♦♦♦	♦♦♦♦♦	♦♦	♦♦♦	♦♦♦♦
City	11	1,348	0	0	n/a	n/a	n/a
Suburbs	1	167	0	0	n/a	n/a	n/a
Total	12	1,515	0	0	n/a	n/a	n/a

Note: n/a not available; classifications range from one diamond (budget properties with basic amenities) to five diamond (luxury properties).
Source: OAG Business Travel Planner, Winter 1999-2000

Estimated Daily Food and Lodging Costs

Area	Food/Other ($/day)	Average Hotel Cost ($/day)
City	34	56
U.S.	30	55

Source: ERI's Relocation Assessor software database, quarterly effective date 4/1/2000

CONVENTION CENTERS

Convention Centers and Event Sites

Name	Guest Rooms	Meeting Space (sq. ft.)	Capacity (Theatre Style)
Assembly Hall	n/a	n/a	78,000
Chancellor Hotel & Convention Center	n/a	n/a	0
Radisson Suite Hotel	199	8,179	500

Note: n/a not available
Source: EventSource.com, 3/15/2000

Living Environment

COST OF LIVING

Cost of Living: Homeowner

Cost Element	U.S. ($)	City ($)	Differential ($)	Percent of U.S. Average
Consumables	14,516	14,721	205	101.4
Transportation	5,957	6,188	231	103.9
Health Services	2,012	2,070	58	102.9
Housing/Utilities/Prop. Tax	16,337	24,786	8,449	151.7
Income+Payroll Taxes	12,615	10,966	-1,649	86.9
Miscellaneous	8,563	8,563	0	100.0
Total Cost of Living	60,000	67,294	7,294	112.2

Note: Figures are based on a single income, four person family with gross annual earnings of $60,000, owning an 1,800 square-foot home, and driving two automobiles worth $22,000 30,000 miles per year.
Source: ERI's Relocation Assessor software database, quarterly effective date 4/1/2000

Cost of Living: Renter

Cost Element	U.S. ($)	City ($)	Differential ($)	Percent of U.S. Average
Consumables	10,486	10,586	100	101.0
Transportation	2,107	2,179	72	103.4
Health Services	1,632	1,672	40	102.5
Rent/Utilities/Insurance	9,299	9,309	10	100.1
Income+Payroll Taxes	8,607	8,303	-304	96.5
Miscellaneous	7,869	7,869	0	100.0
Total Cost of Living	40,000	39,918	-82	99.8

Note: Figures are based on a single income, three person family with gross annual earnings of $40,000, renting a 1,000 square-foot home, and driving one automobile worth $8,000 12,000 miles per year.
Source: ERI's Relocation Assessor software database, quarterly effective date 4/1/2000

HOUSING

Median Home Prices and Housing Affordability

Area	Median Price[2] 4th Qtr. 1999 ($)	HOI[3] 4th Qtr. 1999	Affordability Rank[4]
MSA[1]	93,000	78.8	32
U.S.	139,000	63.8	–

Note: (1) Metropolitan Statistical Area - see Appendix A for areas included; (2) U.S. figures calculated from the sales of 687,516 new and existing homes in 192 markets; (3) Housing Opportunity Index - percent of homes sold that were within the reach of the median income household at the prevailing mortgage interest rate; (4) Rank is from 1-192 with 1 being most affordable
Source: National Association of Home Builders, Housing Opportunity Index, 4th Quarter 1999

Estimated Home Price

Area	Price ($)
City	193,729
U.S.	135,855

Note: Figures are based on an 1,800 square-foot home
Source: ERI's Relocation Assessor software database, quarterly effective date 4/1/2000

Estimated Rent

Area	Rent ($/month)
City	638
U.S.	651

Note: Figures are based on a 1,000 square-foot home
Source: ERI's Relocation Assessor software database, quarterly effective date 4/1/2000

Median Home Price Projection

It is projected that the median home price in the metropolitan area will increase from $90,776 in 1999 to $124,224 in 2010, an increase of 36.8%
Kiplinger's Personal Finance Magazine, January 2000

RESIDENTIAL UTILITIES

Average Residential Utility Costs

Area	All Electric ($/mth)	Part Electric ($/mth)	Other Energy ($/mth)	Phone ($/mth)
City	–	58.82	37.44	21.06
U.S.	99.25	55.47	43.48	20.29

Source: ACCRA, Cost of Living Index, 3rd Quarter 1999

HEALTH CARE

Average Health Care Costs

Area	Hospital ($/day)	Doctor ($/visit)	Dentist ($/visit)
City	516.00	46.95	63.67
U.S.	440.96	53.83	68.42

Note: Hospital—based on a semi-private room; Doctor—based on a general practitioner's routine exam of an established patient; Dentist—based on adult teeth cleaning and periodic oral exam.
Source: ACCRA, Cost of Living Index, 3rd Quarter 1999

Distribution of Office-Based Physicians

Area	Family/Gen. Practitioners	Specialists		
		Medical	Surgical	Other
MSA[1]	46	127	84	102

Note: Data as of 12/31/97; (1) Metropolitan Statistical Area - see Appendix A for areas included
Source: American Medical Assn., Physician Characteristics & Distribution in the U.S., 1999

Hospitals

Champaign has general medical and surgical hospitals, 1 rehabilitation.
AHA Guide to the Healthcare Field, 1999-2000

EDUCATION

Public School District Statistics

District Name	Num. Sch.	Enroll.	Classroom Teachers	Pupils per Teacher	Minority Pupils (%)	Current Exp.[1] ($/pupil)
Champaign Comm. USD 4	17	10,744	621	17.3	n/a	n/a

Note: Data covers the 1997-1998 school year unless otherwise noted; (1) Data covers fiscal year 1996; SD = School District; ISD = Independent School District; n/a not available
Source: National Center for Education Statistics, Common Core of Data Public Education Agency Universe 1997-98; National Center for Education Statistics, Characteristics of the 100 Largest Public Elementary and Secondary School Districts in the United States: 1997-98, July 1999

Educational Quality

School District	Education Quotient[1]	Graduate Outcome[2]	Community Index[3]	Resource Index[4]
Champaign Comm. USD 4	130	143	103	109

Note: Over 1,000 secondary school districts were rated in terms of educational quality. The scores range from a low of 50 to a high of 150; (1) Combination of the Graduate Outcome, Community and Resource indexes weighted to reflect the greater importance of the Graduate Outcome and Resource Index; (2) Based on graduation rates and college board scores (SAT/ACT); (3) Based on the surrounding community's level of affluence and adult education; (4) Based on teacher salaries, per-pupil expenditures and student-teacher ratios.
Source: Expansion Management, Ratings Issue, 1999

Educational Attainment by Race

Area	High School Graduate (%)					Bachelor's Degree (%)				
	Total	White	Black	Other	Hisp.[2]	Total	White	Black	Other	Hisp.[2]
City	88.2	91.3	67.5	91.3	96.2	40.0	43.0	11.5	72.1	71.8
MSA[1]	87.5	88.5	73.5	92.7	91.5	34.1	33.8	14.3	71.4	45.5
U.S.	75.2	77.9	63.1	60.4	49.8	20.3	21.5	11.4	19.4	9.2

Note: Figures shown cover persons 25 years old and over; (1) Metropolitan Statistical Area -
see Appendix A for areas included; (2) people of Hispanic origin can be of any race
Source: 1990 Census of Population and Housing, Summary Tape File 3C

School Enrollment by Type

Area	Preprimary				Elementary/High School			
	Public		Private		Public		Private	
	Enrollment	%	Enrollment	%	Enrollment	%	Enrollment	%
City	611	58.4	435	41.6	6,388	90.6	663	9.4
MSA[1]	2,138	66.1	1,095	33.9	21,523	93.4	1,520	6.6
U.S.	2,679,029	59.5	1,824,256	40.5	38,379,689	90.2	4,187,099	9.8

Note: Figures shown cover persons 3 years old and over;
(1) Metropolitan Statistical Area - see Appendix A for areas included
Source: 1990 Census of Population and Housing, Summary Tape File 3C

School Enrollment by Race

Area	Preprimary (%)				Elementary/High School (%)			
	White	Black	Other	Hisp.[1]	White	Black	Other	Hisp.[1]
City	81.6	16.2	2.2	0.0	68.8	28.7	2.5	0.5
MSA[2]	86.0	9.4	4.6	1.0	80.4	15.9	3.7	1.3
U.S.	80.4	12.5	7.1	7.8	74.1	15.6	10.3	12.5

Note: Figures shown cover persons 3 years old and over; (1) people of Hispanic origin can be of any
race; (2) Metropolitan Statistical Area - see Appendix A for areas included
Source: 1990 Census of Population and Housing, Summary Tape File 3C

Higher Education

Two-Year Colleges		Four-Year Colleges		Medical Schools	Law Schools	Voc/ Tech
Public	Private	Public	Private			
1	0	1	0	0	1	2

Source: College Blue Book, Occupational Education, 1999; Medical School Admission Requirements,
1999-2000; Peterson's Guide to Two-Year Colleges, 2000; Peterson's Guide to Four-Year Colleges,
1999; Barron's Guide to Law Schools, 1999

MAJOR EMPLOYERS

Major Employers

Central Illinois Bank	Champaign National Bank
Champaign News Gazette	Communications Data Group
Great Planes Model Distributors	Myers Management Corp.
Northern Illinois Water Corp.	Regency Associates (real estate)

Note: Companies listed are located in the city
Source: D&B Business Rankings, 1999; Ward's Business Directory, 1999; America's Corporate
Families, 1999

PUBLIC SAFETY

Crime Rate

Area	All Crimes	Violent Crimes				Property Crimes		
		Murder	Forcible Rape	Robbery	Aggrav. Assault	Burglary	Larceny -Theft	Motor Vehicle Theft
City	n/a	n/a	n/a	n/a	n/a	n/a	n/a	n/a
Suburbs[1]	n/a	n/a	n/a	n/a	n/a	n/a	n/a	n/a
MSA[2]	n/a	n/a	n/a	n/a	n/a	n/a	n/a	n/a
U.S.	4,615.5	6.3	34.4	165.2	360.5	862.0	2,728.1	459.0

Note: Crime rate is the number of crimes per 100,000 population; (1) Defined as all areas within the Metropolitan Statistical Area but located outside the central city; (2) Metropolitan Statistical Area - see Appendix A for areas included; n/a not available
Source: FBI Uniform Crime Reports, 1998

RECREATION

Culture and Recreation

Museums	Symphony Orchestras	Opera Companies	Dance Companies	Professional Theatres	Zoos	Pro Sports Teams
2	1	0	0	0	0	0

Source: Musical America, International Directory of the Performing Arts, 1999; Official Museum Directory, 2000; Stern's Performing Arts Directory, 1997; USA Today Four Sport Stadium Guide, 1997; Career Opportunities in Theatre and the Performing Arts, 1999

Library System

The Champaign Public Library has one branchand a budget of $2,982,725 (1997-1998).
American Library Directory, 1999-2000

MEDIA

Newspapers

Name	Type	Freq.	Distribution	Circulation
The Daily Illini	n/a	5x/wk	Camp/Comm	20,000
The News-Gazette	General	7x/wk	Area	46,010

Note: Includes newspapers with circulations of 200 or more located in the city; n/a not available
Source: Burrelle's Media Directory, 1999 Edition

Television Stations

Name	Ch.	Affiliation	Type	Owner
WCIA	n/a	CBST	Commercial	August Meyer, Jr.
WILL	12	PBS	Public	Board of Trustees/University of Illinois
WICD	15	NBCT	Commercial	Gannett Broadcasting
WCCU	27	FBC	Commercial	Bahakel Communications Inc.
WCFN	49	CBST	Commercial	August Meyer, Jr.

Note: Stations included broadcast in the Champaign metro area; n/a not available
Source: Burrelle's Media Directory, 1999 Edition

AM Radio Stations

Call Letters	Freq. (kHz)	Target Audience	Station Format	Music Format
WILL	580	General	M/N/T	Classical
WDWS	1400	General	N/S/T	n/a
WJCI	1460	Religious	M/T	Christian
WBCP	1580	Black	M	Adult Contemporary/Blues/Gospel/Jazz/Urban Contemporary

Note: Stations included broadcast in the Champaign metro area; n/a not available
Target Audience: A=Asian; B=Black; C=Christian; E=Ethnic; F=French; G=General; H=Hispanic; M=Men; N=Native American; R=Religious; S=Senior Citizen; W=Women; Y=Young Adult; Z=Children
Station Format: E=Educational; M=Music; N=News; S=Sports; T=Talk
Source: Burrelle's Media Directory, 1999 Edition

FM Radio Stations

Call Letters	Freq. (mHz)	Target Audience	Station Format	Music Format
WPCD	88.7	General	M/N/S	AOR/Classic Rock/Urban Contemporary
WEFT	90.1	General	M	Adult Contemporary/Christian/Classic Rock
WILL	90.9	General	M	Classical
WBGL	91.7	General	M	Christian
WKIO	92.5	General	M	Oldies
WEBX	93.5	General	M	Alternative/AOR
WLRW	94.5	General	M/N/T	Adult Contemporary/Adult Top 40
WZNF	95.3	General	M	AOR
WQQB	96.1	General	M/N/S	n/a
WHMS	97.5	General	M	Adult Contemporary
WIXY	100.3	General	M/N/T	Country
WGNN	102.5	G/R	E/M	Christian/Classical/Easy Listening/Gospel
WGKC	105.9	General	M	Classic Rock
WPGU	107.1	General	M	Alternative

Note: Stations included broadcast in the Champaign metro area; n/a not available
Station Format: E=Educational; M=Music; N=News; S=Sports; T=Talk
Target Audience: A=Asian; B=Black; C=Christian; E=Ethnic; F=French; G=General; H=Hispanic; M=Men; N=Native American; R=Religious; S=Senior Citizen; W=Women; Y=Young Adult; Z=Children
Music Format: AOR=Album Oriented Rock; MOR=Middle-of-the-Road
Source: Burrelle's Media Directory, 1999 Edition

WEATHER

Temperature/Precipitation/Humidity

	Jan	Feb	Mar	Apr	May	Jun	Jul	Aug	Sep	Oct	Nov	Dec	Yr.
Max. High Temp. (°F)	70	70	85	91	97	103	109	101	101	93	80	70	109
Avg. High Temp. (°F)	35	38	49	62	72	82	86	84	78	66	50	38	62
Avg. Temp. (°F)	27	30	40	51	61	71	75	73	67	55	41	30	52
Avg. Low Temp. (°F)	19	22	31	41	51	61	65	63	56	45	33	23	43
Min. Low Temp. (°F)	-22	-25	-5	19	26	37	41	39	29	13	-5	-20	-25
Avg. Precip. (in.)	2.2	1.9	3.2	3.7	4.1	4.0	3.3	3.3	3.2	2.8	2.4	2.1	36.2
Avg. Snowfall (in.)	4.1	5.1	4.2	0.9	0	0	0	0	0	0	3.4	6.0	23.7
Avg. Rel. Hum. (%)	81	80	75	70	67	68	70	73	67	68	75	80	73

Source: National Climatic Data Center, International Station Meteorological Climate Summary, 3/95

Weather Conditions

Temperature			Precipitation		
0°F & below	32°F & below	90°F & above	0.1 inch or more precip.	1.5 inch or more snow/ice	Thunder-storms
6	120	30	67	6	47

Note: Figures are average number of days per year
Source: National Climatic Data Center, International Station Meteorological Climate Summary, 3/95

AIR & WATER QUALITY

Maximum Pollutant Concentrations

	Particulate Matter (ug/m³)	Carbon Monoxide (ppm)	Sulfur Dioxide (ppm)	Nitrogen Dioxide (ppm)	Ozone (ppm)	Lead (ug/m³)
MSA[1] Level	44	n/a	0.018	n/a	0.09	n/a
NAAQS[2]	150	9	0.140	0.053	0.12	1.50
Met NAAQS	Yes	n/a	Yes	n/a	Yes	n/a

Note: (1) Metropolitan Statistical Area - see Appendix A for areas included; (2) National Ambient Air Quality Standards; ppm = parts per million; ug/m³ = micrograms per cubic meter; n/a not available
Source: EPA, National Air Quality and Emissions Trends Report, 1997

Pollutant Standards Index

Data not available.
EPA, National Air Quality and Emissions Trends Report, 1997

Drinking Water

Water System Name	Pop. Served	Primary Water Source Type	Number of Violations in 1998-99	Type of Violation/ Contaminants
Northern Illinois Water Corp.	110,801	Ground	None	None

Note: Data as of January 19, 2000
Source: EPA, Office of Ground Water and Drinking Water, Safe Drinking Water Information System

Champaign tap water is alkaline, softened, fluoridated and chlorinated.
Editor & Publisher Market Guide, 2000

Chapel Hill, North Carolina

Background

Chapel Hill, North Carolina is located in the north central section of the state, in a region of rolling terrain known as the Piedmont, near Durham and approximately 20 miles from Raleigh. These three communities are known as the Triangle, an area that has experienced rapid growth in educational activity, R&D and technology industries.

Chapel Hill is primarily in Orange County, but a portion lies within neighboing Durham County. The community also encompasses the adjacent town of Carrboro.

The University of North Carolina, opened in Chapel Hill in 1795 and is the nation's oldest public university. The school continues to be the primary focus of Chapel Hill, and a large percentage of city residents are students and staff of the University.

Several Native American tribes lived in the region, including the Occaneechi, prior to European colonization. While North Carolina was among the early areas to be colonized by the British, actual settlement of Chapel Hill coincided with the establishment of the University of North Carolina. Chapel Hill was incorporated as a town in 1819 and is named after the New Hope chapel, which was on the hill at the original crossroads where Chapel Hill is situated.

While its economy has always been oriented to the University, the regional economy of Chapel Hill is also based on textiles and other industries, and agriculture, including tobacco and food products. Neighboring Carrboro was a rail stop for Chapel Hill, and it also contained textile mills.

Although the University of North Carolina remained open during the Civil War, the conflict and the Reconstruction period led to a difficult period for the school and the town. The University was closed from 1870 to 1875.

In 1920, the New York architectural firm of McKim, Mead, and White developed a master plan for the UNC campus, and extensive construction was undertaken in the 1930s. The University experienced a period of significant growth in the latter 20th Century, with the student enrollment increasing from just under 8,800 in 1960 to over 24,000 in 1997. This campus expansion also brought significant growth to Chapel Hill, as did the 1959 opening of Research Triangle, a collaborative campus for academic, government and industrial R&D, which is located between the three communities.

Chapel Hill retains many of the historic features and characteristics of its origins as a small college community, while reflecting the burgeoning growth of the University and the area's economy. Chapel Hill and the Triangle region frequently receive high rankings for quality of life and economic opportunity. While there are still many rural regions nearby, the rapid rate of growth has raised concerns over issues such as congestion and traffic throughout the region.

Chapel Hill is known as a cosmopolitan community, and its residents have access to a wide variety of services and cultural and recreational activities. In addition to the University of North Carolina, there are 16 other colleges and universities in the area. Chapel Hill is also a short drive to the larger city of Durham, which is home to Duke University. The area's recreational amenities include parks, lakes and an extensive network of bicycle paths in Carrboro.

Chapel Hill has a Council-Manager form of government, with an elected Mayor and eight-member City Council, and an appointed Town Manager.

General Rankings and Evaluative Comments

- Chapel Hill was ranked #6 out of 354 metropolitan areas in *Places Rated Almanac*. Criteria: cost of living, climate, crime, transportation, job outlook, education, the arts, health care, and recreation. *Places Rated Almanac, Millennium Edition, 2000*

- Chapel Hill was selected as one of America's best small art towns. The city was ranked #42 out of 100. Criteria: easy and affordable access to the visual arts, performing arts and music, strong sense of community, low crime rate, and full-time population less than 65,000. *The 100 Best Small Art Towns in America: Discover Creative Communities, Fresh Air, and Affordable Living, 1998*

- Chapel Hill was selected as one of America's best places to retire. Criteria: safety, climate, housing, culture and recreation, social compatibility, affordability, medical care, transportation, and jobs and/or volunteer opportunities. *Where to Retire: America's Best and Most Affordable Places, 1998*

- Chapel Hill was selected as one of the best places to retire by *Retirement Places Rated*. Criteria: cost of living, climate, crime, services, working, and leisure living. The city was ranked #71 out of 187. *Retirement Places Rated, 1999*

- Chapel Hill was selected by *Yahoo! Internet Life* as one of "America's Most Wired Cities & Towns." The city ranked #18 out of 50. Criteria: home and work net use, domain density, hosts per capita, directory density, and content quality. *Yahoo! Internet Life, March 1999*

- Cognetics studied 273 metro areas in the United States, ranking them by entrepreneurial activity. Chapel Hill was ranked #4 out of the 50 largest metro areas. Criteria: Significant Starts (firms started in the last 10 years that still employ at least 5 people) and Young Growers (percent of firms 10 years old or less that grew significantly during the last 4 years). *Cognetics, "Entrepreneurial Hot Spots: The Best Places in America to Start and Grow a Company," 1999*

- Chapel Hill was included among *Entrepreneur* magazine's listing of the "20 Best Cities for Small Business." It was ranked #3 among large metro areas and #2 among southern metro areas. Criteria: entrepreneurial activity, small-business growth, economic growth, and risk of failure. *Entrepreneur, October 1999*

- Chapel Hill appeared on *Sales & Marketing Management's* list of the "20 Hottest Cities for Selling." The city ranked #9,999 out of 20. *S&MM* editors looked at Metropolitan Statistical Areas with populations of more than 150,000. The areas were ranked based on population increases, retail sales increases, effective buying income, increase in both residential and commercial building permits issued, unemployment rates, job growth, mix of industries, tax rates, number of corporate relocations, and the number of new corporations. *Sales & Marketing Management, April 1999*

- Reliastar Financial Corporation ranked the 125 largest metropolitan areas according to the general financial security of residents. Chapel Hill was ranked #14 out of 125 with a score of 12.8 (the percentage a metropolitan area is above or below the metropolitan norm; a metro area with a score of 10.6 is 10.6% above the metro average). Criteria: Earnings and Wealth Potential (household income, education, net assets, cost of living); Safety Net (health insurance, retirement savings, life insurance, income support programs); Personal Threats (unemployment rate, low-income households, crime rate); Community Economic Vitality (cost of community services, job quality, job creation, housing costs). *Reliastar Financial Corporation, "The Best Cities to Earn and Save Money: A Ranking of the Largest 125 U.S. Cities," 2000 Edition*

- The Raleigh/Durham/Chapel Hill area was selected as one of "The 50 Most Alive Places to Live" in the U.S. Criteria: ethnic diversity, recreational options, cultural vitality, low crime rate, opportunities for lifelong learning, good hospitals and restaurants, public transportation, walking accessibility, civic activities, and the kitsch factor. The area was ranked #4 out of 10 in the "Big Cities" category. *Modern Maturity, May-June 2000*

Business Environment

STATE ECONOMY

State Economic Profile

"In spite of declines in textiles and apparels, North Carolina has seen impressive job growth in the last few years. As North Carolina continues to diversify its economy away from its traditional manufacturing base and toward its newer high-tech and financial services sectors, job growth will outpace the nation for a number of years to come, albeit at a slightly slower rate than those seen in 1997 and 1998.

Raleigh-Durham has been and will continue to be one of North Carolina's growth engines. High-tech firms in the Research Triangle Park have expanded employment considerably. Cisco Systems, for one, is planning to expand its operations, adding as many as 4,000 jobs over the next three years. Raleigh's housing market has more than doubled in size during the 1990s. Price appreciation has been strong, although homes still remain affordable.

North Carolina's other hot spot has been Charlotte. While many parts of the country have been hurt by consolidation in the financial services industry, many of these jobs have made their way to Charlotte. As this wave of consolidation has slowed, so has job growth in Charlotte, reflected in its 0.6% job growth rate in 1998, far below that of previous years. Continued restructuring in North Carolina's textiles, apparel and furniture industries will slow job growth in the Charlotte area.

The outlook for North Carolina, while a slowdown from its recent pace, is still one of impressive job growth, far outpacing the nation. With its business friendly atmosphere and the decision of Federal Express to locate its Mid-Atlantic hub here, North Carolina will likely attract more corporate relocations. Its affordable housing markets and overall high quality of life will also attract residents, helping fuel job growth." *National Association of Realtors, Economic Profiles: The Fifty States and the District of Columbia, http://nar.realtor.com/databank/profiles.htm*

EXPORTS

Total Export Sales

Area	1995 ($000)	1996 ($000)	1997 ($000)	1998 ($000)	% Chg. 1995-98	% Chg. 1997-98
MSA[1]	2,093,206	2,609,828	2,713,071	2,665,615	27.3	-1.7
U.S.	583,030,524	622,827,063	687,597,999	680,474,251	16.7	-1.0

Note: (1) Metropolitan Statistical Area - see Appendix A for areas included
Source: U.S. Department of Commerce, International Trade Association, Metropolitan Area Exports: An Export Performance Report on Over 250 U.S. Cities, November 10, 1999

CITY FINANCES

City Government Finances

Component	1995 ($million)	1995 (per capita $)
Revenue	19.6	419
Expenditure	8.9	191
Debt Outstanding	8.8	188

Source: 1999 County and City Extra, Annual Metro, City, and County Data Book

City Government Revenue by Source

Source	1995 ($million)	1995 (per capita $)
Intergovernmental	3.4	72
Taxes	13.8	296
Property	12.4	266
Sales and Gross Receipts	0.6	13

Source: 1999 County and City Extra, Annual Metro, City, and County Data Book

City Government Expenditures by Function

Function	1995 ($million)	1995 (per capita $)	1995 (%)
Public Welfare	0.0	0	0.0
Highways	1.3	29	15.3
Parking Facilities	0.0	0	0.0
Education	0.0	0	0.0
Health and Hospitals	<0.1	<1	0.1
Police Protection	2.5	53	28.2
Sewerage and Sanitation	1.1	23	12.5
Parks and Recreation	0.5	12	6.6
Housing and Community Development	0.1	2	1.4
Interest on Debt	0.0	0	0.0

Source: 1999 County and City Extra, Annual Metro, City, and County Data Book

Municipal Bond Ratings

Area	Moody's
City	Aaa

Source: Mergent Bond Record, 2/2000

POPULATION

Population Growth

Area	1980 Census	1990 Census	1999 Estimate	2004 Projection	Population Growth (%) 1990-1999	Population Growth (%) 1999-2004
City	32,461	38,762	45,007	47,036	16.1	4.5
MSA[1]	561,222	735,480	1,101,410	1,203,155	49.8	9.2
U.S.	226,545,805	248,765,170	272,212,864	283,625,312	9.4	4.2

Note: (1) Metropolitan Statistical Area - see Appendix A for areas included
Source: 1990 Census of Population and Housing, Summary Tape File 3C; Claritas, Inc.

Number of Households and Average Household Size

Area	1980 Census	1990 Census	1999 Estimate	2004 Projection	1999 Average Household Size
City	10,593	13,864	16,515	17,377	2.73
MSA[1]	236,385	287,835	433,147	475,321	2.54
U.S.	80,389,592	91,993,582	102,048,200	107,302,392	2.67

Note: (1) Metropolitan Statistical Area - see Appendix A for areas included
Source: 1990 Census of Population and Housing, Summary Tape File 3C; Claritas, Inc.

Race/Ethnicity of City Population

Race/Ethnicity	1990 Census Population	1990 Census %	1999 Estimate Population	1999 Estimate %	% Change 1990-1999
White, Non-Hispanic	31,500	81.3	34,201	76.0	8.6
Black, Non-Hispanic	4,847	12.5	5,805	12.9	19.8
Asian, Non-Hispanic	1,677	4.3	3,207	7.1	91.2
Other, Non-Hispanic	165	0.4	200	0.4	21.2
Hispanic	573	1.5	1,594	3.5	178.2

Source: 1990 Census of Population and Housing, Summary Tape File 3C; Claritas, Inc.

Race/Ethnicity of Metropolitan Statistical Area Population

Race/Ethnicity	1990 Census		1999 Estimate		% Change 1990-1999
	Population	%	Population	%	
White, Non-Hispanic	528,598	71.9	779,653	70.8	47.5
Black, Non-Hispanic	182,435	24.8	261,019	23.7	43.1
Asian, Non-Hispanic	13,877	1.9	28,913	2.6	108.4
Other, Non-Hispanic	2,184	0.3	3,681	0.3	68.5
Hispanic	8,386	1.1	28,144	2.6	235.6

Note: See Appendix A for areas included in the Metropolitan Statistical Area
Source: 1990 Census of Population and Housing, Summary Tape File 3C; Claritas, Inc.

Ancestry

Area	German	Irish	English	Italian	U.S.	French	Polish	Dutch
City	21.9	13.5	23.2	3.7	1.9	3.3	2.3	2.1
MSA[1]	16.3	12.4	19.0	2.6	7.5	2.8	1.7	1.5
U.S.	23.3	15.6	13.1	5.9	5.3	4.2	3.8	2.5

Note: Figures are percentages and include persons that reported multiple ancestry (eg. if a person reported being Irish and Italian, they were included in both columns); (1) Metropolitan Statistical Area - see Appendix A for areas included
Source: 1990 Census of Population and Housing, Summary Tape File 3C

Median Age

Area	1990 Census	1999 Estimate
City	24.9	29.3
MSA[1]	31.2	34.9
U.S.	32.9	35.7

Note: (1) Metropolitan Statistical Area - see Appendix A for areas included
Source: 1990 Census of Population and Housing, Summary Tape File 3C; Claritas, Inc.

Male/Female Population

Area	Number of Males		Number of Females		Males per 100 Females	
	1990	1999	1990	1999	1990	1999
City	17,609	20,723	21,153	24,284	83.2	85.3
MSA[1]	354,235	532,997	381,245	568,413	92.9	93.8
U.S.	121,172,379	132,803,736	127,537,494	139,409,136	95.0	95.3

Note: (1) Metropolitan Statistical Area - see Appendix A for areas included
Source: 1990 Census of Population, General Population Characteristics; Claritas, Inc.

INCOME

Per Capita/Median/Average Income

Area	Per Capita ($)			Median Household ($)			Average Household ($)		
	1989	1999	% Chg.	1989	1999	% Chg.	1989	1999	% Chg.
City	16,288	26,683	63.8	30,489	46,973	54.1	43,781	71,963	64.4
MSA[1]	16,170	24,164	49.4	33,290	46,080	38.4	40,685	60,772	49.4
U.S.	14,420	21,350	48.1	30,056	40,525	34.8	38,453	56,184	46.1

Note: (1) Metropolitan Statistical Area - see Appendix A for areas included; 1989 data is from the 1990 Census; 1999 data is estimated by Claritas, Inc.
Source: 1990 Census of Population, General Population Characteristics; Claritas, Inc.

Household Income Distribution

Area	Percent of Households Earning								
	Under $5,000	$5,000 -14,999	$15,000 -24,999	$25,000 -34,999	$35,000 -49,999	$50,000 -74,999	$75,000 -99,000	$100,000 -149,999	$150,000 and up
City	3.9	10.9	11.7	11.6	14.1	16.4	9.6	9.8	12.0
MSA[1]	3.6	10.5	11.9	11.8	16.0	21.0	11.7	8.3	5.3
U.S.	3.9	13.3	13.8	12.6	16.2	19.4	9.7	6.6	4.6

Note: Data as of 1999; (1) Metropolitan Statistical Area - see Appendix A for areas included
Source: Claritas, Inc.

Effective Buying Income

Area	Per Capita ($)	Median Household ($)	Average Household ($)
City	19,302	36,465	52,556
MSA[1]	19,806	40,513	49,475
U.S.	17,496	36,603	47,036

Note: Data as of 1/1/2000; (1) Metropolitan Statistical Area - see Appendix A for areas included
Source: Standard Rate & Data Service, Newspaper Advertising Source, March 2000

Effective Household Buying Income Distribution

Area	% of Households Earning						
	$10,000 -$19,999	$20,000 -$34,999	$35,000 -$49,999	$50,000 -$74,999	$75,000 -$99,000	$100,000 -$124,999	$125,000 and up
City	14.5	21.2	14.7	15.5	9.8	5.2	6.7
MSA[1]	12.7	20.7	17.9	22.2	10.0	3.6	3.4
U.S.	15.0	21.6	17.6	19.6	8.4	3.0	3.3

Note: Data as of 1/1/2000; (1) Metropolitan Statistical Area - see Appendix A for areas included
Source: Standard Rate & Data Service, Newspaper Advertising Source, March 2000

Poverty Rates by Age

Area	People of All Ages	People Under 18 Years Old	Related Children Age 5-17 in Families in Poverty
City	10.5	n/a	n/a
County	10.4	12.7	12.0
U.S.	13.8	20.8	18.7

Note: Figures show the percent of people living below the poverty line in 1995. The average poverty threshold was $15,569 for a family of four in 1995; n/a not available
Source: Bureau of the Census, Small Area Income and Poverty Estimates Program; U.S. Department of Housing and Urban Development

EMPLOYMENT

Labor Force and Employment

Area	Civilian Labor Force			Workers Employed		
	Dec. 1998	Dec. 1999	% Chg.	Dec. 1998	Dec. 1999	% Chg.
City	24,696	24,939	1.0	24,468	24,675	0.8
MSA[1]	638,967	644,865	0.9	630,924	636,249	0.8
U.S.	138,297,000	139,941,000	1.2	132,732,000	134,696,000	1.5

Note: Data is not seasonally adjusted and covers workers 16 years of age and older;
(1) Metropolitan Statistical Area - see Appendix A for areas included
Source: Bureau of Labor Statistics, http://stats.bls.gov

Unemployment Rate

Area	1999											
	Jan.	Feb.	Mar.	Apr.	May	Jun.	Jul.	Aug.	Sep.	Oct.	Nov.	Dec.
City	1.1	1.1	1.3	0.9	1.3	1.4	1.5	1.5	1.1	1.3	1.2	1.1
MSA[1]	1.6	1.6	1.5	1.3	1.5	1.5	1.6	1.7	1.4	1.5	1.5	1.3
U.S.	4.8	4.7	4.4	4.1	4.0	4.5	4.5	4.2	4.1	3.8	3.8	3.7

Note: Data is not seasonally adjusted and covers workers 16 years of age and older; all figures are percentages; (1) Metropolitan Statistical Area - see Appendix A for areas included
Source: Bureau of Labor Statistics, http://stats.bls.gov

Employment by Industry

Sector	MSA[1]		U.S.
	Number of Employees	Percent of Total	Percent of Total
Services	219,700	32.3	30.2
Retail Trade	113,100	16.6	18.1
Government	127,300	18.7	15.8
Manufacturing	84,100	12.4	14.1
Finance/Insurance/Real Estate	32,000	4.7	5.9
Wholesale Trade	32,400	4.8	5.4
Transportation/Public Utilities	30,300	4.5	5.3
Construction	n/a	n/a	4.8
Mining	n/a	n/a	0.4

Note: Figures cover non-farm employment as of 12/99 and are not seasonally adjusted;
(1) Metropolitan Statistical Area - see Appendix A for areas included; n/a not available
Source: Bureau of Labor Statistics, http://stats.bls.gov

Employment by Occupation

Occupation Category	City (%)	MSA[1] (%)	U.S. (%)
White Collar	80.7	68.9	58.1
Executive/Admin./Management	12.1	14.3	12.3
Professional	34.1	19.3	14.1
Technical & Related Support	8.7	6.5	3.7
Sales	10.5	11.8	11.8
Administrative Support/Clerical	15.3	16.9	16.3
Blue Collar	6.7	18.5	26.2
Precision Production/Craft/Repair	3.1	9.1	11.3
Machine Operators/Assem./Insp.	1.3	4.3	6.8
Transportation/Material Movers	1.1	2.5	4.1
Cleaners/Helpers/Laborers	1.2	2.6	3.9
Services	11.7	11.1	13.2
Farming/Forestry/Fishing	0.9	1.4	2.5

Note: Figures cover workers 16 years of age and older;
(1) Metropolitan Statistical Area - see Appendix A for areas included
Source: 1990 Census of Population and Housing, Summary Tape File 3C

Occupational Employment Projections: 1996 - 2006

Occupations Expected to Have the Largest Job Growth (ranked by numerical growth)	Fast-Growing Occupations[1] (ranked by percent growth)
1. Cashiers	1. Occupational therapy assistants
2. Registered nurses	2. Computer engineers
3. General managers & top executives	3. Database administrators
4. Nursing aides/orderlies/attendants	4. Systems analysts
5. Salespersons, retail	5. Physical therapy assistants and aides
6. Child care workers, private household	6. Physical therapists
7. Food service workers	7. Occupational therapists
8. Marketing & sales, supervisors	8. Home health aides
9. Janitors/cleaners/maids, ex. priv. hshld.	9. Desktop publishers
10. Truck drivers, light	10. Respiratory therapists

Note: Projections cover North Carolina; (1) Excludes occupations with total job growth less than 300
Source: U.S. Department of Labor, Employment and Training Administration, America's Labor Market Information System (ALMIS)

Average Wages

Occupation	$/Hr.	Occupation	$/Hr.
Accountants and Auditors	19.36	Maids and Housekeepers	7.08
Assemblers and Fabricators	9.50	Maintenance Repairers	12.25
Automotive Mechanics	15.32	Marketing/Advertising/PR Managers	30.23
Bookkeepers	12.04	Nurses, Licensed Practical	14.05
Carpenters	11.90	Nurses, Registered	24.41
Cashiers	7.16	Nursing Aides/Orderlies/Attendants	7.70
Clerks, General Office	10.48	Physicians and Surgeons	51.03
Clerks, Shipping/Receiving/Traffic	10.88	Receptionists/Information Clerks	9.34
Computer Programmers	27.78	Sales Reps., Exc. Scientific/Retail	19.27
Computer Support Specialists	19.30	Sales Reps., Scientific, Exc. Retail	-
Cooks, Restaurant	8.60	Salespersons, Retail	9.04
Electricians	13.31	Secretaries, Except Legal/Medical	12.34
Financial Managers	28.23	Stock Clerks, Sales Floor	8.20
First-Line Supervisors/Mgrs., Sales	18.41	Systems Analysts	25.92
Food Preparation Workers	7.36	Teacher Aides	8.93
General Managers/Top Executives	28.81	Teachers, Elementary School	15.70
Guards	8.62	Teachers, Secondary School	15.67
Hand Packers	7.60	Telemarketers	10.59
Janitors and Cleaners	7.64	Truck Drivers, Heavy/Tractor-Trailer	12.68
Laborers, Landscaping	8.23	Truck Drivers, Light	11.16
Lawyers	33.99	Waiters and Waitresses	6.37

Note: Wage data is for 1998 and covers the Metropolitan Statistical Area (see Appendix A for areas included). Hourly wages for elementary and secondary school teachers were calculated by the editors from annual wage data assuming a 40 hour work week; Dashes indicate that data was not available.
Source: Bureau of Labor Statistics, 1998 Metropolitan Area Occupational Employment and Wage Estimates

TAXES

Major State and Local Tax Rates

State Corporate Income (%)	State Personal Income (%)	Residential Property (%)	Sales & Use		State Gasoline (cents/ gallon)	State Cigarette (cents/ pack)
			State (%)	Local (%)		
6.9[a]	6.0 - 7.75	1.78	4.0	2.0	22.25[b]	5.0

Note: Personal/corporate income, sales, gasoline and cigarette tax rates as of January 2000. Property tax rates as of April 2000; (a) Financial institutions are also subject to a tax equal to $30 per one million in assets; (b) Rate is comprised of 22 cents excise and 0.25 cents motor carrier tax
Source: Federation of Tax Administrators, www.taxadmin.org; ERI's Relocation Assessor software database, quarterly effective date 4/1/2000

Total Taxes Per Capita and as a Percent of Income

Area	Per Capita Income ($)	Per Capita Taxes ($)			Percent of Income (%)		
		Total	Federal	State/Local	Total	Federal	State/Local
North Carolina	26,549	8,937	6,132	2,805	33.7	23.1	10.6
U.S.	28,878	10,298	7,026	3,273	35.7	24.3	11.3

Note: Figures are for 1999
Source: Tax Foundation, www.taxfoundation.org

COMMERCIAL UTILITIES

Typical Monthly Electric Bills

Area	Commercial Service ($/month)		Industrial Service ($/month)	
	12 kW demand 1,500 kWh	100 kW demand 30,000 kWh	1,000 kW demand 400,000 kWh	20,000 kW demand 10,000,000 kWh
City	150	1,814	20,801	295,548
U.S.	150	2,174	23,995	508,569

Note: Based on rates in effect January 1, 1999
Source: Edison Electric Institute, Typical Residential, Commercial and Industrial Bills, Winter 1999

TRANSPORTATION

Transportation Statistics

Average minutes to work (1990)	15.6
Interstate highways	I-40; I-85; US-15; US-501
Bus lines	
In-city (1998)	Chapel Hill Transit, 44 buses
Inter-city (1999)	4
Passenger air service	
Airport	Horace Williams Airport; Raleigh-Durham International (15 miles)
Airlines (1999)	n/a
Enplaned passengers (1998)	n/a
Amtrak service	No
Motor freight carriers (1999)	19 (Durham)
Major waterways/ports	None

Source: FAA DOT/TSC CY1998 ACAIS Database; National Transit Database, 1998; Editor & Publisher Market Guide, 2000; Amtrak National Time Table, Fall 1999/Winter 2000; 1990 Census of Population and Housing, STF 3C; Jane's Urban Transport Systems 1999-2000

Means of Transportation to Work

Area	Car/Truck/Van		Public Transportation			Bicycle	Walked	Other Means	Worked at Home
	Drove Alone	Car-pooled	Bus	Subway	Railroad				
City	59.8	10.7	5.3	0.0	0.0	2.7	16.5	1.2	3.8
MSA[1]	78.0	13.3	1.8	0.0	0.0	0.4	3.1	1.0	2.3
U.S.	73.2	13.4	3.0	1.5	0.5	0.4	3.9	1.2	3.0

Note: Figures shown are percentages and only include workers 16 years of age and older;
(1) Metropolitan Statistical Area - see Appendix A for areas included
Source: 1990 Census of Population and Housing, Summary Tape File 3C

BUSINESSES

Major Business Headquarters

Company Name	1999 Rankings	
	Fortune 500	Forbes 500
No companies listed	-	-

Note: Companies listed are located in the city; dashes indicate no ranking
Fortune 500: Companies that produce a 10-K are ranked 1 to 500 based on 1999 revenue
Forbes 500: Private companies are ranked 1 to 500 based on 1998 revenue
Source: Forbes, December 13, 1999; Fortune, April 17, 2000

HOTELS & MOTELS

Hotels/Motels

Area	Hotels/ Motels	Rooms	Luxury-Level Hotels/Motels		Average Minimum Rates ($)		
			♦♦♦♦	♦♦♦♦♦	♦♦	♦♦♦	♦♦♦♦
City	8	809	0	0	n/a	n/a	n/a

Note: n/a not available; classifications range from one diamond (budget properties with basic amenities) to five diamond (luxury properties).
Source: OAG Business Travel Planner, Winter 1999-2000

Estimated Daily Food and Lodging Costs

Area	Food/Other ($/day)	Average Hotel Cost ($/day)
City	38	77
U.S.	30	55

Source: ERI's Relocation Assessor software database, quarterly effective date 4/1/2000

CONVENTION CENTERS

Convention Centers and Event Sites

Name	Guest Rooms	Meeting Space (sq. ft.)	Capacity (Theatre Style)
Dean E. Smith Center	n/a	n/a	21,572
Holiday Inn Chapel Hill	135	n/a	300
Kenan Memorial Stadium	n/a	n/a	52,000
Sheraton Chapel Hill Hotel	n/a	16,000	645
The Carolina Inn	184	n/a	400
The Siena Hotel	80	3,475	250

Note: n/a not available
Source: EventSource.com, 3/15/2000

Living Environment

COST OF LIVING

Cost of Living: Homeowner

Cost Element	U.S. ($)	City ($)	Differential ($)	Percent of U.S. Average
Consumables	14,516	13,802	-714	95.1
Transportation	5,957	5,489	-468	92.1
Health Services	2,012	1,965	-47	97.7
Housing/Utilities/Prop. Tax	16,337	24,848	8,511	152.1
Income+Payroll Taxes	12,615	12,159	-456	96.4
Miscellaneous	8,563	8,563	0	100.0
Total Cost of Living	60,000	66,826	6,826	111.4

Note: Figures are based on a single income, four person family with gross annual earnings of $60,000, owning an 1,800 square-foot home, and driving two automobiles worth $22,000 30,000 miles per year.
Source: ERI's Relocation Assessor software database, quarterly effective date 4/1/2000

Cost of Living: Renter

Cost Element	U.S. ($)	City ($)	Differential ($)	Percent of U.S. Average
Consumables	10,486	10,016	-470	95.5
Transportation	2,107	1,950	-157	92.5
Health Services	1,632	1,602	-30	98.2
Rent/Utilities/Insurance	9,299	10,596	1,297	113.9
Income+Payroll Taxes	8,607	9,217	610	107.1
Miscellaneous	7,869	7,869	0	100.0
Total Cost of Living	40,000	41,250	1,250	103.1

Note: Figures are based on a single income, three person family with gross annual earnings of $40,000, renting a 1,000 square-foot home, and driving one automobile worth $8,000 12,000 miles per year.
Source: ERI's Relocation Assessor software database, quarterly effective date 4/1/2000

HOUSING

Median Home Prices and Housing Affordability

Area	Median Price[2] 4th Qtr. 1999 ($)	HOI[3] 4th Qtr. 1999	Affordability Rank[4]
MSA[1]	160,000	62.5	130
U.S.	139,000	63.8	–

Note: (1) Metropolitan Statistical Area - see Appendix A for areas included; (2) U.S. figures calculated from the sales of 687,516 new and existing homes in 192 markets; (3) Housing Opportunity Index - percent of homes sold that were within the reach of the median income household at the prevailing mortgage interest rate; (4) Rank is from 1-192 with 1 being most affordable
Source: National Association of Home Builders, Housing Opportunity Index, 4th Quarter 1999

Estimated Home Price

Area	Price ($)
City	213,630
U.S.	135,855

Note: Figures are based on an 1,800 square-foot home
Source: ERI's Relocation Assessor software database, quarterly effective date 4/1/2000

Estimated Rent

Area	Rent ($/month)
City	753
U.S.	651

Note: Figures are based on a 1,000 square-foot home
Source: ERI's Relocation Assessor software database, quarterly effective date 4/1/2000

Median Home Price Projection

It is projected that the median home price in the metropolitan area will increase from $164,626 in 1999 to $277,256 in 2010, an increase of 68.4%
Kiplinger's Personal Finance Magazine, January 2000

RESIDENTIAL UTILITIES

Average Residential Utility Costs

Area	All Electric ($/mth)	Part Electric ($/mth)	Other Energy ($/mth)	Phone ($/mth)
City	98.79	–	–	18.33
U.S.	99.25	55.47	43.48	20.29

Source: ACCRA, Cost of Living Index, 3rd Quarter 1999

HEALTH CARE

Average Health Care Costs

Area	Hospital ($/day)	Doctor ($/visit)	Dentist ($/visit)
City	488.00	58.33	80.33
U.S.	440.96	53.83	68.42

Note: Hospital—based on a semi-private room; Doctor—based on a general practitioner's routine exam of an established patient; Dentist—based on adult teeth cleaning and periodic oral exam.
Source: ACCRA, Cost of Living Index, 3rd Quarter 1999

Distribution of Office-Based Physicians

Area	Family/Gen. Practitioners	Specialists		
		Medical	Surgical	Other
MSA[1]	276	922	641	887

Note: Data as of 12/31/97; (1) Metropolitan Statistical Area - see Appendix A for areas included
Source: American Medical Assn., Physician Characteristics & Distribution in the U.S., 1999

Hospitals

Chapel Hill has 1 general medical and surgical hospital.
AHA Guide to the Healthcare Field, 1999-2000

According to *U.S. News and World Report,* Chapel Hill has one of the best hospitals in the U.S.: **University of North Carolina Hospitals**, noted for cancer, endocrinology, gastroenterology, geriatrics, gynecology, neurology, otolaryngology, pulmonology, rheumatology.
U.S. News Online, "America's Best Hospitals," July 19, 1999

EDUCATION

Public School District Statistics

District Name	Num. Sch.	Enroll.	Classroom Teachers	Pupils per Teacher	Minority Pupils (%)	Current Exp.[1] ($/pupil)
Chapel Hill-Carrboro Schools	13	8,225	670	12.3	n/a	n/a

Note: Data covers the 1997-1998 school year unless otherwise noted; (1) Data covers fiscal year 1996; SD = School District; ISD = Independent School District; n/a not available
Source: National Center for Education Statistics, Common Core of Data Public Education Agency Universe 1997-98; National Center for Education Statistics, Characteristics of the 100 Largest Public Elementary and Secondary School Districts in the United States: 1997-98, July 1999

Educational Quality

School District	Education Quotient[1]	Graduate Outcome[2]	Community Index[3]	Resource Index[4]
Chapel Hill-Carboro Schools	133	149	125	104

Note: Over 1,000 secondary school districts were rated in terms of educational quality. The scores range from a low of 50 to a high of 150; (1) Combination of the Graduate Outcome, Community and Resource indexes weighted to reflect the greater importance of the Graduate Outcome and Resource Index; (2) Based on graduation rates and college board scores (SAT/ACT); (3) Based on the surrounding community's level of affluence and adult education; (4) Based on teacher salaries, per-pupil expenditures and student-teacher ratios.
Source: Expansion Management, Ratings Issue, 1999

Educational Attainment by Race

Area	High School Graduate (%)					Bachelor's Degree (%)				
	Total	White	Black	Other	Hisp.[2]	Total	White	Black	Other	Hisp.[2]
City	93.4	97.0	65.4	96.5	84.8	71.2	76.6	28.3	78.6	63.5
MSA[1]	82.4	87.2	66.0	86.3	77.2	34.8	39.2	17.8	55.6	36.6
U.S.	75.2	77.9	63.1	60.4	49.8	20.3	21.5	11.4	19.4	9.2

Note: Figures shown cover persons 25 years old and over; (1) Metropolitan Statistical Area - see Appendix A for areas included; (2) people of Hispanic origin can be of any race
Source: 1990 Census of Population and Housing, Summary Tape File 3C

School Enrollment by Type

Area	Preprimary				Elementary/High School			
	Public		Private		Public		Private	
	Enrollment	%	Enrollment	%	Enrollment	%	Enrollment	%
City	255	36.3	447	63.7	3,108	85.9	511	14.1
MSA[1]	6,751	46.9	7,652	53.1	99,864	92.8	7,735	7.2
U.S.	2,679,029	59.5	1,824,256	40.5	38,379,689	90.2	4,187,099	9.8

Note: Figures shown cover persons 3 years old and over;
(1) Metropolitan Statistical Area - see Appendix A for areas included
Source: 1990 Census of Population and Housing, Summary Tape File 3C

School Enrollment by Race

Area	Preprimary (%)				Elementary/High School (%)			
	White	Black	Other	Hisp.[1]	White	Black	Other	Hisp.[1]
City	82.1	11.5	6.4	3.4	73.6	18.8	7.5	3.1
MSA[2]	78.1	19.4	2.6	1.2	65.4	31.9	2.7	1.2
U.S.	80.4	12.5	7.1	7.8	74.1	15.6	10.3	12.5

Note: Figures shown cover persons 3 years old and over; (1) people of Hispanic origin can be of any race; (2) Metropolitan Statistical Area - see Appendix A for areas included
Source: 1990 Census of Population and Housing, Summary Tape File 3C

Higher Education

Two-Year Colleges		Four-Year Colleges		Medical Schools	Law Schools	Voc/ Tech
Public	Private	Public	Private			
0	0	1	0	1	1	2

Source: College Blue Book, Occupational Education, 1999; Medical School Admission Requirements, 1999-2000; Peterson's Guide to Two-Year Colleges, 2000; Peterson's Guide to Four-Year Colleges, 1999; Barron's Guide to Law Schools, 1999

MAJOR EMPLOYERS

Major Employers

Atwork Corp. (software)	Blue Cross & Blue Shield
Easy Entry Software	FG*ImageWorks (direct mail advertising)
Investors Title Co.	Kenan Transport
Performance Inc. (sporting goods)	Strategic Management Resources
Triangle Laboratories	

Note: Companies listed are located in the city
Source: D&B Business Rankings, 1999; Ward's Business Directory, 1999; America's Corporate Families, 1999

PUBLIC SAFETY

Crime Rate

Area	All Crimes	Violent Crimes				Property Crimes		
		Murder	Forcible Rape	Robbery	Aggrav. Assault	Burglary	Larceny -Theft	Motor Vehicle Theft
City	6,272.2	0.0	17.5	177.3	251.8	853.8	4,645.6	326.2
Suburbs[1]	5,684.4	7.8	33.5	223.4	301.3	1,272.5	3,413.4	432.4
MSA[2]	5,709.6	7.5	32.8	221.4	299.2	1,254.6	3,466.2	427.9
U.S.	4,615.5	6.3	34.4	165.2	360.5	862.0	2,728.1	459.0

Note: Crime rate is the number of crimes per 100,000 population; (1) Defined as all areas within the Metropolitan Statistical Area but located outside the central city; (2) Metropolitan Statistical Area - see Appendix A for areas included
Source: FBI Uniform Crime Reports, 1998

RECREATION

Culture and Recreation

Museums	Symphony Orchestras	Opera Companies	Dance Companies	Professional Theatres	Zoos	Pro Sports Teams
1	1	1	0	1	0	0

Source: Musical America, International Directory of the Performing Arts, 1999; Official Museum Directory, 2000; Stern's Performing Arts Directory, 1997; USA Today Four Sport Stadium Guide, 1997; Career Opportunities in Theatre and the Performing Arts, 1999

Library System

The Chapel Hill Public Library has no branches and holdings of 106,000 volumes.
American Library Directory, 1999-2000

MEDIA

Newspapers

Name	Type	Freq.	Distribution	Circulation
Chapel Hill News	General	3x/wk	Local	22,000
The Daily Tar Heel	n/a	5x/wk	Camp/Comm	20,000

Note: Includes newspapers with circulations of 200 or more located in the city; n/a not available
Source: Burrelle's Media Directory, 1999 Edition

Television Stations

Name	Ch.	Affiliation	Type	Owner

No stations listed.
Note: Stations included broadcast in the Chapel Hill metro area; n/a not available
Source: Burrelle's Media Directory, 1999 Edition

AM Radio Stations

Call Letters	Freq. (kHz)	Target Audience	Station Format	Music Format
WCHL	1360	General	N/S/T	n/a

Note: Stations included broadcast in the Chapel Hill metro area; n/a not available
Station Format: E=Educational; M=Music; N=News; S=Sports; T=Talk
Source: Burrelle's Media Directory, 1999 Edition

FM Radio Stations

Call Letters	Freq. (mHz)	Target Audience	Station Format	Music Format
WXYC	89.3	General	M	Alternative
WUNC	91.5	General	E/M/N	Classical

Note: Stations included broadcast in the Chapel Hill metro area
Station Format: E=Educational; M=Music; N=News; S=Sports; T=Talk
Target Audience: A=Asian; B=Black; C=Christian; E=Ethnic; F=French; G=General; H=Hispanic; M=Men; N=Native American; R=Religious; S=Senior Citizen; W=Women; Y=Young Adult; Z=Children
Source: Burrelle's Media Directory, 1999 Edition

WEATHER

Temperature/Precipitation/Humidity

	Jan	Feb	Mar	Apr	May	Jun	Jul	Aug	Sep	Oct	Nov	Dec	Yr.
Max. High Temp. (°F)	79	84	90	95	97	104	105	105	104	98	88	79	105
Avg. High Temp. (°F)	50	53	61	72	79	86	89	87	81	72	62	53	71
Avg. Temp. (°F)	40	43	50	59	67	75	78	77	71	60	51	42	60
Avg. Low Temp. (°F)	29	31	38	46	55	63	68	67	60	48	39	32	48
Min. Low Temp. (°F)	-9	5	11	23	29	38	48	46	37	19	11	4	-9
Avg. Precip. (in.)	3.4	3.6	3.6	2.9	3.9	3.6	4.4	4.4	3.2	2.9	3.0	3.1	42.0
Avg. Snowfall (in.)	2	3	1	Tr	0	0	0	0	0	0	Tr	1	8
Avg. Rel. Hum. 7am (%)	79	79	79	80	84	86	88	91	91	90	84	81	84
Avg. Rel. Hum. 4pm (%)	53	49	46	43	51	54	57	59	57	53	51	53	52

Note: Tr = Trace amounts (less than 0.05 inches of rain or less than 0.5 inches of snow)
Source: National Climatic Data Center, International Station Meteorological Climate Summary, 3/95

Weather Conditions

Temperature			Precipitation		
5°F & below	32°F & below	90°F & above	0.01 inch or more precip.	1.5 inch or more snow/ice	Thunder-storms
77	160	39	110	3	42

Note: Figures are average number of days per year
Source: National Climatic Data Center, International Station Meteorological Climate Summary, 3/95

AIR & WATER QUALITY

Maximum Pollutant Concentrations

	Particulate Matter (ug/m³)	Carbon Monoxide (ppm)	Sulfur Dioxide (ppm)	Nitrogen Dioxide (ppm)	Ozone (ppm)	Lead (ug/m³)
MSA[1] Level	59	7	n/a	n/a	0.12	0.00
NAAQS[2]	150	9	0.140	0.053	0.12	1.50
Met NAAQS	Yes	Yes	n/a	n/a	Yes	Yes

Note: (1) Metropolitan Statistical Area - see Appendix A for areas included; (2) National Ambient Air Quality Standards; ppm = parts per million; ug/m³ = micrograms per cubic meter; n/a not available
Source: EPA, National Air Quality and Emissions Trends Report, 1997

Pollutant Standards Index

In the Chapel Hill MSA (see Appendix A for areas included), the Pollutant Standards Index (PSI) exceeded 100 on 24 days in 1997. A PSI value greater than 100 indicates that air quality would have been in the unhealthful range on that day.
EPA, National Air Quality and Emissions Trends Report, 1997

Drinking Water

Water System Name	Pop. Served	Primary Water Source Type	Number of Violations in 1998-99	Type of Violation/ Contaminants
Orange Water & Sewer Authority	55,000	Surface	None	None

Note: Data as of January 19, 2000
Source: EPA, Office of Ground Water and Drinking Water, Safe Drinking Water Information System

Chapel Hill tap water is alkaline, soft, and fluoridated.
Editor & Publisher Market Guide, 2000

Charleston, South Carolina

Background

Charleston, South Carolina is located on the state's Atlantic coastline, 110 miles southeast of Columbia and 100 miles north of Savannah, Georgia. The city, named for King Charles II of England, is the county seat of Charleston County. Charleston is on a bay at the end of a peninsula between the Ashley and Cooper rivers. The terrain is low-lying and coastal with nearby islands and inlets.

Charleston is part of a larger metropolitan area that includes North Charleston and Mount Pleasant and covers Charleston, Berkley and Dorchester counties. This area is a regional commercial and cultural center and a southern transportation hub whose port is among the nation's busiest shipping facilities. Other contemporary economic sectors include manufacturing, health care, business and professional services, defense activity, retail and wholesale trade, tourism, education and construction.

Charleston is a popular tourist area, based on its scenery, history and recreation. The city's center is well-known for its historic neighborhoods with distinctive early southern architecture and ambience. As one of the first American cities in the early 20th Century to actively encourage historic restoration and preservation, Charleston has more recently undertaken numerous revitalization initiatives, including the Charleston Place hotel and retail complex and Waterfront Park. North Charleston and other communities are also growing with industry and suburban development.

In 1670, English colonists established a nearby settlement, and subsequently moved to Charleston's present site. Charleston became an early trading center for rice, indigo, cotton and other goods. As the plantation economy grew, Charleston became a slave-trading center. The Civil War started with the firing by the Confederacy on nearby Fort Sumter in 1861. Charleston was under siege during the Civil War, and experienced many difficulties during Reconstruction. Charleston also suffered major damage in an 1886 earthquake. Manufacturing industries including mills and foundries became important in the 19th Century.

The founding of the Charleston Naval Shipyard stimulated a military-based economy after 1901. Numerous other defense facilities were later established, including the Charleston Air Force Base. Several military facilities were closed in the 1990s, although other defense-related operations have remained.

Charleston is a center for health care and medical research. The Medical University of South Carolina, founded in 1824, is the region's largest single employer with approximately 8,000 employees.

Other area educational institutions include The College of Charleston, The Citadel Military College, Trident Technical College, Charleston Southern University, and a campus of Johnson and Wales University offering culinary and hospitality education.

The Charleston area has numerous parks and public waterfront areas. Coastal recreation activities such as boating, swimming, fishing and beaches are popular, as are golf and other land sports. The city is home of the Charleston Riverdogs affiliates of the Tampa Bay Devil Rays baseball team, the Charleston Battery professional soccer team and the Swamp Foxes Arena Football team.

The Charleston Museum is the nation's oldest, founded in 1773. Other attractions include the new South Carolina Aquarium, the American Military Museum, the Drayton Hall plantation museum, the Gibbes Museum of Art and the Karpeles Manuscript Museum. A new North Charleston Convention Center and Performing Arts Center complex opened in 1999. Cultural organizations include the Spoleto Festival USA annual summer arts festival, the Charleston Symphony, and the Charleston Stage Company, among others.

In 1989, Charleston suffered extensive damage from Hurricane Hugo, which required an intensive clean-up and recovery effort.

Charleston is governed by a Mayor and 12-member City Council.

General Rankings and Evaluative Comments

- Charleston was ranked #54 out of 354 metropolitan areas in *Places Rated Almanac*. Criteria: cost of living, climate, crime, transportation, job outlook, education, the arts, health care, and recreation. *Places Rated Almanac, Millennium Edition, 2000*

- Charleston was selected as one of America's best places to retire. Criteria: safety, climate, housing, culture and recreation, social compatibility, affordability, medical care, transportation, and jobs and/or volunteer opportunities. *Where to Retire: America's Best and Most Affordable Places, 1998*

- Charleston appeared on *Travel & Leisure's* list of the world's 100 best cities. It was ranked #46 in the world. Criteria: activities/attractions, culture/arts, restaurants/food, people, and value. *Travel & Leisure, 1999 World's Best Awards*

- *Condé Nast Traveler* polled their readers for travel satisfaction. North American cities were ranked based on the following criteria: people/friendliness, environment/ambiance, cultural enrichment, restaurants, and fun/energy. Charleston appeared in the top 32, ranking number 3. *Condé Nast Traveler, Readers' Choice Poll, May 1999*

- Cognetics studied 273 metro areas in the United States, ranking them by entrepreneurial activity. Charleston was ranked #30 out of 134 smaller metro areas. Criteria: Significant Starts (firms started in the last 10 years that still employ at least 5 people) and Young Growers (percent of firms 10 years old or less that grew significantly during the last 4 years). *Cognetics, "Entrepreneurial Hot Spots: The Best Places in America to Start and Grow a Company," 1999*

- Charleston was included among *Entrepreneur* magazine's listing of the "20 Best Cities for Small Business." It was ranked #4 among mid-sized metro areas. Criteria: entrepreneurial activity, small-business growth, economic growth, and risk of failure. *Entrepreneur, October 1999*

- Charleston was selected as one of the "hottest cities" for expanding or relocating companies. The city ranked #41 out of 50. Criteria: business climate, work force quality, operating costs, incentive programs, and ease of working with local officials. *Expansion Management, January 2000*

- Reliastar Financial Corporation ranked the 125 largest metropolitan areas according to the general financial security of residents. Charleston was ranked #86 out of 125 with a score of -2.0 (the percentage a metropolitan area is above or below the metropolitan norm; a metro area with a score of 10.6 is 10.6% above the metro average). Criteria: Earnings and Wealth Potential (household income, education, net assets, cost of living); Safety Net (health insurance, retirement savings, life insurance, income support programs); Personal Threats (unemployment rate, low-income households, crime rate); Community Economic Vitality (cost of community services, job quality, job creation, housing costs). *Reliastar Financial Corporation, "The Best Cities to Earn and Save Money: A Ranking of the Largest 125 U.S. Cities," 2000 Edition*

Business Environment

STATE ECONOMY

State Economic Profile

"South Carolina has been on a roll and is expected to continue that trend. South Carolina's friendly business environment and high quality of life have attracted an amazing number of businesses and residents. Both the construction and housing markets have been booming. As the US economy cools, its feverish growth will slow; however, South Carolina will remain one of the nation's fastest growing states.

South Carolina non-farm employment grew by 4.0% in 1998. Although manufacturing employment growth slowed to 0.2%, service jobs expanded at 6.1%. Many of these service jobs are in the tourism industry, which benefited in 1998 from the strong US expansion. Other important gains took place in the financial and business services sectors.

South Carolina construction employment grew by 9.8% in 1998, with residential permits growing by 8% and home sales growing by almost 17%. The continued expansion of the Port of Charleston and the strong Charlotte-Gastonia-Rock Hill commercial markets brought a wave of new commercial construction in 1998. Home sales and construction activity are expected to slow in 2000, although still remain strong by national standards.

Unlike many states, South Carolina's strength is spread across the state. Expanding port facilities, fueled by the auto industry, are helping drive job growth in Charleston. Columbia added jobs at a rate of 3% in 1998, below the state average but still high above the national. Employment gains were also strong along the I-85 corridor. The state's real strength has been its ability to attract new residents, both in the form of new workers and retirees. South Carolina's affordable living and pleasant climate will assure continued strong positive migration." *National Association of Realtors, Economic Profiles: The Fifty States and the District of Columbia, http://nar.realtor.com/databank/profiles.htm*

EXPORTS

Total Export Sales

Area	1995 ($000)	1996 ($000)	1997 ($000)	1998 ($000)	% Chg. 1995-98	% Chg. 1997-98
MSA[1]	501,582	595,061	827,611	837,895	67.1	1.2
U.S.	583,030,524	622,827,063	687,597,999	680,474,251	16.7	-1.0

Note: (1) Metropolitan Statistical Area - see Appendix A for areas included
Source: U.S. Department of Commerce, International Trade Association, Metropolitan Area Exports: An Export Performance Report on Over 250 U.S. Cities, November 10, 1999

CITY FINANCES

City Government Finances

Component	1995 ($million)	1995 (per capita $)
Revenue	108.4	1,410
Expenditure	86.8	1,130
Debt Outstanding	329.5	4,287

Source: 1999 County and City Extra, Annual Metro, City, and County Data Book

City Government Revenue by Source

Source	1995 ($million)	1995 (per capita $)
Intergovernmental	14.0	182
Taxes	53.8	699
Property	31.0	404
Sales and Gross Receipts	9.1	119

Source: 1999 County and City Extra, Annual Metro, City, and County Data Book

City Government Expenditures by Function

Function	1995 ($million)	1995 (per capita $)	1995 (%)
Public Welfare	0.8	11	1.0
Highways	2.4	31	2.8
Parking Facilities	1.5	20	1.8
Education	0.0	0	0.0
Health and Hospitals	0.0	0	0.0
Police Protection	13.3	173	15.4
Sewerage and Sanitation	19.7	257	22.8
Parks and Recreation	8.2	107	9.5
Housing and Community Development	3.0	39	3.5
Interest on Debt	4.6	59	5.3

Source: 1999 County and City Extra, Annual Metro, City, and County Data Book

Municipal Bond Ratings

Area	Moody's
City	Aa3

Source: Mergent Bond Record, 2/2000

POPULATION

Population Growth

Area	1980 Census	1990 Census	1999 Estimate	2004 Projection	Population Growth (%) 1990-1999	Population Growth (%) 1999-2004
City	69,510	80,414	77,419	75,989	-3.7	-1.8
MSA[1]	430,462	506,875	544,103	551,139	7.3	1.3
U.S.	226,545,805	248,765,170	272,212,864	283,625,312	9.4	4.2

Note: (1) Metropolitan Statistical Area - see Appendix A for areas included
Source: 1990 Census of Population and Housing, Summary Tape File 3C; Claritas, Inc.

Number of Households and Average Household Size

Area	1980 Census	1990 Census	1999 Estimate	2004 Projection	1999 Average Household Size
City	29,077	30,867	32,296	32,405	2.40
MSA[1]	137,876	177,484	202,311	208,857	2.69
U.S.	80,389,592	91,993,582	102,048,200	107,302,392	2.67

Note: (1) Metropolitan Statistical Area - see Appendix A for areas included
Source: 1990 Census of Population and Housing, Summary Tape File 3C; Claritas, Inc.

Race/Ethnicity of City Population

Race/Ethnicity	1990 Census Population	1990 Census %	1999 Estimate Population	1999 Estimate %	% Change 1990-1999
White, Non-Hispanic	45,740	56.9	42,441	54.8	-7.2
Black, Non-Hispanic	33,424	41.6	32,924	42.5	-1.5
Asian, Non-Hispanic	609	0.8	1,021	1.3	67.7
Other, Non-Hispanic	137	0.2	173	0.2	26.3
Hispanic	504	0.6	860	1.1	70.6

Source: 1990 Census of Population and Housing, Summary Tape File 3C; Claritas, Inc.

Race/Ethnicity of Metropolitan Statistical Area Population

Race/Ethnicity	1990 Census		1999 Estimate		% Change 1990-1999
	Population	%	Population	%	
White, Non-Hispanic	339,953	67.1	353,092	64.9	3.9
Black, Non-Hispanic	152,312	30.0	169,437	31.1	11.2
Asian, Non-Hispanic	5,509	1.1	8,122	1.5	47.4
Other, Non-Hispanic	1,951	0.4	1,951	0.4	0.0
Hispanic	7,150	1.4	11,501	2.1	60.9

Note: See Appendix A for areas included in the Metropolitan Statistical Area
Source: 1990 Census of Population and Housing, Summary Tape File 3C; Claritas, Inc.

Ancestry

Area	German	Irish	English	Italian	U.S.	French	Polish	Dutch
City	13.6	9.6	13.2	2.1	4.9	3.9	1.6	1.1
MSA[1]	17.4	13.5	13.6	2.5	7.3	4.0	1.5	1.6
U.S.	23.3	15.6	13.1	5.9	5.3	4.2	3.8	2.5

Note: Figures are percentages and include persons that reported multiple ancestry (eg. if a person reported being Irish and Italian, they were included in both columns); (1) Metropolitan Statistical Area - see Appendix A for areas included
Source: 1990 Census of Population and Housing, Summary Tape File 3C

Median Age

Area	1990 Census	1999 Estimate
City	30.5	33.9
MSA[1]	29.5	32.4
U.S.	32.9	35.7

Note: (1) Metropolitan Statistical Area - see Appendix A for areas included
Source: 1990 Census of Population and Housing, Summary Tape File 3C; Claritas, Inc.

Male/Female Population

Area	Number of Males		Number of Females		Males per 100 Females	
	1990	1999	1990	1999	1990	1999
City	37,994	36,578	42,420	40,841	89.6	89.6
MSA[1]	252,313	268,708	254,562	275,395	99.1	97.6
U.S.	121,172,379	132,803,736	127,537,494	139,409,136	95.0	95.3

Note: (1) Metropolitan Statistical Area - see Appendix A for areas included
Source: 1990 Census of Population, General Population Characteristics; Claritas, Inc.

INCOME

Per Capita/Median/Average Income

Area	Per Capita ($)			Median Household ($)			Average Household ($)		
	1989	1999	% Chg.	1989	1999	% Chg.	1989	1999	% Chg.
City	14,093	24,630	74.8	25,153	37,286	48.2	35,806	58,162	62.4
MSA[1]	12,334	19,563	58.6	28,066	38,674	37.8	33,865	51,068	50.8
U.S.	14,420	21,350	48.1	30,056	40,525	34.8	38,453	56,184	46.1

Note: (1) Metropolitan Statistical Area - see Appendix A for areas included; 1989 data is from the 1990 Census; 1999 data is estimated by Claritas, Inc.
Source: 1990 Census of Population, General Population Characteristics; Claritas, Inc.

Household Income Distribution

Area	Percent of Households Earning								
	Under $5,000	$5,000 -14,999	$15,000 -24,999	$25,000 -34,999	$35,000 -49,999	$50,000 -74,999	$75,000 -99,000	$100,000 -149,999	$150,000 and up
City	7.5	14.4	13.1	11.6	15.3	16.7	9.1	6.4	6.0
MSA[1]	5.3	11.8	13.5	14.3	17.9	19.9	8.9	5.3	3.2
U.S.	3.9	13.3	13.8	12.6	16.2	19.4	9.7	6.6	4.6

Note: Data as of 1999; (1) Metropolitan Statistical Area - see Appendix A for areas included
Source: Claritas, Inc.

Effective Buying Income

Area	Per Capita ($)	Median Household ($)	Average Household ($)
City	17,118	30,476	43,130
MSA[1]	15,287	33,470	42,141
U.S.	17,496	36,603	47,036

Note: Data as of 1/1/2000; (1) Metropolitan Statistical Area - see Appendix A for areas included
Source: Standard Rate & Data Service, Newspaper Advertising Source, March 2000

Effective Household Buying Income Distribution

Area	% of Households Earning						
	$10,000 -$19,999	$20,000 -$34,999	$35,000 -$49,999	$50,000 -$74,999	$75,000 -$99,000	$100,000 -$124,999	$125,000 and up
City	16.1	21.8	14.8	16.2	7.1	2.1	3.8
MSA[1]	14.9	25.0	19.1	18.5	6.5	1.8	1.8
U.S.	15.0	21.6	17.6	19.6	8.4	3.0	3.3

Note: Data as of 1/1/2000; (1) Metropolitan Statistical Area - see Appendix A for areas included
Source: Standard Rate & Data Service, Newspaper Advertising Source, March 2000

Poverty Rates by Age

Area	People of All Ages	People Under 18 Years Old	Related Children Age 5-17 in Families in Poverty
City	24.5	n/a	n/a
County	18.9	31.9	30.9
U.S.	13.8	20.8	18.7

Note: Figures show the percent of people living below the poverty line in 1995. The average poverty threshold was $15,569 for a family of four in 1995; n/a not available
Source: Bureau of the Census, Small Area Income and Poverty Estimates Program; U.S. Department of Housing and Urban Development

EMPLOYMENT

Labor Force and Employment

Area	Civilian Labor Force			Workers Employed		
	Dec. 1998	Dec. 1999	% Chg.	Dec. 1998	Dec. 1999	% Chg.
City	42,474	44,121	3.9	41,451	42,777	3.2
MSA[1]	263,857	273,729	3.7	257,625	265,864	3.2
U.S.	138,297,000	139,941,000	1.2	132,732,000	134,696,000	1.5

Note: Data is not seasonally adjusted and covers workers 16 years of age and older;
(1) Metropolitan Statistical Area - see Appendix A for areas included
Source: Bureau of Labor Statistics, http://stats.bls.gov

Unemployment Rate

Area	1999											
	Jan.	Feb.	Mar.	Apr.	May	Jun.	Jul.	Aug.	Sep.	Oct.	Nov.	Dec.
City	3.1	3.4	2.3	2.5	2.9	3.5	3.4	3.3	3.3	3.4	3.4	3.0
MSA[1]	2.9	3.2	2.4	2.6	3.0	3.5	3.4	3.2	3.3	3.4	3.2	2.9
U.S.	4.8	4.7	4.4	4.1	4.0	4.5	4.5	4.2	4.1	3.8	3.8	3.7

Note: Data is not seasonally adjusted and covers workers 16 years of age and older; all figures are percentages; (1) Metropolitan Statistical Area - see Appendix A for areas included
Source: Bureau of Labor Statistics, http://stats.bls.gov

Employment by Industry

Sector	MSA[1]		U.S.
	Number of Employees	Percent of Total	Percent of Total
Services	72,800	29.2	30.2
Retail Trade	52,800	21.2	18.1
Government	49,400	19.8	15.8
Manufacturing	22,500	9.0	14.1
Finance/Insurance/Real Estate	8,900	3.6	5.9
Wholesale Trade	10,200	4.1	5.4
Transportation/Public Utilities	13,600	5.5	5.3
Construction	n/a	n/a	4.8
Mining	n/a	n/a	0.4

Note: Figures cover non-farm employment as of 12/99 and are not seasonally adjusted;
(1) Metropolitan Statistical Area - see Appendix A for areas included; n/a not available
Source: Bureau of Labor Statistics, http://stats.bls.gov

Employment by Occupation

Occupation Category	City (%)	MSA[1] (%)	U.S. (%)
White Collar	62.1	55.3	58.1
Executive/Admin./Management	12.2	11.2	12.3
Professional	19.4	13.4	14.1
Technical & Related Support	4.3	4.1	3.7
Sales	12.9	12.5	11.8
Administrative Support/Clerical	13.3	14.1	16.3
Blue Collar	17.6	29.2	26.2
Precision Production/Craft/Repair	8.6	15.1	11.3
Machine Operators/Assem./Insp.	2.8	5.5	6.8
Transportation/Material Movers	3.2	4.4	4.1
Cleaners/Helpers/Laborers	3.1	4.2	3.9
Services	19.3	14.0	13.2
Farming/Forestry/Fishing	1.0	1.4	2.5

Note: Figures cover workers 16 years of age and older;
(1) Metropolitan Statistical Area - see Appendix A for areas included
Source: 1990 Census of Population and Housing, Summary Tape File 3C

Occupational Employment Projections: 1996 - 2006

Occupations Expected to Have the Largest Job Growth (ranked by numerical growth)	Fast-Growing Occupations[1] (ranked by percent growth)
1. Cashiers	1. Desktop publishers
2. Salespersons, retail	2. Database administrators
3. General managers & top executives	3. Computer engineers
4. Marketing & sales, supervisors	4. Paralegals
5. Food preparation workers	5. Systems analysts
6. Truck drivers, light	6. Personal and home care aides
7. Cooks, fast food and short order	7. Medical assistants
8. Food service workers	8. Physical therapy assistants and aides
9. Waiters & waitresses	9. Respiratory therapists
10. Food service and lodging managers	10. Data processing equipment repairers

Note: Projections cover South Carolina; (1) Excludes occupations with total job growth less than 300
Source: U.S. Department of Labor, Employment and Training Administration, America's Labor Market
Information System (ALMIS)

Average Wages

Occupation	$/Hr.	Occupation	$/Hr.
Accountants and Auditors	17.87	Maids and Housekeepers	6.22
Assemblers and Fabricators	11.07	Maintenance Repairers	10.62
Automotive Mechanics	13.50	Marketing/Advertising/PR Managers	21.46
Bookkeepers	10.99	Nurses, Licensed Practical	12.25
Carpenters	11.87	Nurses, Registered	19.92
Cashiers	6.45	Nursing Aides/Orderlies/Attendants	7.16
Clerks, General Office	9.03	Physicians and Surgeons	43.84
Clerks, Shipping/Receiving/Traffic	10.50	Receptionists/Information Clerks	8.45
Computer Programmers	20.61	Sales Reps., Exc. Scientific/Retail	17.99
Computer Support Specialists	16.01	Sales Reps., Scientific, Exc. Retail	19.23
Cooks, Restaurant	8.08	Salespersons, Retail	9.02
Electricians	12.64	Secretaries, Except Legal/Medical	10.25
Financial Managers	25.96	Stock Clerks, Sales Floor	7.52
First-Line Supervisors/Mgrs., Sales	14.72	Systems Analysts	23.01
Food Preparation Workers	6.30	Teacher Aides	7.26
General Managers/Top Executives	25.07	Teachers, Elementary School	15.89
Guards	7.31	Teachers, Secondary School	17.45
Hand Packers	6.82	Telemarketers	-
Janitors and Cleaners	7.06	Truck Drivers, Heavy/Tractor-Trailer	14.41
Laborers, Landscaping	8.01	Truck Drivers, Light	8.77
Lawyers	31.03	Waiters and Waitresses	6.21

Note: Wage data is for 1998 and covers the Metropolitan Statistical Area (see Appendix A for areas
included). Hourly wages for elementary and secondary school teachers were calculated by the editors
from annual wage data assuming a 40 hour work week; Dashes indicate that data was not available.
Source: Bureau of Labor Statistics, 1998 Metropolitan Area Occupational Employment and Wage
Estimates

TAXES

Major State and Local Tax Rates

State Corporate Income (%)	State Personal Income (%)	Residential Property (%)	Sales & Use		State Gasoline (cents/ gallon)	State Cigarette (cents/ pack)
			State (%)	Local (%)		
5.0	2.5 - 7.0	1.27	5.0	1.0	16.0	7.0

Note: Personal/corporate income, sales, gasoline and cigarette tax rates as of January 2000.
Property tax rates as of April 2000.
Source: Federation of Tax Administrators, www.taxadmin.org; ERI's Relocation Assessor software
database, quarterly effective date 4/1/2000

Total Taxes Per Capita and as a Percent of Income

Area	Per Capita Income ($)	Per Capita Taxes ($)			Percent of Income (%)		
		Total	Federal	State/Local	Total	Federal	State/Local
South Carolina	23,601	8,114	5,508	2,606	34.4	23.3	11.0
U.S.	28,878	10,298	7,026	3,273	35.7	24.3	11.3

Note: Figures are for 1999
Source: Tax Foundation, www.taxfoundation.org

COMMERCIAL UTILITIES

Typical Monthly Electric Bills

Area	Commercial Service ($/month)		Industrial Service ($/month)	
	12 kW demand 1,500 kWh	100 kW demand 30,000 kWh	1,000 kW demand 400,000 kWh	20,000 kW demand 10,000,000 kWh
City	122	2,125	19,570	333,900
U.S.	150	2,174	23,995	508,569

Note: Based on rates in effect January 1, 1999
Source: Edison Electric Institute, Typical Residential, Commercial and Industrial Bills, Winter 1999

TRANSPORTATION

Transportation Statistics

Average minutes to work (1990)	18.7
Interstate highways	I-26; I-526; US-17; US-52; US-78
Bus lines	
In-city (1998)	City of Charleston Transit Administration Div., 34 buses
Inter-city (1999)	2
Passenger air service	
Airport	Charleston International
Airlines (1999)	5
Enplaned passengers (1998)	791,566
Amtrak service	Yes
Motor freight carriers (1999)	119
Major waterways/ports	Intracoastal Waterway; Near Atlantic Ocean

Source: FAA DOT/TSC CY1998 ACAIS Database; National Transit Database, 1998; Editor & Publisher Market Guide, 2000; Amtrak National Time Table, Fall 1999/Winter 2000; 1990 Census of Population and Housing, STF 3C; Jane's Urban Transport Systems 1999-2000

Means of Transportation to Work

Area	Car/Truck/Van		Public Transportation			Bicycle	Walked	Other Means	Worked at Home
	Drove Alone	Car-pooled	Bus	Subway	Railroad				
City	68.5	11.9	5.6	0.0	0.0	1.8	8.0	2.1	2.0
MSA[1]	73.0	15.6	1.8	0.0	0.0	0.6	3.1	2.0	3.9
U.S.	73.2	13.4	3.0	1.5	0.5	0.4	3.9	1.2	3.0

Note: Figures shown are percentages and only include workers 16 years of age and older;
(1) Metropolitan Statistical Area - see Appendix A for areas included
Source: 1990 Census of Population and Housing, Summary Tape File 3C

BUSINESSES

Major Business Headquarters

Company Name	1999 Rankings	
	Fortune 500	Forbes 500
Cameron & Barkley	-	357

Note: Companies listed are located in the city; dashes indicate no ranking
Fortune 500: Companies that produce a 10-K are ranked 1 to 500 based on 1999 revenue
Forbes 500: Private companies are ranked 1 to 500 based on 1998 revenue
Source: Forbes, December 13, 1999; Fortune, April 17, 2000

HOTELS & MOTELS

Hotels/Motels

Area	Hotels/ Motels	Rooms	Luxury-Level Hotels/Motels		Average Minimum Rates ($)		
			♦♦♦♦	♦♦♦♦♦	♦♦	♦♦♦	♦♦♦♦
City	39	3,488	1	0	68	101	325
Airport	21	2,544	0	0	n/a	n/a	n/a
Suburbs	16	1,838	0	0	n/a	n/a	n/a
Total	76	7,870	1	0	n/a	n/a	n/a

Note: n/a not available; classifications range from one diamond (budget properties with basic amenities) to five diamond (luxury properties).
Source: OAG Business Travel Planner, Winter 1999-2000

Estimated Daily Food and Lodging Costs

Area	Food/Other ($/day)	Average Hotel Cost ($/day)
City	42	99
U.S.	30	55

Source: ERI's Relocation Assessor software database, quarterly effective date 4/1/2000

Charleston is home to one of the top 100 hotels in the world according to *Travel & Leisure*: Charleston Place (#87) . Criteria: value, rooms/ambience, location, facilities/activities and service. *Travel & Leisure, 1999 World's Best Awards, Best Hotels and Resorts*

CONVENTION CENTERS

Convention Centers and Event Sites

Name	Guest Rooms	Meeting Space (sq. ft.)	Capacity (Theatre Style)
Best Western Charleston Intl Airport	197	n/a	400
Charleston Exhibition Hall	n/a	n/a	0
Charleston Place Hotel	440	25,000	2,000
Dock Street Theatre	n/a	n/a	453
Doubletree Guest Suites Charleston	165	6,362	300
Embassy Suites Historic Charleston	153	4,500	240
Gallard Municipal Auditorium	n/a	n/a	2,734
Garden Theatre	n/a	n/a	500
Holiday Inn Charleston - Airport	260	n/a	125
Holiday Inn Charleston - Mt. Pleasant	158	n/a	300
Holiday Inn Charleston - Riverview	181	1,820	75
Quality Inn Heart of Charleston	126	n/a	250
Quality Suites Charleston	168	n/a	65
Ramada Inn Coliseum	155	n/a	100
Shem Creek Inn - Mt. Pleasant	50	n/a	60
Sheraton Charleston Hotel	333	8,000	700
Sheraton North Charleston	296	12,000	800
The Lodge Alley Inn	40	n/a	100
The Mills House Hotel	214	8,000	350
The Westin Francis Marion	226	14,000	375
Town & Country Inn & Conference Ctr.	122	n/a	275
Wild Dunes Resort	690	16,000	400

Note: n/a not available
Source: EventSource.com, 3/15/2000

Living Environment

COST OF LIVING

Cost of Living: Homeowner

Cost Element	U.S. ($)	City ($)	Differential ($)	Percent of U.S. Average
Consumables	14,516	13,772	-744	94.9
Transportation	5,957	5,388	-569	90.4
Health Services	2,012	2,032	20	101.0
Housing/Utilities/Prop. Tax	16,337	24,693	8,356	151.1
Income+Payroll Taxes	12,615	12,158	-457	96.4
Miscellaneous	8,563	8,563	0	100.0
Total Cost of Living	60,000	66,606	6,606	111.0

Note: Figures are based on a single income, four person family with gross annual earnings of $60,000, owning an 1,800 square-foot home, and driving two automobiles worth $22,000 30,000 miles per year.
Source: ERI's Relocation Assessor software database, quarterly effective date 4/1/2000

Cost of Living: Renter

Cost Element	U.S. ($)	City ($)	Differential ($)	Percent of U.S. Average
Consumables	10,486	9,978	-508	95.2
Transportation	2,107	1,911	-196	90.7
Health Services	1,632	1,654	22	101.3
Rent/Utilities/Insurance	9,299	12,556	3,257	135.0
Income+Payroll Taxes	8,607	9,079	472	105.5
Miscellaneous	7,869	7,869	0	100.0
Total Cost of Living	40,000	43,047	3,047	107.6

Note: Figures are based on a single income, three person family with gross annual earnings of $40,000, renting a 1,000 square-foot home, and driving one automobile worth $8,000 12,000 miles per year.
Source: ERI's Relocation Assessor software database, quarterly effective date 4/1/2000

HOUSING

Median Home Prices and Housing Affordability

Area	Median Price[2] 4th Qtr. 1999 ($)	HOI[3] 4th Qtr. 1999	Affordability Rank[4]
MSA[1]	130,000	54.5	150
U.S.	139,000	63.8	–

Note: (1) Metropolitan Statistical Area - see Appendix A for areas included; (2) U.S. figures calculated from the sales of 687,516 new and existing homes in 192 markets; (3) Housing Opportunity Index - percent of homes sold that were within the reach of the median income household at the prevailing mortgage interest rate; (4) Rank is from 1-192 with 1 being most affordable
Source: National Association of Home Builders, Housing Opportunity Index, 4th Quarter 1999

Estimated Home Price

Area	Price ($)
City	213,701
U.S.	135,855

Note: Figures are based on an 1,800 square-foot home
Source: ERI's Relocation Assessor software database, quarterly effective date 4/1/2000

Estimated Rent

Area	Rent ($/month)
City	902
U.S.	651

Note: Figures are based on a 1,000 square-foot home
Source: ERI's Relocation Assessor software database, quarterly effective date 4/1/2000

Median Home Price Projection

It is projected that the median home price in the metropolitan area will increase from $132,448 in 1999 to $203,571 in 2010, an increase of 53.7%
Kiplinger's Personal Finance Magazine, January 2000

RESIDENTIAL UTILITIES

Average Residential Utility Costs

Area	All Electric ($/mth)	Part Electric ($/mth)	Other Energy ($/mth)	Phone ($/mth)
MSA[1]	118.64	–	–	22.77
U.S.	99.25	55.47	43.48	20.29

Note: (1) Metropolitan Statistical Area - see Appendix A for areas included
Source: ACCRA, Cost of Living Index, 3rd Quarter 1999

HEALTH CARE

Average Health Care Costs

Area	Hospital ($/day)	Doctor ($/visit)	Dentist ($/visit)
MSA[1]	436.00	70.00	73.00
U.S.	440.96	53.83	68.42

Note: Hospital—based on a semi-private room; Doctor—based on a general practitioner's routine exam of an established patient; Dentist—based on adult teeth cleaning and periodic oral exam; (1) Metropolitan Statistical Area - see Appendix A for areas included
Source: ACCRA, Cost of Living Index, 3rd Quarter 1999

Distribution of Office-Based Physicians

Area	Family/Gen. Practitioners	Specialists Medical	Surgical	Other
MSA[1]	124	371	318	379

Note: Data as of 12/31/97; (1) Metropolitan Statistical Area - see Appendix A for areas included
Source: American Medical Assn., Physician Characteristics & Distribution in the U.S., 1999

Hospitals

Charleston has 7 general medical and surgical hospitals, 1 psychiatric.
AHA Guide to the Healthcare Field, 1999-2000

According to *U.S. News and World Report,* Charleston has one of the best hospitals in the U.S.: **Medical University of South Carolina**, noted for gastroenterology.
U.S. News Online, "America's Best Hospitals," July 19, 1999

EDUCATION

Public School District Statistics

District Name	Num. Sch.	Enroll.	Classroom Teachers	Pupils per Teacher	Minority Pupils (%)	Current Exp.[1] ($/pupil)
Charleston County School Dist	74	44,107	2,783	15.8	61.2	4,480

Note: Data covers the 1997-1998 school year unless otherwise noted; (1) Data covers fiscal year 1996; SD = School District; ISD = Independent School District; n/a not available
Source: National Center for Education Statistics, Common Core of Data Public Education Agency Universe 1997-98; National Center for Education Statistics, Characteristics of the 100 Largest Public Elementary and Secondary School Districts in the United States: 1997-98, July 1999

Educational Quality

School District	Education Quotient[1]	Graduate Outcome[2]	Community Index[3]	Resource Index[4]
Charleston Co. School Dist.	75	74	112	70

Note: Over 1,000 secondary school districts were rated in terms of educational quality. The scores range from a low of 50 to a high of 150; (1) Combination of the Graduate Outcome, Community and Resource indexes weighted to reflect the greater importance of the Graduate Outcome and Resource Index; (2) Based on graduation rates and college board scores (SAT/ACT); (3) Based on the surrounding community's level of affluence and adult education; (4) Based on teacher salaries, per-pupil expenditures and student-teacher ratios.
Source: Expansion Management, Ratings Issue, 1999

Educational Attainment by Race

Area	High School Graduate (%)					Bachelor's Degree (%)				
	Total	White	Black	Other	Hisp.[2]	Total	White	Black	Other	Hisp.[2]
City	76.5	89.4	56.4	92.5	82.0	29.4	41.0	11.0	51.9	40.6
MSA[1]	75.7	82.6	57.9	73.7	76.3	18.9	23.0	8.3	21.9	17.3
U.S.	75.2	77.9	63.1	60.4	49.8	20.3	21.5	11.4	19.4	9.2

Note: Figures shown cover persons 25 years old and over; (1) Metropolitan Statistical Area - see Appendix A for areas included; (2) people of Hispanic origin can be of any race
Source: 1990 Census of Population and Housing, Summary Tape File 3C

School Enrollment by Type

Area	Preprimary				Elementary/High School			
	Public		Private		Public		Private	
	Enrollment	%	Enrollment	%	Enrollment	%	Enrollment	%
City	723	55.5	579	44.5	9,648	81.4	2,209	18.6
MSA[1]	4,865	54.6	4,043	45.4	83,505	90.6	8,713	9.4
U.S.	2,679,029	59.5	1,824,256	40.5	38,379,689	90.2	4,187,099	9.8

Note: Figures shown cover persons 3 years old and over;
(1) Metropolitan Statistical Area - see Appendix A for areas included
Source: 1990 Census of Population and Housing, Summary Tape File 3C

School Enrollment by Race

Area	Preprimary (%)				Elementary/High School (%)			
	White	Black	Other	Hisp.[1]	White	Black	Other	Hisp.[1]
City	49.7	49.4	0.9	0.9	37.0	61.7	1.2	0.3
MSA[2]	68.1	30.7	1.2	1.4	58.3	39.5	2.2	1.6
U.S.	80.4	12.5	7.1	7.8	74.1	15.6	10.3	12.5

Note: Figures shown cover persons 3 years old and over; (1) people of Hispanic origin can be of any race; (2) Metropolitan Statistical Area - see Appendix A for areas included
Source: 1990 Census of Population and Housing, Summary Tape File 3C

Higher Education

Two-Year Colleges		Four-Year Colleges		Medical Schools	Law Schools	Voc/ Tech
Public	Private	Public	Private			
1	1	2	2	0	0	5

Source: College Blue Book, Occupational Education, 1999; Medical School Admission Requirements, 1999-2000; Peterson's Guide to Two-Year Colleges, 2000; Peterson's Guide to Four-Year Colleges, 1999; Barron's Guide to Law Schools, 1999

MAJOR EMPLOYERS

Major Employers

Charleston Center (hotels)	Charleston Memorial Hospital
Employee Resource Management	Evening Post Publishing
North Trident Regional Medical Center	Piggly Wiggly Carolina
Roper Hospital	South Carolina State Ports Authority

Note: Companies listed are located in the city
Source: D&B Business Rankings, 1999; Ward's Business Directory, 1999; America's Corporate Families, 1999

PUBLIC SAFETY

Crime Rate

Area	All Crimes	Violent Crimes				Property Crimes		
		Murder	Forcible Rape	Robbery	Aggrav. Assault	Burglary	Larceny -Theft	Motor Vehicle Theft
City	10,410.6	8.2	84.7	333.5	863.8	1,370.9	6,590.5	1,159.0
Suburbs[1]	5,508.3	4.0	45.6	136.5	522.8	977.6	3,279.9	541.8
MSA[2]	6,197.9	4.6	51.1	164.2	570.8	1,032.9	3,745.6	628.7
U.S.	4,615.5	6.3	34.4	165.2	360.5	862.0	2,728.1	459.0

Note: Crime rate is the number of crimes per 100,000 population; (1) Defined as all areas within the Metropolitan Statistical Area but located outside the central city; (2) Metropolitan Statistical Area - see Appendix A for areas included
Source: FBI Uniform Crime Reports, 1998

RECREATION

Culture and Recreation

Museums	Symphony Orchestras	Opera Companies	Dance Companies	Professional Theatres	Zoos	Pro Sports Teams
12	1	1	2	0	1	0

Source: Musical America, International Directory of the Performing Arts, 1999; Official Museum Directory, 2000; Stern's Performing Arts Directory, 1997; USA Today Four Sport Stadium Guide, 1997; Career Opportunities in Theatre and the Performing Arts, 1999

Library System

The Charleston Public Library has 14 branches, holdings of 941,748 volumes, and a budget of $10,482,613 (1997-1998).
American Library Directory, 1999-2000

MEDIA

Newspapers

Name	Type	Freq.	Distribution	Circulation
Airlift Dispatch	General	1x/wk	Local	7,500
Charleston Jewish Journal	Religious	1x/mo	Local	2,600
The Coastal Times	Black	1x/wk	Area	5,000
Hanahan & Goose Creek News	General	1x/wk	Local	21,000
The Post and Courier	n/a	7x/wk	Area	116,000

Note: Includes newspapers with circulations of 200 or more located in the city; n/a not available
Source: Burrelle's Media Directory, 1999 Edition

Television Stations

Name	Ch.	Affiliation	Type	Owner
WCBD	n/a	ABCT	Commercial	Media General Inc.
WCIV	n/a	ABCT	Commercial	Allbritton Communications Company
WCSC	n/a	n/a	Commercial	Jefferson-Pilot Communications Company
WTAT	24	FBC	Commercial	Sinclair Communications Inc.
WMMP	36	UPN	Commercial	Sinclair Communications Inc.

Note: Stations included broadcast in the Charleston metro area; n/a not available
Source: Burrelle's Media Directory, 1999 Edition

AM Radio Stations

Call Letters	Freq. (kHz)	Target Audience	Station Format	Music Format
WPAL	730	General	M	Country
WTMZ	910	n/a	N	n/a
WTMA	1250	General	N/T	n/a
WQSC	1340	General	S	n/a
WXTC	1390	General	M	Oldies

Note: Stations included broadcast in the Charleston metro area; n/a not available
Target Audience: A=Asian; B=Black; C=Christian; E=Ethnic; F=French; G=General; H=Hispanic;
M=Men; N=Native American; R=Religious; S=Senior Citizen; W=Women; Y=Young Adult; Z=Children
Station Format: E=Educational; M=Music; N=News; S=Sports; T=Talk
Source: Burrelle's Media Directory, 1999 Edition

FM Radio Stations

Call Letters	Freq. (mHz)	Target Audience	Station Format	Music Format
WFCH	88.5	General	M	Christian
WWWZ	93.3	General	M	Urban Contemporary
WSSP	94.3	General	M/N/S	Top 40
WSSX	95.1	General	M/N	n/a
WAVF	96.1	General	M/N/T	AOR/Top 40
WSUY	96.9	French	General	M
WYBB	98.1	n/a	M	Adult Contemporary/AOR
WALC	100.5	General	M	Adult Contemporary
WPAL	100.9	n/a	n/a	n/a
WMGL	101.7	General	M	Urban Contemporary
WXLY	102.5	General	M	Oldies
WEZL	103.5	General	M	Country
WRFQ	104.5	General	M	Classic Rock
WCOO	105.3	n/a	M	n/a
WNKT	107.5	General	M/N/S	Country

Note: Stations included broadcast in the Charleston metro area; n/a not available
Station Format: E=Educational; M=Music; N=News; S=Sports; T=Talk
Target Audience: A=Asian; B=Black; C=Christian; E=Ethnic; F=French; G=General; H=Hispanic;
M=Men; N=Native American; R=Religious; S=Senior Citizen; W=Women; Y=Young Adult; Z=Children
Music Format: AOR=Album Oriented Rock; MOR=Middle-of-the-Road
Source: Burrelle's Media Directory, 1999 Edition

WEATHER

Temperature/Precipitation/Humidity

	Jan	Feb	Mar	Apr	May	Jun	Jul	Aug	Sep	Oct	Nov	Dec	Yr.
Max. High Temp. (°F)	83	87	90	94	98	101	104	102	97	94	88	83	104
Avg. High Temp. (°F)	59	62	68	76	83	88	90	89	85	77	69	61	76
Avg. Temp. (°F)	49	51	57	65	73	78	81	80	76	67	58	50	65
Avg. Low Temp. (°F)	37	39	46	53	62	68	72	71	67	56	46	39	55
Min. Low Temp. (°F)	6	12	15	30	36	50	58	56	42	27	15	8	6
Avg. Precip. (in.)	3.2	3.2	4.4	2.8	4.1	5.9	7.4	6.7	5.6	2.9	2.4	3.1	51.8
Avg. Snowfall (in.)	Tr	Tr	Tr	0	0	0	0	0	0	0	Tr	Tr	1
Avg. Rel. Hum. 7am (%)	82	81	83	83	85	86	87	90	91	88	86	83	86
Avg. Rel. Hum. 4pm (%)	55	52	51	51	57	62	66	66	65	57	55	55	58

Note: Tr = Trace amounts (less than 0.05 inches of rain or less than 0.5 inches of snow)
Source: National Climatic Data Center, International Station Meteorological Climate Summary, 3/95

Weather Conditions

Temperature			Precipitation		
10°F & below	32°F & below	90°F & above	0.01 inch or more precip.	1.5 inch or more snow/ice	Thunder-storms
< 0.5	34	52	113	1	58

Note: Figures are average number of days per year
Source: National Climatic Data Center, International Station Meteorological Climate Summary, 3/95

AIR & WATER QUALITY

Maximum Pollutant Concentrations

	Particulate Matter (ug/m³)	Carbon Monoxide (ppm)	Sulfur Dioxide (ppm)	Nitrogen Dioxide (ppm)	Ozone (ppm)	Lead (ug/m³)
MSA[1] Level	49	4	0.022	0.011	0.10	0.01
NAAQS[2]	150	9	0.140	0.053	0.12	1.50
Met NAAQS	Yes	Yes	Yes	Yes	Yes	Yes

Note: (1) Metropolitan Statistical Area - see Appendix A for areas included; (2) National Ambient Air Quality Standards; ppm = parts per million; ug/m³ = micrograms per cubic meter; n/a not available
Source: EPA, National Air Quality and Emissions Trends Report, 1997

Pollutant Standards Index

In the Charleston MSA (see Appendix A for areas included), the Pollutant Standards Index (PSI) exceeded 100 on 3 days in 1997. A PSI value greater than 100 indicates that air quality would have been in the unhealthful range on that day.
EPA, National Air Quality and Emissions Trends Report, 1997

Drinking Water

Water System Name	Pop. Served	Primary Water Source Type	Number of Violations in 1998-99	Type of Violation/ Contaminants
Charleston CPW	180,446	Surface	None	None

Note: Data as of January 19, 2000
Source: EPA, Office of Ground Water and Drinking Water, Safe Drinking Water Information System

Charleston tap water is alkaline, very soft, and fluoridated.
Editor & Publisher Market Guide, 2000

Charleston, West Virginia

Background

Charleston, West Virginia is located in the southwest section of the state, approximately 180 miles south of Wheeling, 50 miles east of Huntington and 340 miles west of Washington, D.C. The state capitol and largest city in West Virginia, Charleston is situated where the Kanawha and Elk rivers intersect.

Charleston is a commercial center and transportation hub for West Virginia and an industrial city especially prominent in chemical manufacturing. Charleston is the capital of Kanawha County, and its metropolitan area includes South Charleston and other communities in Kanawah and Putnam Counties.

The lands of West Virginia were occupied by numerous Native American tribes prior to European colonization. The region was claimed by Britain, and was considered part of colonial Virgina. Settlement was sparse before the late 18th Century because of the mountains and conflicts with the French and Native Americans. The site of Charleston was first settled by George Clendenin, who purchased the site in 1787 and built a military post, Fort Lee. In 1794 the town was chartered as Charles Town, named for Clendenin's father Charles. It was renamed Charleston in 1818. Among the early residents was Daniel Boone.

West Virginia was initially part of the state of Virginia, but after Virginia seceded from the Union during the Civil War, residents of the western region remained in the United States, and West Virginia became its own state in 1863. For several years, the state capital alternated between Wheeling and Charleston, until 1885, when Charleston was permanently established as the capital. After the capitol building burned down in 1921, a new building, designed by Cass Gilbert, was completed in 1932. The limestone structure, topped by a 293-foot-high gold dome, remains a prominent city landmark.

Charleston's river location made it a transportation center for southern West Virginia and for settlers and goods moving west. During the 19th Century Charleston gradually developed an economy based on the rich mineral deposits of West Virginia, including coal and petroleum. The Charleston area also became a center for salt mining. The city experienced significant growth in the early 20th Century in chemical manufacturing and other industries. Improvements to transportation and infrastructure further bolstered the economy.

In the 1950s, Charleston and the state's economy began to decline, leading to revitalization efforts. By the late 1990s there were indications of recovery, including redevelopment of the downtown area and the enclosed Charleston Town Center Mall.

The area's institutions of higher education include the University of Charleston. The Marshall University Graduate College is located in South Charleston, and the West Virginia State College is in nearby Institute.

The city has access to a variety of outdoor recreation activities, including river and mountain sports. Attractions within the city include historic sites and the Capitol complex. The Sunrise Estate houses art and science museums. The West Virginia Center of Arts and Sciences is being developed as a museum and arts center. Recreational attractions include parks, among them the Haddad Riverfront Park, which features an amphitheater. The Capitol Center in Charleston is a cultural center operated by West Virginia State College. Other venues include the Charleston Civic Center and the Municipal Auditorium. Performing arts organizations include the Charleston Civic Chorus, the Charleston Ballet, the Kanawha Players, the West Virginia Symphony, the Charleston Chamber Music Society and Friends of Old Time Music and Dance, among others. The Charleston Alley Cats are Class A baseball team affiliated with the Cincinnati Reds.

Charleston is governed by an elected Mayor and 26-member City Council.

General Rankings and Evaluative Comments

- Charleston was ranked #124 out of 354 metropolitan areas in *Places Rated Almanac*. Criteria: cost of living, climate, crime, transportation, job outlook, education, the arts, health care, and recreation. *Places Rated Almanac, Millennium Edition, 2000*

- Zero Population Growth ranked 229 cities in terms of children's health, safety, and economic well-being. Charleston was ranked #29 out of 112 independent cities (cities with populations greater than 100,000 which were neither Major Cities nor Suburbs/Outer Cities) and was given a grade of B-. Criteria: total population and population change, percent of population under 18 years of age, household language, percent of births to teens, infant mortality rate, percent of low birth weights, dropout rate, enrollment in preprimary school, violent and property crime rates, unemployment rate, percent of children in poverty, percent of owner occupied units, number of bad air days, percent of public transportation commuters, and average travel time to work. *Zero Population Growth, Children's Environmental Index, Fall 1999*

- Cognetics studied 273 metro areas in the United States, ranking them by entrepreneurial activity. Charleston was ranked #56 out of 134 smaller metro areas. Criteria: Significant Starts (firms started in the last 10 years that still employ at least 5 people) and Young Growers (percent of firms 10 years old or less that grew significantly during the last 4 years). *Cognetics, "Entrepreneurial Hot Spots: The Best Places in America to Start and Grow a Company," 1999*

Business Environment

STATE ECONOMY

State Economic Profile

"The West Virginia economy continues to expand slowly. Growth in the services and construction sectors has helped to offset losses in steel and mining. West Virginia's weak demographic outlook will constrain labor force growth and housing demand. West Virginia's growth potential is limited without some fundamental changes to its economy and population structure.

Weak commodity prices have undermined West Virginia's metals and mining sectors. Almost 5% of West Virginia employment are in mining or primary metals, compared to 1% for the US. West Virginia's mining operations have also tended to have among the highest costs in the nation. The growing market share of steel mini-mills has also undercut West Virginia's competitive position. Despite import restrictions, steel prices should remain soft in 2000.

West Virginia is the only state where deaths outnumber births. Coupled with its high rate of out-migration, West Virginia is shrinking. Worse is the fact that the number of person in prime working and home-buying years is shrinking at a rate of almost 1.3% a year. The result has been a shortage of skilled workers and a weak housing market. Residential permits declined 9% in 1998. And although home sales were up in 1998, price appreciation has been weak.

West Virginia has increased its efforts to diversify the economy and attract high-tech jobs. Bell Atlantic has already invested $20 million in high-speed phone lines. This and similar efforts have successfully attracted lower-paying data entry and telephone assistance jobs. Growth should increase after West Virginia's current difficulties have run their course." *National Association of Realtors, Economic Profiles: The Fifty States and the District of Columbia, http://nar.realtor.com/databank/profiles.htm*

EXPORTS

Total Export Sales

Area	1995 ($000)	1996 ($000)	1997 ($000)	1998 ($000)	% Chg. 1995-98	% Chg. 1997-98
MSA[1]	394,362	412,150	393,392	396,693	0.6	0.8
U.S.	583,030,524	622,827,063	687,597,999	680,474,251	16.7	-1.0

Note: (1) Metropolitan Statistical Area - see Appendix A for areas included
Source: U.S. Department of Commerce, International Trade Association, Metropolitan Area Exports: An Export Performance Report on Over 250 U.S. Cities, November 10, 1999

CITY FINANCES

City Government Finances

Component	1995 ($million)	1995 (per capita $)
Revenue	65.0	1,149
Expenditure	66.0	1,168
Debt Outstanding	110.8	1,959

Source: 1999 County and City Extra, Annual Metro, City, and County Data Book

City Government Revenue by Source

Source	1995 ($million)	1995 (per capita $)
Intergovernmental	3.6	63
Taxes	35.6	630
Property	7.9	141
Sales and Gross Receipts	3.6	65

Source: 1999 County and City Extra, Annual Metro, City, and County Data Book

City Government Expenditures by Function

Function	1995 ($million)	1995 (per capita $)	1995 (%)
Public Welfare	0.0	0	0.0
Highways	4.7	84	7.2
Parking Facilities	8.2	145	12.5
Education	0.0	0	0.0
Health and Hospitals	2.5	45	3.9
Police Protection	8.3	148	12.7
Sewerage and Sanitation	8.0	142	12.2
Parks and Recreation	4.4	79	6.8
Housing and Community Development	4.7	84	7.2
Interest on Debt	6.8	121	10.4

Source: 1999 County and City Extra, Annual Metro, City, and County Data Book

Municipal Bond Ratings

Area	Moody's
City	A1

Source: Mergent Bond Record, 2/2000

POPULATION

Population Growth

Area	1980 Census	1990 Census	1999 Estimate	2004 Projection	Population Growth (%) 1990-1999	Population Growth (%) 1999-2004
City	63,968	57,287	54,760	53,273	-4.4	-2.7
MSA[1]	269,595	250,454	253,008	253,123	1.0	0.0
U.S.	226,545,805	248,765,170	272,212,864	283,625,312	9.4	4.2

Note: (1) Metropolitan Statistical Area - see Appendix A for areas included
Source: 1990 Census of Population and Housing, Summary Tape File 3C; Claritas, Inc.

Number of Households and Average Household Size

Area	1980 Census	1990 Census	1999 Estimate	2004 Projection	1999 Average Household Size
City	26,574	25,302	24,824	24,512	2.21
MSA[1]	99,414	100,134	104,556	106,118	2.42
U.S.	80,389,592	91,993,582	102,048,200	107,302,392	2.67

Note: (1) Metropolitan Statistical Area - see Appendix A for areas included
Source: 1990 Census of Population and Housing, Summary Tape File 3C; Claritas, Inc.

Race/Ethnicity of City Population

Race/Ethnicity	1990 Census Population	1990 Census %	1999 Estimate Population	1999 Estimate %	% Change 1990-1999
White, Non-Hispanic	48,015	83.8	45,431	83.0	-5.4
Black, Non-Hispanic	8,106	14.1	8,009	14.6	-1.2
Asian, Non-Hispanic	683	1.2	733	1.3	7.3
Other, Non-Hispanic	154	0.3	151	0.3	-1.9
Hispanic	329	0.6	436	0.8	32.5

Source: 1990 Census of Population and Housing, Summary Tape File 3C; Claritas, Inc.

Race/Ethnicity of Metropolitan Statistical Area Population

Race/Ethnicity	1990 Census		1999 Estimate		% Change 1990-1999
	Population	%	Population	%	
White, Non-Hispanic	233,937	93.4	236,126	93.3	0.9
Black, Non-Hispanic	13,696	5.5	13,736	5.4	0.3
Asian, Non-Hispanic	1,355	0.5	1,440	0.6	6.3
Other, Non-Hispanic	418	0.2	456	0.2	9.1
Hispanic	1,048	0.4	1,250	0.5	19.3

Note: See Appendix A for areas included in the Metropolitan Statistical Area
Source: 1990 Census of Population and Housing, Summary Tape File 3C; Claritas, Inc.

Ancestry

Area	German	Irish	English	Italian	U.S.	French	Polish	Dutch
City	23.1	17.5	19.6	3.6	9.0	2.4	1.5	2.9
MSA[1]	23.0	18.9	18.3	2.7	15.2	2.4	1.0	3.7
U.S.	23.3	15.6	13.1	5.9	5.3	4.2	3.8	2.5

Note: Figures are percentages and include persons that reported multiple ancestry (eg. if a person reported being Irish and Italian, they were included in both columns); (1) Metropolitan Statistical Area - see Appendix A for areas included
Source: 1990 Census of Population and Housing, Summary Tape File 3C

Median Age

Area	1990 Census	1999 Estimate
City	37.5	40.3
MSA[1]	36.2	39.3
U.S.	32.9	35.7

Note: (1) Metropolitan Statistical Area - see Appendix A for areas included
Source: 1990 Census of Population and Housing, Summary Tape File 3C; Claritas, Inc.

Male/Female Population

Area	Number of Males		Number of Females		Males per 100 Females	
	1990	1999	1990	1999	1990	1999
City	26,087	25,077	31,200	29,683	83.6	84.5
MSA[1]	118,861	120,302	131,593	132,706	90.3	90.7
U.S.	121,172,379	132,803,736	127,537,494	139,409,136	95.0	95.3

Note: (1) Metropolitan Statistical Area - see Appendix A for areas included
Source: 1990 Census of Population, General Population Characteristics; Claritas, Inc.

INCOME

Per Capita/Median/Average Income

Area	Per Capita ($)			Median Household ($)			Average Household ($)		
	1989	1999	% Chg.	1989	1999	% Chg.	1989	1999	% Chg.
City	16,067	25,206	56.9	23,584	31,293	32.7	35,886	54,892	53.0
MSA[1]	12,708	20,189	58.9	24,578	34,078	38.7	31,543	48,482	53.7
U.S.	14,420	21,350	48.1	30,056	40,525	34.8	38,453	56,184	46.1

Note: (1) Metropolitan Statistical Area - see Appendix A for areas included; 1989 data is from the 1990 Census; 1999 data is estimated by Claritas, Inc.
Source: 1990 Census of Population, General Population Characteristics; Claritas, Inc.

Household Income Distribution

Area	Percent of Households Earning								
	Under $5,000	$5,000 -14,999	$15,000 -24,999	$25,000 -34,999	$35,000 -49,999	$50,000 -74,999	$75,000 -99,000	$100,000 -149,999	$150,000 and up
City	6.6	18.4	16.8	12.2	12.0	13.8	8.3	6.2	5.7
MSA[1]	4.8	15.7	16.7	13.8	15.3	17.9	8.2	5.0	2.7
U.S.	3.9	13.3	13.8	12.6	16.2	19.4	9.7	6.6	4.6

Note: Data as of 1999; (1) Metropolitan Statistical Area - see Appendix A for areas included
Source: Claritas, Inc.

Effective Buying Income

Area	Per Capita ($)	Median Household ($)	Average Household ($)
City	20,453	30,913	45,194
MSA[1]	17,768	33,348	42,924
U.S.	17,496	36,603	47,036

Note: Data as of 1/1/2000; (1) Metropolitan Statistical Area - see Appendix A for areas included
Source: Standard Rate & Data Service, Newspaper Advertising Source, March 2000

Effective Household Buying Income Distribution

Area	% of Households Earning						
	$10,000 -$19,999	$20,000 -$34,999	$35,000 -$49,999	$50,000 -$74,999	$75,000 -$99,000	$100,000 -$124,999	$125,000 and up
City	18.0	20.5	13.7	15.3	8.1	2.7	5.2
MSA[1]	17.1	22.4	16.4	18.3	8.3	2.4	2.4
U.S.	15.0	21.6	17.6	19.6	8.4	3.0	3.3

Note: Data as of 1/1/2000; (1) Metropolitan Statistical Area - see Appendix A for areas included
Source: Standard Rate & Data Service, Newspaper Advertising Source, March 2000

Poverty Rates by Age

Area	People of All Ages	People Under 18 Years Old	Related Children Age 5-17 in Families in Poverty
City	20.9	n/a	n/a
County	17.1	26.1	21.8
U.S.	13.8	20.8	18.7

Note: Figures show the percent of people living below the poverty line in 1995. The
average poverty threshold was $15,569 for a family of four in 1995; n/a not available
Source: Bureau of the Census, Small Area Income and Poverty Estimates Program;
U.S. Department of Housing and Urban Development

EMPLOYMENT

Labor Force and Employment

Area	Civilian Labor Force			Workers Employed		
	Dec. 1998	Dec. 1999	% Chg.	Dec. 1998	Dec. 1999	% Chg.
City	29,528	30,221	2.3	28,149	28,794	2.3
MSA[1]	131,361	134,448	2.4	125,507	128,385	2.3
U.S.	138,297,000	139,941,000	1.2	132,732,000	134,696,000	1.5

Note: Data is not seasonally adjusted and covers workers 16 years of age and older;
(1) Metropolitan Statistical Area - see Appendix A for areas included
Source: Bureau of Labor Statistics, http://stats.bls.gov

Unemployment Rate

Area	1999											
	Jan.	Feb.	Mar.	Apr.	May	Jun.	Jul.	Aug.	Sep.	Oct.	Nov.	Dec.
City	5.3	5.0	5.2	5.2	4.8	4.6	4.3	4.6	4.7	4.7	4.9	4.7
MSA[1]	5.2	4.8	5.0	4.9	4.6	4.4	4.1	4.3	4.4	4.4	4.7	4.5
U.S.	4.8	4.7	4.4	4.1	4.0	4.5	4.5	4.2	4.1	3.8	3.8	3.7

Note: Data is not seasonally adjusted and covers workers 16 years of age and older; all figures are percentages; (1) Metropolitan Statistical Area - see Appendix A for areas included
Source: Bureau of Labor Statistics, http://stats.bls.gov

Employment by Industry

Sector	MSA[1]		U.S.
	Number of Employees	Percent of Total	Percent of Total
Services	43,100	31.5	30.2
Retail Trade	24,500	17.9	18.1
Government	24,800	18.1	15.8
Manufacturing	10,400	7.6	14.1
Finance/Insurance/Real Estate	7,900	5.8	5.9
Wholesale Trade	7,300	5.3	5.4
Transportation/Public Utilities	9,800	7.2	5.3
Construction	6,700	4.9	4.8
Mining	2,200	1.6	0.4

Note: Figures cover non-farm employment as of 12/99 and are not seasonally adjusted;
(1) Metropolitan Statistical Area - see Appendix A for areas included
Source: Bureau of Labor Statistics, http://stats.bls.gov

Employment by Occupation

Occupation Category	City (%)	MSA[1] (%)	U.S. (%)
White Collar	73.5	62.6	58.1
Executive/Admin./Management	15.3	11.6	12.3
Professional	21.0	14.4	14.1
Technical & Related Support	3.8	4.4	3.7
Sales	14.8	13.3	11.8
Administrative Support/Clerical	18.5	19.0	16.3
Blue Collar	14.5	24.0	26.2
Precision Production/Craft/Repair	6.9	11.6	11.3
Machine Operators/Assem./Insp.	2.3	3.5	6.8
Transportation/Material Movers	2.6	4.8	4.1
Cleaners/Helpers/Laborers	2.6	4.1	3.9
Services	11.6	12.5	13.2
Farming/Forestry/Fishing	0.5	0.9	2.5

Note: Figures cover workers 16 years of age and older;
(1) Metropolitan Statistical Area - see Appendix A for areas included
Source: 1990 Census of Population and Housing, Summary Tape File 3C

Occupational Employment Projections: 1996 - 2006

Occupations Expected to Have the Largest Job Growth (ranked by numerical growth)	Fast-Growing Occupations[1] (ranked by percent growth)
1. General managers & top executives	1. Systems analysts
2. Cashiers	2. Database administrators
3. Salespersons, retail	3. Computer engineers
4. Guards	4. Paralegals
5. Maintenance repairers, general utility	5. Hotel desk clerks
6. Systems analysts	6. Personal and home care aides
7. Hairdressers & cosmetologists	7. Artists and commercial artists
8. Clerical supervisors	8. Counter & rental clerks
9. Counter & rental clerks	9. Cleaners/servants, private home
10. Personal and home care aides	10. Bill and account collectors

Note: Projections cover West Virginia; (1) Excludes occupations with total job growth less than 300
Source: U.S. Department of Labor, Employment and Training Administration, America's Labor Market Information System (ALMIS)

Average Wages

Occupation	$/Hr.	Occupation	$/Hr.
Accountants and Auditors	17.83	Maids and Housekeepers	6.90
Assemblers and Fabricators	10.71	Maintenance Repairers	10.50
Automotive Mechanics	11.68	Marketing/Advertising/PR Managers	23.96
Bookkeepers	9.63	Nurses, Licensed Practical	11.81
Carpenters	15.40	Nurses, Registered	21.01
Cashiers	6.40	Nursing Aides/Orderlies/Attendants	7.30
Clerks, General Office	8.67	Physicians and Surgeons	53.75
Clerks, Shipping/Receiving/Traffic	11.69	Receptionists/Information Clerks	7.87
Computer Programmers	18.06	Sales Reps., Exc. Scientific/Retail	16.82
Computer Support Specialists	17.43	Sales Reps., Scientific, Exc. Retail	22.53
Cooks, Restaurant	6.43	Salespersons, Retail	7.75
Electricians	17.46	Secretaries, Except Legal/Medical	10.10
Financial Managers	23.88	Stock Clerks, Sales Floor	7.62
First-Line Supervisors/Mgrs., Sales	14.31	Systems Analysts	24.06
Food Preparation Workers	6.42	Teacher Aides	-
General Managers/Top Executives	25.93	Teachers, Elementary School	-
Guards	6.41	Teachers, Secondary School	-
Hand Packers	6.14	Telemarketers	-
Janitors and Cleaners	8.04	Truck Drivers, Heavy/Tractor-Trailer	13.17
Laborers, Landscaping	8.43	Truck Drivers, Light	9.68
Lawyers	26.25	Waiters and Waitresses	5.68

Note: Wage data is for 1998 and covers the Metropolitan Statistical Area (see Appendix A for areas included). Hourly wages for elementary and secondary school teachers were calculated by the editors from annual wage data assuming a 40 hour work week; Dashes indicate that data was not available.
Source: Bureau of Labor Statistics, 1998 Metropolitan Area Occupational Employment and Wage Estimates

TAXES

Major State and Local Tax Rates

State Corporate Income (%)	State Personal Income (%)	Residential Property (%)	Sales & Use		State Gasoline (cents/ gallon)	State Cigarette (cents/ pack)
			State (%)	Local (%)		
9.0	3.0 - 6.5	0.91	6.0	None	25.35[a]	17.0

Note: Personal/corporate income, sales, gasoline and cigarette tax rates as of January 2000. Property tax rates as of April 2000; (a) Sales tax added to excise
Source: Federation of Tax Administrators, www.taxadmin.org; ERI's Relocation Assessor software database, quarterly effective date 4/1/2000

Total Taxes Per Capita and as a Percent of Income

Area	Per Capita Income ($)	Per Capita Taxes ($)			Percent of Income (%)		
		Total	Federal	State/Local	Total	Federal	State/Local
West Virginia	20,742	6,798	4,469	2,329	32.8	21.5	11.2
U.S.	28,878	10,298	7,026	3,273	35.7	24.3	11.3

Note: Figures are for 1999
Source: Tax Foundation, www.taxfoundation.org

COMMERCIAL UTILITIES

Typical Monthly Electric Bills

Area	Commercial Service ($/month)		Industrial Service ($/month)	
	12 kW demand 1,500 kWh	100 kW demand 30,000 kWh	1,000 kW demand 400,000 kWh	20,000 kW demand 10,000,000 kWh
City	119	1,658	17,584	275,786
U.S.	150	2,174	23,995	508,569

Note: Based on rates in effect January 1, 1999
Source: Edison Electric Institute, Typical Residential, Commercial and Industrial Bills, Winter 1999

TRANSPORTATION

Transportation Statistics

Average minutes to work (1990)	15.0
Interstate highways	I-64; I-77; I-79; US-60; US-119; US-ALT 60
Bus lines	
In-city (1998)	Kanawha Valley Regional Transportation Authority, 45 buses
Inter-city (1999)	1
Passenger air service	
Airport	Yeager Airport
Airlines (1999)	6
Enplaned passengers (1998)	261,801
Amtrak service	Yes
Motor freight carriers (1999)	30
Major waterways/ports	Kanawha River

Source: FAA DOT/TSC CY1998 ACAIS Database; National Transit Database, 1998; Editor & Publisher Market Guide, 2000; Amtrak National Time Table, Fall 1999/Winter 2000; 1990 Census of Population and Housing, STF 3C; Jane's Urban Transport Systems 1999-2000

Means of Transportation to Work

Area	Car/Truck/Van		Public Transportation			Bicycle	Walked	Other Means	Worked at Home
	Drove Alone	Car-pooled	Bus	Subway	Railroad				
City	71.8	12.6	5.0	0.0	0.0	0.2	6.7	1.1	2.6
MSA[1]	76.6	15.1	2.3	0.0	0.0	0.1	3.3	0.7	2.0
U.S.	73.2	13.4	3.0	1.5	0.5	0.4	3.9	1.2	3.0

Note: Figures shown are percentages and only include workers 16 years of age and older;
(1) Metropolitan Statistical Area - see Appendix A for areas included
Source: 1990 Census of Population and Housing, Summary Tape File 3C

BUSINESSES

Major Business Headquarters

Company Name	1999 Rankings	
	Fortune 500	Forbes 500
McJunkin	-	322

Note: Companies listed are located in the city; dashes indicate no ranking
Fortune 500: Companies that produce a 10-K are ranked 1 to 500 based on 1999 revenue
Forbes 500: Private companies are ranked 1 to 500 based on 1998 revenue
Source: Forbes, December 13, 1999; Fortune, April 17, 2000

HOTELS & MOTELS

Hotels/Motels

Area	Hotels/ Motels	Rooms	Luxury-Level Hotels/Motels		Average Minimum Rates ($)		
			♦♦♦♦	♦♦♦♦♦	♦♦	♦♦♦	♦♦♦♦
City	7	1,231	0	0	n/a	n/a	n/a

Note: n/a not available; classifications range from one diamond (budget properties with basic amenities) to five diamond (luxury properties).
Source: OAG Business Travel Planner, Winter 1999-2000

Estimated Daily Food and Lodging Costs

Area	Food/Other ($/day)	Average Hotel Cost ($/day)
City	38	82
U.S.	30	55

Source: ERI's Relocation Assessor software database, quarterly effective date 4/1/2000

CONVENTION CENTERS

Convention Centers and Event Sites

Name	Guest Rooms	Meeting Space (sq. ft.)	Capacity (Theatre Style)
Charleston Civic Center	n/a	n/a	13,500
Charleston Marriott Town Center	352	n/a	0
Embassy Suites Charleston	253	10,000	0
Laidley Field Athletic & Rec. Ctr.	n/a	n/a	18,600

Note: n/a not available
Source: EventSource.com, 3/15/2000

Living Environment

COST OF LIVING

Cost of Living: Homeowner

Cost Element	U.S. ($)	City ($)	Differential ($)	Percent of U.S. Average
Consumables	14,516	14,960	444	103.1
Transportation	5,957	6,251	294	104.9
Health Services	2,012	1,896	-116	94.2
Housing/Utilities/Prop. Tax	16,337	13,358	-2,979	81.8
Income+Payroll Taxes	12,615	13,026	411	103.3
Miscellaneous	8,563	8,563	0	100.0
Total Cost of Living	60,000	58,054	-1,946	96.8

Note: Figures are based on a single income, four person family with gross annual earnings of $60,000, owning an 1,800 square-foot home, and driving two automobiles worth $22,000 30,000 miles per year.
Source: ERI's Relocation Assessor software database, quarterly effective date 4/1/2000

Cost of Living: Renter

Cost Element	U.S. ($)	City ($)	Differential ($)	Percent of U.S. Average
Consumables	10,486	10,836	350	103.3
Transportation	2,107	2,218	111	105.3
Health Services	1,632	1,542	-90	94.5
Rent/Utilities/Insurance	9,299	7,378	-1,921	79.3
Income+Payroll Taxes	8,607	8,535	-72	99.2
Miscellaneous	7,869	7,869	0	100.0
Total Cost of Living	40,000	38,378	-1,622	95.9

Note: Figures are based on a single income, three person family with gross annual earnings of $40,000, renting a 1,000 square-foot home, and driving one automobile worth $8,000 12,000 miles per year.
Source: ERI's Relocation Assessor software database, quarterly effective date 4/1/2000

HOUSING

Median Home Prices and Housing Affordability

Area	Median Price[2] 4th Qtr. 1999 ($)	HOI[3] 4th Qtr. 1999	Affordability Rank[4]
MSA[1]	n/a	n/a	n/a
U.S.	139,000	63.8	–

Note: (1) Metropolitan Statistical Area - see Appendix A for areas included; (2) U.S. figures calculated from the sales of 687,516 new and existing homes in 192 markets; (3) Housing Opportunity Index - percent of homes sold that were within the reach of the median income household at the prevailing mortgage interest rate; (4) Rank is from 1-192 with 1 being most affordable; n/a not available
Source: National Association of Home Builders, Housing Opportunity Index, 4th Quarter 1999

Estimated Home Price

Area	Price ($)
City	109,848
U.S.	135,855

Note: Figures are based on an 1,800 square-foot home
Source: ERI's Relocation Assessor software database, quarterly effective date 4/1/2000

Estimated Rent

Area	Rent ($/month)
City	489
U.S.	651

Note: Figures are based on a 1,000 square-foot home
Source: ERI's Relocation Assessor software database, quarterly effective date 4/1/2000

Median Home Price Projection

It is projected that the median home price in the metropolitan area will increase from $84,204 in 1999 to $123,812 in 2010, an increase of 47.0%
Kiplinger's Personal Finance Magazine, January 2000

RESIDENTIAL UTILITIES

Average Residential Utility Costs

Area	All Electric ($/mth)	Part Electric ($/mth)	Other Energy ($/mth)	Phone ($/mth)
MSA[1]	–	39.01	47.92	28.59
U.S.	99.25	55.47	43.48	20.29

Note: (1) Metropolitan Statistical Area - see Appendix A for areas included
Source: ACCRA, Cost of Living Index, 3rd Quarter 1999

HEALTH CARE

Average Health Care Costs

Area	Hospital ($/day)	Doctor ($/visit)	Dentist ($/visit)
MSA[1]	258.20	53.80	58.43
U.S.	440.96	53.83	68.42

Note: Hospital—based on a semi-private room; Doctor—based on a general practitioner's routine exam of an established patient; Dentist—based on adult teeth cleaning and periodic oral exam; (1) Metropolitan Statistical Area - see Appendix A for areas included
Source: ACCRA, Cost of Living Index, 3rd Quarter 1999

Distribution of Office-Based Physicians

Area	Family/Gen. Practitioners	Specialists Medical	Specialists Surgical	Specialists Other
MSA[1]	82	164	163	129

Note: Data as of 12/31/97; (1) Metropolitan Statistical Area - see Appendix A for areas included
Source: American Medical Assn., Physician Characteristics & Distribution in the U.S., 1999

Hospitals

Charleston has 2 general medical and surgical hospitals, 1 psychiatric, 1 eye, ear, nose and throat.
AHA Guide to the Healthcare Field, 1999-2000

According to *U.S. News and World Report,* Charleston has one of the best hospitals in the U.S.: **Charleston Area Medical Center**, noted for neurology.
U.S. News Online, "America's Best Hospitals," July 19, 1999

EDUCATION

Public School District Statistics

District Name	Num. Sch.	Enroll.	Classroom Teachers	Pupils per Teacher	Minority Pupils (%)	Current Exp.[1] ($/pupil)
Institutional Programs	7	366	66	5.5	n/a	n/a
Kanawha County School District	90	31,470	1,968	16.0	11.3	5,653

Note: Data covers the 1997-1998 school year unless otherwise noted; (1) Data covers fiscal year 1996; SD = School District; ISD = Independent School District; n/a not available
Source: National Center for Education Statistics, Common Core of Data Public Education Agency Universe 1997-98; National Center for Education Statistics, Characteristics of the 100 Largest Public Elementary and Secondary School Districts in the United States: 1997-98, July 1999

Educational Quality

School District	Education Quotient[1]	Graduate Outcome[2]	Community Index[3]	Resource Index[4]
Kanawha Co. School Dist.	99	103	106	89

Note: Over 1,000 secondary school districts were rated in terms of educational quality. The scores range from a low of 50 to a high of 150; (1) Combination of the Graduate Outcome, Community and Resource indexes weighted to reflect the greater importance of the Graduate Outcome and Resource Index; (2) Based on graduation rates and college board scores (SAT/ACT); (3) Based on the surrounding community's level of affluence and adult education; (4) Based on teacher salaries, per-pupil expenditures and student-teacher ratios.
Source: Expansion Management, Ratings Issue, 1999

Educational Attainment by Race

Area	High School Graduate (%)					Bachelor's Degree (%)				
	Total	White	Black	Other	Hisp.[2]	Total	White	Black	Other	Hisp.[2]
City	77.2	77.6	73.3	88.0	86.5	28.6	30.1	13.7	58.9	41.0
MSA[1]	72.7	72.5	75.3	84.9	76.3	16.9	16.7	16.6	47.7	29.7
U.S.	75.2	77.9	63.1	60.4	49.8	20.3	21.5	11.4	19.4	9.2

Note: Figures shown cover persons 25 years old and over; (1) Metropolitan Statistical Area - see Appendix A for areas included; (2) people of Hispanic origin can be of any race
Source: 1990 Census of Population and Housing, Summary Tape File 3C

School Enrollment by Type

Area	Preprimary				Elementary/High School			
	Public		Private		Public		Private	
	Enrollment	%	Enrollment	%	Enrollment	%	Enrollment	%
City	493	48.7	519	51.3	7,944	93.0	595	7.0
MSA[1]	2,169	60.9	1,394	39.1	40,005	95.4	1,908	4.6
U.S.	2,679,029	59.5	1,824,256	40.5	38,379,689	90.2	4,187,099	9.8

Note: Figures shown cover persons 3 years old and over;
(1) Metropolitan Statistical Area - see Appendix A for areas included
Source: 1990 Census of Population and Housing, Summary Tape File 3C

School Enrollment by Race

Area	Preprimary (%)				Elementary/High School (%)			
	White	Black	Other	Hisp.[1]	White	Black	Other	Hisp.[1]
City	85.4	8.9	5.7	0.8	75.8	21.0	3.2	1.1
MSA[2]	93.3	4.8	1.9	0.8	91.7	6.8	1.5	0.7
U.S.	80.4	12.5	7.1	7.8	74.1	15.6	10.3	12.5

Note: Figures shown cover persons 3 years old and over; (1) people of Hispanic origin can be of any race; (2) Metropolitan Statistical Area - see Appendix A for areas included
Source: 1990 Census of Population and Housing, Summary Tape File 3C

Higher Education

Two-Year Colleges		Four-Year Colleges		Medical Schools	Law Schools	Voc/Tech
Public	Private	Public	Private			
0	1	2	1	1	0	5

Source: College Blue Book, Occupational Education, 1999; Medical School Admission Requirements, 1999-2000; Peterson's Guide to Two-Year Colleges, 2000; Peterson's Guide to Four-Year Colleges, 1999; Barron's Guide to Law Schools, 1999

MAJOR EMPLOYERS

Major Employers

Acordia National (insurance)
Bell-Atlantic WV
Charleston Area Medical Center
Herbert J. Thomas Memorial Hospital
One Valley Bank

Appalachian Tire Products
Camcare (healthcare)
Charleston Hospital
Kanawha Manufacturing (metalworking)

Note: Companies listed are located in the city
Source: D&B Business Rankings, 1999; Ward's Business Directory, 1999; America's Corporate Families, 1999

PUBLIC SAFETY

Crime Rate

Area	All Crimes	Violent Crimes				Property Crimes		
		Murder	Forcible Rape	Robbery	Aggrav. Assault	Burglary	Larceny -Theft	Motor Vehicle Theft
City	10,267.9	14.3	62.5	382.0	555.2	2,085.0	6,156.8	1,012.2
Suburbs[1]	3,007.4	4.1	10.7	28.0	162.7	703.8	1,788.0	310.2
MSA[2]	4,617.2	6.3	22.2	106.5	249.7	1,010.0	2,756.6	465.8
U.S.	4,615.5	6.3	34.4	165.2	360.5	862.0	2,728.1	459.0

Note: Crime rate is the number of crimes per 100,000 population; (1) Defined as all areas within the Metropolitan Statistical Area but located outside the central city; (2) Metropolitan Statistical Area - see Appendix A for areas included
Source: FBI Uniform Crime Reports, 1998

RECREATION

Culture and Recreation

Museums	Symphony Orchestras	Opera Companies	Dance Companies	Professional Theatres	Zoos	Pro Sports Teams
2	2	0	1	0	0	0

Source: Musical America, International Directory of the Performing Arts, 1999; Official Museum Directory, 2000; Stern's Performing Arts Directory, 1997; USA Today Four Sport Stadium Guide, 1997; Career Opportunities in Theatre and the Performing Arts, 1999

Library System

The Kanawha County Public Library has eight branches, holdings of 628,308 volumes, and a budget of $5,305,816 (1997-1998).
American Library Directory, 1999-2000

MEDIA

Newspapers

Name	Type	Freq.	Distribution	Circulation
Charleston Daily Mail	General	7x/wk	Area	44,000
The Charleston Gazette	n/a	7x/wk	Area	54,500
West Virginia Beacon Digest	Black	1x/wk	State	35,000

Note: Includes newspapers with circulations of 200 or more located in the city; n/a not available
Source: Burrelle's Media Directory, 1999 Edition

Television Stations

Name	Ch.	Affiliation	Type	Owner
WCHS	n/a	ABCT	Commercial	Sinclair Communications Inc.

Note: Stations included broadcast in the Charleston metro area; n/a not available
Source: Burrelle's Media Directory, 1999 Edition

AM Radio Stations

Call Letters	Freq. (kHz)	Target Audience	Station Format	Music Format
WCHS	580	General	N/T	n/a
WCAW	680	General	M	Adult Standards
WQBE	950	General	N/S/T	n/a
WVSR	1240	General	M	Adult Contemporary
WCOZ	1300	General	M/N	Classic Rock
WSCW	1410	Religious	M/N/S/T	Christian

Note: Stations included broadcast in the Charleston metro area; n/a not available
Target Audience: A=Asian; B=Black; C=Christian; E=Ethnic; F=French; G=General; H=Hispanic; M=Men; N=Native American; R=Religious; S=Senior Citizen; W=Women; Y=Young Adult; Z=Children
Station Format: E=Educational; M=Music; N=News; S=Sports; T=Talk
Source: Burrelle's Media Directory, 1999 Edition

FM Radio Stations

Call Letters	Freq. (mHz)	Target Audience	Station Format	Music Format
WVPN	88.5	General	M/N	Classical
WVEP	88.9	General	E/M/N	Classical
WVPW	88.9	General	E/M/N	Classical/Jazz
WVNP	89.9	General	E/M/N	Classical
WVWV	89.9	General	M/N	Classical
WVPG	90.3	General	E/M/N	Jazz
WVPM	90.9	General	E/M/N	Jazz
WVPB	91.7	General	E/M/N	Classical
WBES	94.5	General	M	Adult Top 40
WKWS	96.1	General	M	Country
WQBE	97.5	General	M	Country
WVAF	99.9	General	M/N/T	Top 40
WJYP	100.9	Religious	M/N/T	Christian/MOR
WVSR	102.7	General	M	Adult Contemporary
WKLC	105.1	General	M/N	AOR/Classic Rock
WKAZ	107.3	General	M	Oldies

Note: Stations included broadcast in the Charleston metro area
Station Format: E=Educational; M=Music; N=News; S=Sports; T=Talk
Target Audience: A=Asian; B=Black; C=Christian; E=Ethnic; F=French; G=General; H=Hispanic;
M=Men; N=Native American; R=Religious; S=Senior Citizen; W=Women; Y=Young Adult; Z=Children
Music Format: AOR=Album Oriented Rock; MOR=Middle-of-the-Road
Source: Burrelle's Media Directory, 1999 Edition

WEATHER

Temperature/Precipitation/Humidity

	Jan	Feb	Mar	Apr	May	Jun	Jul	Aug	Sep	Oct	Nov	Dec	Yr.
Max. High Temp. (°F)	79	78	89	94	93	98	104	101	102	92	84	80	104
Avg. High Temp. (°F)	43	46	56	67	76	83	86	84	79	68	56	46	66
Avg. Temp. (°F)	34	37	45	55	64	72	75	74	68	57	46	37	55
Avg. Low Temp. (°F)	25	27	34	43	52	60	64	63	56	45	36	28	44
Min. Low Temp. (°F)	-15	-6	0	19	26	33	46	41	34	17	6	-12	-15
Avg. Precip. (in.)	3.4	3.2	3.8	3.3	3.9	3.6	5.1	4.0	3.1	2.7	3.3	3.3	42.8
Avg. Snowfall (in.)	10	9	5	1	Tr	0	0	0	0	Tr	2	5	32
Avg. Rel. Hum. 7am (%)	77	76	74	75	83	86	90	92	91	87	80	77	82
Avg. Rel. Hum. 4pm (%)	59	55	48	44	49	52	56	56	55	51	53	59	53

Note: Tr = Trace amounts (less than 0.05 inches of rain or less than 0.5 inches of snow)
Source: National Climatic Data Center, International Station Meteorological Climate Summary, 3/95

Weather Conditions

Temperature			Precipitation		
10°F & below	32°F & below	90°F & above	0.01 inch or more precip.	1.5 inch or more snow/ice	Thunder-storms
10	100	22	153	7	45

Note: Figures are average number of days per year
Source: National Climatic Data Center, International Station Meteorological Climate Summary, 3/95

AIR & WATER QUALITY

Maximum Pollutant Concentrations

	Particulate Matter (ug/m³)	Carbon Monoxide (ppm)	Sulfur Dioxide (ppm)	Nitrogen Dioxide (ppm)	Ozone (ppm)	Lead (ug/m³)
MSA[1] Level	57	2	0.032	0.020	0.10	0.01
NAAQS[2]	150	9	0.140	0.053	0.12	1.50
Met NAAQS	Yes	Yes	Yes	Yes	Yes	Yes

Note: (1) Metropolitan Statistical Area - see Appendix A for areas included; (2) National Ambient Air
Quality Standards; ppm = parts per million; ug/m³ = micrograms per cubic meter; n/a not available
Source: EPA, National Air Quality and Emissions Trends Report, 1997

Pollutant Standards Index

Data not available.
EPA, National Air Quality and Emissions Trends Report, 1997

Drinking Water

Water System Name	Pop. Served	Primary Water Source Type	Number of Violations in 1998-99	Type of Violation/ Contaminants
WVAWC-Kanawha Valley	173,005	Surface	None	None

Note: Data as of January 19, 2000
Source: EPA, Office of Ground Water and Drinking Water, Safe Drinking Water Information System

Charleston tap water is alkaline, soft, and fluoridated.
Editor & Publisher Market Guide, 2000

Charlottesville, Virginia

Background

Charlottesville, Virginia, rests at the headwaters of the Rivanna River in the foothills of the Blue Ridge Mountains, approximately 70 miles northwest of Richmond and 100 miles southwest of Washington, D.C. As a result of eight annexations, the most recent in 1968, Charlottesville encompasses 10.4 square miles. Interstate 64 and state Route 29 link the city to Richmond and Washington, D.C.

The city's main business is educational services. The University of Virginia, designed and founded by Thomas Jefferson in 1819, has a total enrollment of 18,000 students, the majority of whom study at the College of Arts and Sciences. Other schools include Piedmont Virginia Community College and the Institute of Textile Technology, founded in 1944.

Other economic segments include the manufacture of textiles and elecrical equipment, livestock and racehorse breeding, and farming, mainly apples.

Charlottesville is named for Queen Charlotte Sophia, the young bride of King George III of England. The site was settled in the 1730s, and was established as a town in 1762, thriving as a tobacco trading point and later earning fame as the home of presidents Thomas Jefferson and James Monroe and explorers Meriwether Lewis and George Rogers Clark. That same year, the town's original rectangular tract of 50 acres was separated into lots and sold to farmers who grew tobacco, wheat, Indian corn, barley and oats. Since transportation was difficult between the Shenandoah Valley and Richmond further east, the town became extremely self-sufficient.

Charlottesville has lost none of its self-sufficiency. Although the city lies within Albemarle County, it is autonomous and completely independent of any taxation by, or liability to, any county or school district in the state.

There are many cultural and historical venues in or near the city. Monticello, Thomas Jefferson's home which was also designed by him, overlooks the city. The Jefferson family gravesite has been restored and is maintained as a national shrine. Ash Lawn, the home of James Monroe, is five miles southeast of Charlottesville, and was also designed by Jefferson.

General Rankings and Evaluative Comments

- Charlottesville was ranked #123 out of 354 metropolitan areas in *Places Rated Almanac.* Criteria: cost of living, climate, crime, transportation, job outlook, education, the arts, health care, and recreation. *Places Rated Almanac, Millennium Edition, 2000*

- Charlottesville was selected as one of North America's "Best Small Metro Areas" (population under 250,000). The area ranked #10 out of 20. Criteria: cost of living, climate, crime, transportation, job outlook, education, the arts, health care, and recreation. *Places Rated Almanac, Millennium Edition, 2000*

- Charlottesville was selected as one of America's best small art towns. The city was ranked #25 out of 100. Criteria: easy and affordable access to the visual arts, performing arts and music, strong sense of community, low crime rate, and full-time population less than 65,000. *The 100 Best Small Art Towns in America: Discover Creative Communities, Fresh Air, and Affordable Living, 1998*

- Charlottesville was profiled as one of the "great towns" of America. Criteria: scenic appeal, memorable leisure-time features, natural and/or cultural attractions, pleasant weather, quality restaurants and lodgings, and population under 50,000. *The Great Towns of America: A Guide to the 100 Best Getaways for a Vacation or a Lifetime, 1998*

- Charlottesville was selected as one of America's best places to retire. Criteria: safety, climate, housing, culture and recreation, social compatibility, affordability, medical care, transportation, and jobs and/or volunteer opportunities. *Where to Retire: America's Best and Most Affordable Places, 1998*

- Charlottesville was selected as one of the best places to retire by *Retirement Places Rated.* Criteria: cost of living, climate, crime, services, working, and leisure living. The city was ranked #83 out of 187. *Retirement Places Rated, 1999*

- Charlottesville was selected as one of "America's Best Towns to Raise an Outdoor Family" by *Outdoor Explorer* magazine. Criteria: easy access to the outdoors, quality education and health care, affordable housing, favorable employment opportunities, and low crime rates. The city was ranked #6 out of 25. *Outdoor Explorer, Summer 1999*

- Charlottesville was selected as one of "The 50 Most Alive Places to Live" in the U.S. Criteria: ethnic diversity, recreational options, cultural vitality, low crime rate, opportunities for lifelong learning, good hospitals and restaurants, public transportation, walking accessibility, civic activities, and the kitsch factor. The area was ranked #2 out of 10 in the "College Towns" category. *Modern Maturity, May-June 2000*

Business Environment

STATE ECONOMY

State Economic Profile

"Virginia has begun to slow from its recent expansion. Virginia's above-average growth is largely a result of the expansion of high-tech firms in Northern Virginia. Slower growth in the Hampton Roads and Richmond areas stems from a slowdown in the manufacturing and farm sectors. Virginia's demographic situation is solid, and its housing and construction markets remain vibrant. Although a slowing US economy will be a drag on Virginia, the long-term outlook for Virginia is strong, above-average growth.

Northern Virginia has become less dependent upon defense spending as its economy has diversified into commercial internet and software development. The Tidewater area is a different story. Both consolidation among shipbuilders and declining Naval purchasers are likely to result in job losses in Virginia's shipbuilding industry. Job reductions have also taken place at the Port of Hampton Roads as Virginia's exports have fallen. The opening of the Gateway Plant will diversify southeastern Virginia's economy away from its dependence on military spending.

Virginia's housing market was one of the hottest in 1998. Home sales were up over 25% in 1998 with activity occurring in all parts of the state. Price appreciation was strong in northern, central and southeastern Virginia. While permit activity was flat in Richmond, both northern Virginia and Hampton Roads saw permit activity increase by at least 10%. Sales and starts should moderate slightly in the near future.

Virginia has some of the nation's strongest economic fundamentals: business friendly environment, an educated workforce, strong demographics and a diversified economy. Virginia's most immediate constraint is its tight labor market." *National Association of Realtors, Economic Profiles: The Fifty States and the District of Columbia, http://nar.realtor.com/databank/profiles.htm*

EXPORTS

Total Export Sales

Area	1995 ($000)	1996 ($000)	1997 ($000)	1998 ($000)	% Chg. 1995-98	% Chg. 1997-98
MSA[1]	157,362	140,238	195,369	191,363	21.6	-2.1
U.S.	583,030,524	622,827,063	687,597,999	680,474,251	16.7	-1.0

Note: (1) Metropolitan Statistical Area - see Appendix A for areas included
Source: U.S. Department of Commerce, International Trade Association, Metropolitan Area Exports: An Export Performance Report on Over 250 U.S. Cities, November 10, 1999

CITY FINANCES

City Government Finances

Component	1995 ($million)	1995 (per capita $)
Revenue	97.9	2,385
Expenditure	101.8	2,480
Debt Outstanding	33.7	821

Source: 1999 County and City Extra, Annual Metro, City, and County Data Book

City Government Revenue by Source

Source	1995 ($million)	1995 (per capita $)
Intergovernmental	40.2	979
Taxes	44.1	1,074
Property	25.2	614
Sales and Gross Receipts	15.3	373

Source: 1999 County and City Extra, Annual Metro, City, and County Data Book

City Government Expenditures by Function

Function	1995 ($million)	1995 (per capita $)	1995 (%)
Public Welfare	6.2	151	6.1
Highways	3.7	91	3.7
Parking Facilities	1.7	42	1.7
Education	36.3	885	35.7
Health and Hospitals	0.9	22	0.9
Police Protection	6.0	146	5.9
Sewerage and Sanitation	7.2	176	7.1
Parks and Recreation	3.9	96	3.9
Housing and Community Development	4.1	101	4.1
Interest on Debt	4.0	99	4.0

Source: 1999 County and City Extra, Annual Metro, City, and County Data Book

Municipal Bond Ratings

Area	Moody's
City	Aaa

Source: Mergent Bond Record, 2/2000

POPULATION

Population Growth

Area	1980 Census	1990 Census	1999 Estimate	2004 Projection	Population Growth (%) 1990-1999	Population Growth (%) 1999-2004
City	39,916	40,341	38,357	37,690	-4.9	-1.7
MSA[1]	113,568	131,107	150,961	159,676	15.1	5.8
U.S.	226,545,805	248,765,170	272,212,864	283,625,312	9.4	4.2

Note: (1) Metropolitan Statistical Area - see Appendix A for areas included
Source: 1990 Census of Population and Housing, Summary Tape File 3C; Claritas, Inc.

Number of Households and Average Household Size

Area	1980 Census	1990 Census	1999 Estimate	2004 Projection	1999 Average Household Size
City	15,366	16,099	15,280	15,063	2.51
MSA[1]	40,241	48,718	57,017	61,137	2.65
U.S.	80,389,592	91,993,582	102,048,200	107,302,392	2.67

Note: (1) Metropolitan Statistical Area - see Appendix A for areas included
Source: 1990 Census of Population and Housing, Summary Tape File 3C; Claritas, Inc.

Race/Ethnicity of City Population

Race/Ethnicity	1990 Census Population	1990 Census %	1999 Estimate Population	1999 Estimate %	% Change 1990-1999
White, Non-Hispanic	30,338	75.2	27,083	70.6	-10.7
Black, Non-Hispanic	8,602	21.3	9,362	24.4	8.8
Asian, Non-Hispanic	866	2.1	1,216	3.2	40.4
Other, Non-Hispanic	150	0.4	70	0.2	-53.3
Hispanic	385	1.0	626	1.6	62.6

Source: 1990 Census of Population and Housing, Summary Tape File 3C; Claritas, Inc.

Race/Ethnicity of Metropolitan Statistical Area Population

Race/Ethnicity	1990 Census		1999 Estimate		% Change 1990-1999
	Population	%	Population	%	
White, Non-Hispanic	107,971	82.4	120,175	79.6	11.3
Black, Non-Hispanic	18,950	14.5	24,292	16.1	28.2
Asian, Non-Hispanic	2,505	1.9	3,868	2.6	54.4
Other, Non-Hispanic	315	0.2	314	0.2	-0.3
Hispanic	1,366	1.0	2,312	1.5	69.3

Note: See Appendix A for areas included in the Metropolitan Statistical Area
Source: 1990 Census of Population and Housing, Summary Tape File 3C; Claritas, Inc.

Ancestry

Area	German	Irish	English	Italian	U.S.	French	Polish	Dutch
City	17.7	13.2	19.3	3.0	8.3	2.7	1.6	1.7
MSA[1]	19.7	14.0	20.9	3.3	10.5	2.9	1.8	1.9
U.S.	23.3	15.6	13.1	5.9	5.3	4.2	3.8	2.5

Note: Figures are percentages and include persons that reported multiple ancestry (eg. if a person reported being Irish and Italian, they were included in both columns); (1) Metropolitan Statistical Area - see Appendix A for areas included
Source: 1990 Census of Population and Housing, Summary Tape File 3C

Median Age

Area	1990 Census	1999 Estimate
City	28.8	31.9
MSA[1]	31.0	34.5
U.S.	32.9	35.7

Note: (1) Metropolitan Statistical Area - see Appendix A for areas included
Source: 1990 Census of Population and Housing, Summary Tape File 3C; Claritas, Inc.

Male/Female Population

Area	Number of Males		Number of Females		Males per 100 Females	
	1990	1999	1990	1999	1990	1999
City	18,858	18,123	21,483	20,234	87.8	89.6
MSA[1]	63,490	73,065	67,617	77,896	93.9	93.8
U.S.	121,172,379	132,803,736	127,537,494	139,409,136	95.0	95.3

Note: (1) Metropolitan Statistical Area - see Appendix A for areas included
Source: 1990 Census of Population, General Population Characteristics; Claritas, Inc.

INCOME

Per Capita/Median/Average Income

Area	Per Capita ($)			Median Household ($)			Average Household ($)		
	1989	1999	% Chg.	1989	1999	% Chg.	1989	1999	% Chg.
City	12,928	20,594	59.3	24,190	35,704	47.6	31,238	49,801	59.4
MSA[1]	15,227	23,665	55.4	31,397	44,315	41.1	40,078	61,198	52.7
U.S.	14,420	21,350	48.1	30,056	40,525	34.8	38,453	56,184	46.1

Note: (1) Metropolitan Statistical Area - see Appendix A for areas included; 1989 data is from the 1990 Census; 1999 data is estimated by Claritas, Inc.
Source: 1990 Census of Population, General Population Characteristics; Claritas, Inc.

Household Income Distribution

Area	Percent of Households Earning								
	Under $5,000	$5,000 -14,999	$15,000 -24,999	$25,000 -34,999	$35,000 -49,999	$50,000 -74,999	$75,000 -99,000	$100,000 -149,999	$150,000 and up
City	4.6	16.1	16.1	12.2	16.5	17.4	7.9	5.7	3.5
MSA[1]	3.5	11.2	12.8	11.7	16.6	20.7	10.5	7.4	5.8
U.S.	3.9	13.3	13.8	12.6	16.2	19.4	9.7	6.6	4.6

Note: Data as of 1999; (1) Metropolitan Statistical Area - see Appendix A for areas included
Source: Claritas, Inc.

Effective Buying Income

Area	Per Capita ($)	Median Household ($)	Average Household ($)
City	16,018	29,148	39,018
MSA[1]	18,473	37,522	48,681
U.S.	17,496	36,603	47,036

Note: Data as of 1/1/2000; (1) Metropolitan Statistical Area - see Appendix A for areas included
Source: Standard Rate & Data Service, Newspaper Advertising Source, March 2000

Effective Household Buying Income Distribution

Area	% of Households Earning						
	$10,000 -$19,999	$20,000 -$34,999	$35,000 -$49,999	$50,000 -$74,999	$75,000 -$99,000	$100,000 -$124,999	$125,000 and up
City	19.5	23.6	16.4	14.9	6.1	2.0	1.9
MSA[1]	14.3	21.8	18.6	20.0	8.2	2.9	3.7
U.S.	15.0	21.6	17.6	19.6	8.4	3.0	3.3

Note: Data as of 1/1/2000; (1) Metropolitan Statistical Area - see Appendix A for areas included
Source: Standard Rate & Data Service, Newspaper Advertising Source, March 2000

Poverty Rates by Age

Area	People of All Ages	People Under 18 Years Old	Related Children Age 5-17 in Families in Poverty
City	21.5	n/a	n/a
County	21.5	29.1	32.3
U.S.	13.8	20.8	18.7

Note: Figures show the percent of people living below the poverty line in 1995. The
average poverty threshold was $15,569 for a family of four in 1995; n/a not available
Source: Bureau of the Census, Small Area Income and Poverty Estimates Program;
U.S. Department of Housing and Urban Development

EMPLOYMENT

Labor Force and Employment

Area	Civilian Labor Force			Workers Employed		
	Dec. 1998	Dec. 1999	% Chg.	Dec. 1998	Dec. 1999	% Chg.
City	19,538	19,731	1.0	19,256	19,436	0.9
MSA[1]	76,424	77,190	1.0	75,534	76,243	0.9
U.S.	138,297,000	139,941,000	1.2	132,732,000	134,696,000	1.5

Note: Data is not seasonally adjusted and covers workers 16 years of age and older;
(1) Metropolitan Statistical Area - see Appendix A for areas included
Source: Bureau of Labor Statistics, http://stats.bls.gov

Unemployment Rate

Area	1999											
	Jan.	Feb.	Mar.	Apr.	May	Jun.	Jul.	Aug.	Sep.	Oct.	Nov.	Dec.
City	2.5	1.5	1.2	0.9	1.3	2.2	1.7	2.0	1.6	1.8	1.7	1.5
MSA[1]	1.5	1.1	1.1	0.9	1.2	1.5	1.4	1.5	1.4	1.5	1.3	1.2
U.S.	4.8	4.7	4.4	4.1	4.0	4.5	4.5	4.2	4.1	3.8	3.8	3.7

Note: Data is not seasonally adjusted and covers workers 16 years of age and older; all figures are percentages; (1) Metropolitan Statistical Area - see Appendix A for areas included
Source: Bureau of Labor Statistics, http://stats.bls.gov

Employment by Industry

Sector	MSA[1]		U.S.
	Number of Employees	Percent of Total	Percent of Total
Services	22,200	25.3	30.2
Retail Trade	15,700	17.9	18.1
Government	27,100	30.9	15.8
Manufacturing	8,400	9.6	14.1
Finance/Insurance/Real Estate	4,800	5.5	5.9
Wholesale Trade	2,300	2.6	5.4
Transportation/Public Utilities	2,500	2.9	5.3
Construction	n/a	n/a	4.8
Mining	n/a	n/a	0.4

Note: Figures cover non-farm employment as of 12/99 and are not seasonally adjusted;
(1) Metropolitan Statistical Area - see Appendix A for areas included; n/a not available
Source: Bureau of Labor Statistics, http://stats.bls.gov

Employment by Occupation

Occupation Category	City (%)	MSA[1] (%)	U.S. (%)
White Collar	63.5	64.3	58.1
Executive/Admin./Management	9.6	11.9	12.3
Professional	23.2	20.6	14.1
Technical & Related Support	5.4	5.3	3.7
Sales	9.8	10.7	11.8
Administrative Support/Clerical	15.4	15.8	16.3
Blue Collar	17.1	20.1	26.2
Precision Production/Craft/Repair	8.4	10.7	11.3
Machine Operators/Assem./Insp.	3.5	4.0	6.8
Transportation/Material Movers	2.7	2.9	4.1
Cleaners/Helpers/Laborers	2.5	2.6	3.9
Services	18.3	12.8	13.2
Farming/Forestry/Fishing	1.1	2.8	2.5

Note: Figures cover workers 16 years of age and older;
(1) Metropolitan Statistical Area - see Appendix A for areas included
Source: 1990 Census of Population and Housing, Summary Tape File 3C

Occupational Employment Projections: 1996 - 2006

Occupations Expected to Have the Largest Job Growth (ranked by numerical growth)	Fast-Growing Occupations[1] (ranked by percent growth)
1. Systems analysts	1. Desktop publishers
2. Cashiers	2. Personal and home care aides
3. Computer engineers	3. Physical therapy assistants and aides
4. General managers & top executives	4. Medical assistants
5. Salespersons, retail	5. Physical therapists
6. Janitors/cleaners/maids, ex. priv. hshld.	6. Occupational therapists
7. Database administrators	7. Home health aides
8. Receptionists and information clerks	8. Manicurists
9. Engineering/science/computer sys. mgrs.	9. Paralegals
10. Truck drivers, light	10. Bill and account collectors

Note: Projections cover Virginia; (1) Excludes occupations with total job growth less than 300
Source: U.S. Department of Labor, Employment and Training Administration, America's Labor Market Information System (ALMIS)

Average Wages

Occupation	$/Hr.	Occupation	$/Hr.
Accountants and Auditors	17.84	Maids and Housekeepers	7.25
Assemblers and Fabricators	9.62	Maintenance Repairers	10.86
Automotive Mechanics	14.78	Marketing/Advertising/PR Managers	20.57
Bookkeepers	10.34	Nurses, Licensed Practical	13.46
Carpenters	13.91	Nurses, Registered	-
Cashiers	6.98	Nursing Aides/Orderlies/Attendants	9.28
Clerks, General Office	9.32	Physicians and Surgeons	-
Clerks, Shipping/Receiving/Traffic	11.91	Receptionists/Information Clerks	8.76
Computer Programmers	21.14	Sales Reps., Exc. Scientific/Retail	16.90
Computer Support Specialists	16.36	Sales Reps., Scientific, Exc. Retail	26.18
Cooks, Restaurant	7.62	Salespersons, Retail	8.13
Electricians	13.17	Secretaries, Except Legal/Medical	11.02
Financial Managers	23.52	Stock Clerks, Sales Floor	7.85
First-Line Supervisors/Mgrs., Sales	14.71	Systems Analysts	25.86
Food Preparation Workers	7.02	Teacher Aides	7.74
General Managers/Top Executives	27.87	Teachers, Elementary School	20.52
Guards	7.62	Teachers, Secondary School	19.82
Hand Packers	6.84	Telemarketers	8.14
Janitors and Cleaners	7.68	Truck Drivers, Heavy/Tractor-Trailer	11.68
Laborers, Landscaping	8.74	Truck Drivers, Light	10.36
Lawyers	37.20	Waiters and Waitresses	6.12

Note: Wage data is for 1998 and covers the Metropolitan Statistical Area (see Appendix A for areas included). Hourly wages for elementary and secondary school teachers were calculated by the editors from annual wage data assuming a 40 hour work week; Dashes indicate that data was not available.
Source: Bureau of Labor Statistics, 1998 Metropolitan Area Occupational Employment and Wage Estimates

TAXES

Major State and Local Tax Rates

State Corporate Income (%)	State Personal Income (%)	Residential Property (%)	Sales & Use State (%)	Sales & Use Local (%)	State Gasoline (cents/ gallon)	State Cigarette (cents/ pack)
6.0	2.0 - 5.75	1.11	3.5	1.0	17.5[a]	2.5[b]

Note: Personal/corporate income, sales, gasoline and cigarette tax rates as of January 2000. Property tax rates as of April 2000; (a) Does not include a 2% local option tax. Large trucks pay an additional tax of 3.5 cents; (b) Counties and cities may impose an additional tax of 2 - 15 cents per pack
Source: Federation of Tax Administrators, www.taxadmin.org; ERI's Relocation Assessor software database, quarterly effective date 4/1/2000

Total Taxes Per Capita and as a Percent of Income

Area	Per Capita Income ($)	Per Capita Taxes ($)			Percent of Income (%)		
		Total	Federal	State/Local	Total	Federal	State/Local
Virginia	29,471	10,129	7,057	3,072	34.4	23.9	10.4
U.S.	28,878	10,298	7,026	3,273	35.7	24.3	11.3

Note: Figures are for 1999
Source: Tax Foundation, www.taxfoundation.org

COMMERCIAL UTILITIES

Typical Monthly Electric Bills

Area	Commercial Service ($/month)		Industrial Service ($/month)	
	12 kW demand 1,500 kWh	100 kW demand 30,000 kWh	1,000 kW demand 400,000 kWh	20,000 kW demand 10,000,000 kWh
City	119	1,978	20,383	346,201
U.S.	150	2,174	23,995	508,569

Note: Based on rates in effect January 1, 1999
Source: Edison Electric Institute, Typical Residential, Commercial and Industrial Bills, Winter 1999

TRANSPORTATION

Transportation Statistics

Average minutes to work (1990)	14.0
Interstate highways	I-64; US-250; US-29
Bus lines	
In-city (1998)	Charlottesville Transit Service, 11 buses
Inter-city (1999)	1
Passenger air service	
Airport	Charlottesville-Albemarle Regional Airport
Airlines (1999)	4
Enplaned passengers (1998)	169,369
Amtrak service	Yes
Motor freight carriers (1999)	5
Major waterways/ports	None

Source: FAA DOT/TSC CY1998 ACAIS Database; National Transit Database, 1998; Editor & Publisher Market Guide, 2000; Amtrak National Time Table, Fall 1999/Winter 2000; 1990 Census of Population and Housing, STF 3C; Jane's Urban Transport Systems 1999-2000

Means of Transportation to Work

Area	Car/Truck/Van		Public Transportation			Bicycle	Walked	Other Means	Worked at Home
	Drove Alone	Car-pooled	Bus	Subway	Railroad				
City	60.8	13.4	5.2	0.0	0.0	1.3	14.8	1.6	2.9
MSA[1]	69.6	16.2	2.7	0.1	0.0	0.5	6.5	1.1	3.2
U.S.	73.2	13.4	3.0	1.5	0.5	0.4	3.9	1.2	3.0

Note: Figures shown are percentages and only include workers 16 years of age and older;
(1) Metropolitan Statistical Area - see Appendix A for areas included
Source: 1990 Census of Population and Housing, Summary Tape File 3C

BUSINESSES

Major Business Headquarters

Company Name	1999 Rankings	
	Fortune 500	Forbes 500
No companies listed	-	-

Note: Companies listed are located in the city; dashes indicate no ranking
Fortune 500: Companies that produce a 10-K are ranked 1 to 500 based on 1999 revenue
Forbes 500: Private companies are ranked 1 to 500 based on 1998 revenue
Source: Forbes, December 13, 1999; Fortune, April 17, 2000

HOTELS & MOTELS

Hotels/Motels

Area	Hotels/ Motels	Rooms	Luxury-Level Hotels/Motels		Average Minimum Rates ($)		
			♦♦♦♦	♦♦♦♦♦	♦♦	♦♦♦	♦♦♦♦
City	21	1,629	1	0	64	110	250
Suburbs	4	634	0	0	n/a	n/a	n/a
Total	25	2,263	1	0	n/a	n/a	n/a

Note: n/a not available; classifications range from one diamond (budget properties with basic amenities) to five diamond (luxury properties).
Source: OAG Business Travel Planner, Winter 1999-2000

Estimated Daily Food and Lodging Costs

Area	Food/Other ($/day)	Average Hotel Cost ($/day)
City	42	66
U.S.	30	55

Source: ERI's Relocation Assessor software database, quarterly effective date 4/1/2000

CONVENTION CENTERS

Convention Centers and Event Sites

Name	Guest Rooms	Meeting Space (sq. ft.)	Capacity (Theatre Style)
Four Points Hotel Charlottesville	229	17,000	675
Omni Charlottesville Hotel	204	12,000	660
Sponsors Hall Darden School UVA	114	n/a	0

Note: n/a not available
Source: EventSource.com, 3/15/2000

Living Environment

COST OF LIVING

Cost of Living: Homeowner

Cost Element	U.S. ($)	City ($)	Differential ($)	Percent of U.S. Average
Consumables	14,516	14,101	-415	97.1
Transportation	5,957	6,217	260	104.4
Health Services	2,012	2,095	83	104.1
Housing/Utilities/Prop. Tax	16,337	22,091	5,754	135.2
Income+Payroll Taxes	12,615	12,305	-310	97.5
Miscellaneous	8,563	8,563	0	100.0
Total Cost of Living	60,000	65,372	5,372	109.0

Note: Figures are based on a single income, four person family with gross annual earnings of $60,000, owning an 1,800 square-foot home, and driving two automobiles worth $22,000 30,000 miles per year.
Source: ERI's Relocation Assessor software database, quarterly effective date 4/1/2000

Cost of Living: Renter

Cost Element	U.S. ($)	City ($)	Differential ($)	Percent of U.S. Average
Consumables	10,486	10,195	-291	97.2
Transportation	2,107	2,201	94	104.5
Health Services	1,632	1,701	69	104.2
Rent/Utilities/Insurance	9,299	12,511	3,212	134.5
Income+Payroll Taxes	8,607	8,951	344	104.0
Miscellaneous	7,869	7,869	0	100.0
Total Cost of Living	40,000	43,428	3,428	108.6

Note: Figures are based on a single income, three person family with gross annual earnings of $40,000, renting a 1,000 square-foot home, and driving one automobile worth $8,000 12,000 miles per year.
Source: ERI's Relocation Assessor software database, quarterly effective date 4/1/2000

HOUSING

Median Home Prices and Housing Affordability

Area	Median Price[2] 4th Qtr. 1999 ($)	HOI[3] 4th Qtr. 1999	Affordability Rank[4]
MSA[1]	n/a	n/a	n/a
U.S.	139,000	63.8	–

Note: (1) Metropolitan Statistical Area - see Appendix A for areas included; (2) U.S. figures calculated from the sales of 687,516 new and existing homes in 192 markets; (3) Housing Opportunity Index - percent of homes sold that were within the reach of the median income household at the prevailing mortgage interest rate; (4) Rank is from 1-192 with 1 being most affordable; n/a not available
Source: National Association of Home Builders, Housing Opportunity Index, 4th Quarter 1999

Estimated Home Price

Area	Price ($)
City	192,734
U.S.	135,855

Note: Figures are based on an 1,800 square-foot home
Source: ERI's Relocation Assessor software database, quarterly effective date 4/1/2000

Estimated Rent

Area	Rent ($/month)
City	893
U.S.	651

Note: Figures are based on a 1,000 square-foot home
Source: ERI's Relocation Assessor software database, quarterly effective date 4/1/2000

RESIDENTIAL UTILITIES

Average Residential Utility Costs

Area	All Electric ($/mth)	Part Electric ($/mth)	Other Energy ($/mth)	Phone ($/mth)
City	n/a	n/a	n/a	n/a
U.S.	99.25	55.47	43.48	20.29

Note: n/a not available
Source: ACCRA, Cost of Living Index, 3rd Quarter 1999

HEALTH CARE

Average Health Care Costs

Area	Hospital ($/day)	Doctor ($/visit)	Dentist ($/visit)
City	n/a	n/a	n/a
U.S.	440.96	53.83	68.42

Note: n/a not available
Source: ACCRA, Cost of Living Index, 3rd Quarter 1999

Distribution of Office-Based Physicians

Area	Family/Gen. Practitioners	Specialists		
		Medical	Surgical	Other
MSA[1]	52	218	133	235

Note: Data as of 12/31/97; (1) Metropolitan Statistical Area - see Appendix A for areas included
Source: American Medical Assn., Physician Characteristics & Distribution in the U.S., 1999

Hospitals

Charlottesville has 2 general medical and surgical hospitals, 1 psychiatric.
AHA Guide to the Healthcare Field, 1999-2000

According to *U.S. News and World Report,* Charlottesville has one of the best hospitals in the U.S.: **University of Virginia Health Sciences Center**, noted for cancer, cardiology, endocrinology, gastroenterology, geriatrics, gynecology, neurology, otolaryngology, pulmonology, urology.
U.S. News Online, "America's Best Hospitals," July 19, 1999

EDUCATION

Public School District Statistics

District Name	Num. Sch.	Enroll.	Classroom Teachers	Pupils per Teacher	Minority Pupils (%)	Current Exp.[1] ($/pupil)
Albemarle Co. Public Schools	23	11,644	n/a	n/a	n/a	n/a
Charlottesville City Public	9	4,408	n/a	n/a	n/a	n/a
Charlottsville-Albemarle Tech	1	n/a	n/a	n/a	n/a	n/a
Piedmont Regional Ed.	1	n/a	n/a	n/a	n/a	n/a

Note: Data covers the 1997-1998 school year unless otherwise noted; (1) Data covers fiscal year 1996; SD = School District; ISD = Independent School District; n/a not available
Source: National Center for Education Statistics, Common Core of Data Public Education Agency Universe 1997-98; National Center for Education Statistics, Characteristics of the 100 Largest Public Elementary and Secondary School Districts in the United States: 1997-98, July 1999

Educational Quality

School District	Education Quotient[1]	Graduate Outcome[2]	Community Index[3]	Resource Index[4]
Charlottesville City Public Schools	117	105	86	148

Note: Over 1,000 secondary school districts were rated in terms of educational quality. The scores range from a low of 50 to a high of 150; (1) Combination of the Graduate Outcome, Community and Resource indexes weighted to reflect the greater importance of the Graduate Outcome and Resource Index; (2) Based on graduation rates and college board scores (SAT/ACT); (3) Based on the surrounding community's level of affluence and adult education; (4) Based on teacher salaries, per-pupil expenditures and student-teacher ratios.
Source: Expansion Management, Ratings Issue, 1999

Educational Attainment by Race

Area	High School Graduate (%)					Bachelor's Degree (%)				
	Total	White	Black	Other	Hisp.[2]	Total	White	Black	Other	Hisp.[2]
City	75.5	78.7	61.7	92.5	95.0	34.1	40.7	7.4	52.4	57.3
MSA[1]	76.9	79.8	57.6	92.7	87.0	33.3	36.8	8.1	60.5	44.2
U.S.	75.2	77.9	63.1	60.4	49.8	20.3	21.5	11.4	19.4	9.2

Note: Figures shown cover persons 25 years old and over; (1) Metropolitan Statistical Area - see Appendix A for areas included; (2) people of Hispanic origin can be of any race
Source: 1990 Census of Population and Housing, Summary Tape File 3C

School Enrollment by Type

Area	Preprimary				Elementary/High School			
	Public		Private		Public		Private	
	Enrollment	%	Enrollment	%	Enrollment	%	Enrollment	%
City	322	53.8	276	46.2	4,220	93.9	272	6.1
MSA[1]	1,303	52.0	1,205	48.0	16,572	92.8	1,279	7.2
U.S.	2,679,029	59.5	1,824,256	40.5	38,379,689	90.2	4,187,099	9.8

Note: Figures shown cover persons 3 years old and over;
(1) Metropolitan Statistical Area - see Appendix A for areas included
Source: 1990 Census of Population and Housing, Summary Tape File 3C

School Enrollment by Race

Area	Preprimary (%)				Elementary/High School (%)			
	White	Black	Other	Hisp.[1]	White	Black	Other	Hisp.[1]
City	73.7	24.9	1.3	3.5	58.5	39.7	1.7	0.7
MSA[2]	82.2	16.7	1.2	1.9	78.1	20.2	1.7	1.4
U.S.	80.4	12.5	7.1	7.8	74.1	15.6	10.3	12.5

Note: Figures shown cover persons 3 years old and over; (1) people of Hispanic origin can be of any race; (2) Metropolitan Statistical Area - see Appendix A for areas included
Source: 1990 Census of Population and Housing, Summary Tape File 3C

Higher Education

Two-Year Colleges		Four-Year Colleges		Medical Schools	Law Schools	Voc/Tech
Public	Private	Public	Private			
1	1	1	0	1	1	2

Source: College Blue Book, Occupational Education, 1999; Medical School Admission Requirements, 1999-2000; Peterson's Guide to Two-Year Colleges, 2000; Peterson's Guide to Four-Year Colleges, 1999; Barron's Guide to Law Schools, 1999

MAJOR EMPLOYERS

Major Employers

Comdial Corp. (telephone equipment)
Martha Jefferson Hospital
Nimbus Manufacturing
Sprig Lane Investment Corp.

Jefferson Bankshares
Michie Co. (book publishing)
Sperry Marine
University of Virginia Medical Center

Note: Companies listed are located in the city
Source: D&B Business Rankings, 1999; Ward's Business Directory, 1999; America's Corporate Families, 1999

PUBLIC SAFETY

Crime Rate

Area	All Crimes	Violent Crimes				Property Crimes		
		Murder	Forcible Rape	Robbery	Aggrav. Assault	Burglary	Larceny -Theft	Motor Vehicle Theft
City	7,063.4	2.6	60.2	188.4	941.8	947.0	4,596.5	327.0
Suburbs[1]	2,478.3	2.7	21.9	14.6	125.9	341.1	1,879.9	92.1
MSA[2]	3,663.7	2.7	31.8	59.5	336.8	497.8	2,582.2	152.8
U.S.	4,615.5	6.3	34.4	165.2	360.5	862.0	2,728.1	459.0

Note: Crime rate is the number of crimes per 100,000 population; (1) Defined as all areas within the Metropolitan Statistical Area but located outside the central city; (2) Metropolitan Statistical Area - see Appendix A for areas included
Source: FBI Uniform Crime Reports, 1998

RECREATION

Culture and Recreation

Museums	Symphony Orchestras	Opera Companies	Dance Companies	Professional Theatres	Zoos	Pro Sports Teams
5	1	1	0	0	0	0

Source: Musical America, International Directory of the Performing Arts, 1999; Official Museum Directory, 2000; Stern's Performing Arts Directory, 1997; USA Today Four Sport Stadium Guide, 1997; Career Opportunities in Theatre and the Performing Arts, 1999

Library System

The Jefferson-Madison Regional Library has seven branches, holdings of 439,818 volumes, and a budget of $3,881,736 (1997-1998).
American Library Directory, 1999-2000

MEDIA

Newspapers

Name	Type	Freq.	Distribution	Circulation
The Cavalier Daily	General	5x/wk	Camp/Comm	10,000
The Daily Progress	General	7x/wk	Area	31,500
The University Journal	n/a	5x/wk	Camp/Comm	10,000

Note: Includes newspapers with circulations of 200 or more located in the city; n/a not available
Source: Burrelle's Media Directory, 1999 Edition

Television Stations

Name	Ch.	Affiliation	Type	Owner
WVIR	29	NBCT	Commercial	Waterman Broadcasting
WHTJ	41	PBS	Public	Central Virginia Educational Telecommunications Corp.

Note: Stations included broadcast in the Charlottesville metro area; n/a not available
Source: Burrelle's Media Directory, 1999 Edition

AM Radio Stations

Call Letters	Freq. (kHz)	Target Audience	Station Format	Music Format
WCYK	810	General	M	Country
WINA	1070	General	N/S/T	n/a
WCHV	1260	General	M	Urban Contemporary
WKAV	1400	General	M	Oldies

Note: Stations included broadcast in the Charlottesville metro area; n/a not available
Target Audience: A=Asian; B=Black; C=Christian; E=Ethnic; F=French; G=General; H=Hispanic; M=Men; N=Native American; R=Religious; S=Senior Citizen; W=Women; Y=Young Adult; Z=Children
Station Format: E=Educational; M=Music; N=News; S=Sports; T=Talk
Source: Burrelle's Media Directory, 1999 Edition

FM Radio Stations

Call Letters	Freq. (mHz)	Target Audience	Station Format	Music Format
WTJU	91.1	General	M/N	Alternative/Big Band/Classical/Jazz/Rhythm & Blues
WUVA	92.7	General	M/N/S	Urban Contemporary
WQMZ	95.1	General	M	Adult Contemporary
WWWV	97.5	General	M	AOR
WCYK	99.7	General	M	Country
WVSY	101.9	General	M/N	Oldies/Rhythm & Blues
WVAO	102.3	General	M	Oldies
WLJL	107.5	General	M/N/S	Jazz/Rhythm & Blues

Note: Stations included broadcast in the Charlottesville metro area
Station Format: E=Educational; M=Music; N=News; S=Sports; T=Talk
Target Audience: A=Asian; B=Black; C=Christian; E=Ethnic; F=French; G=General; H=Hispanic; M=Men; N=Native American; R=Religious; S=Senior Citizen; W=Women; Y=Young Adult; Z=Children
Music Format: AOR=Album Oriented Rock; MOR=Middle-of-the-Road
Source: Burrelle's Media Directory, 1999 Edition

WEATHER

Temperature/Precipitation/Humidity

	Jan	Feb	Mar	Apr	May	Jun	Jul	Aug	Sep	Oct	Nov	Dec	Yr.
Max. High Temp. (°F)	76	79	87	91	92	100	103	98	101	93	83	77	103
Avg. High Temp. (°F)	47	49	56	69	76	83	86	85	78	69	57	48	67
Avg. Temp. (°F)	38	39	45	57	65	72	76	75	68	58	47	38	57
Avg. Low Temp. (°F)	29	30	35	46	54	62	66	65	58	48	37	29	47
Min. Low Temp. (°F)	6	2	11	27	32	40	53	48	37	23	11	8	2
Avg. Precip. (in.)	3.0	2.8	3.5	3.2	3.4	3.9	4.1	4.2	3.9	2.4	2.7	3.2	40.4
Avg. Snowfall (in.)	3.9	3.7	4.0	0.2	0	0	0	0	0	0	0.5	2.4	14.7
Avg. Rel. Hum. (%)	68	61	59	58	67	70	71	75	72	66	63	67	66

Source: National Climatic Data Center, International Station Meteorological Climate Summary, 3/95

Weather Conditions

Temperature			Precipitation		
0°F & below	32°F & below	90°F & above	0.1 inch or more precip.	1.5 inch or more snow/ice	Thunder-storms
0	85	30	73	3	35

Note: Figures are average number of days per year
Source: National Climatic Data Center, International Station Meteorological Climate Summary, 3/95

AIR & WATER QUALITY

Maximum Pollutant Concentrations

	Particulate Matter (ug/m³)	Carbon Monoxide (ppm)	Sulfur Dioxide (ppm)	Nitrogen Dioxide (ppm)	Ozone (ppm)	Lead (ug/m³)
MSA[1] Level	42	n/a	n/a	n/a	n/a	n/a
NAAQS[2]	150	9	0.140	0.053	0.12	1.50
Met NAAQS	Yes	n/a	n/a	n/a	n/a	n/a

Note: (1) Metropolitan Statistical Area - see Appendix A for areas included; (2) National Ambient Air Quality Standards; ppm = parts per million; ug/m³ = micrograms per cubic meter; n/a not available
Source: EPA, National Air Quality and Emissions Trends Report, 1997

Pollutant Standards Index

Data not available.
EPA, National Air Quality and Emissions Trends Report, 1997

Drinking Water

Water System Name	Pop. Served	Primary Water Source Type	Number of Violations in 1998-99	Type of Violation/ Contaminants
City of Charlottesville	44,000	Purchased surface	None	None

Note: Data as of January 19, 2000
Source: EPA, Office of Ground Water and Drinking Water, Safe Drinking Water Information System

Charlottesville tap water is pH 7.0, very soft, and fluoridated.
Editor & Publisher Market Guide, 2000

Columbia, Missouri

Background

Columbia, Missouri is located in Boone County, about midway between St. Louis and Kansas City and 30 miles east of Jefferson City.

Columbia is a mix of urban refinement and natural beauty. The city offers affordable housing, diverse shopping, excellent education and health care systems and a healthy environment. Columbia's prominent businesses include health care and retail services, and grain and livestock industries.

The area was originally inhabited by several Native American tribes. White explorers encountered the region's Missouri Indians in the 1600s and trade soon followed. After several transactions between France and Spain, the area became part of the United States in 1803, when President Thomas Jefferson transacted the Louisiana Purchase for $15 million. The twon was established in 1819 as Smithton by settlers from Kentucky but a water shortage in 1821 forced the town to move to Flat Branch. It was reinhabited several years later, incoporporated in 1826 and renamed Columbia.

The city's institutions of higher learning include the University of Missouri, Columbia College, and Stephen's College.

Columbia and the surrounding community offers many recreational attractions including Les Bourgeois Vineyards of Rocheport and Katy Trail State Park, with 185 miles of hiking and biking trails, one of 40 parks in the city. Annual events include the Scott Ragtime Festival in June and the Missouri State Fair in August.

General Rankings and Evaluative Comments

■ Columbia was selected as a "Small City Runner Up" in Money magazine's most recent survey of the best places to live. Criteria: 300 metropolitan areas in the U.S. were ranked on 46 quality-of-life factors including the economy, education, culture, recreation, safety, and clean air and water. *Money, "The Best Places to Live 2000"*

■ Columbia was ranked #116 out of 354 metropolitan areas in *Places Rated Almanac*. Criteria: cost of living, climate, crime, transportation, job outlook, education, the arts, health care, and recreation. *Places Rated Almanac, Millennium Edition, 2000*

■ Columbia was selected as one of North America's "Best Small Metro Areas" (population under 250,000). The area ranked #9 out of 20. Criteria: cost of living, climate, crime, transportation, job outlook, education, the arts, health care, and recreation. *Places Rated Almanac, Millennium Edition, 2000*

■ Columbia was selected as one of America's best places to retire. Criteria: safety, climate, housing, culture and recreation, social compatibility, affordability, medical care, transportation, and jobs and/or volunteer opportunities. *Where to Retire: America's Best and Most Affordable Places, 1998*

■ Columbia was selected as one of the best places to retire by *Retirement Places Rated*. Criteria: cost of living, climate, crime, services, working, and leisure living. The city was ranked #104 out of 187. *Retirement Places Rated, 1999*

■ Columbia was selected as one of "The 50 Most Alive Places to Live" in the U.S. Criteria: ethnic diversity, recreational options, cultural vitality, low crime rate, opportunities for lifelong learning, good hospitals and restaurants, public transportation, walking accessibility, civic activities, and the kitsch factor. The area was ranked #3 out of 10 in the "College Towns" category. *Modern Maturity, May-June 2000*

Business Environment

STATE ECONOMY

State Economic Profile

"St. Louis' weak economy and a slowdown in Kansas City are placing a drag on the Missouri economy. Gross State Product and job growth, after matching or surpassing the national for several years, has slowed. After strong home sales in 1998, Missouri's housing and construction markets will likely slow considerably in the near future.

Like most Plains states, Missouri's significant farm sector has been a drag on the economy. Farm income was down over 20% in 1998 as commodity prices and foreign demand remained weak. With overcapacity in Missouri's beef and grain sectors, a major restructing is in store. Even with a resurgence in Asian demand, the current trend in commodity prices is not likely to reverse.

Manufacturing employment shrank 0.5% in 1998. St. Louis witnessed an even greater decline of 0.9%. With the prospect of job cuts at Boeing's St. Louis facilities, Missouri will likely witness further contraction in manufacturing employment.

An increase in building activity in St. Louis, fueled by corporate relocations, helped to offset declining activity elsewhere in the state. Almost half of the new construction jobs created in Missouri were in St. Louis.

Missouri's relatively high unemployment rate has in some ways been a bonus, helping to attract some corporate relocations. MasterCard and Convergys, for instance, have moved operations to St. Louis to take advantage of the available labor. In spite of these moves, St. Louis should still add little to state GSP and job growth. Gains in Kansas City, Columbia and Springfield will help to offset the weakness in St. Louis and the soft farm economy."
National Association of Realtors, Economic Profiles: The Fifty States and the District of Columbia, http://nar.realtor.com/databank/profiles.htm

EXPORTS

Total Export Sales

Area	1995 ($000)	1996 ($000)	1997 ($000)	1998 ($000)	% Chg. 1995-98	% Chg. 1997-98
MSA[1]	51,134	57,875	74,905	131,476	157.1	75.5
U.S.	583,030,524	622,827,063	687,597,999	680,474,251	16.7	-1.0

Note: (1) Metropolitan Statistical Area - see Appendix A for areas included
Source: U.S. Department of Commerce, International Trade Association, Metropolitan Area Exports: An Export Performance Report on Over 250 U.S. Cities, November 10, 1999

CITY FINANCES

City Government Finances

Component	1995 ($million)	1995 (per capita $)
Revenue	63.5	857
Expenditure	65.1	879
Debt Outstanding	125.4	1,693

Source: 1999 County and City Extra, Annual Metro, City, and County Data Book

City Government Revenue by Source

Source	1995 ($million)	1995 (per capita $)
Intergovernmental	8.5	114
Taxes	26.3	355
Property	4.5	61
Sales and Gross Receipts	21.2	287

Source: 1999 County and City Extra, Annual Metro, City, and County Data Book

City Government Expenditures by Function

Function	1995 ($million)	1995 (per capita $)	1995 (%)
Public Welfare	0.6	8	1.0
Highways	4.6	62	7.1
Parking Facilities	0.3	5	0.6
Education	0.0	0	0.0
Health and Hospitals	2.6	36	4.1
Police Protection	7.7	104	11.9
Sewerage and Sanitation	9.3	125	14.3
Parks and Recreation	7.7	104	11.9
Housing and Community Development	0.1	2	0.3
Interest on Debt	3.3	45	5.2

Source: 1999 County and City Extra, Annual Metro, City, and County Data Book

Municipal Bond Ratings

Area	Moody's
City	Aa2

Source: Mergent Bond Record, 2/2000

POPULATION

Population Growth

Area	1980 Census	1990 Census	1999 Estimate	2004 Projection	Population Growth (%) 1990-1999	Population Growth (%) 1999-2004
City	62,061	69,101	78,482	82,632	13.6	5.3
MSA[1]	100,376	112,379	130,574	138,465	16.2	6.0
U.S.	226,545,805	248,765,170	272,212,864	283,625,312	9.4	4.2

Note: (1) Metropolitan Statistical Area - see Appendix A for areas included
Source: 1990 Census of Population and Housing, Summary Tape File 3C; Claritas, Inc.

Number of Households and Average Household Size

Area	1980 Census	1990 Census	1999 Estimate	2004 Projection	1999 Average Household Size
City	22,270	25,955	29,669	31,428	2.65
MSA[1]	35,296	42,089	48,835	51,940	2.67
U.S.	80,389,592	91,993,582	102,048,200	107,302,392	2.67

Note: (1) Metropolitan Statistical Area - see Appendix A for areas included
Source: 1990 Census of Population and Housing, Summary Tape File 3C; Claritas, Inc.

Race/Ethnicity of City Population

Race/Ethnicity	1990 Census Population	1990 Census %	1999 Estimate Population	1999 Estimate %	% Change 1990-1999
White, Non-Hispanic	58,344	84.4	62,943	80.2	7.9
Black, Non-Hispanic	6,804	9.8	9,212	11.7	35.4
Asian, Non-Hispanic	2,768	4.0	4,508	5.7	62.9
Other, Non-Hispanic	281	0.4	308	0.4	9.6
Hispanic	904	1.3	1,511	1.9	67.1

Source: 1990 Census of Population and Housing, Summary Tape File 3C; Claritas, Inc.

Race/Ethnicity of Metropolitan Statistical Area Population

Race/Ethnicity	1990 Census		1999 Estimate		% Change 1990-1999
	Population	%	Population	%	
White, Non-Hispanic	99,388	88.4	111,579	85.5	12.3
Black, Non-Hispanic	8,279	7.4	11,636	8.9	40.5
Asian, Non-Hispanic	3,095	2.8	4,886	3.7	57.9
Other, Non-Hispanic	387	0.3	527	0.4	36.2
Hispanic	1,230	1.1	1,946	1.5	58.2

Note: See Appendix A for areas included in the Metropolitan Statistical Area
Source: 1990 Census of Population and Housing, Summary Tape File 3C; Claritas, Inc.

Ancestry

Area	German	Irish	English	Italian	U.S.	French	Polish	Dutch
City	36.4	16.5	16.7	2.9	4.0	3.6	2.0	2.4
MSA[1]	36.9	17.5	17.6	2.5	5.9	4.0	1.7	2.8
U.S.	23.3	15.6	13.1	5.9	5.3	4.2	3.8	2.5

Note: Figures are percentages and include persons that reported multiple ancestry (eg. if a person reported being Irish and Italian, they were included in both columns); (1) Metropolitan Statistical Area - see Appendix A for areas included
Source: 1990 Census of Population and Housing, Summary Tape File 3C

Median Age

Area	1990 Census	1999 Estimate
City	25.5	28.7
MSA[1]	27.6	30.8
U.S.	32.9	35.7

Note: (1) Metropolitan Statistical Area - see Appendix A for areas included
Source: 1990 Census of Population and Housing, Summary Tape File 3C; Claritas, Inc.

Male/Female Population

Area	Number of Males		Number of Females		Males per 100 Females	
	1990	1999	1990	1999	1990	1999
City	33,298	37,801	35,803	40,681	93.0	92.9
MSA[1]	54,654	63,306	57,725	67,268	94.7	94.1
U.S.	121,172,379	132,803,736	127,537,494	139,409,136	95.0	95.3

Note: (1) Metropolitan Statistical Area - see Appendix A for areas included
Source: 1990 Census of Population, General Population Characteristics; Claritas, Inc.

INCOME

Per Capita/Median/Average Income

Area	Per Capita ($)			Median Household ($)			Average Household ($)		
	1989	1999	% Chg.	1989	1999	% Chg.	1989	1999	% Chg.
City	12,452	20,477	64.4	22,059	33,864	53.5	31,218	51,799	65.9
MSA[1]	12,707	20,620	62.3	25,647	39,016	52.1	32,704	53,696	64.2
U.S.	14,420	21,350	48.1	30,056	40,525	34.8	38,453	56,184	46.1

Note: (1) Metropolitan Statistical Area - see Appendix A for areas included; 1989 data is from the 1990 Census; 1999 data is estimated by Claritas, Inc.
Source: 1990 Census of Population, General Population Characteristics; Claritas, Inc.

Household Income Distribution

Area	Percent of Households Earning								
	Under $5,000	$5,000 -14,999	$15,000 -24,999	$25,000 -34,999	$35,000 -49,999	$50,000 -74,999	$75,000 -99,000	$100,000 -149,999	$150,000 and up
City	5.9	16.6	16.4	12.1	13.8	14.7	9.2	6.7	4.5
MSA[1]	4.5	13.4	14.5	12.7	15.6	18.9	9.9	6.5	4.0
U.S.	3.9	13.3	13.8	12.6	16.2	19.4	9.7	6.6	4.6

Note: Data as of 1999; (1) Metropolitan Statistical Area - see Appendix A for areas included
Source: Claritas, Inc.

Effective Buying Income

Area	Per Capita ($)	Median Household ($)	Average Household ($)
City	15,896	28,991	42,029
MSA[1]	16,774	33,777	44,652
U.S.	17,496	36,603	47,036

Note: Data as of 1/1/2000; (1) Metropolitan Statistical Area - see Appendix A for areas included
Source: Standard Rate & Data Service, Newspaper Advertising Source, March 2000

Effective Household Buying Income Distribution

Area	% of Households Earning						
	$10,000 -$19,999	$20,000 -$34,999	$35,000 -$49,999	$50,000 -$74,999	$75,000 -$99,000	$100,000 -$124,999	$125,000 and up
City	19.5	20.9	14.1	15.4	7.8	2.5	2.8
MSA[1]	16.4	22.3	16.9	18.0	8.4	2.5	2.6
U.S.	15.0	21.6	17.6	19.6	8.4	3.0	3.3

Note: Data as of 1/1/2000; (1) Metropolitan Statistical Area - see Appendix A for areas included
Source: Standard Rate & Data Service, Newspaper Advertising Source, March 2000

Poverty Rates by Age

Area	People of All Ages	People Under 18 Years Old	Related Children Age 5-17 in Families in Poverty
City	15.7	n/a	n/a
County	12.3	16.1	14.7
U.S.	13.8	20.8	18.7

Note: Figures show the percent of people living below the poverty line in 1995. The
average poverty threshold was $15,569 for a family of four in 1995; n/a not available
Source: Bureau of the Census, Small Area Income and Poverty Estimates Program;
U.S. Department of Housing and Urban Development

EMPLOYMENT

Labor Force and Employment

Area	Civilian Labor Force			Workers Employed		
	Dec. 1998	Dec. 1999	% Chg.	Dec. 1998	Dec. 1999	% Chg.
City	51,315	49,190	-4.1	50,729	48,723	-4.0
MSA[1]	85,610	82,076	-4.1	84,700	81,351	-4.0
U.S.	138,297,000	139,941,000	1.2	132,732,000	134,696,000	1.5

Note: Data is not seasonally adjusted and covers workers 16 years of age and older;
(1) Metropolitan Statistical Area - see Appendix A for areas included
Source: Bureau of Labor Statistics, http://stats.bls.gov

Unemployment Rate

Area	1999											
	Jan.	Feb.	Mar.	Apr.	May	Jun.	Jul.	Aug.	Sep.	Oct.	Nov.	Dec.
City	1.3	1.1	1.1	1.1	1.2	1.7	1.7	1.5	1.2	0.7	0.9	0.9
MSA[1]	1.2	1.1	1.0	1.0	1.1	1.6	1.6	1.4	1.1	0.7	0.8	0.9
U.S.	4.8	4.7	4.4	4.1	4.0	4.5	4.5	4.2	4.1	3.8	3.8	3.7

Note: Data is not seasonally adjusted and covers workers 16 years of age and older; all figures are percentages; (1) Metropolitan Statistical Area - see Appendix A for areas included
Source: Bureau of Labor Statistics, http://stats.bls.gov

Employment by Industry

Sector	MSA[1]		U.S.
	Number of Employees	Percent of Total	Percent of Total
Services	n/a	n/a	30.2
Retail Trade	n/a	n/a	18.1
Government	n/a	n/a	15.8
Manufacturing	n/a	n/a	14.1
Finance/Insurance/Real Estate	n/a	n/a	5.9
Wholesale Trade	n/a	n/a	5.4
Transportation/Public Utilities	n/a	n/a	5.3
Construction	n/a	n/a	4.8
Mining	n/a	n/a	0.4

Note: Figures cover non-farm employment as of 12/99 and are not seasonally adjusted; (1) Metropolitan Statistical Area - see Appendix A for areas included; n/a not available
Source: Bureau of Labor Statistics, http://stats.bls.gov

Employment by Occupation

Occupation Category	City (%)	MSA[1] (%)	U.S. (%)
White Collar	70.5	66.3	58.1
Executive/Admin./Management	11.5	11.7	12.3
Professional	24.4	21.1	14.1
Technical & Related Support	5.8	5.5	3.7
Sales	12.4	11.2	11.8
Administrative Support/Clerical	16.4	16.8	16.3
Blue Collar	12.7	17.5	26.2
Precision Production/Craft/Repair	4.9	7.8	11.3
Machine Operators/Assem./Insp.	2.9	4.1	6.8
Transportation/Material Movers	2.2	2.8	4.1
Cleaners/Helpers/Laborers	2.7	2.9	3.9
Services	15.6	14.4	13.2
Farming/Forestry/Fishing	1.2	1.8	2.5

Note: Figures cover workers 16 years of age and older; (1) Metropolitan Statistical Area - see Appendix A for areas included
Source: 1990 Census of Population and Housing, Summary Tape File 3C

Occupational Employment Projections: 1996 - 2006

Occupations Expected to Have the Largest Job Growth (ranked by numerical growth)	Fast-Growing Occupations[1] (ranked by percent growth)
1. Salespersons, retail	1. Computer engineers
2. Teachers, secondary school	2. Systems analysts
3. Truck drivers, light	3. Desktop publishers
4. General managers & top executives	4. Home health aides
5. Cashiers	5. Teachers, special education
6. Nursing aides/orderlies/attendants	6. Personal and home care aides
7. Child care workers, private household	7. Speech-language pathologists/audiologists
8. Teachers aides, clerical & paraprofess.	8. Paralegals
9. Systems analysts	9. Occupational therapists
10. Marketing & sales, supervisors	10. Physical therapy assistants and aides

Note: Projections cover Missouri; (1) Excludes occupations with total job growth less than 300
Source: U.S. Department of Labor, Employment and Training Administration, America's Labor Market Information System (ALMIS)

Average Wages

Occupation	$/Hr.	Occupation	$/Hr.
Accountants and Auditors	16.85	Maids and Housekeepers	7.20
Assemblers and Fabricators	9.02	Maintenance Repairers	10.35
Automotive Mechanics	13.62	Marketing/Advertising/PR Managers	25.55
Bookkeepers	10.97	Nurses, Licensed Practical	11.05
Carpenters	15.00	Nurses, Registered	18.40
Cashiers	6.62	Nursing Aides/Orderlies/Attendants	7.76
Clerks, General Office	8.83	Physicians and Surgeons	44.73
Clerks, Shipping/Receiving/Traffic	12.01	Receptionists/Information Clerks	7.98
Computer Programmers	21.91	Sales Reps., Exc. Scientific/Retail	16.03
Computer Support Specialists	15.18	Sales Reps., Scientific, Exc. Retail	20.58
Cooks, Restaurant	7.37	Salespersons, Retail	7.76
Electricians	16.69	Secretaries, Except Legal/Medical	9.45
Financial Managers	21.31	Stock Clerks, Sales Floor	7.12
First-Line Supervisors/Mgrs., Sales	13.48	Systems Analysts	23.04
Food Preparation Workers	6.63	Teacher Aides	5.67
General Managers/Top Executives	25.17	Teachers, Elementary School	14.72
Guards	9.44	Teachers, Secondary School	14.56
Hand Packers	6.37	Telemarketers	8.69
Janitors and Cleaners	7.83	Truck Drivers, Heavy/Tractor-Trailer	13.85
Laborers, Landscaping	8.68	Truck Drivers, Light	8.49
Lawyers	26.29	Waiters and Waitresses	5.83

Note: Wage data is for 1998 and covers the Metropolitan Statistical Area (see Appendix A for areas included). Hourly wages for elementary and secondary school teachers were calculated by the editors from annual wage data assuming a 40 hour work week; Dashes indicate that data was not available.
Source: Bureau of Labor Statistics, 1998 Metropolitan Area Occupational Employment and Wage Estimates

TAXES

Major State and Local Tax Rates

State Corporate Income (%)	State Personal Income (%)	Residential Property (%)	Sales & Use		State Gasoline (cents/ gallon)	State Cigarette (cents/ pack)
			State (%)	Local (%)		
6.25	1.5 - 6.0	1.93	4.225	1.75	17.05[a]	17.0[b]

Note: Personal/corporate income, sales, gasoline and cigarette tax rates as of January 2000. Property tax rates as of April 2000; (a) Rate is comprised of 17 cents excise and 0.05 cents motor carrier tax; (b) Counties and cities may impose an additional tax of 4 - 7 cents per pack
Source: Federation of Tax Administrators, www.taxadmin.org; ERI's Relocation Assessor software database, quarterly effective date 4/1/2000

Total Taxes Per Capita and as a Percent of Income

Area	Per Capita Income ($)	Per Capita Taxes ($)			Percent of Income (%)		
		Total	Federal	State/Local	Total	Federal	State/Local
Missouri	27,026	9,186	6,354	2,831	34.0	23.5	10.5
U.S.	28,878	10,298	7,026	3,273	35.7	24.3	11.3

Note: Figures are for 1999
Source: Tax Foundation, www.taxfoundation.org

COMMERCIAL UTILITIES

Typical Monthly Electric Bills

Area	Commercial Service ($/month)		Industrial Service ($/month)	
	12 kW demand 1,500 kWh	100 kW demand 30,000 kWh	1,000 kW demand 400,000 kWh	20,000 kW demand 10,000,000 kWh
City	n/a	n/a	n/a	n/a
U.S.	150	2,174	23,995	508,569

Note: Based on rates in effect January 1, 1999; n/a not available
Source: Edison Electric Institute, Typical Residential, Commercial and Industrial Bills, Winter 1999

TRANSPORTATION

Transportation Statistics

Average minutes to work (1990)	14.1
Interstate highways	I-70; US-40; US-63
Bus lines	
In-city (1998)	Columbia Area Transit System, 9 buses
Inter-city (1999)	2
Passenger air service	
Airport	Columbia Regional
Airlines (1999)	4
Enplaned passengers (1998)	29,282
Amtrak service	No
Motor freight carriers (1999)	20
Major waterways/ports	None

Source: FAA DOT/TSC CY1998 ACAIS Database; National Transit Database, 1998; Editor & Publisher Market Guide, 2000; Amtrak National Time Table, Fall 1999/Winter 2000; 1990 Census of Population and Housing, STF 3C; Jane's Urban Transport Systems 1999-2000

Means of Transportation to Work

Area	Car/Truck/Van		Public Transportation			Bicycle	Walked	Other Means	Worked at Home
	Drove Alone	Car-pooled	Bus	Subway	Railroad				
City	71.3	12.1	1.2	0.0	0.0	1.4	10.3	1.1	2.5
MSA[1]	73.7	14.0	0.8	0.0	0.0	0.9	6.6	0.9	3.2
U.S.	73.2	13.4	3.0	1.5	0.5	0.4	3.9	1.2	3.0

Note: Figures shown are percentages and only include workers 16 years of age and older;
(1) Metropolitan Statistical Area - see Appendix A for areas included
Source: 1990 Census of Population and Housing, Summary Tape File 3C

BUSINESSES

Major Business Headquarters

Company Name	1999 Rankings	
	Fortune 500	Forbes 500
No companies listed	-	-

Note: Companies listed are located in the city; dashes indicate no ranking
Fortune 500: Companies that produce a 10-K are ranked 1 to 500 based on 1999 revenue
Forbes 500: Private companies are ranked 1 to 500 based on 1998 revenue
Source: Forbes, December 13, 1999; Fortune, April 17, 2000

HOTELS & MOTELS

Hotels/Motels

Area	Hotels/ Motels	Rooms	Luxury-Level Hotels/Motels		Average Minimum Rates ($)		
			♦♦♦♦	♦♦♦♦♦	♦♦	♦♦♦	♦♦♦♦
City	16	1,703	0	0	n/a	n/a	n/a

Note: n/a not available; classifications range from one diamond (budget properties with basic amenities) to five diamond (luxury properties).
Source: OAG Business Travel Planner, Winter 1999-2000

Estimated Daily Food and Lodging Costs

Area	Food/Other ($/day)	Average Hotel Cost ($/day)
City	30	55
U.S.	30	55

Source: ERI's Relocation Assessor software database, quarterly effective date 4/1/2000

CONVENTION CENTERS

Convention Centers and Event Sites

Name	Guest Rooms	Meeting Space (sq. ft.)	Capacity (Theatre Style)
Faurot Field	n/a	n/a	70,000
Hearnes Center	n/a	n/a	13,500
Jesse Auditorium	n/a	n/a	1,800

Note: n/a not available
Source: EventSource.com, 3/15/2000

Living Environment

COST OF LIVING

Cost of Living: Homeowner

Cost Element	U.S. ($)	City ($)	Differential ($)	Percent of U.S. Average
Consumables	14,516	13,733	-783	94.6
Transportation	5,957	5,718	-239	96.0
Health Services	2,012	1,935	-77	96.2
Housing/Utilities/Prop. Tax	16,337	12,520	-3,817	76.6
Income+Payroll Taxes	12,615	13,723	1,108	108.8
Miscellaneous	8,563	8,563	0	100.0
Total Cost of Living	60,000	56,192	-3,808	93.7

Note: Figures are based on a single income, four person family with gross annual earnings of $60,000, owning an 1,800 square-foot home, and driving two automobiles worth $22,000 30,000 miles per year.
Source: ERI's Relocation Assessor software database, quarterly effective date 4/1/2000

Cost of Living: Renter

Cost Element	U.S. ($)	City ($)	Differential ($)	Percent of U.S. Average
Consumables	10,486	9,929	-557	94.7
Transportation	2,107	2,024	-83	96.1
Health Services	1,632	1,572	-60	96.3
Rent/Utilities/Insurance	9,299	6,184	-3,115	66.5
Income+Payroll Taxes	8,607	9,135	528	106.1
Miscellaneous	7,869	7,869	0	100.0
Total Cost of Living	40,000	36,713	-3,287	91.8

Note: Figures are based on a single income, three person family with gross annual earnings of $40,000, renting a 1,000 square-foot home, and driving one automobile worth $8,000 12,000 miles per year.
Source: ERI's Relocation Assessor software database, quarterly effective date 4/1/2000

HOUSING

Median Home Prices and Housing Affordability

Area	Median Price[2] 4th Qtr. 1999 ($)	HOI[3] 4th Qtr. 1999	Affordability Rank[4]
MSA[1]	n/a	n/a	n/a
U.S.	139,000	63.8	—

Note: (1) Metropolitan Statistical Area - see Appendix A for areas included; (2) U.S. figures calculated from the sales of 687,516 new and existing homes in 192 markets; (3) Housing Opportunity Index - percent of homes sold that were within the reach of the median income household at the prevailing mortgage interest rate; (4) Rank is from 1-192 with 1 being most affordable; n/a not available
Source: National Association of Home Builders, Housing Opportunity Index, 4th Quarter 1999

Estimated Home Price

Area	Price ($)
City	95,216
U.S.	135,855

Note: Figures are based on an 1,800 square-foot home
Source: ERI's Relocation Assessor software database, quarterly effective date 4/1/2000

Estimated Rent

Area	Rent ($/month)
City	409
U.S.	651

Note: Figures are based on a 1,000 square-foot home
Source: ERI's Relocation Assessor software database, quarterly effective date 4/1/2000

Median Home Price Projection

It is projected that the median home price in the metropolitan area will increase from $119,968 in 1999 to $181,610 in 2010, an increase of 51.4%
Kiplinger's Personal Finance Magazine, January 2000

RESIDENTIAL UTILITIES

Average Residential Utility Costs

Area	All Electric ($/mth)	Part Electric ($/mth)	Other Energy ($/mth)	Phone ($/mth)
City	–	50.16	45.89	14.60
U.S.	99.25	55.47	43.48	20.29

Source: ACCRA, Cost of Living Index, 3rd Quarter 1999

HEALTH CARE

Average Health Care Costs

Area	Hospital ($/day)	Doctor ($/visit)	Dentist ($/visit)
City	506.67	48.43	65.00
U.S.	440.96	53.83	68.42

Note: Hospital—based on a semi-private room; Doctor—based on a general practitioner's routine exam of an established patient; Dentist—based on adult teeth cleaning and periodic oral exam.
Source: ACCRA, Cost of Living Index, 3rd Quarter 1999

Distribution of Office-Based Physicians

Area	Family/Gen. Practitioners	Specialists Medical	Specialists Surgical	Specialists Other
MSA[1]	44	184	142	177

Note: Data as of 12/31/97; (1) Metropolitan Statistical Area - see Appendix A for areas included
Source: American Medical Assn., Physician Characteristics & Distribution in the U.S., 1999

Hospitals

Columbia has 4 general medical and surgical hospitals, 1 psychiatric.
AHA Guide to the Healthcare Field, 1999-2000

According to *U.S. News and World Report,* Columbia has one of the best hospitals in the U.S.:
University Hospitals and Clinics, noted for cancer, pulmonology, rheumatology.
U.S. News Online, "America's Best Hospitals," July 19, 1999

EDUCATION

Public School District Statistics

District Name	Num. Sch.	Enroll.	Classroom Teachers	Pupils per Teacher	Minority Pupils (%)	Current Exp.[1] ($/pupil)
Columbia 93	31	15,957	1,070	14.9	23.0	4,971

Note: Data covers the 1997-1998 school year unless otherwise noted; (1) Data covers fiscal year 1996; SD = School District; ISD = Independent School District; n/a not available
Source: National Center for Education Statistics, Common Core of Data Public Education Agency Universe 1997-98; National Center for Education Statistics, Characteristics of the 100 Largest Public Elementary and Secondary School Districts in the United States: 1997-98, July 1999

Educational Quality

School District	Education Quotient[1]	Graduate Outcome[2]	Community Index[3]	Resource Index[4]
Columbia 93	118	136	105	86

Note: Over 1,000 secondary school districts were rated in terms of educational quality. The scores range from a low of 50 to a high of 150; (1) Combination of the Graduate Outcome, Community and Resource indexes weighted to reflect the greater importance of the Graduate Outcome and Resource Index; (2) Based on graduation rates and college board scores (SAT/ACT); (3) Based on the surrounding community's level of affluence and adult education; (4) Based on teacher salaries, per-pupil expenditures and student-teacher ratios.
Source: Expansion Management, Ratings Issue, 1999

Educational Attainment by Race

Area	High School Graduate (%)					Bachelor's Degree (%)				
	Total	White	Black	Other	Hisp.[2]	Total	White	Black	Other	Hisp.[2]
City	87.2	89.4	68.1	86.2	89.9	45.0	46.5	18.6	67.7	54.3
MSA[1]	84.8	85.9	70.1	86.0	88.6	36.5	36.8	17.6	66.1	44.5
U.S.	75.2	77.9	63.1	60.4	49.8	20.3	21.5	11.4	19.4	9.2

Note: Figures shown cover persons 25 years old and over; (1) Metropolitan Statistical Area - see Appendix A for areas included; (2) people of Hispanic origin can be of any race
Source: 1990 Census of Population and Housing, Summary Tape File 3C

School Enrollment by Type

Area	Preprimary				Elementary/High School			
	Public		Private		Public		Private	
	Enrollment	%	Enrollment	%	Enrollment	%	Enrollment	%
City	620	53.0	549	47.0	7,377	94.9	395	5.1
MSA[1]	1,251	57.9	909	42.1	14,869	95.2	743	4.8
U.S.	2,679,029	59.5	1,824,256	40.5	38,379,689	90.2	4,187,099	9.8

Note: Figures shown cover persons 3 years old and over;
(1) Metropolitan Statistical Area - see Appendix A for areas included
Source: 1990 Census of Population and Housing, Summary Tape File 3C

School Enrollment by Race

Area	Preprimary (%)				Elementary/High School (%)			
	White	Black	Other	Hisp.[1]	White	Black	Other	Hisp.[1]
City	80.7	15.7	3.7	0.4	76.2	19.5	4.3	2.4
MSA[2]	85.8	9.5	4.6	0.5	84.6	12.4	3.0	1.7
U.S.	80.4	12.5	7.1	7.8	74.1	15.6	10.3	12.5

Note: Figures shown cover persons 3 years old and over; (1) people of Hispanic origin can be of any race; (2) Metropolitan Statistical Area - see Appendix A for areas included
Source: 1990 Census of Population and Housing, Summary Tape File 3C

Higher Education

Two-Year Colleges		Four-Year Colleges		Medical Schools	Law Schools	Voc/Tech
Public	Private	Public	Private			
1	1	1	1	1	1	1

Source: College Blue Book, Occupational Education, 1999; Medical School Admission Requirements, 1999-2000; Peterson's Guide to Two-Year Colleges, 2000; Peterson's Guide to Four-Year Colleges, 1999; Barron's Guide to Law Schools, 1999

MAJOR EMPLOYERS

Major Employers

Columbia Insurance Group	Commerce Bank of Columbia
MBS Textbook Exchange	MFA Oil Co.
Regional Alternative Health Services	Semco Inc. (sheetmetal)
Toastmaster Inc.	Tribune Publishing

Note: Companies listed are located in the city
Source: D&B Business Rankings, 1999; Ward's Business Directory, 1999; America's Corporate Families, 1999

PUBLIC SAFETY

Crime Rate

Area	All Crimes	Violent Crimes				Property Crimes		
		Murder	Forcible Rape	Robbery	Aggrav. Assault	Burglary	Larceny -Theft	Motor Vehicle Theft
City	5,592.2	7.6	48.3	97.8	323.9	627.4	4,225.6	261.6
Suburbs[1]	3,095.9	0.0	15.9	15.9	134.8	521.3	2,311.0	97.1
MSA[2]	4,617.3	4.6	35.6	65.8	250.0	586.0	3,477.9	197.4
U.S.	4,615.5	6.3	34.4	165.2	360.5	862.0	2,728.1	459.0

Note: Crime rate is the number of crimes per 100,000 population; (1) Defined as all areas within the Metropolitan Statistical Area but located outside the central city; (2) Metropolitan Statistical Area - see Appendix A for areas included
Source: FBI Uniform Crime Reports, 1998

RECREATION

Culture and Recreation

Museums	Symphony Orchestras	Opera Companies	Dance Companies	Professional Theatres	Zoos	Pro Sports Teams
3	1	0	0	0	0	0

Source: Musical America, International Directory of the Performing Arts, 1999; Official Museum Directory, 2000; Stern's Performing Arts Directory, 1997; USA Today Four Sport Stadium Guide, 1997; Career Opportunities in Theatre and the Performing Arts, 1999

Library System

The Daniel Boone Regional Library has one branch and holdings of 379,349 volumes.
American Library Directory, 1999-2000

MEDIA

Newspapers

Name	Type	Freq.	Distribution	Circulation
Columbia Daily Tribune	General	7x/wk	Area	19,000
Columbia Missourian	General	6x/wk	Local	6,300

Note: Includes newspapers with circulations of 200 or more located in the city;
Source: Burrelle's Media Directory, 1999 Edition

Television Stations

Name	Ch.	Affiliation	Type	Owner
KOMU	n/a	NBCT	Commercial	n/a
KMIZ	17	ABCT	Commercial	Benedek Broadcasting Corporation

Note: Stations included broadcast in the Columbia metro area; n/a not available
Source: Burrelle's Media Directory, 1999 Edition

AM Radio Stations

Call Letters	Freq. (kHz)	Target Audience	Station Format	Music Format
KFRU	1400	General	N/S/T	n/a

Note: Stations included broadcast in the Columbia metro area; n/a not available
Target Audience: A=Asian; B=Black; C=Christian; E=Ethnic; F=French; G=General; H=Hispanic; M=Men; N=Native American; R=Religious; S=Senior Citizen; W=Women; Y=Young Adult; Z=Children
Station Format: E=Educational; M=Music; N=News; S=Sports; T=Talk
Source: Burrelle's Media Directory, 1999 Edition

FM Radio Stations

Call Letters	Freq. (mHz)	Target Audience	Station Format	Music Format
KCOU	88.1	General	E/M/N/S	n/a
KOPN	89.5	General	M/N/T	Adult Contemporary/Country/MOR/Oldies
KWWC	90.5	General	E/M/S	Big Band/Jazz/Rhythm & Blues
KBIA	91.3	General	E/M/N/S/T	Classical/Jazz
KCMQ	96.7	General	M	AOR/Classic Rock
KFMZ	98.3	Alternative	M	Alternative
KCLR	99.3	General	M	Country
KPLA	101.5	General	M/N	Adult Contemporary
KBXR	102.3	General	M/N/S	Alternative
KOQL	106.1	General	N	n/a
KTXY	106.9	General	M	Adult Contemporary

Note: Stations included broadcast in the Columbia metro area; n/a not available
Station Format: E=Educational; M=Music; N=News; S=Sports; T=Talk
Target Audience: A=Asian; B=Black; C=Christian; E=Ethnic; F=French; G=General; H=Hispanic; M=Men; N=Native American; R=Religious; S=Senior Citizen; W=Women; Y=Young Adult; Z=Children
Music Format: AOR=Album Oriented Rock; MOR=Middle-of-the-Road
Source: Burrelle's Media Directory, 1999 Edition

WEATHER

Temperature/Precipitation/Humidity

	Jan	Feb	Mar	Apr	May	Jun	Jul	Aug	Sep	Oct	Nov	Dec	Yr.
Max. High Temp. (°F)	74	75	85	90	90	103	111	110	101	93	83	71	111
Avg. High Temp. (°F)	36	41	54	66	74	83	89	87	79	67	53	40	64
Avg. Temp. (°F)	28	32	44	55	64	73	78	76	68	56	44	32	54
Avg. Low Temp. (°F)	18	23	34	44	53	62	67	65	57	45	34	23	44
Min. Low Temp. (°F)	-19	-15	-5	19	29	43	48	42	32	22	5	-20	-20
Avg. Precip. (in.)	1.5	2.0	3.5	3.9	5.1	3.9	3.6	3.7	3.5	3.2	3.3	2.7	39.9
Avg. Snowfall (in.)	7	8	4	1	0	0	0	0	0	Tr	2	5	27
Avg. Rel. Hum. 6am (%)	78	80	79	78	85	85	86	87	87	84	82	81	83
Avg. Rel. Hum. 3pm (%)	60	59	54	51	56	55	51	52	54	53	58	64	56

Note: Tr = Trace amounts (less than 0.05 inches of rain or less than 0.5 inches of snow)
Source: National Climatic Data Center, International Station Meteorological Climate Summary, 3/95

Weather Conditions

Temperature			Precipitation		
10°F & below	32°F & below	90°F & above	0.01 inch or more precip.	1.5 inch or more snow/ice	Thunder-storms
18	108	37	110	6	52

Note: Figures are average number of days per year
Source: National Climatic Data Center, International Station Meteorological Climate Summary, 3/95

AIR & WATER QUALITY

Maximum Pollutant Concentrations

	Particulate Matter (ug/m³)	Carbon Monoxide (ppm)	Sulfur Dioxide (ppm)	Nitrogen Dioxide (ppm)	Ozone (ppm)	Lead (ug/m³)
MSA[1] Level	n/a	n/a	n/a	n/a	n/a	n/a
NAAQS[2]	150	9	0.140	0.053	0.12	1.50
Met NAAQS	n/a	n/a	n/a	n/a	n/a	n/a

Note: (1) Metropolitan Statistical Area - see Appendix A for areas included; (2) National Ambient Air Quality Standards; ppm = parts per million; ug/m³ = micrograms per cubic meter; n/a not available
Source: EPA, National Air Quality and Emissions Trends Report, 1997

Pollutant Standards Index

Data not available.
EPA, National Air Quality and Emissions Trends Report, 1997

Drinking Water

Water System Name	Pop. Served	Primary Water Source Type	Number of Violations in 1998-99	Type of Violation/ Contaminants
Columbia	64,000	Ground	None	None

Note: Data as of January 19, 2000
Source: EPA, Office of Ground Water and Drinking Water, Safe Drinking Water Information System

Columbia tap water is alkaline and hard.
Editor & Publisher Market Guide, 2000

Davenport, Iowa

Background

Davenport, Iowa is located in the southeast section of the state, approximately 170 miles east of Des Moines and 160 miles southwest of Chicago, Illinois. Davenport is on the Mississippi River, opposite Illinois.

Davenport is the county seat of Scott County. It is part of a larger metropolitan area known as the Quad Cities, which also includes Bettendorf, Rock Island, Moline and East Moline in Illinois and other communities at that section of the river. The I-280 beltway of interstate highway I-80 runs around this area, and I-88 and I-74 connect nearby. The Quad Cities area has a diverse economy that includes manufacturing, transportation, education and other activities. The surrounding region is agricultural. The Quad Cities are also a popular area for tourism, based on local attractions and the Mississippi River.

The region was occupied by Sauk, Fox and other Native Americans. Fort Armstrong was established at the Davenport site after the Black Hawk War between the United States and Native Americans in 1832. The city is named after George Davenport, a prominent trader and soldier on the Mississippi, and was incorporated in 1839. The G.L. Davenport store was its first commercial building. With steam-powered vessels on the Mississippi and other transportation systems, Davenport and the Quad Cities grew as a trading and manufacturing center.

The Quad Cities area manufactures a variety of products, including farm implements, machinery, aluminum and food products, among others. In 1848, John Deere began making plows in Moline, and the John Deere Company is still based there. The Rock Island Arsenal is the site of a military facility operated by the U.S. Army. Other sectors include education, agricultural services, shipping and transportation, business and professional services and health care, among others. It is also a prominent retail and tourism center, and home to several riverboat casinos and non-gaming cruise boats.

Colleges in Davenport include Marycrest International University, St. Ambrose University, Eastern Iowa Community College and Palmer College of Chiropractic, with numerous others in the Quad Cities.

Davenport is known for its traditional and restored historic homes and neighborhoods, including the East Davenport Village historic district. George Davenport's home on Rock Island is a historic museum. Other city museums include the Davenport Museum of Art and the Putnam Museum of Natural History. Others in the Quad Cities include the John Deere Pavilion in Moline, the Rock Island Arsenal Museum and the Hauberg Indian Museum.

The area is home to numerous civic centers and theaters, including the Adler Theater, a restored 1930s Art Deco theater and the John O'Donnell Stadium. Area cultural organizations include the Quad City Symphony, Quad City Music Guild and Playcrafters. Davenport hosts a yearly summer festival to honor local jazz musician Bix Beiderbecke, featuring jazz performances, a running race and other events.

Numerous recreational facilities are available along the Mississippi and inland. There are over 140 parks and recreation areas in the Quad cities, including West Lake Beach in Davenport. The Quad Cities are home to several professional sports teams.

Davenport is governed by a Mayor and City Council.

General Rankings and Evaluative Comments

- Davenport was ranked #128 out of 354 metropolitan areas in *Places Rated Almanac*. Criteria: cost of living, climate, crime, transportation, job outlook, education, the arts, health care, and recreation. *Places Rated Almanac, Millennium Edition, 2000*

- Cognetics studied 273 metro areas in the United States, ranking them by entrepreneurial activity. Davenport was ranked #101 out of 134 smaller metro areas. Criteria: Significant Starts (firms started in the last 10 years that still employ at least 5 people) and Young Growers (percent of firms 10 years old or less that grew significantly during the last 4 years). *Cognetics, "Entrepreneurial Hot Spots: The Best Places in America to Start and Grow a Company," 1999*

Business Environment

STATE ECONOMY

State Economic Profile

"Iowa's economy has seen impressive growth in the last several years. A tight labor market and a softening in both the manufacturing and agriculture sectors will, however, slow Iowa's growth over the next few years.

While low food prices have helped to tame inflation, they have hurt farm income. Depressed commodity prices have hit Iowa's Gross State Product (GSP) particularly hard. Given the current oversupply in many food markets and the weak foreign demand, Iowa's farm economy will remain a drag on its economy.

Services, manufacturing and construction have all provided significant growth, helping to offset the declining farm sector. Business services and high-tech manufacturing, as well as a construction boom, largely contribute to this growth.

Des Moines, the traditional engine of Iowa's non-farm sector employment growth, has actually been growing at a rate below the rest of the state. This is partly due to Des Moines' tight labor market (1.9% unemployment rate) at the end of 1998. Economic growth has instead shifted to Cedar Rapids and Ames, both centers of university-high tech partnerships. Des Moines did, however, witness a building boom in 1998, with single-family permits jumping 35% and construction employment growing almost 12% in 1998.

There have been many bright spots to offset Iowa's hurting farm sector. Unfortunately the continued loss of population and tight labor markets will be a hurdle to companies that want to create jobs." *National Association of Realtors, Economic Profiles: The Fifty States and the District of Columbia, http://nar.realtor.com/databank/profiles.htm*

EXPORTS

Total Export Sales

Area	1995 ($000)	1996 ($000)	1997 ($000)	1998 ($000)	% Chg. 1995-98	% Chg. 1997-98
MSA[1]	1,291,031	1,576,123	1,933,861	1,745,777	35.2	-9.7
U.S.	583,030,524	622,827,063	687,597,999	680,474,251	16.7	-1.0

Note: (1) Metropolitan Statistical Area - see Appendix A for areas included
Source: U.S. Department of Commerce, International Trade Association, Metropolitan Area Exports: An Export Performance Report on Over 250 U.S. Cities, November 10, 1999

CITY FINANCES

City Government Finances

Component	1995 ($million)	1995 (per capita $)
Revenue	100.6	1,037
Expenditure	107.9	1,113
Debt Outstanding	241.7	2,493

Source: 1999 County and City Extra, Annual Metro, City, and County Data Book

City Government Revenue by Source

Source	1995 ($million)	1995 (per capita $)
Intergovernmental	27.8	286
Taxes	37.9	391
Property	29.6	306
Sales and Gross Receipts	7.0	73

Source: 1999 County and City Extra, Annual Metro, City, and County Data Book

City Government Expenditures by Function

Function	1995 ($million)	1995 (per capita $)	1995 (%)
Public Welfare	0.0	0	0.0
Highways	12.1	125	11.3
Parking Facilities	0.7	7	0.7
Education	0.0	0	0.0
Health and Hospitals	0.0	0	0.0
Police Protection	10.8	112	10.1
Sewerage and Sanitation	20.7	213	19.2
Parks and Recreation	9.2	95	8.6
Housing and Community Development	6.3	65	5.9
Interest on Debt	18.0	185	16.7

Source: 1999 County and City Extra, Annual Metro, City, and County Data Book

Municipal Bond Ratings

Area	Moody's
City	Aa2

Source: Mergent Bond Record, 2/2000

POPULATION

Population Growth

Area	1980 Census	1990 Census	1999 Estimate	2004 Projection	Population Growth (%) 1990-1999	Population Growth (%) 1999-2004
City	103,264	95,333	97,284	97,843	2.0	0.6
MSA[1]	383,958	350,861	357,960	359,203	2.0	0.3
U.S.	226,545,805	248,765,170	272,212,864	283,625,312	9.4	4.2

Note: (1) Metropolitan Statistical Area - see Appendix A for areas included
Source: 1990 Census of Population and Housing, Summary Tape File 3C; Claritas, Inc.

Number of Households and Average Household Size

Area	1980 Census	1990 Census	1999 Estimate	2004 Projection	1999 Average Household Size
City	38,009	37,069	38,957	39,709	2.50
MSA[1]	138,256	135,962	143,899	146,831	2.49
U.S.	80,389,592	91,993,582	102,048,200	107,302,392	2.67

Note: (1) Metropolitan Statistical Area - see Appendix A for areas included
Source: 1990 Census of Population and Housing, Summary Tape File 3C; Claritas, Inc.

Race/Ethnicity of City Population

Race/Ethnicity	1990 Census Population	1990 Census %	1999 Estimate Population	1999 Estimate %	% Change 1990-1999
White, Non-Hispanic	83,227	87.3	80,932	83.2	-2.8
Black, Non-Hispanic	7,356	7.7	8,593	8.8	16.8
Asian, Non-Hispanic	882	0.9	1,363	1.4	54.5
Other, Non-Hispanic	511	0.5	480	0.5	-6.1
Hispanic	3,357	3.5	5,916	6.1	76.2

Source: 1990 Census of Population and Housing, Summary Tape File 3C; Claritas, Inc.

Race/Ethnicity of Metropolitan Statistical Area Population

Race/Ethnicity	1990 Census		1999 Estimate		% Change 1990-1999
	Population	%	Population	%	
White, Non-Hispanic	316,105	90.1	311,802	87.1	-1.4
Black, Non-Hispanic	18,550	5.3	21,258	5.9	14.6
Asian, Non-Hispanic	2,236	0.6	3,284	0.9	46.9
Other, Non-Hispanic	1,466	0.4	1,172	0.3	-20.1
Hispanic	12,504	3.6	20,444	5.7	63.5

Note: See Appendix A for areas included in the Metropolitan Statistical Area
Source: 1990 Census of Population and Housing, Summary Tape File 3C; Claritas, Inc.

Ancestry

Area	German	Irish	English	Italian	U.S.	French	Polish	Dutch
City	47.0	20.9	12.3	2.5	3.0	3.4	2.0	3.2
MSA[1]	41.6	19.5	14.0	2.3	3.7	3.5	2.2	3.3
U.S.	23.3	15.6	13.1	5.9	5.3	4.2	3.8	2.5

Note: Figures are percentages and include persons that reported multiple ancestry (eg. if a person reported being Irish and Italian, they were included in both columns); (1) Metropolitan Statistical Area - see Appendix A for areas included
Source: 1990 Census of Population and Housing, Summary Tape File 3C

Median Age

Area	1990 Census	1999 Estimate
City	31.7	34.8
MSA[1]	33.9	36.5
U.S.	32.9	35.7

Note: (1) Metropolitan Statistical Area - see Appendix A for areas included
Source: 1990 Census of Population and Housing, Summary Tape File 3C; Claritas, Inc.

Male/Female Population

Area	Number of Males		Number of Females		Males per 100 Females	
	1990	1999	1990	1999	1990	1999
City	45,517	46,730	49,816	50,554	91.4	92.4
MSA[1]	169,450	173,115	181,411	184,845	93.4	93.7
U.S.	121,172,379	132,803,736	127,537,494	139,409,136	95.0	95.3

Note: (1) Metropolitan Statistical Area - see Appendix A for areas included
Source: 1990 Census of Population, General Population Characteristics; Claritas, Inc.

INCOME

Per Capita/Median/Average Income

Area	Per Capita ($)			Median Household ($)			Average Household ($)		
	1989	1999	% Chg.	1989	1999	% Chg.	1989	1999	% Chg.
City	12,557	18,408	46.6	26,218	34,571	31.9	31,857	44,964	41.1
MSA[1]	13,251	19,602	47.9	27,941	36,538	30.8	33,885	48,074	41.9
U.S.	14,420	21,350	48.1	30,056	40,525	34.8	38,453	56,184	46.1

Note: (1) Metropolitan Statistical Area - see Appendix A for areas included; 1989 data is from the 1990 Census; 1999 data is estimated by Claritas, Inc.
Source: 1990 Census of Population, General Population Characteristics; Claritas, Inc.

Household Income Distribution

Area	Percent of Households Earning								
	Under $5,000	$5,000 -14,999	$15,000 -24,999	$25,000 -34,999	$35,000 -49,999	$50,000 -74,999	$75,000 -99,000	$100,000 -149,999	$150,000 and up
City	5.0	15.9	16.4	13.2	17.2	18.2	8.3	4.3	1.6
MSA[1]	4.0	14.3	15.8	13.6	17.1	19.7	8.7	4.6	2.1
U.S.	3.9	13.3	13.8	12.6	16.2	19.4	9.7	6.6	4.6

Note: Data as of 1999; (1) Metropolitan Statistical Area - see Appendix A for areas included
Source: Claritas, Inc.

Effective Buying Income

Area	Per Capita ($)	Median Household ($)	Average Household ($)
City	15,023	31,435	38,124
MSA[1]	16,236	33,877	41,152
U.S.	17,496	36,603	47,036

Note: Data as of 1/1/2000; (1) Metropolitan Statistical Area - see Appendix A for areas included
Source: Standard Rate & Data Service, Newspaper Advertising Source, March 2000

Effective Household Buying Income Distribution

Area	% of Households Earning						
	$10,000 -$19,999	$20,000 -$34,999	$35,000 -$49,999	$50,000 -$74,999	$75,000 -$99,000	$100,000 -$124,999	$125,000 and up
City	17.7	24.0	18.0	17.7	6.2	1.4	1.4
MSA[1]	16.6	23.2	18.5	19.5	7.0	1.8	1.7
U.S.	15.0	21.6	17.6	19.6	8.4	3.0	3.3

Note: Data as of 1/1/2000; (1) Metropolitan Statistical Area - see Appendix A for areas included
Source: Standard Rate & Data Service, Newspaper Advertising Source, March 2000

Poverty Rates by Age

Area	People of All Ages	People Under 18 Years Old	Related Children Age 5-17 in Families in Poverty
City	15.1	n/a	n/a
County	11.6	17.6	14.6
U.S.	13.8	20.8	18.7

Note: Figures show the percent of people living below the poverty line in 1995. The average poverty threshold was $15,569 for a family of four in 1995; n/a not available
Source: Bureau of the Census, Small Area Income and Poverty Estimates Program; U.S. Department of Housing and Urban Development

EMPLOYMENT

Labor Force and Employment

Area	Civilian Labor Force			Workers Employed		
	Dec. 1998	Dec. 1999	% Chg.	Dec. 1998	Dec. 1999	% Chg.
City	51,530	51,424	-0.2	49,738	49,863	0.3
MSA[1]	185,618	187,335	0.9	179,085	180,431	0.8
U.S.	138,297,000	139,941,000	1.2	132,732,000	134,696,000	1.5

Note: Data is not seasonally adjusted and covers workers 16 years of age and older; (1) Metropolitan Statistical Area - see Appendix A for areas included
Source: Bureau of Labor Statistics, http://stats.bls.gov

Unemployment Rate

| Area | 1999 | | | | | | | | | | | |
	Jan.	Feb.	Mar.	Apr.	May	Jun.	Jul.	Aug.	Sep.	Oct.	Nov.	Dec.
City	4.6	4.6	4.4	4.1	3.8	3.8	3.4	4.1	3.4	2.5	2.9	3.0
MSA[1]	5.6	5.2	4.4	4.0	5.3	4.4	5.1	5.0	4.2	3.5	3.5	3.7
U.S.	4.8	4.7	4.4	4.1	4.0	4.5	4.5	4.2	4.1	3.8	3.8	3.7

Note: Data is not seasonally adjusted and covers workers 16 years of age and older; all figures are percentages; (1) Metropolitan Statistical Area - see Appendix A for areas included
Source: Bureau of Labor Statistics, http://stats.bls.gov

Employment by Industry

| Sector | MSA[1] | | U.S. |
	Number of Employees	Percent of Total	Percent of Total
Services	n/a	n/a	30.2
Retail Trade	n/a	n/a	18.1
Government	n/a	n/a	15.8
Manufacturing	n/a	n/a	14.1
Finance/Insurance/Real Estate	n/a	n/a	5.9
Wholesale Trade	n/a	n/a	5.4
Transportation/Public Utilities	n/a	n/a	5.3
Construction	n/a	n/a	4.8
Mining	n/a	n/a	0.4

Note: Figures cover non-farm employment as of 12/99 and are not seasonally adjusted; (1) Metropolitan Statistical Area - see Appendix A for areas included; n/a not available
Source: Bureau of Labor Statistics, http://stats.bls.gov

Employment by Occupation

Occupation Category	City (%)	MSA[1] (%)	U.S. (%)
White Collar	57.2	55.1	58.1
Executive/Admin./Management	10.8	10.7	12.3
Professional	14.2	13.0	14.1
Technical & Related Support	2.9	2.8	3.7
Sales	13.5	12.5	11.8
Administrative Support/Clerical	15.8	16.2	16.3
Blue Collar	27.2	28.1	26.2
Precision Production/Craft/Repair	10.4	11.3	11.3
Machine Operators/Assem./Insp.	7.1	7.4	6.8
Transportation/Material Movers	4.6	4.7	4.1
Cleaners/Helpers/Laborers	5.1	4.7	3.9
Services	15.0	14.4	13.2
Farming/Forestry/Fishing	0.6	2.3	2.5

Note: Figures cover workers 16 years of age and older; (1) Metropolitan Statistical Area - see Appendix A for areas included
Source: 1990 Census of Population and Housing, Summary Tape File 3C

Occupational Employment Projections: 1996 - 2006

Occupations Expected to Have the Largest Job Growth (ranked by numerical growth)	Fast-Growing Occupations[1] (ranked by percent growth)
1. Truck drivers, light	1. Systems analysts
2. Salespersons, retail	2. Desktop publishers
3. Cashiers	3. Computer engineers
4. General managers & top executives	4. Database administrators
5. Janitors/cleaners/maids, ex. priv. hshld.	5. Emergency medical technicians
6. Registered nurses	6. Respiratory therapists
7. Nursing aides/orderlies/attendants	7. Adjustment clerks
8. Marketing & sales, supervisors	8. Home health aides
9. Hand packers & packagers	9. Human services workers
10. Systems analysts	10. Guards

Note: Projections cover Iowa; (1) Excludes occupations with total job growth less than 300
Source: U.S. Department of Labor, Employment and Training Administration, America's Labor Market Information System (ALMIS)

Average Wages

Occupation	$/Hr.	Occupation	$/Hr.
Accountants and Auditors	18.13	Maids and Housekeepers	6.68
Assemblers and Fabricators	12.72	Maintenance Repairers	10.74
Automotive Mechanics	12.52	Marketing/Advertising/PR Managers	21.66
Bookkeepers	10.47	Nurses, Licensed Practical	10.91
Carpenters	15.51	Nurses, Registered	15.12
Cashiers	6.98	Nursing Aides/Orderlies/Attendants	7.81
Clerks, General Office	10.24	Physicians and Surgeons	57.06
Clerks, Shipping/Receiving/Traffic	11.46	Receptionists/Information Clerks	8.30
Computer Programmers	18.63	Sales Reps., Exc. Scientific/Retail	18.62
Computer Support Specialists	17.39	Sales Reps., Scientific, Exc. Retail	20.07
Cooks, Restaurant	7.22	Salespersons, Retail	9.26
Electricians	19.77	Secretaries, Except Legal/Medical	10.53
Financial Managers	25.33	Stock Clerks, Sales Floor	7.45
First-Line Supervisors/Mgrs., Sales	16.18	Systems Analysts	24.46
Food Preparation Workers	7.06	Teacher Aides	7.52
General Managers/Top Executives	27.12	Teachers, Elementary School	17.91
Guards	8.23	Teachers, Secondary School	18.85
Hand Packers	8.47	Telemarketers	-
Janitors and Cleaners	8.23	Truck Drivers, Heavy/Tractor-Trailer	13.70
Laborers, Landscaping	10.15	Truck Drivers, Light	12.05
Lawyers	26.76	Waiters and Waitresses	6.06

Note: Wage data is for 1998 and covers the Metropolitan Statistical Area (see Appendix A for areas included). Hourly wages for elementary and secondary school teachers were calculated by the editors from annual wage data assuming a 40 hour work week; Dashes indicate that data was not available.
Source: Bureau of Labor Statistics, 1998 Metropolitan Area Occupational Employment and Wage Estimates

TAXES

Major State and Local Tax Rates

State Corporate Income (%)	State Personal Income (%)	Residential Property (%)	Sales & Use		State Gasoline (cents/gallon)	State Cigarette (cents/pack)
			State (%)	Local (%)		
6.0 - 12.0	0.36 - 8.98	3.24	5.0	2.0	20.0	36.0

Note: Personal/corporate income, sales, gasoline and cigarette tax rates as of January 2000. Property tax rates as of April 2000.
Source: Federation of Tax Administrators, www.taxadmin.org; ERI's Relocation Assessor software database, quarterly effective date 4/1/2000

Total Taxes Per Capita and as a Percent of Income

Area	Per Capita Income ($)	Per Capita Taxes ($)			Percent of Income (%)		
		Total	Federal	State/Local	Total	Federal	State/Local
Iowa	26,688	9,097	6,004	3,093	34.1	22.5	11.6
U.S.	28,878	10,298	7,026	3,273	35.7	24.3	11.3

Note: Figures are for 1999
Source: Tax Foundation, www.taxfoundation.org

COMMERCIAL UTILITIES

Typical Monthly Electric Bills

Area	Commercial Service ($/month)		Industrial Service ($/month)	
	12 kW demand 1,500 kWh	100 kW demand 30,000 kWh	1,000 kW demand 400,000 kWh	20,000 kW demand 10,000,000 kWh
City	n/a	n/a	n/a	n/a
U.S.	150	2,174	23,995	508,569

Note: Based on rates in effect January 1, 1999; n/a not available
Source: Edison Electric Institute, Typical Residential, Commercial and Industrial Bills, Winter 1999

TRANSPORTATION

Transportation Statistics

Average minutes to work (1990)	16.1
Interstate highways	I-74; I-80; I-280; US-6; US-61; US-67
Bus lines	
In-city (1998)	Davenport Public Transit, 16 buses
Inter-city (1999)	5
Passenger air service	
Airport	Quad City International
Airlines (1999)	6
Enplaned passengers (1998)	348,114
Amtrak service	Bus Connection
Motor freight carriers (1999)	38
Major waterways/ports	None

Source: FAA DOT/TSC CY1998 ACAIS Database; National Transit Database, 1998; Editor & Publisher Market Guide, 2000; Amtrak National Time Table, Fall 1999/Winter 2000; 1990 Census of Population and Housing, STF 3C; Jane's Urban Transport Systems 1999-2000

Means of Transportation to Work

Area	Car/Truck/Van		Public Transportation			Bicycle	Walked	Other Means	Worked at Home
	Drove Alone	Car-pooled	Bus	Subway	Railroad				
City	80.4	11.7	1.0	0.0	0.0	0.2	3.7	0.6	2.4
MSA[1]	80.9	11.2	0.9	0.0	0.0	0.3	3.2	0.7	2.9
U.S.	73.2	13.4	3.0	1.5	0.5	0.4	3.9	1.2	3.0

Note: Figures shown are percentages and only include workers 16 years of age and older;
(1) Metropolitan Statistical Area - see Appendix A for areas included
Source: 1990 Census of Population and Housing, Summary Tape File 3C

BUSINESSES

Major Business Headquarters

Company Name	1999 Rankings	
	Fortune 500	Forbes 500
No companies listed	-	-

Note: Companies listed are located in the city; dashes indicate no ranking
Fortune 500: Companies that produce a 10-K are ranked 1 to 500 based on 1999 revenue
Forbes 500: Private companies are ranked 1 to 500 based on 1998 revenue
Source: Forbes, December 13, 1999; Fortune, April 17, 2000

HOTELS & MOTELS

Hotels/Motels

Area	Hotels/ Motels	Rooms	Luxury-Level Hotels/Motels		Average Minimum Rates ($)		
			♦♦♦♦	♦♦♦♦♦	♦♦	♦♦♦	♦♦♦♦
City	15	1,563	0	0	n/a	n/a	n/a
Suburbs	3	287	0	0	n/a	n/a	n/a
Total	18	1,850	0	0	n/a	n/a	n/a

Note: n/a not available; classifications range from one diamond (budget properties with basic amenities) to five diamond (luxury properties).
Source: OAG Business Travel Planner, Winter 1999-2000

Estimated Daily Food and Lodging Costs

Area	Food/Other ($/day)	Average Hotel Cost ($/day)
City	30	55
U.S.	30	55

Source: ERI's Relocation Assessor software database, quarterly effective date 4/1/2000

CONVENTION CENTERS

Convention Centers and Event Sites

Name	Guest Rooms	Meeting Space (sq. ft.)	Capacity (Theatre Style)
Palmer Arena Palmer College	n/a	n/a	4,000
Radisson Quad City Plaza Hotel	221	7,800	800
RiverCenter and Adler Theatre	n/a	n/a	3,500

Note: n/a not available
Source: EventSource.com, 3/15/2000

Living Environment

COST OF LIVING

Cost of Living: Homeowner

Cost Element	U.S. ($)	City ($)	Differential ($)	Percent of U.S. Average
Consumables	14,516	15,045	529	103.6
Transportation	5,957	6,146	189	103.2
Health Services	2,012	1,992	-20	99.0
Housing/Utilities/Prop. Tax	16,337	18,649	2,312	114.2
Income+Payroll Taxes	12,615	11,698	-917	92.7
Miscellaneous	8,563	8,563	0	100.0
Total Cost of Living	60,000	62,093	2,093	103.5

Note: Figures are based on a single income, four person family with gross annual earnings of $60,000, owning an 1,800 square-foot home, and driving two automobiles worth $22,000 30,000 miles per year.
Source: ERI's Relocation Assessor software database, quarterly effective date 4/1/2000

Cost of Living: Renter

Cost Element	U.S. ($)	City ($)	Differential ($)	Percent of U.S. Average
Consumables	10,486	10,819	333	103.2
Transportation	2,107	2,164	57	102.7
Health Services	1,632	1,610	-22	98.7
Rent/Utilities/Insurance	9,299	7,917	-1,382	85.1
Income+Payroll Taxes	8,607	8,303	-304	96.5
Miscellaneous	7,869	7,869	0	100.0
Total Cost of Living	40,000	38,682	-1,318	96.7

Note: Figures are based on a single income, three person family with gross annual earnings of $40,000, renting a 1,000 square-foot home, and driving one automobile worth $8,000 12,000 miles per year.
Source: ERI's Relocation Assessor software database, quarterly effective date 4/1/2000

HOUSING

Median Home Prices and Housing Affordability

Area	Median Price[2] 4th Qtr. 1999 ($)	HOI[3] 4th Qtr. 1999	Affordability Rank[4]
MSA[1]	71,000	85.1	9
U.S.	139,000	63.8	–

Note: (1) Metropolitan Statistical Area - see Appendix A for areas included; (2) U.S. figures calculated from the sales of 687,516 new and existing homes in 192 markets; (3) Housing Opportunity Index - percent of homes sold that were within the reach of the median income household at the prevailing mortgage interest rate; (4) Rank is from 1-192 with 1 being most affordable
Source: National Association of Home Builders, Housing Opportunity Index, 4th Quarter 1999

Estimated Home Price

Area	Price ($)
City	133,463
U.S.	135,855

Note: Figures are based on an 1,800 square-foot home
Source: ERI's Relocation Assessor software database, quarterly effective date 4/1/2000

Estimated Rent

Area	Rent ($/month)
City	534
U.S.	651

Note: Figures are based on a 1,000 square-foot home
Source: ERI's Relocation Assessor software database, quarterly effective date 4/1/2000

Median Home Price Projection

It is projected that the median home price in the metropolitan area will increase from $81,882 in 1999 to $82,214 in 2010, an increase of 0.4%
Kiplinger's Personal Finance Magazine, January 2000

RESIDENTIAL UTILITIES

Average Residential Utility Costs

Area	All Electric ($/mth)	Part Electric ($/mth)	Other Energy ($/mth)	Phone ($/mth)
City	n/a	n/a	n/a	n/a
U.S.	99.25	55.47	43.48	20.29

Note: n/a not available
Source: ACCRA, Cost of Living Index, 3rd Quarter 1999

HEALTH CARE

Average Health Care Costs

Area	Hospital ($/day)	Doctor ($/visit)	Dentist ($/visit)
City	n/a	n/a	n/a
U.S.	440.96	53.83	68.42

Note: n/a not available
Source: ACCRA, Cost of Living Index, 3rd Quarter 1999

Distribution of Office-Based Physicians

Area	Family/Gen. Practitioners	Specialists		
		Medical	Surgical	Other
MSA[1]	43	64	75	63

Note: Data as of 12/31/97; (1) Metropolitan Statistical Area - see Appendix A for areas included
Source: American Medical Assn., Physician Characteristics & Distribution in the U.S., 1999

Hospitals

Davenport has 2 general medical and surgical hospitals.
AHA Guide to the Healthcare Field, 1999-2000

EDUCATION

Public School District Statistics

District Name	Num. Sch.	Enroll.	Classroom Teachers	Pupils per Teacher	Minority Pupils (%)	Current Exp.[1] ($/pupil)
Davenport Comm School District	36	17,220	1,246	13.8	27.0	5,408

Note: Data covers the 1997-1998 school year unless otherwise noted; (1) Data covers fiscal year 1996; SD = School District; ISD = Independent School District; n/a not available
Source: National Center for Education Statistics, Common Core of Data Public Education Agency Universe 1997-98; National Center for Education Statistics, Characteristics of the 100 Largest Public Elementary and Secondary School Districts in the United States: 1997-98, July 1999

Educational Quality

School District	Education Quotient[1]	Graduate Outcome[2]	Community Index[3]	Resource Index[4]
Davenport Comm. School Dist.	114	120	103	103

Note: Over 1,000 secondary school districts were rated in terms of educational quality. The scores range from a low of 50 to a high of 150; (1) Combination of the Graduate Outcome, Community and Resource indexes weighted to reflect the greater importance of the Graduate Outcome and Resource Index; (2) Based on graduation rates and college board scores (SAT/ACT); (3) Based on the surrounding community's level of affluence and adult education; (4) Based on teacher salaries, per-pupil expenditures and student-teacher ratios.
Source: Expansion Management, Ratings Issue, 1999

Educational Attainment by Race

Area	High School Graduate (%)					Bachelor's Degree (%)				
	Total	White	Black	Other	Hisp.[2]	Total	White	Black	Other	Hisp.[2]
City	78.8	80.0	63.2	70.2	65.0	20.1	20.7	12.8	17.6	11.3
MSA[1]	79.1	80.0	63.4	66.4	63.5	17.4	17.8	9.7	14.6	10.6
U.S.	75.2	77.9	63.1	60.4	49.8	20.3	21.5	11.4	19.4	9.2

Note: Figures shown cover persons 25 years old and over; (1) Metropolitan Statistical Area - see Appendix A for areas included; (2) people of Hispanic origin can be of any race
Source: 1990 Census of Population and Housing, Summary Tape File 3C

School Enrollment by Type

Area	Preprimary				Elementary/High School			
	Public		Private		Public		Private	
	Enrollment	%	Enrollment	%	Enrollment	%	Enrollment	%
City	1,304	58.4	927	41.6	15,103	89.9	1,699	10.1
MSA[1]	4,788	63.4	2,764	36.6	57,985	92.0	5,018	8.0
U.S.	2,679,029	59.5	1,824,256	40.5	38,379,689	90.2	4,187,099	9.8

Note: Figures shown cover persons 3 years old and over;
(1) Metropolitan Statistical Area - see Appendix A for areas included
Source: 1990 Census of Population and Housing, Summary Tape File 3C

School Enrollment by Race

Area	Preprimary (%)				Elementary/High School (%)			
	White	Black	Other	Hisp.[1]	White	Black	Other	Hisp.[1]
City	87.4	8.2	4.5	5.1	81.7	13.7	4.6	4.8
MSA[2]	90.2	5.9	3.9	5.9	87.8	8.4	3.8	5.4
U.S.	80.4	12.5	7.1	7.8	74.1	15.6	10.3	12.5

Note: Figures shown cover persons 3 years old and over; (1) people of Hispanic origin can be of any race; (2) Metropolitan Statistical Area - see Appendix A for areas included
Source: 1990 Census of Population and Housing, Summary Tape File 3C

Higher Education

Two-Year Colleges		Four-Year Colleges		Medical Schools	Law Schools	Voc/ Tech
Public	Private	Public	Private			
1	1	0	2	0	0	3

Source: College Blue Book, Occupational Education, 1999; Medical School Admission Requirements, 1999-2000; Peterson's Guide to Two-Year Colleges, 2000; Peterson's Guide to Four-Year Colleges, 1999; Barron's Guide to Law Schools, 1999

MAJOR EMPLOYERS

Major Employers

Blackhawk Foundry & Machine
Lee Enterprises (publishing)
Midland Press Corp.
Swiss Valley Farms
Von Maur (department stores)

I&M Rail Link
Lujack Schierbrock Chevrolet
Sears Manufacturing
Tri-City Fabricating & Welding

Note: Companies listed are located in the city
Source: D&B Business Rankings, 1999; Ward's Business Directory, 1999; America's Corporate Families, 1999

PUBLIC SAFETY

Crime Rate

Area	All Crimes	Violent Crimes				Property Crimes		
		Murder	Forcible Rape	Robbery	Aggrav. Assault	Burglary	Larceny -Theft	Motor Vehicle Theft
City	7,261.6	2.0	56.3	225.3	1,124.4	1,413.2	4,044.0	396.3
Suburbs[1]	n/a	n/a	n/a	n/a	n/a	n/a	n/a	n/a
MSA[2]	n/a	n/a	n/a	n/a	n/a	n/a	n/a	n/a
U.S.	4,615.5	6.3	34.4	165.2	360.5	862.0	2,728.1	459.0

Note: Crime rate is the number of crimes per 100,000 population; (1) Defined as all areas within the Metropolitan Statistical Area but located outside the central city; (2) Metropolitan Statistical Area - see Appendix A for areas included; n/a not available
Source: FBI Uniform Crime Reports, 1998

RECREATION

Culture and Recreation

Museums	Symphony Orchestras	Opera Companies	Dance Companies	Professional Theatres	Zoos	Pro Sports Teams
2	2	0	0	0	1	0

Source: Musical America, International Directory of the Performing Arts, 1999; Official Museum Directory, 2000; Stern's Performing Arts Directory, 1997; USA Today Four Sport Stadium Guide, 1997; Career Opportunities in Theatre and the Performing Arts, 1999

Library System

The Davenport Public Library has one branch, holdings of 252,341 volumes, and a budget of $2,868,105 (1997-1998).
American Library Directory, 1999-2000

MEDIA

Newspapers

Name	Type	Freq.	Distribution	Circulation
The Catholic Messenger	Religious	1x/wk	U.S./Int'l.	23,241
The Quad City Advertiser	General	1x/wk	Local	50,000
Quad-City Times	n/a	7x/wk	Area	54,868

Note: Includes newspapers with circulations of 200 or more located in the city; n/a not available
Source: Burrelle's Media Directory, 1999 Edition

Television Stations

Name	Ch.	Affiliation	Type	Owner
KWQC	n/a	NBCT	Commercial	Young Broadcasting Inc.
KLJB	18	FBC	Commercial	Quad Cities TV Acquisition Corp.
KJMH	26	FBC	Commercial	Burlington Television Acquisition Corp.

Note: Stations included broadcast in the Davenport metro area; n/a not available
Source: Burrelle's Media Directory, 1999 Edition

AM Radio Stations

Call Letters	Freq. (kHz)	Target Audience	Station Format	Music Format
KJOC	1170	General	M/S	n/a
WLLR	1230	General	M/S	Country
WKBF	1270	General	M/S	Adult Standards/Big Band
WOC	1420	General	T	n/a

Note: Stations included broadcast in the Davenport metro area; n/a not available
Target Audience: A=Asian; B=Black; C=Christian; E=Ethnic; F=French; G=General; H=Hispanic; M=Men; N=Native American; R=Religious; S=Senior Citizen; W=Women; Y=Young Adult; Z=Children
Station Format: E=Educational; M=Music; N=News; S=Sports; T=Talk
Source: Burrelle's Media Directory, 1999 Edition

FM Radio Stations

Call Letters	Freq. (mHz)	Target Audience	Station Format	Music Format
KALA	88.5	General	M/N/S	n/a
KORB	93.5	General	M/N/S	n/a
KMXG	96.1	General	M	Adult Contemporary
WXLP	96.9	General	M	AOR/Classic Rock
WHTS	98.9	General	M	n/a
KBOB	99.7	General	M/N/T	Country
KUUL	101.3	General	M/N/S	Oldies
WLLR	103.7	General	M	Country
KCQQ	106.5	General	M/N/S	Classic Rock

Note: Stations included broadcast in the Davenport metro area; n/a not available
Station Format: E=Educational; M=Music; N=News; S=Sports; T=Talk
Target Audience: A=Asian; B=Black; C=Christian; E=Ethnic; F=French; G=General; H=Hispanic; M=Men; N=Native American; R=Religious; S=Senior Citizen; W=Women; Y=Young Adult; Z=Children
Music Format: AOR=Album Oriented Rock; MOR=Middle-of-the-Road
Source: Burrelle's Media Directory, 1999 Edition

WEATHER

Temperature/Precipitation/Humidity

	Jan	Feb	Mar	Apr	May	Jun	Jul	Aug	Sep	Oct	Nov	Dec	Yr.
Max. High Temp. (°F)	69	71	88	93	95	101	103	103	99	92	78	69	103
Avg. High Temp. (°F)	29	34	46	61	72	82	86	84	76	65	48	34	60
Avg. Temp. (°F)	21	26	37	51	61	71	75	73	65	54	39	26	50
Avg. Low Temp. (°F)	12	17	28	40	50	60	64	62	53	42	30	18	40
Min. Low Temp. (°F)	-27	-25	-19	7	26	39	46	40	30	16	-9	-24	-27
Avg. Precip. (in.)	1.5	1.4	2.9	3.8	4.1	4.4	4.5	4.0	3.5	2.7	2.2	2.0	37.1
Avg. Snowfall (in.)	8	7	6	1	Tr	0	0	0	0	Tr	3	8	33
Avg. Rel. Hum. 6am (%)	75	77	78	78	79	81	85	89	87	82	79	79	81
Avg. Rel. Hum. 3pm (%)	65	62	57	50	49	50	53	54	52	49	59	67	56

Note: Tr = Trace amounts (less than 0.05 inches of rain or less than 0.5 inches of snow)
Source: National Climatic Data Center, International Station Meteorological Climate Summary, 3/95

Weather Conditions

Temperature			Precipitation		
5°F & below	32°F & below	90°F & above	0.01 inch or more precip.	1.5 inch or more snow/ice	Thunder-storms
23	135	23	113	9	46

Note: Figures are average number of days per year
Source: National Climatic Data Center, International Station Meteorological Climate Summary, 3/95

AIR & WATER QUALITY

Maximum Pollutant Concentrations

	Particulate Matter (ug/m³)	Carbon Monoxide (ppm)	Sulfur Dioxide (ppm)	Nitrogen Dioxide (ppm)	Ozone (ppm)	Lead (ug/m³)
MSA[1] Level	150	n/a	0.020	n/a	0.09	0.02
NAAQS[2]	150	9	0.140	0.053	0.12	1.50
Met NAAQS	Yes	n/a	Yes	n/a	Yes	Yes

Note: (1) Metropolitan Statistical Area - see Appendix A for areas included; (2) National Ambient Air Quality Standards; ppm = parts per million; ug/m³ = micrograms per cubic meter; n/a not available
Source: EPA, National Air Quality and Emissions Trends Report, 1997

Pollutant Standards Index

Data not available.
EPA, National Air Quality and Emissions Trends Report, 1997

Drinking Water

Water System Name	Pop. Served	Primary Water Source Type	Number of Violations in 1998-99	Type of Violation/ Contaminants
Iowa-American Water Corp.	129,516	Surface	None	None

Note: Data as of January 19, 2000
Source: EPA, Office of Ground Water and Drinking Water, Safe Drinking Water Information System

Davenport tap water is neutral, hard, and fluoridated.
Editor & Publisher Market Guide, 2000

Daytona Beach, Florida

Background

Daytona Beach, Florida is located on the Atlantic coast of the state, approximately 60 miles northeast of Orlando. It is situated on the Halifax River, part of the Intracoastal Waterway and known for its white sand beaches.

Daytona Beach is the largest city in Volusia County and a regional commercial center. The city and surrounding area is a popular ocean resort region, with recreational activities that include extensive beaches and water sports, as well as motor sports and golf. The city has 15 marinas. In addition to tourism, the city's economy includes manufacturing of defense systems, mechanical equipment and numerous other products, business services and retail and transportation.

The region was occupied by the Timucuan, Seminole and other Native Americans. It is named after Mathias Day, who laid out the town in 1870. It was incorporated as Daytona in 1876, and renamed Daytona Beach in 1926.

Daytona Beach has been associated with motorsports since the early 20th Century, when its beaches were used as a testing site for races. Today, the Daytona International Speedway hosts the popular Daytona 500 auto race. The headquarters of the National Association for Stock Car Racing are in Daytona Beach, and DAYTONA USA, a motorport theme park is a well known attraction. Motorbike events are also held in the city. Daytona Beach is also the headquarters for the Ladies Professional Golf Association, and the Daytona Cubs are a Class A affiliate of the Chicago Cubs.

Daytona Beach is home to several colleges including Bethune-Cookman College, Embry Riddle Aerospace University, University of Central Florida, Daytona Beach Community College, Keiser Junior College and NOVA Southeastern University.

Museums include the Museum of Arts and Sciences, Southeast Museum of Photography and Haliax Historical Museum. Peabody Auditorium is a cultural center and the summer home of the London Symphony. Ocean Center is a convention and events facility.

Daytona Beach is governed by a City Commission and City Manager.

General Rankings and Evaluative Comments

- Daytona Beach was ranked #115 out of 354 metropolitan areas in *Places Rated Almanac*. Criteria: cost of living, climate, crime, transportation, job outlook, education, the arts, health care, and recreation. *Places Rated Almanac, Millennium Edition, 2000*

- Daytona Beach was selected as one of America's best places to retire. Criteria: safety, climate, housing, culture and recreation, social compatibility, affordability, medical care, transportation, and jobs and/or volunteer opportunities. *Where to Retire: America's Best and Most Affordable Places, 1998*

- Daytona Beach was selected as one of the best places to retire by *Retirement Places Rated*. Criteria: cost of living, climate, crime, services, working, and leisure living. The city was ranked #17 out of 187. *Retirement Places Rated, 1999*

- Cognetics studied 273 metro areas in the United States, ranking them by entrepreneurial activity. Daytona Beach was ranked #78 out of 134 smaller metro areas. Criteria: Significant Starts (firms started in the last 10 years that still employ at least 5 people) and Young Growers (percent of firms 10 years old or less that grew significantly during the last 4 years). *Cognetics, "Entrepreneurial Hot Spots: The Best Places in America to Start and Grow a Company," 1999*

- Reliastar Financial Corporation ranked the 125 largest metropolitan areas according to the general financial security of residents. Daytona Beach was ranked #88 out of 125 with a score of -2.3 (the percentage a metropolitan area is above or below the metropolitan norm; a metro area with a score of 10.6 is 10.6% above the metro average). Criteria: Earnings and Wealth Potential (household income, education, net assets, cost of living); Safety Net (health insurance, retirement savings, life insurance, income support programs); Personal Threats (unemployment rate, low-income households, crime rate); Community Economic Vitality (cost of community services, job quality, job creation, housing costs). *Reliastar Financial Corporation, "The Best Cities to Earn and Save Money: A Ranking of the Largest 125 U.S. Cities," 2000 Edition*

Business Environment

STATE ECONOMY

State Economic Profile

"Florida's economy has been among the nation's strongest in recent years. Job growth has outpaced the nation by a considerable amount since 1992.

While Florida has been able to avoid any significant fallout from the Asian crisis, the weakening of economies in Latin American will dampen both tourism and international trade. 1998 saw the decline in Latin tourism more than offset by domestic visitors. Domestic tourism is projected to soften as U.S. growth cools, offering no offset against the expected decline in Latin tourism. Weaker tourism and trade with Latin American will slow growth in the near future; Florida will still outpace the nation in job growth as Gross State Product growth (GSP) slows.

Over half of Florida's 230,000 new jobs created in 1998 were in the services sector, which grew at 5.2%, more than offsetting a minor decline in manufacturing employment. Much of this growth is taking place in the finance and business services sector.

In spite of strong home sales and a slowing construction market, Florida's price appreciation continued to lag the nation. Although residential permits per 1,000 residents stands at 5.1, well above the national average, this number is only slightly up from 1997 and is poised to decline in the near future.

Growth in Florida, while strong throughout, has been hottest in the Naples, Ft. Myers and Orlando areas. Construction and employment in the construction industry has begun to slow in South Florida. Projected employment and housing gains will be concentrated in Northern and Central Florida. Growing diversification of the economy into financial and business services promises a strong outlook for the years ahead." *National Association of Realtors, Economic Profiles: The Fifty States and the District of Columbia, http://nar.realtor.com/databank/profiles.htm*

EXPORTS

Total Export Sales

Area	1995 ($000)	1996 ($000)	1997 ($000)	1998 ($000)	% Chg. 1995-98	% Chg. 1997-98
MSA[1]	85,855	111,657	137,453	142,793	66.3	3.9
U.S.	583,030,524	622,827,063	687,597,999	680,474,251	16.7	-1.0

Note: (1) Metropolitan Statistical Area - see Appendix A for areas included
Source: U.S. Department of Commerce, International Trade Association, Metropolitan Area Exports: An Export Performance Report on Over 250 U.S. Cities, November 10, 1999

CITY FINANCES

City Government Finances

Component	1995 ($million)	1995 (per capita $)
Revenue	62.0	959
Expenditure	61.3	948
Debt Outstanding	76.1	1,178

Source: 1999 County and City Extra, Annual Metro, City, and County Data Book

City Government Revenue by Source

Source	1995 ($million)	1995 (per capita $)
Intergovernmental	10.7	165
Taxes	24.1	373
Property	12.2	189
Sales and Gross Receipts	10.4	162

Source: 1999 County and City Extra, Annual Metro, City, and County Data Book

City Government Expenditures by Function

Function	1995 ($million)	1995 (per capita $)	1995 (%)
Public Welfare	<0.1	<1	0.1
Highways	6.1	94	10.0
Parking Facilities	0.0	0	0.0
Education	0.0	0	0.0
Health and Hospitals	0.0	0	0.0
Police Protection	16.3	252	26.6
Sewerage and Sanitation	12.0	185	19.6
Parks and Recreation	9.7	150	15.9
Housing and Community Development	2.4	37	4.0
Interest on Debt	1.1	18	1.9

Source: 1999 County and City Extra, Annual Metro, City, and County Data Book

Municipal Bond Ratings

Area	Moody's
City	Aaa

Source: Mergent Bond Record, 2/2000

POPULATION

Population Growth

Area	1980 Census	1990 Census	1999 Estimate	2004 Projection	Population Growth (%) 1990-1999	Population Growth (%) 1999-2004
City	54,176	61,921	63,518	64,659	2.6	1.8
MSA[1]	258,762	370,712	471,864	508,876	27.3	7.8
U.S.	226,545,805	248,765,170	272,212,864	283,625,312	9.4	4.2

Note: (1) Metropolitan Statistical Area - see Appendix A for areas included
Source: 1990 Census of Population and Housing, Summary Tape File 3C; Claritas, Inc.

Number of Households and Average Household Size

Area	1980 Census	1990 Census	1999 Estimate	2004 Projection	1999 Average Household Size
City	23,921	27,328	27,951	28,807	2.27
MSA[1]	110,132	153,315	191,761	208,331	2.46
U.S.	80,389,592	91,993,582	102,048,200	107,302,392	2.67

Note: (1) Metropolitan Statistical Area - see Appendix A for areas included
Source: 1990 Census of Population and Housing, Summary Tape File 3C; Claritas, Inc.

Race/Ethnicity of City Population

Race/Ethnicity	1990 Census Population	1990 Census %	1999 Estimate Population	1999 Estimate %	% Change 1990-1999
White, Non-Hispanic	40,523	65.4	38,017	59.9	-6.2
Black, Non-Hispanic	18,916	30.5	22,037	34.7	16.5
Asian, Non-Hispanic	626	1.0	1,073	1.7	71.4
Other, Non-Hispanic	148	0.2	250	0.4	68.9
Hispanic	1,708	2.8	2,141	3.4	25.4

Source: 1990 Census of Population and Housing, Summary Tape File 3C; Claritas, Inc.

Race/Ethnicity of Metropolitan Statistical Area Population

Race/Ethnicity	1990 Census		1999 Estimate		% Change 1990-1999
	Population	%	Population	%	
White, Non-Hispanic	319,621	86.2	386,284	81.9	20.9
Black, Non-Hispanic	33,005	8.9	51,252	10.9	55.3
Asian, Non-Hispanic	2,159	0.6	5,279	1.1	144.5
Other, Non-Hispanic	1,259	0.3	1,640	0.3	30.3
Hispanic	14,668	4.0	27,409	5.8	86.9

Note: See Appendix A for areas included in the Metropolitan Statistical Area
Source: 1990 Census of Population and Housing, Summary Tape File 3C; Claritas, Inc.

Ancestry

Area	German	Irish	English	Italian	U.S.	French	Polish	Dutch
City	15.6	13.0	13.1	5.2	3.4	3.3	2.5	1.8
MSA[1]	23.1	18.4	19.1	7.4	5.0	5.2	3.4	2.8
U.S.	23.3	15.6	13.1	5.9	5.3	4.2	3.8	2.5

Note: Figures are percentages and include persons that reported multiple ancestry (eg. if a person reported being Irish and Italian, they were included in both columns); (1) Metropolitan Statistical Area - see Appendix A for areas included
Source: 1990 Census of Population and Housing, Summary Tape File 3C

Median Age

Area	1990 Census	1999 Estimate
City	35.0	37.3
MSA[1]	39.3	42.2
U.S.	32.9	35.7

Note: (1) Metropolitan Statistical Area - see Appendix A for areas included
Source: 1990 Census of Population and Housing, Summary Tape File 3C; Claritas, Inc.

Male/Female Population

Area	Number of Males		Number of Females		Males per 100 Females	
	1990	1999	1990	1999	1990	1999
City	30,691	31,652	31,230	31,866	98.3	99.3
MSA[1]	179,549	228,395	191,163	243,469	93.9	93.8
U.S.	121,172,379	132,803,736	127,537,494	139,409,136	95.0	95.3

Note: (1) Metropolitan Statistical Area - see Appendix A for areas included
Source: 1990 Census of Population, General Population Characteristics; Claritas, Inc.

INCOME

Per Capita/Median/Average Income

Area	Per Capita ($)			Median Household ($)			Average Household ($)		
	1989	1999	% Chg.	1989	1999	% Chg.	1989	1999	% Chg.
City	11,901	15,804	32.8	18,631	22,984	23.4	26,152	35,174	34.5
MSA[1]	13,288	17,462	31.4	24,818	30,888	24.5	31,536	42,425	34.5
U.S.	14,420	21,350	48.1	30,056	40,525	34.8	38,453	56,184	46.1

Note: (1) Metropolitan Statistical Area - see Appendix A for areas included; 1989 data is from the 1990 Census; 1999 data is estimated by Claritas, Inc.
Source: 1990 Census of Population, General Population Characteristics; Claritas, Inc.

Household Income Distribution

Area	Percent of Households Earning								
	Under $5,000	$5,000 -14,999	$15,000 -24,999	$25,000 -34,999	$35,000 -49,999	$50,000 -74,999	$75,000 -99,000	$100,000 -149,999	$150,000 and up
City	6.7	24.7	21.9	14.9	14.5	9.9	3.9	2.0	1.5
MSA[1]	4.0	16.2	19.5	16.5	18.6	15.3	5.4	2.6	1.9
U.S.	3.9	13.3	13.8	12.6	16.2	19.4	9.7	6.6	4.6

Note: Data as of 1999; (1) Metropolitan Statistical Area - see Appendix A for areas included
Source: Claritas, Inc.

Effective Buying Income

Area	Per Capita ($)	Median Household ($)	Average Household ($)
City	13,658	21,873	31,059
MSA[1]	15,912	29,527	38,615
U.S.	17,496	36,603	47,036

Note: Data as of 1/1/2000; (1) Metropolitan Statistical Area - see Appendix A for areas included
Source: Standard Rate & Data Service, Newspaper Advertising Source, March 2000

Effective Household Buying Income Distribution

Area	% of Households Earning						
	$10,000 -$19,999	$20,000 -$34,999	$35,000 -$49,999	$50,000 -$74,999	$75,000 -$99,000	$100,000 -$124,999	$125,000 and up
City	25.4	25.7	13.5	9.0	3.4	1.0	1.4
MSA[1]	19.5	27.0	18.1	14.7	5.0	1.5	2.0
U.S.	15.0	21.6	17.6	19.6	8.4	3.0	3.3

Note: Data as of 1/1/2000; (1) Metropolitan Statistical Area - see Appendix A for areas included
Source: Standard Rate & Data Service, Newspaper Advertising Source, March 2000

Poverty Rates by Age

Area	People of All Ages	People Under 18 Years Old	Related Children Age 5-17 in Families in Poverty
City	28.0	n/a	n/a
County	14.8	23.3	20.8
U.S.	13.8	20.8	18.7

Note: Figures show the percent of people living below the poverty line in 1995. The
average poverty threshold was $15,569 for a family of four in 1995; n/a not available
Source: Bureau of the Census, Small Area Income and Poverty Estimates Program;
U.S. Department of Housing and Urban Development

EMPLOYMENT

Labor Force and Employment

Area	Civilian Labor Force			Workers Employed		
	Dec. 1998	Dec. 1999	% Chg.	Dec. 1998	Dec. 1999	% Chg.
City	30,300	30,690	1.3	28,956	29,556	2.1
MSA[1]	191,087	193,948	1.5	184,730	188,557	2.1
U.S.	138,297,000	139,941,000	1.2	132,732,000	134,696,000	1.5

Note: Data is not seasonally adjusted and covers workers 16 years of age and older;
(1) Metropolitan Statistical Area - see Appendix A for areas included
Source: Bureau of Labor Statistics, http://stats.bls.gov

Unemployment Rate

Area	1999											
	Jan.	Feb.	Mar.	Apr.	May	Jun.	Jul.	Aug.	Sep.	Oct.	Nov.	Dec.
City	5.2	4.7	4.6	4.5	4.3	4.1	3.8	3.9	4.1	4.2	4.3	3.7
MSA[1]	4.0	3.5	3.5	3.4	3.3	3.1	2.9	2.9	3.0	3.1	3.2	2.8
U.S.	4.8	4.7	4.4	4.1	4.0	4.5	4.5	4.2	4.1	3.8	3.8	3.7

Note: Data is not seasonally adjusted and covers workers 16 years of age and older; all figures are percentages; (1) Metropolitan Statistical Area - see Appendix A for areas included
Source: Bureau of Labor Statistics, http://stats.bls.gov

Employment by Industry

Sector	MSA[1]		U.S.
	Number of Employees	Percent of Total	Percent of Total
Services	58,300	36.5	30.2
Retail Trade	37,900	23.7	18.1
Government	24,000	15.0	15.8
Manufacturing	12,600	7.9	14.1
Finance/Insurance/Real Estate	6,900	4.3	5.9
Wholesale Trade	5,900	3.7	5.4
Transportation/Public Utilities	5,900	3.7	5.3
Construction	8,200	5.1	4.8
Mining	n/a	n/a	0.4

Note: Figures cover non-farm employment as of 12/99 and are not seasonally adjusted; (1) Metropolitan Statistical Area - see Appendix A for areas included; n/a not available
Source: Bureau of Labor Statistics, http://stats.bls.gov

Employment by Occupation

Occupation Category	City (%)	MSA[1] (%)	U.S. (%)
White Collar	55.1	56.3	58.1
Executive/Admin./Management	11.1	12.2	12.3
Professional	12.5	11.8	14.1
Technical & Related Support	2.9	3.4	3.7
Sales	14.9	14.1	11.8
Administrative Support/Clerical	13.8	14.8	16.3
Blue Collar	18.7	23.8	26.2
Precision Production/Craft/Repair	10.0	12.7	11.3
Machine Operators/Assem./Insp.	3.2	4.1	6.8
Transportation/Material Movers	2.5	3.6	4.1
Cleaners/Helpers/Laborers	3.1	3.4	3.9
Services	24.7	16.7	13.2
Farming/Forestry/Fishing	1.4	3.2	2.5

Note: Figures cover workers 16 years of age and older; (1) Metropolitan Statistical Area - see Appendix A for areas included
Source: 1990 Census of Population and Housing, Summary Tape File 3C

Occupational Employment Projections: 1996 - 2006

Occupations Expected to Have the Largest Job Growth (ranked by numerical growth)	Fast-Growing Occupations[1] (ranked by percent growth)
1. Cashiers	1. Systems analysts
2. Salespersons, retail	2. Physical therapy assistants and aides
3. General managers & top executives	3. Desktop publishers
4. Registered nurses	4. Home health aides
5. Waiters & waitresses	5. Computer engineers
6. Marketing & sales, supervisors	6. Medical assistants
7. Janitors/cleaners/maids, ex. priv. hshld.	7. Physical therapists
8. General office clerks	8. Paralegals
9. Food preparation workers	9. Emergency medical technicians
10. Hand packers & packagers	10. Occupational therapists

Note: Projections cover Florida; (1) Excludes occupations with total job growth less than 300
Source: U.S. Department of Labor, Employment and Training Administration, America's Labor Market Information System (ALMIS)

Average Wages

Occupation	$/Hr.	Occupation	$/Hr.
Accountants and Auditors	15.89	Maids and Housekeepers	6.46
Assemblers and Fabricators	9.37	Maintenance Repairers	9.24
Automotive Mechanics	10.81	Marketing/Advertising/PR Managers	20.57
Bookkeepers	9.86	Nurses, Licensed Practical	12.55
Carpenters	11.01	Nurses, Registered	17.32
Cashiers	6.85	Nursing Aides/Orderlies/Attendants	7.69
Clerks, General Office	8.10	Physicians and Surgeons	55.22
Clerks, Shipping/Receiving/Traffic	10.52	Receptionists/Information Clerks	8.37
Computer Programmers	16.05	Sales Reps., Exc. Scientific/Retail	13.73
Computer Support Specialists	14.39	Sales Reps., Scientific, Exc. Retail	20.06
Cooks, Restaurant	7.83	Salespersons, Retail	8.41
Electricians	11.54	Secretaries, Except Legal/Medical	9.48
Financial Managers	25.46	Stock Clerks, Sales Floor	7.63
First-Line Supervisors/Mgrs., Sales	15.09	Systems Analysts	19.00
Food Preparation Workers	6.34	Teacher Aides	8.83
General Managers/Top Executives	21.25	Teachers, Elementary School	21.19
Guards	6.92	Teachers, Secondary School	-
Hand Packers	6.73	Telemarketers	8.53
Janitors and Cleaners	7.27	Truck Drivers, Heavy/Tractor-Trailer	12.39
Laborers, Landscaping	8.02	Truck Drivers, Light	7.99
Lawyers	34.28	Waiters and Waitresses	5.71

Note: Wage data is for 1998 and covers the Metropolitan Statistical Area (see Appendix A for areas included). Hourly wages for elementary and secondary school teachers were calculated by the editors from annual wage data assuming a 40 hour work week; Dashes indicate that data was not available.
Source: Bureau of Labor Statistics, 1998 Metropolitan Area Occupational Employment and Wage Estimates

TAXES

Major State and Local Tax Rates

State Corporate Income (%)	State Personal Income (%)	Residential Property (%)	Sales & Use		State Gasoline (cents/ gallon)	State Cigarette (cents/ pack)
			State (%)	Local (%)		
5.5[a]	None	2.09	6.0	None	13.3[b]	33.9

Note: Personal/corporate income, sales, gasoline and cigarette tax rates as of January 2000.
Property tax rates as of April 2000; (a) 3.3% Alternative Minimum Tax. An exemption of $5,000 is allowed; (b) Rate is comprised of 4 cents excise and 9.3 cents motor carrier tax. Local taxes vary from 5.5 cents to 17 cents. Plus a 2.07 cent per gallon pollution tax
Source: Federation of Tax Administrators, www.taxadmin.org; ERI's Relocation Assessor software database, quarterly effective date 4/1/2000

Total Taxes Per Capita and as a Percent of Income

Area	Per Capita Income ($)	Per Capita Taxes ($)			Percent of Income (%)		
		Total	Federal	State/ Local	Total	Federal	State/ Local
Florida	28,322	10,333	7,257	3,077	36.5	25.6	10.9
U.S.	28,878	10,298	7,026	3,273	35.7	24.3	11.3

Note: Figures are for 1999
Source: Tax Foundation, www.taxfoundation.org

COMMERCIAL UTILITIES

Typical Monthly Electric Bills

Area	Commercial Service ($/month)		Industrial Service ($/month)	
	12 kW demand 1,500 kWh	100 kW demand 30,000 kWh	1,000 kW demand 400,000 kWh	20,000 kW demand 10,000,000 kWh
City	118	1,993	23,247	387,510
U.S.	150	2,174	23,995	508,569

Note: Based on rates in effect January 1, 1999
Source: Edison Electric Institute, Typical Residential, Commercial and Industrial Bills, Winter 1999

TRANSPORTATION

Transportation Statistics

Average minutes to work (1990)	16.6
Interstate highways	I-4; I-95; US-1; US-92
Bus lines	
In-city (1998)	VOTRAN, 44 buses
Inter-city (1999)	1
Passenger air service	
Airport	Daytona Beach International
Airlines (1999)	3
Enplaned passengers (1998)	303,911
Amtrak service	Bus Connection
Motor freight carriers (1999)	15
Major waterways/ports	Intracoastal Waterway

Source: FAA DOT/TSC CY1998 ACAIS Database; National Transit Database, 1998; Editor & Publisher Market Guide, 2000; Amtrak National Time Table, Fall 1999/Winter 2000; 1990 Census of Population and Housing, STF 3C; Jane's Urban Transport Systems 1999-2000

Means of Transportation to Work

Area	Car/Truck/Van		Public Transportation			Bicycle	Walked	Other Means	Worked at Home
	Drove Alone	Car- pooled	Bus	Subway	Railroad				
City	68.4	15.1	3.4	0.0	0.0	2.0	6.4	2.8	2.0
MSA[1]	76.3	14.9	1.0	0.0	0.0	1.0	2.7	1.8	2.4
U.S.	73.2	13.4	3.0	1.5	0.5	0.4	3.9	1.2	3.0

Note: Figures shown are percentages and only include workers 16 years of age and older;
(1) Metropolitan Statistical Area - see Appendix A for areas included
Source: 1990 Census of Population and Housing, Summary Tape File 3C

BUSINESSES

Major Business Headquarters

Company Name	1999 Rankings	
	Fortune 500	Forbes 500
Budget Group	497	-

Note: Companies listed are located in the city; dashes indicate no ranking
Fortune 500: Companies that produce a 10-K are ranked 1 to 500 based on 1999 revenue
Forbes 500: Private companies are ranked 1 to 500 based on 1998 revenue
Source: Forbes, December 13, 1999; Fortune, April 17, 2000

HOTELS & MOTELS

Hotels/Motels

Area	Hotels/ Motels	Rooms	Luxury-Level Hotels/Motels		Average Minimum Rates ($)		
			♦♦♦♦	♦♦♦♦♦	♦♦	♦♦♦	♦♦♦♦
City	31	3,544	0	0	61	74	n/a
Airport	6	806	0	0	n/a	n/a	n/a
Total	37	4,350	0	0	n/a	n/a	n/a

Note: n/a not available; classifications range from one diamond (budget properties with basic amenities) to five diamond (luxury properties).
Source: OAG Business Travel Planner, Winter 1999-2000

Estimated Daily Food and Lodging Costs

Area	Food/Other ($/day)	Average Hotel Cost ($/day)
City	38	67
U.S.	30	55

Source: ERI's Relocation Assessor software database, quarterly effective date 4/1/2000

CONVENTION CENTERS

Convention Centers and Event Sites

Name	Guest Rooms	Meeting Space (sq. ft.)	Capacity (Theatre Style)
Adam's Mark Daytona Beach Resort	402	16,000	1,200
Best Western Aku Tiki Inn	132	n/a	99
Best Western La Playa Resort	239	3,800	300
Casa del Mar Beach Resort	139	660	70
Castaways Beach Resort	152	850	50
Daytona Beach Hilton	214	16,000	900
Daytona Inn Broadway	80	4,725	400
Daytona International Speedway	n/a	n/a	0
El Caribe Resort & Conference Center	157	8,000	325
Holiday Inn Daytona Beach Shores	196	1,050	180
Holiday Inn Oceanfront	143	532	50
Indigo Lakes Holiday Inn	151	951	125
Ocean Center/Daytona Beach	n/a	n/a	9,500
Peabody Auditorium	n/a	n/a	2,500
Plaza Resort and Spa	323	20,000	1,300
Radisson Resort Daytona Beach	206	6,200	0
Ramada Inn Speedway	127	899	75
Ramada Inn Surfside	119	2,400	200
Ramada Resort Oceanfront	383	870	1,000
Sun Viking lodge	91	360	30
The Aladdin Inn	402	1,035	70
The Granada Inn	194	2,300	135
The Hawaiian Inn	402	8,667	1,200
Treasure Island Inn	228	7,000	450

Note: n/a not available
Source: EventSource.com, 3/15/2000

Living Environment

COST OF LIVING

Cost of Living: Homeowner

Cost Element	U.S. ($)	City ($)	Differential ($)	Percent of U.S. Average
Consumables	14,516	15,209	693	104.8
Transportation	5,957	6,150	193	103.2
Health Services	2,012	2,185	173	108.6
Housing/Utilities/Prop. Tax	16,337	20,463	4,126	125.3
Income+Payroll Taxes	12,615	10,291	-2,324	81.6
Miscellaneous	8,563	8,563	0	100.0
Total Cost of Living	60,000	62,861	2,861	104.8

Note: Figures are based on a single income, four person family with gross annual earnings of $60,000, owning an 1,800 square-foot home, and driving two automobiles worth $22,000 30,000 miles per year.
Source: ERI's Relocation Assessor software database, quarterly effective date 4/1/2000

Cost of Living: Renter

Cost Element	U.S. ($)	City ($)	Differential ($)	Percent of U.S. Average
Consumables	10,486	10,928	442	104.2
Transportation	2,107	2,164	57	102.7
Health Services	1,632	1,764	132	108.1
Rent/Utilities/Insurance	9,299	10,279	980	110.5
Income+Payroll Taxes	8,607	7,183	-1,424	83.5
Miscellaneous	7,869	7,869	0	100.0
Total Cost of Living	40,000	40,187	187	100.5

Note: Figures are based on a single income, three person family with gross annual earnings of $40,000, renting a 1,000 square-foot home, and driving one automobile worth $8,000 12,000 miles per year.
Source: ERI's Relocation Assessor software database, quarterly effective date 4/1/2000

HOUSING

Median Home Prices and Housing Affordability

Area	Median Price[2] 4th Qtr. 1999 ($)	HOI[3] 4th Qtr. 1999	Affordability Rank[4]
MSA[1]	85,000	79.0	31
U.S.	139,000	63.8	–

Note: (1) Metropolitan Statistical Area - see Appendix A for areas included; (2) U.S. figures calculated from the sales of 687,516 new and existing homes in 192 markets; (3) Housing Opportunity Index - percent of homes sold that were within the reach of the median income household at the prevailing mortgage interest rate; (4) Rank is from 1-192 with 1 being most affordable
Source: National Association of Home Builders, Housing Opportunity Index, 4th Quarter 1999

Estimated Home Price

Area	Price ($)
City	159,956
U.S.	135,855

Note: Figures are based on an 1,800 square-foot home
Source: ERI's Relocation Assessor software database, quarterly effective date 4/1/2000

Estimated Rent

Area	Rent ($/month)
City	717
U.S.	651

Note: Figures are based on a 1,000 square-foot home
Source: ERI's Relocation Assessor software database, quarterly effective date 4/1/2000

Median Home Price Projection

It is projected that the median home price in the metropolitan area will increase from $85,955 in 1999 to $134,148 in 2010, an increase of 56.1%
Kiplinger's Personal Finance Magazine, January 2000

RESIDENTIAL UTILITIES

Average Residential Utility Costs

Area	All Electric ($/mth)	Part Electric ($/mth)	Other Energy ($/mth)	Phone ($/mth)
City	106.88	–	–	15.00
U.S.	99.25	55.47	43.48	20.29

Source: ACCRA, Cost of Living Index, 3rd Quarter 1999

HEALTH CARE

Average Health Care Costs

Area	Hospital ($/day)	Doctor ($/visit)	Dentist ($/visit)
City	479.00	53.50	61.62
U.S.	440.96	53.83	68.42

Note: Hospital—based on a semi-private room; Doctor—based on a general practitioner's routine exam of an established patient; Dentist—based on adult teeth cleaning and periodic oral exam.
Source: ACCRA, Cost of Living Index, 3rd Quarter 1999

Distribution of Office-Based Physicians

Area	Family/Gen. Practitioners	Specialists		
		Medical	Surgical	Other
MSA[1]	102	173	168	155

Note: Data as of 12/31/97; (1) Metropolitan Statistical Area - see Appendix A for areas included
Source: American Medical Assn., Physician Characteristics & Distribution in the U.S., 1999

Hospitals

Daytona Beach has 2 general medical and surgical hospitals.
AHA Guide to the Healthcare Field, 1999-2000

EDUCATION

Public School District Statistics

District Name	Num. Sch.	Enroll.	Classroom Teachers	Pupils per Teacher	Minority Pupils (%)	Current Exp.[1] ($/pupil)
Volusia County Sch Dist	82	59,310	3,529	16.8	24.8	4,942

Note: Data covers the 1997-1998 school year unless otherwise noted; (1) Data covers fiscal year 1996; SD = School District; ISD = Independent School District; n/a not available
Source: National Center for Education Statistics, Common Core of Data Public Education Agency Universe 1997-98; National Center for Education Statistics, Characteristics of the 100 Largest Public Elementary and Secondary School Districts in the United States: 1997-98, July 1999

Educational Quality

School District	Education Quotient[1]	Graduate Outcome[2]	Community Index[3]	Resource Index[4]
Volusia County School Dist.	89	93	76	82

Note: Over 1,000 secondary school districts were rated in terms of educational quality. The scores range from a low of 50 to a high of 150; (1) Combination of the Graduate Outcome, Community and Resource indexes weighted to reflect the greater importance of the Graduate Outcome and Resource Index; (2) Based on graduation rates and college board scores (SAT/ACT); (3) Based on the surrounding community's level of affluence and adult education; (4) Based on teacher salaries, per-pupil expenditures and student-teacher ratios.
Source: Expansion Management, Ratings Issue, 1999

Educational Attainment by Race

Area	High School Graduate (%)					Bachelor's Degree (%)				
	Total	White	Black	Other	Hisp.[2]	Total	White	Black	Other	Hisp.[2]
City	73.6	77.0	62.8	70.9	72.4	16.5	16.6	15.8	18.1	21.9
MSA[1]	75.4	76.8	61.2	55.8	58.7	14.8	14.9	13.2	13.8	12.4
U.S.	75.2	77.9	63.1	60.4	49.8	20.3	21.5	11.4	19.4	9.2

Note: Figures shown cover persons 25 years old and over; (1) Metropolitan Statistical Area - see Appendix A for areas included; (2) people of Hispanic origin can be of any race
Source: 1990 Census of Population and Housing, Summary Tape File 3C

School Enrollment by Type

Area	Preprimary				Elementary/High School			
	Public		Private		Public		Private	
	Enrollment	%	Enrollment	%	Enrollment	%	Enrollment	%
City	326	51.3	309	48.7	6,208	90.1	679	9.9
MSA[1]	2,551	50.7	2,480	49.3	44,085	91.4	4,122	8.6
U.S.	2,679,029	59.5	1,824,256	40.5	38,379,689	90.2	4,187,099	9.8

Note: Figures shown cover persons 3 years old and over;
(1) Metropolitan Statistical Area - see Appendix A for areas included
Source: 1990 Census of Population and Housing, Summary Tape File 3C

School Enrollment by Race

Area	Preprimary (%)				Elementary/High School (%)			
	White	Black	Other	Hisp.[1]	White	Black	Other	Hisp.[1]
City	47.4	51.0	1.6	1.6	35.4	63.4	1.1	1.8
MSA[2]	84.0	14.1	1.9	2.5	79.8	15.8	4.3	6.3
U.S.	80.4	12.5	7.1	7.8	74.1	15.6	10.3	12.5

Note: Figures shown cover persons 3 years old and over; (1) people of Hispanic origin can be of any race; (2) Metropolitan Statistical Area - see Appendix A for areas included
Source: 1990 Census of Population and Housing, Summary Tape File 3C

Higher Education

Two-Year Colleges		Four-Year Colleges		Medical Schools	Law Schools	Voc/ Tech
Public	Private	Public	Private			
2	1	0	2	0	0	4

Source: College Blue Book, Occupational Education, 1999; Medical School Admission Requirements, 1999-2000; Peterson's Guide to Two-Year Colleges, 2000; Peterson's Guide to Four-Year Colleges, 1999; Barron's Guide to Law Schools, 1999

MAJOR EMPLOYERS

Major Employers

Budget Group
International Speedway Corp.
National Direct Corp. (electronic parts)
News-Journal Corp.

Falcon International Corp. (detective agency)
Metra Electronics Corp.
News-Journal Corp.
SAC Telemarketing

Note: Companies listed are located in the city
Source: D&B Business Rankings, 1999; Ward's Business Directory, 1999; America's Corporate Families, 1999

PUBLIC SAFETY

Crime Rate

Area	All Crimes	Violent Crimes				Property Crimes		
		Murder	Forcible Rape	Robbery	Aggrav. Assault	Burglary	Larceny -Theft	Motor Vehicle Theft
City	12,281.2	5.9	147.2	693.1	1,179.5	2,988.1	6,019.4	1,247.9
Suburbs[1]	4,695.6	2.5	39.3	82.3	424.1	1,034.8	2,814.6	298.0
MSA[2]	5,770.9	3.0	54.6	168.9	531.1	1,311.7	3,268.9	432.7
U.S.	4,615.5	6.3	34.4	165.2	360.5	862.0	2,728.1	459.0

Note: Crime rate is the number of crimes per 100,000 population; (1) Defined as all areas within the Metropolitan Statistical Area but located outside the central city; (2) Metropolitan Statistical Area - see Appendix A for areas included
Source: FBI Uniform Crime Reports, 1998

RECREATION

Culture and Recreation

Museums	Symphony Orchestras	Opera Companies	Dance Companies	Professional Theatres	Zoos	Pro Sports Teams
3	1	0	1	2	0	0

Source: Musical America, International Directory of the Performing Arts, 1999; Official Museum Directory, 2000; Stern's Performing Arts Directory, 1997; USA Today Four Sport Stadium Guide, 1997; Career Opportunities in Theatre and the Performing Arts, 1999

Library System

The Volusia County Public Library System has 15 branches, holdings of 782,528 volumes, and a budget of $10,361,847 (1997-1998).
American Library Directory, 1999-2000

MEDIA

Newspapers

Name	Type	Freq.	Distribution	Circulation
The Daytona Beach News-Journal	General	7x/wk	Area	101,373

Note: Includes newspapers with circulations of 200 or more located in the city;
Source: Burrelle's Media Directory, 1999 Edition

Television Stations

Name	Ch.	Affiliation	Type	Owner
WCEU	15	PBS	Public	Coastal Educational Broadcasting Corp.

Note: Stations included broadcast in the Daytona Beach metro area; n/a not available
Source: Burrelle's Media Directory, 1999 Edition

AM Radio Stations

Call Letters	Freq. (kHz)	Target Audience	Station Format	Music Format
WROD	1000	General	M	Adult Standards/Big Band/MOR
WNDB	1150	General	N/S/T	n/a
WSBB	1230	General	M/N/S/T	Adult Standards
WYND	1310	General	M/N/T	Christian
WELE	1380	General	N/S/T	n/a
WMFJ	1450	General	E/M	Christian
WXVQ	1490	General	N/S/T	n/a
WPUL	1590	Black	M/N/S	Adult Contemporary/Urban Contemporary

Note: Stations included broadcast in the Daytona Beach metro area; n/a not available
Target Audience: A=Asian; B=Black; C=Christian; E=Ethnic; F=French; G=General; H=Hispanic; M=Men; N=Native American; R=Religious; S=Senior Citizen; W=Women; Y=Young Adult; Z=Children
Station Format: E=Educational; M=Music; N=News; S=Sports; T=Talk
Music Format: AOR=Album Oriented Rock; MOR=Middle-of-the-Road
Source: Burrelle's Media Directory, 1999 Edition

FM Radio Stations

Call Letters	Freq. (mHz)	Target Audience	Station Format	Music Format
WGNE	98.1	General	M	Country
WFKS	99.9	General	M	n/a
WVYB	103.3	Women	M	n/a

Note: Stations included broadcast in the Daytona Beach metro area; n/a not available
Station Format: E=Educational; M=Music; N=News; S=Sports; T=Talk
Source: Burrelle's Media Directory, 1999 Edition

WEATHER

Temperature/Precipitation/Humidity

	Jan	Feb	Mar	Apr	May	Jun	Jul	Aug	Sep	Oct	Nov	Dec	Yr.
Max. High Temp. (°F)	86	89	91	96	100	101	102	100	96	95	89	88	102
Avg. High Temp. (°F)	69	70	75	80	85	88	90	89	87	81	75	70	80
Avg. Temp. (°F)	58	60	64	69	75	80	81	81	80	74	66	60	71
Avg. Low Temp. (°F)	47	49	54	59	65	70	72	73	72	65	56	49	61
Min. Low Temp. (°F)	15	24	26	35	44	52	60	65	52	41	27	19	15
Avg. Precip. (in.)	2.5	3.0	3.2	2.5	3.1	5.7	5.5	6.3	6.7	4.6	2.6	2.4	48.1
Avg. Snowfall (in.)	Tr	Tr	0	0	0	0	0	0	0	0	0	Tr	Tr
Avg. Rel. Hum. 7am (%)	87	86	86	85	84	87	88	90	89	87	87	87	87
Avg. Rel. Hum. 4pm (%)	61	58	57	56	61	67	69	71	70	66	63	63	64

Note: Tr = Trace amounts (less than 0.05 inches of rain or less than 0.5 inches of snow)
Source: National Climatic Data Center, International Station Meteorological Climate Summary, 3/95

Weather Conditions

Temperature			Precipitation		
32°F & below	45°F & below	90°F & above	0.01 inch or more precip.	1.5 inch or more snow/ice	Thunder-storms
6	47	54	112	0	75

Note: Figures are average number of days per year
Source: National Climatic Data Center, International Station Meteorological Climate Summary, 3/95

AIR & WATER QUALITY

Maximum Pollutant Concentrations

	Particulate Matter (ug/m³)	Carbon Monoxide (ppm)	Sulfur Dioxide (ppm)	Nitrogen Dioxide (ppm)	Ozone (ppm)	Lead (ug/m³)
MSA[1] Level	38	n/a	n/a	n/a	0.09	n/a
NAAQS[2]	150	9	0.140	0.053	0.12	1.50
Met NAAQS	Yes	n/a	n/a	n/a	Yes	n/a

Note: (1) Metropolitan Statistical Area - see Appendix A for areas included; (2) National Ambient Air Quality Standards; ppm = parts per million; ug/m³ = micrograms per cubic meter; n/a not available
Source: EPA, National Air Quality and Emissions Trends Report, 1997

Pollutant Standards Index

Data not available. *EPA, National Air Quality and Emissions Trends Report, 1997*

Drinking Water

Water System Name	Pop. Served	Primary Water Source Type	Number of Violations in 1998-99	Type of Violation/ Contaminants
City of Daytona Beach	79,664	Ground	1	(1)

Note: Data as of January 19, 2000; (1) Repeat Major Monitoring (TCR) violation—no follow-up samples collected after a sample that tested positive for total coliform or no speciation under the total coliform rule (1 violation in 1998).
Source: EPA, Office of Ground Water and Drinking Water, Safe Drinking Water Information System

Daytona Beach tap water is alkaline, soft, and fluoridated.
Editor & Publisher Market Guide, 2000

Duluth, Minnesota

Background

Duluth, Minnesota is located in the northeastern portion of the state on the western end of Lake Superior and on the St. Louis River opposite Superior, Wisconsin, and 140 miles northeast of Minneapolis. Duluth is the seat of St. Louis county and the third largest city in Minnesota. It lies at the base of a range of hills that rise abruptly to 800 feet above the level of Lake Superior, then tapers to a slightly rolling plateau.

Duluth and Superior share an excellent harbor that is situated at the head of the Great Lakes system and is linked to the Atlantic Ocean by the Saint Lawrence Seaway. Although the port is closed by ice during the winter months, it is a major outlet for the raw materials of the upper midwestern United States. The principal goods shipped are iron ore, grain, coal, petroleum and lumber.

Important economic segments of the city include meat packing, brewing, wood-products processing, textile manufacturing, iron, steel and cement production, and oil refining. Tourism is also an important industry in Duluth.

When explorers Daniel Greysolon and Sieru Duluth, for whom the city is named, arrived at the site of present day Duluth in 1679, the Sioux and the Chippewa occupied the region. French voyagers and trappers had operated trading posts there for more than a century, including one that became John Jacob Astor's American Fur Company in 1817. In the 1850s, treaties with the Sioux and Chippewa opened the lands for permanent settlement. Duluth was founded in 1856 and incorporated in 1870, the same year in which the railroad entered the city.

Duluth is known as the "Air Conditioned City" in the summer months, when easterly Lake Superior winds cool the city during the day and abate at night, allowing cool lake air to move back onto the city. The proximity of the lake also creates warmer winter temperatures. Outstanding fall colors and scenic lake beauty contribute to Duluth being the gateway for a year-round resort area.

Institutions of higher education include the University of Minnesota at Duluth, the College of St. Scholastica and a community college. Cultural venues include an art institute, ballet company, playhouse, and a symphony orchestra. The 230-foot-high Aerial Lift Bridge, Lake Superior Museum of Transportation and Saint Louis County Historical Museum are popular tourist attractions in Duluth.

Duluth has a Mayor-Council form of government, with the City Administration making policy proposals to a nine-member City Council.

General Rankings and Evaluative Comments

- Duluth was ranked #97 out of 354 metropolitan areas in *Places Rated Almanac*. Criteria: cost of living, climate, crime, transportation, job outlook, education, the arts, health care, and recreation. *Places Rated Almanac, Millennium Edition, 2000*

- Duluth was selected as one of North America's "Best Small Metro Areas" (population under 250,000). The area ranked #4 out of 20. Criteria: cost of living, climate, crime, transportation, job outlook, education, the arts, health care, and recreation. *Places Rated Almanac, Millennium Edition, 2000*

- Cognetics studied 273 metro areas in the United States, ranking them by entrepreneurial activity. Duluth was ranked #76 out of 134 smaller metro areas. Criteria: Significant Starts (firms started in the last 10 years that still employ at least 5 people) and Young Growers (percent of firms 10 years old or less that grew significantly during the last 4 years). *Cognetics, "Entrepreneurial Hot Spots: The Best Places in America to Start and Grow a Company," 1999*

Business Environment

STATE ECONOMY

State Economic Profile

"Minnesota's economy has been a strong performer in recent years. Job growth has been impressive and the construction market has been booming. As the US economy slows in the near future, Minnesota's growth should decelerate.

Minnesota's tight labor market (1.8% unemployment in Minneapolis-St. Paul) and high rate of job creation have allowed the state to weather several layoffs. 3M, Cargill, and Honeywell have all released significant numbers of workers. And while the Northwest strike temporarily hit Minnesota's economy, other sectors have more than offset these concerns.

Minnesota, specifically Minneapolis-St. Paul, experienced a major boom in residential and commercial building in 1998. The 16,811 single-family permits issued in 1998 was the highest level in over a decade. Construction employment increased 6.8% in Minneapolis-St. Paul in 1998. Driving this boom is the impressive levels of price appreciation witnessed in 1998 and the thin inventory of homes for sale. The large volume currently being built will help to moderate price appreciation in 2000.

Among its Midwestern neighbors, Minnesota alone has actually attracted residents from other states. Net migration has been around 10,000 for several years, helping to ease tightness in the labor market and fuel the housing market.

Minnesota will continue to be among the strongest performing Plains state. Labor shortages and the high cost of doing business, however, will limit its growth to below the national average. Most of the action will continue to be concentrated in Minneapolis-St. Paul."
National Association of Realtors, Economic Profiles: The Fifty States and the District of Columbia, http://nar.realtor.com/databank/profiles.htm

EXPORTS

Total Export Sales

Area	1995 ($000)	1996 ($000)	1997 ($000)	1998 ($000)	% Chg. 1995-98	% Chg. 1997-98
MSA[1]	n/a	n/a	n/a	n/a	n/a	n/a
U.S.	583,030,524	622,827,063	687,597,999	680,474,251	16.7	-1.0

Note: (1) Metropolitan Statistical Area - see Appendix A for areas included
Source: U.S. Department of Commerce, International Trade Association, Metropolitan Area Exports: An Export Performance Report on Over 250 U.S. Cities, November 10, 1999

CITY FINANCES

City Government Finances

Component	1995 ($million)	1995 (per capita $)
Revenue	121.3	1,443
Expenditure	118.3	1,408
Debt Outstanding	164.3	1,956

Source: 1999 County and City Extra, Annual Metro, City, and County Data Book

City Government Revenue by Source

Source	1995 ($million)	1995 (per capita $)
Intergovernmental	41.9	498
Taxes	28.7	341
Property	16.3	194
Sales and Gross Receipts	11.9	142

Source: 1999 County and City Extra, Annual Metro, City, and County Data Book

City Government Expenditures by Function

Function	1995 ($million)	1995 (per capita $)	1995 (%)
Public Welfare	0.0	0	0.0
Highways	16.0	191	13.6
Parking Facilities	0.0	0	0.0
Education	0.0	0	0.0
Health and Hospitals	0.0	0	0.0
Police Protection	9.8	116	8.3
Sewerage and Sanitation	11.2	133	9.5
Parks and Recreation	12.8	153	10.9
Housing and Community Development	4.8	57	4.1
Interest on Debt	11.0	130	9.3

Source: 1999 County and City Extra, Annual Metro, City, and County Data Book

Municipal Bond Ratings

Area	Moody's
City	Aaa

Source: Mergent Bond Record, 2/2000

POPULATION

Population Growth

Area	1980 Census	1990 Census	1999 Estimate	2004 Projection	Population Growth (%) 1990-1999	Population Growth (%) 1999-2004
City	92,811	85,493	80,789	80,415	-5.5	-0.5
MSA[1]	266,650	239,971	235,929	238,270	-1.7	1.0
U.S.	226,545,805	248,765,170	272,212,864	283,625,312	9.4	4.2

Note: (1) Metropolitan Statistical Area - see Appendix A for areas included
Source: 1990 Census of Population and Housing, Summary Tape File 3C; Claritas, Inc.

Number of Households and Average Household Size

Area	1980 Census	1990 Census	1999 Estimate	2004 Projection	1999 Average Household Size
City	35,393	34,646	34,395	34,931	2.35
MSA[1]	97,949	95,604	97,692	100,377	2.42
U.S.	80,389,592	91,993,582	102,048,200	107,302,392	2.67

Note: (1) Metropolitan Statistical Area - see Appendix A for areas included
Source: 1990 Census of Population and Housing, Summary Tape File 3C; Claritas, Inc.

Race/Ethnicity of City Population

Race/Ethnicity	1990 Census Population	1990 Census %	1999 Estimate Population	1999 Estimate %	% Change 1990-1999
White, Non-Hispanic	81,438	95.3	76,231	94.4	-6.4
Black, Non-Hispanic	838	1.0	971	1.2	15.9
Asian, Non-Hispanic	810	0.9	1,111	1.4	37.2
Other, Non-Hispanic	1,919	2.2	1,751	2.2	-8.8
Hispanic	488	0.6	725	0.9	48.6

Source: 1990 Census of Population and Housing, Summary Tape File 3C; Claritas, Inc.

Race/Ethnicity of Metropolitan Statistical Area Population

Race/Ethnicity	1990 Census Population	1990 Census %	1999 Estimate Population	1999 Estimate %	% Change 1990-1999
White, Non-Hispanic	231,664	96.5	226,041	95.8	-2.4
Black, Non-Hispanic	1,310	0.5	1,545	0.7	17.9
Asian, Non-Hispanic	1,318	0.5	1,887	0.8	43.2
Other, Non-Hispanic	4,589	1.9	4,805	2.0	4.7
Hispanic	1,090	0.5	1,651	0.7	51.5

Note: See Appendix A for areas included in the Metropolitan Statistical Area
Source: 1990 Census of Population and Housing, Summary Tape File 3C; Claritas, Inc.

Ancestry

Area	German	Irish	English	Italian	U.S.	French	Polish	Dutch
City	26.6	12.3	8.8	5.1	2.2	7.1	7.9	1.5
MSA[1]	25.9	11.0	7.9	5.4	2.6	6.6	7.2	1.4
U.S.	23.3	15.6	13.1	5.9	5.3	4.2	3.8	2.5

Note: Figures are percentages and include persons that reported multiple ancestry (eg. if a person reported being Irish and Italian, they were included in both columns); (1) Metropolitan Statistical Area - see Appendix A for areas included
Source: 1990 Census of Population and Housing, Summary Tape File 3C

Median Age

Area	1990 Census	1999 Estimate
City	34.0	36.1
MSA[1]	35.6	38.0
U.S.	32.9	35.7

Note: (1) Metropolitan Statistical Area - see Appendix A for areas included
Source: 1990 Census of Population and Housing, Summary Tape File 3C; Claritas, Inc.

Male/Female Population

Area	Number of Males 1990	Number of Males 1999	Number of Females 1990	Number of Females 1999	Males per 100 Females 1990	Males per 100 Females 1999
City	40,416	38,309	45,077	42,480	89.7	90.2
MSA[1]	116,882	114,786	123,089	121,143	95.0	94.8
U.S.	121,172,379	132,803,736	127,537,494	139,409,136	95.0	95.3

Note: (1) Metropolitan Statistical Area - see Appendix A for areas included
Source: 1990 Census of Population, General Population Characteristics; Claritas, Inc.

INCOME

Per Capita/Median/Average Income

Area	Per Capita ($) 1989	Per Capita ($) 1999	Per Capita ($) % Chg.	Median Household ($) 1989	Median Household ($) 1999	Median Household ($) % Chg.	Average Household ($) 1989	Average Household ($) 1999	Average Household ($) % Chg.
City	12,484	20,480	64.0	23,370	33,104	41.7	30,224	46,904	55.2
MSA[1]	11,644	18,694	60.5	23,690	33,217	40.2	28,666	44,106	53.9
U.S.	14,420	21,350	48.1	30,056	40,525	34.8	38,453	56,184	46.1

Note: (1) Metropolitan Statistical Area - see Appendix A for areas included; 1989 data is from the 1990 Census; 1999 data is estimated by Claritas, Inc.
Source: 1990 Census of Population, General Population Characteristics; Claritas, Inc.

Household Income Distribution

Area	Percent of Households Earning								
	Under $5,000	$5,000 -14,999	$15,000 -24,999	$25,000 -34,999	$35,000 -49,999	$50,000 -74,999	$75,000 -99,000	$100,000 -149,999	$150,000 and up
City	3.4	18.7	16.5	13.4	15.2	16.8	7.9	5.3	2.8
MSA[1]	3.4	18.2	16.7	13.7	16.0	19.0	7.5	4.0	1.6
U.S.	3.9	13.3	13.8	12.6	16.2	19.4	9.7	6.6	4.6

Note: Data as of 1999; (1) Metropolitan Statistical Area - see Appendix A for areas included
Source: Claritas, Inc.

Effective Buying Income

Area	Per Capita ($)	Median Household ($)	Average Household ($)
City	15,056	28,418	36,570
MSA[1]	14,630	29,271	36,163
U.S.	17,496	36,603	47,036

Note: Data as of 1/1/2000; (1) Metropolitan Statistical Area - see Appendix A for areas included
Source: Standard Rate & Data Service, Newspaper Advertising Source, March 2000

Effective Household Buying Income Distribution

Area	% of Households Earning						
	$10,000 -$19,999	$20,000 -$34,999	$35,000 -$49,999	$50,000 -$74,999	$75,000 -$99,000	$100,000 -$124,999	$125,000 and up
City	20.8	24.2	16.3	15.2	5.9	1.4	1.6
MSA[1]	20.3	23.8	18.2	16.8	5.0	1.2	0.9
U.S.	15.0	21.6	17.6	19.6	8.4	3.0	3.3

Note: Data as of 1/1/2000; (1) Metropolitan Statistical Area - see Appendix A for areas included
Source: Standard Rate & Data Service, Newspaper Advertising Source, March 2000

Poverty Rates by Age

Area	People of All Ages	People Under 18 Years Old	Related Children Age 5-17 in Families in Poverty
City	14.0	n/a	n/a
County	12.0	15.9	13.4
U.S.	13.8	20.8	18.7

Note: Figures show the percent of people living below the poverty line in 1995. The average poverty threshold was $15,569 for a family of four in 1995; n/a not available
Source: Bureau of the Census, Small Area Income and Poverty Estimates Program; U.S. Department of Housing and Urban Development

EMPLOYMENT

Labor Force and Employment

Area	Civilian Labor Force			Workers Employed		
	Dec. 1998	Dec. 1999	% Chg.	Dec. 1998	Dec. 1999	% Chg.
City	44,551	45,127	1.3	43,422	43,997	1.3
MSA[1]	124,776	125,653	0.7	120,550	121,965	1.2
U.S.	138,297,000	139,941,000	1.2	132,732,000	134,696,000	1.5

Note: Data is not seasonally adjusted and covers workers 16 years of age and older; (1) Metropolitan Statistical Area - see Appendix A for areas included
Source: Bureau of Labor Statistics, http://stats.bls.gov

Unemployment Rate

Area	1999											
	Jan.	Feb.	Mar.	Apr.	May	Jun.	Jul.	Aug.	Sep.	Oct.	Nov.	Dec.
City	3.7	3.4	3.2	3.0	2.9	4.0	3.4	2.7	3.3	2.5	2.6	2.5
MSA[1]	4.7	4.4	4.1	3.9	3.4	4.3	3.5	3.7	3.4	2.6	2.9	2.9
U.S.	4.8	4.7	4.4	4.1	4.0	4.5	4.5	4.2	4.1	3.8	3.8	3.7

Note: Data is not seasonally adjusted and covers workers 16 years of age and older; all figures are percentages; (1) Metropolitan Statistical Area - see Appendix A for areas included
Source: Bureau of Labor Statistics, http://stats.bls.gov

Employment by Industry

Sector	MSA[1]		U.S.
	Number of Employees	Percent of Total	Percent of Total
Services	35,300	30.1	30.2
Retail Trade	24,300	20.7	18.1
Government	23,600	20.1	15.8
Manufacturing	8,100	6.9	14.1
Finance/Insurance/Real Estate	3,400	2.9	5.9
Wholesale Trade	4,200	3.6	5.4
Transportation/Public Utilities	8,500	7.2	5.3
Construction	5,300	4.5	4.8
Mining	4,700	4.0	0.4

Note: Figures cover non-farm employment as of 12/99 and are not seasonally adjusted;
(1) Metropolitan Statistical Area - see Appendix A for areas included
Source: Bureau of Labor Statistics, http://stats.bls.gov

Employment by Occupation

Occupation Category	City (%)	MSA[1] (%)	U.S. (%)
White Collar	62.5	54.4	58.1
Executive/Admin./Management	11.0	9.6	12.3
Professional	17.6	14.3	14.1
Technical & Related Support	4.4	3.9	3.7
Sales	13.1	11.9	11.8
Administrative Support/Clerical	16.4	14.7	16.3
Blue Collar	19.0	26.7	26.2
Precision Production/Craft/Repair	7.9	12.2	11.3
Machine Operators/Assem./Insp.	3.5	4.7	6.8
Transportation/Material Movers	4.0	5.6	4.1
Cleaners/Helpers/Laborers	3.5	4.2	3.9
Services	17.8	17.6	13.2
Farming/Forestry/Fishing	0.7	1.3	2.5

Note: Figures cover workers 16 years of age and older;
(1) Metropolitan Statistical Area - see Appendix A for areas included
Source: 1990 Census of Population and Housing, Summary Tape File 3C

Occupational Employment Projections: 1996 - 2006

Occupations Expected to Have the Largest Job Growth (ranked by numerical growth)	Fast-Growing Occupations[1] (ranked by percent growth)
1. General managers & top executives	1. Systems analysts
2. Database administrators	2. Desktop publishers
3. Salespersons, retail	3. Personal and home care aides
4. Cashiers	4. Physical therapy assistants and aides
5. Systems analysts	5. Occupational therapy assistants
6. Truck drivers, light	6. Home health aides
7. Home health aides	7. Human services workers
8. Receptionists and information clerks	8. Data processing equipment repairers
9. Computer engineers	9. Paralegals
10. Marketing & sales, supervisors	10. Surgical technologists

Note: Projections cover Minnesota; (1) Excludes occupations with total job growth less than 300
Source: U.S. Department of Labor, Employment and Training Administration, America's Labor Market Information System (ALMIS)

Average Wages

Occupation	$/Hr.	Occupation	$/Hr.
Accountants and Auditors	17.47	Maids and Housekeepers	7.04
Assemblers and Fabricators	9.47	Maintenance Repairers	11.49
Automotive Mechanics	13.61	Marketing/Advertising/PR Managers	22.44
Bookkeepers	10.55	Nurses, Licensed Practical	12.68
Carpenters	16.35	Nurses, Registered	23.13
Cashiers	7.11	Nursing Aides/Orderlies/Attendants	8.79
Clerks, General Office	9.70	Physicians and Surgeons	56.54
Clerks, Shipping/Receiving/Traffic	11.53	Receptionists/Information Clerks	8.42
Computer Programmers	-	Sales Reps., Exc. Scientific/Retail	17.39
Computer Support Specialists	17.37	Sales Reps., Scientific, Exc. Retail	17.59
Cooks, Restaurant	6.97	Salespersons, Retail	8.17
Electricians	20.92	Secretaries, Except Legal/Medical	10.77
Financial Managers	24.82	Stock Clerks, Sales Floor	7.50
First-Line Supervisors/Mgrs., Sales	13.43	Systems Analysts	23.88
Food Preparation Workers	7.37	Teacher Aides	9.38
General Managers/Top Executives	23.41	Teachers, Elementary School	17.26
Guards	7.61	Teachers, Secondary School	18.82
Hand Packers	7.58	Telemarketers	7.52
Janitors and Cleaners	8.13	Truck Drivers, Heavy/Tractor-Trailer	14.33
Laborers, Landscaping	8.49	Truck Drivers, Light	10.13
Lawyers	30.78	Waiters and Waitresses	5.64

Note: Wage data is for 1998 and covers the Metropolitan Statistical Area (see Appendix A for areas included). Hourly wages for elementary and secondary school teachers were calculated by the editors from annual wage data assuming a 40 hour work week; Dashes indicate that data was not available.
Source: Bureau of Labor Statistics, 1998 Metropolitan Area Occupational Employment and Wage Estimates

TAXES

Major State and Local Tax Rates

State Corporate Income (%)	State Personal Income (%)	Residential Property (%)	Sales & Use		State Gasoline (cents/ gallon)	State Cigarette (cents/ pack)
			State (%)	Local (%)		
9.8[a]	5.5 - 8.0	1.33	6.5	1.0	20.0	48.0

Note: Personal/corporate income, sales, gasoline and cigarette tax rates as of January 2000. Property tax rates as of April 2000; (a) Plus a 5.8% tax on any Alternative Minimum Taxable Income over the base tax
Source: Federation of Tax Administrators, www.taxadmin.org; ERI's Relocation Assessor software database, quarterly effective date 4/1/2000

Total Taxes Per Capita and as a Percent of Income

Area	Per Capita Income ($)	Per Capita Taxes ($)			Percent of Income (%)		
		Total	Federal	State/Local	Total	Federal	State/Local
Minnesota	30,012	11,555	7,601	3,954	38.5	25.3	13.2
U.S.	28,878	10,298	7,026	3,273	35.7	24.3	11.3

Note: Figures are for 1999
Source: Tax Foundation, www.taxfoundation.org

COMMERCIAL UTILITIES

Typical Monthly Electric Bills

Area	Commercial Service ($/month)		Industrial Service ($/month)	
	12 kW demand 1,500 kWh	100 kW demand 30,000 kWh	1,000 kW demand 400,000 kWh	20,000 kW demand 10,000,000 kWh
City	132	1,926	19,855	374,603
U.S.	150	2,174	23,995	508,569

Note: Based on rates in effect January 1, 1999
Source: Edison Electric Institute, Typical Residential, Commercial and Industrial Bills, Winter 1999

TRANSPORTATION

Transportation Statistics

Average minutes to work (1990)	15.5
Interstate highways	I-35; I-535; US-2; US-53
Bus lines	
In-city (1998)	Duluth Transit Authority, 71 buses
Inter-city (1999)	1
Passenger air service	
Airport	Duluth International
Airlines (1999)	2
Enplaned passengers (1998)	113,292
Amtrak service	Bus Connection
Motor freight carriers (1999)	18
Major waterways/ports	Port of Duluth/Superior

Source: FAA DOT/TSC CY1998 ACAIS Database; National Transit Database, 1998; Editor & Publisher Market Guide, 2000; Amtrak National Time Table, Fall 1999/Winter 2000; 1990 Census of Population and Housing, STF 3C; Jane's Urban Transport Systems 1999-2000

Means of Transportation to Work

Area	Car/Truck/Van		Public Transportation			Bicycle	Walked	Other Means	Worked at Home
	Drove Alone	Car-pooled	Bus	Subway	Railroad				
City	70.2	13.5	5.7	0.0	0.0	0.5	6.7	0.7	2.7
MSA[1]	73.2	13.9	2.6	0.0	0.0	0.3	5.9	0.7	3.3
U.S.	73.2	13.4	3.0	1.5	0.5	0.4	3.9	1.2	3.0

Note: Figures shown are percentages and only include workers 16 years of age and older;
(1) Metropolitan Statistical Area - see Appendix A for areas included
Source: 1990 Census of Population and Housing, Summary Tape File 3C

BUSINESSES

Major Business Headquarters

Company Name	1999 Rankings	
	Fortune 500	Forbes 500
No companies listed	-	-

Note: Companies listed are located in the city; dashes indicate no ranking
Fortune 500: Companies that produce a 10-K are ranked 1 to 500 based on 1999 revenue
Forbes 500: Private companies are ranked 1 to 500 based on 1998 revenue
Source: Forbes, December 13, 1999; Fortune, April 17, 2000

HOTELS & MOTELS

Hotels/Motels

Area	Hotels/ Motels	Rooms	Luxury-Level Hotels/Motels		Average Minimum Rates ($)		
			♦♦♦♦	♦♦♦♦♦	♦♦	♦♦♦	♦♦♦♦
City	18	1,516	0	0	46	66	n/a
Airport	3	290	0	0	n/a	n/a	n/a
Suburbs	2	284	0	0	n/a	n/a	n/a
Total	23	2,090	0	0	n/a	n/a	n/a

Note: n/a not available; classifications range from one diamond (budget properties with basic amenities) to five diamond (luxury properties).
Source: OAG Business Travel Planner, Winter 1999-2000

Estimated Daily Food and Lodging Costs

Area	Food/Other ($/day)	Average Hotel Cost ($/day)
City	42	56
U.S.	30	55

Source: ERI's Relocation Assessor software database, quarterly effective date 4/1/2000

CONVENTION CENTERS

Convention Centers and Event Sites

Name	Guest Rooms	Meeting Space (sq. ft.)	Capacity (Theatre Style)
Duluth Entertainment/Convention Ctr.	n/a	n/a	8,000
Radisson Hotel Duluth - Harborview	268	9,000	420

Note: n/a not available
Source: EventSource.com, 3/15/2000

Living Environment

COST OF LIVING

Cost of Living: Homeowner

Cost Element	U.S. ($)	City ($)	Differential ($)	Percent of U.S. Average
Consumables	14,516	14,248	-268	98.2
Transportation	5,957	6,249	292	104.9
Health Services	2,012	2,005	-7	99.7
Housing/Utilities/Prop. Tax	16,337	15,576	-761	95.3
Income+Payroll Taxes	12,615	13,573	958	107.6
Miscellaneous	8,563	8,563	0	100.0
Total Cost of Living	60,000	60,214	214	100.4

Note: Figures are based on a single income, four person family with gross annual earnings of $60,000, owning an 1,800 square-foot home, and driving two automobiles worth $22,000 30,000 miles per year.
Source: ERI's Relocation Assessor software database, quarterly effective date 4/1/2000

Cost of Living: Renter

Cost Element	U.S. ($)	City ($)	Differential ($)	Percent of U.S. Average
Consumables	10,486	10,320	-166	98.4
Transportation	2,107	2,217	110	105.2
Health Services	1,632	1,631	-1	99.9
Rent/Utilities/Insurance	9,299	7,279	-2,020	78.3
Income+Payroll Taxes	8,607	9,135	528	106.1
Miscellaneous	7,869	7,869	0	100.0
Total Cost of Living	40,000	38,451	-1,549	96.1

Note: Figures are based on a single income, three person family with gross annual earnings of $40,000, renting a 1,000 square-foot home, and driving one automobile worth $8,000 12,000 miles per year.
Source: ERI's Relocation Assessor software database, quarterly effective date 4/1/2000

HOUSING

Median Home Prices and Housing Affordability

Area	Median Price[2] 4th Qtr. 1999 ($)	HOI[3] 4th Qtr. 1999	Affordability Rank[4]
MSA[1]	88,000	79.4	29
U.S.	139,000	63.8	–

Note: (1) Metropolitan Statistical Area - see Appendix A for areas included; (2) U.S. figures calculated from the sales of 687,516 new and existing homes in 192 markets; (3) Housing Opportunity Index - percent of homes sold that were within the reach of the median income household at the prevailing mortgage interest rate; (4) Rank is from 1-192 with 1 being most affordable
Source: National Association of Home Builders, Housing Opportunity Index, 4th Quarter 1999

Estimated Home Price

Area	Price ($)
City	117,744
U.S.	135,855

Note: Figures are based on an 1,800 square-foot home
Source: ERI's Relocation Assessor software database, quarterly effective date 4/1/2000

Estimated Rent

Area	Rent ($/month)
City	489
U.S.	651

Note: Figures are based on a 1,000 square-foot home
Source: ERI's Relocation Assessor software database, quarterly effective date 4/1/2000

Median Home Price Projection

It is projected that the median home price in the metropolitan area will increase from $86,328 in 1999 to $87,163 in 2010, an increase of 1.0%
Kiplinger's Personal Finance Magazine, January 2000

RESIDENTIAL UTILITIES

Average Residential Utility Costs

Area	All Electric ($/mth)	Part Electric ($/mth)	Other Energy ($/mth)	Phone ($/mth)
City	n/a	n/a	n/a	n/a
U.S.	99.25	55.47	43.48	20.29

Note: n/a not available
Source: ACCRA, Cost of Living Index, 3rd Quarter 1999

HEALTH CARE

Average Health Care Costs

Area	Hospital ($/day)	Doctor ($/visit)	Dentist ($/visit)
City	n/a	n/a	n/a
U.S.	440.96	53.83	68.42

Note: n/a not available
Source: ACCRA, Cost of Living Index, 3rd Quarter 1999

Distribution of Office-Based Physicians

Area	Family/Gen. Practitioners	Specialists		
		Medical	Surgical	Other
MSA[1]	103	114	112	106

Note: Data as of 12/31/97; (1) Metropolitan Statistical Area - see Appendix A for areas included
Source: American Medical Assn., Physician Characteristics & Distribution in the U.S., 1999

Hospitals

Duluth has 3 general medical and surgical hospitals.
AHA Guide to the Healthcare Field, 1999-2000

EDUCATION

Public School District Statistics

District Name	Num. Sch.	Enroll.	Classroom Teachers	Pupils per Teacher	Minority Pupils (%)	Current Exp.[1] ($/pupil)
Duluth	39	13,631	n/a	n/a	n/a	n/a
Edison Charter School	2	507	n/a	n/a	n/a	n/a

Note: Data covers the 1997-1998 school year unless otherwise noted; (1) Data covers fiscal year 1996; SD = School District; ISD = Independent School District; n/a not available
Source: National Center for Education Statistics, Common Core of Data Public Education Agency Universe 1997-98; National Center for Education Statistics, Characteristics of the 100 Largest Public Elementary and Secondary School Districts in the United States: 1997-98, July 1999

Educational Quality

School District	Education Quotient[1]	Graduate Outcome[2]	Community Index[3]	Resource Index[4]
Duluth	130	142	104	110

Note: Over 1,000 secondary school districts were rated in terms of educational quality. The scores range from a low of 50 to a high of 150; (1) Combination of the Graduate Outcome, Community and Resource indexes weighted to reflect the greater importance of the Graduate Outcome and Resource Index; (2) Based on graduation rates and college board scores (SAT/ACT); (3) Based on the surrounding community's level of affluence and adult education; (4) Based on teacher salaries, per-pupil expenditures and student-teacher ratios.
Source: Expansion Management, Ratings Issue, 1999

Educational Attainment by Race

Area	High School Graduate (%)					Bachelor's Degree (%)				
	Total	White	Black	Other	Hisp.[2]	Total	White	Black	Other	Hisp.[2]
City	81.4	81.5	81.9	76.9	83.4	22.5	22.6	10.2	21.6	24.7
MSA[1]	79.7	79.9	78.4	70.9	76.6	16.8	16.9	12.0	14.1	19.0
U.S.	75.2	77.9	63.1	60.4	49.8	20.3	21.5	11.4	19.4	9.2

Note: Figures shown cover persons 25 years old and over; (1) Metropolitan Statistical Area - see Appendix A for areas included; (2) people of Hispanic origin can be of any race
Source: 1990 Census of Population and Housing, Summary Tape File 3C

School Enrollment by Type

Area	Preprimary				Elementary/High School			
	Public		Private		Public		Private	
	Enrollment	%	Enrollment	%	Enrollment	%	Enrollment	%
City	1,073	73.5	386	26.5	11,830	91.5	1,092	8.5
MSA[1]	3,343	78.8	897	21.2	38,743	94.1	2,419	5.9
U.S.	2,679,029	59.5	1,824,256	40.5	38,379,689	90.2	4,187,099	9.8

Note: Figures shown cover persons 3 years old and over;
(1) Metropolitan Statistical Area - see Appendix A for areas included
Source: 1990 Census of Population and Housing, Summary Tape File 3C

School Enrollment by Race

Area	Preprimary (%)				Elementary/High School (%)			
	White	Black	Other	Hisp.[1]	White	Black	Other	Hisp.[1]
City	94.2	1.1	4.7	2.0	92.8	1.5	5.7	0.8
MSA[2]	95.5	0.4	4.1	1.1	95.3	0.7	4.0	0.8
U.S.	80.4	12.5	7.1	7.8	74.1	15.6	10.3	12.5

Note: Figures shown cover persons 3 years old and over; (1) people of Hispanic origin can be of any race; (2) Metropolitan Statistical Area - see Appendix A for areas included
Source: 1990 Census of Population and Housing, Summary Tape File 3C

Higher Education

Two-Year Colleges		Four-Year Colleges		Medical Schools	Law Schools	Voc/ Tech
Public	Private	Public	Private			
1	0	1	1	1	0	1

Source: College Blue Book, Occupational Education, 1999; Medical School Admission Requirements, 1999-2000; Peterson's Guide to Two-Year Colleges, 2000; Peterson's Guide to Four-Year Colleges, 1999; Barron's Guide to Law Schools, 1999

MAJOR EMPLOYERS

Major Employers

Duluth Clinic	Duluth Entertainment Convention Center
Lake Superior Paper Industries	Louis Kemp Seafood
Miller-Dwon Medical Center	Minnesota Power & Light
St. Luke's Hospital	St. Mary's Medical Center

Note: Companies listed are located in the city
Source: D&B Business Rankings, 1999; Ward's Business Directory, 1999; America's Corporate Families, 1999

PUBLIC SAFETY

Crime Rate

Area	All Crimes	Violent Crimes				Property Crimes		
		Murder	Forcible Rape	Robbery	Aggrav. Assault	Burglary	Larceny -Theft	Motor Vehicle Theft
City	4,832.1	0.0	105.3	91.1	236.6	673.1	3,441.0	285.1
Suburbs[1]	n/a	n/a	n/a	n/a	n/a	n/a	n/a	n/a
MSA[2]	n/a	n/a	n/a	n/a	n/a	n/a	n/a	n/a
U.S.	4,615.5	6.3	34.4	165.2	360.5	862.0	2,728.1	459.0

Note: Crime rate is the number of crimes per 100,000 population; (1) Defined as all areas within the Metropolitan Statistical Area but located outside the central city; (2) Metropolitan Statistical Area - see Appendix A for areas included; n/a not available
Source: FBI Uniform Crime Reports, 1998

RECREATION

Culture and Recreation

Museums	Symphony Orchestras	Opera Companies	Dance Companies	Professional Theatres	Zoos	Pro Sports Teams
4	1	0	1	0	1	0

Source: Musical America, International Directory of the Performing Arts, 1999; Official Museum Directory, 2000; Stern's Performing Arts Directory, 1997; USA Today Four Sport Stadium Guide, 1997; Career Opportunities in Theatre and the Performing Arts, 1999

Library System

The Duluth Public Library has three branches, holdings of 363,882 volumes, and a budget of $3,260,067 (1997-1998).
American Library Directory, 1999-2000

MEDIA

Newspapers

Name	Type	Freq.	Distribution	Circulation
Direct Mail Advertiser	General	1x/mo	Local	16,000
Duluth News-Tribune	General	7x/wk	Area	65,000
Skyworld Duluth News	General	1x/mo	Local	11,500

Note: Includes newspapers with circulations of 200 or more located in the city;
Source: Burrelle's Media Directory, 1999 Edition

Television Stations

Name	Ch.	Affiliation	Type	Owner
KDLH	n/a	CBST	Commercial	Benedek Broadcasting Corporation
KBJR	n/a	n/a	Commercial	Granite Broadcasting Corporation
WDSE	n/a	n/a	Public	Duluth-Superior Area Educational TV
WDIO	10	ABCR/ABCT	Commercial	Hubbard Broadcasting Inc.
WIRT	13	ABCT	Commercial	Hubbard Broadcasting Inc.

Note: Stations included broadcast in the Duluth metro area; n/a not available
Source: Burrelle's Media Directory, 1999 Edition

AM Radio Stations

Call Letters	Freq. (kHz)	Target Audience	Station Format	Music Format
WEBC	560	General	N/S/T	n/a
KDAL	610	General	M/N/S	n/a
WDSM	710	Men	S	n/a
WWJC	850	General	M/N/S	Christian
KXTP	970	Children	M/N/S	Country
KQDS	1490	General	M	Classic Rock

Note: Stations included broadcast in the Duluth metro area; n/a not available
Target Audience: A=Asian; B=Black; C=Christian; E=Ethnic; F=French; G=General; H=Hispanic; M=Men; N=Native American; R=Religious; S=Senior Citizen; W=Women; Y=Young Adult; Z=Children
Station Format: E=Educational; M=Music; N=News; S=Sports; T=Talk
Source: Burrelle's Media Directory, 1999 Edition

FM Radio Stations

Call Letters	Freq. (mHz)	Target Audience	Station Format	Music Format
WNCB	89.3	General	M	Christian
KDNI	90.5	Religious	M/N/S	Christian/Oldies
WIRN	90.9	n/a	N/T	n/a
WIRR	90.9	General	M/N	Classic Rock/Classical
WSCD	92.9	General	M	Classical
KQDS	94.9	Men	M	AOR/Classic Rock
KDAL	95.7	General	M	Adult Contemporary
KDNW	97.3	General	M/N/S	Christian/Easy Listening/MOR
KTCO	98.9	General	M/N/S	Country
WSCN	100.5	General	N	n/a
KLDJ	101.7	General	M/N/T	Oldies
KRBR	102.5	General	M	AOR
KUMD	103.3	General	E/M/N/T	Alternative/Rhythm & Blues
KKCB	105.1	General	N/S	n/a

Note: Stations included broadcast in the Duluth metro area; n/a not available
Station Format: E=Educational; M=Music; N=News; S=Sports; T=Talk
Target Audience: A=Asian; B=Black; C=Christian; E=Ethnic; F=French; G=General; H=Hispanic; M=Men; N=Native American; R=Religious; S=Senior Citizen; W=Women; Y=Young Adult; Z=Children
Music Format: AOR=Album Oriented Rock; MOR=Middle-of-the-Road
Source: Burrelle's Media Directory, 1999 Edition

WEATHER

Temperature/Precipitation/Humidity

	Jan	Feb	Mar	Apr	May	Jun	Jul	Aug	Sep	Oct	Nov	Dec	Yr.
Max. High Temp. (°F)	47	55	71	88	90	93	97	95	95	86	70	55	97
Avg. High Temp. (°F)	16	22	32	48	62	71	77	74	64	53	35	21	48
Avg. Temp. (°F)	8	13	23	39	51	60	66	64	54	44	28	14	39
Avg. Low Temp. (°F)	-1	3	14	29	39	48	55	53	44	35	21	5	29
Min. Low Temp. (°F)	-39	-33	-29	-5	17	27	35	32	23	8	-23	-34	-39
Avg. Precip. (in.)	1.2	0.8	1.8	2.3	3.1	4.0	3.9	3.9	3.5	2.4	1.8	1.3	30.2
Avg. Snowfall (in.)	17	11	14	7	1	0	0	0	Tr	1	11	16	79
Avg. Rel. Hum. 6am (%)	76	77	79	77	77	82	86	89	89	83	82	79	81
Avg. Rel. Hum. 3pm (%)	66	62	61	52	50	56	55	59	60	58	67	70	60

Note: Tr = Trace amounts (less than 0.05 inches of rain or less than 0.5 inches of snow)
Source: National Climatic Data Center, International Station Meteorological Climate Summary, 3/95

Weather Conditions

Temperature			Precipitation		
5°F & below	32°F & below	90°F & above	0.01 inch or more precip.	1.5 inch or more snow/ice	Thunder-storms
63	186	2	136	15	34

Note: Figures are average number of days per year
Source: National Climatic Data Center, International Station Meteorological Climate Summary, 3/95

AIR & WATER QUALITY

Maximum Pollutant Concentrations

	Particulate Matter (ug/m³)	Carbon Monoxide (ppm)	Sulfur Dioxide (ppm)	Nitrogen Dioxide (ppm)	Ozone (ppm)	Lead (ug/m³)
MSA[1] Level	47	3	n/a	n/a	0.08	n/a
NAAQS[2]	150	9	0.140	0.053	0.12	1.50
Met NAAQS	Yes	Yes	n/a	n/a	Yes	n/a

Note: (1) Metropolitan Statistical Area - see Appendix A for areas included; (2) National Ambient Air Quality Standards; ppm = parts per million; ug/m³ = micrograms per cubic meter; n/a not available
Source: EPA, National Air Quality and Emissions Trends Report, 1997

Pollutant Standards Index

Data not available.
EPA, National Air Quality and Emissions Trends Report, 1997

Drinking Water

Water System Name	Pop. Served	Primary Water Source Type	Number of Violations in 1998-99	Type of Violation/ Contaminants
Duluth	85,511	Surface	None	None

Note: Data as of January 19, 2000
Source: EPA, Office of Ground Water and Drinking Water, Safe Drinking Water Information System

Duluth tap water is neutral, very soft, fluoridated, and filtered.
Editor & Publisher Market Guide, 2000

Eau Claire, Wisconsin

Background

Eau Claire, Wisconsin is situated in the west-central portion of the state, 80 miles east of Minneapolis/St. Paul at the confluence of the Eau Claire and Chippewa Rivers. It was named "Clear Water" by 18th century French trappers and traders.

Eau Claire enjoys a mix of both urban culture and rural tranquility. The city offers high quality medical care, excellent schools and transportation, affordable housing, low crime, low traffic and cost of living, and clean air and water.

It was settled in the 1840s by Germans, Irish and Scandinavians who developed a lumber economy from the region's abundance of white pine, the largest tract in North America. When the supply was depleted in the 1890s, rubber manufacturing, dairy and food processing industries took over. Uniroyal Goodrich Tire Company was a major employer in the area until its closing in 1992.

Since then, Eau Claire has been expanding its business base while attracting new businesses such as Hutchinson Technology, Inc., W.L. Gore and Associates, Pleasant Company and Intek Plastics.

Area institutions of higher learning include the University of Wisconsin-Eau Claire, which is among the top three public regional universities in the Midwest, the University of Wisconsin-Stout, the Chippewa Valley Technical College, the National Technological University (NTU), Lakeland College and Immanuel Lutheran College.

Carson Park, a peninsula on Half Moon Lake, houses the Chippewa Valley Museum and the Paul Bunyan Logging Camp—a reproduction of the city's lumber era.

General Rankings and Evaluative Comments

- Eau Claire was ranked #153 out of 354 metropolitan areas in *Places Rated Almanac*. Criteria: cost of living, climate, crime, transportation, job outlook, education, the arts, health care, and recreation. *Places Rated Almanac, Millennium Edition, 2000*

- Eau Claire was selected as one of North America's "Best Small Metro Areas" (population under 250,000). The area ranked #17 out of 20. Criteria: cost of living, climate, crime, transportation, job outlook, education, the arts, health care, and recreation. *Places Rated Almanac, Millennium Edition, 2000*

Business Environment

STATE ECONOMY

State Economic Profile

"Wisconsin's expansion has begun to slow. For the first time in some years, 1998 saw Wisconsin grow at a rate below the national. Wisconsin's manufacturing sector remains stagnant and its farm sector struggling. Wisconsin's tight labor market will help to absorb some of these declines. An unsustainable increase in construction has driven job growth. Wisconsin's economy should trail the nation for some years before rebounding in 2001.

Wisconsin's construction industry remains a lone bright spot. Several commercial projects are under way in Milwaukee, such as the new convention center and baseball park. In addition, industrial and office construction is picking up in the suburbs. Public construction is also set to rise as the new federal transportation regulation raised Wisconsin's federal transportation funding by 48% to $520 million.

Wisconsin's residential market remains healthy with residential permits growing at a torrid pace in 1998. Existing home sales along with house prices are rising. Despite recent price appreciation, affordability still exceeds the national average. In the long run, however, the fast pace of construction will slow as residential construction is outpacing household formation in the state.

Wisconsin exports a large share of its manufacturing and agricultural output. Weak export demand is resulting in cutbacks to its papermaking, pulp, and equipment manufacturing industries. Farm income also dropped by over 90% in 1998 as commodity prices tumbled and export demand shrank. Commodity prices will remain weak, leaving little promise of a resurgence in Wisconsin's farm sector (outside of dairy, which is performing well). Slowing population growth, especially among younger households, will slow long-run growth. Wisconsin's high exposure to manufacturing and agriculture will continue to create downside risks for the state. Wisconsin will moderately underperform the nation in the near term."
National Association of Realtors, Economic Profiles: The Fifty States and the District of Columbia, http://nar.realtor.com/databank/profiles.htm

EXPORTS

Total Export Sales

Area	1995 ($000)	1996 ($000)	1997 ($000)	1998 ($000)	% Chg. 1995-98	% Chg. 1997-98
MSA[1]	399,923	320,596	507,339	583,376	45.9	15.0
U.S.	583,030,524	622,827,063	687,597,999	680,474,251	16.7	-1.0

Note: (1) Metropolitan Statistical Area - see Appendix A for areas included
Source: U.S. Department of Commerce, International Trade Association, Metropolitan Area Exports: An Export Performance Report on Over 250 U.S. Cities, November 10, 1999

CITY FINANCES

City Government Finances

Component	1995 ($million)	1995 (per capita $)
Revenue	49.9	853
Expenditure	49.5	847
Debt Outstanding	43.8	748

Source: 1999 County and City Extra, Annual Metro, City, and County Data Book

City Government Revenue by Source

Source	1995 ($million)	1995 (per capita $)
Intergovernmental	19.4	331
Taxes	12.0	206
Property	9.9	170
Sales and Gross Receipts	0.7	13

Source: 1999 County and City Extra, Annual Metro, City, and County Data Book

City Government Expenditures by Function

Function	1995 ($million)	1995 (per capita $)	1995 (%)
Public Welfare	0.0	0	0.0
Highways	11.0	188	22.3
Parking Facilities	0.2	4	0.5
Education	0.0	0	0.0
Health and Hospitals	3.0	51	6.1
Police Protection	7.2	123	14.6
Sewerage and Sanitation	4.7	81	9.6
Parks and Recreation	4.4	75	8.9
Housing and Community Development	0.7	13	1.6
Interest on Debt	2.4	41	4.9

Source: 1999 County and City Extra, Annual Metro, City, and County Data Book

Municipal Bond Ratings

Area	Moody's
City	Aa2

Source: Mergent Bond Record, 2/2000

POPULATION

Population Growth

Area	1980 Census	1990 Census	1999 Estimate	2004 Projection	Population Growth (%) 1990-1999	Population Growth (%) 1999-2004
City	51,516	56,930	58,679	59,583	3.1	1.5
MSA[1]	130,932	137,543	144,180	147,380	4.8	2.2
U.S.	226,545,805	248,765,170	272,212,864	283,625,312	9.4	4.2

Note: (1) Metropolitan Statistical Area - see Appendix A for areas included
Source: 1990 Census of Population and Housing, Summary Tape File 3C; Claritas, Inc.

Number of Households and Average Household Size

Area	1980 Census	1990 Census	1999 Estimate	2004 Projection	1999 Average Household Size
City	18,851	21,258	22,304	22,905	2.63
MSA[1]	44,511	50,502	54,487	56,535	2.65
U.S.	80,389,592	91,993,582	102,048,200	107,302,392	2.67

Note: (1) Metropolitan Statistical Area - see Appendix A for areas included
Source: 1990 Census of Population and Housing, Summary Tape File 3C; Claritas, Inc.

Race/Ethnicity of City Population

Race/Ethnicity	1990 Census Population	1990 Census %	1999 Estimate Population	1999 Estimate %	% Change 1990-1999
White, Non-Hispanic	53,820	94.5	54,258	92.5	0.8
Black, Non-Hispanic	312	0.5	250	0.4	-19.9
Asian, Non-Hispanic	2,246	3.9	3,248	5.5	44.6
Other, Non-Hispanic	288	0.5	409	0.7	42.0
Hispanic	264	0.5	514	0.9	94.7

Source: 1990 Census of Population and Housing, Summary Tape File 3C; Claritas, Inc.

Race/Ethnicity of Metropolitan Statistical Area Population

Race/Ethnicity	1990 Census		1999 Estimate		% Change 1990-1999
	Population	%	Population	%	
White, Non-Hispanic	133,491	97.1	138,640	96.2	3.9
Black, Non-Hispanic	387	0.3	297	0.2	-23.3
Asian, Non-Hispanic	2,458	1.8	3,578	2.5	45.6
Other, Non-Hispanic	721	0.5	746	0.5	3.5
Hispanic	486	0.4	919	0.6	89.1

Note: See Appendix A for areas included in the Metropolitan Statistical Area
Source: 1990 Census of Population and Housing, Summary Tape File 3C; Claritas, Inc.

Ancestry

Area	German	Irish	English	Italian	U.S.	French	Polish	Dutch
City	51.6	12.9	9.2	1.8	1.9	5.6	5.8	2.0
MSA[1]	55.9	12.5	8.5	1.4	2.0	6.5	5.9	2.0
U.S.	23.3	15.6	13.1	5.9	5.3	4.2	3.8	2.5

Note: Figures are percentages and include persons that reported multiple ancestry (eg. if a person reported being Irish and Italian, they were included in both columns); (1) Metropolitan Statistical Area - see Appendix A for areas included
Source: 1990 Census of Population and Housing, Summary Tape File 3C

Median Age

Area	1990 Census	1999 Estimate
City	28.4	31.5
MSA[1]	31.5	34.1
U.S.	32.9	35.7

Note: (1) Metropolitan Statistical Area - see Appendix A for areas included
Source: 1990 Census of Population and Housing, Summary Tape File 3C; Claritas, Inc.

Male/Female Population

Area	Number of Males		Number of Females		Males per 100 Females	
	1990	1999	1990	1999	1990	1999
City	26,623	27,670	30,307	31,009	87.8	89.2
MSA[1]	66,615	69,836	70,928	74,344	93.9	93.9
U.S.	121,172,379	132,803,736	127,537,494	139,409,136	95.0	95.3

Note: (1) Metropolitan Statistical Area - see Appendix A for areas included
Source: 1990 Census of Population, General Population Characteristics; Claritas, Inc.

INCOME

Per Capita/Median/Average Income

Area	Per Capita ($)			Median Household ($)			Average Household ($)		
	1989	1999	% Chg.	1989	1999	% Chg.	1989	1999	% Chg.
City	11,426	18,718	63.8	24,735	36,445	47.3	29,820	47,774	60.2
MSA[1]	11,560	18,583	60.8	25,876	37,085	43.3	30,989	48,202	55.5
U.S.	14,420	21,350	48.1	30,056	40,525	34.8	38,453	56,184	46.1

Note: (1) Metropolitan Statistical Area - see Appendix A for areas included; 1989 data is from the 1990 Census; 1999 data is estimated by Claritas, Inc.
Source: 1990 Census of Population, General Population Characteristics; Claritas, Inc.

Household Income Distribution

Area	Percent of Households Earning								
	Under $5,000	$5,000 -14,999	$15,000 -24,999	$25,000 -34,999	$35,000 -49,999	$50,000 -74,999	$75,000 -99,000	$100,000 -149,999	$150,000 and up
City	2.7	15.1	16.1	14.0	17.4	19.5	8.5	4.2	2.5
MSA[1]	2.4	14.6	16.0	14.0	17.9	20.4	8.1	4.1	2.4
U.S.	3.9	13.3	13.8	12.6	16.2	19.4	9.7	6.6	4.6

Note: Data as of 1999; (1) Metropolitan Statistical Area - see Appendix A for areas included
Source: Claritas, Inc.

Effective Buying Income

Area	Per Capita ($)	Median Household ($)	Average Household ($)
City	14,096	30,193	37,303
MSA[1]	14,546	31,911	39,063
U.S.	17,496	36,603	47,036

Note: Data as of 1/1/2000; (1) Metropolitan Statistical Area - see Appendix A for areas included
Source: Standard Rate & Data Service, Newspaper Advertising Source, March 2000

Effective Household Buying Income Distribution

Area	% of Households Earning						
	$10,000 -$19,999	$20,000 -$34,999	$35,000 -$49,999	$50,000 -$74,999	$75,000 -$99,000	$100,000 -$124,999	$125,000 and up
City	19.7	25.9	18.8	16.3	4.6	1.2	1.2
MSA[1]	18.8	25.1	19.7	17.6	5.0	1.4	1.5
U.S.	15.0	21.6	17.6	19.6	8.4	3.0	3.3

Note: Data as of 1/1/2000; (1) Metropolitan Statistical Area - see Appendix A for areas included
Source: Standard Rate & Data Service, Newspaper Advertising Source, March 2000

Poverty Rates by Age

Area	People of All Ages	People Under 18 Years Old	Related Children Age 5-17 in Families in Poverty
City	13.0	n/a	n/a
County	11.2	16.2	15.0
U.S.	13.8	20.8	18.7

Note: Figures show the percent of people living below the poverty line in 1995. The average poverty threshold was $15,569 for a family of four in 1995; n/a not available
Source: Bureau of the Census, Small Area Income and Poverty Estimates Program; U.S. Department of Housing and Urban Development

EMPLOYMENT

Labor Force and Employment

Area	Civilian Labor Force			Workers Employed		
	Dec. 1998	Dec. 1999	% Chg.	Dec. 1998	Dec. 1999	% Chg.
City	35,040	34,457	-1.7	33,961	33,578	-1.1
MSA[1]	84,294	82,988	-1.5	81,526	80,608	-1.1
U.S.	138,297,000	139,941,000	1.2	132,732,000	134,696,000	1.5

Note: Data is not seasonally adjusted and covers workers 16 years of age and older;
(1) Metropolitan Statistical Area - see Appendix A for areas included
Source: Bureau of Labor Statistics, http://stats.bls.gov

Unemployment Rate

Area	1999											
	Jan.	Feb.	Mar.	Apr.	May	Jun.	Jul.	Aug.	Sep.	Oct.	Nov.	Dec.
City	3.9	3.8	3.5	4.1	3.5	3.5	2.9	2.8	1.9	2.2	2.4	2.6
MSA[1]	4.4	4.3	3.9	4.1	3.3	3.1	2.6	2.4	1.6	1.9	2.2	2.9
U.S.	4.8	4.7	4.4	4.1	4.0	4.5	4.5	4.2	4.1	3.8	3.8	3.7

Note: Data is not seasonally adjusted and covers workers 16 years of age and older; all figures are percentages; (1) Metropolitan Statistical Area - see Appendix A for areas included
Source: Bureau of Labor Statistics, http://stats.bls.gov

Employment by Industry

Sector	MSA[1]		U.S.
	Number of Employees	Percent of Total	Percent of Total
Services	21,900	28.0	30.2
Retail Trade	18,600	23.8	18.1
Government	12,200	15.6	15.8
Manufacturing	13,600	17.4	14.1
Finance/Insurance/Real Estate	2,400	3.1	5.9
Wholesale Trade	3,000	3.8	5.4
Transportation/Public Utilities	3,600	4.6	5.3
Construction	n/a	n/a	4.8
Mining	n/a	n/a	0.4

Note: Figures cover non-farm employment as of 12/99 and are not seasonally adjusted; (1) Metropolitan Statistical Area - see Appendix A for areas included; n/a not available
Source: Bureau of Labor Statistics, http://stats.bls.gov

Employment by Occupation

Occupation Category	City (%)	MSA[1] (%)	U.S. (%)
White Collar	60.8	50.9	58.1
Executive/Admin./Management	9.9	8.8	12.3
Professional	16.6	13.4	14.1
Technical & Related Support	3.8	3.4	3.7
Sales	14.0	11.3	11.8
Administrative Support/Clerical	16.4	14.0	16.3
Blue Collar	21.2	26.5	26.2
Precision Production/Craft/Repair	7.8	9.9	11.3
Machine Operators/Assem./Insp.	5.9	7.6	6.8
Transportation/Material Movers	3.3	4.6	4.1
Cleaners/Helpers/Laborers	4.3	4.5	3.9
Services	17.2	16.5	13.2
Farming/Forestry/Fishing	0.8	6.0	2.5

Note: Figures cover workers 16 years of age and older; (1) Metropolitan Statistical Area - see Appendix A for areas included
Source: 1990 Census of Population and Housing, Summary Tape File 3C

Occupational Employment Projections: 1996 - 2006

Occupations Expected to Have the Largest Job Growth (ranked by numerical growth)	Fast-Growing Occupations[1] (ranked by percent growth)
1. Janitors/cleaners/maids, ex. priv. hshld.	1. Systems analysts
2. General managers & top executives	2. Desktop publishers
3. Cashiers	3. Personal and home care aides
4. Truck drivers, light	4. Database administrators
5. Salespersons, retail	5. Paralegals
6. Systems analysts	6. Securities, financial services sales
7. Home health aides	7. Occupational therapists
8. Teachers aides, clerical & paraprofess.	8. Home health aides
9. Registered nurses	9. Teachers, special education
10. Waiters & waitresses	10. Medical assistants

Note: Projections cover Wisconsin; (1) Excludes occupations with total job growth less than 300
Source: U.S. Department of Labor, Employment and Training Administration, America's Labor Market Information System (ALMIS)

Average Wages

Occupation	$/Hr.	Occupation	$/Hr.
Accountants and Auditors	19.03	Maids and Housekeepers	6.78
Assemblers and Fabricators	8.18	Maintenance Repairers	10.41
Automotive Mechanics	11.24	Marketing/Advertising/PR Managers	26.92
Bookkeepers	9.86	Nurses, Licensed Practical	12.89
Carpenters	14.81	Nurses, Registered	19.20
Cashiers	6.25	Nursing Aides/Orderlies/Attendants	8.93
Clerks, General Office	9.32	Physicians and Surgeons	56.70
Clerks, Shipping/Receiving/Traffic	11.40	Receptionists/Information Clerks	8.49
Computer Programmers	21.62	Sales Reps., Exc. Scientific/Retail	18.74
Computer Support Specialists	14.83	Sales Reps., Scientific, Exc. Retail	21.53
Cooks, Restaurant	7.29	Salespersons, Retail	7.85
Electricians	16.68	Secretaries, Except Legal/Medical	10.01
Financial Managers	23.63	Stock Clerks, Sales Floor	6.97
First-Line Supervisors/Mgrs., Sales	12.08	Systems Analysts	23.07
Food Preparation Workers	6.57	Teacher Aides	8.41
General Managers/Top Executives	27.89	Teachers, Elementary School	18.26
Guards	7.95	Teachers, Secondary School	17.44
Hand Packers	7.38	Telemarketers	8.98
Janitors and Cleaners	8.83	Truck Drivers, Heavy/Tractor-Trailer	14.31
Laborers, Landscaping	10.12	Truck Drivers, Light	8.37
Lawyers	40.49	Waiters and Waitresses	5.59

Note: Wage data is for 1998 and covers the Metropolitan Statistical Area (see Appendix A for areas included). Hourly wages for elementary and secondary school teachers were calculated by the editors from annual wage data assuming a 40 hour work week; Dashes indicate that data was not available.
Source: Bureau of Labor Statistics, 1998 Metropolitan Area Occupational Employment and Wage Estimates

TAXES

Major State and Local Tax Rates

State Corporate Income (%)	State Personal Income (%)	Residential Property (%)	Sales & Use		State Gasoline (cents/ gallon)	State Cigarette (cents/ pack)
			State (%)	Local (%)		
7.9	4.73 - 6.75[a]	2.25	5.0	None	25.8[b]	59.0

Note: Personal/corporate income, sales, gasoline and cigarette tax rates as of January 2000. Property tax rates as of April 2000; (a) Tax rates scheduled to decrease for tax years 2001 and beyond (ranging from 4.6% to 6.75%). Personal exemption amounts scheduled to increase to $700 for tax year 2001; (b) Portion of the rate is adjustable based on maintenance costs, sales volume, or cost of fuel to state government
Source: Federation of Tax Administrators, www.taxadmin.org; ERI's Relocation Assessor software database, quarterly effective date 4/1/2000

Total Taxes Per Capita and as a Percent of Income

Area	Per Capita Income ($)	Per Capita Taxes ($)			Percent of Income (%)		
		Total	Federal	State/Local	Total	Federal	State/Local
Wisconsin	27,342	10,308	6,546	3,761	37.7	23.9	13.8
U.S.	28,878	10,298	7,026	3,273	35.7	24.3	11.3

Note: Figures are for 1999
Source: Tax Foundation, www.taxfoundation.org

COMMERCIAL UTILITIES

Typical Monthly Electric Bills

Area	Commercial Service ($/month)		Industrial Service ($/month)	
	12 kW demand 1,500 kWh	100 kW demand 30,000 kWh	1,000 kW demand 400,000 kWh	20,000 kW demand 10,000,000 kWh
City	108	1,731	19,340	323,654
U.S.	150	2,174	23,995	508,569

Note: Based on rates in effect January 1, 1999
Source: Edison Electric Institute, Typical Residential, Commercial and Industrial Bills, Winter 1999

TRANSPORTATION

Transportation Statistics

Average minutes to work (1990)	14.3
Interstate highways	I-94; US-53; US-12
Bus lines	
In-city (1998)	Eau Claire Transit System, 16 buses
Inter-city (1999)	3
Passenger air service	
Airport	Chippewa Valley Regional
Airlines (1999)	1
Enplaned passengers (1998)	20,346
Amtrak service	Bus Connection
Motor freight carriers (1999)	31
Major waterways/ports	None

Source: FAA DOT/TSC CY1998 ACAIS Database; National Transit Database, 1998; Editor & Publisher Market Guide, 2000; Amtrak National Time Table, Fall 1999/Winter 2000; 1990 Census of Population and Housing, STF 3C; Jane's Urban Transport Systems 1999-2000

Means of Transportation to Work

Area	Car/Truck/Van		Public Transportation			Bicycle	Walked	Other Means	Worked at Home
	Drove Alone	Car-pooled	Bus	Subway	Railroad				
City	74.5	9.4	1.2	0.0	0.0	1.1	10.4	0.7	2.7
MSA[1]	75.0	9.8	0.7	0.0	0.0	0.5	6.7	0.9	6.3
U.S.	73.2	13.4	3.0	1.5	0.5	0.4	3.9	1.2	3.0

Note: Figures shown are percentages and only include workers 16 years of age and older;
(1) Metropolitan Statistical Area - see Appendix A for areas included
Source: 1990 Census of Population and Housing, Summary Tape File 3C

BUSINESSES

Major Business Headquarters

Company Name	1999 Rankings	
	Fortune 500	Forbes 500
Menard	-	27

Note: Companies listed are located in the city; dashes indicate no ranking
Fortune 500: Companies that produce a 10-K are ranked 1 to 500 based on 1999 revenue
Forbes 500: Private companies are ranked 1 to 500 based on 1998 revenue
Source: Forbes, December 13, 1999; Fortune, April 17, 2000

HOTELS & MOTELS

Hotels/Motels

Area	Hotels/ Motels	Rooms	Luxury-Level Hotels/Motels		Average Minimum Rates ($)		
			♦♦♦♦	♦♦♦♦♦	♦♦	♦♦♦	♦♦♦♦
City	16	1,314	0	0	49	69	n/a
Airport	1	56	0	0	n/a	n/a	n/a
Suburbs	2	122	0	0	n/a	n/a	n/a
Total	19	1,492	0	0	n/a	n/a	n/a

Note: n/a not available; classifications range from one diamond (budget properties with basic amenities) to five diamond (luxury properties).
Source: OAG Business Travel Planner, Winter 1999-2000

Estimated Daily Food and Lodging Costs

Area	Food/Other ($/day)	Average Hotel Cost ($/day)
City	30	55
U.S.	30	55

Source: ERI's Relocation Assessor software database, quarterly effective date 4/1/2000

CONVENTION CENTERS

Convention Centers and Event Sites

Name	Guest Rooms	Meeting Space (sq. ft.)	Capacity (Theatre Style)
Holiday Inn Convention Center	122	n/a	0

Note: n/a not available
Source: EventSource.com, 3/15/2000

Living Environment

COST OF LIVING

Cost of Living: Homeowner

Cost Element	U.S. ($)	City ($)	Differential ($)	Percent of U.S. Average
Consumables	14,516	14,475	-41	99.7
Transportation	5,957	5,981	24	100.4
Health Services	2,012	1,960	-52	97.4
Housing/Utilities/Prop. Tax	16,337	21,294	4,957	130.3
Income+Payroll Taxes	12,615	13,043	428	103.4
Miscellaneous	8,563	8,563	0	100.0
Total Cost of Living	60,000	65,316	5,316	108.9

Note: Figures are based on a single income, four person family with gross annual earnings of $60,000, owning an 1,800 square-foot home, and driving two automobiles worth $22,000 30,000 miles per year.
Source: ERI's Relocation Assessor software database, quarterly effective date 4/1/2000

Cost of Living: Renter

Cost Element	U.S. ($)	City ($)	Differential ($)	Percent of U.S. Average
Consumables	10,486	10,468	-18	99.8
Transportation	2,107	2,118	11	100.5
Health Services	1,632	1,592	-40	97.5
Rent/Utilities/Insurance	9,299	10,135	836	109.0
Income+Payroll Taxes	8,607	9,663	1,056	112.3
Miscellaneous	7,869	7,869	0	100.0
Total Cost of Living	40,000	41,845	1,845	104.6

Note: Figures are based on a single income, three person family with gross annual earnings of $40,000, renting a 1,000 square-foot home, and driving one automobile worth $8,000 12,000 miles per year.
Source: ERI's Relocation Assessor software database, quarterly effective date 4/1/2000

HOUSING

Median Home Prices and Housing Affordability

Area	Median Price[2] 4th Qtr. 1999 ($)	HOI[3] 4th Qtr. 1999	Affordability Rank[4]
MSA[1]	n/a	n/a	n/a
U.S.	139,000	63.8	–

Note: (1) Metropolitan Statistical Area - see Appendix A for areas included; (2) U.S. figures calculated from the sales of 687,516 new and existing homes in 192 markets; (3) Housing Opportunity Index - percent of homes sold that were within the reach of the median income household at the prevailing mortgage interest rate; (4) Rank is from 1-192 with 1 being most affordable; n/a not available
Source: National Association of Home Builders, Housing Opportunity Index, 4th Quarter 1999

Estimated Home Price

Area	Price ($)
City	170,864
U.S.	135,855

Note: Figures are based on an 1,800 square-foot home
Source: ERI's Relocation Assessor software database, quarterly effective date 4/1/2000

Estimated Rent

Area	Rent ($/month)
City	732
U.S.	651

Note: Figures are based on a 1,000 square-foot home
Source: ERI's Relocation Assessor software database, quarterly effective date 4/1/2000

Median Home Price Projection

It is projected that the median home price in the metropolitan area will increase from $102,471 in 1999 to $142,386 in 2010, an increase of 39.0%
Kiplinger's Personal Finance Magazine, January 2000

RESIDENTIAL UTILITIES

Average Residential Utility Costs

Area	All Electric ($/mth)	Part Electric ($/mth)	Other Energy ($/mth)	Phone ($/mth)
City	–	47.52	78.25	16.34
U.S.	99.25	55.47	43.48	20.29

Source: ACCRA, Cost of Living Index, 3rd Quarter 1999

HEALTH CARE

Average Health Care Costs

Area	Hospital ($/day)	Doctor ($/visit)	Dentist ($/visit)
City	320.00	73.16	70.62
U.S.	440.96	53.83	68.42

Note: Hospital—based on a semi-private room; Doctor—based on a general practitioner's routine exam of an established patient; Dentist—based on adult teeth cleaning and periodic oral exam.
Source: ACCRA, Cost of Living Index, 3rd Quarter 1999

Distribution of Office-Based Physicians

Area	Family/Gen. Practitioners	Specialists		
		Medical	Surgical	Other
MSA[1]	62	77	82	73

Note: Data as of 12/31/97; (1) Metropolitan Statistical Area - see Appendix A for areas included
Source: American Medical Assn., Physician Characteristics & Distribution in the U.S., 1999

Hospitals

Eau Claire has 2 general medical and surgical hospitals.
AHA Guide to the Healthcare Field, 1999-2000

EDUCATION

Public School District Statistics

District Name	Num. Sch.	Enroll.	Classroom Teachers	Pupils per Teacher	Minority Pupils (%)	Current Exp.[1] ($/pupil)
Eau Claire Area Sch Dist	23	11,496	724	15.9	n/a	n/a

Note: Data covers the 1997-1998 school year unless otherwise noted; (1) Data covers fiscal year 1996; SD = School District; ISD = Independent School District; n/a not available
Source: National Center for Education Statistics, Common Core of Data Public Education Agency Universe 1997-98; National Center for Education Statistics, Characteristics of the 100 Largest Public Elementary and Secondary School Districts in the United States: 1997-98, July 1999

Educational Quality

School District	Education Quotient[1]	Graduate Outcome[2]	Community Index[3]	Resource Index[4]
Eau Claire Area School Dist.	135	144	122	121

Note: Over 1,000 secondary school districts were rated in terms of educational quality. The scores range from a low of 50 to a high of 150; (1) Combination of the Graduate Outcome, Community and Resource indexes weighted to reflect the greater importance of the Graduate Outcome and Resource Index; (2) Based on graduation rates and college board scores (SAT/ACT); (3) Based on the surrounding community's level of affluence and adult education; (4) Based on teacher salaries, per-pupil expenditures and student-teacher ratios.
Source: Expansion Management, Ratings Issue, 1999

Educational Attainment by Race

Area	High School Graduate (%)					Bachelor's Degree (%)				
	Total	White	Black	Other	Hisp.[2]	Total	White	Black	Other	Hisp.[2]
City	84.8	85.5	78.1	57.6	100.0	23.3	23.4	22.9	20.1	22.6
MSA[1]	79.6	79.8	80.2	65.3	80.1	16.9	16.8	28.6	19.1	12.2
U.S.	75.2	77.9	63.1	60.4	49.8	20.3	21.5	11.4	19.4	9.2

Note: Figures shown cover persons 25 years old and over; (1) Metropolitan Statistical Area - see Appendix A for areas included; (2) people of Hispanic origin can be of any race
Source: 1990 Census of Population and Housing, Summary Tape File 3C

School Enrollment by Type

Area	Preprimary				Elementary/High School			
	Public		Private		Public		Private	
	Enrollment	%	Enrollment	%	Enrollment	%	Enrollment	%
City	742	64.1	416	35.9	7,708	89.5	907	10.5
MSA[1]	1,817	70.5	759	29.5	20,926	88.3	2,761	11.7
U.S.	2,679,029	59.5	1,824,256	40.5	38,379,689	90.2	4,187,099	9.8

Note: Figures shown cover persons 3 years old and over;
(1) Metropolitan Statistical Area - see Appendix A for areas included
Source: 1990 Census of Population and Housing, Summary Tape File 3C

School Enrollment by Race

Area	Preprimary (%)				Elementary/High School (%)			
	White	Black	Other	Hisp.[1]	White	Black	Other	Hisp.[1]
City	89.7	0.0	10.3	1.0	88.6	1.4	10.1	1.1
MSA[2]	94.6	0.5	5.0	0.5	94.8	0.6	4.6	0.8
U.S.	80.4	12.5	7.1	7.8	74.1	15.6	10.3	12.5

Note: Figures shown cover persons 3 years old and over; (1) people of Hispanic origin can be of any race; (2) Metropolitan Statistical Area - see Appendix A for areas included
Source: 1990 Census of Population and Housing, Summary Tape File 3C

Higher Education

Two-Year Colleges		Four-Year Colleges		Medical Schools	Law Schools	Voc/ Tech
Public	Private	Public	Private			
1	0	1	0	0	0	2

Source: College Blue Book, Occupational Education, 1999; Medical School Admission Requirements, 1999-2000; Peterson's Guide to Two-Year Colleges, 2000; Peterson's Guide to Four-Year Colleges, 1999; Barron's Guide to Law Schools, 1999

MAJOR EMPLOYERS

Major Employers

Chippewa Valley Country Music Festival
Hutchinson Technology (computer storage)
Menard (lumber)
National Presto Industries (appliances)
Owen Aynes & Associates (engineering services)

Huntsinger Farms
Luther Hospital
Middlefort Clinic - Mayo Health Systems
Northern States Power Co.

Note: Companies listed are located in the city
Source: D&B Business Rankings, 1999; Ward's Business Directory, 1999; America's Corporate Families, 1999

PUBLIC SAFETY

Crime Rate

Area	All Crimes	Violent Crimes				Property Crimes		
		Murder	Forcible Rape	Robbery	Aggrav. Assault	Burglary	Larceny -Theft	Motor Vehicle Theft
City	4,648.2	0.0	18.5	55.5	215.2	759.8	3,439.5	159.7
Suburbs1	2,340.3	2.4	9.4	5.9	56.5	376.9	1,776.1	113.1
MSA2	3,291.1	1.4	13.2	26.3	121.9	534.7	2,461.4	132.3
U.S.	4,930.0	6.8	35.9	186.3	382.3	919.4	2,893.4	506.0

Note: Crime rate is the number of crimes per 100,000 population; (1) Defined as all areas within the Metropolitan Statistical Area but located outside the central city; (2) Metropolitan Statistical Area - see Appendix A for areas included
Source: FBI Uniform Crime Reports, 1997

RECREATION

Culture and Recreation

Museums	Symphony Orchestras	Opera Companies	Dance Companies	Professional Theatres	Zoos	Pro Sports Teams
2	2	0	0	1	0	0

Source: Musical America, International Directory of the Performing Arts, 1999; Official Museum Directory, 2000; Stern's Performing Arts Directory, 1997; USA Today Four Sport Stadium Guide, 1997; Career Opportunities in Theatre and the Performing Arts, 1999

Library System

The L.E. Philips Memorial Public Library has no branches and holdings of 211,389 volumes.
American Library Directory, 1999-2000

MEDIA

Newspapers

Name	Type	Freq.	Distribution	Circulation
Leader-Telegram	General	7x/wk	Area	32,000

Note: Includes newspapers with circulations of 200 or more located in the city;
Source: Burrelle's Media Directory, 1999 Edition

Television Stations

Name	Ch.	Affiliation	Type	Owner
WEAU	13	NBCT	Commercial	Gray Communications Inc.
WQOW	18	ABCT	Commercial	Shockley Communications Corporation
WEUX	48	FBC	Commercial	Grant Media Inc.

Note: Stations included broadcast in the Eau Claire metro area; n/a not available
Source: Burrelle's Media Directory, 1999 Edition

AM Radio Stations

Call Letters	Freq. (kHz)	Target Audience	Station Format	Music Format
WAYY	790	General	N/T	n/a
WEIO	1050	B/G	E/M/N/S/T	Classic Rock
WEAQ	1150	General	M	Adult Standards
WBIZ	1400	Men	S/T	n/a

Note: Stations included broadcast in the Eau Claire metro area; n/a not available
Target Audience: A=Asian; B=Black; C=Christian; E=Ethnic; F=French; G=General; H=Hispanic; M=Men; N=Native American; R=Religious; S=Senior Citizen; W=Women; Y=Young Adult; Z=Children
Station Format: E=Educational; M=Music; N=News; S=Sports; T=Talk
Source: Burrelle's Media Directory, 1999 Edition

FM Radio Stations

Call Letters	Freq. (mHz)	Target Audience	Station Format	Music Format
WHWC	88.3	General	E/T	n/a
WUEC	89.7	General	E/M/N	Blues/Classical/Jazz/World Music
WVSS	90.7	General	E/M/N	Classical
WIAL	94.1	General	M	Adult Contemporary
WQRB	95.1	General	M/N/T	Country
WISM	98.1	General	M	Classic Rock
WBIZ	100.7	General	M/N/S/T	Adult Contemporary
WAXX	104.5	General	M/N	Country
WATQ	106.7	General	M	Country

Note: Stations included broadcast in the Eau Claire metro area; n/a not available
Station Format: E=Educational; M=Music; N=News; S=Sports; T=Talk
Target Audience: A=Asian; B=Black; C=Christian; E=Ethnic; F=French; G=General; H=Hispanic; M=Men; N=Native American; R=Religious; S=Senior Citizen; W=Women; Y=Young Adult; Z=Children
Source: Burrelle's Media Directory, 1999 Edition

WEATHER

Temperature/Precipitation/Humidity

	Jan	Feb	Mar	Apr	May	Jun	Jul	Aug	Sep	Oct	Nov	Dec	Yr.
Max. High Temp. (°F)	55	61	82	92	107	105	111	104	101	89	79	59	111
Avg. High Temp. (°F)	24	27	40	57	70	79	84	82	73	60	41	28	55
Avg. Temp. (°F)	14	17	30	45	58	67	72	70	61	49	33	20	44
Avg. Low Temp. (°F)	5	7	20	34	46	56	61	58	50	39	25	12	34
Min. Low Temp. (°F)	-45	-40	-21	0	20	25	41	36	22	7	-15	-30	-45
Avg. Precip. (in.)	1.1	1.1	1.8	2.7	4.0	4.7	3.4	3.7	3.6	2.5	1.7	1.2	31.5
Avg. Snowfall (in.)	6.2	6.2	8.9	1.8	0.1	0	0	0	0	0.2	4.7	7.0	35.1
Avg. Rel. Hum. (%)	71	72	70	63	63	68	70	73	73	70	72	74	70

Source: National Climatic Data Center, International Station Meteorological Climate Summary, 3/95

Weather Conditions

Temperature			Precipitation		
0°F & below	32°F & below	90°F & above	0.1 inch or more precip.	1.5 inch or more snow/ice	Thunder-storms
41	174	8	60	8	40

Note: Figures are average number of days per year
Source: National Climatic Data Center, International Station Meteorological Climate Summary, 3/95

AIR & WATER QUALITY

Maximum Pollutant Concentrations

	Particulate Matter (ug/m³)	Carbon Monoxide (ppm)	Sulfur Dioxide (ppm)	Nitrogen Dioxide (ppm)	Ozone (ppm)	Lead (ug/m³)
MSA[1] Level	n/a	n/a	n/a	n/a	n/a	n/a
NAAQS[2]	150	9	0.140	0.053	0.12	1.50
Met NAAQS	n/a	n/a	n/a	n/a	n/a	n/a

Note: (1) Metropolitan Statistical Area - see Appendix A for areas included; (2) National Ambient Air Quality Standards; ppm = parts per million; ug/m³ = micrograms per cubic meter; n/a not available
Source: EPA, National Air Quality and Emissions Trends Report, 1997

Pollutant Standards Index

Data not available.
EPA, National Air Quality and Emissions Trends Report, 1997

Drinking Water

Water System Name	Pop. Served	Primary Water Source Type	Number of Violations in 1998-99	Type of Violation/ Contaminants
Eau Claire Waterworks	65,000	Ground	2	(1), (2)

Note: Data as of January 19, 2000; (1) Monthly Maximum Contaminant Level (TCR) violation—for systems testing more than 40 samples, more than five percent tested positive for Total Coliform or for those systems testing less than 40 samples more than one sample tested positive for Total Coliform (1 violation in 1999); (2) Regular Monitoring violation—failure to conduct initial or repeat sampling, or to accurately report an analytical result for fluoride (1 violation in 1999).
Source: EPA, Office of Ground Water and Drinking Water, Safe Drinking Water Information System

Eau Claire tap water is neutral, soft, and fluoridated.
Editor & Publisher Market Guide, 2000

Fargo, North Dakota

Background

Fargo, North Dakota is situated in Cass County on the west bank of the Red River. It is the largest city in the state.

Fargo's recent economy has been expanding rapidly due in large part to its pro-business climate, with the lowest corporate income taxes in the Upper Midwest, a five-year corporate income tax exemption, no sales tax on manufacturing equipment, and no personal property or inventory taxes. Major industries include health care, education and legal services. There are numerous industrial parks and research centers in the city, including Fargo Industrial Park and Sheyenne Industrial Park. West Fargo is home to the country's largest stockyards and meat-packing plants.

Native hunting and gathering and farming societies occupied the region until 1860, when the first white explorers arrived. Cree, Blackfeet and Crow also frequented the western buffalo ranges. The town was founded in 1871 by the Northern Pacific Railway as an outfitting post for settlers. Named for William George Fargo, founder of Wells Fargo and Company, it developed into a transportation, marketing and distribution center and was incorporated as a city in 1875. Between 1879 and 1905 many Germans and Norwegians settled in the area.

Along with crop failures and dust storms, the 1930s also brought modernization. Federal relief improved roads, schools and city services. By the 1950s, prosperity and expansion came through state government developing airports and highways.

North Dakota State University, founded in 1890 as an agricultural college, remains an influential agricultural research center. The Cass County Historical Society and the Forsberg House both exhibit extensive collections of pioneer artifacts. Bonanzaville, near West Fargo, is a replica of the region's nineteenth century farming boom.

General Rankings and Evaluative Comments

■ Fargo was ranked #81 out of 354 metropolitan areas in *Places Rated Almanac*. Criteria: cost of living, climate, crime, transportation, job outlook, education, the arts, health care, and recreation. *Places Rated Almanac, Millennium Edition, 2000*

■ Fargo was selected as one of North America's "Best Small Metro Areas" (population under 250,000). The area ranked #2 out of 20. Criteria: cost of living, climate, crime, transportation, job outlook, education, the arts, health care, and recreation. *Places Rated Almanac, Millennium Edition, 2000*

■ *Ladies Home Journal* ranked America's 200 largest cities based on the qualities women care about most. Fargo ranked #12 out of 200. Criteria: low crime rate, well-paying jobs, quality health and child care, good public schools, the presence of women in government, size of the gender wage gap, number of sexual-harassment and discrimination complaints filed, unemployment and divorce rates, commute times, population density, number of houses of worship, parks and cultural offerings, number of women's health specialists, how well women cared for themselves, complexion kindness index based on UV radiation levels, odds of finding affordable fashions, rental rates for romance movies, champagne sales, and other matters of the heart. *Ladies Home Journal, November 1998*

■ Zero Population Growth ranked 229 cities in terms of children's health, safety, and economic well-being. Fargo was ranked #1 out of 112 independent cities (cities with populations greater than 100,000 which were neither Major Cities nor Suburbs/Outer Cities) and was given a grade of A+. Criteria: total population and population change, percent of population under 18 years of age, household language, percent of births to teens, infant mortality rate, percent of low birth weights, dropout rate, enrollment in preprimary school, violent and property crime rates, unemployment rate, percent of children in poverty, percent of owner occupied units, number of bad air days, percent of public transportation commuters, and average travel time to work. *Zero Population Growth, Children's Environmental Index, Fall 1999*

■ Cognetics studied 273 metro areas in the United States, ranking them by entrepreneurial activity. Fargo was ranked #3 out of 134 smaller metro areas. Criteria: Significant Starts (firms started in the last 10 years that still employ at least 5 people) and Young Growers (percent of firms 10 years old or less that grew significantly during the last 4 years). *Cognetics, "Entrepreneurial Hot Spots: The Best Places in America to Start and Grow a Company," 1999*

■ Fargo, ND/Moorhead, MN was given an Outstanding Achievement Award for The Cultural Diversity Project by the U.S Conference of Mayors and Waste Management as part of their 1999 City Livability Awards Program. The program honors mayors and their city governments for developing programs that enhance the quality of life in urban areas. The awards are given annually to ten mayors and their cities—a first-place award and four Outstanding Achievement Awards for cities under 100,000 population, and a first-place and four Outstanding Achievement Awards for cities of 100,000 or more inhabitants.

Business Environment

STATE ECONOMY

State Economic Profile

"North Dakota has been trailing the nation for the last several years, a trend that will only worsen in 2000-2001. Weak and declining commodity prices have made North Dakota's dependence on agriculture and oil production a liability. Job growth in finance, insurance and real estate (FIRE) has absorbed job losses elsewhere; however, North Dakota's low unemployment rate, shortage of skilled workers and weak population outlook will limit job growth in the near future.

North Dakota is one of the nation's most agriculture-dependent states, accounting for over 10% of Gross State Product. Weak global demand and over-capacity in US agriculture have made 1998 a difficult year for North Dakota's farmers. Farm income is down, and the number of farm-related business liquidations is up. Closely related industries, such as food-processing, are also having considerable difficulty. Even if global demand for US farm products picks up, the long-term trend for farm products is down. Similar problems plague North Dakota's oil industry, which will likely see negative employment growth as rigs are shut down and exploration curtailed.

Symptomatic of its difficulties is North Dakota's stagnant population growth. In 1997 and 1998, the state lost, on net, a sizable amount of its population. More importantly is its continued loss of younger households, who are needed to fuel the housing and labor markets. While 1998's housing market saw robust sales and strong price appreciation, 2000 will see weaker sales, new construction and softer home price appreciation.

North Dakota's low business costs and affordable living have attracted jobs in its FIRE sectors. These gains, however, will not likely offset losses in agriculture and oil." *National Association of Realtors, Economic Profiles: The Fifty States and the District of Columbia, http://nar.realtor.com/databank/profiles.htm*

EXPORTS

Total Export Sales

Area	1995 ($000)	1996 ($000)	1997 ($000)	1998 ($000)	% Chg. 1995-98	% Chg. 1997-98
MSA[1]	155,010	181,892	208,530	158,071	2.0	-24.2
U.S.	583,030,524	622,827,063	687,597,999	680,474,251	16.7	-1.0

Note: (1) Metropolitan Statistical Area - see Appendix A for areas included
Source: U.S. Department of Commerce, International Trade Association, Metropolitan Area Exports: An Export Performance Report on Over 250 U.S. Cities, November 10, 1999

CITY FINANCES

City Government Finances

Component	1995 ($million)	1995 (per capita $)
Revenue	62.6	784
Expenditure	60.9	763
Debt Outstanding	194.7	2,442

Source: 1999 County and City Extra, Annual Metro, City, and County Data Book

City Government Revenue by Source

Source	1995 ($million)	1995 (per capita $)
Intergovernmental	8.7	109
Taxes	21.4	269
Property	7.5	95
Sales and Gross Receipts	12.6	158

Source: 1999 County and City Extra, Annual Metro, City, and County Data Book

City Government Expenditures by Function

Function	1995 ($million)	1995 (per capita $)	1995 (%)
Public Welfare	0.2	3	0.4
Highways	2.9	37	4.9
Parking Facilities	0.2	3	0.4
Education	0.0	0	0.0
Health and Hospitals	2.0	25	3.3
Police Protection	5.4	68	9.0
Sewerage and Sanitation	6.4	80	10.6
Parks and Recreation	3.4	42	5.6
Housing and Community Development	1.0	12	1.7
Interest on Debt	7.8	98	12.9

Source: 1999 County and City Extra, Annual Metro, City, and County Data Book

Municipal Bond Ratings

Area	Moody's
City	Aa2

Source: Mergent Bond Record, 2/2000

POPULATION

Population Growth

Area	1980 Census	1990 Census	1999 Estimate	2004 Projection	Population Growth (%) 1990-1999	Population Growth (%) 1999-2004
City	61,383	74,115	87,891	91,532	18.6	4.1
MSA[1]	137,574	153,296	169,446	172,538	10.5	1.8
U.S.	226,545,805	248,765,170	272,212,864	283,625,312	9.4	4.2

Note: (1) Metropolitan Statistical Area - see Appendix A for areas included
Source: 1990 Census of Population and Housing, Summary Tape File 3C; Claritas, Inc.

Number of Households and Average Household Size

Area	1980 Census	1990 Census	1999 Estimate	2004 Projection	1999 Average Household Size
City	23,908	30,340	35,955	37,550	2.44
MSA[1]	48,812	57,892	64,605	65,983	2.62
U.S.	80,389,592	91,993,582	102,048,200	107,302,392	2.67

Note: (1) Metropolitan Statistical Area - see Appendix A for areas included
Source: 1990 Census of Population and Housing, Summary Tape File 3C; Claritas, Inc.

Race/Ethnicity of City Population

Race/Ethnicity	1990 Census Population	1990 Census %	1999 Estimate Population	1999 Estimate %	% Change 1990-1999
White, Non-Hispanic	71,835	96.9	83,822	95.4	16.7
Black, Non-Hispanic	255	0.3	377	0.4	47.8
Asian, Non-Hispanic	760	1.0	1,581	1.8	108.0
Other, Non-Hispanic	773	1.0	1,070	1.2	38.4
Hispanic	492	0.7	1,041	1.2	111.6

Source: 1990 Census of Population and Housing, Summary Tape File 3C; Claritas, Inc.

Race/Ethnicity of Metropolitan Statistical Area Population

Race/Ethnicity	1990 Census		1999 Estimate		% Change 1990-1999
	Population	%	Population	%	
White, Non-Hispanic	148,470	96.9	161,533	95.3	8.8
Black, Non-Hispanic	415	0.3	623	0.4	50.1
Asian, Non-Hispanic	1,198	0.8	2,226	1.3	85.8
Other, Non-Hispanic	1,521	1.0	1,903	1.1	25.1
Hispanic	1,692	1.1	3,161	1.9	86.8

Note: See Appendix A for areas included in the Metropolitan Statistical Area
Source: 1990 Census of Population and Housing, Summary Tape File 3C; Claritas, Inc.

Ancestry

Area	German	Irish	English	Italian	U.S.	French	Polish	Dutch
City	48.7	10.3	7.1	1.2	0.9	5.7	2.8	1.9
MSA[1]	47.9	9.5	6.8	1.0	1.2	5.1	2.7	1.7
U.S.	23.3	15.6	13.1	5.9	5.3	4.2	3.8	2.5

Note: Figures are percentages and include persons that reported multiple ancestry (eg. if a person reported being Irish and Italian, they were included in both columns); (1) Metropolitan Statistical Area - see Appendix A for areas included
Source: 1990 Census of Population and Housing, Summary Tape File 3C

Median Age

Area	1990 Census	1999 Estimate
City	29.4	33.0
MSA[1]	29.7	32.5
U.S.	32.9	35.7

Note: (1) Metropolitan Statistical Area - see Appendix A for areas included
Source: 1990 Census of Population and Housing, Summary Tape File 3C; Claritas, Inc.

Male/Female Population

Area	Number of Males		Number of Females		Males per 100 Females	
	1990	1999	1990	1999	1990	1999
City	36,756	43,641	37,359	44,250	98.4	98.6
MSA[1]	75,352	83,354	77,944	86,092	96.7	96.8
U.S.	121,172,379	132,803,736	127,537,494	139,409,136	95.0	95.3

Note: (1) Metropolitan Statistical Area - see Appendix A for areas included
Source: 1990 Census of Population, General Population Characteristics; Claritas, Inc.

INCOME

Per Capita/Median/Average Income

Area	Per Capita ($)			Median Household ($)			Average Household ($)		
	1989	1999	% Chg.	1989	1999	% Chg.	1989	1999	% Chg.
City	13,554	22,595	66.7	25,326	39,914	57.6	32,283	53,998	67.3
MSA[1]	12,449	20,712	66.4	26,551	40,886	54.0	32,261	53,381	65.5
U.S.	14,420	21,350	48.1	30,056	40,525	34.8	38,453	56,184	46.1

Note: (1) Metropolitan Statistical Area - see Appendix A for areas included; 1989 data is from the 1990 Census; 1999 data is estimated by Claritas, Inc.
Source: 1990 Census of Population, General Population Characteristics; Claritas, Inc.

Household Income Distribution

Area	Percent of Households Earning								
	Under $5,000	$5,000 -14,999	$15,000 -24,999	$25,000 -34,999	$35,000 -49,999	$50,000 -74,999	$75,000 -99,000	$100,000 -149,999	$150,000 and up
City	3.2	13.3	14.7	12.7	16.4	20.2	9.5	5.5	4.4
MSA[1]	3.0	13.1	14.5	12.3	16.5	21.5	10.1	5.4	3.6
U.S.	3.9	13.3	13.8	12.6	16.2	19.4	9.7	6.6	4.6

Note: Data as of 1999; (1) Metropolitan Statistical Area - see Appendix A for areas included
Source: Claritas, Inc.

Effective Buying Income

Area	Per Capita ($)	Median Household ($)	Average Household ($)
City	18,772	34,862	45,062
MSA[1]	17,827	36,850	46,060
U.S.	17,496	36,603	47,036

Note: Data as of 1/1/2000; (1) Metropolitan Statistical Area - see Appendix A for areas included
Source: Standard Rate & Data Service, Newspaper Advertising Source, March 2000

Effective Household Buying Income Distribution

Area	% of Households Earning						
	$10,000 -$19,999	$20,000 -$34,999	$35,000 -$49,999	$50,000 -$74,999	$75,000 -$99,000	$100,000 -$124,999	$125,000 and up
City	16.5	23.0	17.8	18.1	7.8	2.6	3.5
MSA[1]	15.9	21.6	18.2	20.5	8.1	2.8	2.8
U.S.	15.0	21.6	17.6	19.6	8.4	3.0	3.3

Note: Data as of 1/1/2000; (1) Metropolitan Statistical Area - see Appendix A for areas included
Source: Standard Rate & Data Service, Newspaper Advertising Source, March 2000

Poverty Rates by Age

Area	People of All Ages	People Under 18 Years Old	Related Children Age 5-17 in Families in Poverty
City	10.0	n/a	n/a
County	8.9	11.0	9.7
U.S.	13.8	20.8	18.7

Note: Figures show the percent of people living below the poverty line in 1995. The average poverty threshold was $15,569 for a family of four in 1995; n/a not available
Source: Bureau of the Census, Small Area Income and Poverty Estimates Program; U.S. Department of Housing and Urban Development

EMPLOYMENT

Labor Force and Employment

Area	Civilian Labor Force			Workers Employed		
	Dec. 1998	Dec. 1999	% Chg.	Dec. 1998	Dec. 1999	% Chg.
City	53,308	52,792	-1.0	52,551	51,984	-1.1
MSA[1]	102,972	101,931	-1.0	101,390	100,206	-1.2
U.S.	138,297,000	139,941,000	1.2	132,732,000	134,696,000	1.5

Note: Data is not seasonally adjusted and covers workers 16 years of age and older;
(1) Metropolitan Statistical Area - see Appendix A for areas included
Source: Bureau of Labor Statistics, http://stats.bls.gov

Unemployment Rate

Area	1999											
	Jan.	Feb.	Mar.	Apr.	May	Jun.	Jul.	Aug.	Sep.	Oct.	Nov.	Dec.
City	1.7	1.8	1.8	1.4	1.3	1.5	1.7	1.2	1.3	1.1	1.4	1.5
MSA[1]	2.1	2.0	2.0	1.5	1.4	1.8	1.9	1.4	1.5	1.1	1.4	1.7
U.S.	4.8	4.7	4.4	4.1	4.0	4.5	4.5	4.2	4.1	3.8	3.8	3.7

Note: Data is not seasonally adjusted and covers workers 16 years of age and older; all figures are percentages; (1) Metropolitan Statistical Area - see Appendix A for areas included
Source: Bureau of Labor Statistics, http://stats.bls.gov

Employment by Industry

Sector	MSA[1]		U.S.
	Number of Employees	Percent of Total	Percent of Total
Services	31,300	30.7	30.2
Retail Trade	20,800	20.4	18.1
Government	15,500	15.2	15.8
Manufacturing	7,800	7.7	14.1
Finance/Insurance/Real Estate	7,100	7.0	5.9
Wholesale Trade	8,700	8.5	5.4
Transportation/Public Utilities	5,200	5.1	5.3
Construction	n/a	n/a	4.8
Mining	n/a	n/a	0.4

Note: Figures cover non-farm employment as of 12/99 and are not seasonally adjusted; (1) Metropolitan Statistical Area - see Appendix A for areas included; n/a not available
Source: Bureau of Labor Statistics, http://stats.bls.gov

Employment by Occupation

Occupation Category	City (%)	MSA[1] (%)	U.S. (%)
White Collar	65.1	60.1	58.1
Executive/Admin./Management	12.5	11.3	12.3
Professional	16.9	14.8	14.1
Technical & Related Support	4.2	3.6	3.7
Sales	15.0	13.8	11.8
Administrative Support/Clerical	16.5	16.7	16.3
Blue Collar	18.6	20.3	26.2
Precision Production/Craft/Repair	7.2	8.5	11.3
Machine Operators/Assem./Insp.	3.9	3.9	6.8
Transportation/Material Movers	4.1	4.3	4.1
Cleaners/Helpers/Laborers	3.4	3.6	3.9
Services	15.3	16.5	13.2
Farming/Forestry/Fishing	1.0	3.1	2.5

Note: Figures cover workers 16 years of age and older; (1) Metropolitan Statistical Area - see Appendix A for areas included
Source: 1990 Census of Population and Housing, Summary Tape File 3C

Occupational Employment Projections: 1996 - 2006

Occupations Expected to Have the Largest Job Growth (ranked by numerical growth)	Fast-Growing Occupations[1] (ranked by percent growth)
1. Truck drivers, light	1. Database administrators
2. Cashiers	2. Systems analysts
3. Salespersons, retail	3. Home health aides
4. Nursing aides/orderlies/attendants	4. Adjustment clerks
5. Registered nurses	5. Human services workers
6. General managers & top executives	6. Personal and home care aides
7. Waiters & waitresses	7. Food service and lodging managers
8. Child care workers, private household	8. Child care workers, private household
9. Database administrators	9. Sales agents, real estate
10. Hairdressers & cosmetologists	10. Guards

Note: Projections cover North Dakota; (1) Excludes occupations with total job growth less than 300
Source: U.S. Department of Labor, Employment and Training Administration, America's Labor Market Information System (ALMIS)

Average Wages

Occupation	$/Hr.	Occupation	$/Hr.
Accountants and Auditors	16.90	Maids and Housekeepers	6.81
Assemblers and Fabricators	8.73	Maintenance Repairers	10.12
Automotive Mechanics	11.64	Marketing/Advertising/PR Managers	24.27
Bookkeepers	10.04	Nurses, Licensed Practical	11.31
Carpenters	12.92	Nurses, Registered	19.62
Cashiers	6.64	Nursing Aides/Orderlies/Attendants	8.04
Clerks, General Office	8.83	Physicians and Surgeons	-
Clerks, Shipping/Receiving/Traffic	10.77	Receptionists/Information Clerks	8.46
Computer Programmers	19.87	Sales Reps., Exc. Scientific/Retail	16.20
Computer Support Specialists	14.81	Sales Reps., Scientific, Exc. Retail	22.17
Cooks, Restaurant	7.28	Salespersons, Retail	8.64
Electricians	14.71	Secretaries, Except Legal/Medical	9.60
Financial Managers	25.75	Stock Clerks, Sales Floor	7.27
First-Line Supervisors/Mgrs., Sales	17.44	Systems Analysts	15.56
Food Preparation Workers	6.73	Teacher Aides	9.49
General Managers/Top Executives	29.11	Teachers, Elementary School	16.57
Guards	7.94	Teachers, Secondary School	17.40
Hand Packers	6.62	Telemarketers	10.04
Janitors and Cleaners	7.99	Truck Drivers, Heavy/Tractor-Trailer	14.17
Laborers, Landscaping	9.08	Truck Drivers, Light	10.45
Lawyers	31.83	Waiters and Waitresses	5.73

Note: Wage data is for 1998 and covers the Metropolitan Statistical Area (see Appendix A for areas included). Hourly wages for elementary and secondary school teachers were calculated by the editors from annual wage data assuming a 40 hour work week; Dashes indicate that data was not available.
Source: Bureau of Labor Statistics, 1998 Metropolitan Area Occupational Employment and Wage Estimates

TAXES

Major State and Local Tax Rates

State Corporate Income (%)	State Personal Income (%)	Residential Property (%)	Sales & Use		State Gasoline (cents/ gallon)	State Cigarette (cents/ pack)
			State (%)	Local (%)		
3.0 - 10.5	2.67 - 12.0[a]	1.94	5.0	1.5	21.0	44.0

Note: Personal/corporate income, sales, gasoline and cigarette tax rates as of January 2000. Property tax rates as of April 2000; (a) Taxpayers have the option of paying 14% of the adjusted federal income tax liability, without a deduction of federal taxes. An additional $300 personal exemption is allowed for joint returns or unmarried head of households
Source: Federation of Tax Administrators, www.taxadmin.org; ERI's Relocation Assessor software database, quarterly effective date 4/1/2000

Total Taxes Per Capita and as a Percent of Income

Area	Per Capita Income ($)	Per Capita Taxes ($)			Percent of Income (%)		
		Total	Federal	State/Local	Total	Federal	State/Local
North Dakota	22,420	7,696	5,260	2,436	34.3	23.5	10.9
U.S.	28,878	10,298	7,026	3,273	35.7	24.3	11.3

Note: Figures are for 1999
Source: Tax Foundation, www.taxfoundation.org

COMMERCIAL UTILITIES

Typical Monthly Electric Bills

Area	Commercial Service ($/month)		Industrial Service ($/month)	
	12 kW demand 1,500 kWh	100 kW demand 30,000 kWh	1,000 kW demand 400,000 kWh	20,000 kW demand 10,000,000 kWh
City	89	1,555	17,749	293,975
U.S.	150	2,174	23,995	508,569

Note: Based on rates in effect January 1, 1999
Source: Edison Electric Institute, Typical Residential, Commercial and Industrial Bills, Winter 1999

TRANSPORTATION

Transportation Statistics

Average minutes to work (1990)	13.4
Interstate highways	I-29; I-94; US-10; US-52; US-75
Bus lines	
In-city (1998)	Fargo Metropolitan Area Transit, 10 buses
Inter-city (1999)	3
Passenger air service	
Airport	Hector International
Airlines (1999)	5
Enplaned passengers (1998)	196,956
Amtrak service	Yes
Motor freight carriers (1999)	94
Major waterways/ports	None

Source: FAA DOT/TSC CY1998 ACAIS Database; National Transit Database, 1998; Editor & Publisher Market Guide, 2000; Amtrak National Time Table, Fall 1999/Winter 2000; 1990 Census of Population and Housing, STF 3C; Jane's Urban Transport Systems 1999-2000

Means of Transportation to Work

Area	Car/Truck/Van		Public Transportation			Bicycle	Walked	Other Means	Worked at Home
	Drove Alone	Car-pooled	Bus	Subway	Railroad				
City	78.9	10.0	1.3	0.0	0.0	0.7	6.1	0.5	2.6
MSA[1]	75.7	10.7	0.9	0.0	0.0	0.5	7.3	0.6	4.3
U.S.	73.2	13.4	3.0	1.5	0.5	0.4	3.9	1.2	3.0

Note: Figures shown are percentages and only include workers 16 years of age and older;
(1) Metropolitan Statistical Area - see Appendix A for areas included
Source: 1990 Census of Population and Housing, Summary Tape File 3C

BUSINESSES

Major Business Headquarters

Company Name	1999 Rankings	
	Fortune 500	Forbes 500
No companies listed	-	-

Note: Companies listed are located in the city; dashes indicate no ranking
Fortune 500: Companies that produce a 10-K are ranked 1 to 500 based on 1999 revenue
Forbes 500: Private companies are ranked 1 to 500 based on 1998 revenue
Source: Forbes, December 13, 1999; Fortune, April 17, 2000

HOTELS & MOTELS

Hotels/Motels

Area	Hotels/ Motels	Rooms	Luxury-Level Hotels/Motels		Average Minimum Rates ($)		
			♦♦♦♦	♦♦♦♦♦	♦♦	♦♦♦	♦♦♦♦
City	18	1,822	0	0	59	82	n/a
Airport	1	75	0	0	n/a	n/a	n/a
Total	19	1,897	0	0	n/a	n/a	n/a

Note: n/a not available; classifications range from one diamond (budget properties with basic amenities) to five diamond (luxury properties).
Source: OAG Business Travel Planner, Winter 1999-2000

Estimated Daily Food and Lodging Costs

Area	Food/Other ($/day)	Average Hotel Cost ($/day)
City	30	55
U.S.	30	55

Source: ERI's Relocation Assessor software database, quarterly effective date 4/1/2000

CONVENTION CENTERS

Convention Centers and Event Sites

Name	Guest Rooms	Meeting Space (sq. ft.)	Capacity (Theatre Style)
Fargo Civic Memorial Auditorium	n/a	n/a	3,330
Fargodome	n/a	n/a	28,000
Radisson Hotel	151	n/a	340

Note: n/a not available
Source: EventSource.com, 3/15/2000

Living Environment

COST OF LIVING

Cost of Living: Homeowner

Cost Element	U.S. ($)	City ($)	Differential ($)	Percent of U.S. Average
Consumables	14,516	15,011	495	103.4
Transportation	5,957	5,817	-140	97.6
Health Services	2,012	2,121	109	105.4
Housing/Utilities/Prop. Tax	16,337	16,495	158	101.0
Income+Payroll Taxes	12,615	11,579	-1,036	91.8
Miscellaneous	8,563	8,563	0	100.0
Total Cost of Living	60,000	59,586	-414	99.3

Note: Figures are based on a single income, four person family with gross annual earnings of $60,000, owning an 1,800 square-foot home, and driving two automobiles worth $22,000 30,000 miles per year.
Source: ERI's Relocation Assessor software database, quarterly effective date 4/1/2000

Cost of Living: Renter

Cost Element	U.S. ($)	City ($)	Differential ($)	Percent of U.S. Average
Consumables	10,486	10,847	361	103.4
Transportation	2,107	2,059	-48	97.7
Health Services	1,632	1,721	89	105.5
Rent/Utilities/Insurance	9,299	7,902	-1,397	85.0
Income+Payroll Taxes	8,607	7,719	-888	89.7
Miscellaneous	7,869	7,869	0	100.0
Total Cost of Living	40,000	38,117	-1,883	95.3

Note: Figures are based on a single income, three person family with gross annual earnings of $40,000, renting a 1,000 square-foot home, and driving one automobile worth $8,000 12,000 miles per year.
Source: ERI's Relocation Assessor software database, quarterly effective date 4/1/2000

HOUSING

Median Home Prices and Housing Affordability

Area	Median Price[2] 4th Qtr. 1999 ($)	HOI[3] 4th Qtr. 1999	Affordability Rank[4]
MSA[1]	n/a	n/a	n/a
U.S.	139,000	63.8	–

Note: (1) Metropolitan Statistical Area - see Appendix A for areas included; (2) U.S. figures calculated from the sales of 687,516 new and existing homes in 192 markets; (3) Housing Opportunity Index - percent of homes sold that were within the reach of the median income household at the prevailing mortgage interest rate; (4) Rank is from 1-192 with 1 being most affordable; n/a not available
Source: National Association of Home Builders, Housing Opportunity Index, 4th Quarter 1999

Estimated Home Price

Area	Price ($)
City	123,797
U.S.	135,855

Note: Figures are based on an 1,800 square-foot home
Source: ERI's Relocation Assessor software database, quarterly effective date 4/1/2000

Estimated Rent

Area	Rent ($/month)
City	545
U.S.	651

Note: Figures are based on a 1,000 square-foot home
Source: ERI's Relocation Assessor software database, quarterly effective date 4/1/2000

RESIDENTIAL UTILITIES

Average Residential Utility Costs

Area	All Electric ($/mth)	Part Electric ($/mth)	Other Energy ($/mth)	Phone ($/mth)
MSA[1]	–	41.31	44.26	20.29
U.S.	99.25	55.47	43.48	20.29

Note: (1) Metropolitan Statistical Area - see Appendix A for areas included
Source: ACCRA, Cost of Living Index, 3rd Quarter 1999

HEALTH CARE

Average Health Care Costs

Area	Hospital ($/day)	Doctor ($/visit)	Dentist ($/visit)
MSA[1]	430.50	57.00	70.91
U.S.	440.96	53.83	68.42

Note: Hospital—based on a semi-private room; Doctor—based on a general practitioner's routine exam of an established patient; Dentist—based on adult teeth cleaning and periodic oral exam; (1) Metropolitan Statistical Area - see Appendix A for areas included
Source: ACCRA, Cost of Living Index, 3rd Quarter 1999

Distribution of Office-Based Physicians

Area	Family/Gen. Practitioners	Specialists		
		Medical	Surgical	Other
MSA[1]	53	120	88	92

Note: Data as of 12/31/97; (1) Metropolitan Statistical Area - see Appendix A for areas included
Source: American Medical Assn., Physician Characteristics & Distribution in the U.S., 1999

Hospitals

Fargo has 1 general medical and surgical hospital.
AHA Guide to the Healthcare Field, 1999-2000

According to *U.S. News and World Report,* Fargo has one of the best hospitals in the U.S.:
Meritcare Health System, noted for cancer.
U.S. News Online, "America's Best Hospitals," July 19, 1999

EDUCATION

Public School District Statistics

District Name	Num. Sch.	Enroll.	Classroom Teachers	Pupils per Teacher	Minority Pupils (%)	Current Exp.[1] ($/pupil)
Fargo 1	23	11,759	681	17.3	n/a	n/a
Fargo Special Ed Unit	1	n/a	n/a	n/a	n/a	n/a
Rural Cass Special Ed Unit	1	n/a	11	0.0	n/a	n/a

Note: Data covers the 1997-1998 school year unless otherwise noted; (1) Data covers fiscal year 1996; SD = School District; ISD = Independent School District; n/a not available
Source: National Center for Education Statistics, Common Core of Data Public Education Agency Universe 1997-98; National Center for Education Statistics, Characteristics of the 100 Largest Public Elementary and Secondary School Districts in the United States: 1997-98, July 1999

Educational Quality

School District	Education Quotient[1]	Graduate Outcome[2]	Community Index[3]	Resource Index[4]
Fargo 1	130	146	105	104

Note: Over 1,000 secondary school districts were rated in terms of educational quality. The scores range from a low of 50 to a high of 150; (1) Combination of the Graduate Outcome, Community and Resource indexes weighted to reflect the greater importance of the Graduate Outcome and Resource Index; (2) Based on graduation rates and college board scores (SAT/ACT); (3) Based on the surrounding community's level of affluence and adult education; (4) Based on teacher salaries, per-pupil expenditures and student-teacher ratios.
Source: Expansion Management, Ratings Issue, 1999

Educational Attainment by Race

Area	High School Graduate (%)					Bachelor's Degree (%)				
	Total	White	Black	Other	Hisp.[2]	Total	White	Black	Other	Hisp.[2]
City	88.7	88.7	91.1	88.2	70.5	30.2	30.0	42.5	39.5	22.0
MSA[1]	85.1	85.2	88.2	77.5	54.7	25.0	24.9	43.6	27.8	8.9
U.S.	75.2	77.9	63.1	60.4	49.8	20.3	21.5	11.4	19.4	9.2

Note: Figures shown cover persons 25 years old and over; (1) Metropolitan Statistical Area - see Appendix A for areas included; (2) people of Hispanic origin can be of any race
Source: 1990 Census of Population and Housing, Summary Tape File 3C

School Enrollment by Type

Area	Preprimary				Elementary/High School			
	Public		Private		Public		Private	
	Enrollment	%	Enrollment	%	Enrollment	%	Enrollment	%
City	826	61.6	515	38.4	9,338	91.7	842	8.3
MSA[1]	1,934	69.5	847	30.5	23,158	93.8	1,538	6.2
U.S.	2,679,029	59.5	1,824,256	40.5	38,379,689	90.2	4,187,099	9.8

Note: Figures shown cover persons 3 years old and over;
(1) Metropolitan Statistical Area - see Appendix A for areas included
Source: 1990 Census of Population and Housing, Summary Tape File 3C

School Enrollment by Race

Area	Preprimary (%)				Elementary/High School (%)			
	White	Black	Other	Hisp.[1]	White	Black	Other	Hisp.[1]
City	96.5	0.6	2.9	1.4	97.0	0.3	2.7	1.4
MSA[2]	96.1	0.4	3.5	2.2	96.4	0.5	3.1	2.0
U.S.	80.4	12.5	7.1	7.8	74.1	15.6	10.3	12.5

Note: Figures shown cover persons 3 years old and over; (1) people of Hispanic origin can be of any race; (2) Metropolitan Statistical Area - see Appendix A for areas included
Source: 1990 Census of Population and Housing, Summary Tape File 3C

Higher Education

Two-Year Colleges		Four-Year Colleges		Medical Schools	Law Schools	Voc/ Tech
Public	Private	Public	Private			
0	0	1	0	0	0	8

Source: College Blue Book, Occupational Education, 1999; Medical School Admission Requirements, 1999-2000; Peterson's Guide to Two-Year Colleges, 2000; Peterson's Guide to Four-Year Colleges, 1999; Barron's Guide to Law Schools, 1999

MAJOR EMPLOYERS

Major Employers

American Lutheran Homes	Bethany Homes
Blue Cross & Blue Shield of ND	Dakota Clinic
Dakota Heartland Health System	Forum Communications
Great Plains Software	Meritcare Health System
Villa Nazareth	World Properties (hotels)

Note: Companies listed are located in the city
Source: D&B Business Rankings, 1999; Ward's Business Directory, 1999; America's Corporate Families, 1999

PUBLIC SAFETY

Crime Rate

Area	All Crimes	Violent Crimes				Property Crimes		
		Murder	Forcible Rape	Robbery	Aggrav. Assault	Burglary	Larceny -Theft	Motor Vehicle Theft
City	3,502.2	0.0	54.3	15.4	55.5	361.4	2,769.8	245.7
Suburbs[1]	2,676.7	1.2	41.6	18.4	95.4	320.5	2,022.2	177.4
MSA[2]	3,096.7	0.6	48.1	16.8	75.1	341.3	2,402.6	212.1
U.S.	4,615.5	6.3	34.4	165.2	360.5	862.0	2,728.1	459.0

Note: Crime rate is the number of crimes per 100,000 population; (1) Defined as all areas within the Metropolitan Statistical Area but located outside the central city; (2) Metropolitan Statistical Area - see Appendix A for areas included
Source: FBI Uniform Crime Reports, 1998

RECREATION

Culture and Recreation

Museums	Symphony Orchestras	Opera Companies	Dance Companies	Professional Theatres	Zoos	Pro Sports Teams
2	1	1	2	3	0	0

Source: Musical America, International Directory of the Performing Arts, 1999; Official Museum Directory, 2000; Stern's Performing Arts Directory, 1997; USA Today Four Sport Stadium Guide, 1997; Career Opportunities in Theatre and the Performing Arts, 1999

Library System

The Fargo Public Library has no branchesand a budget of $1,328,400 (1997-1998).
American Library Directory, 1999-2000

MEDIA

Newspapers

Name	Type	Freq.	Distribution	Circulation
Forum	General	7x/wk	Area	57,000
West Fargo Pioneer	General	1x/wk	Local	3,500

Note: Includes newspapers with circulations of 200 or more located in the city;
Source: Burrelle's Media Directory, 1999 Edition

Television Stations

Name	Ch.	Affiliation	Type	Owner
KGFE	n/a	PBS	Public	Prairie Public Broadcasting Inc.
KBME	n/a	PBS	Public	Prairie Public Broadcasting Inc.
KWSE	n/a	PBS	Public	Prairie Public Broadcasting Inc.
KSRE	n/a	PBS	Public	Prairie Public Broadcasting Inc.
WDAY	n/a	ABCT	Commercial	Forum Communications Company
KJRR	n/a	n/a	Commercial	Red River Broadcast Corporation
KDSE	n/a	PBS	Public	Prairie Public Broadcasting Inc.
KBRR	10	n/a	Commercial	Red River Broadcast Corporation
KVLY	11	n/a	Commercial	Meyer Communications
KNRR	12	FBC	Commercial	Red River Broadcast Corporation
KFME	13	PBS	Public	Prairie Public Broadcasting Inc.
KVRR	15	n/a	Commercial	Red River Broadcast Corporation
KJRE	19	PBS	Public	Prairie Public Broadcasting Inc.

Note: Stations included broadcast in the Fargo metro area; n/a not available
Source: Burrelle's Media Directory, 1999 Edition

AM Radio Stations

Call Letters	Freq. (kHz)	Target Audience	Station Format	Music Format
KFGO	790	General	M/N/S/T	Country
WDAY	970	General	N/S/T	n/a
KFNW	1200	Religious	M/N/T	Christian
KVOX	1280	General	N/S	n/a
KQWB	1550	General	M	Adult Standards

Note: Stations included broadcast in the Fargo metro area; n/a not available
Target Audience: A=Asian; B=Black; C=Christian; E=Ethnic; F=French; G=General; H=Hispanic; M=Men; N=Native American; R=Religious; S=Senior Citizen; W=Women; Y=Young Adult; Z=Children
Station Format: E=Educational; M=Music; N=News; S=Sports; T=Talk
Source: Burrelle's Media Directory, 1999 Edition

FM Radio Stations

Call Letters	Freq. (mHz)	Target Audience	Station Format	Music Format
KPHT	92.7	G/M/W	M/N/S	Christian/Oldies
WDAY	93.7	General	M	n/a
KFNW	97.9	Religious	M/N/T	Christian
KQWB	98.7	General	M	AOR
KVOX	99.9	General	M	Country
KFGO	101.9	General	M	Country
KLTA	105.1	General	M	Adult Contemporary

Note: Stations included broadcast in the Fargo metro area; n/a not available
Station Format: E=Educational; M=Music; N=News; S=Sports; T=Talk
Target Audience: A=Asian; B=Black; C=Christian; E=Ethnic; F=French; G=General; H=Hispanic; M=Men; N=Native American; R=Religious; S=Senior Citizen; W=Women; Y=Young Adult; Z=Children
Music Format: AOR=Album Oriented Rock; MOR=Middle-of-the-Road
Source: Burrelle's Media Directory, 1999 Edition

WEATHER

Temperature/Precipitation/Humidity

	Jan	Feb	Mar	Apr	May	Jun	Jul	Aug	Sep	Oct	Nov	Dec	Yr.
Max. High Temp. (°F)	52	66	78	100	98	99	106	106	102	93	74	57	106
Avg. High Temp. (°F)	15	21	34	53	68	77	83	81	70	57	37	21	52
Avg. Temp. (°F)	6	12	25	43	56	66	71	69	58	46	28	13	41
Avg. Low Temp. (°F)	-3	2	16	32	44	54	59	57	46	35	20	4	31
Min. Low Temp. (°F)	-36	-34	-34	-7	20	30	36	33	19	5	-24	-32	-36
Avg. Precip. (in.)	0.6	0.4	0.9	1.7	2.3	3.0	3.1	2.4	1.8	1.5	0.8	0.6	19.3
Avg. Snowfall (in.)	9	6	7	3	Tr	0	0	0	Tr	1	5	7	38
Avg. Rel. Hum. 6am (%)	74	77	81	79	76	82	85	86	85	80	81	78	81
Avg. Rel. Hum. 3pm (%)	70	71	68	52	45	50	49	47	50	51	65	72	57

Note: Tr = Trace amounts (less than 0.05 inches of rain or less than 0.5 inches of snow)
Source: National Climatic Data Center, International Station Meteorological Climate Summary, 3/95

Weather Conditions

Temperature			Precipitation		
5°F & below	32°F & below	90°F & above	0.01 inch or more precip.	1.5 inch or more snow/ice	Thunder-storms
66	180	15	99	8	31

Note: Figures are average number of days per year
Source: National Climatic Data Center, International Station Meteorological Climate Summary, 3/95

AIR & WATER QUALITY

Maximum Pollutant Concentrations

	Particulate Matter (ug/m³)	Carbon Monoxide (ppm)	Sulfur Dioxide (ppm)	Nitrogen Dioxide (ppm)	Ozone (ppm)	Lead (ug/m³)
MSA[1] Level	63	n/a	0.008	0.008	0.07	n/a
NAAQS[2]	150	9	0.140	0.053	0.12	1.50
Met NAAQS	Yes	n/a	Yes	Yes	Yes	n/a

Note: (1) Metropolitan Statistical Area - see Appendix A for areas included; (2) National Ambient Air Quality Standards; ppm = parts per million; ug/m³ = micrograms per cubic meter; n/a not available Source: EPA, National Air Quality and Emissions Trends Report, 1997

Pollutant Standards Index

Data not available.
EPA, National Air Quality and Emissions Trends Report, 1997

Drinking Water

Water System Name	Pop. Served	Primary Water Source Type	Number of Violations in 1998-99	Type of Violation/ Contaminants
City of Fargo	74,111	Surface	None	None

Note: Data as of January 19, 2000
Source: EPA, Office of Ground Water and Drinking Water, Safe Drinking Water Information System

Fargo tap water is alkaline, soft, and fluoridated.
Editor & Publisher Market Guide, 2000

Fayetteville, Arkansas

Background

Fayetteville, Arkansas is in the northwest section of the state, about 30 miles east of Oklahoma and 50 miles south of Missouri. The city is in Washington County and encompasses 43.39 square miles. Its proximity to the tallest of the Ozark Mountains dramatically sets off the four seasons that attract both visitors and professionals looking to relocate.

Incorporated as a city in 1903, Fayetteville is an agricultural and resort area with farm-based industries, aluminum products, tools, clothing and food processing.

The University of Arkansas contributes to the city's economic prosperity by attracting new industry and serving as a highly educated labor resource, while its teaching and research programs stimulate the area's educational and cultural life. It houses the Walton Arts Center, comprising three theatres, an art gallery, dance and art studios and an outdoor pavilion.

The first European American to visit the area was hunter and trapper Frank Pierce, in 1819. By 1828, several families had begun migrating to the region, and the city grew rapidly. Sophia Sawyer's Fayetteville Female Seminary opened in 1839 and in 1852, the state's first degree-granting institution, Arkansas College, was established, although the latter was destroyed during the Civil War, which devastated the city.

Fayetteville housed both Union and Confederate troops during the war. The battles of Pea Ridge and Prairie Grove were fought nearby. After the Battle of Fayetteville, the city was occupied by Union troops until the end of the war.

Although recovery was slow, Fayetteville was incorporated as a town in 1870, and chosen as the site for the Arkansas Industrial University, which opened in 1872, becoming the University of Arkansas in 1899.

Between 1960 and 1990, Fayetteville's population more than doubled, making it the fifth largest city in Arkansas. Historically, unemployment has been low, and the city is headquarters to several major corporations, including Wal-Mart, Tyson Foods and J.B. Hunt Transport. Business initiatives such as the Capital Improvements Program, a five-year business plan, are in place to direct and enhance the city's economic infrastructure.

The region's ample highway system has undergone continuing development as well. Transportation service is accessible through the Arkansas and Missouri Railroad, daily bus service, and the five airlines operating out of Drake Field. Fifteen miles to the south is the Ozark National Forest. Fayetteville's Parks and Recreation Division maintains not only area parks and ball fields, but also many large recreational facilities and three lakes.

At night during the winter holiday season, merchants and residents create a magical display of over 350 miles of lights for the "Lights of the Ozarks Festival."

General Rankings and Evaluative Comments

■ Fayetteville was ranked #91 out of 354 metropolitan areas in *Places Rated Almanac*. Criteria: cost of living, climate, crime, transportation, job outlook, education, the arts, health care, and recreation. *Places Rated Almanac, Millennium Edition, 2000*

■ Fayetteville was selected as one of America's best places to retire. Criteria: safety, climate, housing, culture and recreation, social compatibility, affordability, medical care, transportation, and jobs and/or volunteer opportunities. *Where to Retire: America's Best and Most Affordable Places, 1998*

■ Fayetteville was selected as one of the best places to retire by *Retirement Places Rated*. Criteria: cost of living, climate, crime, services, working, and leisure living. The city was ranked #21 out of 187. *Retirement Places Rated, 1999*

Business Environment

STATE ECONOMY

State Economic Profile

"Arkansas' economy has trailed the nation's over the last several years. This trend should not change in the near future. A heavy dependence on manufacturing and agriculture leaves Arkansas with a fragile economy. Although its cost structure is very favorable, its shortage of an educated and skilled labor force hampers its potential for growth.

Low foreign demand and a shortage of skilled workers are currently hampering Arkansas' manufacturing sector. The apparel industry is suffering from both foreign competition and a decline in foreign demand. Even with a rebound in demand, its future looks dim. While several food processors, one of Arkansas key industries, increased payrolls in 1998, their long-term future remains uncertain.

While 1998 was a banner year for many industries, agriculture was not one of them. Commodity prices have continued to soften in the face of weak foreign demand. Arkansas' rice, hog and soybean producers have been hit particularly hard by falling prices. However, its poultry industry has not suffered as much as the others and still faces strong domestic demand. Consolidation among producers in both the poultry and hog industries, however, makes it unlikely that these sectors will provide much, if any, employment growth in the near term.

Home sales have been strong in recent years with some rebound in price appreciation in 1998. However, population growth among the "typical buyers" of housing will be negative over the next few years, raising some concern over the future strength of Arkansas' housing market."
National Association of Realtors, Economic Profiles: The Fifty States and the District of Columbia, http://nar.realtor.com/databank/profiles.htm

EXPORTS

Total Export Sales

Area	1995 ($000)	1996 ($000)	1997 ($000)	1998 ($000)	% Chg. 1995-98	% Chg. 1997-98
MSA[1]	669,265	801,203	732,763	597,658	-10.7	-18.4
U.S.	583,030,524	622,827,063	687,597,999	680,474,251	16.7	-1.0

Note: (1) Metropolitan Statistical Area - see Appendix A for areas included
Source: U.S. Department of Commerce, International Trade Association, Metropolitan Area Exports: An Export Performance Report on Over 250 U.S. Cities, November 10, 1999

CITY FINANCES

City Government Finances

Component	1995 ($million)	1995 (per capita $)
Revenue	41.8	849
Expenditure	35.4	720
Debt Outstanding	72.3	1,469

Source: 1999 County and City Extra, Annual Metro, City, and County Data Book

City Government Revenue by Source

Source	1995 ($million)	1995 (per capita $)
Intergovernmental	5.3	107
Taxes	17.0	345
Property	0.0	1
Sales and Gross Receipts	16.4	334

Source: 1999 County and City Extra, Annual Metro, City, and County Data Book

City Government Expenditures by Function

Function	1995 ($million)	1995 (per capita $)	1995 (%)
Public Welfare	0.0	0	0.0
Highways	3.1	63	8.8
Parking Facilities	0.1	2	0.3
Education	0.0	0	0.0
Health and Hospitals	0.1	2	0.4
Police Protection	4.4	89	12.5
Sewerage and Sanitation	8.5	173	24.1
Parks and Recreation	1.0	21	3.0
Housing and Community Development	1.1	23	3.3
Interest on Debt	3.9	80	11.2

Source: 1999 County and City Extra, Annual Metro, City, and County Data Book

Municipal Bond Ratings

Area	Moody's
City	Aaa

Source: Mergent Bond Record, 2/2000

POPULATION

Population Growth

Area	1980 Census	1990 Census	1999 Estimate	2004 Projection	Population Growth (%) 1990-1999	Population Growth (%) 1999-2004
City	36,608	42,095	55,001	58,489	30.7	6.3
MSA[1]	178,609	113,409	278,016	296,970	145.1	6.8
U.S.	226,545,805	248,765,170	272,212,864	283,625,312	9.4	4.2

Note: (1) Metropolitan Statistical Area - see Appendix A for areas included
Source: 1990 Census of Population and Housing, Summary Tape File 3C; Claritas, Inc.

Number of Households and Average Household Size

Area	1980 Census	1990 Census	1999 Estimate	2004 Projection	1999 Average Household Size
City	13,653	17,009	22,259	23,615	2.47
MSA[1]	64,696	43,655	106,245	113,390	2.62
U.S.	80,389,592	91,993,582	102,048,200	107,302,392	2.67

Note: (1) Metropolitan Statistical Area - see Appendix A for areas included
Source: 1990 Census of Population and Housing, Summary Tape File 3C; Claritas, Inc.

Race/Ethnicity of City Population

Race/Ethnicity	1990 Census Population	1990 Census %	1999 Estimate Population	1999 Estimate %	% Change 1990-1999
White, Non-Hispanic	38,830	92.2	49,276	89.6	26.9
Black, Non-Hispanic	1,476	3.5	2,330	4.2	57.9
Asian, Non-Hispanic	642	1.5	1,091	2.0	69.9
Other, Non-Hispanic	533	1.3	570	1.0	6.9
Hispanic	614	1.5	1,734	3.2	182.4

Source: 1990 Census of Population and Housing, Summary Tape File 3C; Claritas, Inc.

Race/Ethnicity of Metropolitan Statistical Area Population

Race/Ethnicity	1990 Census		1999 Estimate		% Change 1990-1999
	Population	%	Population	%	
White, Non-Hispanic	107,778	95.0	260,246	93.6	141.5
Black, Non-Hispanic	1,540	1.4	2,596	0.9	68.6
Asian, Non-Hispanic	1,026	0.9	2,479	0.9	141.6
Other, Non-Hispanic	1,588	1.4	3,409	1.2	114.7
Hispanic	1,477	1.3	9,286	3.3	528.7

Note: See Appendix A for areas included in the Metropolitan Statistical Area
Source: 1990 Census of Population and Housing, Summary Tape File 3C; Claritas, Inc.

Ancestry

Area	German	Irish	English	Italian	U.S.	French	Polish	Dutch
City	24.4	20.2	20.0	2.2	6.6	4.6	1.1	3.4
MSA[1]	23.3	22.4	17.4	2.2	11.7	4.3	1.0	4.2
U.S.	23.3	15.6	13.1	5.9	5.3	4.2	3.8	2.5

Note: Figures are percentages and include persons that reported multiple ancestry (eg. if a person reported being Irish and Italian, they were included in both columns); (1) Metropolitan Statistical Area - see Appendix A for areas included
Source: 1990 Census of Population and Housing, Summary Tape File 3C

Median Age

Area	1990 Census	1999 Estimate
City	26.7	31.1
MSA[1]	30.7	36.1
U.S.	32.9	35.7

Note: (1) Metropolitan Statistical Area - see Appendix A for areas included
Source: 1990 Census of Population and Housing, Summary Tape File 3C; Claritas, Inc.

Male/Female Population

Area	Number of Males		Number of Females		Males per 100 Females	
	1990	1999	1990	1999	1990	1999
City	21,072	27,557	21,023	27,444	100.2	100.4
MSA[1]	56,086	136,404	57,323	141,612	97.8	96.3
U.S.	121,172,379	132,803,736	127,537,494	139,409,136	95.0	95.3

Note: (1) Metropolitan Statistical Area - see Appendix A for areas included
Source: 1990 Census of Population, General Population Characteristics; Claritas, Inc.

INCOME

Per Capita/Median/Average Income

Area	Per Capita ($)			Median Household ($)			Average Household ($)		
	1989	1999	% Chg.	1989	1999	% Chg.	1989	1999	% Chg.
City	12,184	18,957	55.6	21,202	30,622	44.4	29,617	46,895	58.3
MSA[1]	11,625	18,228	56.8	23,124	35,233	52.4	30,010	47,643	58.8
U.S.	14,420	21,350	48.1	30,056	40,525	34.8	38,453	56,184	46.1

Note: (1) Metropolitan Statistical Area - see Appendix A for areas included; 1989 data is from the 1990 Census; 1999 data is estimated by Claritas, Inc.
Source: 1990 Census of Population, General Population Characteristics; Claritas, Inc.

Household Income Distribution

Area	Percent of Households Earning								
	Under $5,000	$5,000 -14,999	$15,000 -24,999	$25,000 -34,999	$35,000 -49,999	$50,000 -74,999	$75,000 -99,000	$100,000 -149,999	$150,000 and up
City	6.5	17.9	17.8	13.7	14.5	14.5	7.0	4.5	3.5
MSA[1]	3.7	13.1	17.2	15.6	19.0	18.6	6.5	3.9	2.4
U.S.	3.9	13.3	13.8	12.6	16.2	19.4	9.7	6.6	4.6

Note: Data as of 1999; (1) Metropolitan Statistical Area - see Appendix A for areas included
Source: Claritas, Inc.

Effective Buying Income

Area	Per Capita ($)	Median Household ($)	Average Household ($)
City	16,224	28,349	38,952
MSA[1]	16,489	33,420	42,091
U.S.	17,496	36,603	47,036

Note: Data as of 1/1/2000; (1) Metropolitan Statistical Area - see Appendix A for areas included
Source: Standard Rate & Data Service, Newspaper Advertising Source, March 2000

Effective Household Buying Income Distribution

Area	% of Households Earning						
	$10,000 -$19,999	$20,000 -$34,999	$35,000 -$49,999	$50,000 -$74,999	$75,000 -$99,000	$100,000 -$124,999	$125,000 and up
City	19.5	23.5	15.1	14.6	5.9	2.0	2.6
MSA[1]	16.5	25.9	19.3	17.9	6.0	2.0	2.2
U.S.	15.0	21.6	17.6	19.6	8.4	3.0	3.3

Note: Data as of 1/1/2000; (1) Metropolitan Statistical Area - see Appendix A for areas included
Source: Standard Rate & Data Service, Newspaper Advertising Source, March 2000

Poverty Rates by Age

Area	People of All Ages	People Under 18 Years Old	Related Children Age 5-17 in Families in Poverty
City	15.2	n/a	n/a
County	12.4	17.4	16.3
U.S.	13.8	20.8	18.7

Note: Figures show the percent of people living below the poverty line in 1995. The average poverty threshold was $15,569 for a family of four in 1995; n/a not available
Source: Bureau of the Census, Small Area Income and Poverty Estimates Program; U.S. Department of Housing and Urban Development

EMPLOYMENT

Labor Force and Employment

Area	Civilian Labor Force			Workers Employed		
	Dec. 1998	Dec. 1999	% Chg.	Dec. 1998	Dec. 1999	% Chg.
City	29,220	30,159	3.2	28,253	29,411	4.1
MSA[1]	143,802	148,826	3.5	139,779	145,509	4.1
U.S.	138,297,000	139,941,000	1.2	132,732,000	134,696,000	1.5

Note: Data is not seasonally adjusted and covers workers 16 years of age and older;
(1) Metropolitan Statistical Area - see Appendix A for areas included
Source: Bureau of Labor Statistics, http://stats.bls.gov

Unemployment Rate

Area	1999											
	Jan.	Feb.	Mar.	Apr.	May	Jun.	Jul.	Aug.	Sep.	Oct.	Nov.	Dec.
City	3.7	3.3	2.8	2.4	2.5	3.0	3.3	3.2	2.6	2.4	2.3	2.5
MSA[1]	3.3	3.0	2.6	2.3	2.3	2.6	2.8	2.8	2.3	2.1	2.1	2.2
U.S.	4.8	4.7	4.4	4.1	4.0	4.5	4.5	4.2	4.1	3.8	3.8	3.7

Note: Data is not seasonally adjusted and covers workers 16 years of age and older; all figures are percentages; (1) Metropolitan Statistical Area - see Appendix A for areas included
Source: Bureau of Labor Statistics, http://stats.bls.gov

Employment by Industry

Sector	MSA[1]		U.S.
	Number of Employees	Percent of Total	Percent of Total
Services	30,500	20.1	30.2
Retail Trade	38,400	25.3	18.1
Government	19,900	13.1	15.8
Manufacturing	35,100	23.1	14.1
Finance/Insurance/Real Estate	5,500	3.6	5.9
Wholesale Trade	5,500	3.6	5.4
Transportation/Public Utilities	10,800	7.1	5.3
Construction	n/a	n/a	4.8
Mining	n/a	n/a	0.4

Note: Figures cover non-farm employment as of 12/99 and are not seasonally adjusted; (1) Metropolitan Statistical Area - see Appendix A for areas included; n/a not available
Source: Bureau of Labor Statistics, http://stats.bls.gov

Employment by Occupation

Occupation Category	City (%)	MSA[1] (%)	U.S. (%)
White Collar	65.7	53.3	58.1
Executive/Admin./Management	12.7	10.6	12.3
Professional	20.6	13.0	14.1
Technical & Related Support	4.1	3.3	3.7
Sales	14.2	12.6	11.8
Administrative Support/Clerical	14.1	13.8	16.3
Blue Collar	19.4	30.0	26.2
Precision Production/Craft/Repair	7.2	11.6	11.3
Machine Operators/Assem./Insp.	6.0	8.3	6.8
Transportation/Material Movers	2.9	5.0	4.1
Cleaners/Helpers/Laborers	3.4	5.2	3.9
Services	13.3	12.1	13.2
Farming/Forestry/Fishing	1.6	4.5	2.5

Note: Figures cover workers 16 years of age and older; (1) Metropolitan Statistical Area - see Appendix A for areas included
Source: 1990 Census of Population and Housing, Summary Tape File 3C

Occupational Employment Projections: 1996 - 2006

Occupations Expected to Have the Largest Job Growth (ranked by numerical growth)	Fast-Growing Occupations[1] (ranked by percent growth)
1. Truck drivers, light	1. Database administrators
2. Salespersons, retail	2. Systems analysts
3. Cashiers	3. Personal and home care aides
4. Nursing aides/orderlies/attendants	4. Occupational therapists
5. Registered nurses	5. Physical therapy assistants and aides
6. General managers & top executives	6. Home health aides
7. Child care workers, private household	7. Computer engineers
8. Home health aides	8. Respiratory therapists
9. Marketing & sales, supervisors	9. Physical therapists
10. Teachers, secondary school	10. Medical records technicians

Note: Projections cover Arkansas; (1) Excludes occupations with total job growth less than 300
Source: U.S. Department of Labor, Employment and Training Administration, America's Labor Market Information System (ALMIS)

Average Wages

Occupation	$/Hr.	Occupation	$/Hr.
Accountants and Auditors	18.16	Maids and Housekeepers	6.30
Assemblers and Fabricators	8.08	Maintenance Repairers	9.84
Automotive Mechanics	11.69	Marketing/Advertising/PR Managers	24.69
Bookkeepers	9.61	Nurses, Licensed Practical	11.20
Carpenters	11.56	Nurses, Registered	16.63
Cashiers	7.12	Nursing Aides/Orderlies/Attendants	7.13
Clerks, General Office	8.76	Physicians and Surgeons	50.45
Clerks, Shipping/Receiving/Traffic	10.21	Receptionists/Information Clerks	7.98
Computer Programmers	22.64	Sales Reps., Exc. Scientific/Retail	17.08
Computer Support Specialists	16.16	Sales Reps., Scientific, Exc. Retail	24.30
Cooks, Restaurant	7.26	Salespersons, Retail	8.29
Electricians	12.30	Secretaries, Except Legal/Medical	8.85
Financial Managers	22.74	Stock Clerks, Sales Floor	7.11
First-Line Supervisors/Mgrs., Sales	13.36	Systems Analysts	21.96
Food Preparation Workers	6.37	Teacher Aides	6.12
General Managers/Top Executives	24.65	Teachers, Elementary School	18.58
Guards	7.44	Teachers, Secondary School	18.08
Hand Packers	7.22	Telemarketers	7.82
Janitors and Cleaners	7.20	Truck Drivers, Heavy/Tractor-Trailer	13.09
Laborers, Landscaping	7.79	Truck Drivers, Light	8.46
Lawyers	21.24	Waiters and Waitresses	5.81

Note: Wage data is for 1998 and covers the Metropolitan Statistical Area (see Appendix A for areas included). Hourly wages for elementary and secondary school teachers were calculated by the editors from annual wage data assuming a 40 hour work week; Dashes indicate that data was not available.
Source: Bureau of Labor Statistics, 1998 Metropolitan Area Occupational Employment and Wage Estimates

TAXES

Major State and Local Tax Rates

State Corporate Income (%)	State Personal Income (%)	Residential Property (%)	Sales & Use		State Gasoline (cents/ gallon)	State Cigarette (cents/ pack)
			State (%)	Local (%)		
1.0 - 6.5	1.0 - 7.0[a]	1.03	4.625	1.875	19.7[b]	31.5[c]

Note: Personal/corporate income, sales, gasoline and cigarette tax rates as of January 2000. Property tax rates as of April 2000; (a) A special tax table is available for low income taxpayers reducing their tax payments; (b) Rate is comprised of 19.5 cents excise plus 0.2 cent motor carrier tax. The tax rate will increase to 20.5 cents on July 1, 2000; (c) A $1.25/1,000 cigarette fee is imposed
Source: Federation of Tax Administrators, www.taxadmin.org; ERI's Relocation Assessor software database, quarterly effective date 4/1/2000

Total Taxes Per Capita and as a Percent of Income

Area	Per Capita Income ($)	Per Capita Taxes ($)			Percent of Income (%)		
		Total	Federal	State/Local	Total	Federal	State/Local
Arkansas	22,051	7,219	4,852	2,367	32.7	22.0	10.7
U.S.	28,878	10,298	7,026	3,273	35.7	24.3	11.3

Note: Figures are for 1999
Source: Tax Foundation, www.taxfoundation.org

COMMERCIAL UTILITIES

Typical Monthly Electric Bills

Area	Commercial Service ($/month)		Industrial Service ($/month)	
	12 kW demand 1,500 kWh	100 kW demand 30,000 kWh	1,000 kW demand 400,000 kWh	20,000 kW demand 10,000,000 kWh
City	n/a	n/a	n/a	n/a
U.S.	150	2,174	23,995	508,569

Note: Based on rates in effect January 1, 1999; n/a not available
Source: Edison Electric Institute, Typical Residential, Commercial and Industrial Bills, Winter 1999

TRANSPORTATION

Transportation Statistics

Average minutes to work (1990)	13.7
Interstate highways	US-71; US-62
Bus lines	
In-city (1998)	Community Resource Group, 27 demand response vehicles
Inter-city (1999)	1
Passenger air service	
Airport	Northwest Arkansas Regional
Airlines (1999)	5
Enplaned passengers (1998)	27,026
Amtrak service	No
Motor freight carriers (1999)	4
Major waterways/ports	None

Source: FAA DOT/TSC CY1998 ACAIS Database; National Transit Database, 1998; Editor & Publisher Market Guide, 2000; Amtrak National Time Table, Fall 1999/Winter 2000; 1990 Census of Population and Housing, STF 3C; Jane's Urban Transport Systems 1999-2000

Means of Transportation to Work

Area	Car/Truck/Van		Public Transportation			Bicycle	Walked	Other Means	Worked at Home
	Drove Alone	Car-pooled	Bus	Subway	Railroad				
City	77.5	12.6	0.9	0.0	0.0	0.2	5.4	0.7	2.6
MSA[1]	77.7	13.7	0.4	0.0	0.0	0.2	3.2	0.9	4.0
U.S.	73.2	13.4	3.0	1.5	0.5	0.4	3.9	1.2	3.0

Note: Figures shown are percentages and only include workers 16 years of age and older;
(1) Metropolitan Statistical Area - see Appendix A for areas included
Source: 1990 Census of Population and Housing, Summary Tape File 3C

BUSINESSES

Major Business Headquarters

Company Name	1999 Rankings	
	Fortune 500	Forbes 500
No companies listed	-	-

Note: Companies listed are located in the city; dashes indicate no ranking
Fortune 500: Companies that produce a 10-K are ranked 1 to 500 based on 1999 revenue
Forbes 500: Private companies are ranked 1 to 500 based on 1998 revenue
Source: Forbes, December 13, 1999; Fortune, April 17, 2000

HOTELS & MOTELS

Hotels/Motels

Area	Hotels/ Motels	Rooms	Luxury-Level Hotels/Motels		Average Minimum Rates ($)		
			♦♦♦♦	♦♦♦♦♦	♦♦	♦♦♦	♦♦♦♦
City	9	1,048	0	0	n/a	n/a	n/a
Suburbs	1	120	0	0	n/a	n/a	n/a
Total	10	1,168	0	0	n/a	n/a	n/a

Note: n/a not available; classifications range from one diamond (budget properties with basic amenities) to five diamond (luxury properties).
Source: OAG Business Travel Planner, Winter 1999-2000

Estimated Daily Food and Lodging Costs

Area	Food/Other ($/day)	Average Hotel Cost ($/day)
City	30	55
U.S.	30	55

Source: ERI's Relocation Assessor software database, quarterly effective date 4/1/2000

CONVENTION CENTERS

Convention Centers and Event Sites

Name	Guest Rooms	Meeting Space (sq. ft.)	Capacity (Theatre Style)
Clarion Fayetteville	197	n/a	400
Fayetteville Hilton	235	13,000	700
Univ. of Ark. Center for Continuing Ed.	n/a	n/a	0

Note: n/a not available
Source: EventSource.com, 3/15/2000

Living Environment

COST OF LIVING

Cost of Living: Homeowner

Cost Element	U.S. ($)	City ($)	Differential ($)	Percent of U.S. Average
Consumables	14,516	13,422	-1,094	92.5
Transportation	5,957	5,362	-595	90.0
Health Services	2,012	1,857	-155	92.3
Housing/Utilities/Prop. Tax	16,337	15,006	-1,331	91.9
Income+Payroll Taxes	12,615	13,623	1,008	108.0
Miscellaneous	8,563	8,563	0	100.0
Total Cost of Living	60,000	57,833	-2,167	96.4

Note: Figures are based on a single income, four person family with gross annual earnings of $60,000, owning an 1,800 square-foot home, and driving two automobiles worth $22,000 30,000 miles per year.
Source: ERI's Relocation Assessor software database, quarterly effective date 4/1/2000

Cost of Living: Renter

Cost Element	U.S. ($)	City ($)	Differential ($)	Percent of U.S. Average
Consumables	10,486	9,736	-750	92.8
Transportation	2,107	1,904	-203	90.4
Health Services	1,632	1,513	-119	92.7
Rent/Utilities/Insurance	9,299	7,459	-1,840	80.2
Income+Payroll Taxes	8,607	9,191	584	106.8
Miscellaneous	7,869	7,869	0	100.0
Total Cost of Living	40,000	37,672	-2,328	94.2

Note: Figures are based on a single income, three person family with gross annual earnings of $40,000, renting a 1,000 square-foot home, and driving one automobile worth $8,000 12,000 miles per year.
Source: ERI's Relocation Assessor software database, quarterly effective date 4/1/2000

HOUSING

Median Home Prices and Housing Affordability

Area	Median Price[2] 4th Qtr. 1999 ($)	HOI[3] 4th Qtr. 1999	Affordability Rank[4]
MSA[1]	n/a	n/a	n/a
U.S.	139,000	63.8	–

Note: (1) Metropolitan Statistical Area - see Appendix A for areas included; (2) U.S. figures calculated from the sales of 687,516 new and existing homes in 192 markets; (3) Housing Opportunity Index - percent of homes sold that were within the reach of the median income household at the prevailing mortgage interest rate; (4) Rank is from 1-192 with 1 being most affordable; n/a not available
Source: National Association of Home Builders, Housing Opportunity Index, 4th Quarter 1999

Estimated Home Price

Area	Price ($)
City	127,327
U.S.	135,855

Note: Figures are based on an 1,800 square-foot home
Source: ERI's Relocation Assessor software database, quarterly effective date 4/1/2000

Estimated Rent

Area	Rent ($/month)
City	504
U.S.	651

Note: Figures are based on a 1,000 square-foot home
Source: ERI's Relocation Assessor software database, quarterly effective date 4/1/2000

Median Home Price Projection

It is projected that the median home price in the metropolitan area will increase from $134,649 in 1999 to $200,008 in 2010, an increase of 48.5%
Kiplinger's Personal Finance Magazine, January 2000

RESIDENTIAL UTILITIES

Average Residential Utility Costs

Area	All Electric ($/mth)	Part Electric ($/mth)	Other Energy ($/mth)	Phone ($/mth)
City	–	49.36	33.71	22.80
U.S.	99.25	55.47	43.48	20.29

Source: ACCRA, Cost of Living Index, 3rd Quarter 1999

HEALTH CARE

Average Health Care Costs

Area	Hospital ($/day)	Doctor ($/visit)	Dentist ($/visit)
City	265.00	48.20	69.75
U.S.	440.96	53.83	68.42

Note: Hospital—based on a semi-private room; Doctor—based on a general practitioner's routine exam of an established patient; Dentist—based on adult teeth cleaning and periodic oral exam.
Source: ACCRA, Cost of Living Index, 3rd Quarter 1999

Distribution of Office-Based Physicians

Area	Family/Gen. Practitioners	Specialists Medical	Specialists Surgical	Specialists Other
MSA[1]	97	93	102	88

Note: Data as of 12/31/97; (1) Metropolitan Statistical Area - see Appendix A for areas included
Source: American Medical Assn., Physician Characteristics & Distribution in the U.S., 1999

Hospitals

Fayetteville has 2 general medical and surgical hospitals, 1 psychiatric, 1 rehabilitation.
AHA Guide to the Healthcare Field, 1999-2000

EDUCATION

Public School District Statistics

District Name	Num. Sch.	Enroll.	Classroom Teachers	Pupils per Teacher	Minority Pupils (%)	Current Exp.[1] ($/pupil)
Fayetteville School District	14	7,742	429	18.0	n/a	n/a

Note: Data covers the 1997-1998 school year unless otherwise noted; (1) Data covers fiscal year 1996; SD = School District; ISD = Independent School District; n/a not available
Source: National Center for Education Statistics, Common Core of Data Public Education Agency Universe 1997-98; National Center for Education Statistics, Characteristics of the 100 Largest Public Elementary and Secondary School Districts in the United States: 1997-98, July 1999

Educational Quality

School District	Education Quotient[1]	Graduate Outcome[2]	Community Index[3]	Resource Index[4]
Fayetteville School Dist.	112	138	84	66

Note: Over 1,000 secondary school districts were rated in terms of educational quality. The scores range from a low of 50 to a high of 150; (1) Combination of the Graduate Outcome, Community and Resource indexes weighted to reflect the greater importance of the Graduate Outcome and Resource Index; (2) Based on graduation rates and college board scores (SAT/ACT); (3) Based on the surrounding community's level of affluence and adult education; (4) Based on teacher salaries, per-pupil expenditures and student-teacher ratios.
Source: Expansion Management, Ratings Issue, 1999

Educational Attainment by Race

Area	High School Graduate (%)					Bachelor's Degree (%)				
	Total	White	Black	Other	Hisp.[2]	Total	White	Black	Other	Hisp.[2]
City	84.3	84.5	78.7	81.3	75.5	36.0	36.3	22.5	38.1	22.4
MSA[1]	73.2	73.2	79.0	72.4	63.4	20.0	19.8	23.0	27.0	17.2
U.S.	75.2	77.9	63.1	60.4	49.8	20.3	21.5	11.4	19.4	9.2

Note: Figures shown cover persons 25 years old and over; (1) Metropolitan Statistical Area - see Appendix A for areas included; (2) people of Hispanic origin can be of any race
Source: 1990 Census of Population and Housing, Summary Tape File 3C

School Enrollment by Type

Area	Preprimary				Elementary/High School			
	Public		Private		Public		Private	
	Enrollment	%	Enrollment	%	Enrollment	%	Enrollment	%
City	338	48.6	358	51.4	4,946	94.5	289	5.5
MSA[1]	873	55.1	710	44.9	17,397	95.3	850	4.7
U.S.	2,679,029	59.5	1,824,256	40.5	38,379,689	90.2	4,187,099	9.8

Note: Figures shown cover persons 3 years old and over;
(1) Metropolitan Statistical Area - see Appendix A for areas included
Source: 1990 Census of Population and Housing, Summary Tape File 3C

School Enrollment by Race

Area	Preprimary (%)				Elementary/High School (%)			
	White	Black	Other	Hisp.[1]	White	Black	Other	Hisp.[1]
City	90.7	6.8	2.6	0.0	93.1	3.9	3.0	3.2
MSA[2]	94.8	3.1	2.1	2.3	95.7	1.2	3.1	2.1
U.S.	80.4	12.5	7.1	7.8	74.1	15.6	10.3	12.5

Note: Figures shown cover persons 3 years old and over; (1) people of Hispanic origin can be of any race; (2) Metropolitan Statistical Area - see Appendix A for areas included
Source: 1990 Census of Population and Housing, Summary Tape File 3C

Higher Education

Two-Year Colleges		Four-Year Colleges		Medical Schools	Law Schools	Voc/ Tech
Public	Private	Public	Private			
0	1	1	0	0	1	4

Source: College Blue Book, Occupational Education, 1999; Medical School Admission Requirements, 1999-2000; Peterson's Guide to Two-Year Colleges, 2000; Peterson's Guide to Four-Year Colleges, 1999; Barron's Guide to Law Schools, 1999

MAJOR EMPLOYERS

Major Employers

Arkansas Book Store	Arkansas Western Gas
Lewis Management	Pace Industries (aluminum die casting)
Southwestern Energy	Staffmark (employment agency)
Twin Rivers Group (poultry)	Washington Regional Medical Center

Note: Companies listed are located in the city
Source: D&B Business Rankings, 1999; Ward's Business Directory, 1999; America's Corporate Families, 1999

PUBLIC SAFETY

Crime Rate

Area	All Crimes	Violent Crimes				Property Crimes		
		Murder	Forcible Rape	Robbery	Aggrav. Assault	Burglary	Larceny -Theft	Motor Vehicle Theft
City	4,770.5	1.9	54.2	69.2	222.5	916.3	3,310.0	196.4
Suburbs[1]	n/a	n/a	n/a	n/a	n/a	n/a	n/a	n/a
MSA[2]	n/a	n/a	n/a	n/a	n/a	n/a	n/a	n/a
U.S.	4,615.5	6.3	34.4	165.2	360.5	862.0	2,728.1	459.0

Note: Crime rate is the number of crimes per 100,000 population; (1) Defined as all areas within the Metropolitan Statistical Area but located outside the central city; (2) Metropolitan Statistical Area - see Appendix A for areas included; n/a not available
Source: FBI Uniform Crime Reports, 1998

RECREATION

Culture and Recreation

Museums	Symphony Orchestras	Opera Companies	Dance Companies	Professional Theatres	Zoos	Pro Sports Teams
2	1	0	0	0	0	0

Source: Musical America, International Directory of the Performing Arts, 1999; Official Museum Directory, 2000; Stern's Performing Arts Directory, 1997; USA Today Four Sport Stadium Guide, 1997; Career Opportunities in Theatre and the Performing Arts, 1999

Library System

The Fayetteville Public Library has no branches, holdings of 120,000 volumes, and a budget of $952,362 (1997-1998).
American Library Directory, 1999-2000

MEDIA

Newspapers

Name	Type	Freq.	Distribution	Circulation
Northwest Arkansas Times	General	7x/wk	Area	15,121

Note: Includes newspapers with circulations of 200 or more located in the city;
Source: Burrelle's Media Directory, 1999 Edition

Television Stations

Name	Ch.	Affiliation	Type	Owner
KHOG	29	n/a	Commercial	Hearst-Argyle Broadcasting
KSBN	57	n/a	Commercial	Total Life Community Educational Foundation Inc.

Note: Stations included broadcast in the Fayetteville metro area; n/a not available
Source: Burrelle's Media Directory, 1999 Edition

AM Radio Stations

Call Letters	Freq. (kHz)	Target Audience	Station Format	Music Format
KFAY	1030	General	N/S/T	n/a
KOFC	1250	Religious	E/M/N/S/T	Christian
KREB	1390	General	M	n/a
KZRA	1590	G/H	n/a	n/a

Note: Stations included broadcast in the Fayetteville metro area; n/a not available
Target Audience: A=Asian; B=Black; C=Christian; E=Ethnic; F=French; G=General; H=Hispanic; M=Men; N=Native American; R=Religious; S=Senior Citizen; W=Women; Y=Young Adult; Z=Children
Station Format: E=Educational; M=Music; N=News; S=Sports; T=Talk
Source: Burrelle's Media Directory, 1999 Edition

FM Radio Stations

Call Letters	Freq. (mHz)	Target Audience	Station Format	Music Format
KUAF	91.3	General	E/M/N	Classical/Jazz/Rhythm & Blues
KKEG	92.1	Men	M	AOR/Classic Rock
KJEM	93.3	General	M/N/S/T	Classic Rock
KDAB	94.9	Religious	E/M/N	Christian
KFAY	98.3	General	M	Country
KREB	99.5	General	S	n/a
KMXF	101.9	General	M	Adult Top 40
KKIX	103.9	General	M/N	Country
KBRS	104.9	General	M	Alternative
KMCK	105.7	General	M	n/a
KEZA	107.9	General	M/N/S	Adult Contemporary/Oldies

Note: Stations included broadcast in the Fayetteville metro area; n/a not available
Station Format: E=Educational; M=Music; N=News; S=Sports; T=Talk
Target Audience: A=Asian; B=Black; C=Christian; E=Ethnic; F=French; G=General; H=Hispanic; M=Men; N=Native American; R=Religious; S=Senior Citizen; W=Women; Y=Young Adult; Z=Children
Music Format: AOR=Album Oriented Rock; MOR=Middle-of-the-Road
Source: Burrelle's Media Directory, 1999 Edition

WEATHER

Temperature/Precipitation/Humidity

	Jan	Feb	Mar	Apr	May	Jun	Jul	Aug	Sep	Oct	Nov	Dec	Yr.
Max. High Temp. (°F)	77	83	85	90	92	101	110	105	102	96	82	78	110
Avg. High Temp. (°F)	49	52	57	69	77	86	89	89	84	73	59	51	70
Avg. Temp. (°F)	37	40	45	57	65	74	78	76	70	59	45	38	57
Avg. Low Temp. (°F)	26	29	34	45	54	63	67	64	56	45	32	26	45
Min. Low Temp. (°F)	-6	-15	8	19	30	41	50	45	34	17	9	-7	-15
Avg. Precip. (in.)	2.3	3.3	3.5	4.8	7.0	4.6	5.4	3.2	3.5	3.0	2.9	2.2	45.5
Avg. Snowfall (in.)	3.0	2.7	1.2	0.1	0	0	0	0	0	0	0.7	0.9	8.6
Avg. Rel. Hum. (%)	72	67	62	63	71	71	71	71	69	70	64	68	68

Source: National Climatic Data Center, International Station Meteorological Climate Summary, 3/95

Weather Conditions

Temperature			Precipitation		
0°F & below	32°F & below	90°F & above	0.1 inch or more precip.	1.5 inch or more snow/ice	Thunder-storms
1	105	57	75	2	56

Note: Figures are average number of days per year
Source: National Climatic Data Center, International Station Meteorological Climate Summary, 3/95

AIR & WATER QUALITY

Maximum Pollutant Concentrations

	Particulate Matter (ug/m³)	Carbon Monoxide (ppm)	Sulfur Dioxide (ppm)	Nitrogen Dioxide (ppm)	Ozone (ppm)	Lead (ug/m³)
MSA[1] Level	36	n/a	n/a	n/a	n/a	n/a
NAAQS[2]	150	9	0.140	0.053	0.12	1.50
Met NAAQS	Yes	n/a	n/a	n/a	n/a	n/a

Note: (1) Metropolitan Statistical Area - see Appendix A for areas included; (2) National Ambient Air Quality Standards; ppm = parts per million; ug/m³ = micrograms per cubic meter; n/a not available
Source: EPA, National Air Quality and Emissions Trends Report, 1997

Pollutant Standards Index

Data not available.
EPA, National Air Quality and Emissions Trends Report, 1997

Drinking Water

Water System Name	Pop. Served	Primary Water Source Type	Number of Violations in 1998-99	Type of Violation/ Contaminants
Fayetteville Waterworks	56,918	Purchased surface	1	(1)

Note: Data as of January 19, 2000; (1) Monthly Maximum Contaminant Level (TCR) violation—for systems testing more than 40 samples, more than five percent tested positive for Total Coliform or for those systems testing less than 40 samples more than one sample tested positive for Total Coliform (1 violation in 1999).
Source: EPA, Office of Ground Water and Drinking Water, Safe Drinking Water Information System

Fayetteville tap water is alkaline and soft.
Editor & Publisher Market Guide, 2000

Fort Myers, Florida

Background

Fort Myers, Florida is located in southwest Florida, about 150 miles west of Miami. It is situated on the Caloosahatchee River, an inlet of the Gulf of Mexico, which is about 15 wiles west of the city. Fort Meyers is between the river and waters of the Gulf of Mexico that include harbors, bays and inlets, with numerous islands nearby.

Fort Myers is the county seat of Lee County. With Cape Coral and other nearby communities it is a commercial and population center in southwest Florida, with a regional economy based on agriculture, manufacturing, business services and other activities. It is also popular for tourism and retirement and seasonal homes, with numerous beaches, golf courses and other waterfront and inland recreational facilities, and other attractions.

During wars with the Seminoles, a riverfront U.S. military post was established at the city's site in 1841, later named after Colonel Abraham C. Myers. The post was intermittently used, and was closed after the Civil War. Scattered settlement developed at the site, and the town was established in 1876. It was originally named Meyers, before being changed back to Fort Meyers in 1901. It evolved as a trade center for the region. Regional agriculture including citrus and flowers became important activities. Thomas Edison established a home and laboratory there in the early 1880s. Henry Ford also spent time in Fort Meyers. The area subsequently became popular with vacationers, seasonal residents and retirees.

In the 20th Century, presence of military facilities in the region stimulated growth and development. The region has experienced growth of other activities related to electronics and other technology, health care and medical services and other industries. Other activities include manufacturing, business and professional services, construction and retailing, among others.

Fort Meyers is a mix of newer development and older neighborhoods, including the historic downtown district. Fort Meyers Historical Museum and the homes of Henry Ford and Thomas Edison are among the historical attractions. The Harborside Convention Center is a multi-use facility. Imaginarium is a museum for young people. The area has numerous parks and other facilities for golf, boating, fishing and other recreational activities. Exploration and sightseeing in regional swampland and other sites are also popular.

Fort Meyers has an elected Mayor and City Council.

General Rankings and Evaluative Comments

- Fort Myers was ranked #92 out of 354 metropolitan areas in *Places Rated Almanac*. Criteria: cost of living, climate, crime, transportation, job outlook, education, the arts, health care, and recreation. *Places Rated Almanac, Millennium Edition, 2000*

- Fort Myers was selected as one of America's best places to retire. Criteria: safety, climate, housing, culture and recreation, social compatibility, affordability, medical care, transportation, and jobs and/or volunteer opportunities. *Where to Retire: America's Best and Most Affordable Places, 1998*

- Fort Myers was selected as one of the best places to retire by *Retirement Places Rated*. Criteria: cost of living, climate, crime, services, working, and leisure living. The city was ranked #10 out of 187. *Retirement Places Rated, 1999*

- Cognetics studied 273 metro areas in the United States, ranking them by entrepreneurial activity. Fort Myers was ranked #45 out of 134 smaller metro areas. Criteria: Significant Starts (firms started in the last 10 years that still employ at least 5 people) and Young Growers (percent of firms 10 years old or less that grew significantly during the last 4 years). *Cognetics, "Entrepreneurial Hot Spots: The Best Places in America to Start and Grow a Company," 1999*

- Reliastar Financial Corporation ranked the 125 largest metropolitan areas according to the general financial security of residents. Fort Myers was ranked #55 out of 125 with a score of 3.9 (the percentage a metropolitan area is above or below the metropolitan norm; a metro area with a score of 10.6 is 10.6% above the metro average). Criteria: Earnings and Wealth Potential (household income, education, net assets, cost of living); Safety Net (health insurance, retirement savings, life insurance, income support programs); Personal Threats (unemployment rate, low-income households, crime rate); Community Economic Vitality (cost of community services, job quality, job creation, housing costs). Reliastar Financial Corporation, "The Best Cities to Earn and Save Money: A Ranking of the Largest 125 U.S. Cities," 2000 Edition

- Fort Myers was selected as a first-round winner in the small city category for its Neighborhood Shade Tree Program by the U.S Conference of Mayors and Waste Management as part of their 2000 City Livability Awards Program. The program honors mayors and their city governments for developing programs that enhance the quality of life in urban areas. The awards are given annually to ten mayors and their cities—a first-place award and four Outstanding Achievement Awards for cities under 100,000 population, and a first-place and four Outstanding Achievement Awards for cities of 100,000 or more inhabitants.

Business Environment

STATE ECONOMY

State Economic Profile

"Florida's economy has been among the nation's strongest in recent years. Job growth has outpaced the nation by a considerable amount since 1992.

While Florida has been able to avoid any significant fallout from the Asian crisis, the weakening of economies in Latin American will dampen both tourism and international trade. 1998 saw the decline in Latin tourism more than offset by domestic visitors. Domestic tourism is projected to soften as U.S. growth cools, offering no offset against the expected decline in Latin tourism. Weaker tourism and trade with Latin American will slow growth in the near future; Florida will still outpace the nation in job growth as Gross State Product growth (GSP) slows.

Over half of Florida's 230,000 new jobs created in 1998 were in the services sector, which grew at 5.2%, more than offsetting a minor decline in manufacturing employment. Much of this growth is taking place in the finance and business services sector.

In spite of strong home sales and a slowing construction market, Florida's price appreciation continued to lag the nation. Although residential permits per 1,000 residents stands at 5.1, well above the national average, this number is only slightly up from 1997 and is poised to decline in the near future.

Growth in Florida, while strong throughout, has been hottest in the Naples, Ft. Myers and Orlando areas. Construction and employment in the construction industry has begun to slow in South Florida. Projected employment and housing gains will be concentrated in Northern and Central Florida. Growing diversification of the economy into financial and business services promises a strong outlook for the years ahead." *National Association of Realtors, Economic Profiles: The Fifty States and the District of Columbia, http://nar.realtor.com/databank/profiles.htm*

EXPORTS

Total Export Sales

Area	1995 ($000)	1996 ($000)	1997 ($000)	1998 ($000)	% Chg. 1995-98	% Chg. 1997-98
MSA[1]	n/a	n/a	n/a	n/a	n/a	n/a
U.S.	583,030,524	622,827,063	687,597,999	680,474,251	16.7	-1.0

Note: (1) Metropolitan Statistical Area - see Appendix A for areas included
Source: U.S. Department of Commerce, International Trade Association, Metropolitan Area Exports: An Export Performance Report on Over 250 U.S. Cities, November 10, 1999

CITY FINANCES

City Government Finances

Component	1995 ($million)	1995 (per capita $)
Revenue	74.5	1,475
Expenditure	74.2	1,469
Debt Outstanding	236.2	4,677

Source: 1999 County and City Extra, Annual Metro, City, and County Data Book

City Government Revenue by Source

Source	1995 ($million)	1995 (per capita $)
Intergovernmental	8.3	164
Taxes	22.4	444
Property	9.6	191
Sales and Gross Receipts	10.7	213

Source: 1999 County and City Extra, Annual Metro, City, and County Data Book

City Government Expenditures by Function

Function	1995 ($million)	1995 (per capita $)	1995 (%)
Public Welfare	0.0	0	0.0
Highways	4.3	86	5.9
Parking Facilities	<0.1	1	0.1
Education	0.0	0	0.0
Health and Hospitals	0.0	0	0.0
Police Protection	10.7	213	14.5
Sewerage and Sanitation	10.3	204	13.9
Parks and Recreation	22.3	442	30.1
Housing and Community Development	3.1	61	4.2
Interest on Debt	0.8	16	1.1

Source: 1999 County and City Extra, Annual Metro, City, and County Data Book

Municipal Bond Ratings

Area	Moody's
City	Aaa

Source: Mergent Bond Record, 2/2000

POPULATION

Population Growth

Area	1980 Census	1990 Census	1999 Estimate	2004 Projection	Population Growth (%) 1990-1999	Population Growth (%) 1999-2004
City	36,638	45,206	44,013	44,468	-2.6	1.0
MSA[1]	205,266	335,113	403,863	435,111	20.5	7.7
U.S.	226,545,805	248,765,170	272,212,864	283,625,312	9.4	4.2

Note: (1) Metropolitan Statistical Area - see Appendix A for areas included
Source: 1990 Census of Population and Housing, Summary Tape File 3C; Claritas, Inc.

Number of Households and Average Household Size

Area	1980 Census	1990 Census	1999 Estimate	2004 Projection	1999 Average Household Size
City	15,245	18,134	17,726	18,085	2.48
MSA[1]	82,507	140,046	167,676	182,107	2.41
U.S.	80,389,592	91,993,582	102,048,200	107,302,392	2.67

Note: (1) Metropolitan Statistical Area - see Appendix A for areas included
Source: 1990 Census of Population and Housing, Summary Tape File 3C; Claritas, Inc.

Race/Ethnicity of City Population

Race/Ethnicity	1990 Census Population	1990 Census %	1999 Estimate Population	1999 Estimate %	% Change 1990-1999
White, Non-Hispanic	27,133	60.0	20,650	46.9	-23.9
Black, Non-Hispanic	14,166	31.3	17,733	40.3	25.2
Asian, Non-Hispanic	415	0.9	468	1.1	12.8
Other, Non-Hispanic	209	0.5	131	0.3	-37.3
Hispanic	3,283	7.3	5,031	11.4	53.2

Source: 1990 Census of Population and Housing, Summary Tape File 3C; Claritas, Inc.

Race/Ethnicity of Metropolitan Statistical Area Population

Race/Ethnicity	1990 Census		1999 Estimate		% Change 1990-1999
	Population	%	Population	%	
White, Non-Hispanic	296,163	88.4	339,906	84.2	14.8
Black, Non-Hispanic	21,416	6.4	31,889	7.9	48.9
Asian, Non-Hispanic	1,571	0.5	3,413	0.8	117.3
Other, Non-Hispanic	1,114	0.3	1,239	0.3	11.2
Hispanic	14,849	4.4	27,416	6.8	84.6

Note: See Appendix A for areas included in the Metropolitan Statistical Area
Source: 1990 Census of Population and Housing, Summary Tape File 3C; Claritas, Inc.

Ancestry

Area	German	Irish	English	Italian	U.S.	French	Polish	Dutch
City	18.7	12.5	13.6	3.7	3.5	3.9	1.9	2.0
MSA[1]	27.6	18.0	18.5	7.2	4.5	5.4	3.8	3.1
U.S.	23.3	15.6	13.1	5.9	5.3	4.2	3.8	2.5

Note: Figures are percentages and include persons that reported multiple ancestry (eg. if a person reported being Irish and Italian, they were included in both columns); (1) Metropolitan Statistical Area - see Appendix A for areas included
Source: 1990 Census of Population and Housing, Summary Tape File 3C

Median Age

Area	1990 Census	1999 Estimate
City	32.0	34.1
MSA[1]	42.0	43.7
U.S.	32.9	35.7

Note: (1) Metropolitan Statistical Area - see Appendix A for areas included
Source: 1990 Census of Population and Housing, Summary Tape File 3C; Claritas, Inc.

Male/Female Population

Area	Number of Males		Number of Females		Males per 100 Females	
	1990	1999	1990	1999	1990	1999
City	22,081	21,561	23,125	22,452	95.5	96.0
MSA[1]	162,110	195,316	173,003	208,547	93.7	93.7
U.S.	121,172,379	132,803,736	127,537,494	139,409,136	95.0	95.3

Note: (1) Metropolitan Statistical Area - see Appendix A for areas included
Source: 1990 Census of Population, General Population Characteristics; Claritas, Inc.

INCOME

Per Capita/Median/Average Income

Area	Per Capita ($)			Median Household ($)			Average Household ($)		
	1989	1999	% Chg.	1989	1999	% Chg.	1989	1999	% Chg.
City	12,329	16,866	36.8	22,102	28,362	28.3	29,577	40,468	36.8
MSA[1]	15,623	21,568	38.1	28,448	36,842	29.5	36,939	51,619	39.7
U.S.	14,420	21,350	48.1	30,056	40,525	34.8	38,453	56,184	46.1

Note: (1) Metropolitan Statistical Area - see Appendix A for areas included; 1989 data is from the 1990 Census; 1999 data is estimated by Claritas, Inc.
Source: 1990 Census of Population, General Population Characteristics; Claritas, Inc.

Household Income Distribution

Area	Percent of Households Earning								
	Under $5,000	$5,000 -14,999	$15,000 -24,999	$25,000 -34,999	$35,000 -49,999	$50,000 -74,999	$75,000 -99,000	$100,000 -149,999	$150,000 and up
City	5.7	18.4	19.8	15.5	17.5	13.6	4.9	2.3	2.4
MSA[1]	2.6	11.5	16.6	16.0	19.6	19.1	7.0	4.0	3.6
U.S.	3.9	13.3	13.8	12.6	16.2	19.4	9.7	6.6	4.6

Note: Data as of 1999; (1) Metropolitan Statistical Area - see Appendix A for areas included
Source: Claritas, Inc.

Effective Buying Income

Area	Per Capita ($)	Median Household ($)	Average Household ($)
City	14,177	25,712	35,702
MSA[1]	18,290	33,637	44,358
U.S.	17,496	36,603	47,036

Note: Data as of 1/1/2000; (1) Metropolitan Statistical Area - see Appendix A for areas included
Source: Standard Rate & Data Service, Newspaper Advertising Source, March 2000

Effective Household Buying Income Distribution

Area	% of Households Earning						
	$10,000 -$19,999	$20,000 -$34,999	$35,000 -$49,999	$50,000 -$74,999	$75,000 -$99,000	$100,000 -$124,999	$125,000 and up
City	21.6	26.6	16.6	11.4	3.6	1.1	2.4
MSA[1]	16.7	26.8	19.6	17.1	5.8	2.1	3.2
U.S.	15.0	21.6	17.6	19.6	8.4	3.0	3.3

Note: Data as of 1/1/2000; (1) Metropolitan Statistical Area - see Appendix A for areas included
Source: Standard Rate & Data Service, Newspaper Advertising Source, March 2000

Poverty Rates by Age

Area	People of All Ages	People Under 18 Years Old	Related Children Age 5-17 in Families in Poverty
City	28.0	n/a	n/a
County	11.6	19.8	17.4
U.S.	13.8	20.8	18.7

Note: Figures show the percent of people living below the poverty line in 1995. The average poverty threshold was $15,569 for a family of four in 1995; n/a not available
Source: Bureau of the Census, Small Area Income and Poverty Estimates Program; U.S. Department of Housing and Urban Development

EMPLOYMENT

Labor Force and Employment

Area	Civilian Labor Force			Workers Employed		
	Dec. 1998	Dec. 1999	% Chg.	Dec. 1998	Dec. 1999	% Chg.
City	25,608	25,854	1.0	24,696	24,970	1.1
MSA[1]	177,572	179,358	1.0	173,089	175,011	1.1
U.S.	138,297,000	139,941,000	1.2	132,732,000	134,696,000	1.5

Note: Data is not seasonally adjusted and covers workers 16 years of age and older; (1) Metropolitan Statistical Area - see Appendix A for areas included
Source: Bureau of Labor Statistics, http://stats.bls.gov

Unemployment Rate

Area	1999											
	Jan.	Feb.	Mar.	Apr.	May	Jun.	Jul.	Aug.	Sep.	Oct.	Nov.	Dec.
City	4.3	3.7	3.6	3.6	3.6	4.1	3.8	3.8	3.9	4.0	4.0	3.4
MSA[1]	3.0	2.6	2.6	2.5	2.6	2.9	2.7	2.7	2.8	2.8	2.8	2.4
U.S.	4.8	4.7	4.4	4.1	4.0	4.5	4.5	4.2	4.1	3.8	3.8	3.7

Note: Data is not seasonally adjusted and covers workers 16 years of age and older; all figures are percentages; (1) Metropolitan Statistical Area - see Appendix A for areas included
Source: Bureau of Labor Statistics, http://stats.bls.gov

Employment by Industry

Sector	MSA[1]		U.S.
	Number of Employees	Percent of Total	Percent of Total
Services	52,800	31.3	30.2
Retail Trade	42,000	24.9	18.1
Government	26,900	15.9	15.8
Manufacturing	7,100	4.2	14.1
Finance/Insurance/Real Estate	9,700	5.7	5.9
Wholesale Trade	6,200	3.7	5.4
Transportation/Public Utilities	8,300	4.9	5.3
Construction	15,500	9.2	4.8
Mining	n/a	n/a	0.4

Note: Figures cover non-farm employment as of 12/99 and are not seasonally adjusted;
(1) Metropolitan Statistical Area - see Appendix A for areas included; n/a not available
Source: Bureau of Labor Statistics, http://stats.bls.gov

Employment by Occupation

Occupation Category	City (%)	MSA[1] (%)	U.S. (%)
White Collar	52.3	57.5	58.1
Executive/Admin./Management	9.5	12.1	12.3
Professional	12.3	10.6	14.1
Technical & Related Support	3.6	3.0	3.7
Sales	13.7	16.3	11.8
Administrative Support/Clerical	13.2	15.5	16.3
Blue Collar	25.3	24.4	26.2
Precision Production/Craft/Repair	11.7	13.3	11.3
Machine Operators/Assem./Insp.	3.9	3.0	6.8
Transportation/Material Movers	5.3	4.1	4.1
Cleaners/Helpers/Laborers	4.4	4.0	3.9
Services	19.1	15.2	13.2
Farming/Forestry/Fishing	3.3	2.9	2.5

Note: Figures cover workers 16 years of age and older;
(1) Metropolitan Statistical Area - see Appendix A for areas included
Source: 1990 Census of Population and Housing, Summary Tape File 3C

Occupational Employment Projections: 1996 - 2006

Occupations Expected to Have the Largest Job Growth (ranked by numerical growth)	Fast-Growing Occupations[1] (ranked by percent growth)
1. Cashiers	1. Systems analysts
2. Salespersons, retail	2. Physical therapy assistants and aides
3. General managers & top executives	3. Desktop publishers
4. Registered nurses	4. Home health aides
5. Waiters & waitresses	5. Computer engineers
6. Marketing & sales, supervisors	6. Medical assistants
7. Janitors/cleaners/maids, ex. priv. hshld.	7. Physical therapists
8. General office clerks	8. Paralegals
9. Food preparation workers	9. Emergency medical technicians
10. Hand packers & packagers	10. Occupational therapists

Note: Projections cover Florida; (1) Excludes occupations with total job growth less than 300
Source: U.S. Department of Labor, Employment and Training Administration, America's Labor Market Information System (ALMIS)

Average Wages

Occupation	$/Hr.	Occupation	$/Hr.
Accountants and Auditors	21.04	Maids and Housekeepers	6.87
Assemblers and Fabricators	9.13	Maintenance Repairers	10.22
Automotive Mechanics	14.49	Marketing/Advertising/PR Managers	22.30
Bookkeepers	10.73	Nurses, Licensed Practical	12.23
Carpenters	12.30	Nurses, Registered	17.78
Cashiers	7.05	Nursing Aides/Orderlies/Attendants	7.83
Clerks, General Office	9.35	Physicians and Surgeons	54.68
Clerks, Shipping/Receiving/Traffic	11.65	Receptionists/Information Clerks	8.82
Computer Programmers	23.09	Sales Reps., Exc. Scientific/Retail	16.41
Computer Support Specialists	15.42	Sales Reps., Scientific, Exc. Retail	23.39
Cooks, Restaurant	8.06	Salespersons, Retail	9.20
Electricians	11.04	Secretaries, Except Legal/Medical	10.29
Financial Managers	22.39	Stock Clerks, Sales Floor	7.88
First-Line Supervisors/Mgrs., Sales	14.70	Systems Analysts	22.38
Food Preparation Workers	7.42	Teacher Aides	11.41
General Managers/Top Executives	24.93	Teachers, Elementary School	-
Guards	6.92	Teachers, Secondary School	-
Hand Packers	6.66	Telemarketers	9.18
Janitors and Cleaners	7.76	Truck Drivers, Heavy/Tractor-Trailer	10.90
Laborers, Landscaping	8.08	Truck Drivers, Light	9.89
Lawyers	38.60	Waiters and Waitresses	6.02

Note: Wage data is for 1998 and covers the Metropolitan Statistical Area (see Appendix A for areas included). Hourly wages for elementary and secondary school teachers were calculated by the editors from annual wage data assuming a 40 hour work week; Dashes indicate that data was not available.
Source: Bureau of Labor Statistics, 1998 Metropolitan Area Occupational Employment and Wage Estimates

TAXES

Major State and Local Tax Rates

State Corporate Income (%)	State Personal Income (%)	Residential Property (%)	Sales & Use		State Gasoline (cents/ gallon)	State Cigarette (cents/ pack)
			State (%)	Local (%)		
5.5[a]	None	1.91	6.0	None	13.3[b]	33.9

Note: Personal/corporate income, sales, gasoline and cigarette tax rates as of January 2000. Property tax rates as of April 2000; (a) 3.3% Alternative Minimum Tax. An exemption of $5,000 is allowed; (b) Rate is comprised of 4 cents excise and 9.3 cents motor carrier tax. Local taxes vary from 5.5 cents to 17 cents. Plus a 2.07 cent per gallon pollution tax
Source: Federation of Tax Administrators, www.taxadmin.org; ERI's Relocation Assessor software database, quarterly effective date 4/1/2000

Total Taxes Per Capita and as a Percent of Income

Area	Per Capita Income ($)	Per Capita Taxes ($)			Percent of Income (%)		
		Total	Federal	State/Local	Total	Federal	State/Local
Florida	28,322	10,333	7,257	3,077	36.5	25.6	10.9
U.S.	28,878	10,298	7,026	3,273	35.7	24.3	11.3

Note: Figures are for 1999
Source: Tax Foundation, www.taxfoundation.org

COMMERCIAL UTILITIES

Typical Monthly Electric Bills

Area	Commercial Service ($/month)		Industrial Service ($/month)	
	12 kW demand 1,500 kWh	100 kW demand 30,000 kWh	1,000 kW demand 400,000 kWh	20,000 kW demand 10,000,000 kWh
City	118	1,993	23,247	387,510
U.S.	150	2,174	23,995	508,569

Note: Based on rates in effect January 1, 1999
Source: Edison Electric Institute, Typical Residential, Commercial and Industrial Bills, Winter 1999

TRANSPORTATION

Transportation Statistics

Average minutes to work (1990)	18.8
Interstate highways	I-75; US-41
Bus lines	
In-city (1998)	Lee County Transit, 41 buses
Inter-city (1999)	1
Passenger air service	
Airport	Southwest Florida International
Airlines (1999)	32
Enplaned passengers (1998)	2,284,930
Amtrak service	Bus Connection
Motor freight carriers (1999)	20
Major waterways/ports	Port Boca Grand (Gulf); Caloosahatchee River

Source: FAA DOT/TSC CY1998 ACAIS Database; National Transit Database, 1998; Editor & Publisher Market Guide, 2000; Amtrak National Time Table, Fall 1999/Winter 2000; 1990 Census of Population and Housing, STF 3C; Jane's Urban Transport Systems 1999-2000

Means of Transportation to Work

Area	Car/Truck/Van		Public Transportation			Bicycle	Walked	Other Means	Worked at Home
	Drove Alone	Car-pooled	Bus	Subway	Railroad				
City	69.6	18.7	1.9	0.0	0.0	1.1	4.5	2.4	1.9
MSA[1]	77.4	15.3	0.8	0.0	0.0	0.7	2.0	1.6	2.2
U.S.	73.2	13.4	3.0	1.5	0.5	0.4	3.9	1.2	3.0

Note: Figures shown are percentages and only include workers 16 years of age and older;
(1) Metropolitan Statistical Area - see Appendix A for areas included
Source: 1990 Census of Population and Housing, Summary Tape File 3C

BUSINESSES

Major Business Headquarters

Company Name	1999 Rankings	
	Fortune 500	Forbes 500
No companies listed	-	-

Note: Companies listed are located in the city; dashes indicate no ranking
Fortune 500: Companies that produce a 10-K are ranked 1 to 500 based on 1999 revenue
Forbes 500: Private companies are ranked 1 to 500 based on 1998 revenue
Source: Forbes, December 13, 1999; Fortune, April 17, 2000

HOTELS & MOTELS

Hotels/Motels

Area	Hotels/ Motels	Rooms	Luxury-Level Hotels/Motels		Average Minimum Rates ($)		
			♦♦♦♦	♦♦♦♦♦	♦♦	♦♦♦	♦♦♦♦
City	16	2,185	1	0	59	87	195
Airport	6	687	0	0	n/a	n/a	n/a
Suburbs	55	4,382	0	0	n/a	n/a	n/a
Total	77	7,254	1	0	n/a	n/a	n/a

Note: n/a not available; classifications range from one diamond (budget properties with basic amenities) to five diamond (luxury properties).
Source: OAG Business Travel Planner, Winter 1999-2000

Estimated Daily Food and Lodging Costs

Area	Food/Other ($/day)	Average Hotel Cost ($/day)
City	42	70
U.S.	30	55

Source: ERI's Relocation Assessor software database, quarterly effective date 4/1/2000

CONVENTION CENTERS

Convention Centers and Event Sites

Name	Guest Rooms	Meeting Space (sq. ft.)	Capacity (Theatre Style)
Sanibel Harbour Resort and Spa	240	18,000	672
Amtel Hotel & Suites	417	18,563	870
Best Western Pink Shell Beach Resort	208	1,620	50
Diamond Head Beach Resort	124	6,000	0
Fort Myers Harborside Convention Complex	n/a	30,000	0
Holiday Inn Central	116	2,037	50
Holiday Inn Select Bell Tower	223	5,312	30
Holiday Inn Sunpree Resort	152	3,513	100
Radisson Inn Fort Myers	192	4,080	500
Radisson Inn Sanibel Gateway	157	680	50

Note: n/a not available
Source: EventSource.com, 3/15/2000

Living Environment

COST OF LIVING

Cost of Living: Homeowner

Cost Element	U.S. ($)	City ($)	Differential ($)	Percent of U.S. Average
Consumables	14,516	15,134	618	104.3
Transportation	5,957	6,451	494	108.3
Health Services	2,012	2,105	93	104.6
Housing/Utilities/Prop. Tax	16,337	20,168	3,831	123.4
Income+Payroll Taxes	12,615	10,346	-2,269	82.0
Miscellaneous	8,563	8,563	0	100.0
Total Cost of Living	60,000	62,767	2,767	104.6

Note: Figures are based on a single income, four person family with gross annual earnings of $60,000, owning an 1,800 square-foot home, and driving two automobiles worth $22,000 30,000 miles per year.
Source: ERI's Relocation Assessor software database, quarterly effective date 4/1/2000

Cost of Living: Renter

Cost Element	U.S. ($)	City ($)	Differential ($)	Percent of U.S. Average
Consumables	10,486	10,873	387	103.7
Transportation	2,107	2,269	162	107.7
Health Services	1,632	1,698	66	104.0
Rent/Utilities/Insurance	9,299	10,244	945	110.2
Income+Payroll Taxes	8,607	7,183	-1,424	83.5
Miscellaneous	7,869	7,869	0	100.0
Total Cost of Living	40,000	40,136	136	100.3

Note: Figures are based on a single income, three person family with gross annual earnings of $40,000, renting a 1,000 square-foot home, and driving one automobile worth $8,000 12,000 miles per year.
Source: ERI's Relocation Assessor software database, quarterly effective date 4/1/2000

HOUSING

Median Home Prices and Housing Affordability

Area	Median Price[2] 4th Qtr. 1999 ($)	HOI[3] 4th Qtr. 1999	Affordability Rank[4]
MSA[1]	101,000	76.0	53
U.S.	139,000	63.8	–

Note: (1) Metropolitan Statistical Area - see Appendix A for areas included; (2) U.S. figures calculated from the sales of 687,516 new and existing homes in 192 markets; (3) Housing Opportunity Index - percent of homes sold that were within the reach of the median income household at the prevailing mortgage interest rate; (4) Rank is from 1-192 with 1 being most affordable
Source: National Association of Home Builders, Housing Opportunity Index, 4th Quarter 1999

Estimated Home Price

Area	Price ($)
City	158,211
U.S.	135,855

Note: Figures are based on an 1,800 square-foot home
Source: ERI's Relocation Assessor software database, quarterly effective date 4/1/2000

Estimated Rent

Area	Rent ($/month)
City	719
U.S.	651

Note: Figures are based on a 1,000 square-foot home
Source: ERI's Relocation Assessor software database, quarterly effective date 4/1/2000

Median Home Price Projection

It is projected that the median home price in the metropolitan area will increase from $94,103 in 1999 to $156,193 in 2010, an increase of 66.0%
Kiplinger's Personal Finance Magazine, January 2000

RESIDENTIAL UTILITIES

Average Residential Utility Costs

Area	All Electric ($/mth)	Part Electric ($/mth)	Other Energy ($/mth)	Phone ($/mth)
MSA[1]	125.19	–	–	16.85
U.S.	99.25	55.47	43.48	20.29

Note: (1) Metropolitan Statistical Area - see Appendix A for areas included
Source: ACCRA, Cost of Living Index, 3rd Quarter 1999

HEALTH CARE

Average Health Care Costs

Area	Hospital ($/day)	Doctor ($/visit)	Dentist ($/visit)
MSA[1]	396.90	58.20	62.90
U.S.	440.96	53.83	68.42

Note: Hospital—based on a semi-private room; Doctor—based on a general practitioner's routine exam of an established patient; Dentist—based on adult teeth cleaning and periodic oral exam; (1) Metropolitan Statistical Area - see Appendix A for areas included
Source: ACCRA, Cost of Living Index, 3rd Quarter 1999

Distribution of Office-Based Physicians

Area	Family/Gen. Practitioners	Specialists		
		Medical	Surgical	Other
MSA[1]	68	210	193	154

Note: Data as of 12/31/97; (1) Metropolitan Statistical Area - see Appendix A for areas included
Source: American Medical Assn., Physician Characteristics & Distribution in the U.S., 1999

Hospitals

Fort Myers has 3 general medical and surgical hospitals, 1 psychiatric.
AHA Guide to the Healthcare Field, 1999-2000

EDUCATION

Public School District Statistics

District Name	Num. Sch.	Enroll.	Classroom Teachers	Pupils per Teacher	Minority Pupils (%)	Current Exp.[1] ($/pupil)
Lee County Sch Dist	72	53,790	2,958	18.2	29.5	5,440

Note: Data covers the 1997-1998 school year unless otherwise noted; (1) Data covers fiscal year 1996; SD = School District; ISD = Independent School District; n/a not available
Source: National Center for Education Statistics, Common Core of Data Public Education Agency Universe 1997-98; National Center for Education Statistics, Characteristics of the 100 Largest Public Elementary and Secondary School Districts in the United States: 1997-98, July 1999

Educational Quality

School District	Education Quotient[1]	Graduate Outcome[2]	Community Index[3]	Resource Index[4]
Lee County School Dist.	88	79	102	102

Note: Over 1,000 secondary school districts were rated in terms of educational quality. The scores range from a low of 50 to a high of 150; (1) Combination of the Graduate Outcome, Community and Resource indexes weighted to reflect the greater importance of the Graduate Outcome and Resource Index; (2) Based on graduation rates and college board scores (SAT/ACT); (3) Based on the surrounding community's level of affluence and adult education; (4) Based on teacher salaries, per-pupil expenditures and student-teacher ratios.
Source: Expansion Management, Ratings Issue, 1999

Educational Attainment by Race

Area	High School Graduate (%)					Bachelor's Degree (%)				
	Total	White	Black	Other	Hisp.[2]	Total	White	Black	Other	Hisp.[2]
City	68.4	76.8	45.0	48.4	42.1	16.1	19.7	5.5	13.0	3.6
MSA[1]	76.9	78.7	47.6	53.4	46.7	16.4	17.0	6.0	13.4	6.5
U.S.	75.2	77.9	63.1	60.4	49.8	20.3	21.5	11.4	19.4	9.2

Note: Figures shown cover persons 25 years old and over; (1) Metropolitan Statistical Area - see Appendix A for areas included; (2) people of Hispanic origin can be of any race
Source: 1990 Census of Population and Housing, Summary Tape File 3C

School Enrollment by Type

Area	Preprimary				Elementary/High School			
	Public		Private		Public		Private	
	Enrollment	%	Enrollment	%	Enrollment	%	Enrollment	%
City	410	57.7	301	42.3	6,654	91.4	630	8.6
MSA[1]	2,293	51.8	2,132	48.2	38,909	91.3	3,691	8.7
U.S.	2,679,029	59.5	1,824,256	40.5	38,379,689	90.2	4,187,099	9.8

Note: Figures shown cover persons 3 years old and over;
(1) Metropolitan Statistical Area - see Appendix A for areas included
Source: 1990 Census of Population and Housing, Summary Tape File 3C

School Enrollment by Race

Area	Preprimary (%)				Elementary/High School (%)			
	White	Black	Other	Hisp.[1]	White	Black	Other	Hisp.[1]
City	51.1	47.3	1.7	9.3	41.4	52.9	5.7	9.7
MSA[2]	87.0	9.9	3.1	5.8	82.2	13.8	4.0	8.0
U.S.	80.4	12.5	7.1	7.8	74.1	15.6	10.3	12.5

Note: Figures shown cover persons 3 years old and over; (1) people of Hispanic origin can be of any race; (2) Metropolitan Statistical Area - see Appendix A for areas included
Source: 1990 Census of Population and Housing, Summary Tape File 3C

Higher Education

Two-Year Colleges		Four-Year Colleges		Medical Schools	Law Schools	Voc/ Tech
Public	Private	Public	Private			
1	1	1	0	0	0	7

Source: College Blue Book, Occupational Education, 1999; Medical School Admission Requirements, 1999-2000; Peterson's Guide to Two-Year Colleges, 2000; Peterson's Guide to Four-Year Colleges, 1999; Barron's Guide to Law Schools, 1999

MAJOR EMPLOYERS

Major Employers

Chico's FAS	Client Business Services
Doctors Osteopathic Medical Center	Hospital Board of Directors of Lee Co.
News-Press Publishing	South Seas Resorts
Southwest Florida Regional Medical Center	Sunshine Masonry

Note: Companies listed are located in the city
Source: D&B Business Rankings, 1999; Ward's Business Directory, 1999; America's Corporate Families, 1999

PUBLIC SAFETY

Crime Rate

Area	All Crimes	Violent Crimes				Property Crimes		
		Murder	Forcible Rape	Robbery	Aggrav. Assault	Burglary	Larceny -Theft	Motor Vehicle Theft
City	12,765.6	29.5	67.4	762.2	1,446.5	2,061.3	5,920.6	2,478.2
Suburbs[1]	4,240.5	4.9	55.4	77.9	244.1	1,027.7	2,345.6	484.8
MSA[2]	5,268.1	7.9	56.9	160.4	389.1	1,152.2	2,776.6	725.1
U.S.	4,615.5	6.3	34.4	165.2	360.5	862.0	2,728.1	459.0

Note: Crime rate is the number of crimes per 100,000 population; (1) Defined as all areas within the Metropolitan Statistical Area but located outside the central city; (2) Metropolitan Statistical Area - see Appendix A for areas included
Source: FBI Uniform Crime Reports, 1998

RECREATION

Culture and Recreation

Museums	Symphony Orchestras	Opera Companies	Dance Companies	Professional Theatres	Zoos	Pro Sports Teams
3	1	0	1	1	0	0

Source: Musical America, International Directory of the Performing Arts, 1999; Official Museum Directory, 2000; Stern's Performing Arts Directory, 1997; USA Today Four Sport Stadium Guide, 1997; Career Opportunities in Theatre and the Performing Arts, 1999

Library System

The Lee County Library System has 10 branches, holdings of 208,018 volumes, and a budget of $13,104,490 (1997-1998).
American Library Directory, 1999-2000

MEDIA

Newspapers

Name	Type	Freq.	Distribution	Circulation
Get Up & Go - Charlotte County Edition	Sen Citizen	1x/mo	Local	18,000
Get Up & Go - Lee County Edition	n/a	1x/mo	Local	50,000
Get Up & Go - Sarasota Edition	n/a	1x/mo	Area	150,000
News-Press	General	7x/wk	Local	90,650

Note: Includes newspapers with circulations of 200 or more located in the city; n/a not available
Source: Burrelle's Media Directory, 1999 Edition

Television Stations

Name	Ch.	Affiliation	Type	Owner
WINK	11	CBST	Commercial	Fort Myers Broadcasting Company
WBBH	20	NBCT	Commercial	Waterman Broadcasting Corporation
WGCU	30	PBS	Public	State of Florida Board of Regents
WFTX	36	FBC	Commercial	Wabash Valley Broadcasting Corp.
WTVK	46	UPN	Commercial	Acme Broadcasting Inc.
WRXY	49	n/a	Commercial	West Coast Christian TV Inc.

Note: Stations included broadcast in the Fort Myers metro area; n/a not available
Source: Burrelle's Media Directory, 1999 Edition

AM Radio Stations

Call Letters	Freq. (kHz)	Target Audience	Station Format	Music Format
WWCN	770	G/H	N/T	n/a
WLBE	790	General	M/N/S	Adult Standards/Big Band/Christian/Oldies
WTLQ	1200	n/a	T	n/a
WINK	1240	General	N/T	n/a
WNOG	1270	General	N/T	n/a
WMYR	1410	General	M	Country
WQBQ	1410	General	M/N/S/T	Country

Note: Stations included broadcast in the Fort Myers metro area; n/a not available
Target Audience: A=Asian; B=Black; C=Christian; E=Ethnic; F=French; G=General; H=Hispanic;
M=Men; N=Native American; R=Religious; S=Senior Citizen; W=Women; Y=Young Adult; Z=Children
Station Format: E=Educational; M=Music; N=News; S=Sports; T=Talk
Source: Burrelle's Media Directory, 1999 Edition

FM Radio Stations

Call Letters	Freq. (mHz)	Target Audience	Station Format	Music Format
WAYJ	88.7	General	E/M	Christian
WGCU	90.1	General	E/M/N/T	Classical/Jazz
WMKO	91.7	General	E/M/N/T	Classical/Jazz
WNLE	91.7	Religious	E/M/N/S	Christian
WTLT	93.5	General	M/N/T	Adult Contemporary
WARO	94.5	General	M/N	Classic Rock
WOLZ	95.3	General	M	Oldies
WRXK	96.1	General	M	AOR
WINK	96.9	General	M/N/S	Adult Contemporary
WDRR	98.5	General	M	Jazz
WJBX	99.3	General	M	Adult Contemporary
WOST	100.1	G/W	M	Adult Contemporary
WWGR	101.9	General	M	Country
WXKB	103.9	General	M	n/a

Note: Stations included broadcast in the Fort Myers metro area; n/a not available
Station Format: E=Educational; M=Music; N=News; S=Sports; T=Talk
Target Audience: A=Asian; B=Black; C=Christian; E=Ethnic; F=French; G=General; H=Hispanic;
M=Men; N=Native American; R=Religious; S=Senior Citizen; W=Women; Y=Young Adult; Z=Children
Music Format: AOR=Album Oriented Rock; MOR=Middle-of-the-Road
Source: Burrelle's Media Directory, 1999 Edition

WEATHER

Temperature/Precipitation/Humidity

	Jan	Feb	Mar	Apr	May	Jun	Jul	Aug	Sep	Oct	Nov	Dec	Yr.
Max. High Temp. (°F)	88	91	93	96	99	103	98	98	96	95	95	90	103
Avg. High Temp. (°F)	75	76	80	85	89	91	91	92	90	86	80	76	84
Avg. Temp. (°F)	64	65	70	73	78	82	83	83	82	77	71	66	75
Avg. Low Temp. (°F)	53	54	58	62	67	73	74	75	74	68	60	55	65
Min. Low Temp. (°F)	28	32	33	39	52	60	66	67	67	48	34	26	26
Avg. Precip. (in.)	1.7	2.1	2.7	1.3	3.7	9.0	8.5	9.0	8.3	3.5	1.5	1.5	52.8
Avg. Snowfall (in.)	0	0	0	0	0	0	0	0	0	0	0	0	0
Avg. Rel. Hum. 7am (%)	90	89	89	88	87	88	89	91	92	90	90	90	89
Avg. Rel. Hum. 4pm (%)	55	54	52	50	53	64	68	67	66	60	57	57	59

Note: Tr = Trace amounts (less than 0.05 inches of rain or less than 0.5 inches of snow)
Source: National Climatic Data Center, International Station Meteorological Climate Summary, 3/95

Weather Conditions

Temperature			Precipitation		
32°F & below	45°F & below	90°F & above	0.01 inch or more precip.	1.5 inch or more snow/ice	Thunder-storms
1	19	114	108	0	89

Note: Figures are average number of days per year
Source: National Climatic Data Center, International Station Meteorological Climate Summary, 3/95

AIR & WATER QUALITY

Maximum Pollutant Concentrations

	Particulate Matter (ug/m³)	Carbon Monoxide (ppm)	Sulfur Dioxide (ppm)	Nitrogen Dioxide (ppm)	Ozone (ppm)	Lead (ug/m³)
MSA[1] Level	33	n/a	n/a	n/a	0.08	n/a
NAAQS[2]	150	9	0.140	0.053	0.12	1.50
Met NAAQS	Yes	n/a	n/a	n/a	Yes	n/a

Note: (1) Metropolitan Statistical Area - see Appendix A for areas included; (2) National Ambient Air Quality Standards; ppm = parts per million; ug/m³ = micrograms per cubic meter; n/a not available
Source: EPA, National Air Quality and Emissions Trends Report, 1997

Pollutant Standards Index

Data not available.
EPA, National Air Quality and Emissions Trends Report, 1997

Drinking Water

Water System Name	Pop. Served	Primary Water Source Type	Number of Violations in 1998-99	Type of Violation/ Contaminants
Fort Myers Water Dept.	47,500	Groundwater under direct influence of surfacewater	None	None

Note: Data as of January 19, 2000
Source: EPA, Office of Ground Water and Drinking Water, Safe Drinking Water Information System

Fort Myers tap water is alkaline, soft, and not fluoridated.
Editor & Publisher Market Guide, 2000

Gainesville, Florida

Background

Gainesville, Florida is located in north central Florida, about 70 miles southwest of Jacksonville. In addition to developed areas, the surrounding region includes numerous lakes and woods.

Gainesville is the county seat of Alachua County, and a regional commercial center. It is the home of the University of Florida, which is the area's major employer. Other economic sectors include technology, health-care and related activities, manufacturing, business and professional services, among others. Tourism and services for university visitors are also a significant activity. Interstate highway I-75 runs by the city.

The area of Gainesville was once occupied by Timucuans, It was claimed by Spain in the colonial era and granted to a merchant in 1817. Florida became a state in 1845. Gainesville was established in 1853 as a stop on the Florida Railroad and as the county seat, named after General Edmund P. Gaines, a military hero. The town became a commercial center for the region, which was agricultural with crops that included cotton and citrus among other products. During the Civil War, skirmishes occurred in the area. Other industries included lumber and phosphate. The University of Florida began operating in 1906. The economy became oriented to education and related activities, and diversified with other new services and industries.

Gainesville maintains about 30 parks and recreation facilities. There are numerous state parks and other recreational and nature centers in the region.

The University of Florida provides a variety of cultural and other activities and facilities, including the Center for the Performing Arts, and Florida Museum of Natural History. The Hippodrome Theater is a state supported theatrical and cultural venue. Other community organizations include Gainesville Civic Chorus, Gainesville Ballet Theater, Gainesville Symphony Orchestra and others. Gainesville has several historic districts. The Thomas Center is a historic hotel and cultural center. The Marjorie Kinnan Rawlings State Historical Site is the home of the author of "The Yearling."

In addition to the University of Florida, Gainesville is home to City College and Santa Fe Community College.

Gainesville is governed by a City Manager and City Commission and an elected Mayor/Commissioner.

General Rankings and Evaluative Comments

- Gainesville was ranked #99 out of 354 metropolitan areas in *Places Rated Almanac*. Criteria: cost of living, climate, crime, transportation, job outlook, education, the arts, health care, and recreation. *Places Rated Almanac, Millennium Edition, 2000*

- Gainesville was selected as one of North America's "Best Small Metro Areas" (population under 250,000). The area ranked #5 out of 20. Criteria: cost of living, climate, crime, transportation, job outlook, education, the arts, health care, and recreation. *Places Rated Almanac, Millennium Edition, 2000*

- Gainesville was selected as one of America's best places to retire. Criteria: safety, climate, housing, culture and recreation, social compatibility, affordability, medical care, transportation, and jobs and/or volunteer opportunities. *Where to Retire: America's Best and Most Affordable Places, 1998*

- Gainesville was selected as one of the best places to retire by *Retirement Places Rated*. Criteria: cost of living, climate, crime, services, working, and leisure living. The city was ranked #19 out of 187. *Retirement Places Rated, 1999*

- Gainesville was selected as one of "America's Best Towns to Raise an Outdoor Family" by *Outdoor Explorer* magazine. Criteria: easy access to the outdoors, quality education and health care, affordable housing, favorable employment opportunities, and low crime rates. The city was ranked #10 out of 25. *Outdoor Explorer, Summer 1999*

- Cognetics studied 273 metro areas in the United States, ranking them by entrepreneurial activity. Gainesville was ranked #36 out of 134 smaller metro areas. Criteria: Significant Starts (firms started in the last 10 years that still employ at least 5 people) and Young Growers (percent of firms 10 years old or less that grew significantly during the last 4 years). *Cognetics, "Entrepreneurial Hot Spots: The Best Places in America to Start and Grow a Company," 1999*

Business Environment

STATE ECONOMY

State Economic Profile

"Florida's economy has been among the nation's strongest in recent years. Job growth has outpaced the nation by a considerable amount since 1992.

While Florida has been able to avoid any significant fallout from the Asian crisis, the weakening of economies in Latin American will dampen both tourism and international trade. 1998 saw the decline in Latin tourism more than offset by domestic visitors. Domestic tourism is projected to soften as U.S. growth cools, offering no offset against the expected decline in Latin tourism. Weaker tourism and trade with Latin American will slow growth in the near future; Florida will still outpace the nation in job growth as Gross State Product growth (GSP) slows.

Over half of Florida's 230,000 new jobs created in 1998 were in the services sector, which grew at 5.2%, more than offsetting a minor decline in manufacturing employment. Much of this growth is taking place in the finance and business services sector.

In spite of strong home sales and a slowing construction market, Florida's price appreciation continued to lag the nation. Although residential permits per 1,000 residents stands at 5.1, well above the national average, this number is only slightly up from 1997 and is poised to decline in the near future.

Growth in Florida, while strong throughout, has been hottest in the Naples, Ft. Myers and Orlando areas. Construction and employment in the construction industry has begun to slow in South Florida. Projected employment and housing gains will be concentrated in Northern and Central Florida. Growing diversification of the economy into financial and business services promises a strong outlook for the years ahead." *National Association of Realtors, Economic Profiles: The Fifty States and the District of Columbia, http://nar.realtor.com/databank/profiles.htm*

EXPORTS

Total Export Sales

Area	1995 ($000)	1996 ($000)	1997 ($000)	1998 ($000)	% Chg. 1995-98	% Chg. 1997-98
MSA[1]	91,619	88,265	79,609	70,187	-23.4	-11.8
U.S.	583,030,524	622,827,063	687,597,999	680,474,251	16.7	-1.0

Note: (1) Metropolitan Statistical Area - see Appendix A for areas included
Source: U.S. Department of Commerce, International Trade Association, Metropolitan Area Exports: An Export Performance Report on Over 250 U.S. Cities, November 10, 1999

CITY FINANCES

City Government Finances

Component	1995 ($million)	1995 (per capita $)
Revenue	75.8	863
Expenditure	85.2	970
Debt Outstanding	480.7	5,474

Source: 1999 County and City Extra, Annual Metro, City, and County Data Book

City Government Revenue by Source

Source	1995 ($million)	1995 (per capita $)
Intergovernmental	12.4	141
Taxes	20.3	232
Property	8.8	101
Sales and Gross Receipts	9.9	113

Source: 1999 County and City Extra, Annual Metro, City, and County Data Book

City Government Expenditures by Function

Function	1995 ($million)	1995 (per capita $)	1995 (%)
Public Welfare	0.0	0	0.0
Highways	5.3	61	6.3
Parking Facilities	0.0	0	0.0
Education	0.0	0	0.0
Health and Hospitals	0.1	1	0.2
Police Protection	16.8	192	19.8
Sewerage and Sanitation	19.7	225	23.2
Parks and Recreation	4.2	48	5.0
Housing and Community Development	2.3	26	2.7
Interest on Debt	5.6	64	6.6

Source: 1999 County and City Extra, Annual Metro, City, and County Data Book

Municipal Bond Ratings

Area	Moody's
City	Aaa

Source: Mergent Bond Record, 2/2000

POPULATION

Population Growth

Area	1980 Census	1990 Census	1999 Estimate	2004 Projection	Population Growth (%) 1990-1999	Population Growth (%) 1999-2004
City	81,371	84,770	83,246	83,603	-1.8	0.4
MSA[1]	151,348	204,111	206,306	218,296	1.1	5.8
U.S.	226,545,805	248,765,170	272,212,864	283,625,312	9.4	4.2

Note: (1) Metropolitan Statistical Area - see Appendix A for areas included
Source: 1990 Census of Population and Housing, Summary Tape File 3C; Claritas, Inc.

Number of Households and Average Household Size

Area	1980 Census	1990 Census	1999 Estimate	2004 Projection	1999 Average Household Size
City	27,557	31,955	31,188	31,704	2.67
MSA[1]	54,607	78,493	81,779	87,883	2.52
U.S.	80,389,592	91,993,582	102,048,200	107,302,392	2.67

Note: (1) Metropolitan Statistical Area - see Appendix A for areas included
Source: 1990 Census of Population and Housing, Summary Tape File 3C; Claritas, Inc.

Race/Ethnicity of City Population

Race/Ethnicity	1990 Census Population	1990 Census %	1999 Estimate Population	1999 Estimate %	% Change 1990-1999
White, Non-Hispanic	59,401	70.1	51,761	62.2	-12.9
Black, Non-Hispanic	18,028	21.3	20,997	25.2	16.5
Asian, Non-Hispanic	3,270	3.9	4,779	5.7	46.1
Other, Non-Hispanic	298	0.4	311	0.4	4.4
Hispanic	3,773	4.5	5,398	6.5	43.1

Source: 1990 Census of Population and Housing, Summary Tape File 3C; Claritas, Inc.

Race/Ethnicity of Metropolitan Statistical Area Population

Race/Ethnicity	1990 Census		1999 Estimate		% Change 1990-1999
	Population	%	Population	%	
White, Non-Hispanic	153,294	75.1	140,315	68.0	-8.5
Black, Non-Hispanic	38,778	19.0	47,061	22.8	21.4
Asian, Non-Hispanic	4,514	2.2	7,454	3.6	65.1
Other, Non-Hispanic	538	0.3	708	0.3	31.6
Hispanic	6,987	3.4	10,768	5.2	54.1

Note: See Appendix A for areas included in the Metropolitan Statistical Area
Source: 1990 Census of Population and Housing, Summary Tape File 3C; Claritas, Inc.

Ancestry

Area	German	Irish	English	Italian	U.S.	French	Polish	Dutch
City	18.3	13.5	15.8	4.5	5.0	3.5	2.7	1.8
MSA[1]	18.2	14.6	16.5	4.0	7.5	3.7	2.3	1.9
U.S.	23.3	15.6	13.1	5.9	5.3	4.2	3.8	2.5

Note: Figures are percentages and include persons that reported multiple ancestry (eg. if a person reported being Irish and Italian, they were included in both columns); (1) Metropolitan Statistical Area - see Appendix A for areas included
Source: 1990 Census of Population and Housing, Summary Tape File 3C

Median Age

Area	1990 Census	1999 Estimate
City	26.6	29.4
MSA[1]	28.9	31.4
U.S.	32.9	35.7

Note: (1) Metropolitan Statistical Area - see Appendix A for areas included
Source: 1990 Census of Population and Housing, Summary Tape File 3C; Claritas, Inc.

Male/Female Population

Area	Number of Males		Number of Females		Males per 100 Females	
	1990	1999	1990	1999	1990	1999
City	41,593	41,173	43,177	42,073	96.3	97.9
MSA[1]	101,247	101,199	102,864	105,107	98.4	96.3
U.S.	121,172,379	132,803,736	127,537,494	139,409,136	95.0	95.3

Note: (1) Metropolitan Statistical Area - see Appendix A for areas included
Source: 1990 Census of Population, General Population Characteristics; Claritas, Inc.

INCOME

Per Capita/Median/Average Income

Area	Per Capita ($)			Median Household ($)			Average Household ($)		
	1989	1999	% Chg.	1989	1999	% Chg.	1989	1999	% Chg.
City	11,549	16,674	44.4	21,077	28,869	37.0	29,843	43,113	44.5
MSA[1]	12,035	18,446	53.3	22,279	30,669	37.7	30,532	45,781	49.9
U.S.	14,420	21,350	48.1	30,056	40,525	34.8	38,453	56,184	46.1

Note: (1) Metropolitan Statistical Area - see Appendix A for areas included; 1989 data is from the 1990 Census; 1999 data is estimated by Claritas, Inc.
Source: 1990 Census of Population, General Population Characteristics; Claritas, Inc.

Household Income Distribution

| Area | Percent of Households Earning | | | | | | | | |
	Under $5,000	$5,000 -14,999	$15,000 -24,999	$25,000 -34,999	$35,000 -49,999	$50,000 -74,999	$75,000 -99,000	$100,000 -149,999	$150,000 and up
City	7.5	19.8	17.8	13.2	13.6	13.7	6.8	5.1	2.7
MSA[1]	7.0	18.8	16.5	13.3	14.2	15.1	7.2	4.9	3.1
U.S.	3.9	13.3	13.8	12.6	16.2	19.4	9.7	6.6	4.6

Note: Data as of 1999; (1) Metropolitan Statistical Area - see Appendix A for areas included
Source: Claritas, Inc.

Effective Buying Income

Area	Per Capita ($)	Median Household ($)	Average Household ($)
City	13,830	25,301	36,632
MSA[1]	15,338	27,214	38,633
U.S.	17,496	36,603	47,036

Note: Data as of 1/1/2000; (1) Metropolitan Statistical Area - see Appendix A for areas included
Source: Standard Rate & Data Service, Newspaper Advertising Source, March 2000

Effective Household Buying Income Distribution

| Area | % of Households Earning | | | | | | |
	$10,000 -$19,999	$20,000 -$34,999	$35,000 -$49,999	$50,000 -$74,999	$75,000 -$99,000	$100,000 -$124,999	$125,000 and up
City	20.0	21.8	13.7	13.0	6.1	2.2	2.4
MSA[1]	18.8	22.2	14.2	14.7	6.1	2.2	2.6
U.S.	15.0	21.6	17.6	19.6	8.4	3.0	3.3

Note: Data as of 1/1/2000; (1) Metropolitan Statistical Area - see Appendix A for areas included
Source: Standard Rate & Data Service, Newspaper Advertising Source, March 2000

Poverty Rates by Age

Area	People of All Ages	People Under 18 Years Old	Related Children Age 5-17 in Families in Poverty
City	21.3	n/a	n/a
County	19.2	24.9	22.4
U.S.	13.8	20.8	18.7

Note: Figures show the percent of people living below the poverty line in 1995. The average poverty threshold was $15,569 for a family of four in 1995; n/a not available
Source: Bureau of the Census, Small Area Income and Poverty Estimates Program; U.S. Department of Housing and Urban Development

EMPLOYMENT

Labor Force and Employment

| Area | Civilian Labor Force | | | Workers Employed | | |
	Dec. 1998	Dec. 1999	% Chg.	Dec. 1998	Dec. 1999	% Chg.
City	47,326	48,393	2.3	46,155	47,276	2.4
MSA[1]	104,398	106,781	2.3	102,231	104,713	2.4
U.S.	138,297,000	139,941,000	1.2	132,732,000	134,696,000	1.5

Note: Data is not seasonally adjusted and covers workers 16 years of age and older; (1) Metropolitan Statistical Area - see Appendix A for areas included
Source: Bureau of Labor Statistics, http://stats.bls.gov

Unemployment Rate

Area	1999											
	Jan.	Feb.	Mar.	Apr.	May	Jun.	Jul.	Aug.	Sep.	Oct.	Nov.	Dec.
City	3.1	2.8	2.7	2.7	2.8	2.9	2.6	2.5	2.5	2.5	2.6	2.3
MSA[1]	2.6	2.3	2.3	2.3	2.3	2.4	2.2	2.1	2.1	2.1	2.2	1.9
U.S.	4.8	4.7	4.4	4.1	4.0	4.5	4.5	4.2	4.1	3.8	3.8	3.7

Note: Data is not seasonally adjusted and covers workers 16 years of age and older; all figures are percentages; (1) Metropolitan Statistical Area - see Appendix A for areas included
Source: Bureau of Labor Statistics, http://stats.bls.gov

Employment by Industry

Sector	MSA[1]		U.S.
	Number of Employees	Percent of Total	Percent of Total
Services	37,400	30.8	30.2
Retail Trade	23,200	19.1	18.1
Government	40,300	33.2	15.8
Manufacturing	5,400	4.4	14.1
Finance/Insurance/Real Estate	5,300	4.4	5.9
Wholesale Trade	2,500	2.1	5.4
Transportation/Public Utilities	2,500	2.1	5.3
Construction	4,800	4.0	4.8
Mining	n/a	n/a	0.4

Note: Figures cover non-farm employment as of 12/99 and are not seasonally adjusted;
(1) Metropolitan Statistical Area - see Appendix A for areas included; n/a not available
Source: Bureau of Labor Statistics, http://stats.bls.gov

Employment by Occupation

Occupation Category	City (%)	MSA[1] (%)	U.S. (%)
White Collar	72.0	67.3	58.1
Executive/Admin./Management	12.2	12.1	12.3
Professional	26.3	22.5	14.1
Technical & Related Support	6.5	5.5	3.7
Sales	11.0	11.4	11.8
Administrative Support/Clerical	16.0	15.9	16.3
Blue Collar	11.7	16.0	26.2
Precision Production/Craft/Repair	5.6	8.2	11.3
Machine Operators/Assem./Insp.	2.0	2.6	6.8
Transportation/Material Movers	1.9	2.6	4.1
Cleaners/Helpers/Laborers	2.2	2.7	3.9
Services	15.1	14.6	13.2
Farming/Forestry/Fishing	1.1	2.2	2.5

Note: Figures cover workers 16 years of age and older;
(1) Metropolitan Statistical Area - see Appendix A for areas included
Source: 1990 Census of Population and Housing, Summary Tape File 3C

Occupational Employment Projections: 1996 - 2006

Occupations Expected to Have the Largest Job Growth (ranked by numerical growth)	Fast-Growing Occupations[1] (ranked by percent growth)
1. Cashiers	1. Systems analysts
2. Salespersons, retail	2. Physical therapy assistants and aides
3. General managers & top executives	3. Desktop publishers
4. Registered nurses	4. Home health aides
5. Waiters & waitresses	5. Computer engineers
6. Marketing & sales, supervisors	6. Medical assistants
7. Janitors/cleaners/maids, ex. priv. hshld.	7. Physical therapists
8. General office clerks	8. Paralegals
9. Food preparation workers	9. Emergency medical technicians
10. Hand packers & packagers	10. Occupational therapists

Note: Projections cover Florida; (1) Excludes occupations with total job growth less than 300
Source: U.S. Department of Labor, Employment and Training Administration, America's Labor Market Information System (ALMIS)

Average Wages

Occupation	$/Hr.	Occupation	$/Hr.
Accountants and Auditors	16.83	Maids and Housekeepers	6.23
Assemblers and Fabricators	9.09	Maintenance Repairers	9.01
Automotive Mechanics	13.98	Marketing/Advertising/PR Managers	19.49
Bookkeepers	9.86	Nurses, Licensed Practical	12.94
Carpenters	10.59	Nurses, Registered	19.96
Cashiers	6.90	Nursing Aides/Orderlies/Attendants	7.96
Clerks, General Office	8.55	Physicians and Surgeons	43.82
Clerks, Shipping/Receiving/Traffic	12.72	Receptionists/Information Clerks	7.95
Computer Programmers	20.91	Sales Reps., Exc. Scientific/Retail	18.93
Computer Support Specialists	16.84	Sales Reps., Scientific, Exc. Retail	25.00
Cooks, Restaurant	7.20	Salespersons, Retail	8.18
Electricians	11.15	Secretaries, Except Legal/Medical	9.23
Financial Managers	22.02	Stock Clerks, Sales Floor	8.04
First-Line Supervisors/Mgrs., Sales	13.73	Systems Analysts	21.93
Food Preparation Workers	7.09	Teacher Aides	8.24
General Managers/Top Executives	24.40	Teachers, Elementary School	16.43
Guards	7.94	Teachers, Secondary School	17.21
Hand Packers	6.75	Telemarketers	8.79
Janitors and Cleaners	7.03	Truck Drivers, Heavy/Tractor-Trailer	10.45
Laborers, Landscaping	8.02	Truck Drivers, Light	10.51
Lawyers	31.93	Waiters and Waitresses	6.18

Note: Wage data is for 1998 and covers the Metropolitan Statistical Area (see Appendix A for areas included). Hourly wages for elementary and secondary school teachers were calculated by the editors from annual wage data assuming a 40 hour work week; Dashes indicate that data was not available.
Source: Bureau of Labor Statistics, 1998 Metropolitan Area Occupational Employment and Wage Estimates

TAXES

Major State and Local Tax Rates

State Corporate Income (%)	State Personal Income (%)	Residential Property (%)	Sales & Use		State Gasoline (cents/ gallon)	State Cigarette (cents/ pack)
			State (%)	Local (%)		
5.5[a]	None	2.38	6.0	None	13.3[b]	33.9

Note: Personal/corporate income, sales, gasoline and cigarette tax rates as of January 2000. Property tax rates as of April 2000; (a) 3.3% Alternative Minimum Tax. An exemption of $5,000 is allowed; (b) Rate is comprised of 4 cents excise and 9.3 cents motor carrier tax. Local taxes vary from 5.5 cents to 17 cents. Plus a 2.07 cent per gallon pollution tax
Source: Federation of Tax Administrators, www.taxadmin.org; ERI's Relocation Assessor software database, quarterly effective date 4/1/2000

Total Taxes Per Capita and as a Percent of Income

Area	Per Capita Income ($)	Per Capita Taxes ($)			Percent of Income (%)		
		Total	Federal	State/Local	Total	Federal	State/Local
Florida	28,322	10,333	7,257	3,077	36.5	25.6	10.9
U.S.	28,878	10,298	7,026	3,273	35.7	24.3	11.3

Note: Figures are for 1999
Source: Tax Foundation, www.taxfoundation.org

COMMERCIAL UTILITIES

Typical Monthly Electric Bills

Area	Commercial Service ($/month)		Industrial Service ($/month)	
	12 kW demand 1,500 kWh	100 kW demand 30,000 kWh	1,000 kW demand 400,000 kWh	20,000 kW demand 10,000,000 kWh
City	n/a	n/a	n/a	n/a
U.S.	150	2,174	23,995	508,569

Note: Based on rates in effect January 1, 1999; n/a not available
Source: Edison Electric Institute, Typical Residential, Commercial and Industrial Bills, Winter 1999

TRANSPORTATION

Transportation Statistics

Average minutes to work (1990)	15.9
Interstate highways	I-75; US-441
Bus lines	
In-city (1998)	Gainesville Regional Transit System, 49 buses
Inter-city (1999)	1
Passenger air service	
Airport	Gainesville Regional
Airlines (1999)	3
Enplaned passengers (1998)	142,995
Amtrak service	Bus Connection
Motor freight carriers (1999)	13
Major waterways/ports	None

Source: FAA DOT/TSC CY1998 ACAIS Database; National Transit Database, 1998; Editor & Publisher Market Guide, 2000; Amtrak National Time Table, Fall 1999/Winter 2000; 1990 Census of Population and Housing, STF 3C; Jane's Urban Transport Systems 1999-2000

Means of Transportation to Work

Area	Car/Truck/Van		Public Transportation			Bicycle	Walked	Other Means	Worked at Home
	Drove Alone	Car-pooled	Bus	Subway	Railroad				
City	66.5	12.8	2.6	0.0	0.0	6.5	7.7	1.3	2.7
MSA[1]	72.5	14.1	1.6	0.0	0.0	3.6	4.1	1.2	2.8
U.S.	73.2	13.4	3.0	1.5	0.5	0.4	3.9	1.2	3.0

Note: Figures shown are percentages and only include workers 16 years of age and older;
(1) Metropolitan Statistical Area - see Appendix A for areas included
Source: 1990 Census of Population and Housing, Summary Tape File 3C

BUSINESSES

Major Business Headquarters

Company Name	1999 Rankings	
	Fortune 500	Forbes 500
No companies listed	-	-

Note: Companies listed are located in the city; dashes indicate no ranking
Fortune 500: Companies that produce a 10-K are ranked 1 to 500 based on 1999 revenue
Forbes 500: Private companies are ranked 1 to 500 based on 1998 revenue
Source: Forbes, December 13, 1999; Fortune, April 17, 2000

HOTELS & MOTELS

Hotels/Motels

Area	Hotels/ Motels	Rooms	Luxury-Level Hotels/Motels		Average Minimum Rates ($)		
			♦♦♦♦	♦♦♦♦♦	♦♦	♦♦♦	♦♦♦♦
City	14	1,446	0	0	59	69	n/a
Airport	1	152	0	0	n/a	n/a	n/a
Suburbs	2	288	0	0	n/a	n/a	n/a
Total	17	1,886	0	0	n/a	n/a	n/a

Note: n/a not available; classifications range from one diamond (budget properties with basic amenities) to five diamond (luxury properties).
Source: OAG Business Travel Planner, Winter 1999-2000

Estimated Daily Food and Lodging Costs

Area	Food/Other ($/day)	Average Hotel Cost ($/day)
City	34	61
U.S.	30	55

Source: ERI's Relocation Assessor software database, quarterly effective date 4/1/2000

CONVENTION CENTERS

Convention Centers and Event Sites

Name	Guest Rooms	Meeting Space (sq. ft.)	Capacity (Theatre Style)
Univ. of Fla. Center for the Performing Arts	n/a	n/a	1,800
Sheraton Gainesville Hotel	n/a	12,468	800
Stephen C. O'Connell Center	n/a	n/a	12,000

Note: n/a not available
Source: EventSource.com, 3/15/2000

Living Environment

COST OF LIVING

Cost of Living: Homeowner

Cost Element	U.S. ($)	City ($)	Differential ($)	Percent of U.S. Average
Consumables	14,516	15,179	663	104.6
Transportation	5,957	6,476	519	108.7
Health Services	2,012	2,092	80	104.0
Housing/Utilities/Prop. Tax	16,337	16,400	63	100.4
Income+Payroll Taxes	12,615	10,670	-1,945	84.6
Miscellaneous	8,563	8,563	0	100.0
Total Cost of Living	60,000	59,380	-620	99.0

Note: Figures are based on a single income, four person family with gross annual earnings of $60,000, owning an 1,800 square-foot home, and driving two automobiles worth $22,000 30,000 miles per year.
Source: ERI's Relocation Assessor software database, quarterly effective date 4/1/2000

Cost of Living: Renter

Cost Element	U.S. ($)	City ($)	Differential ($)	Percent of U.S. Average
Consumables	10,486	10,906	420	104.0
Transportation	2,107	2,278	171	108.1
Health Services	1,632	1,689	57	103.5
Rent/Utilities/Insurance	9,299	8,858	-441	95.3
Income+Payroll Taxes	8,607	7,183	-1,424	83.5
Miscellaneous	7,869	7,869	0	100.0
Total Cost of Living	40,000	38,783	-1,217	97.0

Note: Figures are based on a single income, three person family with gross annual earnings of $40,000, renting a 1,000 square-foot home, and driving one automobile worth $8,000 12,000 miles per year.
Source: ERI's Relocation Assessor software database, quarterly effective date 4/1/2000

HOUSING

Median Home Prices and Housing Affordability

Area	Median Price[2] 4th Qtr. 1999 ($)	HOI[3] 4th Qtr. 1999	Affordability Rank[4]
MSA[1]	101,000	73.7	75
U.S.	139,000	63.8	–

Note: (1) Metropolitan Statistical Area - see Appendix A for areas included; (2) U.S. figures calculated from the sales of 687,516 new and existing homes in 192 markets; (3) Housing Opportunity Index - percent of homes sold that were within the reach of the median income household at the prevailing mortgage interest rate; (4) Rank is from 1-192 with 1 being most affordable
Source: National Association of Home Builders, Housing Opportunity Index, 4th Quarter 1999

Estimated Home Price

Area	Price ($)
City	121,583
U.S.	135,855

Note: Figures are based on an 1,800 square-foot home
Source: ERI's Relocation Assessor software database, quarterly effective date 4/1/2000

Estimated Rent

Area	Rent ($/month)
City	617
U.S.	651

Note: Figures are based on a 1,000 square-foot home
Source: ERI's Relocation Assessor software database, quarterly effective date 4/1/2000

Median Home Price Projection

It is projected that the median home price in the metropolitan area will increase from $107,735 in 1999 to $171,282 in 2010, an increase of 59.0%
Kiplinger's Personal Finance Magazine, January 2000

RESIDENTIAL UTILITIES

Average Residential Utility Costs

Area	All Electric ($/mth)	Part Electric ($/mth)	Other Energy ($/mth)	Phone ($/mth)
City	–	71.11	24.52	15.90
U.S.	99.25	55.47	43.48	20.29

Source: ACCRA, Cost of Living Index, 3rd Quarter 1999

HEALTH CARE

Average Health Care Costs

Area	Hospital ($/day)	Doctor ($/visit)	Dentist ($/visit)
City	536.33	50.00	62.20
U.S.	440.96	53.83	68.42

Note: Hospital—based on a semi-private room; Doctor—based on a general practitioner's routine exam of an established patient; Dentist—based on adult teeth cleaning and periodic oral exam.
Source: ACCRA, Cost of Living Index, 3rd Quarter 1999

Distribution of Office-Based Physicians

Area	Family/Gen. Practitioners	Specialists Medical	Specialists Surgical	Specialists Other
MSA[1]	93	238	189	242

Note: Data as of 12/31/97; (1) Metropolitan Statistical Area - see Appendix A for areas included
Source: American Medical Assn., Physician Characteristics & Distribution in the U.S., 1999

Hospitals

Gainesville has 4 general medical and surgical hospitals, 1 rehabilitation.
AHA Guide to the Healthcare Field, 1999-2000

According to *U.S. News and World Report*, Gainesville has one of the best hospitals in the U.S.: **Shands Hospital at the University of Florida**, noted for cancer, gastroenterology, gynecology, orthopedics, otolaryngology.
U.S. News Online, "America's Best Hospitals," July 19, 1999

EDUCATION

Public School District Statistics

District Name	Num. Sch.	Enroll.	Classroom Teachers	Pupils per Teacher	Minority Pupils (%)	Current Exp.[1] ($/pupil)
Alachua County Sch Dist	50	30,062	1,701	17.7	43.2	4,764
University of Florida Lab Sch	1	961	n/a	n/a	n/a	n/a

Note: Data covers the 1997-1998 school year unless otherwise noted; (1) Data covers fiscal year 1996; SD = School District; ISD = Independent School District; n/a not available
Source: National Center for Education Statistics, Common Core of Data Public Education Agency Universe 1997-98; National Center for Education Statistics, Characteristics of the 100 Largest Public Elementary and Secondary School Districts in the United States: 1997-98, July 1999

Educational Quality

School District	Education Quotient[1]	Graduate Outcome[2]	Community Index[3]	Resource Index[4]
Alachua Co. School Dist.	100	112	115	73

Note: Over 1,000 secondary school districts were rated in terms of educational quality. The scores range from a low of 50 to a high of 150; (1) Combination of the Graduate Outcome, Community and Resource indexes weighted to reflect the greater importance of the Graduate Outcome and Resource Index; (2) Based on graduation rates and college board scores (SAT/ACT); (3) Based on the surrounding community's level of affluence and adult education; (4) Based on teacher salaries, per-pupil expenditures and student-teacher ratios.
Source: Expansion Management, Ratings Issue, 1999

Educational Attainment by Race

Area	High School Graduate (%)					Bachelor's Degree (%)				
	Total	White	Black	Other	Hisp.[2]	Total	White	Black	Other	Hisp.[2]
City	84.8	89.9	63.0	96.3	88.8	40.5	45.7	12.4	74.5	51.7
MSA[1]	80.5	84.3	61.0	93.2	85.6	31.2	34.5	11.0	65.4	41.0
U.S.	75.2	77.9	63.1	60.4	49.8	20.3	21.5	11.4	19.4	9.2

Note: Figures shown cover persons 25 years old and over; (1) Metropolitan Statistical Area - see Appendix A for areas included; (2) people of Hispanic origin can be of any race
Source: 1990 Census of Population and Housing, Summary Tape File 3C

School Enrollment by Type

Area	Preprimary				Elementary/High School			
	Public		Private		Public		Private	
	Enrollment	%	Enrollment	%	Enrollment	%	Enrollment	%
City	1,074	54.4	901	45.6	9,521	91.4	897	8.6
MSA[1]	2,420	56.6	1,858	43.4	26,776	92.2	2,275	7.8
U.S.	2,679,029	59.5	1,824,256	40.5	38,379,689	90.2	4,187,099	9.8

Note: Figures shown cover persons 3 years old and over;
(1) Metropolitan Statistical Area - see Appendix A for areas included
Source: 1990 Census of Population and Housing, Summary Tape File 3C

School Enrollment by Race

Area	Preprimary (%)				Elementary/High School (%)			
	White	Black	Other	Hisp.[1]	White	Black	Other	Hisp.[1]
City	68.3	23.8	7.9	6.2	58.1	38.9	3.1	5.4
MSA[2]	71.4	24.0	4.5	3.8	67.5	30.6	1.9	3.1
U.S.	80.4	12.5	7.1	7.8	74.1	15.6	10.3	12.5

Note: Figures shown cover persons 3 years old and over; (1) people of Hispanic origin can be of any race; (2) Metropolitan Statistical Area - see Appendix A for areas included
Source: 1990 Census of Population and Housing, Summary Tape File 3C

Higher Education

Two-Year Colleges		Four-Year Colleges		Medical Schools	Law Schools	Voc/ Tech
Public	Private	Public	Private			
1	1	1	0	1	1	2

Source: College Blue Book, Occupational Education, 1999; Medical School Admission Requirements, 1999-2000; Peterson's Guide to Two-Year Colleges, 2000; Peterson's Guide to Four-Year Colleges, 1999; Barron's Guide to Law Schools, 1999

MAJOR EMPLOYERS

Major Employers

AV-Med	Barnett Bank of Alachua Co.
Cox Cable University City	Energizer Power Systems
Florida Farm Bureau Federation	Gainesville Sun Publishing
Perma-Fix Environmental Services	Shands Teaching Hospital
Wellness Inc.	

Note: Companies listed are located in the city
Source: D&B Business Rankings, 1999; Ward's Business Directory, 1999; America's Corporate Families, 1999

PUBLIC SAFETY

Crime Rate

Area	All Crimes	Violent Crimes				Property Crimes		
		Murder	Forcible Rape	Robbery	Aggrav. Assault	Burglary	Larceny -Theft	Motor Vehicle Theft
City	10,640.8	1.1	78.4	336.1	956.8	1,997.5	6,670.4	600.5
Suburbs[1]	8,540.8	2.7	101.2	137.6	904.0	1,920.8	4,937.3	537.2
MSA[2]	9,469.4	2.0	91.1	225.4	927.3	1,954.7	5,703.6	565.2
U.S.	4,615.5	6.3	34.4	165.2	360.5	862.0	2,728.1	459.0

Note: Crime rate is the number of crimes per 100,000 population; (1) Defined as all areas within the Metropolitan Statistical Area but located outside the central city; (2) Metropolitan Statistical Area - see Appendix A for areas included
Source: FBI Uniform Crime Reports, 1998

RECREATION

Culture and Recreation

Museums	Symphony Orchestras	Opera Companies	Dance Companies	Professional Theatres	Zoos	Pro Sports Teams
3	1	0	1	2	0	0

Source: Musical America, International Directory of the Performing Arts, 1999; Official Museum Directory, 2000; Stern's Performing Arts Directory, 1997; USA Today Four Sport Stadium Guide, 1997; Career Opportunities in Theatre and the Performing Arts, 1999

Library System

The Alachua County Library District has 10 branches, holdings of 709,463 volumes, and a budget of $7,530,274 (1997-1998).
American Library Directory, 1999-2000

MEDIA

Newspapers

Name	Type	Freq.	Distribution	Circulation
Gainesville Buyers Guide	General	1x/wk	Area	62,000
The Gainesville Sun	General	7x/wk	Area	54,041
The Independent Florida Alligator	n/a	5x/wk	Camp/Comm	35,000
The Record (Alachua County Edition)	General	1x/wk	U.S.	5,000
The Record (Farm & Ranch Edition)	General	1x/wk	Local	5,000

Note: Includes newspapers with circulations of 200 or more located in the city; n/a not available
Source: Burrelle's Media Directory, 1999 Edition

Television Stations

Name	Ch.	Affiliation	Type	Owner
WUFT	n/a	PBS	Public	Board of Regents/State of Florida
WCJB	20	ABCT	Commercial	Diversified Communications
WGFL	53	WB	n/a	Budd Broadcasting Company

Note: Stations included broadcast in the Gainesville metro area; n/a not available
Source: Burrelle's Media Directory, 1999 Edition

AM Radio Stations

Call Letters	Freq. (kHz)	Target Audience	Station Format	Music Format
WRUF	850	General	N/S/T	n/a
WLUS	980	General	M/N/S/T	Big Band/MOR/Oldies
WGGG	1230	General	S	n/a
WAJD	1390	General	M/N/T	Alternative

Note: Stations included broadcast in the Gainesville metro area; n/a not available
Target Audience: A=Asian; B=Black; C=Christian; E=Ethnic; F=French; G=General; H=Hispanic; M=Men; N=Native American; R=Religious; S=Senior Citizen; W=Women; Y=Young Adult; Z=Children
Station Format: E=Educational; M=Music; N=News; S=Sports; T=Talk
Music Format: AOR=Album Oriented Rock; MOR=Middle-of-the-Road
Source: Burrelle's Media Directory, 1999 Edition

FM Radio Stations

Call Letters	Freq. (mHz)	Target Audience	Station Format	Music Format
WUFT	89.1	General	M/N	Blues/Classical/Jazz/Reggae/Rhythm & Blues/World Music
WJUF	90.1	General	M/N	Classical/Jazz
WYFB	90.5	General	E/M	Christian
WSKY	97.3	n/a	N/T	n/a
WKTK	98.5	General	M	Adult Contemporary
WYGC	100.9	General	M	Country
WRUF	103.7	General	M/S	AOR
WRKG	104.9	General	M/N/S	Classic Rock
WYKS	105.3	General	M	n/a

Note: Stations included broadcast in the Gainesville metro area; n/a not available
Station Format: E=Educational; M=Music; N=News; S=Sports; T=Talk
Target Audience: A=Asian; B=Black; C=Christian; E=Ethnic; F=French; G=General; H=Hispanic; M=Men; N=Native American; R=Religious; S=Senior Citizen; W=Women; Y=Young Adult; Z=Children
Music Format: AOR=Album Oriented Rock; MOR=Middle-of-the-Road
Source: Burrelle's Media Directory, 1999 Edition

WEATHER

Temperature/Precipitation/Humidity

	Jan	Feb	Mar	Apr	May	Jun	Jul	Aug	Sep	Oct	Nov	Dec	Yr.
Max. High Temp. (°F)	89	89	96	95	101	104	102	100	99	96	90	87	104
Avg. High Temp. (°F)	69	71	76	81	87	90	91	91	89	83	75	69	81
Avg. Temp. (°F)	58	59	64	69	75	79	81	81	79	72	63	58	70
Avg. Low Temp. (°F)	47	48	53	58	64	69	71	71	70	61	52	47	59
Min. Low Temp. (°F)	14	6	24	32	43	54	60	60	48	33	22	12	6
Avg. Precip. (in.)	3.0	3.0	3.4	2.9	3.2	6.7	7.3	7.1	5.5	3.3	1.9	3.0	50.2
Avg. Snowfall (in.)	0	0	0	0	0	0	0	0	0	0	0	0	0
Avg. Rel. Hum. (%)	75	73	71	70	72	76	79	80	82	78	77	76	76

Source: National Climatic Data Center, International Station Meteorological Climate Summary, 3/95

Weather Conditions

Temperature			Precipitation		
0°F & below	32°F & below	90°F & above	0.1 inch or more precip.	1.5 inch or more snow/ice	Thunder-storms
0	12	79	83	0	69

Note: Figures are average number of days per year
Source: National Climatic Data Center, International Station Meteorological Climate Summary, 3/95

AIR & WATER QUALITY

Maximum Pollutant Concentrations

	Particulate Matter (ug/m³)	Carbon Monoxide (ppm)	Sulfur Dioxide (ppm)	Nitrogen Dioxide (ppm)	Ozone (ppm)	Lead (ug/m³)
MSA[1] Level	41	n/a	n/a	n/a	0.09	n/a
NAAQS[2]	150	9	0.140	0.053	0.12	1.50
Met NAAQS	Yes	n/a	n/a	n/a	Yes	n/a

Note: (1) Metropolitan Statistical Area - see Appendix A for areas included; (2) National Ambient Air Quality Standards; ppm = parts per million; ug/m³ = micrograms per cubic meter; n/a not available
Source: EPA, National Air Quality and Emissions Trends Report, 1997

Pollutant Standards Index

Data not available.
EPA, National Air Quality and Emissions Trends Report, 1997

Drinking Water

Water System Name	Pop. Served	Primary Water Source Type	Number of Violations in 1998-99	Type of Violation/ Contaminants
Gainesville (Murphree WTP)	150,000	Ground	None	None

Note: Data as of January 19, 2000
Source: EPA, Office of Ground Water and Drinking Water, Safe Drinking Water Information System

Gainesville tap water is alkaline and soft.
Editor & Publisher Market Guide, 2000

Greenville, South Carolina

Background

Greenville, South Carolina is located in the northwest section of the state in the foothills of the Blue Ridge Mountains. The city sits on the Reedy River, and is a short drive from Asheville and about 25 miles southeast from Sassafras Mountain, the highest point in South Carolina at 3,560 feet.

Commercial activity is dominated by the textile industry, although dairy production, cattle farming and peach growing are also important economic segments. Greenville also manufactures chemicals, paper, plastic film, machinery, tires, electronics and aircraft.

The city was first called Pleasantville by settlers in the 1760s, and renamed Greenville in 1821, probably for an early settler named Isaac Green. It was chartered as a village in 1831, soon developing into a summer resort community, thanks to its riverfront location.

The power of the Reedy River was harnessed after the Civil War to create the area's thriving textile industry. More recently, the entire southern Appalachian Mountain area in South Carolina has become one the fastest growing economies in the southeastern U.S. That, along with the region's beautiful scenery and almost year-round sunshine, lures businesses and professionals to its booming job market, making Greenville an exciting place to live.

The city is home to several colleges including Furman University, founded in 1826 as a Baptist theological school. Cultural and entertainment venues include the Bi-Lo Center, a new 16,000-seat entertainment complex, the Palmetto International Exposition Center, a symphony orchestra, several theatre organizations and a county art museum.

General Rankings and Evaluative Comments

- Greenville was ranked #75 out of 354 metropolitan areas in *Places Rated Almanac*. Criteria: cost of living, climate, crime, transportation, job outlook, education, the arts, health care, and recreation. *Places Rated Almanac, Millennium Edition, 2000*

- Cognetics studied 273 metro areas in the United States, ranking them by entrepreneurial activity. Greenville was ranked #23 out of 134 smaller metro areas. Criteria: Significant Starts (firms started in the last 10 years that still employ at least 5 people) and Young Growers (percent of firms 10 years old or less that grew significantly during the last 4 years). *Cognetics, "Entrepreneurial Hot Spots: The Best Places in America to Start and Grow a Company," 1999*

- Reliastar Financial Corporation ranked the 125 largest metropolitan areas according to the general financial security of residents. Greenville was ranked #58 out of 125 with a score of 3.6 (the percentage a metropolitan area is above or below the metropolitan norm; a metro area with a score of 10.6 is 10.6% above the metro average). Criteria: Earnings and Wealth Potential (household income, education, net assets, cost of living); Safety Net (health insurance, retirement savings, life insurance, income support programs); Personal Threats (unemployment rate, low-income households, crime rate); Community Economic Vitality (cost of community services, job quality, job creation, housing costs). *Reliastar Financial Corporation, "The Best Cities to Earn and Save Money: A Ranking of the Largest 125 U.S. Cities," 2000 Edition*

Business Environment

STATE ECONOMY

State Economic Profile

"South Carolina has been on a roll and is expected to continue that trend. South Carolina's friendly business environment and high quality of life have attracted an amazing number of businesses and residents. Both the construction and housing markets have been booming. As the US economy cools, its feverish growth will slow; however, South Carolina will remain one of the nation's fastest growing states.

South Carolina non-farm employment grew by 4.0% in 1998. Although manufacturing employment growth slowed to 0.2%, service jobs expanded at 6.1%. Many of these service jobs are in the tourism industry, which benefited in 1998 from the strong US expansion. Other important gains took place in the financial and business services sectors.

South Carolina construction employment grew by 9.8% in 1998, with residential permits growing by 8% and home sales growing by almost 17%. The continued expansion of the Port of Charleston and the strong Charlotte-Gastonia-Rock Hill commercial markets brought a wave of new commercial construction in 1998. Home sales and construction activity are expected to slow in 2000, although still remain strong by national standards.

Unlike many states, South Carolina's strength is spread across the state. Expanding port facilities, fueled by the auto industry, are helping drive job growth in Charleston. Columbia added jobs at a rate of 3% in 1998, below the state average but still high above the national. Employment gains were also strong along the I-85 corridor. The state's real strength has been its ability to attract new residents, both in the form of new workers and retirees. South Carolina's affordable living and pleasant climate will assure continued strong positive migration." *National Association of Realtors, Economic Profiles: The Fifty States and the District of Columbia, http://nar.realtor.com/databank/profiles.htm*

EXPORTS

Total Export Sales

Area	1995 ($000)	1996 ($000)	1997 ($000)	1998 ($000)	% Chg. 1995-98	% Chg. 1997-98
MSA[1]	2,305,311	2,720,417	3,076,918	3,124,156	35.5	1.5
U.S.	583,030,524	622,827,063	687,597,999	680,474,251	16.7	-1.0

Note: (1) Metropolitan Statistical Area - see Appendix A for areas included
Source: U.S. Department of Commerce, International Trade Association, Metropolitan Area Exports: An Export Performance Report on Over 250 U.S. Cities, November 10, 1999

CITY FINANCES

City Government Finances

Component	1995 ($million)	1995 (per capita $)
Revenue	53.7	898
Expenditure	51.9	868
Debt Outstanding	36.0	602

Source: 1999 County and City Extra, Annual Metro, City, and County Data Book

City Government Revenue by Source

Source	1995 ($million)	1995 (per capita $)
Intergovernmental	6.6	110
Taxes	33.2	556
Property	18.9	317
Sales and Gross Receipts	3.2	55

Source: 1999 County and City Extra, Annual Metro, City, and County Data Book

City Government Expenditures by Function

Function	1995 ($million)	1995 (per capita $)	1995 (%)
Public Welfare	0.0	0	0.0
Highways	2.3	39	4.6
Parking Facilities	0.3	5	0.6
Education	0.0	0	0.0
Health and Hospitals	0.5	9	1.1
Police Protection	8.9	150	17.3
Sewerage and Sanitation	4.8	80	9.3
Parks and Recreation	3.9	66	7.7
Housing and Community Development	1.6	26	3.1
Interest on Debt	0.9	16	1.9

Source: 1999 County and City Extra, Annual Metro, City, and County Data Book

Municipal Bond Ratings

Area	Moody's
City	Aa3

Source: Mergent Bond Record, 2/2000

POPULATION

Population Growth

Area	1980 Census	1990 Census	1999 Estimate	2004 Projection	Population Growth (%) 1990-1999	Population Growth (%) 1999-2004
City	58,242	58,282	55,965	55,324	-4.0	-1.1
MSA[1]	570,211	640,861	926,654	964,352	44.6	4.1
U.S.	226,545,805	248,765,170	272,212,864	283,625,312	9.4	4.2

Note: (1) Metropolitan Statistical Area - see Appendix A for areas included
Source: 1990 Census of Population and Housing, Summary Tape File 3C; Claritas, Inc.

Number of Households and Average Household Size

Area	1980 Census	1990 Census	1999 Estimate	2004 Projection	1999 Average Household Size
City	22,890	24,124	24,163	24,360	2.32
MSA[1]	258,127	240,878	361,078	381,792	2.57
U.S.	80,389,592	91,993,582	102,048,200	107,302,392	2.67

Note: (1) Metropolitan Statistical Area - see Appendix A for areas included
Source: 1990 Census of Population and Housing, Summary Tape File 3C; Claritas, Inc.

Race/Ethnicity of City Population

Race/Ethnicity	1990 Census Population	1990 Census %	1999 Estimate Population	1999 Estimate %	% Change 1990-1999
White, Non-Hispanic	36,808	63.2	34,012	60.8	-7.6
Black, Non-Hispanic	20,452	35.1	20,274	36.2	-0.9
Asian, Non-Hispanic	364	0.6	638	1.1	75.3
Other, Non-Hispanic	91	0.2	108	0.2	18.7
Hispanic	567	1.0	933	1.7	64.6

Source: 1990 Census of Population and Housing, Summary Tape File 3C; Claritas, Inc.

Race/Ethnicity of Metropolitan Statistical Area Population

Race/Ethnicity	1990 Census Population	%	1999 Estimate Population	%	% Change 1990-1999
White, Non-Hispanic	519,406	81.0	740,994	80.0	42.7
Black, Non-Hispanic	111,262	17.4	166,021	17.9	49.2
Asian, Non-Hispanic	4,074	0.6	7,575	0.8	85.9
Other, Non-Hispanic	1,117	0.2	1,625	0.2	45.5
Hispanic	5,002	0.8	10,439	1.1	108.7

Note: See Appendix A for areas included in the Metropolitan Statistical Area
Source: 1990 Census of Population and Housing, Summary Tape File 3C; Claritas, Inc.

Ancestry

Area	German	Irish	English	Italian	U.S.	French	Polish	Dutch
City	13.8	12.0	16.7	1.7	6.3	2.9	1.0	1.6
MSA[1]	14.7	17.5	16.1	1.7	11.9	2.5	0.8	2.1
U.S.	23.3	15.6	13.1	5.9	5.3	4.2	3.8	2.5

Note: Figures are percentages and include persons that reported multiple ancestry (eg. if a person reported being Irish and Italian, they were included in both columns); (1) Metropolitan Statistical Area - see Appendix A for areas included
Source: 1990 Census of Population and Housing, Summary Tape File 3C

Median Age

Area	1990 Census	1999 Estimate
City	32.6	35.5
MSA[1]	33.1	36.4
U.S.	32.9	35.7

Note: (1) Metropolitan Statistical Area - see Appendix A for areas included
Source: 1990 Census of Population and Housing, Summary Tape File 3C; Claritas, Inc.

Male/Female Population

Area	Number of Males 1990	1999	Number of Females 1990	1999	Males per 100 Females 1990	1999
City	26,604	25,664	31,678	30,301	84.0	84.7
MSA[1]	309,136	447,404	331,725	479,250	93.2	93.4
U.S.	121,172,379	132,803,736	127,537,494	139,409,136	95.0	95.3

Note: (1) Metropolitan Statistical Area - see Appendix A for areas included
Source: 1990 Census of Population, General Population Characteristics; Claritas, Inc.

INCOME

Per Capita/Median/Average Income

Area	Per Capita ($) 1989	1999	% Chg.	Median Household ($) 1989	1999	% Chg.	Average Household ($) 1989	1999	% Chg.
City	14,708	23,970	63.0	23,963	35,502	48.2	34,382	53,360	55.2
MSA[1]	12,952	19,760	52.6	27,840	37,825	35.9	33,994	50,044	47.2
U.S.	14,420	21,350	48.1	30,056	40,525	34.8	38,453	56,184	46.1

Note: (1) Metropolitan Statistical Area - see Appendix A for areas included; 1989 data is from the 1990 Census; 1999 data is estimated by Claritas, Inc.
Source: 1990 Census of Population, General Population Characteristics; Claritas, Inc.

Household Income Distribution

Area	Percent of Households Earning								
	Under $5,000	$5,000 -14,999	$15,000 -24,999	$25,000 -34,999	$35,000 -49,999	$50,000 -74,999	$75,000 -99,000	$100,000 -149,999	$150,000 and up
City	5.9	15.9	14.4	13.1	15.9	17.4	7.5	4.9	4.9
MSA[1]	4.0	14.5	14.6	13.2	17.0	20.0	8.5	5.4	2.7
U.S.	3.9	13.3	13.8	12.6	16.2	19.4	9.7	6.6	4.6

Note: Data as of 1999; (1) Metropolitan Statistical Area - see Appendix A for areas included
Source: Claritas, Inc.

Effective Buying Income

Area	Per Capita ($)	Median Household ($)	Average Household ($)
City	17,259	28,793	40,676
MSA[1]	15,356	33,112	40,485
U.S.	17,496	36,603	47,036

Note: Data as of 1/1/2000; (1) Metropolitan Statistical Area - see Appendix A for areas included
Source: Standard Rate & Data Service, Newspaper Advertising Source, March 2000

Effective Household Buying Income Distribution

Area	% of Households Earning						
	$10,000 -$19,999	$20,000 -$34,999	$35,000 -$49,999	$50,000 -$74,999	$75,000 -$99,000	$100,000 -$124,999	$125,000 and up
City	18.2	23.3	16.0	14.3	5.3	2.0	3.8
MSA[1]	16.5	23.5	18.7	18.5	6.5	1.9	1.7
U.S.	15.0	21.6	17.6	19.6	8.4	3.0	3.3

Note: Data as of 1/1/2000; (1) Metropolitan Statistical Area - see Appendix A for areas included
Source: Standard Rate & Data Service, Newspaper Advertising Source, March 2000

Poverty Rates by Age

Area	People of All Ages	People Under 18 Years Old	Related Children Age 5-17 in Families in Poverty
City	18.7	n/a	n/a
County	10.7	17.2	14.8
U.S.	13.8	20.8	18.7

Note: Figures show the percent of people living below the poverty line in 1995. The average poverty threshold was $15,569 for a family of four in 1995; n/a not available
Source: Bureau of the Census, Small Area Income and Poverty Estimates Program; U.S. Department of Housing and Urban Development

EMPLOYMENT

Labor Force and Employment

Area	Civilian Labor Force			Workers Employed		
	Dec. 1998	Dec. 1999	% Chg.	Dec. 1998	Dec. 1999	% Chg.
City	34,103	34,541	1.3	33,329	33,669	1.0
MSA[1]	489,095	495,052	1.2	477,063	481,931	1.0
U.S.	138,297,000	139,941,000	1.2	132,732,000	134,696,000	1.5

Note: Data is not seasonally adjusted and covers workers 16 years of age and older; (1) Metropolitan Statistical Area - see Appendix A for areas included
Source: Bureau of Labor Statistics, http://stats.bls.gov

Unemployment Rate

Area	1999											
	Jan.	Feb.	Mar.	Apr.	May	Jun.	Jul.	Aug.	Sep.	Oct.	Nov.	Dec.
City	2.7	3.0	2.3	2.5	2.8	3.0	2.8	2.6	2.8	3.1	2.9	2.5
MSA[1]	3.0	3.2	2.5	2.8	2.8	3.2	3.4	2.8	3.0	3.1	3.0	2.7
U.S.	4.8	4.7	4.4	4.1	4.0	4.5	4.5	4.2	4.1	3.8	3.8	3.7

Note: Data is not seasonally adjusted and covers workers 16 years of age and older; all figures are percentages; (1) Metropolitan Statistical Area - see Appendix A for areas included
Source: Bureau of Labor Statistics, http://stats.bls.gov

Employment by Industry

Sector	MSA[1]		U.S.
	Number of Employees	Percent of Total	Percent of Total
Services	109,800	22.6	30.2
Retail Trade	97,800	20.2	18.1
Government	60,400	12.4	15.8
Manufacturing	118,200	24.4	14.1
Finance/Insurance/Real Estate	16,500	3.4	5.9
Wholesale Trade	29,300	6.0	5.4
Transportation/Public Utilities	20,700	4.3	5.3
Construction	n/a	n/a	4.8
Mining	n/a	n/a	0.4

Note: Figures cover non-farm employment as of 12/99 and are not seasonally adjusted; (1) Metropolitan Statistical Area - see Appendix A for areas included; n/a not available
Source: Bureau of Labor Statistics, http://stats.bls.gov

Employment by Occupation

Occupation Category	City (%)	MSA[1] (%)	U.S. (%)
White Collar	60.2	52.6	58.1
Executive/Admin./Management	12.7	10.7	12.3
Professional	17.5	12.6	14.1
Technical & Related Support	3.5	3.8	3.7
Sales	14.2	11.7	11.8
Administrative Support/Clerical	12.3	13.8	16.3
Blue Collar	22.6	35.2	26.2
Precision Production/Craft/Repair	7.3	13.1	11.3
Machine Operators/Assem./Insp.	8.3	13.6	6.8
Transportation/Material Movers	3.1	4.0	4.1
Cleaners/Helpers/Laborers	3.9	4.4	3.9
Services	16.3	11.2	13.2
Farming/Forestry/Fishing	0.9	1.0	2.5

Note: Figures cover workers 16 years of age and older; (1) Metropolitan Statistical Area - see Appendix A for areas included
Source: 1990 Census of Population and Housing, Summary Tape File 3C

Occupational Employment Projections: 1996 - 2006

Occupations Expected to Have the Largest Job Growth (ranked by numerical growth)	Fast-Growing Occupations[1] (ranked by percent growth)
1. Cashiers	1. Desktop publishers
2. Salespersons, retail	2. Database administrators
3. General managers & top executives	3. Computer engineers
4. Marketing & sales, supervisors	4. Paralegals
5. Food preparation workers	5. Systems analysts
6. Truck drivers, light	6. Personal and home care aides
7. Cooks, fast food and short order	7. Medical assistants
8. Food service workers	8. Physical therapy assistants and aides
9. Waiters & waitresses	9. Respiratory therapists
10. Food service and lodging managers	10. Data processing equipment repairers

Note: Projections cover South Carolina; (1) Excludes occupations with total job growth less than 300
Source: U.S. Department of Labor, Employment and Training Administration, America's Labor Market Information System (ALMIS)

Average Wages

Occupation	$/Hr.	Occupation	$/Hr.
Accountants and Auditors	18.52	Maids and Housekeepers	6.74
Assemblers and Fabricators	10.36	Maintenance Repairers	12.41
Automotive Mechanics	12.47	Marketing/Advertising/PR Managers	26.64
Bookkeepers	10.66	Nurses, Licensed Practical	11.60
Carpenters	10.67	Nurses, Registered	18.75
Cashiers	6.62	Nursing Aides/Orderlies/Attendants	7.36
Clerks, General Office	9.23	Physicians and Surgeons	52.55
Clerks, Shipping/Receiving/Traffic	10.57	Receptionists/Information Clerks	8.75
Computer Programmers	20.98	Sales Reps., Exc. Scientific/Retail	18.84
Computer Support Specialists	17.10	Sales Reps., Scientific, Exc. Retail	22.82
Cooks, Restaurant	7.82	Salespersons, Retail	9.32
Electricians	14.41	Secretaries, Except Legal/Medical	10.81
Financial Managers	26.77	Stock Clerks, Sales Floor	7.87
First-Line Supervisors/Mgrs., Sales	14.97	Systems Analysts	24.72
Food Preparation Workers	6.64	Teacher Aides	6.85
General Managers/Top Executives	27.82	Teachers, Elementary School	16.48
Guards	8.66	Teachers, Secondary School	16.50
Hand Packers	7.59	Telemarketers	9.78
Janitors and Cleaners	6.96	Truck Drivers, Heavy/Tractor-Trailer	13.77
Laborers, Landscaping	8.60	Truck Drivers, Light	10.14
Lawyers	42.27	Waiters and Waitresses	6.35

Note: Wage data is for 1998 and covers the Metropolitan Statistical Area (see Appendix A for areas included). Hourly wages for elementary and secondary school teachers were calculated by the editors from annual wage data assuming a 40 hour work week; Dashes indicate that data was not available.
Source: Bureau of Labor Statistics, 1998 Metropolitan Area Occupational Employment and Wage Estimates

TAXES

Major State and Local Tax Rates

State Corporate Income (%)	State Personal Income (%)	Residential Property (%)	Sales & Use		State Gasoline (cents/ gallon)	State Cigarette (cents/ pack)
			State (%)	Local (%)		
5.0	2.5 - 7.0	1.34	5.0	None	16.0	7.0

Note: Personal/corporate income, sales, gasoline and cigarette tax rates as of January 2000. Property tax rates as of April 2000.
Source: Federation of Tax Administrators, www.taxadmin.org; ERI's Relocation Assessor software database, quarterly effective date 4/1/2000

Total Taxes Per Capita and as a Percent of Income

Area	Per Capita Income ($)	Per Capita Taxes ($)			Percent of Income (%)		
		Total	Federal	State/Local	Total	Federal	State/Local
South Carolina	23,601	8,114	5,508	2,606	34.4	23.3	11.0
U.S.	28,878	10,298	7,026	3,273	35.7	24.3	11.3

Note: Figures are for 1999
Source: Tax Foundation, www.taxfoundation.org

COMMERCIAL UTILITIES

Typical Monthly Electric Bills

Area	Commercial Service ($/month)		Industrial Service ($/month)	
	12 kW demand 1,500 kWh	100 kW demand 30,000 kWh	1,000 kW demand 400,000 kWh	20,000 kW demand 10,000,000 kWh
City	150	1,784	20,348	275,692
U.S.	150	2,174	23,995	508,569

Note: Based on rates in effect January 1, 1999
Source: Edison Electric Institute, Typical Residential, Commercial and Industrial Bills, Winter 1999

TRANSPORTATION

Transportation Statistics

Average minutes to work (1990)	15.3
Interstate highways	I-85; I-385; US-25; US-29; US-123; U.
Bus lines	
In-city (1998)	Greenville Transit Authority, 8 buses
Inter-city (1999)	2
Passenger air service	
Airport	Greenville-Spartanburg International Airport
Airlines (1999)	8
Enplaned passengers (1998)	714,362
Amtrak service	Yes
Motor freight carriers (1999)	50
Major waterways/ports	None

Source: FAA DOT/TSC CY1998 ACAIS Database; National Transit Database, 1998; Editor & Publisher Market Guide, 2000; Amtrak National Time Table, Fall 1999/Winter 2000; 1990 Census of Population and Housing, STF 3C; Jane's Urban Transport Systems 1999-2000

Means of Transportation to Work

Area	Car/Truck/Van		Public Transportation			Bicycle	Walked	Other Means	Worked at Home
	Drove Alone	Car-pooled	Bus	Subway	Railroad				
City	71.6	13.8	2.3	0.0	0.0	0.2	9.1	1.0	2.0
MSA[1]	80.2	14.0	0.6	0.0	0.0	0.2	2.8	0.9	1.5
U.S.	73.2	13.4	3.0	1.5	0.5	0.4	3.9	1.2	3.0

Note: Figures shown are percentages and only include workers 16 years of age and older;
(1) Metropolitan Statistical Area - see Appendix A for areas included
Source: 1990 Census of Population and Housing, Summary Tape File 3C

BUSINESSES

Major Business Headquarters

Company Name	1999 Rankings	
	Fortune 500	Forbes 500
Builder Marts of America	-	389

Note: Companies listed are located in the city; dashes indicate no ranking
Fortune 500: Companies that produce a 10-K are ranked 1 to 500 based on 1999 revenue
Forbes 500: Private companies are ranked 1 to 500 based on 1998 revenue
Source: Forbes, December 13, 1999; Fortune, April 17, 2000

HOTELS & MOTELS

Hotels/Motels

Area	Hotels/ Motels	Rooms	Luxury-Level Hotels/Motels		Average Minimum Rates ($)		
			♦♦♦♦	♦♦♦♦♦	♦♦	♦♦♦	♦♦♦♦
City	34	3,198	0	0	59	91	n/a
Airport	9	1,215	0	0	n/a	n/a	n/a
Suburbs	6	879	0	0	n/a	n/a	n/a
Total	49	5,292	0	0	n/a	n/a	n/a

Note: n/a not available; classifications range from one diamond (budget properties with basic amenities) to five diamond (luxury properties).
Source: OAG Business Travel Planner, Winter 1999-2000

Estimated Daily Food and Lodging Costs

Area	Food/Other ($/day)	Average Hotel Cost ($/day)
City	38	62
U.S.	30	55

Source: ERI's Relocation Assessor software database, quarterly effective date 4/1/2000

CONVENTION CENTERS

Convention Centers and Event Sites

Name	Guest Rooms	Meeting Space (sq. ft.)	Capacity (Theatre Style)
Bi - Lo Center	n/a	n/a	16,000
Comfort Inn Executive Center	191	n/a	50
Embassy Suites Golf Resort	268	n/a	1,050
Furman University	n/a	n/a	1,800
Greenville - Spartanburg Airport Marriott	204	n/a	500
Greenville Convention Center	n/a	n/a	0
Greenville Hilton & Towers	256	n/a	500
Greenville Memorial Auditorium	n/a	n/a	7,200
Greenville-Spartanburg Airport Marriott	204	n/a	0
Holiday Inn	153	n/a	400
Holiday Inn Select	208	n/a	600
Hyatt Regency	327	14,800	2,400
Palmetto Expo Center	n/a	n/a	2,400
Palmetto International Exposition Center	n/a	n/a	3,000
Ramada Hotel Downtown/Medical Ctr.	142	n/a	725
The Phoenix - Greenville's Inn	185	n/a	300
Timmons Arena	n/a	n/a	6,000

Note: n/a not available
Source: EventSource.com, 3/15/2000

Living Environment

COST OF LIVING

Cost of Living: Homeowner

Cost Element	U.S. ($)	City ($)	Differential ($)	Percent of U.S. Average
Consumables	14,516	14,086	-430	97.0
Transportation	5,957	5,359	-598	90.0
Health Services	2,012	1,917	-95	95.3
Housing/Utilities/Prop. Tax	16,337	18,533	2,196	113.4
Income+Payroll Taxes	12,615	12,974	359	102.8
Miscellaneous	8,563	8,563	0	100.0
Total Cost of Living	60,000	61,432	1,432	102.4

Note: Figures are based on a single income, four person family with gross annual earnings of $60,000, owning an 1,800 square-foot home, and driving two automobiles worth $22,000 30,000 miles per year.
Source: ERI's Relocation Assessor software database, quarterly effective date 4/1/2000

Cost of Living: Renter

Cost Element	U.S. ($)	City ($)	Differential ($)	Percent of U.S. Average
Consumables	10,486	10,205	-281	97.3
Transportation	2,107	1,901	-206	90.2
Health Services	1,632	1,560	-72	95.6
Rent/Utilities/Insurance	9,299	10,324	1,025	111.0
Income+Payroll Taxes	8,607	9,079	472	105.5
Miscellaneous	7,869	7,869	0	100.0
Total Cost of Living	40,000	40,938	938	102.3

Note: Figures are based on a single income, three person family with gross annual earnings of $40,000, renting a 1,000 square-foot home, and driving one automobile worth $8,000 12,000 miles per year.
Source: ERI's Relocation Assessor software database, quarterly effective date 4/1/2000

HOUSING

Median Home Prices and Housing Affordability

Area	Median Price[2] 4th Qtr. 1999 ($)	HOI[3] 4th Qtr. 1999	Affordability Rank[4]
MSA[1]	109,000	74.0	68
U.S.	139,000	63.8	–

Note: (1) Metropolitan Statistical Area - see Appendix A for areas included; (2) U.S. figures calculated from the sales of 687,516 new and existing homes in 192 markets; (3) Housing Opportunity Index - percent of homes sold that were within the reach of the median income household at the prevailing mortgage interest rate; (4) Rank is from 1-192 with 1 being most affordable
Source: National Association of Home Builders, Housing Opportunity Index, 4th Quarter 1999

Estimated Home Price

Area	Price ($)
City	155,098
U.S.	135,855

Note: Figures are based on an 1,800 square-foot home
Source: ERI's Relocation Assessor software database, quarterly effective date 4/1/2000

Estimated Rent

Area	Rent ($/month)
City	735
U.S.	651

Note: Figures are based on a 1,000 square-foot home
Source: ERI's Relocation Assessor software database, quarterly effective date 4/1/2000

Median Home Price Projection

It is projected that the median home price in the metropolitan area will increase from $109,682 in 1999 to $168,473 in 2010, an increase of 53.6%
Kiplinger's Personal Finance Magazine, January 2000

RESIDENTIAL UTILITIES

Average Residential Utility Costs

Area	All Electric ($/mth)	Part Electric ($/mth)	Other Energy ($/mth)	Phone ($/mth)
City	n/a	n/a	n/a	n/a
U.S.	99.25	55.47	43.48	20.29

Note: n/a not available
Source: ACCRA, Cost of Living Index, 3rd Quarter 1999

HEALTH CARE

Average Health Care Costs

Area	Hospital ($/day)	Doctor ($/visit)	Dentist ($/visit)
City	n/a	n/a	n/a
U.S.	440.96	53.83	68.42

Note: n/a not available
Source: ACCRA, Cost of Living Index, 3rd Quarter 1999

Distribution of Office-Based Physicians

Area	Family/Gen. Practitioners	Specialists		
		Medical	Surgical	Other
MSA[1]	265	365	397	325

Note: Data as of 12/31/97; (1) Metropolitan Statistical Area - see Appendix A for areas included
Source: American Medical Assn., Physician Characteristics & Distribution in the U.S., 1999

Hospitals

Greenville has 2 general medical and surgical hospitals, 1 other specialty, 1 children's orthopedic.
AHA Guide to the Healthcare Field, 1999-2000

EDUCATION

Public School District Statistics

District Name	Num. Sch.	Enroll.	Classroom Teachers	Pupils per Teacher	Minority Pupils (%)	Current Exp.[1] ($/pupil)
Greenville County School Dist	91	56,967	3,418	16.7	29.9	4,532

Note: Data covers the 1997-1998 school year unless otherwise noted; (1) Data covers fiscal year 1996; SD = School District; ISD = Independent School District; n/a not available
Source: National Center for Education Statistics, Common Core of Data Public Education Agency Universe 1997-98; National Center for Education Statistics, Characteristics of the 100 Largest Public Elementary and Secondary School Districts in the United States: 1997-98, July 1999

Educational Quality

School District	Education Quotient[1]	Graduate Outcome[2]	Community Index[3]	Resource Index[4]
Greenville Co. School Dist.	89	102	83	63

Note: Over 1,000 secondary school districts were rated in terms of educational quality. The scores range from a low of 50 to a high of 150; (1) Combination of the Graduate Outcome, Community and Resource indexes weighted to reflect the greater importance of the Graduate Outcome and Resource Index; (2) Based on graduation rates and college board scores (SAT/ACT); (3) Based on the surrounding community's level of affluence and adult education; (4) Based on teacher salaries, per-pupil expenditures and student-teacher ratios.
Source: Expansion Management, Ratings Issue, 1999

Educational Attainment by Race

Area	High School Graduate (%)					Bachelor's Degree (%)				
	Total	White	Black	Other	Hisp.[2]	Total	White	Black	Other	Hisp.[2]
City	72.5	85.4	44.2	65.6	72.7	29.3	40.2	5.2	30.5	33.2
MSA[1]	67.7	70.6	51.6	72.1	66.3	18.0	19.8	7.4	34.6	29.4
U.S.	75.2	77.9	63.1	60.4	49.8	20.3	21.5	11.4	19.4	9.2

Note: Figures shown cover persons 25 years old and over; (1) Metropolitan Statistical Area - see Appendix A for areas included; (2) people of Hispanic origin can be of any race
Source: 1990 Census of Population and Housing, Summary Tape File 3C

School Enrollment by Type

Area	Preprimary				Elementary/High School			
	Public		Private		Public		Private	
	Enrollment	%	Enrollment	%	Enrollment	%	Enrollment	%
City	343	40.2	511	59.8	7,494	84.7	1,349	15.3
MSA[1]	5,164	51.6	4,850	48.4	99,780	92.3	8,302	7.7
U.S.	2,679,029	59.5	1,824,256	40.5	38,379,689	90.2	4,187,099	9.8

Note: Figures shown cover persons 3 years old and over;
(1) Metropolitan Statistical Area - see Appendix A for areas included
Source: 1990 Census of Population and Housing, Summary Tape File 3C

School Enrollment by Race

Area	Preprimary (%)				Elementary/High School (%)			
	White	Black	Other	Hisp.[1]	White	Black	Other	Hisp.[1]
City	67.2	32.1	0.7	1.8	46.3	52.7	1.0	0.8
MSA[2]	80.7	18.4	0.9	1.5	75.4	23.4	1.2	1.0
U.S.	80.4	12.5	7.1	7.8	74.1	15.6	10.3	12.5

Note: Figures shown cover persons 3 years old and over; (1) people of Hispanic origin can be of any race; (2) Metropolitan Statistical Area - see Appendix A for areas included
Source: 1990 Census of Population and Housing, Summary Tape File 3C

Higher Education

Two-Year Colleges		Four-Year Colleges		Medical Schools	Law Schools	Voc/ Tech
Public	Private	Public	Private			
1	1	0	1	0	0	7

Source: College Blue Book, Occupational Education, 1999; Medical School Admission Requirements, 1999-2000; Peterson's Guide to Two-Year Colleges, 2000; Peterson's Guide to Four-Year Colleges, 1999; Barron's Guide to Law Schools, 1999

MAJOR EMPLOYERS

Major Employers

Insignia Financial Group
Lockheed Martin Aircraft Center
Michelin Americas R&D Corp.
St. Francis Hospital
Umbro International (men's clothing)

Liberty Life Insurance
Metromont Prestress Co. (concrete products)
Michelin North America
Sterling Diagnostic Imaging

Note: Companies listed are located in the city
Source: D&B Business Rankings, 1999; Ward's Business Directory, 1999; America's Corporate Families, 1999

PUBLIC SAFETY

Crime Rate

Area	All Crimes	Violent Crimes				Property Crimes		
		Murder	Forcible Rape	Robbery	Aggrav. Assault	Burglary	Larceny -Theft	Motor Vehicle Theft
City	9,967.6	17.0	79.8	371.8	986.4	1,455.0	6,468.5	589.1
Suburbs[1]	5,023.2	5.9	38.9	144.4	599.6	1,073.7	2,816.4	344.3
MSA[2]	5,338.4	6.6	41.6	158.9	624.3	1,098.0	3,049.2	359.9
U.S.	4,615.5	6.3	34.4	165.2	360.5	862.0	2,728.1	459.0

Note: Crime rate is the number of crimes per 100,000 population; (1) Defined as all areas within the Metropolitan Statistical Area but located outside the central city; (2) Metropolitan Statistical Area - see Appendix A for areas included
Source: FBI Uniform Crime Reports, 1998

RECREATION

Culture and Recreation

Museums	Symphony Orchestras	Opera Companies	Dance Companies	Professional Theatres	Zoos	Pro Sports Teams
2	2	0	1	0	1	0

Source: Musical America, International Directory of the Performing Arts, 1999; Official Museum Directory, 2000; Stern's Performing Arts Directory, 1997; USA Today Four Sport Stadium Guide, 1997; Career Opportunities in Theatre and the Performing Arts, 1999

Library System

The Greenville County Library has 11 branches, holdings of 969,038 volumes, and a budget of $7,672,877 (1997-1998).
American Library Directory, 1999-2000

MEDIA

Newspapers

Name	Type	Freq.	Distribution	Circulation
The Baptist Courier	Religious	1x/wk	State	98,000
The Greenville News	General	7x/wk	Area	100,000

Note: Includes newspapers with circulations of 200 or more located in the city;
Source: Burrelle's Media Directory, 1999 Edition

Television Stations

Name	Ch.	Affiliation	Type	Owner
WYFF	n/a	NBCT	Commercial	Hearst-Argyle Broadcasting
WGGS	16	n/a	Commercial	Carolina Christian Broadcasting
WHNS	21	FBC	Commercial	Meredith Corporation
WFBC	40	n/a	Commercial	Glencairn Communications

Note: Stations included broadcast in the Greenville metro area; n/a not available
Source: Burrelle's Media Directory, 1999 Edition

AM Radio Stations

Call Letters	Freq. (kHz)	Target Audience	Station Format	Music Format
WESC	660	General	M	Oldies
WPJM	800	General	E/M/N/S/T	Adult Contemp./Christian/Oldies/Urban Contemp.
WORD	910	General	N/T	n/a
WMUU	1260	R/S	M	Christian
WCKI	1300	General	M/N	Christian
WYRD	1330	n/a	n/a	n/a
WGVL	1440	General	M	Country
WFIS	1600	General	M/N/S/T	Adult Contemporary

Note: Stations included broadcast in the Greenville metro area; n/a not available
Target Audience: A=Asian; B=Black; C=Christian; E=Ethnic; F=French; G=General; H=Hispanic;
M=Men; N=Native American; R=Religious; S=Senior Citizen; W=Women; Y=Young Adult; Z=Children
Station Format: E=Educational; M=Music; N=News; S=Sports; T=Talk
Source: Burrelle's Media Directory, 1999 Edition

FM Radio Stations

Call Letters	Freq. (mHz)	Target Audience	Station Format	Music Format
WLFJ	89.3	Religious	M/N/S	Adult Contemporary/Christian
WESC	92.5	General	M	Country
WTPT	93.3	General	n/a	n/a
WFBC	93.7	General	M	Top 40
WMUU	94.5	General	M	Christian/Classical/Easy Listening
WPLS	96.7	General	M/N/S	n/a
WPEK	98.1	General	N/S/T	n/a
WSPA	98.9	General	M/N	Adult Contemporary/Jazz
WSSL	100.5	General	M	Country
WROQ	101.1	General	M	Classic Rock
WMYI	102.5	General	M	Adult Contemporary
WOLT	103.3	General	M	Oldies
WOLI	103.9	General	M	Oldies
WJMZ	107.3	Black	M	Urban Contemporary

Note: Stations included broadcast in the Greenville metro area; n/a not available
Station Format: E=Educational; M=Music; N=News; S=Sports; T=Talk
Target Audience: A=Asian; B=Black; C=Christian; E=Ethnic; F=French; G=General; H=Hispanic;
M=Men; N=Native American; R=Religious; S=Senior Citizen; W=Women; Y=Young Adult; Z=Children
Source: Burrelle's Media Directory, 1999 Edition

WEATHER

Temperature/Precipitation/Humidity

	Jan	Feb	Mar	Apr	May	Jun	Jul	Aug	Sep	Oct	Nov	Dec	Yr.
Max. High Temp. (°F)	79	79	88	93	97	100	103	103	96	92	85	76	103
Avg. High Temp. (°F)	50	54	64	72	79	86	88	87	81	72	62	53	71
Avg. Temp. (°F)	40	43	52	60	68	75	78	77	71	61	52	44	60
Avg. Low Temp. (°F)	30	32	40	48	56	64	68	67	61	49	40	33	49
Min. Low Temp. (°F)	-6	8	11	25	31	40	54	52	36	25	12	5	-6
Avg. Precip. (in.)	4.0	4.2	5.4	3.7	4.5	4.5	4.7	3.8	4.1	4.1	3.6	3.9	50.6
Avg. Snowfall (in.)	3	2	1	Tr	0	0	0	0	0	Tr	1	6
Avg. Rel. Hum. 7am (%)	76	75	77	77	83	84	87	89	89	85	81	78	82
Avg. Rel. Hum. 4pm (%)	51	47	45	43	51	53	58	58	57	50	51	53	52

Note: Tr = Trace amounts (less than 0.05 inches of rain or less than 0.5 inches of snow)
Source: National Climatic Data Center, International Station Meteorological Climate Summary, 3/95

Weather Conditions

Temperature			Precipitation		
10°F & below	32°F & below	90°F & above	0.01 inch or more precip.	1.5 inch or more snow/ice	Thunder-storms
1	66	35	118	2	44

Note: Figures are average number of days per year
Source: National Climatic Data Center, International Station Meteorological Climate Summary, 3/95

AIR & WATER QUALITY

Maximum Pollutant Concentrations

	Particulate Matter (ug/m³)	Carbon Monoxide (ppm)	Sulfur Dioxide (ppm)	Nitrogen Dioxide (ppm)	Ozone (ppm)	Lead (ug/m³)
MSA[1] Level	53	6	0.014	0.017	0.11	0.01
NAAQS[2]	150	9	0.140	0.053	0.12	1.50
Met NAAQS	Yes	Yes	Yes	Yes	Yes	Yes

Note: (1) Metropolitan Statistical Area - see Appendix A for areas included; (2) National Ambient Air Quality Standards; ppm = parts per million; ug/m³ = micrograms per cubic meter; n/a not available
Source: EPA, National Air Quality and Emissions Trends Report, 1997

Pollutant Standards Index

In the Greenville MSA (see Appendix A for areas included), the Pollutant Standards Index (PSI) exceeded 100 on 10 days in 1997. A PSI value greater than 100 indicates that air quality would have been in the unhealthful range on that day.
EPA, National Air Quality and Emissions Trends Report, 1997

Drinking Water

Water System Name	Pop. Served	Primary Water Source Type	Number of Violations in 1998-99	Type of Violation/ Contaminants
Greenville Water System	273,000	Surface	None	None

Note: Data as of January 19, 2000
Source: EPA, Office of Ground Water and Drinking Water, Safe Drinking Water Information System

Greenville tap water is alkaline, very soft, and fluoridated.
Editor & Publisher Market Guide, 2000

Harrisburg, Pennsylvania

Background

Harrisburg, Pennsylvania is located in the south-central section of the state, on the east bank of the Susquehanna River, 115 miles west of Philadephia and 85 miles northwest of Baltimore, Maryland. The city is the state capital and the county seat of Dauphin County. The terrain around Harrisburg includes rolling countryside and the Blue Ridge and Appalachian mountains.

Harrisburg is a commercial and cultural center for south and central Pennsylvania. The greater metropolitan and suburban area of Harrisburg covers both sides of the mile-wide Susquehanna River, and nearby Steelton, New Cumberland and other communities.

Primary employers include the Commonwealth of Pennsylvania, Dauphin County and the Federal government. Several defense-related facilities are located in the region, including a Defense Distribution Center in New Cumberland and the U.S. Army War College in Carlisle. Other primary economic sectors of Harrisburg and the surrounding area include transportation and trade, manufacturing of steel, textiles and food products, insurance and other financial, business, and professional services, health care and retail and wholesale trade and tourism.

Various Native American tribes originally resided in the region. In 1718 an English colonist, John Harris, established a settlement near the present site of the city. His son, John Harris Jr. carried on operations, which included a river ferry. The Harris property eventually grew to the current site of Harrisburg. Harris Jr. laid out the community in 1785. In 1812 the legislature designated Harrisburg as Pennsylvania's capital. The town grew as a trading center for riverboat traffic on the Susquehanna, which flows into the Chesapeake Bay, and was connected to the Pennsylvania canal system. Rail lines and road systems also converge in Harrisburg, which encouraged the area to develop as a manufacturing center.

In the mid-20th Century, several of Pennsylvania's traditional industries, including iron and steel, experienced declines, causing a downturn in the Harrisburg economy. More recently, however, the city has experienced growth and diversification with economic development and revitalization initiatives, including the New Baldwin Corridor Enterprise Zone which extends over seven municipalities.

Institutions of higher education in the Harrisburg area include Harrisburg Community College and Widener University School of Law. The Dixon University Center operates as an educational consortium by the 14 universities of the State System of Higher Education and by affiliate members Duquesne University, Elizabethtown College and Philadelphia College of Osteopathic Medicine. The Pennsylvania State University has area branches in downtown Harrisburg, Eastgate, and at Penn State Harrisburg, an undergraduate transfer college and graduate school in Middleburg. Temple University operates a satellite campus in Harrisburg. Central Pennsylvania College is located in Summerdale.

Parks and recreation areas include Italian Lake and the Wildwood Lake Sanctuary. On the Sasquahana, are Riverfront Park and City Island, which includes the home stadium of the Harrisburg Senators, a Class AA baseball team of the Montreal Expos. The city is also home of the Harrisburg Heat soccer team.

The state government complex is a prominent landmark and attraction. It includes the State Museum of Pennsylvania. The Italian Renaissance-style State Capitol building, which was opened in 1906, is topped by a Vatican-styled gold dome. Other cultural venues include the multipurpose Whitaker Center for Science and the Arts, and the John Harris/Simon Cameron Mansion museum in the home of the city's founder. The city is home to the Art Association of Harrisburg and various performing arts groups.

Harrisburg is governed by a Mayor and City Council.

General Rankings and Evaluative Comments

- Harrisburg was ranked #60 out of 354 metropolitan areas in *Places Rated Almanac*. Criteria: cost of living, climate, crime, transportation, job outlook, education, the arts, health care, and recreation. *Places Rated Almanac, Millennium Edition, 2000*

- Cognetics studied 273 metro areas in the United States, ranking them by entrepreneurial activity. Harrisburg was ranked #125 out of 134 smaller metro areas. Criteria: Significant Starts (firms started in the last 10 years that still employ at least 5 people) and Young Growers (percent of firms 10 years old or less that grew significantly during the last 4 years). *Cognetics, "Entrepreneurial Hot Spots: The Best Places in America to Start and Grow a Company," 1999*

- Reliastar Financial Corporation ranked the 125 largest metropolitan areas according to the general financial security of residents. Harrisburg was ranked #15 out of 125 with a score of 12.4 (the percentage a metropolitan area is above or below the metropolitan norm; a metro area with a score of 10.6 is 10.6% above the metro average). Criteria: Earnings and Wealth Potential (household income, education, net assets, cost of living); Safety Net (health insurance, retirement savings, life insurance, income support programs); Personal Threats (unemployment rate, low-income households, crime rate); Community Economic Vitality (cost of community services, job quality, job creation, housing costs). *Reliastar Financial Corporation, "The Best Cities to Earn and Save Money: A Ranking of the Largest 125 U.S. Cities," 2000 Edition*

Business Environment

STATE ECONOMY

State Economic Profile

"Pennsylvania's economy has lagged the nation for several years, a trend that will only get worse. While Philadelphia has seen some resurgence, it has not been enough to offset declines in the rest of the state. Pennsylvania's poor demographic outlook will confine it to slow growth at best in 2000. Expansions by high-tech and biotech firms, such as Lucent, SAP and SmithKline Beecham, will help Pennsylvania's weak job outlook, although these gains will be limited to the eastern part of the state.

Pennsylvania employment grew at the low rate of 0.8% in 1998, driven largely by the 1.0% increase in Philadelphia. In contrast, Pittsburgh lost jobs at a rate of 0.1%. While many areas of the country are experiencing declining manufacturing employment, due to weak export demand and long-term restructuring, Pittsburgh is one of the few urban areas that is also losing service jobs, at a rate of 0.4% in 1998. Services employment for Pennsylvania grew 1.3% and 1.9% for Philadelphia in 1998.

Some of western Pennsylvania's problems stem from its declining steel sector. Weak steel prices, over capacity and a flood of cheap imports have undermined Pennsylvania's steel industry. Even with import restraints and renewed world demand, the outlook for Pennsylvania's steel industry remains bleak. Pennsylvania's steel producers' biggest problem is US mini-mills that are sweeping the industry. Further declines in Pennsylvania's steel industry are likely in 2000.

Few states lose more residents every year than Pennsylvania. Its continued loss of younger households will constrain labor market growth and pose problems for its housing market. Home sales were flat in 1998, and residential permits were up only 3%. Both sales and starts should contract in the near future." *National Association of Realtors, Economic Profiles: The Fifty States and the District of Columbia, http://nar.realtor.com/databank/profiles.htm*

EXPORTS

Total Export Sales

Area	1995 ($000)	1996 ($000)	1997 ($000)	1998 ($000)	% Chg. 1995-98	% Chg. 1997-98
MSA[1]	600,973	775,520	964,423	952,919	58.6	-1.2
U.S.	583,030,524	622,827,063	687,597,999	680,474,251	16.7	-1.0

Note: (1) Metropolitan Statistical Area - see Appendix A for areas included
Source: U.S. Department of Commerce, International Trade Association, Metropolitan Area Exports: An Export Performance Report on Over 250 U.S. Cities, November 10, 1999

CITY FINANCES

City Government Finances

Component	1995 ($million)	1995 (per capita $)
Revenue	57.6	1,060
Expenditure	57.5	1,060
Debt Outstanding	12.3	226

Source: 1999 County and City Extra, Annual Metro, City, and County Data Book

City Government Revenue by Source

Source	1995 ($million)	1995 (per capita $)
Intergovernmental	12.1	222
Taxes	16.8	310
Property	11.2	207
Sales and Gross Receipts	0.0	0

Source: 1999 County and City Extra, Annual Metro, City, and County Data Book

City Government Expenditures by Function

Function	1995 ($million)	1995 (per capita $)	1995 (%)
Public Welfare	0.0	0	0.0
Highways	4.6	84	8.0
Parking Facilities	0.0	0	0.0
Education	0.0	0	0.0
Health and Hospitals	0.0	0	0.0
Police Protection	10.2	188	17.8
Sewerage and Sanitation	16.1	297	28.1
Parks and Recreation	3.7	68	6.5
Housing and Community Development	3.2	60	5.7
Interest on Debt	0.8	14	1.4

Source: 1999 County and City Extra, Annual Metro, City, and County Data Book

Municipal Bond Ratings

Area	Moody's
City	Aaa

Source: Mergent Bond Record, 2/2000

POPULATION

Population Growth

Area	1980 Census	1990 Census	1999 Estimate	2004 Projection	Population Growth (%) 1990-1999	Population Growth (%) 1999-2004
City	53,264	52,376	49,326	47,161	-5.8	-4.4
MSA[1]	555,158	587,986	617,166	620,421	5.0	0.5
U.S.	226,545,805	248,765,170	272,212,864	283,625,312	9.4	4.2

Note: (1) Metropolitan Statistical Area - see Appendix A for areas included
Source: 1990 Census of Population and Housing, Summary Tape File 3C; Claritas, Inc.

Number of Households and Average Household Size

Area	1980 Census	1990 Census	1999 Estimate	2004 Projection	1999 Average Household Size
City	22,029	21,450	20,638	19,885	2.39
MSA[1]	201,169	226,267	240,650	243,495	2.56
U.S.	80,389,592	91,993,582	102,048,200	107,302,392	2.67

Note: (1) Metropolitan Statistical Area - see Appendix A for areas included
Source: 1990 Census of Population and Housing, Summary Tape File 3C; Claritas, Inc.

Race/Ethnicity of City Population

Race/Ethnicity	1990 Census Population	1990 Census %	1999 Estimate Population	1999 Estimate %	% Change 1990-1999
White, Non-Hispanic	21,275	40.6	14,828	30.1	-30.3
Black, Non-Hispanic	26,205	50.0	27,627	56.0	5.4
Asian, Non-Hispanic	821	1.6	890	1.8	8.4
Other, Non-Hispanic	337	0.6	277	0.6	-17.8
Hispanic	3,738	7.1	5,704	11.6	52.6

Source: 1990 Census of Population and Housing, Summary Tape File 3C; Claritas, Inc.

Race/Ethnicity of Metropolitan Statistical Area Population

Race/Ethnicity	1990 Census		1999 Estimate		% Change 1990-1999
	Population	%	Population	%	
White, Non-Hispanic	532,983	90.6	545,522	88.4	2.4
Black, Non-Hispanic	38,617	6.6	46,104	7.5	19.4
Asian, Non-Hispanic	5,901	1.0	9,242	1.5	56.6
Other, Non-Hispanic	1,149	0.2	1,349	0.2	17.4
Hispanic	9,336	1.6	14,949	2.4	60.1

Note: See Appendix A for areas included in the Metropolitan Statistical Area
Source: 1990 Census of Population and Housing, Summary Tape File 3C; Claritas, Inc.

Ancestry

Area	German	Irish	English	Italian	U.S.	French	Polish	Dutch
City	17.8	7.6	4.5	4.0	2.1	1.0	1.4	1.8
MSA[1]	52.2	14.4	9.3	6.1	3.2	2.2	3.2	3.6
U.S.	23.3	15.6	13.1	5.9	5.3	4.2	3.8	2.5

Note: Figures are percentages and include persons that reported multiple ancestry (eg. if a person reported being Irish and Italian, they were included in both columns); (1) Metropolitan Statistical Area - see Appendix A for areas included
Source: 1990 Census of Population and Housing, Summary Tape File 3C

Median Age

Area	1990 Census	1999 Estimate
City	31.7	34.2
MSA[1]	34.8	37.8
U.S.	32.9	35.7

Note: (1) Metropolitan Statistical Area - see Appendix A for areas included
Source: 1990 Census of Population and Housing, Summary Tape File 3C; Claritas, Inc.

Male/Female Population

Area	Number of Males		Number of Females		Males per 100 Females	
	1990	1999	1990	1999	1990	1999
City	24,436	23,141	27,940	26,185	87.5	88.4
MSA[1]	284,409	297,957	303,577	319,209	93.7	93.3
U.S.	121,172,379	132,803,736	127,537,494	139,409,136	95.0	95.3

Note: (1) Metropolitan Statistical Area - see Appendix A for areas included
Source: 1990 Census of Population, General Population Characteristics; Claritas, Inc.

INCOME

Per Capita/Median/Average Income

Area	Per Capita ($)			Median Household ($)			Average Household ($)		
	1989	1999	% Chg.	1989	1999	% Chg.	1989	1999	% Chg.
City	11,037	15,928	44.3	20,329	26,685	31.3	26,385	37,394	41.7
MSA[1]	14,659	22,056	50.5	31,637	44,240	39.8	37,459	55,498	48.2
U.S.	14,420	21,350	48.1	30,056	40,525	34.8	38,453	56,184	46.1

Note: (1) Metropolitan Statistical Area - see Appendix A for areas included; 1989 data is from the 1990 Census; 1999 data is estimated by Claritas, Inc.
Source: 1990 Census of Population, General Population Characteristics; Claritas, Inc.

Household Income Distribution

Area	Percent of Households Earning								
	Under $5,000	$5,000 -14,999	$15,000 -24,999	$25,000 -34,999	$35,000 -49,999	$50,000 -74,999	$75,000 -99,000	$100,000 -149,999	$150,000 and up
City	7.4	21.0	18.8	13.4	16.6	13.4	5.2	3.0	1.2
MSA[1]	2.2	10.1	12.6	13.3	18.7	23.4	10.4	6.4	3.0
U.S.	3.9	13.3	13.8	12.6	16.2	19.4	9.7	6.6	4.6

Note: Data as of 1999; (1) Metropolitan Statistical Area - see Appendix A for areas included
Source: Claritas, Inc.

Effective Buying Income

Area	Per Capita ($)	Median Household ($)	Average Household ($)
City	14,549	26,921	35,415
MSA[1]	19,720	42,452	50,699
U.S.	17,496	36,603	47,036

Note: Data as of 1/1/2000; (1) Metropolitan Statistical Area - see Appendix A for areas included
Source: Standard Rate & Data Service, Newspaper Advertising Source, March 2000

Effective Household Buying Income Distribution

Area	% of Households Earning						
	$10,000 -$19,999	$20,000 -$34,999	$35,000 -$49,999	$50,000 -$74,999	$75,000 -$99,000	$100,000 -$124,999	$125,000 and up
City	20.3	24.2	16.1	13.7	5.1	1.5	1.6
MSA[1]	12.1	21.0	19.7	23.9	10.1	3.4	3.0
U.S.	15.0	21.6	17.6	19.6	8.4	3.0	3.3

Note: Data as of 1/1/2000; (1) Metropolitan Statistical Area - see Appendix A for areas included
Source: Standard Rate & Data Service, Newspaper Advertising Source, March 2000

Poverty Rates by Age

Area	People of All Ages	People Under 18 Years Old	Related Children Age 5-17 in Families in Poverty
City	28.2	n/a	n/a
County	9.9	15.7	13.7
U.S.	13.8	20.8	18.7

Note: Figures show the percent of people living below the poverty line in 1995. The
average poverty threshold was $15,569 for a family of four in 1995; n/a not available
Source: Bureau of the Census, Small Area Income and Poverty Estimates Program;
U.S. Department of Housing and Urban Development

EMPLOYMENT

Labor Force and Employment

Area	Civilian Labor Force			Workers Employed		
	Dec. 1998	Dec. 1999	% Chg.	Dec. 1998	Dec. 1999	% Chg.
City	25,011	24,869	-0.6	24,125	24,021	-0.4
MSA[1]	349,956	348,503	-0.4	341,345	339,884	-0.4
U.S.	138,297,000	139,941,000	1.2	132,732,000	134,696,000	1.5

Note: Data is not seasonally adjusted and covers workers 16 years of age and older;
(1) Metropolitan Statistical Area - see Appendix A for areas included
Source: Bureau of Labor Statistics, http://stats.bls.gov

Unemployment Rate

Area	1999											
	Jan.	Feb.	Mar.	Apr.	May	Jun.	Jul.	Aug.	Sep.	Oct.	Nov.	Dec.
City	4.2	4.5	4.6	4.1	4.0	4.1	4.3	4.3	4.3	3.4	3.7	3.4
MSA[1]	3.2	3.3	3.3	2.9	3.1	3.4	3.5	3.6	3.5	2.9	3.0	2.5
U.S.	4.8	4.7	4.4	4.1	4.0	4.5	4.5	4.2	4.1	3.8	3.8	3.7

Note: Data is not seasonally adjusted and covers workers 16 years of age and older; all figures are percentages; (1) Metropolitan Statistical Area - see Appendix A for areas included
Source: Bureau of Labor Statistics, http://stats.bls.gov

Employment by Industry

Sector	MSA[1]		U.S.
	Number of Employees	Percent of Total	Percent of Total
Services	102,900	28.6	30.2
Retail Trade	60,600	16.8	18.1
Government	67,400	18.7	15.8
Manufacturing	44,200	12.3	14.1
Finance/Insurance/Real Estate	24,400	6.8	5.9
Wholesale Trade	22,200	6.2	5.4
Transportation/Public Utilities	24,900	6.9	5.3
Construction	n/a	n/a	4.8
Mining	n/a	n/a	0.4

Note: Figures cover non-farm employment as of 12/99 and are not seasonally adjusted; (1) Metropolitan Statistical Area - see Appendix A for areas included; n/a not available
Source: Bureau of Labor Statistics, http://stats.bls.gov

Employment by Occupation

Occupation Category	City (%)	MSA[1] (%)	U.S. (%)
White Collar	57.8	57.7	58.1
Executive/Admin./Management	10.4	11.6	12.3
Professional	12.3	13.2	14.1
Technical & Related Support	3.5	4.0	3.7
Sales	7.8	9.9	11.8
Administrative Support/Clerical	23.7	19.1	16.3
Blue Collar	23.3	28.2	26.2
Precision Production/Craft/Repair	7.8	10.8	11.3
Machine Operators/Assem./Insp.	5.5	6.7	6.8
Transportation/Material Movers	4.3	4.6	4.1
Cleaners/Helpers/Laborers	5.7	6.0	3.9
Services	18.8	12.3	13.2
Farming/Forestry/Fishing	0.2	1.8	2.5

Note: Figures cover workers 16 years of age and older;
(1) Metropolitan Statistical Area - see Appendix A for areas included
Source: 1990 Census of Population and Housing, Summary Tape File 3C

Occupational Employment Projections: 1994 - 2005

High Demand Occupations (ranked by annual openings)	Fast-Growing Occupations[1] (ranked by percent growth)
1. Cashiers	1. Personal and home care aides
2. Salespersons, retail	2. Electronic pagination systems workers
3. Waiters & waitresses	3. Computer engineers
4. Registered nurses	4. Systems analysts
5. General managers & top executives	5. Home health aides
6. Janitors/cleaners/maids, ex. priv. hshld.	6. Human services workers
7. Secretaries, except legal & medical	7. Teachers, preschool and kindergarten
8. General office clerks	8. Computer support specialists
9. Teachers, secondary school	9. Physical therapists
10. Marketing & sales, supervisors	10. Residential counselors

Note: Projections cover Pennsylvania; (1) Excludes occupations with total job growth less than 300
Source: Pennsylvania Workforce 2005, Winter 1997-98

Average Wages

Occupation	$/Hr.	Occupation	$/Hr.
Accountants and Auditors	19.59	Maids and Housekeepers	7.61
Assemblers and Fabricators	9.17	Maintenance Repairers	12.81
Automotive Mechanics	13.12	Marketing/Advertising/PR Managers	25.06
Bookkeepers	11.37	Nurses, Licensed Practical	14.13
Carpenters	13.39	Nurses, Registered	20.60
Cashiers	6.62	Nursing Aides/Orderlies/Attendants	9.71
Clerks, General Office	11.18	Physicians and Surgeons	55.66
Clerks, Shipping/Receiving/Traffic	11.93	Receptionists/Information Clerks	9.22
Computer Programmers	23.76	Sales Reps., Exc. Scientific/Retail	18.72
Computer Support Specialists	25.00	Sales Reps., Scientific, Exc. Retail	22.75
Cooks, Restaurant	8.11	Salespersons, Retail	8.63
Electricians	16.33	Secretaries, Except Legal/Medical	11.37
Financial Managers	24.84	Stock Clerks, Sales Floor	6.63
First-Line Supervisors/Mgrs., Sales	15.06	Systems Analysts	23.79
Food Preparation Workers	6.85	Teacher Aides	7.61
General Managers/Top Executives	28.48	Teachers, Elementary School	20.08
Guards	8.26	Teachers, Secondary School	21.11
Hand Packers	9.03	Telemarketers	-
Janitors and Cleaners	8.28	Truck Drivers, Heavy/Tractor-Trailer	15.89
Laborers, Landscaping	8.48	Truck Drivers, Light	13.24
Lawyers	30.84	Waiters and Waitresses	5.82

Note: Wage data is for 1998 and covers the Metropolitan Statistical Area (see Appendix A for areas included). Hourly wages for elementary and secondary school teachers were calculated by the editors from annual wage data assuming a 40 hour work week; Dashes indicate that data was not available.
Source: Bureau of Labor Statistics, 1998 Metropolitan Area Occupational Employment and Wage Estimates

TAXES

Major State and Local Tax Rates

State Corporate Income (%)	State Personal Income (%)	Residential Property (%)	Sales & Use		State Gasoline (cents/ gallon)	State Cigarette (cents/ pack)
			State (%)	Local (%)		
9.99	2.8	3.74	6.0	None	25.9[a]	31.0

Note: Personal/corporate income, sales, gasoline and cigarette tax rates as of January 2000. Property tax rates as of April 2000; (a) Rate is comprised of 12 cents excise and 13.9 cents motor carrier tax.
Source: Federation of Tax Administrators, www.taxadmin.org; ERI's Relocation Assessor software database, quarterly effective date 4/1/2000

Total Taxes Per Capita and as a Percent of Income

Area	Per Capita Income ($)	Per Capita Taxes ($)			Percent of Income (%)		
		Total	Federal	State/Local	Total	Federal	State/Local
Pennsylvania	29,059	10,185	6,991	3,195	35.1	24.1	11.0
U.S.	28,878	10,298	7,026	3,273	35.7	24.3	11.3

Note: Figures are for 1999
Source: Tax Foundation, www.taxfoundation.org

COMMERCIAL UTILITIES

Typical Monthly Electric Bills

Area	Commercial Service ($/month)		Industrial Service ($/month)	
	12 kW demand 1,500 kWh	100 kW demand 30,000 kWh	1,000 kW demand 400,000 kWh	20,000 kW demand 10,000,000 kWh
City	170	2,388	27,078	413,040
U.S.	150	2,174	23,995	508,569

Note: Based on rates in effect January 1, 1999
Source: Edison Electric Institute, Typical Residential, Commercial and Industrial Bills, Winter 1999

TRANSPORTATION

Transportation Statistics

Average minutes to work (1990)	17.2
Interstate highways	I-76; I-81; I-83; I-283; US-11; US-15; US-22; US-322
Bus lines	
In-city (1998)	Capital Area Transit, 50 buses
Inter-city (1999)	4
Passenger air service	
Airport	Harrisburg International
Airlines (1999)	14
Enplaned passengers (1998)	742,322
Amtrak service	Yes
Motor freight carriers (1999)	100
Major waterways/ports	Susquehanna River

Source: FAA DOT/TSC CY1998 ACAIS Database; National Transit Database, 1998; Editor & Publisher Market Guide, 2000; Amtrak National Time Table, Fall 1999/Winter 2000; 1990 Census of Population and Housing, STF 3C; Jane's Urban Transport Systems 1999-2000

Means of Transportation to Work

Area	Car/Truck/Van		Public Transportation			Bicycle	Walked	Other Means	Worked at Home
	Drove Alone	Car-pooled	Bus	Subway	Railroad				
City	53.1	19.2	12.1	0.1	0.1	0.5	11.2	1.7	2.1
MSA[1]	75.0	14.4	1.8	0.0	0.0	0.2	5.0	0.8	2.8
U.S.	73.2	13.4	3.0	1.5	0.5	0.4	3.9	1.2	3.0

Note: Figures shown are percentages and only include workers 16 years of age and older;
(1) Metropolitan Statistical Area - see Appendix A for areas included
Source: 1990 Census of Population and Housing, Summary Tape File 3C

BUSINESSES

Major Business Headquarters

Company Name	1999 Rankings	
	Fortune 500	Forbes 500
No companies listed	-	-

Note: Companies listed are located in the city; dashes indicate no ranking
Fortune 500: Companies that produce a 10-K are ranked 1 to 500 based on 1999 revenue
Forbes 500: Private companies are ranked 1 to 500 based on 1998 revenue
Source: Forbes, December 13, 1999; Fortune, April 17, 2000

HOTELS & MOTELS

Hotels/Motels

Area	Hotels/ Motels	Rooms	Luxury-Level Hotels/Motels		Average Minimum Rates ($)		
			♦♦♦♦	♦♦♦♦♦	♦♦	♦♦♦	♦♦♦♦
City	23	2,948	0	0	69	112	n/a
Airport	8	696	0	0	n/a	n/a	n/a
Suburbs	46	4,778	1	0	n/a	n/a	n/a
Total	77	8,422	1	0	n/a	n/a	n/a

Note: n/a not available; classifications range from one diamond (budget properties with basic amenities) to five diamond (luxury properties).
Source: OAG Business Travel Planner, Winter 1999-2000

Estimated Daily Food and Lodging Costs

Area	Food/Other ($/day)	Average Hotel Cost ($/day)
City	42	61
U.S.	30	55

Source: ERI's Relocation Assessor software database, quarterly effective date 4/1/2000

CONVENTION CENTERS

Convention Centers and Event Sites

Name	Guest Rooms	Meeting Space (sq. ft.)	Capacity (Theatre Style)
Harrisburg Hilton and Towers	341	17,000	1,360
Harrisburg Marriott	348	7,623	1,000
Holiday Inn Harrisburg East	299	27,000	790
Sheraton Inn Harrisburg	174	9,960	1,000
State Farm Show Complex	n/a	n/a	2,000
Wildwood Conference Center	n/a	9,000	0

Note: n/a not available
Source: EventSource.com, 3/15/2000

Living Environment

COST OF LIVING

Cost of Living: Homeowner

Cost Element	U.S. ($)	City ($)	Differential ($)	Percent of U.S. Average
Consumables	14,516	14,206	-310	97.9
Transportation	5,957	6,563	606	110.2
Health Services	2,012	2,059	47	102.3
Housing/Utilities/Prop. Tax	16,337	19,836	3,499	121.4
Income+Payroll Taxes	12,615	11,599	-1,016	91.9
Miscellaneous	8,563	8,563	0	100.0
Total Cost of Living	60,000	62,826	2,826	104.7

Note: Figures are based on a single income, four person family with gross annual earnings of $60,000, owning an 1,800 square-foot home, and driving two automobiles worth $22,000 30,000 miles per year.
Source: ERI's Relocation Assessor software database, quarterly effective date 4/1/2000

Cost of Living: Renter

Cost Element	U.S. ($)	City ($)	Differential ($)	Percent of U.S. Average
Consumables	10,486	10,216	-270	97.4
Transportation	2,107	2,311	204	109.7
Health Services	1,632	1,664	32	102.0
Rent/Utilities/Insurance	9,299	8,610	-689	92.6
Income+Payroll Taxes	8,607	8,303	-304	96.5
Miscellaneous	7,869	7,869	0	100.0
Total Cost of Living	40,000	38,973	-1,027	97.4

Note: Figures are based on a single income, three person family with gross annual earnings of $40,000, renting a 1,000 square-foot home, and driving one automobile worth $8,000 12,000 miles per year.
Source: ERI's Relocation Assessor software database, quarterly effective date 4/1/2000

HOUSING

Median Home Prices and Housing Affordability

Area	Median Price[2] 4th Qtr. 1999 ($)	HOI[3] 4th Qtr. 1999	Affordability Rank[4]
MSA[1]	105,000	76.6	47
U.S.	139,000	63.8	–

Note: (1) Metropolitan Statistical Area - see Appendix A for areas included; (2) U.S. figures calculated from the sales of 687,516 new and existing homes in 192 markets; (3) Housing Opportunity Index - percent of homes sold that were within the reach of the median income household at the prevailing mortgage interest rate; (4) Rank is from 1-192 with 1 being most affordable
Source: National Association of Home Builders, Housing Opportunity Index, 4th Quarter 1999

Estimated Home Price

Area	Price ($)
City	133,227
U.S.	135,855

Note: Figures are based on an 1,800 square-foot home
Source: ERI's Relocation Assessor software database, quarterly effective date 4/1/2000

Estimated Rent

Area	Rent ($/month)
City	575
U.S.	651

Note: Figures are based on a 1,000 square-foot home
Source: ERI's Relocation Assessor software database, quarterly effective date 4/1/2000

Median Home Price Projection

It is projected that the median home price in the metropolitan area will increase from $126,792 in 1999 to $178,604 in 2010, an increase of 40.9%
Kiplinger's Personal Finance Magazine, January 2000

RESIDENTIAL UTILITIES

Average Residential Utility Costs

Area	All Electric ($/mth)	Part Electric ($/mth)	Other Energy ($/mth)	Phone ($/mth)
City	105.51	–	–	19.49
U.S.	99.25	55.47	43.48	20.29

Source: ACCRA, Cost of Living Index, 3rd Quarter 1999

HEALTH CARE

Average Health Care Costs

Area	Hospital ($/day)	Doctor ($/visit)	Dentist ($/visit)
City	668.00	42.80	53.80
U.S.	440.96	53.83	68.42

Note: Hospital—based on a semi-private room; Doctor—based on a general practitioner's routine exam of an established patient; Dentist—based on adult teeth cleaning and periodic oral exam.
Source: ACCRA, Cost of Living Index, 3rd Quarter 1999

Distribution of Office-Based Physicians

Area	Family/Gen. Practitioners	Specialists Medical	Specialists Surgical	Specialists Other
MSA[1]	174	335	305	288

Note: Data as of 12/31/97; (1) Metropolitan Statistical Area - see Appendix A for areas included
Source: American Medical Assn., Physician Characteristics & Distribution in the U.S., 1999

Hospitals

Harrisburg has 1 general medical and surgical hospital, 2 psychiatric.
AHA Guide to the Healthcare Field, 1999-2000

EDUCATION

Public School District Statistics

District Name	Num. Sch.	Enroll.	Classroom Teachers	Pupils per Teacher	Minority Pupils (%)	Current Exp.[1] ($/pupil)
Central Dauphin SD	20	10,746	693	15.5	n/a	n/a
Dauphin Co Avts	1	792	59	13.4	n/a	n/a
Harrisburg City SD	15	9,169	530	17.3	n/a	n/a
Susquehanna Township SD	5	2,854	161	17.7	n/a	n/a

Note: Data covers the 1997-1998 school year unless otherwise noted; (1) Data covers fiscal year 1996; SD = School District; ISD = Independent School District; n/a not available
Source: National Center for Education Statistics, Common Core of Data Public Education Agency Universe 1997-98; National Center for Education Statistics, Characteristics of the 100 Largest Public Elementary and Secondary School Districts in the United States: 1997-98, July 1999

Educational Quality

School District	Education Quotient[1]	Graduate Outcome[2]	Community Index[3]	Resource Index[4]
Central Dauphin School Dist.	120	117	121	126

Note: Over 1,000 secondary school districts were rated in terms of educational quality. The scores range from a low of 50 to a high of 150; (1) Combination of the Graduate Outcome, Community and Resource indexes weighted to reflect the greater importance of the Graduate Outcome and Resource Index; (2) Based on graduation rates and college board scores (SAT/ACT); (3) Based on the surrounding community's level of affluence and adult education; (4) Based on teacher salaries, per-pupil expenditures and student-teacher ratios.
Source: Expansion Management, Ratings Issue, 1999

Educational Attainment by Race

Area	High School Graduate (%)					Bachelor's Degree (%)				
	Total	White	Black	Other	Hisp.[2]	Total	White	Black	Other	Hisp.[2]
City	67.2	73.3	62.0	51.3	40.8	14.0	20.8	7.2	5.5	1.9
MSA[1]	76.9	77.7	66.2	65.6	53.0	18.0	18.4	10.3	20.4	9.9
U.S.	75.2	77.9	63.1	60.4	49.8	20.3	21.5	11.4	19.4	9.2

Note: Figures shown cover persons 25 years old and over; (1) Metropolitan Statistical Area - see Appendix A for areas included; (2) people of Hispanic origin can be of any race
Source: 1990 Census of Population and Housing, Summary Tape File 3C

School Enrollment by Type

Area	Preprimary				Elementary/High School			
	Public		Private		Public		Private	
	Enrollment	%	Enrollment	%	Enrollment	%	Enrollment	%
City	576	78.5	158	21.5	8,136	88.2	1,084	11.8
MSA[1]	5,349	56.3	4,154	43.7	81,876	90.5	8,545	9.5
U.S.	2,679,029	59.5	1,824,256	40.5	38,379,689	90.2	4,187,099	9.8

Note: Figures shown cover persons 3 years old and over;
(1) Metropolitan Statistical Area - see Appendix A for areas included
Source: 1990 Census of Population and Housing, Summary Tape File 3C

School Enrollment by Race

Area	Preprimary (%)				Elementary/High School (%)			
	White	Black	Other	Hisp.[1]	White	Black	Other	Hisp.[1]
City	35.3	49.7	15.0	17.6	22.2	65.2	12.6	14.0
MSA[2]	90.5	6.0	3.5	2.9	87.4	9.1	3.5	3.0
U.S.	80.4	12.5	7.1	7.8	74.1	15.6	10.3	12.5

Note: Figures shown cover persons 3 years old and over; (1) people of Hispanic origin can be of any race; (2) Metropolitan Statistical Area - see Appendix A for areas included
Source: 1990 Census of Population and Housing, Summary Tape File 3C

Higher Education

Two-Year Colleges		Four-Year Colleges		Medical Schools	Law Schools	Voc/ Tech
Public	Private	Public	Private			
1	2	0	0	0	1	5

Source: College Blue Book, Occupational Education, 1999; Medical School Admission Requirements, 1999-2000; Peterson's Guide to Two-Year Colleges, 2000; Peterson's Guide to Four-Year Colleges, 1999; Barron's Guide to Law Schools, 1999

MAJOR EMPLOYERS

Major Employers

Community General Osteopathic Hospital
Patriot New Co.
Penn National Security Insurance
Pinnacle Health System
Synertech Health System Solutions

Keystone Financial
Penn National Mutual Casualty Insurance
Penn. Higher Education Assistance Agency
Super Rite Foods

Note: Companies listed are located in the city
Source: D&B Business Rankings, 1999; Ward's Business Directory, 1999; America's Corporate Families, 1999

PUBLIC SAFETY

Crime Rate

Area	All Crimes	Violent Crimes				Property Crimes		
		Murder	Forcible Rape	Robbery	Aggrav. Assault	Burglary	Larceny -Theft	Motor Vehicle Theft
City	7,204.9	18.4	116.1	792.6	436.8	1,446.9	3,306.6	1,087.5
Suburbs[1]	2,829.6	2.5	21.0	63.6	108.7	392.4	2,072.9	168.5
MSA[2]	3,218.2	3.9	29.5	128.3	137.8	486.0	2,182.5	250.1
U.S.	5,086.6	7.4	36.3	201.9	390.9	944.8	2,979.7	525.6

Note: Crime rate is the number of crimes per 100,000 population; (1) Defined as all areas within the Metropolitan Statistical Area but located outside the central city; (2) Metropolitan Statistical Area - see Appendix A for areas included
Source: FBI Uniform Crime Reports, 1996

RECREATION

Culture and Recreation

Museums	Symphony Orchestras	Opera Companies	Dance Companies	Professional Theatres	Zoos	Pro Sports Teams
3	1	1	1	0	1	0

Source: Musical America, International Directory of the Performing Arts, 1999; Official Museum Directory, 2000; Stern's Performing Arts Directory, 1997; USA Today Four Sport Stadium Guide, 1997; Career Opportunities in Theatre and the Performing Arts, 1999

Library System

The Dauphin County Library System has nine branches, holdings of 287,254 volumes, and a budget of $2,733,725 (1997-1998).
American Library Directory, 1999-2000

MEDIA

Newspapers

Name	Type	Freq.	Distribution	Circulation
The Catholic Witness	n/a	2x/mo	Local	70,000
The Patriot-News	General	7x/wk	Area	102,060
Paxton Herald	General	1x/wk	Local	30,000

Note: Includes newspapers with circulations of 200 or more located in the city; n/a not available
Source: Burrelle's Media Directory, 1999 Edition

Television Stations

Name	Ch.	Affiliation	Type	Owner
WLYH	15	UPN	Commercial	Gateway Communications Inc.
WHP	21	CBST	Commercial	Clear Channel Broadcasting Inc.
WHTM	27	ABCT	Commercial	Allbritton Communications Company
WITF	33	PBS	Public	WITF Inc.

Note: Stations included broadcast in the Harrisburg metro area; n/a not available
Source: Burrelle's Media Directory, 1999 Edition

AM Radio Stations

Call Letters	Freq. (kHz)	Target Audience	Station Format	Music Format
WHP	580	General	T	n/a
WKBO	1230	General	M/N/S	Adult Standards/Oldies
WTCY	1400	B/G	M/N/S	Urban Contemporary
WWKL	1460	General	M	Oldies

Note: Stations included broadcast in the Harrisburg metro area; n/a not available
Target Audience: A=Asian; B=Black; C=Christian; E=Ethnic; F=French; G=General; H=Hispanic; M=Men; N=Native American; R=Religious; S=Senior Citizen; W=Women; Y=Young Adult; Z=Children
Station Format: E=Educational; M=Music; N=News; S=Sports; T=Talk
Source: Burrelle's Media Directory, 1999 Edition

FM Radio Stations

Call Letters	Freq. (mHz)	Target Audience	Station Format	Music Format
WITF	89.5	General	M/N	Classical
WMSS	91.1	General	M/N/S	Alternative/Classical/Urban Contemporary
WRBT	94.9	General	M	Country
WRVV	97.3	General	M/N/S	Adult Contemporary/Alternative/Classic Rock
WWKL	99.3	General	M	Oldies
WNNK	104.1	General	M/N/S	n/a

Note: Stations included broadcast in the Harrisburg metro area; n/a not available
Station Format: E=Educational; M=Music; N=News; S=Sports; T=Talk
Target Audience: A=Asian; B=Black; C=Christian; E=Ethnic; F=French; G=General; H=Hispanic; M=Men; N=Native American; R=Religious; S=Senior Citizen; W=Women; Y=Young Adult; Z=Children
Source: Burrelle's Media Directory, 1999 Edition

WEATHER

Temperature/Precipitation/Humidity

	Jan	Feb	Mar	Apr	May	Jun	Jul	Aug	Sep	Oct	Nov	Dec	Yr.
Max. High Temp. (°F)	73	75	84	93	95	100	107	100	102	90	84	75	107
Avg. High Temp. (°F)	37	40	50	62	72	81	86	84	76	65	53	41	62
Avg. Temp. (°F)	30	32	41	52	62	71	76	74	67	55	44	34	53
Avg. Low Temp. (°F)	22	24	32	42	51	61	65	64	56	45	36	26	44
Min. Low Temp. (°F)	-9	-5	5	19	31	40	50	45	30	23	13	-8	-9
Avg. Precip. (in.)	2.8	2.8	3.3	3.2	4.1	3.6	3.5	3.3	3.3	2.8	3.3	3.2	39.1
Avg. Snowfall (in.)	10	10	6	1	Tr	0	0	0	0	Tr	2	7	35
Avg. Rel. Hum. 7am (%)	71	71	71	70	75	77	79	84	85	82	77	72	76
Avg. Rel. Hum. 4pm (%)	56	54	49	47	51	52	52	54	56	53	56	58	53

Note: Tr = Trace amounts (less than 0.05 inches of rain or less than 0.5 inches of snow)
Source: National Climatic Data Center, International Station Meteorological Climate Summary, 3/95

Weather Conditions

Temperature			Precipitation		
5°F & below	32°F & below	90°F & above	0.01 inch or more precip.	1.5 inch or more snow/ice	Thunder-storms
3	106	21	125	7	31

Note: Figures are average number of days per year
Source: National Climatic Data Center, International Station Meteorological Climate Summary, 3/95

AIR & WATER QUALITY

Maximum Pollutant Concentrations

	Particulate Matter (ug/m³)	Carbon Monoxide (ppm)	Sulfur Dioxide (ppm)	Nitrogen Dioxide (ppm)	Ozone (ppm)	Lead (ug/m³)
MSA[1] Level	67	3	0.022	0.019	0.12	0.04
NAAQS[2]	150	9	0.140	0.053	0.12	1.50
Met NAAQS	Yes	Yes	Yes	Yes	Yes	Yes

Note: (1) Metropolitan Statistical Area - see Appendix A for areas included; (2) National Ambient Air Quality Standards; ppm = parts per million; ug/m³ = micrograms per cubic meter; n/a not available
Source: EPA, National Air Quality and Emissions Trends Report, 1997

Pollutant Standards Index

In the Harrisburg MSA (see Appendix A for areas included), the Pollutant Standards Index (PSI) exceeded 100 on 9 days in 1997. A PSI value greater than 100 indicates that air quality would have been in the unhealthful range on that day.
EPA, National Air Quality and Emissions Trends Report, 1997

Drinking Water

Water System Name	Pop. Served	Primary Water Source Type	Number of Violations in 1998-99	Type of Violation/ Contaminants
Harrisburg Municipal Water Auth.	65,691	Surface	None	None

Note: Data as of January 19, 2000
Source: EPA, Office of Ground Water and Drinking Water, Safe Drinking Water Information System

Harrisburg tap water is alkaline, soft, and fluoridated.
Editor & Publisher Market Guide, 2000

Hattiesburg, Mississippi

Background

Hattiesburg, Mississippi is located in the south east section of the state, approximately 65 miles north of the Mississippi Gulf Coast, 90 miles southeast of Jackson and 125 miles northeast of New Orleans. It is situated on the fork of the Leaf River and Bouie Creek, in a section of the state characterized by large pine forests.

Hattiesburg is the county seat of Forrest County. The metropolitan area, which also extends into Lamar County, includes adjacent Petal and other nearby communities. This comprises an economic center that experienced growth in the 1990s. Hattiesburg has been rated highly in national rankings for quality of life, medical care and other factors. Originally a lumber town, Hattiesburg is nicknamed "The Hub City" because of traditional role as a railroad intersection. Today, it is also a meeting point for several major highways, including Interstate 59 and U.S. highways 49, 98 and 11.

The economy and community are based on a mix of activities. Hattiesburg is an educational and medical center. Colleges include the University of Southern Mississippi, William Carey College, and Pearl River Community College. It also has a military economy with Camp Shelby, a state-owned 135,000-acre facility that is home to the 177th Armored Brigade, and a training site for National Guardsmen and reservists. Other regional activities include manufacturing, health-care, business and professional services, retail and wholesale trades, construction and agriculture. Goods produced include wood, electronic and mechanical products, and poultry and other foods, among others. The area has also become a popular home for retirees.

The Choctaws originally occupied the region. William Hardy established the community in 1882, as a railroad stop and lumber town. The town was incorporated in 1884, and is named for Hardy's wife, Hattie. With the opening of railroad lines through Hattiesburg to New Orleans and the Gulf Coast in the 1880s and 1890s, the lumber industry grew and Hattiesburg became a trading center for other enterprises. In 1898, the town had to rebuild much of its center after a fire. Forrest County was incorporated in 1909.

In the 20th Century, as the original nearby timber was harvested, efforts to diversify the economy were undertaken. This included other wood products operations and other products. In 1906, Mississippi Women's College was founded, which in 1954 became co-educational and was renamed William Carey College. In 1912, Mississippi Normal College was opened, which today is the University of Southern Mississippi, a multi-program state university. Camp Shelby was established in 1917 as a training center for troops in World War One.

Hattiesburg includes areas of new development and traditional neighborhoods. Within the city is the 115-acre Hattiesburg Neighborhood Historic District, with architectural styles from the late 19th Century through 1930. There are several other historic districts and sites within the city.

Among the local parks and recreation areas is Kamper Park, which is also site of the Hattiesburg Zoo. Hattiesburg is located near the DeSoto National Forest. Golf and water sports are popular pastimes.

The colleges, which include an arts school at the University of Southern Mississippi University, provide a variety of cultural and other activities, including the USM Museum of Art. Local cultural organizations and facilities include The Hattiesburg Arts Council Gallery, The Studio Gallery, Just Over the Rainbow Theater, and The Hattiesburg Civic Light Opera, among others. The Saenger Theatre is a historic theater used for performances. The Hattiesburg Lake Terrace Convention Center is a newly opened multi-use facility. The Interaction Factory is a children's museum. The Armed Forces Gallery at Camp Shelby features displays from military history.

Hattiesburg is governed by a Mayor and City Council.

General Rankings and Evaluative Comments

■ Hattiesburg was ranked #169 out of 354 metropolitan areas in *Places Rated Almanac*. Criteria: cost of living, climate, crime, transportation, job outlook, education, the arts, health care, and recreation. *Places Rated Almanac, Millennium Edition, 2000*

■ Hattiesburg was selected as one of America's best places to retire. Criteria: safety, climate, housing, culture and recreation, social compatibility, affordability, medical care, transportation, and jobs and/or volunteer opportunities. *Where to Retire: America's Best and Most Affordable Places, 1998*

■ Hattiesburg was selected as one of the best places to retire by *Retirement Places Rated*. Criteria: cost of living, climate, crime, services, working, and leisure living. The city was ranked #143 out of 187. *Retirement Places Rated, 1999*

■ Hattiesburg was selected as one of "America's Top 100 Small Towns for Corporate Facilities." Criteria: new and expanded facilities from 1989 to present. *Site Selection, March 2000*

Business Environment

STATE ECONOMY

State Economic Profile

"Mississippi's economy continues to lag the nation and is projected to slow further in 2000. Mississippi's manufacturing sector continues to shed jobs, which are not being offset by the slow growth in the services sector. Mississippi's healthiest sectors remain gaming and construction, neither of which is expected to provide significant long-term job growth.

The textiles and apparel industries have lost 35% of their employment base in the last five years. Falling trade barriers have allowed much of low-skilled manufacturing to shift offshore. The weakness in Asian currencies has made Mississippi much less cost effective.

The damage inflicted by Hurricane George and the expansion of the gaming industry have resulted in a significant increase in construction activity. Construction employment increased almost 10% in 1998. Residential permits were up 28%, driven by a boom in multifamily construction activity. In addition highway projects in Tunica County and along the Gulf have added to construction employment. Most of this activity should taper off in 2000.

Mississippi's growth engine has been the gaming industry. The $650 million Beau Rivage Resort recently opened in Biloxi. With its 1,780 hotel rooms and 25,000 sq. ft. retail complex, the development will boost tax revenues, employment and tourism dollars. Gaming, however, is very sensitive to the business cycle. A weakening US economy in 2000 will dampen gaming revenues.

Mississippi's dependence on gaming and construction does not leave it well positioned to weather the next downturn. Mississippi's outlook for the near future is one of slowing economic growth and housing markets." *National Association of Realtors, Economic Profiles: The Fifty States and the District of Columbia, http://nar.realtor.com/databank/profiles.htm*

EXPORTS

Total Export Sales

Area	1995 ($000)	1996 ($000)	1997 ($000)	1998 ($000)	% Chg. 1995-98	% Chg. 1997-98
MSA[1]	n/a	n/a	n/a	n/a	n/a	n/a
U.S.	583,030,524	622,827,063	687,597,999	680,474,251	16.7	-1.0

Note: (1) Metropolitan Statistical Area - see Appendix A for areas included
Source: U.S. Department of Commerce, International Trade Association, Metropolitan Area Exports: An Export Performance Report on Over 250 U.S. Cities, November 10, 1999

CITY FINANCES

City Government Finances

Component	1995 ($million)	1995 (per capita $)
Revenue	32.3	677
Expenditure	30.1	632
Debt Outstanding	59.3	1,244

Source: 1999 County and City Extra, Annual Metro, City, and County Data Book

City Government Revenue by Source

Source	1995 ($million)	1995 (per capita $)
Intergovernmental	11.5	241
Taxes	10.8	227
Property	7.7	163
Sales and Gross Receipts	2.8	60

Source: 1999 County and City Extra, Annual Metro, City, and County Data Book

City Government Expenditures by Function

Function	1995 ($million)	1995 (per capita $)	1995 (%)
Public Welfare	0.0	0	0.0
Highways	3.3	70	11.2
Parking Facilities	0.1	3	0.6
Education	0.0	0	0.0
Health and Hospitals	0.3	6	1.0
Police Protection	4.3	90	14.4
Sewerage and Sanitation	4.8	101	16.1
Parks and Recreation	2.1	44	7.0
Housing and Community Development	0.2	5	0.8
Interest on Debt	3.6	77	12.2

Source: 1999 County and City Extra, Annual Metro, City, and County Data Book

Municipal Bond Ratings

Area	Moody's
City	A2

Source: Mergent Bond Record, 2/2000

POPULATION

Population Growth

Area	1980 Census	1990 Census	1999 Estimate	2004 Projection	Population Growth (%) 1990-1999	Population Growth (%) 1999-2004
City	40,829	41,891	45,842	47,330	9.4	3.2
MSA[1]	n/a	n/a	112,544	118,907	n/a	5.7
U.S.	226,545,805	248,765,170	272,212,864	283,625,312	9.4	4.2

Note: (1) Metropolitan Statistical Area - see Appendix A for areas included; n/a not available
Source: 1990 Census of Population and Housing, Summary Tape File 3C; Claritas, Inc.

Number of Households and Average Household Size

Area	1980 Census	1990 Census	1999 Estimate	2004 Projection	1999 Average Household Size
City	14,786	15,808	17,676	18,455	2.59
MSA[1]	n/a	n/a	41,791	44,607	2.69
U.S.	80,389,592	91,993,582	102,048,200	107,302,392	2.67

Note: (1) Metropolitan Statistical Area - see Appendix A for areas included; n/a not available
Source: 1990 Census of Population and Housing, Summary Tape File 3C; Claritas, Inc.

Race/Ethnicity of City Population

Race/Ethnicity	1990 Census Population	1990 Census %	1999 Estimate Population	1999 Estimate %	% Change 1990-1999
White, Non-Hispanic	24,001	57.3	24,903	54.3	3.8
Black, Non-Hispanic	16,856	40.2	19,455	42.4	15.4
Asian, Non-Hispanic	459	1.1	686	1.5	49.5
Other, Non-Hispanic	56	0.1	80	0.2	42.9
Hispanic	519	1.2	718	1.6	38.3

Source: 1990 Census of Population and Housing, Summary Tape File 3C; Claritas, Inc.

Race/Ethnicity of Metropolitan Statistical Area Population

Race/Ethnicity	1990 Census		1999 Estimate		% Change 1990-1999
	Population	%	Population	%	
White, Non-Hispanic	n/a	n/a	80,846	71.8	n/a
Black, Non-Hispanic	n/a	n/a	29,439	26.2	n/a
Asian, Non-Hispanic	n/a	n/a	890	0.8	n/a
Other, Non-Hispanic	n/a	n/a	222	0.2	n/a
Hispanic	n/a	n/a	1,147	1.0	n/a

Note: See Appendix A for areas included in the Metropolitan Statistical Area; n/a not available
Source: 1990 Census of Population and Housing, Summary Tape File 3C; Claritas, Inc.

Ancestry

Area	German	Irish	English	Italian	U.S.	French	Polish	Dutch
City	9.7	12.4	11.2	2.0	9.5	3.9	0.3	0.9
MSA[1]	n/a	n/a	n/a	n/a	n/a	n/a	n/a	n/a
U.S.	23.3	15.6	13.1	5.9	5.3	4.2	3.8	2.5

Note: Figures are percentages and include persons that reported multiple ancestry (eg. if a person reported being Irish and Italian, they were included in both columns); (1) Metropolitan Statistical Area - see Appendix A for areas included; n/a not available
Source: 1990 Census of Population and Housing, Summary Tape File 3C

Median Age

Area	1990 Census	1999 Estimate
City	27.1	29.4
MSA[1]	n/a	31.8
U.S.	32.9	35.7

Note: (1) Metropolitan Statistical Area - see Appendix A for areas included; n/a not available
Source: 1990 Census of Population and Housing, Summary Tape File 3C; Claritas, Inc.

Male/Female Population

Area	Number of Males		Number of Females		Males per 100 Females	
	1990	1999	1990	1999	1990	1999
City	19,031	21,275	22,860	24,567	83.3	86.6
MSA[1]	n/a	53,478	n/a	59,066	n/a	90.5
U.S.	121,172,379	132,803,736	127,537,494	139,409,136	95.0	95.3

Note: (1) Metropolitan Statistical Area - see Appendix A for areas included; n/a not available
Source: 1990 Census of Population, General Population Characteristics; Claritas, Inc.

INCOME

Per Capita/Median/Average Income

Area	Per Capita ($)			Median Household ($)			Average Household ($)		
	1989	1999	% Chg.	1989	1999	% Chg.	1989	1999	% Chg.
City	10,013	15,333	53.1	15,576	21,031	35.0	25,773	38,517	49.4
MSA[1]	n/a	16,147	n/a	n/a	27,611	n/a	n/a	42,910	n/a
U.S.	14,420	21,350	48.1	30,056	40,525	34.8	38,453	56,184	46.1

Note: (1) Metropolitan Statistical Area - see Appendix A for areas included; 1989 data is from the 1990 Census; 1999 data is estimated by Claritas, Inc.; n/a not available
Source: 1990 Census of Population, General Population Characteristics; Claritas, Inc.

Household Income Distribution

Area	Under $5,000	$5,000 -14,999	$15,000 -24,999	$25,000 -34,999	$35,000 -49,999	$50,000 -74,999	$75,000 -99,000	$100,000 -149,999	$150,000 and up
				Percent of Households Earning					
City	11.4	26.0	18.7	11.2	11.7	10.0	5.2	3.2	2.6
MSA[1]	7.9	20.4	17.7	12.8	14.4	13.9	6.3	4.1	2.5
U.S.	3.9	13.3	13.8	12.6	16.2	19.4	9.7	6.6	4.6

Note: Data as of 1999; (1) Metropolitan Statistical Area - see Appendix A for areas included
Source: Claritas, Inc.

Effective Buying Income

Area	Per Capita ($)	Median Household ($)	Average Household ($)
City	13,331	20,926	34,467
MSA[1]	14,400	27,273	38,646
U.S.	17,496	36,603	47,036

Note: Data as of 1/1/2000; (1) Metropolitan Statistical Area - see Appendix A for areas included
Source: Standard Rate & Data Service, Newspaper Advertising Source, March 2000

Effective Household Buying Income Distribution

Area	$10,000 -$19,999	$20,000 -$34,999	$35,000 -$49,999	$50,000 -$74,999	$75,000 -$99,000	$100,000 -$124,999	$125,000 and up
			% of Households Earning				
City	22.3	20.0	10.5	11.5	5.1	1.8	2.5
MSA[1]	19.3	21.9	14.0	14.2	6.7	2.3	2.3
U.S.	15.0	21.6	17.6	19.6	8.4	3.0	3.3

Note: Data as of 1/1/2000; (1) Metropolitan Statistical Area - see Appendix A for areas included
Source: Standard Rate & Data Service, Newspaper Advertising Source, March 2000

Poverty Rates by Age

Area	People of All Ages	People Under 18 Years Old	Related Children Age 5-17 in Families in Poverty
City	25.4	n/a	n/a
County	21.5	30.2	25.6
U.S.	13.8	20.8	18.7

Note: Figures show the percent of people living below the poverty line in 1995. The average poverty threshold was $15,569 for a family of four in 1995; n/a not available
Source: Bureau of the Census, Small Area Income and Poverty Estimates Program; U.S. Department of Housing and Urban Development

EMPLOYMENT

Labor Force and Employment

Area	Civilian Labor Force			Workers Employed		
	Dec. 1998	Dec. 1999	% Chg.	Dec. 1998	Dec. 1999	% Chg.
City	22,205	21,978	-1.0	21,555	21,009	-2.5
MSA[1]	51,752	50,872	-1.7	50,531	49,249	-2.5
U.S.	138,297,000	139,941,000	1.2	132,732,000	134,696,000	1.5

Note: Data is not seasonally adjusted and covers workers 16 years of age and older;
(1) Metropolitan Statistical Area - see Appendix A for areas included
Source: Bureau of Labor Statistics, http://stats.bls.gov

Unemployment Rate

Area	1999											
	Jan.	Feb.	Mar.	Apr.	May	Jun.	Jul.	Aug.	Sep.	Oct.	Nov.	Dec.
City	4.1	3.0	3.6	2.9	3.9	4.5	3.8	4.2	3.7	4.1	3.4	4.4
MSA[1]	3.4	2.4	3.0	2.5	3.2	3.6	3.1	3.1	3.0	3.4	2.9	3.2
U.S.	4.8	4.7	4.4	4.1	4.0	4.5	4.5	4.2	4.1	3.8	3.8	3.7

Note: Data is not seasonally adjusted and covers workers 16 years of age and older; all figures are percentages; (1) Metropolitan Statistical Area - see Appendix A for areas included
Source: Bureau of Labor Statistics, http://stats.bls.gov

Employment by Industry

Sector	MSA[1]		U.S.
	Number of Employees	Percent of Total	Percent of Total
Services	n/a	n/a	30.2
Retail Trade	n/a	n/a	18.1
Government	n/a	n/a	15.8
Manufacturing	n/a	n/a	14.1
Finance/Insurance/Real Estate	n/a	n/a	5.9
Wholesale Trade	n/a	n/a	5.4
Transportation/Public Utilities	n/a	n/a	5.3
Construction	n/a	n/a	4.8
Mining	n/a	n/a	0.4

Note: Figures cover non-farm employment as of 12/99 and are not seasonally adjusted; (1) Metropolitan Statistical Area - see Appendix A for areas included; n/a not available
Source: Bureau of Labor Statistics, http://stats.bls.gov

Employment by Occupation

Occupation Category	City (%)	MSA[1] (%)	U.S. (%)
White Collar	63.9	n/a	58.1
Executive/Admin./Management	10.2	n/a	12.3
Professional	20.3	n/a	14.1
Technical & Related Support	3.7	n/a	3.7
Sales	14.0	n/a	11.8
Administrative Support/Clerical	15.8	n/a	16.3
Blue Collar	18.7	n/a	26.2
Precision Production/Craft/Repair	6.8	n/a	11.3
Machine Operators/Assem./Insp.	5.0	n/a	6.8
Transportation/Material Movers	3.5	n/a	4.1
Cleaners/Helpers/Laborers	3.4	n/a	3.9
Services	16.2	n/a	13.2
Farming/Forestry/Fishing	1.1	n/a	2.5

Note: Figures cover workers 16 years of age and older; n/a not available (1) Metropolitan Statistical Area - see Appendix A for areas included
Source: 1990 Census of Population and Housing, Summary Tape File 3C

Occupational Employment Projections: 1996 - 2006

Occupations Expected to Have the Largest Job Growth (ranked by numerical growth)	Fast-Growing Occupations[1] (ranked by percent growth)
1. Salespersons, retail	1. Database administrators
2. Cashiers	2. Paralegals
3. General managers & top executives	3. Systems analysts
4. Truck drivers, light	4. Home health aides
5. Teachers aides, clerical & paraprofess.	5. Physical therapy assistants and aides
6. Marketing & sales, supervisors	6. Medical assistants
7. Nursing aides/orderlies/attendants	7. Physical therapists
8. Registered nurses	8. Emergency medical technicians
9. Maintenance repairers, general utility	9. Teachers, special education
10. Home health aides	10. Medical records technicians

Note: Projections cover Mississippi; (1) Excludes occupations with total job growth less than 300
Source: U.S. Department of Labor, Employment and Training Administration, America's Labor Market Information System (ALMIS)

Average Wages

Occupation	$/Hr.	Occupation	$/Hr.
Accountants and Auditors	17.28	Maids and Housekeepers	5.95
Assemblers and Fabricators	7.19	Maintenance Repairers	9.36
Automotive Mechanics	11.49	Marketing/Advertising/PR Managers	17.97
Bookkeepers	9.32	Nurses, Licensed Practical	10.28
Carpenters	11.00	Nurses, Registered	-
Cashiers	6.56	Nursing Aides/Orderlies/Attendants	6.14
Clerks, General Office	7.83	Physicians and Surgeons	-
Clerks, Shipping/Receiving/Traffic	8.77	Receptionists/Information Clerks	7.48
Computer Programmers	15.25	Sales Reps., Exc. Scientific/Retail	14.87
Computer Support Specialists	14.33	Sales Reps., Scientific, Exc. Retail	18.07
Cooks, Restaurant	7.20	Salespersons, Retail	8.07
Electricians	13.60	Secretaries, Except Legal/Medical	8.60
Financial Managers	22.54	Stock Clerks, Sales Floor	6.84
First-Line Supervisors/Mgrs., Sales	13.73	Systems Analysts	21.76
Food Preparation Workers	6.25	Teacher Aides	5.63
General Managers/Top Executives	24.59	Teachers, Elementary School	13.77
Guards	7.39	Teachers, Secondary School	13.46
Hand Packers	6.71	Telemarketers	-
Janitors and Cleaners	6.71	Truck Drivers, Heavy/Tractor-Trailer	11.81
Laborers, Landscaping	7.19	Truck Drivers, Light	10.16
Lawyers	32.47	Waiters and Waitresses	5.66

Note: Wage data is for 1998 and covers the Metropolitan Statistical Area (see Appendix A for areas included). Hourly wages for elementary and secondary school teachers were calculated by the editors from annual wage data assuming a 40 hour work week; Dashes indicate that data was not available.
Source: Bureau of Labor Statistics, 1998 Metropolitan Area Occupational Employment and Wage Estimates

TAXES

Major State and Local Tax Rates

State Corporate Income (%)	State Personal Income (%)	Residential Property (%)	Sales & Use		State Gasoline (cents/ gallon)	State Cigarette (cents/ pack)
			State (%)	Local (%)		
3.0 - 5.0	3.0 - 5.0	1.18	7.0	None	18.4[a]	18.0

Note: Personal/corporate income, sales, gasoline and cigarette tax rates as of January 2000. Property tax rates as of April 2000; (a) Rate is comprised of 18 cents excise and 0.4 cents motor carrier tax
Source: Federation of Tax Administrators, www.taxadmin.org; ERI's Relocation Assessor software database, quarterly effective date 4/1/2000

Total Taxes Per Capita and as a Percent of Income

Area	Per Capita Income ($)	Per Capita Taxes ($)			Percent of Income (%)		
		Total	Federal	State/Local	Total	Federal	State/Local
Mississippi	20,422	6,923	4,567	2,356	33.9	22.4	11.5
U.S.	28,878	10,298	7,026	3,273	35.7	24.3	11.3

Note: Figures are for 1999
Source: Tax Foundation, www.taxfoundation.org

COMMERCIAL UTILITIES

Typical Monthly Electric Bills

Area	Commercial Service ($/month)		Industrial Service ($/month)	
	12 kW demand 1,500 kWh	100 kW demand 30,000 kWh	1,000 kW demand 400,000 kWh	20,000 kW demand 10,000,000 kWh
City	152	1,999	19,870	283,966
U.S.	150	2,174	23,995	508,569

Note: Based on rates in effect January 1, 1999
Source: Edison Electric Institute, Typical Residential, Commercial and Industrial Bills, Winter 1999

TRANSPORTATION

Transportation Statistics

Average minutes to work (1990)	14.6
Interstate highways	I-59; US-11; US-49; US-98
Bus lines	
In-city (1998)	Not available
Inter-city (1999)	1
Passenger air service	
Airport	Hattiesburg-Laurel Regional
Airlines (1999)	2
Enplaned passengers (1998)	12,221
Amtrak service	Yes
Motor freight carriers (1999)	18
Major waterways/ports	None

Source: FAA DOT/TSC CY1998 ACAIS Database; National Transit Database, 1998; Editor & Publisher Market Guide, 2000; Amtrak National Time Table, Fall 1999/Winter 2000; 1990 Census of Population and Housing, STF 3C; Jane's Urban Transport Systems 1999-2000

Means of Transportation to Work

Area	Car/Truck/Van		Public Transportation			Bicycle	Walked	Other Means	Worked at Home
	Drove Alone	Car-pooled	Bus	Subway	Railroad				
City	76.8	13.1	0.6	0.0	0.0	0.6	6.0	1.5	1.4
MSA[1]	n/a	n/a	n/a	n/a	n/a	n/a	n/a	n/a	n/a
U.S.	73.2	13.4	3.0	1.5	0.5	0.4	3.9	1.2	3.0

Note: Figures shown are percentages and only include workers 16 years of age and older;
(1) Metropolitan Statistical Area - see Appendix A for areas included; n/a not available
Source: 1990 Census of Population and Housing, Summary Tape File 3C

BUSINESSES

Major Business Headquarters

Company Name	1999 Rankings	
	Fortune 500	Forbes 500
No companies listed	-	-

Note: Companies listed are located in the city; dashes indicate no ranking
Fortune 500: Companies that produce a 10-K are ranked 1 to 500 based on 1999 revenue
Forbes 500: Private companies are ranked 1 to 500 based on 1998 revenue
Source: Forbes, December 13, 1999; Fortune, April 17, 2000

HOTELS & MOTELS

Hotels/Motels

Area	Hotels/ Motels	Rooms	Luxury-Level Hotels/Motels		Average Minimum Rates ($)		
			♦♦♦♦	♦♦♦♦♦	♦♦	♦♦♦	♦♦♦♦
City	14	1,682	0	0	n/a	n/a	n/a
Suburbs	1	138	0	0	n/a	n/a	n/a
Total	15	1,820	0	0	n/a	n/a	n/a

Note: n/a not available; classifications range from one diamond (budget properties with basic amenities) to five diamond (luxury properties).
Source: OAG Business Travel Planner, Winter 1999-2000

Estimated Daily Food and Lodging Costs

Area	Food/Other ($/day)	Average Hotel Cost ($/day)
City	30	55
U.S.	30	55

Source: ERI's Relocation Assessor software database, quarterly effective date 4/1/2000

CONVENTION CENTERS

Convention Centers and Event Sites

Name	Guest Rooms	Meeting Space (sq. ft.)	Capacity (Theatre Style)
Comfort Inn On The Hill	119	n/a	400
Hattiesburg Convention Center	n/a	n/a	0
Holiday Inn Hattiesburg	125	n/a	220
Quality Inn	142	n/a	150
Ramada Limited	92	n/a	250

Note: n/a not available
Source: EventSource.com, 3/15/2000

Living Environment

COST OF LIVING

Cost of Living: Homeowner

Cost Element	U.S. ($)	City ($)	Differential ($)	Percent of U.S. Average
Consumables	14,516	14,470	-46	99.7
Transportation	5,957	5,744	-213	96.4
Health Services	2,012	1,941	-71	96.5
Housing/Utilities/Prop. Tax	16,337	13,324	-3,013	81.6
Income+Payroll Taxes	12,615	13,384	769	106.1
Miscellaneous	8,563	8,563	0	100.0
Total Cost of Living	60,000	57,426	-2,574	95.7

Note: Figures are based on a single income, four person family with gross annual earnings of $60,000, owning an 1,800 square-foot home, and driving two automobiles worth $22,000 30,000 miles per year.
Source: ERI's Relocation Assessor software database, quarterly effective date 4/1/2000

Cost of Living: Renter

Cost Element	U.S. ($)	City ($)	Differential ($)	Percent of U.S. Average
Consumables	10,486	10,439	-47	99.6
Transportation	2,107	2,029	-78	96.3
Health Services	1,632	1,573	-59	96.4
Rent/Utilities/Insurance	9,299	7,532	-1,767	81.0
Income+Payroll Taxes	8,607	8,871	264	103.1
Miscellaneous	7,869	7,869	0	100.0
Total Cost of Living	40,000	38,313	-1,687	95.8

Note: Figures are based on a single income, three person family with gross annual earnings of $40,000, renting a 1,000 square-foot home, and driving one automobile worth $8,000 12,000 miles per year.
Source: ERI's Relocation Assessor software database, quarterly effective date 4/1/2000

HOUSING

Median Home Prices and Housing Affordability

Area	Median Price[2] 4th Qtr. 1999 ($)	HOI[3] 4th Qtr. 1999	Affordability Rank[4]
MSA[1]	91,000	61.2	135
U.S.	139,000	63.8	–

Note: (1) Metropolitan Statistical Area - see Appendix A for areas included; (2) U.S. figures calculated from the sales of 687,516 new and existing homes in 192 markets; (3) Housing Opportunity Index - percent of homes sold that were within the reach of the median income household at the prevailing mortgage interest rate; (4) Rank is from 1-192 with 1 being most affordable
Source: National Association of Home Builders, Housing Opportunity Index, 4th Quarter 1999

Estimated Home Price

Area	Price ($)
City	98,726
U.S.	135,855

Note: Figures are based on an 1,800 square-foot home
Source: ERI's Relocation Assessor software database, quarterly effective date 4/1/2000

Estimated Rent

Area	Rent ($/month)
City	489
U.S.	651

Note: Figures are based on a 1,000 square-foot home
Source: ERI's Relocation Assessor software database, quarterly effective date 4/1/2000

Median Home Price Projection

It is projected that the median home price in the metropolitan area will increase from $106,818 in 1999 to $163,913 in 2010, an increase of 53.5%
Kiplinger's Personal Finance Magazine, January 2000

RESIDENTIAL UTILITIES

Average Residential Utility Costs

Area	All Electric ($/mth)	Part Electric ($/mth)	Other Energy ($/mth)	Phone ($/mth)
City	101.14	–	–	24.65
U.S.	99.25	55.47	43.48	20.29

Source: ACCRA, Cost of Living Index, 3rd Quarter 1999

HEALTH CARE

Average Health Care Costs

Area	Hospital ($/day)	Doctor ($/visit)	Dentist ($/visit)
City	237.00	49.50	70.83
U.S.	440.96	53.83	68.42

Note: Hospital—based on a semi-private room; Doctor—based on a general practitioner's routine exam of an established patient; Dentist—based on adult teeth cleaning and periodic oral exam.
Source: ACCRA, Cost of Living Index, 3rd Quarter 1999

Distribution of Office-Based Physicians

Area	Family/Gen. Practitioners	Specialists		
		Medical	Surgical	Other
MSA[1]	34	70	84	63

Note: Data as of 12/31/97; (1) Metropolitan Statistical Area - see Appendix A for areas included
Source: American Medical Assn., Physician Characteristics & Distribution in the U.S., 1999

Hospitals

Hattiesburg has 2 general medical and surgical hospitals.
AHA Guide to the Healthcare Field, 1999-2000

EDUCATION

Public School District Statistics

District Name	Num. Sch.	Enroll.	Classroom Teachers	Pupils per Teacher	Minority Pupils (%)	Current Exp.[1] ($/pupil)
Forrest County School District	6	2,574	178	14.5	n/a	n/a
Hattiesburg Public School Dist	8	5,262	336	15.7	n/a	n/a

Note: Data covers the 1997-1998 school year unless otherwise noted; (1) Data covers fiscal year 1996; SD = School District; ISD = Independent School District; n/a not available
Source: National Center for Education Statistics, Common Core of Data Public Education Agency Universe 1997-98; National Center for Education Statistics, Characteristics of the 100 Largest Public Elementary and Secondary School Districts in the United States: 1997-98, July 1999

Educational Quality

School District	Education Quotient[1]	Graduate Outcome[2]	Community Index[3]	Resource Index[4]
Hattiesburg Public School Dist.	68	70	80	63

Note: Over 1,000 secondary school districts were rated in terms of educational quality. The scores range from a low of 50 to a high of 150; (1) Combination of the Graduate Outcome, Community and Resource indexes weighted to reflect the greater importance of the Graduate Outcome and Resource Index; (2) Based on graduation rates and college board scores (SAT/ACT); (3) Based on the surrounding community's level of affluence and adult education; (4) Based on teacher salaries, per-pupil expenditures and student-teacher ratios.
Source: Expansion Management, Ratings Issue, 1999

Educational Attainment by Race

Area	High School Graduate (%)					Bachelor's Degree (%)				
	Total	White	Black	Other	Hisp.[2]	Total	White	Black	Other	Hisp.[2]
City	74.0	84.6	54.2	93.4	84.8	27.0	37.0	7.6	67.2	40.9
MSA[1]	n/a	n/a	n/a	n/a	n/a	n/a	n/a	n/a	n/a	n/a
U.S.	75.2	77.9	63.1	60.4	49.8	20.3	21.5	11.4	19.4	9.2

Note: Figures shown cover persons 25 years old and over; (1) Metropolitan Statistical Area -
see Appendix A for areas included; (2) people of Hispanic origin can be of any race; n/a not available
Source: 1990 Census of Population and Housing, Summary Tape File 3C

School Enrollment by Type

Area	Preprimary				Elementary/High School			
	Public		Private		Public		Private	
	Enrollment	%	Enrollment	%	Enrollment	%	Enrollment	%
City	500	62.3	303	37.7	6,092	92.7	479	7.3
MSA[1]	n/a	n/a	n/a	n/a	n/a	n/a	n/a	n/a
U.S.	2,679,029	59.5	1,824,256	40.5	38,379,689	90.2	4,187,099	9.8

Note: Figures shown cover persons 3 years old and over; (1) Metropolitan Statistical Area - see
Appendix A for areas included; n/a not available
Source: 1990 Census of Population and Housing, Summary Tape File 3C

School Enrollment by Race

Area	Preprimary (%)				Elementary/High School (%)			
	White	Black	Other	Hisp.[1]	White	Black	Other	Hisp.[1]
City	46.8	52.1	1.1	0.0	36.9	62.0	1.1	0.9
MSA[2]	n/a	n/a	n/a	n/a	n/a	n/a	n/a	n/a
U.S.	80.4	12.5	7.1	7.8	74.1	15.6	10.3	12.5

Note: Figures shown cover persons 3 years old and over; (1) people of Hispanic origin can be of any
race; (2) Metropolitan Statistical Area - see Appendix A for areas included; n/a not available
Source: 1990 Census of Population and Housing, Summary Tape File 3C

Higher Education

Two-Year Colleges		Four-Year Colleges		Medical	Law	Voc/
Public	Private	Public	Private	Schools	Schools	Tech
0	0	1	1	0	0	1

Source: College Blue Book, Occupational Education, 1999; Medical School Admission Requirements,
1999-2000; Peterson's Guide to Two-Year Colleges, 2000; Peterson's Guide to Four-Year Colleges,
1999; Barron's Guide to Law Schools, 1999

MAJOR EMPLOYERS

Major Employers

Forrest County General Hospital
Magnolia Federal Bank
Merchant Co. (groceries)
South Mississippi Electric Power Assn.

Hattiesburg Clinic Professional Association
Medical Systems
Murray Envelope Corp.
Wesley Health Systems

Note: Companies listed are located in the city
Source: D&B Business Rankings, 1999; Ward's Business Directory, 1999; America's Corporate
Families, 1999

PUBLIC SAFETY

Crime Rate

Area	All Crimes	Violent Crimes				Property Crimes		
		Murder	Forcible Rape	Robbery	Aggrav. Assault	Burglary	Larceny -Theft	Motor Vehicle Theft
City	8,074.2	8.2	45.3	185.4	222.5	2,152.4	5,102.0	358.4
Suburbs[1]	n/a	n/a	n/a	n/a	n/a	n/a	n/a	n/a
MSA[2]	n/a	n/a	n/a	n/a	n/a	n/a	n/a	n/a
U.S.	4,615.5	6.3	34.4	165.2	360.5	862.0	2,728.1	459.0

Note: Crime rate is the number of crimes per 100,000 population; (1) Defined as all areas within the Metropolitan Statistical Area but located outside the central city; (2) Metropolitan Statistical Area - see Appendix A for areas included; n/a not available
Source: FBI Uniform Crime Reports, 1998

RECREATION

Culture and Recreation

Museums	Symphony Orchestras	Opera Companies	Dance Companies	Professional Theatres	Zoos	Pro Sports Teams
1	1	1	0	0	1	0

Source: Musical America, International Directory of the Performing Arts, 1999; Official Museum Directory, 2000; Stern's Performing Arts Directory, 1997; USA Today Four Sport Stadium Guide, 1997; Career Opportunities in Theatre and the Performing Arts, 1999

Library System

The The Library of Hattiesburg has one branch, holdings of 107,376 volumes, and a budget of $1,172,802 (1997-1998).
American Library Directory, 1999-2000

MEDIA

Newspapers

Name	Type	Freq.	Distribution	Circulation
Hattiesburg American	General	7x/wk	Area	26,706

Note: Includes newspapers with circulations of 200 or more located in the city;
Source: Burrelle's Media Directory, 1999 Edition

Television Stations

Name	Ch.	Affiliation	Type	Owner
WDAM	n/a	NBCT	Commercial	Raycom Media Inc.
WHLT	22	CBST	Commercial	Media General Inc.

Note: Stations included broadcast in the Hattiesburg metro area; n/a not available
Source: Burrelle's Media Directory, 1999 Edition

AM Radio Stations

Call Letters	Freq. (kHz)	Target Audience	Station Format	Music Format
WBKH	950	Religious	M	Christian
WFOR	1400	General	M	Christian
WORV	1580	General	M	Christian

Note: Stations included broadcast in the Hattiesburg metro area
Target Audience: A=Asian; B=Black; C=Christian; E=Ethnic; F=French; G=General; H=Hispanic; M=Men; N=Native American; R=Religious; S=Senior Citizen; W=Women; Y=Young Adult; Z=Children
Station Format: E=Educational; M=Music; N=News; S=Sports; T=Talk
Source: Burrelle's Media Directory, 1999 Edition

FM Radio Stations

Call Letters	Freq. (mHz)	Target Audience	Station Format	Music Format
WUSM	88.5	General	E/M/N	Alternative/Classic Rock/Jazz/Rhythm & Blues
WJMG	92.1	General	M	Urban Contemporary
WHER	103.7	General	M	Country/Oldies
WMFM	106.3	General	M/N/S	Adult Contemporary/Classic Rock/Easy Listening
WKNZ	107.1	General	M/N/S	Classic Rock

Note: Stations included broadcast in the Hattiesburg metro area
Station Format: E=Educational; M=Music; N=News; S=Sports; T=Talk
Source: Burrelle's Media Directory, 1999 Edition

WEATHER

Temperature/Precipitation/Humidity

	Jan	Feb	Mar	Apr	May	Jun	Jul	Aug	Sep	Oct	Nov	Dec	Yr.
Max. High Temp. (°F)	87	86	91	95	104	106	105	106	102	99	89	85	106
Avg. High Temp. (°F)	62	65	72	79	86	92	93	93	89	81	70	63	79
Avg. Temp. (°F)	50	53	60	66	73	80	82	82	77	67	57	51	67
Avg. Low Temp. (°F)	39	41	48	54	61	69	71	71	66	53	45	40	55
Min. Low Temp. (°F)	8	-1	17	29	39	49	54	51	35	23	18	13	-1
Avg. Precip. (in.)	5.1	5.4	6.1	5.1	5.0	4.7	6.6	5.1	3.9	2.6	3.8	5.4	58.7
Avg. Snowfall (in.)	0	0.2	0.1	0	0	0	0	0	0	0	0	0.1	0.4
Avg. Rel. Hum. (%)	79	76	77	74	75	76	77	81	81	78	78	78	78

Source: National Climatic Data Center, International Station Meteorological Climate Summary, 3/95

Weather Conditions

Temperature			Precipitation		
0°F & below	32°F & below	90°F & above	0.1 inch or more precip.	1.5 inch or more snow/ice	Thunder-storms
0	35	0	90	0	76

Note: Figures are average number of days per year
Source: National Climatic Data Center, International Station Meteorological Climate Summary, 3/95

AIR & WATER QUALITY

Maximum Pollutant Concentrations

	Particulate Matter (ug/m³)	Carbon Monoxide (ppm)	Sulfur Dioxide (ppm)	Nitrogen Dioxide (ppm)	Ozone (ppm)	Lead (ug/m³)
MSA[1] Level	n/a	n/a	n/a	n/a	n/a	n/a
NAAQS[2]	150	9	0.140	0.053	0.12	1.50
Met NAAQS	n/a	n/a	n/a	n/a	n/a	n/a

Note: (1) Metropolitan Statistical Area - see Appendix A for areas included; (2) National Ambient Air Quality Standards; ppm = parts per million; ug/m³ = micrograms per cubic meter; n/a not available
Source: EPA, National Air Quality and Emissions Trends Report, 1997

Pollutant Standards Index

Data not available. *EPA, National Air Quality and Emissions Trends Report, 1997*

Drinking Water

Water System Name	Pop. Served	Primary Water Source Type	Number of Violations in 1998-99	Type of Violation/ Contaminants
City of Hattiesburg	46,500	Ground	None	None

Note: Data as of January 19, 2000
Source: EPA, Office of Ground Water and Drinking Water, Safe Drinking Water Information System

Hattiesburg tap water is neutral and very soft.
Editor & Publisher Market Guide, 2000

Hickory, North Carolina

Background

Hickory, North Carolina is located in the western section of the state, approximately 75 miles east of Asheville, 50 miles northwest of Charlotte, and 70 miles southwest of Winston Salem. It is in the piedmont region of North Carolina, near the Blue Ridge Mountains. The surrounding area is rural and includes farmland. The region contains numerous creeks, rivers and large lakes, including Lake Hickory north of the city.

Hickory is located on Interstate 40 in Catawba County, with some portions of the metropolitan area in Burke and Caldwell counties. This is a growing area, with an economy based primarily on manufacturing, education, retailing, agriculture, tourism and services. It has two colleges, Lenoir-Rhyne College and Catawba Valley Community College. Hickory has been rated highly by numerous sources for quality of life and as an entrepreneurial environment.

The county is named after the Catawba, who were among the Native Americans who occupied the region. Around 1745, settlers began to arrive. A number of early settlers migrated from Pennsylvania. A roadside stop, Hickory Tavern was established. The community grew as a trading center. The regional economy was primarily agricultural. Gold was also mined in the region. Catawba County was established in 1842. The town was chartered as Hickory Tavern in 1863. Its name was changed to Hickory after it was incorporated in 1870. The opening of railroad lines through the community in the 1850s and 1880s stimulated the growth of industries and trade. In 1891, Lenoir-Rhymes College was founded as Highland Academy by Lutheran pastors.

In the 20th Century, Hickory grew steadily. It became a national center for the manufacture of furniture and for hosiery and textiles. These continue to be important industries. The Hickory area today is also a center for the manufacture of fiber-optic and telecommunications cable and related equipment. Other regional industries include agricultural services and food products, health care, retail and wholesale trades, education, business services and construction. Other economic segments include tourism, based on its scenic surroundings, historical and recreational attractions, and retailing, with outlets for the furniture and textile industries.

Hickory maintains approximately 20 city parks and recreation facilities. Water-based activities are popular on local and regional lakes and waterways, including Lake Hickory, Lake James, and Lake Rhodhiss. Catawba County operates Riverbend Park on the Catawba River. There are state parks in the region. Golf is a popular pastime. The Hickory Motor Speedway is one of the oldest NASCAR sanctioned tracks in the U.S. The Hickory Crawdads is a Class A baseball team.

Hickory has several designated historic districts. There are numerous other historic sites and museums in the city and surrounding area including Murray's Mill (a restored agricultural mill complex), The Catawba County Museum of History and The Catawba Furniture Museum, among others.

The Arts and Sciences Center of Catawba Valley is a multi-use cultural facility in a building that was redeveloped in the 1980s and 1990s. It includes The Catawba County Council for the Arts, Hickory Museum of Art and The Catawba Science Center. Cultural activities include those offered by area colleges and by other organizations such as the Acoustic Stage performance series, Hickory Community Theater, the Green Room community theater, Hickory Choral Society and Western Piedmont Symphony, among others. The Hickory Metro Convention Center is a multi-use facility.

In 1913, Hickory became one of the earliest cities to adopt a charter form of government, with an elected Mayor and Council, and an appointed City Manager who serves as a chief executive officer.

General Rankings and Evaluative Comments

■ Hickory was ranked #180 out of 354 metropolitan areas in *Places Rated Almanac*. Criteria: cost of living, climate, crime, transportation, job outlook, education, the arts, health care, and recreation. *Places Rated Almanac, Millennium Edition, 2000*

■ Cognetics studied 273 metro areas in the United States, ranking them by entrepreneurial activity. Hickory was ranked #28 out of 134 smaller metro areas. Criteria: Significant Starts (firms started in the last 10 years that still employ at least 5 people) and Young Growers (percent of firms 10 years old or less that grew significantly during the last 4 years). *Cognetics, "Entrepreneurial Hot Spots: The Best Places in America to Start and Grow a Company," 1999*

Business Environment

STATE ECONOMY

State Economic Profile

"In spite of declines in textiles and apparels, North Carolina has seen impressive job growth in the last few years. As North Carolina continues to diversify its economy away from its traditional manufacturing base and toward its newer high-tech and financial services sectors, job growth will outpace the nation for a number of years to come, albeit at a slightly slower rate than those seen in 1997 and 1998.

Raleigh-Durham has been and will continue to be one of North Carolina's growth engines. High-tech firms in the Research Triangle Park have expanded employment considerably. Cisco Systems, for one, is planning to expand its operations, adding as many as 4,000 jobs over the next three years. Raleigh's housing market has more than doubled in size during the 1990s. Price appreciation has been strong, although homes still remain affordable.

North Carolina's other hot spot has been Charlotte. While many parts of the country have been hurt by consolidation in the financial services industry, many of these jobs have made their way to Charlotte. As this wave of consolidation has slowed, so has job growth in Charlotte, reflected in its 0.6% job growth rate in 1998, far below that of previous years. Continued restructuring in North Carolina's textiles, apparel and furniture industries will slow job growth in the Charlotte area.

The outlook for North Carolina, while a slowdown from its recent pace, is still one of impressive job growth, far outpacing the nation. With its business friendly atmosphere and the decision of Federal Express to locate its Mid-Atlantic hub here, North Carolina will likely attract more corporate relocations. Its affordable housing markets and overall high quality of life will also attract residents, helping fuel job growth." *National Association of Realtors, Economic Profiles: The Fifty States and the District of Columbia, http://nar.realtor.com/databank/profiles.htm*

EXPORTS

Total Export Sales

Area	1995 ($000)	1996 ($000)	1997 ($000)	1998 ($000)	% Chg. 1995-98	% Chg. 1997-98
MSA[1]	476,069	464,329	501,193	529,898	11.3	5.7
U.S.	583,030,524	622,827,063	687,597,999	680,474,251	16.7	-1.0

Note: (1) Metropolitan Statistical Area - see Appendix A for areas included
Source: U.S. Department of Commerce, International Trade Association, Metropolitan Area Exports: An Export Performance Report on Over 250 U.S. Cities, November 10, 1999

CITY FINANCES

City Government Finances

Component	1995 ($million)	1995 (per capita $)
Revenue	46.8	1,580
Expenditure	34.4	1,162
Debt Outstanding	20.3	685

Source: 1999 County and City Extra, Annual Metro, City, and County Data Book

City Government Revenue by Source

Source	1995 ($million)	1995 (per capita $)
Intergovernmental	21.4	722
Taxes	13.6	458
Property	12.2	415
Sales and Gross Receipts	0.5	19

Source: 1999 County and City Extra, Annual Metro, City, and County Data Book

City Government Expenditures by Function

Function	1995 ($million)	1995 (per capita $)	1995 (%)
Public Welfare	0.0	0	0.0
Highways	3.0	103	8.9
Parking Facilities	0.0	0	0.0
Education	0.0	0	0.0
Health and Hospitals	<0.1	1	0.1
Police Protection	6.4	218	18.8
Sewerage and Sanitation	9.1	307	26.5
Parks and Recreation	1.7	60	5.2
Housing and Community Development	0.4	16	1.4
Interest on Debt	0.4	16	1.4

Source: 1999 County and City Extra, Annual Metro, City, and County Data Book

Municipal Bond Ratings

Area	Moody's
City	Aa3

Source: Mergent Bond Record, 2/2000

POPULATION

Population Growth

Area	1980 Census	1990 Census	1999 Estimate	2004 Projection	Population Growth (%) 1990-1999	Population Growth (%) 1999-2004
City	20,753	28,337	30,310	31,941	7.0	5.4
MSA[1]	270,457	221,700	325,596	346,185	46.9	6.3
U.S.	226,545,805	248,765,170	272,212,864	283,625,312	9.4	4.2

Note: (1) Metropolitan Statistical Area - see Appendix A for areas included
Source: 1990 Census of Population and Housing, Summary Tape File 3C; Claritas, Inc.

Number of Households and Average Household Size

Area	1980 Census	1990 Census	1999 Estimate	2004 Projection	1999 Average Household Size
City	10,098	11,796	12,803	13,583	2.37
MSA[1]	94,505	85,393	126,702	135,757	2.57
U.S.	80,389,592	91,993,582	102,048,200	107,302,392	2.67

Note: (1) Metropolitan Statistical Area - see Appendix A for areas included
Source: 1990 Census of Population and Housing, Summary Tape File 3C; Claritas, Inc.

Race/Ethnicity of City Population

Race/Ethnicity	1990 Census Population	1990 Census %	1999 Estimate Population	1999 Estimate %	% Change 1990-1999
White, Non-Hispanic	22,928	80.9	23,789	78.5	3.8
Black, Non-Hispanic	4,812	17.0	5,374	17.7	11.7
Asian, Non-Hispanic	319	1.1	534	1.8	67.4
Other, Non-Hispanic	91	0.3	97	0.3	6.6
Hispanic	187	0.7	516	1.7	175.9

Source: 1990 Census of Population and Housing, Summary Tape File 3C; Claritas, Inc.

Race/Ethnicity of Metropolitan Statistical Area Population

Race/Ethnicity	1990 Census		1999 Estimate		% Change 1990-1999
	Population	%	Population	%	
White, Non-Hispanic	201,255	90.8	292,500	89.8	45.3
Black, Non-Hispanic	17,386	7.8	24,707	7.6	42.1
Asian, Non-Hispanic	1,499	0.7	3,240	1.0	116.1
Other, Non-Hispanic	492	0.2	853	0.3	73.4
Hispanic	1,068	0.5	4,296	1.3	302.2

Note: See Appendix A for areas included in the Metropolitan Statistical Area
Source: 1990 Census of Population and Housing, Summary Tape File 3C; Claritas, Inc.

Ancestry

Area	German	Irish	English	Italian	U.S.	French	Polish	Dutch
City	32.1	12.6	14.6	1.4	8.0	2.2	0.5	4.0
MSA[1]	30.4	13.3	11.3	1.6	14.7	1.8	0.4	5.0
U.S.	23.3	15.6	13.1	5.9	5.3	4.2	3.8	2.5

Note: Figures are percentages and include persons that reported multiple ancestry (eg. if a person reported being Irish and Italian, they were included in both columns); (1) Metropolitan Statistical Area - see Appendix A for areas included
Source: 1990 Census of Population and Housing, Summary Tape File 3C

Median Age

Area	1990 Census	1999 Estimate
City	34.3	37.8
MSA[1]	34.5	37.8
U.S.	32.9	35.7

Note: (1) Metropolitan Statistical Area - see Appendix A for areas included
Source: 1990 Census of Population and Housing, Summary Tape File 3C; Claritas, Inc.

Male/Female Population

Area	Number of Males		Number of Females		Males per 100 Females	
	1990	1999	1990	1999	1990	1999
City	13,344	14,276	14,993	16,034	89.0	89.0
MSA[1]	108,321	159,106	113,379	166,490	95.5	95.6
U.S.	121,172,379	132,803,736	127,537,494	139,409,136	95.0	95.3

Note: (1) Metropolitan Statistical Area - see Appendix A for areas included
Source: 1990 Census of Population, General Population Characteristics; Claritas, Inc.

INCOME

Per Capita/Median/Average Income

Area	Per Capita ($)			Median Household ($)			Average Household ($)		
	1989	1999	% Chg.	1989	1999	% Chg.	1989	1999	% Chg.
City	15,433	21,895	41.9	27,212	35,791	31.5	36,627	50,964	39.1
MSA[1]	12,760	18,150	42.2	27,675	36,487	31.8	32,831	46,197	40.7
U.S.	14,420	21,350	48.1	30,056	40,525	34.8	38,453	56,184	46.1

Note: (1) Metropolitan Statistical Area - see Appendix A for areas included; 1989 data is from the 1990 Census; 1999 data is estimated by Claritas, Inc.
Source: 1990 Census of Population, General Population Characteristics; Claritas, Inc.

Household Income Distribution

Area	Percent of Households Earning								
	Under $5,000	$5,000 -14,999	$15,000 -24,999	$25,000 -34,999	$35,000 -49,999	$50,000 -74,999	$75,000 -99,000	$100,000 -149,999	$150,000 and up
City	3.9	14.6	16.1	14.2	18.9	17.0	6.8	4.5	4.2
MSA[1]	3.5	13.5	16.0	14.7	20.1	20.0	6.9	3.5	1.8
U.S.	3.9	13.3	13.8	12.6	16.2	19.4	9.7	6.6	4.6

Note: Data as of 1999; (1) Metropolitan Statistical Area - see Appendix A for areas included
Source: Claritas, Inc.

Effective Buying Income

Area	Per Capita ($)	Median Household ($)	Average Household ($)
City	17,810	31,893	42,347
MSA[1]	15,183	32,951	38,962
U.S.	17,496	36,603	47,036

Note: Data as of 1/1/2000; (1) Metropolitan Statistical Area - see Appendix A for areas included
Source: Standard Rate & Data Service, Newspaper Advertising Source, March 2000

Effective Household Buying Income Distribution

Area	% of Households Earning						
	$10,000 -$19,999	$20,000 -$34,999	$35,000 -$49,999	$50,000 -$74,999	$75,000 -$99,000	$100,000 -$124,999	$125,000 and up
City	17.0	26.5	18.1	14.9	6.5	1.7	3.6
MSA[1]	16.7	26.1	21.4	17.6	4.9	1.3	1.4
U.S.	15.0	21.6	17.6	19.6	8.4	3.0	3.3

Note: Data as of 1/1/2000; (1) Metropolitan Statistical Area - see Appendix A for areas included
Source: Standard Rate & Data Service, Newspaper Advertising Source, March 2000

Poverty Rates by Age

Area	People of All Ages	People Under 18 Years Old	Related Children Age 5-17 in Families in Poverty
City	14.3	n/a	n/a
County	9.2	13.7	11.4
U.S.	13.8	20.8	18.7

Note: Figures show the percent of people living below the poverty line in 1995. The average poverty threshold was $15,569 for a family of four in 1995; n/a not available
Source: Bureau of the Census, Small Area Income and Poverty Estimates Program; U.S. Department of Housing and Urban Development

EMPLOYMENT

Labor Force and Employment

Area	Civilian Labor Force			Workers Employed		
	Dec. 1998	Dec. 1999	% Chg.	Dec. 1998	Dec. 1999	% Chg.
City	16,872	17,150	1.6	16,431	16,763	2.0
MSA[1]	170,507	173,533	1.8	167,298	170,676	2.0
U.S.	138,297,000	139,941,000	1.2	132,732,000	134,696,000	1.5

Note: Data is not seasonally adjusted and covers workers 16 years of age and older;
(1) Metropolitan Statistical Area - see Appendix A for areas included
Source: Bureau of Labor Statistics, http://stats.bls.gov

Unemployment Rate

Area	1999											
	Jan.	Feb.	Mar.	Apr.	May	Jun.	Jul.	Aug.	Sep.	Oct.	Nov.	Dec.
City	3.1	3.2	3.1	2.1	3.0	2.6	2.9	2.7	2.3	2.5	2.4	2.3
MSA[1]	2.5	2.5	2.2	1.7	2.0	1.9	2.1	2.0	1.6	1.8	1.8	1.6
U.S.	4.8	4.7	4.4	4.1	4.0	4.5	4.5	4.2	4.1	3.8	3.8	3.7

Note: Data is not seasonally adjusted and covers workers 16 years of age and older; all figures are percentages; (1) Metropolitan Statistical Area - see Appendix A for areas included
Source: Bureau of Labor Statistics, http://stats.bls.gov

Employment by Industry

Sector	MSA[1]		U.S.
	Number of Employees	Percent of Total	Percent of Total
Services	n/a	n/a	30.2
Retail Trade	n/a	n/a	18.1
Government	n/a	n/a	15.8
Manufacturing	n/a	n/a	14.1
Finance/Insurance/Real Estate	n/a	n/a	5.9
Wholesale Trade	n/a	n/a	5.4
Transportation/Public Utilities	n/a	n/a	5.3
Construction	n/a	n/a	4.8
Mining	n/a	n/a	0.4

Note: Figures cover non-farm employment as of 12/99 and are not seasonally adjusted; (1) Metropolitan Statistical Area - see Appendix A for areas included; n/a not available
Source: Bureau of Labor Statistics, http://stats.bls.gov

Employment by Occupation

Occupation Category	City (%)	MSA[1] (%)	U.S. (%)
White Collar	54.9	40.8	58.1
Executive/Admin./Management	12.9	8.5	12.3
Professional	11.4	8.8	14.1
Technical & Related Support	2.0	2.4	3.7
Sales	14.5	9.3	11.8
Administrative Support/Clerical	14.1	11.8	16.3
Blue Collar	33.1	48.0	26.2
Precision Production/Craft/Repair	9.0	15.3	11.3
Machine Operators/Assem./Insp.	17.3	23.4	6.8
Transportation/Material Movers	2.7	4.3	4.1
Cleaners/Helpers/Laborers	4.2	5.0	3.9
Services	11.2	9.8	13.2
Farming/Forestry/Fishing	0.8	1.4	2.5

Note: Figures cover workers 16 years of age and older; (1) Metropolitan Statistical Area - see Appendix A for areas included
Source: 1990 Census of Population and Housing, Summary Tape File 3C

Occupational Employment Projections: 1996 - 2006

Occupations Expected to Have the Largest Job Growth (ranked by numerical growth)	Fast-Growing Occupations[1] (ranked by percent growth)
1. Cashiers	1. Occupational therapy assistants
2. Registered nurses	2. Computer engineers
3. General managers & top executives	3. Database administrators
4. Nursing aides/orderlies/attendants	4. Systems analysts
5. Salespersons, retail	5. Physical therapy assistants and aides
6. Child care workers, private household	6. Physical therapists
7. Food service workers	7. Occupational therapists
8. Marketing & sales, supervisors	8. Home health aides
9. Janitors/cleaners/maids, ex. priv. hshld.	9. Desktop publishers
10. Truck drivers, light	10. Respiratory therapists

Note: Projections cover North Carolina; (1) Excludes occupations with total job growth less than 300
Source: U.S. Department of Labor, Employment and Training Administration, America's Labor Market Information System (ALMIS)

Average Wages

Occupation	$/Hr.	Occupation	$/Hr.
Accountants and Auditors	18.91	Maids and Housekeepers	6.90
Assemblers and Fabricators	9.42	Maintenance Repairers	11.43
Automotive Mechanics	12.65	Marketing/Advertising/PR Managers	27.66
Bookkeepers	10.84	Nurses, Licensed Practical	13.37
Carpenters	11.03	Nurses, Registered	19.09
Cashiers	6.73	Nursing Aides/Orderlies/Attendants	7.50
Clerks, General Office	9.13	Physicians and Surgeons	57.68
Clerks, Shipping/Receiving/Traffic	10.18	Receptionists/Information Clerks	8.86
Computer Programmers	21.01	Sales Reps., Exc. Scientific/Retail	19.70
Computer Support Specialists	16.44	Sales Reps., Scientific, Exc. Retail	22.97
Cooks, Restaurant	7.89	Salespersons, Retail	9.56
Electricians	12.68	Secretaries, Except Legal/Medical	10.13
Financial Managers	26.61	Stock Clerks, Sales Floor	7.74
First-Line Supervisors/Mgrs., Sales	16.48	Systems Analysts	21.37
Food Preparation Workers	6.64	Teacher Aides	7.97
General Managers/Top Executives	27.33	Teachers, Elementary School	14.93
Guards	7.46	Teachers, Secondary School	14.26
Hand Packers	8.28	Telemarketers	-
Janitors and Cleaners	7.54	Truck Drivers, Heavy/Tractor-Trailer	16.90
Laborers, Landscaping	8.73	Truck Drivers, Light	10.07
Lawyers	33.72	Waiters and Waitresses	5.76

Note: Wage data is for 1998 and covers the Metropolitan Statistical Area (see Appendix A for areas included). Hourly wages for elementary and secondary school teachers were calculated by the editors from annual wage data assuming a 40 hour work week; Dashes indicate that data was not available.
Source: Bureau of Labor Statistics, 1998 Metropolitan Area Occupational Employment and Wage Estimates

TAXES

Major State and Local Tax Rates

State Corporate Income (%)	State Personal Income (%)	Residential Property (%)	Sales & Use		State Gasoline (cents/ gallon)	State Cigarette (cents/ pack)
			State (%)	Local (%)		
6.9[a]	6.0 - 7.75	1.11	4.0	2.0	22.25[b]	5.0

Note: Personal/corporate income, sales, gasoline and cigarette tax rates as of January 2000. Property tax rates as of April 2000; (a) Financial institutions are also subject to a tax equal to $30 per one million in assets; (b) Rate is comprised of 22 cents excise and 0.25 cents motor carrier tax
Source: Federation of Tax Administrators, www.taxadmin.org; ERI's Relocation Assessor software database, quarterly effective date 4/1/2000

Total Taxes Per Capita and as a Percent of Income

Area	Per Capita Income ($)	Per Capita Taxes ($)			Percent of Income (%)		
		Total	Federal	State/Local	Total	Federal	State/Local
North Carolina	26,549	8,937	6,132	2,805	33.7	23.1	10.6
U.S.	28,878	10,298	7,026	3,273	35.7	24.3	11.3

Note: Figures are for 1999
Source: Tax Foundation, www.taxfoundation.org

COMMERCIAL UTILITIES

Typical Monthly Electric Bills

Area	Commercial Service ($/month)		Industrial Service ($/month)	
	12 kW demand 1,500 kWh	100 kW demand 30,000 kWh	1,000 kW demand 400,000 kWh	20,000 kW demand 10,000,000 kWh
City	150	1,814	20,801	295,548
U.S.	150	2,174	23,995	508,569

Note: Based on rates in effect January 1, 1999
Source: Edison Electric Institute, Typical Residential, Commercial and Industrial Bills, Winter 1999

TRANSPORTATION

Transportation Statistics

Average minutes to work (1990)	14.7
Interstate highways	I-40; US-70; US-321; US-ALT 64
Bus lines	
In-city (1998)	Not available
Inter-city (1999)	1
Passenger air service	
Airport	Hickory Regional
Airlines (1999)	1
Enplaned passengers (1998)	26,856
Amtrak service	No
Motor freight carriers (1999)	42
Major waterways/ports	None

Source: FAA DOT/TSC CY1998 ACAIS Database; National Transit Database, 1998; Editor & Publisher Market Guide, 2000; Amtrak National Time Table, Fall 1999/Winter 2000; 1990 Census of Population and Housing, STF 3C; Jane's Urban Transport Systems 1999-2000

Means of Transportation to Work

Area	Car/Truck/Van		Public Transportation			Bicycle	Walked	Other Means	Worked at Home
	Drove Alone	Car-pooled	Bus	Subway	Railroad				
City	77.1	15.6	0.3	0.0	0.0	0.2	4.5	1.2	1.2
MSA[1]	79.0	16.4	0.1	0.0	0.0	0.1	1.9	0.8	1.7
U.S.	73.2	13.4	3.0	1.5	0.5	0.4	3.9	1.2	3.0

Note: Figures shown are percentages and only include workers 16 years of age and older;
(1) Metropolitan Statistical Area - see Appendix A for areas included
Source: 1990 Census of Population and Housing, Summary Tape File 3C

BUSINESSES

Major Business Headquarters

Company Name	1999 Rankings	
	Fortune 500	Forbes 500
Alex Lee	-	101

Note: Companies listed are located in the city; dashes indicate no ranking
Fortune 500: Companies that produce a 10-K are ranked 1 to 500 based on 1999 revenue
Forbes 500: Private companies are ranked 1 to 500 based on 1998 revenue
Source: Forbes, December 13, 1999; Fortune, April 17, 2000

HOTELS & MOTELS

Hotels/Motels

Area	Hotels/Motels	Rooms	Luxury-Level Hotels/Motels		Average Minimum Rates ($)		
			♦♦♦♦	♦♦♦♦♦	♦♦	♦♦♦	♦♦♦♦
City	10	818	0	0	n/a	n/a	n/a
Suburbs	1	201	0	0	n/a	n/a	n/a
Total	11	1,019	0	0	n/a	n/a	n/a

Note: n/a not available; classifications range from one diamond (budget properties with basic amenities) to five diamond (luxury properties).
Source: OAG Business Travel Planner, Winter 1999-2000

Estimated Daily Food and Lodging Costs

Area	Food/Other ($/day)	Average Hotel Cost ($/day)
City	30	55
U.S.	30	55

Source: ERI's Relocation Assessor software database, quarterly effective date 4/1/2000

CONVENTION CENTERS

Convention Centers and Event Sites

Name	Guest Rooms	Meeting Space (sq. ft.)	Capacity (Theatre Style)
Holiday Inn Piedmont Center	200	n/a	400

Note: n/a not available
Source: EventSource.com, 3/15/2000

Living Environment

COST OF LIVING

Cost of Living: Homeowner

Cost Element	U.S. ($)	City ($)	Differential ($)	Percent of U.S. Average
Consumables	14,516	13,802	-714	95.1
Transportation	5,957	5,489	-468	92.1
Health Services	2,012	1,965	-47	97.7
Housing/Utilities/Prop. Tax	16,337	16,487	150	100.9
Income+Payroll Taxes	12,615	13,465	850	106.7
Miscellaneous	8,563	8,563	0	100.0
Total Cost of Living	60,000	59,771	-229	99.6

Note: Figures are based on a single income, four person family with gross annual earnings of $60,000, owning an 1,800 square-foot home, and driving two automobiles worth $22,000 30,000 miles per year.
Source: ERI's Relocation Assessor software database, quarterly effective date 4/1/2000

Cost of Living: Renter

Cost Element	U.S. ($)	City ($)	Differential ($)	Percent of U.S. Average
Consumables	10,486	10,016	-470	95.5
Transportation	2,107	1,950	-157	92.5
Health Services	1,632	1,602	-30	98.2
Rent/Utilities/Insurance	9,299	9,285	-14	99.8
Income+Payroll Taxes	8,607	9,217	610	107.1
Miscellaneous	7,869	7,869	0	100.0
Total Cost of Living	40,000	39,939	-61	99.8

Note: Figures are based on a single income, three person family with gross annual earnings of $40,000, renting a 1,000 square-foot home, and driving one automobile worth $8,000 12,000 miles per year.
Source: ERI's Relocation Assessor software database, quarterly effective date 4/1/2000

HOUSING

Median Home Prices and Housing Affordability

Area	Median Price[2] 4th Qtr. 1999 ($)	HOI[3] 4th Qtr. 1999	Affordability Rank[4]
MSA[1]	n/a	n/a	n/a
U.S.	139,000	63.8	–

Note: (1) Metropolitan Statistical Area - see Appendix A for areas included; (2) U.S. figures calculated from the sales of 687,516 new and existing homes in 192 markets; (3) Housing Opportunity Index - percent of homes sold that were within the reach of the median income household at the prevailing mortgage interest rate; (4) Rank is from 1-192 with 1 being most affordable; n/a not available
Source: National Association of Home Builders, Housing Opportunity Index, 4th Quarter 1999

Estimated Home Price

Area	Price ($)
City	140,477
U.S.	135,855

Note: Figures are based on an 1,800 square-foot home
Source: ERI's Relocation Assessor software database, quarterly effective date 4/1/2000

Estimated Rent

Area	Rent ($/month)
City	644
U.S.	651

Note: Figures are based on a 1,000 square-foot home
Source: ERI's Relocation Assessor software database, quarterly effective date 4/1/2000

Median Home Price Projection

It is projected that the median home price in the metropolitan area will increase from $118,476 in 1999 to $167,455 in 2010, an increase of 41.3%
Kiplinger's Personal Finance Magazine, January 2000

RESIDENTIAL UTILITIES

Average Residential Utility Costs

Area	All Electric ($/mth)	Part Electric ($/mth)	Other Energy ($/mth)	Phone ($/mth)
City	97.33	–	–	17.65
U.S.	99.25	55.47	43.48	20.29

Source: ACCRA, Cost of Living Index, 3rd Quarter 1999

HEALTH CARE

Average Health Care Costs

Area	Hospital ($/day)	Doctor ($/visit)	Dentist ($/visit)
City	295.00	46.75	56.00
U.S.	440.96	53.83	68.42

Note: Hospital—based on a semi-private room; Doctor—based on a general practitioner's routine exam of an established patient; Dentist—based on adult teeth cleaning and periodic oral exam.
Source: ACCRA, Cost of Living Index, 3rd Quarter 1999

Distribution of Office-Based Physicians

Area	Family/Gen. Practitioners	Specialists		
		Medical	Surgical	Other
MSA[1]	99	86	124	107

Note: Data as of 12/31/97; (1) Metropolitan Statistical Area - see Appendix A for areas included
Source: American Medical Assn., Physician Characteristics & Distribution in the U.S., 1999

Hospitals

Hickory has 2 general medical and surgical hospitals.
AHA Guide to the Healthcare Field, 1999-2000

EDUCATION

Public School District Statistics

District Name	Num. Sch.	Enroll.	Classroom Teachers	Pupils per Teacher	Minority Pupils (%)	Current Exp.[1] ($/pupil)
Hickory City Schools	10	4,506	309	14.6	n/a	n/a

Note: Data covers the 1997-1998 school year unless otherwise noted; (1) Data covers fiscal year 1996; SD = School District; ISD = Independent School District; n/a not available
Source: National Center for Education Statistics, Common Core of Data Public Education Agency Universe 1997-98; National Center for Education Statistics, Characteristics of the 100 Largest Public Elementary and Secondary School Districts in the United States: 1997-98, July 1999

Educational Quality

School District	Education Quotient[1]	Graduate Outcome[2]	Community Index[3]	Resource Index[4]
Hickory School Dist.	n/a	n/a	n/a	n/a

Note: Over 1,000 secondary school districts were rated in terms of educational quality. The scores range from a low of 50 to a high of 150; (1) Combination of the Graduate Outcome, Community and Resource indexes weighted to reflect the greater importance of the Graduate Outcome and Resource Index; (2) Based on graduation rates and college board scores (SAT/ACT); (3) Based on the surrounding community's level of affluence and adult education; (4) Based on teacher salaries, per-pupil expenditures and student-teacher ratios.
Source: Expansion Management, Ratings Issue, 1999

Educational Attainment by Race

Area	High School Graduate (%)					Bachelor's Degree (%)				
	Total	White	Black	Other	Hisp.[2]	Total	White	Black	Other	Hisp.[2]
City	72.1	75.6	51.6	57.6	67.8	23.4	26.0	7.6	20.3	32.2
MSA[1]	63.5	64.3	54.0	53.8	63.5	12.2	12.6	5.8	15.4	19.8
U.S.	75.2	77.9	63.1	60.4	49.8	20.3	21.5	11.4	19.4	9.2

Note: Figures shown cover persons 25 years old and over; (1) Metropolitan Statistical Area - see Appendix A for areas included; (2) people of Hispanic origin can be of any race
Source: 1990 Census of Population and Housing, Summary Tape File 3C

School Enrollment by Type

Area	Preprimary				Elementary/High School			
	Public		Private		Public		Private	
	Enrollment	%	Enrollment	%	Enrollment	%	Enrollment	%
City	234	60.0	156	40.0	3,792	95.6	175	4.4
MSA[1]	1,744	65.1	937	34.9	35,391	97.1	1,074	2.9
U.S.	2,679,029	59.5	1,824,256	40.5	38,379,689	90.2	4,187,099	9.8

Note: Figures shown cover persons 3 years old and over;
(1) Metropolitan Statistical Area - see Appendix A for areas included
Source: 1990 Census of Population and Housing, Summary Tape File 3C

School Enrollment by Race

Area	Preprimary (%)				Elementary/High School (%)			
	White	Black	Other	Hisp.[1]	White	Black	Other	Hisp.[1]
City	80.8	16.7	2.6	0.0	70.0	28.1	2.0	1.4
MSA[2]	91.2	6.2	2.7	0.3	88.5	10.2	1.3	0.5
U.S.	80.4	12.5	7.1	7.8	74.1	15.6	10.3	12.5

Note: Figures shown cover persons 3 years old and over; (1) people of Hispanic origin can be of any race; (2) Metropolitan Statistical Area - see Appendix A for areas included
Source: 1990 Census of Population and Housing, Summary Tape File 3C

Higher Education

Two-Year Colleges		Four-Year Colleges		Medical Schools	Law Schools	Voc/ Tech
Public	Private	Public	Private			
1	0	0	1	0	0	0

Source: College Blue Book, Occupational Education, 1999; Medical School Admission Requirements, 1999-2000; Peterson's Guide to Two-Year Colleges, 2000; Peterson's Guide to Four-Year Colleges, 1999; Barron's Guide to Law Schools, 1999

MAJOR EMPLOYERS

Major Employers

Alcatel (telecommunications cable)
Ellis Hosiery Mills
Hickory Springs Manufacturing
STM Industries (textiles)
Siecor Corp. (fiber optic cable)

Catawba Memorial Hospital
FRYE Regional Medical Center
Moose Products (alarm products)
Sherrill Furniture Co.

Note: Companies listed are located in the city
Source: D&B Business Rankings, 1999; Ward's Business Directory, 1999; America's Corporate Families, 1999

PUBLIC SAFETY

Crime Rate

Area	All Crimes	Violent Crimes				Property Crimes		
		Murder	Forcible Rape	Robbery	Aggrav. Assault	Burglary	Larceny -Theft	Motor Vehicle Theft
City	10,379.7	25.5	41.4	245.1	404.2	2,018.0	7,040.8	604.8
Suburbs[1]	3,351.8	5.5	21.2	34.2	220.4	935.5	1,953.2	181.8
MSA[2]	4,034.2	7.4	23.2	54.7	238.3	1,040.6	2,447.2	222.8
U.S.	4,615.5	6.3	34.4	165.2	360.5	862.0	2,728.1	459.0

Note: Crime rate is the number of crimes per 100,000 population; (1) Defined as all areas within the Metropolitan Statistical Area but located outside the central city; (2) Metropolitan Statistical Area - see Appendix A for areas included
Source: FBI Uniform Crime Reports, 1998

RECREATION

Culture and Recreation

Museums	Symphony Orchestras	Opera Companies	Dance Companies	Professional Theatres	Zoos	Pro Sports Teams
2	1	0	0	0	0	0

Source: Musical America, International Directory of the Performing Arts, 1999; Official Museum Directory, 2000; Stern's Performing Arts Directory, 1997; USA Today Four Sport Stadium Guide, 1997; Career Opportunities in Theatre and the Performing Arts, 1999

Library System

The Hickory Public Library has one branchand a budget of $1,360,222 (1996-1997).
American Library Directory, 1999-2000

MEDIA

Newspapers

Name	Type	Freq.	Distribution	Circulation
The Hickory Daily Record	General	7x/wk	Area	21,280

Note: Includes newspapers with circulations of 200 or more located in the city;
Source: Burrelle's Media Directory, 1999 Edition

Television Stations

Name	Ch.	Affiliation	Type	Owner
WHKY	14	n/a	Commercial	Long Family Partnership

Note: Stations included broadcast in the Hickory metro area; n/a not available
Source: Burrelle's Media Directory, 1999 Edition

AM Radio Stations

Call Letters	Freq. (kHz)	Target Audience	Station Format	Music Format
WIRC	630	General	M/N/S/T	Country
WCXN	1170	H/R	M/N/S	Latin
WNNC	1230	General	M/N/S	Adult Contemporary
WHKY	1290	General	N/T	n/a

Note: Stations included broadcast in the Hickory metro area; n/a not available
Target Audience: A=Asian; B=Black; C=Christian; E=Ethnic; F=French; G=General; H=Hispanic; M=Men; N=Native American; R=Religious; S=Senior Citizen; W=Women; Y=Young Adult; Z=Children
Station Format: E=Educational; M=Music; N=News; S=Sports; T=Talk
Source: Burrelle's Media Directory, 1999 Edition

FM Radio Stations

Call Letters	Freq. (mHz)	Target Audience	Station Format	Music Format
WPIR	88.1	Religious	M/N	Christian/Gospel

Note: Stations included broadcast in the Hickory metro area
Station Format: E=Educational; M=Music; N=News; S=Sports; T=Talk
Target Audience: A=Asian; B=Black; C=Christian; E=Ethnic; F=French; G=General; H=Hispanic; M=Men; N=Native American; R=Religious; S=Senior Citizen; W=Women; Y=Young Adult; Z=Children
Source: Burrelle's Media Directory, 1999 Edition

WEATHER

Temperature/Precipitation/Humidity

	Jan	Feb	Mar	Apr	May	Jun	Jul	Aug	Sep	Oct	Nov	Dec	Yr.
Max. High Temp. (°F)	80	82	90	94	98	104	105	106	102	96	86	76	106
Avg. High Temp. (°F)	51	54	61	71	79	86	88	87	82	73	61	52	70
Avg. Temp. (°F)	41	43	49	58	67	74	77	76	70	60	49	41	59
Avg. Low Temp. (°F)	31	32	37	46	55	63	66	65	59	48	37	31	48
Min. Low Temp. (°F)	1	2	6	21	30	45	50	50	34	23	10	-5	-5
Avg. Precip. (in.)	4.2	4.0	4.6	3.7	3.5	4.0	5.3	5.4	3.8	3.6	2.9	4.2	49.3
Avg. Snowfall (in.)	1.9	2.1	0	0	0	0	0	0	0	0	0.1	0.7	4.8
Avg. Rel. Hum. (%)	74	67	64	62	68	71	73	76	74	70	69	73	70

Source: National Climatic Data Center, International Station Meteorological Climate Summary, 3/95

Weather Conditions

Temperature			Precipitation		
0°F & below	32°F & below	90°F & above	0.1 inch or more precip.	1.5 inch or more snow/ice	Thunder-storms
0	78	39	83	1	45

Note: Figures are average number of days per year
Source: National Climatic Data Center, International Station Meteorological Climate Summary, 3/95

AIR & WATER QUALITY

Maximum Pollutant Concentrations

	Particulate Matter (ug/m³)	Carbon Monoxide (ppm)	Sulfur Dioxide (ppm)	Nitrogen Dioxide (ppm)	Ozone (ppm)	Lead (ug/m³)
MSA[1] Level	60	n/a	n/a	n/a	0.10	0.04
NAAQS[2]	150	9	0.140	0.053	0.12	1.50
Met NAAQS	Yes	n/a	n/a	n/a	Yes	Yes

Note: (1) Metropolitan Statistical Area - see Appendix A for areas included; (2) National Ambient Air Quality Standards; ppm = parts per million; ug/m³ = micrograms per cubic meter; n/a not available
Source: EPA, National Air Quality and Emissions Trends Report, 1997

Pollutant Standards Index

Data not available.
EPA, National Air Quality and Emissions Trends Report, 1997

Drinking Water

Water System Name	Pop. Served	Primary Water Source Type	Number of Violations in 1998-99	Type of Violation/ Contaminants
City of Hickory	38,700	Surface	None	None

Note: Data as of January 19, 2000
Source: EPA, Office of Ground Water and Drinking Water, Safe Drinking Water Information System

Hickory tap water is slightly acid, soft, and fluoridated.
Editor & Publisher Market Guide, 2000

Huntington, West Virginia

Background

Huntington, West Virginia is located in the southwest section of the state where West Virginia, Kentucky and Ohio intersect. It is 50 miles west of Charleston and 140 miles southeast of Columbus, Ohio. Huntington is on the north bank of the Ohio River, with several other rivers nearby. The terrain around the lower riverbank area includes rolling land and hills.

Huntington is the county seat of Cabell County, with portions in Wayne County. The cities of Huntington, Barboursville, Milton and other nearby communities form a metropolitan area that is a regional commercial center and transportation hub. Huntington was founded as a railroad terminus, and interstate highway I-64 goes through the city today. Huntington is also home to Marshall University, founded in 1837, which is an important presence in the city.

Significant European colonization did not occur at the site until the latter 18th Century, due to the mountain barrier and conflicts stemming from the French and Indian Wars. In 1869, railroad tycoon Colis P. Huntington, acquired the Chesapeake and Ohio Railway in Virginia, and selected the site of Huntington as the riverside terminal. In 1871 the community was incorporated and named after him. Huntington became a transfer point for a variety of goods, including coal and other minerals mined in West Virginia. The city's economic segments also included the manufacture and processing of transported resources, as well as railroad equipment and other goods. Meanwhile, Marshall University grew into a large university. In the early 20th Century, recurrent problems with flooding prompted construction of a floodwall in the city.

In the mid-20th Century, Huntington faced challenges stemming from economic changes, and regional trends in the region and its traditional industries. The area diversified, and in the 1990s has been experiencing new growth. Primary current employers include health care, manufacturing, education, transportation and distribution services, retail and wholesale trades, and business and professional services.

Early in 2000, online merchant Amazon.com opened an East Coast customer service center in Huntington. Goods produced in the area include steel products, machinery, electronic equipment and petroleum and chemical products, among others. The region is also known for glassmaking.

Huntington's parks include the large Ritter Park, which extends along the city's length, and includes a jogging path, a Rose Garden and an innovative childrens' playground, among other features. State parks and other recreational activities are available in the region, including Wayne National Forest in Ohio. The Huntington Blizzards is a professional hockey team.

The city and surrounding area has numerous points of historic interest, including Heritage Village a downtown historic and retail complex around a redeveloped railway station, and Heritage Farm Museum, a recreated agricultural village. A more recent local landmark is the East End Bridge over the Ohio River, which opened in 1985 after ten years of construction. It is characterized by a distinctive cable design.

The Huntington Civic Arena is a multi-purpose facility. Keith-Albee Theater is a restored 1920s venue. The Huntington Museum of Art features a variety of exhibits and facilities. Marshall University sponsors numerous cultural activities, including the Marshall Artists performance series. The Huntington Symphony, the Huntington Chamber Orchestra and other area music and theater organizations are also active.

Huntington is governed by an elected Mayor and City Council.

General Rankings and Evaluative Comments

- Huntington was ranked #126 out of 354 metropolitan areas in *Places Rated Almanac*. Criteria: cost of living, climate, crime, transportation, job outlook, education, the arts, health care, and recreation. *Places Rated Almanac, Millennium Edition, 2000*

- Zero Population Growth ranked 229 cities in terms of children's health, safety, and economic well-being. Huntington was ranked #39 out of 112 independent cities (cities with populations greater than 100,000 which were neither Major Cities nor Suburbs/Outer Cities) and was given a grade of C+. Criteria: total population and population change, percent of population under 18 years of age, household language, percent of births to teens, infant mortality rate, percent of low birth weights, dropout rate, enrollment in preprimary school, violent and property crime rates, unemployment rate, percent of children in poverty, percent of owner occupied units, number of bad air days, percent of public transportation commuters, and average travel time to work. *Zero Population Growth, Children's Environmental Index, Fall 1999*

- Cognetics studied 273 metro areas in the United States, ranking them by entrepreneurial activity. Huntington was ranked #68 out of 134 smaller metro areas. Criteria: Significant Starts (firms started in the last 10 years that still employ at least 5 people) and Young Growers (percent of firms 10 years old or less that grew significantly during the last 4 years). *Cognetics, "Entrepreneurial Hot Spots: The Best Places in America to Start and Grow a Company," 1999*

Business Environment

STATE ECONOMY

State Economic Profile

"The West Virginia economy continues to expand slowly. Growth in the services and construction sectors has helped to offset losses in steel and mining. West Virginia's weak demographic outlook will constrain labor force growth and housing demand. West Virginia's growth potential is limited without some fundamental changes to its economy and population structure.

Weak commodity prices have undermined West Virginia's metals and mining sectors. Almost 5% of West Virginia employment are in mining or primary metals, compared to 1% for the US. West Virginia's mining operations have also tended to have among the highest costs in the nation. The growing market share of steel mini-mills has also undercut West Virginia's competitive position. Despite import restrictions, steel prices should remain soft in 2000.

West Virginia is the only state where deaths outnumber births. Coupled with its high rate of out-migration, West Virginia is shrinking. Worse is the fact that the number of person in prime working and home-buying years is shrinking at a rate of almost 1.3% a year. The result has been a shortage of skilled workers and a weak housing market. Residential permits declined 9% in 1998. And although home sales were up in 1998, price appreciation has been weak.

West Virginia has increased its efforts to diversify the economy and attract high-tech jobs. Bell Atlantic has already invested $20 million in high-speed phone lines. This and similar efforts have successfully attracted lower-paying data entry and telephone assistance jobs. Growth should increase after West Virginia's current difficulties have run their course." *National Association of Realtors, Economic Profiles: The Fifty States and the District of Columbia, http://nar.realtor.com/databank/profiles.htm*

EXPORTS

Total Export Sales

Area	1995 ($000)	1996 ($000)	1997 ($000)	1998 ($000)	% Chg. 1995-98	% Chg. 1997-98
MSA[1]	237,186	193,938	218,721	138,892	-41.4	-36.5
U.S.	583,030,524	622,827,063	687,597,999	680,474,251	16.7	-1.0

Note: (1) Metropolitan Statistical Area - see Appendix A for areas included
Source: U.S. Department of Commerce, International Trade Association, Metropolitan Area Exports: An Export Performance Report on Over 250 U.S. Cities, November 10, 1999

CITY FINANCES

City Government Finances

Component	1995 ($million)	1995 (per capita $)
Revenue	37.8	702
Expenditure	37.5	697
Debt Outstanding	68.6	1,275

Source: 1999 County and City Extra, Annual Metro, City, and County Data Book

City Government Revenue by Source

Source	1995 ($million)	1995 (per capita $)
Intergovernmental	3.8	70
Taxes	17.1	318
Property	4.0	76
Sales and Gross Receipts	2.2	41

Source: 1999 County and City Extra, Annual Metro, City, and County Data Book

City Government Expenditures by Function

Function	1995 ($million)	1995 (per capita $)	1995 (%)
Public Welfare	0.0	0	0.0
Highways	1.6	31	4.5
Parking Facilities	0.7	14	2.1
Education	0.0	0	0.0
Health and Hospitals	0.1	2	0.3
Police Protection	4.9	91	13.1
Sewerage and Sanitation	6.3	118	17.0
Parks and Recreation	2.8	52	7.6
Housing and Community Development	3.6	67	9.7
Interest on Debt	4.4	82	11.9

Source: 1999 County and City Extra, Annual Metro, City, and County Data Book

Municipal Bond Ratings

Area	Moody's
City	Baa1

Source: Mergent Bond Record, 2/2000

POPULATION

Population Growth

Area	1980 Census	1990 Census	1999 Estimate	2004 Projection	Population Growth (%) 1990-1999	Population Growth (%) 1999-2004
City	63,684	54,844	52,481	51,493	-4.3	-1.9
MSA[1]	336,410	312,529	313,439	314,904	0.3	0.5
U.S.	226,545,805	248,765,170	272,212,864	283,625,312	9.4	4.2

Note: (1) Metropolitan Statistical Area - see Appendix A for areas included
Source: 1990 Census of Population and Housing, Summary Tape File 3C; Claritas, Inc.

Number of Households and Average Household Size

Area	1980 Census	1990 Census	1999 Estimate	2004 Projection	1999 Average Household Size
City	25,520	23,427	22,748	22,554	2.31
MSA[1]	119,006	119,654	123,695	126,191	2.53
U.S.	80,389,592	91,993,582	102,048,200	107,302,392	2.67

Note: (1) Metropolitan Statistical Area - see Appendix A for areas included
Source: 1990 Census of Population and Housing, Summary Tape File 3C; Claritas, Inc.

Race/Ethnicity of City Population

Race/Ethnicity	1990 Census Population	1990 Census %	1999 Estimate Population	1999 Estimate %	% Change 1990-1999
White, Non-Hispanic	50,596	92.3	48,184	91.8	-4.8
Black, Non-Hispanic	3,658	6.7	3,615	6.9	-1.2
Asian, Non-Hispanic	228	0.4	235	0.4	3.1
Other, Non-Hispanic	152	0.3	104	0.2	-31.6
Hispanic	210	0.4	343	0.7	63.3

Source: 1990 Census of Population and Housing, Summary Tape File 3C; Claritas, Inc.

Race/Ethnicity of Metropolitan Statistical Area Population

Race/Ethnicity	1990 Census		1999 Estimate		% Change 1990-1999
	Population	%	Population	%	
White, Non-Hispanic	303,412	97.1	303,229	96.7	-0.1
Black, Non-Hispanic	6,419	2.1	7,004	2.2	9.1
Asian, Non-Hispanic	1,109	0.4	963	0.3	-13.2
Other, Non-Hispanic	476	0.2	514	0.2	8.0
Hispanic	1,113	0.4	1,729	0.6	55.3

Note: See Appendix A for areas included in the Metropolitan Statistical Area
Source: 1990 Census of Population and Housing, Summary Tape File 3C; Claritas, Inc.

Ancestry

Area	German	Irish	English	Italian	U.S.	French	Polish	Dutch
City	22.4	19.9	20.4	3.1	10.7	3.0	0.8	3.6
MSA[1]	20.9	19.7	16.9	1.8	14.8	2.4	0.5	3.5
U.S.	23.3	15.6	13.1	5.9	5.3	4.2	3.8	2.5

Note: Figures are percentages and include persons that reported multiple ancestry (eg. if a person reported being Irish and Italian, they were included in both columns); (1) Metropolitan Statistical Area - see Appendix A for areas included
Source: 1990 Census of Population and Housing, Summary Tape File 3C

Median Age

Area	1990 Census	1999 Estimate
City	36.7	38.7
MSA[1]	35.3	38.0
U.S.	32.9	35.7

Note: (1) Metropolitan Statistical Area - see Appendix A for areas included
Source: 1990 Census of Population and Housing, Summary Tape File 3C; Claritas, Inc.

Male/Female Population

Area	Number of Males		Number of Females		Males per 100 Females	
	1990	1999	1990	1999	1990	1999
City	24,793	23,950	30,051	28,531	82.5	83.9
MSA[1]	149,216	149,875	163,313	163,564	91.4	91.6
U.S.	121,172,379	132,803,736	127,537,494	139,409,136	95.0	95.3

Note: (1) Metropolitan Statistical Area - see Appendix A for areas included
Source: 1990 Census of Population, General Population Characteristics; Claritas, Inc.

INCOME

Per Capita/Median/Average Income

Area	Per Capita ($)			Median Household ($)			Average Household ($)		
	1989	1999	% Chg.	1989	1999	% Chg.	1989	1999	% Chg.
City	12,005	17,933	49.4	18,276	23,973	31.2	27,507	40,635	47.7
MSA[1]	10,744	15,389	43.2	21,058	26,541	26.0	27,782	38,337	38.0
U.S.	14,420	21,350	48.1	30,056	40,525	34.8	38,453	56,184	46.1

Note: (1) Metropolitan Statistical Area - see Appendix A for areas included; 1989 data is from the 1990 Census; 1999 data is estimated by Claritas, Inc.
Source: 1990 Census of Population, General Population Characteristics; Claritas, Inc.

Household Income Distribution

Area	Percent of Households Earning								
	Under $5,000	$5,000 -14,999	$15,000 -24,999	$25,000 -34,999	$35,000 -49,999	$50,000 -74,999	$75,000 -99,000	$100,000 -149,999	$150,000 and up
City	8.4	24.1	18.9	12.4	13.8	11.6	4.8	3.1	3.0
MSA[1]	7.2	22.4	18.0	13.4	14.9	15.0	5.4	2.4	1.4
U.S.	3.9	13.3	13.8	12.6	16.2	19.4	9.7	6.6	4.6

Note: Data as of 1999; (1) Metropolitan Statistical Area - see Appendix A for areas included
Source: Claritas, Inc.

Effective Buying Income

Area	Per Capita ($)	Median Household ($)	Average Household ($)
City	14,874	22,547	34,016
MSA[1]	13,838	26,529	35,128
U.S.	17,496	36,603	47,036

Note: Data as of 1/1/2000; (1) Metropolitan Statistical Area - see Appendix A for areas included
Source: Standard Rate & Data Service, Newspaper Advertising Source, March 2000

Effective Household Buying Income Distribution

Area	% of Households Earning						
	$10,000 -$19,999	$20,000 -$34,999	$35,000 -$49,999	$50,000 -$74,999	$75,000 -$99,000	$100,000 -$124,999	$125,000 and up
City	23.2	21.5	13.5	11.2	4.2	1.4	2.5
MSA[1]	20.5	22.1	15.8	15.2	5.0	1.3	1.4
U.S.	15.0	21.6	17.6	19.6	8.4	3.0	3.3

Note: Data as of 1/1/2000; (1) Metropolitan Statistical Area - see Appendix A for areas included
Source: Standard Rate & Data Service, Newspaper Advertising Source, March 2000

Poverty Rates by Age

Area	People of All Ages	People Under 18 Years Old	Related Children Age 5-17 in Families in Poverty
City	23.4	n/a	n/a
County	19.5	29.4	24.9
U.S.	13.8	20.8	18.7

Note: Figures show the percent of people living below the poverty line in 1995. The
average poverty threshold was $15,569 for a family of four in 1995; n/a not available
Source: Bureau of the Census, Small Area Income and Poverty Estimates Program;
U.S. Department of Housing and Urban Development

EMPLOYMENT

Labor Force and Employment

Area	Civilian Labor Force			Workers Employed		
	Dec. 1998	Dec. 1999	% Chg.	Dec. 1998	Dec. 1999	% Chg.
City	23,194	23,735	2.3	21,899	22,390	2.2
MSA[1]	138,411	140,312	1.4	130,365	132,182	1.4
U.S.	138,297,000	139,941,000	1.2	132,732,000	134,696,000	1.5

Note: Data is not seasonally adjusted and covers workers 16 years of age and older;
(1) Metropolitan Statistical Area - see Appendix A for areas included
Source: Bureau of Labor Statistics, http://stats.bls.gov

Unemployment Rate

Area	1999											
	Jan.	Feb.	Mar.	Apr.	May	Jun.	Jul.	Aug.	Sep.	Oct.	Nov.	Dec.
City	6.5	5.8	6.5	6.5	6.0	5.9	5.8	5.8	6.1	6.5	6.5	5.7
MSA[1]	7.5	7.3	6.8	6.5	6.4	6.8	6.1	6.3	6.3	5.8	5.7	5.8
U.S.	4.8	4.7	4.4	4.1	4.0	4.5	4.5	4.2	4.1	3.8	3.8	3.7

Note: Data is not seasonally adjusted and covers workers 16 years of age and older; all figures are percentages; (1) Metropolitan Statistical Area - see Appendix A for areas included
Source: Bureau of Labor Statistics, http://stats.bls.gov

Employment by Industry

Sector	MSA[1]		U.S.
	Number of Employees	Percent of Total	Percent of Total
Services	38,000	30.0	30.2
Retail Trade	27,200	21.5	18.1
Government	22,400	17.7	15.8
Manufacturing	15,300	12.1	14.1
Finance/Insurance/Real Estate	5,000	3.9	5.9
Wholesale Trade	5,300	4.2	5.4
Transportation/Public Utilities	6,700	5.3	5.3
Construction	5,700	4.5	4.8
Mining	1,000	0.8	0.4

Note: Figures cover non-farm employment as of 12/99 and are not seasonally adjusted;
(1) Metropolitan Statistical Area - see Appendix A for areas included
Source: Bureau of Labor Statistics, http://stats.bls.gov

Employment by Occupation

Occupation Category	City (%)	MSA[1] (%)	U.S. (%)
White Collar	64.2	52.4	58.1
Executive/Admin./Management	12.1	8.9	12.3
Professional	20.0	13.8	14.1
Technical & Related Support	3.8	3.5	3.7
Sales	13.8	12.3	11.8
Administrative Support/Clerical	14.5	14.0	16.3
Blue Collar	19.4	32.6	26.2
Precision Production/Craft/Repair	7.6	13.4	11.3
Machine Operators/Assem./Insp.	4.6	7.1	6.8
Transportation/Material Movers	3.5	6.3	4.1
Cleaners/Helpers/Laborers	3.7	5.8	3.9
Services	15.7	13.5	13.2
Farming/Forestry/Fishing	0.7	1.5	2.5

Note: Figures cover workers 16 years of age and older;
(1) Metropolitan Statistical Area - see Appendix A for areas included
Source: 1990 Census of Population and Housing, Summary Tape File 3C

Occupational Employment Projections: 1996 - 2006

Occupations Expected to Have the Largest Job Growth (ranked by numerical growth)	Fast-Growing Occupations[1] (ranked by percent growth)
1. General managers & top executives	1. Systems analysts
2. Cashiers	2. Database administrators
3. Salespersons, retail	3. Computer engineers
4. Guards	4. Paralegals
5. Maintenance repairers, general utility	5. Hotel desk clerks
6. Systems analysts	6. Personal and home care aides
7. Hairdressers & cosmetologists	7. Artists and commercial artists
8. Clerical supervisors	8. Counter & rental clerks
9. Counter & rental clerks	9. Cleaners/servants, private home
10. Personal and home care aides	10. Bill and account collectors

Note: Projections cover West Virginia; (1) Excludes occupations with total job growth less than 300
Source: U.S. Department of Labor, Employment and Training Administration, America's Labor Market Information System (ALMIS)

Average Wages

Occupation	$/Hr.	Occupation	$/Hr.
Accountants and Auditors	15.41	Maids and Housekeepers	6.25
Assemblers and Fabricators	10.22	Maintenance Repairers	10.35
Automotive Mechanics	10.65	Marketing/Advertising/PR Managers	20.27
Bookkeepers	9.28	Nurses, Licensed Practical	11.12
Carpenters	12.60	Nurses, Registered	17.16
Cashiers	6.31	Nursing Aides/Orderlies/Attendants	7.07
Clerks, General Office	8.39	Physicians and Surgeons	55.18
Clerks, Shipping/Receiving/Traffic	10.59	Receptionists/Information Clerks	7.83
Computer Programmers	18.52	Sales Reps., Exc. Scientific/Retail	16.28
Computer Support Specialists	14.15	Sales Reps., Scientific, Exc. Retail	18.32
Cooks, Restaurant	6.41	Salespersons, Retail	7.56
Electricians	16.10	Secretaries, Except Legal/Medical	9.21
Financial Managers	22.00	Stock Clerks, Sales Floor	6.96
First-Line Supervisors/Mgrs., Sales	12.97	Systems Analysts	19.38
Food Preparation Workers	6.34	Teacher Aides	7.57
General Managers/Top Executives	23.49	Teachers, Elementary School	17.32
Guards	6.41	Teachers, Secondary School	17.64
Hand Packers	6.56	Telemarketers	8.05
Janitors and Cleaners	7.69	Truck Drivers, Heavy/Tractor-Trailer	13.04
Laborers, Landscaping	8.59	Truck Drivers, Light	9.30
Lawyers	27.16	Waiters and Waitresses	5.91

Note: Wage data is for 1998 and covers the Metropolitan Statistical Area (see Appendix A for areas included). Hourly wages for elementary and secondary school teachers were calculated by the editors from annual wage data assuming a 40 hour work week; Dashes indicate that data was not available.
Source: Bureau of Labor Statistics, 1998 Metropolitan Area Occupational Employment and Wage Estimates

TAXES

Major State and Local Tax Rates

State Corporate Income (%)	State Personal Income (%)	Residential Property (%)	Sales & Use		State Gasoline (cents/ gallon)	State Cigarette (cents/ pack)
			State (%)	Local (%)		
9.0	3.0 - 6.5	1.04	6.0	None	25.35[a]	17.0

Note: Personal/corporate income, sales, gasoline and cigarette tax rates as of January 2000. Property tax rates as of April 2000; (a) Sales tax added to excise
Source: Federation of Tax Administrators, www.taxadmin.org; ERI's Relocation Assessor software database, quarterly effective date 4/1/2000

Total Taxes Per Capita and as a Percent of Income

Area	Per Capita Income ($)	Per Capita Taxes ($)			Percent of Income (%)		
		Total	Federal	State/Local	Total	Federal	State/Local
West Virginia	20,742	6,798	4,469	2,329	32.8	21.5	11.2
U.S.	28,878	10,298	7,026	3,273	35.7	24.3	11.3

Note: Figures are for 1999
Source: Tax Foundation, www.taxfoundation.org

COMMERCIAL UTILITIES

Typical Monthly Electric Bills

Area	Commercial Service ($/month)		Industrial Service ($/month)	
	12 kW demand 1,500 kWh	100 kW demand 30,000 kWh	1,000 kW demand 400,000 kWh	20,000 kW demand 10,000,000 kWh
City	n/a	n/a	n/a	n/a
U.S.	150	2,174	23,995	508,569

Note: Based on rates in effect January 1, 1999; n/a not available
Source: Edison Electric Institute, Typical Residential, Commercial and Industrial Bills, Winter 1999

TRANSPORTATION

Transportation Statistics

Average minutes to work (1990)	15.1
Interstate highways	I-64; US-23; US-52; US-60
Bus lines	
In-city (1998)	The Tri-State Transit Authority, 21 buses
Inter-city (1999)	2
Passenger air service	
Airport	Tri-State/Milton J. Ferguson Field
Airlines (1999)	5
Enplaned passengers (1998)	70,675
Amtrak service	Yes
Motor freight carriers (1999)	30
Major waterways/ports	Ohio River

Source: FAA DOT/TSC CY1998 ACAIS Database; National Transit Database, 1998; Editor & Publisher Market Guide, 2000; Amtrak National Time Table, Fall 1999/Winter 2000; 1990 Census of Population and Housing, STF 3C; Jane's Urban Transport Systems 1999-2000

Means of Transportation to Work

Area	Car/Truck/Van		Public Transportation			Bicycle	Walked	Other Means	Worked at Home
	Drove Alone	Car-pooled	Bus	Subway	Railroad				
City	71.9	12.8	1.6	0.0	0.0	0.4	10.0	1.4	2.0
MSA[1]	79.8	12.8	0.5	0.0	0.0	0.1	4.1	0.9	1.8
U.S.	73.2	13.4	3.0	1.5	0.5	0.4	3.9	1.2	3.0

Note: Figures shown are percentages and only include workers 16 years of age and older;
(1) Metropolitan Statistical Area - see Appendix A for areas included
Source: 1990 Census of Population and Housing, Summary Tape File 3C

BUSINESSES

Major Business Headquarters

Company Name	1999 Rankings	
	Fortune 500	Forbes 500
No companies listed	-	-

Note: Companies listed are located in the city; dashes indicate no ranking
Fortune 500: Companies that produce a 10-K are ranked 1 to 500 based on 1999 revenue
Forbes 500: Private companies are ranked 1 to 500 based on 1998 revenue
Source: Forbes, December 13, 1999; Fortune, April 17, 2000

HOTELS & MOTELS

Hotels/Motels

Area	Hotels/ Motels	Rooms	Luxury-Level Hotels/Motels		Average Minimum Rates ($)		
			♦♦♦♦	♦♦♦♦♦	♦♦	♦♦♦	♦♦♦♦
City	6	721	0	0	n/a	n/a	n/a

Note: n/a not available; classifications range from one diamond (budget properties with basic amenities) to five diamond (luxury properties).
Source: OAG Business Travel Planner, Winter 1999-2000

Estimated Daily Food and Lodging Costs

Area	Food/Other ($/day)	Average Hotel Cost ($/day)
City	30	55
U.S.	30	55

Source: ERI's Relocation Assessor software database, quarterly effective date 4/1/2000

CONVENTION CENTERS

Convention Centers and Event Sites

Name	Guest Rooms	Meeting Space (sq. ft.)	Capacity (Theatre Style)
Cabell-Huntington Convention Center	n/a	n/a	0
Huntington Civic Arena	n/a	n/a	0
Huntington Civic Center	n/a	n/a	11,000
Radisson Hotel Huntington	200	10,350	1,200
Veterans Memorial Field House	n/a	n/a	6,500

Note: n/a not available
Source: EventSource.com, 3/15/2000

Living Environment

COST OF LIVING

Cost of Living: Homeowner

Cost Element	U.S. ($)	City ($)	Differential ($)	Percent of U.S. Average
Consumables	14,516	14,973	457	103.1
Transportation	5,957	6,120	163	102.7
Health Services	2,012	1,930	-82	95.9
Housing/Utilities/Prop. Tax	16,337	20,737	4,400	126.9
Income+Payroll Taxes	12,615	12,052	-563	95.5
Miscellaneous	8,563	8,563	0	100.0
Total Cost of Living	60,000	64,375	4,375	107.3

Note: Figures are based on a single income, four person family with gross annual earnings of $60,000, owning an 1,800 square-foot home, and driving two automobiles worth $22,000 30,000 miles per year.
Source: ERI's Relocation Assessor software database, quarterly effective date 4/1/2000

Cost of Living: Renter

Cost Element	U.S. ($)	City ($)	Differential ($)	Percent of U.S. Average
Consumables	10,486	10,846	360	103.4
Transportation	2,107	2,171	64	103.0
Health Services	1,632	1,570	-62	96.2
Rent/Utilities/Insurance	9,299	11,639	2,340	125.2
Income+Payroll Taxes	8,607	8,535	-72	99.2
Miscellaneous	7,869	7,869	0	100.0
Total Cost of Living	40,000	42,630	2,630	106.6

Note: Figures are based on a single income, three person family with gross annual earnings of $40,000, renting a 1,000 square-foot home, and driving one automobile worth $8,000 12,000 miles per year.
Source: ERI's Relocation Assessor software database, quarterly effective date 4/1/2000

HOUSING

Median Home Prices and Housing Affordability

Area	Median Price[2] 4th Qtr. 1999 ($)	HOI[3] 4th Qtr. 1999	Affordability Rank[4]
MSA[1]	n/a	n/a	n/a
U.S.	139,000	63.8	—

Note: (1) Metropolitan Statistical Area - see Appendix A for areas included; (2) U.S. figures calculated from the sales of 687,516 new and existing homes in 192 markets; (3) Housing Opportunity Index - percent of homes sold that were within the reach of the median income household at the prevailing mortgage interest rate; (4) Rank is from 1-192 with 1 being most affordable; n/a not available
Source: National Association of Home Builders, Housing Opportunity Index, 4th Quarter 1999

Estimated Home Price

Area	Price ($)
City	184,173
U.S.	135,855

Note: Figures are based on an 1,800 square-foot home
Source: ERI's Relocation Assessor software database, quarterly effective date 4/1/2000

Estimated Rent

Area	Rent ($/month)
City	843
U.S.	651

Note: Figures are based on a 1,000 square-foot home
Source: ERI's Relocation Assessor software database, quarterly effective date 4/1/2000

Median Home Price Projection

It is projected that the median home price in the metropolitan area will increase from $97,511 in 1999 to $97,533 in 2010, an increase of 0.0%
Kiplinger's Personal Finance Magazine, January 2000

RESIDENTIAL UTILITIES

Average Residential Utility Costs

Area	All Electric ($/mth)	Part Electric ($/mth)	Other Energy ($/mth)	Phone ($/mth)
City	n/a	n/a	n/a	n/a
U.S.	99.25	55.47	43.48	20.29

Note: n/a not available
Source: ACCRA, Cost of Living Index, 3rd Quarter 1999

HEALTH CARE

Average Health Care Costs

Area	Hospital ($/day)	Doctor ($/visit)	Dentist ($/visit)
City	n/a	n/a	n/a
U.S.	440.96	53.83	68.42

Note: n/a not available
Source: ACCRA, Cost of Living Index, 3rd Quarter 1999

Distribution of Office-Based Physicians

Area	Family/Gen. Practitioners	Specialists		
		Medical	Surgical	Other
MSA[1]	56	132	92	88

Note: Data as of 12/31/97; (1) Metropolitan Statistical Area - see Appendix A for areas included
Source: American Medical Assn., Physician Characteristics & Distribution in the U.S., 1999

Hospitals

Huntington has 2 general medical and surgical hospitals, 1 psychiatric, 1 rehabilitation.
AHA Guide to the Healthcare Field, 1999-2000

EDUCATION

Public School District Statistics

District Name	Num. Sch.	Enroll.	Classroom Teachers	Pupils per Teacher	Minority Pupils (%)	Current Exp.[1] ($/pupil)
Cabell County School District	34	13,548	986	13.7	n/a	n/a

Note: Data covers the 1997-1998 school year unless otherwise noted; (1) Data covers fiscal year 1996; SD = School District; ISD = Independent School District; n/a not available
Source: National Center for Education Statistics, Common Core of Data Public Education Agency Universe 1997-98; National Center for Education Statistics, Characteristics of the 100 Largest Public Elementary and Secondary School Districts in the United States: 1997-98, July 1999

Educational Quality

School District	Education Quotient[1]	Graduate Outcome[2]	Community Index[3]	Resource Index[4]
Cabell Co. School Dist.	100	101	92	101

Note: Over 1,000 secondary school districts were rated in terms of educational quality. The scores range from a low of 50 to a high of 150; (1) Combination of the Graduate Outcome, Community and Resource indexes weighted to reflect the greater importance of the Graduate Outcome and Resource Index; (2) Based on graduation rates and college board scores (SAT/ACT); (3) Based on the surrounding community's level of affluence and adult education; (4) Based on teacher salaries, per-pupil expenditures and student-teacher ratios.
Source: Expansion Management, Ratings Issue, 1999

Educational Attainment by Race

Area	High School Graduate (%)					Bachelor's Degree (%)				
	Total	White	Black	Other	Hisp.[2]	Total	White	Black	Other	Hisp.[2]
City	72.4	72.4	72.6	81.1	85.6	20.8	21.2	12.9	48.3	30.8
MSA[1]	66.7	66.6	69.7	80.3	68.9	12.6	12.5	9.5	44.9	13.7
U.S.	75.2	77.9	63.1	60.4	49.8	20.3	21.5	11.4	19.4	9.2

Note: Figures shown cover persons 25 years old and over; (1) Metropolitan Statistical Area - see Appendix A for areas included; (2) people of Hispanic origin can be of any race
Source: 1990 Census of Population and Housing, Summary Tape File 3C

School Enrollment by Type

Area	Preprimary				Elementary/High School			
	Public		Private		Public		Private	
	Enrollment	%	Enrollment	%	Enrollment	%	Enrollment	%
City	431	62.4	260	37.6	6,991	92.9	536	7.1
MSA[1]	2,602	74.4	893	25.6	53,477	96.9	1,705	3.1
U.S.	2,679,029	59.5	1,824,256	40.5	38,379,689	90.2	4,187,099	9.8

Note: Figures shown cover persons 3 years old and over;
(1) Metropolitan Statistical Area - see Appendix A for areas included
Source: 1990 Census of Population and Housing, Summary Tape File 3C

School Enrollment by Race

Area	Preprimary (%)				Elementary/High School (%)			
	White	Black	Other	Hisp.[1]	White	Black	Other	Hisp.[1]
City	90.3	9.7	0.0	0.0	89.5	9.8	0.7	0.6
MSA[2]	96.9	2.8	0.3	0.0	97.0	2.4	0.6	0.4
U.S.	80.4	12.5	7.1	7.8	74.1	15.6	10.3	12.5

Note: Figures shown cover persons 3 years old and over; (1) people of Hispanic origin can be of any race; (2) Metropolitan Statistical Area - see Appendix A for areas included
Source: 1990 Census of Population and Housing, Summary Tape File 3C

Higher Education

Two-Year Colleges		Four-Year Colleges		Medical Schools	Law Schools	Voc/ Tech
Public	Private	Public	Private			
1	1	0	0	1	0	3

Source: College Blue Book, Occupational Education, 1999; Medical School Admission Requirements, 1999-2000; Peterson's Guide to Two-Year Colleges, 2000; Peterson's Guide to Four-Year Colleges, 1999; Barron's Guide to Law Schools, 1999

MAJOR EMPLOYERS

Major Employers

Arthur's Enterprises (electrical supplies)
Champion Industries (printing)
Logan Corp. (machinery)
SWVA Inc. (blast furnaces)
Tri Cities Health Services Corp.

Cabell Huntington Hospital
Inco Alloys International
Namaco Industries (mattresses)
St. Mary's Hospital

Note: Companies listed are located in the city
Source: D&B Business Rankings, 1999; Ward's Business Directory, 1999; America's Corporate Families, 1999

PUBLIC SAFETY

Crime Rate

Area	All Crimes	Violent Crimes				Property Crimes		
		Murder	Forcible Rape	Robbery	Aggrav. Assault	Burglary	Larceny -Theft	Motor Vehicle Theft
City	6,243.1	13.1	95.7	184.0	210.2	2,378.2	3,042.7	319.1
Suburbs[1]	n/a	n/a	n/a	n/a	n/a	n/a	n/a	n/a
MSA[2]	n/a	n/a	n/a	n/a	n/a	n/a	n/a	n/a
U.S.	4,615.5	6.3	34.4	165.2	360.5	862.0	2,728.1	459.0

Note: Crime rate is the number of crimes per 100,000 population; (1) Defined as all areas within the Metropolitan Statistical Area but located outside the central city; (2) Metropolitan Statistical Area - see Appendix A for areas included; n/a not available
Source: FBI Uniform Crime Reports, 1998

RECREATION

Culture and Recreation

Museums	Symphony Orchestras	Opera Companies	Dance Companies	Professional Theatres	Zoos	Pro Sports Teams
2	1	0	1	0	0	0

Source: Musical America, International Directory of the Performing Arts, 1999; Official Museum Directory, 2000; Stern's Performing Arts Directory, 1997; USA Today Four Sport Stadium Guide, 1997; Career Opportunities in Theatre and the Performing Arts, 1999

Library System

The Cabell County Public Library has six branches, holdings of 356,160 volumes, and a budget of $2,296,398 (1997-1998).
American Library Directory, 1999-2000

MEDIA

Newspapers

Name	Type	Freq.	Distribution	Circulation
Herald-Dispatch	General	7x/wk	Regional	40,975

Note: Includes newspapers with circulations of 200 or more located in the city;
Source: Burrelle's Media Directory, 1999 Edition

Television Stations

Name	Ch.	Affiliation	Type	Owner
WSAZ	n/a	NBCT	Commercial	Lee Enterprises Inc.
WOWK	13	CBST	Commercial	Gateway Communications Inc.
WPBY	33	PBS	Public	WV Educational Broadcasting Authority

Note: Stations included broadcast in the Huntington metro area; n/a not available
Source: Burrelle's Media Directory, 1999 Edition

AM Radio Stations

Call Letters	Freq. (kHz)	Target Audience	Station Format	Music Format
WKEE	800	General	M/N/S	Adult Standards/Big Band/Easy Listening
WRVC	930	General	T	n/a
WTCR	1420	General	M	Country
WZZW	1600	General	M/N/S	n/a

Note: Stations included broadcast in the Huntington metro area; n/a not available
Target Audience: A=Asian; B=Black; C=Christian; E=Ethnic; F=French; G=General; H=Hispanic; M=Men; N=Native American; R=Religious; S=Senior Citizen; W=Women; Y=Young Adult; Z=Children
Station Format: E=Educational; M=Music; N=News; S=Sports; T=Talk
Source: Burrelle's Media Directory, 1999 Edition

FM Radio Stations

Call Letters	Freq. (mHz)	Target Audience	Station Format	Music Format
WMEJ	91.9	General	E/M	Christian/Easy Listening
WRVC	92.7	General	M	Oldies
WDGG	93.7	General	M	Country
WKEE	100.5	General	M/N/S	Adult Contemporary
WTCR	103.3	General	M	Country
WFXN	107.1	General	M/N/S	Classic Rock
WEMM	107.9	Religious	M/N	Christian

Note: Stations included broadcast in the Huntington metro area
Station Format: E=Educational; M=Music; N=News; S=Sports; T=Talk
Target Audience: A=Asian; B=Black; C=Christian; E=Ethnic; F=French; G=General; H=Hispanic;
M=Men; N=Native American; R=Religious; S=Senior Citizen; W=Women; Y=Young Adult; Z=Children
Source: Burrelle's Media Directory, 1999 Edition

WEATHER

Temperature/Precipitation/Humidity

	Jan	Feb	Mar	Apr	May	Jun	Jul	Aug	Sep	Oct	Nov	Dec	Yr.
Max. High Temp. (°F)	74	79	86	92	92	100	102	100	97	86	82	80	102
Avg. High Temp. (°F)	40	44	57	67	75	82	85	84	78	67	56	45	65
Avg. Temp. (°F)	32	35	46	56	64	72	75	74	68	56	47	37	55
Avg. Low Temp. (°F)	23	26	35	44	52	61	65	64	57	45	37	28	45
Min. Low Temp. (°F)	-16	-6	-2	20	27	40	46	43	31	16	8	-13	-16
Avg. Precip. (in.)	2.8	2.9	3.6	3.4	4.3	3.3	4.6	3.9	3.0	2.8	3.3	3.4	41.4
Avg. Snowfall (in.)	9	7	4	1	Tr	0	0	0	0	Tr	1	4	26
Avg. Rel. Hum. 7am (%)	77	76	75	76	84	88	90	92	92	87	80	78	83
Avg. Rel. Hum. 4pm (%)	60	56	49	45	51	55	58	58	57	51	56	62	55

Note: Tr = Trace amounts (less than 0.05 inches of rain or less than 0.5 inches of snow)
Source: National Climatic Data Center, International Station Meteorological Climate Summary, 3/95

Weather Conditions

Temperature			Precipitation		
10°F & below	32°F & below	90°F & above	0.01 inch or more precip.	1.5 inch or more snow/ice	Thunder-storms
11	97	19	142	7	42

Note: Figures are average number of days per year
Source: National Climatic Data Center, International Station Meteorological Climate Summary, 3/95

AIR & WATER QUALITY

Maximum Pollutant Concentrations

	Particulate Matter (ug/m³)	Carbon Monoxide (ppm)	Sulfur Dioxide (ppm)	Nitrogen Dioxide (ppm)	Ozone (ppm)	Lead (ug/m³)
MSA[1] Level	94	4	0.046	0.015	0.12	0.02
NAAQS[2]	150	9	0.140	0.053	0.12	1.50
Met NAAQS	Yes	Yes	Yes	Yes	Yes	Yes

Note: (1) Metropolitan Statistical Area - see Appendix A for areas included; (2) National Ambient Air Quality Standards; ppm = parts per million; ug/m³ = micrograms per cubic meter; n/a not available
Source: EPA, National Air Quality and Emissions Trends Report, 1997

Pollutant Standards Index

Data not available.
EPA, National Air Quality and Emissions Trends Report, 1997

Drinking Water

Water System Name	Pop. Served	Primary Water Source Type	Number of Violations in 1998-99	Type of Violation/ Contaminants
WVAWC-Huntington District	84,718	Surface	None	None

Note: Data as of January 19, 2000
Source: EPA, Office of Ground Water and Drinking Water, Safe Drinking Water Information System

Huntington tap water is alkaline, soft, and not fluoridated.
Editor & Publisher Market Guide, 2000

Iowa City, Iowa

Background

Iowa City, Iowa is located in the southeast section of the state, approximately 110 miles east of Des Moines, 25 miles south of Cedar Rapids and 60 miles northwest of Davenport. The city is on the Iowa River, just south of the river dam that creates Coralville Lake. The surrounding area is farmland. Iowa City is on the interstate east-west highway I-80, at a point where several major roads intersect.

Iowa City and neighboring Coralville are often considered to be a single metropolitan area, although they are separate municipalities. Iowa City is the county seat of Johnson County. The University of Iowa is a significant social, cultural and economic presence, and the city's largest single employer. The region is heavily oriented to agriculture, and other economic segments include manufacturing, health care, business and professional services, and retail and wholesale trades.

The population of Iowa City and Johnson County have increased steadily since the 1970s, and that trend is projected to continue.

The Sauk, the Mesquaki and other Native Americans originally inhabited the region. It was explored by the French during the early colonial period, and was part of territory France sold to the United States in the Lousiana Purchase. Iowa City was established in 1838-1839 as the capital of the Iowa Territory, and saw construction of a Capital building in 1840. In the 1850s, due to the emergence of railroads, the city became a trade and services center for west bound settlers. In 1857, however, the state capital was moved to Des Moines, and the former Capitol building in Iowa City became the site of the University of Iowa. The building was refurbished in the early 1990s, and houses a historic museum.

Among other settlers, the Amish established themselves in nearby Kalona, where a sizable Amish community still exists. In the 1850s, the communal society of the Amana colonies developed nearby, as did the organization of Mormon expeditions to the west. Although the Amana society disbanded in the 1930s, its influence remains in the area.

The University of Iowa provides the area with a variety of cultural activities and facilities, including the University of Iowa Museum of Art, Hancher Auditorium, Mabie Theater, Iowa Hall Museum of Natural History and the UIHC Medical Museum. The university's Writers' Workshop is regarded as one of the nation's leading centers for creative writing. Other cultural activities and venues in Iowa City include The Iowa City Community Theater, Riverside Theater, Dreamwell Theater and Arts Iowa City, among others. The Iowa Children's Museum recently opened.

Historic attractions include the Johnson County Heritage Museum in Coralville. The Plum Grove Historic Farm, built in 1844, was the retirement home of territorial Governor Robert Lucas and is now a museum. The Herbert Hoover Presidential Library and Museum is located in President Hoover's boyhood residence in West Branch. A museum in Amana preserves the history of that early community.

Iowa City maintains over 30 local parks. Coralville Lake is maintained by the U.S. Army Corps of Engineers and is available for public recreation. Lake McBride is a nearby state park.

Iowa City is governed under a Home Rule charter. An elected City Council and Mayor appoint a City Manager.

General Rankings and Evaluative Comments

■ Iowa City was ranked #183 out of 354 metropolitan areas in *Places Rated Almanac*. Criteria: cost of living, climate, crime, transportation, job outlook, education, the arts, health care, and recreation. *Places Rated Almanac, Millennium Edition, 2000*

■ Iowa City was selected as one of America's best small art towns. The city was ranked #75 out of 100. Criteria: easy and affordable access to the visual arts, performing arts and music, strong sense of community, low crime rate, and full-time population less than 65,000. *The 100 Best Small Art Towns in America: Discover Creative Communities, Fresh Air, and Affordable Living, 1998*

■ Iowa City was selected as one of the best places to retire by *Retirement Places Rated*. Criteria: cost of living, climate, crime, services, working, and leisure living. The city was ranked #116 out of 187. *Retirement Places Rated, 1999*

■ Cognetics studied 273 metro areas in the United States, ranking them by entrepreneurial activity. Iowa City was ranked #59 out of 134 smaller metro areas. Criteria: Significant Starts (firms started in the last 10 years that still employ at least 5 people) and Young Growers (percent of firms 10 years old or less that grew significantly during the last 4 years). *Cognetics, "Entrepreneurial Hot Spots: The Best Places in America to Start and Grow a Company," 1999*

■ Iowa City was selected as one of "The 50 Most Alive Places to Live" in the U.S. Criteria: ethnic diversity, recreational options, cultural vitality, low crime rate, opportunities for lifelong learning, good hospitals and restaurants, public transportation, walking accessibility, civic activities, and the kitsch factor. The area was ranked #6 out of 10 in the "College Towns" category. *Modern Maturity, May-June 2000*

Business Environment

STATE ECONOMY

State Economic Profile

"Iowa's economy has seen impressive growth in the last several years. A tight labor market and a softening in both the manufacturing and agriculture sectors will, however, slow Iowa's growth over the next few years.

While low food prices have helped to tame inflation, they have hurt farm income. Depressed commodity prices have hit Iowa's Gross State Product (GSP) particularly hard. Given the current oversupply in many food markets and the weak foreign demand, Iowa's farm economy will remain a drag on its economy.

Services, manufacturing and construction have all provided significant growth, helping to offset the declining farm sector. Business services and high-tech manufacturing, as well as a construction boom, largely contribute to this growth.

Des Moines, the traditional engine of Iowa's non-farm sector employment growth, has actually been growing at a rate below the rest of the state. This is partly due to Des Moines' tight labor market (1.9% unemployment rate) at the end of 1998. Economic growth has instead shifted to Cedar Rapids and Ames, both centers of university-high tech partnerships. Des Moines did, however, witness a building boom in 1998, with single-family permits jumping 35% and construction employment growing almost 12% in 1998.

There have been many bright spots to offset Iowa's hurting farm sector. Unfortunately the continued loss of population and tight labor markets will be a hurdle to companies that want to create jobs." *National Association of Realtors, Economic Profiles: The Fifty States and the District of Columbia, http://nar.realtor.com/databank/profiles.htm*

EXPORTS

Total Export Sales

Area	1995 ($000)	1996 ($000)	1997 ($000)	1998 ($000)	% Chg. 1995-98	% Chg. 1997-98
MSA[1]	n/a	n/a	n/a	n/a	n/a	n/a
U.S.	583,030,524	622,827,063	687,597,999	680,474,251	16.7	-1.0

Note: (1) Metropolitan Statistical Area - see Appendix A for areas included
Source: U.S. Department of Commerce, International Trade Association, Metropolitan Area Exports: An Export Performance Report on Over 250 U.S. Cities, November 10, 1999

CITY FINANCES

City Government Finances

Component	1995 ($million)	1995 (per capita $)
Revenue	57.8	952
Expenditure	54.8	903
Debt Outstanding	96.2	1,586

Source: 1999 County and City Extra, Annual Metro, City, and County Data Book

City Government Revenue by Source

Source	1995 ($million)	1995 (per capita $)
Intergovernmental	14.1	232
Taxes	19.5	322
Property	18.4	304
Sales and Gross Receipts	0.4	8

Source: 1999 County and City Extra, Annual Metro, City, and County Data Book

City Government Expenditures by Function

Function	1995 ($million)	1995 (per capita $)	1995 (%)
Public Welfare	0.0	0	0.0
Highways	6.2	102	11.4
Parking Facilities	4.0	66	7.4
Education	0.0	0	0.0
Health and Hospitals	0.2	3	0.4
Police Protection	4.8	79	8.8
Sewerage and Sanitation	9.6	158	17.6
Parks and Recreation	3.2	53	5.9
Housing and Community Development	7.1	118	13.1
Interest on Debt	6.3	104	11.6

Source: 1999 County and City Extra, Annual Metro, City, and County Data Book

Municipal Bond Ratings

Area	Moody's
City	Aaa

Source: Mergent Bond Record, 2/2000

POPULATION

Population Growth

Area	1980 Census	1990 Census	1999 Estimate	2004 Projection	Population Growth (%) 1990-1999	Population Growth (%) 1999-2004
City	50,508	59,738	61,401	61,361	2.8	-0.1
MSA[1]	81,717	96,119	103,232	104,793	7.4	1.5
U.S.	226,545,805	248,765,170	272,212,864	283,625,312	9.4	4.2

Note: (1) Metropolitan Statistical Area - see Appendix A for areas included
Source: 1990 Census of Population and Housing, Summary Tape File 3C; Claritas, Inc.

Number of Households and Average Household Size

Area	1980 Census	1990 Census	1999 Estimate	2004 Projection	1999 Average Household Size
City	18,712	21,964	21,957	21,837	2.80
MSA[1]	30,220	36,118	37,824	38,253	2.73
U.S.	80,389,592	91,993,582	102,048,200	107,302,392	2.67

Note: (1) Metropolitan Statistical Area - see Appendix A for areas included
Source: 1990 Census of Population and Housing, Summary Tape File 3C; Claritas, Inc.

Race/Ethnicity of City Population

Race/Ethnicity	1990 Census Population	1990 Census %	1999 Estimate Population	1999 Estimate %	% Change 1990-1999
White, Non-Hispanic	54,017	90.4	52,761	85.9	-2.3
Black, Non-Hispanic	1,475	2.5	1,722	2.8	16.7
Asian, Non-Hispanic	3,282	5.5	4,783	7.8	45.7
Other, Non-Hispanic	49	0.1	164	0.3	234.7
Hispanic	915	1.5	1,971	3.2	115.4

Source: 1990 Census of Population and Housing, Summary Tape File 3C; Claritas, Inc.

Race/Ethnicity of Metropolitan Statistical Area Population

Race/Ethnicity	1990 Census		1999 Estimate		% Change 1990-1999
	Population	%	Population	%	
White, Non-Hispanic	89,109	92.7	92,434	89.5	3.7
Black, Non-Hispanic	1,993	2.1	2,289	2.2	14.9
Asian, Non-Hispanic	3,705	3.9	5,540	5.4	49.5
Other, Non-Hispanic	126	0.1	268	0.3	112.7
Hispanic	1,186	1.2	2,701	2.6	127.7

Note: See Appendix A for areas included in the Metropolitan Statistical Area
Source: 1990 Census of Population and Housing, Summary Tape File 3C; Claritas, Inc.

Ancestry

Area	German	Irish	English	Italian	U.S.	French	Polish	Dutch
City	44.1	20.6	13.9	2.8	1.7	3.7	2.5	4.1
MSA[1]	46.3	20.6	14.4	2.4	1.9	3.4	2.3	4.3
U.S.	23.3	15.6	13.1	5.9	5.3	4.2	3.8	2.5

Note: Figures are percentages and include persons that reported multiple ancestry (eg. if a person reported being Irish and Italian, they were included in both columns); (1) Metropolitan Statistical Area - see Appendix A for areas included
Source: 1990 Census of Population and Housing, Summary Tape File 3C

Median Age

Area	1990 Census	1999 Estimate
City	24.8	27.0
MSA[1]	27.1	30.0
U.S.	32.9	35.7

Note: (1) Metropolitan Statistical Area - see Appendix A for areas included
Source: 1990 Census of Population and Housing, Summary Tape File 3C; Claritas, Inc.

Male/Female Population

Area	Number of Males		Number of Females		Males per 100 Females	
	1990	1999	1990	1999	1990	1999
City	29,677	30,465	30,061	30,936	98.7	98.5
MSA[1]	47,609	51,167	48,510	52,065	98.1	98.3
U.S.	121,172,379	132,803,736	127,537,494	139,409,136	95.0	95.3

Note: (1) Metropolitan Statistical Area - see Appendix A for areas included
Source: 1990 Census of Population, General Population Characteristics; Claritas, Inc.

INCOME

Per Capita/Median/Average Income

Area	Per Capita ($)			Median Household ($)			Average Household ($)		
	1989	1999	% Chg.	1989	1999	% Chg.	1989	1999	% Chg.
City	13,277	20,981	58.0	24,565	36,675	49.3	34,803	57,076	64.0
MSA[1]	14,113	22,494	59.4	27,862	42,339	52.0	36,625	60,448	65.0
U.S.	14,420	21,350	48.1	30,056	40,525	34.8	38,453	56,184	46.1

Note: (1) Metropolitan Statistical Area - see Appendix A for areas included; 1989 data is from the 1990 Census; 1999 data is estimated by Claritas, Inc.
Source: 1990 Census of Population, General Population Characteristics; Claritas, Inc.

Household Income Distribution

Area	Percent of Households Earning							
	Under $5,000	$5,000 -14,999	$15,000 -24,999	$25,000 -34,999	$35,000 -49,999	$50,000 -74,999	$75,000 -99,000	$100,000 -149,999	$150,000 and up
City	4.5	15.7	16.0	11.8	13.6	16.0	9.8	6.3	6.5
MSA[1]	3.4	12.5	13.8	11.3	15.6	18.7	11.2	7.1	6.5
U.S.	3.9	13.3	13.8	12.6	16.2	19.4	9.7	6.6	4.6

Note: Data as of 1999; (1) Metropolitan Statistical Area - see Appendix A for areas included
Source: Claritas, Inc.

Effective Buying Income

Area	Per Capita ($)	Median Household ($)	Average Household ($)
City	16,805	31,929	45,613
MSA[1]	18,493	36,972	49,250
U.S.	17,496	36,603	47,036

Note: Data as of 1/1/2000; (1) Metropolitan Statistical Area - see Appendix A for areas included
Source: Standard Rate & Data Service, Newspaper Advertising Source, March 2000

Effective Household Buying Income Distribution

Area	% of Households Earning						
	$10,000 -$19,999	$20,000 -$34,999	$35,000 -$49,999	$50,000 -$74,999	$75,000 -$99,000	$100,000 -$124,999	$125,000 and up
City	18.6	21.8	14.8	16.0	7.7	2.9	4.6
MSA[1]	15.5	21.2	16.7	18.9	9.1	3.3	4.5
U.S.	15.0	21.6	17.6	19.6	8.4	3.0	3.3

Note: Data as of 1/1/2000; (1) Metropolitan Statistical Area - see Appendix A for areas included
Source: Standard Rate & Data Service, Newspaper Advertising Source, March 2000

Poverty Rates by Age

Area	People of All Ages	People Under 18 Years Old	Related Children Age 5-17 in Families in Poverty
City	12.7	n/a	n/a
County	9.5	9.8	8.3
U.S.	13.8	20.8	18.7

Note: Figures show the percent of people living below the poverty line in 1995. The average poverty threshold was $15,569 for a family of four in 1995; n/a not available
Source: Bureau of the Census, Small Area Income and Poverty Estimates Program; U.S. Department of Housing and Urban Development

EMPLOYMENT

Labor Force and Employment

Area	Civilian Labor Force			Workers Employed		
	Dec. 1998	Dec. 1999	% Chg.	Dec. 1998	Dec. 1999	% Chg.
City	40,242	40,602	0.9	39,423	39,944	1.3
MSA[1]	65,577	66,177	0.9	64,311	65,160	1.3
U.S.	138,297,000	139,941,000	1.2	132,732,000	134,696,000	1.5

Note: Data is not seasonally adjusted and covers workers 16 years of age and older; (1) Metropolitan Statistical Area - see Appendix A for areas included
Source: Bureau of Labor Statistics, http://stats.bls.gov

Unemployment Rate

Area	1999											
	Jan.	Feb.	Mar.	Apr.	May	Jun.	Jul.	Aug.	Sep.	Oct.	Nov.	Dec.
City	2.4	2.4	2.4	2.3	2.1	2.5	2.5	2.4	2.1	1.7	1.7	1.6
MSA[1]	2.3	2.3	2.3	2.1	1.9	2.4	2.4	2.3	2.0	1.6	1.6	1.5
U.S.	4.8	4.7	4.4	4.1	4.0	4.5	4.5	4.2	4.1	3.8	3.8	3.7

Note: Data is not seasonally adjusted and covers workers 16 years of age and older; all figures are percentages; (1) Metropolitan Statistical Area - see Appendix A for areas included
Source: Bureau of Labor Statistics, http://stats.bls.gov

Employment by Industry

Sector	MSA[1]		U.S.
	Number of Employees	Percent of Total	Percent of Total
Services	16,100	22.0	30.2
Retail Trade	13,300	18.2	18.1
Government	29,000	39.7	15.8
Manufacturing	5,600	7.7	14.1
Finance/Insurance/Real Estate	2,600	3.6	5.9
Wholesale Trade	1,700	2.3	5.4
Transportation/Public Utilities	2,500	3.4	5.3
Construction	n/a	n/a	4.8
Mining	n/a	n/a	0.4

Note: Figures cover non-farm employment as of 12/99 and are not seasonally adjusted;
(1) Metropolitan Statistical Area - see Appendix A for areas included; n/a not available
Source: Bureau of Labor Statistics, http://stats.bls.gov

Employment by Occupation

Occupation Category	City (%)	MSA[1] (%)	U.S. (%)
White Collar	70.0	66.1	58.1
Executive/Admin./Management	9.3	10.0	12.3
Professional	27.1	24.7	14.1
Technical & Related Support	6.7	6.1	3.7
Sales	11.2	10.1	11.8
Administrative Support/Clerical	15.7	15.1	16.3
Blue Collar	11.9	14.8	26.2
Precision Production/Craft/Repair	4.6	6.3	11.3
Machine Operators/Assem./Insp.	2.7	3.3	6.8
Transportation/Material Movers	2.2	2.5	4.1
Cleaners/Helpers/Laborers	2.4	2.7	3.9
Services	17.4	16.5	13.2
Farming/Forestry/Fishing	0.6	2.6	2.5

Note: Figures cover workers 16 years of age and older;
(1) Metropolitan Statistical Area - see Appendix A for areas included
Source: 1990 Census of Population and Housing, Summary Tape File 3C

Occupational Employment Projections: 1996 - 2006

Occupations Expected to Have the Largest Job Growth (ranked by numerical growth)	Fast-Growing Occupations[1] (ranked by percent growth)
1. Truck drivers, light	1. Systems analysts
2. Salespersons, retail	2. Desktop publishers
3. Cashiers	3. Computer engineers
4. General managers & top executives	4. Database administrators
5. Janitors/cleaners/maids, ex. priv. hshld.	5. Emergency medical technicians
6. Registered nurses	6. Respiratory therapists
7. Nursing aides/orderlies/attendants	7. Adjustment clerks
8. Marketing & sales, supervisors	8. Home health aides
9. Hand packers & packagers	9. Human services workers
10. Systems analysts	10. Guards

Note: Projections cover Iowa; (1) Excludes occupations with total job growth less than 300
Source: U.S. Department of Labor, Employment and Training Administration, America's Labor Market Information System (ALMIS)

Average Wages

Occupation	$/Hr.	Occupation	$/Hr.
Accountants and Auditors	17.24	Maids and Housekeepers	8.23
Assemblers and Fabricators	9.33	Maintenance Repairers	12.12
Automotive Mechanics	12.45	Marketing/Advertising/PR Managers	19.39
Bookkeepers	10.85	Nurses, Licensed Practical	12.77
Carpenters	13.17	Nurses, Registered	-
Cashiers	7.18	Nursing Aides/Orderlies/Attendants	-
Clerks, General Office	11.33	Physicians and Surgeons	-
Clerks, Shipping/Receiving/Traffic	12.59	Receptionists/Information Clerks	8.91
Computer Programmers	20.45	Sales Reps., Exc. Scientific/Retail	18.32
Computer Support Specialists	-	Sales Reps., Scientific, Exc. Retail	20.60
Cooks, Restaurant	7.78	Salespersons, Retail	7.77
Electricians	13.77	Secretaries, Except Legal/Medical	-
Financial Managers	25.76	Stock Clerks, Sales Floor	6.98
First-Line Supervisors/Mgrs., Sales	13.38	Systems Analysts	-
Food Preparation Workers	6.47	Teacher Aides	6.91
General Managers/Top Executives	24.06	Teachers, Elementary School	16.03
Guards	10.20	Teachers, Secondary School	17.86
Hand Packers	8.51	Telemarketers	8.30
Janitors and Cleaners	-	Truck Drivers, Heavy/Tractor-Trailer	13.56
Laborers, Landscaping	10.41	Truck Drivers, Light	9.36
Lawyers	21.42	Waiters and Waitresses	5.88

Note: Wage data is for 1998 and covers the Metropolitan Statistical Area (see Appendix A for areas included). Hourly wages for elementary and secondary school teachers were calculated by the editors from annual wage data assuming a 40 hour work week; Dashes indicate that data was not available.
Source: Bureau of Labor Statistics, 1998 Metropolitan Area Occupational Employment and Wage Estimates

TAXES

Major State and Local Tax Rates

State Corporate Income (%)	State Personal Income (%)	Residential Property (%)	Sales & Use		State Gasoline (cents/ gallon)	State Cigarette (cents/ pack)
			State (%)	Local (%)		
6.0 - 12.0	0.36 - 8.98	3.02	5.0	2.0	20.0	36.0

Note: Personal/corporate income, sales, gasoline and cigarette tax rates as of January 2000.
Property tax rates as of April 2000.
Source: Federation of Tax Administrators, www.taxadmin.org; ERI's Relocation Assessor software database, quarterly effective date 4/1/2000

Total Taxes Per Capita and as a Percent of Income

Area	Per Capita Income ($)	Per Capita Taxes ($)			Percent of Income (%)		
		Total	Federal	State/Local	Total	Federal	State/Local
Iowa	26,688	9,097	6,004	3,093	34.1	22.5	11.6
U.S.	28,878	10,298	7,026	3,273	35.7	24.3	11.3

Note: Figures are for 1999
Source: Tax Foundation, www.taxfoundation.org

COMMERCIAL UTILITIES

Typical Monthly Electric Bills

Area	Commercial Service ($/month)		Industrial Service ($/month)	
	12 kW demand 1,500 kWh	100 kW demand 30,000 kWh	1,000 kW demand 400,000 kWh	20,000 kW demand 10,000,000 kWh
City	n/a	n/a	n/a	n/a
U.S.	150	2,174	23,995	508,569

Note: Based on rates in effect January 1, 1999; n/a not available
Source: Edison Electric Institute, Typical Residential, Commercial and Industrial Bills, Winter 1999

TRANSPORTATION

Transportation Statistics

Average minutes to work (1990)	14.6
Interstate highways	I-80; I-380; US-6; US-218
Bus lines	
In-city (1998)	Iowa City Transit, 18 buses
Inter-city (1999)	2
Passenger air service	
Airport	Eastern Iowa Airport
Airlines (1999)	3
Enplaned passengers (1998)	462,478
Amtrak service	No
Motor freight carriers (1999)	3
Major waterways/ports	Iowa River

Source: FAA DOT/TSC CY1998 ACAIS Database; National Transit Database, 1998; Editor & Publisher Market Guide, 2000; Amtrak National Time Table, Fall 1999/Winter 2000; 1990 Census of Population and Housing, STF 3C; Jane's Urban Transport Systems 1999-2000

Means of Transportation to Work

Area	Car/Truck/Van		Public Transportation			Bicycle	Walked	Other Means	Worked at Home
	Drove Alone	Car-pooled	Bus	Subway	Railroad				
City	51.7	11.9	10.1	0.0	0.0	2.6	20.0	0.8	2.9
MSA[1]	59.3	13.2	7.5	0.0	0.0	1.7	13.3	0.7	4.2
U.S.	73.2	13.4	3.0	1.5	0.5	0.4	3.9	1.2	3.0

Note: Figures shown are percentages and only include workers 16 years of age and older;
(1) Metropolitan Statistical Area - see Appendix A for areas included
Source: 1990 Census of Population and Housing, Summary Tape File 3C

BUSINESSES

Major Business Headquarters

Company Name	1999 Rankings	
	Fortune 500	Forbes 500
No companies listed	-	-

Note: Companies listed are located in the city; dashes indicate no ranking
Fortune 500: Companies that produce a 10-K are ranked 1 to 500 based on 1999 revenue
Forbes 500: Private companies are ranked 1 to 500 based on 1998 revenue
Source: Forbes, December 13, 1999; Fortune, April 17, 2000

HOTELS & MOTELS

Hotels/Motels

Area	Hotels/Motels	Rooms	Luxury-Level Hotels/Motels		Average Minimum Rates ($)		
			♦♦♦♦	♦♦♦♦♦	♦♦	♦♦♦	♦♦♦♦
City	4	511	0	0	n/a	n/a	n/a

Note: n/a not available; classifications range from one diamond (budget properties with basic amenities) to five diamond (luxury properties).
Source: OAG Business Travel Planner, Winter 1999-2000

Estimated Daily Food and Lodging Costs

Area	Food/Other ($/day)	Average Hotel Cost ($/day)
City	30	55
U.S.	30	55

Source: ERI's Relocation Assessor software database, quarterly effective date 4/1/2000

CONVENTION CENTERS

Convention Centers and Event Sites

Name	Guest Rooms	Meeting Space (sq. ft.)	Capacity (Theatre Style)
Alexis Park Inn	27	n/a	0
Carver-Hawkeye Arena	n/a	n/a	15,750
Country Inn	80	n/a	0
Hancher Auditorium	n/a	n/a	2,533
Holiday Inn	236	n/a	0
Iowa House Hotel	100	n/a	0
Kinnick Stadium	n/a	n/a	70,356
Radisson Hotel Iowa City	96	14,106	0
University of Iowa	n/a	n/a	2,533

Note: n/a not available
Source: EventSource.com, 3/15/2000

Living Environment

COST OF LIVING

Cost of Living: Homeowner

Cost Element	U.S. ($)	City ($)	Differential ($)	Percent of U.S. Average
Consumables	14,516	13,160	-1,356	90.7
Transportation	5,957	5,943	-14	99.8
Health Services	2,012	1,979	-33	98.4
Housing/Utilities/Prop. Tax	16,337	19,504	3,167	119.4
Income+Payroll Taxes	12,615	12,798	183	101.5
Miscellaneous	8,563	8,563	0	100.0
Total Cost of Living	60,000	61,947	1,947	103.2

Note: Figures are based on a single income, four person family with gross annual earnings of $60,000, owning an 1,800 square-foot home, and driving two automobiles worth $22,000 30,000 miles per year.
Source: ERI's Relocation Assessor software database, quarterly effective date 4/1/2000

Cost of Living: Renter

Cost Element	U.S. ($)	City ($)	Differential ($)	Percent of U.S. Average
Consumables	10,486	9,550	-936	91.1
Transportation	2,107	2,111	4	100.2
Health Services	1,632	1,614	-18	98.9
Rent/Utilities/Insurance	9,299	11,058	1,759	118.9
Income+Payroll Taxes	8,607	9,095	488	105.7
Miscellaneous	7,869	7,869	0	100.0
Total Cost of Living	40,000	41,297	1,297	103.2

Note: Figures are based on a single income, three person family with gross annual earnings of $40,000, renting a 1,000 square-foot home, and driving one automobile worth $8,000 12,000 miles per year.
Source: ERI's Relocation Assessor software database, quarterly effective date 4/1/2000

HOUSING

Median Home Prices and Housing Affordability

Area	Median Price[2] 4th Qtr. 1999 ($)	HOI[3] 4th Qtr. 1999	Affordability Rank[4]
MSA[1]	n/a	n/a	n/a
U.S.	139,000	63.8	–

Note: (1) Metropolitan Statistical Area - see Appendix A for areas included; (2) U.S. figures calculated from the sales of 687,516 new and existing homes in 192 markets; (3) Housing Opportunity Index - percent of homes sold that were within the reach of the median income household at the prevailing mortgage interest rate; (4) Rank is from 1-192 with 1 being most affordable; n/a not available
Source: National Association of Home Builders, Housing Opportunity Index, 4th Quarter 1999

Estimated Home Price

Area	Price ($)
City	142,824
U.S.	135,855

Note: Figures are based on an 1,800 square-foot home
Source: ERI's Relocation Assessor software database, quarterly effective date 4/1/2000

Estimated Rent

Area	Rent ($/month)
City	799
U.S.	651

Note: Figures are based on a 1,000 square-foot home
Source: ERI's Relocation Assessor software database, quarterly effective date 4/1/2000

Median Home Price Projection

It is projected that the median home price in the metropolitan area will increase from $118,116 in 1999 to $172,377 in 2010, an increase of 45.9%
Kiplinger's Personal Finance Magazine, January 2000

RESIDENTIAL UTILITIES

Average Residential Utility Costs

Area	All Electric ($/mth)	Part Electric ($/mth)	Other Energy ($/mth)	Phone ($/mth)
City	n/a	n/a	n/a	n/a
U.S.	99.25	55.47	43.48	20.29

Note: n/a not available
Source: ACCRA, Cost of Living Index, 3rd Quarter 1999

HEALTH CARE

Average Health Care Costs

Area	Hospital ($/day)	Doctor ($/visit)	Dentist ($/visit)
City	n/a	n/a	n/a
U.S.	440.96	53.83	68.42

Note: n/a not available
Source: ACCRA, Cost of Living Index, 3rd Quarter 1999

Distribution of Office-Based Physicians

Area	Family/Gen. Practitioners	Specialists		
		Medical	Surgical	Other
MSA[1]	40	176	149	189

Note: Data as of 12/31/97; (1) Metropolitan Statistical Area - see Appendix A for areas included
Source: American Medical Assn., Physician Characteristics & Distribution in the U.S., 1999

Hospitals

Iowa City has 3 general medical and surgical hospitals.
AHA Guide to the Healthcare Field, 1999-2000

According to *U.S. News and World Report*, Iowa City has one of the best hospitals in the U.S.:
University of Iowa Hospitals and Clinics, noted for cancer, endocrinology, gastroenterology, geriatrics, gynecology, neurology, ophthalmology, orthopedics, otolaryngology, rheumatology.
U.S. News Online, "America's Best Hospitals," July 19, 1999

EDUCATION

Public School District Statistics

District Name	Num. Sch.	Enroll.	Classroom Teachers	Pupils per Teacher	Minority Pupils (%)	Current Exp.[1] ($/pupil)
Iowa City Comm School District	22	10,424	556	18.7	n/a	n/a

Note: Data covers the 1997-1998 school year unless otherwise noted; (1) Data covers fiscal year 1996; SD = School District; ISD = Independent School District; n/a not available
Source: National Center for Education Statistics, Common Core of Data Public Education Agency Universe 1997-98; National Center for Education Statistics, Characteristics of the 100 Largest Public Elementary and Secondary School Districts in the United States: 1997-98, July 1999

Educational Quality

School District	Education Quotient[1]	Graduate Outcome[2]	Community Index[3]	Resource Index[4]
Iowa City Comm. School Dist.	132	150	128	98

Note: Over 1,000 secondary school districts were rated in terms of educational quality. The scores range from a low of 50 to a high of 150; (1) Combination of the Graduate Outcome, Community and Resource indexes weighted to reflect the greater importance of the Graduate Outcome and Resource Index; (2) Based on graduation rates and college board scores (SAT/ACT); (3) Based on the surrounding community's level of affluence and adult education; (4) Based on teacher salaries, per-pupil expenditures and student-teacher ratios.
Source: Expansion Management, Ratings Issue, 1999

Educational Attainment by Race

Area	High School Graduate (%)					Bachelor's Degree (%)				
	Total	White	Black	Other	Hisp.[2]	Total	White	Black	Other	Hisp.[2]
City	93.9	93.8	91.0	95.8	84.5	53.7	51.5	53.3	82.6	55.0
MSA[1]	90.6	90.4	89.8	94.8	80.6	44.0	42.1	52.6	78.6	52.7
U.S.	75.2	77.9	63.1	60.4	49.8	20.3	21.5	11.4	19.4	9.2

Note: Figures shown cover persons 25 years old and over; (1) Metropolitan Statistical Area - see Appendix A for areas included; (2) people of Hispanic origin can be of any race
Source: 1990 Census of Population and Housing, Summary Tape File 3C

School Enrollment by Type

Area	Preprimary				Elementary/High School			
	Public		Private		Public		Private	
	Enrollment	%	Enrollment	%	Enrollment	%	Enrollment	%
City	614	52.4	558	47.6	5,427	93.1	400	6.9
MSA[1]	1,165	57.4	864	42.6	10,715	93.0	809	7.0
U.S.	2,679,029	59.5	1,824,256	40.5	38,379,689	90.2	4,187,099	9.8

Note: Figures shown cover persons 3 years old and over;
(1) Metropolitan Statistical Area - see Appendix A for areas included
Source: 1990 Census of Population and Housing, Summary Tape File 3C

School Enrollment by Race

Area	Preprimary (%)				Elementary/High School (%)			
	White	Black	Other	Hisp.[1]	White	Black	Other	Hisp.[1]
City	88.7	2.6	8.6	2.5	91.4	4.5	4.2	2.3
MSA[2]	91.7	2.1	6.2	1.9	94.0	2.8	3.2	1.4
U.S.	80.4	12.5	7.1	7.8	74.1	15.6	10.3	12.5

Note: Figures shown cover persons 3 years old and over; (1) people of Hispanic origin can be of any race; (2) Metropolitan Statistical Area - see Appendix A for areas included
Source: 1990 Census of Population and Housing, Summary Tape File 3C

Higher Education

Two-Year Colleges		Four-Year Colleges		Medical Schools	Law Schools	Voc/ Tech
Public	Private	Public	Private			
0	0	1	0	1	1	4

Source: College Blue Book, Occupational Education, 1999; Medical School Admission Requirements, 1999-2000; Peterson's Guide to Two-Year Colleges, 2000; Peterson's Guide to Four-Year Colleges, 1999; Barron's Guide to Law Schools, 1999

MAJOR EMPLOYERS

Major Employers

Act Inc. (business consulting)
Heartland Express of Iowa (trucking)
Press Citizen Co.
University of Iowa Hospitals & Clinics

First National Bank - Iowa City
Iowa Book & Supply Co.
State University of Iowa Foundation

Note: Companies listed are located in the city
Source: D&B Business Rankings, 1999; Ward's Business Directory, 1999; America's Corporate Families, 1999

PUBLIC SAFETY

Crime Rate

Area	All Crimes	Violent Crimes				Property Crimes		
		Murder	Forcible Rape	Robbery	Aggrav. Assault	Burglary	Larceny -Theft	Motor Vehicle Theft
City	4,035.7	0.0	53.6	45.5	638.2	760.0	2,400.3	138.0
Suburbs[1]	3,578.9	2.4	56.0	17.0	187.3	627.7	2,547.3	141.1
MSA[2]	3,852.9	1.0	54.5	34.1	457.7	707.1	2,459.2	139.3
U.S.	4,615.5	6.3	34.4	165.2	360.5	862.0	2,728.1	459.0

Note: Crime rate is the number of crimes per 100,000 population; (1) Defined as all areas within the Metropolitan Statistical Area but located outside the central city; (2) Metropolitan Statistical Area - see Appendix A for areas included
Source: FBI Uniform Crime Reports, 1998

RECREATION

Culture and Recreation

Museums	Symphony Orchestras	Opera Companies	Dance Companies	Professional Theatres	Zoos	Pro Sports Teams
3	0	0	0	1	0	0

Source: Musical America, International Directory of the Performing Arts, 1999; Official Museum Directory, 2000; Stern's Performing Arts Directory, 1997; USA Today Four Sport Stadium Guide, 1997; Career Opportunities in Theatre and the Performing Arts, 1999

Library System

The Iowa City Public Library has no branches and holdings of 165,000 volumes.
American Library Directory, 1999-2000

MEDIA

Newspapers

Name	Type	Freq.	Distribution	Circulation
The Daily Iowan	General	5x/wk	Camp/Comm	20,000
Iowa City Press-Citizen	General	6x/wk	Area	17,500

Note: Includes newspapers with circulations of 200 or more located in the city;
Source: Burrelle's Media Directory, 1999 Edition

Television Stations

Name	Ch.	Affiliation	Type	Owner

No stations listed.
Note: Stations included broadcast in the Iowa City metro area; n/a not available
Source: Burrelle's Media Directory, 1999 Edition

AM Radio Stations

Call Letters	Freq. (kHz)	Target Audience	Station Format	Music Format
KXIC	800	General	N/T	n/a
WSUI	910	General	M/N/T	Jazz
KCJJ	1560	General	M/N/S/T	Adult Contemporary/Jazz

Note: Stations included broadcast in the Iowa City metro area; n/a not available
Target Audience: A=Asian; B=Black; C=Christian; E=Ethnic; F=French; G=General; H=Hispanic; M=Men; N=Native American; R=Religious; S=Senior Citizen; W=Women; Y=Young Adult; Z=Children
Station Format: E=Educational; M=Music; N=News; S=Sports; T=Talk
Source: Burrelle's Media Directory, 1999 Edition

FM Radio Stations

Call Letters	Freq. (mHz)	Target Audience	Station Format	Music Format
KRUI	89.7	General	E/M/N/S	Alternative
KSUI	91.7	General	M	Classical
KRNA	94.1	General	M/N/T	AOR
KKRQ	100.7	General	M/N/S	Classic Rock

Note: Stations included broadcast in the Iowa City metro area
Station Format: E=Educational; M=Music; N=News; S=Sports; T=Talk
Target Audience: A=Asian; B=Black; C=Christian; E=Ethnic; F=French; G=General; H=Hispanic;
M=Men; N=Native American; R=Religious; S=Senior Citizen; W=Women; Y=Young Adult; Z=Children
Music Format: AOR=Album Oriented Rock; MOR=Middle-of-the-Road
Source: Burrelle's Media Directory, 1999 Edition

WEATHER

Temperature/Precipitation/Humidity

	Jan	Feb	Mar	Apr	May	Jun	Jul	Aug	Sep	Oct	Nov	Dec	Yr.
Max. High Temp. (°F)	61	66	84	92	105	105	109	108	99	94	81	67	109
Avg. High Temp. (°F)	32	35	46	61	73	82	87	85	78	67	49	36	61
Avg. Temp. (°F)	23	26	36	50	61	71	75	73	65	54	39	27	50
Avg. Low Temp. (°F)	15	18	27	39	50	60	64	62	53	42	29	19	40
Min. Low Temp. (°F)	-23	-23	-16	13	27	37	45	39	24	11	-4	-19	-23
Avg. Precip. (in.)	1.5	1.4	2.3	3.0	4.2	4.7	4.1	3.9	3.8	2.7	2.1	1.6	35.2
Avg. Snowfall (in.)	7.7	6.7	5.0	1.0	0	0	0	0	0	0.2	1.8	6.0	28.4
Avg. Rel. Hum. (%)	79	78	75	67	70	75	76	77	75	69	72	78	74

Source: National Climatic Data Center, International Station Meteorological Climate Summary, 3/95

Weather Conditions

Temperature			Precipitation		
0°F & below	32°F & below	90°F & above	0.1 inch or more precip.	1.5 inch or more snow/ice	Thunderstorms
19	158	21	65	7	45

Note: Figures are average number of days per year
Source: National Climatic Data Center, International Station Meteorological Climate Summary, 3/95

AIR & WATER QUALITY

Maximum Pollutant Concentrations

	Particulate Matter (ug/m³)	Carbon Monoxide (ppm)	Sulfur Dioxide (ppm)	Nitrogen Dioxide (ppm)	Ozone (ppm)	Lead (ug/m³)
MSA[1] Level	n/a	n/a	n/a	n/a	n/a	n/a
NAAQS[2]	150	9	0.140	0.053	0.12	1.50
Met NAAQS	n/a	n/a	n/a	n/a	n/a	n/a

Note: (1) Metropolitan Statistical Area - see Appendix A for areas included; (2) National Ambient Air
Quality Standards; ppm = parts per million; ug/m³ = micrograms per cubic meter; n/a not available
Source: EPA, National Air Quality and Emissions Trends Report, 1997

Pollutant Standards Index

Data not available. *EPA, National Air Quality and Emissions Trends Report, 1997*

Drinking Water

Water System Name	Pop. Served	Primary Water Source Type	Number of Violations in 1998-99	Type of Violation/ Contaminants
Iowa City Water Dept.	54,231	Surface	None	None

Note: Data as of January 19, 2000
Source: EPA, Office of Ground Water and Drinking Water, Safe Drinking Water Information System

Iowa City tap water is neutral, very hard, and fluoridated.
Editor & Publisher Market Guide, 2000

Johnson City, Tennessee

Background

Johnson City, Tennessee is situated in the northeastern section of the state, in the Great Appalachian Valley, about 98 miles east-northeast of Knoxville. Its landscape is mostly rolling hills.

The city's major industry is agriculture, dominated by cattle, poultry and tobacco. Other important economic segments include the manufacture of telephone and electrical equipment, textiles, chemicals, furniture, tools and building materials. Mining and limestone quarrying are present as well.

The area was settled in the 1760s by farmers and iron-makers. When the East Tennessee and Virginia Railroad arrived 100 years later, a settlement called Johnson's Depot, after first town postmaster Henry Johnson, developed around the town water tank. In 1859, the town was renamed Haynesville for Landon C. Haynes, a Confederate senator, but again became Johnson in 1861.

Johnson City is in a region rich in natural beauty and offers much in the way of outdoor recreation. Named the top city for jogging by The Runner magazine, it is also an ideal place for hiking and camping. The Tennessee Valley Authority system of lakes offers boating, water-skiing, whitewater rafting and fishing. Nearby Cherokee National Forest, with over 30 miles of trails, pristine waterfalls, and trout streams, is a paradise for nature lovers. The city experiences little snowfall, unlike the surrounding mountains, which are often snow-covered throughout the winter and offer gorgeous scenery and superb skiing.

Higher educational facilities in Johnson City include East Tennessee State University and Milligan College. The city has extensive public and community services, and has benefitted from intelligent urban planning.

Nearby Jonesborough is Tennessee's oldest town and a National Historic Site. It was restored in the 1960s and, as the first capital of the Lost State of Franklin, it hosts approximately 8,000 people each October during the National Storytelling Festival. President Andrew Jackson, who once practiced law in Johnson City, stayed at Jonesborough's Chester Inn, the town's oldest frame structure, built in 1797.

General Rankings and Evaluative Comments

■ Johnson City was ranked #73 out of 354 metropolitan areas in *Places Rated Almanac*. Criteria: cost of living, climate, crime, transportation, job outlook, education, the arts, health care, and recreation. *Places Rated Almanac, Millennium Edition, 2000*

■ Cognetics studied 273 metro areas in the United States, ranking them by entrepreneurial activity. Johnson City was ranked #95 out of 134 smaller metro areas. Criteria: Significant Starts (firms started in the last 10 years that still employ at least 5 people) and Young Growers (percent of firms 10 years old or less that grew significantly during the last 4 years). *Cognetics, "Entrepreneurial Hot Spots: The Best Places in America to Start and Grow a Company," 1999*

■ Reliastar Financial Corporation ranked the 125 largest metropolitan areas according to the general financial security of residents. Johnson City was ranked #98 out of 125 with a score of -3.7 (the percentage a metropolitan area is above or below the metropolitan norm; a metro area with a score of 10.6 is 10.6% above the metro average). Criteria: Earnings and Wealth Potential (household income, education, net assets, cost of living); Safety Net (health insurance, retirement savings, life insurance, income support programs); Personal Threats (unemployment rate, low-income households, crime rate); Community Economic Vitality (cost of community services, job quality, job creation, housing costs). *Reliastar Financial Corporation, "The Best Cities to Earn and Save Money: A Ranking of the Largest 125 U.S. Cities," 2000 Edition*

Business Environment

STATE ECONOMY

State Economic Profile

"Tennessee's economy has been decelerating for almost three years now, a trend that should continue into 2000. Tennessee continues to shed jobs in its manufacturing sector, specifically textiles and apparels. In previous years, growth in other sectors was enough to offset these losses. Now growth in these other sectors has slowed. Tennessee's demographics are still strong, and Tennessee continues to have one of the lowest business costs in the country. The Tennessee outlook is one of moderating growth.

Tennessee's manufacturing employment shed some 11,500 jobs in 1998, a decline of 2.2%. Weak export demand and a strong dollar have undermined the apparel industry's competitive position. Soft commodity prices have also hurt Tennessee's metals industry. Neither of these situations will reverse in the near future.

Job growth across Tennessee has been mixed. Declines in manufacturing have hit central and eastern Tennessee harder than the west. Memphis' distribution and transportation sectors, located along the Mississippi, have continued to provide job growth even as the manufacturing sector stumbles. Federal Express and United Parcel Service continue to expand operations. A slowing of the US economy in 2000 will weaken the demand for distribution services, although less so than in most industries.

Nashville's economic outlook is less bright. Almost half of 1998's employment gains were in the construction industry. The city's tourism and convention industry remain strong, although it appears likely that commercial construction, especially hotel, has outpaced demand. Construction employment should contract. The slowing US economy will also place a drag on tourism." *National Association of Realtors, Economic Profiles: The Fifty States and the District of Columbia, http://nar.realtor.com/databank/profiles.htm*

EXPORTS

Total Export Sales

Area	1995 ($000)	1996 ($000)	1997 ($000)	1998 ($000)	% Chg. 1995-98	% Chg. 1997-98
MSA[1]	1,677,497	1,566,532	1,698,562	1,587,388	-5.4	-6.5
U.S.	583,030,524	622,827,063	687,597,999	680,474,251	16.7	-1.0

Note: (1) Metropolitan Statistical Area - see Appendix A for areas included
Source: U.S. Department of Commerce, International Trade Association, Metropolitan Area Exports: An Export Performance Report on Over 250 U.S. Cities, November 10, 1999

CITY FINANCES

City Government Finances

Component	1995 ($million)	1995 (per capita $)
Revenue	86.3	1,673
Expenditure	116.3	2,256
Debt Outstanding	124.8	2,419

Source: 1999 County and City Extra, Annual Metro, City, and County Data Book

City Government Revenue by Source

Source	1995 ($million)	1995 (per capita $)
Intergovernmental	40.0	775
Taxes	24.2	469
Property	20.3	394
Sales and Gross Receipts	3.4	67

Source: 1999 County and City Extra, Annual Metro, City, and County Data Book

City Government Expenditures by Function

Function	1995 ($million)	1995 (per capita $)	1995 (%)
Public Welfare	0.1	2	0.1
Highways	5.4	105	4.7
Parking Facilities	0.0	0	0.0
Education	41.2	800	35.5
Health and Hospitals	0.4	9	0.4
Police Protection	6.8	133	5.9
Sewerage and Sanitation	12.7	248	11.0
Parks and Recreation	2.9	56	2.5
Housing and Community Development	1.0	20	0.9
Interest on Debt	2.4	47	2.1

Source: 1999 County and City Extra, Annual Metro, City, and County Data Book

Municipal Bond Ratings

Area	Moody's
City	Aaa

Source: Mergent Bond Record, 2/2000

POPULATION

Population Growth

Area	1980 Census	1990 Census	1999 Estimate	2004 Projection	Population Growth (%) 1990-1999	Population Growth (%) 1999-2004
City	39,738	49,178	56,012	60,221	13.9	7.5
MSA[1]	433,638	436,047	464,210	483,333	6.5	4.1
U.S.	226,545,805	248,765,170	272,212,864	283,625,312	9.4	4.2

Note: (1) Metropolitan Statistical Area - see Appendix A for areas included
Source: 1990 Census of Population and Housing, Summary Tape File 3C; Claritas, Inc.

Number of Households and Average Household Size

Area	1980 Census	1990 Census	1999 Estimate	2004 Projection	1999 Average Household Size
City	17,860	19,577	23,749	26,178	2.36
MSA[1]	154,169	170,626	190,273	202,477	2.44
U.S.	80,389,592	91,993,582	102,048,200	107,302,392	2.67

Note: (1) Metropolitan Statistical Area - see Appendix A for areas included
Source: 1990 Census of Population and Housing, Summary Tape File 3C; Claritas, Inc.

Race/Ethnicity of City Population

Race/Ethnicity	1990 Census Population	1990 Census %	1999 Estimate Population	1999 Estimate %	% Change 1990-1999
White, Non-Hispanic	45,586	92.7	50,974	91.0	11.8
Black, Non-Hispanic	2,761	5.6	3,694	6.6	33.8
Asian, Non-Hispanic	305	0.6	528	0.9	73.1
Other, Non-Hispanic	138	0.3	142	0.3	2.9
Hispanic	388	0.8	674	1.2	73.7

Source: 1990 Census of Population and Housing, Summary Tape File 3C; Claritas, Inc.

Race/Ethnicity of Metropolitan Statistical Area Population

Race/Ethnicity	1990 Census		1999 Estimate		% Change 1990-1999
	Population	%	Population	%	
White, Non-Hispanic	423,765	97.2	447,413	96.4	5.6
Black, Non-Hispanic	8,464	1.9	10,798	2.3	27.6
Asian, Non-Hispanic	1,224	0.3	1,814	0.4	48.2
Other, Non-Hispanic	1,112	0.3	1,039	0.2	-6.6
Hispanic	1,482	0.3	3,146	0.7	112.3

Note: See Appendix A for areas included in the Metropolitan Statistical Area
Source: 1990 Census of Population and Housing, Summary Tape File 3C; Claritas, Inc.

Ancestry

Area	German	Irish	English	Italian	U.S.	French	Polish	Dutch
City	20.2	17.7	18.2	1.6	10.7	2.7	1.1	3.6
MSA[1]	18.9	18.2	15.9	1.2	15.3	2.0	0.6	3.7
U.S.	23.3	15.6	13.1	5.9	5.3	4.2	3.8	2.5

Note: Figures are percentages and include persons that reported multiple ancestry (eg. if a person reported being Irish and Italian, they were included in both columns); (1) Metropolitan Statistical Area - see Appendix A for areas included
Source: 1990 Census of Population and Housing, Summary Tape File 3C

Median Age

Area	1990 Census	1999 Estimate
City	34.5	37.8
MSA[1]	36.3	39.4
U.S.	32.9	35.7

Note: (1) Metropolitan Statistical Area - see Appendix A for areas included
Source: 1990 Census of Population and Housing, Summary Tape File 3C; Claritas, Inc.

Male/Female Population

Area	Number of Males		Number of Females		Males per 100 Females	
	1990	1999	1990	1999	1990	1999
City	23,721	26,801	25,457	29,211	93.2	91.7
MSA[1]	210,026	223,419	226,021	240,791	92.9	92.8
U.S.	121,172,379	132,803,736	127,537,494	139,409,136	95.0	95.3

Note: (1) Metropolitan Statistical Area - see Appendix A for areas included
Source: 1990 Census of Population, General Population Characteristics; Claritas, Inc.

INCOME

Per Capita/Median/Average Income

Area	Per Capita ($)			Median Household ($)			Average Household ($)		
	1989	1999	% Chg.	1989	1999	% Chg.	1989	1999	% Chg.
City	13,071	20,913	60.0	23,053	31,978	38.7	32,037	48,422	51.1
MSA[1]	11,427	17,468	52.9	22,386	30,163	34.7	28,897	41,869	44.9
U.S.	14,420	21,350	48.1	30,056	40,525	34.8	38,453	56,184	46.1

Note: (1) Metropolitan Statistical Area - see Appendix A for areas included; 1989 data is from the 1990 Census; 1999 data is estimated by Claritas, Inc.
Source: 1990 Census of Population, General Population Characteristics; Claritas, Inc.

Household Income Distribution

Area	Percent of Households Earning								
	Under $5,000	$5,000 -14,999	$15,000 -24,999	$25,000 -34,999	$35,000 -49,999	$50,000 -74,999	$75,000 -99,000	$100,000 -149,999	$150,000 and up
City	5.9	19.1	15.1	12.9	15.1	15.2	8.6	4.5	3.5
MSA[1]	5.6	18.8	17.9	14.3	16.0	16.1	6.2	3.2	1.8
U.S.	3.9	13.3	13.8	12.6	16.2	19.4	9.7	6.6	4.6

Note: Data as of 1999; (1) Metropolitan Statistical Area - see Appendix A for areas included
Source: Claritas, Inc.

Effective Buying Income

Area	Per Capita ($)	Median Household ($)	Average Household ($)
City	17,336	30,697	42,791
MSA[1]	15,628	29,587	38,973
U.S.	17,496	36,603	47,036

Note: Data as of 1/1/2000; (1) Metropolitan Statistical Area - see Appendix A for areas included
Source: Standard Rate & Data Service, Newspaper Advertising Source, March 2000

Effective Household Buying Income Distribution

Area	% of Households Earning						
	$10,000 -$19,999	$20,000 -$34,999	$35,000 -$49,999	$50,000 -$74,999	$75,000 -$99,000	$100,000 -$124,999	$125,000 and up
City	17.8	20.9	15.6	16.4	6.3	2.6	3.7
MSA[1]	19.0	23.1	16.3	16.3	6.1	2.0	2.0
U.S.	15.0	21.6	17.6	19.6	8.4	3.0	3.3

Note: Data as of 1/1/2000; (1) Metropolitan Statistical Area - see Appendix A for areas included
Source: Standard Rate & Data Service, Newspaper Advertising Source, March 2000

Poverty Rates by Age

Area	People of All Ages	People Under 18 Years Old	Related Children Age 5-17 in Families in Poverty
City	14.4	n/a	n/a
County	13.9	21.4	18.8
U.S.	13.8	20.8	18.7

Note: Figures show the percent of people living below the poverty line in 1995. The
average poverty threshold was $15,569 for a family of four in 1995; n/a not available
Source: Bureau of the Census, Small Area Income and Poverty Estimates Program;
U.S. Department of Housing and Urban Development

EMPLOYMENT

Labor Force and Employment

Area	Civilian Labor Force			Workers Employed		
	Dec. 1998	Dec. 1999	% Chg.	Dec. 1998	Dec. 1999	% Chg.
City	26,792	26,825	0.1	26,051	25,976	-0.3
MSA[1]	227,259	223,197	-1.8	216,970	215,809	-0.5
U.S.	138,297,000	139,941,000	1.2	132,732,000	134,696,000	1.5

Note: Data is not seasonally adjusted and covers workers 16 years of age and older;
(1) Metropolitan Statistical Area - see Appendix A for areas included
Source: Bureau of Labor Statistics, http://stats.bls.gov

Unemployment Rate

Area	1999											
	Jan.	Feb.	Mar.	Apr.	May	Jun.	Jul.	Aug.	Sep.	Oct.	Nov.	Dec.
City	4.7	4.6	4.4	4.2	3.5	3.7	3.3	3.5	3.3	2.9	3.1	3.2
MSA[1]	5.1	4.9	4.8	4.4	4.2	4.4	4.2	4.3	3.7	3.5	3.6	3.3
U.S.	4.8	4.7	4.4	4.1	4.0	4.5	4.5	4.2	4.1	3.8	3.8	3.7

Note: Data is not seasonally adjusted and covers workers 16 years of age and older; all figures are percentages; (1) Metropolitan Statistical Area - see Appendix A for areas included
Source: Bureau of Labor Statistics, http://stats.bls.gov

Employment by Industry

Sector	MSA[1]		U.S.
	Number of Employees	Percent of Total	Percent of Total
Services	48,200	24.1	30.2
Retail Trade	37,900	18.9	18.1
Government	30,300	15.1	15.8
Manufacturing	47,300	23.6	14.1
Finance/Insurance/Real Estate	7,900	3.9	5.9
Wholesale Trade	8,900	4.4	5.4
Transportation/Public Utilities	8,300	4.1	5.3
Construction	n/a	n/a	4.8
Mining	n/a	n/a	0.4

Note: Figures cover non-farm employment as of 12/99 and are not seasonally adjusted;
(1) Metropolitan Statistical Area - see Appendix A for areas included; n/a not available
Source: Bureau of Labor Statistics, http://stats.bls.gov

Employment by Occupation

Occupation Category	City (%)	MSA[1] (%)	U.S. (%)
White Collar	63.4	49.0	58.1
Executive/Admin./Management	12.0	8.6	12.3
Professional	17.6	11.8	14.1
Technical & Related Support	4.2	3.8	3.7
Sales	14.9	11.5	11.8
Administrative Support/Clerical	14.7	13.4	16.3
Blue Collar	22.3	36.2	26.2
Precision Production/Craft/Repair	8.7	13.7	11.3
Machine Operators/Assem./Insp.	7.4	12.7	6.8
Transportation/Material Movers	2.9	4.9	4.1
Cleaners/Helpers/Laborers	3.4	5.0	3.9
Services	13.6	12.6	13.2
Farming/Forestry/Fishing	0.7	2.2	2.5

Note: Figures cover workers 16 years of age and older;
(1) Metropolitan Statistical Area - see Appendix A for areas included
Source: 1990 Census of Population and Housing, Summary Tape File 3C

Occupational Employment Projections: 1996 - 2006

Occupations Expected to Have the Largest Job Growth (ranked by numerical growth)	Fast-Growing Occupations[1] (ranked by percent growth)
1. Salespersons, retail	1. Personal and home care aides
2. Truck drivers, light	2. Systems analysts
3. Cashiers	3. Paralegals
4. General managers & top executives	4. Respiratory therapists
5. Janitors/cleaners/maids, ex. priv. hshld.	5. Home health aides
6. Food service workers	6. Directors, religious activities & educ.
7. Child care workers, private household	7. Computer engineers
8. Cooks, fast food and short order	8. Child care workers, private household
9. Registered nurses	9. Corrections officers & jailers
10. Waiters & waitresses	10. Emergency medical technicians

Note: Projections cover Tennessee; (1) Excludes occupations with total job growth less than 300
Source: U.S. Department of Labor, Employment and Training Administration, America's Labor Market Information System (ALMIS)

Average Wages

Occupation	$/Hr.	Occupation	$/Hr.
Accountants and Auditors	15.66	Maids and Housekeepers	6.26
Assemblers and Fabricators	9.48	Maintenance Repairers	10.69
Automotive Mechanics	10.01	Marketing/Advertising/PR Managers	30.24
Bookkeepers	9.68	Nurses, Licensed Practical	10.06
Carpenters	11.39	Nurses, Registered	18.93
Cashiers	6.48	Nursing Aides/Orderlies/Attendants	7.39
Clerks, General Office	8.57	Physicians and Surgeons	47.80
Clerks, Shipping/Receiving/Traffic	10.45	Receptionists/Information Clerks	8.05
Computer Programmers	21.39	Sales Reps., Exc. Scientific/Retail	16.61
Computer Support Specialists	13.40	Sales Reps., Scientific, Exc. Retail	20.70
Cooks, Restaurant	7.13	Salespersons, Retail	8.15
Electricians	14.03	Secretaries, Except Legal/Medical	9.90
Financial Managers	25.16	Stock Clerks, Sales Floor	6.79
First-Line Supervisors/Mgrs., Sales	14.08	Systems Analysts	20.73
Food Preparation Workers	6.29	Teacher Aides	7.32
General Managers/Top Executives	24.67	Teachers, Elementary School	16.19
Guards	7.60	Teachers, Secondary School	16.68
Hand Packers	8.17	Telemarketers	-
Janitors and Cleaners	8.01	Truck Drivers, Heavy/Tractor-Trailer	12.45
Laborers, Landscaping	7.93	Truck Drivers, Light	8.85
Lawyers	38.00	Waiters and Waitresses	5.94

Note: Wage data is for 1998 and covers the Metropolitan Statistical Area (see Appendix A for areas included). Hourly wages for elementary and secondary school teachers were calculated by the editors from annual wage data assuming a 40 hour work week; Dashes indicate that data was not available.
Source: Bureau of Labor Statistics, 1998 Metropolitan Area Occupational Employment and Wage Estimates

TAXES

Major State and Local Tax Rates

State Corporate Income (%)	State Personal Income (%)	Residential Property (%)	Sales & Use		State Gasoline (cents/ gallon)	State Cigarette (cents/ pack)
			State (%)	Local (%)		
6.0	6.0[a]	1.10	6.0	2.5	21.4[b]	13.0[c]

Note: Personal/corporate income, sales, gasoline and cigarette tax rates as of January 2000. Property tax rates as of April 2000; (a) Applies to interest and dividend income only; (b) Rate is comprised of 20 cents excise and 1.4 cent motor carrier tax. Does not include a 1 cent local option tax; (c) Counties and cities may impose an additional tax of 1 cent per pack. Dealers pay a additional enforcement and admin. fee of 0.05 cent per pack
Source: Federation of Tax Administrators, www.taxadmin.org; ERI's Relocation Assessor software database, quarterly effective date 4/1/2000

Total Taxes Per Capita and as a Percent of Income

Area	Per Capita Income ($)	Per Capita Taxes ($)			Percent of Income (%)		
		Total	Federal	State/Local	Total	Federal	State/Local
Tennessee	25,347	8,481	6,088	2,393	33.5	24.0	9.4
U.S.	28,878	10,298	7,026	3,273	35.7	24.3	11.3

Note: Figures are for 1999
Source: Tax Foundation, www.taxfoundation.org

COMMERCIAL UTILITIES

Typical Monthly Electric Bills

Area	Commercial Service ($/month)		Industrial Service ($/month)	
	12 kW demand 1,500 kWh	100 kW demand 30,000 kWh	1,000 kW demand 400,000 kWh	20,000 kW demand 10,000,000 kWh
City	n/a	n/a	n/a	n/a
U.S.	150	2,174	23,995	508,569

Note: Based on rates in effect January 1, 1999; n/a not available
Source: Edison Electric Institute, Typical Residential, Commercial and Industrial Bills, Winter 1999

TRANSPORTATION

Transportation Statistics

Average minutes to work (1990)	16.0
Interstate highways	I-81; I-181; US-23; US-321; US-19W; U
Bus lines	
In-city (1998)	Johnson City Transit System, 6 buses
Inter-city (1999)	2
Passenger air service	
Airport	Tri-Cities Regional TN/VA
Airlines (1999)	2
Enplaned passengers (1998)	219,639
Amtrak service	No
Motor freight carriers (1999)	20
Major waterways/ports	None

Source: FAA DOT/TSC CY1998 ACAIS Database; National Transit Database, 1998; Editor & Publisher Market Guide, 2000; Amtrak National Time Table, Fall 1999/Winter 2000; 1990 Census of Population and Housing, STF 3C; Jane's Urban Transport Systems 1999-2000

Means of Transportation to Work

Area	Car/Truck/Van		Public Transportation			Bicycle	Walked	Other Means	Worked at Home
	Drove Alone	Car-pooled	Bus	Subway	Railroad				
City	82.9	10.2	0.8	0.0	0.0	0.1	2.9	1.0	2.1
MSA[1]	82.3	12.1	0.3	0.0	0.0	0.0	2.1	0.9	2.3
U.S.	73.2	13.4	3.0	1.5	0.5	0.4	3.9	1.2	3.0

Note: Figures shown are percentages and only include workers 16 years of age and older;
(1) Metropolitan Statistical Area - see Appendix A for areas included
Source: 1990 Census of Population and Housing, Summary Tape File 3C

BUSINESSES

Major Business Headquarters

Company Name	1999 Rankings	
	Fortune 500	Forbes 500
No companies listed	-	-

Note: Companies listed are located in the city; dashes indicate no ranking
Fortune 500: Companies that produce a 10-K are ranked 1 to 500 based on 1999 revenue
Forbes 500: Private companies are ranked 1 to 500 based on 1998 revenue
Source: Forbes, December 13, 1999; Fortune, April 17, 2000

HOTELS & MOTELS

Hotels/Motels

Area	Hotels/ Motels	Rooms	Luxury-Level Hotels/Motels		Average Minimum Rates ($)		
			♦♦♦♦	♦♦♦♦♦	♦♦	♦♦♦	♦♦♦♦
City	10	1,099	0	0	n/a	n/a	n/a
Suburbs	1	186	0	0	n/a	n/a	n/a
Total	11	1,285	0	0	n/a	n/a	n/a

Note: n/a not available; classifications range from one diamond (budget properties with basic amenities) to five diamond (luxury properties).
Source: OAG Business Travel Planner, Winter 1999-2000

Estimated Daily Food and Lodging Costs

Area	Food/Other ($/day)	Average Hotel Cost ($/day)
City	30	55
U.S.	30	55

Source: ERI's Relocation Assessor software database, quarterly effective date 4/1/2000

CONVENTION CENTERS

Convention Centers and Event Sites

Name	Guest Rooms	Meeting Space (sq. ft.)	Capacity (Theatre Style)
Freedom Hall Civic Center	n/a	n/a	8,500
Garden Plaza	187	n/a	200
Holiday Inn	205	n/a	600
Quality Inn	195	n/a	275

Note: n/a not available
Source: EventSource.com, 3/15/2000

Living Environment

COST OF LIVING

Cost of Living: Homeowner

Cost Element	U.S. ($)	City ($)	Differential ($)	Percent of U.S. Average
Consumables	14,516	14,813	297	102.0
Transportation	5,957	5,818	-139	97.7
Health Services	2,012	2,114	102	105.1
Housing/Utilities/Prop. Tax	16,337	12,638	-3,699	77.4
Income+Payroll Taxes	12,615	11,076	-1,539	87.8
Miscellaneous	8,563	8,563	0	100.0
Total Cost of Living	60,000	55,022	-4,978	91.7

Note: Figures are based on a single income, four person family with gross annual earnings of $60,000, owning an 1,800 square-foot home, and driving two automobiles worth $22,000 30,000 miles per year.
Source: ERI's Relocation Assessor software database, quarterly effective date 4/1/2000

Cost of Living: Renter

Cost Element	U.S. ($)	City ($)	Differential ($)	Percent of U.S. Average
Consumables	10,486	10,643	157	101.5
Transportation	2,107	2,047	-60	97.2
Health Services	1,632	1,706	74	104.5
Rent/Utilities/Insurance	9,299	6,036	-3,263	64.9
Income+Payroll Taxes	8,607	7,183	-1,424	83.5
Miscellaneous	7,869	7,869	0	100.0
Total Cost of Living	40,000	35,484	-4,516	88.7

Note: Figures are based on a single income, three person family with gross annual earnings of $40,000, renting a 1,000 square-foot home, and driving one automobile worth $8,000 12,000 miles per year.
Source: ERI's Relocation Assessor software database, quarterly effective date 4/1/2000

HOUSING

Median Home Prices and Housing Affordability

Area	Median Price[2] 4th Qtr. 1999 ($)	HOI[3] 4th Qtr. 1999	Affordability Rank[4]
MSA[1]	77,000	80.4	23
U.S.	139,000	63.8	–

Note: (1) Metropolitan Statistical Area - see Appendix A for areas included; (2) U.S. figures calculated from the sales of 687,516 new and existing homes in 192 markets; (3) Housing Opportunity Index - percent of homes sold that were within the reach of the median income household at the prevailing mortgage interest rate; (4) Rank is from 1-192 with 1 being most affordable
Source: National Association of Home Builders, Housing Opportunity Index, 4th Quarter 1999

Estimated Home Price

Area	Price ($)
City	100,057
U.S.	135,855

Note: Figures are based on an 1,800 square-foot home
Source: ERI's Relocation Assessor software database, quarterly effective date 4/1/2000

Estimated Rent

Area	Rent ($/month)
City	379
U.S.	651

Note: Figures are based on a 1,000 square-foot home
Source: ERI's Relocation Assessor software database, quarterly effective date 4/1/2000

Median Home Price Projection

It is projected that the median home price in the metropolitan area will increase from $92,155 in 1999 to $93,172 in 2010, an increase of 1.1%
Kiplinger's Personal Finance Magazine, January 2000

RESIDENTIAL UTILITIES

Average Residential Utility Costs

Area	All Electric ($/mth)	Part Electric ($/mth)	Other Energy ($/mth)	Phone ($/mth)
City	–	45.01	46.03	19.70
U.S.	99.25	55.47	43.48	20.29

Source: ACCRA, Cost of Living Index, 3rd Quarter 1999

HEALTH CARE

Average Health Care Costs

Area	Hospital ($/day)	Doctor ($/visit)	Dentist ($/visit)
City	309.50	51.50	49.75
U.S.	440.96	53.83	68.42

Note: Hospital—based on a semi-private room; Doctor—based on a general practitioner's routine exam of an established patient; Dentist—based on adult teeth cleaning and periodic oral exam.
Source: ACCRA, Cost of Living Index, 3rd Quarter 1999

Distribution of Office-Based Physicians

Area	Family/Gen. Practitioners	Specialists		
		Medical	Surgical	Other
MSA[1]	165	295	244	239

Note: Data as of 12/31/97; (1) Metropolitan Statistical Area - see Appendix A for areas included
Source: American Medical Assn., Physician Characteristics & Distribution in the U.S., 1999

Hospitals

Johnson City has 1 general medical and surgical hospital, 1 psychiatric, 1 eye, ear, nose and throat, 1 rehabilitation.
AHA Guide to the Healthcare Field, 1999-2000

EDUCATION

Public School District Statistics

District Name	Num. Sch.	Enroll.	Classroom Teachers	Pupils per Teacher	Minority Pupils (%)	Current Exp.[1] ($/pupil)
Johnson City School District	10	6,694	n/a	n/a	n/a	n/a

Note: Data covers the 1997-1998 school year unless otherwise noted; (1) Data covers fiscal year 1996; SD = School District; ISD = Independent School District; n/a not available
Source: National Center for Education Statistics, Common Core of Data Public Education Agency Universe 1997-98; National Center for Education Statistics, Characteristics of the 100 Largest Public Elementary and Secondary School Districts in the United States: 1997-98, July 1999

Educational Quality

School District	Education Quotient[1]	Graduate Outcome[2]	Community Index[3]	Resource Index[4]
Johnson City School Dist.	96	104	71	84

Note: Over 1,000 secondary school districts were rated in terms of educational quality. The scores range from a low of 50 to a high of 150; (1) Combination of the Graduate Outcome, Community and Resource indexes weighted to reflect the greater importance of the Graduate Outcome and Resource Index; (2) Based on graduation rates and college board scores (SAT/ACT); (3) Based on the surrounding community's level of affluence and adult education; (4) Based on teacher salaries, per-pupil expenditures and student-teacher ratios.
Source: Expansion Management, Ratings Issue, 1999

Educational Attainment by Race

Area	High School Graduate (%)					Bachelor's Degree (%)				
	Total	White	Black	Other	Hisp.[2]	Total	White	Black	Other	Hisp.[2]
City	71.1	71.6	60.8	70.0	76.1	25.9	26.8	7.2	40.8	36.8
MSA[1]	63.1	63.0	63.6	69.0	69.3	13.8	13.8	9.9	25.3	23.1
U.S.	75.2	77.9	63.1	60.4	49.8	20.3	21.5	11.4	19.4	9.2

Note: Figures shown cover persons 25 years old and over; (1) Metropolitan Statistical Area - see Appendix A for areas included; (2) people of Hispanic origin can be of any race
Source: 1990 Census of Population and Housing, Summary Tape File 3C

School Enrollment by Type

Area	Preprimary				Elementary/High School			
	Public		Private		Public		Private	
	Enrollment	%	Enrollment	%	Enrollment	%	Enrollment	%
City	394	53.9	337	46.1	6,374	96.9	207	3.1
MSA[1]	3,596	65.1	1,931	34.9	65,968	96.7	2,228	3.3
U.S.	2,679,029	59.5	1,824,256	40.5	38,379,689	90.2	4,187,099	9.8

Note: Figures shown cover persons 3 years old and over;
(1) Metropolitan Statistical Area - see Appendix A for areas included
Source: 1990 Census of Population and Housing, Summary Tape File 3C

School Enrollment by Race

Area	Preprimary (%)				Elementary/High School (%)			
	White	Black	Other	Hisp.[1]	White	Black	Other	Hisp.[1]
City	94.7	5.3	0.0	2.6	88.8	10.1	1.0	0.9
MSA[2]	95.8	3.0	1.2	1.0	96.8	2.4	0.7	0.4
U.S.	80.4	12.5	7.1	7.8	74.1	15.6	10.3	12.5

Note: Figures shown cover persons 3 years old and over; (1) people of Hispanic origin can be of any race; (2) Metropolitan Statistical Area - see Appendix A for areas included
Source: 1990 Census of Population and Housing, Summary Tape File 3C

Higher Education

Two-Year Colleges		Four-Year Colleges		Medical Schools	Law Schools	Voc/ Tech
Public	Private	Public	Private			
0	0	1	0	1	0	2

Source: College Blue Book, Occupational Education, 1999; Medical School Admission Requirements, 1999-2000; Peterson's Guide to Two-Year Colleges, 2000; Peterson's Guide to Four-Year Colleges, 1999; Barron's Guide to Law Schools, 1999

MAJOR EMPLOYERS

Major Employers

Accurate Machine Products
Denise Lingerie Corp.
Leon-Ferenbach Co. (yarns)
TPI Corp. (heating equipment)

American Water Heater Group
Harris-Tarkett (hardwood floors)
Press Inc. (newspapers)
Tennessee Motor Co.

Note: Companies listed are located in the city
Source: D&B Business Rankings, 1999; Ward's Business Directory, 1999; America's Corporate Families, 1999

PUBLIC SAFETY

Crime Rate

Area	All Crimes	Violent Crimes				Property Crimes		
		Murder	Forcible Rape	Robbery	Aggrav. Assault	Burglary	Larceny -Theft	Motor Vehicle Theft
City	5,546.5	1.8	56.1	101.7	404.9	818.7	3,793.5	369.9
Suburbs[1]	2,570.0	2.9	28.4	19.4	281.9	500.8	1,584.6	152.0
MSA[2]	2,935.2	2.8	31.8	29.5	297.0	539.8	1,855.6	178.7
U.S.	4,615.5	6.3	34.4	165.2	360.5	862.0	2,728.1	459.0

Note: Crime rate is the number of crimes per 100,000 population; (1) Defined as all areas within the Metropolitan Statistical Area but located outside the central city; (2) Metropolitan Statistical Area - see Appendix A for areas included
Source: FBI Uniform Crime Reports, 1998

RECREATION

Culture and Recreation

Museums	Symphony Orchestras	Opera Companies	Dance Companies	Professional Theatres	Zoos	Pro Sports Teams
3	1	0	1	1	0	0

Source: Musical America, International Directory of the Performing Arts, 1999; Official Museum Directory, 2000; Stern's Performing Arts Directory, 1997; USA Today Four Sport Stadium Guide, 1997; Career Opportunities in Theatre and the Performing Arts, 1999

Library System

The Johnson City Public Library has no branches, holdings of 95,985 volumes, and a budget of $835,764 (1997-1998).
American Library Directory, 1999-2000

MEDIA

Newspapers

Name	Type	Freq.	Distribution	Circulation
Johnson City Press	General	7x/wk	Area	31,031

Note: Includes newspapers with circulations of 200 or more located in the city;
Source: Burrelle's Media Directory, 1999 Edition

Television Stations

Name	Ch.	Affiliation	Type	Owner
WJHL	11	CBST	Commercial	Media General Inc.
WEMT	39	FBC	Commercial	Sinclair Communications Inc.

Note: Stations included broadcast in the Johnson City metro area; n/a not available
Source: Burrelle's Media Directory, 1999 Edition

AM Radio Stations

Call Letters	Freq. (kHz)	Target Audience	Station Format	Music Format
WETB	790	General	M/N/S	Christian
WJCW	910	General	M/N/S/T	Classic Rock/Oldies
WKIN	1320	General	T	n/a

Note: Stations included broadcast in the Johnson City metro area; n/a not available
Target Audience: A=Asian; B=Black; C=Christian; E=Ethnic; F=French; G=General; H=Hispanic; M=Men; N=Native American; R=Religious; S=Senior Citizen; W=Women; Y=Young Adult; Z=Children
Station Format: E=Educational; M=Music; N=News; S=Sports; T=Talk
Source: Burrelle's Media Directory, 1999 Edition

FM Radio Stations

Call Letters	Freq. (mHz)	Target Audience	Station Format	Music Format
WETS	89.5	General	E/M/N	n/a
WQUT	101.5	General	M	Classic Rock
WXIS	103.9	General	M	n/a
WKOS	104.9	General	M	Oldies

Note: Stations included broadcast in the Johnson City metro area; n/a not available
Station Format: E=Educational; M=Music; N=News; S=Sports; T=Talk
Source: Burrelle's Media Directory, 1999 Edition

WEATHER

Temperature/Precipitation/Humidity

	Jan	Feb	Mar	Apr	May	Jun	Jul	Aug	Sep	Oct	Nov	Dec	Yr.
Max. High Temp. (°F)	79	80	85	89	92	97	102	101	100	90	81	78	102
Avg. High Temp. (°F)	45	49	58	68	76	83	85	85	80	69	58	48	67
Avg. Temp. (°F)	35	39	47	56	64	72	75	74	68	57	47	38	56
Avg. Low Temp. (°F)	26	28	35	44	52	60	64	63	57	45	35	28	45
Min. Low Temp. (°F)	-21	-5	-2	21	30	38	48	43	34	20	5	-9	-21
Avg. Precip. (in.)	3.4	3.5	3.9	3.4	3.8	3.5	4.5	3.4	3.0	2.4	3.0	3.4	41.3
Avg. Snowfall (in.)	6	5	2	1	Tr	0	0	0	0	Tr	1	3	18
Avg. Rel. Hum. 7am (%)	81	80	80	80	87	88	90	92	92	89	84	82	85
Avg. Rel. Hum. 4pm (%)	59	54	49	46	52	54	57	56	54	50	53	59	54

Note: Tr = Trace amounts (less than 0.05 inches of rain or less than 0.5 inches of snow)
Source: National Climatic Data Center, International Station Meteorological Climate Summary, 3/95

Weather Conditions

Temperature			Precipitation		
10°F & below	32°F & below	90°F & above	0.01 inch or more precip.	1.5 inch or more snow/ice	Thunder-storms
7	96	17	134	4	42

Note: Figures are average number of days per year
Source: National Climatic Data Center, International Station Meteorological Climate Summary, 3/95

AIR & WATER QUALITY

Maximum Pollutant Concentrations

	Particulate Matter (ug/m³)	Carbon Monoxide (ppm)	Sulfur Dioxide (ppm)	Nitrogen Dioxide (ppm)	Ozone (ppm)	Lead (ug/m³)
MSA[1] Level	56	4	0.069	0.018	0.11	0.20
NAAQS[2]	150	9	0.140	0.053	0.12	1.50
Met NAAQS	Yes	Yes	Yes	Yes	Yes	Yes

Note: (1) Metropolitan Statistical Area - see Appendix A for areas included; (2) National Ambient Air Quality Standards; ppm = parts per million; ug/m³ = micrograms per cubic meter; n/a not available
Source: EPA, National Air Quality and Emissions Trends Report, 1997

Pollutant Standards Index

Data not available. *EPA, National Air Quality and Emissions Trends Report, 1997*

Drinking Water

Water System Name	Pop. Served	Primary Water Source Type	Number of Violations in 1998-99	Type of Violation/ Contaminants
Johnson City Water Dept.	78,231	Surface	None	None

Note: Data as of January 19, 2000
Source: EPA, Office of Ground Water and Drinking Water, Safe Drinking Water Information System

Johnson City tap water is alkaline, very soft, and fluoridated.
Editor & Publisher Market Guide, 2000

Kalamazoo, Michigan

Background

Kalamazoo, Michigan is situated in the southwestern section of the state along the Kalamazoo River, which links the city to Lake Michigan.

Called Kee-Kalamazoo, meaning "mirage" or "reflecting river," the site was a fur-trading post where Native Americans lived in several settlements. In 1829, a white settler named Titus Bronson built a cabin there, thus establishing a settlement that was originally known as Bronson, but renamed Kalamazoo in 1836.

Most of the area's early pioneers came from New York and New England to settle the "West." Kalamazoo was surrounded by hills, swamp and marshlands, the last of which were cultivated by the Dutch, who made the region famous for the celery they discovered could be grown in the muddy soil. However, most settlers made their homes in the flatland surrounding the central city, and were either industrialists who built mills and factories or immigrants who worked in them.

In 1846, with the arrival of the Michigan Central Railroad, and Kalamazoo a stop between Detroit and Chicago, the city was transformed from an agricultural village to a bustling town and political center. In the 19th Century, Kalamazoo spawned four U.S. senators and a state governor. In 1856, then-lawyer Abraham Lincoln spoke at a political rally in Bronson Park.

Today, Kalamazoo's economic segments include the manufacture of paper, pharmaceuticals, transportation equipment and metal products.

Contributing to the city's energy and diversity are many colleges including the Kalamazoo Institute of Arts, Western Michigan University and Kalamazoo Valley Community College. Kalamazoo College, founded by Baptists in 1833, has international study programs with centers in Kenya, Senegal, Sierre Leone, Swaziland, Ecuador, Mexico, Spain, France, Germany and China.

Architects Dankmar Adler, Louis Sullivan and Frank Lloyd Wright all designed buildings in Kalamazoo. The city also claims as a native the Pulitzer Prize-winning author Edna Ferber.

General Rankings and Evaluative Comments

- Kalamazoo was ranked #130 out of 354 metropolitan areas in *Places Rated Almanac*. Criteria: cost of living, climate, crime, transportation, job outlook, education, the arts, health care, and recreation. *Places Rated Almanac, Millennium Edition, 2000*

- Cognetics studied 273 metro areas in the United States, ranking them by entrepreneurial activity. Kalamazoo was ranked #79 out of 134 smaller metro areas. Criteria: Significant Starts (firms started in the last 10 years that still employ at least 5 people) and Young Growers (percent of firms 10 years old or less that grew significantly during the last 4 years). *Cognetics, "Entrepreneurial Hot Spots: The Best Places in America to Start and Grow a Company," 1999*

- Reliastar Financial Corporation ranked the 125 largest metropolitan areas according to the general financial security of residents. Kalamazoo was ranked #45 out of 125 with a score of 5.5 (the percentage a metropolitan area is above or below the metropolitan norm; a metro area with a score of 10.6 is 10.6% above the metro average). Criteria: Earnings and Wealth Potential (household income, education, net assets, cost of living); Safety Net (health insurance, retirement savings, life insurance, income support programs); Personal Threats (unemployment rate, low-income households, crime rate); Community Economic Vitality (cost of community services, job quality, job creation, housing costs). *Reliastar Financial Corporation, "The Best Cities to Earn and Save Money: A Ranking of the Largest 125 U.S. Cities," 2000 Edition*

Business Environment

STATE ECONOMY

State Economic Profile

"Although the Michigan economy bounced back quickly from the GM strike, it is losing much of its mid-1990s momentum. Strong auto sales have not translated into employment gains in the auto industry. Canada's weak economy has caused a drop in Michigan's exports. And what constrains Michigan the most is its demographic situation. The next several years should see a slowing economy.

In spite of the GM strike and booming automobile sales, GM has not increased employment and is currently planning to close plants in Kalamazoo and Flint. In addition, some 1,000 office jobs are targeted for elimination at the Detroit headquarters; Ford is currently planning to cut jobs within the state. Auto sales 2000 should fall below 1998, only adding to Detroit's need for employment reductions.

Construction activity added significantly to job growth in 1998, with construction employment growing 2.5% for the state and 8.3% for Detroit. Almost 1,800 commercial/industrial developments were undertaken in 1998. With the slowing economy, construction activity is likely to contract, undermining one of Michigan's bright spots. Residential starts, up 7% in 1998, should decline in the near future.

Michigan's tight labor markets have helped to absorb downsizing in the auto industry, keeping the unemployment rate manageable. Labor availability has, however, started to become a problem for the state's information technology firms. The state's weak population growth, especially its continuing loss of young households, will dampen the high home price appreciation witnessed in recent years, as well as limit job entry-level job growth." *National Association of Realtors, Economic Profiles: The Fifty States and the District of Columbia, http://nar.realtor.com/databank/profiles.htm*

EXPORTS

Total Export Sales

Area	1995 ($000)	1996 ($000)	1997 ($000)	1998 ($000)	% Chg. 1995-98	% Chg. 1997-98
MSA[1]	897,345	836,062	919,453	929,692	3.6	1.1
U.S.	583,030,524	622,827,063	687,597,999	680,474,251	16.7	-1.0

Note: (1) Metropolitan Statistical Area - see Appendix A for areas included
Source: U.S. Department of Commerce, International Trade Association, Metropolitan Area Exports: An Export Performance Report on Over 250 U.S. Cities, November 10, 1999

CITY FINANCES

City Government Finances

Component	1995 ($million)	1995 (per capita $)
Revenue	101.9	1,248
Expenditure	92.6	1,134
Debt Outstanding	377.1	4,619

Source: 1999 County and City Extra, Annual Metro, City, and County Data Book

City Government Revenue by Source

Source	1995 ($million)	1995 (per capita $)
Intergovernmental	22.5	275
Taxes	23.3	286
Property	22.4	275
Sales and Gross Receipts	0.0	0

Source: 1999 County and City Extra, Annual Metro, City, and County Data Book

City Government Expenditures by Function

Function	1995 ($million)	1995 (per capita $)	1995 (%)
Public Welfare	0.0	0	0.0
Highways	7.3	89	7.9
Parking Facilities	0.0	0	0.0
Education	0.0	0	0.0
Health and Hospitals	0.0	0	0.0
Police Protection	21.9	268	23.7
Sewerage and Sanitation	16.2	198	17.5
Parks and Recreation	0.8	10	0.9
Housing and Community Development	0.0	0	0.0
Interest on Debt	26.2	320	28.3

Source: 1999 County and City Extra, Annual Metro, City, and County Data Book

Municipal Bond Ratings

Area	Moody's
City	Aa3

Source: Mergent Bond Record, 2/2000

POPULATION

Population Growth

Area	1980 Census	1990 Census	1999 Estimate	2004 Projection	Population Growth (%) 1990-1999	Population Growth (%) 1999-2004
City	79,722	80,277	75,445	73,766	-6.0	-2.2
MSA[1]	212,378	223,411	446,939	454,847	100.1	1.8
U.S.	226,545,805	248,765,170	272,212,864	283,625,312	9.4	4.2

Note: (1) Metropolitan Statistical Area - see Appendix A for areas included
Source: 1990 Census of Population and Housing, Summary Tape File 3C; Claritas, Inc.

Number of Households and Average Household Size

Area	1980 Census	1990 Census	1999 Estimate	2004 Projection	1999 Average Household Size
City	28,430	29,534	28,203	27,732	2.68
MSA[1]	149,649	84,021	170,284	174,509	2.62
U.S.	80,389,592	91,993,582	102,048,200	107,302,392	2.67

Note: (1) Metropolitan Statistical Area - see Appendix A for areas included
Source: 1990 Census of Population and Housing, Summary Tape File 3C; Claritas, Inc.

Race/Ethnicity of City Population

Race/Ethnicity	1990 Census Population	1990 Census %	1999 Estimate Population	1999 Estimate %	% Change 1990-1999
White, Non-Hispanic	61,129	76.1	54,763	72.6	-10.4
Black, Non-Hispanic	14,964	18.6	15,689	20.8	4.8
Asian, Non-Hispanic	1,679	2.1	1,811	2.4	7.9
Other, Non-Hispanic	434	0.5	523	0.7	20.5
Hispanic	2,071	2.6	2,659	3.5	28.4

Source: 1990 Census of Population and Housing, Summary Tape File 3C; Claritas, Inc.

Race/Ethnicity of Metropolitan Statistical Area Population

Race/Ethnicity	1990 Census		1999 Estimate		% Change 1990-1999
	Population	%	Population	%	
White, Non-Hispanic	195,737	87.6	383,046	85.7	95.7
Black, Non-Hispanic	19,759	8.8	43,296	9.7	119.1
Asian, Non-Hispanic	3,423	1.5	6,313	1.4	84.4
Other, Non-Hispanic	899	0.4	2,706	0.6	201.0
Hispanic	3,593	1.6	11,578	2.6	222.2

Note: See Appendix A for areas included in the Metropolitan Statistical Area
Source: 1990 Census of Population and Housing, Summary Tape File 3C; Claritas, Inc.

Ancestry

Area	German	Irish	English	Italian	U.S.	French	Polish	Dutch
City	26.3	14.6	14.4	3.0	2.8	4.2	5.0	10.8
MSA[1]	30.8	16.1	18.5	2.8	3.6	5.2	4.9	16.0
U.S.	23.3	15.6	13.1	5.9	5.3	4.2	3.8	2.5

Note: Figures are percentages and include persons that reported multiple ancestry (eg. if a person reported being Irish and Italian, they were included in both columns); (1) Metropolitan Statistical Area - see Appendix A for areas included
Source: 1990 Census of Population and Housing, Summary Tape File 3C

Median Age

Area	1990 Census	1999 Estimate
City	26.7	29.1
MSA[1]	31.0	35.1
U.S.	32.9	35.7

Note: (1) Metropolitan Statistical Area - see Appendix A for areas included
Source: 1990 Census of Population and Housing, Summary Tape File 3C; Claritas, Inc.

Male/Female Population

Area	Number of Males		Number of Females		Males per 100 Females	
	1990	1999	1990	1999	1990	1999
City	37,574	35,571	42,703	39,874	88.0	89.2
MSA[1]	107,255	216,188	116,156	230,751	92.3	93.7
U.S.	121,172,379	132,803,736	127,537,494	139,409,136	95.0	95.3

Note: (1) Metropolitan Statistical Area - see Appendix A for areas included
Source: 1990 Census of Population, General Population Characteristics; Claritas, Inc.

INCOME

Per Capita/Median/Average Income

Area	Per Capita ($)			Median Household ($)			Average Household ($)		
	1989	1999	% Chg.	1989	1999	% Chg.	1989	1999	% Chg.
City	11,956	17,676	47.8	23,207	30,725	32.4	31,276	45,351	45.0
MSA[1]	14,548	20,407	40.3	31,060	40,095	29.1	38,109	52,862	38.7
U.S.	14,420	21,350	48.1	30,056	40,525	34.8	38,453	56,184	46.1

Note: (1) Metropolitan Statistical Area - see Appendix A for areas included; 1989 data is from the 1990 Census; 1999 data is estimated by Claritas, Inc.
Source: 1990 Census of Population, General Population Characteristics; Claritas, Inc.

Household Income Distribution

Area	Percent of Households Earning								
	Under $5,000	$5,000 -14,999	$15,000 -24,999	$25,000 -34,999	$35,000 -49,999	$50,000 -74,999	$75,000 -99,000	$100,000 -149,999	$150,000 and up
City	5.9	20.4	16.7	11.7	15.4	15.9	7.0	4.0	3.1
MSA[1]	3.5	13.8	14.5	12.3	16.7	19.9	9.7	6.4	3.2
U.S.	3.9	13.3	13.8	12.6	16.2	19.4	9.7	6.6	4.6

Note: Data as of 1999; (1) Metropolitan Statistical Area - see Appendix A for areas included
Source: Claritas, Inc.

Effective Buying Income

Area	Per Capita ($)	Median Household ($)	Average Household ($)
City	14,249	27,872	38,428
MSA[1]	16,470	35,453	43,479
U.S.	17,496	36,603	47,036

Note: Data as of 1/1/2000; (1) Metropolitan Statistical Area - see Appendix A for areas included
Source: Standard Rate & Data Service, Newspaper Advertising Source, March 2000

Effective Household Buying Income Distribution

Area	% of Households Earning						
	$10,000 -$19,999	$20,000 -$34,999	$35,000 -$49,999	$50,000 -$74,999	$75,000 -$99,000	$100,000 -$124,999	$125,000 and up
City	20.2	21.3	16.4	14.3	5.2	2.0	2.4
MSA[1]	16.1	21.8	18.1	20.0	7.9	2.4	2.2
U.S.	15.0	21.6	17.6	19.6	8.4	3.0	3.3

Note: Data as of 1/1/2000; (1) Metropolitan Statistical Area - see Appendix A for areas included
Source: Standard Rate & Data Service, Newspaper Advertising Source, March 2000

Poverty Rates by Age

Area	People of All Ages	People Under 18 Years Old	Related Children Age 5-17 in Families in Poverty
City	21.5	n/a	n/a
County	11.3	16.6	14.5
U.S.	13.8	20.8	18.7

Note: Figures show the percent of people living below the poverty line in 1995. The
average poverty threshold was $15,569 for a family of four in 1995; n/a not available
Source: Bureau of the Census, Small Area Income and Poverty Estimates Program;
U.S. Department of Housing and Urban Development

EMPLOYMENT

Labor Force and Employment

Area	Civilian Labor Force			Workers Employed		
	Dec. 1998	Dec. 1999	% Chg.	Dec. 1998	Dec. 1999	% Chg.
City	41,547	41,940	0.9	39,976	40,402	1.1
MSA[1]	230,575	232,890	1.0	223,107	225,481	1.1
U.S.	138,297,000	139,941,000	1.2	132,732,000	134,696,000	1.5

Note: Data is not seasonally adjusted and covers workers 16 years of age and older;
(1) Metropolitan Statistical Area - see Appendix A for areas included
Source: Bureau of Labor Statistics, http://stats.bls.gov

Unemployment Rate

Area	1999											
	Jan.	Feb.	Mar.	Apr.	May	Jun.	Jul.	Aug.	Sep.	Oct.	Nov.	Dec.
City	4.6	4.8	4.5	4.4	4.4	5.4	4.6	3.8	4.2	4.2	4.0	3.7
MSA[1]	4.0	4.1	4.0	3.4	3.3	3.8	3.8	2.8	3.1	3.2	3.4	3.2
U.S.	4.8	4.7	4.4	4.1	4.0	4.5	4.5	4.2	4.1	3.8	3.8	3.7

Note: Data is not seasonally adjusted and covers workers 16 years of age and older; all figures are percentages; (1) Metropolitan Statistical Area - see Appendix A for areas included
Source: Bureau of Labor Statistics, http://stats.bls.gov

Employment by Industry

Sector	MSA[1]		U.S.
	Number of Employees	Percent of Total	Percent of Total
Services	55,800	25.5	30.2
Retail Trade	42,900	19.6	18.1
Government	36,400	16.6	15.8
Manufacturing	48,700	22.3	14.1
Finance/Insurance/Real Estate	10,700	4.9	5.9
Wholesale Trade	7,500	3.4	5.4
Transportation/Public Utilities	7,700	3.5	5.3
Construction	n/a	n/a	4.8
Mining	n/a	n/a	0.4

Note: Figures cover non-farm employment as of 12/99 and are not seasonally adjusted; (1) Metropolitan Statistical Area - see Appendix A for areas included; n/a not available
Source: Bureau of Labor Statistics, http://stats.bls.gov

Employment by Occupation

Occupation Category	City (%)	MSA[1] (%)	U.S. (%)
White Collar	59.4	60.4	58.1
Executive/Admin./Management	11.3	12.2	12.3
Professional	17.5	16.6	14.1
Technical & Related Support	4.2	4.2	3.7
Sales	12.0	12.1	11.8
Administrative Support/Clerical	14.4	15.3	16.3
Blue Collar	19.8	23.3	26.2
Precision Production/Craft/Repair	6.8	9.1	11.3
Machine Operators/Assem./Insp.	6.5	7.7	6.8
Transportation/Material Movers	2.6	3.0	4.1
Cleaners/Helpers/Laborers	3.9	3.5	3.9
Services	19.5	14.6	13.2
Farming/Forestry/Fishing	1.3	1.7	2.5

Note: Figures cover workers 16 years of age and older; (1) Metropolitan Statistical Area - see Appendix A for areas included
Source: 1990 Census of Population and Housing, Summary Tape File 3C

Occupational Employment Projections: 1994 - 2005

Occupations Expected to Have the Largest Job Growth (ranked by numerical growth)	Fast-Growing Occupations[1] (ranked by percent growth)
1. Waiters & waitresses	1. Computer engineers
2. Cashiers	2. Home health aides
3. All other helper, laborer, mover	3. Systems analysts
4. Systems analysts	4. Personal and home care aides
5. Home health aides	5. Electronic pagination systems workers
6. General managers & top executives	6. All other computer scientists
7. All other profess., paraprofess., tech.	7. Physical therapists
8. Registered nurses	8. All other therapists
9. All other sales reps. & services	9. Electronics repairers, comm. & indust.
10. Salespersons, retail	10. Occupational therapists

Note: Projections cover Michigan; (1) Excludes occupations with total job growth less than 300
Source: Office of Labor Market Information, Occupational Employment Forecasts, 1994-2005

Average Wages

Occupation	$/Hr.	Occupation	$/Hr.
Accountants and Auditors	17.52	Maids and Housekeepers	7.57
Assemblers and Fabricators	10.74	Maintenance Repairers	12.55
Automotive Mechanics	12.90	Marketing/Advertising/PR Managers	23.76
Bookkeepers	11.05	Nurses, Licensed Practical	13.81
Carpenters	13.81	Nurses, Registered	20.21
Cashiers	7.33	Nursing Aides/Orderlies/Attendants	8.92
Clerks, General Office	9.52	Physicians and Surgeons	56.54
Clerks, Shipping/Receiving/Traffic	12.29	Receptionists/Information Clerks	8.65
Computer Programmers	22.75	Sales Reps., Exc. Scientific/Retail	18.99
Computer Support Specialists	17.37	Sales Reps., Scientific, Exc. Retail	32.23
Cooks, Restaurant	7.47	Salespersons, Retail	8.28
Electricians	18.35	Secretaries, Except Legal/Medical	11.18
Financial Managers	27.72	Stock Clerks, Sales Floor	7.53
First-Line Supervisors/Mgrs., Sales	15.23	Systems Analysts	24.69
Food Preparation Workers	7.27	Teacher Aides	8.12
General Managers/Top Executives	29.31	Teachers, Elementary School	19.91
Guards	9.02	Teachers, Secondary School	19.35
Hand Packers	6.61	Telemarketers	9.56
Janitors and Cleaners	9.36	Truck Drivers, Heavy/Tractor-Trailer	13.51
Laborers, Landscaping	10.70	Truck Drivers, Light	9.97
Lawyers	31.22	Waiters and Waitresses	5.78

Note: Wage data is for 1998 and covers the Metropolitan Statistical Area (see Appendix A for areas included). Hourly wages for elementary and secondary school teachers were calculated by the editors from annual wage data assuming a 40 hour work week; Dashes indicate that data was not available.
Source: Bureau of Labor Statistics, 1998 Metropolitan Area Occupational Employment and Wage Estimates

TAXES

Major State and Local Tax Rates

State Corporate Income (%)	State Personal Income (%)	Residential Property (%)	Sales & Use		State Gasoline (cents/ gallon)	State Cigarette (cents/ pack)
			State (%)	Local (%)		
2.2[a]	4.3[b]	2.57	6.0	None	19.0[c]	75.0

Note: Personal/corporate income, sales, gasoline and cigarette tax rates as of January 2000.
Property tax rates as of April 2000; (b) Tax rate scheduled to decrease to 4.2% for tax year 2001; (a) Value added tax imposed on the sum of federal taxable income of the business, compensation paid to employees, dividends, interest, royalties paid and other items; (c) Sales tax applicable
Source: Federation of Tax Administrators, www.taxadmin.org; ERI's Relocation Assessor software database, quarterly effective date 4/1/2000

Total Taxes Per Capita and as a Percent of Income

Area	Per Capita Income ($)	Per Capita Taxes ($)			Percent of Income (%)		
		Total	Federal	State/Local	Total	Federal	State/Local
Michigan	28,685	10,510	7,235	3,274	36.6	25.2	11.4
U.S.	28,878	10,298	7,026	3,273	35.7	24.3	11.3

Note: Figures are for 1999
Source: Tax Foundation, www.taxfoundation.org

COMMERCIAL UTILITIES

Typical Monthly Electric Bills

Area	Commercial Service ($/month)		Industrial Service ($/month)	
	12 kW demand 1,500 kWh	100 kW demand 30,000 kWh	1,000 kW demand 400,000 kWh	20,000 kW demand 10,000,000 kWh
City	153	2,081	23,525	396,252
U.S.	150	2,174	23,995	508,569

Note: Based on rates in effect January 1, 1999
Source: Edison Electric Institute, Typical Residential, Commercial and Industrial Bills, Winter 1999

TRANSPORTATION

Transportation Statistics

Average minutes to work (1990)	15.0
Interstate highways	I-94; US-131
Bus lines	
In-city (1998)	Kalamazoo Metro Transit System, 29 buses
Inter-city (1999)	2
Passenger air service	
Airport	Kalamazoo/Battle Creek International
Airlines (1999)	6
Enplaned passengers (1998)	280,301
Amtrak service	Yes
Motor freight carriers (1999)	22
Major waterways/ports	None

Source: FAA DOT/TSC CY1998 ACAIS Database; National Transit Database, 1998; Editor & Publisher Market Guide, 2000; Amtrak National Time Table, Fall 1999/Winter 2000; 1990 Census of Population and Housing, STF 3C; Jane's Urban Transport Systems 1999-2000

Means of Transportation to Work

Area	Car/Truck/Van		Public Transportation			Bicycle	Walked	Other Means	Worked at Home
	Drove Alone	Car-pooled	Bus	Subway	Railroad				
City	72.1	11.2	2.4	0.0	0.0	0.8	9.9	1.0	2.5
MSA[1]	81.5	9.5	1.0	0.0	0.0	0.4	4.4	0.6	2.5
U.S.	73.2	13.4	3.0	1.5	0.5	0.4	3.9	1.2	3.0

Note: Figures shown are percentages and only include workers 16 years of age and older;
(1) Metropolitan Statistical Area - see Appendix A for areas included
Source: 1990 Census of Population and Housing, Summary Tape File 3C

BUSINESSES

Major Business Headquarters

Company Name	1999 Rankings	
	Fortune 500	Forbes 500
No companies listed	-	-

Note: Companies listed are located in the city; dashes indicate no ranking
Fortune 500: Companies that produce a 10-K are ranked 1 to 500 based on 1999 revenue
Forbes 500: Private companies are ranked 1 to 500 based on 1998 revenue
Source: Forbes, December 13, 1999; Fortune, April 17, 2000

HOTELS & MOTELS

Hotels/Motels

Area	Hotels/ Motels	Rooms	Luxury-Level Hotels/Motels		Average Minimum Rates ($)		
			◆◆◆◆	◆◆◆◆◆	◆◆	◆◆◆	◆◆◆◆
City	10	1,187	0	0	n/a	n/a	n/a
Airport	8	774	0	0	n/a	n/a	n/a
Total	18	1,961	0	0	n/a	n/a	n/a

Note: n/a not available; classifications range from one diamond (budget properties with basic amenities) to five diamond (luxury properties).
Source: OAG Business Travel Planner, Winter 1999-2000

Estimated Daily Food and Lodging Costs

Area	Food/Other ($/day)	Average Hotel Cost ($/day)
City	30	55
U.S.	30	55

Source: ERI's Relocation Assessor software database, quarterly effective date 4/1/2000

CONVENTION CENTERS

Convention Centers and Event Sites

Name	Guest Rooms	Meeting Space (sq. ft.)	Capacity (Theatre Style)
Fetzer Center	n/a	n/a	0
Howard Chenery Auditorium	n/a	n/a	2,500
James W. Miller Auditorium	n/a	n/a	3,497
Radisson Plaza Hotel at Kalamazoo Center	281	35,000	1,080
Wings Stadium	n/a	n/a	8,113

Note: n/a not available
Source: EventSource.com, 3/15/2000

Living Environment

COST OF LIVING

Cost of Living: Homeowner

Cost Element	U.S. ($)	City ($)	Differential ($)	Percent of U.S. Average
Consumables	14,516	15,050	534	103.7
Transportation	5,957	5,854	-103	98.3
Health Services	2,012	1,960	-52	97.4
Housing/Utilities/Prop. Tax	16,337	20,514	4,177	125.6
Income+Payroll Taxes	12,615	12,434	-181	98.6
Miscellaneous	8,563	8,563	0	100.0
Total Cost of Living	60,000	64,375	4,375	107.3

Note: Figures are based on a single income, four person family with gross annual earnings of $60,000, owning an 1,800 square-foot home, and driving two automobiles worth $22,000 30,000 miles per year.
Source: ERI's Relocation Assessor software database, quarterly effective date 4/1/2000

Cost of Living: Renter

Cost Element	U.S. ($)	City ($)	Differential ($)	Percent of U.S. Average
Consumables	10,486	10,845	359	103.4
Transportation	2,107	2,066	-41	98.1
Health Services	1,632	1,587	-45	97.2
Rent/Utilities/Insurance	9,299	10,443	1,144	112.3
Income+Payroll Taxes	8,607	9,047	440	105.1
Miscellaneous	7,869	7,869	0	100.0
Total Cost of Living	40,000	41,857	1,857	104.6

Note: Figures are based on a single income, three person family with gross annual earnings of $40,000, renting a 1,000 square-foot home, and driving one automobile worth $8,000 12,000 miles per year.
Source: ERI's Relocation Assessor software database, quarterly effective date 4/1/2000

HOUSING

Median Home Prices and Housing Affordability

Area	Median Price[2] 4th Qtr. 1999 ($)	HOI[3] 4th Qtr. 1999	Affordability Rank[4]
MSA[1]	107,000	63.8	125
U.S.	139,000	63.8	–

Note: (1) Metropolitan Statistical Area - see Appendix A for areas included; (2) U.S. figures calculated from the sales of 687,516 new and existing homes in 192 markets; (3) Housing Opportunity Index - percent of homes sold that were within the reach of the median income household at the prevailing mortgage interest rate; (4) Rank is from 1-192 with 1 being most affordable
Source: National Association of Home Builders, Housing Opportunity Index, 4th Quarter 1999

Estimated Home Price

Area	Price ($)
City	154,113
U.S.	135,855

Note: Figures are based on an 1,800 square-foot home
Source: ERI's Relocation Assessor software database, quarterly effective date 4/1/2000

Estimated Rent

Area	Rent ($/month)
City	758
U.S.	651

Note: Figures are based on a 1,000 square-foot home
Source: ERI's Relocation Assessor software database, quarterly effective date 4/1/2000

Median Home Price Projection

It is projected that the median home price in the metropolitan area will increase from $110,931 in 1999 to $141,095 in 2010, an increase of 27.2%
Kiplinger's Personal Finance Magazine, January 2000

RESIDENTIAL UTILITIES

Average Residential Utility Costs

Area	All Electric ($/mth)	Part Electric ($/mth)	Other Energy ($/mth)	Phone ($/mth)
City	n/a	n/a	n/a	n/a
U.S.	99.25	55.47	43.48	20.29

Note: n/a not available
Source: ACCRA, Cost of Living Index, 3rd Quarter 1999

HEALTH CARE

Average Health Care Costs

Area	Hospital ($/day)	Doctor ($/visit)	Dentist ($/visit)
City	n/a	n/a	n/a
U.S.	440.96	53.83	68.42

Note: n/a not available
Source: ACCRA, Cost of Living Index, 3rd Quarter 1999

Distribution of Office-Based Physicians

Area	Family/Gen. Practitioners	Specialists		
		Medical	Surgical	Other
MSA[1]	104	225	185	185

Note: Data as of 12/31/97; (1) Metropolitan Statistical Area - see Appendix A for areas included
Source: American Medical Assn., Physician Characteristics & Distribution in the U.S., 1999

Hospitals

Kalamazoo has 2 general medical and surgical hospitals, 1 psychiatric.
AHA Guide to the Healthcare Field, 1999-2000

EDUCATION

Public School District Statistics

District Name	Num. Sch.	Enroll.	Classroom Teachers	Pupils per Teacher	Minority Pupils (%)	Current Exp.[1] ($/pupil)
Comstock Public Schools	7	3,051	174	17.5	n/a	n/a
Kalamazoo Public School Distri	30	12,001	728	16.5	n/a	n/a

Note: Data covers the 1997-1998 school year unless otherwise noted; (1) Data covers fiscal year 1996; SD = School District; ISD = Independent School District; n/a not available
Source: National Center for Education Statistics, Common Core of Data Public Education Agency Universe 1997-98; National Center for Education Statistics, Characteristics of the 100 Largest Public Elementary and Secondary School Districts in the United States: 1997-98, July 1999

Educational Quality

School District	Education Quotient[1]	Graduate Outcome[2]	Community Index[3]	Resource Index[4]
Kalamazoo Public School Dist.	122	129	128	106

Note: Over 1,000 secondary school districts were rated in terms of educational quality. The scores range from a low of 50 to a high of 150; (1) Combination of the Graduate Outcome, Community and Resource indexes weighted to reflect the greater importance of the Graduate Outcome and Resource Index; (2) Based on graduation rates and college board scores (SAT/ACT); (3) Based on the surrounding community's level of affluence and adult education; (4) Based on teacher salaries, per-pupil expenditures and student-teacher ratios.
Source: Expansion Management, Ratings Issue, 1999

Educational Attainment by Race

Area	High School Graduate (%)					Bachelor's Degree (%)				
	Total	White	Black	Other	Hisp.[2]	Total	White	Black	Other	Hisp.[2]
City	79.6	82.5	66.6	72.3	55.2	29.8	33.4	9.1	41.9	13.6
MSA[1]	83.4	84.5	71.7	78.4	63.9	27.1	27.7	14.2	43.7	17.4
U.S.	75.2	77.9	63.1	60.4	49.8	20.3	21.5	11.4	19.4	9.2

Note: Figures shown cover persons 25 years old and over; (1) Metropolitan Statistical Area - see Appendix A for areas included; (2) people of Hispanic origin can be of any race
Source: 1990 Census of Population and Housing, Summary Tape File 3C

School Enrollment by Type

Area	Preprimary				Elementary/High School			
	Public		Private		Public		Private	
	Enrollment	%	Enrollment	%	Enrollment	%	Enrollment	%
City	1,035	66.6	518	33.4	9,726	89.7	1,113	10.3
MSA[1]	3,009	65.7	1,568	34.3	31,871	90.6	3,314	9.4
U.S.	2,679,029	59.5	1,824,256	40.5	38,379,689	90.2	4,187,099	9.8

Note: Figures shown cover persons 3 years old and over;
(1) Metropolitan Statistical Area - see Appendix A for areas included
Source: 1990 Census of Population and Housing, Summary Tape File 3C

School Enrollment by Race

Area	Preprimary (%)				Elementary/High School (%)			
	White	Black	Other	Hisp.[1]	White	Black	Other	Hisp.[1]
City	73.5	22.7	3.8	2.1	58.6	35.0	6.5	4.2
MSA[2]	87.5	9.7	2.8	1.5	82.8	13.8	3.5	2.5
U.S.	80.4	12.5	7.1	7.8	74.1	15.6	10.3	12.5

Note: Figures shown cover persons 3 years old and over; (1) people of Hispanic origin can be of any race; (2) Metropolitan Statistical Area - see Appendix A for areas included
Source: 1990 Census of Population and Housing, Summary Tape File 3C

Higher Education

Two-Year Colleges		Four-Year Colleges		Medical Schools	Law Schools	Voc/Tech
Public	Private	Public	Private			
1	1	1	1	0	0	6

Source: College Blue Book, Occupational Education, 1999; Medical School Admission Requirements, 1999-2000; Peterson's Guide to Two-Year Colleges, 2000; Peterson's Guide to Four-Year Colleges, 1999; Barron's Guide to Law Schools, 1999

MAJOR EMPLOYERS

Major Employers

Borgess Medical Center
Flowserve Red Corp. (rubber products)
Humphrey Products
Summit Polymers
Wells Aluminum

Bronson Methodist Hospital
Gilmore Bros. (department stores)
Stryker Corp. (medical instruments)
Upjohn International

Note: Companies listed are located in the city
Source: D&B Business Rankings, 1999; Ward's Business Directory, 1999; America's Corporate Families, 1999

PUBLIC SAFETY

Crime Rate

Area	All Crimes	Violent Crimes				Property Crimes		
		Murder	Forcible Rape	Robbery	Aggrav. Assault	Burglary	Larceny -Theft	Motor Vehicle Theft
City	7,014.4	2.6	87.3	285.1	679.5	1,392.3	4,103.8	463.7
Suburbs[1]	n/a	n/a	n/a	n/a	n/a	n/a	n/a	n/a
MSA[2]	n/a	n/a	n/a	n/a	n/a	n/a	n/a	n/a
U.S.	4,615.5	6.3	34.4	165.2	360.5	862.0	2,728.1	459.0

Note: Crime rate is the number of crimes per 100,000 population; (1) Defined as all areas within the Metropolitan Statistical Area but located outside the central city; (2) Metropolitan Statistical Area - see Appendix A for areas included; n/a not available
Source: FBI Uniform Crime Reports, 1998

RECREATION

Culture and Recreation

Museums	Symphony Orchestras	Opera Companies	Dance Companies	Professional Theatres	Zoos	Pro Sports Teams
3	1	0	1	1	2	0

Source: Musical America, International Directory of the Performing Arts, 1999; Official Museum Directory, 2000; Stern's Performing Arts Directory, 1997; USA Today Four Sport Stadium Guide, 1997; Career Opportunities in Theatre and the Performing Arts, 1999

Library System

The Kalamazoo Public Library has four branches, holdings of 435,660 volumes, and a budget of $9,033,581 (1997-1998).
American Library Directory, 1999-2000

MEDIA

Newspapers

Name	Type	Freq.	Distribution	Circulation
The Hometown Gazette	n/a	1x/wk	Local	99,000
Kalamazoo Gazette	General	7x/wk	Area	65,000

Note: Includes newspapers with circulations of 200 or more located in the city; n/a not available
Source: Burrelle's Media Directory, 1999 Edition

Television Stations

Name	Ch.	Affiliation	Type	Owner
WWMT	n/a	CBST	Commercial	Freedom Broadcasting
WLLA	64	WB	Commercial	Christian Faith Broadcasting Inc.

Note: Stations included broadcast in the Kalamazoo metro area; n/a not available
Source: Burrelle's Media Directory, 1999 Edition

AM Radio Stations

Call Letters	Freq. (kHz)	Target Audience	Station Format	Music Format
WKZO	590	General	N/T	n/a
WKMI	1360	General	N/S/T	n/a
WKPR	1420	Religious	E/M/N/S	Christian
WNWN	1560	Black	M/N/S	Rhythm & Blues
WQSN	1660	General	S	n/a

Note: Stations included broadcast in the Kalamazoo metro area; n/a not available
Target Audience: A=Asian; B=Black; C=Christian; E=Ethnic; F=French; G=General; H=Hispanic; M=Men; N=Native American; R=Religious; S=Senior Citizen; W=Women; Y=Young Adult; Z=Children
Station Format: E=Educational; M=Music; N=News; S=Sports; T=Talk
Source: Burrelle's Media Directory, 1999 Edition

FM Radio Stations

Call Letters	Freq. (mHz)	Target Audience	Station Format	Music Format
WAYK	88.3	General	M	Christian
WIDR	89.1	General	M/N/S	Alternative/Big Band/Blues/Christian/Classical/ Country/Gospel/Jazz/Latin/Modern Rock/ Reggae/Rhythm & Blues/Urban Contemporary
WFAT	96.5	General	M/N/S	Adult Contemporary
WNWN	98.5	General	M/N/S	Country
WMUK	102.1	G/H	E/M/N/S	Classical/Jazz
WKFR	103.3	General	M/N	n/a
WQLR	106.5	General	M/N	Adult Contemporary
WRKR	107.7	General	M/N/S	AOR/Classic Rock

Note: Stations included broadcast in the Kalamazoo metro area; n/a not available
Station Format: E=Educational; M=Music; N=News; S=Sports; T=Talk
Target Audience: A=Asian; B=Black; C=Christian; E=Ethnic; F=French; G=General; H=Hispanic; M=Men; N=Native American; R=Religious; S=Senior Citizen; W=Women; Y=Young Adult; Z=Children
Music Format: AOR=Album Oriented Rock; MOR=Middle-of-the-Road
Source: Burrelle's Media Directory, 1999 Edition

WEATHER

Temperature/Precipitation/Humidity

	Jan	Feb	Mar	Apr	May	Jun	Jul	Aug	Sep	Oct	Nov	Dec	Yr.
Max. High Temp. (°F)	67	68	83	89	93	100	109	102	100	90	81	69	109
Avg. High Temp. (°F)	32	33	43	58	69	80	84	82	75	62	46	34	58
Avg. Temp. (°F)	24	25	34	46	58	68	72	70	64	52	38	28	48
Avg. Low Temp. (°F)	17	17	25	35	48	57	61	59	53	42	31	22	39
Min. Low Temp. (°F)	-20	-25	-14	6	24	34	42	39	29	17	-7	-19	-25
Avg. Precip. (in.)	2.2	2.1	2.5	2.9	3.9	3.8	3.1	2.8	3.2	2.9	2.8	2.5	34.7
Avg. Snowfall (in.)	9.6	8.9	6.6	1.3	0.2	0	0	0	0	0.2	4.1	8.9	39.8
Avg. Rel. Hum. (%)	78	75	72	68	67	70	67	70	71	72	77	77	72

Source: National Climatic Data Center, International Station Meteorological Climate Summary, 3/95

Weather Conditions

Temperature			Precipitation		
0°F & below	32°F & below	90°F & above	0.1 inch or more precip.	1.5 inch or more snow/ice	Thunder-storms
4	138	24	66	8	36

Note: Figures are average number of days per year
Source: National Climatic Data Center, International Station Meteorological Climate Summary, 3/95

AIR & WATER QUALITY

Maximum Pollutant Concentrations

	Particulate Matter (ug/m³)	Carbon Monoxide (ppm)	Sulfur Dioxide (ppm)	Nitrogen Dioxide (ppm)	Ozone (ppm)	Lead (ug/m³)
MSA[1] Level	48	n/a	n/a	n/a	0.10	n/a
NAAQS[2]	150	9	0.140	0.053	0.12	1.50
Met NAAQS	Yes	n/a	n/a	n/a	Yes	n/a

Note: (1) Metropolitan Statistical Area - see Appendix A for areas included; (2) National Ambient Air Quality Standards; ppm = parts per million; ug/m³ = micrograms per cubic meter; n/a not available
Source: EPA, National Air Quality and Emissions Trends Report, 1997

Pollutant Standards Index

Data not available.
EPA, National Air Quality and Emissions Trends Report, 1997

Drinking Water

Water System Name	Pop. Served	Primary Water Source Type	Number of Violations in 1998-99	Type of Violation/ Contaminants
Kalamazoo	150,000	Ground	None	None

Note: Data as of January 19, 2000
Source: EPA, Office of Ground Water and Drinking Water, Safe Drinking Water Information System

Kalamazoo tap water is alkaline, very hard, and fluoridated.
Editor & Publisher Market Guide, 2000

La Crosse, Wisconsin

Background

La Crosse, Wisconsin lies along the Mississippi River at the influx of the Black and La Crosse Rivers in western Wisconsin, 129 miles northwest of Madison. The city's strategic location near the center of the tri-state area (Wisconsin, Minnesota, Iowa) is ideal for business and industry. La Crosse's metro area includes Onalaska and La Crescent.

In the late 1700s, French explorers and fur traders named the site Prairie La Crosse after the game of lacrosse played by the Iroquois who lived in the area. Incorporated in 1856, the city became a transportation and sawmilling center, expanding with the arrival of the railroad in 1858. As lumber resources were depleted in the early 1900s, La Crosse's industries diversified to include rubber footwear, air-conditioning systems, sausage and beer.

Institutions of higher learning include Western Wisconsin Technical College, the University of Wisconsin-La Crosse and Viterbo College. The city is also home to the Wisconsin Regional Art Program, La Crosse Community Theatre and an annual Oktoberfest.

La Crosse affords many outdoor recreational opportunities, including bird-watching, with a large, year-round population of eagles, and La Crosse River Trail Prairie State Natural Area, which preserves an expanse of native plants and flowers. The Upper Mississippi Valley, in general, offers woods and rocky bluffs overlooking the river and its backwaters, and provides fishing, hunting, boating and skiing.

General Rankings and Evaluative Comments

■ La Crosse was ranked #136 out of 354 metropolitan areas in *Places Rated Almanac*. Criteria: cost of living, climate, crime, transportation, job outlook, education, the arts, health care, and recreation. *Places Rated Almanac, Millennium Edition, 2000*

■ La Crosse was selected as one of North America's "Best Small Metro Areas" (population under 250,000). The area ranked #12 out of 20. Criteria: cost of living, climate, crime, transportation, job outlook, education, the arts, health care, and recreation. *Places Rated Almanac, Millennium Edition, 2000*

Business Environment

STATE ECONOMY

State Economic Profile

"Wisconsin's expansion has begun to slow. For the first time in some years, 1998 saw Wisconsin grow at a rate below the national. Wisconsin's manufacturing sector remains stagnant and its farm sector struggling. Wisconsin's tight labor market will help to absorb some of these declines. An unsustainable increase in construction has driven job growth. Wisconsin's economy should trail the nation for some years before rebounding in 2001.

Wisconsin's construction industry remains a lone bright spot. Several commercial projects are under way in Milwaukee, such as the new convention center and baseball park. In addition, industrial and office construction is picking up in the suburbs. Public construction is also set to rise as the new federal transportation regulation raised Wisconsin's federal transportation funding by 48% to $520 million.

Wisconsin's residential market remains healthy with residential permits growing at a torrid pace in 1998. Existing home sales along with house prices are rising. Despite recent price appreciation, affordability still exceeds the national average. In the long run, however, the fast pace of construction will slow as residential construction is outpacing household formation in the state.

Wisconsin exports a large share of its manufacturing and agricultural output. Weak export demand is resulting in cutbacks to its papermaking, pulp, and equipment manufacturing industries. Farm income also dropped by over 90% in 1998 as commodity prices tumbled and export demand shrank. Commodity prices will remain weak, leaving little promise of a resurgence in Wisconsin's farm sector (outside of dairy, which is performing well). Slowing population growth, especially among younger households, will slow long-run growth. Wisconsin's high exposure to manufacturing and agriculture will continue to create downside risks for the state. Wisconsin will moderately underperform the nation in the near term."
National Association of Realtors, Economic Profiles: The Fifty States and the District of Columbia, http://nar.realtor.com/databank/profiles.htm

EXPORTS

Total Export Sales

Area	1995 ($000)	1996 ($000)	1997 ($000)	1998 ($000)	% Chg. 1995-98	% Chg. 1997-98
MSA[1]	276,217	273,185	297,792	229,955	-16.7	-22.8
U.S.	583,030,524	622,827,063	687,597,999	680,474,251	16.7	-1.0

Note: (1) Metropolitan Statistical Area - see Appendix A for areas included
Source: U.S. Department of Commerce, International Trade Association, Metropolitan Area Exports: An Export Performance Report on Over 250 U.S. Cities, November 10, 1999

CITY FINANCES

City Government Finances

Component	1995 ($million)	1995 (per capita $)
Revenue	49.1	964
Expenditure	53.9	1,059
Debt Outstanding	70.5	1,386

Source: 1999 County and City Extra, Annual Metro, City, and County Data Book

City Government Revenue by Source

Source	1995 ($million)	1995 (per capita $)
Intergovernmental	17.5	343
Taxes	14.2	280
Property	12.7	250
Sales and Gross Receipts	0.7	14

Source: 1999 County and City Extra, Annual Metro, City, and County Data Book

City Government Expenditures by Function

Function	1995 ($million)	1995 (per capita $)	1995 (%)
Public Welfare	<0.1	1	0.1
Highways	6.6	130	12.3
Parking Facilities	0.5	11	1.1
Education	0.0	0	0.0
Health and Hospitals	0.1	2	0.2
Police Protection	6.9	136	12.9
Sewerage and Sanitation	7.0	137	13.0
Parks and Recreation	6.3	123	11.7
Housing and Community Development	1.1	22	2.1
Interest on Debt	5.9	117	11.1

Source: 1999 County and City Extra, Annual Metro, City, and County Data Book

Municipal Bond Ratings

Area	Moody's
City	Aa3

Source: Mergent Bond Record, 2/2000

POPULATION

Population Growth

Area	1980 Census	1990 Census	1999 Estimate	2004 Projection	Population Growth (%) 1990-1999	Population Growth (%) 1999-2004
City	48,347	51,003	48,121	47,094	-5.7	-2.1
MSA[1]	91,056	97,904	122,061	124,600	24.7	2.1
U.S.	226,545,805	248,765,170	272,212,864	283,625,312	9.4	4.2

Note: (1) Metropolitan Statistical Area - see Appendix A for areas included
Source: 1990 Census of Population and Housing, Summary Tape File 3C; Claritas, Inc.

Number of Households and Average Household Size

Area	1980 Census	1990 Census	1999 Estimate	2004 Projection	1999 Average Household Size
City	18,447	20,003	19,421	19,294	2.48
MSA[1]	38,353	36,847	46,882	48,500	2.60
U.S.	80,389,592	91,993,582	102,048,200	107,302,392	2.67

Note: (1) Metropolitan Statistical Area - see Appendix A for areas included
Source: 1990 Census of Population and Housing, Summary Tape File 3C; Claritas, Inc.

Race/Ethnicity of City Population

Race/Ethnicity	1990 Census Population	1990 Census %	1999 Estimate Population	1999 Estimate %	% Change 1990-1999
White, Non-Hispanic	47,546	93.2	43,227	89.8	-9.1
Black, Non-Hispanic	293	0.6	425	0.9	45.1
Asian, Non-Hispanic	2,387	4.7	3,509	7.3	47.0
Other, Non-Hispanic	321	0.6	281	0.6	-12.5
Hispanic	456	0.9	679	1.4	48.9

Source: 1990 Census of Population and Housing, Summary Tape File 3C; Claritas, Inc.

Race/Ethnicity of Metropolitan Statistical Area Population

Race/Ethnicity	1990 Census		1999 Estimate		% Change 1990-1999
	Population	%	Population	%	
White, Non-Hispanic	93,663	95.7	116,027	95.1	23.9
Black, Non-Hispanic	411	0.4	540	0.4	31.4
Asian, Non-Hispanic	2,662	2.7	3,868	3.2	45.3
Other, Non-Hispanic	467	0.5	550	0.5	17.8
Hispanic	701	0.7	1,076	0.9	53.5

Note: See Appendix A for areas included in the Metropolitan Statistical Area
Source: 1990 Census of Population and Housing, Summary Tape File 3C; Claritas, Inc.

Ancestry

Area	German	Irish	English	Italian	U.S.	French	Polish	Dutch
City	54.4	16.1	8.0	2.2	1.0	4.0	6.1	1.7
MSA[1]	56.4	14.7	8.3	2.0	1.2	4.0	5.8	1.7
U.S.	23.3	15.6	13.1	5.9	5.3	4.2	3.8	2.5

Note: Figures are percentages and include persons that reported multiple ancestry (eg. if a person reported being Irish and Italian, they were included in both columns); (1) Metropolitan Statistical Area - see Appendix A for areas included
Source: 1990 Census of Population and Housing, Summary Tape File 3C

Median Age

Area	1990 Census	1999 Estimate
City	29.3	32.3
MSA[1]	31.1	34.5
U.S.	32.9	35.7

Note: (1) Metropolitan Statistical Area - see Appendix A for areas included
Source: 1990 Census of Population and Housing, Summary Tape File 3C; Claritas, Inc.

Male/Female Population

Area	Number of Males		Number of Females		Males per 100 Females	
	1990	1999	1990	1999	1990	1999
City	23,586	22,377	27,417	25,744	86.0	86.9
MSA[1]	46,986	58,957	50,918	63,104	92.3	93.4
U.S.	121,172,379	132,803,736	127,537,494	139,409,136	95.0	95.3

Note: (1) Metropolitan Statistical Area - see Appendix A for areas included
Source: 1990 Census of Population, General Population Characteristics; Claritas, Inc.

INCOME

Per Capita/Median/Average Income

Area	Per Capita ($)			Median Household ($)			Average Household ($)		
	1989	1999	% Chg.	1989	1999	% Chg.	1989	1999	% Chg.
City	10,898	16,846	54.6	21,947	30,321	38.2	27,063	40,148	48.3
MSA[1]	12,141	18,988	56.4	26,857	37,722	40.5	31,826	48,512	52.4
U.S.	14,420	21,350	48.1	30,056	40,525	34.8	38,453	56,184	46.1

Note: (1) Metropolitan Statistical Area - see Appendix A for areas included; 1989 data is from the 1990 Census; 1999 data is estimated by Claritas, Inc.
Source: 1990 Census of Population, General Population Characteristics; Claritas, Inc.

Household Income Distribution

Area	Percent of Households Earning								
	Under $5,000	$5,000 -14,999	$15,000 -24,999	$25,000 -34,999	$35,000 -49,999	$50,000 -74,999	$75,000 -99,000	$100,000 -149,999	$150,000 and up
City	2.4	19.9	19.2	14.9	17.5	16.4	5.4	2.7	1.5
MSA[1]	2.1	14.3	16.1	13.7	18.0	20.9	8.2	4.3	2.2
U.S.	3.9	13.3	13.8	12.6	16.2	19.4	9.7	6.6	4.6

Note: Data as of 1999; (1) Metropolitan Statistical Area - see Appendix A for areas included
Source: Claritas, Inc.

Effective Buying Income

Area	Per Capita ($)	Median Household ($)	Average Household ($)
City	13,572	26,758	33,931
MSA[1]	15,080	32,606	39,502
U.S.	17,496	36,603	47,036

Note: Data as of 1/1/2000; (1) Metropolitan Statistical Area - see Appendix A for areas included
Source: Standard Rate & Data Service, Newspaper Advertising Source, March 2000

Effective Household Buying Income Distribution

Area	% of Households Earning						
	$10,000 -$19,999	$20,000 -$34,999	$35,000 -$49,999	$50,000 -$74,999	$75,000 -$99,000	$100,000 -$124,999	$125,000 and up
City	23.7	26.4	17.6	13.5	3.3	1.2	0.8
MSA[1]	18.6	24.8	19.7	18.5	5.3	1.4	1.5
U.S.	15.0	21.6	17.6	19.6	8.4	3.0	3.3

Note: Data as of 1/1/2000; (1) Metropolitan Statistical Area - see Appendix A for areas included
Source: Standard Rate & Data Service, Newspaper Advertising Source, March 2000

Poverty Rates by Age

Area	People of All Ages	People Under 18 Years Old	Related Children Age 5-17 in Families in Poverty
City	15.5	n/a	n/a
County	9.7	13.7	12.7
U.S.	13.8	20.8	18.7

Note: Figures show the percent of people living below the poverty line in 1995. The
average poverty threshold was $15,569 for a family of four in 1995; n/a not available
Source: Bureau of the Census, Small Area Income and Poverty Estimates Program;
U.S. Department of Housing and Urban Development

EMPLOYMENT

Labor Force and Employment

Area	Civilian Labor Force			Workers Employed		
	Dec. 1998	Dec. 1999	% Chg.	Dec. 1998	Dec. 1999	% Chg.
City	28,954	29,172	0.8	28,018	28,190	0.6
MSA[1]	72,836	73,534	1.0	70,918	71,482	0.8
U.S.	138,297,000	139,941,000	1.2	132,732,000	134,696,000	1.5

Note: Data is not seasonally adjusted and covers workers 16 years of age and older;
(1) Metropolitan Statistical Area - see Appendix A for areas included
Source: Bureau of Labor Statistics, http://stats.bls.gov

Unemployment Rate

Area	1999											
	Jan.	Feb.	Mar.	Apr.	May	Jun.	Jul.	Aug.	Sep.	Oct.	Nov.	Dec.
City	4.3	4.6	3.8	3.5	3.7	4.0	3.3	3.9	3.0	3.3	3.3	3.4
MSA[1]	3.8	3.9	3.2	2.6	2.6	3.0	2.6	3.0	2.4	2.5	2.6	2.8
U.S.	4.8	4.7	4.4	4.1	4.0	4.5	4.5	4.2	4.1	3.8	3.8	3.7

Note: Data is not seasonally adjusted and covers workers 16 years of age and older; all figures are
percentages; (1) Metropolitan Statistical Area - see Appendix A for areas included
Source: Bureau of Labor Statistics, http://stats.bls.gov

Employment by Industry

Sector	MSA[1]		U.S.
	Number of Employees	Percent of Total	Percent of Total
Services	22,100	30.7	30.2
Retail Trade	14,500	20.2	18.1
Government	11,000	15.3	15.8
Manufacturing	11,200	15.6	14.1
Finance/Insurance/Real Estate	2,700	3.8	5.9
Wholesale Trade	4,000	5.6	5.4
Transportation/Public Utilities	3,500	4.9	5.3
Construction	n/a	n/a	4.8
Mining	n/a	n/a	0.4

Note: Figures cover non-farm employment as of 12/99 and are not seasonally adjusted;
(1) Metropolitan Statistical Area - see Appendix A for areas included; n/a not available
Source: Bureau of Labor Statistics, http://stats.bls.gov

Employment by Occupation

Occupation Category	City (%)	MSA[1] (%)	U.S. (%)
White Collar	54.9	54.3	58.1
Executive/Admin./Management	8.4	9.3	12.3
Professional	16.4	15.4	14.1
Technical & Related Support	3.2	3.2	3.7
Sales	12.6	12.5	11.8
Administrative Support/Clerical	14.2	13.8	16.3
Blue Collar	23.3	26.0	26.2
Precision Production/Craft/Repair	7.4	9.2	11.3
Machine Operators/Assem./Insp.	7.2	7.4	6.8
Transportation/Material Movers	3.8	4.6	4.1
Cleaners/Helpers/Laborers	5.0	4.8	3.9
Services	20.7	17.2	13.2
Farming/Forestry/Fishing	1.1	2.6	2.5

Note: Figures cover workers 16 years of age and older;
(1) Metropolitan Statistical Area - see Appendix A for areas included
Source: 1990 Census of Population and Housing, Summary Tape File 3C

Occupational Employment Projections: 1996 - 2006

Occupations Expected to Have the Largest Job Growth (ranked by numerical growth)	Fast-Growing Occupations[1] (ranked by percent growth)
1. Janitors/cleaners/maids, ex. priv. hshld.	1. Systems analysts
2. General managers & top executives	2. Desktop publishers
3. Cashiers	3. Personal and home care aides
4. Truck drivers, light	4. Database administrators
5. Salespersons, retail	5. Paralegals
6. Systems analysts	6. Securities, financial services sales
7. Home health aides	7. Occupational therapists
8. Teachers aides, clerical & paraprofess.	8. Home health aides
9. Registered nurses	9. Teachers, special education
10. Waiters & waitresses	10. Medical assistants

Note: Projections cover Wisconsin; (1) Excludes occupations with total job growth less than 300
Source: U.S. Department of Labor, Employment and Training Administration, America's Labor Market Information System (ALMIS)

Average Wages

Occupation	$/Hr.	Occupation	$/Hr.
Accountants and Auditors	15.49	Maids and Housekeepers	7.58
Assemblers and Fabricators	-	Maintenance Repairers	11.77
Automotive Mechanics	9.87	Marketing/Advertising/PR Managers	24.50
Bookkeepers	9.70	Nurses, Licensed Practical	12.75
Carpenters	13.62	Nurses, Registered	18.33
Cashiers	6.86	Nursing Aides/Orderlies/Attendants	8.60
Clerks, General Office	9.03	Physicians and Surgeons	26.24
Clerks, Shipping/Receiving/Traffic	11.20	Receptionists/Information Clerks	8.62
Computer Programmers	18.13	Sales Reps., Exc. Scientific/Retail	19.21
Computer Support Specialists	14.64	Sales Reps., Scientific, Exc. Retail	19.01
Cooks, Restaurant	7.81	Salespersons, Retail	8.94
Electricians	18.42	Secretaries, Except Legal/Medical	10.73
Financial Managers	25.12	Stock Clerks, Sales Floor	7.37
First-Line Supervisors/Mgrs., Sales	14.79	Systems Analysts	22.72
Food Preparation Workers	6.37	Teacher Aides	8.29
General Managers/Top Executives	23.56	Teachers, Elementary School	17.46
Guards	8.46	Teachers, Secondary School	17.38
Hand Packers	8.10	Telemarketers	9.17
Janitors and Cleaners	8.25	Truck Drivers, Heavy/Tractor-Trailer	13.72
Laborers, Landscaping	9.44	Truck Drivers, Light	9.17
Lawyers	29.51	Waiters and Waitresses	5.82

Note: Wage data is for 1998 and covers the Metropolitan Statistical Area (see Appendix A for areas included). Hourly wages for elementary and secondary school teachers were calculated by the editors from annual wage data assuming a 40 hour work week; Dashes indicate that data was not available.
Source: Bureau of Labor Statistics, 1998 Metropolitan Area Occupational Employment and Wage Estimates

TAXES

Major State and Local Tax Rates

State Corporate Income (%)	State Personal Income (%)	Residential Property (%)	Sales & Use		State Gasoline (cents/ gallon)	State Cigarette (cents/ pack)
			State (%)	Local (%)		
7.9	4.73 - 6.75[a]	2.67	5.0	None	25.8[b]	59.0

Note: Personal/corporate income, sales, gasoline and cigarette tax rates as of January 2000. Property tax rates as of April 2000; (a) Tax rates scheduled to decrease for tax years 2001 and beyond (ranging from 4.6% to 6.75%). Personal exemption amounts scheduled to increase to $700 for tax year 2001; (b) Portion of the rate is adjustable based on maintenance costs, sales volume, or cost of fuel to state government
Source: Federation of Tax Administrators, www.taxadmin.org; ERI's Relocation Assessor software database, quarterly effective date 4/1/2000

Total Taxes Per Capita and as a Percent of Income

Area	Per Capita Income ($)	Per Capita Taxes ($)			Percent of Income (%)		
		Total	Federal	State/Local	Total	Federal	State/Local
Wisconsin	27,342	10,308	6,546	3,761	37.7	23.9	13.8
U.S.	28,878	10,298	7,026	3,273	35.7	24.3	11.3

Note: Figures are for 1999
Source: Tax Foundation, www.taxfoundation.org

COMMERCIAL UTILITIES

Typical Monthly Electric Bills

Area	Commercial Service ($/month)		Industrial Service ($/month)	
	12 kW demand 1,500 kWh	100 kW demand 30,000 kWh	1,000 kW demand 400,000 kWh	20,000 kW demand 10,000,000 kWh
City	108	1,731	19,340	323,654
U.S.	150	2,174	23,995	508,569

Note: Based on rates in effect January 1, 1999
Source: Edison Electric Institute, Typical Residential, Commercial and Industrial Bills, Winter 1999

TRANSPORTATION

Transportation Statistics

Average minutes to work (1990)	13.0
Interstate highways	I-90; US-53; US-14; US-61
Bus lines	
In-city (1998)	La Crosse Municipal Transit Utility, 13 buses
Inter-city (1999)	4
Passenger air service	
Airport	La Crosse Municipal
Airlines (1999)	3
Enplaned passengers (1998)	115,291
Amtrak service	Yes
Motor freight carriers (1999)	23
Major waterways/ports	Mississippi River

Source: FAA DOT/TSC CY1998 ACAIS Database; National Transit Database, 1998; Editor & Publisher Market Guide, 2000; Amtrak National Time Table, Fall 1999/Winter 2000; 1990 Census of Population and Housing, STF 3C; Jane's Urban Transport Systems 1999-2000

Means of Transportation to Work

Area	Car/Truck/Van		Public Transportation			Bicycle	Walked	Other Means	Worked at Home
	Drove Alone	Car-pooled	Bus	Subway	Railroad				
City	69.1	10.8	3.1	0.0	0.0	1.6	12.4	1.0	2.0
MSA[1]	74.2	11.3	1.6	0.0	0.0	0.9	7.8	0.8	3.3
U.S.	73.2	13.4	3.0	1.5	0.5	0.4	3.9	1.2	3.0

Note: Figures shown are percentages and only include workers 16 years of age and older;
(1) Metropolitan Statistical Area - see Appendix A for areas included
Source: 1990 Census of Population and Housing, Summary Tape File 3C

BUSINESSES

Major Business Headquarters

Company Name	1999 Rankings	
	Fortune 500	Forbes 500
No companies listed	-	-

Note: Companies listed are located in the city; dashes indicate no ranking
Fortune 500: Companies that produce a 10-K are ranked 1 to 500 based on 1999 revenue
Forbes 500: Private companies are ranked 1 to 500 based on 1998 revenue
Source: Forbes, December 13, 1999; Fortune, April 17, 2000

HOTELS & MOTELS

Hotels/Motels

Area	Hotels/ Motels	Rooms	Luxury-Level Hotels/Motels		Average Minimum Rates ($)		
			♦♦♦♦	♦♦♦♦♦	♦♦	♦♦♦	♦♦♦♦
City	13	1,240	0	0	47	87	n/a
Airport	2	221	0	0	n/a	n/a	n/a
Suburbs	1	110	0	0	n/a	n/a	n/a
Total	16	1,571	0	0	n/a	n/a	n/a

Note: n/a not available; classifications range from one diamond (budget properties with basic amenities) to five diamond (luxury properties).
Source: OAG Business Travel Planner, Winter 1999-2000

Estimated Daily Food and Lodging Costs

Area	Food/Other ($/day)	Average Hotel Cost ($/day)
City	30	55
U.S.	30	55

Source: ERI's Relocation Assessor software database, quarterly effective date 4/1/2000

CONVENTION CENTERS

Convention Centers and Event Sites

Name	Guest Rooms	Meeting Space (sq. ft.)	Capacity (Theatre Style)
La Crosse Center	n/a	n/a	8,000
Radisson Hotel	169	7,748	400

Note: n/a not available
Source: EventSource.com, 3/15/2000

Living Environment

COST OF LIVING

Cost of Living: Homeowner

Cost Element	U.S. ($)	City ($)	Differential ($)	Percent of U.S. Average
Consumables	14,516	14,082	-434	97.0
Transportation	5,957	5,808	-149	97.5
Health Services	2,012	1,911	-101	95.0
Housing/Utilities/Prop. Tax	16,337	18,913	2,576	115.8
Income+Payroll Taxes	12,615	13,426	811	106.4
Miscellaneous	8,563	8,563	0	100.0
Total Cost of Living	60,000	62,703	2,703	104.5

Note: Figures are based on a single income, four person family with gross annual earnings of $60,000, owning an 1,800 square-foot home, and driving two automobiles worth $22,000 30,000 miles per year.
Source: ERI's Relocation Assessor software database, quarterly effective date 4/1/2000

Cost of Living: Renter

Cost Element	U.S. ($)	City ($)	Differential ($)	Percent of U.S. Average
Consumables	10,486	10,184	-302	97.1
Transportation	2,107	2,056	-51	97.6
Health Services	1,632	1,553	-79	95.2
Rent/Utilities/Insurance	9,299	8,148	-1,151	87.6
Income+Payroll Taxes	8,607	9,663	1,056	112.3
Miscellaneous	7,869	7,869	0	100.0
Total Cost of Living	40,000	39,473	-527	98.7

Note: Figures are based on a single income, three person family with gross annual earnings of $40,000, renting a 1,000 square-foot home, and driving one automobile worth $8,000 12,000 miles per year.
Source: ERI's Relocation Assessor software database, quarterly effective date 4/1/2000

HOUSING

Median Home Prices and Housing Affordability

Area	Median Price[2] 4th Qtr. 1999 ($)	HOI[3] 4th Qtr. 1999	Affordability Rank[4]
MSA[1]	n/a	n/a	n/a
U.S.	139,000	63.8	–

Note: (1) Metropolitan Statistical Area - see Appendix A for areas included; (2) U.S. figures calculated from the sales of 687,516 new and existing homes in 192 markets; (3) Housing Opportunity Index - percent of homes sold that were within the reach of the median income household at the prevailing mortgage interest rate; (4) Rank is from 1-192 with 1 being most affordable; n/a not available
Source: National Association of Home Builders, Housing Opportunity Index, 4th Quarter 1999

Estimated Home Price

Area	Price ($)
City	141,882
U.S.	135,855

Note: Figures are based on an 1,800 square-foot home
Source: ERI's Relocation Assessor software database, quarterly effective date 4/1/2000

Estimated Rent

Area	Rent ($/month)
City	571
U.S.	651

Note: Figures are based on a 1,000 square-foot home
Source: ERI's Relocation Assessor software database, quarterly effective date 4/1/2000

Median Home Price Projection

It is projected that the median home price in the metropolitan area will increase from $107,534 in 1999 to $108,567 in 2010, an increase of 1.0%
Kiplinger's Personal Finance Magazine, January 2000

RESIDENTIAL UTILITIES

Average Residential Utility Costs

Area	All Electric ($/mth)	Part Electric ($/mth)	Other Energy ($/mth)	Phone ($/mth)
City	n/a	n/a	n/a	n/a
U.S.	99.25	55.47	43.48	20.29

Note: n/a not available
Source: ACCRA, Cost of Living Index, 3rd Quarter 1999

HEALTH CARE

Average Health Care Costs

Area	Hospital ($/day)	Doctor ($/visit)	Dentist ($/visit)
City	n/a	n/a	n/a
U.S.	440.96	53.83	68.42

Note: n/a not available
Source: ACCRA, Cost of Living Index, 3rd Quarter 1999

Distribution of Office-Based Physicians

Area	Family/Gen. Practitioners	Specialists		
		Medical	Surgical	Other
MSA[1]	38	119	89	106

Note: Data as of 12/31/97; (1) Metropolitan Statistical Area - see Appendix A for areas included
Source: American Medical Assn., Physician Characteristics & Distribution in the U.S., 1999

Hospitals

La Crosse has 2 general medical and surgical hospitals.
AHA Guide to the Healthcare Field, 1999-2000

EDUCATION

Public School District Statistics

District Name	Num. Sch.	Enroll.	Classroom Teachers	Pupils per Teacher	Minority Pupils (%)	Current Exp.[1] ($/pupil)
La Crosse Sch Dist	20	7,959	n/a	n/a	n/a	n/a

Note: Data covers the 1997-1998 school year unless otherwise noted; (1) Data covers fiscal year 1996; SD = School District; ISD = Independent School District; n/a not available
Source: National Center for Education Statistics, Common Core of Data Public Education Agency Universe 1997-98; National Center for Education Statistics, Characteristics of the 100 Largest Public Elementary and Secondary School Districts in the United States: 1997-98, July 1999

Educational Quality

School District	Education Quotient[1]	Graduate Outcome[2]	Community Index[3]	Resource Index[4]
La Crosse School Dist.	134	139	106	130

Note: Over 1,000 secondary school districts were rated in terms of educational quality. The scores range from a low of 50 to a high of 150; (1) Combination of the Graduate Outcome, Community and Resource indexes weighted to reflect the greater importance of the Graduate Outcome and Resource Index; (2) Based on graduation rates and college board scores (SAT/ACT); (3) Based on the surrounding community's level of affluence and adult education; (4) Based on teacher salaries, per-pupil expenditures and student-teacher ratios.
Source: Expansion Management, Ratings Issue, 1999

Educational Attainment by Race

Area	High School Graduate (%)					Bachelor's Degree (%)				
	Total	White	Black	Other	Hisp.[2]	Total	White	Black	Other	Hisp.[2]
City	80.7	81.5	69.6	57.1	95.1	21.4	21.7	27.0	13.5	33.7
MSA[1]	82.6	83.0	76.5	60.9	92.2	21.1	21.1	20.4	18.9	31.8
U.S.	75.2	77.9	63.1	60.4	49.8	20.3	21.5	11.4	19.4	9.2

Note: Figures shown cover persons 25 years old and over; (1) Metropolitan Statistical Area - see Appendix A for areas included; (2) people of Hispanic origin can be of any race
Source: 1990 Census of Population and Housing, Summary Tape File 3C

School Enrollment by Type

Area	Preprimary				Elementary/High School			
	Public		Private		Public		Private	
	Enrollment	%	Enrollment	%	Enrollment	%	Enrollment	%
City	566	64.0	318	36.0	5,161	80.2	1,273	19.8
MSA[1]	1,126	63.5	647	36.5	13,387	84.5	2,461	15.5
U.S.	2,679,029	59.5	1,824,256	40.5	38,379,689	90.2	4,187,099	9.8

Note: Figures shown cover persons 3 years old and over;
(1) Metropolitan Statistical Area - see Appendix A for areas included
Source: 1990 Census of Population and Housing, Summary Tape File 3C

School Enrollment by Race

Area	Preprimary (%)				Elementary/High School (%)			
	White	Black	Other	Hisp.[1]	White	Black	Other	Hisp.[1]
City	88.1	2.5	9.4	4.3	83.5	1.5	15.0	1.5
MSA[2]	93.2	1.2	5.6	2.1	92.3	0.9	6.8	1.3
U.S.	80.4	12.5	7.1	7.8	74.1	15.6	10.3	12.5

Note: Figures shown cover persons 3 years old and over; (1) people of Hispanic origin can be of any race; (2) Metropolitan Statistical Area - see Appendix A for areas included
Source: 1990 Census of Population and Housing, Summary Tape File 3C

Higher Education

Two-Year Colleges		Four-Year Colleges		Medical Schools	Law Schools	Voc/Tech
Public	Private	Public	Private			
0	1	1	1	0	0	2

Source: College Blue Book, Occupational Education, 1999; Medical School Admission Requirements, 1999-2000; Peterson's Guide to Two-Year Colleges, 2000; Peterson's Guide to Four-Year Colleges, 1999; Barron's Guide to Law Schools, 1999

MAJOR EMPLOYERS

Major Employers

None listed in city

Source: D&B Business Rankings, 1999; Ward's Business Directory, 1999; America's Corporate Families, 1999

PUBLIC SAFETY

Crime Rate

Area	All Crimes	Violent Crimes				Property Crimes		
		Murder	Forcible Rape	Robbery	Aggrav. Assault	Burglary	Larceny -Theft	Motor Vehicle Theft
City	4,909.5	0.0	13.5	44.4	63.8	427.0	4,183.0	177.8
Suburbs[1]	2,187.1	1.4	18.4	4.2	182.7	223.8	1,678.6	77.9
MSA[2]	3,338.7	0.8	16.3	21.2	132.4	309.8	2,738.0	120.1
U.S.	4,930.0	6.8	35.9	186.3	382.3	919.4	2,893.4	506.0

Note: Crime rate is the number of crimes per 100,000 population; (1) Defined as all areas within the Metropolitan Statistical Area but located outside the central city; (2) Metropolitan Statistical Area - see Appendix A for areas included
Source: FBI Uniform Crime Reports, 1997

RECREATION

Culture and Recreation

Museums	Symphony Orchestras	Opera Companies	Dance Companies	Professional Theatres	Zoos	Pro Sports Teams
4	1	0	0	1	1	0

Source: Musical America, International Directory of the Performing Arts, 1999; Official Museum Directory, 2000; Stern's Performing Arts Directory, 1997; USA Today Four Sport Stadium Guide, 1997; Career Opportunities in Theatre and the Performing Arts, 1999

Library System

The La Crosse Public Library has two branches, holdings of 209,999 volumes, and a budget of $3,293,685 (1997-1998).
American Library Directory, 1999-2000

MEDIA

Newspapers

Name	Type	Freq.	Distribution	Circulation
The Buyer Express	General	1x/wk	Local	20,000
La Crosse Tribune	General	7x/wk	Area	34,840

Note: Includes newspapers with circulations of 200 or more located in the city;
Source: Burrelle's Media Directory, 1999 Edition

Television Stations

Name	Ch.	Affiliation	Type	Owner
WKBT	n/a	CBST	Commercial	Young Broadcasting Inc.
WLAX	25	FBC	Commercial	Grant Media Inc.

Note: Stations included broadcast in the La Crosse metro area; n/a not available
Source: Burrelle's Media Directory, 1999 Edition

AM Radio Stations

Call Letters	Freq. (kHz)	Target Audience	Station Format	Music Format
WKTY	580	General	S	n/a
WIZM	1410	General	N/T	n/a
WLFN	1490	General	M/N/S	Classic Rock/Oldies
WKBH	1570	General	S/T	n/a

Note: Stations included broadcast in the La Crosse metro area; n/a not available
Target Audience: A=Asian; B=Black; C=Christian; E=Ethnic; F=French; G=General; H=Hispanic; M=Men; N=Native American; R=Religious; S=Senior Citizen; W=Women; Y=Young Adult; Z=Children
Station Format: E=Educational; M=Music; N=News; S=Sports; T=Talk
Source: Burrelle's Media Directory, 1999 Edition

FM Radio Stations

Call Letters	Freq. (mHz)	Target Audience	Station Format	Music Format
WLSU	88.9	General	E/M/N	Classical/Jazz
WHLA	90.3	General	E/T	n/a
WIZM	93.3	General	M	Adult Contemporary
WRQT	95.7	General	M	Country
WKBH	100.1	Men	M	Classic Rock
KQEG	102.7	General	M/N/S	Oldies
WLXR	104.9	General	M/N/S	Adult Contemporary
WFBZ	105.5	General	M/N/S	Classic Rock
WQCC	106.3	n/a	M/N	Country

Note: Stations included broadcast in the La Crosse metro area; n/a not available
Station Format: E=Educational; M=Music; N=News; S=Sports; T=Talk
Target Audience: A=Asian; B=Black; C=Christian; E=Ethnic; F=French; G=General; H=Hispanic; M=Men; N=Native American; R=Religious; S=Senior Citizen; W=Women; Y=Young Adult; Z=Children
Source: Burrelle's Media Directory, 1999 Edition

WEATHER

Temperature/Precipitation/Humidity

	Jan	Feb	Mar	Apr	May	Jun	Jul	Aug	Sep	Oct	Nov	Dec	Yr.
Max. High Temp. (°F)	46	60	70	92	92	98	101	103	100	86	74	61	103
Avg. High Temp. (°F)	25	31	38	56	69	79	82	81	72	61	42	30	56
Avg. Temp. (°F)	16	21	29	46	59	68	72	71	62	51	34	22	46
Avg. Low Temp. (°F)	7	12	20	37	49	58	63	61	52	41	26	14	37
Min. Low Temp. (°F)	-37	-26	-18	10	28	41	49	36	29	19	-10	-22	-37
Avg. Precip. (in.)	0.8	0.9	2.1	3.1	3.7	4.1	4.2	3.5	2.8	1.9	1.6	0.9	29.5
Avg. Snowfall (in.)	7.2	7.7	12.4	1.7	0.1	0	0	0	0	0.1	5.6	8.0	42.8
Avg. Rel. Hum. (%)	73	73	71	63	64	69	72	75	73	69	72	75	71

Source: National Climatic Data Center, International Station Meteorological Climate Summary, 3/95

Weather Conditions

Temperature			Precipitation		
0°F & below	32°F & below	90°F & above	0.1 inch or more precip.	1.5 inch or more snow/ice	Thunder-storms
24	154	13	61	9	44

Note: Figures are average number of days per year
Source: National Climatic Data Center, International Station Meteorological Climate Summary, 3/95

AIR & WATER QUALITY

Maximum Pollutant Concentrations

	Particulate Matter (ug/m³)	Carbon Monoxide (ppm)	Sulfur Dioxide (ppm)	Nitrogen Dioxide (ppm)	Ozone (ppm)	Lead (ug/m³)
MSA[1] Level	n/a	n/a	n/a	n/a	n/a	n/a
NAAQS[2]	150	9	0.140	0.053	0.12	1.50
Met NAAQS	n/a	n/a	n/a	n/a	n/a	n/a

Note: (1) Metropolitan Statistical Area - see Appendix A for areas included; (2) National Ambient Air Quality Standards; ppm = parts per million; ug/m³ = micrograms per cubic meter; n/a not available
Source: EPA, National Air Quality and Emissions Trends Report, 1997

Pollutant Standards Index

Data not available.
EPA, National Air Quality and Emissions Trends Report, 1997

Drinking Water

Water System Name	Pop. Served	Primary Water Source Type	Number of Violations in 1998-99	Type of Violation/ Contaminants
La Crosse Waterworks	53,000	Ground	None	None

Note: Data as of January 19, 2000
Source: EPA, Office of Ground Water and Drinking Water, Safe Drinking Water Information System

La Crosse tap water is alkaline, hard, and fluoridated.
Editor & Publisher Market Guide, 2000

Lafayette, Indiana

Background

Lafayette, Indiana is located in Tippecanoe County on the Wabash River in the west-central portion of the state, 63 miles northwest of Indianapolis. Named for the Marquis de Lafayette, who was making his last trip to America, it was laid out in 1825 by William Digby and incorporated in 1853.

The area has become highly urbanized with the growth of Purdue University, established in 1869 through a gift from John Purdue, a local businessman. The region's economy is dominated by educational services generated by the university, now the county's largest employer. Secondary businesses are manufacturing and retail, including aluminum, rubber, electrical and grain products, and pharmaceuticals. Major firms in Lafayette include ALCOA, Eli Lilly and Company, Caterpillar Tractor Company and Subaru-Isuzu. As a result of its diverse economy, Lafayette's unemployment rate remains below the state average.

Steeped in history, Lafayette is situated four miles northeast of the area's first white settlement, Fort Ouiatanon, built by the French in 1719 as an Indian fur-trading post. It was lost to the English in 1763 during the French and Indian War, and later to the Americans in 1779. Tippecanoe County is famous for the Battle of Tippecanoe in 1811, in which then-Governor William Henry Harrison's small army defeated a confederacy led by Shawnee prophet Tenskwatana, brother of Tecumseh.

In the 1960s Lafayette's downtown district became congested and depressed, but has since undergone major revitalization as a result of a Redevelopment Commission formed in 1966. The waterfront was dredged and a riverside park complex was created. Commercial buildings were restored and renovated, as were historical landmarks.

Purdue University has spawned many astronauts, as well as Nobel Prize winners Dr. Herbert C. Brown, Edward M. Purcell, Julian C. Schwinger and Ben Roy Mottelson. Famous Lafayette residents include Alva Roebuck, cofounder of Sears, Roebuck and Company, and the father of the Mayo brothers, founders of the Mayo Clinic.

General Rankings and Evaluative Comments

- Lafayette was ranked #199 out of 354 metropolitan areas in *Places Rated Almanac*. Criteria: cost of living, climate, crime, transportation, job outlook, education, the arts, health care, and recreation. *Places Rated Almanac, Millennium Edition, 2000*

- Cognetics studied 273 metro areas in the United States, ranking them by entrepreneurial activity. Lafayette was ranked #86 out of 134 smaller metro areas. Criteria: Significant Starts (firms started in the last 10 years that still employ at least 5 people) and Young Growers (percent of firms 10 years old or less that grew significantly during the last 4 years). *Cognetics, "Entrepreneurial Hot Spots: The Best Places in America to Start and Grow a Company," 1999*

Business Environment

STATE ECONOMY

State Economic Profile

"Indiana is lagging the nation in both job and Gross State Product (GSP) growth. While US job growth in 1998 was 2.0%, Indiana's was only 0.4%. Indiana's primary obstacle to growth is its lack of workers. The state unemployment rate is below the national, and its population growth rate is barely above zero.

Indiana's manufacturing base is much stronger than its neighbors, actually adding manufacturing jobs in 1998. The recent surge in automobile sales has helped boost employment in Indiana's auto sector, with some gains projected in the near future. Even if auto sales continue at the current pace, which is unlikely, Indiana auto plants would have a hard time finding workers to fill those jobs.

Demographic forces have restrained Indiana's housing and construction markets. Construction employment was down 2% in 1998, even though residential permits were up 15%. Home sales have been at the highest level in years, although new construction and slow population growth have kept price appreciation below the national.

Much of Indiana's economic strength has been in Indianapolis. Job growth in Indianapolis was 2.7% in 1998, almost 8 times the state average. Construction employment was up 7% in Indianapolis, while down for the state as a whole. Indianapolis' housing market has also witnessed price appreciation and new construction above the rest of the state.

While low foreign demand for manufacturing goods has hit Indiana as hard as other states in the region, its tight labor markets and a surge in auto sales have minimized job losses. These same tight labor markets, however, constrain Indiana to a moderate to slow growth path."
National Association of Realtors, Economic Profiles: The Fifty States and the District of Columbia, http://nar.realtor.com/databank/profiles.htm

EXPORTS

Total Export Sales

Area	1995 ($000)	1996 ($000)	1997 ($000)	1998 ($000)	% Chg. 1995-98	% Chg. 1997-98
MSA[1]	116,206	133,218	172,701	289,098	148.8	67.4
U.S.	583,030,524	622,827,063	687,597,999	680,474,251	16.7	-1.0

Note: (1) Metropolitan Statistical Area - see Appendix A for areas included
Source: U.S. Department of Commerce, International Trade Association, Metropolitan Area Exports: An Export Performance Report on Over 250 U.S. Cities, November 10, 1999

CITY FINANCES

City Government Finances

Component	1995 ($million)	1995 (per capita $)
Revenue	43.2	942
Expenditure	36.0	785
Debt Outstanding	12.1	264

Source: 1999 County and City Extra, Annual Metro, City, and County Data Book

City Government Revenue by Source

Source	1995 ($million)	1995 (per capita $)
Intergovernmental	12.3	268
Taxes	16.6	362
Property	11.0	241
Sales and Gross Receipts	0.0	0

Source: 1999 County and City Extra, Annual Metro, City, and County Data Book

City Government Expenditures by Function

Function	1995 ($million)	1995 (per capita $)	1995 (%)
Public Welfare	0.0	0	0.0
Highways	6.2	135	17.3
Parking Facilities	<0.1	<1	0.1
Education	0.0	0	0.0
Health and Hospitals	0.0	0	0.0
Police Protection	4.1	91	11.6
Sewerage and Sanitation	5.4	118	15.1
Parks and Recreation	2.3	51	6.6
Housing and Community Development	1.8	40	5.2
Interest on Debt	0.1	3	0.5

Source: 1999 County and City Extra, Annual Metro, City, and County Data Book

Municipal Bond Ratings

Area	Moody's
City	Aaa

Source: Mergent Bond Record, 2/2000

POPULATION

Population Growth

Area	1980 Census	1990 Census	1999 Estimate	2004 Projection	Population Growth (%) 1990-1999	1999-2004
City	43,011	43,764	42,176	41,538	-3.6	-1.5
MSA[1]	121,702	130,598	172,920	177,404	32.4	2.6
U.S.	226,545,805	248,765,170	272,212,864	283,625,312	9.4	4.2

Note: (1) Metropolitan Statistical Area - see Appendix A for areas included
Source: 1990 Census of Population and Housing, Summary Tape File 3C; Claritas, Inc.

Number of Households and Average Household Size

Area	1980 Census	1990 Census	1999 Estimate	2004 Projection	1999 Average Household Size
City	17,592	18,017	17,548	17,353	2.40
MSA[1]	52,005	45,509	61,625	63,334	2.81
U.S.	80,389,592	91,993,582	102,048,200	107,302,392	2.67

Note: (1) Metropolitan Statistical Area - see Appendix A for areas included
Source: 1990 Census of Population and Housing, Summary Tape File 3C; Claritas, Inc.

Race/Ethnicity of City Population

Race/Ethnicity	1990 Census Population	%	1999 Estimate Population	%	% Change 1990-1999
White, Non-Hispanic	41,733	95.4	39,132	92.8	-6.2
Black, Non-Hispanic	818	1.9	1,112	2.6	35.9
Asian, Non-Hispanic	572	1.3	645	1.5	12.8
Other, Non-Hispanic	69	0.2	168	0.4	143.5
Hispanic	572	1.3	1,119	2.7	95.6

Source: 1990 Census of Population and Housing, Summary Tape File 3C; Claritas, Inc.

Race/Ethnicity of Metropolitan Statistical Area Population

Race/Ethnicity	1990 Census		1999 Estimate		% Change 1990-1999
	Population	%	Population	%	
White, Non-Hispanic	121,222	92.8	158,580	91.7	30.8
Black, Non-Hispanic	2,470	1.9	3,125	1.8	26.5
Asian, Non-Hispanic	4,905	3.8	6,773	3.9	38.1
Other, Non-Hispanic	246	0.2	493	0.3	100.4
Hispanic	1,755	1.3	3,949	2.3	125.0

Note: See Appendix A for areas included in the Metropolitan Statistical Area
Source: 1990 Census of Population and Housing, Summary Tape File 3C; Claritas, Inc.

Ancestry

Area	German	Irish	English	Italian	U.S.	French	Polish	Dutch
City	38.5	19.7	14.1	2.3	7.6	4.7	1.5	7.5
MSA[1]	39.7	18.2	14.5	2.7	5.5	4.3	2.7	5.9
U.S.	23.3	15.6	13.1	5.9	5.3	4.2	3.8	2.5

Note: Figures are percentages and include persons that reported multiple ancestry (eg. if a person reported being Irish and Italian, they were included in both columns); (1) Metropolitan Statistical Area - see Appendix A for areas included
Source: 1990 Census of Population and Housing, Summary Tape File 3C

Median Age

Area	1990 Census	1999 Estimate
City	32.4	36.0
MSA[1]	26.6	31.2
U.S.	32.9	35.7

Note: (1) Metropolitan Statistical Area - see Appendix A for areas included
Source: 1990 Census of Population and Housing, Summary Tape File 3C; Claritas, Inc.

Male/Female Population

Area	Number of Males		Number of Females		Males per 100 Females	
	1990	1999	1990	1999	1990	1999
City	21,291	20,465	22,473	21,711	94.7	94.3
MSA[1]	66,174	86,703	64,424	86,217	102.7	100.6
U.S.	121,172,379	132,803,736	127,537,494	139,409,136	95.0	95.3

Note: (1) Metropolitan Statistical Area - see Appendix A for areas included
Source: 1990 Census of Population, General Population Characteristics; Claritas, Inc.

INCOME

Per Capita/Median/Average Income

Area	Per Capita ($)			Median Household ($)			Average Household ($)		
	1989	1999	% Chg.	1989	1999	% Chg.	1989	1999	% Chg.
City	13,468	21,929	62.8	27,023	41,068	52.0	32,391	52,386	61.7
MSA[1]	12,570	19,962	58.8	27,630	40,869	47.9	34,591	54,507	57.6
U.S.	14,420	21,350	48.1	30,056	40,525	34.8	38,453	56,184	46.1

Note: (1) Metropolitan Statistical Area - see Appendix A for areas included; 1989 data is from the 1990 Census; 1999 data is estimated by Claritas, Inc.
Source: 1990 Census of Population, General Population Characteristics; Claritas, Inc.

Household Income Distribution

Area	Percent of Households Earning								
	Under $5,000	$5,000 -14,999	$15,000 -24,999	$25,000 -34,999	$35,000 -49,999	$50,000 -74,999	$75,000 -99,000	$100,000 -149,999	$150,000 and up
City	2.4	10.6	14.5	14.0	19.0	22.7	9.1	4.4	3.4
MSA[1]	3.1	12.3	14.0	13.3	16.4	20.6	10.3	6.2	3.9
U.S.	3.9	13.3	13.8	12.6	16.2	19.4	9.7	6.6	4.6

Note: Data as of 1999; (1) Metropolitan Statistical Area - see Appendix A for areas included
Source: Claritas, Inc.

Effective Buying Income

Area	Per Capita ($)	Median Household ($)	Average Household ($)
City	17,894	34,907	42,240
MSA[1]	17,320	36,950	47,445
U.S.	17,496	36,603	47,036

Note: Data as of 1/1/2000; (1) Metropolitan Statistical Area - see Appendix A for areas included
Source: Standard Rate & Data Service, Newspaper Advertising Source, March 2000

Effective Household Buying Income Distribution

Area	% of Households Earning						
	$10,000 -$19,999	$20,000 -$34,999	$35,000 -$49,999	$50,000 -$74,999	$75,000 -$99,000	$100,000 -$124,999	$125,000 and up
City	15.5	26.2	21.8	18.6	5.5	1.6	2.4
MSA[1]	15.0	22.7	17.8	20.1	8.8	2.9	2.9
U.S.	15.0	21.6	17.6	19.6	8.4	3.0	3.3

Note: Data as of 1/1/2000; (1) Metropolitan Statistical Area - see Appendix A for areas included
Source: Standard Rate & Data Service, Newspaper Advertising Source, March 2000

Poverty Rates by Age

Area	People of All Ages	People Under 18 Years Old	Related Children Age 5-17 in Families in Poverty
City	7.0	n/a	n/a
County	9.8	11.5	9.9
U.S.	13.8	20.8	18.7

Note: Figures show the percent of people living below the poverty line in 1995. The average poverty threshold was $15,569 for a family of four in 1995; n/a not available
Source: Bureau of the Census, Small Area Income and Poverty Estimates Program; U.S. Department of Housing and Urban Development

EMPLOYMENT

Labor Force and Employment

Area	Civilian Labor Force			Workers Employed		
	Dec. 1998	Dec. 1999	% Chg.	Dec. 1998	Dec. 1999	% Chg.
City	26,581	26,733	0.6	26,072	26,257	0.7
MSA[1]	91,456	91,890	0.5	89,528	90,163	0.7
U.S.	138,297,000	139,941,000	1.2	132,732,000	134,696,000	1.5

Note: Data is not seasonally adjusted and covers workers 16 years of age and older;
(1) Metropolitan Statistical Area - see Appendix A for areas included
Source: Bureau of Labor Statistics, http://stats.bls.gov

Unemployment Rate

Area	1999											
	Jan.	Feb.	Mar.	Apr.	May	Jun.	Jul.	Aug.	Sep.	Oct.	Nov.	Dec.
City	2.4	2.3	2.1	1.9	2.3	2.4	1.7	1.8	1.8	1.6	1.7	1.8
MSA[1]	2.6	2.5	2.2	2.0	2.4	2.5	1.7	1.8	1.8	1.7	1.8	1.9
U.S.	4.8	4.7	4.4	4.1	4.0	4.5	4.5	4.2	4.1	3.8	3.8	3.7

Note: Data is not seasonally adjusted and covers workers 16 years of age and older; all figures are percentages; (1) Metropolitan Statistical Area - see Appendix A for areas included
Source: Bureau of Labor Statistics, http://stats.bls.gov

Employment by Industry

Sector	MSA[1]		U.S.
	Number of Employees	Percent of Total	Percent of Total
Services	19,600	19.4	30.2
Retail Trade	18,600	18.5	18.1
Government	26,100	25.9	15.8
Manufacturing	23,800	23.6	14.1
Finance/Insurance/Real Estate	3,800	3.8	5.9
Wholesale Trade	2,400	2.4	5.4
Transportation/Public Utilities	2,400	2.4	5.3
Construction	n/a	n/a	4.8
Mining	n/a	n/a	0.4

Note: Figures cover non-farm employment as of 12/99 and are not seasonally adjusted; (1) Metropolitan Statistical Area - see Appendix A for areas included; n/a not available
Source: Bureau of Labor Statistics, http://stats.bls.gov

Employment by Occupation

Occupation Category	City (%)	MSA[1] (%)	U.S. (%)
White Collar	54.5	60.1	58.1
Executive/Admin./Management	10.8	10.5	12.3
Professional	13.1	19.2	14.1
Technical & Related Support	4.5	5.5	3.7
Sales	11.0	10.3	11.8
Administrative Support/Clerical	15.1	14.5	16.3
Blue Collar	28.0	22.1	26.2
Precision Production/Craft/Repair	11.1	9.1	11.3
Machine Operators/Assem./Insp.	9.4	6.7	6.8
Transportation/Material Movers	3.3	2.9	4.1
Cleaners/Helpers/Laborers	4.2	3.5	3.9
Services	16.9	15.9	13.2
Farming/Forestry/Fishing	0.5	1.9	2.5

Note: Figures cover workers 16 years of age and older; (1) Metropolitan Statistical Area - see Appendix A for areas included
Source: 1990 Census of Population and Housing, Summary Tape File 3C

Occupational Employment Projections: 1994 - 2005

Projections not available at time of publication.

Average Wages

Occupation	$/Hr.	Occupation	$/Hr.
Accountants and Auditors	16.94	Maids and Housekeepers	6.72
Assemblers and Fabricators	12.69	Maintenance Repairers	11.21
Automotive Mechanics	12.66	Marketing/Advertising/PR Managers	26.17
Bookkeepers	10.19	Nurses, Licensed Practical	13.01
Carpenters	13.58	Nurses, Registered	17.88
Cashiers	6.79	Nursing Aides/Orderlies/Attendants	7.78
Clerks, General Office	8.46	Physicians and Surgeons	53.38
Clerks, Shipping/Receiving/Traffic	11.78	Receptionists/Information Clerks	8.05
Computer Programmers	17.96	Sales Reps., Exc. Scientific/Retail	18.08
Computer Support Specialists	16.96	Sales Reps., Scientific, Exc. Retail	25.23
Cooks, Restaurant	8.24	Salespersons, Retail	8.95
Electricians	17.44	Secretaries, Except Legal/Medical	10.53
Financial Managers	27.13	Stock Clerks, Sales Floor	7.40
First-Line Supervisors/Mgrs., Sales	15.89	Systems Analysts	25.37
Food Preparation Workers	6.89	Teacher Aides	8.48
General Managers/Top Executives	29.74	Teachers, Elementary School	20.33
Guards	7.90	Teachers, Secondary School	20.16
Hand Packers	7.59	Telemarketers	-
Janitors and Cleaners	8.37	Truck Drivers, Heavy/Tractor-Trailer	13.85
Laborers, Landscaping	8.23	Truck Drivers, Light	11.05
Lawyers	-	Waiters and Waitresses	5.79

Note: Wage data is for 1998 and covers the Metropolitan Statistical Area (see Appendix A for areas included). Hourly wages for elementary and secondary school teachers were calculated by the editors from annual wage data assuming a 40 hour work week; Dashes indicate that data was not available.
Source: Bureau of Labor Statistics, 1998 Metropolitan Area Occupational Employment and Wage Estimates

TAXES

Major State and Local Tax Rates

State Corporate Income (%)	State Personal Income (%)	Residential Property (%)	Sales & Use		State Gasoline (cents/gallon)	State Cigarette (cents/pack)
			State (%)	Local (%)		
7.9[a]	3.4	2.91	5.0	None	15.0[b]	15.5

Note: Personal/corporate income, sales, gasoline and cigarette tax rates as of January 2000. Property tax rates as of April 2000; (a) Consists of 3.4% on income from sources within the state plus a 4.5% supplemental income tax; (b) Carriers pay an additional surcharge of 11 cents. Sales tax applicable
Source: Federation of Tax Administrators, www.taxadmin.org; ERI's Relocation Assessor software database, quarterly effective date 4/1/2000

Total Taxes Per Capita and as a Percent of Income

Area	Per Capita Income ($)	Per Capita Taxes ($)			Percent of Income (%)		
		Total	Federal	State/Local	Total	Federal	State/Local
Indiana	25,904	9,059	6,178	2,881	35.0	23.8	11.1
U.S.	28,878	10,298	7,026	3,273	35.7	24.3	11.3

Note: Figures are for 1999
Source: Tax Foundation, www.taxfoundation.org

COMMERCIAL UTILITIES

Typical Monthly Electric Bills

Area	Commercial Service ($/month)		Industrial Service ($/month)	
	12 kW demand 1,500 kWh	100 kW demand 30,000 kWh	1,000 kW demand 400,000 kWh	20,000 kW demand 10,000,000 kWh
City	n/a	n/a	n/a	n/a
U.S.	150	2,174	23,995	508,569

Note: Based on rates in effect January 1, 1999; n/a not available
Source: Edison Electric Institute, Typical Residential, Commercial and Industrial Bills, Winter 1999

TRANSPORTATION

Transportation Statistics

Average minutes to work (1990)	14.7
Interstate highways	I-65; US-52; US-231
Bus lines	
In-city (1998)	Greater Lafayette Public Transportation Corp., 38 buses
Inter-city (1999)	1
Passenger air service	
Airport	Purdue University
Airlines (1999)	2
Enplaned passengers (1998)	19,584
Amtrak service	Yes
Motor freight carriers (1999)	10
Major waterways/ports	None

Source: FAA DOT/TSC CY1998 ACAIS Database; National Transit Database, 1998; Editor & Publisher Market Guide, 2000; Amtrak National Time Table, Fall 1999/Winter 2000; 1990 Census of Population and Housing, STF 3C; Jane's Urban Transport Systems 1999-2000

Means of Transportation to Work

Area	Car/Truck/Van		Public Transportation			Bicycle	Walked	Other Means	Worked at Home
	Drove Alone	Car-pooled	Bus	Subway	Railroad				
City	79.9	12.4	1.7	0.0	0.0	0.4	3.0	0.5	2.0
MSA[1]	73.1	11.4	1.1	0.0	0.0	0.7	10.3	0.5	2.8
U.S.	73.2	13.4	3.0	1.5	0.5	0.4	3.9	1.2	3.0

Note: Figures shown are percentages and only include workers 16 years of age and older; (1) Metropolitan Statistical Area - see Appendix A for areas included
Source: 1990 Census of Population and Housing, Summary Tape File 3C

BUSINESSES

Major Business Headquarters

Company Name	1999 Rankings	
	Fortune 500	Forbes 500
No companies listed	-	-

Note: Companies listed are located in the city; dashes indicate no ranking
Fortune 500: Companies that produce a 10-K are ranked 1 to 500 based on 1999 revenue
Forbes 500: Private companies are ranked 1 to 500 based on 1998 revenue
Source: Forbes, December 13, 1999; Fortune, April 17, 2000

HOTELS & MOTELS

Hotels/Motels

Area	Hotels/ Motels	Rooms	Luxury-Level Hotels/Motels		Average Minimum Rates ($)		
			♦♦♦♦	♦♦♦♦♦	♦♦	♦♦♦	♦♦♦♦
City	7	554	0	0	n/a	n/a	n/a
Suburbs	2	205	0	0	n/a	n/a	n/a
Total	9	759	0	0	n/a	n/a	n/a

Note: n/a not available; classifications range from one diamond (budget properties with basic amenities) to five diamond (luxury properties).
Source: OAG Business Travel Planner, Winter 1999-2000

Estimated Daily Food and Lodging Costs

Area	Food/Other ($/day)	Average Hotel Cost ($/day)
City	30	62
U.S.	30	55

Source: ERI's Relocation Assessor software database, quarterly effective date 4/1/2000

CONVENTION CENTERS

Convention Centers and Event Sites

Name	Guest Rooms	Meeting Space (sq. ft.)	Capacity (Theatre Style)
Radisson Inn	126	6,668	450

Source: EventSource.com, 3/15/2000

Living Environment

COST OF LIVING

Cost of Living: Homeowner

Cost Element	U.S. ($)	City ($)	Differential ($)	Percent of U.S. Average
Consumables	14,516	14,023	-493	96.6
Transportation	5,957	5,810	-147	97.5
Health Services	2,012	1,949	-63	96.9
Housing/Utilities/Prop. Tax	16,337	14,483	-1,854	88.7
Income+Payroll Taxes	12,615	12,437	-178	98.6
Miscellaneous	8,563	8,563	0	100.0
Total Cost of Living	60,000	57,265	-2,735	95.4

Note: Figures are based on a single income, four person family with gross annual earnings of $60,000, owning an 1,800 square-foot home, and driving two automobiles worth $22,000 30,000 miles per year.
Source: ERI's Relocation Assessor software database, quarterly effective date 4/1/2000

Cost of Living: Renter

Cost Element	U.S. ($)	City ($)	Differential ($)	Percent of U.S. Average
Consumables	10,486	10,093	-393	96.3
Transportation	2,107	2,048	-59	97.2
Health Services	1,632	1,575	-57	96.5
Rent/Utilities/Insurance	9,299	10,617	1,318	114.2
Income+Payroll Taxes	8,607	8,428	-179	97.9
Miscellaneous	7,869	7,869	0	100.0
Total Cost of Living	40,000	40,630	630	101.6

Note: Figures are based on a single income, three person family with gross annual earnings of $40,000, renting a 1,000 square-foot home, and driving one automobile worth $8,000 12,000 miles per year.
Source: ERI's Relocation Assessor software database, quarterly effective date 4/1/2000

HOUSING

Median Home Prices and Housing Affordability

Area	Median Price[2] 4th Qtr. 1999 ($)	HOI[3] 4th Qtr. 1999	Affordability Rank[4]
MSA[1]	124,000	74.3	63
U.S.	139,000	63.8	–

Note: (1) Metropolitan Statistical Area - see Appendix A for areas included; (2) U.S. figures calculated from the sales of 687,516 new and existing homes in 192 markets; (3) Housing Opportunity Index - percent of homes sold that were within the reach of the median income household at the prevailing mortgage interest rate; (4) Rank is from 1-192 with 1 being most affordable
Source: National Association of Home Builders, Housing Opportunity Index, 4th Quarter 1999

Estimated Home Price

Area	Price ($)
City	100,651
U.S.	135,855

Note: Figures are based on an 1,800 square-foot home
Source: ERI's Relocation Assessor software database, quarterly effective date 4/1/2000

Estimated Rent

Area	Rent ($/month)
City	762
U.S.	651

Note: Figures are based on a 1,000 square-foot home
Source: ERI's Relocation Assessor software database, quarterly effective date 4/1/2000

Median Home Price Projection

It is projected that the median home price in the metropolitan area will increase from $94,088 in 1999 to $136,190 in 2010, an increase of 44.7%
Kiplinger's Personal Finance Magazine, January 2000

RESIDENTIAL UTILITIES

Average Residential Utility Costs

Area	All Electric ($/mth)	Part Electric ($/mth)	Other Energy ($/mth)	Phone ($/mth)
City	–	51.57	53.91	22.76
U.S.	99.25	55.47	43.48	20.29

Source: ACCRA, Cost of Living Index, 3rd Quarter 1999

HEALTH CARE

Average Health Care Costs

Area	Hospital ($/day)	Doctor ($/visit)	Dentist ($/visit)
City	411.50	53.00	68.40
U.S.	440.96	53.83	68.42

Note: Hospital—based on a semi-private room; Doctor—based on a general practitioner's routine exam of an established patient; Dentist—based on adult teeth cleaning and periodic oral exam.
Source: ACCRA, Cost of Living Index, 3rd Quarter 1999

Distribution of Office-Based Physicians

Area	Family/Gen. Practitioners	Specialists		
		Medical	Surgical	Other
MSA[1]	33	80	69	79

Note: Data as of 12/31/97; (1) Metropolitan Statistical Area - see Appendix A for areas included
Source: American Medical Assn., Physician Characteristics & Distribution in the U.S., 1999

Hospitals

Lafayette has 2 general medical and surgical hospitals, 1 psychiatric.
AHA Guide to the Healthcare Field, 1999-2000

EDUCATION

Public School District Statistics

District Name	Num. Sch.	Enroll.	Classroom Teachers	Pupils per Teacher	Minority Pupils (%)	Current Exp.[1] ($/pupil)
Lafayette School Corporation	15	7,524	522	14.4	n/a	n/a
Tippecanoe School Corp	14	8,807	464	19.0	n/a	n/a

Note: Data covers the 1997-1998 school year unless otherwise noted; (1) Data covers fiscal year 1996; SD = School District; ISD = Independent School District; n/a not available
Source: National Center for Education Statistics, Common Core of Data Public Education Agency Universe 1997-98; National Center for Education Statistics, Characteristics of the 100 Largest Public Elementary and Secondary School Districts in the United States: 1997-98, July 1999

Educational Quality

School District	Education Quotient[1]	Graduate Outcome[2]	Community Index[3]	Resource Index[4]
Lafayette School Corp.	92	104	103	67

Note: Over 1,000 secondary school districts were rated in terms of educational quality. The scores range from a low of 50 to a high of 150; (1) Combination of the Graduate Outcome, Community and Resource indexes weighted to reflect the greater importance of the Graduate Outcome and Resource Index; (2) Based on graduation rates and college board scores (SAT/ACT); (3) Based on the surrounding community's level of affluence and adult education; (4) Based on teacher salaries, per-pupil expenditures and student-teacher ratios.
Source: Expansion Management, Ratings Issue, 1999

Educational Attainment by Race

Area	High School Graduate (%)					Bachelor's Degree (%)				
	Total	White	Black	Other	Hisp.[2]	Total	White	Black	Other	Hisp.[2]
City	80.5	80.7	72.2	78.4	47.9	21.4	21.1	19.1	41.2	20.1
MSA[1]	85.2	85.0	76.8	91.9	73.5	30.7	28.7	29.4	71.3	45.8
U.S.	75.2	77.9	63.1	60.4	49.8	20.3	21.5	11.4	19.4	9.2

Note: Figures shown cover persons 25 years old and over; (1) Metropolitan Statistical Area - see Appendix A for areas included; (2) people of Hispanic origin can be of any race
Source: 1990 Census of Population and Housing, Summary Tape File 3C

School Enrollment by Type

Area	Preprimary				Elementary/High School			
	Public		Private		Public		Private	
	Enrollment	%	Enrollment	%	Enrollment	%	Enrollment	%
City	456	53.3	400	46.7	5,672	87.6	806	12.4
MSA[1]	1,297	53.5	1,126	46.5	15,750	90.5	1,645	9.5
U.S.	2,679,029	59.5	1,824,256	40.5	38,379,689	90.2	4,187,099	9.8

Note: Figures shown cover persons 3 years old and over;
(1) Metropolitan Statistical Area - see Appendix A for areas included
Source: 1990 Census of Population and Housing, Summary Tape File 3C

School Enrollment by Race

Area	Preprimary (%)				Elementary/High School (%)			
	White	Black	Other	Hisp.[1]	White	Black	Other	Hisp.[1]
City	93.0	3.9	3.2	2.7	94.1	2.9	3.0	2.1
MSA[2]	90.6	3.0	6.4	2.5	94.7	1.6	3.7	1.6
U.S.	80.4	12.5	7.1	7.8	74.1	15.6	10.3	12.5

Note: Figures shown cover persons 3 years old and over; (1) people of Hispanic origin can be of any race; (2) Metropolitan Statistical Area - see Appendix A for areas included
Source: 1990 Census of Population and Housing, Summary Tape File 3C

Higher Education

Two-Year Colleges		Four-Year Colleges		Medical Schools	Law Schools	Voc/ Tech
Public	Private	Public	Private			
1	1	0	0	0	0	3

Source: College Blue Book, Occupational Education, 1999; Medical School Admission Requirements, 1999-2000; Peterson's Guide to Two-Year Colleges, 2000; Peterson's Guide to Four-Year Colleges, 1999; Barron's Guide to Law Schools, 1999

MAJOR EMPLOYERS

Major Employers

Grauel Enterprises (appliance rentals)
North Central Health Services
Tippecanoe Laboratories

Lafayette Home Hospital
Phycor-Lafayette (management services)
Wabash National Corp. (truck trailers)

Note: Companies listed are located in the city
Source: D&B Business Rankings, 1999; Ward's Business Directory, 1999; America's Corporate Families, 1999

PUBLIC SAFETY

Crime Rate

Area	All Crimes	Violent Crimes				Property Crimes		
		Murder	Forcible Rape	Robbery	Aggrav. Assault	Burglary	Larceny -Theft	Motor Vehicle Theft
City	6,933.2	0.0	69.4	73.9	351.6	1,081.6	5,038.6	318.0
Suburbs[1]	2,632.8	3.0	21.9	15.9	128.3	350.1	1,981.3	132.3
MSA[2]	3,955.4	2.1	36.5	33.7	197.0	575.1	2,921.6	189.4
U.S.	4,615.5	6.3	34.4	165.2	360.5	862.0	2,728.1	459.0

Note: Crime rate is the number of crimes per 100,000 population; (1) Defined as all areas within the Metropolitan Statistical Area but located outside the central city; (2) Metropolitan Statistical Area - see Appendix A for areas included
Source: FBI Uniform Crime Reports, 1998

RECREATION

Culture and Recreation

Museums	Symphony Orchestras	Opera Companies	Dance Companies	Professional Theatres	Zoos	Pro Sports Teams
3	1	0	0	1	1	0

Source: Musical America, International Directory of the Performing Arts, 1999; Official Museum Directory, 2000; Stern's Performing Arts Directory, 1997; USA Today Four Sport Stadium Guide, 1997; Career Opportunities in Theatre and the Performing Arts, 1999

Library System

The Tippecanoe County Public Library has no branches and holdings of 266,444 volumes.
American Library Directory, 1999-2000

MEDIA

Newspapers

Name	Type	Freq.	Distribution	Circulation
Journal and Courier	General	7x/wk	Local	38,567
The Purdue Exponent	n/a	5x/wk	Camp/Comm	20,000

Note: Includes newspapers with circulations of 200 or more located in the city; n/a not available
Source: Burrelle's Media Directory, 1999 Edition

Television Stations

Name	Ch.	Affiliation	Type	Owner
WLFI	18	CBST	Commercial	Blade Communications Inc.

Note: Stations included broadcast in the Lafayette metro area; n/a not available
Source: Burrelle's Media Directory, 1999 Edition

AM Radio Stations

Call Letters	Freq. (kHz)	Target Audience	Station Format	Music Format
WBAA	920	General	M/N/T	Jazz
WAZY	1410	n/a	n/a	n/a
WASK	1450	General	M/N/S	Oldies

Note: Stations included broadcast in the Lafayette metro area; n/a not available
Target Audience: A=Asian; B=Black; C=Christian; E=Ethnic; F=French; G=General; H=Hispanic; M=Men; N=Native American; R=Religious; S=Senior Citizen; W=Women; Y=Young Adult; Z=Children
Station Format: E=Educational; M=Music; N=News; S=Sports; T=Talk
Source: Burrelle's Media Directory, 1999 Edition

FM Radio Stations

Call Letters	Freq. (mHz)	Target Audience	Station Format	Music Format
WHPL	89.9	General	E/M/N/T	Christian
WJEF	91.9	General	M	Oldies
WKHY	93.5	General	M	AOR/Classic Rock
WEZV	95.3	General	M/N/S	Easy Listening
WGBD	95.7	Men	M/N/S	Alternative
WAZY	96.5	General	M/N/S	Adult Contemporary
WASK	98.7	General	M/N/S	Oldies
WBAA	101.3	General	M	Classical
WKOA	105.3	General	M/N	Country

Note: Stations included broadcast in the Lafayette metro area
Station Format: E=Educational; M=Music; N=News; S=Sports; T=Talk
Target Audience: A=Asian; B=Black; C=Christian; E=Ethnic; F=French; G=General; H=Hispanic; M=Men; N=Native American; R=Religious; S=Senior Citizen; W=Women; Y=Young Adult; Z=Children
Music Format: AOR=Album Oriented Rock; MOR=Middle-of-the-Road
Source: Burrelle's Media Directory, 1999 Edition

WEATHER

Temperature/Precipitation/Humidity

	Jan	Feb	Mar	Apr	May	Jun	Jul	Aug	Sep	Oct	Nov	Dec	Yr.
Max. High Temp. (°F)	61	67	78	86	90	98	97	96	93	87	76	64	98
Avg. High Temp. (°F)	31	35	44	60	72	80	82	82	76	66	50	35	59
Avg. Temp. (°F)	23	27	36	50	61	69	72	71	65	54	41	27	50
Avg. Low Temp. (°F)	16	20	28	40	51	59	62	61	54	43	32	20	41
Min. Low Temp. (°F)	-19	-11	-4	19	29	40	44	37	33	20	-1	-14	-19
Avg. Precip. (in.)	1.8	2.2	2.7	3.9	3.6	4.6	4.6	3.0	2.0	1.9	2.4	1.8	34.5
Avg. Snowfall (in.)	5.4	7.1	4.0	1.9	0	0	0	0	0	0	1.5	6.3	26.2
Avg. Rel. Hum. (%)	77	79	74	68	67	68	72	73	70	68	73	78	72

Source: National Climatic Data Center, International Station Meteorological Climate Summary, 3/95

Weather Conditions

Temperature			Precipitation		
0°F & below	32°F & below	90°F & above	0.1 inch or more precip.	1.5 inch or more snow/ice	Thunder-storms
10	129	11	64	6	43

Note: Figures are average number of days per year
Source: National Climatic Data Center, International Station Meteorological Climate Summary, 3/95

AIR & WATER QUALITY

Maximum Pollutant Concentrations

	Particulate Matter (ug/m^3)	Carbon Monoxide (ppm)	Sulfur Dioxide (ppm)	Nitrogen Dioxide (ppm)	Ozone (ppm)	Lead (ug/m^3)
MSA[1] Level	n/a	n/a	n/a	n/a	n/a	n/a
NAAQS[2]	150	9	0.140	0.053	0.12	1.50
Met NAAQS	n/a	n/a	n/a	n/a	n/a	n/a

Note: (1) Metropolitan Statistical Area - see Appendix A for areas included; (2) National Ambient Air Quality Standards; ppm = parts per million; ug/m^3 = micrograms per cubic meter; n/a not available
Source: EPA, National Air Quality and Emissions Trends Report, 1997

Pollutant Standards Index

Data not available.
EPA, National Air Quality and Emissions Trends Report, 1997

Drinking Water

Water System Name	Pop. Served	Primary Water Source Type	Number of Violations in 1998-99	Type of Violation/ Contaminants
Lafayette Water Works	50,525	Ground	None	None

Note: Data as of January 19, 2000
Source: EPA, Office of Ground Water and Drinking Water, Safe Drinking Water Information System

Lafayette tap water is alkaline, very hard, and fluoridated.
Editor & Publisher Market Guide, 2000

Lancaster, Pennsylvania

Background

Lancaster, Pennsylvania is located in the southeast section of the state, approximately 75 miles west of Philadelphia and 45 miles southeast of Harrisburg. Lancaster is the county seat of Lancaster County. The city is close to the Susquehanna River, in a valley characterized by rolling countryside with large areas of farmland.

Lancaster and nearby communities form the county's metropolitan center. Trade and manufacturing are primary economic activities. Lancaster County is known for its fertile soil, making it a valuable agricultural region. It is also a popular tourist area, based on its scenic qualities, historic sites and other attractions. The city and surrounding areas are closely associated with early American history and with the Pennsylvania Dutch culture. Lancaster County is also known for the community of Amish farmers who live very traditionally. At the same time, Lancaster and the county have experienced significant modern growth and development.

Several colleges in the Lancaster community include Franklin and Marshall College, which was founded in 1787 with Benjamin Franklin as an original benefactor, Millersville University, Lancaster Theological Seminary, Pennsylvania School of Art and Design and Elizabethtown College.

The Conestogas and other Native American groups occupied the region in the late 17th and early 18th Centuries. Colonial settlement of the Lancaster area began around 1717. In 1729, Lancaster County was established, named for a community in England. Lancaster was designated as the county seat. It became a borough in 1742 and a city in 1818.

Lancaster was an early center for trade and manufacturing, including guns and wagons. It was the site of several important political events in the 18th Century, including a brief stay by the Continental Congress in 1777. Lancaster was the state capital from 1799 to 1812. Followers of Anabaptist religious beliefs were among the settlers of Lancaster County. Many became assimilated into the larger society, but the Amish resisted modern technology to retain their traditional lifestyles.

Lancaster and the region grew steadily in the 19th and 20th Centuries. In the 1980s and 1990s, the area entered a growth period, which is projected to continue. Lancaster is the headquarters of Armstrong World Industries Inc., a global flooring and ceiling manufacturer. Regional products also include farm equipment and other machinery, electric and electronic equipment, metals, clothing, foods and commercial printing, among others. Agriculture continues to be a mainstay. Other significant economic sectors include health-care, wholesale and retail trades, tourism, education, finance, services and construction.

An underlying shift in population and economic growth from the city to outlying communities has prompted urban revitalization and redevelopment efforts, including projects initiated by a coalition of business leaders. Concerns about sprawl, meanwhile, have prompted efforts to protect farmland and the area's rural qualities through planning and preservation initiatives.

Lancaster contains a large downtown historic district, in addition to other individual historic buildings, neighborhoods and museums. Penn Square is a section of the city that includes the Heritage Center Museum and the nearby Central Market, a farmer's market established in the 18th Century. Wheatland in Lancaster Township is a museum at the home of President James Buchanan.

The Fulton Opera House, built in 1852, is a restored downtown venue for concerts and other events. Other venues and cultural organizations include the Lancaster Museum of Art, Lancaster Symphony Orchestra, Lancaster Opera Company, American Music Theater, Dutch Apple Dinner Theater and the activities of area colleges.

Parks in Lancaster include Conestoga Pines Park and Lancaster County Central Park, among others. Lancaster is also accessible to state parks and other recreation areas in the region.

Lancaster is governed by a Mayor and City Council.

General Rankings and Evaluative Comments

- Lancaster was ranked #171 out of 354 metropolitan areas in *Places Rated Almanac*. Criteria: cost of living, climate, crime, transportation, job outlook, education, the arts, health care, and recreation. *Places Rated Almanac, Millennium Edition, 2000*

- Cognetics studied 273 metro areas in the United States, ranking them by entrepreneurial activity. Lancaster was ranked #110 out of 134 smaller metro areas. Criteria: Significant Starts (firms started in the last 10 years that still employ at least 5 people) and Young Growers (percent of firms 10 years old or less that grew significantly during the last 4 years). *Cognetics, "Entrepreneurial Hot Spots: The Best Places in America to Start and Grow a Company," 1999*

- Reliastar Financial Corporation ranked the 125 largest metropolitan areas according to the general financial security of residents. Lancaster was ranked #8 out of 125 with a score of 15.0 (the percentage a metropolitan area is above or below the metropolitan norm; a metro area with a score of 10.6 is 10.6% above the metro average). Criteria: Earnings and Wealth Potential (household income, education, net assets, cost of living); Safety Net (health insurance, retirement savings, life insurance, income support programs); Personal Threats (unemployment rate, low-income households, crime rate); Community Economic Vitality (cost of community services, job quality, job creation, housing costs). *Reliastar Financial Corporation, "The Best Cities to Earn and Save Money: A Ranking of the Largest 125 U.S. Cities," 2000 Edition*

Business Environment

STATE ECONOMY

State Economic Profile

"Pennsylvania's economy has lagged the nation for several years, a trend that will only get worse. While Philadelphia has seen some resurgence, it has not been enough to offset declines in the rest of the state. Pennsylvania's poor demographic outlook will confine it to slow growth at best in 2000. Expansions by high-tech and biotech firms, such as Lucent, SAP and SmithKline Beecham, will help Pennsylvania's weak job outlook, although these gains will be limited to the eastern part of the state.

Pennsylvania employment grew at the low rate of 0.8% in 1998, driven largely by the 1.0% increase in Philadelphia. In contrast, Pittsburgh lost jobs at a rate of 0.1%. While many areas of the country are experiencing declining manufacturing employment, due to weak export demand and long-term restructuring, Pittsburgh is one of the few urban areas that is also losing service jobs, at a rate of 0.4% in 1998. Services employment for Pennsylvania grew 1.3% and 1.9% for Philadelphia in 1998.

Some of western Pennsylvania's problems stem from its declining steel sector. Weak steel prices, over capacity and a flood of cheap imports have undermined Pennsylvania's steel industry. Even with import restraints and renewed world demand, the outlook for Pennsylvania's steel industry remains bleak. Pennsylvania's steel producers' biggest problem is US mini-mills that are sweeping the industry. Further declines in Pennsylvania's steel industry are likely in 2000.

Few states lose more residents every year than Pennsylvania. Its continued loss of younger households will constrain labor market growth and pose problems for its housing market. Home sales were flat in 1998, and residential permits were up only 3%. Both sales and starts should contract in the near future." National Association of Realtors, Economic Profiles: The Fifty States and the District of Columbia, http://nar.realtor.com/databank/profiles.htm

EXPORTS

Total Export Sales

Area	1995 ($000)	1996 ($000)	1997 ($000)	1998 ($000)	% Chg. 1995-98	% Chg. 1997-98
MSA[1]	581,528	626,225	620,250	591,005	1.6	-4.7
U.S.	583,030,524	622,827,063	687,597,999	680,474,251	16.7	-1.0

Note: (1) Metropolitan Statistical Area - see Appendix A for areas included
Source: U.S. Department of Commerce, International Trade Association, Metropolitan Area Exports: An Export Performance Report on Over 250 U.S. Cities, November 10, 1999

CITY FINANCES

City Government Finances

Component	1995 ($million)	1995 (per capita $)
Revenue	27.6	477
Expenditure	35.4	613
Debt Outstanding	6.6	114

Source: 1999 County and City Extra, Annual Metro, City, and County Data Book

City Government Revenue by Source

Source	1995 ($million)	1995 (per capita $)
Intergovernmental	5.8	100
Taxes	11.5	200
Property	7.7	134
Sales and Gross Receipts	0.0	0

Source: 1999 County and City Extra, Annual Metro, City, and County Data Book

City Government Expenditures by Function

Function	1995 ($million)	1995 (per capita $)	1995 (%)
Public Welfare	0.0	0	0.0
Highways	2.1	37	6.2
Parking Facilities	0.0	0	0.0
Education	0.0	0	0.0
Health and Hospitals	0.1	2	0.4
Police Protection	6.3	110	18.0
Sewerage and Sanitation	8.5	147	24.1
Parks and Recreation	1.3	23	3.8
Housing and Community Development	2.5	44	7.2
Interest on Debt	0.2	4	0.8

Source: 1999 County and City Extra, Annual Metro, City, and County Data Book

Municipal Bond Ratings

Area	Moody's
City	A1

Source: Mergent Bond Record, 2/2000

POPULATION

Population Growth

Area	1980 Census	1990 Census	1999 Estimate	2004 Projection	Population Growth (%) 1990-1999	Population Growth (%) 1999-2004
City	54,725	55,551	51,935	49,728	-6.5	-4.2
MSA[1]	362,346	422,822	458,907	465,904	8.5	1.5
U.S.	226,545,805	248,765,170	272,212,864	283,625,312	9.4	4.2

Note: (1) Metropolitan Statistical Area - see Appendix A for areas included
Source: 1990 Census of Population and Housing, Summary Tape File 3C; Claritas, Inc.

Number of Households and Average Household Size

Area	1980 Census	1990 Census	1999 Estimate	2004 Projection	1999 Average Household Size
City	20,486	21,203	19,678	18,806	2.64
MSA[1]	123,865	151,352	162,803	165,146	2.82
U.S.	80,389,592	91,993,582	102,048,200	107,302,392	2.67

Note: (1) Metropolitan Statistical Area - see Appendix A for areas included
Source: 1990 Census of Population and Housing, Summary Tape File 3C; Claritas, Inc.

Race/Ethnicity of City Population

Race/Ethnicity	1990 Census Population	1990 Census %	1999 Estimate Population	1999 Estimate %	% Change 1990-1999
White, Non-Hispanic	37,170	66.9	28,307	54.5	-23.8
Black, Non-Hispanic	6,105	11.0	6,384	12.3	4.6
Asian, Non-Hispanic	1,042	1.9	1,232	2.4	18.2
Other, Non-Hispanic	253	0.5	195	0.4	-22.9
Hispanic	10,981	19.8	15,817	30.5	44.0

Source: 1990 Census of Population and Housing, Summary Tape File 3C; Claritas, Inc.

Race/Ethnicity of Metropolitan Statistical Area Population

Race/Ethnicity	1990 Census		1999 Estimate		% Change 1990-1999
	Population	%	Population	%	
White, Non-Hispanic	393,751	93.1	416,137	90.7	5.7
Black, Non-Hispanic	8,821	2.1	11,057	2.4	25.3
Asian, Non-Hispanic	4,676	1.1	7,046	1.5	50.7
Other, Non-Hispanic	732	0.2	783	0.2	7.0
Hispanic	14,842	3.5	23,884	5.2	60.9

Note: See Appendix A for areas included in the Metropolitan Statistical Area
Source: 1990 Census of Population and Housing, Summary Tape File 3C; Claritas, Inc.

Ancestry

Area	German	Irish	English	Italian	U.S.	French	Polish	Dutch
City	39.1	12.0	6.8	4.4	3.1	1.9	1.7	1.6
MSA[1]	58.9	12.8	8.9	4.4	3.9	2.4	2.4	2.4
U.S.	23.3	15.6	13.1	5.9	5.3	4.2	3.8	2.5

Note: Figures are percentages and include persons that reported multiple ancestry (eg. if a person reported being Irish and Italian, they were included in both columns); (1) Metropolitan Statistical Area - see Appendix A for areas included
Source: 1990 Census of Population and Housing, Summary Tape File 3C

Median Age

Area	1990 Census	1999 Estimate
City	29.7	32.7
MSA[1]	32.8	35.9
U.S.	32.9	35.7

Note: (1) Metropolitan Statistical Area - see Appendix A for areas included
Source: 1990 Census of Population and Housing, Summary Tape File 3C; Claritas, Inc.

Male/Female Population

Area	Number of Males		Number of Females		Males per 100 Females	
	1990	1999	1990	1999	1990	1999
City	26,901	25,164	28,650	26,771	93.9	94.0
MSA[1]	205,296	222,498	217,526	236,409	94.4	94.1
U.S.	121,172,379	132,803,736	127,537,494	139,409,136	95.0	95.3

Note: (1) Metropolitan Statistical Area - see Appendix A for areas included
Source: 1990 Census of Population, General Population Characteristics; Claritas, Inc.

INCOME

Per Capita/Median/Average Income

Area	Per Capita ($)			Median Household ($)			Average Household ($)		
	1989	1999	% Chg.	1989	1999	% Chg.	1989	1999	% Chg.
City	10,693	15,162	41.8	22,210	29,305	31.9	27,292	38,998	42.9
MSA[1]	14,235	20,169	41.7	33,255	44,912	35.1	39,237	56,288	43.5
U.S.	14,420	21,350	48.1	30,056	40,525	34.8	38,453	56,184	46.1

Note: (1) Metropolitan Statistical Area - see Appendix A for areas included; 1989 data is from the 1990 Census; 1999 data is estimated by Claritas, Inc.
Source: 1990 Census of Population, General Population Characteristics; Claritas, Inc.

Household Income Distribution

Area	Percent of Households Earning								
	Under $5,000	$5,000 -14,999	$15,000 -24,999	$25,000 -34,999	$35,000 -49,999	$50,000 -74,999	$75,000 -99,000	$100,000 -149,999	$150,000 and up
City	4.3	19.5	19.0	15.6	16.9	15.9	5.3	2.4	1.1
MSA[1]	2.0	9.4	12.6	12.9	19.3	24.7	10.2	5.8	3.2
U.S.	3.9	13.3	13.8	12.6	16.2	19.4	9.7	6.6	4.6

Note: Data as of 1999; (1) Metropolitan Statistical Area - see Appendix A for areas included
Source: Claritas, Inc.

Effective Buying Income

Area	Per Capita ($)	Median Household ($)	Average Household ($)
City	13,475	27,748	35,141
MSA[1]	18,322	42,633	50,455
U.S.	17,496	36,603	47,036

Note: Data as of 1/1/2000; (1) Metropolitan Statistical Area - see Appendix A for areas included
Source: Standard Rate & Data Service, Newspaper Advertising Source, March 2000

Effective Household Buying Income Distribution

Area	% of Households Earning						
	$10,000 -$19,999	$20,000 -$34,999	$35,000 -$49,999	$50,000 -$74,999	$75,000 -$99,000	$100,000 -$124,999	$125,000 and up
City	20.9	26.3	17.8	14.8	4.0	1.0	1.0
MSA[1]	11.9	21.0	20.8	24.8	9.2	2.9	3.0
U.S.	15.0	21.6	17.6	19.6	8.4	3.0	3.3

Note: Data as of 1/1/2000; (1) Metropolitan Statistical Area - see Appendix A for areas included
Source: Standard Rate & Data Service, Newspaper Advertising Source, March 2000

Poverty Rates by Age

Area	People of All Ages	People Under 18 Years Old	Related Children Age 5-17 in Families in Poverty
City	22.0	n/a	n/a
County	7.8	12.4	10.8
U.S.	13.8	20.8	18.7

Note: Figures show the percent of people living below the poverty line in 1995. The
average poverty threshold was $15,569 for a family of four in 1995; n/a not available
Source: Bureau of the Census, Small Area Income and Poverty Estimates Program;
U.S. Department of Housing and Urban Development

EMPLOYMENT

Labor Force and Employment

Area	Civilian Labor Force			Workers Employed		
	Dec. 1998	Dec. 1999	% Chg.	Dec. 1998	Dec. 1999	% Chg.
City	25,905	25,952	0.2	24,984	25,037	0.2
MSA[1]	241,760	242,013	0.1	236,334	236,843	0.2
U.S.	138,297,000	139,941,000	1.2	132,732,000	134,696,000	1.5

Note: Data is not seasonally adjusted and covers workers 16 years of age and older;
(1) Metropolitan Statistical Area - see Appendix A for areas included
Source: Bureau of Labor Statistics, http://stats.bls.gov

Unemployment Rate

Area	1999											
	Jan.	Feb.	Mar.	Apr.	May	Jun.	Jul.	Aug.	Sep.	Oct.	Nov.	Dec.
City	4.8	4.7	4.5	4.1	4.1	4.8	4.5	4.1	4.4	3.9	4.1	3.5
MSA[1]	3.0	3.0	2.8	2.3	2.4	2.7	2.8	2.7	2.8	2.5	2.5	2.1
U.S.	4.8	4.7	4.4	4.1	4.0	4.5	4.5	4.2	4.1	3.8	3.8	3.7

Note: Data is not seasonally adjusted and covers workers 16 years of age and older; all figures are percentages; (1) Metropolitan Statistical Area - see Appendix A for areas included
Source: Bureau of Labor Statistics, http://stats.bls.gov

Employment by Industry

Sector	MSA[1]		U.S.
	Number of Employees	Percent of Total	Percent of Total
Services	58,000	25.7	30.2
Retail Trade	42,100	18.7	18.1
Government	19,600	8.7	15.8
Manufacturing	57,200	25.4	14.1
Finance/Insurance/Real Estate	10,400	4.6	5.9
Wholesale Trade	15,000	6.7	5.4
Transportation/Public Utilities	8,800	3.9	5.3
Construction	13,800	6.1	4.8
Mining	400	0.2	0.4

Note: Figures cover non-farm employment as of 12/99 and are not seasonally adjusted;
(1) Metropolitan Statistical Area - see Appendix A for areas included
Source: Bureau of Labor Statistics, http://stats.bls.gov

Employment by Occupation

Occupation Category	City (%)	MSA[1] (%)	U.S. (%)
White Collar	46.0	48.3	58.1
Executive/Admin./Management	8.4	9.8	12.3
Professional	10.6	11.2	14.1
Technical & Related Support	2.9	3.0	3.7
Sales	9.6	10.5	11.8
Administrative Support/Clerical	14.5	13.8	16.3
Blue Collar	36.3	35.4	26.2
Precision Production/Craft/Repair	10.5	13.6	11.3
Machine Operators/Assem./Insp.	14.2	10.7	6.8
Transportation/Material Movers	4.2	5.1	4.1
Cleaners/Helpers/Laborers	7.4	6.0	3.9
Services	16.6	12.4	13.2
Farming/Forestry/Fishing	1.1	3.9	2.5

Note: Figures cover workers 16 years of age and older;
(1) Metropolitan Statistical Area - see Appendix A for areas included
Source: 1990 Census of Population and Housing, Summary Tape File 3C

Occupational Employment Projections: 1994 - 2005

High Demand Occupations (ranked by annual openings)	Fast-Growing Occupations[1] (ranked by percent growth)
1. Cashiers	1. Personal and home care aides
2. Salespersons, retail	2. Electronic pagination systems workers
3. Waiters & waitresses	3. Computer engineers
4. Registered nurses	4. Systems analysts
5. General managers & top executives	5. Home health aides
6. Janitors/cleaners/maids, ex. priv. hshld.	6. Human services workers
7. Secretaries, except legal & medical	7. Teachers, preschool and kindergarten
8. General office clerks	8. Computer support specialists
9. Teachers, secondary school	9. Physical therapists
10. Marketing & sales, supervisors	10. Residential counselors

Note: Projections cover Pennsylvania; (1) Excludes occupations with total job growth less than 300
Source: Pennsylvania Workforce 2005, Winter 1997-98

Average Wages

Occupation	$/Hr.	Occupation	$/Hr.
Accountants and Auditors	18.09	Maids and Housekeepers	7.59
Assemblers and Fabricators	10.75	Maintenance Repairers	12.15
Automotive Mechanics	12.93	Marketing/Advertising/PR Managers	28.27
Bookkeepers	11.34	Nurses, Licensed Practical	12.81
Carpenters	13.52	Nurses, Registered	17.98
Cashiers	6.87	Nursing Aides/Orderlies/Attendants	9.34
Clerks, General Office	9.08	Physicians and Surgeons	51.41
Clerks, Shipping/Receiving/Traffic	12.14	Receptionists/Information Clerks	9.05
Computer Programmers	21.03	Sales Reps., Exc. Scientific/Retail	19.71
Computer Support Specialists	16.53	Sales Reps., Scientific, Exc. Retail	20.31
Cooks, Restaurant	8.01	Salespersons, Retail	8.79
Electricians	16.42	Secretaries, Except Legal/Medical	10.81
Financial Managers	27.21	Stock Clerks, Sales Floor	7.75
First-Line Supervisors/Mgrs., Sales	15.33	Systems Analysts	22.43
Food Preparation Workers	7.03	Teacher Aides	-
General Managers/Top Executives	28.27	Teachers, Elementary School	22.00
Guards	9.32	Teachers, Secondary School	22.96
Hand Packers	9.25	Telemarketers	9.07
Janitors and Cleaners	8.80	Truck Drivers, Heavy/Tractor-Trailer	13.97
Laborers, Landscaping	8.95	Truck Drivers, Light	10.19
Lawyers	26.54	Waiters and Waitresses	6.36

Note: Wage data is for 1998 and covers the Metropolitan Statistical Area (see Appendix A for areas included). Hourly wages for elementary and secondary school teachers were calculated by the editors from annual wage data assuming a 40 hour work week; Dashes indicate that data was not available.
Source: Bureau of Labor Statistics, 1998 Metropolitan Area Occupational Employment and Wage Estimates

TAXES

Major State and Local Tax Rates

State Corporate Income (%)	State Personal Income (%)	Residential Property (%)	Sales & Use		State Gasoline (cents/ gallon)	State Cigarette (cents/ pack)
			State (%)	Local (%)		
9.99	2.8	2.45	6.0	None	25.9[a]	31.0

Note: Personal/corporate income, sales, gasoline and cigarette tax rates as of January 2000.
Property tax rates as of April 2000; (a) Rate is comprised of 12 cents excise and 13.9 cents motor carrier tax.
Source: Federation of Tax Administrators, www.taxadmin.org; ERI's Relocation Assessor software database, quarterly effective date 4/1/2000

Total Taxes Per Capita and as a Percent of Income

Area	Per Capita Income ($)	Per Capita Taxes ($)			Percent of Income (%)		
		Total	Federal	State/Local	Total	Federal	State/Local
Pennsylvania	29,059	10,185	6,991	3,195	35.1	24.1	11.0
U.S.	28,878	10,298	7,026	3,273	35.7	24.3	11.3

Note: Figures are for 1999
Source: Tax Foundation, www.taxfoundation.org

COMMERCIAL UTILITIES

Typical Monthly Electric Bills

Area	Commercial Service ($/month)		Industrial Service ($/month)	
	12 kW demand 1,500 kWh	100 kW demand 30,000 kWh	1,000 kW demand 400,000 kWh	20,000 kW demand 10,000,000 kWh
City	170	2,388	27,078	413,040
U.S.	150	2,174	23,995	508,569

Note: Based on rates in effect January 1, 1999
Source: Edison Electric Institute, Typical Residential, Commercial and Industrial Bills, Winter 1999

TRANSPORTATION

Transportation Statistics

Average minutes to work (1990)	17.0
Interstate highways	US-30; US-222
Bus lines	
In-city (1998)	Red Rose Transit Authority, 33 buses
Inter-city (1999)	1
Passenger air service	
Airport	Lancaster Airport
Airlines (1999)	n/a
Enplaned passengers (1998)	26,609
Amtrak service	Yes
Motor freight carriers (1999)	20
Major waterways/ports	None

Source: FAA DOT/TSC CY1998 ACAIS Database; National Transit Database, 1998; Editor & Publisher Market Guide, 2000; Amtrak National Time Table, Fall 1999/Winter 2000; 1990 Census of Population and Housing, STF 3C; Jane's Urban Transport Systems 1999-2000

Means of Transportation to Work

Area	Car/Truck/Van		Public Transportation			Bicycle	Walked	Other Means	Worked at Home
	Drove Alone	Car-pooled	Bus	Subway	Railroad				
City	61.0	15.9	5.1	0.1	0.1	0.8	13.8	1.3	1.9
MSA[1]	75.0	12.0	1.0	0.0	0.1	0.5	5.7	1.0	4.8
U.S.	73.2	13.4	3.0	1.5	0.5	0.4	3.9	1.2	3.0

Note: Figures shown are percentages and only include workers 16 years of age and older;
(1) Metropolitan Statistical Area - see Appendix A for areas included
Source: 1990 Census of Population and Housing, Summary Tape File 3C

BUSINESSES

Major Business Headquarters

Company Name	1999 Rankings	
	Fortune 500	Forbes 500
Armstrong World Industries	449	-

Note: Companies listed are located in the city; dashes indicate no ranking
Fortune 500: Companies that produce a 10-K are ranked 1 to 500 based on 1999 revenue
Forbes 500: Private companies are ranked 1 to 500 based on 1998 revenue
Source: Forbes, December 13, 1999; Fortune, April 17, 2000

HOTELS & MOTELS

Hotels/Motels

Area	Hotels/ Motels	Rooms	Luxury-Level Hotels/Motels		Average Minimum Rates ($)		
			♦♦♦♦	♦♦♦♦♦	♦♦	♦♦♦	♦♦♦♦
City	29	3,519	0	0	64	92	n/a
Suburbs	2	70	0	0	n/a	n/a	n/a
Total	31	3,589	0	0	n/a	n/a	n/a

Note: n/a not available; classifications range from one diamond (budget properties with basic amenities) to five diamond (luxury properties).
Source: OAG Business Travel Planner, Winter 1999-2000

Estimated Daily Food and Lodging Costs

Area	Food/Other ($/day)	Average Hotel Cost ($/day)
City	38	69
U.S.	30	55

Source: ERI's Relocation Assessor software database, quarterly effective date 4/1/2000

CONVENTION CENTERS

Convention Centers and Event Sites

Name	Guest Rooms	Meeting Space (sq. ft.)	Capacity (Theatre Style)
Lancaster Hilton Garden Inn	156	1,300	25
Lancaster Host Resort & Conference Ctr.	330	75,000	0

Source: EventSource.com, 3/15/2000

Living Environment

COST OF LIVING

Cost of Living: Homeowner

Cost Element	U.S. ($)	City ($)	Differential ($)	Percent of U.S. Average
Consumables	14,516	14,559	43	100.3
Transportation	5,957	6,436	479	108.0
Health Services	2,012	2,051	39	101.9
Housing/Utilities/Prop. Tax	16,337	18,605	2,268	113.9
Income+Payroll Taxes	12,615	11,813	-802	93.6
Miscellaneous	8,563	8,563	0	100.0
Total Cost of Living	60,000	62,027	2,027	103.4

Note: Figures are based on a single income, four person family with gross annual earnings of $60,000, owning an 1,800 square-foot home, and driving two automobiles worth $22,000 30,000 miles per year.
Source: ERI's Relocation Assessor software database, quarterly effective date 4/1/2000

Cost of Living: Renter

Cost Element	U.S. ($)	City ($)	Differential ($)	Percent of U.S. Average
Consumables	10,486	10,470	-16	99.8
Transportation	2,107	2,266	159	107.5
Health Services	1,632	1,657	25	101.5
Rent/Utilities/Insurance	9,299	10,453	1,154	112.4
Income+Payroll Taxes	8,607	8,303	-304	96.5
Miscellaneous	7,869	7,869	0	100.0
Total Cost of Living	40,000	41,018	1,018	102.5

Note: Figures are based on a single income, three person family with gross annual earnings of $40,000, renting a 1,000 square-foot home, and driving one automobile worth $8,000 12,000 miles per year.
Source: ERI's Relocation Assessor software database, quarterly effective date 4/1/2000

HOUSING

Median Home Prices and Housing Affordability

Area	Median Price[2] 4th Qtr. 1999 ($)	HOI[3] 4th Qtr. 1999	Affordability Rank[4]
MSA[1]	111,000	77.0	44
U.S.	139,000	63.8	–

Note: (1) Metropolitan Statistical Area - see Appendix A for areas included; (2) U.S. figures calculated from the sales of 687,516 new and existing homes in 192 markets; (3) Housing Opportunity Index - percent of homes sold that were within the reach of the median income household at the prevailing mortgage interest rate; (4) Rank is from 1-192 with 1 being most affordable
Source: National Association of Home Builders, Housing Opportunity Index, 4th Quarter 1999

Estimated Home Price

Area	Price ($)
City	136,640
U.S.	135,855

Note: Figures are based on an 1,800 square-foot home
Source: ERI's Relocation Assessor software database, quarterly effective date 4/1/2000

Estimated Rent

Area	Rent ($/month)
City	724
U.S.	651

Note: Figures are based on a 1,000 square-foot home
Source: ERI's Relocation Assessor software database, quarterly effective date 4/1/2000

Median Home Price Projection

It is projected that the median home price in the metropolitan area will increase from $125,117 in 1999 to $167,906 in 2010, an increase of 34.2%
Kiplinger's Personal Finance Magazine, January 2000

RESIDENTIAL UTILITIES

Average Residential Utility Costs

Area	All Electric ($/mth)	Part Electric ($/mth)	Other Energy ($/mth)	Phone ($/mth)
City	–	52.35	65.91	17.46
U.S.	99.25	55.47	43.48	20.29

Source: ACCRA, Cost of Living Index, 3rd Quarter 1999

HEALTH CARE

Average Health Care Costs

Area	Hospital ($/day)	Doctor ($/visit)	Dentist ($/visit)
City	340.00	50.75	65.00
U.S.	440.96	53.83	68.42

Note: Hospital—based on a semi-private room; Doctor—based on a general practitioner's routine exam of an established patient; Dentist—based on adult teeth cleaning and periodic oral exam.
Source: ACCRA, Cost of Living Index, 3rd Quarter 1999

Distribution of Office-Based Physicians

Area	Family/Gen. Practitioners	Specialists		
		Medical	Surgical	Other
MSA[1]	166	122	132	125

Note: Data as of 12/31/97; (1) Metropolitan Statistical Area - see Appendix A for areas included
Source: American Medical Assn., Physician Characteristics & Distribution in the U.S., 1999

Hospitals

Lancaster has 3 general medical and surgical hospitals.
AHA Guide to the Healthcare Field, 1999-2000

EDUCATION

Public School District Statistics

District Name	Num. Sch.	Enroll.	Classroom Teachers	Pupils per Teacher	Minority Pupils (%)	Current Exp.[1] ($/pupil)
Conestoga Valley SD	7	3,599	216	16.7	n/a	n/a
Lancaster County Academy	1	70	n/a	n/a	n/a	n/a
Lancaster SD	19	10,997	636	17.3	n/a	n/a
Manheim Township SD	8	4,779	273	17.5	n/a	n/a

Note: Data covers the 1997-1998 school year unless otherwise noted; (1) Data covers fiscal year 1996; SD = School District; ISD = Independent School District; n/a not available
Source: National Center for Education Statistics, Common Core of Data Public Education Agency Universe 1997-98; National Center for Education Statistics, Characteristics of the 100 Largest Public Elementary and Secondary School Districts in the United States: 1997-98, July 1999

Educational Quality

School District	Education Quotient[1]	Graduate Outcome[2]	Community Index[3]	Resource Index[4]
Manheim Township School Dist.	132	136	120	126

Note: Over 1,000 secondary school districts were rated in terms of educational quality. The scores range from a low of 50 to a high of 150; (1) Combination of the Graduate Outcome, Community and Resource indexes weighted to reflect the greater importance of the Graduate Outcome and Resource Index; (2) Based on graduation rates and college board scores (SAT/ACT); (3) Based on the surrounding community's level of affluence and adult education; (4) Based on teacher salaries, per-pupil expenditures and student-teacher ratios.
Source: Expansion Management, Ratings Issue, 1999

Educational Attainment by Race

Area	High School Graduate (%)					Bachelor's Degree (%)				
	Total	White	Black	Other	Hisp.[2]	Total	White	Black	Other	Hisp.[2]
City	61.4	66.6	48.9	36.2	35.5	13.5	15.7	5.6	4.7	2.9
MSA[1]	70.5	71.3	56.6	46.2	43.6	16.7	17.0	9.4	9.7	5.0
U.S.	75.2	77.9	63.1	60.4	49.8	20.3	21.5	11.4	19.4	9.2

*Note: Figures shown cover persons 25 years old and over; (1) Metropolitan Statistical Area -
see Appendix A for areas included; (2) people of Hispanic origin can be of any race*
Source: 1990 Census of Population and Housing, Summary Tape File 3C

School Enrollment by Type

Area	Preprimary				Elementary/High School			
	Public		Private		Public		Private	
	Enrollment	%	Enrollment	%	Enrollment	%	Enrollment	%
City	746	76.0	235	24.0	8,390	91.6	771	8.4
MSA[1]	4,636	61.5	2,900	38.5	56,861	82.6	11,978	17.4
U.S.	2,679,029	59.5	1,824,256	40.5	38,379,689	90.2	4,187,099	9.8

Note: Figures shown cover persons 3 years old and over;
(1) Metropolitan Statistical Area - see Appendix A for areas included
Source: 1990 Census of Population and Housing, Summary Tape File 3C

School Enrollment by Race

Area	Preprimary (%)				Elementary/High School (%)			
	White	Black	Other	Hisp.[1]	White	Black	Other	Hisp.[1]
City	68.1	12.2	19.7	20.2	50.6	19.5	29.9	35.5
MSA[2]	93.6	2.8	3.7	4.2	90.2	3.4	6.4	6.1
U.S.	80.4	12.5	7.1	7.8	74.1	15.6	10.3	12.5

*Note: Figures shown cover persons 3 years old and over; (1) people of Hispanic origin can be of any
race; (2) Metropolitan Statistical Area - see Appendix A for areas included*
Source: 1990 Census of Population and Housing, Summary Tape File 3C

Higher Education

Two-Year Colleges		Four-Year Colleges		Medical Schools	Law Schools	Voc/ Tech
Public	Private	Public	Private			
1	2	0	1	0	0	7

*Source: College Blue Book, Occupational Education, 1999; Medical School Admission Requirements,
1999-2000; Peterson's Guide to Two-Year Colleges, 2000; Peterson's Guide to Four-Year Colleges,
1999; Barron's Guide to Law Schools, 1999*

MAJOR EMPLOYERS

Major Employers

Armstrong World Industries	Brethren Village
Community Hospital of Lancaster	Ferranti Technologies (circuit boards)
Lancaster General Hospital	Lancaster Newspapers
Pennfield Corp. (dairy feeds)	St. Joseph Hospital
Sterling Financial Corp.	

Note: Companies listed are located in the city
*Source: D&B Business Rankings, 1999; Ward's Business Directory, 1999; America's Corporate
Families, 1999*

PUBLIC SAFETY

Crime Rate

Area	All Crimes	Violent Crimes				Property Crimes		
		Murder	Forcible Rape	Robbery	Aggrav. Assault	Burglary	Larceny -Theft	Motor Vehicle Theft
City	7,651.3	12.2	94.0	423.0	320.3	1,688.7	4,465.5	647.6
Suburbs[1]	2,350.1	1.1	10.8	30.1	95.0	421.9	1,631.9	159.4
MSA[2]	3,047.8	2.5	21.8	81.8	124.6	588.6	2,004.8	223.6
U.S.	5,373.5	9.0	39.3	237.7	427.6	1,042.0	3,026.7	591.3

Note: Crime rate is the number of crimes per 100,000 population; (1) Defined as all areas within the Metropolitan Statistical Area but located outside the central city; (2) Metropolitan Statistical Area - see Appendix A for areas included
Source: FBI Uniform Crime Reports, 1994

RECREATION

Culture and Recreation

Museums	Symphony Orchestras	Opera Companies	Dance Companies	Professional Theatres	Zoos	Pro Sports Teams
4	1	1	0	1	0	0

Source: Musical America, International Directory of the Performing Arts, 1999; Official Museum Directory, 2000; Stern's Performing Arts Directory, 1997; USA Today Four Sport Stadium Guide, 1997; Career Opportunities in Theatre and the Performing Arts, 1999

Library System

The Lancaster County Library has three branches.
American Library Directory, 1999-2000

MEDIA

Newspapers

Name	Type	Freq.	Distribution	Circulation
Intelligencer Journal	General	6x/wk	Local	43,151
Lancaster New Era	General	6x/wk	Local	46,249

Note: Includes newspapers with circulations of 200 or more located in the city;
Source: Burrelle's Media Directory, 1999 Edition

Television Stations

Name	Ch.	Affiliation	Type	Owner
WGAL	n/a	NBCT	Commercial	Hearst-Argyle Broadcasting

Note: Stations included broadcast in the Lancaster metro area; n/a not available
Source: Burrelle's Media Directory, 1999 Edition

AM Radio Stations

Call Letters	Freq. (kHz)	Target Audience	Station Format	Music Format
WIOV	1240	G/H	M/N/S/T	Country
WQXA	1250	General	M/N/S	Adult Standards
WLAN	1390	General	M/N/T	MOR
WLPA	1490	General	N/S/T	n/a
WPDC	1600	General	S	n/a

Note: Stations included broadcast in the Lancaster metro area; n/a not available
Target Audience: A=Asian; B=Black; C=Christian; E=Ethnic; F=French; G=General; H=Hispanic; M=Men; N=Native American; R=Religious; S=Senior Citizen; W=Women; Y=Young Adult; Z=Children
Station Format: E=Educational; M=Music; N=News; S=Sports; T=Talk
Music Format: AOR=Album Oriented Rock; MOR=Middle-of-the-Road
Source: Burrelle's Media Directory, 1999 Edition

FM Radio Stations

Call Letters	Freq. (mHz)	Target Audience	Station Format	Music Format
WWEC	88.3	General	M/N/S	Alternative/Classic Rock/Classical/Jazz/Modern Rock/Oldies/Rhythm & Blues/Top 40
WFNM	89.1	General	E/M/T	Alternative/Big Band/Classic Rock/Classical/ Jazz/ Latin/MOR/Oldies/Rhythm & Blues/Urban Contemp.
WJTL	90.3	General	M	Christian
WIXQ	91.7	General	E/M/N/S/T	Alternative/AOR/Classic Rock/Country/MOR/Oldies
WEGK	92.7	General	M/T	Classic Rock
WDAC	94.5	General	M/N/S	Christian
WLAN	96.9	General	M	n/a
WROZ	101.3	General	M	Easy Listening
WIOV	105.1	General	M	Country
WQXA	105.7	General	M/N/S	Alternative
WRKZ	106.7	General	M	Country

Note: Stations included broadcast in the Lancaster metro area; n/a not available
Station Format: E=Educational; M=Music; N=News; S=Sports; T=Talk
Target Audience: A=Asian; B=Black; C=Christian; E=Ethnic; F=French; G=General; H=Hispanic; M=Men; N=Native American; R=Religious; S=Senior Citizen; W=Women; Y=Young Adult; Z=Children
Music Format: AOR=Album Oriented Rock; MOR=Middle-of-the-Road
Source: Burrelle's Media Directory, 1999 Edition

WEATHER

Temperature/Precipitation/Humidity

	Jan	Feb	Mar	Apr	May	Jun	Jul	Aug	Sep	Oct	Nov	Dec	Yr.
Max. High Temp. (°F)	77	78	88	94	98	103	104	107	99	95	82	73	107
Avg. High Temp. (°F)	40	42	53	65	76	83	87	85	79	68	55	42	65
Avg. Temp. (°F)	30	32	41	51	62	70	74	72	66	54	43	32	52
Avg. Low Temp. (°F)	21	22	29	38	48	57	61	60	53	41	32	23	40
Min. Low Temp. (°F)	-27	-18	0	11	27	33	42	39	27	19	-7	-9	-27
Avg. Precip. (in.)	3.1	2.6	3.5	3.5	3.5	3.9	4.3	4.3	3.4	3.2	2.8	3.1	41.4
Avg. Snowfall (in.)	7.2	7.5	6.1	1.3	0	0	0	0	0	0.1	0.9	4.4	27.5
Avg. Rel. Hum. (%)	64	63	59	59	63	65	66	70	71	69	66	66	65

Source: National Climatic Data Center, International Station Meteorological Climate Summary, 3/95

Weather Conditions

Temperature			Precipitation		
0°F & below	32°F & below	90°F & above	0.1 inch or more precip.	1.5 inch or more snow/ice	Thunder-storms
1	123	18	74	6	33

Note: Figures are average number of days per year
Source: National Climatic Data Center, International Station Meteorological Climate Summary, 3/95

AIR & WATER QUALITY

Maximum Pollutant Concentrations

	Particulate Matter (ug/m^3)	Carbon Monoxide (ppm)	Sulfur Dioxide (ppm)	Nitrogen Dioxide (ppm)	Ozone (ppm)	Lead (ug/m^3)
MSA[1] Level	83	3	0.023	0.016	0.13	0.04
NAAQS[2]	150	9	0.140	0.053	0.12	1.50
Met NAAQS	Yes	Yes	Yes	Yes	No	Yes

Note: (1) Metropolitan Statistical Area - see Appendix A for areas included; (2) National Ambient Air Quality Standards; ppm = parts per million; ug/m^3 = micrograms per cubic meter; n/a not available
Source: EPA, National Air Quality and Emissions Trends Report, 1997

Pollutant Standards Index

Data not available.
EPA, National Air Quality and Emissions Trends Report, 1997

Drinking Water

Water System Name	Pop. Served	Primary Water Source Type	Number of Violations in 1998-99	Type of Violation/ Contaminants
Lancaster City Authority	108,000	Surface	None	None

Note: Data as of January 19, 2000
Source: EPA, Office of Ground Water and Drinking Water, Safe Drinking Water Information System

Lancaster tap water is alkaline, hard, and fluoridated.
Editor & Publisher Market Guide, 2000

Melbourne, Florida

Background

Melbourne, Florida is located in southern Brevard County on the central section of the state's Atlantic coastline. It is 75 miles southeast of Orlando, 170 miles north of Miami and 40 miles south of the Kennedy Space Center and Cape Canaveral complex. The city is situated on a natural harbor of the Indian River Lagoon, part of the Intercoastal Waterway. A long narrow barrier island across the lagoon separates most of Melbourne from the ocean, but two high-rise bridges connect the two.

The city covers about 33 square miles and is part of a larger population center that includes Palm Bay, Melbourne Beach, Indialantic, Suntree, Viera and several other communities nearby. This is also part of a larger region known as the Space Coast, a center for space flight, electronics and aerospace industries, and also a popular area for tourists and retirees.

Present day Melbourne was the site of a small settlement established at the harbor when Indian River Lagoon was the primary transportation route in eastern Florida. The region was sparsely populated through the latter 19th Century, with fishing and agriculture among the primary activities. In 1888, residents incorporated the settlement, and named it for Melbourne, Australia. In 1893 railroad service arrived. In the latter 19th Century, the first winter resorts were established in the region.

In 1919 a fire burned much of Melbourne's original waterfront business district.

The presence of the U.S. space program brought major changes after the 1950s. In 1969 Melbourne merged with a neighboring community to the north, Eau Gallie, which gave the city two distinct town centers. In the latter 20th Century, the Space Coast experienced rapid growth, which is expected to continue.

Presently, the Space Coast region's modern economic activity includes the U.S. space program and research, manufacturing and services for the aerospace, electronics and technology industries. Patrick Air Force Base is also nearby. Among Melbourne's largest employers is Harris Electronics and the Bombardier Corporation, makers of Sea-Doo and Ski-Doo water craft, who is headquartered in Melbourne. The city holds a 1,200-acre technology and industrial park around Melbourne International Airport. Retailing, wholesale and other services, including tourism, are also major sectors of the region's economy.

The Space Coast includes about 70 miles of beachfront. Tourists and new residents are attracted by the coastal lifestyle, the space center complex and the proximity to Disney World and other destinations in central Florida. Despite modern growth, this section of the coastline is less developed than Florida's largest resort areas. There are about 250 square miles of protected wildlife refuges in the region, and in certain areas nature-oriented ecotourism is emphasized. While approximately 75 percent of land within Melbourne is developed, the city has approximately 555 acres of public parkland, athletic facilities and scenic corridors. Area marinas offer boat and fishing charters, airboat rides and other activities. The city operates two public golf courses, with numerous other private courses in the area. Other recreational activities include horseback riding, indoor ice skating and the Andretti Thrill Park.

Venues for concerts, sports and other events include Melbourne Auditorium, the Eau Gallie Civic Center and the Maxwell King Center for the Performing Arts. The nearby Space Coast Stadium is the spring training facility for the Florida Marlins major league baseball team, and home of a minor league affiliate. Other attractions and organizations in and around Melbourne include the Brevard Zoo, Henegar Center for the Arts, Alpha Center Phoenix Theater, Brevard Museum of Art and Science, and the Honor America-Liberty Bell Memorial Museum.

Melbourne has a Council-Manager form of government with an elected Mayor and a six-member City Council.

General Rankings and Evaluative Comments

■ Melbourne was ranked #119 out of 354 metropolitan areas in *Places Rated Almanac*. Criteria: cost of living, climate, crime, transportation, job outlook, education, the arts, health care, and recreation. *Places Rated Almanac, Millennium Edition, 2000*

■ Melbourne was selected as one of America's best places to retire. Criteria: safety, climate, housing, culture and recreation, social compatibility, affordability, medical care, transportation, and jobs and/or volunteer opportunities. *Where to Retire: America's Best and Most Affordable Places, 1998*

■ Melbourne was selected as one of the best places to retire by *Retirement Places Rated*. Criteria: cost of living, climate, crime, services, working, and leisure living. The city was ranked #26 out of 187. *Retirement Places Rated, 1999*

■ Cognetics studied 273 metro areas in the United States, ranking them by entrepreneurial activity. Melbourne was ranked #65 out of 134 smaller metro areas. Criteria: Significant Starts (firms started in the last 10 years that still employ at least 5 people) and Young Growers (percent of firms 10 years old or less that grew significantly during the last 4 years). *Cognetics, "Entrepreneurial Hot Spots: The Best Places in America to Start and Grow a Company," 1999*

■ Reliastar Financial Corporation ranked the 125 largest metropolitan areas according to the general financial security of residents. Melbourne was ranked #65 out of 125 with a score of 2.5 (the percentage a metropolitan area is above or below the metropolitan norm; a metro area with a score of 10.6 is 10.6% above the metro average). Criteria: Earnings and Wealth Potential (household income, education, net assets, cost of living); Safety Net (health insurance, retirement savings, life insurance, income support programs); Personal Threats (unemployment rate, low-income households, crime rate); Community Economic Vitality (cost of community services, job quality, job creation, housing costs). *Reliastar Financial Corporation, "The Best Cities to Earn and Save Money: A Ranking of the Largest 125 U.S. Cities," 2000 Edition*

Business Environment

STATE ECONOMY

State Economic Profile

"Florida's economy has been among the nation's strongest in recent years. Job growth has outpaced the nation by a considerable amount since 1992.

While Florida has been able to avoid any significant fallout from the Asian crisis, the weakening of economies in Latin American will dampen both tourism and international trade. 1998 saw the decline in Latin tourism more than offset by domestic visitors. Domestic tourism is projected to soften as U.S. growth cools, offering no offset against the expected decline in Latin tourism. Weaker tourism and trade with Latin American will slow growth in the near future; Florida will still outpace the nation in job growth as Gross State Product growth (GSP) slows.

Over half of Florida's 230,000 new jobs created in 1998 were in the services sector, which grew at 5.2%, more than offsetting a minor decline in manufacturing employment. Much of this growth is taking place in the finance and business services sector.

In spite of strong home sales and a slowing construction market, Florida's price appreciation continued to lag the nation. Although residential permits per 1,000 residents stands at 5.1, well above the national average, this number is only slightly up from 1997 and is poised to decline in the near future.

Growth in Florida, while strong throughout, has been hottest in the Naples, Ft. Myers and Orlando areas. Construction and employment in the construction industry has begun to slow in South Florida. Projected employment and housing gains will be concentrated in Northern and Central Florida. Growing diversification of the economy into financial and business services promises a strong outlook for the years ahead." *National Association of Realtors, Economic Profiles: The Fifty States and the District of Columbia, http://nar.realtor.com/databank/profiles.htm*

EXPORTS

Total Export Sales

Area	1995 ($000)	1996 ($000)	1997 ($000)	1998 ($000)	% Chg. 1995-98	% Chg. 1997-98
MSA[1]	310,089	634,964	408,798	538,531	73.7	31.7
U.S.	583,030,524	622,827,063	687,597,999	680,474,251	16.7	-1.0

Note: (1) Metropolitan Statistical Area - see Appendix A for areas included
Source: U.S. Department of Commerce, International Trade Association, Metropolitan Area Exports: An Export Performance Report on Over 250 U.S. Cities, November 10, 1999

CITY FINANCES

City Government Finances

Component	1995 ($million)	1995 (per capita $)
Revenue	51.3	754
Expenditure	43.6	642
Debt Outstanding	93.3	1,371

Source: 1999 County and City Extra, Annual Metro, City, and County Data Book

City Government Revenue by Source

Source	1995 ($million)	1995 (per capita $)
Intergovernmental	6.3	92
Taxes	20.2	298
Property	7.4	109
Sales and Gross Receipts	11.1	164

Source: 1999 County and City Extra, Annual Metro, City, and County Data Book

City Government Expenditures by Function

Function	1995 ($million)	1995 (per capita $)	1995 (%)
Public Welfare	0.0	0	0.0
Highways	3.1	46	7.3
Parking Facilities	0.0	0	0.0
Education	0.0	0	0.0
Health and Hospitals	0.0	0	0.0
Police Protection	10.5	154	24.1
Sewerage and Sanitation	5.4	80	12.5
Parks and Recreation	7.4	110	17.2
Housing and Community Development	0.5	8	1.3
Interest on Debt	1.4	21	3.4

Source: 1999 County and City Extra, Annual Metro, City, and County Data Book

Municipal Bond Ratings

Area	Moody's
City	Aaa

Source: Mergent Bond Record, 2/2000

POPULATION

Population Growth

Area	1980 Census	1990 Census	1999 Estimate	2004 Projection	Population Growth (%) 1990-1999	Population Growth (%) 1999-2004
City	46,497	59,646	68,939	73,308	15.6	6.3
MSA[1]	272,959	398,978	470,027	503,067	17.8	7.0
U.S.	226,545,805	248,765,170	272,212,864	283,625,312	9.4	4.2

Note: (1) Metropolitan Statistical Area - see Appendix A for areas included
Source: 1990 Census of Population and Housing, Summary Tape File 3C; Claritas, Inc.

Number of Households and Average Household Size

Area	1980 Census	1990 Census	1999 Estimate	2004 Projection	1999 Average Household Size
City	17,911	25,176	29,562	31,976	2.33
MSA[1]	101,783	161,928	192,449	208,917	2.44
U.S.	80,389,592	91,993,582	102,048,200	107,302,392	2.67

Note: (1) Metropolitan Statistical Area - see Appendix A for areas included
Source: 1990 Census of Population and Housing, Summary Tape File 3C; Claritas, Inc.

Race/Ethnicity of City Population

Race/Ethnicity	1990 Census Population	1990 Census %	1999 Estimate Population	1999 Estimate %	% Change 1990-1999
White, Non-Hispanic	50,631	84.9	54,299	78.8	7.2
Black, Non-Hispanic	5,554	9.3	8,320	12.1	49.8
Asian, Non-Hispanic	1,135	1.9	2,154	3.1	89.8
Other, Non-Hispanic	242	0.4	265	0.4	9.5
Hispanic	2,084	3.5	3,901	5.7	87.2

Source: 1990 Census of Population and Housing, Summary Tape File 3C; Claritas, Inc.

Race/Ethnicity of Metropolitan Statistical Area Population

Race/Ethnicity	1990 Census		1999 Estimate		% Change 1990-1999
	Population	%	Population	%	
White, Non-Hispanic	349,297	87.5	391,224	83.2	12.0
Black, Non-Hispanic	30,842	7.7	45,018	9.6	46.0
Asian, Non-Hispanic	4,955	1.2	9,577	2.0	93.3
Other, Non-Hispanic	1,605	0.4	2,169	0.5	35.1
Hispanic	12,279	3.1	22,039	4.7	79.5

Note: See Appendix A for areas included in the Metropolitan Statistical Area
Source: 1990 Census of Population and Housing, Summary Tape File 3C; Claritas, Inc.

Ancestry

Area	German	Irish	English	Italian	U.S.	French	Polish	Dutch
City	23.2	18.0	17.3	6.7	7.6	5.0	3.7	2.3
MSA[1]	25.5	18.8	19.1	7.4	6.2	5.2	3.4	2.8
U.S.	23.3	15.6	13.1	5.9	5.3	4.2	3.8	2.5

Note: Figures are percentages and include persons that reported multiple ancestry (eg. if a person reported being Irish and Italian, they were included in both columns); (1) Metropolitan Statistical Area - see Appendix A for areas included
Source: 1990 Census of Population and Housing, Summary Tape File 3C

Median Age

Area	1990 Census	1999 Estimate
City	34.6	37.9
MSA[1]	36.1	39.3
U.S.	32.9	35.7

Note: (1) Metropolitan Statistical Area - see Appendix A for areas included
Source: 1990 Census of Population and Housing, Summary Tape File 3C; Claritas, Inc.

Male/Female Population

Area	Number of Males		Number of Females		Males per 100 Females	
	1990	1999	1990	1999	1990	1999
City	29,123	33,642	30,523	35,297	95.4	95.3
MSA[1]	197,032	231,491	201,946	238,536	97.6	97.0
U.S.	121,172,379	132,803,736	127,537,494	139,409,136	95.0	95.3

Note: (1) Metropolitan Statistical Area - see Appendix A for areas included
Source: 1990 Census of Population, General Population Characteristics; Claritas, Inc.

INCOME

Per Capita/Median/Average Income

Area	Per Capita ($)			Median Household ($)			Average Household ($)		
	1989	1999	% Chg.	1989	1999	% Chg.	1989	1999	% Chg.
City	13,224	16,697	26.3	25,893	30,334	17.2	30,920	38,476	24.4
MSA[1]	15,093	18,914	25.3	30,534	35,224	15.4	36,898	45,883	24.3
U.S.	14,420	21,350	48.1	30,056	40,525	34.8	38,453	56,184	46.1

Note: (1) Metropolitan Statistical Area - see Appendix A for areas included; 1989 data is from the 1990 Census; 1999 data is estimated by Claritas, Inc.
Source: 1990 Census of Population, General Population Characteristics; Claritas, Inc.

Household Income Distribution

| Area | Percent of Households Earning | | | | | | | |
	Under $5,000	$5,000 -14,999	$15,000 -24,999	$25,000 -34,999	$35,000 -49,999	$50,000 -74,999	$75,000 -99,000	$100,000 -149,999	$150,000 and up
City	4.6	18.5	17.7	16.6	17.6	17.0	4.8	2.3	0.8
MSA[1]	3.2	13.7	16.6	16.1	18.5	19.2	7.2	3.8	1.7
U.S.	3.9	13.3	13.8	12.6	16.2	19.4	9.7	6.6	4.6

Note: Data as of 1999; (1) Metropolitan Statistical Area - see Appendix A for areas included
Source: Claritas, Inc.

Effective Buying Income

Area	Per Capita ($)	Median Household ($)	Average Household ($)
City	14,374	27,805	33,746
MSA[1]	16,644	33,355	40,626
U.S.	17,496	36,603	47,036

Note: Data as of 1/1/2000; (1) Metropolitan Statistical Area - see Appendix A for areas included
Source: Standard Rate & Data Service, Newspaper Advertising Source, March 2000

Effective Household Buying Income Distribution

| Area | % of Households Earning | | | | | | |
	$10,000 -$19,999	$20,000 -$34,999	$35,000 -$49,999	$50,000 -$74,999	$75,000 -$99,000	$100,000 -$124,999	$125,000 and up
City	19.9	27.0	18.9	13.8	3.6	0.9	0.9
MSA[1]	17.0	25.4	19.4	18.3	6.3	1.8	1.7
U.S.	15.0	21.6	17.6	19.6	8.4	3.0	3.3

Note: Data as of 1/1/2000; (1) Metropolitan Statistical Area - see Appendix A for areas included
Source: Standard Rate & Data Service, Newspaper Advertising Source, March 2000

Poverty Rates by Age

Area	People of All Ages	People Under 18 Years Old	Related Children Age 5-17 in Families in Poverty
City	15.9	n/a	n/a
County	11.4	17.7	16.0
U.S.	13.8	20.8	18.7

Note: Figures show the percent of people living below the poverty line in 1995. The average poverty threshold was $15,569 for a family of four in 1995; n/a not available
Source: Bureau of the Census, Small Area Income and Poverty Estimates Program; U.S. Department of Housing and Urban Development

EMPLOYMENT

Labor Force and Employment

| Area | Civilian Labor Force | | | Workers Employed | | |
	Dec. 1998	Dec. 1999	% Chg.	Dec. 1998	Dec. 1999	% Chg.
City	31,493	31,794	1.0	29,999	30,505	1.7
MSA[1]	207,674	209,854	1.0	199,090	202,450	1.7
U.S.	138,297,000	139,941,000	1.2	132,732,000	134,696,000	1.5

Note: Data is not seasonally adjusted and covers workers 16 years of age and older; (1) Metropolitan Statistical Area - see Appendix A for areas included
Source: Bureau of Labor Statistics, http://stats.bls.gov

Unemployment Rate

Area	1999											
	Jan.	Feb.	Mar.	Apr.	May	Jun.	Jul.	Aug.	Sep.	Oct.	Nov.	Dec.
City	5.7	5.1	4.8	4.8	4.5	4.4	4.2	4.4	4.4	4.5	4.7	4.1
MSA[1]	5.0	4.4	4.1	4.1	3.9	3.9	3.6	3.8	3.9	4.0	4.1	3.5
U.S.	4.8	4.7	4.4	4.1	4.0	4.5	4.5	4.2	4.1	3.8	3.8	3.7

Note: Data is not seasonally adjusted and covers workers 16 years of age and older; all figures are percentages; (1) Metropolitan Statistical Area - see Appendix A for areas included
Source: Bureau of Labor Statistics, http://stats.bls.gov

Employment by Industry

Sector	MSA[1]		U.S.
	Number of Employees	Percent of Total	Percent of Total
Services	67,200	35.5	30.2
Retail Trade	40,800	21.6	18.1
Government	25,700	13.6	15.8
Manufacturing	25,800	13.6	14.1
Finance/Insurance/Real Estate	6,300	3.3	5.9
Wholesale Trade	6,500	3.4	5.4
Transportation/Public Utilities	6,100	3.2	5.3
Construction	10,800	5.7	4.8
Mining	n/a	n/a	0.4

Note: Figures cover non-farm employment as of 12/99 and are not seasonally adjusted; (1) Metropolitan Statistical Area - see Appendix A for areas included; n/a not available
Source: Bureau of Labor Statistics, http://stats.bls.gov

Employment by Occupation

Occupation Category	City (%)	MSA[1] (%)	U.S. (%)
White Collar	59.9	61.4	58.1
Executive/Admin./Management	11.9	12.9	12.3
Professional	15.0	16.4	14.1
Technical & Related Support	5.7	5.4	3.7
Sales	12.7	12.1	11.8
Administrative Support/Clerical	14.7	14.6	16.3
Blue Collar	25.0	23.0	26.2
Precision Production/Craft/Repair	13.5	12.8	11.3
Machine Operators/Assem./Insp.	4.7	3.8	6.8
Transportation/Material Movers	3.3	3.1	4.1
Cleaners/Helpers/Laborers	3.4	3.2	3.9
Services	13.5	13.8	13.2
Farming/Forestry/Fishing	1.6	1.8	2.5

Note: Figures cover workers 16 years of age and older; (1) Metropolitan Statistical Area - see Appendix A for areas included
Source: 1990 Census of Population and Housing, Summary Tape File 3C

Occupational Employment Projections: 1996 - 2006

Occupations Expected to Have the Largest Job Growth (ranked by numerical growth)	Fast-Growing Occupations[1] (ranked by percent growth)
1. Cashiers	1. Systems analysts
2. Salespersons, retail	2. Physical therapy assistants and aides
3. General managers & top executives	3. Desktop publishers
4. Registered nurses	4. Home health aides
5. Waiters & waitresses	5. Computer engineers
6. Marketing & sales, supervisors	6. Medical assistants
7. Janitors/cleaners/maids, ex. priv. hshld.	7. Physical therapists
8. General office clerks	8. Paralegals
9. Food preparation workers	9. Emergency medical technicians
10. Hand packers & packagers	10. Occupational therapists

Note: Projections cover Florida; (1) Excludes occupations with total job growth less than 300
Source: U.S. Department of Labor, Employment and Training Administration, America's Labor Market Information System (ALMIS)

Average Wages

Occupation	$/Hr.	Occupation	$/Hr.
Accountants and Auditors	18.86	Maids and Housekeepers	6.85
Assemblers and Fabricators	7.55	Maintenance Repairers	10.98
Automotive Mechanics	13.27	Marketing/Advertising/PR Managers	23.23
Bookkeepers	10.13	Nurses, Licensed Practical	13.68
Carpenters	11.76	Nurses, Registered	17.83
Cashiers	6.62	Nursing Aides/Orderlies/Attendants	7.92
Clerks, General Office	9.45	Physicians and Surgeons	53.75
Clerks, Shipping/Receiving/Traffic	11.26	Receptionists/Information Clerks	8.58
Computer Programmers	22.58	Sales Reps., Exc. Scientific/Retail	16.38
Computer Support Specialists	16.34	Sales Reps., Scientific, Exc. Retail	19.72
Cooks, Restaurant	8.03	Salespersons, Retail	8.47
Electricians	11.50	Secretaries, Except Legal/Medical	10.91
Financial Managers	25.11	Stock Clerks, Sales Floor	6.82
First-Line Supervisors/Mgrs., Sales	15.41	Systems Analysts	23.75
Food Preparation Workers	7.21	Teacher Aides	7.58
General Managers/Top Executives	25.22	Teachers, Elementary School	14.99
Guards	7.23	Teachers, Secondary School	17.29
Hand Packers	6.21	Telemarketers	9.54
Janitors and Cleaners	7.11	Truck Drivers, Heavy/Tractor-Trailer	12.06
Laborers, Landscaping	7.88	Truck Drivers, Light	8.94
Lawyers	37.51	Waiters and Waitresses	5.74

Note: Wage data is for 1998 and covers the Metropolitan Statistical Area (see Appendix A for areas included). Hourly wages for elementary and secondary school teachers were calculated by the editors from annual wage data assuming a 40 hour work week; Dashes indicate that data was not available.
Source: Bureau of Labor Statistics, 1998 Metropolitan Area Occupational Employment and Wage Estimates

TAXES

Major State and Local Tax Rates

State Corporate Income (%)	State Personal Income (%)	Residential Property (%)	Sales & Use		State Gasoline (cents/ gallon)	State Cigarette (cents/ pack)
			State (%)	Local (%)		
5.5[a]	None	1.73	6.0	None	13.3[b]	33.9

Note: Personal/corporate income, sales, gasoline and cigarette tax rates as of January 2000. Property tax rates as of April 2000; (a) 3.3% Alternative Minimum Tax. An exemption of $5,000 is allowed; (b) Rate is comprised of 4 cents excise and 9.3 cents motor carrier tax. Local taxes vary from 5.5 cents to 17 cents. Plus a 2.07 cent per gallon pollution tax
Source: Federation of Tax Administrators, www.taxadmin.org; ERI's Relocation Assessor software database, quarterly effective date 4/1/2000

Total Taxes Per Capita and as a Percent of Income

Area	Per Capita Income ($)	Per Capita Taxes ($)			Percent of Income (%)		
		Total	Federal	State/Local	Total	Federal	State/Local
Florida	28,322	10,333	7,257	3,077	36.5	25.6	10.9
U.S.	28,878	10,298	7,026	3,273	35.7	24.3	11.3

Note: Figures are for 1999
Source: Tax Foundation, www.taxfoundation.org

COMMERCIAL UTILITIES

Typical Monthly Electric Bills

Area	Commercial Service ($/month)		Industrial Service ($/month)	
	12 kW demand 1,500 kWh	100 kW demand 30,000 kWh	1,000 kW demand 400,000 kWh	20,000 kW demand 10,000,000 kWh
City	118	1,993	23,247	387,510
U.S.	150	2,174	23,995	508,569

Note: Based on rates in effect January 1, 1999
Source: Edison Electric Institute, Typical Residential, Commercial and Industrial Bills, Winter 1999

TRANSPORTATION

Transportation Statistics

Average minutes to work (1990)	18.2
Interstate highways	I-95; US-192
Bus lines	
In-city (1998)	Space Coast Area Transit, 18 buses
Inter-city (1999)	4
Passenger air service	
Airport	Melbourne International
Airlines (1999)	4
Enplaned passengers (1998)	259,426
Amtrak service	No
Motor freight carriers (1999)	11
Major waterways/ports	Intracoastal Waterway; Atlantic Ocean

Source: FAA DOT/TSC CY1998 ACAIS Database; National Transit Database, 1998; Editor & Publisher Market Guide, 2000; Amtrak National Time Table, Fall 1999/Winter 2000; 1990 Census of Population and Housing, STF 3C; Jane's Urban Transport Systems 1999-2000

Means of Transportation to Work

Area	Car/Truck/Van		Public Transportation			Bicycle	Walked	Other Means	Worked at Home
	Drove Alone	Car-pooled	Bus	Subway	Railroad				
City	79.9	13.7	0.1	0.0	0.0	1.3	2.4	1.0	1.6
MSA[1]	80.6	13.0	0.2	0.0	0.0	0.9	1.9	1.3	2.1
U.S.	73.2	13.4	3.0	1.5	0.5	0.4	3.9	1.2	3.0

Note: Figures shown are percentages and only include workers 16 years of age and older;
(1) Metropolitan Statistical Area - see Appendix A for areas included
Source: 1990 Census of Population and Housing, Summary Tape File 3C

BUSINESSES

Major Business Headquarters

Company Name	1999 Rankings	
	Fortune 500	Forbes 500
Harris	427	-

Note: Companies listed are located in the city; dashes indicate no ranking
Fortune 500: Companies that produce a 10-K are ranked 1 to 500 based on 1999 revenue
Forbes 500: Private companies are ranked 1 to 500 based on 1998 revenue
Source: Forbes, December 13, 1999; Fortune, April 17, 2000

HOTELS & MOTELS

Hotels/Motels

Area	Hotels/Motels	Rooms	Luxury-Level Hotels/Motels		Average Minimum Rates ($)		
			♦♦♦♦	♦♦♦♦♦	♦♦	♦♦♦	♦♦♦♦
City	9	738	0	0	n/a	n/a	n/a
Airport	3	459	0	0	n/a	n/a	n/a
Total	12	1,197	0	0	n/a	n/a	n/a

Note: n/a not available; classifications range from one diamond (budget properties with basic amenities) to five diamond (luxury properties).
Source: OAG Business Travel Planner, Winter 1999-2000

Estimated Daily Food and Lodging Costs

Area	Food/Other ($/day)	Average Hotel Cost ($/day)
City	30	55
U.S.	30	55

Source: ERI's Relocation Assessor software database, quarterly effective date 4/1/2000

CONVENTION CENTERS

Convention Centers and Event Sites

Name	Guest Rooms	Meeting Space (sq. ft.)	Capacity (Theatre Style)
Hilton Melbourne Airport	237	12,000	830
King Center for the Performing Arts	n/a	n/a	1,200
King Center for the Performing Arts	n/a	n/a	2,001
Melbourne Auditorium	n/a	n/a	1,400
Radisson Suite Hotel Oceanfront	168	7,500	400

Note: n/a not available
Source: EventSource.com, 3/15/2000

Living Environment

COST OF LIVING

Cost of Living: Homeowner

Cost Element	U.S. ($)	City ($)	Differential ($)	Percent of U.S. Average
Consumables	14,516	15,286	770	105.3
Transportation	5,957	6,407	450	107.6
Health Services	2,012	2,112	100	105.0
Housing/Utilities/Prop. Tax	16,337	16,187	-150	99.1
Income+Payroll Taxes	12,615	10,707	-1,908	84.9
Miscellaneous	8,563	8,563	0	100.0
Total Cost of Living	60,000	59,262	-738	98.8

Note: Figures are based on a single income, four person family with gross annual earnings of $60,000, owning an 1,800 square-foot home, and driving two automobiles worth $22,000 30,000 miles per year.
Source: ERI's Relocation Assessor software database, quarterly effective date 4/1/2000

Cost of Living: Renter

Cost Element	U.S. ($)	City ($)	Differential ($)	Percent of U.S. Average
Consumables	10,486	10,983	497	104.7
Transportation	2,107	2,254	147	107.0
Health Services	1,632	1,705	73	104.5
Rent/Utilities/Insurance	9,299	9,042	-257	97.2
Income+Payroll Taxes	8,607	7,183	-1,424	83.5
Miscellaneous	7,869	7,869	0	100.0
Total Cost of Living	40,000	39,036	-964	97.6

Note: Figures are based on a single income, three person family with gross annual earnings of $40,000, renting a 1,000 square-foot home, and driving one automobile worth $8,000 12,000 miles per year.
Source: ERI's Relocation Assessor software database, quarterly effective date 4/1/2000

HOUSING

Median Home Prices and Housing Affordability

Area	Median Price[2] 4th Qtr. 1999 ($)	HOI[3] 4th Qtr. 1999	Affordability Rank[4]
MSA[1]	90,000	84.3	12
U.S.	139,000	63.8	–

Note: (1) Metropolitan Statistical Area - see Appendix A for areas included; (2) U.S. figures calculated from the sales of 687,516 new and existing homes in 192 markets; (3) Housing Opportunity Index - percent of homes sold that were within the reach of the median income household at the prevailing mortgage interest rate; (4) Rank is from 1-192 with 1 being most affordable
Source: National Association of Home Builders, Housing Opportunity Index, 4th Quarter 1999

Estimated Home Price

Area	Price ($)
City	127,517
U.S.	135,855

Note: Figures are based on an 1,800 square-foot home
Source: ERI's Relocation Assessor software database, quarterly effective date 4/1/2000

Estimated Rent

Area	Rent ($/month)
City	628
U.S.	651

Note: Figures are based on a 1,000 square-foot home
Source: ERI's Relocation Assessor software database, quarterly effective date 4/1/2000

Median Home Price Projection

It is projected that the median home price in the metropolitan area will increase from $94,095 in 1999 to $149,318 in 2010, an increase of 58.7%
Kiplinger's Personal Finance Magazine, January 2000

RESIDENTIAL UTILITIES

Average Residential Utility Costs

Area	All Electric ($/mth)	Part Electric ($/mth)	Other Energy ($/mth)	Phone ($/mth)
City	n/a	n/a	n/a	n/a
U.S.	99.25	55.47	43.48	20.29

Note: n/a not available
Source: ACCRA, Cost of Living Index, 3rd Quarter 1999

HEALTH CARE

Average Health Care Costs

Area	Hospital ($/day)	Doctor ($/visit)	Dentist ($/visit)
City	n/a	n/a	n/a
U.S.	440.96	53.83	68.42

Note: n/a not available
Source: ACCRA, Cost of Living Index, 3rd Quarter 1999

Distribution of Office-Based Physicians

Area	Family/Gen. Practitioners	Specialists Medical	Specialists Surgical	Specialists Other
MSA[1]	109	238	177	171

Note: Data as of 12/31/97; (1) Metropolitan Statistical Area - see Appendix A for areas included
Source: American Medical Assn., Physician Characteristics & Distribution in the U.S., 1999

Hospitals

Melbourne has 1 general medical and surgical hospital, 1 psychiatric, 1 rehabilitation, 1 children's psychiatric.
AHA Guide to the Healthcare Field, 1999-2000

EDUCATION

Public School District Statistics

District Name	Num. Sch.	Enroll.	Classroom Teachers	Pupils per Teacher	Minority Pupils (%)	Current Exp.[1] ($/pupil)
Brevard County Sch Dist	90	67,879	3,945	17.2	20.2	4,561

Note: Data covers the 1997-1998 school year unless otherwise noted; (1) Data covers fiscal year 1996; SD = School District; ISD = Independent School District; n/a not available
Source: National Center for Education Statistics, Common Core of Data Public Education Agency Universe 1997-98; National Center for Education Statistics, Characteristics of the 100 Largest Public Elementary and Secondary School Districts in the United States: 1997-98, July 1999

Educational Quality

School District	Education Quotient[1]	Graduate Outcome[2]	Community Index[3]	Resource Index[4]
Brevard Co. School Dist.	93	97	115	81

Note: Over 1,000 secondary school districts were rated in terms of educational quality. The scores range from a low of 50 to a high of 150; (1) Combination of the Graduate Outcome, Community and Resource indexes weighted to reflect the greater importance of the Graduate Outcome and Resource Index; (2) Based on graduation rates and college board scores (SAT/ACT); (3) Based on the surrounding community's level of affluence and adult education; (4) Based on teacher salaries, per-pupil expenditures and student-teacher ratios.
Source: Expansion Management, Ratings Issue, 1999

Educational Attainment by Race

Area	High School Graduate (%)					Bachelor's Degree (%)				
	Total	White	Black	Other	Hisp.[2]	Total	White	Black	Other	Hisp.[2]
City	79.2	81.0	57.2	78.3	77.5	18.8	19.0	10.6	32.7	23.0
MSA[1]	82.3	83.6	64.2	80.5	76.3	20.4	20.8	11.7	26.5	20.7
U.S.	75.2	77.9	63.1	60.4	49.8	20.3	21.5	11.4	19.4	9.2

Note: Figures shown cover persons 25 years old and over; (1) Metropolitan Statistical Area -
see Appendix A for areas included; (2) people of Hispanic origin can be of any race
Source: 1990 Census of Population and Housing, Summary Tape File 3C

School Enrollment by Type

Area	Preprimary				Elementary/High School			
	Public		Private		Public		Private	
	Enrollment	%	Enrollment	%	Enrollment	%	Enrollment	%
City	546	57.7	401	42.3	7,087	90.6	731	9.4
MSA[1]	3,730	51.2	3,561	48.8	51,090	91.7	4,650	8.3
U.S.	2,679,029	59.5	1,824,256	40.5	38,379,689	90.2	4,187,099	9.8

Note: Figures shown cover persons 3 years old and over;
(1) Metropolitan Statistical Area - see Appendix A for areas included
Source: 1990 Census of Population and Housing, Summary Tape File 3C

School Enrollment by Race

Area	Preprimary (%)				Elementary/High School (%)			
	White	Black	Other	Hisp.[1]	White	Black	Other	Hisp.[1]
City	91.7	5.3	3.1	0.6	79.7	16.4	3.9	4.8
MSA[2]	86.2	12.0	1.9	3.6	83.6	13.7	2.6	4.3
U.S.	80.4	12.5	7.1	7.8	74.1	15.6	10.3	12.5

Note: Figures shown cover persons 3 years old and over; (1) people of Hispanic origin can be of any
race; (2) Metropolitan Statistical Area - see Appendix A for areas included
Source: 1990 Census of Population and Housing, Summary Tape File 3C

Higher Education

Two-Year Colleges		Four-Year Colleges		Medical Schools	Law Schools	Voc/ Tech
Public	Private	Public	Private			
0	1	0	1	0	0	7

Source: College Blue Book, Occupational Education, 1999; Medical School Admission Requirements,
1999-2000; Peterson's Guide to Two-Year Colleges, 2000; Peterson's Guide to Four-Year Colleges,
1999; Barron's Guide to Law Schools, 1999

MAJOR EMPLOYERS

Major Employers

Adage Inc. (communications equipment)   Cape Publications
Florida Institute of Technology (flying instruction) Goldfield Corp. (powerline construction)
Harris Air Traffic Control Systems   Harris Corp. (communications)
Holmes Regional Medical Center   USA Insurance Group

Note: Companies listed are located in the city
Source: D&B Business Rankings, 1999; Ward's Business Directory, 1999; America's Corporate
Families, 1999

PUBLIC SAFETY

Crime Rate

Area	All Crimes	Violent Crimes				Property Crimes		
		Murder	Forcible Rape	Robbery	Aggrav. Assault	Burglary	Larceny -Theft	Motor Vehicle Theft
City	7,866.1	5.7	55.9	249.2	790.6	1,373.6	5,047.3	343.7
Suburbs[1]	4,560.8	3.5	44.6	88.9	506.8	936.9	2,720.6	259.6
MSA[2]	5,052.7	3.8	46.2	112.7	549.0	1,001.9	3,066.8	272.2
U.S.	4,615.5	6.3	34.4	165.2	360.5	862.0	2,728.1	459.0

Note: Crime rate is the number of crimes per 100,000 population; (1) Defined as all areas within the Metropolitan Statistical Area but located outside the central city; (2) Metropolitan Statistical Area - see Appendix A for areas included
Source: FBI Uniform Crime Reports, 1998

RECREATION

Culture and Recreation

Museums	Symphony Orchestras	Opera Companies	Dance Companies	Professional Theatres	Zoos	Pro Sports Teams
1	1	0	0	0	0	0

Source: Musical America, International Directory of the Performing Arts, 1999; Official Museum Directory, 2000; Stern's Performing Arts Directory, 1997; USA Today Four Sport Stadium Guide, 1997; Career Opportunities in Theatre and the Performing Arts, 1999

Library System

The Melbourne Public Library has no branches, holdings of 124,304 volumes, and a budget of $954,188 (1997-1998).
American Library Directory, 1999-2000

MEDIA

Newspapers

Name	Type	Freq.	Distribution	Circulation
Bay Bulletin	General	1x/wk	Local	30,524
Florida Today	General	7x/wk	Local	84,365
The Times	General	1x/wk	Local	52,778
The Tribune	n/a	1x/wk	Local	38,022

Note: Includes newspapers with circulations of 200 or more located in the city; n/a not available
Source: Burrelle's Media Directory, 1999 Edition

Television Stations

Name	Ch.	Affiliation	Type	Owner
WBSF	43	n/a	Commercial	USA Broadcasting Group
WBCC	68	n/a	Non-comm.	Brevard Community College

Note: Stations included broadcast in the Melbourne metro area; n/a not available
Source: Burrelle's Media Directory, 1999 Edition

AM Radio Stations

Call Letters	Freq. (kHz)	Target Audience	Station Format	Music Format
WPGS	840	General	M/N/T	MOR
WRFB	860	General	M	Easy Listening
WMEL	920	General	N/S/T	n/a
WMMB	1240	General	M/N	Adult Standards/Big Band/MOR
WMMV	1350	General	M/N/S	Adult Standards/Big Band/MOR/Oldies
WWBC	1510	General	M/T	Christian
WTMS	1560	General	M/N/S	Oldies

Note: Stations included broadcast in the Melbourne metro area; n/a not available
Target Audience: A=Asian; B=Black; C=Christian; E=Ethnic; F=French; G=General; H=Hispanic; M=Men; N=Native American; R=Religious; S=Senior Citizen; W=Women; Y=Young Adult; Z=Children
Station Format: E=Educational; M=Music; N=News; S=Sports; T=Talk
Music Format: AOR=Album Oriented Rock; MOR=Middle-of-the-Road
Source: Burrelle's Media Directory, 1999 Edition

FM Radio Stations

Call Letters	Freq. (mHz)	Target Audience	Station Format	Music Format
WPIO	89.3	General	M	Christian
WFIT	89.5	General	M/N/S	Adult Contemporary/Alternative/AOR/Jazz
WMIE	91.5	General	M	Christian
WBVD	95.1	General	M/N/T	Classic Rock
WLRQ	99.3	General	M/N/S	Adult Contemporary
WAOA	107.1	General	M/N	n/a

Note: Stations included broadcast in the Melbourne metro area; n/a not available
Station Format: E=Educational; M=Music; N=News; S=Sports; T=Talk
Target Audience: A=Asian; B=Black; C=Christian; E=Ethnic; F=French; G=General; H=Hispanic; M=Men; N=Native American; R=Religious; S=Senior Citizen; W=Women; Y=Young Adult; Z=Children
Music Format: AOR=Album Oriented Rock; MOR=Middle-of-the-Road
Source: Burrelle's Media Directory, 1999 Edition

WEATHER

Temperature/Precipitation/Humidity

	Jan	Feb	Mar	Apr	May	Jun	Jul	Aug	Sep	Oct	Nov	Dec	Yr.
Max. High Temp. (°F)	89	91	91	94	97	100	99	100	97	96	89	90	100
Avg. High Temp. (°F)	72	73	77	81	85	88	90	90	88	83	77	73	81
Avg. Temp. (°F)	62	63	67	72	76	79	81	81	80	75	68	63	72
Avg. Low Temp. (°F)	52	54	57	63	67	71	73	73	73	68	59	54	64
Min. Low Temp. (°F)	22	28	31	38	50	62	66	65	57	41	30	26	22
Avg. Precip. (in.)	2.1	2.5	3.5	2.8	3.6	5.8	6.3	5.1	8.7	6.3	2.6	1.9	51.2
Avg. Snowfall (in.)	0	0	0	0	0	0	0	0	0	0	0	0	0
Avg. Rel. Hum. (%)	80	78	75	75	74	79	82	82	82	79	77	81	79

Source: National Climatic Data Center, International Station Meteorological Climate Summary, 3/95

Weather Conditions

Temperature			Precipitation		
0°F & below	32°F & below	90°F & above	0.1 inch or more precip.	1.5 inch or more snow/ice	Thunderstorms
0	0	51	85	0	85

Note: Figures are average number of days per year
Source: National Climatic Data Center, International Station Meteorological Climate Summary, 3/95

AIR & WATER QUALITY

Maximum Pollutant Concentrations

	Particulate Matter (ug/m³)	Carbon Monoxide (ppm)	Sulfur Dioxide (ppm)	Nitrogen Dioxide (ppm)	Ozone (ppm)	Lead (ug/m³)
MSA[1] Level	38	n/a	n/a	n/a	0.09	n/a
NAAQS[2]	150	9	0.140	0.053	0.12	1.50
Met NAAQS	Yes	n/a	n/a	n/a	Yes	n/a

Note: (1) Metropolitan Statistical Area - see Appendix A for areas included; (2) National Ambient Air Quality Standards; ppm = parts per million; ug/m³ = micrograms per cubic meter; n/a not available
Source: EPA, National Air Quality and Emissions Trends Report, 1997

Pollutant Standards Index

Data not available.
EPA, National Air Quality and Emissions Trends Report, 1997

Drinking Water

Water System Name	Pop. Served	Primary Water Source Type	Number of Violations in 1998-99	Type of Violation/ Contaminants
City of Melbourne	131,374	Surface	1	(1)

Note: Data as of January 19, 2000; (1) Routine Major Monitoring (TCR) violation—no samples collected for a period under the total coliform rule (1 violation in 1999).
Source: EPA, Office of Ground Water and Drinking Water, Safe Drinking Water Information System

Data on Melbourne tap water was not available.
Editor & Publisher Market Guide, 2000

Missoula, Montana

Background

Missoula, Montana is located in the Rocky Mountains in the western section of the state, 170 miles southwest of Great Falls and 110 miles northwest of Helena. The city is situated on a dry lakebed at a geographic focal point for several valleys. The Clark Fork and other rivers run through or near Missoula. The terrain is open land that rises to foothills, canyons and mountain ranges, including the Bitterroots. A significant amount of the surrounding land is within large national parks and forests.

Missoula is a regional economic center, the county seat of Missoula County and is known as a community of people with diverse interests and lifestyles. The city is a transportation hub situated on a historic route for east-west travel through the wilderness. Today, Interstate 90 runs through Missoula. The traditional economy is based on agriculture and forestry and related industries. Missoula's contemporary economy includes health care, financial and business services and tourism. The University of Montana in Missoula also plays an important economic and social role.

Originally occupied by the Salish and other Native Americans, the area remained largely unpopulated by whites until the Gold Rush of the middle 19th Century. In 1860, Christopher Higgins and Francis Worden opened a trading post and mill, known as Hell Gate, later changed to Missoula, believed to be a Salish description of the area. Missoula grew as a commercial and industrial center. In 1877, the Army established and maintained Fort Missoula until 1947. The opening of the Northern Pacific Railroad in the 1880s brought further growth and the town was incorporated in 1883.

In 1895, The University of Montana opened. In 1908, the U.S. Forest Service established its northern regional headquarters and a firefighting school in Missoula in 1908. Local resident Janette Rankin became the first woman elected to the U.S. Congress in 1916.

In the 1970s, the region went through challenging economic transitions due to changes in the forestry and wood-products industry. While Missoula's traditional industries continue to be important, there has been a shift towards other economic activities.

Throughout the 1980s and 1990s, western Montana's beauty and rural lifestyle attracted an increasing number of new residents and vacationers. Many newcomers are also drawn to Missoula's urban attributes and cultural life. This in-migration prompted debates and concerns over development and other issues. Initiatives for sustainable growth have been undertaken, including preservation of the historic city center.

Missoula is accessible to outdoor recreation in numerous local and national parks and forests including Greenough Park, Lolo National Forest, Rattlesnake Wilderness Area, and the Lee Metcalf Wildlife Refuge, among others. The Marshall Mountain and Montana Snow Bowl ski areas are nearby. Bicycling is especially popular in Missoula.

Cultural venues include the Missoula Children's Theater, Missoula Symphony, the Crystal Theater moviehouse, the Montana Repertory Theater, the International Choral festival and the Art Museum of Missoula. The University of Montana sponsors many cultural activities.

Other local attractions include a carousel in Caras Park, the Fort Missoula historic park and the Smokejumper Visitors' Center.

In 1997, Missoula adopted a new city government charter and now has an elected Mayor, a 12-member City Council, and an appointed Chief Administrative Officer.

General Rankings and Evaluative Comments

- Missoula was ranked #185 out of 354 metropolitan areas in *Places Rated Almanac*. Criteria: cost of living, climate, crime, transportation, job outlook, education, the arts, health care, and recreation. *Places Rated Almanac, Millennium Edition, 2000*

- Missoula was selected as one of America's best small art towns. The city was ranked #37 out of 100. Criteria: easy and affordable access to the visual arts, performing arts and music, strong sense of community, low crime rate, and full-time population less than 65,000. *The 100 Best Small Art Towns in America: Discover Creative Communities, Fresh Air, and Affordable Living, 1998*

- Missoula was selected as one of "America's Best Towns to Raise an Outdoor Family" by Outdoor Explorer magazine. Criteria: easy access to the outdoors, quality education and health care, affordable housing, favorable employment opportunities, and low crime rates. The city was ranked #5 out of 25. Outdoor Explorer, Summer 1999

Business Environment

STATE ECONOMY

State Economic Profile

"Montana's economy continued to slow in 1998. Employment growth was barely positive. Montana's primary industries, agriculture and mining, are both plagued by over capacity and weak commodity prices. Residential construction has practically come to a standstill, and the state continues to lose a significant share of its younger population.

Wheat and wheat products constitute 28% of Montana's exports. The falloff in Asian demand has hit Montana's farm sector particularly hard. Although a federal aid package has reduced some of the pain, Montana's farm sector will continue to be plagued by declining commodity prices in the absence of major restructuring.

While low and declining food prices have crippled Montana's farm sector, declining metals prices have weakened Montana's mining sector. Metals prices should continue declining, potentially resulting in a loss of employment in that sector.

Although homes sales were robust in 1998, permit activity held steady, while construction employment declined almost 4%; declining starts should follow. Price appreciation has been weak, but should pick up in the near future. Constraining housing market growth will be Montana's slow population growth and the continuing loss of "typical buyer" households.

Montana's short-term prospects are not bright. Weakness in its agriculture and mining sectors is unlikely to reverse in the near term. Some gains in its tourism and gaming sectors should offset other employment losses. Its below average business costs and high quality of life could attract some corporate relocations." National Association of Realtors, Economic Profiles: The Fifty States and the District of Columbia, http://nar.realtor.com/databank/profiles.htm

EXPORTS

Total Export Sales

Area	1995 ($000)	1996 ($000)	1997 ($000)	1998 ($000)	% Chg. 1995-98	% Chg. 1997-98
MSA[1]	n/a	n/a	n/a	n/a	n/a	n/a
U.S.	583,030,524	622,827,063	687,597,999	680,474,251	16.7	-1.0

Note: (1) Metropolitan Statistical Area - see Appendix A for areas included
Source: U.S. Department of Commerce, International Trade Association, Metropolitan Area Exports: An Export Performance Report on Over 250 U.S. Cities, November 10, 1999

CITY FINANCES

City Government Finances

Component	1995 ($million)	1995 (per capita $)
Revenue	27.9	615
Expenditure	25.7	568
Debt Outstanding	56.0	1,235

Source: 1999 County and City Extra, Annual Metro, City, and County Data Book

City Government Revenue by Source

Source	1995 ($million)	1995 (per capita $)
Intergovernmental	4.1	90
Taxes	13.0	287
Property	11.3	251
Sales and Gross Receipts	0.1	4

Source: 1999 County and City Extra, Annual Metro, City, and County Data Book

City Government Expenditures by Function

Function	1995 ($million)	1995 (per capita $)	1995 (%)
Public Welfare	0.0	0	0.0
Highways	2.5	56	10.0
Parking Facilities	0.5	11	2.1
Education	0.0	0	0.0
Health and Hospitals	0.8	18	3.3
Police Protection	3.8	85	15.0
Sewerage and Sanitation	2.3	52	9.2
Parks and Recreation	1.3	28	5.1
Housing and Community Development	0.4	10	1.9
Interest on Debt	3.9	86	15.2

Source: 1999 County and City Extra, Annual Metro, City, and County Data Book

Municipal Bond Ratings

Area	Moody's
City	n/a

Note: n/a not available
Source: Mergent Bond Record, 2/2000

POPULATION

Population Growth

Area	1980 Census	1990 Census	1999 Estimate	2004 Projection	Population Growth (%) 1990-1999	Population Growth (%) 1999-2004
City	33,387	42,918	53,027	56,762	23.6	7.0
MSA[1]	n/a	n/a	n/a	n/a	n/a	4.6
U.S.	226,545,805	248,765,170	272,212,864	283,625,312	9.4	4.2

Note: (1) Metropolitan Statistical Area - see Appendix A for areas included; n/a not available
Source: 1990 Census of Population and Housing, Summary Tape File 3C; Claritas, Inc.

Number of Households and Average Household Size

Area	1980 Census	1990 Census	1999 Estimate	2004 Projection	1999 Average Household Size
City	16,746	17,765	22,242	24,046	2.38
MSA[1]	n/a	n/a	35,782	37,806	2.50
U.S.	80,389,592	91,993,582	102,048,200	107,302,392	2.67

Note: (1) Metropolitan Statistical Area - see Appendix A for areas included; n/a not available
Source: 1990 Census of Population and Housing, Summary Tape File 3C; Claritas, Inc.

Race/Ethnicity of City Population

Race/Ethnicity	1990 Census Population	1990 Census %	1999 Estimate Population	1999 Estimate %	% Change 1990-1999
White, Non-Hispanic	40,725	94.9	49,850	94.0	22.4
Black, Non-Hispanic	120	0.3	199	0.4	65.8
Asian, Non-Hispanic	602	1.4	743	1.4	23.4
Other, Non-Hispanic	892	2.1	1,390	2.6	55.8
Hispanic	579	1.3	845	1.6	45.9

Source: 1990 Census of Population and Housing, Summary Tape File 3C; Claritas, Inc.

Race/Ethnicity of Metropolitan Statistical Area Population

Race/Ethnicity	1990 Census		1999 Estimate		% Change 1990-1999
	Population	%	Population	%	
White, Non-Hispanic	n/a	n/a	84,981	94.9	n/a
Black, Non-Hispanic	n/a	n/a	234	0.3	n/a
Asian, Non-Hispanic	n/a	n/a	951	1.1	n/a
Other, Non-Hispanic	n/a	n/a	2,177	2.4	n/a
Hispanic	n/a	n/a	1,246	1.4	n/a

Note: See Appendix A for areas included in the Metropolitan Statistical Area; n/a not available
Source: 1990 Census of Population and Housing, Summary Tape File 3C; Claritas, Inc.

Ancestry

Area	German	Irish	English	Italian	U.S.	French	Polish	Dutch
City	36.8	20.0	17.7	3.5	1.1	7.3	2.6	2.8
MSA[1]	n/a	n/a	n/a	n/a	n/a	n/a	n/a	n/a
U.S.	23.3	15.6	13.1	5.9	5.3	4.2	3.8	2.5

Note: Figures are percentages and include persons that reported multiple ancestry (eg. if a person reported being Irish and Italian, they were included in both columns); (1) Metropolitan Statistical Area - see Appendix A for areas included; n/a not available
Source: 1990 Census of Population and Housing, Summary Tape File 3C

Median Age

Area	1990 Census	1999 Estimate
City	30.7	34.7
MSA[1]	n/a	35.0
U.S.	32.9	35.7

Note: (1) Metropolitan Statistical Area - see Appendix A for areas included; n/a not available
Source: 1990 Census of Population and Housing, Summary Tape File 3C; Claritas, Inc.

Male/Female Population

Area	Number of Males		Number of Females		Males per 100 Females	
	1990	1999	1990	1999	1990	1999
City	20,817	25,773	22,101	27,254	94.2	94.6
MSA[1]	n/a	43,937	n/a	45,652	n/a	96.2
U.S.	121,172,379	132,803,736	127,537,494	139,409,136	95.0	95.3

Note: (1) Metropolitan Statistical Area - see Appendix A for areas included; n/a not available
Source: 1990 Census of Population, General Population Characteristics; Claritas, Inc.

INCOME

Per Capita/Median/Average Income

Area	Per Capita ($)			Median Household ($)			Average Household ($)		
	1989	1999	% Chg.	1989	1999	% Chg.	1989	1999	% Chg.
City	11,759	19,462	65.5	21,033	31,313	48.9	27,825	45,555	63.7
MSA[1]	n/a	19,816	n/a	n/a	35,394	n/a	n/a	49,053	n/a
U.S.	14,420	21,350	48.1	30,056	40,525	34.8	38,453	56,184	46.1

Note: (1) Metropolitan Statistical Area - see Appendix A for areas included; 1989 data is from the 1990 Census; 1999 data is estimated by Claritas, Inc.; n/a not available
Source: 1990 Census of Population, General Population Characteristics; Claritas, Inc.

Household Income Distribution

Area	Percent of Households Earning								
	Under $5,000	$5,000 -14,999	$15,000 -24,999	$25,000 -34,999	$35,000 -49,999	$50,000 -74,999	$75,000 -99,000	$100,000 -149,999	$150,000 and up
City	5.3	17.9	17.9	13.2	14.6	16.1	7.3	4.6	2.9
MSA[1]	4.5	15.3	16.6	13.1	15.8	18.5	8.5	4.7	3.1
U.S.	3.9	13.3	13.8	12.6	16.2	19.4	9.7	6.6	4.6

Note: Data as of 1999; (1) Metropolitan Statistical Area - see Appendix A for areas included
Source: Claritas, Inc.

Effective Buying Income

Area	Per Capita ($)	Median Household ($)	Average Household ($)
City	15,252	27,368	36,711
MSA[1]	16,043	31,427	40,651
U.S.	17,496	36,603	47,036

Note: Data as of 1/1/2000; (1) Metropolitan Statistical Area - see Appendix A for areas included
Source: Standard Rate & Data Service, Newspaper Advertising Source, March 2000

Effective Household Buying Income Distribution

Area	% of Households Earning						
	$10,000 -$19,999	$20,000 -$34,999	$35,000 -$49,999	$50,000 -$74,999	$75,000 -$99,000	$100,000 -$124,999	$125,000 and up
City	20.9	23.7	15.1	14.8	5.4	1.6	1.7
MSA[1]	18.3	23.2	16.8	17.6	6.4	2.1	2.1
U.S.	15.0	21.6	17.6	19.6	8.4	3.0	3.3

Note: Data as of 1/1/2000; (1) Metropolitan Statistical Area - see Appendix A for areas included
Source: Standard Rate & Data Service, Newspaper Advertising Source, March 2000

Poverty Rates by Age

Area	People of All Ages	People Under 18 Years Old	Related Children Age 5-17 in Families in Poverty
City	16.9	n/a	n/a
County	16.3	22.2	19.6
U.S.	13.8	20.8	18.7

Note: Figures show the percent of people living below the poverty line in 1995. The
average poverty threshold was $15,569 for a family of four in 1995; n/a not available
Source: Bureau of the Census, Small Area Income and Poverty Estimates Program;
U.S. Department of Housing and Urban Development

EMPLOYMENT

Labor Force and Employment

Area	Civilian Labor Force			Workers Employed		
	Dec. 1998	Dec. 1999	% Chg.	Dec. 1998	Dec. 1999	% Chg.
City	29,021	29,518	1.7	27,686	28,211	1.9
MSA[1]	52,752	53,664	1.7	50,542	51,500	1.9
U.S.	138,297,000	139,941,000	1.2	132,732,000	134,696,000	1.5

Note: Data is not seasonally adjusted and covers workers 16 years of age and older;
(1) Metropolitan Statistical Area - see Appendix A for areas included
Source: Bureau of Labor Statistics, http://stats.bls.gov

Unemployment Rate

Area	1999											
	Jan.	Feb.	Mar.	Apr.	May	Jun.	Jul.	Aug.	Sep.	Oct.	Nov.	Dec.
City	5.3	5.3	5.0	4.3	3.5	3.3	3.2	3.2	3.4	3.5	3.7	4.4
MSA[1]	4.9	4.8	4.6	3.9	3.2	3.0	2.9	2.9	3.1	3.2	3.4	4.0
U.S.	4.8	4.7	4.4	4.1	4.0	4.5	4.5	4.2	4.1	3.8	3.8	3.7

Note: Data is not seasonally adjusted and covers workers 16 years of age and older; all figures are percentages; (1) Metropolitan Statistical Area - see Appendix A for areas included
Source: Bureau of Labor Statistics, http://stats.bls.gov

Employment by Industry

Sector	MSA[1]		U.S.
	Number of Employees	Percent of Total	Percent of Total
Services	n/a	n/a	30.2
Retail Trade	n/a	n/a	18.1
Government	n/a	n/a	15.8
Manufacturing	n/a	n/a	14.1
Finance/Insurance/Real Estate	n/a	n/a	5.9
Wholesale Trade	n/a	n/a	5.4
Transportation/Public Utilities	n/a	n/a	5.3
Construction	n/a	n/a	4.8
Mining	n/a	n/a	0.4

Note: Figures cover non-farm employment as of 12/99 and are not seasonally adjusted;
(1) Metropolitan Statistical Area - see Appendix A for areas included; n/a not available
Source: Bureau of Labor Statistics, http://stats.bls.gov

Employment by Occupation

Occupation Category	City (%)	MSA[1] (%)	U.S. (%)
White Collar	63.6	n/a	58.1
Executive/Admin./Management	11.7	n/a	12.3
Professional	19.6	n/a	14.1
Technical & Related Support	4.3	n/a	3.7
Sales	13.4	n/a	11.8
Administrative Support/Clerical	14.7	n/a	16.3
Blue Collar	17.5	n/a	26.2
Precision Production/Craft/Repair	6.7	n/a	11.3
Machine Operators/Assem./Insp.	3.4	n/a	6.8
Transportation/Material Movers	4.0	n/a	4.1
Cleaners/Helpers/Laborers	3.4	n/a	3.9
Services	17.2	n/a	13.2
Farming/Forestry/Fishing	1.7	n/a	2.5

Note: Figures cover workers 16 years of age and older; n/a not available
(1) Metropolitan Statistical Area - see Appendix A for areas included
Source: 1990 Census of Population and Housing, Summary Tape File 3C

Occupational Employment Projections: 1996 - 2006

Occupations Expected to Have the Largest Job Growth (ranked by numerical growth)	Fast-Growing Occupations[1] (ranked by percent growth)
1. Salespersons, retail	1. Home health aides
2. Carpenters, including brattice builders	2. Corrections officers & jailers
3. Janitors/cleaners/maids, ex. priv. hshld.	3. Teachers, special education
4. Child care workers, private household	4. Residential counselors
5. Waiters & waitresses	5. Amusement and recreation attendants
6. Marketing & sales, supervisors	6. Cooks, restaurant
7. Cashiers	7. Child care workers, private household
8. Truck drivers, light	8. Animal caretakers, exc. farm
9. Bookkeeping, accounting & auditing clerks	9. Guards
10. General managers & top executives	10. Personal and home care aides

Note: Projections cover Montana; (1) Excludes occupations with total job growth less than 300
Source: U.S. Department of Labor, Employment and Training Administration, America's Labor Market Information System (ALMIS)

Average Wages

Occupation	$/Hr.	Occupation	$/Hr.
Accountants and Auditors	-	Maids and Housekeepers	-
Assemblers and Fabricators	-	Maintenance Repairers	-
Automotive Mechanics	-	Marketing/Advertising/PR Managers	-
Bookkeepers	-	Nurses, Licensed Practical	-
Carpenters	-	Nurses, Registered	-
Cashiers	-	Nursing Aides/Orderlies/Attendants	-
Clerks, General Office	-	Physicians and Surgeons	-
Clerks, Shipping/Receiving/Traffic	-	Receptionists/Information Clerks	-
Computer Programmers	-	Sales Reps., Exc. Scientific/Retail	-
Computer Support Specialists	-	Sales Reps., Scientific, Exc. Retail	-
Cooks, Restaurant	-	Salespersons, Retail	-
Electricians	-	Secretaries, Except Legal/Medical	-
Financial Managers	-	Stock Clerks, Sales Floor	-
First-Line Supervisors/Mgrs., Sales	-	Systems Analysts	-
Food Preparation Workers	-	Teacher Aides	-
General Managers/Top Executives	-	Teachers, Elementary School	-
Guards	-	Teachers, Secondary School	-
Hand Packers	-	Telemarketers	-
Janitors and Cleaners	-	Truck Drivers, Heavy/Tractor-Trailer	-
Laborers, Landscaping	-	Truck Drivers, Light	-
Lawyers	-	Waiters and Waitresses	-

Note: Wage data is for 1998 and covers the Metropolitan Statistical Area (see Appendix A for areas included). Hourly wages for elementary and secondary school teachers were calculated by the editors from annual wage data assuming a 40 hour work week; Dashes indicate that data was not available.
Source: Bureau of Labor Statistics, 1998 Metropolitan Area Occupational Employment and Wage Estimates

TAXES

Major State and Local Tax Rates

State Corporate Income (%)	State Personal Income (%)	Residential Property (%)	Sales & Use		State Gasoline (cents/gallon)	State Cigarette (cents/pack)
			State (%)	Local (%)		
6.75[a]	2.0 - 11.0	2.19	None	None	27.0	18.0

Note: Personal/corporate income, sales, gasoline and cigarette tax rates as of January 2000. Property tax rates as of April 2000; (a) A 7% tax on taxpayers using water's edge combination. Minimum tax is $50
Source: Federation of Tax Administrators, www.taxadmin.org; ERI's Relocation Assessor software database, quarterly effective date 4/1/2000

Total Taxes Per Capita and as a Percent of Income

Area	Per Capita Income ($)	Per Capita Taxes ($)			Percent of Income (%)		
		Total	Federal	State/Local	Total	Federal	State/Local
Montana	21,186	7,196	4,843	2,353	34.0	22.9	11.1
U.S.	28,878	10,298	7,026	3,273	35.7	24.3	11.3

Note: Figures are for 1999
Source: Tax Foundation, www.taxfoundation.org

COMMERCIAL UTILITIES

Typical Monthly Electric Bills

Area	Commercial Service ($/month)		Industrial Service ($/month)	
	12 kW demand 1,500 kWh	100 kW demand 30,000 kWh	1,000 kW demand 400,000 kWh	20,000 kW demand 10,000,000 kWh
City	162	2,079	22,236	399,016
U.S.	150	2,174	23,995	508,569

Note: Based on rates in effect January 1, 1999
Source: Edison Electric Institute, Typical Residential, Commercial and Industrial Bills, Winter 1999

TRANSPORTATION

Transportation Statistics

Average minutes to work (1990)	13.0
Interstate highways	I-90; US-12; US-93
Bus lines	
In-city (1998)	Missoula Urban Transportation District, 15 buses
Inter-city (1999)	5
Passenger air service	
Airport	Missoula International
Airlines (1999)	3
Enplaned passengers (1998)	202,947
Amtrak service	No
Motor freight carriers (1999)	13
Major waterways/ports	None

Source: FAA DOT/TSC CY1998 ACAIS Database; National Transit Database, 1998; Editor & Publisher Market Guide, 2000; Amtrak National Time Table, Fall 1999/Winter 2000; 1990 Census of Population and Housing, STF 3C; Jane's Urban Transport Systems 1999-2000

Means of Transportation to Work

Area	Car/Truck/Van		Public Transportation			Bicycle	Walked	Other Means	Worked at Home
	Drove Alone	Car-pooled	Bus	Subway	Railroad				
City	72.4	9.7	1.5	0.0	0.0	4.0	8.2	1.0	3.1
MSA[1]	n/a	n/a	n/a	n/a	n/a	n/a	n/a	n/a	n/a
U.S.	73.2	13.4	3.0	1.5	0.5	0.4	3.9	1.2	3.0

Note: Figures shown are percentages and only include workers 16 years of age and older;
(1) Metropolitan Statistical Area - see Appendix A for areas included; n/a not available
Source: 1990 Census of Population and Housing, Summary Tape File 3C

BUSINESSES

Major Business Headquarters

Company Name	1999 Rankings	
	Fortune 500	Forbes 500
Washington Cos.	-	311

Note: Companies listed are located in the city; dashes indicate no ranking
Fortune 500: Companies that produce a 10-K are ranked 1 to 500 based on 1999 revenue
Forbes 500: Private companies are ranked 1 to 500 based on 1998 revenue
Source: Forbes, December 13, 1999; Fortune, April 17, 2000

HOTELS & MOTELS

Hotels/Motels

Area	Hotels/ Motels	Rooms	Luxury-Level Hotels/Motels		Average Minimum Rates ($)		
			♦♦♦♦	♦♦♦♦♦	♦♦	♦♦♦	♦♦♦♦
City	20	1,433	0	0	60	76	n/a
Airport	6	393	0	0	n/a	n/a	n/a
Total	26	1,826	0	0	n/a	n/a	n/a

Note: n/a not available; classifications range from one diamond (budget properties with basic amenities) to five diamond (luxury properties).
Source: OAG Business Travel Planner, Winter 1999-2000

Estimated Daily Food and Lodging Costs

Area	Food/Other ($/day)	Average Hotel Cost ($/day)
City	30	55
U.S.	30	55

Source: ERI's Relocation Assessor software database, quarterly effective date 4/1/2000

CONVENTION CENTERS

Convention Centers and Event Sites

Name	Guest Rooms	Meeting Space (sq. ft.)	Capacity (Theatre Style)
Doubletree Edgewater	172	n/a	800
Holiday Inn Parkside	200	n/a	600
Montana Sports Complex	n/a	n/a	18,845

Note: n/a not available
Source: EventSource.com, 3/15/2000

Living Environment

COST OF LIVING

Cost of Living: Homeowner

Cost Element	U.S. ($)	City ($)	Differential ($)	Percent of U.S. Average
Consumables	14,516	14,842	326	102.2
Transportation	5,957	6,514	557	109.4
Health Services	2,012	2,048	36	101.8
Housing/Utilities/Prop. Tax	16,337	14,298	-2,039	87.5
Income+Payroll Taxes	12,615	13,287	672	105.3
Miscellaneous	8,563	8,563	0	100.0
Total Cost of Living	60,000	59,552	-448	99.3

Note: Figures are based on a single income, four person family with gross annual earnings of $60,000, owning an 1,800 square-foot home, and driving two automobiles worth $22,000 30,000 miles per year.
Source: ERI's Relocation Assessor software database, quarterly effective date 4/1/2000

Cost of Living: Renter

Cost Element	U.S. ($)	City ($)	Differential ($)	Percent of U.S. Average
Consumables	10,486	10,757	271	102.6
Transportation	2,107	2,311	204	109.7
Health Services	1,632	1,667	35	102.1
Rent/Utilities/Insurance	9,299	6,916	-2,383	74.4
Income+Payroll Taxes	8,607	8,887	280	103.3
Miscellaneous	7,869	7,869	0	100.0
Total Cost of Living	40,000	38,407	-1,593	96.0

Note: Figures are based on a single income, three person family with gross annual earnings of $40,000, renting a 1,000 square-foot home, and driving one automobile worth $8,000 12,000 miles per year.
Source: ERI's Relocation Assessor software database, quarterly effective date 4/1/2000

HOUSING

Median Home Prices and Housing Affordability

Area	Median Price[2] 4th Qtr. 1999 ($)	HOI[3] 4th Qtr. 1999	Affordability Rank[4]
MSA[1]	n/a	n/a	n/a
U.S.	139,000	63.8	–

Note: (1) Metropolitan Statistical Area - see Appendix A for areas included; (2) U.S. figures calculated from the sales of 687,516 new and existing homes in 192 markets; (3) Housing Opportunity Index - percent of homes sold that were within the reach of the median income household at the prevailing mortgage interest rate; (4) Rank is from 1-192 with 1 being most affordable; n/a not available
Source: National Association of Home Builders, Housing Opportunity Index, 4th Quarter 1999

Estimated Home Price

Area	Price ($)
City	106,621
U.S.	135,855

Note: Figures are based on an 1,800 square-foot home
Source: ERI's Relocation Assessor software database, quarterly effective date 4/1/2000

Estimated Rent

Area	Rent ($/month)
City	469
U.S.	651

Note: Figures are based on a 1,000 square-foot home
Source: ERI's Relocation Assessor software database, quarterly effective date 4/1/2000

RESIDENTIAL UTILITIES

Average Residential Utility Costs

Area	All Electric ($/mth)	Part Electric ($/mth)	Other Energy ($/mth)	Phone ($/mth)
City	–	35.62	48.44	25.08
U.S.	99.25	55.47	43.48	20.29

Source: ACCRA, Cost of Living Index, 3rd Quarter 1999

HEALTH CARE

Average Health Care Costs

Area	Hospital ($/day)	Doctor ($/visit)	Dentist ($/visit)
City	416.00	51.00	72.00
U.S.	440.96	53.83	68.42

Note: Hospital—based on a semi-private room; Doctor—based on a general practitioner's routine exam of an established patient; Dentist—based on adult teeth cleaning and periodic oral exam.
Source: ACCRA, Cost of Living Index, 3rd Quarter 1999

Distribution of Office-Based Physicians

Area	Family/Gen. Practitioners	Specialists		
		Medical	Surgical	Other
MSA[1]	0	0	0	0

Note: Data as of 12/31/97; (1) Metropolitan Statistical Area - see Appendix A for areas included
Source: American Medical Assn., Physician Characteristics & Distribution in the U.S., 1999

Hospitals

Missoula has 2 general medical and surgical hospitals.
AHA Guide to the Healthcare Field, 1999-2000

EDUCATION

Public School District Statistics

District Name	Num. Sch.	Enroll.	Classroom Teachers	Pupils per Teacher	Minority Pupils (%)	Current Exp.[1] ($/pupil)
Desmet Elementary	2	146	13	11.2	n/a	n/a
Hellgate Elementary	2	1,221	65	18.8	n/a	n/a
Missoula Area Coop	n/a	n/a	n/a	n/a	n/a	n/a
Missoula Elementary	16	5,683	331	17.2	n/a	n/a
Missoula High School	4	3,926	242	16.2	n/a	n/a
Target Range Elementary	2	465	25	18.6	n/a	n/a

Note: Data covers the 1997-1998 school year unless otherwise noted; (1) Data covers fiscal year 1996; SD = School District; ISD = Independent School District; n/a not available
Source: National Center for Education Statistics, Common Core of Data Public Education Agency Universe 1997-98; National Center for Education Statistics, Characteristics of the 100 Largest Public Elementary and Secondary School Districts in the United States: 1997-98, July 1999

Educational Quality

School District	Education Quotient[1]	Graduate Outcome[2]	Community Index[3]	Resource Index[4]
Missoula School Dist.	n/a	n/a	n/a	n/a

Note: Over 1,000 secondary school districts were rated in terms of educational quality. The scores range from a low of 50 to a high of 150; (1) Combination of the Graduate Outcome, Community and Resource indexes weighted to reflect the greater importance of the Graduate Outcome and Resource Index; (2) Based on graduation rates and college board scores (SAT/ACT); (3) Based on the surrounding community's level of affluence and adult education; (4) Based on teacher salaries, per-pupil expenditures and student-teacher ratios.
Source: Expansion Management, Ratings Issue, 1999

Educational Attainment by Race

Area	High School Graduate (%)					Bachelor's Degree (%)				
	Total	White	Black	Other	Hisp.[2]	Total	White	Black	Other	Hisp.[2]
City	87.2	87.4	100.0	81.7	82.7	33.4	33.5	18.6	29.9	19.1
MSA[1]	n/a	n/a	n/a	n/a	n/a	n/a	n/a	n/a	n/a	n/a
U.S.	75.2	77.9	63.1	60.4	49.8	20.3	21.5	11.4	19.4	9.2

Note: Figures shown cover persons 25 years old and over; (1) Metropolitan Statistical Area -
see Appendix A for areas included; (2) people of Hispanic origin can be of any race; n/a not available
Source: 1990 Census of Population and Housing, Summary Tape File 3C

School Enrollment by Type

Area	Preprimary				Elementary/High School			
	Public		Private		Public		Private	
	Enrollment	%	Enrollment	%	Enrollment	%	Enrollment	%
City	482	60.9	310	39.1	6,021	94.9	326	5.1
MSA[1]	n/a	n/a	n/a	n/a	n/a	n/a	n/a	n/a
U.S.	2,679,029	59.5	1,824,256	40.5	38,379,689	90.2	4,187,099	9.8

Note: Figures shown cover persons 3 years old and over; n/a not available; (1) Metropolitan Statistical
Area - see Appendix A for areas included
Source: 1990 Census of Population and Housing, Summary Tape File 3C

School Enrollment by Race

Area	Preprimary (%)				Elementary/High School (%)			
	White	Black	Other	Hisp.[1]	White	Black	Other	Hisp.[1]
City	95.5	1.1	3.4	1.0	94.7	0.0	5.3	2.1
MSA[2]	n/a	n/a	n/a	n/a	n/a	n/a	n/a	n/a
U.S.	80.4	12.5	7.1	7.8	74.1	15.6	10.3	12.5

Note: Figures shown cover persons 3 years old and over; (1) people of Hispanic origin can be of any
race; (2) Metropolitan Statistical Area - see Appendix A for areas included; n/a not available
Source: 1990 Census of Population and Housing, Summary Tape File 3C

Higher Education

Two-Year Colleges		Four-Year Colleges		Medical Schools	Law Schools	Voc/ Tech
Public	Private	Public	Private			
0	0	1	0	0	1	5

Source: College Blue Book, Occupational Education, 1999; Medical School Admission Requirements,
1999-2000; Peterson's Guide to Two-Year Colleges, 2000; Peterson's Guide to Four-Year Colleges,
1999; Barron's Guide to Law Schools, 1999

MAJOR EMPLOYERS

Major Employers

Community Medical Center
Montana Rail Link
St. Patrick Hospital
Washington Corporations (construction)
Western Montana Clinic

Missoula White Pine Sash
SEA Trucking
Sun Mountain Sports
Western Federal Savings

Note: Companies listed are located in the city
Source: D&B Business Rankings, 1999; Ward's Business Directory, 1999; America's Corporate
Families, 1999

PUBLIC SAFETY

Crime Rate

Area	All Crimes	Violent Crimes				Property Crimes		
		Murder	Forcible Rape	Robbery	Aggrav. Assault	Burglary	Larceny -Theft	Motor Vehicle Theft
City	8,931.6	6.5	30.4	62.9	164.8	770.0	7,528.3	368.7
Suburbs[1]	n/a	n/a	n/a	n/a	n/a	n/a	n/a	n/a
MSA[2]	n/a	n/a	n/a	n/a	n/a	n/a	n/a	n/a
U.S.	5,275.9	8.2	37.1	220.9	418.3	987.1	3,043.8	560.4

Note: Crime rate is the number of crimes per 100,000 population; (1) Defined as all areas within the Metropolitan Statistical Area but located outside the central city; (2) Metropolitan Statistical Area - see Appendix A for areas included; n/a not available
Source: FBI Uniform Crime Reports, 1995

RECREATION

Culture and Recreation

Museums	Symphony Orchestras	Opera Companies	Dance Companies	Professional Theatres	Zoos	Pro Sports Teams
4	1	0	0	1	0	0

Source: Musical America, International Directory of the Performing Arts, 1999; Official Museum Directory, 2000; Stern's Performing Arts Directory, 1997; USA Today Four Sport Stadium Guide, 1997; Career Opportunities in Theatre and the Performing Arts, 1999

Library System

The Missoula Public Library has two branches, holdings of 193,909 volumes, and a budget of $1,056,171 (1997-1998).
American Library Directory, 1999-2000

MEDIA

Newspapers

Name	Type	Freq.	Distribution	Circulation
Missoulian	General	7x/wk	Area	32,711
Montana Kaimin	n/a	4x/wk	Camp/Comm	6,000
The Western Montana Messenger	General	1x/wk	Local	35,000

Note: Includes newspapers with circulations of 200 or more located in the city; n/a not available
Source: Burrelle's Media Directory, 1999 Edition

Television Stations

Name	Ch.	Affiliation	Type	Owner
KPAX	n/a	CBST	Commercial	KPAX Communications
KECI	13	NBCT	Commercial	Lamco Communications
KTMF	23	ABCT	Commercial	Continental Television Network Inc.

Note: Stations included broadcast in the Missoula metro area; n/a not available
Source: Burrelle's Media Directory, 1999 Edition

AM Radio Stations

Call Letters	Freq. (kHz)	Target Audience	Station Format	Music Format
KLCY	930	General	E/N/S/T	n/a
KGVO	1290	General	N/S/T	n/a
KYLT	1340	General	M/N/S	Oldies
KGRZ	1450	Men	S/T	n/a

Note: Stations included broadcast in the Missoula metro area; n/a not available
Target Audience: A=Asian; B=Black; C=Christian; E=Ethnic; F=French; G=General; H=Hispanic; M=Men; N=Native American; R=Religious; S=Senior Citizen; W=Women; Y=Young Adult; Z=Children
Station Format: E=Educational; M=Music; N=News; S=Sports; T=Talk
Source: Burrelle's Media Directory, 1999 Edition

FM Radio Stations

Call Letters	Freq. (mHz)	Target Audience	Station Format	Music Format
KUFM	89.1	General	M	n/a
KBGA	89.9	General	n/a	n/a
KGGL	93.3	General	M	Country
KYSS	94.9	General	M/N/S	Country
KZOQ	100.1	General	M	AOR
KMSO	102.5	General	M	Adult Contemporary/Classic Rock/Oldies/Top 40

Note: Stations included broadcast in the Missoula metro area; n/a not available
Station Format: E=Educational; M=Music; N=News; S=Sports; T=Talk
Target Audience: A=Asian; B=Black; C=Christian; E=Ethnic; F=French; G=General; H=Hispanic;
M=Men; N=Native American; R=Religious; S=Senior Citizen; W=Women; Y=Young Adult; Z=Children
Music Format: AOR=Album Oriented Rock; MOR=Middle-of-the-Road
Source: Burrelle's Media Directory, 1999 Edition

WEATHER

Temperature/Precipitation/Humidity

	Jan	Feb	Mar	Apr	May	Jun	Jul	Aug	Sep	Oct	Nov	Dec	Yr.
Max. High Temp. (°F)	59	60	75	87	95	98	105	105	99	85	66	60	105
Avg. High Temp. (°F)	29	36	45	57	66	74	84	83	71	57	41	31	56
Avg. Temp. (°F)	22	28	35	45	53	60	67	66	56	44	32	24	44
Avg. Low Temp. (°F)	14	19	25	32	39	46	50	49	40	31	24	16	32
Min. Low Temp. (°F)	-33	-27	-13	14	21	31	31	32	20	0	-23	-30	-33
Avg. Precip. (in.)	1.2	0.8	0.9	1.0	1.8	1.8	0.9	1.0	1.1	0.8	0.9	1.1	13.4
Avg. Snowfall (in.)	13	8	6	2	1	Tr	0	0	Tr	1	6	11	48
Avg. Rel. Hum. 5am (%)	85	85	83	79	82	83	77	75	81	85	86	86	82
Avg. Rel. Hum. 5pm (%)	76	67	52	41	42	42	30	31	38	50	71	79	51

Note: Tr = Trace amounts (less than 0.05 inches of rain or less than 0.5 inches of snow)
Source: National Climatic Data Center, International Station Meteorological Climate Summary, 3/95

Weather Conditions

Temperature			Precipitation		
5°F & below	32°F & below	90°F & above	0.01 inch or more precip.	1.5 inch or more snow/ice	Thunder-storms
18	183	21	124	10	23

Note: Figures are average number of days per year
Source: National Climatic Data Center, International Station Meteorological Climate Summary, 3/95

AIR & WATER QUALITY

Maximum Pollutant Concentrations

	Particulate Matter (ug/m³)	Carbon Monoxide (ppm)	Sulfur Dioxide (ppm)	Nitrogen Dioxide (ppm)	Ozone (ppm)	Lead (ug/m³)
MSA[1] Level	n/a	n/a	n/a	n/a	n/a	n/a
NAAQS[2]	150	9	0.140	0.053	0.12	1.50
Met NAAQS	n/a	n/a	n/a	n/a	n/a	n/a

Note: (1) Metropolitan Statistical Area - see Appendix A for areas included; (2) National Ambient Air Quality Standards; ppm = parts per million; ug/m³ = micrograms per cubic meter; n/a not available
Source: EPA, National Air Quality and Emissions Trends Report, 1997

Pollutant Standards Index

Data not available.
EPA, National Air Quality and Emissions Trends Report, 1997

Drinking Water

Water System Name	Pop. Served	Primary Water Source Type	Number of Violations in 1998-99	Type of Violation/ Contaminants
Mountain Water Company MWC	55,500	Ground	None	None

Note: Data as of January 19, 2000
Source: EPA, Office of Ground Water and Drinking Water, Safe Drinking Water Information System

Missoula tap water is neutral, soft, and not fluoridated.
Editor & Publisher Market Guide, 2000

Napa, California

Background

Napa, California is in the northern section of the state, 50 miles northeast of San Francisco. It is located in the southern portion of Napa Valley on the Napa River, which flows into the San Pueblo and San Francisco bays. The Napa Valley has varied terrain that includes level land, rolling hills and higher mountains toward the north.

The county seat of Napa County, Napa is the primary commercial and population center for the Napa Valley region. The city's economy is based on manufacturing and a variety of other activities, including its well-known grape growing and wine-producing industry, due to the area's unusual soil and favorable weather conditions. Napa Valley is also a popular tourist region, based on its winery tours, the region's scenic qualities and other attractions. Napa is located near interstate highway I-80.

The Wappo occupied the region, and the name Napa is based on a Native American word. In the colonial era, Spain and Mexico originally claimed the area. The first known non-native visitors arrived in 1823, led by missionary Father Jose Altimura. Nicholas Coombs, who had purchased the site from Nicolas Higuerra, laid out Napa in 1848 and the first business was opened in 1849. Napa County was established in 1850, when the California became a state. The region's economy was based on ranching, logging and various agriculture. Napa served as a port for the Napa Valley and nearby areas, providing access to San Francisco Bay and the Pacific Ocean via the river. A gold and silver rush stimulated Napa's early growth and in the late 1850s, it boomed with businesses to serve miners and prospectors, who established a large tent city. Silver mining became an important regional industry.

In the 20th Century, the wine industry, including growing grapes, wine production, tourism and related goods and services, became a mainstay of the Napa Valley economy. Today, Napa industries include manufacture of building materials, pharmaceuticals, electronic and mechanical equipment, clothing and other products. Additional economic segments include retail and wholesale, business and professional services, health care, construction and transport.

Because of its low-lying topography (17 feet above sea level), Napa is prone to flooding, and has experienced several severe floods throughout its history. In the 1990s, the city initiated an extensive flood control system, which Napa River Voters approved in 1998. In addition, Napa undertook an ambitious revitalization plan that includes new construction, restoration of historic structures, downtown and waterfront redevelopment, and natural habitat restoration projects.

Winery tours and wine tastings are popular activities for visitors. The Napa Wine Train offers dining service and passenger tours. Napa Valley Museum in Yountsville offers regional exhibits. Arts organizations in Napa include the Napa Valley Symphony and Dreamweavers Theater, among others.

Napa parks include John F. Kennedy Memorial Park, Alston Park, Fuller Park and Skyline Wilderness Park. Napa is known for having a significant number of historic houses and neighborhoods from the Victorian and early 20th Century. The Napa Valley Historical Society operates a museum in the Goodman Library.

Napa is governed by an elected Mayor and four-member City Council, with a City Manager.

General Rankings and Evaluative Comments

- Napa was ranked #202 out of 354 metropolitan areas in *Places Rated Almanac*. Criteria: cost of living, climate, crime, transportation, job outlook, education, the arts, health care, and recreation. *Places Rated Almanac, Millennium Edition, 2000*

- Cognetics studied 273 metro areas in the United States, ranking them by entrepreneurial activity. Napa was ranked #31 out of the 50 largest metro areas. Criteria: Significant Starts (firms started in the last 10 years that still employ at least 5 people) and Young Growers (percent of firms 10 years old or less that grew significantly during the last 4 years). *Cognetics, "Entrepreneurial Hot Spots: The Best Places in America to Start and Grow a Company," 1999*

- Reliastar Financial Corporation ranked the 125 largest metropolitan areas according to the general financial security of residents. Napa was ranked #96 out of 125 with a score of -3.3 (the percentage a metropolitan area is above or below the metropolitan norm; a metro area with a score of 10.6 is 10.6% above the metro average). Criteria: Earnings and Wealth Potential (household income, education, net assets, cost of living); Safety Net (health insurance, retirement savings, life insurance, income support programs); Personal Threats (unemployment rate, low-income households, crime rate); Community Economic Vitality (cost of community services, job quality, job creation, housing costs). *Reliastar Financial Corporation, "The Best Cities to Earn and Save Money: A Ranking of the Largest 125 U.S. Cities," 2000 Edition*

Business Environment

STATE ECONOMY

State Economic Profile

"California has been on a roll. Its economic strength under almost any measure has surged ahead of the national rate during the last two years. If there was any doubt whether California had climbed out of the hole it was in during the early 1990s, those doubts have since passed. That roll has, however, begun to lose a little of its momentum. In short, California should outpace the nation over the next few years, albeit at a slower rate.

The Asian economic crisis has hit California hard. State's exports to Asia fell nearly 10% over 1998. Most of this decline has been in the high-tech electronics sector, which provided much of the job growth in recent years.

With some over capacity, California's high-tech industries will remain flat until the troubles in Asia have passed. Job growth in several of California's other industries, such as tourism and entertainment, should be strong over the next few years.

Most importantly, California has seen its mass exodus of residents come to an end. While several areas, such as Los Angeles, continue to see domestic losses, offset only by foreign immigrants, most of California will see strong population growth over the next few years.

Housing will remain a mixed bag in California. A shortage of developable land, caused by tight land use controls, will restrain new construction. Residential permits per 1,000 persons should be just over 2, below the national average of 3.5. California will continue to see above average price appreciation in many markets. While remaining a seller's market, several California metro areas will continue to be among the nation's least affordable markets."
National Association of Realtors, Economic Profiles: The Fifty States and the District of Columbia, http://nar.realtor.com/databank/profiles.htm

EXPORTS

Total Export Sales

Area	1995 ($000)	1996 ($000)	1997 ($000)	1998 ($000)	% Chg. 1995-98	% Chg. 1997-98
MSA[1]	238,118	277,981	384,854	398,845	67.5	3.6
U.S.	583,030,524	622,827,063	687,597,999	680,474,251	16.7	-1.0

Note: (1) Metropolitan Statistical Area - see Appendix A for areas included
Source: U.S. Department of Commerce, International Trade Association, Metropolitan Area Exports: An Export Performance Report on Over 250 U.S. Cities, November 10, 1999

CITY FINANCES

City Government Finances

Component	1995 ($million)	1995 (per capita $)
Revenue	36.4	573
Expenditure	33.0	520
Debt Outstanding	40.1	632

Source: 1999 County and City Extra, Annual Metro, City, and County Data Book

City Government Revenue by Source

Source	1995 ($million)	1995 (per capita $)
Intergovernmental	6.7	105
Taxes	21.3	335
Property	8.0	126
Sales and Gross Receipts	9.1	144

Source: 1999 County and City Extra, Annual Metro, City, and County Data Book

City Government Expenditures by Function

Function	1995 ($million)	1995 (per capita $)	1995 (%)
Public Welfare	0.0	0	0.0
Highways	4.2	67	12.9
Parking Facilities	0.1	2	0.5
Education	0.0	0	0.0
Health and Hospitals	0.7	11	2.2
Police Protection	7.0	110	21.3
Sewerage and Sanitation	2.5	40	7.8
Parks and Recreation	3.3	53	10.2
Housing and Community Development	1.9	30	5.9
Interest on Debt	1.2	20	3.9

Source: 1999 County and City Extra, Annual Metro, City, and County Data Book

Municipal Bond Ratings

Area	Moody's
City	n/a

Note: n/a not available
Source: Mergent Bond Record, 2/2000

POPULATION

Population Growth

Area	1980 Census	1990 Census	1999 Estimate	2004 Projection	Population Growth (%) 1990-1999	Population Growth (%) 1999-2004
City	50,879	61,842	68,555	71,686	10.9	4.6
MSA[1]	334,402	451,186	503,800	530,151	11.7	5.2
U.S.	226,545,805	248,765,170	272,212,864	283,625,312	9.4	4.2

Note: (1) Metropolitan Statistical Area - see Appendix A for areas included
Source: 1990 Census of Population and Housing, Summary Tape File 3C; Claritas, Inc.

Number of Households and Average Household Size

Area	1980 Census	1990 Census	1999 Estimate	2004 Projection	1999 Average Household Size
City	21,100	23,830	27,775	29,788	2.47
MSA[1]	117,049	154,822	176,100	187,254	2.86
U.S.	80,389,592	91,993,582	102,048,200	107,302,392	2.67

Note: (1) Metropolitan Statistical Area - see Appendix A for areas included
Source: 1990 Census of Population and Housing, Summary Tape File 3C; Claritas, Inc.

Race/Ethnicity of City Population

Race/Ethnicity	1990 Census Population	1990 Census %	1999 Estimate Population	1999 Estimate %	% Change 1990-1999
White, Non-Hispanic	50,751	82.1	51,786	75.5	2.0
Black, Non-Hispanic	100	0.2	203	0.3	103.0
Asian, Non-Hispanic	1,307	2.1	1,632	2.4	24.9
Other, Non-Hispanic	431	0.7	475	0.7	10.2
Hispanic	9,253	15.0	14,459	21.1	56.3

Source: 1990 Census of Population and Housing, Summary Tape File 3C; Claritas, Inc.

Race/Ethnicity of Metropolitan Statistical Area Population

Race/Ethnicity	1990 Census		1999 Estimate		% Change 1990-1999
	Population	%	Population	%	
White, Non-Hispanic	297,688	66.0	297,039	59.0	-0.2
Black, Non-Hispanic	45,242	10.0	49,975	9.9	10.5
Asian, Non-Hispanic	44,433	9.8	62,229	12.4	40.1
Other, Non-Hispanic	4,247	0.9	3,988	0.8	-6.1
Hispanic	59,576	13.2	90,569	18.0	52.0

Note: See Appendix A for areas included in the Metropolitan Statistical Area
Source: 1990 Census of Population and Housing, Summary Tape File 3C; Claritas, Inc.

Ancestry

Area	German	Irish	English	Italian	U.S.	French	Polish	Dutch
City	24.2	17.4	18.3	8.5	3.4	5.1	1.8	2.7
MSA[1]	20.1	14.2	14.3	6.0	2.5	4.3	1.8	2.2
U.S.	23.3	15.6	13.1	5.9	5.3	4.2	3.8	2.5

Note: Figures are percentages and include persons that reported multiple ancestry (eg. if a person reported being Irish and Italian, they were included in both columns); (1) Metropolitan Statistical Area - see Appendix A for areas included
Source: 1990 Census of Population and Housing, Summary Tape File 3C

Median Age

Area	1990 Census	1999 Estimate
City	34.7	37.2
MSA[1]	32.0	34.7
U.S.	32.9	35.7

Note: (1) Metropolitan Statistical Area - see Appendix A for areas included
Source: 1990 Census of Population and Housing, Summary Tape File 3C; Claritas, Inc.

Male/Female Population

Area	Number of Males		Number of Females		Males per 100 Females	
	1990	1999	1990	1999	1990	1999
City	29,738	33,334	32,104	35,221	92.6	94.6
MSA[1]	229,161	253,682	222,025	250,118	103.2	101.4
U.S.	121,172,379	132,803,736	127,537,494	139,409,136	95.0	95.3

Note: (1) Metropolitan Statistical Area - see Appendix A for areas included
Source: 1990 Census of Population, General Population Characteristics; Claritas, Inc.

INCOME

Per Capita/Median/Average Income

Area	Per Capita ($)			Median Household ($)			Average Household ($)		
	1989	1999	% Chg.	1989	1999	% Chg.	1989	1999	% Chg.
City	16,219	23,677	46.0	35,479	45,806	29.1	41,795	57,335	37.2
MSA[1]	15,522	20,527	32.2	38,454	46,834	21.8	44,383	57,753	30.1
U.S.	14,420	21,350	48.1	30,056	40,525	34.8	38,453	56,184	46.1

Note: (1) Metropolitan Statistical Area - see Appendix A for areas included; 1989 data is from the 1990 Census; 1999 data is estimated by Claritas, Inc.
Source: 1990 Census of Population, General Population Characteristics; Claritas, Inc.

Household Income Distribution

Area	Percent of Households Earning								
	Under $5,000	$5,000 -14,999	$15,000 -24,999	$25,000 -34,999	$35,000 -49,999	$50,000 -74,999	$75,000 -99,000	$100,000 -149,999	$150,000 and up
City	1.8	10.8	12.5	12.8	16.1	22.5	12.4	7.2	3.8
MSA[1]	1.9	10.1	11.9	12.0	17.3	24.1	12.4	7.1	3.3
U.S.	3.9	13.3	13.8	12.6	16.2	19.4	9.7	6.6	4.6

Note: Data as of 1999; (1) Metropolitan Statistical Area - see Appendix A for areas included
Source: Claritas, Inc.

Effective Buying Income

Area	Per Capita ($)	Median Household ($)	Average Household ($)
City	17,552	38,825	45,482
MSA[1]	16,492	41,927	48,311
U.S.	17,496	36,603	47,036

Note: Data as of 1/1/2000; (1) Metropolitan Statistical Area - see Appendix A for areas included
Source: Standard Rate & Data Service, Newspaper Advertising Source, March 2000

Effective Household Buying Income Distribution

Area	% of Households Earning						
	$10,000 -$19,999	$20,000 -$34,999	$35,000 -$49,999	$50,000 -$74,999	$75,000 -$99,000	$100,000 -$124,999	$125,000 and up
City	14.7	21.8	20.1	23.0	7.8	2.5	1.9
MSA[1]	12.7	20.5	20.7	24.9	9.4	2.5	2.1
U.S.	15.0	21.6	17.6	19.6	8.4	3.0	3.3

Note: Data as of 1/1/2000; (1) Metropolitan Statistical Area - see Appendix A for areas included
Source: Standard Rate & Data Service, Newspaper Advertising Source, March 2000

Poverty Rates by Age

Area	People of All Ages	People Under 18 Years Old	Related Children Age 5-17 in Families in Poverty
City	9.9	n/a	n/a
County	8.5	13.0	11.6
U.S.	13.8	20.8	18.7

Note: Figures show the percent of people living below the poverty line in 1995. The average poverty threshold was $15,569 for a family of four in 1995; n/a not available
Source: Bureau of the Census, Small Area Income and Poverty Estimates Program; U.S. Department of Housing and Urban Development

EMPLOYMENT

Labor Force and Employment

Area	Civilian Labor Force			Workers Employed		
	Dec. 1998	Dec. 1999	% Chg.	Dec. 1998	Dec. 1999	% Chg.
City	35,176	35,824	1.8	33,398	34,427	3.1
MSA[1]	243,692	248,865	2.1	232,553	239,719	3.1
U.S.	138,297,000	139,941,000	1.2	132,732,000	134,696,000	1.5

Note: Data is not seasonally adjusted and covers workers 16 years of age and older;
(1) Metropolitan Statistical Area - see Appendix A for areas included
Source: Bureau of Labor Statistics, http://stats.bls.gov

Unemployment Rate

Area	1999											
	Jan.	Feb.	Mar.	Apr.	May	Jun.	Jul.	Aug.	Sep.	Oct.	Nov.	Dec.
City	5.3	4.8	4.6	4.3	3.2	3.6	3.7	3.5	2.8	2.7	3.8	3.9
MSA[1]	5.6	5.2	5.0	4.6	4.0	4.4	4.6	4.1	3.8	3.6	3.8	3.7
U.S.	4.8	4.7	4.4	4.1	4.0	4.5	4.5	4.2	4.1	3.8	3.8	3.7

Note: Data is not seasonally adjusted and covers workers 16 years of age and older; all figures are percentages; (1) Metropolitan Statistical Area - see Appendix A for areas included
Source: Bureau of Labor Statistics, http://stats.bls.gov

Employment by Industry

Sector	MSA[1]		U.S.
	Number of Employees	Percent of Total	Percent of Total
Services	44,900	26.6	30.2
Retail Trade	36,900	21.9	18.1
Government	34,100	20.2	15.8
Manufacturing	20,800	12.3	14.1
Finance/Insurance/Real Estate	6,800	4.0	5.9
Wholesale Trade	6,500	3.9	5.4
Transportation/Public Utilities	5,800	3.4	5.3
Construction	12,500	7.4	4.8
Mining	500	0.3	0.4

Note: Figures cover non-farm employment as of 12/99 and are not seasonally adjusted; (1) Metropolitan Statistical Area - see Appendix A for areas included
Source: Bureau of Labor Statistics, http://stats.bls.gov

Employment by Occupation

Occupation Category	City (%)	MSA[1] (%)	U.S. (%)
White Collar	55.0	57.1	58.1
Executive/Admin./Management	11.7	12.2	12.3
Professional	14.6	13.0	14.1
Technical & Related Support	3.9	4.1	3.7
Sales	10.7	11.6	11.8
Administrative Support/Clerical	14.0	16.2	16.3
Blue Collar	24.9	25.5	26.2
Precision Production/Craft/Repair	13.2	13.4	11.3
Machine Operators/Assem./Insp.	4.9	4.3	6.8
Transportation/Material Movers	2.6	3.6	4.1
Cleaners/Helpers/Laborers	4.1	4.1	3.9
Services	16.0	14.6	13.2
Farming/Forestry/Fishing	4.1	2.8	2.5

Note: Figures cover workers 16 years of age and older; (1) Metropolitan Statistical Area - see Appendix A for areas included
Source: 1990 Census of Population and Housing, Summary Tape File 3C

Occupational Employment Projections: 1996 - 2006

Occupations Expected to Have the Largest Job Growth (ranked by numerical growth)	Fast-Growing Occupations[1] (ranked by percent growth)
1. Cashiers	1. Home health aides
2. General managers & top executives	2. Physical therapy assistants and aides
3. Teachers aides, clerical & paraprofess.	3. Occupational therapy assistants
4. Salespersons, retail	4. Personal and home care aides
5. Truck drivers, light	5. Plasterers
6. Guards	6. Occupational therapists
7. Receptionists and information clerks	7. Teachers, special education
8. General office clerks	8. Bricklayers and stone masons
9. Food service workers	9. Medical assistants
10. Systems analysts	10. Ceiling tile installers/acoust. carpenters

Note: Projections cover California; (1) Excludes occupations with total job growth less than 300
Source: U.S. Department of Labor, Employment and Training Administration, America's Labor Market Information System (ALMIS)

Average Wages

Occupation	$/Hr.	Occupation	$/Hr.
Accountants and Auditors	-	Maids and Housekeepers	-
Assemblers and Fabricators	-	Maintenance Repairers	-
Automotive Mechanics	-	Marketing/Advertising/PR Managers	-
Bookkeepers	-	Nurses, Licensed Practical	-
Carpenters	-	Nurses, Registered	-
Cashiers	-	Nursing Aides/Orderlies/Attendants	-
Clerks, General Office	-	Physicians and Surgeons	-
Clerks, Shipping/Receiving/Traffic	-	Receptionists/Information Clerks	-
Computer Programmers	-	Sales Reps., Exc. Scientific/Retail	-
Computer Support Specialists	-	Sales Reps., Scientific, Exc. Retail	-
Cooks, Restaurant	-	Salespersons, Retail	-
Electricians	-	Secretaries, Except Legal/Medical	-
Financial Managers	-	Stock Clerks, Sales Floor	-
First-Line Supervisors/Mgrs., Sales	-	Systems Analysts	-
Food Preparation Workers	-	Teacher Aides	-
General Managers/Top Executives	-	Teachers, Elementary School	-
Guards	-	Teachers, Secondary School	-
Hand Packers	-	Telemarketers	-
Janitors and Cleaners	-	Truck Drivers, Heavy/Tractor-Trailer	-
Laborers, Landscaping	-	Truck Drivers, Light	-
Lawyers	-	Waiters and Waitresses	-

Note: Wage data is for 1998 and covers the Metropolitan Statistical Area (see Appendix A for areas included). Hourly wages for elementary and secondary school teachers were calculated by the editors from annual wage data assuming a 40 hour work week; Dashes indicate that data was not available.
Source: Bureau of Labor Statistics, 1998 Metropolitan Area Occupational Employment and Wage Estimates

TAXES

Major State and Local Tax Rates

State Corporate Income (%)	State Personal Income (%)	Residential Property (%)	Sales & Use		State Gasoline (cents/ gallon)	State Cigarette (cents/ pack)
			State (%)	Local (%)		
8.84[a]	1.0 - 9.3	1.02	6.0	1.75	18.0[b]	87.0

Note: Personal/corporate income, sales, gasoline and cigarette tax rates as of January 2000.
Property tax rates as of April 2000; (a) Minimum tax is $800. The tax rate on S-Corporations is 1.5% (3.5% for banks); (b) Does not include local option tax
Source: Federation of Tax Administrators, www.taxadmin.org; ERI's Relocation Assessor software database, quarterly effective date 4/1/2000

Total Taxes Per Capita and as a Percent of Income

Area	Per Capita Income ($)	Per Capita Taxes ($)			Percent of Income (%)		
		Total	Federal	State/Local	Total	Federal	State/Local
California	30,415	10,875	7,438	3,437	35.8	24.5	11.3
U.S.	28,878	10,298	7,026	3,273	35.7	24.3	11.3

Note: Figures are for 1999
Source: Tax Foundation, www.taxfoundation.org

COMMERCIAL UTILITIES

Typical Monthly Electric Bills

Area	Commercial Service ($/month)		Industrial Service ($/month)	
	12 kW demand 1,500 kWh	100 kW demand 30,000 kWh	1,000 kW demand 400,000 kWh	20,000 kW demand 10,000,000 kWh
City	n/a	n/a	n/a	n/a
U.S.	150	2,174	23,995	508,569

Note: Based on rates in effect January 1, 1999; n/a not available
Source: Edison Electric Institute, Typical Residential, Commercial and Industrial Bills, Winter 1999

TRANSPORTATION

Transportation Statistics

Average minutes to work (1990)	20.9
Interstate highways	I-80
Bus lines	
In-city (1998)	City of Napa, Napa Valley Transit-The VINE, 13 buses
Inter-city (1999)	1
Passenger air service	
Airport	Napa County Airport; Oakland International Airport (35 miles)
Airlines (1999)	n/a
Enplaned passengers (1998)	n/a
Amtrak service	Bus Connection
Motor freight carriers (1999)	2
Major waterways/ports	Near San Pablo Bay/Pacific Ocean

Source: FAA DOT/TSC CY1998 ACAIS Database; National Transit Database, 1998; Editor & Publisher Market Guide, 2000; Amtrak National Time Table, Fall 1999/Winter 2000; 1990 Census of Population and Housing, STF 3C; Jane's Urban Transport Systems 1999-2000

Means of Transportation to Work

Area	Car/Truck/Van		Public Transportation			Bicycle	Walked	Other Means	Worked at Home
	Drove Alone	Car-pooled	Bus	Subway	Railroad				
City	78.6	12.8	1.5	0.1	0.0	1.5	2.4	0.8	2.4
MSA[1]	72.8	17.1	1.3	0.4	0.0	0.9	3.1	1.6	2.9
U.S.	73.2	13.4	3.0	1.5	0.5	0.4	3.9	1.2	3.0

Note: Figures shown are percentages and only include workers 16 years of age and older;
(1) Metropolitan Statistical Area - see Appendix A for areas included
Source: 1990 Census of Population and Housing, Summary Tape File 3C

BUSINESSES

Major Business Headquarters

Company Name	1999 Rankings	
	Fortune 500	Forbes 500
No companies listed	-	-

Note: Companies listed are located in the city; dashes indicate no ranking
Fortune 500: Companies that produce a 10-K are ranked 1 to 500 based on 1999 revenue
Forbes 500: Private companies are ranked 1 to 500 based on 1998 revenue
Source: Forbes, December 13, 1999; Fortune, April 17, 2000

HOTELS & MOTELS

Hotels/Motels

Area	Hotels/ Motels	Rooms	Luxury-Level Hotels/Motels		Average Minimum Rates ($)		
			♦♦♦♦	♦♦♦♦♦	♦♦	♦♦♦	♦♦♦♦
City	15	1,066	0	0	n/a	n/a	n/a
Airport	1	59	0	0	n/a	n/a	n/a
Total	16	1,125	0	0	n/a	n/a	n/a

Note: n/a not available; classifications range from one diamond (budget properties with basic amenities) to five diamond (luxury properties).
Source: OAG Business Travel Planner, Winter 1999-2000

Estimated Daily Food and Lodging Costs

Area	Food/Other ($/day)	Average Hotel Cost ($/day)
City	42	100
U.S.	30	55

Source: ERI's Relocation Assessor software database, quarterly effective date 4/1/2000

CONVENTION CENTERS

Convention Centers and Event Sites

Name	Guest Rooms	Meeting Space (sq. ft.)	Capacity (Theatre Style)
Best Western Inn	68	n/a	50
Chateau Hotel	115	n/a	80
Christian Brothers Retreat & Conf. Ctr.	16	3,146	100
Domaine Carneros Winery	n/a	n/a	200
Elm House	16	n/a	25
Embassy Suites Napa Valley	205	8,500	250
Hakusan Sake Gardens	n/a	n/a	100
Jarvis Conservatory	n/a	n/a	250
John Muir Inn	60	n/a	36
Mumm Napa Valley	n/a	n/a	250
Napa Valley Marriott	191	8,500	500
Silverado Country Club & Resort	280	15,000	450

Note: n/a not available
Source: EventSource.com, 3/15/2000

Living Environment

COST OF LIVING

Cost of Living: Homeowner

Cost Element	U.S. ($)	City ($)	Differential ($)	Percent of U.S. Average
Consumables	14,516	17,629	3,113	121.4
Transportation	5,957	7,372	1,415	123.8
Health Services	2,012	2,798	786	139.1
Housing/Utilities/Prop. Tax	16,337	27,932	11,595	171.0
Income+Payroll Taxes	12,615	11,161	-1,454	88.5
Miscellaneous	8,563	8,563	0	100.0
Total Cost of Living	60,000	75,455	15,455	125.8

Note: Figures are based on a single income, four person family with gross annual earnings of $60,000, owning an 1,800 square-foot home, and driving two automobiles worth $22,000 30,000 miles per year.
Source: ERI's Relocation Assessor software database, quarterly effective date 4/1/2000

Cost of Living: Renter

Cost Element	U.S. ($)	City ($)	Differential ($)	Percent of U.S. Average
Consumables	10,486	12,849	2,363	122.5
Transportation	2,107	2,646	539	125.6
Health Services	1,632	2,289	657	140.3
Rent/Utilities/Insurance	9,299	12,164	2,865	130.8
Income+Payroll Taxes	8,607	8,392	-215	97.5
Miscellaneous	7,869	7,869	0	100.0
Total Cost of Living	40,000	46,209	6,209	115.5

Note: Figures are based on a single income, three person family with gross annual earnings of $40,000, renting a 1,000 square-foot home, and driving one automobile worth $8,000 12,000 miles per year.
Source: ERI's Relocation Assessor software database, quarterly effective date 4/1/2000

HOUSING

Median Home Prices and Housing Affordability

Area	Median Price[2] 4th Qtr. 1999 ($)	HOI[3] 4th Qtr. 1999	Affordability Rank[4]
MSA[1]	189,000	41.3	177
U.S.	139,000	63.8	–

Note: (1) Metropolitan Statistical Area - see Appendix A for areas included; (2) U.S. figures calculated from the sales of 687,516 new and existing homes in 192 markets; (3) Housing Opportunity Index - percent of homes sold that were within the reach of the median income household at the prevailing mortgage interest rate; (4) Rank is from 1-192 with 1 being most affordable
Source: National Association of Home Builders, Housing Opportunity Index, 4th Quarter 1999

Estimated Home Price

Area	Price ($)
City	258,846
U.S.	135,855

Note: Figures are based on an 1,800 square-foot home
Source: ERI's Relocation Assessor software database, quarterly effective date 4/1/2000

Estimated Rent

Area	Rent ($/month)
City	887
U.S.	651

Note: Figures are based on a 1,000 square-foot home
Source: ERI's Relocation Assessor software database, quarterly effective date 4/1/2000

Median Home Price Projection

It is projected that the median home price in the metropolitan area will increase from $232,299 in 1999 to $347,514 in 2010, an increase of 49.6%
Kiplinger's Personal Finance Magazine, January 2000

RESIDENTIAL UTILITIES

Average Residential Utility Costs

Area	All Electric ($/mth)	Part Electric ($/mth)	Other Energy ($/mth)	Phone ($/mth)
City	n/a	n/a	n/a	n/a
U.S.	99.25	55.47	43.48	20.29

Note: n/a not available
Source: ACCRA, Cost of Living Index, 3rd Quarter 1999

HEALTH CARE

Average Health Care Costs

Area	Hospital ($/day)	Doctor ($/visit)	Dentist ($/visit)
City	n/a	n/a	n/a
U.S.	440.96	53.83	68.42

Note: n/a not available
Source: ACCRA, Cost of Living Index, 3rd Quarter 1999

Distribution of Office-Based Physicians

Area	Family/Gen. Practitioners	Specialists		
		Medical	Surgical	Other
MSA[1]	110	227	157	179

Note: Data as of 12/31/97; (1) Metropolitan Statistical Area - see Appendix A for areas included
Source: American Medical Assn., Physician Characteristics & Distribution in the U.S., 1999

Hospitals

Napa has 1 general medical and surgical hospital, 1 psychiatric.
AHA Guide to the Healthcare Field, 1999-2000

EDUCATION

Public School District Statistics

District Name	Num. Sch.	Enroll.	Classroom Teachers	Pupils per Teacher	Minority Pupils (%)	Current Exp.[1] ($/pupil)
Napa Valley Unified	30	16,045	737	21.8	33.0	4,146

Note: Data covers the 1997-1998 school year unless otherwise noted; (1) Data covers fiscal year
1996; SD = School District; ISD = Independent School District; n/a not available
Source: National Center for Education Statistics, Common Core of Data Public Education Agency
Universe 1997-98; National Center for Education Statistics, Characteristics of the 100 Largest Public
Elementary and Secondary School Districts in the United States: 1997-98, July 1999

Educational Quality

School District	Education Quotient[1]	Graduate Outcome[2]	Community Index[3]	Resource Index[4]
Napa Valley Unified	n/a	n/a	n/a	n/a

Note: Over 1,000 secondary school districts were rated in terms of educational quality. The scores
range from a low of 50 to a high of 150; (1) Combination of the Graduate Outcome, Community and
Resource indexes weighted to reflect the greater importance of the Graduate Outcome and Resource
Index; (2) Based on graduation rates and college board scores (SAT/ACT); (3) Based on the
surrounding community's level of affluence and adult education; (4) Based on teacher salaries,
per-pupil expenditures and student-teacher ratios.
Source: Expansion Management, Ratings Issue, 1999

Educational Attainment by Race

Area	High School Graduate (%)					Bachelor's Degree (%)				
	Total	White	Black	Other	Hisp.[2]	Total	White	Black	Other	Hisp.[2]
City	80.8	83.0	95.2	52.2	46.7	19.2	19.8	25.4	11.8	6.3
MSA[1]	82.2	84.2	81.0	72.8	61.0	19.7	20.1	14.4	20.8	9.3
U.S.	75.2	77.9	63.1	60.4	49.8	20.3	21.5	11.4	19.4	9.2

Note: Figures shown cover persons 25 years old and over; (1) Metropolitan Statistical Area - see Appendix A for areas included; (2) people of Hispanic origin can be of any race
Source: 1990 Census of Population and Housing, Summary Tape File 3C

School Enrollment by Type

Area	Preprimary				Elementary/High School			
	Public		Private		Public		Private	
	Enrollment	%	Enrollment	%	Enrollment	%	Enrollment	%
City	901	61.7	559	38.3	9,045	90.8	919	9.2
MSA[1]	5,583	60.9	3,588	39.1	73,826	91.9	6,476	8.1
U.S.	2,679,029	59.5	1,824,256	40.5	38,379,689	90.2	4,187,099	9.8

Note: Figures shown cover persons 3 years old and over;
(1) Metropolitan Statistical Area - see Appendix A for areas included
Source: 1990 Census of Population and Housing, Summary Tape File 3C

School Enrollment by Race

Area	Preprimary (%)				Elementary/High School (%)			
	White	Black	Other	Hisp.[1]	White	Black	Other	Hisp.[1]
City	91.6	0.0	8.4	16.8	87.9	0.2	11.9	21.3
MSA[2]	72.3	10.8	17.0	14.4	65.5	12.9	21.6	16.8
U.S.	80.4	12.5	7.1	7.8	74.1	15.6	10.3	12.5

Note: Figures shown cover persons 3 years old and over; (1) people of Hispanic origin can be of any race; (2) Metropolitan Statistical Area - see Appendix A for areas included
Source: 1990 Census of Population and Housing, Summary Tape File 3C

Higher Education

Two-Year Colleges		Four-Year Colleges		Medical Schools	Law Schools	Voc/ Tech
Public	Private	Public	Private			
2	0	0	0	0	0	2

Source: College Blue Book, Occupational Education, 1999; Medical School Admission Requirements, 1999-2000; Peterson's Guide to Two-Year Colleges, 2000; Peterson's Guide to Four-Year Colleges, 1999; Barron's Guide to Law Schools, 1999

MAJOR EMPLOYERS

Major Employers

Beringer Wine Estates
Doctor's Co. (interinsurance exchange)
NTX Inc. (telephone communication)
Napa Pipe Corp.
Oddzon Inc. (toys)

Cultured Stone Corp.
Marine Industries
Napa Nursing Center
Oakville Grocery Corp.
Queen of the Valley Hospital

Note: Companies listed are located in the city
Source: D&B Business Rankings, 1999; Ward's Business Directory, 1999; America's Corporate Families, 1999

PUBLIC SAFETY

Crime Rate

Area	All Crimes	Violent Crimes				Property Crimes		
		Murder	Forcible Rape	Robbery	Aggrav. Assault	Burglary	Larceny -Theft	Motor Vehicle Theft
City	4,062.6	1.5	26.9	71.9	272.4	755.9	2,719.9	214.1
Suburbs[1]	4,424.7	3.3	34.2	158.8	494.5	893.7	2,427.0	413.2
MSA[2]	4,375.9	3.0	33.2	147.1	464.6	875.2	2,466.4	386.4
U.S.	4,615.5	6.3	34.4	165.2	360.5	862.0	2,728.1	459.0

Note: Crime rate is the number of crimes per 100,000 population; (1) Defined as all areas within the Metropolitan Statistical Area but located outside the central city; (2) Metropolitan Statistical Area - see Appendix A for areas included
Source: FBI Uniform Crime Reports, 1998

RECREATION

Culture and Recreation

Museums	Symphony Orchestras	Opera Companies	Dance Companies	Professional Theatres	Zoos	Pro Sports Teams
1	1	0	0	0	0	0

Source: Musical America, International Directory of the Performing Arts, 1999; Official Museum Directory, 2000; Stern's Performing Arts Directory, 1997; USA Today Four Sport Stadium Guide, 1997; Career Opportunities in Theatre and the Performing Arts, 1999

Library System

The Napa City-County Library has two branches, holdings of 149,020 volumes, and a budget of $2,493,313 (1997-1998).
American Library Directory, 1999-2000

MEDIA

Newspapers

Name	Type	Freq.	Distribution	Circulation
The Napa Valley Register	General	7x/wk	Local	20,017
Positive Living	General	1x/mo	n/a	6,000

Note: Includes newspapers with circulations of 200 or more located in the city; n/a not available
Source: Burrelle's Media Directory, 1999 Edition

Television Stations

Name	Ch.	Affiliation	Type	Owner

No stations listed.
Note: Stations included broadcast in the Napa metro area; n/a not available
Source: Burrelle's Media Directory, 1999 Edition

AM Radio Stations

Call Letters	Freq. (kHz)	Target Audience	Station Format	Music Format
KVON	1440	General	N/S/T	n/a

Note: Stations included broadcast in the Napa metro area; n/a not available
Target Audience: A=Asian; B=Black; C=Christian; E=Ethnic; F=French; G=General; H=Hispanic; M=Men; N=Native American; R=Religious; S=Senior Citizen; W=Women; Y=Young Adult; Z=Children
Station Format: E=Educational; M=Music; N=News; S=Sports; T=Talk
Source: Burrelle's Media Directory, 1999 Edition

FM Radio Stations

Call Letters	Freq. (mHz)	Target Audience	Station Format	Music Format
KNDL	89.9	Religious	M	Christian
KVYN	99.3	General	M	Adult Contemporary

Note: Stations included broadcast in the Napa metro area
Station Format: E=Educational; M=Music; N=News; S=Sports; T=Talk
Target Audience: A=Asian; B=Black; C=Christian; E=Ethnic; F=French; G=General; H=Hispanic;
M=Men; N=Native American; R=Religious; S=Senior Citizen; W=Women; Y=Young Adult; Z=Children
Source: Burrelle's Media Directory, 1999 Edition

WEATHER

Temperature/Precipitation/Humidity

	Jan	Feb	Mar	Apr	May	Jun	Jul	Aug	Sep	Oct	Nov	Dec	Yr.
Max. High Temp. (°F)	83	86	92	95	104	110	110	110	110	103	89	77	110
Avg. High Temp. (°F)	56	61	64	69	73	79	81	81	82	76	67	58	71
Avg. Temp. (°F)	47	50	52	56	60	64	66	66	66	61	54	48	58
Avg. Low Temp. (°F)	38	40	41	43	47	50	52	52	50	47	42	39	45
Min. Low Temp. (°F)	19	23	23	24	32	34	38	37	36	28	25	17	17
Avg. Precip. (in.)	4.9	4.2	3.3	1.7	0.8	0.2	0.0	0.0	0.4	1.2	2.4	4.4	23.5
Avg. Snowfall (in.)	-	-	-	-	0	0	0	0	0	-	-	-	-
Avg. Rel. Hum. (%)	85	74	70	69	68	63	71	68	66	74	81	82	73

Source: National Climatic Data Center, International Station Meteorological Climate Summary, 3/95

Weather Conditions

Temperature			Precipitation		
0°F & below	32°F & below	90°F & above	0.1 inch or more precip.	1.5 inch or more snow/ice	Thunder-storms
0	23	25	46	0	2

Note: Figures are average number of days per year
Source: National Climatic Data Center, International Station Meteorological Climate Summary, 3/95

AIR & WATER QUALITY

Maximum Pollutant Concentrations

	Particulate Matter (ug/m³)	Carbon Monoxide (ppm)	Sulfur Dioxide (ppm)	Nitrogen Dioxide (ppm)	Ozone (ppm)	Lead (ug/m³)
MSA[1] Level	n/a	n/a	n/a	n/a	n/a	n/a
NAAQS[2]	150	9	0.140	0.053	0.12	1.50
Met NAAQS	n/a	n/a	n/a	n/a	n/a	n/a

Note: (1) Metropolitan Statistical Area - see Appendix A for areas included; (2) National Ambient Air Quality Standards; ppm = parts per million; ug/m³ = micrograms per cubic meter; n/a not available
Source: EPA, National Air Quality and Emissions Trends Report, 1997

Pollutant Standards Index

Data not available.
EPA, National Air Quality and Emissions Trends Report, 1997

Drinking Water

Water System Name	Pop. Served	Primary Water Source Type	Number of Violations in 1998-99	Type of Violation/ Contaminants
City of Napa	70,500	Surface	None	None

Note: Data as of January 19, 2000
Source: EPA, Office of Ground Water and Drinking Water, Safe Drinking Water Information System

Napa tap water is hard and not fluoridated.
Editor & Publisher Market Guide, 2000

Ogden, Utah

Background

Ogden Utah is located in the northern section of the state, approximately 30 miles north of Salt Lake City. It is on the Ogden and Weber Rivers at the western base of the Wasatch Mountains, by the Wasatch-Cache National Forest. The Great Salt Lake is to the west of Ogden. The area's terrain includes level land, which rises to the mountains, with valleys and canyons.

Ogden is the county seat of Weber County. The city of Ogden and South Ogden, Roy and other nearby communities form a metropolitan area that is a regional commercial and transportation center. The economy is based on a variety of activities including industry and government services. Ogden's original growth was due to a national railroad terminus, and Interstate 84 connects Ogden to other highways today. The area is also a destination for tourism and outdoor recreation. Ogden is the home of Weber State University, founded in 1889, which is a significant influence in the economy and culture of the city.

The region was originally occupied by Ute and other Native Americans. Fur traders were among the first white explorers in the early 19th Century. The earliest known settler of the area was a trapper, Miles Goodyear. Members of the Mormon community arrived in Utah in 1848, and a group was established at the site of Ogden, which was incorporated in 1851. It was named for Peter Ogden, an early fur trader.

The community's economy was originally primarily agricultural. Things began to change in 1869, when the Union Pacific and the Central Pacific railroads were joined to create the transcontinental railroad, and a ceremonial gold spike was driven at nearby Promontory. Ogden became a major railroad hub, nicknamed "Junction City," which stimulated significant growth of trade and industry in the 19th and 20th Centuries. In 1939 Hill Air Force Base was established near Ogden, which also brought defense-related industries to the area.

Ogden's industrial segments produce a variety of goods including mineral and chemical products, machinery, computer and electronic equipment and aerospace products, among others. Government agencies and services include regional centers of the Internal Revenue Service and the U.S. Forest Service. Other important sectors are information technology services, wholesale and retail trade, education, health care, business and professional services, construction and tourism and recreation.

The mountains and the Great Salt Lake provide many outdoor recreational opportunities in the region. In addition to the Wasatch-Cache National Forest, Ogden has numerous local parks and state parks. Recreation sites include Willard Bay State Park, Pineview Reservoir, and Ogden Nature Center. Antelope Island is a nature preserve and recreation area in the Great Salt Lake. There are several ski areas nearby, including Snow Basin, Nordic Valley and Powder Mountain. The Ogden Raptors are a minor league baseball team.

Downtown points of interest include the 25th Street historic district and the Mormon Temple and Tabernacle. Union Station is a historic former railroad station that houses several individual museums and shops, related to firearms, railroads, cars and natural history. Fort Buenaventura in West Ogden is a recreation of Miles Goodyear's original fort and cabin. The George S. Eccles Dinosaur Park features exhibits and recreations of prehistoric creatures. Other local attractions include the Treehouse Children's Museum, Hill Aerospace Museum in Roy and the Ogden River Parkway.

The David Eccles Conference Center is a multi-use facility. The Egyptian is a 1920s theater still in use. Cultural activities sponsored by Weber State University and community organizations include Utah Musical Theater, Terrace Plaza Playhouse, the Ogden Symphony Ballet series, and Eccles Community Arts Center, among others.

Ogden is governed by an elected City Council and a full-time elected Mayor.

General Rankings and Evaluative Comments

■ Ogden was ranked #1 out of 354 metropolitan areas in *Places Rated Almanac*. Criteria: cost of living, climate, crime, transportation, job outlook, education, the arts, health care, and recreation. *Places Rated Almanac, Millennium Edition, 2000*

■ Ogden was selected by *Yahoo! Internet Life* as one of "America's Most Wired Cities & Towns." The city ranked #25 out of 50. Criteria: home and work net use, domain density, hosts per capita, directory density, and content quality. *Yahoo! Internet Life, March 1999*

■ Cognetics studied 273 metro areas in the United States, ranking them by entrepreneurial activity. Ogden was ranked #2 out of the 50 largest metro areas. Criteria: Significant Starts (firms started in the last 10 years that still employ at least 5 people) and Young Growers (percent of firms 10 years old or less that grew significantly during the last 4 years). *Cognetics, "Entrepreneurial Hot Spots: The Best Places in America to Start and Grow a Company," 1999*

■ Ogden was included among *Entrepreneur* magazine's listing of the "20 Best Cities for Small Business." It was ranked #2 among large metro areas and #1 among mountain metro areas. Criteria: entrepreneurial activity, small-business growth, economic growth, and risk of failure. *Entrepreneur, October 1999*

■ Reliastar Financial Corporation ranked the 125 largest metropolitan areas according to the general financial security of residents. Ogden was ranked #13 out of 125 with a score of 12.9 (the percentage a metropolitan area is above or below the metropolitan norm; a metro area with a score of 10.6 is 10.6% above the metro average). Criteria: Earnings and Wealth Potential (household income, education, net assets, cost of living); Safety Net (health insurance, retirement savings, life insurance, income support programs); Personal Threats (unemployment rate, low-income households, crime rate); Community Economic Vitality (cost of community services, job quality, job creation, housing costs). *Reliastar Financial Corporation, "The Best Cities to Earn and Save Money: A Ranking of the Largest 125 U.S. Cities," 2000 Edition*

Business Environment

STATE ECONOMY

State Economic Profile

"After several years of rapid growth, the Utah economy has begun to slow. Manufacturing employment remains weak, and population growth has slowed as migration from California has fallen. Even with a deceleration in growth, Utah will remain one of the nation's strongest performers in the next several years.

During the 1990s, Utah was one of the nation's fastest growing states. Most of this increase was the result of migration from California, driven by California's then weak economy. Recently California has rebounded, and migration to Utah from CA has declined. Despite a current population growth rate below that of the early 1990s, Utah will remain one of the fastest growing states over the next several years.

Utah's economy is still deeply rooted in natural resources. Weak commodity prices have undermined the strength of many Utah employers. Geneva Steel laid off hundreds of workers in the state. Copper prices have also started to go the way of steel, forcing cutbacks among Utah mining firms. The long-term outlook for Utah's mining and metals industry is not bright. Soft prices and over-capacity will constraint growth and force some cutbacks in the years ahead.

Business migration has been centered around Salt Lake City, where affordable business costs have attracted several hi-tech firms and corporate back-office operations. The Provo-Orem/Utah Valley area is also one of the nation's largest concentrations of software development. A high quality of life and low business costs will continue to attract firms to the area. New construction and employment due to the 2002 Olympics will offset losses elsewhere." *National Association of Realtors, Economic Profiles: The Fifty States and the District of Columbia, http://nar.realtor.com/databank/profiles.htm*

EXPORTS

Total Export Sales

Area	1995 ($000)	1996 ($000)	1997 ($000)	1998 ($000)	% Chg. 1995-98	% Chg. 1997-98
MSA[1]	1,838,151	2,111,534	2,593,603	2,494,809	35.7	-3.8
U.S.	583,030,524	622,827,063	687,597,999	680,474,251	16.7	-1.0

Note: (1) Metropolitan Statistical Area - see Appendix A for areas included
Source: U.S. Department of Commerce, International Trade Association, Metropolitan Area Exports: An Export Performance Report on Over 250 U.S. Cities, November 10, 1999

CITY FINANCES

City Government Finances

Component	1995 ($million)	1995 (per capita $)
Revenue	50.1	739
Expenditure	46.8	691
Debt Outstanding	45.9	678

Source: 1999 County and City Extra, Annual Metro, City, and County Data Book

City Government Revenue by Source

Source	1995 ($million)	1995 (per capita $)
Intergovernmental	8.8	129
Taxes	23.8	352
Property	9.4	139
Sales and Gross Receipts	8.9	132

Source: 1999 County and City Extra, Annual Metro, City, and County Data Book

City Government Expenditures by Function

Function	1995 ($million)	1995 (per capita $)	1995 (%)
Public Welfare	0.0	0	0.0
Highways	4.1	60	8.8
Parking Facilities	0.0	0	0.0
Education	0.0	0	0.0
Health and Hospitals	1.4	20	3.0
Police Protection	7.1	105	15.3
Sewerage and Sanitation	4.9	73	10.6
Parks and Recreation	5.4	80	11.7
Housing and Community Development	3.6	53	7.8
Interest on Debt	3.7	55	8.0

Source: 1999 County and City Extra, Annual Metro, City, and County Data Book

Municipal Bond Ratings

Area	Moody's
City	Aaa

Source: Mergent Bond Record, 2/2000

POPULATION

Population Growth

Area	1980 Census	1990 Census	1999 Estimate	2004 Projection	Population Growth (%) 1990-1999	Population Growth (%) 1999-2004
City	64,407	63,909	67,514	70,801	5.6	4.9
MSA[1]	910,222	1,072,227	1,281,817	1,399,266	19.5	9.2
U.S.	226,545,805	248,765,170	272,212,864	283,625,312	9.4	4.2

Note: (1) Metropolitan Statistical Area - see Appendix A for areas included
Source: 1990 Census of Population and Housing, Summary Tape File 3C; Claritas, Inc.

Number of Households and Average Household Size

Area	1980 Census	1990 Census	1999 Estimate	2004 Projection	1999 Average Household Size
City	23,974	24,259	27,040	29,081	2.50
MSA[1]	289,381	347,121	433,796	483,559	2.95
U.S.	80,389,592	91,993,582	102,048,200	107,302,392	2.67

Note: (1) Metropolitan Statistical Area - see Appendix A for areas included
Source: 1990 Census of Population and Housing, Summary Tape File 3C; Claritas, Inc.

Race/Ethnicity of City Population

Race/Ethnicity	1990 Census Population	1990 Census %	1999 Estimate Population	1999 Estimate %	% Change 1990-1999
White, Non-Hispanic	52,859	82.7	51,520	76.3	-2.5
Black, Non-Hispanic	1,535	2.4	2,176	3.2	41.8
Asian, Non-Hispanic	1,181	1.8	1,515	2.2	28.3
Other, Non-Hispanic	781	1.2	660	1.0	-15.5
Hispanic	7,553	11.8	11,643	17.2	54.2

Source: 1990 Census of Population and Housing, Summary Tape File 3C; Claritas, Inc.

Race/Ethnicity of Metropolitan Statistical Area Population

Race/Ethnicity	1990 Census		1999 Estimate		% Change 1990-1999
	Population	%	Population	%	
White, Non-Hispanic	968,466	90.3	1,114,867	87.0	15.1
Black, Non-Hispanic	9,372	0.9	14,267	1.1	52.2
Asian, Non-Hispanic	24,633	2.3	38,502	3.0	56.3
Other, Non-Hispanic	8,487	0.8	8,778	0.7	3.4
Hispanic	61,269	5.7	105,403	8.2	72.0

Note: See Appendix A for areas included in the Metropolitan Statistical Area
Source: 1990 Census of Population and Housing, Summary Tape File 3C; Claritas, Inc.

Ancestry

Area	German	Irish	English	Italian	U.S.	French	Polish	Dutch
City	16.8	9.6	34.2	3.4	4.0	3.1	0.9	4.3
MSA[1]	18.3	8.5	41.2	3.0	3.7	3.1	1.0	3.7
U.S.	23.3	15.6	13.1	5.9	5.3	4.2	3.8	2.5

Note: Figures are percentages and include persons that reported multiple ancestry (eg. if a person reported being Irish and Italian, they were included in both columns); (1) Metropolitan Statistical Area - see Appendix A for areas included
Source: 1990 Census of Population and Housing, Summary Tape File 3C

Median Age

Area	1990 Census	1999 Estimate
City	30.0	32.9
MSA[1]	27.5	30.2
U.S.	32.9	35.7

Note: (1) Metropolitan Statistical Area - see Appendix A for areas included
Source: 1990 Census of Population and Housing, Summary Tape File 3C; Claritas, Inc.

Male/Female Population

Area	Number of Males		Number of Females		Males per 100 Females	
	1990	1999	1990	1999	1990	1999
City	31,105	32,954	32,804	34,560	94.8	95.4
MSA[1]	532,133	635,295	540,094	646,522	98.5	98.3
U.S.	121,172,379	132,803,736	127,537,494	139,409,136	95.0	95.3

Note: (1) Metropolitan Statistical Area - see Appendix A for areas included
Source: 1990 Census of Population, General Population Characteristics; Claritas, Inc.

INCOME

Per Capita/Median/Average Income

Area	Per Capita ($)			Median Household ($)			Average Household ($)		
	1989	1999	% Chg.	1989	1999	% Chg.	1989	1999	% Chg.
City	10,754	15,966	48.5	23,487	30,332	29.1	27,886	39,066	40.1
MSA[1]	12,029	20,393	69.5	30,882	46,674	51.1	36,866	59,523	61.5
U.S.	14,420	21,350	48.1	30,056	40,525	34.8	38,453	56,184	46.1

Note: (1) Metropolitan Statistical Area - see Appendix A for areas included; 1989 data is from the 1990 Census; 1999 data is estimated by Claritas, Inc.
Source: 1990 Census of Population, General Population Characteristics; Claritas, Inc.

Household Income Distribution

Area	Percent of Households Earning							
	Under $5,000	$5,000 -14,999	$15,000 -24,999	$25,000 -34,999	$35,000 -49,999	$50,000 -74,999	$75,000 -99,000	$100,000 -149,999	$150,000 and up
City	4.9	18.3	17.8	16.1	18.1	15.0	5.5	2.8	1.5
MSA[1]	2.4	9.0	11.8	12.2	18.0	23.5	11.9	7.0	4.3
U.S.	3.9	13.3	13.8	12.6	16.2	19.4	9.7	6.6	4.6

Note: Data as of 1999; (1) Metropolitan Statistical Area - see Appendix A for areas included
Source: Claritas, Inc.

Effective Buying Income

Area	Per Capita ($)	Median Household ($)	Average Household ($)
City	12,944	28,085	33,587
MSA[1]	15,896	39,923	47,792
U.S.	17,496	36,603	47,036

Note: Data as of 1/1/2000; (1) Metropolitan Statistical Area - see Appendix A for areas included
Source: Standard Rate & Data Service, Newspaper Advertising Source, March 2000

Effective Household Buying Income Distribution

Area	% of Households Earning						
	$10,000 -$19,999	$20,000 -$34,999	$35,000 -$49,999	$50,000 -$74,999	$75,000 -$99,000	$100,000 -$124,999	$125,000 and up
City	19.7	27.7	19.0	13.9	3.3	0.9	0.9
MSA[1]	12.7	22.6	20.3	22.6	8.9	2.8	2.7
U.S.	15.0	21.6	17.6	19.6	8.4	3.0	3.3

Note: Data as of 1/1/2000; (1) Metropolitan Statistical Area - see Appendix A for areas included
Source: Standard Rate & Data Service, Newspaper Advertising Source, March 2000

Poverty Rates by Age

Area	People of All Ages	People Under 18 Years Old	Related Children Age 5-17 in Families in Poverty
City	18.1	n/a	n/a
County	10.3	12.1	9.1
U.S.	13.8	20.8	18.7

Note: Figures show the percent of people living below the poverty line in 1995. The average poverty threshold was $15,569 for a family of four in 1995; n/a not available
Source: Bureau of the Census, Small Area Income and Poverty Estimates Program; U.S. Department of Housing and Urban Development

EMPLOYMENT

Labor Force and Employment

Area	Civilian Labor Force			Workers Employed		
	Dec. 1998	Dec. 1999	% Chg.	Dec. 1998	Dec. 1999	% Chg.
City	39,663	39,897	0.6	37,603	38,023	1.1
MSA[1]	699,827	706,366	0.9	682,129	689,743	1.1
U.S.	138,297,000	139,941,000	1.2	132,732,000	134,696,000	1.5

Note: Data is not seasonally adjusted and covers workers 16 years of age and older; (1) Metropolitan Statistical Area - see Appendix A for areas included
Source: Bureau of Labor Statistics, http://stats.bls.gov

Unemployment Rate

| Area | 1999 | | | | | | | | | | | |
	Jan.	Feb.	Mar.	Apr.	May	Jun.	Jul.	Aug.	Sep.	Oct.	Nov.	Dec.
City	5.9	5.6	5.3	4.6	4.8	6.1	6.4	7.0	6.5	6.6	5.4	4.7
MSA[1]	3.1	3.2	3.1	2.8	2.9	3.7	3.4	3.6	3.3	3.3	2.7	2.4
U.S.	4.8	4.7	4.4	4.1	4.0	4.5	4.5	4.2	4.1	3.8	3.8	3.7

Note: Data is not seasonally adjusted and covers workers 16 years of age and older; all figures are
percentages; (1) Metropolitan Statistical Area - see Appendix A for areas included
Source: Bureau of Labor Statistics, http://stats.bls.gov

Employment by Industry

| | MSA[1] | | U.S. |
Sector	Number of Employees	Percent of Total	Percent of Total
Services	196,400	27.3	30.2
Retail Trade	134,100	18.7	18.1
Government	116,100	16.2	15.8
Manufacturing	84,800	11.8	14.1
Finance/Insurance/Real Estate	47,800	6.7	5.9
Wholesale Trade	40,300	5.6	5.4
Transportation/Public Utilities	47,200	6.6	5.3
Construction	49,000	6.8	4.8
Mining	2,900	0.4	0.4

Note: Figures cover non-farm employment as of 12/99 and are not seasonally adjusted;
(1) Metropolitan Statistical Area - see Appendix A for areas included
Source: Bureau of Labor Statistics, http://stats.bls.gov

Employment by Occupation

Occupation Category	City (%)	MSA[1] (%)	U.S. (%)
White Collar	55.3	62.6	58.1
Executive/Admin./Management	12.0	13.3	12.3
Professional	12.0	14.4	14.1
Technical & Related Support	3.8	4.3	3.7
Sales	10.5	12.6	11.8
Administrative Support/Clerical	17.0	18.1	16.3
Blue Collar	28.9	24.3	26.2
Precision Production/Craft/Repair	11.8	11.0	11.3
Machine Operators/Assem./Insp.	8.5	6.0	6.8
Transportation/Material Movers	3.6	3.7	4.1
Cleaners/Helpers/Laborers	5.1	3.7	3.9
Services	14.8	12.1	13.2
Farming/Forestry/Fishing	1.1	1.0	2.5

Note: Figures cover workers 16 years of age and older;
(1) Metropolitan Statistical Area - see Appendix A for areas included
Source: 1990 Census of Population and Housing, Summary Tape File 3C

Occupational Employment Projections: 1996 - 2006

Occupations Expected to Have the Largest Job Growth (ranked by numerical growth)	Fast-Growing Occupations[1] (ranked by percent growth)
1. Salespersons, retail	1. Systems analysts
2. Truck drivers, light	2. Computer engineers
3. Cashiers	3. Respiratory therapists
4. Marketing & sales, supervisors	4. Directors, religious activities & educ.
5. Janitors/cleaners/maids, ex. priv. hshld.	5. Physical therapy assistants and aides
6. General managers & top executives	6. Emergency medical technicians
7. Registered nurses	7. Paralegals
8. Carpenters, including brattice builders	8. Medical assistants
9. Food preparation workers	9. Medical records technicians
10. General office clerks	10. Home health aides

Note: Projections cover Utah; (1) Excludes occupations with total job growth less than 300
Source: U.S. Department of Labor, Employment and Training Administration, America's Labor Market Information System (ALMIS)

Average Wages

Occupation	$/Hr.	Occupation	$/Hr.
Accountants and Auditors	18.24	Maids and Housekeepers	6.93
Assemblers and Fabricators	9.35	Maintenance Repairers	11.56
Automotive Mechanics	13.28	Marketing/Advertising/PR Managers	28.53
Bookkeepers	10.52	Nurses, Licensed Practical	13.12
Carpenters	14.12	Nurses, Registered	20.87
Cashiers	7.58	Nursing Aides/Orderlies/Attendants	8.14
Clerks, General Office	9.66	Physicians and Surgeons	45.48
Clerks, Shipping/Receiving/Traffic	11.01	Receptionists/Information Clerks	8.43
Computer Programmers	22.75	Sales Reps., Exc. Scientific/Retail	19.54
Computer Support Specialists	16.09	Sales Reps., Scientific, Exc. Retail	26.24
Cooks, Restaurant	8.01	Salespersons, Retail	8.99
Electricians	16.93	Secretaries, Except Legal/Medical	11.02
Financial Managers	25.57	Stock Clerks, Sales Floor	8.59
First-Line Supervisors/Mgrs., Sales	16.42	Systems Analysts	23.44
Food Preparation Workers	6.92	Teacher Aides	8.18
General Managers/Top Executives	29.11	Teachers, Elementary School	15.93
Guards	8.52	Teachers, Secondary School	16.62
Hand Packers	7.00	Telemarketers	7.82
Janitors and Cleaners	7.71	Truck Drivers, Heavy/Tractor-Trailer	14.82
Laborers, Landscaping	8.18	Truck Drivers, Light	9.52
Lawyers	36.34	Waiters and Waitresses	6.08

Note: Wage data is for 1998 and covers the Metropolitan Statistical Area (see Appendix A for areas included). Hourly wages for elementary and secondary school teachers were calculated by the editors from annual wage data assuming a 40 hour work week; Dashes indicate that data was not available.
Source: Bureau of Labor Statistics, 1998 Metropolitan Area Occupational Employment and Wage Estimates

TAXES

Major State and Local Tax Rates

State Corporate Income (%)	State Personal Income (%)	Residential Property (%)	Sales & Use		State Gasoline (cents/ gallon)	State Cigarette (cents/ pack)
			State (%)	Local (%)		
5.0[a]	2.3 - 7.0	0.80	4.75	1.5	24.75[b]	51.5

Note: Personal/corporate income, sales, gasoline and cigarette tax rates as of January 2000.
Property tax rates as of April 2000; (a) Minimum tax $100; (b) Rate is comprised of 24.5 cents excise and 0.25 cent motor carrier tax
Source: Federation of Tax Administrators, www.taxadmin.org; ERI's Relocation Assessor software database, quarterly effective date 4/1/2000

Total Taxes Per Capita and as a Percent of Income

Area	Per Capita Income ($)	Per Capita Taxes ($)			Percent of Income (%)		
		Total	Federal	State/Local	Total	Federal	State/Local
Utah	23,138	8,028	5,433	2,596	34.7	23.5	11.2
U.S.	28,878	10,298	7,026	3,273	35.7	24.3	11.3

Note: Figures are for 1999
Source: Tax Foundation, www.taxfoundation.org

COMMERCIAL UTILITIES

Typical Monthly Electric Bills

Area	Commercial Service ($/month)		Industrial Service ($/month)	
	12 kW demand 1,500 kWh	100 kW demand 30,000 kWh	1,000 kW demand 400,000 kWh	20,000 kW demand 10,000,000 kWh
City	n/a	n/a	n/a	n/a
U.S.	150	2,174	23,995	508,569

Note: Based on rates in effect January 1, 1999; n/a not available
Source: Edison Electric Institute, Typical Residential, Commercial and Industrial Bills, Winter 1999

TRANSPORTATION

Transportation Statistics

Average minutes to work (1990)	19.2
Interstate highways	I-15; I-84; US-89
Bus lines	
In-city (1998)	Utah Transit Authority (Salt Lake City area), 513 buses
Inter-city (1999)	2
Passenger air service	
Airport	Ogden Municipal Airport; Salt Lake City International (30 miles)
Airlines (1999)	n/a
Enplaned passengers (1998)	n/a
Amtrak service	No
Motor freight carriers (1999)	21
Major waterways/ports	None

Source: FAA DOT/TSC CY1998 ACAIS Database; National Transit Database, 1998; Editor & Publisher Market Guide, 2000; Amtrak National Time Table, Fall 1999/Winter 2000; 1990 Census of Population and Housing, STF 3C; Jane's Urban Transport Systems 1999-2000

Means of Transportation to Work

Area	Car/Truck/Van		Public Transportation			Bicycle	Walked	Other Means	Worked at Home
	Drove Alone	Car-pooled	Bus	Subway	Railroad				
City	72.9	17.7	2.8	0.0	0.0	0.7	2.8	1.3	1.9
MSA[1]	76.3	14.0	2.9	0.0	0.0	0.5	2.3	0.9	3.1
U.S.	73.2	13.4	3.0	1.5	0.5	0.4	3.9	1.2	3.0

Note: Figures shown are percentages and only include workers 16 years of age and older;
(1) Metropolitan Statistical Area - see Appendix A for areas included
Source: 1990 Census of Population and Housing, Summary Tape File 3C

BUSINESSES

Major Business Headquarters

Company Name	1999 Rankings	
	Fortune 500	Forbes 500
Autoliv	422	-

Note: Companies listed are located in the city; dashes indicate no ranking
Fortune 500: Companies that produce a 10-K are ranked 1 to 500 based on 1999 revenue
Forbes 500: Private companies are ranked 1 to 500 based on 1998 revenue
Source: Forbes, December 13, 1999; Fortune, April 17, 2000

HOTELS & MOTELS

Hotels/Motels

Area	Hotels/Motels	Rooms	Luxury-Level Hotels/Motels		Average Minimum Rates ($)		
			♦♦♦♦	♦♦♦♦♦	♦♦	♦♦♦	♦♦♦♦
City	11	1,108	0	0	n/a	n/a	n/a

Note: n/a not available; classifications range from one diamond (budget properties with basic amenities) to five diamond (luxury properties).
Source: OAG Business Travel Planner, Winter 1999-2000

Estimated Daily Food and Lodging Costs

Area	Food/Other ($/day)	Average Hotel Cost ($/day)
City	34	69
U.S.	30	55

Source: ERI's Relocation Assessor software database, quarterly effective date 4/1/2000

CONVENTION CENTERS

Convention Centers and Event Sites

Name	Guest Rooms	Meeting Space (sq. ft.)	Capacity (Theatre Style)
Best Western Odgen Park Hotel	288	n/a	1,000
Dee Events Center Weber State Univ.	n/a	n/a	11,615
Historic Radisson Suite Hotel	144	n/a	350
Ogden Egyptian Center	n/a	n/a	825

Note: n/a not available
Source: EventSource.com, 3/15/2000

Living Environment

COST OF LIVING

Cost of Living: Homeowner

Cost Element	U.S. ($)	City ($)	Differential ($)	Percent of U.S. Average
Consumables	14,516	14,898	382	102.6
Transportation	5,957	6,178	221	103.7
Health Services	2,012	2,022	10	100.5
Housing/Utilities/Prop. Tax	16,337	16,711	374	102.3
Income+Payroll Taxes	12,615	13,183	568	104.5
Miscellaneous	8,563	8,563	0	100.0
Total Cost of Living	60,000	61,555	1,555	102.6

Note: Figures are based on a single income, four person family with gross annual earnings of $60,000, owning an 1,800 square-foot home, and driving two automobiles worth $22,000 30,000 miles per year.
Source: ERI's Relocation Assessor software database, quarterly effective date 4/1/2000

Cost of Living: Renter

Cost Element	U.S. ($)	City ($)	Differential ($)	Percent of U.S. Average
Consumables	10,486	10,779	293	102.8
Transportation	2,107	2,189	82	103.9
Health Services	1,632	1,643	11	100.7
Rent/Utilities/Insurance	9,299	9,589	290	103.1
Income+Payroll Taxes	8,607	9,119	512	105.9
Miscellaneous	7,869	7,869	0	100.0
Total Cost of Living	40,000	41,188	1,188	103.0

Note: Figures are based on a single income, three person family with gross annual earnings of $40,000, renting a 1,000 square-foot home, and driving one automobile worth $8,000 12,000 miles per year.
Source: ERI's Relocation Assessor software database, quarterly effective date 4/1/2000

HOUSING

Median Home Prices and Housing Affordability

Area	Median Price[2] 4th Qtr. 1999 ($)	HOI[3] 4th Qtr. 1999	Affordability Rank[4]
MSA[1]	145,000	59.3	140
U.S.	139,000	63.8	–

Note: (1) Metropolitan Statistical Area - see Appendix A for areas included; (2) U.S. figures calculated from the sales of 687,516 new and existing homes in 192 markets; (3) Housing Opportunity Index - percent of homes sold that were within the reach of the median income household at the prevailing mortgage interest rate; (4) Rank is from 1-192 with 1 being most affordable
Source: National Association of Home Builders, Housing Opportunity Index, 4th Quarter 1999

Estimated Home Price

Area	Price ($)
City	150,605
U.S.	135,855

Note: Figures are based on an 1,800 square-foot home
Source: ERI's Relocation Assessor software database, quarterly effective date 4/1/2000

Estimated Rent

Area	Rent ($/month)
City	694
U.S.	651

Note: Figures are based on a 1,000 square-foot home
Source: ERI's Relocation Assessor software database, quarterly effective date 4/1/2000

Median Home Price Projection

It is projected that the median home price in the metropolitan area will increase from $138,689 in 1999 to $200,104 in 2010, an increase of 44.3%
Kiplinger's Personal Finance Magazine, January 2000

RESIDENTIAL UTILITIES

Average Residential Utility Costs

Area	All Electric ($/mth)	Part Electric ($/mth)	Other Energy ($/mth)	Phone ($/mth)
City	n/a	n/a	n/a	n/a
U.S.	99.25	55.47	43.48	20.29

Note: n/a not available
Source: ACCRA, Cost of Living Index, 3rd Quarter 1999

HEALTH CARE

Average Health Care Costs

Area	Hospital ($/day)	Doctor ($/visit)	Dentist ($/visit)
City	n/a	n/a	n/a
U.S.	440.96	53.83	68.42

Note: n/a not available
Source: ACCRA, Cost of Living Index, 3rd Quarter 1999

Distribution of Office-Based Physicians

Area	Family/Gen. Practitioners	Specialists		
		Medical	Surgical	Other
MSA[1]	237	670	603	631

Note: Data as of 12/31/97; (1) Metropolitan Statistical Area - see Appendix A for areas included
Source: American Medical Assn., Physician Characteristics & Distribution in the U.S., 1999

Hospitals

Ogden has 2 general medical and surgical hospitals.
AHA Guide to the Healthcare Field, 1999-2000

EDUCATION

Public School District Statistics

District Name	Num. Sch.	Enroll.	Classroom Teachers	Pupils per Teacher	Minority Pupils (%)	Current Exp.[1] ($/pupil)
Ogden School District	24	13,069	681	19.2	n/a	n/a
School For The Blind	1	409	39	10.5	n/a	n/a
School For The Deaf	1	520	78	6.7	n/a	n/a
Weber School District	39	28,129	1,280	22.0	7.4	3,473

Note: Data covers the 1997-1998 school year unless otherwise noted; (1) Data covers fiscal year 1996; SD = School District; ISD = Independent School District; n/a not available
Source: National Center for Education Statistics, Common Core of Data Public Education Agency Universe 1997-98; National Center for Education Statistics, Characteristics of the 100 Largest Public Elementary and Secondary School Districts in the United States: 1997-98, July 1999

Educational Quality

School District	Education Quotient[1]	Graduate Outcome[2]	Community Index[3]	Resource Index[4]
Ogden School Dist.	89	81	76	108

Note: Over 1,000 secondary school districts were rated in terms of educational quality. The scores range from a low of 50 to a high of 150; (1) Combination of the Graduate Outcome, Community and Resource indexes weighted to reflect the greater importance of the Graduate Outcome and Resource Index; (2) Based on graduation rates and college board scores (SAT/ACT); (3) Based on the surrounding community's level of affluence and adult education; (4) Based on teacher salaries, per-pupil expenditures and student-teacher ratios.
Source: Expansion Management, Ratings Issue, 1999

Educational Attainment by Race

Area	High School Graduate (%)					Bachelor's Degree (%)				
	Total	White	Black	Other	Hisp.[2]	Total	White	Black	Other	Hisp.[2]
City	75.1	77.8	63.8	49.0	44.2	16.2	17.2	5.4	9.1	5.8
MSA[1]	85.6	86.6	76.1	68.4	62.1	22.9	23.4	15.5	15.5	8.9
U.S.	75.2	77.9	63.1	60.4	49.8	20.3	21.5	11.4	19.4	9.2

Note: Figures shown cover persons 25 years old and over; (1) Metropolitan Statistical Area - see Appendix A for areas included; (2) people of Hispanic origin can be of any race
Source: 1990 Census of Population and Housing, Summary Tape File 3C

School Enrollment by Type

Area	Preprimary				Elementary/High School			
	Public		Private		Public		Private	
	Enrollment	%	Enrollment	%	Enrollment	%	Enrollment	%
City	908	70.7	376	29.3	11,063	96.1	448	3.9
MSA[1]	17,219	63.6	9,848	36.4	246,375	96.8	8,205	3.2
U.S.	2,679,029	59.5	1,824,256	40.5	38,379,689	90.2	4,187,099	9.8

Note: Figures shown cover persons 3 years old and over;
(1) Metropolitan Statistical Area - see Appendix A for areas included
Source: 1990 Census of Population and Housing, Summary Tape File 3C

School Enrollment by Race

Area	Preprimary (%)				Elementary/High School (%)			
	White	Black	Other	Hisp.[1]	White	Black	Other	Hisp.[1]
City	87.8	3.3	9.0	14.0	84.5	2.7	12.8	16.6
MSA[2]	94.5	1.1	4.4	5.2	93.2	0.9	6.0	6.4
U.S.	80.4	12.5	7.1	7.8	74.1	15.6	10.3	12.5

Note: Figures shown cover persons 3 years old and over; (1) people of Hispanic origin can be of any race; (2) Metropolitan Statistical Area - see Appendix A for areas included
Source: 1990 Census of Population and Housing, Summary Tape File 3C

Higher Education

Two-Year Colleges		Four-Year Colleges		Medical Schools	Law Schools	Voc/ Tech
Public	Private	Public	Private			
1	1	1	0	0	0	4

Source: College Blue Book, Occupational Education, 1999; Medical School Admission Requirements, 1999-2000; Peterson's Guide to Two-Year Colleges, 2000; Peterson's Guide to Four-Year Colleges, 1999; Barron's Guide to Law Schools, 1999

MAJOR EMPLOYERS

Major Employers

Amalgamated Sugar	Autoliv ASP (machinery)
Big D Construction Corp.	Bourns Integrated Technologies
Marketstar Corp.	Ogden Medical Center
Technology Advancement Corp.	Thiokol Corp. (rocket motors)

Note: Companies listed are located in the city
Source: D&B Business Rankings, 1999; Ward's Business Directory, 1999; America's Corporate Families, 1999

PUBLIC SAFETY

Crime Rate

Area	All Crimes	Violent Crimes				Property Crimes		
		Murder	Forcible Rape	Robbery	Aggrav. Assault	Burglary	Larceny -Theft	Motor Vehicle Theft
City	8,908.7	10.3	101.3	183.5	339.2	1,387.6	6,371.3	515.4
Suburbs[1]	6,015.1	2.1	42.6	84.6	236.4	876.7	4,326.9	445.8
MSA[2]	6,170.0	2.5	45.7	89.9	241.9	904.1	4,436.3	449.5
U.S.	4,615.5	6.3	34.4	165.2	360.5	862.0	2,728.1	459.0

Note: Crime rate is the number of crimes per 100,000 population; (1) Defined as all areas within the Metropolitan Statistical Area but located outside the central city; (2) Metropolitan Statistical Area - see Appendix A for areas included
Source: FBI Uniform Crime Reports, 1998

RECREATION

Culture and Recreation

Museums	Symphony Orchestras	Opera Companies	Dance Companies	Professional Theatres	Zoos	Pro Sports Teams
1	1	0	0	0	1	0

Source: Musical America, International Directory of the Performing Arts, 1999; Official Museum Directory, 2000; Stern's Performing Arts Directory, 1997; USA Today Four Sport Stadium Guide, 1997; Career Opportunities in Theatre and the Performing Arts, 1999

Library System

The Weber County Library has four branches, holdings of 370,832 volumes, and a budget of $3,905,793 (1997-1998).
American Library Directory, 1999-2000

MEDIA

Newspapers

Name	Type	Freq.	Distribution	Circulation
Standard-Examiner	General	7x/wk	Local	62,000

Note: Includes newspapers with circulations of 200 or more located in the city;
Source: Burrelle's Media Directory, 1999 Edition

Television Stations

Name	Ch.	Affiliation	Type	Owner
KUPX	16	PAXTV	Commercial	Paxson Communications Corporation

Note: Stations included broadcast in the Ogden metro area; n/a not available
Source: Burrelle's Media Directory, 1999 Edition

AM Radio Stations

Call Letters	Freq. (kHz)	Target Audience	Station Format	Music Format
KSVN	730	Hispanic	M	n/a
KSOS	800	General	M	Oldies
KLO	1430	General	M/N/S	MOR/Oldies
KYFO	1490	General	M	Christian/Latin
KXOL	1660	n/a	M	Oldies

Note: Stations included broadcast in the Ogden metro area; n/a not available
Target Audience: A=Asian; B=Black; C=Christian; E=Ethnic; F=French; G=General; H=Hispanic; M=Men; N=Native American; R=Religious; S=Senior Citizen; W=Women; Y=Young Adult; Z=Children
Station Format: E=Educational; M=Music; N=News; S=Sports; T=Talk
Music Format: AOR=Album Oriented Rock; MOR=Middle-of-the-Road
Source: Burrelle's Media Directory, 1999 Edition

FM Radio Stations

Call Letters	Freq. (mHz)	Target Audience	Station Format	Music Format
KWCR	88.1	General	M/N/S	Adult Contemporary/Alternative/Christian
KYFO	95.5	General	n/a	n/a
KLZX	106.9	General	M	Classic Rock

Note: Stations included broadcast in the Ogden metro area; n/a not available
Station Format: E=Educational; M=Music; N=News; S=Sports; T=Talk
Target Audience: A=Asian; B=Black; C=Christian; E=Ethnic; F=French; G=General; H=Hispanic;
M=Men; N=Native American; R=Religious; S=Senior Citizen; W=Women; Y=Young Adult; Z=Children
Source: Burrelle's Media Directory, 1999 Edition

WEATHER

Temperature/Precipitation/Humidity

	Jan	Feb	Mar	Apr	May	Jun	Jul	Aug	Sep	Oct	Nov	Dec	Yr.
Max. High Temp. (°F)	62	69	78	85	93	104	107	104	100	89	75	67	107
Avg. High Temp. (°F)	37	43	52	62	72	83	93	90	80	66	50	38	64
Avg. Temp. (°F)	28	34	41	50	59	69	78	76	65	53	40	30	52
Avg. Low Temp. (°F)	19	24	31	38	46	54	62	61	51	40	30	22	40
Min. Low Temp. (°F)	-22	-14	2	15	25	35	40	37	27	16	-14	-15	-22
Avg. Precip. (in.)	1.3	1.2	1.8	2.0	1.7	0.9	0.8	0.9	1.1	1.3	1.3	1.4	15.6
Avg. Snowfall (in.)	13	10	11	6	1	Tr	0	0	Tr	2	6	13	63
Avg. Rel. Hum. 5am (%)	79	77	71	67	66	60	53	54	60	68	75	79	67
Avg. Rel. Hum. 5pm (%)	69	59	47	38	33	26	22	23	28	40	59	71	43

Note: Tr = Trace amounts (less than 0.05 inches of rain or less than 0.5 inches of snow)
Source: National Climatic Data Center, International Station Meteorological Climate Summary, 3/95

Weather Conditions

Temperature			Precipitation		
5°F & below	32°F & below	90°F & above	0.01 inch or more precip.	1.5 inch or more snow/ice	Thunder-storms
7	128	56	92	14	38

Note: Figures are average number of days per year
Source: National Climatic Data Center, International Station Meteorological Climate Summary, 3/95

AIR & WATER QUALITY

Maximum Pollutant Concentrations

	Particulate Matter (ug/m³)	Carbon Monoxide (ppm)	Sulfur Dioxide (ppm)	Nitrogen Dioxide (ppm)	Ozone (ppm)	Lead (ug/m³)
MSA[1] Level	108	7	0.011	0.027	0.10	0.10
NAAQS[2]	150	9	0.140	0.053	0.12	1.50
Met NAAQS	Yes	Yes	Yes	Yes	Yes	Yes

Note: (1) Metropolitan Statistical Area - see Appendix A for areas included; (2) National Ambient Air Quality Standards; ppm = parts per million; ug/m³ = micrograms per cubic meter; n/a not available
Source: EPA, National Air Quality and Emissions Trends Report, 1997

Pollutant Standards Index

In the Ogden MSA (see Appendix A for areas included), the Pollutant Standards Index (PSI) exceeded 100 on 2 days in 1997. A PSI value greater than 100 indicates that air quality would have been in the unhealthful range on that day.
EPA, National Air Quality and Emissions Trends Report, 1997

Drinking Water

Water System Name	Pop. Served	Primary Water Source Type	Number of Violations in 1998-99	Type of Violation/ Contaminants
Ogden City	65,000	Surface	None	None

Note: Data as of January 19, 2000
Source: EPA, Office of Ground Water and Drinking Water, Safe Drinking Water Information System

Ogden tap water is alkaline, hard, and not fluoridated.
Editor & Publisher Market Guide, 2000

Olympia, Washington

Background

Olympia, Washington is situated on a peninsula 60 miles southwest of Seattle at the southernmost tip of Puget Sound. It was known as "the black bear place" by the Native Americans who had occupied the region for generations before the first white settlers arrived in the 18th Century.

Since the 1960s, state government has expanded to become Olympia's primary business, spurring growth that has affected the surrounding area as well. Other successful industries include lumber, plastics and oyster fishing. The city also harbors a large merchant reserve fleet.

The Coastal Range allows for Olympia's gentle climate of warm, dry summers and wet, mild winters. Scenic Olympia National Park and Olympia National Forest afford outdoor activities such as hiking and camping, while the harbor provides a perfect setting for sailing enthusiasts.

Although Spaniards had already sailed along Washington's coast, a wealth of sea otter skins bought from the Indians by Captain James Cook in 1778 marked the beginning of intense exploration and fur trade.

In 1792, Peter Puget of the British Vancouver Expedition visited the site, as did George Vancouver, sent by Britain to find the mythical Northwest Passage. The first American settlers were Levi Lathrop Smith and Edmund Sylvester, who officially laid out the town site in 1850. A native of Maine, Sylvester plotted a New England-style town complete with a town square, tree-lined streets, land for schools, a Masonic hall and capital grounds. A local resident, Isaac Ebey, used the nearby Olympic Mountains as inspiration for the town's name.

By 1853, Olympia was named as the capital of the newly formed Washington Territory. Its waterfront quickly became a hub of maritime commerce in the region, whose prosperity increased further when Washington became a state in 1889. An opera house was built, along with a streetcar line, a city water system, and a new hotel. Also in 1853, the Washington State Library became the state's first library, launching the creation of a public system of over 250 libraries.

A dredging and filling project in 1912 created 22 extra city blocks as well as a deep water harbor. In the years following World War I, Olympia became a lumber processing center. New building efforts helped develop its downtown and residential areas, culminating in the construction of a great domed legislative building in 1927.

General Rankings and Evaluative Comments

■ Olympia was ranked #170 out of 354 metropolitan areas in *Places Rated Almanac*. Criteria: cost of living, climate, crime, transportation, job outlook, education, the arts, health care, and recreation. *Places Rated Almanac, Millennium Edition, 2000*

■ Olympia was selected as one of America's best small art towns. The city was ranked #53 out of 100. Criteria: easy and affordable access to the visual arts, performing arts and music, strong sense of community, low crime rate, and full-time population less than 65,000. *The 100 Best Small Art Towns in America: Discover Creative Communities, Fresh Air, and Affordable Living, 1998*

■ Olympia was selected as one of America's best places to retire. Criteria: safety, climate, housing, culture and recreation, social compatibility, affordability, medical care, transportation, and jobs and/or volunteer opportunities. *Where to Retire: America's Best and Most Affordable Places, 1998*

Business Environment

STATE ECONOMY

State Economic Profile

"After some recent years of very strong growth, the Washington economy is quickly losing steam. Washington's manufacturing employment shrank in 1998, mostly as the result of continued layoffs by Boeing.

Further layoffs and a slowing US economy will dampen the Washington economy. Strong migration and a young, educated workforce will lead to strong long-term growth for Washington after its current problems have run their course.

Spokane's employment base shrank by almost 2% in 1998, shedding some 3,700 jobs on net. The bulk of these were in manufacturing, where employment declined by 13.7%, losing 3,100 jobs on net. Construction employment also declined by 11.2%, even as multifamily housing permits increased by 69% and single family permits by 19%. Given its current economic contract, both Spokane' residential and commercial properties markets are facing increasing inventories and rising vacancies. While the rest of the nation enjoyed a booming housing market, home price appreciation in Spokane was negative in 1998. The housing market should stabilize, but remain weak in the near future.

The Puget Sound economy fared well in 1998 in light of the expected Boeing cutbacks. The employment base expanded by 2.7% in 1998, even as manufacturing declined by 0.6%. An increase of 3.4% in services and 6.6% in construction helped to offset losses in manufacturing. With the manufacturing sector declining even further, the current level of construction is not sustainable, and construction employment should contract in 2000. Home price appreciation in Seattle was weak in 1998 at around 2%, and both volume and prices in Seattle should decline in 2000.

Washington's economy is headed for a substantial turbulence in the near term. Fortunately, the economy is mostly in good shape, which will help with the absorption of workers leaving Boeing. Long term, stabilization at Boeing, the ongoing expansion of the software industry, and a rebound in migration will lead to above-average growth." *National Association of Realtors, Economic Profiles: The Fifty States and the District of Columbia, http://nar.realtor.com/databank/profiles.htm*

EXPORTS

Total Export Sales

Area	1995 ($000)	1996 ($000)	1997 ($000)	1998 ($000)	% Chg. 1995-98	% Chg. 1997-98
MSA[1]	n/a	n/a	n/a	n/a	n/a	n/a
U.S.	583,030,524	622,827,063	687,597,999	680,474,251	16.7	-1.0

Note: (1) Metropolitan Statistical Area - see Appendix A for areas included
Source: U.S. Department of Commerce, International Trade Association, Metropolitan Area Exports: An Export Performance Report on Over 250 U.S. Cities, November 10, 1999

CITY FINANCES

City Government Finances

Component	1995 ($million)	1995 (per capita $)
Revenue	57.2	1,439
Expenditure	54.3	1,367
Debt Outstanding	28.5	717

Source: 1999 County and City Extra, Annual Metro, City, and County Data Book

City Government Revenue by Source

Source	1995 ($million)	1995 (per capita $)
Intergovernmental	10.4	261
Taxes	23.8	599
Property	7.5	191
Sales and Gross Receipts	13.1	330

Source: 1999 County and City Extra, Annual Metro, City, and County Data Book

City Government Expenditures by Function

Function	1995 ($million)	1995 (per capita $)	1995 (%)
Public Welfare	0.2	6	0.5
Highways	4.5	113	8.3
Parking Facilities	<0.1	1	0.1
Education	0.0	0	0.0
Health and Hospitals	0.3	9	0.7
Police Protection	5.5	139	10.2
Sewerage and Sanitation	14.2	359	26.3
Parks and Recreation	4.3	109	8.0
Housing and Community Development	1.2	31	2.3
Interest on Debt	2.0	52	3.8

Source: 1999 County and City Extra, Annual Metro, City, and County Data Book

Municipal Bond Ratings

Area	Moody's
City	A1

Source: Mergent Bond Record, 2/2000

POPULATION

Population Growth

Area	1980 Census	1990 Census	1999 Estimate	2004 Projection	Population Growth (%) 1990-1999	Population Growth (%) 1999-2004
City	27,447	33,840	38,946	40,683	15.1	4.5
MSA[1]	124,264	161,238	204,043	219,633	26.5	7.6
U.S.	226,545,805	248,765,170	272,212,864	283,625,312	9.4	4.2

Note: (1) Metropolitan Statistical Area - see Appendix A for areas included
Source: 1990 Census of Population and Housing, Summary Tape File 3C; Claritas, Inc.

Number of Households and Average Household Size

Area	1980 Census	1990 Census	1999 Estimate	2004 Projection	1999 Average Household Size
City	12,028	14,958	17,626	18,602	2.21
MSA[1]	46,376	62,047	80,155	87,033	2.55
U.S.	80,389,592	91,993,582	102,048,200	107,302,392	2.67

Note: (1) Metropolitan Statistical Area - see Appendix A for areas included
Source: 1990 Census of Population and Housing, Summary Tape File 3C; Claritas, Inc.

Race/Ethnicity of City Population

Race/Ethnicity	1990 Census Population	1990 Census %	1999 Estimate Population	1999 Estimate %	% Change 1990-1999
White, Non-Hispanic	30,687	90.7	33,870	87.0	10.4
Black, Non-Hispanic	386	1.1	537	1.4	39.1
Asian, Non-Hispanic	1,613	4.8	2,478	6.4	53.6
Other, Non-Hispanic	359	1.1	472	1.2	31.5
Hispanic	795	2.3	1,589	4.1	99.9

Source: 1990 Census of Population and Housing, Summary Tape File 3C; Claritas, Inc.

Race/Ethnicity of Metropolitan Statistical Area Population

Race/Ethnicity	1990 Census		1999 Estimate		% Change 1990-1999
	Population	%	Population	%	
White, Non-Hispanic	146,042	90.6	177,978	87.2	21.9
Black, Non-Hispanic	2,602	1.6	4,123	2.0	58.5
Asian, Non-Hispanic	5,894	3.7	9,668	4.7	64.0
Other, Non-Hispanic	2,423	1.5	2,962	1.5	22.2
Hispanic	4,277	2.7	9,312	4.6	117.7

Note: See Appendix A for areas included in the Metropolitan Statistical Area
Source: 1990 Census of Population and Housing, Summary Tape File 3C; Claritas, Inc.

Ancestry

Area	German	Irish	English	Italian	U.S.	French	Polish	Dutch
City	28.4	17.7	21.3	2.8	4.1	4.9	2.1	4.0
MSA[1]	30.5	17.6	19.8	2.9	4.3	5.5	2.3	3.6
U.S.	23.3	15.6	13.1	5.9	5.3	4.2	3.8	2.5

Note: Figures are percentages and include persons that reported multiple ancestry (eg. if a person reported being Irish and Italian, they were included in both columns); (1) Metropolitan Statistical Area - see Appendix A for areas included
Source: 1990 Census of Population and Housing, Summary Tape File 3C

Median Age

Area	1990 Census	1999 Estimate
City	35.0	38.0
MSA[1]	33.7	36.5
U.S.	32.9	35.7

Note: (1) Metropolitan Statistical Area - see Appendix A for areas included
Source: 1990 Census of Population and Housing, Summary Tape File 3C; Claritas, Inc.

Male/Female Population

Area	Number of Males		Number of Females		Males per 100 Females	
	1990	1999	1990	1999	1990	1999
City	16,073	18,490	17,767	20,456	90.5	90.4
MSA[1]	78,590	99,247	82,648	104,796	95.1	94.7
U.S.	121,172,379	132,803,736	127,537,494	139,409,136	95.0	95.3

Note: (1) Metropolitan Statistical Area - see Appendix A for areas included
Source: 1990 Census of Population, General Population Characteristics; Claritas, Inc.

INCOME

Per Capita/Median/Average Income

Area	Per Capita ($)			Median Household ($)			Average Household ($)		
	1989	1999	% Chg.	1989	1999	% Chg.	1989	1999	% Chg.
City	15,502	22,850	47.4	27,785	37,469	34.9	34,579	49,625	43.5
MSA[1]	13,901	20,453	47.1	30,976	41,578	34.2	35,772	51,622	44.3
U.S.	14,420	21,350	48.1	30,056	40,525	34.8	38,453	56,184	46.1

Note: (1) Metropolitan Statistical Area - see Appendix A for areas included; 1989 data is from the 1990 Census; 1999 data is estimated by Claritas, Inc.
Source: 1990 Census of Population, General Population Characteristics; Claritas, Inc.

Household Income Distribution

Area	Percent of Households Earning								
	Under $5,000	$5,000 -14,999	$15,000 -24,999	$25,000 -34,999	$35,000 -49,999	$50,000 -74,999	$75,000 -99,000	$100,000 -149,999	$150,000 and up
City	3.5	15.2	13.8	13.3	17.4	20.5	8.5	5.4	2.4
MSA[1]	2.5	11.0	13.7	13.9	18.4	22.6	9.9	5.8	2.1
U.S.	3.9	13.3	13.8	12.6	16.2	19.4	9.7	6.6	4.6

Note: Data as of 1999; (1) Metropolitan Statistical Area - see Appendix A for areas included
Source: Claritas, Inc.

Effective Buying Income

Area	Per Capita ($)	Median Household ($)	Average Household ($)
City	19,929	36,700	45,007
MSA[1]	18,743	41,708	48,633
U.S.	17,496	36,603	47,036

Note: Data as of 1/1/2000; (1) Metropolitan Statistical Area - see Appendix A for areas included
Source: Standard Rate & Data Service, Newspaper Advertising Source, March 2000

Effective Household Buying Income Distribution

Area	% of Households Earning						
	$10,000 -$19,999	$20,000 -$34,999	$35,000 -$49,999	$50,000 -$74,999	$75,000 -$99,000	$100,000 -$124,999	$125,000 and up
City	14.9	21.9	18.4	19.7	8.7	2.8	2.6
MSA[1]	12.5	21.4	19.1	23.0	10.5	3.5	2.6
U.S.	15.0	21.6	17.6	19.6	8.4	3.0	3.3

Note: Data as of 1/1/2000; (1) Metropolitan Statistical Area - see Appendix A for areas included
Source: Standard Rate & Data Service, Newspaper Advertising Source, March 2000

Poverty Rates by Age

Area	People of All Ages	People Under 18 Years Old	Related Children Age 5-17 in Families in Poverty
City	12.6	n/a	n/a
County	9.4	13.1	10.8
U.S.	13.8	20.8	18.7

Note: Figures show the percent of people living below the poverty line in 1995. The average poverty threshold was $15,569 for a family of four in 1995; n/a not available
Source: Bureau of the Census, Small Area Income and Poverty Estimates Program; U.S. Department of Housing and Urban Development

EMPLOYMENT

Labor Force and Employment

Area	Civilian Labor Force			Workers Employed		
	Dec. 1998	Dec. 1999	% Chg.	Dec. 1998	Dec. 1999	% Chg.
City	22,250	22,693	2.0	21,234	21,787	2.6
MSA[1]	101,131	103,128	2.0	96,423	98,931	2.6
U.S.	138,297,000	139,941,000	1.2	132,732,000	134,696,000	1.5

Note: Data is not seasonally adjusted and covers workers 16 years of age and older;
(1) Metropolitan Statistical Area - see Appendix A for areas included
Source: Bureau of Labor Statistics, http://stats.bls.gov

Unemployment Rate

Area	1999											
	Jan.	Feb.	Mar.	Apr.	May	Jun.	Jul.	Aug.	Sep.	Oct.	Nov.	Dec.
City	5.1	5.2	4.6	4.0	4.1	4.4	4.5	4.2	4.4	4.7	4.0	4.0
MSA[1]	5.2	5.3	4.7	4.1	4.2	4.5	4.6	4.3	4.5	4.8	4.0	4.1
U.S.	4.8	4.7	4.4	4.1	4.0	4.5	4.5	4.2	4.1	3.8	3.8	3.7

Note: Data is not seasonally adjusted and covers workers 16 years of age and older; all figures are percentages; (1) Metropolitan Statistical Area - see Appendix A for areas included
Source: Bureau of Labor Statistics, http://stats.bls.gov

Employment by Industry

Sector	MSA[1]		U.S.
	Number of Employees	Percent of Total	Percent of Total
Services	n/a	n/a	30.2
Retail Trade	n/a	n/a	18.1
Government	n/a	n/a	15.8
Manufacturing	n/a	n/a	14.1
Finance/Insurance/Real Estate	n/a	n/a	5.9
Wholesale Trade	n/a	n/a	5.4
Transportation/Public Utilities	n/a	n/a	5.3
Construction	n/a	n/a	4.8
Mining	n/a	n/a	0.4

Note: Figures cover non-farm employment as of 12/99 and are not seasonally adjusted; (1) Metropolitan Statistical Area - see Appendix A for areas included; n/a not available
Source: Bureau of Labor Statistics, http://stats.bls.gov

Employment by Occupation

Occupation Category	City (%)	MSA[1] (%)	U.S. (%)
White Collar	71.5	64.4	58.1
Executive/Admin./Management	18.0	15.3	12.3
Professional	20.1	16.3	14.1
Technical & Related Support	5.2	4.8	3.7
Sales	10.6	10.2	11.8
Administrative Support/Clerical	17.5	17.8	16.3
Blue Collar	15.1	20.7	26.2
Precision Production/Craft/Repair	6.9	9.6	11.3
Machine Operators/Assem./Insp.	3.5	3.6	6.8
Transportation/Material Movers	2.0	4.2	4.1
Cleaners/Helpers/Laborers	2.7	3.3	3.9
Services	11.7	12.0	13.2
Farming/Forestry/Fishing	1.6	2.9	2.5

Note: Figures cover workers 16 years of age and older; (1) Metropolitan Statistical Area - see Appendix A for areas included
Source: 1990 Census of Population and Housing, Summary Tape File 3C

Occupational Employment Projections: 1996 - 2006

Occupations Expected to Have the Largest Job Growth (ranked by numerical growth)	Fast-Growing Occupations[1] (ranked by percent growth)
1. Salespersons, retail	1. Personal and home care aides
2. Cashiers	2. Systems analysts
3. Child care workers, private household	3. Paralegals
4. General managers & top executives	4. Electronic semiconductor processors
5. Computer engineers	5. Directors, religious activities & educ.
6. Systems analysts	6. Physical therapy assistants and aides
7. Database administrators	7. Respiratory therapists
8. Food service workers	8. Human services workers
9. Truck drivers, light	9. Medical assistants
10. Janitors/cleaners/maids, ex. priv. hshld.	10. Medical records technicians

Note: Projections cover Washington; (1) Excludes occupations with total job growth less than 300
Source: U.S. Department of Labor, Employment and Training Administration, America's Labor Market Information System (ALMIS)

Average Wages

Occupation	$/Hr.	Occupation	$/Hr.
Accountants and Auditors	-	Maids and Housekeepers	7.84
Assemblers and Fabricators	8.03	Maintenance Repairers	11.01
Automotive Mechanics	14.36	Marketing/Advertising/PR Managers	22.11
Bookkeepers	11.81	Nurses, Licensed Practical	12.55
Carpenters	17.26	Nurses, Registered	21.03
Cashiers	8.82	Nursing Aides/Orderlies/Attendants	8.55
Clerks, General Office	-	Physicians and Surgeons	53.11
Clerks, Shipping/Receiving/Traffic	11.53	Receptionists/Information Clerks	9.31
Computer Programmers	34.49	Sales Reps., Exc. Scientific/Retail	15.44
Computer Support Specialists	-	Sales Reps., Scientific, Exc. Retail	15.70
Cooks, Restaurant	8.00	Salespersons, Retail	9.47
Electricians	18.22	Secretaries, Except Legal/Medical	12.38
Financial Managers	25.54	Stock Clerks, Sales Floor	9.16
First-Line Supervisors/Mgrs., Sales	16.37	Systems Analysts	-
Food Preparation Workers	7.49	Teacher Aides	9.25
General Managers/Top Executives	27.16	Teachers, Elementary School	17.97
Guards	8.63	Teachers, Secondary School	17.96
Hand Packers	8.50	Telemarketers	-
Janitors and Cleaners	7.77	Truck Drivers, Heavy/Tractor-Trailer	14.93
Laborers, Landscaping	10.01	Truck Drivers, Light	9.22
Lawyers	-	Waiters and Waitresses	6.03

Note: Wage data is for 1998 and covers the Metropolitan Statistical Area (see Appendix A for areas included). Hourly wages for elementary and secondary school teachers were calculated by the editors from annual wage data assuming a 40 hour work week; Dashes indicate that data was not available.
Source: Bureau of Labor Statistics, 1998 Metropolitan Area Occupational Employment and Wage Estimates

TAXES

Major State and Local Tax Rates

State Corporate Income (%)	State Personal Income (%)	Residential Property (%)	Sales & Use		State Gasoline (cents/ gallon)	State Cigarette (cents/ pack)
			State (%)	Local (%)		
None	None	1.38	6.5	2.1	23.0	82.5

Note: Personal/corporate income, sales, gasoline and cigarette tax rates as of January 2000. Property tax rates as of April 2000.
Source: Federation of Tax Administrators, www.taxadmin.org; ERI's Relocation Assessor software database, quarterly effective date 4/1/2000

Total Taxes Per Capita and as a Percent of Income

Area	Per Capita Income ($)	Per Capita Taxes ($)			Percent of Income (%)		
		Total	Federal	State/Local	Total	Federal	State/Local
Washington	30,430	11,355	7,688	3,667	37.3	25.3	12.0
U.S.	28,878	10,298	7,026	3,273	35.7	24.3	11.3

Note: Figures are for 1999
Source: Tax Foundation, www.taxfoundation.org

COMMERCIAL UTILITIES

Typical Monthly Electric Bills

Area	Commercial Service ($/month)		Industrial Service ($/month)	
	12 kW demand 1,500 kWh	100 kW demand 30,000 kWh	1,000 kW demand 400,000 kWh	20,000 kW demand 10,000,000 kWh
City	114	2,013	23,085	328,663
U.S.	150	2,174	23,995	508,569

Note: Based on rates in effect January 1, 1999
Source: Edison Electric Institute, Typical Residential, Commercial and Industrial Bills, Winter 1999

TRANSPORTATION

Transportation Statistics

Average minutes to work (1990)	16.9
Interstate highways	I-5; US-101
Bus lines	
In-city (1998)	Intercity Transit, 64 buses
Inter-city (1999)	6
Passenger air service	
Airport	Olympia Airport; Seattle-Tacoma International Airport (55 miles)
Airlines (1999)	n/a
Enplaned passengers (1998)	n/a
Amtrak service	Yes
Motor freight carriers (1999)	11
Major waterways/ports	Port of Olympia; South Puget Sound

Source: FAA DOT/TSC CY1998 ACAIS Database; National Transit Database, 1998; Editor & Publisher Market Guide, 2000; Amtrak National Time Table, Fall 1999/Winter 2000; 1990 Census of Population and Housing, STF 3C; Jane's Urban Transport Systems 1999-2000

Means of Transportation to Work

Area	Car/Truck/Van		Public Transportation			Bicycle	Walked	Other Means	Worked at Home
	Drove Alone	Car-pooled	Bus	Subway	Railroad				
City	74.5	12.3	3.2	0.0	0.0	1.3	5.3	0.8	2.7
MSA[1]	78.7	12.1	1.4	0.0	0.0	0.7	2.7	0.9	3.5
U.S.	73.2	13.4	3.0	1.5	0.5	0.4	3.9	1.2	3.0

Note: Figures shown are percentages and only include workers 16 years of age and older;
(1) Metropolitan Statistical Area - see Appendix A for areas included
Source: 1990 Census of Population and Housing, Summary Tape File 3C

BUSINESSES

Major Business Headquarters

Company Name	1999 Rankings	
	Fortune 500	Forbes 500
No companies listed	-	-

Note: Companies listed are located in the city; dashes indicate no ranking
Fortune 500: Companies that produce a 10-K are ranked 1 to 500 based on 1999 revenue
Forbes 500: Private companies are ranked 1 to 500 based on 1998 revenue
Source: Forbes, December 13, 1999; Fortune, April 17, 2000

HOTELS & MOTELS

Hotels/Motels

Area	Hotels/ Motels	Rooms	Luxury-Level Hotels/Motels		Average Minimum Rates ($)		
			♦♦♦♦	♦♦♦♦♦	♦♦	♦♦♦	♦♦♦♦
City	4	436	0	0	n/a	n/a	n/a
Suburbs	1	62	0	0	n/a	n/a	n/a
Total	5	498	0	0	n/a	n/a	n/a

Note: n/a not available; classifications range from one diamond (budget properties with basic amenities) to five diamond (luxury properties).
Source: OAG Business Travel Planner, Winter 1999-2000

Estimated Daily Food and Lodging Costs

Area	Food/Other ($/day)	Average Hotel Cost ($/day)
City	38	58
U.S.	30	55

Source: ERI's Relocation Assessor software database, quarterly effective date 4/1/2000

CONVENTION CENTERS

Convention Centers and Event Sites

Name	Guest Rooms	Meeting Space (sq. ft.)	Capacity (Theatre Style)
Holiday Inn Select	191	n/a	1,100
Ramada Inn Governor House Hotel	123	7,000	0
WestCoast Tyee Hotel	146	17,000	0

Note: n/a not available
Source: EventSource.com, 3/15/2000

Living Environment

COST OF LIVING

Cost of Living: Homeowner

Cost Element	U.S. ($)	City ($)	Differential ($)	Percent of U.S. Average
Consumables	14,516	15,911	1,395	109.6
Transportation	5,957	6,213	256	104.3
Health Services	2,012	2,423	411	120.4
Housing/Utilities/Prop. Tax	16,337	23,617	7,280	144.6
Income+Payroll Taxes	12,615	9,837	-2,778	78.0
Miscellaneous	8,563	8,563	0	100.0
Total Cost of Living	60,000	66,564	6,564	110.9

Note: Figures are based on a single income, four person family with gross annual earnings of $60,000, owning an 1,800 square-foot home, and driving two automobiles worth $22,000 30,000 miles per year.
Source: ERI's Relocation Assessor software database, quarterly effective date 4/1/2000

Cost of Living: Renter

Cost Element	U.S. ($)	City ($)	Differential ($)	Percent of U.S. Average
Consumables	10,486	11,432	946	109.0
Transportation	2,107	2,186	79	103.7
Health Services	1,632	1,956	324	119.9
Rent/Utilities/Insurance	9,299	12,753	3,454	137.1
Income+Payroll Taxes	8,607	7,183	-1,424	83.5
Miscellaneous	7,869	7,869	0	100.0
Total Cost of Living	40,000	43,379	3,379	108.4

Note: Figures are based on a single income, three person family with gross annual earnings of $40,000, renting a 1,000 square-foot home, and driving one automobile worth $8,000 12,000 miles per year.
Source: ERI's Relocation Assessor software database, quarterly effective date 4/1/2000

HOUSING

Median Home Prices and Housing Affordability

Area	Median Price[2] 4th Qtr. 1999 ($)	HOI[3] 4th Qtr. 1999	Affordability Rank[4]
MSA[1]	n/a	n/a	n/a
U.S.	139,000	63.8	–

Note: (1) Metropolitan Statistical Area - see Appendix A for areas included; (2) U.S. figures calculated from the sales of 687,516 new and existing homes in 192 markets; (3) Housing Opportunity Index - percent of homes sold that were within the reach of the median income household at the prevailing mortgage interest rate; (4) Rank is from 1-192 with 1 being most affordable; n/a not available
Source: National Association of Home Builders, Housing Opportunity Index, 4th Quarter 1999

Estimated Home Price

Area	Price ($)
City	218,599
U.S.	135,855

Note: Figures are based on an 1,800 square-foot home
Source: ERI's Relocation Assessor software database, quarterly effective date 4/1/2000

Estimated Rent

Area	Rent ($/month)
City	976
U.S.	651

Note: Figures are based on a 1,000 square-foot home
Source: ERI's Relocation Assessor software database, quarterly effective date 4/1/2000

Median Home Price Projection

It is projected that the median home price in the metropolitan area will increase from $163,641 in 1999 to $250,606 in 2010, an increase of 53.1%
Kiplinger's Personal Finance Magazine, January 2000

RESIDENTIAL UTILITIES

Average Residential Utility Costs

Area	All Electric ($/mth)	Part Electric ($/mth)	Other Energy ($/mth)	Phone ($/mth)
City	–	33.98	34.61	17.46
U.S.	99.25	55.47	43.48	20.29

Source: ACCRA, Cost of Living Index, 3rd Quarter 1999

HEALTH CARE

Average Health Care Costs

Area	Hospital ($/day)	Doctor ($/visit)	Dentist ($/visit)
City	629.00	57.44	108.44
U.S.	440.96	53.83	68.42

Note: Hospital—based on a semi-private room; Doctor—based on a general practitioner's routine exam of an established patient; Dentist—based on adult teeth cleaning and periodic oral exam.
Source: ACCRA, Cost of Living Index, 3rd Quarter 1999

Distribution of Office-Based Physicians

Area	Family/Gen. Practitioners	Specialists Medical	Surgical	Other
MSA[1]	65	87	82	98

Note: Data as of 12/31/97; (1) Metropolitan Statistical Area - see Appendix A for areas included
Source: American Medical Assn., Physician Characteristics & Distribution in the U.S., 1999

Hospitals

Olympia has 2 general medical and surgical hospitals.
AHA Guide to the Healthcare Field, 1999-2000

EDUCATION

Public School District Statistics

District Name	Num. Sch.	Enroll.	Classroom Teachers	Pupils per Teacher	Minority Pupils (%)	Current Exp.[1] ($/pupil)
E.S.D. #113	1	n/a	5	0.0	n/a	n/a
Griffin	1	643	31	20.7	n/a	n/a
Olympia	20	9,021	442	20.4	n/a	n/a

Note: Data covers the 1997-1998 school year unless otherwise noted; (1) Data covers fiscal year 1996; SD = School District; ISD = Independent School District; n/a not available
Source: National Center for Education Statistics, Common Core of Data Public Education Agency Universe 1997-98; National Center for Education Statistics, Characteristics of the 100 Largest Public Elementary and Secondary School Districts in the United States: 1997-98, July 1999

Educational Quality

School District	Education Quotient[1]	Graduate Outcome[2]	Community Index[3]	Resource Index[4]
Olympia	125	133	122	111

Note: Over 1,000 secondary school districts were rated in terms of educational quality. The scores range from a low of 50 to a high of 150; (1) Combination of the Graduate Outcome, Community and Resource indexes weighted to reflect the greater importance of the Graduate Outcome and Resource Index; (2) Based on graduation rates and college board scores (SAT/ACT); (3) Based on the surrounding community's level of affluence and adult education; (4) Based on teacher salaries, per-pupil expenditures and student-teacher ratios.
Source: Expansion Management, Ratings Issue, 1999

Educational Attainment by Race

Area	High School Graduate (%)					Bachelor's Degree (%)				
	Total	White	Black	Other	Hisp.[2]	Total	White	Black	Other	Hisp.[2]
City	88.9	89.3	99.1	81.4	82.1	33.1	33.5	41.6	25.2	23.1
MSA[1]	86.5	87.0	94.5	74.9	78.7	24.7	25.1	27.2	18.0	20.6
U.S.	75.2	77.9	63.1	60.4	49.8	20.3	21.5	11.4	19.4	9.2

Note: Figures shown cover persons 25 years old and over; (1) Metropolitan Statistical Area - see Appendix A for areas included; (2) people of Hispanic origin can be of any race
Source: 1990 Census of Population and Housing, Summary Tape File 3C

School Enrollment by Type

Area	Preprimary				Elementary/High School			
	Public		Private		Public		Private	
	Enrollment	%	Enrollment	%	Enrollment	%	Enrollment	%
City	345	53.7	298	46.3	4,664	95.2	237	4.8
MSA[1]	2,182	65.1	1,172	34.9	27,661	95.0	1,444	5.0
U.S.	2,679,029	59.5	1,824,256	40.5	38,379,689	90.2	4,187,099	9.8

Note: Figures shown cover persons 3 years old and over;
(1) Metropolitan Statistical Area - see Appendix A for areas included
Source: 1990 Census of Population and Housing, Summary Tape File 3C

School Enrollment by Race

Area	Preprimary (%)				Elementary/High School (%)			
	White	Black	Other	Hisp.[1]	White	Black	Other	Hisp.[1]
City	85.7	2.6	11.7	3.0	87.6	1.2	11.3	3.3
MSA[2]	87.5	3.0	9.6	4.6	89.1	2.1	8.8	3.9
U.S.	80.4	12.5	7.1	7.8	74.1	15.6	10.3	12.5

Note: Figures shown cover persons 3 years old and over; (1) people of Hispanic origin can be of any race; (2) Metropolitan Statistical Area - see Appendix A for areas included
Source: 1990 Census of Population and Housing, Summary Tape File 3C

Higher Education

Two-Year Colleges		Four-Year Colleges		Medical Schools	Law Schools	Voc/ Tech
Public	Private	Public	Private			
1	0	1	0	0	0	3

Source: College Blue Book, Occupational Education, 1999; Medical School Admission Requirements, 1999-2000; Peterson's Guide to Two-Year Colleges, 2000; Peterson's Guide to Four-Year Colleges, 1999; Barron's Guide to Law Schools, 1999

MAJOR EMPLOYERS

Major Employers

Columbia Capital Medical Center
Lumbermen's of Washington
Olympia Hospital Corp.
Washington State Employers Credit Union

Heritage Financial Corp.
Memorial Clinic
Sisters of Providence in Washington

Note: Companies listed are located in the city
Source: D&B Business Rankings, 1999; Ward's Business Directory, 1999; America's Corporate Families, 1999

PUBLIC SAFETY

Crime Rate

Area	All Crimes	Violent Crimes				Property Crimes		
		Murder	Forcible Rape	Robbery	Aggrav. Assault	Burglary	Larceny -Theft	Motor Vehicle Theft
City	7,453.5	0.0	74.5	166.3	131.5	1,084.6	5,445.5	551.0
Suburbs[1]	3,372.2	3.1	35.6	35.0	135.7	883.4	2,013.0	266.4
MSA[2]	4,181.5	2.5	43.3	61.0	134.9	923.3	2,693.6	322.9
U.S.	4,615.5	6.3	34.4	165.2	360.5	862.0	2,728.1	459.0

Note: Crime rate is the number of crimes per 100,000 population; (1) Defined as all areas within the Metropolitan Statistical Area but located outside the central city; (2) Metropolitan Statistical Area - see Appendix A for areas included
Source: FBI Uniform Crime Reports, 1998

RECREATION

Culture and Recreation

Museums	Symphony Orchestras	Opera Companies	Dance Companies	Professional Theatres	Zoos	Pro Sports Teams
3	1	0	0	0	0	0

Source: Musical America, International Directory of the Performing Arts, 1999; Official Museum Directory, 2000; Stern's Performing Arts Directory, 1997; USA Today Four Sport Stadium Guide, 1997; Career Opportunities in Theatre and the Performing Arts, 1999

Library System

The Timberland Regional Library has 27 branches, holdings of 355,674 volumes, and a budget of $13,326,242 (1997-1998).
American Library Directory, 1999-2000

MEDIA

Newspapers

Name	Type	Freq.	Distribution	Circulation
The Olympian	General	7x/wk	Area	38,584

Note: Includes newspapers with circulations of 200 or more located in the city;
Source: Burrelle's Media Directory, 1999 Edition

Television Stations

Name	Ch.	Affiliation	Type	Owner
No stations listed.				

Note: Stations included broadcast in the Olympia metro area; n/a not available
Source: Burrelle's Media Directory, 1999 Edition

AM Radio Stations

Call Letters	Freq. (kHz)	Target Audience	Station Format	Music Format
KBRD	680	General	M	Big Band
KGY	1240	General	M/N/S	Adult Contemporary
KLDY	1280	General	M	Classical
KVSN	1340	General	M/N/S	Christian

Note: Stations included broadcast in the Olympia metro area
Target Audience: A=Asian; B=Black; C=Christian; E=Ethnic; F=French; G=General; H=Hispanic; M=Men; N=Native American; R=Religious; S=Senior Citizen; W=Women; Y=Young Adult; Z=Children
Station Format: E=Educational; M=Music; N=News; S=Sports; T=Talk
Source: Burrelle's Media Directory, 1999 Edition

FM Radio Stations

Call Letters	Freq. (mHz)	Target Audience	Station Format	Music Format
KAOS	89.3	G/H	E/M/N	Adult Standards/Alternative/Big Band/Classical
KRXY	94.5	General	M	Adult Top 40
KXXO	96.1	General	M/N/S	Adult Contemporary
KGY	96.9	General	M/N	Country

Note: Stations included broadcast in the Olympia metro area
Station Format: E=Educational; M=Music; N=News; S=Sports; T=Talk
Target Audience: A=Asian; B=Black; C=Christian; E=Ethnic; F=French; G=General; H=Hispanic;
M=Men; N=Native American; R=Religious; S=Senior Citizen; W=Women; Y=Young Adult; Z=Children
Source: Burrelle's Media Directory, 1999 Edition

WEATHER

Temperature/Precipitation/Humidity

	Jan	Feb	Mar	Apr	May	Jun	Jul	Aug	Sep	Oct	Nov	Dec	Yr.
Max. High Temp. (°F)	61	73	76	87	96	98	100	104	98	90	74	64	104
Avg. High Temp. (°F)	44	49	53	59	66	71	77	77	71	61	50	45	60
Avg. Temp. (°F)	38	41	43	48	54	59	63	63	58	50	43	39	50
Avg. Low Temp. (°F)	31	33	33	36	41	47	49	49	45	40	35	33	39
Min. Low Temp. (°F)	-8	-1	9	23	25	30	35	33	25	20	-1	-7	-8
Avg. Precip. (in.)	8.0	6.0	5.0	3.2	2.0	1.6	0.8	1.2	2.2	4.8	8.2	8.3	51.3
Avg. Snowfall (in.)	8	4	2	Tr	Tr	Tr	0	0	0	Tr	1	4	20
Avg. Rel. Hum. 7am (%)	91	91	91	88	83	82	83	87	92	94	92	92	89
Avg. Rel. Hum. 4pm (%)	80	71	62	55	53	54	49	50	55	68	80	84	63

Note: Tr = Trace amounts (less than 0.05 inches of rain or less than 0.5 inches of snow)
Source: National Climatic Data Center, International Station Meteorological Climate Summary, 3/95

Weather Conditions

Temperature			Precipitation		
5°F & below	32°F & below	90°F & above	0.01 inch or more precip.	1.5 inch or more snow/ice	Thunder-storms
1	85	6	165	5	4

Note: Figures are average number of days per year
Source: National Climatic Data Center, International Station Meteorological Climate Summary, 3/95

AIR & WATER QUALITY

Maximum Pollutant Concentrations

	Particulate Matter (ug/m^3)	Carbon Monoxide (ppm)	Sulfur Dioxide (ppm)	Nitrogen Dioxide (ppm)	Ozone (ppm)	Lead (ug/m^3)
MSA[1] Level	58	7	n/a	n/a	n/a	n/a
NAAQS[2]	150	9	0.140	0.053	0.12	1.50
Met NAAQS	Yes	Yes	n/a	n/a	n/a	n/a

Note: (1) Metropolitan Statistical Area - see Appendix A for areas included; (2) National Ambient Air Quality Standards; ppm = parts per million; ug/m^3 = micrograms per cubic meter; n/a not available
Source: EPA, National Air Quality and Emissions Trends Report, 1997

Pollutant Standards Index

Data not available.
EPA, National Air Quality and Emissions Trends Report, 1997

Drinking Water

Water System Name	Pop. Served	Primary Water Source Type	Number of Violations in 1998-99	Type of Violation/ Contaminants
City of Olympia	36,047	Surface	1	(1)

Note: Data as of January 19, 2000; (1) Repeat Major Monitoring (TCR) violation—no follow-up samples collected after a sample that tested positive for total coliform or no speciation under the total coliform rule (1 violation in 1998).
Source: EPA, Office of Ground Water and Drinking Water, Safe Drinking Water Information System

Olympia tap water is alkaline, very soft, and not fluoridated.
Editor & Publisher Market Guide, 2000

Pensacola, Florida

Background

Pensacola, Florida is situated in the northwest corner of the state, 200 miles west of Tallahassee, 55 miles southeast of Mobile, Alabama and 6 miles from the Gulf of Mexico. The city is a port of entry on Pensacola Bay, Florida's largest landlocked harbor.

Pensacola was founded in 1559 by Don Tristan de Luna, under King Phillip of Spain. Two years later, the settlement was abandoned due to dissension among its inhabitants. The city was resettled 137 years later by the Spanish until 1719, when the French gained control. In 1722, control again went to the Spanish, which continued until 1763 when, due to a European agreement, Pensacola was passed to the British.

During the Civil War, Pensacola again changed hands when city forces evacuated. In 1862, the Confederate army abandoned the city to Union forces and, once again, Pensacola flew the United States flag. It was ceded to the United States in 1821 and was charted as a city in 1822. Pensacola is known as "The City of Five Flags," due to the fact that during its more than 400 years of history, the city changed hands 13 times, and the flags of five different nations have flown over its ports.

Pensacola's Spanish heritage is evident throughout the city. Much of the downtown area has been designated a national historic landmark, with many architectural and other reminders of the city's Spanish roots and rich history.

Pensacola's primary economic segments include the manufacture of nylon, paper and chemicals. Tourism is also an important element of the city's economy due, in part, to its near perfect climate; the nearby Gulf of Mexico tempers the winters and cools the summers.

Pensacola and the Florida Panhandle comprise one of the most industrially significant areas of the state. The region is home to many industry giants, including Monsanto, Champion International, Armstrong World Industries and Westinghouse. The city's contemporary economy is moving toward telecommunications and financial service operations.

General Rankings and Evaluative Comments

■ Pensacola was ranked #147 out of 354 metropolitan areas in *Places Rated Almanac*. Criteria: cost of living, climate, crime, transportation, job outlook, education, the arts, health care, and recreation. *Places Rated Almanac, Millennium Edition, 2000*

■ Pensacola was selected as one of America's best places to retire. Criteria: safety, climate, housing, culture and recreation, social compatibility, affordability, medical care, transportation, and jobs and/or volunteer opportunities. *Where to Retire: America's Best and Most Affordable Places, 1998*

■ Pensacola was selected as one of the best places to retire by *Retirement Places Rated*. Criteria: cost of living, climate, crime, services, working, and leisure living. The city was ranked #50 out of 187. *Retirement Places Rated, 1999*

■ Cognetics studied 273 metro areas in the United States, ranking them by entrepreneurial activity. Pensacola was ranked #22 out of 134 smaller metro areas. Criteria: Significant Starts (firms started in the last 10 years that still employ at least 5 people) and Young Growers (percent of firms 10 years old or less that grew significantly during the last 4 years). *Cognetics, "Entrepreneurial Hot Spots: The Best Places in America to Start and Grow a Company," 1999*

■ Reliastar Financial Corporation ranked the 125 largest metropolitan areas according to the general financial security of residents. Pensacola was ranked #79 out of 125 with a score of 0.2 (the percentage a metropolitan area is above or below the metropolitan norm; a metro area with a score of 10.6 is 10.6% above the metro average). Criteria: Earnings and Wealth Potential (household income, education, net assets, cost of living); Safety Net (health insurance, retirement savings, life insurance, income support programs); Personal Threats (unemployment rate, low-income households, crime rate); Community Economic Vitality (cost of community services, job quality, job creation, housing costs). *Reliastar Financial Corporation, "The Best Cities to Earn and Save Money: A Ranking of the Largest 125 U.S. Cities," 2000 Edition*

Business Environment

STATE ECONOMY

State Economic Profile

"Florida's economy has been among the nation's strongest in recent years. Job growth has outpaced the nation by a considerable amount since 1992.

While Florida has been able to avoid any significant fallout from the Asian crisis, the weakening of economies in Latin American will dampen both tourism and international trade. 1998 saw the decline in Latin tourism more than offset by domestic visitors. Domestic tourism is projected to soften as U.S. growth cools, offering no offset against the expected decline in Latin tourism. Weaker tourism and trade with Latin American will slow growth in the near future; Florida will still outpace the nation in job growth as Gross State Product growth (GSP) slows.

Over half of Florida's 230,000 new jobs created in 1998 were in the services sector, which grew at 5.2%, more than offsetting a minor decline in manufacturing employment. Much of this growth is taking place in the finance and business services sector.

In spite of strong home sales and a slowing construction market, Florida's price appreciation continued to lag the nation. Although residential permits per 1,000 residents stands at 5.1, well above the national average, this number is only slightly up from 1997 and is poised to decline in the near future.

Growth in Florida, while strong throughout, has been hottest in the Naples, Ft. Myers and Orlando areas. Construction and employment in the construction industry has begun to slow in South Florida. Projected employment and housing gains will be concentrated in Northern and Central Florida. Growing diversification of the economy into financial and business services promises a strong outlook for the years ahead." *National Association of Realtors, Economic Profiles: The Fifty States and the District of Columbia, http://nar.realtor.com/databank/profiles.htm*

EXPORTS

Total Export Sales

Area	1995 ($000)	1996 ($000)	1997 ($000)	1998 ($000)	% Chg. 1995-98	% Chg. 1997-98
MSA[1]	32,207	36,836	59,842	47,881	48.7	-20.0
U.S.	583,030,524	622,827,063	687,597,999	680,474,251	16.7	-1.0

Note: (1) Metropolitan Statistical Area - see Appendix A for areas included
Source: U.S. Department of Commerce, International Trade Association, Metropolitan Area Exports: An Export Performance Report on Over 250 U.S. Cities, November 10, 1999

CITY FINANCES

City Government Finances

Component	1995 ($million)	1995 (per capita $)
Revenue	62.7	1,044
Expenditure	67.2	1,119
Debt Outstanding	144.2	2,402

Source: 1999 County and City Extra, Annual Metro, City, and County Data Book

City Government Revenue by Source

Source	1995 ($million)	1995 (per capita $)
Intergovernmental	11.5	191
Taxes	25.8	430
Property	7.5	126
Sales and Gross Receipts	16.9	283

Source: 1999 County and City Extra, Annual Metro, City, and County Data Book

City Government Expenditures by Function

Function	1995 ($million)	1995 (per capita $)	1995 (%)
Public Welfare	0.0	0	0.0
Highways	4.0	68	6.1
Parking Facilities	0.0	0	0.0
Education	0.0	0	0.0
Health and Hospitals	0.1	2	0.2
Police Protection	9.4	156	14.0
Sewerage and Sanitation	3.1	52	4.7
Parks and Recreation	7.4	124	11.1
Housing and Community Development	4.9	82	7.4
Interest on Debt	9.4	156	14.0

Source: 1999 County and City Extra, Annual Metro, City, and County Data Book

Municipal Bond Ratings

Area	Moody's
City	Aaa

Source: Mergent Bond Record, 2/2000

POPULATION

Population Growth

Area	1980 Census	1990 Census	1999 Estimate	2004 Projection	Population Growth (%) 1990-1999	Population Growth (%) 1999-2004
City	57,619	58,165	57,582	58,731	-1.0	2.0
MSA[1]	289,782	344,406	405,930	442,314	17.9	9.0
U.S.	226,545,805	248,765,170	272,212,864	283,625,312	9.4	4.2

Note: (1) Metropolitan Statistical Area - see Appendix A for areas included
Source: 1990 Census of Population and Housing, Summary Tape File 3C; Claritas, Inc.

Number of Households and Average Household Size

Area	1980 Census	1990 Census	1999 Estimate	2004 Projection	1999 Average Household Size
City	21,776	24,055	23,939	24,726	2.41
MSA[1]	99,662	128,776	153,378	169,544	2.65
U.S.	80,389,592	91,993,582	102,048,200	107,302,392	2.67

Note: (1) Metropolitan Statistical Area - see Appendix A for areas included
Source: 1990 Census of Population and Housing, Summary Tape File 3C; Claritas, Inc.

Race/Ethnicity of City Population

Race/Ethnicity	1990 Census Population	1990 Census %	1999 Estimate Population	1999 Estimate %	% Change 1990-1999
White, Non-Hispanic	37,546	64.6	33,554	58.3	-10.6
Black, Non-Hispanic	18,418	31.7	20,880	36.3	13.4
Asian, Non-Hispanic	959	1.6	1,449	2.5	51.1
Other, Non-Hispanic	248	0.4	330	0.6	33.1
Hispanic	994	1.7	1,369	2.4	37.7

Source: 1990 Census of Population and Housing, Summary Tape File 3C; Claritas, Inc.

Race/Ethnicity of Metropolitan Statistical Area Population

Race/Ethnicity	1990 Census		1999 Estimate		% Change 1990-1999
	Population	%	Population	%	
White, Non-Hispanic	273,693	79.5	305,038	75.1	11.5
Black, Non-Hispanic	55,550	16.1	74,940	18.5	34.9
Asian, Non-Hispanic	5,521	1.6	10,112	2.5	83.2
Other, Non-Hispanic	3,414	1.0	4,727	1.2	38.5
Hispanic	6,228	1.8	11,113	2.7	78.4

Note: See Appendix A for areas included in the Metropolitan Statistical Area
Source: 1990 Census of Population and Housing, Summary Tape File 3C; Claritas, Inc.

Ancestry

Area	German	Irish	English	Italian	U.S.	French	Polish	Dutch
City	15.7	13.8	16.2	3.4	4.9	3.9	1.3	1.4
MSA[1]	17.5	18.0	14.6	3.4	8.5	4.2	1.4	2.3
U.S.	23.3	15.6	13.1	5.9	5.3	4.2	3.8	2.5

Note: Figures are percentages and include persons that reported multiple ancestry (eg. if a person reported being Irish and Italian, they were included in both columns); (1) Metropolitan Statistical Area - see Appendix A for areas included
Source: 1990 Census of Population and Housing, Summary Tape File 3C

Median Age

Area	1990 Census	1999 Estimate
City	35.7	38.3
MSA[1]	32.4	35.5
U.S.	32.9	35.7

Note: (1) Metropolitan Statistical Area - see Appendix A for areas included
Source: 1990 Census of Population and Housing, Summary Tape File 3C; Claritas, Inc.

Male/Female Population

Area	Number of Males		Number of Females		Males per 100 Females	
	1990	1999	1990	1999	1990	1999
City	26,631	26,798	31,534	30,784	84.5	87.1
MSA[1]	167,835	198,023	176,571	207,907	95.1	95.2
U.S.	121,172,379	132,803,736	127,537,494	139,409,136	95.0	95.3

Note: (1) Metropolitan Statistical Area - see Appendix A for areas included
Source: 1990 Census of Population, General Population Characteristics; Claritas, Inc.

INCOME

Per Capita/Median/Average Income

Area	Per Capita ($)			Median Household ($)			Average Household ($)		
	1989	1999	% Chg.	1989	1999	% Chg.	1989	1999	% Chg.
City	14,795	22,450	51.7	25,066	33,693	34.4	35,158	53,072	51.0
MSA[1]	12,278	18,114	47.5	25,736	34,802	35.2	32,104	46,971	46.3
U.S.	14,420	21,350	48.1	30,056	40,525	34.8	38,453	56,184	46.1

Note: (1) Metropolitan Statistical Area - see Appendix A for areas included; 1989 data is from the 1990 Census; 1999 data is estimated by Claritas, Inc.
Source: 1990 Census of Population, General Population Characteristics; Claritas, Inc.

Household Income Distribution

Area	Percent of Households Earning								
	Under $5,000	$5,000 -14,999	$15,000 -24,999	$25,000 -34,999	$35,000 -49,999	$50,000 -74,999	$75,000 -99,000	$100,000 -149,999	$150,000 and up
City	6.3	15.4	15.6	14.0	13.9	16.2	8.2	6.0	4.4
MSA[1]	4.8	14.5	16.1	14.8	17.6	18.4	7.3	4.2	2.2
U.S.	3.9	13.3	13.8	12.6	16.2	19.4	9.7	6.6	4.6

Note: Data as of 1999; (1) Metropolitan Statistical Area - see Appendix A for areas included
Source: Claritas, Inc.

Effective Buying Income

Area	Per Capita ($)	Median Household ($)	Average Household ($)
City	16,526	28,802	40,411
MSA[1]	14,613	31,107	40,051
U.S.	17,496	36,603	47,036

Note: Data as of 1/1/2000; (1) Metropolitan Statistical Area - see Appendix A for areas included
Source: Standard Rate & Data Service, Newspaper Advertising Source, March 2000

Effective Household Buying Income Distribution

Area	% of Households Earning						
	$10,000 -$19,999	$20,000 -$34,999	$35,000 -$49,999	$50,000 -$74,999	$75,000 -$99,000	$100,000 -$124,999	$125,000 and up
City	17.9	22.9	15.4	15.3	6.5	1.7	3.3
MSA[1]	17.4	24.6	17.8	16.9	5.9	1.7	2.0
U.S.	15.0	21.6	17.6	19.6	8.4	3.0	3.3

Note: Data as of 1/1/2000; (1) Metropolitan Statistical Area - see Appendix A for areas included
Source: Standard Rate & Data Service, Newspaper Advertising Source, March 2000

Poverty Rates by Age

Area	People of All Ages	People Under 18 Years Old	Related Children Age 5-17 in Families in Poverty
City	22.2	n/a	n/a
County	19.0	30.1	27.0
U.S.	13.8	20.8	18.7

Note: Figures show the percent of people living below the poverty line in 1995. The average poverty threshold was $15,569 for a family of four in 1995; n/a not available
Source: Bureau of the Census, Small Area Income and Poverty Estimates Program; U.S. Department of Housing and Urban Development

EMPLOYMENT

Labor Force and Employment

Area	Civilian Labor Force			Workers Employed		
	Dec. 1998	Dec. 1999	% Chg.	Dec. 1998	Dec. 1999	% Chg.
City	27,392	27,887	1.8	26,382	26,859	1.8
MSA[1]	174,592	177,785	1.8	168,521	171,567	1.8
U.S.	138,297,000	139,941,000	1.2	132,732,000	134,696,000	1.5

Note: Data is not seasonally adjusted and covers workers 16 years of age and older; (1) Metropolitan Statistical Area - see Appendix A for areas included
Source: Bureau of Labor Statistics, http://stats.bls.gov

Unemployment Rate

Area	1999											
	Jan.	Feb.	Mar.	Apr.	May	Jun.	Jul.	Aug.	Sep.	Oct.	Nov.	Dec.
City	4.6	4.0	3.8	3.9	3.9	4.2	3.9	3.8	3.8	3.9	4.2	3.7
MSA[1]	4.3	3.7	3.6	3.5	3.5	3.9	3.7	3.7	3.8	3.9	4.1	3.5
U.S.	4.8	4.7	4.4	4.1	4.0	4.5	4.5	4.2	4.1	3.8	3.8	3.7

Note: Data is not seasonally adjusted and covers workers 16 years of age and older; all figures are percentages; (1) Metropolitan Statistical Area - see Appendix A for areas included
Source: Bureau of Labor Statistics, http://stats.bls.gov

Employment by Industry

Sector	MSA[1]		U.S.
	Number of Employees	Percent of Total	Percent of Total
Services	55,800	34.9	30.2
Retail Trade	33,400	20.9	18.1
Government	29,500	18.4	15.8
Manufacturing	9,300	5.8	14.1
Finance/Insurance/Real Estate	6,300	3.9	5.9
Wholesale Trade	6,500	4.1	5.4
Transportation/Public Utilities	7,900	4.9	5.3
Construction	11,100	6.9	4.8
Mining	n/a	n/a	0.4

Note: Figures cover non-farm employment as of 12/99 and are not seasonally adjusted; (1) Metropolitan Statistical Area - see Appendix A for areas included; n/a not available
Source: Bureau of Labor Statistics, http://stats.bls.gov

Employment by Occupation

Occupation Category	City (%)	MSA[1] (%)	U.S. (%)
White Collar	67.1	58.0	58.1
Executive/Admin./Management	13.8	10.9	12.3
Professional	20.6	13.6	14.1
Technical & Related Support	4.3	4.5	3.7
Sales	13.1	13.9	11.8
Administrative Support/Clerical	15.3	15.1	16.3
Blue Collar	16.2	25.8	26.2
Precision Production/Craft/Repair	7.5	13.5	11.3
Machine Operators/Assem./Insp.	2.9	4.7	6.8
Transportation/Material Movers	3.3	4.2	4.1
Cleaners/Helpers/Laborers	2.5	3.5	3.9
Services	15.8	14.5	13.2
Farming/Forestry/Fishing	0.9	1.6	2.5

Note: Figures cover workers 16 years of age and older; (1) Metropolitan Statistical Area - see Appendix A for areas included
Source: 1990 Census of Population and Housing, Summary Tape File 3C

Occupational Employment Projections: 1996 - 2006

Occupations Expected to Have the Largest Job Growth (ranked by numerical growth)	Fast-Growing Occupations[1] (ranked by percent growth)
1. Cashiers	1. Systems analysts
2. Salespersons, retail	2. Physical therapy assistants and aides
3. General managers & top executives	3. Desktop publishers
4. Registered nurses	4. Home health aides
5. Waiters & waitresses	5. Computer engineers
6. Marketing & sales, supervisors	6. Medical assistants
7. Janitors/cleaners/maids, ex. priv. hshld.	7. Physical therapists
8. General office clerks	8. Paralegals
9. Food preparation workers	9. Emergency medical technicians
10. Hand packers & packagers	10. Occupational therapists

Note: Projections cover Florida; (1) Excludes occupations with total job growth less than 300
Source: U.S. Department of Labor, Employment and Training Administration, America's Labor Market Information System (ALMIS)

Average Wages

Occupation	$/Hr.	Occupation	$/Hr.
Accountants and Auditors	16.12	Maids and Housekeepers	6.17
Assemblers and Fabricators	7.69	Maintenance Repairers	11.64
Automotive Mechanics	13.16	Marketing/Advertising/PR Managers	20.01
Bookkeepers	10.25	Nurses, Licensed Practical	10.54
Carpenters	11.43	Nurses, Registered	19.32
Cashiers	6.64	Nursing Aides/Orderlies/Attendants	6.91
Clerks, General Office	8.64	Physicians and Surgeons	59.24
Clerks, Shipping/Receiving/Traffic	10.73	Receptionists/Information Clerks	7.84
Computer Programmers	16.05	Sales Reps., Exc. Scientific/Retail	15.15
Computer Support Specialists	15.63	Sales Reps., Scientific, Exc. Retail	16.69
Cooks, Restaurant	7.84	Salespersons, Retail	8.57
Electricians	12.21	Secretaries, Except Legal/Medical	9.22
Financial Managers	19.12	Stock Clerks, Sales Floor	7.35
First-Line Supervisors/Mgrs., Sales	14.99	Systems Analysts	-
Food Preparation Workers	6.22	Teacher Aides	-
General Managers/Top Executives	22.05	Teachers, Elementary School	13.46
Guards	6.55	Teachers, Secondary School	16.23
Hand Packers	6.50	Telemarketers	10.46
Janitors and Cleaners	6.84	Truck Drivers, Heavy/Tractor-Trailer	10.63
Laborers, Landscaping	7.57	Truck Drivers, Light	9.50
Lawyers	29.98	Waiters and Waitresses	5.75

Note: Wage data is for 1998 and covers the Metropolitan Statistical Area (see Appendix A for areas included). Hourly wages for elementary and secondary school teachers were calculated by the editors from annual wage data assuming a 40 hour work week; Dashes indicate that data was not available.
Source: Bureau of Labor Statistics, 1998 Metropolitan Area Occupational Employment and Wage Estimates

TAXES

Major State and Local Tax Rates

State Corporate Income (%)	State Personal Income (%)	Residential Property (%)	Sales & Use		State Gasoline (cents/ gallon)	State Cigarette (cents/ pack)
			State (%)	Local (%)		
5.5[a]	None	1.74	6.0	None	13.3[b]	33.9

Note: Personal/corporate income, sales, gasoline and cigarette tax rates as of January 2000. Property tax rates as of April 2000; (a) 3.3% Alternative Minimum Tax. An exemption of $5,000 is allowed; (b) Rate is comprised of 4 cents excise and 9.3 cents motor carrier tax. Local taxes vary from 5.5 cents to 17 cents. Plus a 2.07 cent per gallon pollution tax
Source: Federation of Tax Administrators, www.taxadmin.org; ERI's Relocation Assessor software database, quarterly effective date 4/1/2000

Total Taxes Per Capita and as a Percent of Income

Area	Per Capita Income ($)	Per Capita Taxes ($)			Percent of Income (%)		
		Total	Federal	State/Local	Total	Federal	State/Local
Florida	28,322	10,333	7,257	3,077	36.5	25.6	10.9
U.S.	28,878	10,298	7,026	3,273	35.7	24.3	11.3

Note: Figures are for 1999
Source: Tax Foundation, www.taxfoundation.org

COMMERCIAL UTILITIES

Typical Monthly Electric Bills

Area	Commercial Service ($/month)		Industrial Service ($/month)	
	12 kW demand 1,500 kWh	100 kW demand 30,000 kWh	1,000 kW demand 400,000 kWh	20,000 kW demand 10,000,000 kWh
City	118	1,993	23,247	387,510
U.S.	150	2,174	23,995	508,569

Note: Based on rates in effect January 1, 1999
Source: Edison Electric Institute, Typical Residential, Commercial and Industrial Bills, Winter 1999

TRANSPORTATION

Transportation Statistics

Average minutes to work (1990)	18.2
Interstate highways	I-10; I-110; US-90; US-98; US-29
Bus lines	
In-city (1998)	Escambia County Area Transit, 32 buses
Inter-city (1999)	2
Passenger air service	
Airport	Pensacola Regional
Airlines (1999)	8
Enplaned passengers (1998)	570,833
Amtrak service	Yes
Motor freight carriers (1999)	27
Major waterways/ports	Port of Pensacola; Escambia Bay; Gulf of Mexico

Source: FAA DOT/TSC CY1998 ACAIS Database; National Transit Database, 1998; Editor & Publisher Market Guide, 2000; Amtrak National Time Table, Fall 1999/Winter 2000; 1990 Census of Population and Housing, STF 3C; Jane's Urban Transport Systems 1999-2000

Means of Transportation to Work

Area	Car/Truck/Van		Public Transportation			Bicycle	Walked	Other Means	Worked at Home
	Drove Alone	Car-pooled	Bus	Subway	Railroad				
City	80.4	11.8	1.7	0.0	0.0	0.4	2.2	1.7	1.8
MSA[1]	78.5	12.6	0.8	0.0	0.0	0.4	3.6	1.5	2.4
U.S.	73.2	13.4	3.0	1.5	0.5	0.4	3.9	1.2	3.0

Note: Figures shown are percentages and only include workers 16 years of age and older;
(1) Metropolitan Statistical Area - see Appendix A for areas included
Source: 1990 Census of Population and Housing, Summary Tape File 3C

BUSINESSES

Major Business Headquarters

Company Name	1999 Rankings	
	Fortune 500	Forbes 500
No companies listed	-	-

Note: Companies listed are located in the city; dashes indicate no ranking
Fortune 500: Companies that produce a 10-K are ranked 1 to 500 based on 1999 revenue
Forbes 500: Private companies are ranked 1 to 500 based on 1998 revenue
Source: Forbes, December 13, 1999; Fortune, April 17, 2000

HOTELS & MOTELS

Hotels/Motels

Area	Hotels/Motels	Rooms	Luxury-Level Hotels/Motels		Average Minimum Rates ($)		
			♦♦♦♦	♦♦♦♦♦	♦♦	♦♦♦	♦♦♦♦
City	26	2,710	0	0	60	71	n/a
Airport	1	126	0	0	n/a	n/a	n/a
Suburbs	1	101	0	0	n/a	n/a	n/a
Total	28	2,937	0	0	n/a	n/a	n/a

Note: n/a not available; classifications range from one diamond (budget properties with basic amenities) to five diamond (luxury properties).
Source: OAG Business Travel Planner, Winter 1999-2000

Estimated Daily Food and Lodging Costs

Area	Food/Other ($/day)	Average Hotel Cost ($/day)
City	30	55
U.S.	30	55

Source: ERI's Relocation Assessor software database, quarterly effective date 4/1/2000

CONVENTION CENTERS

Convention Centers and Event Sites

Name	Guest Rooms	Meeting Space (sq. ft.)	Capacity (Theatre Style)
Bayfront Auditorium	n/a	n/a	2,612
Pensacola Civic Center	n/a	n/a	10,268
Saenger Theatre	n/a	n/a	1,802

Note: n/a not available
Source: EventSource.com, 3/15/2000

Living Environment

COST OF LIVING

Cost of Living: Homeowner

Cost Element	U.S. ($)	City ($)	Differential ($)	Percent of U.S. Average
Consumables	14,516	15,408	892	106.1
Transportation	5,957	6,219	262	104.4
Health Services	2,012	2,164	152	107.6
Housing/Utilities/Prop. Tax	16,337	13,397	-2,940	82.0
Income+Payroll Taxes	12,615	10,997	-1,618	87.2
Miscellaneous	8,563	8,563	0	100.0
Total Cost of Living	60,000	56,748	-3,252	94.6

Note: Figures are based on a single income, four person family with gross annual earnings of $60,000, owning an 1,800 square-foot home, and driving two automobiles worth $22,000 30,000 miles per year.
Source: ERI's Relocation Assessor software database, quarterly effective date 4/1/2000

Cost of Living: Renter

Cost Element	U.S. ($)	City ($)	Differential ($)	Percent of U.S. Average
Consumables	10,486	11,071	585	105.6
Transportation	2,107	2,188	81	103.8
Health Services	1,632	1,746	114	107.0
Rent/Utilities/Insurance	9,299	7,280	-2,019	78.3
Income+Payroll Taxes	8,607	7,183	-1,424	83.5
Miscellaneous	7,869	7,869	0	100.0
Total Cost of Living	40,000	37,337	-2,663	93.3

Note: Figures are based on a single income, three person family with gross annual earnings of $40,000, renting a 1,000 square-foot home, and driving one automobile worth $8,000 12,000 miles per year.
Source: ERI's Relocation Assessor software database, quarterly effective date 4/1/2000

HOUSING

Median Home Prices and Housing Affordability

Area	Median Price[2] 4th Qtr. 1999 ($)	HOI[3] 4th Qtr. 1999	Affordability Rank[4]
MSA[1]	97,000	79.7	26
U.S.	139,000	63.8	–

Note: (1) Metropolitan Statistical Area - see Appendix A for areas included; (2) U.S. figures calculated from the sales of 687,516 new and existing homes in 192 markets; (3) Housing Opportunity Index - percent of homes sold that were within the reach of the median income household at the prevailing mortgage interest rate; (4) Rank is from 1-192 with 1 being most affordable
Source: National Association of Home Builders, Housing Opportunity Index, 4th Quarter 1999

Estimated Home Price

Area	Price ($)
City	99,969
U.S.	135,855

Note: Figures are based on an 1,800 square-foot home
Source: ERI's Relocation Assessor software database, quarterly effective date 4/1/2000

Estimated Rent

Area	Rent ($/month)
City	488
U.S.	651

Note: Figures are based on a 1,000 square-foot home
Source: ERI's Relocation Assessor software database, quarterly effective date 4/1/2000

Median Home Price Projection

It is projected that the median home price in the metropolitan area will increase from $99,478 in 1999 to $152,746 in 2010, an increase of 53.5%
Kiplinger's Personal Finance Magazine, January 2000

RESIDENTIAL UTILITIES

Average Residential Utility Costs

Area	All Electric ($/mth)	Part Electric ($/mth)	Other Energy ($/mth)	Phone ($/mth)
City	–	57.17	39.44	13.18
U.S.	99.25	55.47	43.48	20.29

Source: ACCRA, Cost of Living Index, 3rd Quarter 1999

HEALTH CARE

Average Health Care Costs

Area	Hospital ($/day)	Doctor ($/visit)	Dentist ($/visit)
City	562.00	56.00	65.00
U.S.	440.96	53.83	68.42

Note: Hospital—based on a semi-private room; Doctor—based on a general practitioner's routine exam of an established patient; Dentist—based on adult teeth cleaning and periodic oral exam.
Source: ACCRA, Cost of Living Index, 3rd Quarter 1999

Distribution of Office-Based Physicians

Area	Family/Gen. Practitioners	Specialists		
		Medical	Surgical	Other
MSA[1]	93	186	176	173

Note: Data as of 12/31/97; (1) Metropolitan Statistical Area - see Appendix A for areas included
Source: American Medical Assn., Physician Characteristics & Distribution in the U.S., 1999

Hospitals

Pensacola has 4 general medical and surgical hospitals.
AHA Guide to the Healthcare Field, 1999-2000

EDUCATION

Public School District Statistics

District Name	Num. Sch.	Enroll.	Classroom Teachers	Pupils per Teacher	Minority Pupils (%)	Current Exp.[1] ($/pupil)
Escambia County Sch Dist	81	46,083	2,662	17.3	40.3	5,146

Note: Data covers the 1997-1998 school year unless otherwise noted; (1) Data covers fiscal year 1996; SD = School District; ISD = Independent School District; n/a not available
Source: National Center for Education Statistics, Common Core of Data Public Education Agency Universe 1997-98; National Center for Education Statistics, Characteristics of the 100 Largest Public Elementary and Secondary School Districts in the United States: 1997-98, July 1999

Educational Quality

School District	Education Quotient[1]	Graduate Outcome[2]	Community Index[3]	Resource Index[4]
Escambia Co. School Dist.	91	103	94	66

Note: Over 1,000 secondary school districts were rated in terms of educational quality. The scores range from a low of 50 to a high of 150; (1) Combination of the Graduate Outcome, Community and Resource indexes weighted to reflect the greater importance of the Graduate Outcome and Resource Index; (2) Based on graduation rates and college board scores (SAT/ACT); (3) Based on the surrounding community's level of affluence and adult education; (4) Based on teacher salaries, per-pupil expenditures and student-teacher ratios.
Source: Expansion Management, Ratings Issue, 1999

Educational Attainment by Race

Area	High School Graduate (%)					Bachelor's Degree (%)				
	Total	White	Black	Other	Hisp.[2]	Total	White	Black	Other	Hisp.[2]
City	79.1	86.8	59.5	80.6	84.7	28.1	35.3	8.8	41.2	32.8
MSA[1]	76.7	79.3	61.7	74.0	81.2	18.3	20.0	8.0	17.0	18.8
U.S.	75.2	77.9	63.1	60.4	49.8	20.3	21.5	11.4	19.4	9.2

Note: Figures shown cover persons 25 years old and over; (1) Metropolitan Statistical Area - see Appendix A for areas included; (2) people of Hispanic origin can be of any race
Source: 1990 Census of Population and Housing, Summary Tape File 3C

School Enrollment by Type

Area	Preprimary				Elementary/High School			
	Public		Private		Public		Private	
	Enrollment	%	Enrollment	%	Enrollment	%	Enrollment	%
City	608	56.0	478	44.0	8,089	87.2	1,183	12.8
MSA[1]	3,778	64.1	2,113	35.9	53,162	92.1	4,568	7.9
U.S.	2,679,029	59.5	1,824,256	40.5	38,379,689	90.2	4,187,099	9.8

Note: Figures shown cover persons 3 years old and over;
(1) Metropolitan Statistical Area - see Appendix A for areas included
Source: 1990 Census of Population and Housing, Summary Tape File 3C

School Enrollment by Race

Area	Preprimary (%)				Elementary/High School (%)			
	White	Black	Other	Hisp.[1]	White	Black	Other	Hisp.[1]
City	60.5	37.8	1.7	0.6	51.5	44.8	3.7	1.9
MSA[2]	77.5	20.9	1.5	2.3	72.8	23.0	4.2	2.1
U.S.	80.4	12.5	7.1	7.8	74.1	15.6	10.3	12.5

Note: Figures shown cover persons 3 years old and over; (1) people of Hispanic origin can be of any race; (2) Metropolitan Statistical Area - see Appendix A for areas included
Source: 1990 Census of Population and Housing, Summary Tape File 3C

Higher Education

Two-Year Colleges		Four-Year Colleges		Medical Schools	Law Schools	Voc/ Tech
Public	Private	Public	Private			
1	0	1	0	0	0	11

Source: College Blue Book, Occupational Education, 1999; Medical School Admission Requirements, 1999-2000; Peterson's Guide to Two-Year Colleges, 2000; Peterson's Guide to Four-Year Colleges, 1999; Barron's Guide to Law Schools, 1999

MAJOR EMPLOYERS

Major Employers

Baptist Health Care Corp.	Baptist Hospital
Cox Communications	Gulf Power
Lakeview Center	Pensacola News-Journal
Sacred Heart Hospital of Pensacola	West Florida Regional Medical Center

Note: Companies listed are located in the city
Source: D&B Business Rankings, 1999; Ward's Business Directory, 1999; America's Corporate Families, 1999

PUBLIC SAFETY

Crime Rate

Area	All Crimes	Violent Crimes				Property Crimes		
		Murder	Forcible Rape	Robbery	Aggrav. Assault	Burglary	Larceny -Theft	Motor Vehicle Theft
City	6,128.7	3.3	39.2	231.6	551.4	1,208.8	3,717.7	376.8
Suburbs[1]	4,783.8	6.7	60.7	149.9	576.3	1,074.1	2,674.1	242.1
MSA[2]	4,987.8	6.2	57.4	162.3	572.5	1,094.5	2,832.4	262.5
U.S.	4,615.5	6.3	34.4	165.2	360.5	862.0	2,728.1	459.0

Note: Crime rate is the number of crimes per 100,000 population; (1) Defined as all areas within the Metropolitan Statistical Area but located outside the central city; (2) Metropolitan Statistical Area - see Appendix A for areas included
Source: FBI Uniform Crime Reports, 1998

RECREATION

Culture and Recreation

Museums	Symphony Orchestras	Opera Companies	Dance Companies	Professional Theatres	Zoos	Pro Sports Teams
4	1	0	1	1	0	0

Source: Musical America, International Directory of the Performing Arts, 1999; Official Museum Directory, 2000; Stern's Performing Arts Directory, 1997; USA Today Four Sport Stadium Guide, 1997; Career Opportunities in Theatre and the Performing Arts, 1999

Library System

The West Florida Regional Library has six branches, holdings of 295,425 volumes, and a budget of $2,553,807 (1997-1998).
American Library Directory, 1999-2000

MEDIA

Newspapers

Name	Type	Freq.	Distribution	Circulation
Escambia Sun Press	General	1x/wk	Local	4,800
New American Press	General	1x/wk	Local	36,000
Pensacola News Journal	General	7x/wk	Local	64,200
Pensacola Voice	Black	1x/wk	Local	36,151

Note: Includes newspapers with circulations of 200 or more located in the city;
Source: Burrelle's Media Directory, 1999 Edition

Television Stations

Name	Ch.	Affiliation	Type	Owner
WEAR	n/a	ABCT	Commercial	Sinclair Communications Inc.
WSRE	23	PBS	Public	n/a

Note: Stations included broadcast in the Pensacola metro area; n/a not available
Source: Burrelle's Media Directory, 1999 Edition

AM Radio Stations

Call Letters	Freq. (kHz)	Target Audience	Station Format	Music Format
WVTJ	610	General	M/T	Christian/Gospel
WSWL	790	General	N	n/a
WRNE	980	n/a	n/a	n/a
WZNO	1230	General	M/N	Christian/Gospel
WCOA	1370	General	N/S/T	n/a
WBSR	1450	General	M	Adult Contemporary
WRFP	1610	G/R	N/S/T	n/a

Note: Stations included broadcast in the Pensacola metro area; n/a not available
Target Audience: A=Asian; B=Black; C=Christian; E=Ethnic; F=French; G=General; H=Hispanic; M=Men; N=Native American; R=Religious; S=Senior Citizen; W=Women; Y=Young Adult; Z=Children
Station Format: E=Educational; M=Music; N=News; S=Sports; T=Talk
Source: Burrelle's Media Directory, 1999 Edition

FM Radio Stations

Call Letters	Freq. (mHz)	Target Audience	Station Format	Music Format
WUWF	88.1	General	E/M/N	Alternative/Classical/Jazz
WPCS	89.5	General	E/M/N	Christian
WEGS	91.7	General	M	Christian
WWRO	100.7	General	M	Classic Rock
WTKX	101.5	General	M/N/S	Alternative/AOR/Classic Rock
WYCL	107.3	General	M	Oldies

Note: Stations included broadcast in the Pensacola metro area
Station Format: E=Educational; M=Music; N=News; S=Sports; T=Talk
Target Audience: A=Asian; B=Black; C=Christian; E=Ethnic; F=French; G=General;
M=Men; N=Native American; R=Religious; S=Senior Citizen; W=Women; Y=Young Adult; Z=Children
Music Format: AOR=Album Oriented Rock; MOR=Middle-of-the-Road
Source: Burrelle's Media Directory, 1999 Edition

WEATHER

Temperature/Precipitation/Humidity

	Jan	Feb	Mar	Apr	May	Jun	Jul	Aug	Sep	Oct	Nov	Dec	Yr.
Max. High Temp. (°F)	81	82	85	96	102	101	106	104	98	95	85	81	106
Avg. High Temp. (°F)	61	63	69	77	83	89	90	90	86	80	70	63	77
Avg. Temp. (°F)	52	54	61	68	75	81	82	82	79	70	60	54	68
Avg. Low Temp. (°F)	43	45	51	59	66	72	74	74	70	60	50	45	59
Min. Low Temp. (°F)	5	13	22	33	47	56	61	63	43	34	22	11	5
Avg. Precip. (in.)	4.2	5.1	5.7	4.1	4.4	6.3	7.4	6.9	5.8	3.8	3.4	4.4	61.4
Avg. Snowfall (in.)	Tr	Tr	Tr	0	0	0	0	0	0	0	0	Tr	Tr
Avg. Rel. Hum. 7am (%)	86	84	78	76	75	75	77	78	80	77	78	83	79
Avg. Rel. Hum. 4pm (%)	70	63	60	60	60	61	66	65	65	58	60	68	63

Note: Tr = Trace amounts (less than 0.05 inches of rain or less than 0.5 inches of snow)
Source: National Climatic Data Center, International Station Meteorological Climate Summary, 3/95

Weather Conditions

Temperature			Precipitation		
32°F & below	45°F & below	90°F & above	0.01 inch or more precip.	1.5 inch or more snow/ice	Thunder-storms
15	74	61	108	1	68

Note: Figures are average number of days per year
Source: National Climatic Data Center, International Station Meteorological Climate Summary, 3/95

AIR & WATER QUALITY

Maximum Pollutant Concentrations

	Particulate Matter (ug/m³)	Carbon Monoxide (ppm)	Sulfur Dioxide (ppm)	Nitrogen Dioxide (ppm)	Ozone (ppm)	Lead (ug/m³)
MSA[1] Level	56	n/a	0.033	n/a	0.11	n/a
NAAQS[2]	150	9	0.140	0.053	0.12	1.50
Met NAAQS	Yes	n/a	Yes	n/a	Yes	n/a

Note: (1) Metropolitan Statistical Area - see Appendix A for areas included; (2) National Ambient Air
Quality Standards; ppm = parts per million; ug/m³ = micrograms per cubic meter; n/a not available
Source: EPA, National Air Quality and Emissions Trends Report, 1997

Pollutant Standards Index

Data not available.
EPA, National Air Quality and Emissions Trends Report, 1997

Drinking Water

Water System Name	Pop. Served	Primary Water Source Type	Number of Violations in 1998-99	Type of Violation/ Contaminants
Escambia Co. Utility Authority	269,545	Ground	None	None

Note: Data as of January 19, 2000
Source: EPA, Office of Ground Water and Drinking Water, Safe Drinking Water Information System

Pensacola tap water is very soft.
Editor & Publisher Market Guide, 2000

Portland, Maine

Background

Portland, Maine is located on the southern Atlantic coastline, about 100 miles north of Boston, Massachusetts. On Casco Bay, the city sits on a peninsula comprised of numerous inlets, coves and islands. Portland is the largest city in Maine, the county seat of Cumberland County and an important East Coast port.

Portland is part of a metropolitan area that includes Cape Elizabeth, Falmouth and other communities. This area comprises one of Maine's primary population, commercial and transportation centers. Portland's traditional and contemporary economy includes shipping and related transportation, manufacturing, fishing, wholesale and retail trades, business and other services, and forestry. Southeast Maine is also a popular area for tourism, based on local coastal scenery, recreation and historic attractions, and as an entry point to Maine's northern coast and interior. Since the 1980s the traditional economy of southern Maine has diversified, and now includes new technology and services companies.

The British first settled the Casco Peninsula in 1632. Raids by hostile Native Americans and other problems hindered the settlement until the 18th Century. The region was part of Massachusetts during its early history. Cumberland County was established in 1760. The port suffered extensive damage during the Revolutionary War. After the war, Portland began to experience significant growth, despite some difficult times during the War of 1812. Portland served as the state capital until 1831, and was incorporated as a city in 1832. In the mid-19th Century, Portland's role was enhanced by linkages with railroads and other transportation systems to the interior and to Canada. In 1866, a serious fire damaged much of the city, which prompted major reconstruction.

During World Wars I and II, Portland was a military shipbuilding center, and in World Wart II it was the home port for the Navy's North Atlantic Fleet. Changes in regional industries, shipping and other trends created economic challenges in the mid-20th Century. A variety of revitalization initiatives were undertaken, including urban redevelopment, upgrades in port facilities and other activities. This helped to stimulate the economy and, in the 1990s, southern Maine experienced significant growth and diversification, stimulated by growth in southeast New Hampshire and the Boston area.

There are many individual historic districts, landmarks and museums in Portland and the surrounding area. Since 1960, an emphasis has been placed on redevelopment and historic preservation in Portland, such as the Old Port Exchange retail district. Fort Williams Park in Cape Elizabeth, includes the 1791 Portland Head Light, the first lighthouse on the East Coast. The Wadsworth Longfellow House is a museum in the boyhood home of poet Henry Wadsworth Longfellow.

The Cumberland County Civic Center is a downtown multi-use facility. Merrill Auditorium is a venue for concerts and other events, including the PCA Great Performances series. Other area cultural organizations include the Portland Opera Repertory Theater, Portland Symphony Orchestra, Portland Stage Company, and Portland Museum of Art.

The numerous schools and colleges in the region include the Maine College of Art, Andover College, Westbrook College and a campus of the University of Maine.

The Portland area contains many parks and beaches for waterfront and aquatic activities. It is also a short drive from other sections of the Maine coast and inland mountains and recreation areas. Sports teams include the Portland Seadogs Class A baseball team and the Portland Pirates Hockey Club.

Portland has an elected City Council and Mayor and a City Manager.

General Rankings and Evaluative Comments

- Portland was ranked #72 out of 354 metropolitan areas in *Places Rated Almanac*. Criteria: cost of living, climate, crime, transportation, job outlook, education, the arts, health care, and recreation. *Places Rated Almanac, Millennium Edition, 2000*

- Portland was selected as one of North America's "Best Small Metro Areas" (population under 250,000). The area ranked #1 out of 20. Criteria: cost of living, climate, crime, transportation, job outlook, education, the arts, health care, and recreation. *Places Rated Almanac, Millennium Edition, 2000*

- Portland was selected as one of America's best small art towns. The city was ranked #4 out of 100. Criteria: easy and affordable access to the visual arts, performing arts and music, strong sense of community, low crime rate, and full-time population less than 65,000. *The 100 Best Small Art Towns in America: Discover Creative Communities, Fresh Air, and Affordable Living, 1998*

- *Ladies Home Journal* ranked America's 200 largest cities based on the qualities women care about most. Portland ranked #83 out of 200. Criteria: low crime rate, well-paying jobs, quality health and child care, good public schools, the presence of women in government, size of the gender wage gap, number of sexual-harassment and discrimination complaints filed, unemployment and divorce rates, commute times, population density, number of houses of worship, parks and cultural offerings, number of women's health specialists, how well women cared for themselves, complexion kindness index based on UV radiation levels, odds of finding affordable fashions, rental rates for romance movies, champagne sales, and other matters of the heart. *Ladies Home Journal, November 1998*

- Portland was selected as one of "America's Best Towns to Raise an Outdoor Family" by *Outdoor Explorer* magazine. Criteria: easy access to the outdoors, quality education and health care, affordable housing, favorable employment opportunities, and low crime rates. The city was ranked #8 out of 25. *Outdoor Explorer, Summer 1999*

- Cognetics studied 273 metro areas in the United States, ranking them by entrepreneurial activity. Portland was ranked #64 out of 134 smaller metro areas. Criteria: Significant Starts (firms started in the last 10 years that still employ at least 5 people) and Young Growers (percent of firms 10 years old or less that grew significantly during the last 4 years). *Cognetics, "Entrepreneurial Hot Spots: The Best Places in America to Start and Grow a Company," 1999*

Business Environment

STATE ECONOMY

State Economic Profile

"Maine continues to grow along its traditional stable, yet slow, growth path. Job losses in Maine's resources and manufacturing sectors have been more than balanced by job growth in the services sector, particularly telemarketing. Weak demographics, specifically low in-migration and the loss of younger households, will constrain Maine's housing and construction markets to slow growth.

Maine's service's sector added jobs at 4.0% during 1998, twice the overall rate of state job growth. MBNA, which expanded its telemarketing call centers in the state, plans to add more jobs in the near future. Several other telemarketers, such as ICT Telemarketing, are also planning to expand operations in Maine. A boom in tourism has also added to Maine's services and retails sectors.

Manufacturing employment continued its long-term decline, shedding over 2,000 jobs in 1998. Maine's textile and paper products industries have been hurt by both weak foreign demand and strong foreign competition. Maine's cost structure in these industries makes it uncompetitive with textile and paper products produced elsewhere in the US, not to mention lower-cost overseas producers. Manufacturing employment should continue to contract in the near term.

Construction employment provided a much needed boost in 1998, providing almost 1 in 5 new non-farm jobs created. Although home sales were at record levels in 1998, the state's weak demographics and current level of construction, indicate a contraction in construction activity. These same factors will moderate the unusually high level of home price appreciation witnessed in 1998." *National Association of Realtors, Economic Profiles: The Fifty States and the District of Columbia, http://nar.realtor.com/databank/profiles.htm*

EXPORTS

Total Export Sales

Area	1995 ($000)	1996 ($000)	1997 ($000)	1998 ($000)	% Chg. 1995-98	% Chg. 1997-98
MSA[1]	373,121	339,152	617,447	755,580	102.5	22.4
U.S.	583,030,524	622,827,063	687,597,999	680,474,251	16.7	-1.0

Note: (1) Metropolitan Statistical Area - see Appendix A for areas included
Source: U.S. Department of Commerce, International Trade Association, Metropolitan Area Exports: An Export Performance Report on Over 250 U.S. Cities, November 10, 1999

CITY FINANCES

City Government Finances

Component	1995 ($million)	1995 (per capita $)
Revenue	161.4	2,604
Expenditure	162.5	2,622
Debt Outstanding	106.9	1,725

Source: 1999 County and City Extra, Annual Metro, City, and County Data Book

City Government Revenue by Source

Source	1995 ($million)	1995 (per capita $)
Intergovernmental	26.6	429
Taxes	85.1	1,374
Property	83.4	1,347
Sales and Gross Receipts	0.0	0

Source: 1999 County and City Extra, Annual Metro, City, and County Data Book

City Government Expenditures by Function

Function	1995 ($million)	1995 (per capita $)	1995 (%)
Public Welfare	14.6	235	9.0
Highways	6.9	112	4.3
Parking Facilities	0.0	0	0.0
Education	56.3	909	34.7
Health and Hospitals	0.6	10	0.4
Police Protection	7.1	115	4.4
Sewerage and Sanitation	10.7	173	6.6
Parks and Recreation	3.5	57	2.2
Housing and Community Development	1.9	31	1.2
Interest on Debt	8.6	138	5.3

Source: 1999 County and City Extra, Annual Metro, City, and County Data Book

Municipal Bond Ratings

Area	Moody's
City	Aa1

Source: Mergent Bond Record, 2/2000

POPULATION

Population Growth

Area	1980 Census	1990 Census	1999 Estimate	2004 Projection	Population Growth (%) 1990-1999	Population Growth (%) 1999-2004
City	61,572	64,358	62,955	61,880	-2.2	-1.7
MSA[1]	198,277	215,481	232,708	235,722	8.0	1.3
U.S.	226,545,805	248,765,170	272,212,864	283,625,312	9.4	4.2

Note: (1) Metropolitan Statistical Area - see Appendix A for areas included
Source: 1990 Census of Population and Housing, Summary Tape File 3C; Claritas, Inc.

Number of Households and Average Household Size

Area	1980 Census	1990 Census	1999 Estimate	2004 Projection	1999 Average Household Size
City	25,419	28,230	28,887	28,882	2.18
MSA[1]	72,701	84,809	94,175	96,666	2.47
U.S.	80,389,592	91,993,582	102,048,200	107,302,392	2.67

Note: (1) Metropolitan Statistical Area - see Appendix A for areas included
Source: 1990 Census of Population and Housing, Summary Tape File 3C; Claritas, Inc.

Race/Ethnicity of City Population

Race/Ethnicity	1990 Census Population	1990 Census %	1999 Estimate Population	1999 Estimate %	% Change 1990-1999
White, Non-Hispanic	61,845	96.1	59,677	94.8	-3.5
Black, Non-Hispanic	658	1.0	804	1.3	22.2
Asian, Non-Hispanic	966	1.5	1,350	2.1	39.8
Other, Non-Hispanic	294	0.5	293	0.5	-0.3
Hispanic	595	0.9	831	1.3	39.7

Source: 1990 Census of Population and Housing, Summary Tape File 3C; Claritas, Inc.

Race/Ethnicity of Metropolitan Statistical Area Population

Race/Ethnicity	1990 Census		1999 Estimate		% Change 1990-1999
	Population	%	Population	%	
White, Non-Hispanic	210,196	97.5	226,394	97.3	7.7
Black, Non-Hispanic	1,300	0.6	1,333	0.6	2.5
Asian, Non-Hispanic	1,896	0.9	2,390	1.0	26.1
Other, Non-Hispanic	698	0.3	694	0.3	-0.6
Hispanic	1,391	0.6	1,897	0.8	36.4

Note: See Appendix A for areas included in the Metropolitan Statistical Area
Source: 1990 Census of Population and Housing, Summary Tape File 3C; Claritas, Inc.

Ancestry

Area	German	Irish	English	Italian	U.S.	French	Polish	Dutch
City	8.9	26.4	25.0	11.6	3.9	14.2	3.0	1.4
MSA[1]	9.5	23.2	30.2	8.3	5.1	15.6	2.8	1.4
U.S.	23.3	15.6	13.1	5.9	5.3	4.2	3.8	2.5

Note: Figures are percentages and include persons that reported multiple ancestry (eg. if a person reported being Irish and Italian, they were included in both columns); (1) Metropolitan Statistical Area - see Appendix A for areas included
Source: 1990 Census of Population and Housing, Summary Tape File 3C

Median Age

Area	1990 Census	1999 Estimate
City	32.8	36.5
MSA[1]	33.7	36.9
U.S.	32.9	35.7

Note: (1) Metropolitan Statistical Area - see Appendix A for areas included
Source: 1990 Census of Population and Housing, Summary Tape File 3C; Claritas, Inc.

Male/Female Population

Area	Number of Males		Number of Females		Males per 100 Females	
	1990	1999	1990	1999	1990	1999
City	29,854	29,565	34,504	33,390	86.5	88.5
MSA[1]	103,088	112,003	112,393	120,705	91.7	92.8
U.S.	121,172,379	132,803,736	127,537,494	139,409,136	95.0	95.3

Note: (1) Metropolitan Statistical Area - see Appendix A for areas included
Source: 1990 Census of Population, General Population Characteristics; Claritas, Inc.

INCOME

Per Capita/Median/Average Income

Area	Per Capita ($)			Median Household ($)			Average Household ($)		
	1989	1999	% Chg.	1989	1999	% Chg.	1989	1999	% Chg.
City	14,914	21,176	42.0	26,576	33,254	25.1	33,559	45,061	34.3
MSA[1]	16,120	22,696	40.8	32,776	42,228	28.8	40,590	55,304	36.2
U.S.	14,420	21,350	48.1	30,056	40,525	34.8	38,453	56,184	46.1

Note: (1) Metropolitan Statistical Area - see Appendix A for areas included; 1989 data is from the 1990 Census; 1999 data is estimated by Claritas, Inc.
Source: 1990 Census of Population, General Population Characteristics; Claritas, Inc.

Household Income Distribution

Area	Percent of Households Earning								
	Under $5,000	$5,000 -14,999	$15,000 -24,999	$25,000 -34,999	$35,000 -49,999	$50,000 -74,999	$75,000 -99,000	$100,000 -149,999	$150,000 and up
City	4.1	18.5	15.9	13.3	16.2	18.3	7.4	4.0	2.4
MSA[1]	2.4	12.2	12.9	12.7	18.1	22.4	9.9	5.4	3.9
U.S.	3.9	13.3	13.8	12.6	16.2	19.4	9.7	6.6	4.6

Note: Data as of 1999; (1) Metropolitan Statistical Area - see Appendix A for areas included
Source: Claritas, Inc.

Effective Buying Income

Area	Per Capita ($)	Median Household ($)	Average Household ($)
City	17,594	31,236	39,463
MSA[1]	19,072	38,896	47,801
U.S.	17,496	36,603	47,036

Note: Data as of 1/1/2000; (1) Metropolitan Statistical Area - see Appendix A for areas included
Source: Standard Rate & Data Service, Newspaper Advertising Source, March 2000

Effective Household Buying Income Distribution

Area	% of Households Earning						
	$10,000 -$19,999	$20,000 -$34,999	$35,000 -$49,999	$50,000 -$74,999	$75,000 -$99,000	$100,000 -$124,999	$125,000 and up
City	18.4	23.3	18.7	16.6	5.7	1.8	1.9
MSA[1]	13.7	22.2	19.7	22.0	8.0	2.7	3.1
U.S.	15.0	21.6	17.6	19.6	8.4	3.0	3.3

Note: Data as of 1/1/2000; (1) Metropolitan Statistical Area - see Appendix A for areas included
Source: Standard Rate & Data Service, Newspaper Advertising Source, March 2000

Poverty Rates by Age

Area	People of All Ages	People Under 18 Years Old	Related Children Age 5-17 in Families in Poverty
City	17.0	n/a	n/a
County	9.2	12.3	10.8
U.S.	13.8	20.8	18.7

Note: Figures show the percent of people living below the poverty line in 1995. The
average poverty threshold was $15,569 for a family of four in 1995; n/a not available
Source: Bureau of the Census, Small Area Income and Poverty Estimates Program;
U.S. Department of Housing and Urban Development

EMPLOYMENT

Labor Force and Employment

Area	Civilian Labor Force			Workers Employed		
	Dec. 1998	Dec. 1999	% Chg.	Dec. 1998	Dec. 1999	% Chg.
City	37,884	39,078	3.2	37,189	38,350	3.1
MSA[1]	136,967	141,490	3.3	134,749	138,957	3.1
U.S.	138,297,000	139,941,000	1.2	132,732,000	134,696,000	1.5

Note: Data is not seasonally adjusted and covers workers 16 years of age and older;
(1) Metropolitan Statistical Area - see Appendix A for areas included
Source: Bureau of Labor Statistics, http://stats.bls.gov

Unemployment Rate

Area	1999											
	Jan.	Feb.	Mar.	Apr.	May	Jun.	Jul.	Aug.	Sep.	Oct.	Nov.	Dec.
City	2.4	2.4	2.3	2.0	2.4	2.9	2.4	2.4	2.1	2.1	2.1	1.9
MSA[1]	2.1	2.2	2.0	1.7	1.8	2.2	1.8	1.9	1.9	2.0	2.0	1.8
U.S.	4.8	4.7	4.4	4.1	4.0	4.5	4.5	4.2	4.1	3.8	3.8	3.7

Note: Data is not seasonally adjusted and covers workers 16 years of age and older; all figures are percentages; (1) Metropolitan Statistical Area - see Appendix A for areas included
Source: Bureau of Labor Statistics, http://stats.bls.gov

Employment by Industry

Sector	MSA[1]		U.S.
	Number of Employees	Percent of Total	Percent of Total
Services	45,800	29.9	30.2
Retail Trade	35,800	23.4	18.1
Government	19,500	12.7	15.8
Manufacturing	14,900	9.7	14.1
Finance/Insurance/Real Estate	14,000	9.1	5.9
Wholesale Trade	9,200	6.0	5.4
Transportation/Public Utilities	6,800	4.4	5.3
Construction	7,100	4.6	4.8
Mining	n/a	n/a	0.4

Note: Figures cover non-farm employment as of 12/99 and are not seasonally adjusted; (1) Metropolitan Statistical Area - see Appendix A for areas included; n/a not available
Source: Bureau of Labor Statistics, http://stats.bls.gov

Employment by Occupation

Occupation Category	City (%)	MSA[1] (%)	U.S. (%)
White Collar	65.3	64.0	58.1
Executive/Admin./Management	13.9	13.7	12.3
Professional	17.6	16.4	14.1
Technical & Related Support	3.6	3.6	3.7
Sales	12.6	13.2	11.8
Administrative Support/Clerical	17.7	17.0	16.3
Blue Collar	18.4	22.0	26.2
Precision Production/Craft/Repair	8.1	10.0	11.3
Machine Operators/Assem./Insp.	4.1	4.9	6.8
Transportation/Material Movers	3.0	3.6	4.1
Cleaners/Helpers/Laborers	3.2	3.5	3.9
Services	15.3	12.7	13.2
Farming/Forestry/Fishing	1.0	1.3	2.5

Note: Figures cover workers 16 years of age and older; (1) Metropolitan Statistical Area - see Appendix A for areas included
Source: 1990 Census of Population and Housing, Summary Tape File 3C

Occupational Employment Projections: 1996 - 2006

Occupations Expected to Have the Largest Job Growth (ranked by numerical growth)	Fast-Growing Occupations[1] (ranked by percent growth)
1. Home health aides	1. Database administrators
2. Registered nurses	2. Adjustment clerks
3. Nursing aides/orderlies/attendants	3. Personal and home care aides
4. General managers & top executives	4. Physical therapists
5. Truck drivers, light	5. Medical assistants
6. Cashiers	6. Home health aides
7. Salespersons, retail	7. Systems analysts
8. Child care workers, private household	8. Human services workers
9. Marketing & sales, supervisors	9. Bill and account collectors
10. Food service workers	10. Dental hygienists

Note: Projections cover Maine; (1) Excludes occupations with total job growth less than 300
Source: U.S. Department of Labor, Employment and Training Administration, America's Labor Market Information System (ALMIS)

Average Wages

Occupation	$/Hr.	Occupation	$/Hr.
Accountants and Auditors	18.64	Maids and Housekeepers	7.94
Assemblers and Fabricators	9.50	Maintenance Repairers	11.61
Automotive Mechanics	12.46	Marketing/Advertising/PR Managers	27.76
Bookkeepers	10.97	Nurses, Licensed Practical	12.59
Carpenters	12.63	Nurses, Registered	18.57
Cashiers	7.47	Nursing Aides/Orderlies/Attendants	8.92
Clerks, General Office	9.72	Physicians and Surgeons	56.70
Clerks, Shipping/Receiving/Traffic	10.11	Receptionists/Information Clerks	9.31
Computer Programmers	22.20	Sales Reps., Exc. Scientific/Retail	18.26
Computer Support Specialists	16.06	Sales Reps., Scientific, Exc. Retail	23.30
Cooks, Restaurant	8.68	Salespersons, Retail	8.93
Electricians	17.61	Secretaries, Except Legal/Medical	11.17
Financial Managers	26.61	Stock Clerks, Sales Floor	8.47
First-Line Supervisors/Mgrs., Sales	16.58	Systems Analysts	26.70
Food Preparation Workers	7.74	Teacher Aides	8.75
General Managers/Top Executives	30.27	Teachers, Elementary School	16.72
Guards	7.95	Teachers, Secondary School	15.05
Hand Packers	7.82	Telemarketers	10.20
Janitors and Cleaners	8.38	Truck Drivers, Heavy/Tractor-Trailer	13.80
Laborers, Landscaping	8.88	Truck Drivers, Light	12.54
Lawyers	30.81	Waiters and Waitresses	6.18

Note: Wage data is for 1998 and covers the Metropolitan Statistical Area (see Appendix A for areas included). Hourly wages for elementary and secondary school teachers were calculated by the editors from annual wage data assuming a 40 hour work week; Dashes indicate that data was not available.
Source: Bureau of Labor Statistics, 1998 Metropolitan Area Occupational Employment and Wage Estimates

TAXES

Major State and Local Tax Rates

State Corporate Income (%)	State Personal Income (%)	Residential Property (%)	Sales & Use		State Gasoline (cents/ gallon)	State Cigarette (cents/ pack)
			State (%)	Local (%)		
3.5 - 8.93[a]	2.0 - 8.5	2.44	5.5	0.5	22.0	74.0

Note: Personal/corporate income, sales, gasoline and cigarette tax rates as of January 2000. Property tax rates as of April 2000; (a) Or a 27% tax on Federal Alternative Minimum Taxable Income
Source: Federation of Tax Administrators, www.taxadmin.org; ERI's Relocation Assessor software database, quarterly effective date 4/1/2000

Total Taxes Per Capita and as a Percent of Income

Area	Per Capita Income ($)	Per Capita Taxes ($)			Percent of Income (%)		
		Total	Federal	State/Local	Total	Federal	State/Local
Maine	24,930	9,048	5,602	3,446	36.3	22.5	13.8
U.S.	28,878	10,298	7,026	3,273	35.7	24.3	11.3

Note: Figures are for 1999
Source: Tax Foundation, www.taxfoundation.org

COMMERCIAL UTILITIES

Typical Monthly Electric Bills

Area	Commercial Service ($/month)		Industrial Service ($/month)	
	12 kW demand 1,500 kWh	100 kW demand 30,000 kWh	1,000 kW demand 400,000 kWh	20,000 kW demand 10,000,000 kWh
City	153	3,714	50,127	582,003
U.S.	150	2,174	23,995	508,569

Note: Based on rates in effect January 1, 1999
Source: Edison Electric Institute, Typical Residential, Commercial and Industrial Bills, Winter 1999

TRANSPORTATION

Transportation Statistics

Average minutes to work (1990)	15.8
Interstate highways	I-95; I-295; I-495; US-1; US-302
Bus lines	
In-city (1998)	Greater Portland Transit District, 22 buses
Inter-city (1999)	3
Passenger air service	
Airport	Portland International
Airlines (1999)	14
Enplaned passengers (1998)	651,491
Amtrak service	No
Motor freight carriers (1999)	30
Major waterways/ports	Casco Bay; Atlantic Ocean

Source: FAA DOT/TSC CY1998 ACAIS Database; National Transit Database, 1998; Editor & Publisher Market Guide, 2000; Amtrak National Time Table, Fall 1999/Winter 2000; 1990 Census of Population and Housing, STF 3C; Jane's Urban Transport Systems 1999-2000

Means of Transportation to Work

Area	Car/Truck/Van		Public Transportation			Bicycle	Walked	Other Means	Worked at Home
	Drove Alone	Car-pooled	Bus	Subway	Railroad				
City	67.8	11.7	3.1	0.0	0.0	0.9	12.4	1.4	2.7
MSA[1]	76.9	11.5	1.5	0.0	0.0	0.4	5.5	0.9	3.4
U.S.	73.2	13.4	3.0	1.5	0.5	0.4	3.9	1.2	3.0

Note: Figures shown are percentages and only include workers 16 years of age and older;
(1) Metropolitan Statistical Area - see Appendix A for areas included
Source: 1990 Census of Population and Housing, Summary Tape File 3C

BUSINESSES

Major Business Headquarters

Company Name	1999 Rankings	
	Fortune 500	Forbes 500
Unumprovident	184	-

Note: Companies listed are located in the city; dashes indicate no ranking
Fortune 500: Companies that produce a 10-K are ranked 1 to 500 based on 1999 revenue
Forbes 500: Private companies are ranked 1 to 500 based on 1998 revenue
Source: Forbes, December 13, 1999; Fortune, April 17, 2000

HOTELS & MOTELS

Hotels/Motels

Area	Hotels/ Motels	Rooms	Luxury-Level Hotels/Motels		Average Minimum Rates ($)		
			♦♦♦♦	♦♦♦♦♦	♦♦	♦♦♦	♦♦♦♦
City	13	1,183	0	0	80	109	n/a
Airport	8	1,258	0	0	n/a	n/a	n/a
Suburbs	2	252	0	0	n/a	n/a	n/a
Total	23	2,693	0	0	n/a	n/a	n/a

Note: n/a not available; classifications range from one diamond (budget properties with basic amenities) to five diamond (luxury properties).
Source: OAG Business Travel Planner, Winter 1999-2000

Estimated Daily Food and Lodging Costs

Area	Food/Other ($/day)	Average Hotel Cost ($/day)
City	38	80
U.S.	30	55

Source: ERI's Relocation Assessor software database, quarterly effective date 4/1/2000

CONVENTION CENTERS

Convention Centers and Event Sites

Name	Guest Rooms	Meeting Space (sq. ft.)	Capacity (Theatre Style)
Cumberland County Civic Center	n/a	n/a	8,798
Embassy Suites Portland	n/a	2,000	0
Holiday Inn By The Bay	239	12,500	1,500
Portland Expo/Hadlock Field	n/a	n/a	6,650
Portland Regency Hotel	95	n/a	0
Radisson Eastland Hotel Portland	204	18,000	600

Note: n/a not available
Source: EventSource.com, 3/15/2000

Living Environment

COST OF LIVING

Cost of Living: Homeowner

Cost Element	U.S. ($)	City ($)	Differential ($)	Percent of U.S. Average
Consumables	14,516	16,711	2,195	115.1
Transportation	5,957	7,548	1,591	126.7
Health Services	2,012	2,287	275	113.7
Housing/Utilities/Prop. Tax	16,337	19,465	3,128	119.1
Income+Payroll Taxes	12,615	12,854	239	101.9
Miscellaneous	8,563	8,563	0	100.0
Total Cost of Living	60,000	67,428	7,428	112.4

Note: Figures are based on a single income, four person family with gross annual earnings of $60,000, owning an 1,800 square-foot home, and driving two automobiles worth $22,000 30,000 miles per year.
Source: ERI's Relocation Assessor software database, quarterly effective date 4/1/2000

Cost of Living: Renter

Cost Element	U.S. ($)	City ($)	Differential ($)	Percent of U.S. Average
Consumables	10,486	12,133	1,647	115.7
Transportation	2,107	2,723	616	129.2
Health Services	1,632	1,864	232	114.2
Rent/Utilities/Insurance	9,299	9,969	670	107.2
Income+Payroll Taxes	8,607	8,847	240	102.8
Miscellaneous	7,869	7,869	0	100.0
Total Cost of Living	40,000	43,405	3,405	108.5

Note: Figures are based on a single income, three person family with gross annual earnings of $40,000, renting a 1,000 square-foot home, and driving one automobile worth $8,000 12,000 miles per year.
Source: ERI's Relocation Assessor software database, quarterly effective date 4/1/2000

HOUSING

Median Home Prices and Housing Affordability

Area	Median Price[2] 4th Qtr. 1999 ($)	HOI[3] 4th Qtr. 1999	Affordability Rank[4]
MSA[1]	n/a	n/a	n/a
U.S.	139,000	63.8	–

Note: (1) Metropolitan Statistical Area - see Appendix A for areas included; (2) U.S. figures calculated from the sales of 687,516 new and existing homes in 192 markets; (3) Housing Opportunity Index - percent of homes sold that were within the reach of the median income household at the prevailing mortgage interest rate; (4) Rank is from 1-192 with 1 being most affordable; n/a not available
Source: National Association of Home Builders, Housing Opportunity Index, 4th Quarter 1999

Estimated Home Price

Area	Price ($)
City	132,835
U.S.	135,855

Note: Figures are based on an 1,800 square-foot home
Source: ERI's Relocation Assessor software database, quarterly effective date 4/1/2000

Estimated Rent

Area	Rent ($/month)
City	660
U.S.	651

Note: Figures are based on a 1,000 square-foot home
Source: ERI's Relocation Assessor software database, quarterly effective date 4/1/2000

Median Home Price Projection

It is projected that the median home price in the metropolitan area will increase from $146,804 in 1999 to $234,894 in 2010, an increase of 60.0%
Kiplinger's Personal Finance Magazine, January 2000

RESIDENTIAL UTILITIES

Average Residential Utility Costs

Area	All Electric ($/mth)	Part Electric ($/mth)	Other Energy ($/mth)	Phone ($/mth)
City	n/a	n/a	n/a	n/a
U.S.	99.25	55.47	43.48	20.29

Note: n/a not available
Source: ACCRA, Cost of Living Index, 3rd Quarter 1999

HEALTH CARE

Average Health Care Costs

Area	Hospital ($/day)	Doctor ($/visit)	Dentist ($/visit)
City	n/a	n/a	n/a
U.S.	440.96	53.83	68.42

Note: n/a not available
Source: ACCRA, Cost of Living Index, 3rd Quarter 1999

Distribution of Office-Based Physicians

Area	Family/Gen. Practitioners	Specialists		
		Medical	Surgical	Other
MSA[1]	73	222	166	173

Note: Data as of 12/31/97; (1) Metropolitan Statistical Area - see Appendix A for areas included
Source: American Medical Assn., Physician Characteristics & Distribution in the U.S., 1999

Hospitals

Portland has 2 general medical and surgical hospitals, 1 rehabilitation.
AHA Guide to the Healthcare Field, 1999-2000

EDUCATION

Public School District Statistics

District Name	Num. Sch.	Enroll.	Classroom Teachers	Pupils per Teacher	Minority Pupils (%)	Current Exp.[1] ($/pupil)
Gov Baxter Sch for the Deaf	1	62	32	1.9	n/a	n/a
Portland	19	8,224	599	13.7	n/a	n/a

Note: Data covers the 1997-1998 school year unless otherwise noted; (1) Data covers fiscal year 1996; SD = School District; ISD = Independent School District; n/a not available
Source: National Center for Education Statistics, Common Core of Data Public Education Agency Universe 1997-98; National Center for Education Statistics, Characteristics of the 100 Largest Public Elementary and Secondary School Districts in the United States: 1997-98, July 1999

Educational Quality

School District	Education Quotient[1]	Graduate Outcome[2]	Community Index[3]	Resource Index[4]
Portland School Dist.	n/a	n/a	n/a	n/a

Note: Over 1,000 secondary school districts were rated in terms of educational quality. The scores range from a low of 50 to a high of 150; (1) Combination of the Graduate Outcome, Community and Resource indexes weighted to reflect the greater importance of the Graduate Outcome and Resource Index; (2) Based on graduation rates and college board scores (SAT/ACT); (3) Based on the surrounding community's level of affluence and adult education; (4) Based on teacher salaries, per-pupil expenditures and student-teacher ratios.
Source: Expansion Management, Ratings Issue, 1999

Educational Attainment by Race

Area	High School Graduate (%)					Bachelor's Degree (%)				
	Total	White	Black	Other	Hisp.[2]	Total	White	Black	Other	Hisp.[2]
City	83.2	83.6	72.3	66.4	73.1	29.6	30.1	7.6	12.8	22.2
MSA[1]	85.1	85.2	83.9	72.0	84.1	27.7	27.8	19.9	20.7	23.4
U.S.	75.2	77.9	63.1	60.4	49.8	20.3	21.5	11.4	19.4	9.2

Note: Figures shown cover persons 25 years old and over; (1) Metropolitan Statistical Area - see Appendix A for areas included; (2) people of Hispanic origin can be of any race
Source: 1990 Census of Population and Housing, Summary Tape File 3C

School Enrollment by Type

Area	Preprimary				Elementary/High School			
	Public		Private		Public		Private	
	Enrollment	%	Enrollment	%	Enrollment	%	Enrollment	%
City	905	66.9	447	33.1	7,042	92.7	558	7.3
MSA[1]	2,712	61.2	1,718	38.8	30,160	93.7	2,030	6.3
U.S.	2,679,029	59.5	1,824,256	40.5	38,379,689	90.2	4,187,099	9.8

Note: Figures shown cover persons 3 years old and over;
(1) Metropolitan Statistical Area - see Appendix A for areas included
Source: 1990 Census of Population and Housing, Summary Tape File 3C

School Enrollment by Race

Area	Preprimary (%)				Elementary/High School (%)			
	White	Black	Other	Hisp.[1]	White	Black	Other	Hisp.[1]
City	97.8	0.4	1.8	2.1	93.8	1.5	4.7	0.8
MSA[2]	97.5	0.9	1.6	1.0	97.0	0.7	2.4	1.0
U.S.	80.4	12.5	7.1	7.8	74.1	15.6	10.3	12.5

Note: Figures shown cover persons 3 years old and over; (1) people of Hispanic origin can be of any race; (2) Metropolitan Statistical Area - see Appendix A for areas included
Source: 1990 Census of Population and Housing, Summary Tape File 3C

Higher Education

Two-Year Colleges		Four-Year Colleges		Medical Schools	Law Schools	Voc/ Tech
Public	Private	Public	Private			
0	2	0	1	0	1	5

Source: College Blue Book, Occupational Education, 1999; Medical School Admission Requirements, 1999-2000; Peterson's Guide to Two-Year Colleges, 2000; Peterson's Guide to Four-Year Colleges, 1999; Barron's Guide to Law Schools, 1999

MAJOR EMPLOYERS

Major Employers

Consumers Water Co.

Guy Gannett Communications

Mercy Hospital

Sky Media

Unum Life Insurance

Cumberland County Recreation District

Maine Medical Center

New England Rehabilitation Hospital

Talk America

Note: Companies listed are located in the city
Source: D&B Business Rankings, 1999; Ward's Business Directory, 1999; America's Corporate Families, 1999

PUBLIC SAFETY

Crime Rate

Area	All Crimes	Violent Crimes				Property Crimes		
		Murder	Forcible Rape	Robbery	Aggrav. Assault	Burglary	Larceny -Theft	Motor Vehicle Theft
City	5,750.7	4.7	81.8	128.9	314.5	1,371.2	3,648.3	201.3
Suburbs[1]	3,152.7	2.8	11.3	14.6	48.4	599.1	2,365.0	111.5
MSA[2]	3,837.7	3.3	29.9	44.8	118.6	802.7	2,703.3	135.2
U.S.	4,615.5	6.3	34.4	165.2	360.5	862.0	2,728.1	459.0

Note: Crime rate is the number of crimes per 100,000 population; (1) Defined as all areas within the Metropolitan Statistical Area but located outside the central city; (2) Metropolitan Statistical Area - see Appendix A for areas included
Source: FBI Uniform Crime Reports, 1998

RECREATION

Culture and Recreation

Museums	Symphony Orchestras	Opera Companies	Dance Companies	Professional Theatres	Zoos	Pro Sports Teams
6	1	0	0	1	0	0

Source: Musical America, International Directory of the Performing Arts, 1999; Official Museum Directory, 2000; Stern's Performing Arts Directory, 1997; USA Today Four Sport Stadium Guide, 1997; Career Opportunities in Theatre and the Performing Arts, 1999

Library System

The Portland Public Library has five branches, holdings of 317,259 volumes, and a budget of $2,965,197 (1997-1998).
American Library Directory, 1999-2000

MEDIA

Newspapers

Name	Type	Freq.	Distribution	Circulation
Casco Bay Weekly	General	1x/wk	Local	30,000
The Munjoy Hill Observer	General	10x/yr	Local	3,000
Portland Press Herald	General	7x/wk	Area	76,021
The Wise Guide	General	1x/wk	Area	30,000

Note: Includes newspapers with circulations of 200 or more located in the city;
Source: Burrelle's Media Directory, 1999 Edition

Television Stations

Name	Ch.	Affiliation	Type	Owner
WCSH	n/a	NBCT	Commercial	Gannett Broadcasting
WGME	13	CBST	Commercial	Sinclair Communications
WPXT	51	FBC/UPN	Commercial	Pegasus Media & Communications Inc.

Note: Stations included broadcast in the Portland metro area; n/a not available
Source: Burrelle's Media Directory, 1999 Edition

AM Radio Stations

Call Letters	Freq. (kHz)	Target Audience	Station Format	Music Format
WGAN	560	General	N/S/T	n/a
WCLZ	900	General	T	n/a
WZAN	970	General	S/T	n/a
WLOB	1310	G/R	M/T	Christian
WJAE	1440	Men	S/T	n/a
WPOR	1490	General	M	Country

Note: Stations included broadcast in the Portland metro area; n/a not available
Target Audience: A=Asian; B=Black; C=Christian; E=Ethnic; F=French; G=General; H=Hispanic; M=Men; N=Native American; R=Religious; S=Senior Citizen; W=Women; Y=Young Adult; Z=Children
Station Format: E=Educational; M=Music; N=News; S=Sports; T=Talk
Source: Burrelle's Media Directory, 1999 Edition

FM Radio Stations

Call Letters	Freq. (mHz)	Target Audience	Station Format	Music Format
WMSJ	89.3	General	M/N	Adult Contemporary/Christian
WMPG	90.9	General	M/N	Alternative
WBOR	91.1	General	E/M/N/S/T	Adult Contemporary/Adult Standards/Alternative/AOR/Big Band/Jazz/Rhythm & Blues/Urban Contemporary
WSJB	91.5	General	M/N/S	Alternative
WMGX	93.1	General	M/N/S	Adult Top 40
WCYY	94.3	Young Adult	M	Alternative
WHOM	94.9	General	M	Adult Contemporary
WJBQ	97.9	General	M	Top 40
WCLZ	98.9	General	M/N/T	Adult Standards/Alternative/AOR
WYNZ	100.9	General	M	Oldies
WPOR	101.9	General	M	Country
WBLM	102.9	General	M/N/T	Classic Rock
WPKM	106.3	General	M/N	Classical
WTHT	107.5	n/a	M	Country

Note: Stations included broadcast in the Portland metro area; n/a not available
Station Format: E=Educational; M=Music; N=News; S=Sports; T=Talk
Target Audience: A=Asian; B=Black; C=Christian; E=Ethnic; F=French; G=General; H=Hispanic; M=Men; N=Native American; R=Religious; S=Senior Citizen; W=Women; Y=Young Adult; Z=Children
Music Format: AOR=Album Oriented Rock; MOR=Middle-of-the-Road
Source: Burrelle's Media Directory, 1999 Edition

WEATHER

Temperature/Precipitation/Humidity

	Jan	Feb	Mar	Apr	May	Jun	Jul	Aug	Sep	Oct	Nov	Dec	Yr.
Max. High Temp. (°F)	64	64	77	85	94	97	99	103	95	88	74	69	103
Avg. High Temp. (°F)	31	34	41	53	63	73	79	78	70	59	47	35	55
Avg. Temp. (°F)	22	24	32	43	53	63	69	67	59	49	39	27	46
Avg. Low Temp. (°F)	12	14	23	33	43	52	58	56	48	38	30	17	35
Min. Low Temp. (°F)	-26	-25	-21	8	23	35	40	33	26	15	3	-21	-26
Avg. Precip. (in.)	3.7	3.4	3.8	3.9	3.7	3.2	2.9	2.7	3.2	3.7	5.0	4.3	43.5
Avg. Snowfall (in.)	20	17	13	3	Tr	0	0	0	Tr	Tr	3	15	71
Avg. Rel. Hum. 7am (%)	75	75	74	73	75	79	80	83	86	84	82	78	79
Avg. Rel. Hum. 4pm (%)	62	60	60	58	61	63	62	63	64	64	67	65	62

Note: Tr = Trace amounts (less than 0.05 inches of rain or less than 0.5 inches of snow)
Source: National Climatic Data Center, International Station Meteorological Climate Summary, 3/95

Weather Conditions

Temperature			Precipitation		
5°F & below	32°F & below	90°F & above	0.01 inch or more precip.	1.5 inch or more snow/ice	Thunder-storms
23	156	5	129	15	16

Note: Figures are average number of days per year
Source: National Climatic Data Center, International Station Meteorological Climate Summary, 3/95

AIR & WATER QUALITY

Maximum Pollutant Concentrations

	Particulate Matter (ug/m³)	Carbon Monoxide (ppm)	Sulfur Dioxide (ppm)	Nitrogen Dioxide (ppm)	Ozone (ppm)	Lead (ug/m³)
MSA[1] Level	81	n/a	0.023	n/a	0.13	n/a
NAAQS[2]	150	9	0.140	0.053	0.12	1.50
Met NAAQS	Yes	n/a	Yes	n/a	No	n/a

Note: (1) Metropolitan Statistical Area - see Appendix A for areas included; (2) National Ambient Air Quality Standards; ppm = parts per million; ug/m³ = micrograms per cubic meter; n/a not available
Source: EPA, National Air Quality and Emissions Trends Report, 1997

Pollutant Standards Index

Data not available.
EPA, National Air Quality and Emissions Trends Report, 1997

Drinking Water

Water System Name	Pop. Served	Primary Water Source Type	Number of Violations in 1998-99	Type of Violation/ Contaminants
Greater Portland Water District	113,560	Surface	None	None

Note: Data as of January 19, 2000
Source: EPA, Office of Ground Water and Drinking Water, Safe Drinking Water Information System

Portland tap water is neutral, very soft, and not fluoridated.
Editor & Publisher Market Guide, 2000

Provo, Utah

Background

Provo, Utah is located in the Wasatch Mountains in the north-central section of the state, along the Provo River and 40 miles from Salt Lake City. It sits at a elevation of 4,549 feet.

Since 1980, Provo has been one of the fastest growing cities in the country and is ranked the sixth most productive city in the United States. With its five business and research parks, the Provo/Salt Lake City area has the world's second largest concentration of software and computer engineering firms—over 80. Other important economic segments include the steel and iron industries, clothing manufacture and food processing.

Originally called Fort Utah after the Ute Indians, the city's name was changed in 1850 to honor Etienne Provost, a French-Canadian trapper. In the 1870s, railroads stimulated industrial development in Provo, which became a center for silver, lead, copper and gold mining as well as steel and textile manufacturing. The city also prospered from the 1875 founding of Brigham Young Academy, which became a university in 1903.

Recreational activities in the region include the Timpanagos Cave Monument, which houses a state fish hatchery and bird refuge, Provo Peak for hikers, and Uinta National Forest.

General Rankings and Evaluative Comments

- Provo was ranked #161 out of 354 metropolitan areas in *Places Rated Almanac*. Criteria: cost of living, climate, crime, transportation, job outlook, education, the arts, health care, and recreation. *Places Rated Almanac, Millennium Edition, 2000*

- Provo was selected as one of America's best places to retire. Criteria: safety, climate, housing, culture and recreation, social compatibility, affordability, medical care, transportation, and jobs and/or volunteer opportunities. *Where to Retire: America's Best and Most Affordable Places, 1998*

- Provo was selected as one of "America's Best Towns to Raise an Outdoor Family" by *Outdoor Explorer* magazine. Criteria: easy access to the outdoors, quality education and health care, affordable housing, favorable employment opportunities, and low crime rates. The city was ranked #12 out of 25. *Outdoor Explorer, Summer 1999*

- Cognetics studied 273 metro areas in the United States, ranking them by entrepreneurial activity. Provo was ranked #2 out of the 50 largest metro areas. Criteria: Significant Starts (firms started in the last 10 years that still employ at least 5 people) and Young Growers (percent of firms 10 years old or less that grew significantly during the last 4 years). *Cognetics, "Entrepreneurial Hot Spots: The Best Places in America to Start and Grow a Company," 1999*

Business Environment

STATE ECONOMY

State Economic Profile

"After several years of rapid growth, the Utah economy has begun to slow. Manufacturing employment remains weak, and population growth has slowed as migration from California has fallen. Even with a deceleration in growth, Utah will remain one of the nation's strongest performers in the next several years.

During the 1990s, Utah was one of the nation's fastest growing states. Most of this increase was the result of migration from California, driven by California's then weak economy. Recently California has rebounded, and migration to Utah from CA has declined. Despite a current population growth rate below that of the early 1990s, Utah will remain one of the fastest growing states over the next several years.

Utah's economy is still deeply rooted in natural resources. Weak commodity prices have undermined the strength of many Utah employers. Geneva Steel laid off hundreds of workers in the state. Copper prices have also started to go the way of steel, forcing cutbacks among Utah mining firms. The long-term outlook for Utah's mining and metals industry is not bright. Soft prices and over-capacity will constraint growth and force some cutbacks in the years ahead.

Business migration has been centered around Salt Lake City, where affordable business costs have attracted several hi-tech firms and corporate back-office operations. The Provo-Orem/Utah Valley area is also one of the nation's largest concentrations of software development. A high quality of life and low business costs will continue to attract firms to the area. New construction and employment due to the 2002 Olympics will offset losses elsewhere." *National Association of Realtors, Economic Profiles: The Fifty States and the District of Columbia, http://nar.realtor.com/databank/profiles.htm*

EXPORTS

Total Export Sales

Area	1995 ($000)	1996 ($000)	1997 ($000)	1998 ($000)	% Chg. 1995-98	% Chg. 1997-98
MSA[1]	201,586	301,871	360,463	320,369	58.9	-11.1
U.S.	583,030,524	622,827,063	687,597,999	680,474,251	16.7	-1.0

Note: (1) Metropolitan Statistical Area - see Appendix A for areas included
Source: U.S. Department of Commerce, International Trade Association, Metropolitan Area Exports: An Export Performance Report on Over 250 U.S. Cities, November 10, 1999

CITY FINANCES

City Government Finances

Component	1995 ($million)	1995 (per capita $)
Revenue	40.9	462
Expenditure	41.9	474
Debt Outstanding	118.5	1,339

Source: 1999 County and City Extra, Annual Metro, City, and County Data Book

City Government Revenue by Source

Source	1995 ($million)	1995 (per capita $)
Intergovernmental	5.3	59
Taxes	20.4	230
Property	6.1	69
Sales and Gross Receipts	13.6	154

Source: 1999 County and City Extra, Annual Metro, City, and County Data Book

City Government Expenditures by Function

Function	1995 ($million)	1995 (per capita $)	1995 (%)
Public Welfare	0.0	0	0.0
Highways	2.1	24	5.1
Parking Facilities	0.0	0	0.0
Education	0.0	0	0.0
Health and Hospitals	0.0	0	0.0
Police Protection	6.9	79	16.7
Sewerage and Sanitation	5.2	59	12.5
Parks and Recreation	3.6	41	8.8
Housing and Community Development	2.7	31	6.6
Interest on Debt	4.1	46	9.9

Source: 1999 County and City Extra, Annual Metro, City, and County Data Book

Municipal Bond Ratings

Area	Moody's
City	Aaa

Source: Mergent Bond Record, 2/2000

POPULATION

Population Growth

Area	1980 Census	1990 Census	1999 Estimate	2004 Projection	Population Growth (%) 1990-1999	Population Growth (%) 1999-2004
City	74,108	86,848	102,534	110,799	18.1	8.1
MSA[1]	218,106	263,590	340,913	378,894	29.3	11.1
U.S.	226,545,805	248,765,170	272,212,864	283,625,312	9.4	4.2

Note: (1) Metropolitan Statistical Area - see Appendix A for areas included
Source: 1990 Census of Population and Housing, Summary Tape File 3C; Claritas, Inc.

Number of Households and Average Household Size

Area	1980 Census	1990 Census	1999 Estimate	2004 Projection	1999 Average Household Size
City	20,114	23,713	28,828	31,416	3.56
MSA[1]	58,515	70,011	91,399	101,878	3.73
U.S.	80,389,592	91,993,582	102,048,200	107,302,392	2.67

Note: (1) Metropolitan Statistical Area - see Appendix A for areas included
Source: 1990 Census of Population and Housing, Summary Tape File 3C; Claritas, Inc.

Race/Ethnicity of City Population

Race/Ethnicity	1990 Census Population	1990 Census %	1999 Estimate Population	1999 Estimate %	% Change 1990-1999
White, Non-Hispanic	80,067	92.2	91,222	89.0	13.9
Black, Non-Hispanic	149	0.2	330	0.3	121.5
Asian, Non-Hispanic	2,250	2.6	3,721	3.6	65.4
Other, Non-Hispanic	806	0.9	998	1.0	23.8
Hispanic	3,576	4.1	6,263	6.1	75.1

Source: 1990 Census of Population and Housing, Summary Tape File 3C; Claritas, Inc.

Race/Ethnicity of Metropolitan Statistical Area Population

Race/Ethnicity	1990 Census		1999 Estimate		% Change 1990-1999
	Population	%	Population	%	
White, Non-Hispanic	249,952	94.8	316,229	92.8	26.5
Black, Non-Hispanic	251	0.1	523	0.2	108.4
Asian, Non-Hispanic	3,801	1.4	6,531	1.9	71.8
Other, Non-Hispanic	1,675	0.6	2,157	0.6	28.8
Hispanic	7,911	3.0	15,473	4.5	95.6

Note: See Appendix A for areas included in the Metropolitan Statistical Area
Source: 1990 Census of Population and Housing, Summary Tape File 3C; Claritas, Inc.

Ancestry

Area	German	Irish	English	Italian	U.S.	French	Polish	Dutch
City	17.7	6.9	43.6	2.0	2.8	3.3	0.9	2.3
MSA[1]	17.4	6.5	50.1	2.0	2.9	3.5	0.7	2.7
U.S.	23.3	15.6	13.1	5.9	5.3	4.2	3.8	2.5

Note: Figures are percentages and include persons that reported multiple ancestry (eg. if a person reported being Irish and Italian, they were included in both columns); (1) Metropolitan Statistical Area - see Appendix A for areas included
Source: 1990 Census of Population and Housing, Summary Tape File 3C

Median Age

Area	1990 Census	1999 Estimate
City	22.6	23.5
MSA[1]	22.5	23.9
U.S.	32.9	35.7

Note: (1) Metropolitan Statistical Area - see Appendix A for areas included
Source: 1990 Census of Population and Housing, Summary Tape File 3C; Claritas, Inc.

Male/Female Population

Area	Number of Males		Number of Females		Males per 100 Females	
	1990	1999	1990	1999	1990	1999
City	42,122	49,787	44,726	52,747	94.2	94.4
MSA[1]	130,236	168,143	133,354	172,770	97.7	97.3
U.S.	121,172,379	132,803,736	127,537,494	139,409,136	95.0	95.3

Note: (1) Metropolitan Statistical Area - see Appendix A for areas included
Source: 1990 Census of Population, General Population Characteristics; Claritas, Inc.

INCOME

Per Capita/Median/Average Income

Area	Per Capita ($)			Median Household ($)			Average Household ($)		
	1989	1999	% Chg.	1989	1999	% Chg.	1989	1999	% Chg.
City	8,408	14,902	77.2	21,162	32,959	55.7	29,604	51,075	72.5
MSA[1]	9,051	16,059	77.4	27,432	45,078	64.3	33,532	59,161	76.4
U.S.	14,420	21,350	48.1	30,056	40,525	34.8	38,453	56,184	46.1

Note: (1) Metropolitan Statistical Area - see Appendix A for areas included; 1989 data is from the 1990 Census; 1999 data is estimated by Claritas, Inc.
Source: 1990 Census of Population, General Population Characteristics; Claritas, Inc.

Household Income Distribution

Area	Percent of Households Earning								
	Under $5,000	$5,000 -14,999	$15,000 -24,999	$25,000 -34,999	$35,000 -49,999	$50,000 -74,999	$75,000 -99,000	$100,000 -149,999	$150,000 and up
City	3.4	14.8	20.1	13.8	16.1	14.7	7.3	5.6	4.2
MSA[1]	2.3	9.4	13.9	12.5	17.2	22.7	11.1	6.6	4.2
U.S.	3.9	13.3	13.8	12.6	16.2	19.4	9.7	6.6	4.6

Note: Data as of 1999; (1) Metropolitan Statistical Area - see Appendix A for areas included
Source: Claritas, Inc.

Effective Buying Income

Area	Per Capita ($)	Median Household ($)	Average Household ($)
City	10,863	27,705	39,447
MSA[1]	12,409	36,872	45,338
U.S.	17,496	36,603	47,036

Note: Data as of 1/1/2000; (1) Metropolitan Statistical Area - see Appendix A for areas included
Source: Standard Rate & Data Service, Newspaper Advertising Source, March 2000

Effective Household Buying Income Distribution

Area	% of Households Earning						
	$10,000 -$19,999	$20,000 -$34,999	$35,000 -$49,999	$50,000 -$74,999	$75,000 -$99,000	$100,000 -$124,999	$125,000 and up
City	23.2	26.6	16.2	13.0	5.7	1.8	2.1
MSA[1]	15.7	23.9	20.0	20.4	7.7	2.5	2.1
U.S.	15.0	21.6	17.6	19.6	8.4	3.0	3.3

Note: Data as of 1/1/2000; (1) Metropolitan Statistical Area - see Appendix A for areas included
Source: Standard Rate & Data Service, Newspaper Advertising Source, March 2000

Poverty Rates by Age

Area	People of All Ages	People Under 18 Years Old	Related Children Age 5-17 in Families in Poverty
City	20.3	n/a	n/a
County	10.8	10.0	7.1
U.S.	13.8	20.8	18.7

Note: Figures show the percent of people living below the poverty line in 1995. The average poverty threshold was $15,569 for a family of four in 1995; n/a not available
Source: Bureau of the Census, Small Area Income and Poverty Estimates Program; U.S. Department of Housing and Urban Development

EMPLOYMENT

Labor Force and Employment

Area	Civilian Labor Force			Workers Employed		
	Dec. 1998	Dec. 1999	% Chg.	Dec. 1998	Dec. 1999	% Chg.
City	58,997	60,623	2.8	57,422	59,390	3.4
MSA[1]	163,471	168,097	2.8	159,585	165,055	3.4
U.S.	138,297,000	139,941,000	1.2	132,732,000	134,696,000	1.5

Note: Data is not seasonally adjusted and covers workers 16 years of age and older; (1) Metropolitan Statistical Area - see Appendix A for areas included
Source: Bureau of Labor Statistics, http://stats.bls.gov

Unemployment Rate

| Area | 1999 | | | | | | | | | | | |
	Jan.	Feb.	Mar.	Apr.	May	Jun.	Jul.	Aug.	Sep.	Oct.	Nov.	Dec.
City	3.3	3.5	3.4	3.0	3.1	3.8	3.3	3.4	3.0	2.9	2.3	2.0
MSA[1]	3.0	3.1	3.1	2.6	2.8	3.4	3.0	3.0	2.7	2.6	2.0	1.8
U.S.	4.8	4.7	4.4	4.1	4.0	4.5	4.5	4.2	4.1	3.8	3.8	3.7

Note: Data is not seasonally adjusted and covers workers 16 years of age and older; all figures are percentages; (1) Metropolitan Statistical Area - see Appendix A for areas included
Source: Bureau of Labor Statistics, http://stats.bls.gov

Employment by Industry

| Sector | MSA[1] | | U.S. |
	Number of Employees	Percent of Total	Percent of Total
Services	59,100	39.1	30.2
Retail Trade	30,000	19.9	18.1
Government	20,200	13.4	15.8
Manufacturing	18,400	12.2	14.1
Finance/Insurance/Real Estate	4,600	3.0	5.9
Wholesale Trade	5,800	3.8	5.4
Transportation/Public Utilities	2,400	1.6	5.3
Construction	n/a	n/a	4.8
Mining	n/a	n/a	0.4

Note: Figures cover non-farm employment as of 12/99 and are not seasonally adjusted; (1) Metropolitan Statistical Area - see Appendix A for areas included; n/a not available
Source: Bureau of Labor Statistics, http://stats.bls.gov

Employment by Occupation

Occupation Category	City (%)	MSA[1] (%)	U.S. (%)
White Collar	65.4	59.4	58.1
Executive/Admin./Management	8.8	10.2	12.3
Professional	20.9	17.6	14.1
Technical & Related Support	4.9	4.3	3.7
Sales	11.6	11.1	11.8
Administrative Support/Clerical	19.2	16.3	16.3
Blue Collar	17.8	24.0	26.2
Precision Production/Craft/Repair	6.8	10.2	11.3
Machine Operators/Assem./Insp.	5.6	7.0	6.8
Transportation/Material Movers	2.1	3.1	4.1
Cleaners/Helpers/Laborers	3.2	3.8	3.9
Services	15.3	14.3	13.2
Farming/Forestry/Fishing	1.5	2.3	2.5

Note: Figures cover workers 16 years of age and older; (1) Metropolitan Statistical Area - see Appendix A for areas included
Source: 1990 Census of Population and Housing, Summary Tape File 3C

Occupational Employment Projections: 1996 - 2006

Occupations Expected to Have the Largest Job Growth (ranked by numerical growth)	Fast-Growing Occupations[1] (ranked by percent growth)
1. Salespersons, retail	1. Systems analysts
2. Truck drivers, light	2. Computer engineers
3. Cashiers	3. Respiratory therapists
4. Marketing & sales, supervisors	4. Directors, religious activities & educ.
5. Janitors/cleaners/maids, ex. priv. hshld.	5. Physical therapy assistants and aides
6. General managers & top executives	6. Emergency medical technicians
7. Registered nurses	7. Paralegals
8. Carpenters, including brattice builders	8. Medical assistants
9. Food preparation workers	9. Medical records technicians
10. General office clerks	10. Home health aides

Note: Projections cover Utah; (1) Excludes occupations with total job growth less than 300
Source: U.S. Department of Labor, Employment and Training Administration, America's Labor Market Information System (ALMIS)

Average Wages

Occupation	$/Hr.	Occupation	$/Hr.
Accountants and Auditors	17.60	Maids and Housekeepers	6.77
Assemblers and Fabricators	8.14	Maintenance Repairers	10.34
Automotive Mechanics	15.29	Marketing/Advertising/PR Managers	27.56
Bookkeepers	9.98	Nurses, Licensed Practical	11.72
Carpenters	12.73	Nurses, Registered	-
Cashiers	7.08	Nursing Aides/Orderlies/Attendants	7.74
Clerks, General Office	9.00	Physicians and Surgeons	55.24
Clerks, Shipping/Receiving/Traffic	10.05	Receptionists/Information Clerks	8.00
Computer Programmers	23.71	Sales Reps., Exc. Scientific/Retail	19.19
Computer Support Specialists	14.85	Sales Reps., Scientific, Exc. Retail	20.15
Cooks, Restaurant	8.60	Salespersons, Retail	8.63
Electricians	14.80	Secretaries, Except Legal/Medical	9.80
Financial Managers	27.01	Stock Clerks, Sales Floor	7.85
First-Line Supervisors/Mgrs., Sales	15.46	Systems Analysts	21.36
Food Preparation Workers	6.98	Teacher Aides	-
General Managers/Top Executives	29.00	Teachers, Elementary School	-
Guards	8.13	Teachers, Secondary School	16.28
Hand Packers	6.46	Telemarketers	7.89
Janitors and Cleaners	8.03	Truck Drivers, Heavy/Tractor-Trailer	13.89
Laborers, Landscaping	8.24	Truck Drivers, Light	9.69
Lawyers	25.38	Waiters and Waitresses	6.15

Note: Wage data is for 1998 and covers the Metropolitan Statistical Area (see Appendix A for areas included). Hourly wages for elementary and secondary school teachers were calculated by the editors from annual wage data assuming a 40 hour work week; Dashes indicate that data was not available.
Source: Bureau of Labor Statistics, 1998 Metropolitan Area Occupational Employment and Wage Estimates

TAXES

Major State and Local Tax Rates

State Corporate Income (%)	State Personal Income (%)	Residential Property (%)	Sales & Use		State Gasoline (cents/ gallon)	State Cigarette (cents/ pack)
			State (%)	Local (%)		
5.0[a]	2.3 - 7.0	0.61	4.75	1.5	24.75[b]	51.5

Note: Personal/corporate income, sales, gasoline and cigarette tax rates as of January 2000. Property tax rates as of April 2000; (a) Minimum tax $100; (b) Rate is comprised of 24.5 cents excise and 0.25 cent motor carrier tax
Source: Federation of Tax Administrators, www.taxadmin.org; ERI's Relocation Assessor software database, quarterly effective date 4/1/2000

Total Taxes Per Capita and as a Percent of Income

Area	Per Capita Income ($)	Per Capita Taxes ($)			Percent of Income (%)		
		Total	Federal	State/Local	Total	Federal	State/Local
Utah	23,138	8,028	5,433	2,596	34.7	23.5	11.2
U.S.	28,878	10,298	7,026	3,273	35.7	24.3	11.3

Note: Figures are for 1999
Source: Tax Foundation, www.taxfoundation.org

COMMERCIAL UTILITIES

Typical Monthly Electric Bills

Area	Commercial Service ($/month)		Industrial Service ($/month)	
	12 kW demand 1,500 kWh	100 kW demand 30,000 kWh	1,000 kW demand 400,000 kWh	20,000 kW demand 10,000,000 kWh
City	n/a	n/a	n/a	n/a
U.S.	150	2,174	23,995	508,569

Note: Based on rates in effect January 1, 1999; n/a not available
Source: Edison Electric Institute, Typical Residential, Commercial and Industrial Bills, Winter 1999

TRANSPORTATION

Transportation Statistics

Average minutes to work (1990)	13.9
Interstate highways	I-15; US-189; US-89
Bus lines	
In-city (1998)	Utah Transit Authority (Salt Lake City area), 513 buses
Inter-city (1999)	2
Passenger air service	
Airport	Provo Municipal Airport; Salt Lake City International (50 miles)
Airlines (1999)	n/a
Enplaned passengers (1998)	n/a
Amtrak service	Yes
Motor freight carriers (1999)	8
Major waterways/ports	None

Source: FAA DOT/TSC CY1998 ACAIS Database; National Transit Database, 1998; Editor & Publisher Market Guide, 2000; Amtrak National Time Table, Fall 1999/Winter 2000; 1990 Census of Population and Housing, STF 3C; Jane's Urban Transport Systems 1999-2000

Means of Transportation to Work

Area	Car/Truck/Van		Public Transportation			Bicycle	Walked	Other Means	Worked at Home
	Drove Alone	Car-pooled	Bus	Subway	Railroad				
City	61.4	15.1	2.6	0.0	0.0	2.4	12.9	1.3	4.2
MSA[1]	69.9	15.9	1.8	0.0	0.0	1.2	6.0	0.9	4.4
U.S.	73.2	13.4	3.0	1.5	0.5	0.4	3.9	1.2	3.0

Note: Figures shown are percentages and only include workers 16 years of age and older;
(1) Metropolitan Statistical Area - see Appendix A for areas included
Source: 1990 Census of Population and Housing, Summary Tape File 3C

BUSINESSES

Major Business Headquarters

Company Name	1999 Rankings	
	Fortune 500	Forbes 500
No companies listed	-	-

Note: Companies listed are located in the city; dashes indicate no ranking
Fortune 500: Companies that produce a 10-K are ranked 1 to 500 based on 1999 revenue
Forbes 500: Private companies are ranked 1 to 500 based on 1998 revenue
Source: Forbes, December 13, 1999; Fortune, April 17, 2000

HOTELS & MOTELS

Hotels/Motels

Area	Hotels/ Motels	Rooms	Luxury-Level Hotels/Motels		Average Minimum Rates ($)		
			◆◆◆◆	◆◆◆◆◆	◆◆	◆◆◆	◆◆◆◆
City	11	442	0	0	n/a	n/a	n/a
Suburbs	1	100	0	0	n/a	n/a	n/a
Total	12	542	0	0	n/a	n/a	n/a

Note: n/a not available; classifications range from one diamond (budget properties with basic amenities) to five diamond (luxury properties).
Source: OAG Business Travel Planner, Winter 1999-2000

Estimated Daily Food and Lodging Costs

Area	Food/Other ($/day)	Average Hotel Cost ($/day)
City	38	60
U.S.	30	55

Source: ERI's Relocation Assessor software database, quarterly effective date 4/1/2000

CONVENTION CENTERS

Convention Centers and Event Sites

Name	Guest Rooms	Meeting Space (sq. ft.)	Capacity (Theatre Style)
Marriott Center/Cougar Stadium	n/a	n/a	65,000
Provo Park Hotel	333	n/a	700

Note: n/a not available
Source: EventSource.com, 3/15/2000

Living Environment

COST OF LIVING

Cost of Living: Homeowner

Cost Element	U.S. ($)	City ($)	Differential ($)	Percent of U.S. Average
Consumables	14,516	13,843	-673	95.4
Transportation	5,957	6,272	315	105.3
Health Services	2,012	2,024	12	100.6
Housing/Utilities/Prop. Tax	16,337	16,633	296	101.8
Income+Payroll Taxes	12,615	13,195	580	104.6
Miscellaneous	8,563	8,563	0	100.0
Total Cost of Living	60,000	60,530	530	100.9

Note: Figures are based on a single income, four person family with gross annual earnings of $60,000, owning an 1,800 square-foot home, and driving two automobiles worth $22,000 30,000 miles per year.
Source: ERI's Relocation Assessor software database, quarterly effective date 4/1/2000

Cost of Living: Renter

Cost Element	U.S. ($)	City ($)	Differential ($)	Percent of U.S. Average
Consumables	10,486	10,016	-470	95.5
Transportation	2,107	2,222	115	105.5
Health Services	1,632	1,645	13	100.8
Rent/Utilities/Insurance	9,299	10,055	756	108.1
Income+Payroll Taxes	8,607	9,119	512	105.9
Miscellaneous	7,869	7,869	0	100.0
Total Cost of Living	40,000	40,926	926	102.3

Note: Figures are based on a single income, three person family with gross annual earnings of $40,000, renting a 1,000 square-foot home, and driving one automobile worth $8,000 12,000 miles per year.
Source: ERI's Relocation Assessor software database, quarterly effective date 4/1/2000

HOUSING

Median Home Prices and Housing Affordability

Area	Median Price[2] 4th Qtr. 1999 ($)	HOI[3] 4th Qtr. 1999	Affordability Rank[4]
MSA[1]	152,000	46.3	169
U.S.	139,000	63.8	–

Note: (1) Metropolitan Statistical Area - see Appendix A for areas included; (2) U.S. figures calculated from the sales of 687,516 new and existing homes in 192 markets; (3) Housing Opportunity Index - percent of homes sold that were within the reach of the median income household at the prevailing mortgage interest rate; (4) Rank is from 1-192 with 1 being most affordable
Source: National Association of Home Builders, Housing Opportunity Index, 4th Quarter 1999

Estimated Home Price

Area	Price ($)
City	153,536
U.S.	135,855

Note: Figures are based on an 1,800 square-foot home
Source: ERI's Relocation Assessor software database, quarterly effective date 4/1/2000

Estimated Rent

Area	Rent ($/month)
City	735
U.S.	651

Note: Figures are based on a 1,000 square-foot home
Source: ERI's Relocation Assessor software database, quarterly effective date 4/1/2000

Median Home Price Projection

It is projected that the median home price in the metropolitan area will increase from $152,284 in 1999 to $251,923 in 2010, an increase of 65.4%
Kiplinger's Personal Finance Magazine, January 2000

RESIDENTIAL UTILITIES

Average Residential Utility Costs

Area	All Electric ($/mth)	Part Electric ($/mth)	Other Energy ($/mth)	Phone ($/mth)
City	–	41.81	33.03	21.49
U.S.	99.25	55.47	43.48	20.29

Source: ACCRA, Cost of Living Index, 3rd Quarter 1999

HEALTH CARE

Average Health Care Costs

Area	Hospital ($/day)	Doctor ($/visit)	Dentist ($/visit)
City	278.00	47.75	60.75
U.S.	440.96	53.83	68.42

Note: Hospital—based on a semi-private room; Doctor—based on a general practitioner's routine exam of an established patient; Dentist—based on adult teeth cleaning and periodic oral exam.
Source: ACCRA, Cost of Living Index, 3rd Quarter 1999

Distribution of Office-Based Physicians

| Area | Family/Gen. Practitioners | Specialists | | |
		Medical	Surgical	Other
MSA[1]	70	86	109	76

Note: Data as of 12/31/97; (1) Metropolitan Statistical Area - see Appendix A for areas included
Source: American Medical Assn., Physician Characteristics & Distribution in the U.S., 1999

Hospitals

Provo has 1 general medical and surgical hospital, 1 psychiatric.
AHA Guide to the Healthcare Field, 1999-2000

EDUCATION

Public School District Statistics

District Name	Num. Sch.	Enroll.	Classroom Teachers	Pupils per Teacher	Minority Pupils (%)	Current Exp.[1] ($/pupil)
Provo School District	24	13,723	696	19.7	n/a	n/a

Note: Data covers the 1997-1998 school year unless otherwise noted; (1) Data covers fiscal year 1996; SD = School District; ISD = Independent School District; n/a not available
Source: National Center for Education Statistics, Common Core of Data Public Education Agency Universe 1997-98; National Center for Education Statistics, Characteristics of the 100 Largest Public Elementary and Secondary School Districts in the United States: 1997-98, July 1999

Educational Quality

School District	Education Quotient[1]	Graduate Outcome[2]	Community Index[3]	Resource Index[4]
Provo School Dist.	122	130	130	105

Note: Over 1,000 secondary school districts were rated in terms of educational quality. The scores range from a low of 50 to a high of 150; (1) Combination of the Graduate Outcome, Community and Resource indexes weighted to reflect the greater importance of the Graduate Outcome and Resource Index; (2) Based on graduation rates and college board scores (SAT/ACT); (3) Based on the surrounding community's level of affluence and adult education; (4) Based on teacher salaries, per-pupil expenditures and student-teacher ratios.
Source: Expansion Management, Ratings Issue, 1999

Educational Attainment by Race

Area	High School Graduate (%)					Bachelor's Degree (%)				
	Total	White	Black	Other	Hisp.[2]	Total	White	Black	Other	Hisp.[2]
City	89.8	90.2	100.0	84.6	82.5	34.5	34.3	45.3	37.8	19.4
MSA[1]	87.9	88.3	84.5	75.9	68.2	26.2	26.1	34.5	28.8	15.9
U.S.	75.2	77.9	63.1	60.4	49.8	20.3	21.5	11.4	19.4	9.2

Note: Figures shown cover persons 25 years old and over; (1) Metropolitan Statistical Area - see Appendix A for areas included; (2) people of Hispanic origin can be of any race
Source: 1990 Census of Population and Housing, Summary Tape File 3C

School Enrollment by Type

Area	Preprimary				Elementary/High School			
	Public		Private		Public		Private	
	Enrollment	%	Enrollment	%	Enrollment	%	Enrollment	%
City	773	60.7	501	39.3	12,192	95.7	544	4.3
MSA[1]	4,278	67.3	2,082	32.7	63,767	97.8	1,414	2.2
U.S.	2,679,029	59.5	1,824,256	40.5	38,379,689	90.2	4,187,099	9.8

Note: Figures shown cover persons 3 years old and over;
(1) Metropolitan Statistical Area - see Appendix A for areas included
Source: 1990 Census of Population and Housing, Summary Tape File 3C

School Enrollment by Race

Area	Preprimary (%)				Elementary/High School (%)			
	White	Black	Other	Hisp.[1]	White	Black	Other	Hisp.[1]
City	92.6	0.5	6.8	4.1	94.1	0.1	5.7	4.8
MSA[2]	95.8	0.3	3.9	3.3	96.4	0.1	3.6	3.1
U.S.	80.4	12.5	7.1	7.8	74.1	15.6	10.3	12.5

Note: Figures shown cover persons 3 years old and over; (1) people of Hispanic origin can be of any race; (2) Metropolitan Statistical Area - see Appendix A for areas included
Source: 1990 Census of Population and Housing, Summary Tape File 3C

Higher Education

Two-Year Colleges		Four-Year Colleges		Medical Schools	Law Schools	Voc/ Tech
Public	Private	Public	Private			
0	1	0	1	0	1	4

Source: College Blue Book, Occupational Education, 1999; Medical School Admission Requirements, 1999-2000; Peterson's Guide to Two-Year Colleges, 2000; Peterson's Guide to Four-Year Colleges, 1999; Barron's Guide to Law Schools, 1999

MAJOR EMPLOYERS

Major Employers

Ameritech Library Services (computer systems)
Eyering Corp. (software)
Novell
Sears Roebuck & Co.

Birrell Bottling Co.
Nature's Sunshine Products
NuSkin Enterprises
Western Wats Center (business services)

Note: Companies listed are located in the city
Source: D&B Business Rankings, 1999; Ward's Business Directory, 1999; America's Corporate Families, 1999

PUBLIC SAFETY

Crime Rate

Area	All Crimes	Violent Crimes				Property Crimes		
		Murder	Forcible Rape	Robbery	Aggrav. Assault	Burglary	Larceny -Theft	Motor Vehicle Theft
City	3,591.9	2.9	38.4	26.9	71.1	640.8	2,617.8	194.1
Suburbs[1]	4,087.5	1.3	21.7	18.2	107.1	465.3	3,272.2	201.7
MSA[2]	3,933.4	1.8	26.9	20.9	95.9	519.9	3,068.6	199.3
U.S.	4,615.5	6.3	34.4	165.2	360.5	862.0	2,728.1	459.0

Note: Crime rate is the number of crimes per 100,000 population; (1) Defined as all areas within the Metropolitan Statistical Area but located outside the central city; (2) Metropolitan Statistical Area - see Appendix A for areas included
Source: FBI Uniform Crime Reports, 1998

RECREATION

Culture and Recreation

Museums	Symphony Orchestras	Opera Companies	Dance Companies	Professional Theatres	Zoos	Pro Sports Teams
5	1	0	1	1	0	0

Source: Musical America, International Directory of the Performing Arts, 1999; Official Museum Directory, 2000; Stern's Performing Arts Directory, 1997; USA Today Four Sport Stadium Guide, 1997; Career Opportunities in Theatre and the Performing Arts, 1999

Library System

The Provo City Library has no branchesand a budget of $1,800,000 (1997-1998).
American Library Directory, 1999-2000

MEDIA

Newspapers

Name	Type	Freq.	Distribution	Circulation
The Daily Herald	General	7x/wk	Local	32,005
The Daily Universe	General	5x/wk	Campus	18,500

Note: Includes newspapers with circulations of 200 or more located in the city;
Source: Burrelle's Media Directory, 1999 Edition

Television Stations

Name	Ch.	Affiliation	Type	Owner
KBYU	11	PBS	Public	Brigham Young University

Note: Stations included broadcast in the Provo metro area; n/a not available
Source: Burrelle's Media Directory, 1999 Edition

AM Radio Stations

Call Letters	Freq. (kHz)	Target Audience	Station Format	Music Format
KOVO	960	General	M	Big Band/Oldies
KEYY	1450	Religious	E/M/N/T	Christian
KHQN	1480	R/S	M	n/a

Note: Stations included broadcast in the Provo metro area; n/a not available
Target Audience: A=Asian; B=Black; C=Christian; E=Ethnic; F=French; G=General; H=Hispanic; M=Men; N=Native American; R=Religious; S=Senior Citizen; W=Women; Y=Young Adult; Z=Children
Station Format: E=Educational; M=Music; N=News; S=Sports; T=Talk
Source: Burrelle's Media Directory, 1999 Edition

FM Radio Stations

Call Letters	Freq. (mHz)	Target Audience	Station Format	Music Format
KPGR	88.1	General	E/M	AOR/Classic Rock/MOR
KBYU	89.1	General	E/M	Classical
KOHS	91.7	General	M/N/S	Alternative

Note: Stations included broadcast in the Provo metro area
Station Format: E=Educational; M=Music; N=News; S=Sports; T=Talk
Target Audience: A=Asian; B=Black; C=Christian; E=Ethnic; F=French; G=General; H=Hispanic; M=Men; N=Native American; R=Religious; S=Senior Citizen; W=Women; Y=Young Adult; Z=Children
Music Format: AOR=Album Oriented Rock; MOR=Middle-of-the-Road
Source: Burrelle's Media Directory, 1999 Edition

WEATHER

Temperature/Precipitation/Humidity

	Jan	Feb	Mar	Apr	May	Jun	Jul	Aug	Sep	Oct	Nov	Dec	Yr.
Max. High Temp. (°F)	60	68	78	85	93	104	107	103	98	88	74	66	107
Avg. High Temp. (°F)	36	42	51	62	72	82	92	90	80	66	49	40	64
Avg. Temp. (°F)	27	33	40	50	58	67	76	75	65	53	38	31	51
Avg. Low Temp. (°F)	18	24	30	38	45	53	61	60	50	40	28	22	39
Min. Low Temp. (°F)	-22	-30	5	14	27	35	41	39	30	18	-14	-21	-30
Avg. Precip. (in.)	1.3	1.2	1.6	1.8	1.4	0.9	0.6	0.9	0.6	1.2	1.3	1.2	13.9
Avg. Snowfall (in.)	13.6	9.3	8.2	3.2	0.2	0	0	0	0	0.5	6.1	10.3	51.4
Avg. Rel. Hum. (%)	73	70	60	52	48	40	36	39	43	53	67	77	55

Source: National Climatic Data Center, International Station Meteorological Climate Summary, 3/95

Weather Conditions

Temperature			Precipitation		
0°F & below	32°F & below	90°F & above	0.1 inch or more precip.	1.5 inch or more snow/ice	Thunder-storms
2	135	57	35	13	35

Note: Figures are average number of days per year
Source: National Climatic Data Center, International Station Meteorological Climate Summary, 3/95

AIR & WATER QUALITY

Maximum Pollutant Concentrations

	Particulate Matter (ug/m^3)	Carbon Monoxide (ppm)	Sulfur Dioxide (ppm)	Nitrogen Dioxide (ppm)	Ozone (ppm)	Lead (ug/m^3)
MSA[1] Level	115	6	n/a	0.023	0.10	n/a
NAAQS[2]	150	9	0.140	0.053	0.12	1.50
Met NAAQS	Yes	Yes	n/a	Yes	Yes	n/a

Note: (1) Metropolitan Statistical Area - see Appendix A for areas included; (2) National Ambient Air Quality Standards; ppm = parts per million; ug/m^3 = micrograms per cubic meter; n/a not available
Source: EPA, National Air Quality and Emissions Trends Report, 1997

Pollutant Standards Index

Data not available.
EPA, National Air Quality and Emissions Trends Report, 1997

Drinking Water

Water System Name	Pop. Served	Primary Water Source Type	Number of Violations in 1998-99	Type of Violation/ Contaminants
Provo City	95,000	Ground	None	None

Note: Data as of January 19, 2000
Source: EPA, Office of Ground Water and Drinking Water, Safe Drinking Water Information System

Provo tap water is alkaline and hard.
Editor & Publisher Market Guide, 2000

Roanoke, Virginia

Background

Roanoke, Virginia is located on the Roanoke River in southwestern Virginia, 148 miles west of Richmond, between the Blue Ridge and the Allegheny Mountains. Known as the "Capital of the Blue Ridge," Roanoke is a center for trade, manufacturing, and distribution of metal and steel products, electrical equipment, clothing, chemicals and furniture.

In the 1740s, Mark Evans and Tasker Tosh came from Pennsylvania to settle near the salt marches, or "licks," which were a gathering place for deer, elk and buffalo. Known originally as Gainsborough, then Old Lick, the town moved in 1874 several miles from its original location to where the new railroad had established a station stop. The new location became Big Lick until 1882, when it was renamed Roanoke after "rawrenock," the Indian word for the shell beads they traded.

Roanoke became a crossroads for the Shenandoah Valley Railroad, which would eventually become the Norfolk and Western Railway. The town grew rapidly, and was chartered as a city in 1884. Roanoke became a hub of commerce as large railroad shops and offices were built. In the early 1900s, fabricated steel and textile companies were established. The city's marketplace, one of the oldest in the country, is still active today.

Roanoke offers cultural attractions such as the Center-in-the-Square — a theatre, planetarium and museum complex. Opportunities for outdoor recreation are plentiful including George Washington National Forest and Jefferson National Forest with outstanding scenery and hiking trails, Blue Ridge Parkway with incredible mountain views, and Mill Mountain on top of which sits a a 100-foot illuminated star, symbolizing 40 years of progress and serves as a beacon for airplanes, earning Roanoke the name "Star City of the South."

Institutions of higher learning include the National Business College, Virginia Western Community College, Hollins University and Roanoke College. The Booker T. Washington National Monument is 18 miles from the city.

Called "Festival City," Roanoke hosts the Roanoke Festival in the Park, Downtown Roanoke's Railway Festival, Vinton's Dogwood Festival and the Strawberry Festival, among others.

General Rankings and Evaluative Comments

■ Roanoke was ranked #84 out of 354 metropolitan areas in *Places Rated Almanac*. Criteria: cost of living, climate, crime, transportation, job outlook, education, the arts, health care, and recreation. *Places Rated Almanac, Millennium Edition, 2000*

■ Roanoke was selected as one of North America's "Best Small Metro Areas" (population under 250,000). The area ranked #3 out of 20. Criteria: cost of living, climate, crime, transportation, job outlook, education, the arts, health care, and recreation. *Places Rated Almanac, Millennium Edition, 2000*

■ Cognetics studied 273 metro areas in the United States, ranking them by entrepreneurial activity. Roanoke was ranked #71 out of 134 smaller metro areas. Criteria: Significant Starts (firms started in the last 10 years that still employ at least 5 people) and Young Growers (percent of firms 10 years old or less that grew significantly during the last 4 years). *Cognetics, "Entrepreneurial Hot Spots: The Best Places in America to Start and Grow a Company," 1999*

Business Environment

STATE ECONOMY

State Economic Profile

"Virginia has begun to slow from its recent expansion. Virginia's above-average growth is largely a result of the expansion of high-tech firms in Northern Virginia. Slower growth in the Hampton Roads and Richmond areas stems from a slowdown in the manufacturing and farm sectors. Virginia's demographic situation is solid, and its housing and construction markets remain vibrant. Although a slowing US economy will be a drag on Virginia, the long-term outlook for Virginia is strong, above-average growth.

Northern Virginia has become less dependent upon defense spending as its economy has diversified into commercial internet and software development. The Tidewater area is a different story. Both consolidation among shipbuilders and declining Naval purchasers are likely to result in job losses in Virginia's shipbuilding industry. Job reductions have also taken place at the Port of Hampton Roads as Virginia's exports have fallen. The opening of the Gateway Plant will diversify southeastern Virginia's economy away from its dependence on military spending.

Virginia's housing market was one of the hottest in 1998. Home sales were up over 25% in 1998 with activity occurring in all parts of the state. Price appreciation was strong in northern, central and southeastern Virginia. While permit activity was flat in Richmond, both northern Virginia and Hampton Roads saw permit activity increase by at least 10%. Sales and starts should moderate slightly in the near future.

Virginia has some of the nation's strongest economic fundamentals: business friendly environment, an educated workforce, strong demographics and a diversified economy. Virginia's most immediate constraint is its tight labor market." *National Association of Realtors, Economic Profiles: The Fifty States and the District of Columbia, http://nar.realtor.com/databank/profiles.htm*

EXPORTS

Total Export Sales

Area	1995 ($000)	1996 ($000)	1997 ($000)	1998 ($000)	% Chg. 1995-98	% Chg. 1997-98
MSA[1]	231,349	238,327	285,157	436,741	88.8	53.2
U.S.	583,030,524	622,827,063	687,597,999	680,474,251	16.7	-1.0

Note: (1) Metropolitan Statistical Area - see Appendix A for areas included
Source: U.S. Department of Commerce, International Trade Association, Metropolitan Area Exports: An Export Performance Report on Over 250 U.S. Cities, November 10, 1999

CITY FINANCES

City Government Finances

Component	1995 ($million)	1995 (per capita $)
Revenue	233.1	2,411
Expenditure	233.5	2,416
Debt Outstanding	326.3	3,376

Source: 1999 County and City Extra, Annual Metro, City, and County Data Book

City Government Revenue by Source

Source	1995 ($million)	1995 (per capita $)
Intergovernmental	91.2	943
Taxes	104.4	1,080
Property	58.1	602
Sales and Gross Receipts	34.7	360

Source: 1999 County and City Extra, Annual Metro, City, and County Data Book

City Government Expenditures by Function

Function	1995 ($million)	1995 (per capita $)	1995 (%)
Public Welfare	17.2	178	7.4
Highways	8.4	86	3.6
Parking Facilities	0.4	4	0.2
Education	85.9	889	36.8
Health and Hospitals	3.0	31	1.3
Police Protection	12.3	128	5.3
Sewerage and Sanitation	14.4	149	6.2
Parks and Recreation	5.3	55	2.3
Housing and Community Development	18.6	193	8.0
Interest on Debt	22.8	236	9.8

Source: 1999 County and City Extra, Annual Metro, City, and County Data Book

Municipal Bond Ratings

Area	Moody's
City	Aa2

Source: Mergent Bond Record, 2/2000

POPULATION

Population Growth

Area	1980 Census	1990 Census	1999 Estimate	2004 Projection	Population Growth (%) 1990-1999	Population Growth (%) 1999-2004
City	100,220	96,397	93,288	93,728	-3.2	0.5
MSA[1]	224,341	224,477	227,408	233,763	1.3	2.8
U.S.	226,545,805	248,765,170	272,212,864	283,625,312	9.4	4.2

Note: (1) Metropolitan Statistical Area - see Appendix A for areas included
Source: 1990 Census of Population and Housing, Summary Tape File 3C; Claritas, Inc.

Number of Households and Average Household Size

Area	1980 Census	1990 Census	1999 Estimate	2004 Projection	1999 Average Household Size
City	40,023	41,064	40,605	41,330	2.30
MSA[1]	81,878	89,617	93,767	97,966	2.43
U.S.	80,389,592	91,993,582	102,048,200	107,302,392	2.67

Note: (1) Metropolitan Statistical Area - see Appendix A for areas included
Source: 1990 Census of Population and Housing, Summary Tape File 3C; Claritas, Inc.

Race/Ethnicity of City Population

Race/Ethnicity	1990 Census Population	1990 Census %	1999 Estimate Population	1999 Estimate %	% Change 1990-1999
White, Non-Hispanic	71,590	74.3	65,538	70.3	-8.5
Black, Non-Hispanic	23,073	23.9	25,625	27.5	11.1
Asian, Non-Hispanic	775	0.8	915	1.0	18.1
Other, Non-Hispanic	240	0.2	238	0.3	-0.8
Hispanic	719	0.7	972	1.0	35.2

Source: 1990 Census of Population and Housing, Summary Tape File 3C; Claritas, Inc.

Race/Ethnicity of Metropolitan Statistical Area Population

Race/Ethnicity	1990 Census		1999 Estimate		% Change 1990-1999
	Population	%	Population	%	
White, Non-Hispanic	193,819	86.3	191,790	84.3	-1.0
Black, Non-Hispanic	27,243	12.1	30,916	13.6	13.5
Asian, Non-Hispanic	1,754	0.8	2,150	0.9	22.6
Other, Non-Hispanic	390	0.2	403	0.2	3.3
Hispanic	1,271	0.6	2,149	0.9	69.1

Note: See Appendix A for areas included in the Metropolitan Statistical Area
Source: 1990 Census of Population and Housing, Summary Tape File 3C; Claritas, Inc.

Ancestry

Area	German	Irish	English	Italian	U.S.	French	Polish	Dutch
City	18.1	12.8	14.9	2.2	12.3	2.5	0.8	2.3
MSA[1]	23.0	15.5	18.4	2.2	11.6	2.9	1.1	2.7
U.S.	23.3	15.6	13.1	5.9	5.3	4.2	3.8	2.5

Note: Figures are percentages and include persons that reported multiple ancestry (eg. if a person reported being Irish and Italian, they were included in both columns); (1) Metropolitan Statistical Area - see Appendix A for areas included
Source: 1990 Census of Population and Housing, Summary Tape File 3C

Median Age

Area	1990 Census	1999 Estimate
City	35.2	38.0
MSA[1]	36.3	39.4
U.S.	32.9	35.7

Note: (1) Metropolitan Statistical Area - see Appendix A for areas included
Source: 1990 Census of Population and Housing, Summary Tape File 3C; Claritas, Inc.

Male/Female Population

Area	Number of Males		Number of Females		Males per 100 Females	
	1990	1999	1990	1999	1990	1999
City	44,622	43,419	51,775	49,869	86.2	87.1
MSA[1]	105,899	107,674	118,578	119,734	89.3	89.9
U.S.	121,172,379	132,803,736	127,537,494	139,409,136	95.0	95.3

Note: (1) Metropolitan Statistical Area - see Appendix A for areas included
Source: 1990 Census of Population, General Population Characteristics; Claritas, Inc.

INCOME

Per Capita/Median/Average Income

Area	Per Capita ($)			Median Household ($)			Average Household ($)		
	1989	1999	% Chg.	1989	1999	% Chg.	1989	1999	% Chg.
City	12,513	18,672	49.2	22,591	30,688	35.8	29,057	42,081	44.8
MSA[1]	14,318	21,720	51.7	28,944	39,483	36.4	35,412	51,643	45.8
U.S.	14,420	21,350	48.1	30,056	40,525	34.8	38,453	56,184	46.1

Note: (1) Metropolitan Statistical Area - see Appendix A for areas included; 1989 data is from the 1990 Census; 1999 data is estimated by Claritas, Inc.
Source: 1990 Census of Population, General Population Characteristics; Claritas, Inc.

Household Income Distribution

Area	Percent of Households Earning								
	Under $5,000	$5,000 -14,999	$15,000 -24,999	$25,000 -34,999	$35,000 -49,999	$50,000 -74,999	$75,000 -99,000	$100,000 -149,999	$150,000 and up
City	5.3	17.5	18.1	15.1	17.5	16.2	5.2	2.9	2.1
MSA[1]	3.4	12.8	14.7	13.5	17.5	20.7	9.0	5.4	3.0
U.S.	3.9	13.3	13.8	12.6	16.2	19.4	9.7	6.6	4.6

Note: Data as of 1999; (1) Metropolitan Statistical Area - see Appendix A for areas included
Source: Claritas, Inc.

Effective Buying Income

Area	Per Capita ($)	Median Household ($)	Average Household ($)
City	14,793	26,135	33,970
MSA[1]	18,261	35,832	44,671
U.S.	17,496	36,603	47,036

Note: Data as of 1/1/2000; (1) Metropolitan Statistical Area - see Appendix A for areas included
Source: Standard Rate & Data Service, Newspaper Advertising Source, March 2000

Effective Household Buying Income Distribution

Area	% of Households Earning						
	$10,000 -$19,999	$20,000 -$34,999	$35,000 -$49,999	$50,000 -$74,999	$75,000 -$99,000	$100,000 -$124,999	$125,000 and up
City	21.4	26.1	18.0	11.9	3.4	1.1	1.6
MSA[1]	15.7	22.6	18.5	19.8	7.8	2.4	2.6
U.S.	15.0	21.6	17.6	19.6	8.4	3.0	3.3

Note: Data as of 1/1/2000; (1) Metropolitan Statistical Area - see Appendix A for areas included
Source: Standard Rate & Data Service, Newspaper Advertising Source, March 2000

Poverty Rates by Age

Area	People of All Ages	People Under 18 Years Old	Related Children Age 5-17 in Families in Poverty
City	20.0	n/a	n/a
County	20.0	32.1	33.1
U.S.	13.8	20.8	18.7

Note: Figures show the percent of people living below the poverty line in 1995. The average poverty threshold was $15,569 for a family of four in 1995; n/a not available
Source: Bureau of the Census, Small Area Income and Poverty Estimates Program; U.S. Department of Housing and Urban Development

EMPLOYMENT

Labor Force and Employment

Area	Civilian Labor Force			Workers Employed		
	Dec. 1998	Dec. 1999	% Chg.	Dec. 1998	Dec. 1999	% Chg.
City	51,307	51,291	0.0	49,979	50,254	0.6
MSA[1]	132,712	132,751	0.0	130,020	130,735	0.5
U.S.	138,297,000	139,941,000	1.2	132,732,000	134,696,000	1.5

Note: Data is not seasonally adjusted and covers workers 16 years of age and older;
(1) Metropolitan Statistical Area - see Appendix A for areas included
Source: Bureau of Labor Statistics, http://stats.bls.gov

Unemployment Rate

Area	1999											
	Jan.	Feb.	Mar.	Apr.	May	Jun.	Jul.	Aug.	Sep.	Oct.	Nov.	Dec.
City	2.6	2.5	2.2	2.2	2.7	2.8	2.7	2.9	2.9	2.4	2.1	2.0
MSA[1]	2.1	1.8	1.6	1.6	2.0	2.1	1.9	2.0	2.1	1.8	1.6	1.5
U.S.	4.8	4.7	4.4	4.1	4.0	4.5	4.5	4.2	4.1	3.8	3.8	3.7

Note: Data is not seasonally adjusted and covers workers 16 years of age and older; all figures are percentages; (1) Metropolitan Statistical Area - see Appendix A for areas included
Source: Bureau of Labor Statistics, http://stats.bls.gov

Employment by Industry

Sector	MSA[1]		U.S.
	Number of Employees	Percent of Total	Percent of Total
Services	43,100	29.6	30.2
Retail Trade	29,100	20.0	18.1
Government	17,400	12.0	15.8
Manufacturing	19,000	13.1	14.1
Finance/Insurance/Real Estate	10,200	7.0	5.9
Wholesale Trade	8,700	6.0	5.4
Transportation/Public Utilities	8,900	6.1	5.3
Construction	n/a	n/a	4.8
Mining	n/a	n/a	0.4

Note: Figures cover non-farm employment as of 12/99 and are not seasonally adjusted; (1) Metropolitan Statistical Area - see Appendix A for areas included; n/a not available
Source: Bureau of Labor Statistics, http://stats.bls.gov

Employment by Occupation

Occupation Category	City (%)	MSA[1] (%)	U.S. (%)
White Collar	55.0	60.4	58.1
Executive/Admin./Management	8.8	11.5	12.3
Professional	12.0	13.3	14.1
Technical & Related Support	3.8	3.6	3.7
Sales	12.7	13.8	11.8
Administrative Support/Clerical	17.8	18.1	16.3
Blue Collar	28.1	26.1	26.2
Precision Production/Craft/Repair	10.4	10.4	11.3
Machine Operators/Assem./Insp.	8.5	7.1	6.8
Transportation/Material Movers	4.5	4.6	4.1
Cleaners/Helpers/Laborers	4.6	4.0	3.9
Services	15.8	12.2	13.2
Farming/Forestry/Fishing	1.2	1.2	2.5

Note: Figures cover workers 16 years of age and older; (1) Metropolitan Statistical Area - see Appendix A for areas included
Source: 1990 Census of Population and Housing, Summary Tape File 3C

Occupational Employment Projections: 1996 - 2006

Occupations Expected to Have the Largest Job Growth (ranked by numerical growth)	Fast-Growing Occupations[1] (ranked by percent growth)
1. Systems analysts	1. Desktop publishers
2. Cashiers	2. Personal and home care aides
3. Computer engineers	3. Physical therapy assistants and aides
4. General managers & top executives	4. Medical assistants
5. Salespersons, retail	5. Physical therapists
6. Janitors/cleaners/maids, ex. priv. hshld.	6. Occupational therapists
7. Database administrators	7. Home health aides
8. Receptionists and information clerks	8. Manicurists
9. Engineering/science/computer sys. mgrs.	9. Paralegals
10. Truck drivers, light	10. Bill and account collectors

Note: Projections cover Virginia; (1) Excludes occupations with total job growth less than 300
Source: U.S. Department of Labor, Employment and Training Administration, America's Labor Market Information System (ALMIS)

Average Wages

Occupation	$/Hr.	Occupation	$/Hr.
Accountants and Auditors	16.41	Maids and Housekeepers	6.59
Assemblers and Fabricators	8.21	Maintenance Repairers	11.43
Automotive Mechanics	12.61	Marketing/Advertising/PR Managers	24.72
Bookkeepers	10.24	Nurses, Licensed Practical	13.16
Carpenters	10.95	Nurses, Registered	18.09
Cashiers	6.70	Nursing Aides/Orderlies/Attendants	7.83
Clerks, General Office	9.13	Physicians and Surgeons	47.87
Clerks, Shipping/Receiving/Traffic	9.68	Receptionists/Information Clerks	8.12
Computer Programmers	19.14	Sales Reps., Exc. Scientific/Retail	18.12
Computer Support Specialists	16.34	Sales Reps., Scientific, Exc. Retail	21.60
Cooks, Restaurant	7.27	Salespersons, Retail	8.51
Electricians	13.37	Secretaries, Except Legal/Medical	10.05
Financial Managers	24.22	Stock Clerks, Sales Floor	8.14
First-Line Supervisors/Mgrs., Sales	14.96	Systems Analysts	23.28
Food Preparation Workers	6.53	Teacher Aides	6.42
General Managers/Top Executives	26.91	Teachers, Elementary School	17.74
Guards	7.87	Teachers, Secondary School	18.46
Hand Packers	6.32	Telemarketers	8.04
Janitors and Cleaners	7.14	Truck Drivers, Heavy/Tractor-Trailer	13.47
Laborers, Landscaping	8.49	Truck Drivers, Light	9.62
Lawyers	40.31	Waiters and Waitresses	6.17

Note: Wage data is for 1998 and covers the Metropolitan Statistical Area (see Appendix A for areas included). Hourly wages for elementary and secondary school teachers were calculated by the editors from annual wage data assuming a 40 hour work week; Dashes indicate that data was not available.
Source: Bureau of Labor Statistics, 1998 Metropolitan Area Occupational Employment and Wage Estimates

TAXES

Major State and Local Tax Rates

State Corporate Income (%)	State Personal Income (%)	Residential Property (%)	Sales & Use		State Gasoline (cents/ gallon)	State Cigarette (cents/ pack)
			State (%)	Local (%)		
6.0	2.0 - 5.75	1.23	3.5	1.0	17.5[a]	2.5[b]

Note: Personal/corporate income, sales, gasoline and cigarette tax rates as of January 2000. Property tax rates as of April 2000; (a) Does not include a 2% local option tax. Large trucks pay an additional tax of 3.5 cents; (b) Counties and cities may impose an additional tax of 2 - 15 cents per pack
Source: Federation of Tax Administrators, www.taxadmin.org; ERI's Relocation Assessor software database, quarterly effective date 4/1/2000

Total Taxes Per Capita and as a Percent of Income

Area	Per Capita Income ($)	Per Capita Taxes ($)			Percent of Income (%)		
		Total	Federal	State/Local	Total	Federal	State/Local
Virginia	29,471	10,129	7,057	3,072	34.4	23.9	10.4
U.S.	28,878	10,298	7,026	3,273	35.7	24.3	11.3

Note: Figures are for 1999
Source: Tax Foundation, www.taxfoundation.org

COMMERCIAL UTILITIES

Typical Monthly Electric Bills

Area	Commercial Service ($/month)		Industrial Service ($/month)	
	12 kW demand 1,500 kWh	100 kW demand 30,000 kWh	1,000 kW demand 400,000 kWh	20,000 kW demand 10,000,000 kWh
City	87	1,590	16,412	260,986
U.S.	150	2,174	23,995	508,569

Note: Based on rates in effect January 1, 1999
Source: Edison Electric Institute, Typical Residential, Commercial and Industrial Bills, Winter 1999

TRANSPORTATION

Transportation Statistics

Average minutes to work (1990)	16.8
Interstate highways	I-81; US-220; US-460; US-221; US-11
Bus lines	
In-city (1998)	Valley Metro, 30 buses
Inter-city (1999)	5
Passenger air service	
Airport	Roanoke Regional/Woodrum Field
Airlines (1999)	6
Enplaned passengers (1998)	340,653
Amtrak service	No
Motor freight carriers (1999)	58
Major waterways/ports	None

Source: FAA DOT/TSC CY1998 ACAIS Database; National Transit Database, 1998; Editor & Publisher Market Guide, 2000; Amtrak National Time Table, Fall 1999/Winter 2000; 1990 Census of Population and Housing, STF 3C; Jane's Urban Transport Systems 1999-2000

Means of Transportation to Work

Area	Car/Truck/Van		Public Transportation			Bicycle	Walked	Other Means	Worked at Home
	Drove Alone	Car-pooled	Bus	Subway	Railroad				
City	77.2	14.5	2.9	0.0	0.0	0.2	2.9	1.0	1.3
MSA[1]	82.1	11.6	1.3	0.0	0.0	0.1	2.3	0.7	2.0
U.S.	73.2	13.4	3.0	1.5	0.5	0.4	3.9	1.2	3.0

Note: Figures shown are percentages and only include workers 16 years of age and older;
(1) Metropolitan Statistical Area - see Appendix A for areas included
Source: 1990 Census of Population and Housing, Summary Tape File 3C

BUSINESSES

Major Business Headquarters

Company Name	1999 Rankings	
	Fortune 500	Forbes 500
Advance Holding	-	148

Note: Companies listed are located in the city; dashes indicate no ranking
Fortune 500: Companies that produce a 10-K are ranked 1 to 500 based on 1999 revenue
Forbes 500: Private companies are ranked 1 to 500 based on 1998 revenue
Source: Forbes, December 13, 1999; Fortune, April 17, 2000

HOTELS & MOTELS

Hotels/Motels

Area	Hotels/ Motels	Rooms	Luxury-Level Hotels/Motels		Average Minimum Rates ($)		
			♦♦♦♦	♦♦♦♦♦	♦♦	♦♦♦	♦♦♦♦
City	16	1,684	0	0	53	106	n/a
Airport	6	670	0	0	n/a	n/a	n/a
Suburbs	1	196	0	0	n/a	n/a	n/a
Total	23	2,550	0	0	n/a	n/a	n/a

Note: n/a not available; classifications range from one diamond (budget properties with basic amenities) to five diamond (luxury properties).
Source: OAG Business Travel Planner, Winter 1999-2000

Estimated Daily Food and Lodging Costs

Area	Food/Other ($/day)	Average Hotel Cost ($/day)
City	34	59
U.S.	30	55

Source: ERI's Relocation Assessor software database, quarterly effective date 4/1/2000

CONVENTION CENTERS

Convention Centers and Event Sites

Name	Guest Rooms	Meeting Space (sq. ft.)	Capacity (Theatre Style)
Roanoke Airport Marriott	320	6,435	900
Roanoke Civic Center	n/a	n/a	25,000
The Conference Center of Roanoke	332	63,000	0

Note: n/a not available
Source: EventSource.com, 3/15/2000

Living Environment

COST OF LIVING

Cost of Living: Homeowner

Cost Element	U.S. ($)	City ($)	Differential ($)	Percent of U.S. Average
Consumables	14,516	13,914	-602	95.9
Transportation	5,957	5,339	-618	89.6
Health Services	2,012	1,889	-123	93.9
Housing/Utilities/Prop. Tax	16,337	17,276	939	105.7
Income+Payroll Taxes	12,615	12,819	204	101.6
Miscellaneous	8,563	8,563	0	100.0
Total Cost of Living	60,000	59,800	-200	99.7

Note: Figures are based on a single income, four person family with gross annual earnings of $60,000, owning an 1,800 square-foot home, and driving two automobiles worth $22,000 30,000 miles per year.
Source: ERI's Relocation Assessor software database, quarterly effective date 4/1/2000

Cost of Living: Renter

Cost Element	U.S. ($)	City ($)	Differential ($)	Percent of U.S. Average
Consumables	10,486	10,060	-426	95.9
Transportation	2,107	1,890	-217	89.7
Health Services	1,632	1,534	-98	94.0
Rent/Utilities/Insurance	9,299	10,717	1,418	115.2
Income+Payroll Taxes	8,607	8,951	344	104.0
Miscellaneous	7,869	7,869	0	100.0
Total Cost of Living	40,000	41,021	1,021	102.6

Note: Figures are based on a single income, three person family with gross annual earnings of $40,000, renting a 1,000 square-foot home, and driving one automobile worth $8,000 12,000 miles per year.
Source: ERI's Relocation Assessor software database, quarterly effective date 4/1/2000

HOUSING

Median Home Prices and Housing Affordability

Area	Median Price[2] 4th Qtr. 1999 ($)	HOI[3] 4th Qtr. 1999	Affordability Rank[4]
MSA[1]	128,000	65.7	118
U.S.	139,000	63.8	–

Note: (1) Metropolitan Statistical Area - see Appendix A for areas included; (2) U.S. figures calculated from the sales of 687,516 new and existing homes in 192 markets; (3) Housing Opportunity Index - percent of homes sold that were within the reach of the median income household at the prevailing mortgage interest rate; (4) Rank is from 1-192 with 1 being most affordable
Source: National Association of Home Builders, Housing Opportunity Index, 4th Quarter 1999

Estimated Home Price

Area	Price ($)
City	152,600
U.S.	135,855

Note: Figures are based on an 1,800 square-foot home
Source: ERI's Relocation Assessor software database, quarterly effective date 4/1/2000

Estimated Rent

Area	Rent ($/month)
City	785
U.S.	651

Note: Figures are based on a 1,000 square-foot home
Source: ERI's Relocation Assessor software database, quarterly effective date 4/1/2000

Median Home Price Projection

It is projected that the median home price in the metropolitan area will increase from $168,269 in 1999 to $247,293 in 2010, an increase of 47.0%
Kiplinger's Personal Finance Magazine, January 2000

RESIDENTIAL UTILITIES

Average Residential Utility Costs

Area	All Electric ($/mth)	Part Electric ($/mth)	Other Energy ($/mth)	Phone ($/mth)
City	78.95	–	–	20.09
U.S.	99.25	55.47	43.48	20.29

Source: ACCRA, Cost of Living Index, 3rd Quarter 1999

HEALTH CARE

Average Health Care Costs

Area	Hospital ($/day)	Doctor ($/visit)	Dentist ($/visit)
City	347.67	57.40	61.67
U.S.	440.96	53.83	68.42

Note: Hospital—based on a semi-private room; Doctor—based on a general practitioner's routine exam of an established patient; Dentist—based on adult teeth cleaning and periodic oral exam.
Source: ACCRA, Cost of Living Index, 3rd Quarter 1999

Distribution of Office-Based Physicians

Area	Family/Gen. Practitioners	Specialists		
		Medical	Surgical	Other
MSA[1]	71	163	163	175

Note: Data as of 12/31/97; (1) Metropolitan Statistical Area - see Appendix A for areas included
Source: American Medical Assn., Physician Characteristics & Distribution in the U.S., 1999

Hospitals

Roanoke has 1 general medical and surgical hospital.
AHA Guide to the Healthcare Field, 1999-2000

According to *U.S. News and World Report*, Roanoke has one of the best hospitals in the U.S.: **Carilion Medical Center**, noted for cardiology.
U.S. News Online, "America's Best Hospitals," July 19, 1999

EDUCATION

Public School District Statistics

District Name	Num. Sch.	Enroll.	Classroom Teachers	Pupils per Teacher	Minority Pupils (%)	Current Exp.[1] ($/pupil)
Roanoke City Public Schls	30	13,514	n/a	n/a	n/a	n/a
Roanoke Co. Public Schls	28	13,976	n/a	n/a	n/a	n/a

Note: Data covers the 1997-1998 school year unless otherwise noted; (1) Data covers fiscal year 1996; SD = School District; ISD = Independent School District; n/a not available
Source: National Center for Education Statistics, Common Core of Data Public Education Agency Universe 1997-98; National Center for Education Statistics, Characteristics of the 100 Largest Public Elementary and Secondary School Districts in the United States: 1997-98, July 1999

Educational Quality

School District	Education Quotient[1]	Graduate Outcome[2]	Community Index[3]	Resource Index[4]
Roanoke City Public Schools	99	78	61	147

Note: Over 1,000 secondary school districts were rated in terms of educational quality. The scores range from a low of 50 to a high of 150; (1) Combination of the Graduate Outcome, Community and Resource indexes weighted to reflect the greater importance of the Graduate Outcome and Resource Index; (2) Based on graduation rates and college board scores (SAT/ACT); (3) Based on the surrounding community's level of affluence and adult education; (4) Based on teacher salaries, per-pupil expenditures and student-teacher ratios.
Source: Expansion Management, Ratings Issue, 1999

Educational Attainment by Race

Area	High School Graduate (%)					Bachelor's Degree (%)				
	Total	White	Black	Other	Hisp.[2]	Total	White	Black	Other	Hisp.[2]
City	68.0	69.5	62.0	69.5	61.8	15.6	17.8	7.0	26.9	11.4
MSA[1]	73.4	74.7	62.4	79.2	66.4	18.1	19.2	8.1	33.0	18.8
U.S.	75.2	77.9	63.1	60.4	49.8	20.3	21.5	11.4	19.4	9.2

Note: Figures shown cover persons 25 years old and over; (1) Metropolitan Statistical Area - see Appendix A for areas included; (2) people of Hispanic origin can be of any race
Source: 1990 Census of Population and Housing, Summary Tape File 3C

School Enrollment by Type

Area	Preprimary				Elementary/High School			
	Public		Private		Public		Private	
	Enrollment	%	Enrollment	%	Enrollment	%	Enrollment	%
City	923	60.8	594	39.2	13,107	95.2	655	4.8
MSA[1]	2,422	58.8	1,696	41.2	31,867	95.1	1,625	4.9
U.S.	2,679,029	59.5	1,824,256	40.5	38,379,689	90.2	4,187,099	9.8

Note: Figures shown cover persons 3 years old and over;
(1) Metropolitan Statistical Area - see Appendix A for areas included
Source: 1990 Census of Population and Housing, Summary Tape File 3C

School Enrollment by Race

Area	Preprimary (%)				Elementary/High School (%)			
	White	Black	Other	Hisp.[1]	White	Black	Other	Hisp.[1]
City	73.8	26.2	0.0	0.9	63.0	35.0	2.0	1.1
MSA[2]	89.2	10.2	0.6	0.5	81.7	16.5	1.8	0.8
U.S.	80.4	12.5	7.1	7.8	74.1	15.6	10.3	12.5

Note: Figures shown cover persons 3 years old and over; (1) people of Hispanic origin can be of any race; (2) Metropolitan Statistical Area - see Appendix A for areas included
Source: 1990 Census of Population and Housing, Summary Tape File 3C

Higher Education

Two-Year Colleges		Four-Year Colleges		Medical Schools	Law Schools	Voc/ Tech
Public	Private	Public	Private			
1	2	0	1	0	0	5

Source: College Blue Book, Occupational Education, 1999; Medical School Admission Requirements, 1999-2000; Peterson's Guide to Two-Year Colleges, 2000; Peterson's Guide to Four-Year Colleges, 1999; Barron's Guide to Law Schools, 1999

MAJOR EMPLOYERS

Major Employers

Appalachian Power
First Union Corp. of Virginia
HCMF Corp. (management services)
Petroleum Marketers
Rubatex Corp. (gaskets)

BellSouth Communications Systems
Grand Piano & Furniture Co.
Maid Bess Corp.
RPS Teleservice Center
Times World Corp.

Note: Companies listed are located in the city
Source: D&B Business Rankings, 1999; Ward's Business Directory, 1999; America's Corporate Families, 1999

PUBLIC SAFETY

Crime Rate

Area	All Crimes	Violent Crimes				Property Crimes		
		Murder	Forcible Rape	Robbery	Aggrav. Assault	Burglary	Larceny -Theft	Motor Vehicle Theft
City	5,649.3	15.8	44.2	262.2	247.5	815.2	3,950.5	313.8
Suburbs[1]	2,119.3	3.0	21.4	23.6	132.1	256.8	1,596.1	86.3
MSA[2]	3,573.6	8.2	30.8	121.9	179.6	486.8	2,566.1	180.1
U.S.	4,615.5	6.3	34.4	165.2	360.5	862.0	2,728.1	459.0

Note: Crime rate is the number of crimes per 100,000 population; (1) Defined as all areas within the Metropolitan Statistical Area but located outside the central city; (2) Metropolitan Statistical Area - see Appendix A for areas included
Source: FBI Uniform Crime Reports, 1998

RECREATION

Culture and Recreation

Museums	Symphony Orchestras	Opera Companies	Dance Companies	Professional Theatres	Zoos	Pro Sports Teams
4	1	1	1	1	1	0

Source: Musical America, International Directory of the Performing Arts, 1999; Official Museum Directory, 2000; Stern's Performing Arts Directory, 1997; USA Today Four Sport Stadium Guide, 1997; Career Opportunities in Theatre and the Performing Arts, 1999

Library System

The Roanoke City Public Library System has six branches, holdings of 335,851 volumes, and a budget of $2,889,210 (1997-1998).
American Library Directory, 1999-2000

MEDIA

Newspapers

Name	Type	Freq.	Distribution	Circulation
The Roanoke Times	General	7x/wk	Area	113,054
Roanoke Tribune	Black	1x/wk	Area	5,600

Note: Includes newspapers with circulations of 200 or more located in the city;
Source: Burrelle's Media Directory, 1999 Edition

Television Stations

Name	Ch.	Affiliation	Type	Owner
WDBJ	n/a	CBST	Commercial	WDBJ Television Inc.
WSLS	10	NBCT	Commercial	Media General Inc.
WBRA	15	PBS	Public	Blue Ridge Public TV
WJPR	21	FBC	Commercial	Milton Grant Broadcasting Inc.
WDRL	24	UPN	Commercial	TMC
WFXR	27	FBC	Commercial	Milton Grant Broadcasting Inc.
WPXR	38	PAXTV	Commercial	Paxson Broadcasting
WSBN	47	PBS	Public	Blue Ridge Public TV
WMSY	52	PBS	Public	Blue Ridge Public TV

Note: Stations included broadcast in the Roanoke metro area; n/a not available
Source: Burrelle's Media Directory, 1999 Edition

AM Radio Stations

Call Letters	Freq. (kHz)	Target Audience	Station Format	Music Format
WSLC	610	General	M/N/S	Country/Gospel
WRNL	910	General	N/S	n/a
WWWR	910	Religious	M/N/S	Gospel
WFIR	960	General	N/S	n/a
WKPA	1170	General	M/N/S	Christian
WROV	1240	General	M/N/S	AOR
WRIS	1410	Religious	M/N	Adult Standards/Christian
WTOY	1480	Black	M/N/S	Christian/Gospel/Urban Contemporary
WKBA	1550	General	M	Christian

Note: Stations included broadcast in the Roanoke metro area; n/a not available
Target Audience: A=Asian; B=Black; C=Christian; E=Ethnic; F=French; G=General; H=Hispanic;
M=Men; N=Native American; R=Religious; S=Senior Citizen; W=Women; Y=Young Adult; Z=Children
Station Format: E=Educational; M=Music; N=News; S=Sports; T=Talk
Music Format: AOR=Album Oriented Rock; MOR=Middle-of-the-Road
Source: Burrelle's Media Directory, 1999 Edition

FM Radio Stations

Call Letters	Freq. (mHz)	Target Audience	Station Format	Music Format
WVTW	88.5	General	E/M/N	Classical/Jazz
WVTF	89.1	General	M/N/T	Classical/Jazz
WVTU	89.3	General	M/N/T	Classical/Jazz
WRXT	90.3	n/a	n/a	n/a
WVTR	91.9	General	M/N/T	Classical/Jazz
WXLK	92.3	General	M/N/T	Top 40
WJLM	93.5	General	M/N/S	Country
WPVR	94.9	General	M	Classic Rock
WROV	96.3	General	M/N/S	AOR
WSLQ	99.1	General	M/N/S	Adult Contemporary
WLYK	100.1	General	M/N	Adult Contemporary/Top 40
WZZI	101.5	General	M	Modern Rock

Note: Stations included broadcast in the Roanoke metro area; n/a not available
Station Format: E=Educational; M=Music; N=News; S=Sports; T=Talk
Target Audience: A=Asian; B=Black; C=Christian; E=Ethnic; F=French; G=General; H=Hispanic;
M=Men; N=Native American; R=Religious; S=Senior Citizen; W=Women; Y=Young Adult; Z=Children
Music Format: AOR=Album Oriented Rock; MOR=Middle-of-the-Road
Source: Burrelle's Media Directory, 1999 Edition

WEATHER

Temperature/Precipitation/Humidity

	Jan	Feb	Mar	Apr	May	Jun	Jul	Aug	Sep	Oct	Nov	Dec	Yr.
Max. High Temp. (°F)	78	80	87	95	96	100	104	105	101	93	83	76	105
Avg. High Temp. (°F)	45	48	57	68	76	84	87	86	79	69	57	48	67
Avg. Temp. (°F)	36	38	46	56	65	72	76	75	68	57	47	39	57
Avg. Low Temp. (°F)	26	28	35	44	53	61	65	64	57	46	37	29	46
Min. Low Temp. (°F)	-11	1	10	20	31	39	47	42	34	22	9	-4	-11
Avg. Precip. (in.)	2.7	3.2	3.5	3.3	4.0	3.3	3.7	4.2	3.4	3.5	2.9	3.0	40.9
Avg. Snowfall (in.)	7	8	4	Tr	Tr	0	0	0	0	Tr	2	4	24
Avg. Rel. Hum. 7am (%)	70	70	70	70	78	81	83	86	88	83	75	72	77
Avg. Rel. Hum. 4pm (%)	51	48	45	43	50	52	54	54	54	50	50	52	50

Note: Tr = Trace amounts (less than 0.05 inches of rain or less than 0.5 inches of snow)
Source: National Climatic Data Center, International Station Meteorological Climate Summary, 3/95

Weather Conditions

Temperature			Precipitation		
10°F & below	32°F & below	90°F & above	0.01 inch or more precip.	1.5 inch or more snow/ice	Thunder-storms
4	90	31	120	5	35

Note: Figures are average number of days per year
Source: National Climatic Data Center, International Station Meteorological Climate Summary, 3/95

AIR & WATER QUALITY

Maximum Pollutant Concentrations

	Particulate Matter (ug/m^3)	Carbon Monoxide (ppm)	Sulfur Dioxide (ppm)	Nitrogen Dioxide (ppm)	Ozone (ppm)	Lead (ug/m^3)
MSA[1] Level	95	4	0.013	0.013	0.10	n/a
NAAQS[2]	150	9	0.140	0.053	0.12	1.50
Met NAAQS	Yes	Yes	Yes	Yes	Yes	n/a

Note: (1) Metropolitan Statistical Area - see Appendix A for areas included; (2) National Ambient Air Quality Standards; ppm = parts per million; ug/m^3 = micrograms per cubic meter; n/a not available
Source: EPA, National Air Quality and Emissions Trends Report, 1997

Pollutant Standards Index

Data not available.
EPA, National Air Quality and Emissions Trends Report, 1997

Drinking Water

Water System Name	Pop. Served	Primary Water Source Type	Number of Violations in 1998-99	Type of Violation/ Contaminants
Roanoke City Water Dept.	158,000	Surface	None	None

Note: Data as of January 19, 2000
Source: EPA, Office of Ground Water and Drinking Water, Safe Drinking Water Information System

Roanoke tap water is alkaline, soft, and fluoridated.
Editor & Publisher Market Guide, 2000

Rochester, Minnesota

Background

Rochester, Minnesota is located in the southeast section of the state, about 80 miles south of Minneapolis. The city is located on a branch of the Zumbro River and is in the Zumbro River Valley. The terrain is rolling.

Rochester is the county seat of Olmstead County. It is best known as the home of the prominent Mayo Clinic medical complex, which is a major employer and significant presence. The clinics attracts many visitors from around the world. Rochester is also home to IBM operations, and other industries and services.

The region was inhabited by various Native Americans including the Winnebago, Dakota Sioux and Ojibway. In 1853 the Sioux ceded claims to the territory which opened the land to white settlement. Olmstead County was created in 1855. Rochester was a wagon stop and crossroads. The town was incorporated in 1858. George Head, one of the earliest settlers named Rochester after Rochester, N.Y. and established one of the first businesses, a tavern, and initiated other development of the community. It grew as a commercial and services area.

In 1883, a tornado created significant destruction. In the aftermath, Mother Alfred Moes, a Franciscan sister, and Dr. William W. Mayo founded Saint Mary's Hospital. His sons, William J. and Charles H. Mayo joined their father's practice. The Mayos group medical practice developed innovative medical and administrative models. In 1919 the practice was turned over to the non-profit Mayo Foundation. The Mayo Clinic grew to become a leading center for medical care, research and education. The Mayo Clinic is also a major element of the economy, including its operations and services for visitors.

Parks include Quarry Hill Nature Center, Silver Lake Park and Soldiers Memorial Park, among others. The Mayo Civic Center is a multi-use facility for public events. The Mayo Clinic and Mayowood Mansion, the family home of the Mayos, are open for tours. The Olmstead County Historical Society and Museum presents the region's history.

Colleges include schools affiliated with the Mayo Clinic, Rochester Community and Technical College, Minnesota Bible College and campuses of the University of Minnesota and Winona State University.

Cultural organizations include Civic Music, Choral Arts Ensemble, The Lyra Concert, Masque Youth Theater, Rochester Civic Theater, Rochester Orchestra and Chorale, Rochester Repertory Theater, among others. The Rochester Civic Center is a multi-purpose event facility.

Rochester is governed by a Mayor and City Council, with an appointed City Administrator.

General Rankings and Evaluative Comments

- Rochester was selected as the "Best Small City" in *Money* magazine's most recent survey of the best places to live. Criteria: 300 metropolitan areas in the U.S. were ranked on 46 quality-of-life factors including the economy, education, culture, recreation, safety, and clean air and water. *Money, "The Best Places to Live 2000"*

- Rochester was ranked #224 out of 354 metropolitan areas in *Places Rated Almanac*. Criteria: cost of living, climate, crime, transportation, job outlook, education, the arts, health care, and recreation. *Places Rated Almanac, Millennium Edition, 2000*

- Rochester appeared on *New Mobility's* list of "10 Disability Friendly Cities." The city ranked #8 out of 10. Criteria: affordable and accessible housing, transportation, quality medical care, personal assistance services, and strong advocacy. *New Mobility, December 1997*

- Cognetics studied 273 metro areas in the United States, ranking them by entrepreneurial activity. Rochester was ranked #85 out of 134 smaller metro areas. Criteria: Significant Starts (firms started in the last 10 years that still employ at least 5 people) and Young Growers (percent of firms 10 years old or less that grew significantly during the last 4 years). *Cognetics, "Entrepreneurial Hot Spots: The Best Places in America to Start and Grow a Company," 1999*

Business Environment

STATE ECONOMY

State Economic Profile

"Minnesota's economy has been a strong performer in recent years. Job growth has been impressive and the construction market has been booming. As the US economy slows in the near future, Minnesota's growth should decelerate.

Minnesota's tight labor market (1.8% unemployment in Minneapolis-St. Paul) and high rate of job creation have allowed the state to weather several layoffs. 3M, Cargill, and Honeywell have all released significant numbers of workers. And while the Northwest strike temporarily hit Minnesota's economy, other sectors have more than offset these concerns.

Minnesota, specifically Minneapolis-St. Paul, experienced a major boom in residential and commercial building in 1998. The 16,811 single-family permits issued in 1998 was the highest level in over a decade. Construction employment increased 6.8% in Minneapolis-St. Paul in 1998. Driving this boom is the impressive levels of price appreciation witnessed in 1998 and the thin inventory of homes for sale. The large volume currently being built will help to moderate price appreciation in 2000.

Among its Midwestern neighbors, Minnesota alone has actually attracted residents from other states. Net migration has been around 10,000 for several years, helping to ease tightness in the labor market and fuel the housing market.

Minnesota will continue to be among the strongest performing Plains state. Labor shortages and the high cost of doing business, however, will limit its growth to below the national average. Most of the action will continue to be concentrated in Minneapolis-St. Paul."
National Association of Realtors, Economic Profiles: The Fifty States and the District of Columbia, http://nar.realtor.com/databank/profiles.htm

EXPORTS

Total Export Sales

Area	1995 ($000)	1996 ($000)	1997 ($000)	1998 ($000)	% Chg. 1995-98	% Chg. 1997-98
MSA[1]	93,938	92,866	131,825	171,985	83.1	30.5
U.S.	583,030,524	622,827,063	687,597,999	680,474,251	16.7	-1.0

Note: (1) Metropolitan Statistical Area - see Appendix A for areas included
Source: U.S. Department of Commerce, International Trade Association, Metropolitan Area Exports: An Export Performance Report on Over 250 U.S. Cities, November 10, 1999

CITY FINANCES

City Government Finances

Component	1995 ($million)	1995 (per capita $)
Revenue	73.2	965
Expenditure	83.9	1,107
Debt Outstanding	78.3	1,033

Source: 1999 County and City Extra, Annual Metro, City, and County Data Book

City Government Revenue by Source

Source	1995 ($million)	1995 (per capita $)
Intergovernmental	20.8	274
Taxes	24.3	321
Property	16.5	218
Sales and Gross Receipts	6.1	81

Source: 1999 County and City Extra, Annual Metro, City, and County Data Book

City Government Expenditures by Function

Function	1995 ($million)	1995 (per capita $)	1995 (%)
Public Welfare	0.0	0	0.0
Highways	11.7	154	14.0
Parking Facilities	6.6	87	7.9
Education	0.0	0	0.0
Health and Hospitals	<0.1	1	0.1
Police Protection	9.3	122	11.1
Sewerage and Sanitation	6.0	79	7.2
Parks and Recreation	7.5	99	9.0
Housing and Community Development	2.8	37	3.4
Interest on Debt	6.4	85	7.7

Source: 1999 County and City Extra, Annual Metro, City, and County Data Book

Municipal Bond Ratings

Area	Moody's
City	Aaa

Source: Mergent Bond Record, 2/2000

POPULATION

Population Growth

Area	1980 Census	1990 Census	1999 Estimate	2004 Projection	Population Growth (%) 1990-1999	Population Growth (%) 1999-2004
City	57,890	70,745	78,393	80,788	10.8	3.1
MSA[1]	92,006	106,470	117,605	121,002	10.5	2.9
U.S.	226,545,805	248,765,170	272,212,864	283,625,312	9.4	4.2

Note: (1) Metropolitan Statistical Area - see Appendix A for areas included
Source: 1990 Census of Population and Housing, Summary Tape File 3C; Claritas, Inc.

Number of Households and Average Household Size

Area	1980 Census	1990 Census	1999 Estimate	2004 Projection	1999 Average Household Size
City	22,750	27,973	31,203	32,307	2.51
MSA[1]	32,677	40,161	44,717	46,240	2.63
U.S.	80,389,592	91,993,582	102,048,200	107,302,392	2.67

Note: (1) Metropolitan Statistical Area - see Appendix A for areas included
Source: 1990 Census of Population and Housing, Summary Tape File 3C; Claritas, Inc.

Race/Ethnicity of City Population

Race/Ethnicity	1990 Census Population	1990 Census %	1999 Estimate Population	1999 Estimate %	% Change 1990-1999
White, Non-Hispanic	66,376	93.8	70,738	90.2	6.6
Black, Non-Hispanic	760	1.1	1,085	1.4	42.8
Asian, Non-Hispanic	2,804	4.0	4,903	6.3	74.9
Other, Non-Hispanic	136	0.2	274	0.3	101.5
Hispanic	669	0.9	1,393	1.8	108.2

Source: 1990 Census of Population and Housing, Summary Tape File 3C; Claritas, Inc.

Race/Ethnicity of Metropolitan Statistical Area Population

Race/Ethnicity	1990 Census		1999 Estimate		% Change 1990-1999
	Population	%	Population	%	
White, Non-Hispanic	101,508	95.3	109,040	92.7	7.4
Black, Non-Hispanic	784	0.7	1,159	1.0	47.8
Asian, Non-Hispanic	3,121	2.9	5,388	4.6	72.6
Other, Non-Hispanic	213	0.2	398	0.3	86.9
Hispanic	844	0.8	1,620	1.4	91.9

Note: See Appendix A for areas included in the Metropolitan Statistical Area
Source: 1990 Census of Population and Housing, Summary Tape File 3C; Claritas, Inc.

Ancestry

Area	German	Irish	English	Italian	U.S.	French	Polish	Dutch
City	49.3	16.5	11.5	2.0	1.5	4.0	3.8	2.8
MSA[1]	52.0	16.3	11.7	1.8	1.6	4.0	3.6	3.0
U.S.	23.3	15.6	13.1	5.9	5.3	4.2	3.8	2.5

Note: Figures are percentages and include persons that reported multiple ancestry (eg. if a person reported being Irish and Italian, they were included in both columns); (1) Metropolitan Statistical Area - see Appendix A for areas included
Source: 1990 Census of Population and Housing, Summary Tape File 3C

Median Age

Area	1990 Census	1999 Estimate
City	31.4	34.6
MSA[1]	31.5	34.6
U.S.	32.9	35.7

Note: (1) Metropolitan Statistical Area - see Appendix A for areas included
Source: 1990 Census of Population and Housing, Summary Tape File 3C; Claritas, Inc.

Male/Female Population

Area	Number of Males		Number of Females		Males per 100 Females	
	1990	1999	1990	1999	1990	1999
City	33,816	37,658	36,929	40,735	91.6	92.4
MSA[1]	51,688	57,146	54,782	60,459	94.4	94.5
U.S.	121,172,379	132,803,736	127,537,494	139,409,136	95.0	95.3

Note: (1) Metropolitan Statistical Area - see Appendix A for areas included
Source: 1990 Census of Population, General Population Characteristics; Claritas, Inc.

INCOME

Per Capita/Median/Average Income

Area	Per Capita ($)			Median Household ($)			Average Household ($)		
	1989	1999	% Chg.	1989	1999	% Chg.	1989	1999	% Chg.
City	16,533	23,942	44.8	34,922	48,233	38.1	40,989	58,847	43.6
MSA[1]	16,214	24,500	51.1	35,789	51,067	42.7	42,412	63,462	49.6
U.S.	14,420	21,350	48.1	30,056	40,525	34.8	38,453	56,184	46.1

Note: (1) Metropolitan Statistical Area - see Appendix A for areas included; 1989 data is from the 1990 Census; 1999 data is estimated by Claritas, Inc.
Source: 1990 Census of Population, General Population Characteristics; Claritas, Inc.

Household Income Distribution

Area	Percent of Households Earning								
	Under $5,000	$5,000 -14,999	$15,000 -24,999	$25,000 -34,999	$35,000 -49,999	$50,000 -74,999	$75,000 -99,000	$100,000 -149,999	$150,000 and up
City	2.3	10.1	11.4	11.3	16.5	23.4	13.0	7.5	4.4
MSA[1]	2.1	9.2	10.8	10.8	15.9	23.5	13.7	8.5	5.5
U.S.	3.9	13.3	13.8	12.6	16.2	19.4	9.7	6.6	4.6

Note: Data as of 1999; (1) Metropolitan Statistical Area - see Appendix A for areas included
Source: Claritas, Inc.

Effective Buying Income

Area	Per Capita ($)	Median Household ($)	Average Household ($)
City	19,049	40,823	47,838
MSA[1]	19,360	43,156	50,665
U.S.	17,496	36,603	47,036

Note: Data as of 1/1/2000; (1) Metropolitan Statistical Area - see Appendix A for areas included
Source: Standard Rate & Data Service, Newspaper Advertising Source, March 2000

Effective Household Buying Income Distribution

Area	% of Households Earning						
	$10,000 -$19,999	$20,000 -$34,999	$35,000 -$49,999	$50,000 -$74,999	$75,000 -$99,000	$100,000 -$124,999	$125,000 and up
City	12.7	20.6	20.2	24.3	8.6	2.3	3.2
MSA[1]	12.0	19.7	19.7	25.3	9.5	2.7	3.9
U.S.	15.0	21.6	17.6	19.6	8.4	3.0	3.3

Note: Data as of 1/1/2000; (1) Metropolitan Statistical Area - see Appendix A for areas included
Source: Standard Rate & Data Service, Newspaper Advertising Source, March 2000

Poverty Rates by Age

Area	People of All Ages	People Under 18 Years Old	Related Children Age 5-17 in Families in Poverty
City	7.4	n/a	n/a
County	6.6	8.3	7.4
U.S.	13.8	20.8	18.7

Note: Figures show the percent of people living below the poverty line in 1995. The average poverty threshold was $15,569 for a family of four in 1995; n/a not available
Source: Bureau of the Census, Small Area Income and Poverty Estimates Program; U.S. Department of Housing and Urban Development

EMPLOYMENT

Labor Force and Employment

Area	Civilian Labor Force			Workers Employed		
	Dec. 1998	Dec. 1999	% Chg.	Dec. 1998	Dec. 1999	% Chg.
City	46,992	48,233	2.6	46,433	47,372	2.0
MSA[1]	70,301	72,020	2.4	69,425	70,828	2.0
U.S.	138,297,000	139,941,000	1.2	132,732,000	134,696,000	1.5

Note: Data is not seasonally adjusted and covers workers 16 years of age and older; (1) Metropolitan Statistical Area - see Appendix A for areas included
Source: Bureau of Labor Statistics, http://stats.bls.gov

Unemployment Rate

Area	1999											
	Jan.	Feb.	Mar.	Apr.	May	Jun.	Jul.	Aug.	Sep.	Oct.	Nov.	Dec.
City	1.9	1.7	1.7	1.6	1.5	2.4	2.1	1.9	2.4	1.8	1.9	1.8
MSA[1]	2.0	1.9	1.8	1.5	1.4	2.2	1.9	1.7	2.2	1.6	1.7	1.7
U.S.	4.8	4.7	4.4	4.1	4.0	4.5	4.5	4.2	4.1	3.8	3.8	3.7

Note: Data is not seasonally adjusted and covers workers 16 years of age and older; all figures are percentages; (1) Metropolitan Statistical Area - see Appendix A for areas included
Source: Bureau of Labor Statistics, http://stats.bls.gov

Employment by Industry

Sector	MSA[1]		U.S.
	Number of Employees	Percent of Total	Percent of Total
Services	38,400	46.3	30.2
Retail Trade	13,900	16.8	18.1
Government	7,700	9.3	15.8
Manufacturing	12,800	15.4	14.1
Finance/Insurance/Real Estate	2,500	3.0	5.9
Wholesale Trade	1,900	2.3	5.4
Transportation/Public Utilities	2,500	3.0	5.3
Construction	n/a	n/a	4.8
Mining	n/a	n/a	0.4

Note: Figures cover non-farm employment as of 12/99 and are not seasonally adjusted; (1) Metropolitan Statistical Area - see Appendix A for areas included; n/a not available
Source: Bureau of Labor Statistics, http://stats.bls.gov

Employment by Occupation

Occupation Category	City (%)	MSA[1] (%)	U.S. (%)
White Collar	68.9	64.9	58.1
Executive/Admin./Management	10.0	9.5	12.3
Professional	23.0	20.9	14.1
Technical & Related Support	10.5	9.7	3.7
Sales	11.2	10.9	11.8
Administrative Support/Clerical	14.2	13.8	16.3
Blue Collar	14.4	16.8	26.2
Precision Production/Craft/Repair	6.3	7.6	11.3
Machine Operators/Assem./Insp.	3.4	3.9	6.8
Transportation/Material Movers	2.2	2.6	4.1
Cleaners/Helpers/Laborers	2.5	2.7	3.9
Services	16.1	15.9	13.2
Farming/Forestry/Fishing	0.6	2.4	2.5

Note: Figures cover workers 16 years of age and older; (1) Metropolitan Statistical Area - see Appendix A for areas included
Source: 1990 Census of Population and Housing, Summary Tape File 3C

Occupational Employment Projections: 1996 - 2006

Occupations Expected to Have the Largest Job Growth (ranked by numerical growth)	Fast-Growing Occupations[1] (ranked by percent growth)
1. General managers & top executives	1. Systems analysts
2. Database administrators	2. Desktop publishers
3. Salespersons, retail	3. Personal and home care aides
4. Cashiers	4. Physical therapy assistants and aides
5. Systems analysts	5. Occupational therapy assistants
6. Truck drivers, light	6. Home health aides
7. Home health aides	7. Human services workers
8. Receptionists and information clerks	8. Data processing equipment repairers
9. Computer engineers	9. Paralegals
10. Marketing & sales, supervisors	10. Surgical technologists

Note: Projections cover Minnesota; (1) Excludes occupations with total job growth less than 300
Source: U.S. Department of Labor, Employment and Training Administration, America's Labor Market Information System (ALMIS)

Average Wages

Occupation	$/Hr.	Occupation	$/Hr.
Accountants and Auditors	17.65	Maids and Housekeepers	7.61
Assemblers and Fabricators	10.26	Maintenance Repairers	12.45
Automotive Mechanics	12.78	Marketing/Advertising/PR Managers	25.68
Bookkeepers	11.92	Nurses, Licensed Practical	13.99
Carpenters	16.72	Nurses, Registered	23.88
Cashiers	6.93	Nursing Aides/Orderlies/Attendants	9.73
Clerks, General Office	11.40	Physicians and Surgeons	53.34
Clerks, Shipping/Receiving/Traffic	10.58	Receptionists/Information Clerks	11.09
Computer Programmers	18.49	Sales Reps., Exc. Scientific/Retail	17.80
Computer Support Specialists	16.87	Sales Reps., Scientific, Exc. Retail	21.04
Cooks, Restaurant	8.04	Salespersons, Retail	8.61
Electricians	19.47	Secretaries, Except Legal/Medical	11.57
Financial Managers	27.60	Stock Clerks, Sales Floor	7.76
First-Line Supervisors/Mgrs., Sales	14.93	Systems Analysts	20.74
Food Preparation Workers	7.96	Teacher Aides	-
General Managers/Top Executives	26.85	Teachers, Elementary School	15.64
Guards	9.32	Teachers, Secondary School	16.55
Hand Packers	7.81	Telemarketers	10.91
Janitors and Cleaners	8.71	Truck Drivers, Heavy/Tractor-Trailer	14.14
Laborers, Landscaping	9.82	Truck Drivers, Light	10.34
Lawyers	35.44	Waiters and Waitresses	5.70

Note: Wage data is for 1998 and covers the Metropolitan Statistical Area (see Appendix A for areas included). Hourly wages for elementary and secondary school teachers were calculated by the editors from annual wage data assuming a 40 hour work week; Dashes indicate that data was not available.
Source: Bureau of Labor Statistics, 1998 Metropolitan Area Occupational Employment and Wage Estimates

TAXES

Major State and Local Tax Rates

State Corporate Income (%)	State Personal Income (%)	Residential Property (%)	Sales & Use		State Gasoline (cents/ gallon)	State Cigarette (cents/ pack)
			State (%)	Local (%)		
9.8[a]	5.5 - 8.0	1.29	6.5	1.0	20.0	48.0

Note: Personal/corporate income, sales, gasoline and cigarette tax rates as of January 2000. Property tax rates as of April 2000; (a) Plus a 5.8% tax on any Alternative Minimum Taxable Income over the base tax
Source: Federation of Tax Administrators, www.taxadmin.org; ERI's Relocation Assessor software database, quarterly effective date 4/1/2000

Total Taxes Per Capita and as a Percent of Income

Area	Per Capita Income ($)	Per Capita Taxes ($)			Percent of Income (%)		
		Total	Federal	State/Local	Total	Federal	State/Local
Minnesota	30,012	11,555	7,601	3,954	38.5	25.3	13.2
U.S.	28,878	10,298	7,026	3,273	35.7	24.3	11.3

Note: Figures are for 1999
Source: Tax Foundation, www.taxfoundation.org

COMMERCIAL UTILITIES

Typical Monthly Electric Bills

Area	Commercial Service ($/month)		Industrial Service ($/month)	
	12 kW demand 1,500 kWh	100 kW demand 30,000 kWh	1,000 kW demand 400,000 kWh	20,000 kW demand 10,000,000 kWh
City	n/a	n/a	n/a	n/a
U.S.	150	2,174	23,995	508,569

Note: Based on rates in effect January 1, 1999; n/a not available
Source: Edison Electric Institute, Typical Residential, Commercial and Industrial Bills, Winter 1999

TRANSPORTATION

Transportation Statistics

Average minutes to work (1990)	13.3
Interstate highways	I-90; US-14; US-52; US-63
Bus lines	
In-city (1998)	City of Rochester, 21 buses
Inter-city (1999)	4
Passenger air service	
Airport	Rochester International
Airlines (1999)	3
Enplaned passengers (1998)	156,897
Amtrak service	No
Motor freight carriers (1999)	22
Major waterways/ports	None

Source: FAA DOT/TSC CY1998 ACAIS Database; National Transit Database, 1998; Editor & Publisher Market Guide, 2000; Amtrak National Time Table, Fall 1999/Winter 2000; 1990 Census of Population and Housing, STF 3C; Jane's Urban Transport Systems 1999-2000

Means of Transportation to Work

Area	Car/Truck/Van		Public Transportation			Bicycle	Walked	Other Means	Worked at Home
	Drove Alone	Car-pooled	Bus	Subway	Railroad				
City	75.1	10.9	3.6	0.0	0.0	0.6	7.0	0.4	2.4
MSA[1]	75.1	12.0	2.6	0.0	0.0	0.5	5.6	0.4	3.9
U.S.	73.2	13.4	3.0	1.5	0.5	0.4	3.9	1.2	3.0

Note: Figures shown are percentages and only include workers 16 years of age and older;
(1) Metropolitan Statistical Area - see Appendix A for areas included
Source: 1990 Census of Population and Housing, Summary Tape File 3C

BUSINESSES

Major Business Headquarters

Company Name	1999 Rankings	
	Fortune 500	Forbes 500
No companies listed	-	-

Note: Companies listed are located in the city; dashes indicate no ranking
Fortune 500: Companies that produce a 10-K are ranked 1 to 500 based on 1999 revenue
Forbes 500: Private companies are ranked 1 to 500 based on 1998 revenue
Source: Forbes, December 13, 1999; Fortune, April 17, 2000

HOTELS & MOTELS

Hotels/Motels

Area	Hotels/ Motels	Rooms	Luxury-Level Hotels/Motels		Average Minimum Rates ($)		
			♦♦♦♦	♦♦♦♦♦	♦♦	♦♦♦	♦♦♦♦
City	36	4,011	0	0	61	96	n/a
Airport	1	44	0	0	n/a	n/a	n/a
Total	37	4,055	0	0	n/a	n/a	n/a

Note: n/a not available; classifications range from one diamond (budget properties with basic amenities) to five diamond (luxury properties).
Source: OAG Business Travel Planner, Winter 1999-2000

Estimated Daily Food and Lodging Costs

Area	Food/Other ($/day)	Average Hotel Cost ($/day)
City	34	72
U.S.	30	55

Source: ERI's Relocation Assessor software database, quarterly effective date 4/1/2000

CONVENTION CENTERS

Convention Centers and Event Sites

Name	Guest Rooms	Meeting Space (sq. ft.)	Capacity (Theatre Style)
Mayo Civic Center	n/a	n/a	7,200
Radisson Plaza Hotel	212	9,950	500
Rochester Marriott at Mayo Clinic	194	10,021	300

Note: n/a not available
Source: EventSource.com, 3/15/2000

Living Environment

COST OF LIVING

Cost of Living: Homeowner

Cost Element	U.S. ($)	City ($)	Differential ($)	Percent of U.S. Average
Consumables	14,516	14,221	-295	98.0
Transportation	5,957	6,325	368	106.2
Health Services	2,012	2,027	15	100.7
Housing/Utilities/Prop. Tax	16,337	14,393	-1,944	88.1
Income+Payroll Taxes	12,615	13,656	1,041	108.3
Miscellaneous	8,563	8,563	0	100.0
Total Cost of Living	60,000	59,185	-815	98.6

Note: Figures are based on a single income, four person family with gross annual earnings of $60,000, owning an 1,800 square-foot home, and driving two automobiles worth $22,000 30,000 miles per year.
Source: ERI's Relocation Assessor software database, quarterly effective date 4/1/2000

Cost of Living: Renter

Cost Element	U.S. ($)	City ($)	Differential ($)	Percent of U.S. Average
Consumables	10,486	10,299	-187	98.2
Transportation	2,107	2,244	137	106.5
Health Services	1,632	1,649	17	101.0
Rent/Utilities/Insurance	9,299	12,848	3,549	138.2
Income+Payroll Taxes	8,607	9,135	528	106.1
Miscellaneous	7,869	7,869	0	100.0
Total Cost of Living	40,000	44,044	4,044	110.1

Note: Figures are based on a single income, three person family with gross annual earnings of $40,000, renting a 1,000 square-foot home, and driving one automobile worth $8,000 12,000 miles per year.
Source: ERI's Relocation Assessor software database, quarterly effective date 4/1/2000

HOUSING

Median Home Prices and Housing Affordability

Area	Median Price[2] 4th Qtr. 1999 ($)	HOI[3] 4th Qtr. 1999	Affordability Rank[4]
MSA[1]	n/a	n/a	n/a
U.S.	139,000	63.8	–

Note: (1) Metropolitan Statistical Area - see Appendix A for areas included; (2) U.S. figures calculated from the sales of 687,516 new and existing homes in 192 markets; (3) Housing Opportunity Index - percent of homes sold that were within the reach of the median income household at the prevailing mortgage interest rate; (4) Rank is from 1-192 with 1 being most affordable; n/a not available
Source: National Association of Home Builders, Housing Opportunity Index, 4th Quarter 1999

Estimated Home Price

Area	Price ($)
City	112,481
U.S.	135,855

Note: Figures are based on an 1,800 square-foot home
Source: ERI's Relocation Assessor software database, quarterly effective date 4/1/2000

Estimated Rent

Area	Rent ($/month)
City	954
U.S.	651

Note: Figures are based on a 1,000 square-foot home
Source: ERI's Relocation Assessor software database, quarterly effective date 4/1/2000

Median Home Price Projection

It is projected that the median home price in the metropolitan area will increase from $128,813 in 1999 to $192,890 in 2010, an increase of 49.7%
Kiplinger's Personal Finance Magazine, January 2000

RESIDENTIAL UTILITIES

Average Residential Utility Costs

Area	All Electric ($/mth)	Part Electric ($/mth)	Other Energy ($/mth)	Phone ($/mth)
City	n/a	n/a	n/a	n/a
U.S.	99.25	55.47	43.48	20.29

Note: n/a not available
Source: ACCRA, Cost of Living Index, 3rd Quarter 1999

HEALTH CARE

Average Health Care Costs

Area	Hospital ($/day)	Doctor ($/visit)	Dentist ($/visit)
City	n/a	n/a	n/a
U.S.	440.96	53.83	68.42

Note: n/a not available
Source: ACCRA, Cost of Living Index, 3rd Quarter 1999

Distribution of Office-Based Physicians

Area	Family/Gen. Practitioners	Specialists		
		Medical	Surgical	Other
MSA[1]	37	481	217	367

Note: Data as of 12/31/97; (1) Metropolitan Statistical Area - see Appendix A for areas included
Source: American Medical Assn., Physician Characteristics & Distribution in the U.S., 1999

Hospitals

Rochester has 3 general medical and surgical hospitals.
AHA Guide to the Healthcare Field, 1999-2000

According to *U.S. News and World Report,* Rochester has one of the best hospitals in the U.S.: **Mayo Clinic**, noted for cancer, cardiology, endocrinology, gastroenterology, geriatrics, gynecology, neurology, ophthalmology, orthopedics, otolaryngology, pediatrics, psychiatry, pulmonology, rehabilitation, rheumatology, urology.
U.S. News Online, "America's Best Hospitals," July 19, 1999

EDUCATION

Public School District Statistics

District Name	Num. Sch.	Enroll.	Classroom Teachers	Pupils per Teacher	Minority Pupils (%)	Current Exp.[1] ($/pupil)
Rochester	31	15,814	n/a	n/a	15.7	5,511

Note: Data covers the 1997-1998 school year unless otherwise noted; (1) Data covers fiscal year 1996; SD = School District; ISD = Independent School District; n/a not available
Source: National Center for Education Statistics, Common Core of Data Public Education Agency Universe 1997-98; National Center for Education Statistics, Characteristics of the 100 Largest Public Elementary and Secondary School Districts in the United States: 1997-98, July 1999

Educational Quality

School District	Education Quotient[1]	Graduate Outcome[2]	Community Index[3]	Resource Index[4]
Rochester	133	145	121	110

Note: Over 1,000 secondary school districts were rated in terms of educational quality. The scores range from a low of 50 to a high of 150; (1) Combination of the Graduate Outcome, Community and Resource indexes weighted to reflect the greater importance of the Graduate Outcome and Resource Index; (2) Based on graduation rates and college board scores (SAT/ACT); (3) Based on the surrounding community's level of affluence and adult education; (4) Based on teacher salaries, per-pupil expenditures and student-teacher ratios.
Source: Expansion Management, Ratings Issue, 1999

Educational Attainment by Race

Area	High School Graduate (%)					Bachelor's Degree (%)				
	Total	White	Black	Other	Hisp.[2]	Total	White	Black	Other	Hisp.[2]
City	89.1	89.8	95.6	66.0	82.1	33.2	32.8	34.7	43.2	33.7
MSA[1]	88.0	88.5	94.7	66.9	77.3	29.5	29.1	34.1	43.6	29.0
U.S.	75.2	77.9	63.1	60.4	49.8	20.3	21.5	11.4	19.4	9.2

*Note: Figures shown cover persons 25 years old and over; (1) Metropolitan Statistical Area -
see Appendix A for areas included; (2) people of Hispanic origin can be of any race*
Source: 1990 Census of Population and Housing, Summary Tape File 3C

School Enrollment by Type

Area	Preprimary				Elementary/High School			
	Public		Private		Public		Private	
	Enrollment	%	Enrollment	%	Enrollment	%	Enrollment	%
City	1,008	55.2	817	44.8	9,242	85.4	1,585	14.6
MSA[1]	1,630	59.7	1,102	40.3	16,014	88.3	2,118	11.7
U.S.	2,679,029	59.5	1,824,256	40.5	38,379,689	90.2	4,187,099	9.8

Note: Figures shown cover persons 3 years old and over;
(1) Metropolitan Statistical Area - see Appendix A for areas included
Source: 1990 Census of Population and Housing, Summary Tape File 3C

School Enrollment by Race

Area	Preprimary (%)				Elementary/High School (%)			
	White	Black	Other	Hisp.[1]	White	Black	Other	Hisp.[1]
City	90.8	1.2	8.0	0.4	91.1	1.7	7.3	0.6
MSA[2]	93.5	0.8	5.7	0.8	93.8	1.0	5.1	0.7
U.S.	80.4	12.5	7.1	7.8	74.1	15.6	10.3	12.5

*Note: Figures shown cover persons 3 years old and over; (1) people of Hispanic origin can be of any
race; (2) Metropolitan Statistical Area - see Appendix A for areas included*
Source: 1990 Census of Population and Housing, Summary Tape File 3C

Higher Education

Two-Year Colleges		Four-Year Colleges		Medical Schools	Law Schools	Voc/ Tech
Public	Private	Public	Private			
2	0	0	1	1	0	2

*Source: College Blue Book, Occupational Education, 1999; Medical School Admission Requirements,
1999-2000; Peterson's Guide to Two-Year Colleges, 2000; Peterson's Guide to Four-Year Colleges,
1999; Barron's Guide to Law Schools, 1999*

MAJOR EMPLOYERS

Major Employers

Crenlo (metal stampings)	Kahler Corp. (hotels)
Mayo Foundation for Medical Education & Research	Mayo Medical Center
Metafile Information Systems	Pace Dairy Foods
Post Bulletin	Rochester Methodist Hospital

Note: Companies listed are located in the city
*Source: D&B Business Rankings, 1999; Ward's Business Directory, 1999; America's Corporate
Families, 1999*

PUBLIC SAFETY

Crime Rate

Area	All Crimes	Violent Crimes				Property Crimes		
		Murder	Forcible Rape	Robbery	Aggrav. Assault	Burglary	Larceny -Theft	Motor Vehicle Theft
City	3,673.7	1.3	72.5	64.7	194.2	511.3	2,654.9	174.8
Suburbs[1]	1,234.3	0.0	47.0	0.0	86.1	297.5	715.0	88.7
MSA[2]	2,864.9	0.9	64.0	43.3	158.3	440.4	2,011.7	146.2
U.S.	4,615.5	6.3	34.4	165.2	360.5	862.0	2,728.1	459.0

Note: Crime rate is the number of crimes per 100,000 population; (1) Defined as all areas within the Metropolitan Statistical Area but located outside the central city; (2) Metropolitan Statistical Area - see Appendix A for areas included
Source: FBI Uniform Crime Reports, 1998

RECREATION

Culture and Recreation

Museums	Symphony Orchestras	Opera Companies	Dance Companies	Professional Theatres	Zoos	Pro Sports Teams
1	1	0	1	1	0	0

Source: Musical America, International Directory of the Performing Arts, 1999; Official Museum Directory, 2000; Stern's Performing Arts Directory, 1997; USA Today Four Sport Stadium Guide, 1997; Career Opportunities in Theatre and the Performing Arts, 1999

Library System

The Rochester Public Library has no branches, holdings of 295,182 volumes, and a budget of $3,484,994 (1997-1998).
American Library Directory, 1999-2000

MEDIA

Newspapers

Name	Type	Freq.	Distribution	Circulation
Post-Bulletin	General	6x/wk	Area	42,000

Note: Includes newspapers with circulations of 200 or more located in the city;
Source: Burrelle's Media Directory, 1999 Edition

Television Stations

Name	Ch.	Affiliation	Type	Owner
KTTC	10	n/a	Commercial	Quincy Newspapers Inc.
KXLT	47	n/a	Commercial	Shockley Communications Corporation

Note: Stations included broadcast in the Rochester metro area; n/a not available
Source: Burrelle's Media Directory, 1999 Edition

AM Radio Stations

Call Letters	Freq. (kHz)	Target Audience	Station Format	Music Format
KWEB	1270	General	S/T	n/a
KROC	1340	General	N/T	n/a
KOLM	1520	General	M/N/S/T	Oldies

Note: Stations included broadcast in the Rochester metro area; n/a not available
Target Audience: A=Asian; B=Black; C=Christian; E=Ethnic; F=French; G=General; H=Hispanic; M=Men; N=Native American; R=Religious; S=Senior Citizen; W=Women; Y=Young Adult; Z=Children
Station Format: E=Educational; M=Music; N=News; S=Sports; T=Talk
Source: Burrelle's Media Directory, 1999 Edition

FM Radio Stations

Call Letters	Freq. (mHz)	Target Audience	Station Format	Music Format
KLCD	89.5	General	M/N	Classical
KZSE	90.7	General	M/N	Classical
KXLC	91.1	General	N	n/a
KLSE	91.7	General	M/N	Classical
KFSI	92.9	Religious	M/N	Christian
KWWK	96.5	General	M/N/S	Country
KRCH	101.7	General	M/N/S	Classic Rock
KMFX	102.5	General	M	Country
KYBA	105.3	General	M/N/S	Adult Contemporary
KROC	106.9	General	M	Top 40
KLCX	107.7	General	M	Classic Rock

Note: Stations included broadcast in the Rochester metro area; n/a not available
Station Format: E=Educational; M=Music; N=News; S=Sports; T=Talk
Target Audience: A=Asian; B=Black; C=Christian; E=Ethnic; F=French; G=General; H=Hispanic;
M=Men; N=Native American; R=Religious; S=Senior Citizen; W=Women; Y=Young Adult; Z=Children
Source: Burrelle's Media Directory, 1999 Edition

WEATHER

Temperature/Precipitation/Humidity

	Jan	Feb	Mar	Apr	May	Jun	Jul	Aug	Sep	Oct	Nov	Dec	Yr.
Max. High Temp. (°F)	55	63	79	91	92	101	102	100	97	90	74	62	102
Avg. High Temp. (°F)	21	26	37	55	68	78	82	80	70	59	41	26	54
Avg. Temp. (°F)	12	18	29	45	57	67	71	69	60	49	33	18	44
Avg. Low Temp. (°F)	3	8	20	34	46	55	60	58	48	38	24	10	34
Min. Low Temp. (°F)	-40	-29	-31	5	21	35	42	35	23	11	-20	-33	-40
Avg. Precip. (in.)	0.8	0.8	1.8	2.6	3.4	4.1	4.1	3.8	3.1	2.1	1.5	1.0	29.0
Avg. Snowfall (in.)	9	8	10	4	Tr	0	0	0	Tr	1	5	10	46
Avg. Rel. Hum. 6am (%)	79	80	81	80	79	82	85	88	87	82	82	83	82
Avg. Rel. Hum. 3pm (%)	71	68	65	54	52	53	55	56	56	54	65	74	60

Note: Tr = Trace amounts (less than 0.05 inches of rain or less than 0.5 inches of snow)
Source: National Climatic Data Center, International Station Meteorological Climate Summary, 3/95

Weather Conditions

Temperature			Precipitation		
5°F & below	32°F & below	90°F & above	0.01 inch or more precip.	1.5 inch or more snow/ice	Thunderstorms
47	165	10	113	10	41

Note: Figures are average number of days per year
Source: National Climatic Data Center, International Station Meteorological Climate Summary, 3/95

AIR & WATER QUALITY

Maximum Pollutant Concentrations

	Particulate Matter (ug/m³)	Carbon Monoxide (ppm)	Sulfur Dioxide (ppm)	Nitrogen Dioxide (ppm)	Ozone (ppm)	Lead (ug/m³)
MSA[1] Level	38	n/a	n/a	n/a	n/a	n/a
NAAQS[2]	150	9	0.140	0.053	0.12	1.50
Met NAAQS	Yes	n/a	n/a	n/a	n/a	n/a

Note: (1) Metropolitan Statistical Area - see Appendix A for areas included; (2) National Ambient Air Quality Standards; ppm = parts per million; ug/m³ = micrograms per cubic meter; n/a not available
Source: EPA, National Air Quality and Emissions Trends Report, 1997

Pollutant Standards Index

Data not available.
EPA, National Air Quality and Emissions Trends Report, 1997

Drinking Water

Water System Name	Pop. Served	Primary Water Source Type	Number of Violations in 1998-99	Type of Violation/ Contaminants
Rochester	77,000	Ground	None	None

Note: Data as of January 19, 2000
Source: EPA, Office of Ground Water and Drinking Water, Safe Drinking Water Information System

Rochester tap water is hard, fluoridated and chlorinated.
Editor & Publisher Market Guide, 2000

Saginaw, Michigan

Background

Saginaw, Michigan is located in the east central section of the state, 40 miles north of Flint and 100 miles northwest of Detroit. The city is on both banks of the Saginaw River, about 20 miles south of Bay City, where the Saginaw Bay of Lake Huron flows into the river. The region is a mix of urban and rural areas.

Saginaw is the county seat and largest city in Saginaw County. It is also the largest city in a region that is sometimes referred to as the "Tri-Cities," which also includes Bay City and Midland and smaller communities. Manufacturing, particularly for the automotive industry, is the most prominent economic activity in Saginaw. Agriculture and food products, retail and wholesale trades, transportation, health care, education, business and other services and tourism are among the other primary economic activities in the city and Saginaw County.

The Chippewa were among the Native Americans who occupied the region at the time of European colonization. The name Saginaw is based on Chippewa phrase. France claimed the region before ceding it to Britain after 1760 with the end of the French and Indian Wars. The region became a United States territory in 1796, and the Chippewa ceded claims in the early 19th Century. In 1812 a fur trading post was established on the Saginaw River. Saginaw County was established in 1835. During the 19th Century, the Saginaw Valley economy was based primarily on logging. Saginaw City was founded on the west bank of the river in 1836. East Saginaw was founded on the opposite bank shortly thereafter. The two initially were rivals, but united as one city, Saginaw, in 1890.

By the 20th Century, the lumber industry had declined, as the forests were cut. With the invention of the automobile and Michigan's emergence as a center for automobile manufacturing, Saginaw's economy, too, became oriented to manufacturing of automotive products. This continues to be a mainstay of the economy. A variety of other products including mechanical and electronic equipment are also manufactured. In recent years, the city has undertaken a number of economic development and diversification initiatives, including receiving Renaissance Zone designation for certain area to encourage their redevelopment.

Area colleges include Delta Community College, Saginaw Valley State University and Great Lakes College.

Saginaw has 540 acres of parks, with a variety of attractions and activities. Ojibway Island is a park and gathering place for outdoor concerts and other events. Riverwalk is a park and trail along the Saginaw River. The Anderson Enrichment Center is a building for meetings and events surrounded by formal gardens. The Saginaw Children's Zoo includes a carousel and other activities. The Japanese Culture Center features a tea-house and garden.

Old Saginaw City is a district with turn-of-the-century ambience that includes shopping and other activities. Saginaw has several architecturally distinctive structures from earlier eras. Among them is a water treatment plant with ornate Gothic architecture, which is lit up for the holidays. The Castle Museum of Saginaw County History is located in a structure designed as a French castle, which was originally a post office.

Saginaw Civic Center includes a 2,200-seat theater, 7,000-seat arena and conference rooms. Cultural organizations include the Saginaw Bay Orchestra, Saginaw Choral Society, Pit and Balcony Theater, among others. The Temple Theater is a restored movie palace that shows current and nostalgic films.

Under a charter adopted in 1935, Saginaw has a Council-Manager form of government, with an elected City Council and Mayor and an appointed City Manager.

General Rankings and Evaluative Comments

- Saginaw was ranked #177 out of 354 metropolitan areas in *Places Rated Almanac*. Criteria: cost of living, climate, crime, transportation, job outlook, education, the arts, health care, and recreation. *Places Rated Almanac, Millennium Edition, 2000*

- Cognetics studied 273 metro areas in the United States, ranking them by entrepreneurial activity. Saginaw was ranked #93 out of 134 smaller metro areas. Criteria: Significant Starts (firms started in the last 10 years that still employ at least 5 people) and Young Growers (percent of firms 10 years old or less that grew significantly during the last 4 years). *Cognetics, "Entrepreneurial Hot Spots: The Best Places in America to Start and Grow a Company," 1999*

- Reliastar Financial Corporation ranked the 125 largest metropolitan areas according to the general financial security of residents. Saginaw was ranked #43 out of 125 with a score of 5.8 (the percentage a metropolitan area is above or below the metropolitan norm; a metro area with a score of 10.6 is 10.6% above the metro average). Criteria: Earnings and Wealth Potential (household income, education, net assets, cost of living); Safety Net (health insurance, retirement savings, life insurance, income support programs); Personal Threats (unemployment rate, low-income households, crime rate); Community Economic Vitality (cost of community services, job quality, job creation, housing costs). *Reliastar Financial Corporation, "The Best Cities to Earn and Save Money: A Ranking of the Largest 125 U.S. Cities," 2000 Edition*

Business Environment

STATE ECONOMY

State Economic Profile

"Although the Michigan economy bounced back quickly from the GM strike, it is losing much of its mid-1990s momentum. Strong auto sales have not translated into employment gains in the auto industry. Canada's weak economy has caused a drop in Michigan's exports. And what constrains Michigan the most is its demographic situation. The next several years should see a slowing economy.

In spite of the GM strike and booming automobile sales, GM has not increased employment and is currently planning to close plants in Kalamazoo and Flint. In addition, some 1,000 office jobs are targeted for elimination at the Detroit headquarters; Ford is currently planning to cut jobs within the state. Auto sales 2000 should fall below 1998, only adding to Detroit's need for employment reductions.

Construction activity added significantly to job growth in 1998, with construction employment growing 2.5% for the state and 8.3% for Detroit. Almost 1,800 commercial/industrial developments were undertaken in 1998. With the slowing economy, construction activity is likely to contract, undermining one of Michigan's bright spots. Residential starts, up 7% in 1998, should decline in the near future.

Michigan's tight labor markets have helped to absorb downsizing in the auto industry, keeping the unemployment rate manageable. Labor availability has, however, started to become a problem for the state's information technology firms. The state's weak population growth, especially its continuing loss of young households, will dampen the high home price appreciation witnessed in recent years, as well as limit job entry-level job growth." *National Association of Realtors, Economic Profiles: The Fifty States and the District of Columbia, http://nar.realtor.com/databank/profiles.htm*

EXPORTS

Total Export Sales

Area	1995 ($000)	1996 ($000)	1997 ($000)	1998 ($000)	% Chg. 1995-98	% Chg. 1997-98
MSA[1]	1,035,565	1,254,464	1,654,394	1,557,900	50.4	-5.8
U.S.	583,030,524	622,827,063	687,597,999	680,474,251	16.7	-1.0

Note: (1) Metropolitan Statistical Area - see Appendix A for areas included
Source: U.S. Department of Commerce, International Trade Association, Metropolitan Area Exports: An Export Performance Report on Over 250 U.S. Cities, November 10, 1999

CITY FINANCES

City Government Finances

Component	1995 ($million)	1995 (per capita $)
Revenue	73.8	1,045
Expenditure	111.7	1,582
Debt Outstanding	92.0	1,303

Source: 1999 County and City Extra, Annual Metro, City, and County Data Book

City Government Revenue by Source

Source	1995 ($million)	1995 (per capita $)
Intergovernmental	30.1	426
Taxes	21.0	297
Property	6.2	88
Sales and Gross Receipts	0.0	0

Source: 1999 County and City Extra, Annual Metro, City, and County Data Book

City Government Expenditures by Function

Function	1995 ($million)	1995 (per capita $)	1995 (%)
Public Welfare	0.3	4	0.3
Highways	11.8	167	10.6
Parking Facilities	0.8	12	0.8
Education	0.0	0	0.0
Health and Hospitals	0.0	0	0.0
Police Protection	10.4	148	9.4
Sewerage and Sanitation	55.8	790	50.0
Parks and Recreation	1.2	17	1.1
Housing and Community Development	0.1	1	0.1
Interest on Debt	8.0	113	7.2

Source: 1999 County and City Extra, Annual Metro, City, and County Data Book

Municipal Bond Ratings

Area	Moody's
City	A3

Source: Mergent Bond Record, 2/2000

POPULATION

Population Growth

Area	1980 Census	1990 Census	1999 Estimate	2004 Projection	Population Growth (%) 1990-1999	Population Growth (%) 1999-2004
City	77,508	69,512	62,580	59,812	-10.0	-4.4
MSA[1]	421,518	399,320	401,279	404,712	0.5	0.9
U.S.	226,545,805	248,765,170	272,212,864	283,625,312	9.4	4.2

Note: (1) Metropolitan Statistical Area - see Appendix A for areas included
Source: 1990 Census of Population and Housing, Summary Tape File 3C; Claritas, Inc.

Number of Households and Average Household Size

Area	1980 Census	1990 Census	1999 Estimate	2004 Projection	1999 Average Household Size
City	27,344	26,197	24,526	23,956	2.55
MSA[1]	141,962	148,098	155,503	160,323	2.58
U.S.	80,389,592	91,993,582	102,048,200	107,302,392	2.67

Note: (1) Metropolitan Statistical Area - see Appendix A for areas included
Source: 1990 Census of Population and Housing, Summary Tape File 3C; Claritas, Inc.

Race/Ethnicity of City Population

Race/Ethnicity	1990 Census Population	1990 Census %	1999 Estimate Population	1999 Estimate %	% Change 1990-1999
White, Non-Hispanic	34,028	49.0	26,257	42.0	-22.8
Black, Non-Hispanic	27,778	40.0	27,371	43.7	-1.5
Asian, Non-Hispanic	289	0.4	270	0.4	-6.6
Other, Non-Hispanic	441	0.6	300	0.5	-32.0
Hispanic	6,976	10.0	8,382	13.4	20.2

Source: 1990 Census of Population and Housing, Summary Tape File 3C; Claritas, Inc.

Race/Ethnicity of Metropolitan Statistical Area Population

Race/Ethnicity	1990 Census Population	%	1999 Estimate Population	%	% Change 1990-1999
White, Non-Hispanic	339,813	85.1	334,078	83.3	-1.7
Black, Non-Hispanic	38,348	9.6	40,078	10.0	4.5
Asian, Non-Hispanic	2,462	0.6	3,405	0.8	38.3
Other, Non-Hispanic	1,996	0.5	1,948	0.5	-2.4
Hispanic	16,701	4.2	21,770	5.4	30.4

Note: See Appendix A for areas included in the Metropolitan Statistical Area
Source: 1990 Census of Population and Housing, Summary Tape File 3C; Claritas, Inc.

Ancestry

Area	German	Irish	English	Italian	U.S.	French	Polish	Dutch
City	24.7	8.5	6.9	1.8	2.0	5.7	6.3	1.0
MSA[1]	40.3	13.3	13.5	2.3	2.5	11.6	12.9	3.0
U.S.	23.3	15.6	13.1	5.9	5.3	4.2	3.8	2.5

Note: Figures are percentages and include persons that reported multiple ancestry (eg. if a person reported being Irish and Italian, they were included in both columns); (1) Metropolitan Statistical Area - see Appendix A for areas included
Source: 1990 Census of Population and Housing, Summary Tape File 3C

Median Age

Area	1990 Census	1999 Estimate
City	29.7	30.4
MSA[1]	33.0	35.7
U.S.	32.9	35.7

Note: (1) Metropolitan Statistical Area - see Appendix A for areas included
Source: 1990 Census of Population and Housing, Summary Tape File 3C; Claritas, Inc.

Male/Female Population

Area	Number of Males 1990	1999	Number of Females 1990	1999	Males per 100 Females 1990	1999
City	32,177	29,146	37,335	33,434	86.2	87.2
MSA[1]	192,562	193,542	206,758	207,737	93.1	93.2
U.S.	121,172,379	132,803,736	127,537,494	139,409,136	95.0	95.3

Note: (1) Metropolitan Statistical Area - see Appendix A for areas included
Source: 1990 Census of Population, General Population Characteristics; Claritas, Inc.

INCOME

Per Capita/Median/Average Income

Area	Per Capita ($) 1989	1999	% Chg.	Median Household ($) 1989	1999	% Chg.	Average Household ($) 1989	1999	% Chg.
City	8,944	12,484	39.6	17,736	21,703	22.4	23,529	30,986	31.7
MSA[1]	13,040	20,528	57.4	29,157	39,529	35.6	34,908	52,132	49.3
U.S.	14,420	21,350	48.1	30,056	40,525	34.8	38,453	56,184	46.1

Note: (1) Metropolitan Statistical Area - see Appendix A for areas included; 1989 data is from the 1990 Census; 1999 data is estimated by Claritas, Inc.
Source: 1990 Census of Population, General Population Characteristics; Claritas, Inc.

Household Income Distribution

Area	Percent of Households Earning								
	Under $5,000	$5,000 -14,999	$15,000 -24,999	$25,000 -34,999	$35,000 -49,999	$50,000 -74,999	$75,000 -99,000	$100,000 -149,999	$150,000 and up
City	11.0	26.6	17.8	11.8	13.1	13.0	4.7	1.6	0.4
MSA[1]	4.5	15.0	14.2	11.8	14.7	20.2	10.0	6.6	3.0
U.S.	3.9	13.3	13.8	12.6	16.2	19.4	9.7	6.6	4.6

Note: Data as of 1999; (1) Metropolitan Statistical Area - see Appendix A for areas included
Source: Claritas, Inc.

Effective Buying Income

Area	Per Capita ($)	Median Household ($)	Average Household ($)
City	10,268	20,162	26,938
MSA[1]	16,370	35,559	43,396
U.S.	17,496	36,603	47,036

Note: Data as of 1/1/2000; (1) Metropolitan Statistical Area - see Appendix A for areas included
Source: Standard Rate & Data Service, Newspaper Advertising Source, March 2000

Effective Household Buying Income Distribution

Area	% of Households Earning						
	$10,000 -$19,999	$20,000 -$34,999	$35,000 -$49,999	$50,000 -$74,999	$75,000 -$99,000	$100,000 -$124,999	$125,000 and up
City	22.1	21.2	14.6	11.1	2.5	0.6	0.2
MSA[1]	15.9	20.0	17.2	20.0	8.4	2.7	2.4
U.S.	15.0	21.6	17.6	19.6	8.4	3.0	3.3

Note: Data as of 1/1/2000; (1) Metropolitan Statistical Area - see Appendix A for areas included
Source: Standard Rate & Data Service, Newspaper Advertising Source, March 2000

Poverty Rates by Age

Area	People of All Ages	People Under 18 Years Old	Related Children Age 5-17 in Families in Poverty
City	32.8	n/a	n/a
County	16.9	27.2	24.4
U.S.	13.8	20.8	18.7

Note: Figures show the percent of people living below the poverty line in 1995. The average poverty threshold was $15,569 for a family of four in 1995; n/a not available
Source: Bureau of the Census, Small Area Income and Poverty Estimates Program; U.S. Department of Housing and Urban Development

EMPLOYMENT

Labor Force and Employment

Area	Civilian Labor Force			Workers Employed		
	Dec. 1998	Dec. 1999	% Chg.	Dec. 1998	Dec. 1999	% Chg.
City	27,308	27,448	0.5	25,435	25,686	1.0
MSA[1]	200,439	201,552	0.6	192,595	194,498	1.0
U.S.	138,297,000	139,941,000	1.2	132,732,000	134,696,000	1.5

Note: Data is not seasonally adjusted and covers workers 16 years of age and older; (1) Metropolitan Statistical Area - see Appendix A for areas included
Source: Bureau of Labor Statistics, http://stats.bls.gov

Unemployment Rate

Area	1999											
	Jan.	Feb.	Mar.	Apr.	May	Jun.	Jul.	Aug.	Sep.	Oct.	Nov.	Dec.
City	9.1	9.1	9.3	8.1	7.2	8.3	8.2	6.3	6.8	6.9	7.0	6.4
MSA[1]	5.2	5.3	5.4	4.6	4.0	4.5	3.8	3.2	3.4	3.5	3.7	3.5
U.S.	4.8	4.7	4.4	4.1	4.0	4.5	4.5	4.2	4.1	3.8	3.8	3.7

Note: Data is not seasonally adjusted and covers workers 16 years of age and older; all figures are percentages; (1) Metropolitan Statistical Area - see Appendix A for areas included
Source: Bureau of Labor Statistics, http://stats.bls.gov

Employment by Industry

Sector	MSA[1]		U.S.
	Number of Employees	Percent of Total	Percent of Total
Services	49,400	27.0	30.2
Retail Trade	40,700	22.2	18.1
Government	23,300	12.7	15.8
Manufacturing	39,300	21.5	14.1
Finance/Insurance/Real Estate	6,900	3.8	5.9
Wholesale Trade	6,800	3.7	5.4
Transportation/Public Utilities	6,700	3.7	5.3
Construction	n/a	n/a	4.8
Mining	n/a	n/a	0.4

Note: Figures cover non-farm employment as of 12/99 and are not seasonally adjusted; (1) Metropolitan Statistical Area - see Appendix A for areas included; n/a not available
Source: Bureau of Labor Statistics, http://stats.bls.gov

Employment by Occupation

Occupation Category	City (%)	MSA[1] (%)	U.S. (%)
White Collar	49.6	54.1	58.1
Executive/Admin./Management	7.2	9.5	12.3
Professional	10.3	13.6	14.1
Technical & Related Support	3.1	3.7	3.7
Sales	13.6	12.3	11.8
Administrative Support/Clerical	15.4	15.0	16.3
Blue Collar	29.3	30.0	26.2
Precision Production/Craft/Repair	9.2	12.8	11.3
Machine Operators/Assem./Insp.	11.1	9.1	6.8
Transportation/Material Movers	4.1	4.0	4.1
Cleaners/Helpers/Laborers	4.9	4.1	3.9
Services	20.1	14.5	13.2
Farming/Forestry/Fishing	1.0	1.4	2.5

Note: Figures cover workers 16 years of age and older; (1) Metropolitan Statistical Area - see Appendix A for areas included
Source: 1990 Census of Population and Housing, Summary Tape File 3C

Occupational Employment Projections: 1994 - 2005

Occupations Expected to Have the Largest Job Growth (ranked by numerical growth)	Fast-Growing Occupations[1] (ranked by percent growth)
1. Waiters & waitresses	1. Computer engineers
2. Cashiers	2. Home health aides
3. All other helper, laborer, mover	3. Systems analysts
4. Systems analysts	4. Personal and home care aides
5. Home health aides	5. Electronic pagination systems workers
6. General managers & top executives	6. All other computer scientists
7. All other profess., paraprofess., tech.	7. Physical therapists
8. Registered nurses	8. All other therapists
9. All other sales reps. & services	9. Electronics repairers, comm. & indust.
10. Salespersons, retail	10. Occupational therapists

Note: Projections cover Michigan; (1) Excludes occupations with total job growth less than 300
Source: Office of Labor Market Information, Occupational Employment Forecasts, 1994-2005

Average Wages

Occupation	$/Hr.	Occupation	$/Hr.
Accountants and Auditors	18.76	Maids and Housekeepers	6.50
Assemblers and Fabricators	10.01	Maintenance Repairers	15.50
Automotive Mechanics	13.04	Marketing/Advertising/PR Managers	26.42
Bookkeepers	10.58	Nurses, Licensed Practical	13.87
Carpenters	15.42	Nurses, Registered	19.64
Cashiers	7.13	Nursing Aides/Orderlies/Attendants	8.09
Clerks, General Office	9.45	Physicians and Surgeons	54.29
Clerks, Shipping/Receiving/Traffic	14.44	Receptionists/Information Clerks	8.00
Computer Programmers	21.64	Sales Reps., Exc. Scientific/Retail	17.35
Computer Support Specialists	-	Sales Reps., Scientific, Exc. Retail	25.24
Cooks, Restaurant	6.44	Salespersons, Retail	8.36
Electricians	20.63	Secretaries, Except Legal/Medical	10.98
Financial Managers	25.73	Stock Clerks, Sales Floor	7.47
First-Line Supervisors/Mgrs., Sales	15.30	Systems Analysts	21.17
Food Preparation Workers	7.02	Teacher Aides	8.35
General Managers/Top Executives	27.95	Teachers, Elementary School	21.48
Guards	9.67	Teachers, Secondary School	22.44
Hand Packers	7.94	Telemarketers	7.65
Janitors and Cleaners	9.25	Truck Drivers, Heavy/Tractor-Trailer	13.37
Laborers, Landscaping	8.73	Truck Drivers, Light	8.99
Lawyers	33.18	Waiters and Waitresses	5.72

Note: Wage data is for 1998 and covers the Metropolitan Statistical Area (see Appendix A for areas included). Hourly wages for elementary and secondary school teachers were calculated by the editors from annual wage data assuming a 40 hour work week; Dashes indicate that data was not available.
Source: Bureau of Labor Statistics, 1998 Metropolitan Area Occupational Employment and Wage Estimates

TAXES

Major State and Local Tax Rates

State Corporate Income (%)	State Personal Income (%)	Residential Property (%)	Sales & Use		State Gasoline (cents/ gallon)	State Cigarette (cents/ pack)
			State (%)	Local (%)		
2.2[a]	4.3[b]	2.10	6.0	None	19.0[c]	75.0

Note: Personal/corporate income, sales, gasoline and cigarette tax rates as of January 2000. Property tax rates as of April 2000; (b) Tax rate scheduled to decrease to 4.2% for tax year 2001; (a) Value added tax imposed on the sum of federal taxable income of the business, compensation paid to employees, dividends, interest, royalties paid and other items; (c) Sales tax applicable
Source: Federation of Tax Administrators, www.taxadmin.org; ERI's Relocation Assessor software database, quarterly effective date 4/1/2000

Total Taxes Per Capita and as a Percent of Income

Area	Per Capita Income ($)	Per Capita Taxes ($)			Percent of Income (%)		
		Total	Federal	State/Local	Total	Federal	State/Local
Michigan	28,685	10,510	7,235	3,274	36.6	25.2	11.4
U.S.	28,878	10,298	7,026	3,273	35.7	24.3	11.3

Note: Figures are for 1999
Source: Tax Foundation, www.taxfoundation.org

COMMERCIAL UTILITIES

Typical Monthly Electric Bills

Area	Commercial Service ($/month)		Industrial Service ($/month)	
	12 kW demand 1,500 kWh	100 kW demand 30,000 kWh	1,000 kW demand 400,000 kWh	20,000 kW demand 10,000,000 kWh
City	153	2,081	23,525	396,252
U.S.	150	2,174	23,995	508,569

Note: Based on rates in effect January 1, 1999
Source: Edison Electric Institute, Typical Residential, Commercial and Industrial Bills, Winter 1999

TRANSPORTATION

Transportation Statistics

Average minutes to work (1990)	15.3
Interstate highways	I-75; I-675; US-23
Bus lines	
In-city (1998)	Saginaw Transit System Authority, 32 buses
Inter-city (1999)	2
Passenger air service	
Airport	Midland-Bay City-Saginaw International
Airlines (1999)	4
Enplaned passengers (1998)	295,696
Amtrak service	No
Motor freight carriers (1999)	21
Major waterways/ports	Saginaw River

Source: FAA DOT/TSC CY1998 ACAIS Database; National Transit Database, 1998; Editor & Publisher Market Guide, 2000; Amtrak National Time Table, Fall 1999/Winter 2000; 1990 Census of Population and Housing, STF 3C; Jane's Urban Transport Systems 1999-2000

Means of Transportation to Work

Area	Car/Truck/Van		Public Transportation			Bicycle	Walked	Other Means	Worked at Home
	Drove Alone	Car-pooled	Bus	Subway	Railroad				
City	81.8	10.9	1.6	0.0	0.0	0.2	3.2	1.2	1.1
MSA[1]	85.2	8.9	0.5	0.0	0.0	0.1	2.3	0.6	2.4
U.S.	73.2	13.4	3.0	1.5	0.5	0.4	3.9	1.2	3.0

Note: Figures shown are percentages and only include workers 16 years of age and older;
(1) Metropolitan Statistical Area - see Appendix A for areas included
Source: 1990 Census of Population and Housing, Summary Tape File 3C

BUSINESSES

Major Business Headquarters

Company Name	1999 Rankings	
	Fortune 500	Forbes 500
No companies listed	-	-

Note: Companies listed are located in the city; dashes indicate no ranking
Fortune 500: Companies that produce a 10-K are ranked 1 to 500 based on 1999 revenue
Forbes 500: Private companies are ranked 1 to 500 based on 1998 revenue
Source: Forbes, December 13, 1999; Fortune, April 17, 2000

HOTELS & MOTELS

Hotels/Motels

Area	Hotels/ Motels	Rooms	Luxury-Level Hotels/Motels		Average Minimum Rates ($)		
			♦♦♦♦	♦♦♦♦♦	♦♦	♦♦♦	♦♦♦♦
City	9	957	0	0	n/a	n/a	n/a
Suburbs	2	135	0	0	n/a	n/a	n/a
Total	11	1,092	0	0	n/a	n/a	n/a

Note: n/a not available; classifications range from one diamond (budget properties with basic amenities) to five diamond (luxury properties).
Source: OAG Business Travel Planner, Winter 1999-2000

Estimated Daily Food and Lodging Costs

Area	Food/Other ($/day)	Average Hotel Cost ($/day)
City	30	55
U.S.	30	55

Source: ERI's Relocation Assessor software database, quarterly effective date 4/1/2000

CONVENTION CENTERS

Convention Centers and Event Sites

Name	Guest Rooms	Meeting Space (sq. ft.)	Capacity (Theatre Style)
Four Points Hotel Saginaw	156	3,808	300
Horizons Conference Center	n/a	n/a	0
Saginaw Civic Center	n/a	n/a	7,500

Note: n/a not available
Source: EventSource.com, 3/15/2000

Living Environment

COST OF LIVING

Cost of Living: Homeowner

Cost Element	U.S. ($)	City ($)	Differential ($)	Percent of U.S. Average
Consumables	14,516	14,979	463	103.2
Transportation	5,957	5,813	-144	97.6
Health Services	2,012	1,922	-90	95.5
Housing/Utilities/Prop. Tax	16,337	17,062	725	104.4
Income+Payroll Taxes	12,615	12,846	231	101.8
Miscellaneous	8,563	8,563	0	100.0
Total Cost of Living	60,000	61,185	1,185	102.0

Note: Figures are based on a single income, four person family with gross annual earnings of $60,000, owning an 1,800 square-foot home, and driving two automobiles worth $22,000 30,000 miles per year.
Source: ERI's Relocation Assessor software database, quarterly effective date 4/1/2000

Cost of Living: Renter

Cost Element	U.S. ($)	City ($)	Differential ($)	Percent of U.S. Average
Consumables	10,486	10,794	308	102.9
Transportation	2,107	2,051	-56	97.3
Health Services	1,632	1,555	-77	95.3
Rent/Utilities/Insurance	9,299	8,034	-1,265	86.4
Income+Payroll Taxes	8,607	9,047	440	105.1
Miscellaneous	7,869	7,869	0	100.0
Total Cost of Living	40,000	39,350	-650	98.4

Note: Figures are based on a single income, three person family with gross annual earnings of $40,000, renting a 1,000 square-foot home, and driving one automobile worth $8,000 12,000 miles per year.
Source: ERI's Relocation Assessor software database, quarterly effective date 4/1/2000

HOUSING

Median Home Prices and Housing Affordability

Area	Median Price[2] 4th Qtr. 1999 ($)	HOI[3] 4th Qtr. 1999	Affordability Rank[4]
MSA[1]	78,000	78.6	35
U.S.	139,000	63.8	–

Note: (1) Metropolitan Statistical Area - see Appendix A for areas included; (2) U.S. figures calculated from the sales of 687,516 new and existing homes in 192 markets; (3) Housing Opportunity Index - percent of homes sold that were within the reach of the median income household at the prevailing mortgage interest rate; (4) Rank is from 1-192 with 1 being most affordable
Source: National Association of Home Builders, Housing Opportunity Index, 4th Quarter 1999

Estimated Home Price

Area	Price ($)
City	135,316
U.S.	135,855

Note: Figures are based on an 1,800 square-foot home
Source: ERI's Relocation Assessor software database, quarterly effective date 4/1/2000

Estimated Rent

Area	Rent ($/month)
City	562
U.S.	651

Note: Figures are based on a 1,000 square-foot home
Source: ERI's Relocation Assessor software database, quarterly effective date 4/1/2000

Median Home Price Projection

It is projected that the median home price in the metropolitan area will increase from $83,016 in 1999 to $105,823 in 2010, an increase of 27.5%
Kiplinger's Personal Finance Magazine, January 2000

RESIDENTIAL UTILITIES

Average Residential Utility Costs

Area	All Electric ($/mth)	Part Electric ($/mth)	Other Energy ($/mth)	Phone ($/mth)
City	n/a	n/a	n/a	n/a
U.S.	99.25	55.47	43.48	20.29

Note: n/a not available
Source: ACCRA, Cost of Living Index, 3rd Quarter 1999

HEALTH CARE

Average Health Care Costs

Area	Hospital ($/day)	Doctor ($/visit)	Dentist ($/visit)
City	n/a	n/a	n/a
U.S.	440.96	53.83	68.42

Note: n/a not available
Source: ACCRA, Cost of Living Index, 3rd Quarter 1999

Distribution of Office-Based Physicians

Area	Family/Gen. Practitioners	Specialists		
		Medical	Surgical	Other
MSA[1]	108	156	135	136

Note: Data as of 12/31/97; (1) Metropolitan Statistical Area - see Appendix A for areas included
Source: American Medical Assn., Physician Characteristics & Distribution in the U.S., 1999

Hospitals

Saginaw has 3 general medical and surgical hospitals, 1 other specialty.
AHA Guide to the Healthcare Field, 1999-2000

EDUCATION

Public School District Statistics

District Name	Num. Sch.	Enroll.	Classroom Teachers	Pupils per Teacher	Minority Pupils (%)	Current Exp.[1] ($/pupil)
Buena Vista School District	5	1,648	114	14.5	n/a	n/a
Saginaw City School District	34	12,850	774	16.6	n/a	n/a
Saginaw ISD	1	n/a	33	0.0	n/a	n/a
Saginaw Twp. Comm. Schools	10	4,764	229	20.8	n/a	n/a
Swan Valley School District	4	1,666	84	19.8	n/a	n/a

Note: Data covers the 1997-1998 school year unless otherwise noted; (1) Data covers fiscal year 1996; SD = School District; ISD = Independent School District; n/a not available
Source: National Center for Education Statistics, Common Core of Data Public Education Agency Universe 1997-98; National Center for Education Statistics, Characteristics of the 100 Largest Public Elementary and Secondary School Districts in the United States: 1997-98, July 1999

Educational Quality

School District	Education Quotient[1]	Graduate Outcome[2]	Community Index[3]	Resource Index[4]
Saginaw School Dist.	n/a	n/a	n/a	n/a

Note: Over 1,000 secondary school districts were rated in terms of educational quality. The scores range from a low of 50 to a high of 150; (1) Combination of the Graduate Outcome, Community and Resource indexes weighted to reflect the greater importance of the Graduate Outcome and Resource Index; (2) Based on graduation rates and college board scores (SAT/ACT); (3) Based on the surrounding community's level of affluence and adult education; (4) Based on teacher salaries, per-pupil expenditures and student-teacher ratios.
Source: Expansion Management, Ratings Issue, 1999

Educational Attainment by Race

Area	High School Graduate (%)					Bachelor's Degree (%)				
	Total	White	Black	Other	Hisp.[2]	Total	White	Black	Other	Hisp.[2]
City	68.6	75.6	58.1	58.0	58.5	9.3	12.1	5.2	4.4	3.8
MSA[1]	76.2	77.8	61.1	66.1	62.6	15.1	15.8	7.7	15.3	6.9
U.S.	75.2	77.9	63.1	60.4	49.8	20.3	21.5	11.4	19.4	9.2

Note: Figures shown cover persons 25 years old and over; (1) Metropolitan Statistical Area -
see Appendix A for areas included; (2) people of Hispanic origin can be of any race
Source: 1990 Census of Population and Housing, Summary Tape File 3C

School Enrollment by Type

Area	Preprimary				Elementary/High School			
	Public		Private		Public		Private	
	Enrollment	%	Enrollment	%	Enrollment	%	Enrollment	%
City	1,468	83.4	292	16.6	13,953	91.3	1,335	8.7
MSA[1]	6,097	68.6	2,790	31.4	68,131	89.2	8,291	10.8
U.S.	2,679,029	59.5	1,824,256	40.5	38,379,689	90.2	4,187,099	9.8

Note: Figures shown cover persons 3 years old and over;
(1) Metropolitan Statistical Area - see Appendix A for areas included
Source: 1990 Census of Population and Housing, Summary Tape File 3C

School Enrollment by Race

Area	Preprimary (%)				Elementary/High School (%)			
	White	Black	Other	Hisp.[1]	White	Black	Other	Hisp.[1]
City	43.1	48.3	8.6	11.4	38.2	50.3	11.5	14.9
MSA[2]	84.2	12.2	3.7	5.3	81.1	13.5	5.4	6.6
U.S.	80.4	12.5	7.1	7.8	74.1	15.6	10.3	12.5

Note: Figures shown cover persons 3 years old and over; (1) people of Hispanic origin can be of any
race; (2) Metropolitan Statistical Area - see Appendix A for areas included
Source: 1990 Census of Population and Housing, Summary Tape File 3C

Higher Education

Two-Year Colleges		Four-Year Colleges		Medical Schools	Law Schools	Voc/ Tech
Public	Private	Public	Private			
0	1	0	0	0	0	3

Source: College Blue Book, Occupational Education, 1999; Medical School Admission Requirements,
1999-2000; Peterson's Guide to Two-Year Colleges, 2000; Peterson's Guide to Four-Year Colleges,
1999; Barron's Guide to Law Schools, 1999

MAJOR EMPLOYERS

Major Employers

Healthsource Saginaw
Michigan Sugar Co.
Second National Bank of Saginaw
U.S. Graphite

Means Industries (automotive stampings)
Saginaw Control & Engineering (fluid power values)
Thomson Saginaw Ball Screw
Wright-K Technology (machinery)

Note: Companies listed are located in the city
Source: D&B Business Rankings, 1999; Ward's Business Directory, 1999; America's Corporate
Families, 1999

PUBLIC SAFETY

Crime Rate

Area	All Crimes	Violent Crimes				Property Crimes		
		Murder	Forcible Rape	Robbery	Aggrav. Assault	Burglary	Larceny -Theft	Motor Vehicle Theft
City	7,618.5	30.7	162.7	348.4	1,390.5	1,992.1	3,107.9	586.3
Suburbs[1]	3,383.7	1.8	40.9	35.3	175.2	520.4	2,432.5	177.6
MSA[2]	4,065.5	6.4	60.5	85.7	370.9	757.3	2,541.3	243.4
U.S.	4,615.5	6.3	34.4	165.2	360.5	862.0	2,728.1	459.0

Note: Crime rate is the number of crimes per 100,000 population; (1) Defined as all areas within the Metropolitan Statistical Area but located outside the central city; (2) Metropolitan Statistical Area - see Appendix A for areas included
Source: FBI Uniform Crime Reports, 1998

RECREATION

Culture and Recreation

Museums	Symphony Orchestras	Opera Companies	Dance Companies	Professional Theatres	Zoos	Pro Sports Teams
2	2	0	0	0	1	0

Source: Musical America, International Directory of the Performing Arts, 1999; Official Museum Directory, 2000; Stern's Performing Arts Directory, 1997; USA Today Four Sport Stadium Guide, 1997; Career Opportunities in Theatre and the Performing Arts, 1999

Library System

The Public Libraries of Saginaw has five branches, holdings of 462,079 volumes, and a budget of $5,789,690 (1997-1998).
American Library Directory, 1999-2000

MEDIA

Newspapers

Name	Type	Freq.	Distribution	Circulation
Saginaw News	General	7x/wk	Area	50,821
The Township Times	General	1x/wk	Local	10,000

Note: Includes newspapers with circulations of 200 or more located in the city;
Source: Burrelle's Media Directory, 1999 Edition

Television Stations

Name	Ch.	Affiliation	Type	Owner
WNEM	n/a	CBST	Commercial	Meredith Corporation
WAQP	49	n/a	Commercial	Tri-State Christian TV Inc.

Note: Stations included broadcast in the Saginaw metro area; n/a not available
Source: Burrelle's Media Directory, 1999 Edition

AM Radio Stations

Call Letters	Freq. (kHz)	Target Audience	Station Format	Music Format
WSGW	790	General	N/T	n/a
WKNX	1250	General	M/N	Oldies
WSAM	1400	General	M/N/S	Adult Standards
WMAX	1440	General	S/T	n/a

Note: Stations included broadcast in the Saginaw metro area; n/a not available
Target Audience: A=Asian; B=Black; C=Christian; E=Ethnic; F=French; G=General; H=Hispanic; M=Men; N=Native American; R=Religious; S=Senior Citizen; W=Women; Y=Young Adult; Z=Children
Station Format: E=Educational; M=Music; N=News; S=Sports; T=Talk
Source: Burrelle's Media Directory, 1999 Edition

FM Radio Stations

Call Letters	Freq. (mHz)	Target Audience	Station Format	Music Format
WKQZ	93.3	General	M/N	AOR/Classic Rock
WHNN	96.1	General	M	Oldies
WKCQ	98.1	General	M	Country
WMJK	100.9	General	M/N/T	Oldies
WIOG	102.5	General	M/N/T	Adult Contemporary
WMJA	104.5	General	M/N/T	Oldies
WGER	106.3	General	M/N/T	Adult Contemporary/Classic Rock
WTLZ	107.1	General	M	Adult Contemporary/Urban Contemporary

Note: Stations included broadcast in the Saginaw metro area
Station Format: E=Educational; M=Music; N=News; S=Sports; T=Talk
Target Audience: A=Asian; B=Black; C=Christian; E=Ethnic; F=French; G=General; H=Hispanic;
M=Men; N=Native American; R=Religious; S=Senior Citizen; W=Women; Y=Young Adult; Z=Children
Music Format: AOR=Album Oriented Rock; MOR=Middle-of-the-Road
Source: Burrelle's Media Directory, 1999 Edition

WEATHER

Temperature/Precipitation/Humidity

	Jan	Feb	Mar	Apr	May	Jun	Jul	Aug	Sep	Oct	Nov	Dec	Yr.
Max. High Temp. (°F)	62	56	68	80	88	97	97	96	100	86	80	61	100
Avg. High Temp. (°F)	32	33	38	53	67	79	82	80	71	62	44	34	56
Avg. Temp. (°F)	25	26	30	43	55	67	70	68	59	51	36	27	46
Avg. Low Temp. (°F)	18	19	23	33	44	56	59	56	48	40	29	21	37
Min. Low Temp. (°F)	-17	-13	-1	11	27	33	42	38	29	20	-3	-11	-17
Avg. Precip. (in.)	2.2	2.2	2.3	3.2	1.8	3.1	3.6	2.5	3.4	3.2	2.4	2.5	32.5
Avg. Snowfall (in.)	9.1	10.8	5.7	3.0	0	0	0	0	0	0	6.0	10.7	45.3
Avg. Rel. Hum. (%)	82	80	77	72	69	71	71	74	75	76	79	82	76

Source: National Climatic Data Center, International Station Meteorological Climate Summary, 3/95

Weather Conditions

Temperature			Precipitation		
0°F & below	32°F & below	90°F & above	0.1 inch or more precip.	1.5 inch or more snow/ice	Thunder-storms
5	153	11	74	10	33

Note: Figures are average number of days per year
Source: National Climatic Data Center, International Station Meteorological Climate Summary, 3/95

AIR & WATER QUALITY

Maximum Pollutant Concentrations

	Particulate Matter (ug/m³)	Carbon Monoxide (ppm)	Sulfur Dioxide (ppm)	Nitrogen Dioxide (ppm)	Ozone (ppm)	Lead (ug/m³)
MSA[1] Level	n/a	n/a	n/a	n/a	n/a	n/a
NAAQS[2]	150	9	0.140	0.053	0.12	1.50
Met NAAQS	n/a	n/a	n/a	n/a	n/a	n/a

Note: (1) Metropolitan Statistical Area - see Appendix A for areas included; (2) National Ambient Air Quality Standards; ppm = parts per million; ug/m³ = micrograms per cubic meter; n/a not available
Source: EPA, National Air Quality and Emissions Trends Report, 1997

Pollutant Standards Index

Data not available.
EPA, National Air Quality and Emissions Trends Report, 1997

Drinking Water

Water System Name	Pop. Served	Primary Water Source Type	Number of Violations in 1998-99	Type of Violation/ Contaminants
Saginaw	69,512	Surface	None	None

Note: Data as of January 19, 2000
Source: EPA, Office of Ground Water and Drinking Water, Safe Drinking Water Information System

Saginaw tap water is alkaline, soft, and fluoridated.
Editor & Publisher Market Guide, 2000

Saint Cloud, Minnesota

Background

Saint Cloud, Minnesota is in the south central section of the state. It is located about 60 miles northwest of Minneapolis. The city is located on the Mississippi River, in a region of rolling terrain. Outside the population centers are numerous lakes and wooded areas and agricultural land.

Saint Cloud is the county seat of Stearns County. It and neighboring communities form a regional metropolitan center for an area that includes Stearns, Benton and Sherburne counties. It is known as a center for entrepreneurial activity, and the region has experienced significant growth. The surrounding region is traditionally agricultural.

Ojibwe and Dakota occupied the region. Saint Cloud was a small settlement that incorporated in 1856. It became a city in 1868. Among early activities, it was originally a fur shipping port. The discovery of granite deposits the region in 1868 led to the development of a major industry, and quarries and related operations are still a major industry. The presence of sand prompted the development of a lens industry, which used the material, and there are numerous optical firms in the area. Other activities include manufacturing, agricultural services and food products, catalogue sales, retail and wholesale trades, services, education and health care, among others.

Colleges in and around Saint Cloud include Saint Cloud State University, Saint Cloud Technical College, College of St. Benedict and St. John's University and Abbey. In addition to activities sponsored by area colleges, cultural activities include the County Sterns Theatrical Company, Minnesota Center Chorale and the Chamber Music Society of Saint Cloud, among others. The Saint Cloud Civic Center is a multi-purpose event facility. Stearns County Heritage Center is a regional history museum.

Parks and preserved areas include Sand Prarie Wildlife Management and Educational Center, Heritage Park and Lake George Eastman Park, among others.

Saint Cloud is governed by a Mayor and a City Council.

General Rankings and Evaluative Comments

■ Saint Cloud was ranked #145 out of 354 metropolitan areas in *Places Rated Almanac*. Criteria: cost of living, climate, crime, transportation, job outlook, education, the arts, health care, and recreation. *Places Rated Almanac, Millennium Edition, 2000*

■ Saint Cloud was selected as one of North America's "Best Small Metro Areas" (population under 250,000). The area ranked #14 out of 20. Criteria: cost of living, climate, crime, transportation, job outlook, education, the arts, health care, and recreation. *Places Rated Almanac, Millennium Edition, 2000*

Business Environment

STATE ECONOMY

State Economic Profile

"Minnesota's economy has been a strong performer in recent years. Job growth has been impressive and the construction market has been booming. As the US economy slows in the near future, Minnesota's growth should decelerate.

Minnesota's tight labor market (1.8% unemployment in Minneapolis-St. Paul) and high rate of job creation have allowed the state to weather several layoffs. 3M, Cargill, and Honeywell have all released significant numbers of workers. And while the Northwest strike temporarily hit Minnesota's economy, other sectors have more than offset these concerns.

Minnesota, specifically Minneapolis-St. Paul, experienced a major boom in residential and commercial building in 1998. The 16,811 single-family permits issued in 1998 was the highest level in over a decade. Construction employment increased 6.8% in Minneapolis-St. Paul in 1998. Driving this boom is the impressive levels of price appreciation witnessed in 1998 and the thin inventory of homes for sale. The large volume currently being built will help to moderate price appreciation in 2000.

Among its Midwestern neighbors, Minnesota alone has actually attracted residents from other states. Net migration has been around 10,000 for several years, helping to ease tightness in the labor market and fuel the housing market.

Minnesota will continue to be among the strongest performing Plains state. Labor shortages and the high cost of doing business, however, will limit its growth to below the national average. Most of the action will continue to be concentrated in Minneapolis-St. Paul."
National Association of Realtors, Economic Profiles: The Fifty States and the District of Columbia, http://nar.realtor.com/databank/profiles.htm

EXPORTS

Total Export Sales

Area	1995 ($000)	1996 ($000)	1997 ($000)	1998 ($000)	% Chg. 1995-98	% Chg. 1997-98
MSA[1]	n/a	n/a	n/a	n/a	n/a	n/a
U.S.	583,030,524	622,827,063	687,597,999	680,474,251	16.7	-1.0

Note: (1) Metropolitan Statistical Area - see Appendix A for areas included
Source: U.S. Department of Commerce, International Trade Association, Metropolitan Area Exports: An Export Performance Report on Over 250 U.S. Cities, November 10, 1999

CITY FINANCES

City Government Finances

Component	1995 ($million)	1995 (per capita $)
Revenue	57.5	1,132
Expenditure	57.4	1,130
Debt Outstanding	260.1	5,122

Source: 1999 County and City Extra, Annual Metro, City, and County Data Book

City Government Revenue by Source

Source	1995 ($million)	1995 (per capita $)
Intergovernmental	13.3	261
Taxes	15.1	298
Property	11.7	231
Sales and Gross Receipts	2.5	51

Source: 1999 County and City Extra, Annual Metro, City, and County Data Book

City Government Expenditures by Function

Function	1995 ($million)	1995 (per capita $)	1995 (%)
Public Welfare	0.0	0	0.0
Highways	8.7	171	15.2
Parking Facilities	0.4	9	0.8
Education	0.0	0	0.0
Health and Hospitals	0.8	16	1.5
Police Protection	5.5	108	9.6
Sewerage and Sanitation	4.6	91	8.1
Parks and Recreation	4.7	92	8.2
Housing and Community Development	1.4	29	2.6
Interest on Debt	16.8	331	29.3

Source: 1999 County and City Extra, Annual Metro, City, and County Data Book

Municipal Bond Ratings

Area	Moody's
City	A1 (1998)

Source: Mergent Bond Record, 2/2000

POPULATION

Population Growth

Area	1980 Census	1990 Census	1999 Estimate	2004 Projection	Population Growth (%) 1990-1999	Population Growth (%) 1999-2004
City	42,566	48,812	50,525	51,254	3.5	1.4
MSA[1]	163,256	190,921	163,298	168,480	-14.5	3.2
U.S.	226,545,805	248,765,170	272,212,864	283,625,312	9.4	4.2

Note: (1) Metropolitan Statistical Area - see Appendix A for areas included
Source: 1990 Census of Population and Housing, Summary Tape File 3C; Claritas, Inc.

Number of Households and Average Household Size

Area	1980 Census	1990 Census	1999 Estimate	2004 Projection	1999 Average Household Size
City	13,881	17,746	19,706	20,493	2.56
MSA[1]	40,386	64,335	58,808	62,101	2.78
U.S.	80,389,592	91,993,582	102,048,200	107,302,392	2.67

Note: (1) Metropolitan Statistical Area - see Appendix A for areas included
Source: 1990 Census of Population and Housing, Summary Tape File 3C; Claritas, Inc.

Race/Ethnicity of City Population

Race/Ethnicity	1990 Census Population	1990 Census %	1999 Estimate Population	1999 Estimate %	% Change 1990-1999
White, Non-Hispanic	47,190	96.7	47,952	94.9	1.6
Black, Non-Hispanic	492	1.0	644	1.3	30.9
Asian, Non-Hispanic	406	0.8	1,085	2.1	167.2
Other, Non-Hispanic	441	0.9	356	0.7	-19.3
Hispanic	283	0.6	488	1.0	72.4

Source: 1990 Census of Population and Housing, Summary Tape File 3C; Claritas, Inc.

Race/Ethnicity of Metropolitan Statistical Area Population

Race/Ethnicity	1990 Census		1999 Estimate		% Change 1990-1999
	Population	%	Population	%	
White, Non-Hispanic	187,592	98.3	159,242	97.5	-15.1
Black, Non-Hispanic	750	0.4	681	0.4	-9.2
Asian, Non-Hispanic	769	0.4	1,582	1.0	105.7
Other, Non-Hispanic	890	0.5	582	0.4	-34.6
Hispanic	920	0.5	1,211	0.7	31.6

Note: See Appendix A for areas included in the Metropolitan Statistical Area
Source: 1990 Census of Population and Housing, Summary Tape File 3C; Claritas, Inc.

Ancestry

Area	German	Irish	English	Italian	U.S.	French	Polish	Dutch
City	57.9	11.1	5.1	1.4	1.1	3.8	7.9	1.6
MSA[1]	65.7	10.4	5.1	1.0	1.1	4.7	10.3	1.8
U.S.	23.3	15.6	13.1	5.9	5.3	4.2	3.8	2.5

Note: Figures are percentages and include persons that reported multiple ancestry (eg. if a person reported being Irish and Italian, they were included in both columns); (1) Metropolitan Statistical Area - see Appendix A for areas included
Source: 1990 Census of Population and Housing, Summary Tape File 3C

Median Age

Area	1990 Census	1999 Estimate
City	25.6	30.1
MSA[1]	28.3	31.1
U.S.	32.9	35.7

Note: (1) Metropolitan Statistical Area - see Appendix A for areas included
Source: 1990 Census of Population and Housing, Summary Tape File 3C; Claritas, Inc.

Male/Female Population

Area	Number of Males		Number of Females		Males per 100 Females	
	1990	1999	1990	1999	1990	1999
City	23,955	24,849	24,857	25,676	96.4	96.8
MSA[1]	95,749	81,288	95,172	82,010	100.6	99.1
U.S.	121,172,379	132,803,736	127,537,494	139,409,136	95.0	95.3

Note: (1) Metropolitan Statistical Area - see Appendix A for areas included
Source: 1990 Census of Population, General Population Characteristics; Claritas, Inc.

INCOME

Per Capita/Median/Average Income

Area	Per Capita ($)			Median Household ($)			Average Household ($)		
	1989	1999	% Chg.	1989	1999	% Chg.	1989	1999	% Chg.
City	11,736	17,734	51.1	24,004	31,394	30.8	29,978	42,406	41.5
MSA[1]	11,860	17,588	48.3	29,047	37,236	28.2	34,223	47,419	38.6
U.S.	14,420	21,350	48.1	30,056	40,525	34.8	38,453	56,184	46.1

Note: (1) Metropolitan Statistical Area - see Appendix A for areas included; 1989 data is from the 1990 Census; 1999 data is estimated by Claritas, Inc.
Source: 1990 Census of Population, General Population Characteristics; Claritas, Inc.

Household Income Distribution

Area	Percent of Households Earning								
	Under $5,000	$5,000 -14,999	$15,000 -24,999	$25,000 -34,999	$35,000 -49,999	$50,000 -74,999	$75,000 -99,000	$100,000 -149,999	$150,000 and up
City	3.3	19.1	17.6	15.0	17.5	17.0	5.7	2.8	1.9
MSA[1]	2.9	14.3	15.1	14.2	19.5	20.9	7.2	3.7	2.2
U.S.	3.9	13.3	13.8	12.6	16.2	19.4	9.7	6.6	4.6

Note: Data as of 1999; (1) Metropolitan Statistical Area - see Appendix A for areas included
Source: Claritas, Inc.

Effective Buying Income

Area	Per Capita ($)	Median Household ($)	Average Household ($)
City	13,950	28,887	38,363
MSA[1]	14,176	33,619	41,204
U.S.	17,496	36,603	47,036

Note: Data as of 1/1/2000; (1) Metropolitan Statistical Area - see Appendix A for areas included
Source: Standard Rate & Data Service, Newspaper Advertising Source, March 2000

Effective Household Buying Income Distribution

Area	% of Households Earning						
	$10,000 -$19,999	$20,000 -$34,999	$35,000 -$49,999	$50,000 -$74,999	$75,000 -$99,000	$100,000 -$124,999	$125,000 and up
City	19.9	27.2	17.8	15.3	4.1	1.0	1.6
MSA[1]	16.4	25.6	20.5	19.0	5.2	1.4	1.7
U.S.	15.0	21.6	17.6	19.6	8.4	3.0	3.3

Note: Data as of 1/1/2000; (1) Metropolitan Statistical Area - see Appendix A for areas included
Source: Standard Rate & Data Service, Newspaper Advertising Source, March 2000

Poverty Rates by Age

Area	People of All Ages	People Under 18 Years Old	Related Children Age 5-17 in Families in Poverty
City	14.4	n/a	n/a
County	9.0	9.9	8.7
U.S.	13.8	20.8	18.7

Note: Figures show the percent of people living below the poverty line in 1995. The average poverty threshold was $15,569 for a family of four in 1995; n/a not available
Source: Bureau of the Census, Small Area Income and Poverty Estimates Program; U.S. Department of Housing and Urban Development

EMPLOYMENT

Labor Force and Employment

Area	Civilian Labor Force			Workers Employed		
	Dec. 1998	Dec. 1999	% Chg.	Dec. 1998	Dec. 1999	% Chg.
City	36,436	36,923	1.3	35,670	36,211	1.5
MSA[1]	93,951	95,225	1.4	91,629	93,001	1.5
U.S.	138,297,000	139,941,000	1.2	132,732,000	134,696,000	1.5

Note: Data is not seasonally adjusted and covers workers 16 years of age and older; (1) Metropolitan Statistical Area - see Appendix A for areas included
Source: Bureau of Labor Statistics, http://stats.bls.gov

Unemployment Rate

Area	1999											
	Jan.	Feb.	Mar.	Apr.	May	Jun.	Jul.	Aug.	Sep.	Oct.	Nov.	Dec.
City	3.3	2.8	2.7	2.3	2.3	3.5	3.0	2.6	2.9	2.1	2.0	1.9
MSA[1]	4.1	3.5	3.3	2.5	2.3	3.2	2.7	2.2	2.4	1.8	2.1	2.3
U.S.	4.8	4.7	4.4	4.1	4.0	4.5	4.5	4.2	4.1	3.8	3.8	3.7

Note: Data is not seasonally adjusted and covers workers 16 years of age and older; all figures are percentages; (1) Metropolitan Statistical Area - see Appendix A for areas included
Source: Bureau of Labor Statistics, http://stats.bls.gov

Employment by Industry

Sector	MSA[1]		U.S.
	Number of Employees	Percent of Total	Percent of Total
Services	24,900	26.2	30.2
Retail Trade	22,800	24.0	18.1
Government	14,200	14.9	15.8
Manufacturing	17,300	18.2	14.1
Finance/Insurance/Real Estate	3,500	3.7	5.9
Wholesale Trade	5,000	5.3	5.4
Transportation/Public Utilities	3,600	3.8	5.3
Construction	n/a	n/a	4.8
Mining	n/a	n/a	0.4

Note: Figures cover non-farm employment as of 12/99 and are not seasonally adjusted; (1) Metropolitan Statistical Area - see Appendix A for areas included; n/a not available
Source: Bureau of Labor Statistics, http://stats.bls.gov

Employment by Occupation

Occupation Category	City (%)	MSA[1] (%)	U.S. (%)
White Collar	61.1	51.4	58.1
Executive/Admin./Management	9.2	8.6	12.3
Professional	16.3	12.5	14.1
Technical & Related Support	3.4	3.1	3.7
Sales	14.2	11.2	11.8
Administrative Support/Clerical	18.0	15.9	16.3
Blue Collar	20.0	28.1	26.2
Precision Production/Craft/Repair	6.9	11.6	11.3
Machine Operators/Assem./Insp.	5.6	7.5	6.8
Transportation/Material Movers	3.1	4.5	4.1
Cleaners/Helpers/Laborers	4.4	4.5	3.9
Services	18.6	15.0	13.2
Farming/Forestry/Fishing	0.3	5.5	2.5

Note: Figures cover workers 16 years of age and older; (1) Metropolitan Statistical Area - see Appendix A for areas included
Source: 1990 Census of Population and Housing, Summary Tape File 3C

Occupational Employment Projections: 1996 - 2006

Occupations Expected to Have the Largest Job Growth (ranked by numerical growth)	Fast-Growing Occupations[1] (ranked by percent growth)
1. General managers & top executives	1. Systems analysts
2. Database administrators	2. Desktop publishers
3. Salespersons, retail	3. Personal and home care aides
4. Cashiers	4. Physical therapy assistants and aides
5. Systems analysts	5. Occupational therapy assistants
6. Truck drivers, light	6. Home health aides
7. Home health aides	7. Human services workers
8. Receptionists and information clerks	8. Data processing equipment repairers
9. Computer engineers	9. Paralegals
10. Marketing & sales, supervisors	10. Surgical technologists

Note: Projections cover Minnesota; (1) Excludes occupations with total job growth less than 300
Source: U.S. Department of Labor, Employment and Training Administration, America's Labor Market Information System (ALMIS)

Average Wages

Occupation	$/Hr.	Occupation	$/Hr.
Accountants and Auditors	16.07	Maids and Housekeepers	6.61
Assemblers and Fabricators	-	Maintenance Repairers	12.15
Automotive Mechanics	14.06	Marketing/Advertising/PR Managers	23.61
Bookkeepers	10.05	Nurses, Licensed Practical	12.39
Carpenters	13.32	Nurses, Registered	-
Cashiers	6.75	Nursing Aides/Orderlies/Attendants	8.42
Clerks, General Office	10.08	Physicians and Surgeons	-
Clerks, Shipping/Receiving/Traffic	11.21	Receptionists/Information Clerks	8.61
Computer Programmers	22.37	Sales Reps., Exc. Scientific/Retail	25.79
Computer Support Specialists	14.89	Sales Reps., Scientific, Exc. Retail	19.89
Cooks, Restaurant	7.72	Salespersons, Retail	8.89
Electricians	16.89	Secretaries, Except Legal/Medical	10.31
Financial Managers	23.95	Stock Clerks, Sales Floor	6.81
First-Line Supervisors/Mgrs., Sales	16.00	Systems Analysts	26.96
Food Preparation Workers	6.96	Teacher Aides	8.56
General Managers/Top Executives	23.56	Teachers, Elementary School	18.40
Guards	11.64	Teachers, Secondary School	18.38
Hand Packers	8.42	Telemarketers	8.92
Janitors and Cleaners	7.96	Truck Drivers, Heavy/Tractor-Trailer	13.05
Laborers, Landscaping	8.69	Truck Drivers, Light	9.80
Lawyers	33.49	Waiters and Waitresses	6.10

Note: Wage data is for 1998 and covers the Metropolitan Statistical Area (see Appendix A for areas included). Hourly wages for elementary and secondary school teachers were calculated by the editors from annual wage data assuming a 40 hour work week; Dashes indicate that data was not available.
Source: Bureau of Labor Statistics, 1998 Metropolitan Area Occupational Employment and Wage Estimates

TAXES

Major State and Local Tax Rates

State Corporate Income (%)	State Personal Income (%)	Residential Property (%)	Sales & Use		State Gasoline (cents/ gallon)	State Cigarette (cents/ pack)
			State (%)	Local (%)		
9.8[a]	5.5 - 8.0	1.18	6.5	None	20.0	48.0

Note: Personal/corporate income, sales, gasoline and cigarette tax rates as of January 2000. Property tax rates as of April 2000; (a) Plus a 5.8% tax on any Alternative Minimum Taxable Income over the base tax
Source: Federation of Tax Administrators, www.taxadmin.org; ERI's Relocation Assessor software database, quarterly effective date 4/1/2000

Total Taxes Per Capita and as a Percent of Income

Area	Per Capita Income ($)	Per Capita Taxes ($)			Percent of Income (%)		
		Total	Federal	State/Local	Total	Federal	State/Local
Minnesota	30,012	11,555	7,601	3,954	38.5	25.3	13.2
U.S.	28,878	10,298	7,026	3,273	35.7	24.3	11.3

Note: Figures are for 1999
Source: Tax Foundation, www.taxfoundation.org

COMMERCIAL UTILITIES

Typical Monthly Electric Bills

Area	Commercial Service ($/month)		Industrial Service ($/month)	
	12 kW demand 1,500 kWh	100 kW demand 30,000 kWh	1,000 kW demand 400,000 kWh	20,000 kW demand 10,000,000 kWh
City	107	1,701	18,915	312,867
U.S.	150	2,174	23,995	508,569

Note: Based on rates in effect January 1, 1999
Source: Edison Electric Institute, Typical Residential, Commercial and Industrial Bills, Winter 1999

TRANSPORTATION

Transportation Statistics

Average minutes to work (1990)	14.0
Interstate highways	I-94; US-10
Bus lines	
In-city (1998)	St. Cloud Metropolitan Transit Commission, 19 buses
Inter-city (1999)	2
Passenger air service	
Airport	Saint Cloud Regional
Airlines (1999)	2
Enplaned passengers (1998)	20,968
Amtrak service	Yes
Motor freight carriers (1999)	18
Major waterways/ports	Mississippi River

Source: FAA DOT/TSC CY1998 ACAIS Database; National Transit Database, 1998; Editor & Publisher Market Guide, 2000; Amtrak National Time Table, Fall 1999/Winter 2000; 1990 Census of Population and Housing, STF 3C; Jane's Urban Transport Systems 1999-2000

Means of Transportation to Work

Area	Car/Truck/Van		Public Transportation			Bicycle	Walked	Other Means	Worked at Home
	Drove Alone	Car-pooled	Bus	Subway	Railroad				
City	73.6	9.4	3.4	0.0	0.0	0.4	10.0	0.8	2.3
MSA[1]	72.7	11.5	1.3	0.0	0.0	0.3	6.9	0.6	6.8
U.S.	73.2	13.4	3.0	1.5	0.5	0.4	3.9	1.2	3.0

Note: Figures shown are percentages and only include workers 16 years of age and older;
(1) Metropolitan Statistical Area - see Appendix A for areas included
Source: 1990 Census of Population and Housing, Summary Tape File 3C

BUSINESSES

Major Business Headquarters

Company Name	1999 Rankings	
	Fortune 500	Forbes 500
No companies listed	-	-

Note: Companies listed are located in the city; dashes indicate no ranking
Fortune 500: Companies that produce a 10-K are ranked 1 to 500 based on 1999 revenue
Forbes 500: Private companies are ranked 1 to 500 based on 1998 revenue
Source: Forbes, December 13, 1999; Fortune, April 17, 2000

HOTELS & MOTELS

Hotels/Motels

Area	Hotels/ Motels	Rooms	Luxury-Level Hotels/Motels		Average Minimum Rates ($)		
			♦♦♦♦	♦♦♦♦♦	♦♦	♦♦♦	♦♦♦♦
City	10	645	0	0	n/a	n/a	n/a
Airport	1	64	0	0	n/a	n/a	n/a
Suburbs	2	348	0	0	n/a	n/a	n/a
Total	13	1,057	0	0	n/a	n/a	n/a

Note: n/a not available; classifications range from one diamond (budget properties with basic amenities) to five diamond (luxury properties).
Source: OAG Business Travel Planner, Winter 1999-2000

Estimated Daily Food and Lodging Costs

Area	Food/Other ($/day)	Average Hotel Cost ($/day)
City	30	55
U.S.	30	55

Source: ERI's Relocation Assessor software database, quarterly effective date 4/1/2000

CONVENTION CENTERS

Convention Centers and Event Sites

Name	Guest Rooms	Meeting Space (sq. ft.)	Capacity (Theatre Style)
Radisson Suite Hotel St. Cloud	103	7,200	300
St. Cloud Civic Center	n/a	n/a	2,200

Note: n/a not available
Source: EventSource.com, 3/15/2000

Living Environment

COST OF LIVING

Cost of Living: Homeowner

Cost Element	U.S. ($)	City ($)	Differential ($)	Percent of U.S. Average
Consumables	14,516	14,405	-111	99.2
Transportation	5,957	6,220	263	104.4
Health Services	2,012	1,982	-30	98.5
Housing/Utilities/Prop. Tax	16,337	19,938	3,601	122.0
Income+Payroll Taxes	12,615	12,925	310	102.5
Miscellaneous	8,563	8,563	0	100.0
Total Cost of Living	60,000	64,033	4,033	106.7

Note: Figures are based on a single income, four person family with gross annual earnings of $60,000, owning an 1,800 square-foot home, and driving two automobiles worth $22,000 30,000 miles per year.
Source: ERI's Relocation Assessor software database, quarterly effective date 4/1/2000

Cost of Living: Renter

Cost Element	U.S. ($)	City ($)	Differential ($)	Percent of U.S. Average
Consumables	10,486	10,433	-53	99.5
Transportation	2,107	2,206	99	104.7
Health Services	1,632	1,612	-20	98.8
Rent/Utilities/Insurance	9,299	12,100	2,801	130.1
Income+Payroll Taxes	8,607	9,135	528	106.1
Miscellaneous	7,869	7,869	0	100.0
Total Cost of Living	40,000	43,355	3,355	108.4

Note: Figures are based on a single income, three person family with gross annual earnings of $40,000, renting a 1,000 square-foot home, and driving one automobile worth $8,000 12,000 miles per year.
Source: ERI's Relocation Assessor software database, quarterly effective date 4/1/2000

HOUSING

Median Home Prices and Housing Affordability

Area	Median Price[2] 4th Qtr. 1999 ($)	HOI[3] 4th Qtr. 1999	Affordability Rank[4]
MSA[1]	n/a	n/a	n/a
U.S.	139,000	63.8	–

Note: (1) Metropolitan Statistical Area - see Appendix A for areas included; (2) U.S. figures calculated from the sales of 687,516 new and existing homes in 192 markets; (3) Housing Opportunity Index - percent of homes sold that were within the reach of the median income household at the prevailing mortgage interest rate; (4) Rank is from 1-192 with 1 being most affordable; n/a not available
Source: National Association of Home Builders, Housing Opportunity Index, 4th Quarter 1999

Estimated Home Price

Area	Price ($)
City	165,678
U.S.	135,855

Note: Figures are based on an 1,800 square-foot home
Source: ERI's Relocation Assessor software database, quarterly effective date 4/1/2000

Estimated Rent

Area	Rent ($/month)
City	894
U.S.	651

Note: Figures are based on a 1,000 square-foot home
Source: ERI's Relocation Assessor software database, quarterly effective date 4/1/2000

Median Home Price Projection

It is projected that the median home price in the metropolitan area will increase from $100,117 in 1999 to $145,467 in 2010, an increase of 45.3%
Kiplinger's Personal Finance Magazine, January 2000

RESIDENTIAL UTILITIES

Average Residential Utility Costs

Area	All Electric ($/mth)	Part Electric ($/mth)	Other Energy ($/mth)	Phone ($/mth)
MSA[1]	–	45.19	48.85	25.35
U.S.	99.25	55.47	43.48	20.29

Note: (1) Metropolitan Statistical Area - see Appendix A for areas included
Source: ACCRA, Cost of Living Index, 3rd Quarter 1999

HEALTH CARE

Average Health Care Costs

Area	Hospital ($/day)	Doctor ($/visit)	Dentist ($/visit)
MSA[1]	492.00	55.83	64.25
U.S.	440.96	53.83	68.42

Note: Hospital—based on a semi-private room; Doctor—based on a general practitioner's routine exam of an established patient; Dentist—based on adult teeth cleaning and periodic oral exam; (1) Metropolitan Statistical Area - see Appendix A for areas included
Source: ACCRA, Cost of Living Index, 3rd Quarter 1999

Distribution of Office-Based Physicians

Area	Family/Gen. Practitioners	Specialists		
		Medical	Surgical	Other
MSA[1]	60	66	69	53

Note: Data as of 12/31/97; (1) Metropolitan Statistical Area - see Appendix A for areas included
Source: American Medical Assn., Physician Characteristics & Distribution in the U.S., 1999

Hospitals

Saint Cloud has 1 general medical and surgical hospital, 1 psychiatric.
AHA Guide to the Healthcare Field, 1999-2000

EDUCATION

Public School District Statistics

District Name	Num. Sch.	Enroll.	Classroom Teachers	Pupils per Teacher	Minority Pupils (%)	Current Exp.[1] ($/pupil)
Central Minnesota Deaf School	1	7	n/a	n/a	n/a	n/a
Saint Cloud	20	11,083	n/a	n/a	n/a	n/a

Note: Data covers the 1997-1998 school year unless otherwise noted; (1) Data covers fiscal year 1996; SD = School District; ISD = Independent School District; n/a not available
Source: National Center for Education Statistics, Common Core of Data Public Education Agency Universe 1997-98; National Center for Education Statistics, Characteristics of the 100 Largest Public Elementary and Secondary School Districts in the United States: 1997-98, July 1999

Educational Quality

School District	Education Quotient[1]	Graduate Outcome[2]	Community Index[3]	Resource Index[4]
Saint Cloud	112	116	104	107

Note: Over 1,000 secondary school districts were rated in terms of educational quality. The scores range from a low of 50 to a high of 150; (1) Combination of the Graduate Outcome, Community and Resource indexes weighted to reflect the greater importance of the Graduate Outcome and Resource Index; (2) Based on graduation rates and college board scores (SAT/ACT); (3) Based on the surrounding community's level of affluence and adult education; (4) Based on teacher salaries, per-pupil expenditures and student-teacher ratios.
Source: Expansion Management, Ratings Issue, 1999

Educational Attainment by Race

Area	High School Graduate (%)					Bachelor's Degree (%)				
	Total	White	Black	Other	Hisp.[2]	Total	White	Black	Other	Hisp.[2]
City	84.4	84.9	59.0	65.0	73.8	25.4	25.5	24.9	12.6	7.8
MSA[1]	79.5	79.6	64.4	67.5	76.0	16.9	16.9	24.9	16.3	24.0
U.S.	75.2	77.9	63.1	60.4	49.8	20.3	21.5	11.4	19.4	9.2

Note: Figures shown cover persons 25 years old and over; (1) Metropolitan Statistical Area - see Appendix A for areas included; (2) people of Hispanic origin can be of any race
Source: 1990 Census of Population and Housing, Summary Tape File 3C

School Enrollment by Type

Area	Preprimary				Elementary/High School			
	Public		Private		Public		Private	
	Enrollment	%	Enrollment	%	Enrollment	%	Enrollment	%
City	522	65.1	280	34.9	5,245	82.6	1,107	17.4
MSA[1]	2,644	72.0	1,026	28.0	32,058	87.8	4,468	12.2
U.S.	2,679,029	59.5	1,824,256	40.5	38,379,689	90.2	4,187,099	9.8

Note: Figures shown cover persons 3 years old and over;
(1) Metropolitan Statistical Area - see Appendix A for areas included
Source: 1990 Census of Population and Housing, Summary Tape File 3C

School Enrollment by Race

Area	Preprimary (%)				Elementary/High School (%)			
	White	Black	Other	Hisp.[1]	White	Black	Other	Hisp.[1]
City	96.5	0.5	3.0	1.5	95.4	0.8	3.8	0.9
MSA[2]	98.6	0.2	1.3	0.9	98.2	0.4	1.4	0.6
U.S.	80.4	12.5	7.1	7.8	74.1	15.6	10.3	12.5

Note: Figures shown cover persons 3 years old and over; (1) people of Hispanic origin can be of any race; (2) Metropolitan Statistical Area - see Appendix A for areas included
Source: 1990 Census of Population and Housing, Summary Tape File 3C

Higher Education

Two-Year Colleges		Four-Year Colleges		Medical Schools	Law Schools	Voc/Tech
Public	Private	Public	Private			
1	1	1	0	0	0	3

Source: College Blue Book, Occupational Education, 1999; Medical School Admission Requirements, 1999-2000; Peterson's Guide to Two-Year Colleges, 2000; Peterson's Guide to Four-Year Colleges, 1999; Barron's Guide to Law Schools, 1999

MAJOR EMPLOYERS

Major Employers

Anderson Trucking Service
G.R. Herbergers
Jack Frost
St. Benedict's Center
Stearns Manufacturing

Bankers System
Gold'n Plump Poultry
Merrill/May Inc. (commercial printing)
St. Cloud Hospital

Note: Companies listed are located in the city
Source: D&B Business Rankings, 1999; Ward's Business Directory, 1999; America's Corporate Families, 1999

PUBLIC SAFETY

Crime Rate

Area	All Crimes	Violent Crimes				Property Crimes		
		Murder	Forcible Rape	Robbery	Aggrav. Assault	Burglary	Larceny -Theft	Motor Vehicle Theft
City	5,851.5	0.0	82.9	100.3	183.2	966.2	4,198.6	320.2
Suburbs[1]	1,470.6	0.0	17.2	0.9	33.4	270.1	1,079.5	69.6
MSA[2]	2,868.0	0.0	38.1	32.6	81.2	492.2	2,074.4	149.5
U.S.	4,615.5	6.3	34.4	165.2	360.5	862.0	2,728.1	459.0

Note: Crime rate is the number of crimes per 100,000 population; (1) Defined as all areas within the Metropolitan Statistical Area but located outside the central city; (2) Metropolitan Statistical Area - see Appendix A for areas included
Source: FBI Uniform Crime Reports, 1998

RECREATION

Culture and Recreation

Museums	Symphony Orchestras	Opera Companies	Dance Companies	Professional Theatres	Zoos	Pro Sports Teams
2	1	1	0	1	0	0

Source: Musical America, International Directory of the Performing Arts, 1999; Official Museum Directory, 2000; Stern's Performing Arts Directory, 1997; USA Today Four Sport Stadium Guide, 1997; Career Opportunities in Theatre and the Performing Arts, 1999

Library System

The Great River Regional Library has no branches, holdings of 735,293 volumes, and a budget of $5,161,378 (1997-1998).
American Library Directory, 1999-2000

MEDIA

Newspapers

Name	Type	Freq.	Distribution	Circulation
Saint Cloud Times	n/a	7x/wk	Area	28,780

Note: Includes newspapers with circulations of 200 or more located in the city; n/a not available
Source: Burrelle's Media Directory, 1999 Edition

Television Stations

Name	Ch.	Affiliation	Type	Owner
No stations listed.				

Note: Stations included broadcast in the Saint Cloud metro area; n/a not available
Source: Burrelle's Media Directory, 1999 Edition

AM Radio Stations

Call Letters	Freq. (kHz)	Target Audience	Station Format	Music Format
KASM	1150	General	M/N/S/T	Country
WJON	1240	General	M/N/S/T	Country
KXSS	1390	General	M	Easy Listening/Oldies
KNSI	1450	General	M/N/T	Adult Contemporary

Note: Stations included broadcast in the Saint Cloud metro area
Target Audience: A=Asian; B=Black; C=Christian; E=Ethnic; F=French; G=General; H=Hispanic; M=Men; N=Native American; R=Religious; S=Senior Citizen; W=Women; Y=Young Adult; Z=Children
Station Format: E=Educational; M=Music; N=News; S=Sports; T=Talk
Source: Burrelle's Media Directory, 1999 Edition

FM Radio Stations

Call Letters	Freq. (mHz)	Target Audience	Station Format	Music Format
KVSC	88.1	General	M/N/S	Alternative/Classic Rock/Jazz/Urban Contemporary
KNCM	88.5	General	N	n/a
KWRV	91.9	General	M	Classical
KMSR	94.3	General	M/N/S	Country
KMXK	94.9	General	M/N	Oldies
WWJO	98.1	General	M	Country
KLZZ	103.7	General	M	Classic Rock
KCLD	104.7	General	M	Adult Contemporary

Note: Stations included broadcast in the Saint Cloud metro area; n/a not available
Station Format: E=Educational; M=Music; N=News; S=Sports; T=Talk
Target Audience: A=Asian; B=Black; C=Christian; E=Ethnic; F=French; G=General; H=Hispanic;
M=Men; N=Native American; R=Religious; S=Senior Citizen; W=Women; Y=Young Adult; Z=Children
Source: Burrelle's Media Directory, 1999 Edition

WEATHER

Temperature/Precipitation/Humidity

	Jan	Feb	Mar	Apr	May	Jun	Jul	Aug	Sep	Oct	Nov	Dec	Yr.
Max. High Temp. (°F)	56	57	79	96	97	102	102	100	98	90	74	60	102
Avg. High Temp. (°F)	19	25	37	55	68	77	82	80	69	58	38	24	53
Avg. Temp. (°F)	9	15	27	44	56	65	71	68	58	47	30	15	42
Avg. Low Temp. (°F)	-1	4	17	32	44	53	59	56	46	35	21	6	31
Min. Low Temp. (°F)	-43	-35	-32	-3	19	33	40	33	18	5	-20	-41	-43
Avg. Precip. (in.)	0.8	0.7	1.4	2.3	3.2	4.7	3.3	4.1	2.9	1.9	1.3	0.8	27.4
Avg. Snowfall (in.)	9	7	10	3	Tr	0	0	0	Tr	1	7	8	45
Avg. Rel. Hum. 6am (%)	77	79	81	81	81	85	88	91	90	85	83	80	83
Avg. Rel. Hum. 3pm (%)	66	63	60	48	46	51	51	53	54	52	64	69	57

Note: Tr = Trace amounts (less than 0.05 inches of rain or less than 0.5 inches of snow)
Source: National Climatic Data Center, International Station Meteorological Climate Summary, 3/95

Weather Conditions

Temperature			Precipitation		
32°F & below	45°F & below	90°F & above	0.01 inch or more precip.	1.5 inch or more snow/ice	Thunder-storms
177	246	11	111	9	43

Note: Figures are average number of days per year
Source: National Climatic Data Center, International Station Meteorological Climate Summary, 3/95

AIR & WATER QUALITY

Maximum Pollutant Concentrations

	Particulate Matter (ug/m³)	Carbon Monoxide (ppm)	Sulfur Dioxide (ppm)	Nitrogen Dioxide (ppm)	Ozone (ppm)	Lead (ug/m³)
MSA[1] Level	n/a	4	n/a	n/a	n/a	n/a
NAAQS[2]	150	9	0.140	0.053	0.12	1.50
Met NAAQS	n/a	Yes	n/a	n/a	n/a	n/a

Note: (1) Metropolitan Statistical Area - see Appendix A for areas included; (2) National Ambient Air Quality Standards; ppm = parts per million; ug/m³ = micrograms per cubic meter; n/a not available
Source: EPA, National Air Quality and Emissions Trends Report, 1997

Pollutant Standards Index

Data not available.
EPA, National Air Quality and Emissions Trends Report, 1997

Drinking Water

Water System Name	Pop. Served	Primary Water Source Type	Number of Violations in 1998-99	Type of Violation/ Contaminants
Saint Cloud	58,253	Surface	None	None

Note: Data as of January 19, 2000
Source: EPA, Office of Ground Water and Drinking Water, Safe Drinking Water Information System

Saint Cloud tap water is soft and fluoridated.
Editor & Publisher Market Guide, 2000

San Luis Obispo, California

Background

San Luis Obispo, California is located along the central California coastline, approximately 200 miles northwest of Los Angeles, 235 miles south of San Francisco and eight miles from the Pacific Ocean. The site is 315 feet above sea level and is known for its spectacular scenic qualities, with mountains around the city.

San Luis Obispo is the seat of San Luis Obispo County. It is a regional commercial and cultural center for mid-coastal California. It is home of California Polytechnic Institute, a major presence in the city and its economy. Cuesta College is also located there. It is also a popular area for tourism, with the nearby ocean, inland lakes and numerous parks, golf courses and historic and cultural attractions. The city has diverse industries, including technology and agriculture, among others. San Luis Obispo is located at the intersection of Highway 101 and scenic Highway 1.

The Chumash and Salinan were among the Native Americans in the region. In 1772 Mission San Luis Obispo de Tolosa was established as one of a chain of Spanish mission settlements in California. It is Spanish for "St. Louis the Bishop," whom it is named after. Under Spanish and subsequent Mexican control, settlement and activities, including cattle ranching, developed. In 1850 California became a state. San Luis Obispo was incorporated 1856 and became a charter city in 1876. California Polytechnic was founded in 1901. The area was hard-hit by the Depression of the 1930s, but the presence of military activity during World War II brought new growth and activity.

Mission Plaza is a redeveloped and historic district based around the original mission which include a popular Farmers Market. Museums include the San Luis Obispo Art Center and San Luis Obispo County Historical Museum. California Polytechnic sponsors a variety of community activities. Local cultural organizations include the annual San Luis Obispo Mozart Festival, San Luis Obispo International Film Festival, Civic Ballet of San Luis Obispo, Pacific Repertory Opera and San Luis Obispo Symphony, among others.

San Luis Obispo is a charter city with home rule, with an elected City Council and Mayor and an appointed City Administrative Officer.

General Rankings and Evaluative Comments

- San Luis Obispo was ranked #196 out of 354 metropolitan areas in *Places Rated Almanac*. Criteria: cost of living, climate, crime, transportation, job outlook, education, the arts, health care, and recreation. *Places Rated Almanac, Millennium Edition, 2000*

- San Luis Obispo was profiled as one of the "great towns" of America. Criteria: scenic appeal, memorable leisure-time features, natural and/or cultural attractions, pleasant weather, quality restaurants and lodgings, and population under 50,000. *The Great Towns of America: A Guide to the 100 Best Getaways for a Vacation or a Lifetime, 1998*

- San Luis Obispo was selected as one of America's best places to retire. Criteria: safety, climate, housing, culture and recreation, social compatibility, affordability, medical care, transportation, and jobs and/or volunteer opportunities. *Where to Retire: America's Best and Most Affordable Places, 1998*

- Cognetics studied 273 metro areas in the United States, ranking them by entrepreneurial activity. San Luis Obispo was ranked #99 out of 134 smaller metro areas. Criteria: Significant Starts (firms started in the last 10 years that still employ at least 5 people) and Young Growers (percent of firms 10 years old or less that grew significantly during the last 4 years). *Cognetics, "Entrepreneurial Hot Spots: The Best Places in America to Start and Grow a Company," 1999*

- San Luis Obispo was given an Outstanding Achievement Award for The Prado Day Center by the U.S Conference of Mayors and Waste Management as part of their 1999 City Livability Awards Program. The program honors mayors and their city governments for developing programs that enhance the quality of life in urban areas. The awards are given annually to ten mayors and their cities—a first-place award and four Outstanding Achievement Awards for cities under 100,000 population, and a first-place and four Outstanding Achievement Awards for cities of 100,000 or more inhabitants.

Business Environment

STATE ECONOMY

State Economic Profile

"California has been on a roll. Its economic strength under almost any measure has surged ahead of the national rate during the last two years. If there was any doubt whether California had climbed out of the hole it was in during the early 1990s, those doubts have since passed. That roll has, however, begun to lose a little of its momentum. In short, California should outpace the nation over the next few years, albeit at a slower rate.

The Asian economic crisis has hit California hard. State's exports to Asia fell nearly 10% over 1998. Most of this decline has been in the high-tech electronics sector, which provided much of the job growth in recent years.

With some over capacity, California's high-tech industries will remain flat until the troubles in Asia have passed. Job growth in several of California's other industries, such as tourism and entertainment, should be strong over the next few years.

Most importantly, California has seen its mass exodus of residents come to an end. While several areas, such as Los Angeles, continue to see domestic losses, offset only by foreign immigrants, most of California will see strong population growth over the next few years.

Housing will remain a mixed bag in California. A shortage of developable land, caused by tight land use controls, will restrain new construction. Residential permits per 1,000 persons should be just over 2, below the national average of 3.5. California will continue to see above average price appreciation in many markets. While remaining a seller's market, several California metro areas will continue to be among the nation's least affordable markets."
National Association of Realtors, Economic Profiles: The Fifty States and the District of Columbia, http://nar.realtor.com/databank/profiles.htm

EXPORTS

Total Export Sales

Area	1995 ($000)	1996 ($000)	1997 ($000)	1998 ($000)	% Chg. 1995-98	% Chg. 1997-98
MSA[1]	n/a	n/a	n/a	n/a	n/a	n/a
U.S.	583,030,524	622,827,063	687,597,999	680,474,251	16.7	-1.0

Note: (1) Metropolitan Statistical Area - see Appendix A for areas included; n/a not available
Source: U.S. Department of Commerce, International Trade Association, Metropolitan Area Exports: An Export Performance Report on Over 250 U.S. Cities, November 10, 1999

CITY FINANCES

City Government Finances

Component	1995 ($million)	1995 (per capita $)
Revenue	n/a	n/a
Expenditure	n/a	n/a
Debt Outstanding	n/a	n/a

Note: n/a not available
Source: 1999 County and City Extra, Annual Metro, City, and County Data Book

City Government Revenue by Source

Source	1995 ($million)	1995 (per capita $)
Intergovernmental	n/a	n/a
Taxes	n/a	n/a
Property	n/a	n/a
Sales and Gross Receipts	n/a	n/a

Note: n/a not available
Source: 1999 County and City Extra, Annual Metro, City, and County Data Book

City Government Expenditures by Function

Function	1995 ($million)	1995 (per capita $)	1995 (%)
Public Welfare	n/a	n/a	n/a
Highways	n/a	n/a	n/a
Parking Facilities	n/a	n/a	n/a
Education	n/a	n/a	n/a
Health and Hospitals	n/a	n/a	n/a
Police Protection	n/a	n/a	n/a
Sewerage and Sanitation	n/a	n/a	n/a
Parks and Recreation	n/a	n/a	n/a
Housing and Community Development	n/a	n/a	n/a
Interest on Debt	n/a	n/a	n/a

Note: n/a not available
Source: 1999 County and City Extra, Annual Metro, City, and County Data Book

Municipal Bond Ratings

Area	Moody's
City	Aaa

Source: Mergent Bond Record, 2/2000

POPULATION

Population Growth

Area	1980 Census	1990 Census	1999 Estimate	2004 Projection	Population Growth (%) 1990-1999	Population Growth (%) 1999-2004
City	34,252	41,958	42,058	43,414	0.2	3.2
MSA[1]	n/a	n/a	237,170	252,050	n/a	6.3
U.S.	226,545,805	248,765,170	272,212,864	283,625,312	9.4	4.2

Note: (1) Metropolitan Statistical Area - see Appendix A for areas included; n/a not available
Source: 1990 Census of Population and Housing, Summary Tape File 3C; Claritas, Inc.

Number of Households and Average Household Size

Area	1980 Census	1990 Census	1999 Estimate	2004 Projection	1999 Average Household Size
City	13,758	16,920	17,173	17,895	2.45
MSA[1]	n/a	n/a	87,954	94,240	2.70
U.S.	80,389,592	91,993,582	102,048,200	107,302,392	2.67

Note: (1) Metropolitan Statistical Area - see Appendix A for areas included; n/a not available
Source: 1990 Census of Population and Housing, Summary Tape File 3C; Claritas, Inc.

Race/Ethnicity of City Population

Race/Ethnicity	1990 Census Population	1990 Census %	1999 Estimate Population	1999 Estimate %	% Change 1990-1999
White, Non-Hispanic	35,059	83.6	32,270	76.7	-8.0
Black, Non-Hispanic	784	1.9	929	2.2	18.5
Asian, Non-Hispanic	2,052	4.9	2,643	6.3	28.8
Other, Non-Hispanic	259	0.6	246	0.6	-5.0
Hispanic	3,804	9.1	5,970	14.2	56.9

Source: 1990 Census of Population and Housing, Summary Tape File 3C; Claritas, Inc.

Race/Ethnicity of Metropolitan Statistical Area Population

Race/Ethnicity	1990 Census		1999 Estimate		% Change 1990-1999
	Population	%	Population	%	
White, Non-Hispanic	n/a	n/a	180,267	76.0	n/a
Black, Non-Hispanic	n/a	n/a	4,769	2.0	n/a
Asian, Non-Hispanic	n/a	n/a	7,815	3.3	n/a
Other, Non-Hispanic	n/a	n/a	2,035	0.9	n/a
Hispanic	n/a	n/a	42,284	17.8	n/a

Note: See Appendix A for areas included in the Metropolitan Statistical Area; n/a not available
Source: 1990 Census of Population and Housing, Summary Tape File 3C; Claritas, Inc.

Ancestry

Area	German	Irish	English	Italian	U.S.	French	Polish	Dutch
City	25.1	17.0	19.2	6.4	1.6	4.4	2.4	2.5
MSA[1]	n/a	n/a	n/a	n/a	n/a	n/a	n/a	n/a
U.S.	23.3	15.6	13.1	5.9	5.3	4.2	3.8	2.5

Note: Figures are percentages and include persons that reported multiple ancestry (eg. if a person reported being Irish and Italian, they were included in both columns); (1) Metropolitan Statistical Area - see Appendix A for areas included; n/a not available
Source: 1990 Census of Population and Housing, Summary Tape File 3C

Median Age

Area	1990 Census	1999 Estimate
City	26.6	31.8
MSA[1]	n/a	35.6
U.S.	32.9	35.7

Note: (1) Metropolitan Statistical Area - see Appendix A for areas included; n/a not available
Source: 1990 Census of Population and Housing, Summary Tape File 3C; Claritas, Inc.

Male/Female Population

Area	Number of Males		Number of Females		Males per 100 Females	
	1990	1999	1990	1999	1990	1999
City	21,617	21,529	20,341	20,529	106.3	104.9
MSA[1]	n/a	121,860	n/a	115,310	n/a	105.7
U.S.	121,172,379	132,803,736	127,537,494	139,409,136	95.0	95.3

Note: (1) Metropolitan Statistical Area - see Appendix A for areas included; n/a not available
Source: 1990 Census of Population, General Population Characteristics; Claritas, Inc.

INCOME

Per Capita/Median/Average Income

Area	Per Capita ($)			Median Household ($)			Average Household ($)		
	1989	1999	% Chg.	1989	1999	% Chg.	1989	1999	% Chg.
City	14,760	20,090	36.1	25,982	32,854	26.4	35,612	47,964	34.7
MSA[1]	n/a	20,927	n/a	n/a	40,182	n/a	n/a	54,172	n/a
U.S.	14,420	21,350	48.1	30,056	40,525	34.8	38,453	56,184	46.1

Note: (1) Metropolitan Statistical Area - see Appendix A for areas included; 1989 data is from the 1990 Census; 1999 data is estimated by Claritas, Inc.; n/a not available
Source: 1990 Census of Population, General Population Characteristics; Claritas, Inc.

Household Income Distribution

Area	Percent of Households Earning								
	Under $5,000	$5,000 -14,999	$15,000 -24,999	$25,000 -34,999	$35,000 -49,999	$50,000 -74,999	$75,000 -99,000	$100,000 -149,999	$150,000 and up
City	4.8	17.5	16.9	13.1	16.1	15.0	7.5	5.7	3.3
MSA[1]	2.6	12.8	14.7	13.5	17.6	20.1	9.0	5.8	3.8
U.S.	3.9	13.3	13.8	12.6	16.2	19.4	9.7	6.6	4.6

Note: Data as of 1999; (1) Metropolitan Statistical Area - see Appendix A for areas included
Source: Claritas, Inc.

Effective Buying Income

Area	Per Capita ($)	Median Household ($)	Average Household ($)
City	15,560	28,179	38,558
MSA[1]	16,482	33,809	44,307
U.S.	17,496	36,603	47,036

Note: Data as of 1/1/2000; (1) Metropolitan Statistical Area - see Appendix A for areas included
Source: Standard Rate & Data Service, Newspaper Advertising Source, March 2000

Effective Household Buying Income Distribution

Area	% of Households Earning						
	$10,000 -$19,999	$20,000 -$34,999	$35,000 -$49,999	$50,000 -$74,999	$75,000 -$99,000	$100,000 -$124,999	$125,000 and up
City	20.3	24.3	15.1	14.4	6.6	2.0	1.9
MSA[1]	17.1	24.3	18.8	18.2	6.7	2.3	2.2
U.S.	15.0	21.6	17.6	19.6	8.4	3.0	3.3

Note: Data as of 1/1/2000; (1) Metropolitan Statistical Area - see Appendix A for areas included
Source: Standard Rate & Data Service, Newspaper Advertising Source, March 2000

Poverty Rates by Age

Area	People of All Ages	People Under 18 Years Old	Related Children Age 5-17 in Families in Poverty
City	30.0	n/a	n/a
County	13.2	16.7	15.2
U.S.	13.8	20.8	18.7

Note: Figures show the percent of people living below the poverty line in 1995. The average poverty threshold was $15,569 for a family of four in 1995; n/a not available
Source: Bureau of the Census, Small Area Income and Poverty Estimates Program; U.S. Department of Housing and Urban Development

EMPLOYMENT

Labor Force and Employment

Area	Civilian Labor Force			Workers Employed		
	Dec. 1998	Dec. 1999	% Chg.	Dec. 1998	Dec. 1999	% Chg.
City	23,614	23,827	0.9	22,666	23,044	1.7
MSA[1]	108,830	109,880	1.0	104,809	106,559	1.7
U.S.	138,297,000	139,941,000	1.2	132,732,000	134,696,000	1.5

Note: Data is not seasonally adjusted and covers workers 16 years of age and older; (1) Metropolitan Statistical Area - see Appendix A for areas included
Source: Bureau of Labor Statistics, http://stats.bls.gov

Unemployment Rate

Area	1999											
	Jan.	Feb.	Mar.	Apr.	May	Jun.	Jul.	Aug.	Sep.	Oct.	Nov.	Dec.
City	4.6	4.1	4.0	3.7	3.4	3.8	4.1	3.5	3.2	2.8	3.2	3.3
MSA[1]	4.2	3.8	3.6	3.4	3.1	3.5	3.8	3.3	2.9	2.6	2.9	3.0
U.S.	4.8	4.7	4.4	4.1	4.0	4.5	4.5	4.2	4.1	3.8	3.8	3.7

Note: Data is not seasonally adjusted and covers workers 16 years of age and older; all figures are percentages; (1) Metropolitan Statistical Area - see Appendix A for areas included
Source: Bureau of Labor Statistics, http://stats.bls.gov

Employment by Industry

Sector	MSA[1]		U.S.
	Number of Employees	Percent of Total	Percent of Total
Services	n/a	n/a	30.2
Retail Trade	n/a	n/a	18.1
Government	n/a	n/a	15.8
Manufacturing	n/a	n/a	14.1
Finance/Insurance/Real Estate	n/a	n/a	5.9
Wholesale Trade	n/a	n/a	5.4
Transportation/Public Utilities	n/a	n/a	5.3
Construction	n/a	n/a	4.8
Mining	n/a	n/a	0.4

Note: Figures cover non-farm employment as of 12/99 and are not seasonally adjusted; (1) Metropolitan Statistical Area - see Appendix A for areas included; n/a not available
Source: Bureau of Labor Statistics, http://stats.bls.gov

Employment by Occupation

Occupation Category	City (%)	MSA[1] (%)	U.S. (%)
White Collar	64.1	n/a	58.1
Executive/Admin./Management	11.4	n/a	12.3
Professional	19.0	n/a	14.1
Technical & Related Support	4.5	n/a	3.7
Sales	13.5	n/a	11.8
Administrative Support/Clerical	15.7	n/a	16.3
Blue Collar	15.1	n/a	26.2
Precision Production/Craft/Repair	7.1	n/a	11.3
Machine Operators/Assem./Insp.	2.6	n/a	6.8
Transportation/Material Movers	1.9	n/a	4.1
Cleaners/Helpers/Laborers	3.4	n/a	3.9
Services	18.6	n/a	13.2
Farming/Forestry/Fishing	2.3	n/a	2.5

Note: Figures cover workers 16 years of age and older; n/a not available
(1) Metropolitan Statistical Area - see Appendix A for areas included
Source: 1990 Census of Population and Housing, Summary Tape File 3C

Occupational Employment Projections: 1996 - 2006

Occupations Expected to Have the Largest Job Growth (ranked by numerical growth)	Fast-Growing Occupations[1] (ranked by percent growth)
1. Cashiers	1. Home health aides
2. General managers & top executives	2. Physical therapy assistants and aides
3. Teachers aides, clerical & paraprofess.	3. Occupational therapy assistants
4. Salespersons, retail	4. Personal and home care aides
5. Truck drivers, light	5. Plasterers
6. Guards	6. Occupational therapists
7. Receptionists and information clerks	7. Teachers, special education
8. General office clerks	8. Bricklayers and stone masons
9. Food service workers	9. Medical assistants
10. Systems analysts	10. Ceiling tile installers/acoust. carpenters

Note: Projections cover California; (1) Excludes occupations with total job growth less than 300
Source: U.S. Department of Labor, Employment and Training Administration, America's Labor Market Information System (ALMIS)

Average Wages

Occupation	$/Hr.	Occupation	$/Hr.
Accountants and Auditors	18.79	Maids and Housekeepers	6.84
Assemblers and Fabricators	9.23	Maintenance Repairers	11.07
Automotive Mechanics	15.45	Marketing/Advertising/PR Managers	19.44
Bookkeepers	11.56	Nurses, Licensed Practical	14.44
Carpenters	17.96	Nurses, Registered	21.94
Cashiers	9.13	Nursing Aides/Orderlies/Attendants	7.57
Clerks, General Office	9.41	Physicians and Surgeons	51.89
Clerks, Shipping/Receiving/Traffic	11.21	Receptionists/Information Clerks	8.51
Computer Programmers	21.85	Sales Reps., Exc. Scientific/Retail	17.36
Computer Support Specialists	14.23	Sales Reps., Scientific, Exc. Retail	20.23
Cooks, Restaurant	8.25	Salespersons, Retail	8.21
Electricians	17.81	Secretaries, Except Legal/Medical	11.66
Financial Managers	25.56	Stock Clerks, Sales Floor	10.05
First-Line Supervisors/Mgrs., Sales	15.16	Systems Analysts	20.97
Food Preparation Workers	7.29	Teacher Aides	9.52
General Managers/Top Executives	26.31	Teachers, Elementary School	20.22
Guards	10.63	Teachers, Secondary School	21.07
Hand Packers	7.40	Telemarketers	10.78
Janitors and Cleaners	8.91	Truck Drivers, Heavy/Tractor-Trailer	14.24
Laborers, Landscaping	9.30	Truck Drivers, Light	10.29
Lawyers	37.00	Waiters and Waitresses	5.99

Note: Wage data is for 1998 and covers the Metropolitan Statistical Area (see Appendix A for areas included). Hourly wages for elementary and secondary school teachers were calculated by the editors from annual wage data assuming a 40 hour work week; Dashes indicate that data was not available.
Source: Bureau of Labor Statistics, 1998 Metropolitan Area Occupational Employment and Wage Estimates

TAXES

Major State and Local Tax Rates

State Corporate Income (%)	State Personal Income (%)	Residential Property (%)	Sales & Use		State Gasoline (cents/ gallon)	State Cigarette (cents/ pack)
			State (%)	Local (%)		
8.84[a]	1.0 - 9.3	1.10	6.0	1.25	18.0[b]	87.0

Note: Personal/corporate income, sales, gasoline and cigarette tax rates as of January 2000.
Property tax rates as of April 2000; (a) Minimum tax is $800. The tax rate on S-Corporations is 1.5% (3.5% for banks); (b) Does not include local option tax
Source: Federation of Tax Administrators, www.taxadmin.org; ERI's Relocation Assessor software database, quarterly effective date 4/1/2000

Total Taxes Per Capita and as a Percent of Income

Area	Per Capita Income ($)	Per Capita Taxes ($)			Percent of Income (%)		
		Total	Federal	State/Local	Total	Federal	State/Local
California	30,415	10,875	7,438	3,437	35.8	24.5	11.3
U.S.	28,878	10,298	7,026	3,273	35.7	24.3	11.3

Note: Figures are for 1999
Source: Tax Foundation, www.taxfoundation.org

COMMERCIAL UTILITIES

Typical Monthly Electric Bills

Area	Commercial Service ($/month)		Industrial Service ($/month)	
	12 kW demand 1,500 kWh	100 kW demand 30,000 kWh	1,000 kW demand 400,000 kWh	20,000 kW demand 10,000,000 kWh
City	161	2,424	27,278	283,902
U.S.	150	2,174	23,995	508,569

Note: Based on rates in effect January 1, 1999
Source: Edison Electric Institute, Typical Residential, Commercial and Industrial Bills, Winter 1999

TRANSPORTATION

Transportation Statistics

Average minutes to work (1990)	13.2
Interstate highways	US-101
Bus lines	
In-city (1998)	San Luis Obispo Transit, 10 buses
Inter-city (1999)	1
Passenger air service	
Airport	San Luis Obispo County-McChesney Field
Airlines (1999)	3
Enplaned passengers (1998)	137,247
Amtrak service	Yes
Motor freight carriers (1999)	2
Major waterways/ports	None

Source: FAA DOT/TSC CY1998 ACAIS Database; National Transit Database, 1998; Editor & Publisher Market Guide, 2000; Amtrak National Time Table, Fall 1999/Winter 2000; 1990 Census of Population and Housing, STF 3C; Jane's Urban Transport Systems 1999-2000

Means of Transportation to Work

Area	Car/Truck/Van		Public Transportation			Bicycle	Walked	Other Means	Worked at Home
	Drove Alone	Car-pooled	Bus	Subway	Railroad				
City	71.7	8.7	1.9	0.0	0.0	4.7	7.4	3.1	2.5
MSA[1]	n/a	n/a	n/a	n/a	n/a	n/a	n/a	n/a	n/a
U.S.	73.2	13.4	3.0	1.5	0.5	0.4	3.9	1.2	3.0

Note: Figures shown are percentages and only include workers 16 years of age and older;
(1) Metropolitan Statistical Area - see Appendix A for areas included; n/a not available
Source: 1990 Census of Population and Housing, Summary Tape File 3C

BUSINESSES

Major Business Headquarters

Company Name	1999 Rankings	
	Fortune 500	Forbes 500
No companies listed	-	-

Note: Companies listed are located in the city; dashes indicate no ranking
Fortune 500: Companies that produce a 10-K are ranked 1 to 500 based on 1999 revenue
Forbes 500: Private companies are ranked 1 to 500 based on 1998 revenue
Source: Forbes, December 13, 1999; Fortune, April 17, 2000

HOTELS & MOTELS

Hotels/Motels

Area	Hotels/ Motels	Rooms	Luxury-Level Hotels/Motels		Average Minimum Rates ($)		
			♦♦♦♦	♦♦♦♦♦	♦♦	♦♦♦	♦♦♦♦
City	15	1,009	0	0	65	113	n/a
Airport	1	13	0	0	n/a	n/a	n/a
Suburbs	2	169	0	0	n/a	n/a	n/a
Total	18	1,191	0	0	n/a	n/a	n/a

Note: n/a not available; classifications range from one diamond (budget properties with basic amenities) to five diamond (luxury properties).
Source: OAG Business Travel Planner, Winter 1999-2000

Estimated Daily Food and Lodging Costs

Area	Food/Other ($/day)	Average Hotel Cost ($/day)
City	38	79
U.S.	30	55

Source: ERI's Relocation Assessor software database, quarterly effective date 4/1/2000

CONVENTION CENTERS

Convention Centers and Event Sites

Name	Guest Rooms	Meeting Space (sq. ft.)	Capacity (Theatre Style)
Best Western Royal Oak Motor Hotel	99	n/a	200
Christopher Cohan Performing Arts Ctr.	n/a	n/a	1,313
Embassy Suites	196	12,000	600

Note: n/a not available
Source: EventSource.com, 3/15/2000

Living Environment

COST OF LIVING

Cost of Living: Homeowner

Cost Element	U.S. ($)	City ($)	Differential ($)	Percent of U.S. Average
Consumables	14,516	15,847	1,331	109.2
Transportation	5,957	6,606	649	110.9
Health Services	2,012	2,194	182	109.0
Housing/Utilities/Prop. Tax	16,337	26,878	10,541	164.5
Income+Payroll Taxes	12,615	11,433	-1,182	90.6
Miscellaneous	8,563	8,563	0	100.0
Total Cost of Living	60,000	71,521	11,521	119.2

Note: Figures are based on a single income, four person family with gross annual earnings of $60,000, owning an 1,800 square-foot home, and driving two automobiles worth $22,000 30,000 miles per year.
Source: ERI's Relocation Assessor software database, quarterly effective date 4/1/2000

Cost of Living: Renter

Cost Element	U.S. ($)	City ($)	Differential ($)	Percent of U.S. Average
Consumables	10,486	11,551	1,065	110.2
Transportation	2,107	2,359	252	112.0
Health Services	1,632	1,795	163	110.0
Rent/Utilities/Insurance	9,299	12,912	3,613	138.9
Income+Payroll Taxes	8,607	8,392	-215	97.5
Miscellaneous	7,869	7,869	0	100.0
Total Cost of Living	40,000	44,878	4,878	112.2

Note: Figures are based on a single income, three person family with gross annual earnings of $40,000, renting a 1,000 square-foot home, and driving one automobile worth $8,000 12,000 miles per year.
Source: ERI's Relocation Assessor software database, quarterly effective date 4/1/2000

HOUSING

Median Home Prices and Housing Affordability

Area	Median Price[2] 4th Qtr. 1999 ($)	HOI[3] 4th Qtr. 1999	Affordability Rank[4]
MSA[1]	198,000	29.6	186
U.S.	139,000	63.8	–

Note: (1) Metropolitan Statistical Area - see Appendix A for areas included; (2) U.S. figures calculated from the sales of 687,516 new and existing homes in 192 markets; (3) Housing Opportunity Index - percent of homes sold that were within the reach of the median income household at the prevailing mortgage interest rate; (4) Rank is from 1-192 with 1 being most affordable
Source: National Association of Home Builders, Housing Opportunity Index, 4th Quarter 1999

Estimated Home Price

Area	Price ($)
City	235,175
U.S.	135,855

Note: Figures are based on an 1,800 square-foot home
Source: ERI's Relocation Assessor software database, quarterly effective date 4/1/2000

Estimated Rent

Area	Rent ($/month)
City	927
U.S.	651

Note: Figures are based on a 1,000 square-foot home
Source: ERI's Relocation Assessor software database, quarterly effective date 4/1/2000

RESIDENTIAL UTILITIES

Average Residential Utility Costs

Area	All Electric ($/mth)	Part Electric ($/mth)	Other Energy ($/mth)	Phone ($/mth)
City	n/a	n/a	n/a	n/a
U.S.	99.25	55.47	43.48	20.29

Note: n/a not available
Source: ACCRA, Cost of Living Index, 3rd Quarter 1999

HEALTH CARE

Average Health Care Costs

Area	Hospital ($/day)	Doctor ($/visit)	Dentist ($/visit)
City	n/a	n/a	n/a
U.S.	440.96	53.83	68.42

Note: n/a not available
Source: ACCRA, Cost of Living Index, 3rd Quarter 1999

Distribution of Office-Based Physicians

Area	Family/Gen. Practitioners	Specialists		
		Medical	Surgical	Other
MSA[1]	77	114	101	141

Note: Data as of 12/31/97; (1) Metropolitan Statistical Area - see Appendix A for areas included
Source: American Medical Assn., Physician Characteristics & Distribution in the U.S., 1999

Hospitals

San Luis Obispo has 3 general medical and surgical hospitals, 1 other specialty.
AHA Guide to the Healthcare Field, 1999-2000

EDUCATION

Public School District Statistics

District Name	Num. Sch.	Enroll.	Classroom Teachers	Pupils per Teacher	Minority Pupils (%)	Current Exp.[1] ($/pupil)
San Luis Coastal Unified	19	8,609	395	21.8	n/a	n/a

Note: Data covers the 1997-1998 school year unless otherwise noted; (1) Data covers fiscal year 1996; SD = School District; ISD = Independent School District; n/a not available
Source: National Center for Education Statistics, Common Core of Data Public Education Agency Universe 1997-98; National Center for Education Statistics, Characteristics of the 100 Largest Public Elementary and Secondary School Districts in the United States: 1997-98, July 1999

Educational Quality

School District	Education Quotient[1]	Graduate Outcome[2]	Community Index[3]	Resource Index[4]
San Luis Coastal Unified	132	132	119	135

Note: Over 1,000 secondary school districts were rated in terms of educational quality. The scores range from a low of 50 to a high of 150; (1) Combination of the Graduate Outcome, Community and Resource indexes weighted to reflect the greater importance of the Graduate Outcome and Resource Index; (2) Based on graduation rates and college board scores (SAT/ACT); (3) Based on the surrounding community's level of affluence and adult education; (4) Based on teacher salaries, per-pupil expenditures and student-teacher ratios.
Source: Expansion Management, Ratings Issue, 1999

Educational Attainment by Race

Area	High School Graduate (%)					Bachelor's Degree (%)				
	Total	White	Black	Other	Hisp.[2]	Total	White	Black	Other	Hisp.[2]
City	89.0	89.6	89.9	81.6	71.0	34.9	35.8	15.5	28.3	18.8
MSA[1]	n/a	n/a	n/a	n/a	n/a	n/a	n/a	n/a	n/a	n/a
U.S.	75.2	77.9	63.1	60.4	49.8	20.3	21.5	11.4	19.4	9.2

Note: Figures shown cover persons 25 years old and over; (1) Metropolitan Statistical Area -
see Appendix A for areas included; (2) people of Hispanic origin can be of any race; n/a not available
Source: 1990 Census of Population and Housing, Summary Tape File 3C

School Enrollment by Type

Area	Preprimary				Elementary/High School			
	Public		Private		Public		Private	
	Enrollment	%	Enrollment	%	Enrollment	%	Enrollment	%
City	358	54.9	294	45.1	3,346	91.5	309	8.5
MSA[1]	n/a	n/a	n/a	n/a	n/a	n/a	n/a	n/a
U.S.	2,679,029	59.5	1,824,256	40.5	38,379,689	90.2	4,187,099	9.8

Note: Figures shown cover persons 3 years old and over; n/a not available;
(1) Metropolitan Statistical Area - see Appendix A for areas included
Source: 1990 Census of Population and Housing, Summary Tape File 3C

School Enrollment by Race

Area	Preprimary (%)				Elementary/High School (%)			
	White	Black	Other	Hisp.[1]	White	Black	Other	Hisp.[1]
City	92.8	3.4	3.8	9.7	85.3	4.1	10.6	12.4
MSA[2]	n/a	n/a	n/a	n/a	n/a	n/a	n/a	n/a
U.S.	80.4	12.5	7.1	7.8	74.1	15.6	10.3	12.5

Note: Figures shown cover persons 3 years old and over; (1) people of Hispanic origin can be of any
race; (2) Metropolitan Statistical Area - see Appendix A for areas included; n/a not available
Source: 1990 Census of Population and Housing, Summary Tape File 3C

Higher Education

Two-Year Colleges		Four-Year Colleges		Medical Schools	Law Schools	Voc/ Tech
Public	Private	Public	Private			
1	0	1	0	0	0	5

Source: College Blue Book, Occupational Education, 1999; Medical School Admission Requirements,
1999-2000; Peterson's Guide to Two-Year Colleges, 2000; Peterson's Guide to Four-Year Colleges,
1999; Barron's Guide to Law Schools, 1999

MAJOR EMPLOYERS

Major Employers

French Hospital Medical Center	JBL Scientific
Mission Medical Associates of the Central Coast	San Luis Sourdough
Sierra Vista Hospital	Sonic Cable TV of San Luis Obispo
Wings West Airlines	

Note: Companies listed are located in the city
Source: D&B Business Rankings, 1999; Ward's Business Directory, 1999; America's Corporate
Families, 1999

PUBLIC SAFETY

Crime Rate

Area	All Crimes	Violent Crimes				Property Crimes		
		Murder	Forcible Rape	Robbery	Aggrav. Assault	Burglary	Larceny -Theft	Motor Vehicle Theft
City	5,106.0	2.3	87.2	59.7	220.3	947.8	3,520.3	268.5
Suburbs[1]	2,664.6	3.1	46.2	27.5	266.4	581.5	1,618.9	121.0
MSA[2]	3,115.0	3.0	53.8	33.4	257.9	649.1	1,969.7	148.2
U.S.	4,615.5	6.3	34.4	165.2	360.5	862.0	2,728.1	459.0

Note: Crime rate is the number of crimes per 100,000 population; (1) Defined as all areas within the Metropolitan Statistical Area but located outside the central city; (2) Metropolitan Statistical Area - see Appendix A for areas included
Source: FBI Uniform Crime Reports, 1998

RECREATION

Culture and Recreation

Museums	Symphony Orchestras	Opera Companies	Dance Companies	Professional Theatres	Zoos	Pro Sports Teams
2	1	1	0	0	0	0

Source: Musical America, International Directory of the Performing Arts, 1999; Official Museum Directory, 2000; Stern's Performing Arts Directory, 1997; USA Today Four Sport Stadium Guide, 1997; Career Opportunities in Theatre and the Performing Arts, 1999

Library System

The San Luis Obispo City-County Library has 15 branches, holdings of 387,521 volumes, and a budget of $4,000,199 (1996-1997).
American Library Directory, 1999-2000

MEDIA

Newspapers

Name	Type	Freq.	Distribution	Circulation
Mustang Daily	n/a	5x/wk	Camp/Comm	6,000
San Luis Obispo New Times	General	1x/wk	Area	42,000
San Luis Obispo Telegram-Tribune	General	6x/wk	Local	36,000

Note: Includes newspapers with circulations of 200 or more located in the city; n/a not available
Source: Burrelle's Media Directory, 1999 Edition

Television Stations

Name	Ch.	Affiliation	Type	Owner
KSBY	n/a	NBCT	Commercial	SJL Communications

Note: Stations included broadcast in the San Luis Obispo metro area; n/a not available
Source: Burrelle's Media Directory, 1999 Edition

AM Radio Stations

Call Letters	Freq. (kHz)	Target Audience	Station Format	Music Format
KVEC	920	General	N/S/T	n/a
KPRL	1230	General	N/S/T	n/a
KKAL	1280	C/G/M	M/T	Christian
KGLW	1340	General	N/T	n/a
KKJL	1400	General	M/S	Adult Standards

Note: Stations included broadcast in the San Luis Obispo metro area; n/a not available
Target Audience: A=Asian; B=Black; C=Christian; E=Ethnic; F=French; G=General; H=Hispanic; M=Men; N=Native American; R=Religious; S=Senior Citizen; W=Women; Y=Young Adult; Z=Children
Station Format: E=Educational; M=Music; N=News; S=Sports; T=Talk
Source: Burrelle's Media Directory, 1999 Edition

FM Radio Stations

Call Letters	Freq. (mHz)	Target Audience	Station Format	Music Format
KLFF	89.3	Religious	E/M/N	Christian
KCBX	90.1	General	E/M/N	Big Band/Christian/Classical/Country/Jazz
KCPR	91.3	General	M/N/S	Alternative/Big Band/Jazz/Latin/Rhythm & Blues/Urban Contemporary
KDDB	92.5	General	M/N/S	Country
KZOZ	93.3	G/M	M	Classic Rock
KBZK	94.1	General	M	Adult Contemporary
KOTR	94.9	General	M/N/S	Adult Contemporary/Adult Standards/Alternative
KXTZ	95.3	General	M	Alternative/AOR/Classic Rock
KSLY	96.1	General	M	Adult Contemporary
KKJG	98.1	General	M/N/S	Country
KXFM	99.1	General	M	Adult Contemporary
KWWV	99.7	General	M	Top 40
KSTT	101.3	General	M/N/T	Adult Contemporary
KBZX	103.1	General	M	Adult Contemporary
KIQO	104.5	General	M/N/S	Oldies
KGUR	105.3	General	M	Alternative
KWEZ	106.1	General	M	Easy Listening
KQJZ	107.3	n/a	M	Jazz

Note: Stations included broadcast in the San Luis Obispo metro area; n/a not available
Station Format: E=Educational; M=Music; N=News; S=Sports; T=Talk
Target Audience: A=Asian; B=Black; C=Christian; E=Ethnic; F=French; G=General; H=Hispanic; M=Men; N=Native American; R=Religious; S=Senior Citizen; W=Women; Y=Young Adult; Z=Children
Music Format: AOR=Album Oriented Rock; MOR=Middle-of-the-Road
Source: Burrelle's Media Directory, 1999 Edition

WEATHER

Temperature/Precipitation/Humidity

	Jan	Feb	Mar	Apr	May	Jun	Jul	Aug	Sep	Oct	Nov	Dec	Yr.
Max. High Temp. (°F)	83	87	88	97	93	95	104	103	102	103	93	90	104
Avg. High Temp. (°F)	62	63	64	66	68	70	72	72	74	73	70	65	68
Avg. Temp. (°F)	50	51	53	55	57	59	62	62	62	60	56	52	56
Avg. Low Temp. (°F)	38	40	42	44	47	49	52	52	51	47	42	40	45
Min. Low Temp. (°F)	21	24	25	31	31	36	43	43	36	30	25	24	21
Avg. Precip. (in.)	2.3	2.0	1.9	1.2	0.2	0.0	0.0	0.0	0.1	0.5	1.1	2.0	11.3
Avg. Snowfall (in.)	0	0	0	0	0	0	0	0	0	0	0	0	0
Avg. Rel. Hum. (%)	70	74	73	74	76	78	79	79	78	74	66	67	74

Source: National Climatic Data Center, International Station Meteorological Climate Summary, 3/95

Weather Conditions

Temperature			Precipitation		
0°F & below	32°F & below	90°F & above	0.1 inch or more precip.	1.5 inch or more snow/ice	Thunder-storms
0	19	4	29	0	3

Note: Figures are average number of days per year
Source: National Climatic Data Center, International Station Meteorological Climate Summary, 3/95

AIR & WATER QUALITY

Maximum Pollutant Concentrations

	Particulate Matter (ug/m³)	Carbon Monoxide (ppm)	Sulfur Dioxide (ppm)	Nitrogen Dioxide (ppm)	Ozone (ppm)	Lead (ug/m³)
MSA[1] Level	n/a	n/a	n/a	n/a	n/a	n/a
NAAQS[2]	150	9	0.140	0.053	0.12	1.50
Met NAAQS	n/a	n/a	n/a	n/a	n/a	n/a

Note: (1) Metropolitan Statistical Area - see Appendix A for areas included; (2) National Ambient Air Quality Standards; ppm = parts per million; ug/m³ = micrograms per cubic meter; n/a not available
Source: EPA, National Air Quality and Emissions Trends Report, 1997

Pollutant Standards Index

Data not available.
EPA, National Air Quality and Emissions Trends Report, 1997

Drinking Water

Water System Name	Pop. Served	Primary Water Source Type	Number of Violations in 1998-99	Type of Violation/ Contaminants
San Luis Obispo Water Dept.	42,500	Surface	None	None

Note: Data as of January 19, 2000
Source: EPA, Office of Ground Water and Drinking Water, Safe Drinking Water Information System

San Luis Obispo tap water is alkaline, hard, and fluoridated.
Editor & Publisher Market Guide, 2000

Santa Barbara, California

Background

Santa Barbara, California is situated in the southwestern section of the state, on the Santa Barbara Channel at the foot of the Santa Ynez Mountains. It is 92 miles from Los Angeles and 332 miles from San Francisco. The city is the seat of Santa Barbara County.

Santa Barbara remained a sleepy pueblo until late in the 19 Century, when wealthy easterners were drawn by accounts of the city's wonderful climate, health-giving springs and natural beauty. Resort hotels and cultural opportunities blossomed, drawing celebrity visitors from around the globe, including presidents, opera stars and royalty. Douglas Fairbanks and Mary Pickford owned property in the Santa Barbara hills. In 1928, Charlie Chaplin built the Montecito Inn to cater to the Hollywood crowd. Actor Ronald Colman and Alvin Weingand bought the San Ysidro Ranch in 1935, operating it as an exclusive hideaway for friends and guests. Today, many celebrities maintain Santa Barbara residences, finding this a perfect place to escape the glare of Hollywood, less than two hours away.

In addition to tourism, other economic sectors include electronics and aerospace research, assembling of electronic component parts, fishing and mining petroleum and natural from offshore wells. For a short time, Santa Barbara was the film capital of the world. In 1910 before the motion picture industry centralized in Hollywood, the American Film Company opened the Flying A Studio in Santa Barbara, then the largest studio of its kind. More than 1,200 movies, mostly westerns, were made in the studio's ten-year life span.

Until 1542 and the arrival of the Portuguese explorer Juan Cabrillo, the Chumash Indians inhabited the area along the Santa Barbara coast. The Chumash Indians welcomed the Portuguese travelers and in 1782, Spaniard missionary Father Junipero Serra arrived. He and others founded the city of Santa Barbara and the Spaniards governed the area until 1822, when California became a Mexican territory. In 1846, Colonel John Fremont took Santa Barbara for the United States.

Santa Barbara has retained its Spanish, Mexican and Chumash influences. Old buildings still stand, including the original mission and county courthouse. The city is filled with old adobes with quiet courtyards, streets named for historical figures, and picturesque Mediterranean-style architecture inspired by the city's Spanish history.

Cultural and historical opportunities are plentiful in the city, including 76 designated historic landmarks, an impressive line-up of performing arts venues, museums, galleries and restaurants. Santa Barbara boasts nine beaches, from the beautiful Butterfly Beach, in front of the Four Seasons Biltmore, to the surf-ripe Leadbetter Beach, to West Beach with calm swimming waters and lifeguards on duty.

Other attractions include Chase Palm Park, a $5 million, 10-acre playland, and the ocean at large, offering every physical type of water sports from scuba diving to sailing, parasailing, seasonal whale watching, sunset cruises and kayaking. Santa Barbara has one of the largest sailing rental fleets in the world, with vessels ranging from small craft to large yachts.

Santa Barbara is governed by a Mayor and six-member City Council.

General Rankings and Evaluative Comments

- Santa Barbara was ranked #90 out of 354 metropolitan areas in *Places Rated Almanac*. Criteria: cost of living, climate, crime, transportation, job outlook, education, the arts, health care, and recreation. *Places Rated Almanac, Millennium Edition, 2000*

- Santa Barbara was selected as one of America's best places to retire. Criteria: safety, climate, housing, culture and recreation, social compatibility, affordability, medical care, transportation, and jobs and/or volunteer opportunities. *Where to Retire: America's Best and Most Affordable Places, 1998*

- Santa Barbara was selected as one of the best places to retire by *Retirement Places Rated*. Criteria: cost of living, climate, crime, services, working, and leisure living. The city was ranked #31 out of 187. *Retirement Places Rated, 1999*

- *Condé Nast Traveler* polled their readers for travel satisfaction. North American cities were ranked based on the following criteria: people/friendliness, environment/ambiance, cultural enrichment, restaurants, and fun/energy. Santa Barbara appeared in the top 32, ranking number 24. *Condé Nast Traveler, Readers' Choice Poll, May 1999*

- Cognetics studied 273 metro areas in the United States, ranking them by entrepreneurial activity. Santa Barbara was ranked #99 out of 134 smaller metro areas. Criteria: Significant Starts (firms started in the last 10 years that still employ at least 5 people) and Young Growers (percent of firms 10 years old or less that grew significantly during the last 4 years). *Cognetics, "Entrepreneurial Hot Spots: The Best Places in America to Start and Grow a Company," 1999*

- Reliastar Financial Corporation ranked the 125 largest metropolitan areas according to the general financial security of residents. Santa Barbara was ranked #101 out of 125 with a score of -5.0 (the percentage a metropolitan area is above or below the metropolitan norm; a metro area with a score of 10.6 is 10.6% above the metro average). Criteria: Earnings and Wealth Potential (household income, education, net assets, cost of living); Safety Net (health insurance, retirement savings, life insurance, income support programs); Personal Threats (unemployment rate, low-income households, crime rate); Community Economic Vitality (cost of community services, job quality, job creation, housing costs). *Reliastar Financial Corporation, "The Best Cities to Earn and Save Money: A Ranking of the Largest 125 U.S. Cities," 2000 Edition*

Business Environment

STATE ECONOMY

State Economic Profile

"California has been on a roll. Its economic strength under almost any measure has surged ahead of the national rate during the last two years. If there was any doubt whether California had climbed out of the hole it was in during the early 1990s, those doubts have since passed. That roll has, however, begun to lose a little of its momentum. In short, California should outpace the nation over the next few years, albeit at a slower rate.

The Asian economic crisis has hit California hard. State's exports to Asia fell nearly 10% over 1998. Most of this decline has been in the high-tech electronics sector, which provided much of the job growth in recent years.

With some over capacity, California's high-tech industries will remain flat until the troubles in Asia have passed. Job growth in several of California's other industries, such as tourism and entertainment, should be strong over the next few years.

Most importantly, California has seen its mass exodus of residents come to an end. While several areas, such as Los Angeles, continue to see domestic losses, offset only by foreign immigrants, most of California will see strong population growth over the next few years.

Housing will remain a mixed bag in California. A shortage of developable land, caused by tight land use controls, will restrain new construction. Residential permits per 1,000 persons should be just over 2, below the national average of 3.5. California will continue to see above average price appreciation in many markets. While remaining a seller's market, several California metro areas will continue to be among the nation's least affordable markets."
National Association of Realtors, Economic Profiles: The Fifty States and the District of Columbia, http://nar.realtor.com/databank/profiles.htm

EXPORTS

Total Export Sales

Area	1995 ($000)	1996 ($000)	1997 ($000)	1998 ($000)	% Chg. 1995-98	% Chg. 1997-98
MSA[1]	565,199	647,995	623,344	501,280	-11.3	-19.6
U.S.	583,030,524	622,827,063	687,597,999	680,474,251	16.7	-1.0

Note: (1) Metropolitan Statistical Area - see Appendix A for areas included
Source: U.S. Department of Commerce, International Trade Association, Metropolitan Area Exports: An Export Performance Report on Over 250 U.S. Cities, November 10, 1999

CITY FINANCES

City Government Finances

Component	1995 ($million)	1995 (per capita $)
Revenue	97.1	1,134
Expenditure	91.7	1,072
Debt Outstanding	129.7	1,515

Source: 1999 County and City Extra, Annual Metro, City, and County Data Book

City Government Revenue by Source

Source	1995 ($million)	1995 (per capita $)
Intergovernmental	13.7	160
Taxes	45.7	533
Property	14.2	167
Sales and Gross Receipts	28.3	331

Source: 1999 County and City Extra, Annual Metro, City, and County Data Book

City Government Expenditures by Function

Function	1995 ($million)	1995 (per capita $)	1995 (%)
Public Welfare	0.0	0	0.0
Highways	5.3	62	5.8
Parking Facilities	2.4	28	2.7
Education	0.0	0	0.0
Health and Hospitals	0.2	3	0.3
Police Protection	15.6	183	17.1
Sewerage and Sanitation	7.2	84	7.9
Parks and Recreation	7.7	90	8.4
Housing and Community Development	11.0	128	12.0
Interest on Debt	3.6	42	4.0

Source: 1999 County and City Extra, Annual Metro, City, and County Data Book

Municipal Bond Ratings

Area	Moody's
City	Aaa

Source: Mergent Bond Record, 2/2000

POPULATION

Population Growth

Area	1980 Census	1990 Census	1999 Estimate	2004 Projection	Population Growth (%) 1990-1999	Population Growth (%) 1999-2004
City	74,414	85,571	88,998	92,460	4.0	3.9
MSA[1]	298,694	369,608	397,596	418,340	7.6	5.2
U.S.	226,545,805	248,765,170	272,212,864	283,625,312	9.4	4.2

Note: (1) Metropolitan Statistical Area - see Appendix A for areas included
Source: 1990 Census of Population and Housing, Summary Tape File 3C; Claritas, Inc.

Number of Households and Average Household Size

Area	1980 Census	1990 Census	1999 Estimate	2004 Projection	1999 Average Household Size
City	32,575	34,466	35,546	37,110	2.50
MSA[1]	109,314	130,378	138,946	146,885	2.86
U.S.	80,389,592	91,993,582	102,048,200	107,302,392	2.67

Note: (1) Metropolitan Statistical Area - see Appendix A for areas included
Source: 1990 Census of Population and Housing, Summary Tape File 3C; Claritas, Inc.

Race/Ethnicity of City Population

Race/Ethnicity	1990 Census Population	1990 Census %	1999 Estimate Population	1999 Estimate %	% Change 1990-1999
White, Non-Hispanic	54,744	64.0	48,463	54.5	-11.5
Black, Non-Hispanic	2,050	2.4	1,739	2.0	-15.2
Asian, Non-Hispanic	1,836	2.1	2,389	2.7	30.1
Other, Non-Hispanic	441	0.5	525	0.6	19.0
Hispanic	26,500	31.0	35,882	40.3	35.4

Source: 1990 Census of Population and Housing, Summary Tape File 3C; Claritas, Inc.

Race/Ethnicity of Metropolitan Statistical Area Population

Race/Ethnicity	1990 Census Population	%	1999 Estimate Population	%	% Change 1990-1999
White, Non-Hispanic	245,074	66.3	229,654	57.8	-6.3
Black, Non-Hispanic	9,327	2.5	9,638	2.4	3.3
Asian, Non-Hispanic	15,232	4.1	19,373	4.9	27.2
Other, Non-Hispanic	2,891	0.8	2,696	0.7	-6.7
Hispanic	97,084	26.3	136,235	34.3	40.3

Note: See Appendix A for areas included in the Metropolitan Statistical Area
Source: 1990 Census of Population and Housing, Summary Tape File 3C; Claritas, Inc.

Ancestry

Area	German	Irish	English	Italian	U.S.	French	Polish	Dutch
City	17.7	11.8	15.1	5.2	2.0	3.8	2.2	1.8
MSA[1]	20.0	12.9	15.8	4.8	2.1	4.2	2.2	2.3
U.S.	23.3	15.6	13.1	5.9	5.3	4.2	3.8	2.5

Note: Figures are percentages and include persons that reported multiple ancestry (eg. if a person reported being Irish and Italian, they were included in both columns); (1) Metropolitan Statistical Area - see Appendix A for areas included
Source: 1990 Census of Population and Housing, Summary Tape File 3C

Median Age

Area	1990 Census	1999 Estimate
City	33.9	37.4
MSA[1]	31.6	34.7
U.S.	32.9	35.7

Note: (1) Metropolitan Statistical Area - see Appendix A for areas included
Source: 1990 Census of Population and Housing, Summary Tape File 3C; Claritas, Inc.

Male/Female Population

Area	Number of Males 1990	Number of Males 1999	Number of Females 1990	Number of Females 1999	Males per 100 Females 1990	Males per 100 Females 1999
City	41,985	43,796	43,586	45,202	96.3	96.9
MSA[1]	185,606	199,395	184,002	198,201	100.9	100.6
U.S.	121,172,379	132,803,736	127,537,494	139,409,136	95.0	95.3

Note: (1) Metropolitan Statistical Area - see Appendix A for areas included
Source: 1990 Census of Population, General Population Characteristics; Claritas, Inc.

INCOME

Per Capita/Median/Average Income

Area	Per Capita ($) 1989	1999	% Chg.	Median Household ($) 1989	1999	% Chg.	Average Household ($) 1989	1999	% Chg.
City	18,934	26,493	39.9	33,667	45,220	34.3	45,994	65,384	42.2
MSA[1]	17,155	23,978	39.8	35,677	47,017	31.8	47,247	67,262	42.4
U.S.	14,420	21,350	48.1	30,056	40,525	34.8	38,453	56,184	46.1

Note: (1) Metropolitan Statistical Area - see Appendix A for areas included; 1989 data is from the 1990 Census; 1999 data is estimated by Claritas, Inc.
Source: 1990 Census of Population, General Population Characteristics; Claritas, Inc.

Household Income Distribution

Area	Percent of Households Earning								
	Under $5,000	$5,000 -14,999	$15,000 -24,999	$25,000 -34,999	$35,000 -49,999	$50,000 -74,999	$75,000 -99,000	$100,000 -149,999	$150,000 and up
City	2.3	11.2	12.2	12.3	16.3	18.9	10.7	8.8	7.4
MSA[1]	2.5	10.3	12.2	11.4	15.9	20.5	11.6	8.5	7.0
U.S.	3.9	13.3	13.8	12.6	16.2	19.4	9.7	6.6	4.6

Note: Data as of 1999; (1) Metropolitan Statistical Area - see Appendix A for areas included
Source: Claritas, Inc.

Effective Buying Income

Area	Per Capita ($)	Median Household ($)	Average Household ($)
City	18,489	34,700	46,654
MSA[1]	16,959	37,023	49,303
U.S.	17,496	36,603	47,036

Note: Data as of 1/1/2000; (1) Metropolitan Statistical Area - see Appendix A for areas included
Source: Standard Rate & Data Service, Newspaper Advertising Source, March 2000

Effective Household Buying Income Distribution

Area	% of Households Earning						
	$10,000 -$19,999	$20,000 -$34,999	$35,000 -$49,999	$50,000 -$74,999	$75,000 -$99,000	$100,000 -$124,999	$125,000 and up
City	15.7	24.3	17.3	17.4	7.9	2.8	4.1
MSA[1]	15.0	22.6	18.5	19.9	7.6	2.8	3.9
U.S.	15.0	21.6	17.6	19.6	8.4	3.0	3.3

Note: Data as of 1/1/2000; (1) Metropolitan Statistical Area - see Appendix A for areas included
Source: Standard Rate & Data Service, Newspaper Advertising Source, March 2000

Poverty Rates by Age

Area	People of All Ages	People Under 18 Years Old	Related Children Age 5-17 in Families in Poverty
City	14.4	n/a	n/a
County	13.8	19.3	17.8
U.S.	13.8	20.8	18.7

Note: Figures show the percent of people living below the poverty line in 1995. The average poverty threshold was $15,569 for a family of four in 1995; n/a not available
Source: Bureau of the Census, Small Area Income and Poverty Estimates Program; U.S. Department of Housing and Urban Development

EMPLOYMENT

Labor Force and Employment

Area	Civilian Labor Force			Workers Employed		
	Dec. 1998	Dec. 1999	% Chg.	Dec. 1998	Dec. 1999	% Chg.
City	50,306	51,248	1.9	48,295	49,584	2.7
MSA[1]	195,338	198,711	1.7	186,115	191,079	2.7
U.S.	138,297,000	139,941,000	1.2	132,732,000	134,696,000	1.5

Note: Data is not seasonally adjusted and covers workers 16 years of age and older;
(1) Metropolitan Statistical Area - see Appendix A for areas included
Source: Bureau of Labor Statistics, http://stats.bls.gov

Unemployment Rate

Area	1999											
	Jan.	Feb.	Mar.	Apr.	May	Jun.	Jul.	Aug.	Sep.	Oct.	Nov.	Dec.
City	4.7	4.4	4.1	3.5	2.8	3.0	3.0	2.9	3.0	2.7	3.0	3.2
MSA[1]	5.6	5.2	4.9	4.1	3.3	3.6	3.6	3.4	3.5	3.2	3.5	3.8
U.S.	4.8	4.7	4.4	4.1	4.0	4.5	4.5	4.2	4.1	3.8	3.8	3.7

Note: Data is not seasonally adjusted and covers workers 16 years of age and older; all figures are percentages; (1) Metropolitan Statistical Area - see Appendix A for areas included
Source: Bureau of Labor Statistics, http://stats.bls.gov

Employment by Industry

Sector	MSA[1]		U.S.
	Number of Employees	Percent of Total	Percent of Total
Services	51,100	31.3	30.2
Retail Trade	35,100	21.5	18.1
Government	33,000	20.2	15.8
Manufacturing	16,300	10.0	14.1
Finance/Insurance/Real Estate	7,800	4.8	5.9
Wholesale Trade	5,800	3.6	5.4
Transportation/Public Utilities	5,100	3.1	5.3
Construction	8,000	4.9	4.8
Mining	800	0.5	0.4

Note: Figures cover non-farm employment as of 12/99 and are not seasonally adjusted;
(1) Metropolitan Statistical Area - see Appendix A for areas included
Source: Bureau of Labor Statistics, http://stats.bls.gov

Employment by Occupation

Occupation Category	City (%)	MSA[1] (%)	U.S. (%)
White Collar	61.3	59.5	58.1
Executive/Admin./Management	14.1	12.6	12.3
Professional	17.0	16.3	14.1
Technical & Related Support	3.7	3.9	3.7
Sales	11.7	11.5	11.8
Administrative Support/Clerical	14.7	15.2	16.3
Blue Collar	18.6	20.5	26.2
Precision Production/Craft/Repair	10.1	10.7	11.3
Machine Operators/Assem./Insp.	3.7	3.8	6.8
Transportation/Material Movers	1.8	2.7	4.1
Cleaners/Helpers/Laborers	3.0	3.2	3.9
Services	15.8	13.7	13.2
Farming/Forestry/Fishing	4.4	6.3	2.5

Note: Figures cover workers 16 years of age and older;
(1) Metropolitan Statistical Area - see Appendix A for areas included
Source: 1990 Census of Population and Housing, Summary Tape File 3C

Occupational Employment Projections: 1996 - 2006

Occupations Expected to Have the Largest Job Growth (ranked by numerical growth)	Fast-Growing Occupations[1] (ranked by percent growth)
1. Cashiers	1. Home health aides
2. General managers & top executives	2. Physical therapy assistants and aides
3. Teachers aides, clerical & paraprofess.	3. Occupational therapy assistants
4. Salespersons, retail	4. Personal and home care aides
5. Truck drivers, light	5. Plasterers
6. Guards	6. Occupational therapists
7. Receptionists and information clerks	7. Teachers, special education
8. General office clerks	8. Bricklayers and stone masons
9. Food service workers	9. Medical assistants
10. Systems analysts	10. Ceiling tile installers/acoust. carpenters

Note: Projections cover California; (1) Excludes occupations with total job growth less than 300
Source: U.S. Department of Labor, Employment and Training Administration, America's Labor Market Information System (ALMIS)

Average Wages

Occupation	$/Hr.	Occupation	$/Hr.
Accountants and Auditors	20.35	Maids and Housekeepers	6.64
Assemblers and Fabricators	8.53	Maintenance Repairers	12.41
Automotive Mechanics	13.31	Marketing/Advertising/PR Managers	29.57
Bookkeepers	12.89	Nurses, Licensed Practical	15.26
Carpenters	18.62	Nurses, Registered	23.23
Cashiers	8.64	Nursing Aides/Orderlies/Attendants	8.04
Clerks, General Office	10.19	Physicians and Surgeons	55.98
Clerks, Shipping/Receiving/Traffic	11.56	Receptionists/Information Clerks	10.06
Computer Programmers	28.59	Sales Reps., Exc. Scientific/Retail	19.77
Computer Support Specialists	20.41	Sales Reps., Scientific, Exc. Retail	22.70
Cooks, Restaurant	8.95	Salespersons, Retail	8.61
Electricians	19.99	Secretaries, Except Legal/Medical	12.89
Financial Managers	29.11	Stock Clerks, Sales Floor	9.27
First-Line Supervisors/Mgrs., Sales	17.19	Systems Analysts	27.65
Food Preparation Workers	7.13	Teacher Aides	9.46
General Managers/Top Executives	31.87	Teachers, Elementary School	21.38
Guards	7.68	Teachers, Secondary School	22.46
Hand Packers	7.11	Telemarketers	10.80
Janitors and Cleaners	7.94	Truck Drivers, Heavy/Tractor-Trailer	13.60
Laborers, Landscaping	9.33	Truck Drivers, Light	8.89
Lawyers	40.46	Waiters and Waitresses	6.50

Note: Wage data is for 1998 and covers the Metropolitan Statistical Area (see Appendix A for areas included). Hourly wages for elementary and secondary school teachers were calculated by the editors from annual wage data assuming a 40 hour work week; Dashes indicate that data was not available.
Source: Bureau of Labor Statistics, 1998 Metropolitan Area Occupational Employment and Wage Estimates

TAXES

Major State and Local Tax Rates

State Corporate Income (%)	State Personal Income (%)	Residential Property (%)	Sales & Use		State Gasoline (cents/ gallon)	State Cigarette (cents/ pack)
			State (%)	Local (%)		
8.84[a]	1.0 - 9.3	1.02	6.0	1.75	18.0[b]	87.0

Note: Personal/corporate income, sales, gasoline and cigarette tax rates as of January 2000. Property tax rates as of April 2000; (a) Minimum tax is $800. The tax rate on S-Corporations is 1.5% (3.5% for banks); (b) Does not include local option tax
Source: Federation of Tax Administrators, www.taxadmin.org; ERI's Relocation Assessor software database, quarterly effective date 4/1/2000

Total Taxes Per Capita and as a Percent of Income

Area	Per Capita Income ($)	Per Capita Taxes ($)			Percent of Income (%)		
		Total	Federal	State/Local	Total	Federal	State/Local
California	30,415	10,875	7,438	3,437	35.8	24.5	11.3
U.S.	28,878	10,298	7,026	3,273	35.7	24.3	11.3

Note: Figures are for 1999
Source: Tax Foundation, www.taxfoundation.org

COMMERCIAL UTILITIES

Typical Monthly Electric Bills

Area	Commercial Service ($/month)		Industrial Service ($/month)	
	12 kW demand 1,500 kWh	100 kW demand 30,000 kWh	1,000 kW demand 400,000 kWh	20,000 kW demand 10,000,000 kWh
City	172	2,914	28,291	302,935
U.S.	150	2,174	23,995	508,569

Note: Based on rates in effect January 1, 1999
Source: Edison Electric Institute, Typical Residential, Commercial and Industrial Bills, Winter 1999

TRANSPORTATION

Transportation Statistics

Average minutes to work (1990)	15.9
Interstate highways	US-101
Bus lines	
In-city (1998)	Santa Barbara Metropolitan Transit District, 62 buses
Inter-city (1999)	1
Passenger air service	
Airport	Santa Barbara Municipal
Airlines (1999)	6
Enplaned passengers (1998)	406,199
Amtrak service	Yes
Motor freight carriers (1999)	7
Major waterways/ports	Santa Barbara Channel

Source: FAA DOT/TSC CY1998 ACAIS Database; National Transit Database, 1998; Editor & Publisher Market Guide, 2000; Amtrak National Time Table, Fall 1999/Winter 2000; 1990 Census of Population and Housing, STF 3C; Jane's Urban Transport Systems 1999-2000

Means of Transportation to Work

Area	Car/Truck/Van		Public Transportation			Bicycle	Walked	Other Means	Worked at Home
	Drove Alone	Car-pooled	Bus	Subway	Railroad				
City	68.2	13.1	3.8	0.0	0.0	3.2	5.9	1.8	4.1
MSA[1]	70.4	14.7	1.8	0.0	0.0	3.3	4.5	1.6	3.7
U.S.	73.2	13.4	3.0	1.5	0.5	0.4	3.9	1.2	3.0

Note: Figures shown are percentages and only include workers 16 years of age and older;
(1) Metropolitan Statistical Area - see Appendix A for areas included
Source: 1990 Census of Population and Housing, Summary Tape File 3C

BUSINESSES

Major Business Headquarters

Company Name	1999 Rankings	
	Fortune 500	Forbes 500
Tenet Healthcare	158	-

Note: Companies listed are located in the city; dashes indicate no ranking
Fortune 500: Companies that produce a 10-K are ranked 1 to 500 based on 1999 revenue
Forbes 500: Private companies are ranked 1 to 500 based on 1998 revenue
Source: Forbes, December 13, 1999; Fortune, April 17, 2000

HOTELS & MOTELS

Hotels/Motels

Area	Hotels/Motels	Rooms	Luxury-Level Hotels/Motels		Average Minimum Rates ($)		
			♦♦♦♦	♦♦♦♦♦	♦♦	♦♦♦	♦♦♦♦
City	40	2,767	1	0	81	158	405
Airport	3	126	0	0	n/a	n/a	n/a
Suburbs	1	126	0	0	n/a	n/a	n/a
Total	44	3,019	1	0	n/a	n/a	n/a

Note: n/a not available; classifications range from one diamond (budget properties with basic amenities) to five diamond (luxury properties).
Source: OAG Business Travel Planner, Winter 1999-2000

Estimated Daily Food and Lodging Costs

Area	Food/Other ($/day)	Average Hotel Cost ($/day)
City	38	99
U.S.	30	55

Source: ERI's Relocation Assessor software database, quarterly effective date 4/1/2000

Santa Barbara is home to one of the top 100 hotels in the world according to *Travel & Leisure*: Four Seasons Biltmore (#25). Criteria: value, rooms/ambience, location, facilities/activities and service. *Travel & Leisure, 1999 World's Best Awards, Best Hotels and Resorts*

CONVENTION CENTERS

Convention Centers and Event Sites

Name	Guest Rooms	Meeting Space (sq. ft.)	Capacity (Theatre Style)
Bacara Resort & Spa	311	n/a	220
Best Western Beachside Inn	60	n/a	40
Best Western Pepper Tree Inn	150	n/a	100
Best Western South Coast Inn	121	n/a	50
Cathedral Oaks Lodge	126	n/a	0
El Encanto Hotel and Garden Villas	84	660	60
Fess Parker's Doubletree Resort	360	18,000	1,000
Four Seasons Biltmore Resort	217	15,000	500
Harbor View Inn	9	n/a	0
Montecito Inn	60	n/a	6
Orange Tree Inn	48	n/a	0
Pacifica Suites	87	n/a	0
Radisson Hotel Santa Barbara	173	10,000	300
The Hotel Santa Barbara	45	n/a	0
The Sandman Inn	113	1,507	72
The Santa Barbara Inn	71	5,196	125
The Upham	50	1,940	110
Villa Rosa Inn	18	n/a	0

Note: n/a not available
Source: EventSource.com, 3/15/2000

Living Environment

COST OF LIVING

Cost of Living: Homeowner

Cost Element	U.S. ($)	City ($)	Differential ($)	Percent of U.S. Average
Consumables	14,516	15,760	1,244	108.6
Transportation	5,957	6,528	571	109.6
Health Services	2,012	2,235	223	111.1
Housing/Utilities/Prop. Tax	16,337	33,749	17,412	206.6
Income+Payroll Taxes	12,615	10,331	-2,284	81.9
Miscellaneous	8,563	8,563	0	100.0
Total Cost of Living	60,000	77,166	17,166	128.6

Note: Figures are based on a single income, four person family with gross annual earnings of $60,000, owning an 1,800 square-foot home, and driving two automobiles worth $22,000 30,000 miles per year.
Source: ERI's Relocation Assessor software database, quarterly effective date 4/1/2000

Cost of Living: Renter

Cost Element	U.S. ($)	City ($)	Differential ($)	Percent of U.S. Average
Consumables	10,486	11,487	1,001	109.5
Transportation	2,107	2,332	225	110.7
Health Services	1,632	1,829	197	112.1
Rent/Utilities/Insurance	9,299	16,596	7,297	178.5
Income+Payroll Taxes	8,607	8,392	-215	97.5
Miscellaneous	7,869	7,869	0	100.0
Total Cost of Living	40,000	48,505	8,505	121.3

Note: Figures are based on a single income, three person family with gross annual earnings of $40,000, renting a 1,000 square-foot home, and driving one automobile worth $8,000 12,000 miles per year.
Source: ERI's Relocation Assessor software database, quarterly effective date 4/1/2000

HOUSING

Median Home Prices and Housing Affordability

Area	Median Price[2] 4th Qtr. 1999 ($)	HOI[3] 4th Qtr. 1999	Affordability Rank[4]
MSA[1]	190,000	45.3	170
U.S.	139,000	63.8	–

Note: (1) Metropolitan Statistical Area - see Appendix A for areas included; (2) U.S. figures calculated from the sales of 687,516 new and existing homes in 192 markets; (3) Housing Opportunity Index - percent of homes sold that were within the reach of the median income household at the prevailing mortgage interest rate; (4) Rank is from 1-192 with 1 being most affordable
Source: National Association of Home Builders, Housing Opportunity Index, 4th Quarter 1999

Estimated Home Price

Area	Price ($)
City	323,327
U.S.	135,855

Note: Figures are based on an 1,800 square-foot home
Source: ERI's Relocation Assessor software database, quarterly effective date 4/1/2000

Estimated Rent

Area	Rent ($/month)
City	1,271
U.S.	651

Note: Figures are based on a 1,000 square-foot home
Source: ERI's Relocation Assessor software database, quarterly effective date 4/1/2000

Median Home Price Projection

It is projected that the median home price in the metropolitan area will increase from $250,144 in 1999 to $366,436 in 2010, an increase of 46.5%
Kiplinger's Personal Finance Magazine, January 2000

RESIDENTIAL UTILITIES

Average Residential Utility Costs

Area	All Electric ($/mth)	Part Electric ($/mth)	Other Energy ($/mth)	Phone ($/mth)
City	n/a	n/a	n/a	n/a
U.S.	99.25	55.47	43.48	20.29

Note: n/a not available
Source: ACCRA, Cost of Living Index, 3rd Quarter 1999

HEALTH CARE

Average Health Care Costs

Area	Hospital ($/day)	Doctor ($/visit)	Dentist ($/visit)
City	n/a	n/a	n/a
U.S.	440.96	53.83	68.42

Note: n/a not available
Source: ACCRA, Cost of Living Index, 3rd Quarter 1999

Distribution of Office-Based Physicians

Area	Family/Gen. Practitioners	Specialists		
		Medical	Surgical	Other
MSA[1]	110	265	206	226

Note: Data as of 12/31/97; (1) Metropolitan Statistical Area - see Appendix A for areas included
Source: American Medical Assn., Physician Characteristics & Distribution in the U.S., 1999

Hospitals

Santa Barbara has 3 general medical and surgical hospitals, 1 rehabilitation.
AHA Guide to the Healthcare Field, 1999-2000

EDUCATION

Public School District Statistics

District Name	Num. Sch.	Enroll.	Classroom Teachers	Pupils per Teacher	Minority Pupils (%)	Current Exp.[1] ($/pupil)
Cold Spring Elementary	1	205	11	18.6	n/a	n/a
Hope Elementary	3	1,173	61	19.2	n/a	n/a
Montecito Union Elementary	1	522	29	18.0	n/a	n/a
Santa Barbara Elementary	12	6,118	316	19.4	n/a	n/a
Santa Barbara High	11	9,452	429	22.0	n/a	n/a

Note: Data covers the 1997-1998 school year unless otherwise noted; (1) Data covers fiscal year 1996; SD = School District; ISD = Independent School District; n/a not available
Source: National Center for Education Statistics, Common Core of Data Public Education Agency Universe 1997-98; National Center for Education Statistics, Characteristics of the 100 Largest Public Elementary and Secondary School Districts in the United States: 1997-98, July 1999

Educational Quality

School District	Education Quotient[1]	Graduate Outcome[2]	Community Index[3]	Resource Index[4]
Santa Barbara High	133	135	93	137

Note: Over 1,000 secondary school districts were rated in terms of educational quality. The scores range from a low of 50 to a high of 150; (1) Combination of the Graduate Outcome, Community and Resource indexes weighted to reflect the greater importance of the Graduate Outcome and Resource Index; (2) Based on graduation rates and college board scores (SAT/ACT); (3) Based on the surrounding community's level of affluence and adult education; (4) Based on teacher salaries, per-pupil expenditures and student-teacher ratios.
Source: Expansion Management, Ratings Issue, 1999

Educational Attainment by Race

Area	High School Graduate (%)					Bachelor's Degree (%)				
	Total	White	Black	Other	Hisp.[2]	Total	White	Black	Other	Hisp.[2]
City	79.1	85.2	70.7	46.6	44.4	33.1	37.3	19.8	12.3	7.9
MSA[1]	80.0	85.7	81.3	50.5	46.9	26.6	29.6	17.6	12.6	6.9
U.S.	75.2	77.9	63.1	60.4	49.8	20.3	21.5	11.4	19.4	9.2

Note: Figures shown cover persons 25 years old and over; (1) Metropolitan Statistical Area - see Appendix A for areas included; (2) people of Hispanic origin can be of any race
Source: 1990 Census of Population and Housing, Summary Tape File 3C

School Enrollment by Type

Area	Preprimary				Elementary/High School			
	Public		Private		Public		Private	
	Enrollment	%	Enrollment	%	Enrollment	%	Enrollment	%
City	652	59.4	445	40.6	9,339	90.2	1,009	9.8
MSA[1]	3,440	57.0	2,599	43.0	51,285	91.1	5,023	8.9
U.S.	2,679,029	59.5	1,824,256	40.5	38,379,689	90.2	4,187,099	9.8

Note: Figures shown cover persons 3 years old and over;
(1) Metropolitan Statistical Area - see Appendix A for areas included
Source: 1990 Census of Population and Housing, Summary Tape File 3C

School Enrollment by Race

Area	Preprimary (%)				Elementary/High School (%)			
	White	Black	Other	Hisp.[1]	White	Black	Other	Hisp.[1]
City	78.7	1.7	19.6	30.3	60.4	2.9	36.7	55.7
MSA[2]	80.5	1.5	18.0	25.4	67.0	3.5	29.4	40.8
U.S.	80.4	12.5	7.1	7.8	74.1	15.6	10.3	12.5

Note: Figures shown cover persons 3 years old and over; (1) people of Hispanic origin can be of any race; (2) Metropolitan Statistical Area - see Appendix A for areas included
Source: 1990 Census of Population and Housing, Summary Tape File 3C

Higher Education

Two-Year Colleges		Four-Year Colleges		Medical Schools	Law Schools	Voc/ Tech
Public	Private	Public	Private			
1	0	1	1	0	0	8

Source: College Blue Book, Occupational Education, 1999; Medical School Admission Requirements, 1999-2000; Peterson's Guide to Two-Year Colleges, 2000; Peterson's Guide to Four-Year Colleges, 1999; Barron's Guide to Law Schools, 1999

MAJOR EMPLOYERS

Major Employers

Channel Technologies (electrical supplies)
Jordano's (softdrinks)
Mentor Corp. (surgical appliances)
Teknar Corp. (medical apparatus)

Doubletree Inc. of California
Lafayette Co. (ice cream)
Smith Broadcasting Group
Tenet Health Care Corp.

Note: Companies listed are located in the city
Source: D&B Business Rankings, 1999; Ward's Business Directory, 1999; America's Corporate Families, 1999

PUBLIC SAFETY

Crime Rate

Area	All Crimes	Violent Crimes				Property Crimes		
		Murder	Forcible Rape	Robbery	Aggrav. Assault	Burglary	Larceny -Theft	Motor Vehicle Theft
City	3,828.9	2.3	18.1	91.6	460.4	668.5	2,412.7	175.3
Suburbs[1]	2,925.5	2.9	28.7	60.7	353.5	698.3	1,640.5	140.9
MSA[2]	3,127.7	2.8	26.3	67.6	377.4	691.6	1,813.3	148.6
U.S.	4,615.5	6.3	34.4	165.2	360.5	862.0	2,728.1	459.0

Note: Crime rate is the number of crimes per 100,000 population; (1) Defined as all areas within the Metropolitan Statistical Area but located outside the central city; (2) Metropolitan Statistical Area - see Appendix A for areas included
Source: FBI Uniform Crime Reports, 1998

RECREATION

Culture and Recreation

Museums	Symphony Orchestras	Opera Companies	Dance Companies	Professional Theatres	Zoos	Pro Sports Teams
6	2	0	1	1	1	0

Source: Musical America, International Directory of the Performing Arts, 1999; Official Museum Directory, 2000; Stern's Performing Arts Directory, 1997; USA Today Four Sport Stadium Guide, 1997; Career Opportunities in Theatre and the Performing Arts, 1999

Library System

The Santa Barbara Public Library has seven branches, holdings of 367,578 volumes, and a budget of $3,392,295 (1997-1998).
American Library Directory, 1999-2000

MEDIA

Newspapers

Name	Type	Freq.	Distribution	Circulation
Daily Nexus	n/a	5x/wk	Campus	11,000
Santa Barbara Independent	General	1x/wk	Local	40,000
Santa Barbara News-Press	General	7x/wk	Local	49,000

Note: Includes newspapers with circulations of 200 or more located in the city; n/a not available
Source: Burrelle's Media Directory, 1999 Edition

Television Stations

Name	Ch.	Affiliation	Type	Owner
KEYT	n/a	n/a	Commercial	Smith Broadcasting Company Inc.
KTA	n/a	UNIN	Commercial	R & C Enterprises
KCOY	12	CBST	Commercial	Benedict Communications Inc.

Note: Stations included broadcast in the Santa Barbara metro area; n/a not available
Source: Burrelle's Media Directory, 1999 Edition

AM Radio Stations

Call Letters	Freq. (kHz)	Target Audience	Station Format	Music Format
KGDP	660	Religious	T	n/a
KCLL	960	General	M/N/S	Oldies
KTMS	990	General	N/S/T	n/a
KSMA	1240	General	N/S/T	n/a
KZBN	1290	General	M	Adult Standards
KUHL	1440	General	N/T	n/a
KSBQ	1480	Hispanic	M/N/S	Latin
KBKO	1490	Hispanic	E/M/N/S/T	Latin
KTAP	1600	Hispanic	M/N/S	Latin

Note: Stations included broadcast in the Santa Barbara metro area; n/a not available
Target Audience: A=Asian; B=Black; C=Christian; E=Ethnic; F=French; G=General; H=Hispanic;
M=Men; N=Native American; R=Religious; S=Senior Citizen; W=Women; Y=Young Adult; Z=Children
Station Format: E=Educational; M=Music; N=News; S=Sports; T=Talk
Source: Burrelle's Media Directory, 1999 Edition

FM Radio Stations

Call Letters	Freq. (mHz)	Target Audience	Station Format	Music Format
KCSB	91.9	General	E/M/N/S	AOR/Big Band/Jazz/Latin/Rhythm & Blues/Urban Contemporary
KJEE	92.9	G/M	M	Alternative
KDB	93.7	General	M	Classical
KSPE	94.5	Hispanic	M/N/S/T	n/a
KSYV	96.7	General	M/N	Adult Contemporary
KMGQ	97.5	General	M	Jazz
KTYD	99.9	General	M	Classic Rock
KRQK	100.3	Hispanic	M/N/S	Latin
KSBL	101.7	Hispanic	Women	M/N/S
KSNI	102.5	General	M/S	Country
KRUZ	103.3	General	M/N	Adult Contemporary
KBOX	104.1	General	M	Adult Contemporary
KIST	107.7	General	M	Oldies

Note: Stations included broadcast in the Santa Barbara metro area; n/a not available
Station Format: E=Educational; M=Music; N=News; S=Sports; T=Talk
Target Audience: A=Asian; B=Black; C=Christian; E=Ethnic; F=French; G=General; H=Hispanic;
M=Men; N=Native American; R=Religious; S=Senior Citizen; W=Women; Y=Young Adult; Z=Children
Music Format: AOR=Album Oriented Rock; MOR=Middle-of-the-Road
Source: Burrelle's Media Directory, 1999 Edition

WEATHER

Temperature/Precipitation/Humidity

	Jan	Feb	Mar	Apr	May	Jun	Jul	Aug	Sep	Oct	Nov	Dec	Yr.
Max. High Temp. (°F)	86	85	87	94	95	96	101	94	99	99	96	89	101
Avg. High Temp. (°F)	64	64	66	67	70	72	74	74	75	72	70	66	70
Avg. Temp. (°F)	51	53	55	57	60	62	65	65	65	61	57	53	59
Avg. Low Temp. (°F)	39	42	44	48	50	53	56	56	55	50	44	41	48
Min. Low Temp. (°F)	26	31	31	33	39	41	45	43	42	37	30	28	26
Avg. Precip. (in.)	3.3	2.5	2.2	1.4	0.3	0.0	0.1	0.0	0.1	0.3	1.4	2.7	14.1
Avg. Snowfall (in.)	0	0	0	0	0	0	0	0	0	0	0	0	0
Avg. Rel. Hum. (%)	71	68	70	74	72	73	78	78	78	74	70	70	73

Source: National Climatic Data Center, International Station Meteorological Climate Summary, 3/95

Weather Conditions

Temperature			Precipitation		
0°F & below	32°F & below	90°F & above	0.1 inch or more precip.	1.5 inch or more snow/ice	Thunder-storms
0	6	3	33	0	2

Note: Figures are average number of days per year
Source: National Climatic Data Center, International Station Meteorological Climate Summary, 3/95

AIR & WATER QUALITY

Maximum Pollutant Concentrations

	Particulate Matter (ug/m³)	Carbon Monoxide (ppm)	Sulfur Dioxide (ppm)	Nitrogen Dioxide (ppm)	Ozone (ppm)	Lead (ug/m³)
MSA[1] Level	63	4	0.005	0.019	0.11	0.00
NAAQS[2]	150	9	0.140	0.053	0.12	1.50
Met NAAQS	Yes	Yes	Yes	Yes	Yes	Yes

Note: (1) Metropolitan Statistical Area - see Appendix A for areas included; (2) National Ambient Air Quality Standards; ppm = parts per million; ug/m³ = micrograms per cubic meter; n/a not available
Source: EPA, National Air Quality and Emissions Trends Report, 1997

Pollutant Standards Index

Data not available.
EPA, National Air Quality and Emissions Trends Report, 1997

Drinking Water

Water System Name	Pop. Served	Primary Water Source Type	Number of Violations in 1998-99	Type of Violation/ Contaminants
Santa Barbara Water District	95,064	Purchased surface	None	None

Note: Data as of January 19, 2000
Source: EPA, Office of Ground Water and Drinking Water, Safe Drinking Water Information System

Santa Barbara tap water is alkaline, hard, and not fluoridated.
Editor & Publisher Market Guide, 2000

Santa Fe, New Mexico

Background

Santa Fe, New Mexico is located in the north-central section of the state, approximately 60 miles northeast of Albuquerque and 325 miles north of El Paso, Texas. It is on the Santa Fe River, at 7,000 feet elevation, in a valley at the southern Rocky Mountains. The Sangre de Cristo, the Jemez and other mountain ranges are nearby. The large Santa Fe National Forest is near the city.

Santa Fe is the capital of New Mexico and the seat of Santa Fe County. It is the oldest capital city in the United States and a regional trade center. Santa Fe is a shortened version of the original Spanish name for "City of Holy Faith." Modern Santa Fe is also nicknamed "The City Different." The region's heritage and contemporary life reflect its diverse influences, including the Pueblo Indians and Hispanics, who continue to be a significant segment of the region's modern population.

Santa Fe is a prominent center for the arts, a popular tourist destination, based on its diverse attractions and dramatic landscape. Skiing, hiking and other outdoor activities are nearby in the Santa Fe National Forest and other parks and facilities.

In 1607, during Spanish colonization of New Mexico, Santa Fe was established as a mission and settlement at the site of an abandoned ancient Indian village. In 1610, the territorial capital of New Mexico was moved to Santa Fe. In 1680, the region's Pueblo Indians rebelled and pushed out the Spanish, until 1693, when Spanish control was reestablished. After 1821, Mexico's independence from Spain stimulated New Mexico's trade with the United States on the Santa Fe Trail. In 1850, following war with Mexico, the United States gained New Mexico as a territory, with Santa Fe as its capital.

Santa Fe is a longstanding trade and transportation center. In the early 20th Century, the area attracted a community of creative artists, including painter Georgia O'Keefe. In the 1940s, nuclear research facilities were established at nearby Los Alamos. Beginning in the 1960s, Santa Fe attracted a new generation of artists and alternative lifestylers. In the 1980s, the area experienced significant growth, including diversification with biotechnology and other activities. Primary economic sectors today include government, retail and wholesale trades, business and other services, tourism, construction and education. Local arts and crafts, is an important industry.

Santa Fe is the site of prominent performing arts organizations and festivals. Performance series include the Santa Fe Chamber Music Festival, Santa Fe Opera, Desert Choral, Santa Fe Symphony, Santa Fe Stages, Santa Fe Festival Ballet and numerous others. Museums include the Museum of Fine Arts, Museum of Indian Arts and Culture, Wheelwright Museum of the American Indian and Santa Fe Children's Museum, among others.

The region's distinctive adobe buildings are well-known. Many early structures still exist in the city and the surrounding region, including Santa Fe's original 17th Century central Plaza. It includes the Palace of the Governors, built when Santa Fe was founded, and the nation's oldest public building. The area also has experienced significant new development. Local policies encourage new construction to be compatible with the traditional architectural styles and materials.

Schools of higher education are St. John's College, The College of Santa Fe, Southwestern College, Santa Fe Community College and branch campuses of the University of New Mexico and the University of Phoenix.

Santa Fe is governed by an elected Mayor and City Council and a City Manager.

General Rankings and Evaluative Comments

■ Santa Fe was ranked #175 out of 354 metropolitan areas in *Places Rated Almanac*. Criteria: cost of living, climate, crime, transportation, job outlook, education, the arts, health care, and recreation. *Places Rated Almanac, Millennium Edition, 2000*

■ Santa Fe was selected as one of America's best small art towns. The city was ranked #2 out of 100. Criteria: easy and affordable access to the visual arts, performing arts and music, strong sense of community, low crime rate, and full-time population less than 65,000. *The 100 Best Small Art Towns in America: Discover Creative Communities, Fresh Air, and Affordable Living, 1998*

■ Santa Fe was selected as one of America's best places to retire. Criteria: safety, climate, housing, culture and recreation, social compatibility, affordability, medical care, transportation, and jobs and/or volunteer opportunities. *Where to Retire: America's Best and Most Affordable Places, 1998*

■ Santa Fe was selected as one of the best places to retire by *Retirement Places Rated*. Criteria: cost of living, climate, crime, services, working, and leisure living. The city was ranked #13 out of 187. *Retirement Places Rated, 1999*

■ Santa Fe was selected as one of "America's Best Towns to Raise an Outdoor Family" by *Outdoor Explorer* magazine. Criteria: easy access to the outdoors, quality education and health care, affordable housing, favorable employment opportunities, and low crime rates. The city was ranked #20 out of 25. *Outdoor Explorer, Summer 1999*

■ Santa Fe appeared on *Travel & Leisure's* list of the world's 100 best cities. It was ranked #31 in the world. Criteria: activities/attractions, culture/arts, restaurants/food, people, and value. *Travel & Leisure, 1999 World's Best Awards*

■ *Condé Nast Traveler* polled their readers for travel satisfaction. North American cities were ranked based on the following criteria: people/friendliness, environment/ambiance, cultural enrichment, restaurants, and fun/energy. Santa Fe appeared in the top 32, ranking number 6. *Condé Nast Traveler, Readers' Choice Poll, May 1999*

Business Environment

STATE ECONOMY

State Economic Profile

"New Mexico's reliance on natural resources and federal spending has become a drag on the state economy as commodity prices remain weak and years of federal cutbacks take hold. New Mexico's unemployment rate is currently among the highest in the nation. Its undiversified economy has made it extremely vulnerable to the disruption of a few key sectors. However, New Mexico's high quality of life and affordable business and living environment continue to attract residents, tourists and businesses.

Oil producers account for 4% of New Mexico's output. Weak oil prices have squeezed profits and forced some producers to curtail production. Recent price increases are unlikely to prolong the life of New Mexico's oil industry. Many of the producers are small, high-cost producers, and oil prices are projected to fall from their current levels. Similarly, New Mexico's metals producers have undergone layoffs and curtailed production. The recent layoffs by Phelps Dodge Mining Company is only representative of the industry's troubles. Further declines in metals prices are likely in 2000.

Government's share of New Mexico employment declined in 1998 to about 25% (still far above the US average). Much of this employment is concentrated around the defense industry. Cutbacks in defense-related research have forced some firms, such as Sandia National Laboratories, to look for commercial business. Sandia has teamed with the city of Albuquerque and University of New Mexico in the development of a science and technology park. If these efforts prove successful, the Albuquerque economy may see a rebirth. In addition, New Mexico's low cost of doing business and increasing trade with Mexico are helping to build a stronger economic foundation. Current efforts to diversify the economy may yield dividends in the years ahead." *National Association of Realtors, Economic Profiles: The Fifty States and the District of Columbia, http://nar.realtor.com/databank/profiles.htm*

EXPORTS

Total Export Sales

Area	1995 ($000)	1996 ($000)	1997 ($000)	1998 ($000)	% Chg. 1995-98	% Chg. 1997-98
MSA[1]	n/a	n/a	n/a	n/a	n/a	n/a
U.S.	583,030,524	622,827,063	687,597,999	680,474,251	16.7	-1.0

Note: (1) Metropolitan Statistical Area - see Appendix A for areas included
Source: U.S. Department of Commerce, International Trade Association, Metropolitan Area Exports: An Export Performance Report on Over 250 U.S. Cities, November 10, 1999

CITY FINANCES

City Government Finances

Component	1995 ($million)	1995 (per capita $)
Revenue	85.5	1,367
Expenditure	86.5	1,384
Debt Outstanding	191.8	3,068

Source: 1999 County and City Extra, Annual Metro, City, and County Data Book

City Government Revenue by Source

Source	1995 ($million)	1995 (per capita $)
Intergovernmental	28.7	459
Taxes	33.5	535
Property	0.9	15
Sales and Gross Receipts	31.6	507

Source: 1999 County and City Extra, Annual Metro, City, and County Data Book

City Government Expenditures by Function

Function	1995 ($million)	1995 (per capita $)	1995 (%)
Public Welfare	5.8	94	6.8
Highways	9.4	150	10.9
Parking Facilities	2.1	34	2.5
Education	0.0	0	0.0
Health and Hospitals	0.0	0	0.0
Police Protection	9.0	145	10.5
Sewerage and Sanitation	10.4	167	12.1
Parks and Recreation	8.5	136	9.9
Housing and Community Development	3.9	63	4.6
Interest on Debt	7.9	127	9.2

Source: 1999 County and City Extra, Annual Metro, City, and County Data Book

Municipal Bond Ratings

Area	Moody's
City	A

Source: Mergent Bond Record, 2/2000

POPULATION

Population Growth

Area	1980 Census	1990 Census	1999 Estimate	2004 Projection	Population Growth (%) 1990-1999	Population Growth (%) 1999-2004
City	48,953	55,993	67,096	71,599	19.8	6.7
MSA[1]	92,959	117,043	143,386	153,666	22.5	7.2
U.S.	226,545,805	248,765,170	272,212,864	283,625,312	9.4	4.2

Note: (1) Metropolitan Statistical Area - see Appendix A for areas included
Source: 1990 Census of Population and Housing, Summary Tape File 3C; Claritas, Inc.

Number of Households and Average Household Size

Area	1980 Census	1990 Census	1999 Estimate	2004 Projection	1999 Average Household Size
City	18,073	22,783	28,633	31,304	2.34
MSA[1]	32,570	44,998	57,761	63,341	2.48
U.S.	80,389,592	91,993,582	102,048,200	107,302,392	2.67

Note: (1) Metropolitan Statistical Area - see Appendix A for areas included
Source: 1990 Census of Population and Housing, Summary Tape File 3C; Claritas, Inc.

Race/Ethnicity of City Population

Race/Ethnicity	1990 Census Population	1990 Census %	1999 Estimate Population	1999 Estimate %	% Change 1990-1999
White, Non-Hispanic	27,745	49.6	32,037	47.7	15.5
Black, Non-Hispanic	162	0.3	480	0.7	196.3
Asian, Non-Hispanic	254	0.5	555	0.8	118.5
Other, Non-Hispanic	1,229	2.2	1,437	2.1	16.9
Hispanic	26,603	47.5	32,587	48.6	22.5

Source: 1990 Census of Population and Housing, Summary Tape File 3C; Claritas, Inc.

Race/Ethnicity of Metropolitan Statistical Area Population

Race/Ethnicity	1990 Census		1999 Estimate		% Change 1990-1999
	Population	%	Population	%	
White, Non-Hispanic	62,387	53.3	71,399	49.8	14.4
Black, Non-Hispanic	465	0.4	1,009	0.7	117.0
Asian, Non-Hispanic	838	0.7	1,363	1.0	62.6
Other, Non-Hispanic	2,760	2.4	3,280	2.3	18.8
Hispanic	50,593	43.2	66,335	46.3	31.1

Note: See Appendix A for areas included in the Metropolitan Statistical Area
Source: 1990 Census of Population and Housing, Summary Tape File 3C; Claritas, Inc.

Ancestry

Area	German	Irish	English	Italian	U.S.	French	Polish	Dutch
City	15.0	10.3	12.9	3.0	2.3	3.6	1.9	1.6
MSA[1]	17.4	10.7	14.6	2.9	2.6	3.4	1.9	1.8
U.S.	23.3	15.6	13.1	5.9	5.3	4.2	3.8	2.5

Note: Figures are percentages and include persons that reported multiple ancestry (eg. if a person reported being Irish and Italian, they were included in both columns); (1) Metropolitan Statistical Area - see Appendix A for areas included
Source: 1990 Census of Population and Housing, Summary Tape File 3C

Median Age

Area	1990 Census	1999 Estimate
City	36.1	38.8
MSA[1]	34.9	37.3
U.S.	32.9	35.7

Note: (1) Metropolitan Statistical Area - see Appendix A for areas included
Source: 1990 Census of Population and Housing, Summary Tape File 3C; Claritas, Inc.

Male/Female Population

Area	Number of Males		Number of Females		Males per 100 Females	
	1990	1999	1990	1999	1990	1999
City	26,446	32,032	29,547	35,064	89.5	91.4
MSA[1]	57,869	70,509	59,174	72,877	97.8	96.8
U.S.	121,172,379	132,803,736	127,537,494	139,409,136	95.0	95.3

Note: (1) Metropolitan Statistical Area - see Appendix A for areas included
Source: 1990 Census of Population, General Population Characteristics; Claritas, Inc.

INCOME

Per Capita/Median/Average Income

Area	Per Capita ($)			Median Household ($)			Average Household ($)		
	1989	1999	% Chg.	1989	1999	% Chg.	1989	1999	% Chg.
City	16,554	27,155	64.0	30,023	42,903	42.9	40,370	61,670	52.8
MSA[1]	16,499	26,206	58.8	32,294	46,105	42.8	42,451	63,518	49.6
U.S.	14,420	21,350	48.1	30,056	40,525	34.8	38,453	56,184	46.1

Note: (1) Metropolitan Statistical Area - see Appendix A for areas included; 1989 data is from the 1990 Census; 1999 data is estimated by Claritas, Inc.
Source: 1990 Census of Population, General Population Characteristics; Claritas, Inc.

Household Income Distribution

Area	Percent of Households Earning								
	Under $5,000	$5,000 -14,999	$15,000 -24,999	$25,000 -34,999	$35,000 -49,999	$50,000 -74,999	$75,000 -99,000	$100,000 -149,999	$150,000 and up
City	3.5	10.1	13.5	12.6	17.0	19.6	10.0	6.9	6.7
MSA[1]	3.1	9.1	12.8	12.0	16.6	19.8	11.8	8.6	6.2
U.S.	3.9	13.3	13.8	12.6	16.2	19.4	9.7	6.6	4.6

Note: Data as of 1999; (1) Metropolitan Statistical Area - see Appendix A for areas included
Source: Claritas, Inc.

Effective Buying Income

Area	Per Capita ($)	Median Household ($)	Average Household ($)
City	21,274	38,145	50,662
MSA[1]	21,441	41,038	53,585
U.S.	17,496	36,603	47,036

Note: Data as of 1/1/2000; (1) Metropolitan Statistical Area - see Appendix A for areas included
Source: Standard Rate & Data Service, Newspaper Advertising Source, March 2000

Effective Household Buying Income Distribution

Area	% of Households Earning						
	$10,000 -$19,999	$20,000 -$34,999	$35,000 -$49,999	$50,000 -$74,999	$75,000 -$99,000	$100,000 -$124,999	$125,000 and up
City	14.0	22.7	17.4	19.5	8.8	3.4	4.9
MSA[1]	13.0	21.3	16.9	21.3	10.7	3.9	4.6
U.S.	15.0	21.6	17.6	19.6	8.4	3.0	3.3

Note: Data as of 1/1/2000; (1) Metropolitan Statistical Area - see Appendix A for areas included
Source: Standard Rate & Data Service, Newspaper Advertising Source, March 2000

Poverty Rates by Age

Area	People of All Ages	People Under 18 Years Old	Related Children Age 5-17 in Families in Poverty
City	11.7	n/a	n/a
County	12.4	20.0	17.9
U.S.	13.8	20.8	18.7

Note: Figures show the percent of people living below the poverty line in 1995. The average poverty threshold was $15,569 for a family of four in 1995; n/a not available
Source: Bureau of the Census, Small Area Income and Poverty Estimates Program; U.S. Department of Housing and Urban Development

EMPLOYMENT

Labor Force and Employment

Area	Civilian Labor Force			Workers Employed		
	Dec. 1998	Dec. 1999	% Chg.	Dec. 1998	Dec. 1999	% Chg.
City	37,758	37,537	-0.6	36,645	36,603	-0.1
MSA[1]	74,777	74,344	-0.6	72,490	72,408	-0.1
U.S.	138,297,000	139,941,000	1.2	132,732,000	134,696,000	1.5

Note: Data is not seasonally adjusted and covers workers 16 years of age and older; (1) Metropolitan Statistical Area - see Appendix A for areas included
Source: Bureau of Labor Statistics, http://stats.bls.gov

Unemployment Rate

Area	1999											
	Jan.	Feb.	Mar.	Apr.	May	Jun.	Jul.	Aug.	Sep.	Oct.	Nov.	Dec.
City	3.1	2.8	2.7	2.6	2.7	3.3	3.0	3.0	2.9	2.8	2.6	2.5
MSA[1]	3.2	2.9	2.8	2.7	2.7	3.4	3.1	3.1	3.1	2.9	2.8	2.6
U.S.	4.8	4.7	4.4	4.1	4.0	4.5	4.5	4.2	4.1	3.8	3.8	3.7

Note: Data is not seasonally adjusted and covers workers 16 years of age and older; all figures are percentages; (1) Metropolitan Statistical Area - see Appendix A for areas included
Source: Bureau of Labor Statistics, http://stats.bls.gov

Employment by Industry

Sector	MSA[1]		U.S.
	Number of Employees	Percent of Total	Percent of Total
Services	21,700	29.3	30.2
Retail Trade	14,600	19.7	18.1
Government	25,600	34.5	15.8
Manufacturing	1,800	2.4	14.1
Finance/Insurance/Real Estate	3,600	4.9	5.9
Wholesale Trade	1,500	2.0	5.4
Transportation/Public Utilities	1,200	1.6	5.3
Construction	n/a	n/a	4.8
Mining	n/a	n/a	0.4

Note: Figures cover non-farm employment as of 12/99 and are not seasonally adjusted; (1) Metropolitan Statistical Area - see Appendix A for areas included; n/a not available
Source: Bureau of Labor Statistics, http://stats.bls.gov

Employment by Occupation

Occupation Category	City (%)	MSA[1] (%)	U.S. (%)
White Collar	69.9	69.4	58.1
Executive/Admin./Management	15.7	15.0	12.3
Professional	20.5	21.4	14.1
Technical & Related Support	3.5	6.2	3.7
Sales	14.9	11.8	11.8
Administrative Support/Clerical	15.3	15.0	16.3
Blue Collar	14.7	16.5	26.2
Precision Production/Craft/Repair	7.9	9.2	11.3
Machine Operators/Assem./Insp.	2.8	2.6	6.8
Transportation/Material Movers	1.7	2.3	4.1
Cleaners/Helpers/Laborers	2.3	2.4	3.9
Services	14.3	12.8	13.2
Farming/Forestry/Fishing	1.1	1.2	2.5

Note: Figures cover workers 16 years of age and older; (1) Metropolitan Statistical Area - see Appendix A for areas included
Source: 1990 Census of Population and Housing, Summary Tape File 3C

Occupational Employment Projections: 1996 - 2006

Occupations Expected to Have the Largest Job Growth (ranked by numerical growth)	Fast-Growing Occupations[1] (ranked by percent growth)
1. Salespersons, retail	1. Systems analysts
2. Cashiers	2. Computer engineers
3. General managers & top executives	3. Database administrators
4. Teachers, secondary school	4. Personal and home care aides
5. Teachers aides, clerical & paraprofess.	5. Teachers, special education
6. Waiters & waitresses	6. Corrections officers & jailers
7. Truck drivers, light	7. Geologists/geophysicists/oceanographers
8. Maintenance repairers, general utility	8. Physical therapists
9. Registered nurses	9. Human services workers
10. Secretaries, except legal & medical	10. Chemists, exc. biochemists

Note: Projections cover New Mexico; (1) Excludes occupations with total job growth less than 300
Source: U.S. Department of Labor, Employment and Training Administration, America's Labor Market Information System (ALMIS)

Average Wages

Occupation	$/Hr.	Occupation	$/Hr.
Accountants and Auditors	16.10	Maids and Housekeepers	7.94
Assemblers and Fabricators	10.64	Maintenance Repairers	9.67
Automotive Mechanics	14.20	Marketing/Advertising/PR Managers	21.53
Bookkeepers	12.40	Nurses, Licensed Practical	13.97
Carpenters	14.67	Nurses, Registered	20.74
Cashiers	8.33	Nursing Aides/Orderlies/Attendants	7.23
Clerks, General Office	10.16	Physicians and Surgeons	49.42
Clerks, Shipping/Receiving/Traffic	11.01	Receptionists/Information Clerks	9.83
Computer Programmers	24.74	Sales Reps., Exc. Scientific/Retail	13.27
Computer Support Specialists	17.76	Sales Reps., Scientific, Exc. Retail	22.13
Cooks, Restaurant	8.49	Salespersons, Retail	9.43
Electricians	16.50	Secretaries, Except Legal/Medical	11.04
Financial Managers	22.97	Stock Clerks, Sales Floor	8.14
First-Line Supervisors/Mgrs., Sales	14.93	Systems Analysts	-
Food Preparation Workers	6.81	Teacher Aides	-
General Managers/Top Executives	24.62	Teachers, Elementary School	-
Guards	11.96	Teachers, Secondary School	-
Hand Packers	6.98	Telemarketers	7.38
Janitors and Cleaners	7.74	Truck Drivers, Heavy/Tractor-Trailer	11.46
Laborers, Landscaping	8.93	Truck Drivers, Light	11.18
Lawyers	28.73	Waiters and Waitresses	7.23

Note: Wage data is for 1998 and covers the Metropolitan Statistical Area (see Appendix A for areas included). Hourly wages for elementary and secondary school teachers were calculated by the editors from annual wage data assuming a 40 hour work week; Dashes indicate that data was not available.
Source: Bureau of Labor Statistics, 1998 Metropolitan Area Occupational Employment and Wage Estimates

TAXES

Major State and Local Tax Rates

State Corporate Income (%)	State Personal Income (%)	Residential Property (%)	Sales & Use		State Gasoline (cents/ gallon)	State Cigarette (cents/ pack)
			State (%)	Local (%)		
4.8 - 7.6	1.7 - 8.2	0.45	5.0	1.0625	18.0[a]	21.0

Note: Personal/corporate income, sales, gasoline and cigarette tax rates as of January 2000. Property tax rates as of April 2000; (a) Rate is comprised of 17 cents excise and 1.0 cents motor carrier tax
Source: Federation of Tax Administrators, www.taxadmin.org; ERI's Relocation Assessor software database, quarterly effective date 4/1/2000

Total Taxes Per Capita and as a Percent of Income

Area	Per Capita Income ($)	Per Capita Taxes ($)			Percent of Income (%)		
		Total	Federal	State/Local	Total	Federal	State/Local
New Mexico	21,022	7,397	4,837	2,560	35.2	23.0	12.2
U.S.	28,878	10,298	7,026	3,273	35.7	24.3	11.3

Note: Figures are for 1999
Source: Tax Foundation, www.taxfoundation.org

COMMERCIAL UTILITIES

Typical Monthly Electric Bills

Area	Commercial Service ($/month)		Industrial Service ($/month)	
	12 kW demand 1,500 kWh	100 kW demand 30,000 kWh	1,000 kW demand 400,000 kWh	20,000 kW demand 10,000,000 kWh
City	n/a	n/a	n/a	n/a
U.S.	150	2,174	23,995	508,569

Note: Based on rates in effect January 1, 1999; n/a not available
Source: Edison Electric Institute, Typical Residential, Commercial and Industrial Bills, Winter 1999

TRANSPORTATION

Transportation Statistics

Average minutes to work (1990)	16.1
Interstate highways	I-25; US-84; US-285
Bus lines	
In-city (1998)	Santa Fe Public Works, Transit Services Div., 19 buses
Inter-city (1999)	1
Passenger air service	
Airport	Santa Fe Municipal
Airlines (1999)	n/a
Enplaned passengers (1998)	28,434
Amtrak service	Bus Connection
Motor freight carriers (1999)	3
Major waterways/ports	None

Source: FAA DOT/TSC CY1998 ACAIS Database; National Transit Database, 1998; Editor & Publisher Market Guide, 2000; Amtrak National Time Table, Fall 1999/Winter 2000; 1990 Census of Population and Housing, STF 3C; Jane's Urban Transport Systems 1999-2000

Means of Transportation to Work

Area	Car/Truck/Van		Public Transportation			Bicycle	Walked	Other Means	Worked at Home
	Drove Alone	Car-pooled	Bus	Subway	Railroad				
City	73.4	14.0	0.0	0.0	0.0	1.0	4.6	0.9	6.0
MSA[1]	73.1	15.3	0.3	0.0	0.0	0.6	3.6	1.0	6.0
U.S.	73.2	13.4	3.0	1.5	0.5	0.4	3.9	1.2	3.0

Note: Figures shown are percentages and only include workers 16 years of age and older;
(1) Metropolitan Statistical Area - see Appendix A for areas included
Source: 1990 Census of Population and Housing, Summary Tape File 3C

BUSINESSES

Major Business Headquarters

Company Name	1999 Rankings	
	Fortune 500	Forbes 500
No companies listed	-	-

Note: Companies listed are located in the city; dashes indicate no ranking
Fortune 500: Companies that produce a 10-K are ranked 1 to 500 based on 1999 revenue
Forbes 500: Private companies are ranked 1 to 500 based on 1998 revenue
Source: Forbes, December 13, 1999; Fortune, April 17, 2000

HOTELS & MOTELS

Hotels/Motels

Area	Hotels/ Motels	Rooms	Luxury-Level Hotels/Motels		Average Minimum Rates ($)		
			◆◆◆◆	◆◆◆◆◆	◆◆	◆◆◆	◆◆◆◆
City	45	3,661	0	0	82	140	n/a
Airport	2	203	0	0	n/a	n/a	n/a
Suburbs	3	155	0	0	n/a	n/a	n/a
Total	50	4,019	0	0	n/a	n/a	n/a

Note: n/a not available; classifications range from one diamond (budget properties with basic amenities) to five diamond (luxury properties).
Source: OAG Business Travel Planner, Winter 1999-2000

Estimated Daily Food and Lodging Costs

Area	Food/Other ($/day)	Average Hotel Cost ($/day)
City	46	90
U.S.	30	55

Source: ERI's Relocation Assessor software database, quarterly effective date 4/1/2000

Santa Fe is home to two of the top 100 hotels in the world according to *Travel & Leisure*: Bishop's Lodge (#50) and Inn of the Anasazi (#66) . Criteria: value, rooms/ambience, location, facilities/activities and service. *Travel & Leisure, 1999 World's Best Awards, Best Hotels and Resorts*

CONVENTION CENTERS

Convention Centers and Event Sites

Name	Guest Rooms	Meeting Space (sq. ft.)	Capacity (Theatre Style)
Doubletree Hotel Santa Fe	213	6,500	400
Eldorado Hotel	219	14,000	750
Fort Marcy Hotel & Suites	130	n/a	150
Hilton of Santa Fe	156	240	600
Homewood Suites	105	n/a	0
Hotel Santa Fe	128	4,600	250
Hotel St. Francis-Santa Fe	80	n/a	50
Inn of the Governors	100	832	90
Inn on the Alameda	67	n/a	0
La Fonda Hotel	153	11,500	750
La Posada de Santa Fe	119	4,500	100
Marriott Residence Inn	120	n/a	0
Paolo Soleri Amphitheater	n/a	n/a	2,900
Radisson Hotel and Suites on the Plaza	56	n/a	0
Radisson Hotel Santa Fe	157	2,200	250
Radisson Picasho Hotel	149	n/a	0
Rancho Encantado Resort	80	n/a	70
Sweeney Convention Center	n/a	n/a	1,460
The Bishop's Lodge Santa Fe	88	10,000	200
The Inn at Loretto	141	10,000	400
The Inn of the Anasazi	59	n/a	0

Note: n/a not available
Source: EventSource.com, 3/15/2000

Living Environment

COST OF LIVING

Cost of Living: Homeowner

Cost Element	U.S. ($)	City ($)	Differential ($)	Percent of U.S. Average
Consumables	14,516	14,829	313	102.2
Transportation	5,957	6,632	675	111.3
Health Services	2,012	2,131	119	105.9
Housing/Utilities/Prop. Tax	16,337	20,027	3,690	122.6
Income+Payroll Taxes	12,615	12,021	-594	95.3
Miscellaneous	8,563	8,563	0	100.0
Total Cost of Living	60,000	64,203	4,203	107.0

Note: Figures are based on a single income, four person family with gross annual earnings of $60,000, owning an 1,800 square-foot home, and driving two automobiles worth $22,000 30,000 miles per year.
Source: ERI's Relocation Assessor software database, quarterly effective date 4/1/2000

Cost of Living: Renter

Cost Element	U.S. ($)	City ($)	Differential ($)	Percent of U.S. Average
Consumables	10,486	10,793	307	102.9
Transportation	2,107	2,364	257	112.2
Health Services	1,632	1,742	110	106.7
Rent/Utilities/Insurance	9,299	12,047	2,748	129.6
Income+Payroll Taxes	8,607	8,295	-312	96.4
Miscellaneous	7,869	7,869	0	100.0
Total Cost of Living	40,000	43,110	3,110	107.8

Note: Figures are based on a single income, three person family with gross annual earnings of $40,000, renting a 1,000 square-foot home, and driving one automobile worth $8,000 12,000 miles per year.
Source: ERI's Relocation Assessor software database, quarterly effective date 4/1/2000

HOUSING

Median Home Prices and Housing Affordability

Area	Median Price[2] 4th Qtr. 1999 ($)	HOI[3] 4th Qtr. 1999	Affordability Rank[4]
MSA[1]	n/a	n/a	n/a
U.S.	139,000	63.8	–

Note: (1) Metropolitan Statistical Area - see Appendix A for areas included; (2) U.S. figures calculated from the sales of 687,516 new and existing homes in 192 markets; (3) Housing Opportunity Index - percent of homes sold that were within the reach of the median income household at the prevailing mortgage interest rate; (4) Rank is from 1-192 with 1 being most affordable; n/a not available
Source: National Association of Home Builders, Housing Opportunity Index, 4th Quarter 1999

Estimated Home Price

Area	Price ($)
City	193,215
U.S.	135,855

Note: Figures are based on an 1,800 square-foot home
Source: ERI's Relocation Assessor software database, quarterly effective date 4/1/2000

Estimated Rent

Area	Rent ($/month)
City	885
U.S.	651

Note: Figures are based on a 1,000 square-foot home
Source: ERI's Relocation Assessor software database, quarterly effective date 4/1/2000

Median Home Price Projection

It is projected that the median home price in the metropolitan area will increase from $188,520 in 1999 to $297,613 in 2010, an increase of 57.9%
Kiplinger's Personal Finance Magazine, January 2000

RESIDENTIAL UTILITIES

Average Residential Utility Costs

Area	All Electric ($/mth)	Part Electric ($/mth)	Other Energy ($/mth)	Phone ($/mth)
City	–	50.32	36.83	21.08
U.S.	99.25	55.47	43.48	20.29

Source: ACCRA, Cost of Living Index, 3rd Quarter 1999

HEALTH CARE

Average Health Care Costs

Area	Hospital ($/day)	Doctor ($/visit)	Dentist ($/visit)
City	260.00	60.50	84.00
U.S.	440.96	53.83	68.42

Note: Hospital—based on a semi-private room; Doctor—based on a general practitioner's routine exam of an established patient; Dentist—based on adult teeth cleaning and periodic oral exam.
Source: ACCRA, Cost of Living Index, 3rd Quarter 1999

Distribution of Office-Based Physicians

Area	Family/Gen. Practitioners	Specialists		
		Medical	Surgical	Other
MSA[1]	50	81	72	96

Note: Data as of 12/31/97; (1) Metropolitan Statistical Area - see Appendix A for areas included
Source: American Medical Assn., Physician Characteristics & Distribution in the U.S., 1999

Hospitals

Santa Fe has 2 general medical and surgical hospitals, 1 psychiatric.
AHA Guide to the Healthcare Field, 1999-2000

EDUCATION

Public School District Statistics

District Name	Num. Sch.	Enroll.	Classroom Teachers	Pupils per Teacher	Minority Pupils (%)	Current Exp.[1] ($/pupil)
Pojoaque Valley Public Schools	4	1,990	118	16.9	n/a	n/a
Santa Fe Public Schools	30	13,583	658	20.6	n/a	n/a

Note: Data covers the 1997-1998 school year unless otherwise noted; (1) Data covers fiscal year 1996; SD = School District; ISD = Independent School District; n/a not available
Source: National Center for Education Statistics, Common Core of Data Public Education Agency Universe 1997-98; National Center for Education Statistics, Characteristics of the 100 Largest Public Elementary and Secondary School Districts in the United States: 1997-98, July 1999

Educational Quality

School District	Education Quotient[1]	Graduate Outcome[2]	Community Index[3]	Resource Index[4]
Santa Fe Public Schools	90	88	125	87

Note: Over 1,000 secondary school districts were rated in terms of educational quality. The scores range from a low of 50 to a high of 150; (1) Combination of the Graduate Outcome, Community and Resource indexes weighted to reflect the greater importance of the Graduate Outcome and Resource Index; (2) Based on graduation rates and college board scores (SAT/ACT); (3) Based on the surrounding community's level of affluence and adult education; (4) Based on teacher salaries, per-pupil expenditures and student-teacher ratios.
Source: Expansion Management, Ratings Issue, 1999

Educational Attainment by Race

Area	High School Graduate (%)					Bachelor's Degree (%)				
	Total	White	Black	Other	Hisp.[2]	Total	White	Black	Other	Hisp.[2]
City	84.0	86.4	100.0	70.3	69.0	36.1	40.1	42.2	13.8	14.9
MSA[1]	84.5	86.7	85.3	71.4	69.0	35.7	39.3	27.4	14.9	13.6
U.S.	75.2	77.9	63.1	60.4	49.8	20.3	21.5	11.4	19.4	9.2

Note: Figures shown cover persons 25 years old and over; (1) Metropolitan Statistical Area - see Appendix A for areas included; (2) people of Hispanic origin can be of any race
Source: 1990 Census of Population and Housing, Summary Tape File 3C

School Enrollment by Type

Area	Preprimary				Elementary/High School			
	Public		Private		Public		Private	
	Enrollment	%	Enrollment	%	Enrollment	%	Enrollment	%
City	425	43.5	551	56.5	7,736	89.4	922	10.6
MSA[1]	1,074	50.0	1,075	50.0	18,837	91.4	1,762	8.6
U.S.	2,679,029	59.5	1,824,256	40.5	38,379,689	90.2	4,187,099	9.8

Note: Figures shown cover persons 3 years old and over;
(1) Metropolitan Statistical Area - see Appendix A for areas included
Source: 1990 Census of Population and Housing, Summary Tape File 3C

School Enrollment by Race

Area	Preprimary (%)				Elementary/High School (%)			
	White	Black	Other	Hisp.[1]	White	Black	Other	Hisp.[1]
City	83.6	0.3	16.1	35.6	75.3	0.5	24.1	60.1
MSA[2]	85.1	0.6	14.3	33.9	77.6	0.9	21.5	52.5
U.S.	80.4	12.5	7.1	7.8	74.1	15.6	10.3	12.5

Note: Figures shown cover persons 3 years old and over; (1) people of Hispanic origin can be of any race; (2) Metropolitan Statistical Area - see Appendix A for areas included
Source: 1990 Census of Population and Housing, Summary Tape File 3C

Higher Education

Two-Year Colleges		Four-Year Colleges		Medical Schools	Law Schools	Voc/ Tech
Public	Private	Public	Private			
2	0	0	2	0	0	7

Source: College Blue Book, Occupational Education, 1999; Medical School Admission Requirements, 1999-2000; Peterson's Guide to Two-Year Colleges, 2000; Peterson's Guide to Four-Year Colleges, 1999; Barron's Guide to Law Schools, 1999

MAJOR EMPLOYERS

Major Employers

Camel Rock Gaming Center
Eberline Instrument Corp.
Nambe Mills (metal products)
Security Capital Group
Sunwest Bank of Santa Fe

Corporacion de la Fonda (hotels)
Guardian Santa Fe Partnership (hotels)
Peters Corp. (art dealers)
St. Vincent Hospital

Note: Companies listed are located in the city
Source: D&B Business Rankings, 1999; Ward's Business Directory, 1999; America's Corporate Families, 1999

PUBLIC SAFETY

Crime Rate

Area	All Crimes	Violent Crimes				Property Crimes		
		Murder	Forcible Rape	Robbery	Aggrav. Assault	Burglary	Larceny -Theft	Motor Vehicle Theft
City	n/a	n/a	n/a	n/a	n/a	n/a	n/a	n/a
Suburbs[1]	n/a	n/a	n/a	n/a	n/a	n/a	n/a	n/a
MSA[2]	n/a	n/a	n/a	n/a	n/a	n/a	n/a	n/a
U.S.	4,615.5	6.3	34.4	165.2	360.5	862.0	2,728.1	459.0

Note: Crime rate is the number of crimes per 100,000 population; (1) Defined as all areas within the Metropolitan Statistical Area but located outside the central city; (2) Metropolitan Statistical Area - see Appendix A for areas included; n/a not available
Source: FBI Uniform Crime Reports, 1998

RECREATION

Culture and Recreation

Museums	Symphony Orchestras	Opera Companies	Dance Companies	Professional Theatres	Zoos	Pro Sports Teams
12	2	1	1	1	0	0

Source: Musical America, International Directory of the Performing Arts, 1999; Official Museum Directory, 2000; Stern's Performing Arts Directory, 1997; USA Today Four Sport Stadium Guide, 1997; Career Opportunities in Theatre and the Performing Arts, 1999

Library System

The Santa Fe Public Library has two branches, holdings of 258,000 volumes, and a budget of $1,694,222 (1997-1998).
American Library Directory, 1999-2000

MEDIA

Newspapers

Name	Type	Freq.	Distribution	Circulation
The New Mexican	n/a	7x/wk	Area	24,500

Note: Includes newspapers with circulations of 200 or more located in the city; n/a not available
Source: Burrelle's Media Directory, 1999 Edition

Television Stations

Name	Ch.	Affiliation	Type	Owner
KCHF	11	n/a	Commercial	Son Broadcasting

Note: Stations included broadcast in the Santa Fe metro area; n/a not available
Source: Burrelle's Media Directory, 1999 Edition

AM Radio Stations

Call Letters	Freq. (kHz)	Target Audience	Station Format	Music Format
KSWV	810	G/H	E/M/N/S	Latin
KVSF	1260	General	T	n/a

Note: Stations included broadcast in the Santa Fe metro area; n/a not available
Target Audience: A=Asian; B=Black; C=Christian; E=Ethnic; F=French; G=General; H=Hispanic; M=Men; N=Native American; R=Religious; S=Senior Citizen; W=Women; Y=Young Adult; Z=Children
Station Format: E=Educational; M=Music; N=News; S=Sports; T=Talk
Source: Burrelle's Media Directory, 1999 Edition

FM Radio Stations

Call Letters	Freq. (mHz)	Target Audience	Station Format	Music Format
KSFR	90.7	General	E/M/N	Blues/Classical/Jazz/Latin/Reggae/Rhythm & Blues
KBAC	98.1	General	M	Adult Contemporary
KBOM	106.7	General	M/N/S	Oldies

Note: Stations included broadcast in the Santa Fe metro area
Station Format: E=Educational; M=Music; N=News; S=Sports; T=Talk
Target Audience: A=Asian; B=Black; C=Christian; E=Ethnic; F=French; G=General; H=Hispanic;
M=Men; N=Native American; R=Religious; S=Senior Citizen; W=Women; Y=Young Adult; Z=Children
Source: Burrelle's Media Directory, 1999 Edition

WEATHER

Temperature/Precipitation/Humidity

	Jan	Feb	Mar	Apr	May	Jun	Jul	Aug	Sep	Oct	Nov	Dec	Yr.
Max. High Temp. (°F)	64	68	73	81	92	98	98	95	92	85	71	63	98
Avg. High Temp. (°F)	43	48	54	64	74	84	87	84	81	68	52	45	65
Avg. Temp. (°F)	31	35	40	49	59	68	72	70	65	53	38	32	51
Avg. Low Temp. (°F)	19	22	26	34	44	53	58	56	50	39	24	19	37
Min. Low Temp. (°F)	-8	-10	0	14	27	37	49	45	35	20	-4	-7	-10
Avg. Precip. (in.)	0.5	0.5	0.5	0.4	0.9	0.7	2.0	2.3	0.6	0.6	0.3	0.3	9.8
Avg. Snowfall (in.)	5.2	3.7	2.2	1.5	0.1	0	0	0	0	0	2.3	3.3	18.3
Avg. Rel. Hum. (%)	63	59	50	42	42	36	49	54	46	46	54	60	50

Source: National Climatic Data Center, International Station Meteorological Climate Summary, 3/95

Weather Conditions

Temperature			Precipitation		
0°F & below	32°F & below	90°F & above	0.1 inch or more precip.	1.5 inch or more snow/ice	Thunder-storms
2	157	23	27	4	51

Note: Figures are average number of days per year
Source: National Climatic Data Center, International Station Meteorological Climate Summary, 3/95

AIR & WATER QUALITY

Maximum Pollutant Concentrations

	Particulate Matter (ug/m3)	Carbon Monoxide (ppm)	Sulfur Dioxide (ppm)	Nitrogen Dioxide (ppm)	Ozone (ppm)	Lead (ug/m3)
MSA[1] Level	33	2	n/a	n/a	n/a	n/a
NAAQS[2]	150	9	0.140	0.053	0.12	1.50
Met NAAQS	Yes	Yes	n/a	n/a	n/a	n/a

Note: (1) Metropolitan Statistical Area - see Appendix A for areas included; (2) National Ambient Air Quality Standards; ppm = parts per million; ug/m3 = micrograms per cubic meter; n/a not available
Source: EPA, National Air Quality and Emissions Trends Report, 1997

Pollutant Standards Index

Data not available.
EPA, National Air Quality and Emissions Trends Report, 1997

Drinking Water

Water System Name	Pop. Served	Primary Water Source Type	Number of Violations in 1998-99	Type of Violation/ Contaminants
Sangre de Cristo Water Co.	60,000	Surface	None	None

Note: Data as of January 19, 2000
Source: EPA, Office of Ground Water and Drinking Water, Safe Drinking Water Information System

Santa Fe tap water is neutral, soft in summer, hard in winter.
Editor & Publisher Market Guide, 2000

Sarasota, Florida

Background

Sarasota, Florida is situated in the west-central portion of the state, on Sarasota Bay, an inlet of the Gulf of Mexico, 55 miles south of Tampa. It is the seat of Sarasota county.

The city's major industries are tourism, cattle raising and vegetable farming. Other economic segments include research, boatbuilding and the manufacture of mobile homes. Sarasota is also a popular retirement location.

Scottish settlers arrived in the area 1885. After 1910, Mrs. Potter Palmer, a Chicago socialite, popularized the area as a resort and established a model cattle ranch there. In 1927 John Ringling selected Sarasota as winter headquarters for the Ringling Bros. and Barnum & Bailey Circus, a position relinquished to nearby Venice in 1960.

Cultural venues in the city include the Ringling museums, with their large gallery of Baroque art and renowned Peter Paul Rubens collection, the Asolo Theater, brought from Venice and reassembled by the state of Florida, Ca'd'Zan, the 1925 palatial home of John Ringling, and the Museum of the Circus. The Circus Hall of Fame, Sarasota Jungle Gardens, and the Mayakka River State Park are nearby.

Institutions of higher learning include the University of South Florida, Sarasota campus, and the Ringling School of Art and Design. Sarasota is also home to an opera troupe, several theater and ballet companies and a symphony orchestra.

Sarasota is governed by a Commission Manager form of government. A City Manager is appointed by the elected five-member City Commission, serves as the City's Chief Administrative Officer.

General Rankings and Evaluative Comments

- Sarasota was ranked #55 out of 354 metropolitan areas in *Places Rated Almanac*. Criteria: cost of living, climate, crime, transportation, job outlook, education, the arts, health care, and recreation. Places Rated Almanac, Millennium Edition, 2000

- Sarasota was selected as one of the best places to retire by *Retirement Places Rated*. Criteria: cost of living, climate, crime, services, working, and leisure living. The city was ranked #15 out of 187. *Retirement Places Rated, 1999*

- Cognetics studied 273 metro areas in the United States, ranking them by entrepreneurial activity. Sarasota was ranked #61 out of 134 smaller metro areas. Criteria: Significant Starts (firms started in the last 10 years that still employ at least 5 people) and Young Growers (percent of firms 10 years old or less that grew significantly during the last 4 years). *Cognetics, "Entrepreneurial Hot Spots: The Best Places in America to Start and Grow a Company," 1999*

- Reliastar Financial Corporation ranked the 125 largest metropolitan areas according to the general financial security of residents. Sarasota was ranked #39 out of 125 with a score of 6.1 (the percentage a metropolitan area is above or below the metropolitan norm; a metro area with a score of 10.6 is 10.6% above the metro average). Criteria: Earnings and Wealth Potential (household income, education, net assets, cost of living); Safety Net (health insurance, retirement savings, life insurance, income support programs); Personal Threats (unemployment rate, low-income households, crime rate); Community Economic Vitality (cost of community services, job quality, job creation, housing costs). *Reliastar Financial Corporation, "The Best Cities to Earn and Save Money: A Ranking of the Largest 125 U.S. Cities," 2000 Edition*

- Sarasota was selected as one of "The 50 Most Alive Places to Live" in the U.S. Criteria: ethnic diversity, recreational options, cultural vitality, low crime rate, opportunities for lifelong learning, good hospitals and restaurants, public transportation, walking accessibility, civic activities, and the kitsch factor. The area was ranked #3 out of 10 in the "Big Cities" category. *Modern Maturity, May-June 2000*

Business Environment

STATE ECONOMY

State Economic Profile

"Florida's economy has been among the nation's strongest in recent years. Job growth has outpaced the nation by a considerable amount since 1992.

While Florida has been able to avoid any significant fallout from the Asian crisis, the weakening of economies in Latin American will dampen both tourism and international trade. 1998 saw the decline in Latin tourism more than offset by domestic visitors. Domestic tourism is projected to soften as U.S. growth cools, offering no offset against the expected decline in Latin tourism. Weaker tourism and trade with Latin American will slow growth in the near future; Florida will still outpace the nation in job growth as Gross State Product growth (GSP) slows.

Over half of Florida's 230,000 new jobs created in 1998 were in the services sector, which grew at 5.2%, more than offsetting a minor decline in manufacturing employment. Much of this growth is taking place in the finance and business services sector.

In spite of strong home sales and a slowing construction market, Florida's price appreciation continued to lag the nation. Although residential permits per 1,000 residents stands at 5.1, well above the national average, this number is only slightly up from 1997 and is poised to decline in the near future.

Growth in Florida, while strong throughout, has been hottest in the Naples, Ft. Myers and Orlando areas. Construction and employment in the construction industry has begun to slow in South Florida. Projected employment and housing gains will be concentrated in Northern and Central Florida. Growing diversification of the economy into financial and business services promises a strong outlook for the years ahead." *National Association of Realtors, Economic Profiles: The Fifty States and the District of Columbia, http://nar.realtor.com/databank/profiles.htm*

EXPORTS

Total Export Sales

Area	1995 ($000)	1996 ($000)	1997 ($000)	1998 ($000)	% Chg. 1995-98	% Chg. 1997-98
MSA[1]	182,765	180,243	184,778	208,502	14.1	12.8
U.S.	583,030,524	622,827,063	687,597,999	680,474,251	16.7	-1.0

Note: (1) Metropolitan Statistical Area - see Appendix A for areas included
Source: U.S. Department of Commerce, International Trade Association, Metropolitan Area Exports: An Export Performance Report on Over 250 U.S. Cities, November 10, 1999

CITY FINANCES

City Government Finances

Component	1995 ($million)	1995 (per capita $)
Revenue	73.8	1,355
Expenditure	72.7	1,335
Debt Outstanding	123.5	2,269

Source: 1999 County and City Extra, Annual Metro, City, and County Data Book

City Government Revenue by Source

Source	1995 ($million)	1995 (per capita $)
Intergovernmental	7.4	135
Taxes	33.4	615
Property	16.6	305
Sales and Gross Receipts	15.4	284

Source: 1999 County and City Extra, Annual Metro, City, and County Data Book

City Government Expenditures by Function

Function	1995 ($million)	1995 (per capita $)	1995 (%)
Public Welfare	0.0	0	0.0
Highways	6.4	118	8.9
Parking Facilities	0.3	6	0.5
Education	0.0	0	0.0
Health and Hospitals	0.0	0	0.0
Police Protection	15.2	280	21.0
Sewerage and Sanitation	15.2	280	21.0
Parks and Recreation	8.7	161	12.1
Housing and Community Development	1.5	28	2.1
Interest on Debt	3.5	65	4.9

Source: 1999 County and City Extra, Annual Metro, City, and County Data Book

Municipal Bond Ratings

Area	Moody's
City	Aa3

Source: Mergent Bond Record, 2/2000

POPULATION

Population Growth

Area	1980 Census	1990 Census	1999 Estimate	2004 Projection	Population Growth (%) 1990-1999	Population Growth (%) 1999-2004
City	48,876	50,978	49,713	50,274	-2.5	1.1
MSA[1]	202,251	277,776	557,303	596,184	100.6	7.0
U.S.	226,545,805	248,765,170	272,212,864	283,625,312	9.4	4.2

Note: (1) Metropolitan Statistical Area - see Appendix A for areas included
Source: 1990 Census of Population and Housing, Summary Tape File 3C; Claritas, Inc.

Number of Households and Average Household Size

Area	1980 Census	1990 Census	1999 Estimate	2004 Projection	1999 Average Household Size
City	21,198	22,905	22,139	22,622	2.25
MSA[1]	150,735	125,764	243,384	262,256	2.29
U.S.	80,389,592	91,993,582	102,048,200	107,302,392	2.67

Note: (1) Metropolitan Statistical Area - see Appendix A for areas included
Source: 1990 Census of Population and Housing, Summary Tape File 3C; Claritas, Inc.

Race/Ethnicity of City Population

Race/Ethnicity	1990 Census Population	1990 Census %	1999 Estimate Population	1999 Estimate %	% Change 1990-1999
White, Non-Hispanic	40,166	78.8	35,150	70.7	-12.5
Black, Non-Hispanic	8,083	15.9	9,962	20.0	23.2
Asian, Non-Hispanic	295	0.6	494	1.0	67.5
Other, Non-Hispanic	152	0.3	168	0.3	10.5
Hispanic	2,282	4.5	3,939	7.9	72.6

Source: 1990 Census of Population and Housing, Summary Tape File 3C; Claritas, Inc.

Race/Ethnicity of Metropolitan Statistical Area Population

Race/Ethnicity	1990 Census		1999 Estimate		% Change 1990-1999
	Population	%	Population	%	
White, Non-Hispanic	258,188	92.9	485,619	87.1	88.1
Black, Non-Hispanic	11,672	4.2	39,081	7.0	234.8
Asian, Non-Hispanic	1,327	0.5	4,635	0.8	249.3
Other, Non-Hispanic	679	0.2	1,720	0.3	153.3
Hispanic	5,910	2.1	26,248	4.7	344.1

Note: See Appendix A for areas included in the Metropolitan Statistical Area
Source: 1990 Census of Population and Housing, Summary Tape File 3C; Claritas, Inc.

Ancestry

Area	German	Irish	English	Italian	U.S.	French	Polish	Dutch
City	24.1	14.8	17.4	5.7	4.1	5.4	2.4	2.4
MSA[1]	29.2	17.3	21.4	6.8	4.4	5.8	3.8	3.1
U.S.	23.3	15.6	13.1	5.9	5.3	4.2	3.8	2.5

Note: Figures are percentages and include persons that reported multiple ancestry (eg. if a person reported being Irish and Italian, they were included in both columns); (1) Metropolitan Statistical Area - see Appendix A for areas included
Source: 1990 Census of Population and Housing, Summary Tape File 3C

Median Age

Area	1990 Census	1999 Estimate
City	39.8	41.9
MSA[1]	48.9	47.7
U.S.	32.9	35.7

Note: (1) Metropolitan Statistical Area - see Appendix A for areas included
Source: 1990 Census of Population and Housing, Summary Tape File 3C; Claritas, Inc.

Male/Female Population

Area	Number of Males		Number of Females		Males per 100 Females	
	1990	1999	1990	1999	1990	1999
City	23,943	23,552	27,035	26,161	88.6	90.0
MSA[1]	130,165	262,780	147,611	294,523	88.2	89.2
U.S.	121,172,379	132,803,736	127,537,494	139,409,136	95.0	95.3

Note: (1) Metropolitan Statistical Area - see Appendix A for areas included
Source: 1990 Census of Population, General Population Characteristics; Claritas, Inc.

INCOME

Per Capita/Median/Average Income

Area	Per Capita ($)			Median Household ($)			Average Household ($)		
	1989	1999	% Chg.	1989	1999	% Chg.	1989	1999	% Chg.
City	16,151	23,603	46.1	24,884	34,304	37.9	35,254	52,346	48.5
MSA[1]	18,441	24,514	32.9	29,919	39,427	31.8	40,357	55,877	38.5
U.S.	14,420	21,350	48.1	30,056	40,525	34.8	38,453	56,184	46.1

Note: (1) Metropolitan Statistical Area - see Appendix A for areas included; 1989 data is from the 1990 Census; 1999 data is estimated by Claritas, Inc.
Source: 1990 Census of Population, General Population Characteristics; Claritas, Inc.

Household Income Distribution

Area	Percent of Households Earning								
	Under $5,000	$5,000 -14,999	$15,000 -24,999	$25,000 -34,999	$35,000 -49,999	$50,000 -74,999	$75,000 -99,000	$100,000 -149,999	$150,000 and up
City	3.9	14.0	16.3	16.6	17.3	16.5	6.5	4.5	4.3
MSA[1]	2.5	10.8	15.4	15.3	18.6	19.7	8.1	5.3	4.4
U.S.	3.9	13.3	13.8	12.6	16.2	19.4	9.7	6.6	4.6

Note: Data as of 1999; (1) Metropolitan Statistical Area - see Appendix A for areas included
Source: Claritas, Inc.

Effective Buying Income

Area	Per Capita ($)	Median Household ($)	Average Household ($)
City	18,687	29,185	41,544
MSA[1]	20,270	34,310	46,026
U.S.	17,496	36,603	47,036

Note: Data as of 1/1/2000; (1) Metropolitan Statistical Area - see Appendix A for areas included
Source: Standard Rate & Data Service, Newspaper Advertising Source, March 2000

Effective Household Buying Income Distribution

Area	% of Households Earning						
	$10,000 -$19,999	$20,000 -$34,999	$35,000 -$49,999	$50,000 -$74,999	$75,000 -$99,000	$100,000 -$124,999	$125,000 and up
City	18.8	27.4	16.9	13.4	4.8	2.0	3.7
MSA[1]	16.4	26.0	19.0	17.5	6.4	2.4	3.6
U.S.	15.0	21.6	17.6	19.6	8.4	3.0	3.3

Note: Data as of 1/1/2000; (1) Metropolitan Statistical Area - see Appendix A for areas included
Source: Standard Rate & Data Service, Newspaper Advertising Source, March 2000

Poverty Rates by Age

Area	People of All Ages	People Under 18 Years Old	Related Children Age 5-17 in Families in Poverty
City	18.2	n/a	n/a
County	9.2	16.1	13.9
U.S.	13.8	20.8	18.7

Note: Figures show the percent of people living below the poverty line in 1995. The
average poverty threshold was $15,569 for a family of four in 1995; n/a not available
Source: Bureau of the Census, Small Area Income and Poverty Estimates Program;
U.S. Department of Housing and Urban Development

EMPLOYMENT

Labor Force and Employment

Area	Civilian Labor Force			Workers Employed		
	Dec. 1998	Dec. 1999	% Chg.	Dec. 1998	Dec. 1999	% Chg.
City	30,840	31,395	1.8	30,040	30,679	2.1
MSA[1]	266,373	271,491	1.9	260,889	266,437	2.1
U.S.	138,297,000	139,941,000	1.2	132,732,000	134,696,000	1.5

Note: Data is not seasonally adjusted and covers workers 16 years of age and older;
(1) Metropolitan Statistical Area - see Appendix A for areas included
Source: Bureau of Labor Statistics, http://stats.bls.gov

Unemployment Rate

Area	1999											
	Jan.	Feb.	Mar.	Apr.	May	Jun.	Jul.	Aug.	Sep.	Oct.	Nov.	Dec.
City	3.7	3.0	2.6	3.3	2.6	2.5	2.7	2.4	3.1	2.8	2.8	2.3
MSA[1]	2.7	2.3	2.1	2.4	2.1	2.1	2.4	2.4	2.7	2.4	2.3	1.9
U.S.	4.8	4.7	4.4	4.1	4.0	4.5	4.5	4.2	4.1	3.8	3.8	3.7

Note: Data is not seasonally adjusted and covers workers 16 years of age and older; all figures are percentages; (1) Metropolitan Statistical Area - see Appendix A for areas included
Source: Bureau of Labor Statistics, http://stats.bls.gov

Employment by Industry

Sector	MSA[1]		U.S.
	Number of Employees	Percent of Total	Percent of Total
Services	129,800	47.5	30.2
Retail Trade	56,000	20.5	18.1
Government	24,300	8.9	15.8
Manufacturing	22,100	8.1	14.1
Finance/Insurance/Real Estate	12,000	4.4	5.9
Wholesale Trade	8,500	3.1	5.4
Transportation/Public Utilities	5,400	2.0	5.3
Construction	14,900	5.5	4.8
Mining	n/a	n/a	0.4

Note: Figures cover non-farm employment as of 12/99 and are not seasonally adjusted; (1) Metropolitan Statistical Area - see Appendix A for areas included; n/a not available
Source: Bureau of Labor Statistics, http://stats.bls.gov

Employment by Occupation

Occupation Category	City (%)	MSA[1] (%)	U.S. (%)
White Collar	55.2	59.9	58.1
Executive/Admin./Management	10.8	13.5	12.3
Professional	14.1	13.1	14.1
Technical & Related Support	3.5	3.2	3.7
Sales	13.1	15.9	11.8
Administrative Support/Clerical	13.7	14.2	16.3
Blue Collar	21.2	21.0	26.2
Precision Production/Craft/Repair	11.0	11.8	11.3
Machine Operators/Assem./Insp.	2.8	2.9	6.8
Transportation/Material Movers	3.8	3.0	4.1
Cleaners/Helpers/Laborers	3.5	3.3	3.9
Services	21.0	16.7	13.2
Farming/Forestry/Fishing	2.6	2.3	2.5

Note: Figures cover workers 16 years of age and older; (1) Metropolitan Statistical Area - see Appendix A for areas included
Source: 1990 Census of Population and Housing, Summary Tape File 3C

Occupational Employment Projections: 1996 - 2006

Occupations Expected to Have the Largest Job Growth (ranked by numerical growth)	Fast-Growing Occupations[1] (ranked by percent growth)
1. Cashiers	1. Systems analysts
2. Salespersons, retail	2. Physical therapy assistants and aides
3. General managers & top executives	3. Desktop publishers
4. Registered nurses	4. Home health aides
5. Waiters & waitresses	5. Computer engineers
6. Marketing & sales, supervisors	6. Medical assistants
7. Janitors/cleaners/maids, ex. priv. hshld.	7. Physical therapists
8. General office clerks	8. Paralegals
9. Food preparation workers	9. Emergency medical technicians
10. Hand packers & packagers	10. Occupational therapists

Note: Projections cover Florida; (1) Excludes occupations with total job growth less than 300
Source: U.S. Department of Labor, Employment and Training Administration, America's Labor Market Information System (ALMIS)

Average Wages

Occupation	$/Hr.	Occupation	$/Hr.
Accountants and Auditors	23.00	Maids and Housekeepers	7.32
Assemblers and Fabricators	8.81	Maintenance Repairers	10.32
Automotive Mechanics	14.90	Marketing/Advertising/PR Managers	20.73
Bookkeepers	10.77	Nurses, Licensed Practical	12.75
Carpenters	12.54	Nurses, Registered	18.24
Cashiers	7.12	Nursing Aides/Orderlies/Attendants	8.40
Clerks, General Office	8.71	Physicians and Surgeons	54.00
Clerks, Shipping/Receiving/Traffic	11.19	Receptionists/Information Clerks	8.56
Computer Programmers	22.06	Sales Reps., Exc. Scientific/Retail	14.79
Computer Support Specialists	12.43	Sales Reps., Scientific, Exc. Retail	23.24
Cooks, Restaurant	8.87	Salespersons, Retail	9.06
Electricians	11.99	Secretaries, Except Legal/Medical	10.50
Financial Managers	23.95	Stock Clerks, Sales Floor	7.81
First-Line Supervisors/Mgrs., Sales	15.36	Systems Analysts	19.23
Food Preparation Workers	7.22	Teacher Aides	8.85
General Managers/Top Executives	26.34	Teachers, Elementary School	18.03
Guards	6.80	Teachers, Secondary School	18.67
Hand Packers	6.66	Telemarketers	9.81
Janitors and Cleaners	7.62	Truck Drivers, Heavy/Tractor-Trailer	12.48
Laborers, Landscaping	7.60	Truck Drivers, Light	9.49
Lawyers	27.39	Waiters and Waitresses	6.12

Note: Wage data is for 1998 and covers the Metropolitan Statistical Area (see Appendix A for areas included). Hourly wages for elementary and secondary school teachers were calculated by the editors from annual wage data assuming a 40 hour work week; Dashes indicate that data was not available.
Source: Bureau of Labor Statistics, 1998 Metropolitan Area Occupational Employment and Wage Estimates

TAXES

Major State and Local Tax Rates

State Corporate Income (%)	State Personal Income (%)	Residential Property (%)	Sales & Use		State Gasoline (cents/ gallon)	State Cigarette (cents/ pack)
			State (%)	Local (%)		
5.5[a]	None	1.20	6.0	None	13.3[b]	33.9

Note: Personal/corporate income, sales, gasoline and cigarette tax rates as of January 2000. Property tax rates as of April 2000; (a) 3.3% Alternative Minimum Tax. An exemption of $5,000 is allowed; (b) Rate is comprised of 4 cents excise and 9.3 cents motor carrier tax. Local taxes vary from 5.5 cents to 17 cents. Plus a 2.07 cent per gallon pollution tax
Source: Federation of Tax Administrators, www.taxadmin.org; ERI's Relocation Assessor software database, quarterly effective date 4/1/2000

Total Taxes Per Capita and as a Percent of Income

Area	Per Capita Income ($)	Per Capita Taxes ($)			Percent of Income (%)		
		Total	Federal	State/Local	Total	Federal	State/Local
Florida	28,322	10,333	7,257	3,077	36.5	25.6	10.9
U.S.	28,878	10,298	7,026	3,273	35.7	24.3	11.3

Note: Figures are for 1999
Source: Tax Foundation, www.taxfoundation.org

COMMERCIAL UTILITIES

Typical Monthly Electric Bills

Area	Commercial Service ($/month)		Industrial Service ($/month)	
	12 kW demand 1,500 kWh	100 kW demand 30,000 kWh	1,000 kW demand 400,000 kWh	20,000 kW demand 10,000,000 kWh
City	118	1,993	23,247	387,510
U.S.	150	2,174	23,995	508,569

Note: Based on rates in effect January 1, 1999
Source: Edison Electric Institute, Typical Residential, Commercial and Industrial Bills, Winter 1999

TRANSPORTATION

Transportation Statistics

Average minutes to work (1990)	16.8
Interstate highways	I-75; US-41
Bus lines	
In-city (1998)	Sarasota County Transportation Authority, 25 buses
Inter-city (1999)	1
Passenger air service	
Airport	Sarasota/Bradenton International
Airlines (1999)	11
Enplaned passengers (1998)	775,484
Amtrak service	Bus Connection
Motor freight carriers (1999)	n/a
Major waterways/ports	Port Manatee

Source: FAA DOT/TSC CY1998 ACAIS Database; National Transit Database, 1998; Editor & Publisher Market Guide, 2000; Amtrak National Time Table, Fall 1999/Winter 2000; 1990 Census of Population and Housing, STF 3C; Jane's Urban Transport Systems 1999-2000

Means of Transportation to Work

Area	Car/Truck/Van		Public Transportation			Bicycle	Walked	Other Means	Worked at Home
	Drove Alone	Car-pooled	Bus	Subway	Railroad				
City	73.9	14.3	1.4	0.1	0.0	2.0	3.7	1.8	2.8
MSA[1]	79.8	11.8	0.5	0.0	0.0	1.1	2.1	1.3	3.3
U.S.	73.2	13.4	3.0	1.5	0.5	0.4	3.9	1.2	3.0

Note: Figures shown are percentages and only include workers 16 years of age and older;
(1) Metropolitan Statistical Area - see Appendix A for areas included
Source: 1990 Census of Population and Housing, Summary Tape File 3C

BUSINESSES

Major Business Headquarters

Company Name	1999 Rankings	
	Fortune 500	Forbes 500
No companies listed	-	-

Note: Companies listed are located in the city; dashes indicate no ranking
Fortune 500: Companies that produce a 10-K are ranked 1 to 500 based on 1999 revenue
Forbes 500: Private companies are ranked 1 to 500 based on 1998 revenue
Source: Forbes, December 13, 1999; Fortune, April 17, 2000

HOTELS & MOTELS

Hotels/Motels

Area	Hotels/ Motels	Rooms	Luxury-Level Hotels/Motels		Average Minimum Rates ($)		
			♦♦♦♦	♦♦♦♦♦	♦♦	♦♦♦	♦♦♦♦
City	16	1,644	0	0	79	101	n/a
Airport	8	774	0	0	n/a	n/a	n/a
Suburbs	31	2,735	2	0	n/a	n/a	n/a
Total	55	5,153	2	0	n/a	n/a	n/a

Note: n/a not available; classifications range from one diamond (budget properties with basic amenities) to five diamond (luxury properties).
Source: OAG Business Travel Planner, Winter 1999-2000

Estimated Daily Food and Lodging Costs

Area	Food/Other ($/day)	Average Hotel Cost ($/day)
City	38	79
U.S.	30	55

Source: ERI's Relocation Assessor software database, quarterly effective date 4/1/2000

CONVENTION CENTERS

Convention Centers and Event Sites

Name	Guest Rooms	Meeting Space (sq. ft.)	Capacity (Theatre Style)
Ed Smith Stadium/Sports Complex	n/a	n/a	7,500
Radisson Lido Beach Resort	116	n/a	100
Sarasota Municipal Auditorium	n/a	n/a	1,280

Note: n/a not available
Source: EventSource.com, 3/15/2000

Living Environment

COST OF LIVING

Cost of Living: Homeowner

Cost Element	U.S. ($)	City ($)	Differential ($)	Percent of U.S. Average
Consumables	14,516	15,118	602	104.1
Transportation	5,957	6,150	193	103.2
Health Services	2,012	2,159	147	107.3
Housing/Utilities/Prop. Tax	16,337	20,991	4,654	128.5
Income+Payroll Taxes	12,615	10,254	-2,361	81.3
Miscellaneous	8,563	8,563	0	100.0
Total Cost of Living	60,000	63,235	3,235	105.4

Note: Figures are based on a single income, four person family with gross annual earnings of $60,000, owning an 1,800 square-foot home, and driving two automobiles worth $22,000 30,000 miles per year.
Source: ERI's Relocation Assessor software database, quarterly effective date 4/1/2000

Cost of Living: Renter

Cost Element	U.S. ($)	City ($)	Differential ($)	Percent of U.S. Average
Consumables	10,486	10,862	376	103.6
Transportation	2,107	2,164	57	102.7
Health Services	1,632	1,743	111	106.8
Rent/Utilities/Insurance	9,299	11,637	2,338	125.1
Income+Payroll Taxes	8,607	7,183	-1,424	83.5
Miscellaneous	7,869	7,869	0	100.0
Total Cost of Living	40,000	41,458	1,458	103.6

Note: Figures are based on a single income, three person family with gross annual earnings of $40,000, renting a 1,000 square-foot home, and driving one automobile worth $8,000 12,000 miles per year.
Source: ERI's Relocation Assessor software database, quarterly effective date 4/1/2000

HOUSING

Median Home Prices and Housing Affordability

Area	Median Price[2] 4th Qtr. 1999 ($)	HOI[3] 4th Qtr. 1999	Affordability Rank[4]
MSA[1]	109,000	69.7	96
U.S.	139,000	63.8	–

Note: (1) Metropolitan Statistical Area - see Appendix A for areas included; (2) U.S. figures calculated from the sales of 687,516 new and existing homes in 192 markets; (3) Housing Opportunity Index - percent of homes sold that were within the reach of the median income household at the prevailing mortgage interest rate; (4) Rank is from 1-192 with 1 being most affordable
Source: National Association of Home Builders, Housing Opportunity Index, 4th Quarter 1999

Estimated Home Price

Area	Price ($)
City	181,508
U.S.	135,855

Note: Figures are based on an 1,800 square-foot home
Source: ERI's Relocation Assessor software database, quarterly effective date 4/1/2000

Estimated Rent

Area	Rent ($/month)
City	844
U.S.	651

Note: Figures are based on a 1,000 square-foot home
Source: ERI's Relocation Assessor software database, quarterly effective date 4/1/2000

Median Home Price Projection

It is projected that the median home price in the metropolitan area will increase from $126,141 in 1999 to $194,042 in 2010, an increase of 53.8%
Kiplinger's Personal Finance Magazine, January 2000

RESIDENTIAL UTILITIES

Average Residential Utility Costs

Area	All Electric ($/mth)	Part Electric ($/mth)	Other Energy ($/mth)	Phone ($/mth)
City	105.18	–	–	17.16
U.S.	99.25	55.47	43.48	20.29

Source: ACCRA, Cost of Living Index, 3rd Quarter 1999

HEALTH CARE

Average Health Care Costs

Area	Hospital ($/day)	Doctor ($/visit)	Dentist ($/visit)
City	448.67	56.17	61.40
U.S.	440.96	53.83	68.42

Note: Hospital—based on a semi-private room; Doctor—based on a general practitioner's routine exam of an established patient; Dentist—based on adult teeth cleaning and periodic oral exam.
Source: ACCRA, Cost of Living Index, 3rd Quarter 1999

Distribution of Office-Based Physicians

Area	Family/Gen. Practitioners	Specialists		
		Medical	Surgical	Other
MSA[1]	150	390	327	277

Note: Data as of 12/31/97; (1) Metropolitan Statistical Area - see Appendix A for areas included
Source: American Medical Assn., Physician Characteristics & Distribution in the U.S., 1999

Hospitals

Sarasota has 2 general medical and surgical hospitals, 1 rehabilitation.
AHA Guide to the Healthcare Field, 1999-2000

EDUCATION

Public School District Statistics

District Name	Num. Sch.	Enroll.	Classroom Teachers	Pupils per Teacher	Minority Pupils (%)	Current Exp.[1] ($/pupil)
Sarasota County Sch Dist	43	33,160	1,929	17.2	17.0	5,982

Note: Data covers the 1997-1998 school year unless otherwise noted; (1) Data covers fiscal year 1996; SD = School District; ISD = Independent School District; n/a not available
Source: National Center for Education Statistics, Common Core of Data Public Education Agency Universe 1997-98; National Center for Education Statistics, Characteristics of the 100 Largest Public Elementary and Secondary School Districts in the United States: 1997-98, July 1999

Educational Quality

School District	Education Quotient[1]	Graduate Outcome[2]	Community Index[3]	Resource Index[4]
Sarasota Co. School Dist.	115	120	131	102

Note: Over 1,000 secondary school districts were rated in terms of educational quality. The scores range from a low of 50 to a high of 150; (1) Combination of the Graduate Outcome, Community and Resource indexes weighted to reflect the greater importance of the Graduate Outcome and Resource Index; (2) Based on graduation rates and college board scores (SAT/ACT); (3) Based on the surrounding community's level of affluence and adult education; (4) Based on teacher salaries, per-pupil expenditures and student-teacher ratios.
Source: Expansion Management, Ratings Issue, 1999

Educational Attainment by Race

Area	High School Graduate (%)					Bachelor's Degree (%)				
	Total	White	Black	Other	Hisp.[2]	Total	White	Black	Other	Hisp.[2]
City	76.4	80.2	51.1	51.1	53.0	21.0	22.8	8.6	10.9	9.9
MSA[1]	81.3	82.3	54.5	62.8	63.7	21.9	22.4	9.8	17.2	13.5
U.S.	75.2	77.9	63.1	60.4	49.8	20.3	21.5	11.4	19.4	9.2

Note: Figures shown cover persons 25 years old and over; (1) Metropolitan Statistical Area - see Appendix A for areas included; (2) people of Hispanic origin can be of any race
Source: 1990 Census of Population and Housing, Summary Tape File 3C

School Enrollment by Type

Area	Preprimary				Elementary/High School			
	Public		Private		Public		Private	
	Enrollment	%	Enrollment	%	Enrollment	%	Enrollment	%
City	411	58.5	292	41.5	5,171	92.6	412	7.4
MSA[1]	1,805	49.7	1,827	50.3	25,943	90.6	2,706	9.4
U.S.	2,679,029	59.5	1,824,256	40.5	38,379,689	90.2	4,187,099	9.8

Note: Figures shown cover persons 3 years old and over;
(1) Metropolitan Statistical Area - see Appendix A for areas included
Source: 1990 Census of Population and Housing, Summary Tape File 3C

School Enrollment by Race

Area	Preprimary (%)				Elementary/High School (%)			
	White	Black	Other	Hisp.[1]	White	Black	Other	Hisp.[1]
City	68.1	29.4	2.4	6.3	66.3	30.5	3.2	6.7
MSA[2]	90.7	7.9	1.4	2.9	89.2	8.7	2.2	4.0
U.S.	80.4	12.5	7.1	7.8	74.1	15.6	10.3	12.5

Note: Figures shown cover persons 3 years old and over; (1) people of Hispanic origin can be of any race; (2) Metropolitan Statistical Area - see Appendix A for areas included
Source: 1990 Census of Population and Housing, Summary Tape File 3C

Higher Education

Two-Year Colleges		Four-Year Colleges		Medical Schools	Law Schools	Voc/ Tech
Public	Private	Public	Private			
0	1	1	1	0	0	7

Source: College Blue Book, Occupational Education, 1999; Medical School Admission Requirements, 1999-2000; Peterson's Guide to Two-Year Colleges, 2000; Peterson's Guide to Four-Year Colleges, 1999; Barron's Guide to Law Schools, 1999

MAJOR EMPLOYERS

Major Employers

FCCI Insurance Group
Hi Stat Manufacturing
National Instore Marketing
Sarasota Doctor's Hospital

Florida Employers Insurance Service Corp.
Integrated Health Services at Sarasota
Sarasota Co. Public Hospital Board
Wellcraft Marine Corp.

Note: Companies listed are located in the city
Source: D&B Business Rankings, 1999; Ward's Business Directory, 1999; America's Corporate Families, 1999

PUBLIC SAFETY

Crime Rate

Area	All Crimes	Violent Crimes				Property Crimes		
		Murder	Forcible Rape	Robbery	Aggrav. Assault	Burglary	Larceny -Theft	Motor Vehicle Theft
City	8,799.8	5.7	61.0	449.8	850.1	1,639.1	5,233.8	560.4
Suburbs[1]	4,753.5	3.4	26.6	105.3	421.6	1,068.1	2,867.8	260.7
MSA[2]	5,140.6	3.6	29.9	138.2	462.6	1,122.7	3,094.2	289.4
U.S.	4,615.5	6.3	34.4	165.2	360.5	862.0	2,728.1	459.0

Note: Crime rate is the number of crimes per 100,000 population; (1) Defined as all areas within the Metropolitan Statistical Area but located outside the central city; (2) Metropolitan Statistical Area - see Appendix A for areas included
Source: FBI Uniform Crime Reports, 1998

RECREATION

Culture and Recreation

Museums	Symphony Orchestras	Opera Companies	Dance Companies	Professional Theatres	Zoos	Pro Sports Teams
4	2	1	1	3	0	0

Source: Musical America, International Directory of the Performing Arts, 1999; Official Museum Directory, 2000; Stern's Performing Arts Directory, 1997; USA Today Four Sport Stadium Guide, 1997; Career Opportunities in Theatre and the Performing Arts, 1999

Library System

The Selby Public Library has no branches and holdings of 192,727 volumes.
American Library Directory, 1999-2000

MEDIA

Newspapers

Name	Type	Freq.	Distribution	Circulation
The Bulletin	Black	1x/wk	Local	20,000
Sarasota Herald-Tribune	General	7x/wk	Area	114,450
The Weekly	General	1x/wk	Local	50,000

Note: Includes newspapers with circulations of 200 or more located in the city;
Source: Burrelle's Media Directory, 1999 Edition

Television Stations

Name	Ch.	Affiliation	Type	Owner
WWSB	40	ABCT	Commercial	Southern Broadcasting Corporation
WBSV	62	n/a	Non-comm.	DeSoto Broadcasting Inc.

Note: Stations included broadcast in the Sarasota metro area; n/a not available
Source: Burrelle's Media Directory, 1999 Edition

AM Radio Stations

Call Letters	Freq. (kHz)	Target Audience	Station Format	Music Format
WKXY	930	General	N/T	n/a
WTMY	1280	General	T	n/a
WAMR	1320	Men	S	n/a
WBRD	1420	Religious	M	Christian
WSPB	1450	General	N/T	n/a
WENG	1530	General	E/N/S/T	n/a

Note: Stations included broadcast in the Sarasota metro area; n/a not available
Target Audience: A=Asian; B=Black; C=Christian; E=Ethnic; F=French; G=General; H=Hispanic; M=Men; N=Native American; R=Religious; S=Senior Citizen; W=Women; Y=Young Adult; Z=Children
Station Format: E=Educational; M=Music; N=News; S=Sports; T=Talk
Source: Burrelle's Media Directory, 1999 Edition

FM Radio Stations

Call Letters	Freq. (mHz)	Target Audience	Station Format	Music Format
WCTQ	92.1	Women	M/N/S	Country
WKZM	104.3	General	M	Christian
WYNF	105.9	General	n/a	n/a
WSRZ	106.5	General	M	Oldies

Note: Stations included broadcast in the Sarasota metro area; n/a not available
Station Format: E=Educational; M=Music; N=News; S=Sports; T=Talk
Target Audience: A=Asian; B=Black; C=Christian; E=Ethnic; F=French; G=General; H=Hispanic; M=Men; N=Native American; R=Religious; S=Senior Citizen; W=Women; Y=Young Adult; Z=Children
Source: Burrelle's Media Directory, 1999 Edition

WEATHER

Temperature/Precipitation/Humidity

	Jan	Feb	Mar	Apr	May	Jun	Jul	Aug	Sep	Oct	Nov	Dec	Yr.
Max. High Temp. (°F)	83	85	86	93	96	98	98	97	97	93	89	86	98
Avg. High Temp. (°F)	70	73	75	81	86	90	90	90	89	83	77	71	81
Avg. Temp. (°F)	61	64	67	73	78	82	83	83	82	75	68	62	73
Avg. Low Temp. (°F)	53	56	59	65	70	75	76	76	75	68	60	54	66
Min. Low Temp. (°F)	32	32	37	50	54	66	69	68	65	43	34	29	29
Avg. Precip. (in.)	1.7	2.4	3.1	2.4	2.3	4.3	7.0	5.8	6.2	3.7	1.9	2.0	42.8
Avg. Snowfall (in.)	0	0	0	0	0	0	0	0	0	0	0	0	0
Avg. Rel. Hum. (%)	76	74	73	71	70	73	76	77	78	75	75	75	74

Source: National Climatic Data Center, International Station Meteorological Climate Summary, 3/95

Weather Conditions

Temperature			Precipitation		
0°F & below	32°F & below	90°F & above	0.1 inch or more precip.	1.5 inch or more snow/ice	Thunder-storms
0	0	87	67	0	76

Note: Figures are average number of days per year
Source: National Climatic Data Center, International Station Meteorological Climate Summary, 3/95

AIR & WATER QUALITY

Maximum Pollutant Concentrations

	Particulate Matter (ug/m³)	Carbon Monoxide (ppm)	Sulfur Dioxide (ppm)	Nitrogen Dioxide (ppm)	Ozone (ppm)	Lead (ug/m³)
MSA[1] Level	56	5	0.012	n/a	0.11	n/a
NAAQS[2]	150	9	0.140	0.053	0.12	1.50
Met NAAQS	Yes	Yes	Yes	n/a	Yes	n/a

Note: (1) Metropolitan Statistical Area - see Appendix A for areas included; (2) National Ambient Air Quality Standards; ppm = parts per million; ug/m³ = micrograms per cubic meter; n/a not available
Source: EPA, National Air Quality and Emissions Trends Report, 1997

Pollutant Standards Index

Data not available. *EPA, National Air Quality and Emissions Trends Report, 1997*

Drinking Water

Water System Name	Pop. Served	Primary Water Source Type	Number of Violations in 1998-99	Type of Violation/ Contaminants
City of Sarasota	52,000	Ground	None	None

Note: Data as of January 19, 2000
Source: EPA, Office of Ground Water and Drinking Water, Safe Drinking Water Information System

Sarasota tap water is hard.
Editor & Publisher Market Guide, 2000

Scranton, Pennsylvania

Background

Scranton, Pennsylvania is located in northeast Pennsylvania, about 130 miles north of Philadelphia and 130 miles west of New York City. The city is situated in a valley on the Lackawanna River within in a very mountainous region, with the Pocanos and other ranges nearby. Scranton is at the base of mountains, and the terrain is marked by dramatic changes in elevation.

Scranton is the county seat of Lackawanna County, and was chartered as a city in 1866. It is the largest city in a metropolitan statistical area that includes Wilkes Barre, about 20 miles away, and Hazelton beyond that. The area's history was shaped by the coal, iron and railroad industries. Today Scranton and the surrounding area have a more diverse economy.

A village was established on the site of Scranton in the 1780s, and iron furnaces and metals-processing operations were among its early activities. Around 1840, the community developed into a major center for the iron and steel industry, including the manufacture of steel rails for the railroads. The city, which had several names in its early years, was officially named Scranton in 1851, for George Scranton and his family who were instrumental in local industrial development. The area was also the site of a major deposit of anthracite coal.

In the mid-19th Century, with the increasing demand for the fuel, Scranton also became a center of the coal industry, with underground and above-ground coal mines and processing operations throughout the city and surrounding area. Scranton also became a center for railroading and transport. These industries attracted many immigrants into the area, and miners' wives worked in the lace and textile industry. Scranton, which is sometimes called "Electric City," pioneered in the development of urban electricity in street lighting and trolley systems.

Scranton began to experience serious economic decline after 1920, with changes in the steel industry, the replacement of coal by other fuels and the diminishing role of railroads. Because it experienced the loss of its traditional industrial base earlier than many areas Scranton, in the early 1950s, was among the earliest cities to pursue modern public-private sector partnerships and community-based economic revitalization strategies. Under what is known as the "Scranton Plan," government, the Greater Scranton Chamber of Commerce and others formed non-profit enterprises to invest in industrial sites and offer other incentives to attract new industries and local improvements. Over time, these efforts helped the Scranton area to establish a more diverse economic base. Current economic sectors in Scranton include information-processing and other business-support operations, financial services, manufacturing, government, education and other services.

Although not primarily a resort area, Scranton has also developed a tourism economy. Several major interstate highways connect around Scranton, which is near the Pocono resort region. The city also has several tourist attractions based on the region's history, including museums, tours of old coal mines and processing facilities, and Steamtown, a national park and historic site dedicated to the age of steam railroads. The Houdini Museum, dedicated to the well-known magician is also in Scranton.

Montage Mountain ski resort in Scranton hosts concerts and other events in warm weather. The Scranton Cultural Center is restoration of an elaborate Masonic Temple. The Lackawanna County Multi-Purpose Stadium is home to the Scranton-Wilkes Barre Red Barons, a minor league affiliate of the Philadelphia Phillies.

Colleges within Scranton include the University of Scranton, Marywood University Judson Technical Institute and Lackawanna Junior College. Scranton is also headquarters of the International Correspondence Schools.

General Rankings and Evaluative Comments

- Scranton was ranked #80 out of 354 metropolitan areas in *Places Rated Almanac*. Criteria: cost of living, climate, crime, transportation, job outlook, education, the arts, health care, and recreation. *Places Rated Almanac, Millennium Edition, 2000*

- Cognetics studied 273 metro areas in the United States, ranking them by entrepreneurial activity. Scranton was ranked #132 out of 134 smaller metro areas. Criteria: Significant Starts (firms started in the last 10 years that still employ at least 5 people) and Young Growers (percent of firms 10 years old or less that grew significantly during the last 4 years). *Cognetics, "Entrepreneurial Hot Spots: The Best Places in America to Start and Grow a Company," 1999*

- Reliastar Financial Corporation ranked the 125 largest metropolitan areas according to the general financial security of residents. Scranton was ranked #97 out of 125 with a score of -3.5 (the percentage a metropolitan area is above or below the metropolitan norm; a metro area with a score of 10.6 is 10.6% above the metro average). Criteria: Earnings and Wealth Potential (household income, education, net assets, cost of living); Safety Net (health insurance, retirement savings, life insurance, income support programs); Personal Threats (unemployment rate, low-income households, crime rate); Community Economic Vitality (cost of community services, job quality, job creation, housing costs). Reliastar Financial Corporation, "The Best Cities to Earn and Save Money: A Ranking of the Largest 125 U.S. Cities," 2000 Edition

Business Environment

STATE ECONOMY

State Economic Profile

"Pennsylvania's economy has lagged the nation for several years, a trend that will only get worse. While Philadelphia has seen some resurgence, it has not been enough to offset declines in the rest of the state. Pennsylvania's poor demographic outlook will confine it to slow growth at best in 2000. Expansions by high-tech and biotech firms, such as Lucent, SAP and SmithKline Beecham, will help Pennsylvania's weak job outlook, although these gains will be limited to the eastern part of the state.

Pennsylvania employment grew at the low rate of 0.8% in 1998, driven largely by the 1.0% increase in Philadelphia. In contrast, Pittsburgh lost jobs at a rate of 0.1%. While many areas of the country are experiencing declining manufacturing employment, due to weak export demand and long-term restructuring, Pittsburgh is one of the few urban areas that is also losing service jobs, at a rate of 0.4% in 1998. Services employment for Pennsylvania grew 1.3% and 1.9% for Philadelphia in 1998.

Some of western Pennsylvania's problems stem from its declining steel sector. Weak steel prices, over capacity and a flood of cheap imports have undermined Pennsylvania's steel industry. Even with import restraints and renewed world demand, the outlook for Pennsylvania's steel industry remains bleak. Pennsylvania's steel producers' biggest problem is US mini-mills that are sweeping the industry. Further declines in Pennsylvania's steel industry are likely in 2000.

Few states lose more residents every year than Pennsylvania. Its continued loss of younger households will constrain labor market growth and pose problems for its housing market. Home sales were flat in 1998, and residential permits were up only 3%. Both sales and starts should contract in the near future." *National Association of Realtors, Economic Profiles: The Fifty States and the District of Columbia, http://nar.realtor.com/databank/profiles.htm*

EXPORTS

Total Export Sales

Area	1995 ($000)	1996 ($000)	1997 ($000)	1998 ($000)	% Chg. 1995-98	% Chg. 1997-98
MSA[1]	431,874	391,991	442,414	438,238	1.5	-0.9
U.S.	583,030,524	622,827,063	687,597,999	680,474,251	16.7	-1.0

Note: (1) Metropolitan Statistical Area - see Appendix A for areas included
Source: U.S. Department of Commerce, International Trade Association, Metropolitan Area Exports: An Export Performance Report on Over 250 U.S. Cities, November 10, 1999

CITY FINANCES

City Government Finances

Component	1995 ($million)	1995 (per capita $)
Revenue	42.1	541
Expenditure	45.1	579
Debt Outstanding	8.0	103

Source: 1999 County and City Extra, Annual Metro, City, and County Data Book

City Government Revenue by Source

Source	1995 ($million)	1995 (per capita $)
Intergovernmental	8.4	107
Taxes	29.3	375
Property	9.6	124
Sales and Gross Receipts	0.0	0

Source: 1999 County and City Extra, Annual Metro, City, and County Data Book

City Government Expenditures by Function

Function	1995 ($million)	1995 (per capita $)	1995 (%)
Public Welfare	0.0	0	0.0
Highways	3.6	46	8.0
Parking Facilities	0.9	12	2.1
Education	0.0	0	0.0
Health and Hospitals	<0.1	<1	0.1
Police Protection	9.5	122	21.2
Sewerage and Sanitation	2.5	33	5.7
Parks and Recreation	1.2	16	2.8
Housing and Community Development	3.4	44	7.7
Interest on Debt	0.3	4	0.8

Source: 1999 County and City Extra, Annual Metro, City, and County Data Book

Municipal Bond Ratings

Area	Moody's
City	n/a

Note: n/a not available
Source: Mergent Bond Record, 2/2000

POPULATION

Population Growth

Area	1980 Census	1990 Census	1999 Estimate	2004 Projection	Population Growth (%) 1990-1999	Population Growth (%) 1999-2004
City	88,117	81,805	74,036	70,823	-9.5	-4.3
MSA[1]	659,387	734,175	611,758	600,579	-16.7	-1.8
U.S.	226,545,805	248,765,170	272,212,864	283,625,312	9.4	4.2

Note: (1) Metropolitan Statistical Area - see Appendix A for areas included
Source: 1990 Census of Population and Housing, Summary Tape File 3C; Claritas, Inc.

Number of Households and Average Household Size

Area	1980 Census	1990 Census	1999 Estimate	2004 Projection	1999 Average Household Size
City	33,520	32,648	30,223	29,207	2.45
MSA[1]	238,101	280,648	241,634	239,811	2.53
U.S.	80,389,592	91,993,582	102,048,200	107,302,392	2.67

Note: (1) Metropolitan Statistical Area - see Appendix A for areas included
Source: 1990 Census of Population and Housing, Summary Tape File 3C; Claritas, Inc.

Race/Ethnicity of City Population

Race/Ethnicity	1990 Census Population	1990 Census %	1999 Estimate Population	1999 Estimate %	% Change 1990-1999
White, Non-Hispanic	79,167	96.8	70,832	95.7	-10.5
Black, Non-Hispanic	1,192	1.5	1,348	1.8	13.1
Asian, Non-Hispanic	853	1.0	899	1.2	5.4
Other, Non-Hispanic	73	0.1	177	0.2	142.5
Hispanic	520	0.6	780	1.1	50.0

Source: 1990 Census of Population and Housing, Summary Tape File 3C; Claritas, Inc.

Race/Ethnicity of Metropolitan Statistical Area Population

Race/Ethnicity	1990 Census		1999 Estimate		% Change 1990-1999
	Population	%	Population	%	
White, Non-Hispanic	717,059	97.7	595,781	97.4	-16.9
Black, Non-Hispanic	7,284	1.0	5,991	1.0	-17.8
Asian, Non-Hispanic	3,392	0.5	4,188	0.7	23.5
Other, Non-Hispanic	833	0.1	885	0.1	6.2
Hispanic	5,607	0.8	4,913	0.8	-12.4

Note: See Appendix A for areas included in the Metropolitan Statistical Area
Source: 1990 Census of Population and Housing, Summary Tape File 3C; Claritas, Inc.

Ancestry

Area	German	Irish	English	Italian	U.S.	French	Polish	Dutch
City	21.8	32.3	7.3	20.0	1.6	1.4	16.6	1.2
MSA[1]	25.7	20.6	9.9	16.6	2.1	1.9	19.3	4.0
U.S.	23.3	15.6	13.1	5.9	5.3	4.2	3.8	2.5

Note: Figures are percentages and include persons that reported multiple ancestry (eg. if a person reported being Irish and Italian, they were included in both columns); (1) Metropolitan Statistical Area - see Appendix A for areas included
Source: 1990 Census of Population and Housing, Summary Tape File 3C

Median Age

Area	1990 Census	1999 Estimate
City	37.1	39.1
MSA[1]	36.8	39.7
U.S.	32.9	35.7

Note: (1) Metropolitan Statistical Area - see Appendix A for areas included
Source: 1990 Census of Population and Housing, Summary Tape File 3C; Claritas, Inc.

Male/Female Population

Area	Number of Males		Number of Females		Males per 100 Females	
	1990	1999	1990	1999	1990	1999
City	37,445	34,117	44,360	39,919	84.4	85.5
MSA[1]	348,503	289,161	385,672	322,597	90.4	89.6
U.S.	121,172,379	132,803,736	127,537,494	139,409,136	95.0	95.3

Note: (1) Metropolitan Statistical Area - see Appendix A for areas included
Source: 1990 Census of Population, General Population Characteristics; Claritas, Inc.

INCOME

Per Capita/Median/Average Income

Area	Per Capita ($)			Median Household ($)			Average Household ($)		
	1989	1999	% Chg.	1989	1999	% Chg.	1989	1999	% Chg.
City	11,108	15,691	41.3	21,060	26,328	25.0	27,210	37,192	36.7
MSA[1]	12,216	17,347	42.0	25,229	31,249	23.9	31,490	43,050	36.7
U.S.	14,420	21,350	48.1	30,056	40,525	34.8	38,453	56,184	46.1

Note: (1) Metropolitan Statistical Area - see Appendix A for areas included; 1989 data is from the 1990 Census; 1999 data is estimated by Claritas, Inc.
Source: 1990 Census of Population, General Population Characteristics; Claritas, Inc.

Household Income Distribution

Area	Percent of Households Earning								
	Under $5,000	$5,000 -14,999	$15,000 -24,999	$25,000 -34,999	$35,000 -49,999	$50,000 -74,999	$75,000 -99,000	$100,000 -149,999	$150,000 and up
City	4.8	24.1	19.0	13.5	16.9	13.6	4.5	2.2	1.4
MSA[1]	3.7	19.1	17.9	14.2	17.3	17.0	6.0	3.0	1.8
U.S.	3.9	13.3	13.8	12.6	16.2	19.4	9.7	6.6	4.6

Note: Data as of 1999; (1) Metropolitan Statistical Area - see Appendix A for areas included
Source: Claritas, Inc.

Effective Buying Income

Area	Per Capita ($)	Median Household ($)	Average Household ($)
City	14,179	26,932	35,353
MSA[1]	16,220	31,892	41,091
U.S.	17,496	36,603	47,036

Note: Data as of 1/1/2000; (1) Metropolitan Statistical Area - see Appendix A for areas included
Source: Standard Rate & Data Service, Newspaper Advertising Source, March 2000

Effective Household Buying Income Distribution

Area	% of Households Earning						
	$10,000 -$19,999	$20,000 -$34,999	$35,000 -$49,999	$50,000 -$74,999	$75,000 -$99,000	$100,000 -$124,999	$125,000 and up
City	22.7	23.1	16.7	13.9	4.5	1.3	1.5
MSA[1]	19.0	23.0	17.8	17.8	6.2	1.9	2.0
U.S.	15.0	21.6	17.6	19.6	8.4	3.0	3.3

Note: Data as of 1/1/2000; (1) Metropolitan Statistical Area - see Appendix A for areas included
Source: Standard Rate & Data Service, Newspaper Advertising Source, March 2000

Poverty Rates by Age

Area	People of All Ages	People Under 18 Years Old	Related Children Age 5-17 in Families in Poverty
City	15.9	n/a	n/a
County	11.0	16.2	14.2
U.S.	13.8	20.8	18.7

Note: Figures show the percent of people living below the poverty line in 1995. The average poverty threshold was $15,569 for a family of four in 1995; n/a not available
Source: Bureau of the Census, Small Area Income and Poverty Estimates Program; U.S. Department of Housing and Urban Development

EMPLOYMENT

Labor Force and Employment

Area	Civilian Labor Force			Workers Employed		
	Dec. 1998	Dec. 1999	% Chg.	Dec. 1998	Dec. 1999	% Chg.
City	35,690	35,364	-0.9	33,956	33,983	0.1
MSA[1]	308,972	307,661	-0.4	292,864	293,097	0.1
U.S.	138,297,000	139,941,000	1.2	132,732,000	134,696,000	1.5

Note: Data is not seasonally adjusted and covers workers 16 years of age and older; (1) Metropolitan Statistical Area - see Appendix A for areas included
Source: Bureau of Labor Statistics, http://stats.bls.gov

Unemployment Rate

Area	1999											
	Jan.	Feb.	Mar.	Apr.	May	Jun.	Jul.	Aug.	Sep.	Oct.	Nov.	Dec.
City	5.9	6.2	6.1	6.1	5.6	5.9	6.8	5.8	5.2	4.2	4.3	3.9
MSA[1]	7.0	6.5	6.3	5.3	4.8	5.2	5.5	5.0	5.1	4.5	4.9	4.7
U.S.	4.8	4.7	4.4	4.1	4.0	4.5	4.5	4.2	4.1	3.8	3.8	3.7

Note: Data is not seasonally adjusted and covers workers 16 years of age and older; all figures are percentages; (1) Metropolitan Statistical Area - see Appendix A for areas included
Source: Bureau of Labor Statistics, http://stats.bls.gov

Employment by Industry

Sector	MSA[1]		U.S.
	Number of Employees	Percent of Total	Percent of Total
Services	82,700	29.3	30.2
Retail Trade	53,600	19.0	18.1
Government	35,700	12.7	15.8
Manufacturing	53,500	19.0	14.1
Finance/Insurance/Real Estate	14,200	5.0	5.9
Wholesale Trade	14,900	5.3	5.4
Transportation/Public Utilities	16,500	5.9	5.3
Construction	10,400	3.7	4.8
Mining	400	0.1	0.4

Note: Figures cover non-farm employment as of 12/99 and are not seasonally adjusted;
(1) Metropolitan Statistical Area - see Appendix A for areas included
Source: Bureau of Labor Statistics, http://stats.bls.gov

Employment by Occupation

Occupation Category	City (%)	MSA[1] (%)	U.S. (%)
White Collar	53.5	51.7	58.1
Executive/Admin./Management	9.5	9.4	12.3
Professional	11.6	11.9	14.1
Technical & Related Support	3.3	3.4	3.7
Sales	10.9	11.0	11.8
Administrative Support/Clerical	18.2	16.0	16.3
Blue Collar	30.5	33.3	26.2
Precision Production/Craft/Repair	10.6	12.6	11.3
Machine Operators/Assem./Insp.	10.5	10.5	6.8
Transportation/Material Movers	4.3	4.8	4.1
Cleaners/Helpers/Laborers	5.1	5.4	3.9
Services	15.6	13.9	13.2
Farming/Forestry/Fishing	0.3	1.2	2.5

Note: Figures cover workers 16 years of age and older;
(1) Metropolitan Statistical Area - see Appendix A for areas included
Source: 1990 Census of Population and Housing, Summary Tape File 3C

Occupational Employment Projections: 1994 - 2005

High Demand Occupations (ranked by annual openings)	Fast-Growing Occupations[1] (ranked by percent growth)
1. Cashiers	1. Personal and home care aides
2. Salespersons, retail	2. Electronic pagination systems workers
3. Waiters & waitresses	3. Computer engineers
4. Registered nurses	4. Systems analysts
5. General managers & top executives	5. Home health aides
6. Janitors/cleaners/maids, ex. priv. hshld.	6. Human services workers
7. Secretaries, except legal & medical	7. Teachers, preschool and kindergarten
8. General office clerks	8. Computer support specialists
9. Teachers, secondary school	9. Physical therapists
10. Marketing & sales, supervisors	10. Residential counselors

Note: Projections cover Pennsylvania; (1) Excludes occupations with total job growth less than 300
Source: Pennsylvania Workforce 2005, Winter 1997-98

Average Wages

Occupation	$/Hr.	Occupation	$/Hr.
Accountants and Auditors	15.56	Maids and Housekeepers	7.09
Assemblers and Fabricators	10.30	Maintenance Repairers	11.34
Automotive Mechanics	10.95	Marketing/Advertising/PR Managers	23.46
Bookkeepers	9.77	Nurses, Licensed Practical	12.24
Carpenters	12.54	Nurses, Registered	17.19
Cashiers	6.72	Nursing Aides/Orderlies/Attendants	8.56
Clerks, General Office	8.93	Physicians and Surgeons	42.51
Clerks, Shipping/Receiving/Traffic	11.34	Receptionists/Information Clerks	8.00
Computer Programmers	21.84	Sales Reps., Exc. Scientific/Retail	17.97
Computer Support Specialists	15.02	Sales Reps., Scientific, Exc. Retail	22.40
Cooks, Restaurant	7.93	Salespersons, Retail	8.02
Electricians	17.48	Secretaries, Except Legal/Medical	9.89
Financial Managers	22.69	Stock Clerks, Sales Floor	6.97
First-Line Supervisors/Mgrs., Sales	15.34	Systems Analysts	20.66
Food Preparation Workers	6.81	Teacher Aides	7.89
General Managers/Top Executives	25.74	Teachers, Elementary School	23.50
Guards	9.16	Teachers, Secondary School	23.62
Hand Packers	8.82	Telemarketers	8.36
Janitors and Cleaners	8.45	Truck Drivers, Heavy/Tractor-Trailer	13.99
Laborers, Landscaping	9.34	Truck Drivers, Light	8.91
Lawyers	29.60	Waiters and Waitresses	5.77

Note: Wage data is for 1998 and covers the Metropolitan Statistical Area (see Appendix A for areas included). Hourly wages for elementary and secondary school teachers were calculated by the editors from annual wage data assuming a 40 hour work week; Dashes indicate that data was not available.
Source: Bureau of Labor Statistics, 1998 Metropolitan Area Occupational Employment and Wage Estimates

TAXES

Major State and Local Tax Rates

State Corporate Income (%)	State Personal Income (%)	Residential Property (%)	Sales & Use		State Gasoline (cents/ gallon)	State Cigarette (cents/ pack)
			State (%)	Local (%)		
9.99	2.8	2.41	6.0	None	25.9[a]	31.0

Note: Personal/corporate income, sales, gasoline and cigarette tax rates as of January 2000.
Property tax rates as of April 2000; (a) Rate is comprised of 12 cents excise and 13.9 cents motor carrier tax.
Source: Federation of Tax Administrators, www.taxadmin.org; ERI's Relocation Assessor software database, quarterly effective date 4/1/2000

Total Taxes Per Capita and as a Percent of Income

Area	Per Capita Income ($)	Per Capita Taxes ($)			Percent of Income (%)		
		Total	Federal	State/Local	Total	Federal	State/Local
Pennsylvania	29,059	10,185	6,991	3,195	35.1	24.1	11.0
U.S.	28,878	10,298	7,026	3,273	35.7	24.3	11.3

Note: Figures are for 1999
Source: Tax Foundation, www.taxfoundation.org

COMMERCIAL UTILITIES

Typical Monthly Electric Bills

Area	Commercial Service ($/month)		Industrial Service ($/month)	
	12 kW demand 1,500 kWh	100 kW demand 30,000 kWh	1,000 kW demand 400,000 kWh	20,000 kW demand 10,000,000 kWh
City	170	2,388	27,078	413,040
U.S.	150	2,174	23,995	508,569

Note: Based on rates in effect January 1, 1999
Source: Edison Electric Institute, Typical Residential, Commercial and Industrial Bills, Winter 1999

TRANSPORTATION

Transportation Statistics

Average minutes to work (1990)	15.3
Interstate highways	I-81; I-84; I-380; I-476; US-6; US-11
Bus lines	
In-city (1998)	County of Lackawanna Transit System, 26 buses
Inter-city (1999)	4
Passenger air service	
Airport	Wilkes-Barre/Scranton International
Airlines (1999)	5
Enplaned passengers (1998)	229,848
Amtrak service	No
Motor freight carriers (1999)	41
Major waterways/ports	None

Source: FAA DOT/TSC CY1998 ACAIS Database; National Transit Database, 1998; Editor & Publisher Market Guide, 2000; Amtrak National Time Table, Fall 1999/Winter 2000; 1990 Census of Population and Housing, STF 3C; Jane's Urban Transport Systems 1999-2000

Means of Transportation to Work

Area	Car/Truck/Van		Public Transportation			Bicycle	Walked	Other Means	Worked at Home
	Drove Alone	Car-pooled	Bus	Subway	Railroad				
City	68.7	17.3	2.9	0.0	0.0	0.1	8.2	1.3	1.4
MSA[1]	75.0	15.0	1.5	0.0	0.0	0.1	5.4	0.7	2.2
U.S.	73.2	13.4	3.0	1.5	0.5	0.4	3.9	1.2	3.0

Note: Figures shown are percentages and only include workers 16 years of age and older;
(1) Metropolitan Statistical Area - see Appendix A for areas included
Source: 1990 Census of Population and Housing, Summary Tape File 3C

BUSINESSES

Major Business Headquarters

Company Name	1999 Rankings	
	Fortune 500	Forbes 500
No companies listed	-	-

Note: Companies listed are located in the city; dashes indicate no ranking
Fortune 500: Companies that produce a 10-K are ranked 1 to 500 based on 1999 revenue
Forbes 500: Private companies are ranked 1 to 500 based on 1998 revenue
Source: Forbes, December 13, 1999; Fortune, April 17, 2000

HOTELS & MOTELS

Hotels/Motels

Area	Hotels/ Motels	Rooms	Luxury-Level Hotels/Motels		Average Minimum Rates ($)		
			♦♦♦♦	♦♦♦♦♦	♦♦	♦♦♦	♦♦♦♦
City	6	648	0	0	n/a	n/a	n/a
Airport	1	98	0	0	n/a	n/a	n/a
Total	7	746	0	0	n/a	n/a	n/a

Note: n/a not available; classifications range from one diamond (budget properties with basic amenities) to five diamond (luxury properties).
Source: OAG Business Travel Planner, Winter 1999-2000

Estimated Daily Food and Lodging Costs

Area	Food/Other ($/day)	Average Hotel Cost ($/day)
City	30	60
U.S.	30	55

Source: ERI's Relocation Assessor software database, quarterly effective date 4/1/2000

CONVENTION CENTERS

Convention Centers and Event Sites

Name	Guest Rooms	Meeting Space (sq. ft.)	Capacity (Theatre Style)
Montage Performing Arts Center	n/a	n/a	0
Radisson Lackawanna Station Hotel Scranton	145	12,098	600
Scranton Cultural Center	n/a	n/a	1,836

Note: n/a not available
Source: EventSource.com, 3/15/2000

Living Environment

COST OF LIVING

Cost of Living: Homeowner

Cost Element	U.S. ($)	City ($)	Differential ($)	Percent of U.S. Average
Consumables	14,516	14,712	196	101.4
Transportation	5,957	5,409	-548	90.8
Health Services	2,012	1,918	-94	95.3
Housing/Utilities/Prop. Tax	16,337	17,196	859	105.3
Income+Payroll Taxes	12,615	12,845	230	101.8
Miscellaneous	8,563	8,563	0	100.0
Total Cost of Living	60,000	60,643	643	101.1

Note: Figures are based on a single income, four person family with gross annual earnings of $60,000, owning an 1,800 square-foot home, and driving two automobiles worth $22,000 30,000 miles per year.
Source: ERI's Relocation Assessor software database, quarterly effective date 4/1/2000

Cost of Living: Renter

Cost Element	U.S. ($)	City ($)	Differential ($)	Percent of U.S. Average
Consumables	10,486	10,588	102	101.0
Transportation	2,107	1,906	-201	90.5
Health Services	1,632	1,551	-81	95.0
Rent/Utilities/Insurance	9,299	7,067	-2,232	76.0
Income+Payroll Taxes	8,607	9,103	496	105.8
Miscellaneous	7,869	7,869	0	100.0
Total Cost of Living	40,000	38,084	-1,916	95.2

Note: Figures are based on a single income, three person family with gross annual earnings of $40,000, renting a 1,000 square-foot home, and driving one automobile worth $8,000 12,000 miles per year.
Source: ERI's Relocation Assessor software database, quarterly effective date 4/1/2000

HOUSING

Median Home Prices and Housing Affordability

Area	Median Price[2] 4th Qtr. 1999 ($)	HOI[3] 4th Qtr. 1999	Affordability Rank[4]
MSA[1]	n/a	n/a	n/a
U.S.	139,000	63.8	–

Note: (1) Metropolitan Statistical Area - see Appendix A for areas included; (2) U.S. figures calculated from the sales of 687,516 new and existing homes in 192 markets; (3) Housing Opportunity Index - percent of homes sold that were within the reach of the median income household at the prevailing mortgage interest rate; (4) Rank is from 1-192 with 1 being most affordable; n/a not available
Source: National Association of Home Builders, Housing Opportunity Index, 4th Quarter 1999

Estimated Home Price

Area	Price ($)
City	131,928
U.S.	135,855

Note: Figures are based on an 1,800 square-foot home
Source: ERI's Relocation Assessor software database, quarterly effective date 4/1/2000

Estimated Rent

Area	Rent ($/month)
City	471
U.S.	651

Note: Figures are based on a 1,000 square-foot home
Source: ERI's Relocation Assessor software database, quarterly effective date 4/1/2000

Median Home Price Projection

It is projected that the median home price in the metropolitan area will increase from $98,697 in 1999 to $154,663 in 2010, an increase of 56.7%
Kiplinger's Personal Finance Magazine, January 2000

RESIDENTIAL UTILITIES

Average Residential Utility Costs

Area	All Electric ($/mth)	Part Electric ($/mth)	Other Energy ($/mth)	Phone ($/mth)
City	n/a	n/a	n/a	n/a
U.S.	99.25	55.47	43.48	20.29

Note: n/a not available
Source: ACCRA, Cost of Living Index, 3rd Quarter 1999

HEALTH CARE

Average Health Care Costs

Area	Hospital ($/day)	Doctor ($/visit)	Dentist ($/visit)
City	n/a	n/a	n/a
U.S.	440.96	53.83	68.42

Note: n/a not available
Source: ACCRA, Cost of Living Index, 3rd Quarter 1999

Distribution of Office-Based Physicians

Area	Family/Gen. Practitioners	Specialists Medical	Specialists Surgical	Specialists Other
MSA[1]	180	350	274	210

Note: Data as of 12/31/97; (1) Metropolitan Statistical Area - see Appendix A for areas included
Source: American Medical Assn., Physician Characteristics & Distribution in the U.S., 1999

Hospitals

Scranton has 3 general medical and surgical hospitals, 1 rehabilitation.
AHA Guide to the Healthcare Field, 1999-2000

EDUCATION

Public School District Statistics

District Name	Num. Sch.	Enroll.	Classroom Teachers	Pupils per Teacher	Minority Pupils (%)	Current Exp.[1] ($/pupil)
Scranton SD	18	8,837	537	16.5	n/a	n/a

Note: Data covers the 1997-1998 school year unless otherwise noted; (1) Data covers fiscal year 1996; SD = School District; ISD = Independent School District; n/a not available
Source: National Center for Education Statistics, Common Core of Data Public Education Agency Universe 1997-98; National Center for Education Statistics, Characteristics of the 100 Largest Public Elementary and Secondary School Districts in the United States: 1997-98, July 1999

Educational Quality

School District	Education Quotient[1]	Graduate Outcome[2]	Community Index[3]	Resource Index[4]
Scranton School Dist.	87	68	68	129

Note: Over 1,000 secondary school districts were rated in terms of educational quality. The scores range from a low of 50 to a high of 150; (1) Combination of the Graduate Outcome, Community and Resource indexes weighted to reflect the greater importance of the Graduate Outcome and Resource Index; (2) Based on graduation rates and college board scores (SAT/ACT); (3) Based on the surrounding community's level of affluence and adult education; (4) Based on teacher salaries, per-pupil expenditures and student-teacher ratios.
Source: Expansion Management, Ratings Issue, 1999

Educational Attainment by Race

Area	High School Graduate (%)					Bachelor's Degree (%)				
	Total	White	Black	Other	Hisp.[2]	Total	White	Black	Other	Hisp.[2]
City	70.4	70.5	65.2	70.0	64.3	13.6	13.5	5.7	32.7	20.2
MSA[1]	73.4	73.5	68.2	74.6	70.9	14.1	14.0	8.2	36.7	15.8
U.S.	75.2	77.9	63.1	60.4	49.8	20.3	21.5	11.4	19.4	9.2

Note: Figures shown cover persons 25 years old and over; (1) Metropolitan Statistical Area - see Appendix A for areas included; (2) people of Hispanic origin can be of any race
Source: 1990 Census of Population and Housing, Summary Tape File 3C

School Enrollment by Type

Area	Preprimary				Elementary/High School			
	Public		Private		Public		Private	
	Enrollment	%	Enrollment	%	Enrollment	%	Enrollment	%
City	940	58.8	658	41.2	8,748	77.9	2,480	22.1
MSA[1]	6,683	54.6	5,550	45.4	93,852	86.4	14,823	13.6
U.S.	2,679,029	59.5	1,824,256	40.5	38,379,689	90.2	4,187,099	9.8

Note: Figures shown cover persons 3 years old and over;
(1) Metropolitan Statistical Area - see Appendix A for areas included
Source: 1990 Census of Population and Housing, Summary Tape File 3C

School Enrollment by Race

Area	Preprimary (%)				Elementary/High School (%)			
	White	Black	Other	Hisp.[1]	White	Black	Other	Hisp.[1]
City	95.4	2.1	2.5	1.6	94.4	3.2	2.4	1.2
MSA[2]	98.1	0.6	1.2	1.0	97.2	1.5	1.3	1.4
U.S.	80.4	12.5	7.1	7.8	74.1	15.6	10.3	12.5

Note: Figures shown cover persons 3 years old and over; (1) people of Hispanic origin can be of any race; (2) Metropolitan Statistical Area - see Appendix A for areas included
Source: 1990 Census of Population and Housing, Summary Tape File 3C

Higher Education

Two-Year Colleges		Four-Year Colleges		Medical Schools	Law Schools	Voc/ Tech
Public	Private	Public	Private			
0	3	0	2	0	0	9

Source: College Blue Book, Occupational Education, 1999; Medical School Admission Requirements, 1999-2000; Peterson's Guide to Two-Year Colleges, 2000; Peterson's Guide to Four-Year Colleges, 1999; Barron's Guide to Law Schools, 1999

MAJOR EMPLOYERS

Major Employers

Allied Services Institute of Rehabilitation Medicine
Donlock Ltd. (ambulance service)
Mercy Hospital of Scranton
Paper Magic Group (greeting cards)
United States Postal Service

Community Medical Center
Fleet Pennsylvania Service (banking)
Moses Taylor Hospital
Scranton Lace Co.

Note: Companies listed are located in the city
Source: D&B Business Rankings, 1999; Ward's Business Directory, 1999; America's Corporate Families, 1999

PUBLIC SAFETY

Crime Rate

Area	All Crimes	Violent Crimes				Property Crimes		
		Murder	Forcible Rape	Robbery	Aggrav. Assault	Burglary	Larceny -Theft	Motor Vehicle Theft
City	n/a	n/a	n/a	n/a	n/a	n/a	n/a	n/a
Suburbs[1]	n/a	n/a	n/a	n/a	n/a	n/a	n/a	n/a
MSA[2]	n/a	n/a	n/a	n/a	n/a	n/a	n/a	n/a
U.S.	4,615.5	6.3	34.4	165.2	360.5	862.0	2,728.1	459.0

Note: Crime rate is the number of crimes per 100,000 population; (1) Defined as all areas within the Metropolitan Statistical Area but located outside the central city; (2) Metropolitan Statistical Area - see Appendix A for areas included; n/a not available
Source: FBI Uniform Crime Reports, 1998

RECREATION

Culture and Recreation

Museums	Symphony Orchestras	Opera Companies	Dance Companies	Professional Theatres	Zoos	Pro Sports Teams
5	0	0	1	0	0	0

Source: Musical America, International Directory of the Performing Arts, 1999; Official Museum Directory, 2000; Stern's Performing Arts Directory, 1997; USA Today Four Sport Stadium Guide, 1997; Career Opportunities in Theatre and the Performing Arts, 1999

Library System

The Scranton Public Library has three branches, holdings of 180,000 volumes, and a budget of $2,054,868 (1997-1998).
American Library Directory, 1999-2000

MEDIA

Newspapers

Name	Type	Freq.	Distribution	Circulation
Scranton Times	n/a	7x/wk	Area	43,976
Scranton Tribune	General	5x/wk	Area	30,213
Straz (The Guard)	n/a	1x/wk	U.S.	10,500

Note: Includes newspapers with circulations of 200 or more located in the city; n/a not available
Source: Burrelle's Media Directory, 1999 Edition

Television Stations

Name	Ch.	Affiliation	Type	Owner
WNEP	16	ABCT	Commercial	New York Times Company
WYOU	22	CBST	Commercial	Bastet Broadcasting
WOLF	38	FBC	Commercial	Pegasus Broadcast Television Inc.
WILF	53	FBC	Commercial	Pegasus Broadcast Television Inc.
WWLF	56	FBC	Commercial	Pegasus Broadcast Television Inc.
WQPX	64	n/a	Commercial	Paxson Communications Corporation

Note: Stations included broadcast in the Scranton metro area; n/a not available
Source: Burrelle's Media Directory, 1999 Edition

AM Radio Stations

Call Letters	Freq. (kHz)	Target Audience	Station Format	Music Format
WEJL	630	General	M/N/S	Adult Standards
WAAT	750	G/R	M/T	Christian
WBAX	1240	General	M	Adult Standards
WICK	1400	General	M/N/S	Adult Standards/Easy Listening/MOR/Oldies
WCDL	1440	General	M/N/S	Country
WWCC	1590	General	E/M/N/S/T	Easy Listening/Oldies

Note: Stations included broadcast in the Scranton metro area
Target Audience: A=Asian; B=Black; C=Christian; E=Ethnic; F=French; G=General; H=Hispanic;
M=Men; N=Native American; R=Religious; S=Senior Citizen; W=Women; Y=Young Adult; Z=Children
Station Format: E=Educational; M=Music; N=News; S=Sports; T=Talk
Music Format: AOR=Album Oriented Rock; MOR=Middle-of-the-Road
Source: Burrelle's Media Directory, 1999 Edition

FM Radio Stations

Call Letters	Freq. (mHz)	Target Audience	Station Format	Music Format
WVMW	91.5	General	M/N/S	Alternative
WQFM	92.1	General	M	Oldies
WDLS	93.7	General	M/N/S	Oldies
WWDL	104.9	General	M	Adult Contemporary
WEZX	106.9	General	M	Classic Rock

Note: Stations included broadcast in the Scranton metro area
Station Format: E=Educational; M=Music; N=News; S=Sports; T=Talk
Target Audience: A=Asian; B=Black; C=Christian; E=Ethnic; F=French; G=General; H=Hispanic;
M=Men; N=Native American; R=Religious; S=Senior Citizen; W=Women; Y=Young Adult; Z=Children
Source: Burrelle's Media Directory, 1999 Edition

WEATHER

Temperature/Precipitation/Humidity

	Jan	Feb	Mar	Apr	May	Jun	Jul	Aug	Sep	Oct	Nov	Dec	Yr.
Max. High Temp. (°F)	67	73	83	92	93	97	101	98	101	88	80	67	101
Avg. High Temp. (°F)	33	35	45	58	69	78	82	80	72	62	48	37	58
Avg. Temp. (°F)	26	28	36	48	59	67	72	70	63	52	41	30	50
Avg. Low Temp. (°F)	18	20	28	38	48	57	61	60	53	42	33	23	40
Min. Low Temp. (°F)	-14	-16	-4	14	27	34	43	38	30	19	9	-9	-16
Avg. Precip. (in.)	2.3	2.2	2.5	3.3	3.6	3.8	3.8	3.5	3.3	2.8	3.1	2.6	36.8
Avg. Snowfall (in.)	11	10	8	3	Tr	0	0	0	Tr	Tr	4	9	44
Avg. Rel. Hum. 7am (%)	76	75	74	72	76	81	83	86	87	84	79	77	79
Avg. Rel. Hum. 4pm (%)	64	61	55	50	50	54	54	56	58	56	63	66	57

Note: Tr = Trace amounts (less than 0.05 inches of rain or less than 0.5 inches of snow)
Source: National Climatic Data Center, International Station Meteorological Climate Summary, 3/95

Weather Conditions

Temperature			Precipitation		
5°F & below	32°F & below	90°F & above	0.01 inch or more precip.	1.5 inch or more snow/ice	Thunder-storms
9	127	8	136	11	29

Note: Figures are average number of days per year
Source: National Climatic Data Center, International Station Meteorological Climate Summary, 3/95

AIR & WATER QUALITY

Maximum Pollutant Concentrations

	Particulate Matter (ug/m³)	Carbon Monoxide (ppm)	Sulfur Dioxide (ppm)	Nitrogen Dioxide (ppm)	Ozone (ppm)	Lead (ug/m³)
MSA[1] Level	69	3	0.031	0.018	0.11	n/a
NAAQS[2]	150	9	0.140	0.053	0.12	1.50
Met NAAQS	Yes	Yes	Yes	Yes	Yes	n/a

Note: (1) Metropolitan Statistical Area - see Appendix A for areas included; (2) National Ambient Air Quality Standards; ppm = parts per million; ug/m³ = micrograms per cubic meter; n/a not available
Source: EPA, National Air Quality and Emissions Trends Report, 1997

Pollutant Standards Index

In the Scranton MSA (see Appendix A for areas included), the Pollutant Standards Index (PSI) exceeded 100 on 11 days in 1997. A PSI value greater than 100 indicates that air quality would have been in the unhealthful range on that day.
EPA, National Air Quality and Emissions Trends Report, 1997

Drinking Water

Water System Name	Pop. Served	Primary Water Source Type	Number of Violations in 1998-99	Type of Violation/ Contaminants
PAWC-Lake Scranton	121,995	Surface	None	None

Note: Data as of January 19, 2000
Source: EPA, Office of Ground Water and Drinking Water, Safe Drinking Water Information System

Scranton tap water is slightly acid and very soft.
Editor & Publisher Market Guide, 2000

South Bend, Indiana

Background

South Bend, Indiana is located ten miles south of the Michigan state border, 140 miles north of Indianapolis and 95 miles east of Chicago, Illinois. The city is named for its location on the south bend of the Saint Joseph River, which extends to Lake Michigan.

South Bend is the county seat of St. Joseph County. Its metropolitan area includes the city of Mishawaka and other nearby communities. This is an industrial, commercial and services center for a region known as Michiana, which includes counties in southwest Michigan and north-central Indiana. South Bend is also the home of the University of Notre Dame, which sits adjacent to South Bend, in Notre Dame, Indiana.

In 1681, French explorer Ren-Robert Cavelier, Sieur de La Salle negotiated an alliance with the French and the native Miami and Illinois peoples. Around 1820, Pierre Navarre became the first permanent white settler at the site of South Bend. A settlement was established with a small fur-trading post. The community adopted the name South Bend in 1830 and was incorporated in 1835. It became a city in 1865. A Catholic priest, Father Edward Sorin, established the University of Notre Dame in 1845. In the mid-19th Century, South Bend evolved into an industrial center, manufacturing a variety of products including sewing machine cabinets and farm equipment.

One of the most prominent local companies was established in 1852, when brothers Henry and Clement Studebaker opened a blacksmith shop which built wagons for western pioneers and for the U.S. Army. The Studebaker Manufacturing Company became one of the largest wagon makers in the world. In 1904 Studebaker began making gasoline-powered cars and became a major automotive manufacturer. These industries attracted new residents and immigrants from many ethnic cultures.

South Bend's manufacturing economy began to decline after World War II, which caused difficult times for the city in the middle and latter 20th Century. Studebaker's South Bend plant was closed in 1963, and the company went out of business in 1966, as did other prominent manufacturers in more recent years.

Economic development initiatives have helped the economy to move toward recovery in the 1990s, and there has been significant new construction in the South Bend area. While manufacturing has remained an important sector, its role continues to decline as the economy becomes more diversified. Currently education, health care, construction, business services, retailing, agricultural services and tourism are among the primary economic sectors and employers today.

In addition to Notre Dame, other institutions of higher education in the South Bend area include Holy Cross College, Saint Mary's College, Indiana University South Bend, Ivy Tech State College South Bend and Bethel College in Mishawaka.

South Bend is the home of the College Football Hall of Fame, which opened in 1995. Other local attractions include the South Bend Regional Museum of Art, the Northern Indiana Center for History, the Potawatomi Zoo and the Studebaker National Museum, which commemorates the history of the automotive manufacturer. The East Race Waterway is the first artificial whitewater race course in North America. The city operates about 25 parks, and several public golf courses.

Venues for concerts, sports and other events include the Century Center multi-use facility and the recently restored Morris Performing Arts Center. The Stanley Coveleski Regional Stadium is the home field for the South Bend Silver Hawks, a Class A baseball team. Performing arts organizations include the South Bend Symphony Orchestra, the South Bend Theater League, and the South Bend Civic Theater. South Bend hosts a number of festivals, including an annual ethnic celebration.

South Bend has an elected Mayor and nine-member City Council.

General Rankings and Evaluative Comments

- South Bend was ranked #108 out of 354 metropolitan areas in *Places Rated Almanac*. Criteria: cost of living, climate, crime, transportation, job outlook, education, the arts, health care, and recreation. *Places Rated Almanac, Millennium Edition, 2000*

- *Ladies Home Journal* ranked America's 200 largest cities based on the qualities women care about most. South Bend ranked #182 out of 200. Criteria: low crime rate, well-paying jobs, quality health and child care, good public schools, the presence of women in government, size of the gender wage gap, number of sexual-harassment and discrimination complaints filed, unemployment and divorce rates, commute times, population density, number of houses of worship, parks and cultural offerings, number of women's health specialists, how well women cared for themselves, complexion kindness index based on UV radiation levels, odds of finding affordable fashions, rental rates for romance movies, champagne sales, and other matters of the heart. *Ladies Home Journal, November 1998*

- Zero Population Growth ranked 229 cities in terms of children's health, safety, and economic well-being. South Bend was ranked #57 out of 112 independent cities (cities with populations greater than 100,000 which were neither Major Cities nor Suburbs/Outer Cities) and was given a grade of C. Criteria: total population and population change, percent of population under 18 years of age, household language, percent of births to teens, infant mortality rate, percent of low birth weights, dropout rate, enrollment in preprimary school, violent and property crime rates, unemployment rate, percent of children in poverty, percent of owner occupied units, number of bad air days, percent of public transportation commuters, and average travel time to work. *Zero Population Growth, Children's Environmental Index, Fall 1999*

- Cognetics studied 273 metro areas in the United States, ranking them by entrepreneurial activity. South Bend was ranked #34 out of 134 smaller metro areas. Criteria: Significant Starts (firms started in the last 10 years that still employ at least 5 people) and Young Growers (percent of firms 10 years old or less that grew significantly during the last 4 years). *Cognetics, "Entrepreneurial Hot Spots: The Best Places in America to Start and Grow a Company," 1999*

Business Environment

STATE ECONOMY

State Economic Profile

"Indiana is lagging the nation in both job and Gross State Product (GSP) growth. While US job growth in 1998 was 2.0%, Indiana's was only 0.4%. Indiana's primary obstacle to growth is its lack of workers. The state unemployment rate is below the national, and its population growth rate is barely above zero.

Indiana's manufacturing base is much stronger than its neighbors, actually adding manufacturing jobs in 1998. The recent surge in automobile sales has helped boost employment in Indiana's auto sector, with some gains projected in the near future. Even if auto sales continue at the current pace, which is unlikely, Indiana auto plants would have a hard time finding workers to fill those jobs.

Demographic forces have restrained Indiana's housing and construction markets. Construction employment was down 2% in 1998, even though residential permits were up 15%. Home sales have been at the highest level in years, although new construction and slow population growth have kept price appreciation below the national.

Much of Indiana's economic strength has been in Indianapolis. Job growth in Indianapolis was 2.7% in 1998, almost 8 times the state average. Construction employment was up 7% in Indianapolis, while down for the state as a whole. Indianapolis' housing market has also witnessed price appreciation and new construction above the rest of the state.

While low foreign demand for manufacturing goods has hit Indiana as hard as other states in the region, its tight labor markets and a surge in auto sales have minimized job losses. These same tight labor markets, however, constrain Indiana to a moderate to slow growth path."
National Association of Realtors, Economic Profiles: The Fifty States and the District of Columbia, http://nar.realtor.com/databank/profiles.htm

EXPORTS

Total Export Sales

Area	1995 ($000)	1996 ($000)	1997 ($000)	1998 ($000)	% Chg. 1995-98	% Chg. 1997-98
MSA[1]	389,474	494,800	522,082	586,871	50.7	12.4
U.S.	583,030,524	622,827,063	687,597,999	680,474,251	16.7	-1.0

Note: (1) Metropolitan Statistical Area - see Appendix A for areas included
Source: U.S. Department of Commerce, International Trade Association, Metropolitan Area Exports: An Export Performance Report on Over 250 U.S. Cities, November 10, 1999

CITY FINANCES

City Government Finances

Component	1995 ($million)	1995 (per capita $)
Revenue	88.4	841
Expenditure	91.1	867
Debt Outstanding	76.0	723

Source: 1999 County and City Extra, Annual Metro, City, and County Data Book

City Government Revenue by Source

Source	1995 ($million)	1995 (per capita $)
Intergovernmental	20.1	191
Taxes	35.5	338
Property	34.2	326
Sales and Gross Receipts	0.0	0

Source: 1999 County and City Extra, Annual Metro, City, and County Data Book

City Government Expenditures by Function

Function	1995 ($million)	1995 (per capita $)	1995 (%)
Public Welfare	0.0	0	0.0
Highways	6.9	65	7.6
Parking Facilities	0.5	5	0.6
Education	0.0	0	0.0
Health and Hospitals	2.1	20	2.4
Police Protection	12.2	116	13.4
Sewerage and Sanitation	13.3	126	14.6
Parks and Recreation	10.0	95	11.0
Housing and Community Development	12.1	115	13.3
Interest on Debt	3.1	30	3.5

Source: 1999 County and City Extra, Annual Metro, City, and County Data Book

Municipal Bond Ratings

Area	Moody's
City	n/a

Note: n/a not available
Source: Mergent Bond Record, 2/2000

POPULATION

Population Growth

Area	1980 Census	1990 Census	1999 Estimate	2004 Projection	Population Growth (%) 1990-1999	Population Growth (%) 1999-2004
City	109,727	105,536	99,029	96,810	-6.2	-2.2
MSA[1]	241,617	247,052	258,713	264,432	4.7	2.2
U.S.	226,545,805	248,765,170	272,212,864	283,625,312	9.4	4.2

Note: (1) Metropolitan Statistical Area - see Appendix A for areas included
Source: 1990 Census of Population and Housing, Summary Tape File 3C; Claritas, Inc.

Number of Households and Average Household Size

Area	1980 Census	1990 Census	1999 Estimate	2004 Projection	1999 Average Household Size
City	42,635	42,000	40,520	40,035	2.44
MSA[1]	86,203	92,171	98,075	100,987	2.64
U.S.	80,389,592	91,993,582	102,048,200	107,302,392	2.67

Note: (1) Metropolitan Statistical Area - see Appendix A for areas included
Source: 1990 Census of Population and Housing, Summary Tape File 3C; Claritas, Inc.

Race/Ethnicity of City Population

Race/Ethnicity	1990 Census Population	1990 Census %	1999 Estimate Population	1999 Estimate %	% Change 1990-1999
White, Non-Hispanic	78,950	74.8	67,655	68.3	-14.3
Black, Non-Hispanic	21,974	20.8	24,828	25.1	13.0
Asian, Non-Hispanic	794	0.8	1,102	1.1	38.8
Other, Non-Hispanic	363	0.3	420	0.4	15.7
Hispanic	3,455	3.3	5,024	5.1	45.4

Source: 1990 Census of Population and Housing, Summary Tape File 3C; Claritas, Inc.

Race/Ethnicity of Metropolitan Statistical Area Population

Race/Ethnicity	1990 Census		1999 Estimate		% Change 1990-1999
	Population	%	Population	%	
White, Non-Hispanic	214,978	87.0	218,399	84.4	1.6
Black, Non-Hispanic	23,775	9.6	27,853	10.8	17.2
Asian, Non-Hispanic	2,279	0.9	3,480	1.3	52.7
Other, Non-Hispanic	933	0.4	1,109	0.4	18.9
Hispanic	5,087	2.1	7,872	3.0	54.7

Note: See Appendix A for areas included in the Metropolitan Statistical Area
Source: 1990 Census of Population and Housing, Summary Tape File 3C; Claritas, Inc.

Ancestry

Area	German	Irish	English	Italian	U.S.	French	Polish	Dutch
City	27.7	14.7	8.7	3.3	2.7	3.1	14.5	3.1
MSA[1]	35.1	18.5	10.3	4.1	3.2	3.9	13.7	4.1
U.S.	23.3	15.6	13.1	5.9	5.3	4.2	3.8	2.5

Note: Figures are percentages and include persons that reported multiple ancestry (eg. if a person reported being Irish and Italian, they were included in both columns); (1) Metropolitan Statistical Area - see Appendix A for areas included
Source: 1990 Census of Population and Housing, Summary Tape File 3C

Median Age

Area	1990 Census	1999 Estimate
City	33.2	35.5
MSA[1]	32.9	35.2
U.S.	32.9	35.7

Note: (1) Metropolitan Statistical Area - see Appendix A for areas included
Source: 1990 Census of Population and Housing, Summary Tape File 3C; Claritas, Inc.

Male/Female Population

Area	Number of Males		Number of Females		Males per 100 Females	
	1990	1999	1990	1999	1990	1999
City	49,883	47,020	55,653	52,009	89.6	90.4
MSA[1]	119,029	124,883	128,023	133,830	93.0	93.3
U.S.	121,172,379	132,803,736	127,537,494	139,409,136	95.0	95.3

Note: (1) Metropolitan Statistical Area - see Appendix A for areas included
Source: 1990 Census of Population, General Population Characteristics; Claritas, Inc.

INCOME

Per Capita/Median/Average Income

Area	Per Capita ($)			Median Household ($)			Average Household ($)		
	1989	1999	% Chg.	1989	1999	% Chg.	1989	1999	% Chg.
City	11,949	17,587	47.2	24,131	32,361	34.1	29,638	42,436	43.2
MSA[1]	13,277	20,298	52.9	28,235	39,503	39.9	35,001	52,754	50.7
U.S.	14,420	21,350	48.1	30,056	40,525	34.8	38,453	56,184	46.1

Note: (1) Metropolitan Statistical Area - see Appendix A for areas included; 1989 data is from the 1990 Census; 1999 data is estimated by Claritas, Inc.
Source: 1990 Census of Population, General Population Characteristics; Claritas, Inc.

Household Income Distribution

Area	Percent of Households Earning								
	Under $5,000	$5,000 -14,999	$15,000 -24,999	$25,000 -34,999	$35,000 -49,999	$50,000 -74,999	$75,000 -99,000	$100,000 -149,999	$150,000 and up
City	4.7	16.1	17.5	15.0	17.8	17.9	6.0	3.7	1.3
MSA[1]	3.1	12.2	15.0	14.0	17.6	20.7	8.9	5.8	2.7
U.S.	3.9	13.3	13.8	12.6	16.2	19.4	9.7	6.6	4.6

Note: Data as of 1999; (1) Metropolitan Statistical Area - see Appendix A for areas included
Source: Claritas, Inc.

Effective Buying Income

Area	Per Capita ($)	Median Household ($)	Average Household ($)
City	14,910	29,895	36,705
MSA[1]	16,981	35,503	44,425
U.S.	17,496	36,603	47,036

Note: Data as of 1/1/2000; (1) Metropolitan Statistical Area - see Appendix A for areas included
Source: Standard Rate & Data Service, Newspaper Advertising Source, March 2000

Effective Household Buying Income Distribution

Area	% of Households Earning						
	$10,000 -$19,999	$20,000 -$34,999	$35,000 -$49,999	$50,000 -$74,999	$75,000 -$99,000	$100,000 -$124,999	$125,000 and up
City	19.0	25.9	18.2	15.7	5.1	1.7	1.2
MSA[1]	16.1	23.6	18.7	20.0	7.5	2.3	2.1
U.S.	15.0	21.6	17.6	19.6	8.4	3.0	3.3

Note: Data as of 1/1/2000; (1) Metropolitan Statistical Area - see Appendix A for areas included
Source: Standard Rate & Data Service, Newspaper Advertising Source, March 2000

Poverty Rates by Age

Area	People of All Ages	People Under 18 Years Old	Related Children Age 5-17 in Families in Poverty
City	16.8	n/a	n/a
County	10.3	15.7	13.5
U.S.	13.8	20.8	18.7

Note: Figures show the percent of people living below the poverty line in 1995. The
average poverty threshold was $15,569 for a family of four in 1995; n/a not available
Source: Bureau of the Census, Small Area Income and Poverty Estimates Program;
U.S. Department of Housing and Urban Development

EMPLOYMENT

Labor Force and Employment

Area	Civilian Labor Force			Workers Employed		
	Dec. 1998	Dec. 1999	% Chg.	Dec. 1998	Dec. 1999	% Chg.
City	56,578	55,456	-2.0	54,453	53,064	-2.6
MSA[1]	138,006	135,052	-2.1	134,269	130,845	-2.6
U.S.	138,297,000	139,941,000	1.2	132,732,000	134,696,000	1.5

Note: Data is not seasonally adjusted and covers workers 16 years of age and older;
(1) Metropolitan Statistical Area - see Appendix A for areas included
Source: Bureau of Labor Statistics, http://stats.bls.gov

Unemployment Rate

Area	1999											
	Jan.	Feb.	Mar.	Apr.	May	Jun.	Jul.	Aug.	Sep.	Oct.	Nov.	Dec.
City	4.4	4.3	3.8	3.3	3.8	3.8	4.0	3.9	4.2	3.9	4.3	4.3
MSA[1]	3.2	3.1	2.7	2.4	2.7	2.8	2.9	2.8	3.1	2.8	3.1	3.1
U.S.	4.8	4.7	4.4	4.1	4.0	4.5	4.5	4.2	4.1	3.8	3.8	3.7

Note: Data is not seasonally adjusted and covers workers 16 years of age and older; all figures are percentages; (1) Metropolitan Statistical Area - see Appendix A for areas included
Source: Bureau of Labor Statistics, http://stats.bls.gov

Employment by Industry

Sector	MSA[1]		U.S.
	Number of Employees	Percent of Total	Percent of Total
Services	45,200	32.7	30.2
Retail Trade	27,400	19.8	18.1
Government	14,200	10.3	15.8
Manufacturing	22,900	16.6	14.1
Finance/Insurance/Real Estate	6,800	4.9	5.9
Wholesale Trade	9,300	6.7	5.4
Transportation/Public Utilities	5,500	4.0	5.3
Construction	n/a	n/a	4.8
Mining	n/a	n/a	0.4

Note: Figures cover non-farm employment as of 12/99 and are not seasonally adjusted; (1) Metropolitan Statistical Area - see Appendix A for areas included; n/a not available
Source: Bureau of Labor Statistics, http://stats.bls.gov

Employment by Occupation

Occupation Category	City (%)	MSA[1] (%)	U.S. (%)
White Collar	56.9	57.4	58.1
Executive/Admin./Management	11.1	12.0	12.3
Professional	14.3	13.6	14.1
Technical & Related Support	3.6	3.3	3.7
Sales	11.5	12.2	11.8
Administrative Support/Clerical	16.5	16.3	16.3
Blue Collar	27.4	28.3	26.2
Precision Production/Craft/Repair	9.4	10.8	11.3
Machine Operators/Assem./Insp.	9.8	9.1	6.8
Transportation/Material Movers	3.7	4.2	4.1
Cleaners/Helpers/Laborers	4.5	4.3	3.9
Services	15.2	13.3	13.2
Farming/Forestry/Fishing	0.4	1.0	2.5

Note: Figures cover workers 16 years of age and older; (1) Metropolitan Statistical Area - see Appendix A for areas included
Source: 1990 Census of Population and Housing, Summary Tape File 3C

Occupational Employment Projections: 1994 - 2005

Projections not available at time of publication.

Average Wages

Occupation	$/Hr.	Occupation	$/Hr.
Accountants and Auditors	19.17	Maids and Housekeepers	6.86
Assemblers and Fabricators	9.11	Maintenance Repairers	13.36
Automotive Mechanics	14.21	Marketing/Advertising/PR Managers	24.97
Bookkeepers	10.77	Nurses, Licensed Practical	13.38
Carpenters	15.44	Nurses, Registered	16.92
Cashiers	7.15	Nursing Aides/Orderlies/Attendants	7.68
Clerks, General Office	8.55	Physicians and Surgeons	56.31
Clerks, Shipping/Receiving/Traffic	10.88	Receptionists/Information Clerks	8.91
Computer Programmers	19.35	Sales Reps., Exc. Scientific/Retail	20.35
Computer Support Specialists	16.13	Sales Reps., Scientific, Exc. Retail	21.13
Cooks, Restaurant	7.69	Salespersons, Retail	8.96
Electricians	18.49	Secretaries, Except Legal/Medical	10.37
Financial Managers	25.38	Stock Clerks, Sales Floor	8.44
First-Line Supervisors/Mgrs., Sales	17.44	Systems Analysts	23.75
Food Preparation Workers	6.96	Teacher Aides	8.04
General Managers/Top Executives	30.00	Teachers, Elementary School	17.90
Guards	9.34	Teachers, Secondary School	19.20
Hand Packers	8.10	Telemarketers	9.35
Janitors and Cleaners	8.70	Truck Drivers, Heavy/Tractor-Trailer	15.10
Laborers, Landscaping	8.50	Truck Drivers, Light	10.49
Lawyers	28.60	Waiters and Waitresses	5.88

Note: Wage data is for 1998 and covers the Metropolitan Statistical Area (see Appendix A for areas included). Hourly wages for elementary and secondary school teachers were calculated by the editors from annual wage data assuming a 40 hour work week; Dashes indicate that data was not available.
Source: Bureau of Labor Statistics, 1998 Metropolitan Area Occupational Employment and Wage Estimates

TAXES

Major State and Local Tax Rates

State Corporate Income (%)	State Personal Income (%)	Residential Property (%)	Sales & Use State (%)	Sales & Use Local (%)	State Gasoline (cents/ gallon)	State Cigarette (cents/ pack)
7.9[a]	3.4	5.17	5.0	None	15.0[b]	15.5

Note: Personal/corporate income, sales, gasoline and cigarette tax rates as of January 2000. Property tax rates as of April 2000; (a) Consists of 3.4% on income from sources within the state plus a 4.5% supplemental income tax; (b) Carriers pay an additional surcharge of 11 cents. Sales tax applicable
Source: Federation of Tax Administrators, www.taxadmin.org; ERI's Relocation Assessor software database, quarterly effective date 4/1/2000

Total Taxes Per Capita and as a Percent of Income

Area	Per Capita Income ($)	Per Capita Taxes ($) Total	Per Capita Taxes ($) Federal	Per Capita Taxes ($) State/ Local	Percent of Income (%) Total	Percent of Income (%) Federal	Percent of Income (%) State/ Local
Indiana	25,904	9,059	6,178	2,881	35.0	23.8	11.1
U.S.	28,878	10,298	7,026	3,273	35.7	24.3	11.3

Note: Figures are for 1999
Source: Tax Foundation, www.taxfoundation.org

COMMERCIAL UTILITIES

Typical Monthly Electric Bills

Area	Commercial Service ($/month) 12 kW demand 1,500 kWh	Commercial Service ($/month) 100 kW demand 30,000 kWh	Industrial Service ($/month) 1,000 kW demand 400,000 kWh	Industrial Service ($/month) 20,000 kW demand 10,000,000 kWh
City	153	2,005	23,749	363,979
U.S.	150	2,174	23,995	508,569

Note: Based on rates in effect January 1, 1999
Source: Edison Electric Institute, Typical Residential, Commercial and Industrial Bills, Winter 1999

TRANSPORTATION

Transportation Statistics

Average minutes to work (1990)	17.1
Interstate highways	I-80; I-90; US-20; US-31
Bus lines	
In-city (1998)	South Bend Public Transportation Corp., 43 buses
Inter-city (1999)	2
Passenger air service	
Airport	Michiana Regional Transportation Center
Airlines (1999)	9
Enplaned passengers (1998)	501,618
Amtrak service	Yes
Motor freight carriers (1999)	30
Major waterways/ports	None

Source: FAA DOT/TSC CY1998 ACAIS Database; National Transit Database, 1998; Editor & Publisher Market Guide, 2000; Amtrak National Time Table, Fall 1999/Winter 2000; 1990 Census of Population and Housing, STF 3C; Jane's Urban Transport Systems 1999-2000

Means of Transportation to Work

Area	Car/Truck/Van		Public Transportation			Bicycle	Walked	Other Means	Worked at Home
	Drove Alone	Car-pooled	Bus	Subway	Railroad				
City	77.3	13.2	3.5	0.0	0.0	0.3	3.2	1.0	1.4
MSA[1]	79.6	10.5	1.8	0.0	0.0	0.3	4.7	0.8	2.3
U.S.	73.2	13.4	3.0	1.5	0.5	0.4	3.9	1.2	3.0

Note: Figures shown are percentages and only include workers 16 years of age and older; (1) Metropolitan Statistical Area - see Appendix A for areas included
Source: 1990 Census of Population and Housing, Summary Tape File 3C

BUSINESSES

Major Business Headquarters

Company Name	1999 Rankings	
	Fortune 500	Forbes 500
No companies listed	-	-

Note: Companies listed are located in the city; dashes indicate no ranking
Fortune 500: Companies that produce a 10-K are ranked 1 to 500 based on 1999 revenue
Forbes 500: Private companies are ranked 1 to 500 based on 1998 revenue
Source: Forbes, December 13, 1999; Fortune, April 17, 2000

HOTELS & MOTELS

Hotels/Motels

Area	Hotels/ Motels	Rooms	Luxury-Level Hotels/Motels		Average Minimum Rates ($)		
			♦♦♦♦	♦♦♦♦♦	♦♦	♦♦♦	♦♦♦♦
City	14	1,644	0	0	80	99	n/a
Suburbs	1	123	0	0	n/a	n/a	n/a
Total	15	1,767	0	0	n/a	n/a	n/a

Note: n/a not available; classifications range from one diamond (budget properties with basic amenities) to five diamond (luxury properties).
Source: OAG Business Travel Planner, Winter 1999-2000

Estimated Daily Food and Lodging Costs

Area	Food/Other ($/day)	Average Hotel Cost ($/day)
City	34	58
U.S.	30	55

Source: ERI's Relocation Assessor software database, quarterly effective date 4/1/2000

CONVENTION CENTERS

Convention Centers and Event Sites

Name	Guest Rooms	Meeting Space (sq. ft.)	Capacity (Theatre Style)
Century Center	n/a	n/a	2,590
Morris Civic Auditorium	n/a	n/a	2,400
South Bend Marriott	299	7,000	460

Note: n/a not available
Source: EventSource.com, 3/15/2000

Living Environment

COST OF LIVING

Cost of Living: Homeowner

Cost Element	U.S. ($)	City ($)	Differential ($)	Percent of U.S. Average
Consumables	14,516	13,609	-907	93.8
Transportation	5,957	5,478	-479	92.0
Health Services	2,012	1,934	-78	96.1
Housing/Utilities/Prop. Tax	16,337	17,649	1,312	108.0
Income+Payroll Taxes	12,615	12,021	-594	95.3
Miscellaneous	8,563	8,563	0	100.0
Total Cost of Living	60,000	59,254	-746	98.8

Note: Figures are based on a single income, four person family with gross annual earnings of $60,000, owning an 1,800 square-foot home, and driving two automobiles worth $22,000 30,000 miles per year.
Source: ERI's Relocation Assessor software database, quarterly effective date 4/1/2000

Cost of Living: Renter

Cost Element	U.S. ($)	City ($)	Differential ($)	Percent of U.S. Average
Consumables	10,486	9,796	-690	93.4
Transportation	2,107	1,931	-176	91.6
Health Services	1,632	1,564	-68	95.8
Rent/Utilities/Insurance	9,299	9,916	617	106.6
Income+Payroll Taxes	8,607	8,463	-144	98.3
Miscellaneous	7,869	7,869	0	100.0
Total Cost of Living	40,000	39,539	-461	98.8

Note: Figures are based on a single income, three person family with gross annual earnings of $40,000, renting a 1,000 square-foot home, and driving one automobile worth $8,000 12,000 miles per year.
Source: ERI's Relocation Assessor software database, quarterly effective date 4/1/2000

HOUSING

Median Home Prices and Housing Affordability

Area	Median Price[2] 4th Qtr. 1999 ($)	HOI[3] 4th Qtr. 1999	Affordability Rank[4]
MSA[1]	96,000	78.0	38
U.S.	139,000	63.8	–

Note: (1) Metropolitan Statistical Area - see Appendix A for areas included; (2) U.S. figures calculated from the sales of 687,516 new and existing homes in 192 markets; (3) Housing Opportunity Index - percent of homes sold that were within the reach of the median income household at the prevailing mortgage interest rate; (4) Rank is from 1-192 with 1 being most affordable
Source: National Association of Home Builders, Housing Opportunity Index, 4th Quarter 1999

Estimated Home Price

Area	Price ($)
City	106,102
U.S.	135,855

Note: Figures are based on an 1,800 square-foot home
Source: ERI's Relocation Assessor software database, quarterly effective date 4/1/2000

Estimated Rent

Area	Rent ($/month)
City	710
U.S.	651

Note: Figures are based on a 1,000 square-foot home
Source: ERI's Relocation Assessor software database, quarterly effective date 4/1/2000

Median Home Price Projection

It is projected that the median home price in the metropolitan area will increase from $86,101 in 1999 to $122,731 in 2010, an increase of 42.5%
Kiplinger's Personal Finance Magazine, January 2000

RESIDENTIAL UTILITIES

Average Residential Utility Costs

Area	All Electric ($/mth)	Part Electric ($/mth)	Other Energy ($/mth)	Phone ($/mth)
City	–	54.42	54.11	16.46
U.S.	99.25	55.47	43.48	20.29

Source: ACCRA, Cost of Living Index, 3rd Quarter 1999

HEALTH CARE

Average Health Care Costs

Area	Hospital ($/day)	Doctor ($/visit)	Dentist ($/visit)
City	641.33	48.80	61.80
U.S.	440.96	53.83	68.42

Note: Hospital—based on a semi-private room; Doctor—based on a general practitioner's routine exam of an established patient; Dentist—based on adult teeth cleaning and periodic oral exam.
Source: ACCRA, Cost of Living Index, 3rd Quarter 1999

Distribution of Office-Based Physicians

Area	Family/Gen. Practitioners	Specialists		
		Medical	Surgical	Other
MSA[1]	88	105	100	130

Note: Data as of 12/31/97; (1) Metropolitan Statistical Area - see Appendix A for areas included
Source: American Medical Assn., Physician Characteristics & Distribution in the U.S., 1999

Hospitals

South Bend has 2 general medical and surgical hospitals.
AHA Guide to the Healthcare Field, 1999-2000

EDUCATION

Public School District Statistics

District Name	Num. Sch.	Enroll.	Classroom Teachers	Pupils per Teacher	Minority Pupils (%)	Current Exp.[1] ($/pupil)
South Bend Community Sch Corp	38	20,966	1,242	16.9	43.3	5,682

Note: Data covers the 1997-1998 school year unless otherwise noted; (1) Data covers fiscal year 1996; SD = School District; ISD = Independent School District; n/a not available
Source: National Center for Education Statistics, Common Core of Data Public Education Agency Universe 1997-98; National Center for Education Statistics, Characteristics of the 100 Largest Public Elementary and Secondary School Districts in the United States: 1997-98, July 1999

Educational Quality

School District	Education Quotient[1]	Graduate Outcome[2]	Community Index[3]	Resource Index[4]
South Bend Comm. School Corp.	84	90	103	68

Note: Over 1,000 secondary school districts were rated in terms of educational quality. The scores range from a low of 50 to a high of 150; (1) Combination of the Graduate Outcome, Community and Resource indexes weighted to reflect the greater importance of the Graduate Outcome and Resource Index; (2) Based on graduation rates and college board scores (SAT/ACT); (3) Based on the surrounding community's level of affluence and adult education; (4) Based on teacher salaries, per-pupil expenditures and student-teacher ratios.
Source: Expansion Management, Ratings Issue, 1999

Educational Attainment by Race

Area	High School Graduate (%)					Bachelor's Degree (%)				
	Total	White	Black	Other	Hisp.[2]	Total	White	Black	Other	Hisp.[2]
City	72.0	75.6	56.6	56.7	57.4	18.5	21.2	5.5	18.3	13.3
MSA[1]	76.1	77.9	58.3	66.0	63.5	19.2	20.1	6.8	31.7	19.0
U.S.	75.2	77.9	63.1	60.4	49.8	20.3	21.5	11.4	19.4	9.2

Note: Figures shown cover persons 25 years old and over; (1) Metropolitan Statistical Area - see Appendix A for areas included; (2) people of Hispanic origin can be of any race
Source: 1990 Census of Population and Housing, Summary Tape File 3C

School Enrollment by Type

Area	Preprimary				Elementary/High School			
	Public		Private		Public		Private	
	Enrollment	%	Enrollment	%	Enrollment	%	Enrollment	%
City	1,312	59.9	878	40.1	14,186	81.9	3,131	18.1
MSA[1]	2,710	53.4	2,363	46.6	33,965	83.4	6,772	16.6
U.S.	2,679,029	59.5	1,824,256	40.5	38,379,689	90.2	4,187,099	9.8

Note: Figures shown cover persons 3 years old and over;
(1) Metropolitan Statistical Area - see Appendix A for areas included
Source: 1990 Census of Population and Housing, Summary Tape File 3C

School Enrollment by Race

Area	Preprimary (%)				Elementary/High School (%)			
	White	Black	Other	Hisp.[1]	White	Black	Other	Hisp.[1]
City	70.2	27.5	2.3	6.2	62.9	32.5	4.6	5.4
MSA[2]	85.4	12.8	1.8	3.4	82.2	14.4	3.3	3.0
U.S.	80.4	12.5	7.1	7.8	74.1	15.6	10.3	12.5

Note: Figures shown cover persons 3 years old and over; (1) people of Hispanic origin can be of any race; (2) Metropolitan Statistical Area - see Appendix A for areas included
Source: 1990 Census of Population and Housing, Summary Tape File 3C

Higher Education

Two-Year Colleges		Four-Year Colleges		Medical Schools	Law Schools	Voc/ Tech
Public	Private	Public	Private			
1	1	1	0	0	1	2

Source: College Blue Book, Occupational Education, 1999; Medical School Admission Requirements, 1999-2000; Peterson's Guide to Two-Year Colleges, 2000; Peterson's Guide to Four-Year Colleges, 1999; Barron's Guide to Law Schools, 1999

MAJOR EMPLOYERS

Major Employers

Adams Remco (office equipment)
Holy Cross Health System
Memorial Hospital of South Bend
South Bend Tribune Corp.

Clark Equipment Co. (machinery)
Madison Hospital Corp.
Schurz Communications
St. Joseph's Medical Center

Note: Companies listed are located in the city
Source: D&B Business Rankings, 1999; Ward's Business Directory, 1999; America's Corporate Families, 1999

PUBLIC SAFETY

Crime Rate

Area	All Crimes	Violent Crimes				Property Crimes		
		Murder	Forcible Rape	Robbery	Aggrav. Assault	Burglary	Larceny -Theft	Motor Vehicle Theft
City	8,901.3	13.6	70.9	348.6	328.2	2,005.9	5,400.2	734.0
Suburbs[1]	4,433.0	4.5	28.7	51.1	470.6	639.2	3,031.9	206.9
MSA[2]	6,205.8	8.1	45.5	169.1	414.1	1,181.5	3,971.6	416.0
U.S.	4,615.5	6.3	34.4	165.2	360.5	862.0	2,728.1	459.0

Note: Crime rate is the number of crimes per 100,000 population; (1) Defined as all areas within the Metropolitan Statistical Area but located outside the central city; (2) Metropolitan Statistical Area - see Appendix A for areas included
Source: FBI Uniform Crime Reports, 1998

RECREATION

Culture and Recreation

Museums	Symphony Orchestras	Opera Companies	Dance Companies	Professional Theatres	Zoos	Pro Sports Teams
6	1	0	1	0	1	0

Source: Musical America, International Directory of the Performing Arts, 1999; Official Museum Directory, 2000; Stern's Performing Arts Directory, 1997; USA Today Four Sport Stadium Guide, 1997; Career Opportunities in Theatre and the Performing Arts, 1999

Library System

The St. Joseph County Public Library has seven branches, holdings of 498,100 volumes, and a budget of $7,547,910 (1997-1998).
American Library Directory, 1999-2000

MEDIA

Newspapers

Name	Type	Freq.	Distribution	Circulation
South Bend Tribune	General	7x/wk	Local	79,600
Tri-County News	n/a	1x/wk	Area	1,000

Note: Includes newspapers with circulations of 200 or more located in the city; n/a not available
Source: Burrelle's Media Directory, 1999 Edition

Television Stations

Name	Ch.	Affiliation	Type	Owner
WNDU	16	NBCT	Commercial	Michiana Telecasting Corp.
WSBT	22	CBST	Commercial	Schurz Communications Inc.
WNIT	34	PBS	Public	Michiana Public Broadcasting Corporation
WHME	46	n/a	Commercial	Le Sea Broadcasting Corporation
WBND	58	ABCT	Commercial	Weigel Broadcasting Company

Note: Stations included broadcast in the South Bend metro area; n/a not available
Source: Burrelle's Media Directory, 1999 Edition

AM Radio Stations

Call Letters	Freq. (kHz)	Target Audience	Station Format	Music Format
WSBT	960	General	N/S/T	n/a
WNDU	1490	General	M/S	Oldies

Note: Stations included broadcast in the South Bend metro area; n/a not available
Target Audience: A=Asian; B=Black; C=Christian; E=Ethnic; F=French; G=General; H=Hispanic; M=Men; N=Native American; R=Religious; S=Senior Citizen; W=Women; Y=Young Adult; Z=Children
Station Format: E=Educational; M=Music; N=News; S=Sports; T=Talk
Source: Burrelle's Media Directory, 1999 Edition

FM Radio Stations

Call Letters	Freq. (mHz)	Target Audience	Station Format	Music Format
WVPE	88.1	General	M/N/T	Blues/Jazz
WSND	88.9	General	E/M	Alternative/Classical/Jazz/Reggae/World Music
WNDU	92.9	General	M	Adult Contemporary
WNSN	101.5	General	M	Adult Contemporary
WHME	103.1	General	T	n/a

Note: Stations included broadcast in the South Bend metro area; n/a not available
Station Format: E=Educational; M=Music; N=News; S=Sports; T=Talk
Source: Burrelle's Media Directory, 1999 Edition

WEATHER

Temperature/Precipitation/Humidity

	Jan	Feb	Mar	Apr	May	Jun	Jul	Aug	Sep	Oct	Nov	Dec	Yr.
Max. High Temp. (°F)	68	69	85	89	92	104	100	103	99	92	82	70	104
Avg. High Temp. (°F)	31	34	45	59	70	80	83	81	74	63	48	36	59
Avg. Temp. (°F)	24	27	37	·49	59	69	73	71	64	53	41	29	50
Avg. Low Temp. (°F)	16	19	28	38	48	58	63	61	54	43	33	22	40
Min. Low Temp. (°F)	-21	-17	-2	11	24	35	44	40	32	20	-7	-16	-21
Avg. Precip. (in.)	2.4	2.0	3.0	3.8	3.2	4.0	3.8	3.6	3.3	3.1	3.1	3.0	38.3
Avg. Snowfall (in.)	21	15	9	2	Tr	0	0	0	0	1	9	19	76
Avg. Rel. Hum. 7am (%)	82	82	80	77	76	78	81	85	85	84	82	83	81
Avg. Rel. Hum. 4pm (%)	73	70	62	55	53	53	55	56	56	58	68	75	61

Note: Tr = Trace amounts (less than 0.05 inches of rain or less than 0.5 inches of snow)
Source: National Climatic Data Center, International Station Meteorological Climate Summary, 3/95

Weather Conditions

Temperature			Precipitation		
5°F & below	32°F & below	90°F & above	0.01 inch or more precip.	1.5 inch or more snow/ice	Thunderstorms
14	129	13	144	16	39

Note: Figures are average number of days per year
Source: National Climatic Data Center, International Station Meteorological Climate Summary, 3/95

AIR & WATER QUALITY

Maximum Pollutant Concentrations

	Particulate Matter (ug/m³)	Carbon Monoxide (ppm)	Sulfur Dioxide (ppm)	Nitrogen Dioxide (ppm)	Ozone (ppm)	Lead (ug/m³)
MSA[1] Level	41	n/a	n/a	0.012	0.12	n/a
NAAQS[2]	150	9	0.140	0.053	0.12	1.50
Met NAAQS	Yes	n/a	n/a	Yes	Yes	n/a

Note: (1) Metropolitan Statistical Area - see Appendix A for areas included; (2) National Ambient Air Quality Standards; ppm = parts per million; ug/m³ = micrograms per cubic meter; n/a not available
Source: EPA, National Air Quality and Emissions Trends Report, 1997

Pollutant Standards Index

Data not available.
EPA, National Air Quality and Emissions Trends Report, 1997

Drinking Water

Water System Name	Pop. Served	Primary Water Source Type	Number of Violations in 1998-99	Type of Violation/ Contaminants
South Bend Water Works	108,170	Ground	None	None

Note: Data as of January 19, 2000
Source: EPA, Office of Ground Water and Drinking Water, Safe Drinking Water Information System

South Bend tap water is neutral, hard, and fluoridated.
Editor & Publisher Market Guide, 2000

Trenton, New Jersey

Background

Trenton, New Jersey is in the western section of the state, approximately 50 miles southwest of Newark and 30 miles northeast of Philadelphia, Pennsylvannia. It is on the east bank of the Delaware River, across the river from Pennsylvania.

Trenton is the capital of New Jersey and the county seat of Mercer County. The Trenton metropolitan area is a regional commercial and population center. Trenton has long been a prominent manufacturing center, with both light and heavy industry. While it still has significant manufacturing activity, the emphasis in the local economy has shifted in recent decades to government operations, business services and other economic activities. It is near interstate highway I-95. Trenton and the surrounding area were the site of many historic events in early American history.

The region was originally inhabited by the Delaware and other Native Americans. In 1679, Mahlon Stacy, an English Quaker, established a mill and settlement. In 1714, William Trent, a businessman, purchased the Stacy properties to develop a town. The community was subsequently named Trent's Town, which was later changed to Trenton. An important battle of the Revolutionary War occurred in Trenton in 1776, when George Washington and his troops crossed the Delaware and defeated Hessain troops who fighting for England. In 1784, the Congress held sessions in Trenton. In 1790, Trenton became New Jersey's capital, and was incorporated as a city in 1792.

Trenton became an important industrial area during the 19th Century, including the manufacture of clothing, chemical products, mechanical equipment, rubber items and many other goods. John Robeling founded a company that manufactured the wire cable used to build the Brooklyn Bridge and other structures. Pottery, ceramics and china, are also prominent products of the Trenton area.

In the mid-20th Century, changes in manufacturing and other trends affected Trenton's traditional economy. Numerous industries left, prompting revitalization and redevelopment initiatives. The contemporary economy is based on state government operations and services, manufacturing, trade and transport, retail, business and professional services and other activities.

Colleges in the area include Mercer County Community College, Thomas Edison State College, Princeton University in Princeton, and Rider University in Lawrenceville.

Trenton and the surrounding area contain many historic sites, including the 1719 home of founder William Trent. Mill Hill is a restored colonial neighborhood. The Old Barracks Museum is a military site built in 1758 to defend the region during the French and Indian Wars. The state government district has historic features and landmarks that include the domed State Capitol building.

Museums include The New Jersey State Museum, The Trenton City Museum and the Contemporary Victorian Museum, among others. In 1999, the Sovereign Bank Arena, a facility for sports, concerts and other events was opened. The Trenton War Memorial is a recently restored 1932 community center and theater. Cultural activities include The Greater Trenton Symphony, New Jersey Symphony, Trenton Civic Opera, and Mill Hill Theater, among others. Artworks is a school of visual arts in Trenton.

The Mercer Riverfront Park, Cadwalader Park and Stacy Park are among the local recreational facilities, and the city is accessible to outdoor activities and nearby scenic rural regions. Professional sports activities include Trenton Thunder — a Class AA team affiliated with the Boston Red Sox, Trenton Titans — affiliated with the East Coast Hockey League, and Trenton Stars — members of the International Basketball League.

Trenton is governed by an elected Mayor and a City Council.

General Rankings and Evaluative Comments

■ Trenton was ranked #134 out of 354 metropolitan areas in *Places Rated Almanac*. Criteria: cost of living, climate, crime, transportation, job outlook, education, the arts, health care, and recreation. *Places Rated Almanac, Millennium Edition, 2000*

Business Environment

STATE ECONOMY

State Economic Profile

"While still on a solid footing, the New Jersey economy has begun to decelerate. A decline in exports has added to New Jersey's already declining manufacturing sector. Corporate layoffs and mergers are having a disproportionate influence on the New Jersey economy, as a large share of corporate headquarters are located there.

New Jersey manufacturing employment declined 2.1% in 1998, with almost 90% of the losses concentrated in the northern and central parts of the state. A large share of these job losses were white-collar jobs and high paying, associated with corporate and research operations. These losses are often the result of merger-related downsizing. For instance the Mobil-Exxon merger will result in the closing of Exxon's international operations in New Jersey, with 460 high-paying positions being transferred to Mobil sites in Houston and Fairfax, Virginia. Recent mergers within the pharmaceutical industry will likely result in another round of corporate layoffs in New Jersey.

In spite of a decelerating economy, New Jersey's housing was strong in 1998. Sales were robust across the state and price appreciation strong in the northern and central parts of the state. Construction employment increased 4.7% in 1998 as residential starts increased 13%. Some of the biggest gains came in Hudson and Mercer counties, where construction jumped significantly. The state's weak demographics and moderating economy will constrain home price appreciation and sales in 2000.

New Jersey's fundamental strengths, its central location, skilled workforce and strong transportation network indicate that the state will remain an attractive business location, in spite of its high cost of doing business. The short-term outlook, however, is for slower growth." *National Association of Realtors, Economic Profiles: The Fifty States and the District of Columbia, http://nar.realtor.com/databank/profiles.htm*

EXPORTS

Total Export Sales

Area	1995 ($000)	1996 ($000)	1997 ($000)	1998 ($000)	% Chg. 1995-98	% Chg. 1997-98
MSA[1]	392,472	267,847	343,383	276,918	-29.4	-19.4
U.S.	583,030,524	622,827,063	687,597,999	680,474,251	16.7	-1.0

Note: (1) Metropolitan Statistical Area - see Appendix A for areas included
Source: U.S. Department of Commerce, International Trade Association, Metropolitan Area Exports: An Export Performance Report on Over 250 U.S. Cities, November 10, 1999

CITY FINANCES

City Government Finances

Component	1995 ($million)	1995 (per capita $)
Revenue	277.8	3,289
Expenditure	273.5	3,239
Debt Outstanding	118.6	1,404

Source: 1999 County and City Extra, Annual Metro, City, and County Data Book

City Government Revenue by Source

Source	1995 ($million)	1995 (per capita $)
Intergovernmental	180.2	2,133
Taxes	71.7	849
Property	69.8	827
Sales and Gross Receipts	0.0	0

Source: 1999 County and City Extra, Annual Metro, City, and County Data Book

City Government Expenditures by Function

Function	1995 ($million)	1995 (per capita $)	1995 (%)
Public Welfare	2.4	29	0.9
Highways	1.9	22	0.7
Parking Facilities	1.0	12	0.4
Education	140.5	1,664	51.4
Health and Hospitals	2.7	32	1.0
Police Protection	25.9	307	9.5
Sewerage and Sanitation	18.0	213	6.6
Parks and Recreation	2.7	32	1.0
Housing and Community Development	16.1	191	5.9
Interest on Debt	4.3	51	1.6

Source: 1999 County and City Extra, Annual Metro, City, and County Data Book

Municipal Bond Ratings

Area	Moody's
City	Aaa

Source: Mergent Bond Record, 2/2000

POPULATION

Population Growth

Area	1980 Census	1990 Census	1999 Estimate	2004 Projection	Population Growth (%) 1990-1999	Population Growth (%) 1999-2004
City	92,124	88,675	84,019	82,403	-5.3	-1.9
MSA[1]	307,863	325,824	332,203	336,113	2.0	1.2
U.S.	226,545,805	248,765,170	272,212,864	283,625,312	9.4	4.2

Note: (1) Metropolitan Statistical Area - see Appendix A for areas included
Source: 1990 Census of Population and Housing, Summary Tape File 3C; Claritas, Inc.

Number of Households and Average Household Size

Area	1980 Census	1990 Census	1999 Estimate	2004 Projection	1999 Average Household Size
City	32,463	30,673	29,121	28,567	2.89
MSA[1]	105,819	116,777	119,590	121,185	2.78
U.S.	80,389,592	91,993,582	102,048,200	107,302,392	2.67

Note: (1) Metropolitan Statistical Area - see Appendix A for areas included
Source: 1990 Census of Population and Housing, Summary Tape File 3C; Claritas, Inc.

Race/Ethnicity of City Population

Race/Ethnicity	1990 Census Population	1990 Census %	1999 Estimate Population	1999 Estimate %	% Change 1990-1999
White, Non-Hispanic	33,527	37.8	24,130	28.7	-28.0
Black, Non-Hispanic	42,696	48.1	42,566	50.7	-0.3
Asian, Non-Hispanic	371	0.4	409	0.5	10.2
Other, Non-Hispanic	380	0.4	351	0.4	-7.6
Hispanic	11,701	13.2	16,563	19.7	41.6

Source: 1990 Census of Population and Housing, Summary Tape File 3C; Claritas, Inc.

Race/Ethnicity of Metropolitan Statistical Area Population

Race/Ethnicity	1990 Census		1999 Estimate		% Change 1990-1999
	Population	%	Population	%	
White, Non-Hispanic	236,790	72.7	222,193	66.9	-6.2
Black, Non-Hispanic	59,787	18.3	65,950	19.9	10.3
Asian, Non-Hispanic	9,441	2.9	15,592	4.7	65.2
Other, Non-Hispanic	1,083	0.3	1,044	0.3	-3.6
Hispanic	18,723	5.7	27,424	8.3	46.5

Note: See Appendix A for areas included in the Metropolitan Statistical Area
Source: 1990 Census of Population and Housing, Summary Tape File 3C; Claritas, Inc.

Ancestry

Area	German	Irish	English	Italian	U.S.	French	Polish	Dutch
City	7.9	7.5	4.1	12.0	1.7	0.6	6.2	0.7
MSA[1]	17.9	15.7	11.9	16.6	2.1	2.0	9.7	1.9
U.S.	23.3	15.6	13.1	5.9	5.3	4.2	3.8	2.5

Note: Figures are percentages and include persons that reported multiple ancestry (eg. if a person reported being Irish and Italian, they were included in both columns); (1) Metropolitan Statistical Area - see Appendix A for areas included
Source: 1990 Census of Population and Housing, Summary Tape File 3C

Median Age

Area	1990 Census	1999 Estimate
City	31.2	32.2
MSA[1]	34.0	37.0
U.S.	32.9	35.7

Note: (1) Metropolitan Statistical Area - see Appendix A for areas included
Source: 1990 Census of Population and Housing, Summary Tape File 3C; Claritas, Inc.

Male/Female Population

Area	Number of Males		Number of Females		Males per 100 Females	
	1990	1999	1990	1999	1990	1999
City	42,883	40,981	45,792	43,038	93.6	95.2
MSA[1]	157,112	160,789	168,712	171,414	93.1	93.8
U.S.	121,172,379	132,803,736	127,537,494	139,409,136	95.0	95.3

Note: (1) Metropolitan Statistical Area - see Appendix A for areas included
Source: 1990 Census of Population, General Population Characteristics; Claritas, Inc.

INCOME

Per Capita/Median/Average Income

Area	Per Capita ($)			Median Household ($)			Average Household ($)		
	1989	1999	% Chg.	1989	1999	% Chg.	1989	1999	% Chg.
City	11,018	15,863	44.0	25,719	34,408	33.8	30,890	45,081	45.9
MSA[1]	18,936	29,115	53.8	41,227	59,885	45.3	51,984	80,028	53.9
U.S.	14,420	21,350	48.1	30,056	40,525	34.8	38,453	56,184	46.1

Note: (1) Metropolitan Statistical Area - see Appendix A for areas included; 1989 data is from the 1990 Census; 1999 data is estimated by Claritas, Inc.
Source: 1990 Census of Population, General Population Characteristics; Claritas, Inc.

Household Income Distribution

Area	Percent of Households Earning								
	Under $5,000	$5,000 -14,999	$15,000 -24,999	$25,000 -34,999	$35,000 -49,999	$50,000 -74,999	$75,000 -99,000	$100,000 -149,999	$150,000 and up
City	5.1	17.4	14.2	13.9	15.9	17.9	8.2	5.7	1.6
MSA[1]	2.1	8.4	8.8	9.3	13.6	19.9	13.4	13.6	10.8
U.S.	3.9	13.3	13.8	12.6	16.2	19.4	9.7	6.6	4.6

Note: Data as of 1999; (1) Metropolitan Statistical Area - see Appendix A for areas included
Source: Claritas, Inc.

Effective Buying Income

Area	Per Capita ($)	Median Household ($)	Average Household ($)
City	13,475	31,328	39,132
MSA[1]	22,837	50,497	63,674
U.S.	17,496	36,603	47,036

Note: Data as of 1/1/2000; (1) Metropolitan Statistical Area - see Appendix A for areas included
Source: Standard Rate & Data Service, Newspaper Advertising Source, March 2000

Effective Household Buying Income Distribution

Area	% of Households Earning						
	$10,000 -$19,999	$20,000 -$34,999	$35,000 -$49,999	$50,000 -$74,999	$75,000 -$99,000	$100,000 -$124,999	$125,000 and up
City	17.0	23.2	17.2	17.3	7.2	2.3	1.0
MSA[1]	10.0	16.6	15.7	22.6	14.1	6.7	7.2
U.S.	15.0	21.6	17.6	19.6	8.4	3.0	3.3

Note: Data as of 1/1/2000; (1) Metropolitan Statistical Area - see Appendix A for areas included
Source: Standard Rate & Data Service, Newspaper Advertising Source, March 2000

Poverty Rates by Age

Area	People of All Ages	People Under 18 Years Old	Related Children Age 5-17 in Families in Poverty
City	20.9	n/a	n/a
County	8.2	11.7	11.4
U.S.	13.8	20.8	18.7

Note: Figures show the percent of people living below the poverty line in 1995. The average poverty threshold was $15,569 for a family of four in 1995; n/a not available
Source: Bureau of the Census, Small Area Income and Poverty Estimates Program; U.S. Department of Housing and Urban Development

EMPLOYMENT

Labor Force and Employment

Area	Civilian Labor Force			Workers Employed		
	Dec. 1998	Dec. 1999	% Chg.	Dec. 1998	Dec. 1999	% Chg.
City	39,987	40,155	0.4	36,811	37,422	1.7
MSA[1]	169,147	170,976	1.1	162,871	165,575	1.7
U.S.	138,297,000	139,941,000	1.2	132,732,000	134,696,000	1.5

Note: Data is not seasonally adjusted and covers workers 16 years of age and older; (1) Metropolitan Statistical Area - see Appendix A for areas included
Source: Bureau of Labor Statistics, http://stats.bls.gov

Unemployment Rate

Area	1999											
	Jan.	Feb.	Mar.	Apr.	May	Jun.	Jul.	Aug.	Sep.	Oct.	Nov.	Dec.
City	9.4	8.5	8.9	7.9	8.1	9.0	9.9	8.7	8.5	7.6	7.3	6.8
MSA[1]	4.4	4.0	4.2	3.7	3.8	4.2	4.7	4.1	4.0	3.6	3.4	3.2
U.S.	4.8	4.7	4.4	4.1	4.0	4.5	4.5	4.2	4.1	3.8	3.8	3.7

Note: Data is not seasonally adjusted and covers workers 16 years of age and older; all figures are percentages; (1) Metropolitan Statistical Area - see Appendix A for areas included
Source: Bureau of Labor Statistics, http://stats.bls.gov

Employment by Industry

Sector	MSA[1]		U.S.
	Number of Employees	Percent of Total	Percent of Total
Services	77,100	37.6	30.2
Retail Trade	29,100	14.2	18.1
Government	52,400	25.6	15.8
Manufacturing	16,000	7.8	14.1
Finance/Insurance/Real Estate	11,300	5.5	5.9
Wholesale Trade	6,800	3.3	5.4
Transportation/Public Utilities	7,500	3.7	5.3
Construction	n/a	n/a	4.8
Mining	n/a	n/a	0.4

Note: Figures cover non-farm employment as of 12/99 and are not seasonally adjusted;
(1) Metropolitan Statistical Area - see Appendix A for areas included; n/a not available
Source: Bureau of Labor Statistics, http://stats.bls.gov

Employment by Occupation

Occupation Category	City (%)	MSA[1] (%)	U.S. (%)
White Collar	50.0	68.2	58.1
Executive/Admin./Management	8.4	15.9	12.3
Professional	9.2	18.3	14.1
Technical & Related Support	3.4	4.6	3.7
Sales	6.7	9.5	11.8
Administrative Support/Clerical	22.2	19.9	16.3
Blue Collar	27.2	18.3	26.2
Precision Production/Craft/Repair	8.7	8.0	11.3
Machine Operators/Assem./Insp.	8.6	4.3	6.8
Transportation/Material Movers	4.7	3.0	4.1
Cleaners/Helpers/Laborers	5.2	3.1	3.9
Services	21.7	12.4	13.2
Farming/Forestry/Fishing	1.1	1.0	2.5

Note: Figures cover workers 16 years of age and older;
(1) Metropolitan Statistical Area - see Appendix A for areas included
Source: 1990 Census of Population and Housing, Summary Tape File 3C

Occupational Employment Projections: 1996 - 2006

Occupations Expected to Have the Largest Job Growth (ranked by numerical growth)	Fast-Growing Occupations[1] (ranked by percent growth)
1. Systems analysts	1. Systems analysts
2. Home health aides	2. Database administrators
3. Cashiers	3. Computer engineers
4. Salespersons, retail	4. Personal and home care aides
5. Nursing aides/orderlies/attendants	5. Physical therapy assistants and aides
6. Registered nurses	6. Desktop publishers
7. Truck drivers, light	7. Medical assistants
8. General managers & top executives	8. Home health aides
9. Adjustment clerks	9. Physical therapists
10. Receptionists and information clerks	10. Customer service representatives

Note: Projections cover New Jersey; (1) Excludes occupations with total job growth less than 300
Source: U.S. Department of Labor, Employment and Training Administration, America's Labor Market Information System (ALMIS)

Average Wages

Occupation	$/Hr.	Occupation	$/Hr.
Accountants and Auditors	24.19	Maids and Housekeepers	8.07
Assemblers and Fabricators	12.28	Maintenance Repairers	15.32
Automotive Mechanics	17.17	Marketing/Advertising/PR Managers	37.23
Bookkeepers	13.86	Nurses, Licensed Practical	15.65
Carpenters	24.51	Nurses, Registered	22.26
Cashiers	7.57	Nursing Aides/Orderlies/Attendants	9.59
Clerks, General Office	11.46	Physicians and Surgeons	55.05
Clerks, Shipping/Receiving/Traffic	14.26	Receptionists/Information Clerks	10.77
Computer Programmers	26.96	Sales Reps., Exc. Scientific/Retail	22.47
Computer Support Specialists	23.35	Sales Reps., Scientific, Exc. Retail	27.51
Cooks, Restaurant	10.09	Salespersons, Retail	9.44
Electricians	21.50	Secretaries, Except Legal/Medical	15.04
Financial Managers	33.71	Stock Clerks, Sales Floor	8.31
First-Line Supervisors/Mgrs., Sales	20.31	Systems Analysts	27.15
Food Preparation Workers	7.71	Teacher Aides	9.90
General Managers/Top Executives	43.42	Teachers, Elementary School	24.74
Guards	11.03	Teachers, Secondary School	24.01
Hand Packers	8.32	Telemarketers	10.27
Janitors and Cleaners	9.46	Truck Drivers, Heavy/Tractor-Trailer	14.98
Laborers, Landscaping	10.49	Truck Drivers, Light	13.44
Lawyers	36.10	Waiters and Waitresses	6.14

Note: Wage data is for 1998 and covers the Metropolitan Statistical Area (see Appendix A for areas included). Hourly wages for elementary and secondary school teachers were calculated by the editors from annual wage data assuming a 40 hour work week; Dashes indicate that data was not available.
Source: Bureau of Labor Statistics, 1998 Metropolitan Area Occupational Employment and Wage Estimates

TAXES

Major State and Local Tax Rates

State Corporate Income (%)	State Personal Income (%)	Residential Property (%)	Sales & Use		State Gasoline (cents/ gallon)	State Cigarette (cents/ pack)
			State (%)	Local (%)		
9.0[a]	1.4 - 6.37	3.35	6.0	None	10.5[b]	80.0

Note: Personal/corporate income, sales, gasoline and cigarette tax rates as of January 2000. Property tax rates as of April 2000; (a) Business franchise tax rate ($200 min. tax). Corporations not subject to the franchise tax are subject to a 7.25% income tax. S-Corporations are subject to an entity level tax of 2.0%. Corporations with net income under $100,000 are taxed at 7.5%zz

; (b) Plus a 2.75% GRT
Source: Federation of Tax Administrators, www.taxadmin.org; ERI's Relocation Assessor software database, quarterly effective date 4/1/2000

Total Taxes Per Capita and as a Percent of Income

Area	Per Capita Income ($)	Per Capita Taxes ($)			Percent of Income (%)		
		Total	Federal	State/Local	Total	Federal	State/Local
New Jersey	36,685	13,780	9,532	4,248	37.6	26.0	11.6
U.S.	28,878	10,298	7,026	3,273	35.7	24.3	11.3

Note: Figures are for 1999
Source: Tax Foundation, www.taxfoundation.org

COMMERCIAL UTILITIES

Typical Monthly Electric Bills

Area	Commercial Service ($/month)		Industrial Service ($/month)	
	12 kW demand 1,500 kWh	100 kW demand 30,000 kWh	1,000 kW demand 400,000 kWh	20,000 kW demand 10,000,000 kWh
City	212	3,121	33,990	512,619
U.S.	150	2,174	23,995	508,569

Note: Based on rates in effect January 1, 1999
Source: Edison Electric Institute, Typical Residential, Commercial and Industrial Bills, Winter 1999

TRANSPORTATION

Transportation Statistics

Average minutes to work (1990)	19.6
Interstate highways	I-95; I-195; I-295; US-1; US-13; US-130; US-206
Bus lines	
In-city (1998)	New Jersey Transit Corp., 66 buses
Inter-city (1999)	7
Passenger air service	
Airport	Trenton Mercer County Airport
Airlines (1999)	3
Enplaned passengers (1998)	92,472
Amtrak service	Yes
Motor freight carriers (1999)	100
Major waterways/ports	Delaware River

Source: FAA DOT/TSC CY1998 ACAIS Database; National Transit Database, 1998; Editor & Publisher Market Guide, 2000; Amtrak National Time Table, Fall 1999/Winter 2000; 1990 Census of Population and Housing, STF 3C; Jane's Urban Transport Systems 1999-2000

Means of Transportation to Work

Area	Car/Truck/Van		Public Transportation			Bicycle	Walked	Other Means	Worked at Home
	Drove Alone	Car-pooled	Bus	Subway	Railroad				
City	60.9	18.7	8.7	0.2	1.0	0.5	7.4	1.6	1.1
MSA[1]	71.5	12.7	3.1	0.1	2.9	0.5	5.9	0.8	2.5
U.S.	73.2	13.4	3.0	1.5	0.5	0.4	3.9	1.2	3.0

Note: Figures shown are percentages and only include workers 16 years of age and older;
(1) Metropolitan Statistical Area - see Appendix A for areas included
Source: 1990 Census of Population and Housing, Summary Tape File 3C

BUSINESSES

Major Business Headquarters

Company Name	1999 Rankings	
	Fortune 500	Forbes 500
No companies listed	-	-

Note: Companies listed are located in the city; dashes indicate no ranking
Fortune 500: Companies that produce a 10-K are ranked 1 to 500 based on 1999 revenue
Forbes 500: Private companies are ranked 1 to 500 based on 1998 revenue
Source: Forbes, December 13, 1999; Fortune, April 17, 2000

HOTELS & MOTELS

Hotels/Motels

Area	Hotels/ Motels	Rooms	Luxury-Level Hotels/Motels		Average Minimum Rates ($)		
			♦♦♦♦	♦♦♦♦♦	♦♦	♦♦♦	♦♦♦♦
City	4	-1	0	0	n/a	n/a	n/a
Suburbs	5	563	0	0	n/a	n/a	n/a
Total	9	562	0	0	n/a	n/a	n/a

Note: n/a not available; classifications range from one diamond (budget properties with basic amenities) to five diamond (luxury properties).
Source: OAG Business Travel Planner, Winter 1999-2000

Estimated Daily Food and Lodging Costs

Area	Food/Other ($/day)	Average Hotel Cost ($/day)
City	38	84
U.S.	30	55

Source: ERI's Relocation Assessor software database, quarterly effective date 4/1/2000

CONVENTION CENTERS

Convention Centers and Event Sites

Name	Guest Rooms	Meeting Space (sq. ft.)	Capacity (Theatre Style)
Mercer County Improvement Authority	n/a	n/a	10,000

Note: n/a not available
Source: EventSource.com, 3/15/2000

Living Environment

COST OF LIVING

Cost of Living: Homeowner

Cost Element	U.S. ($)	City ($)	Differential ($)	Percent of U.S. Average
Consumables	14,516	16,604	2,088	114.4
Transportation	5,957	6,558	601	110.1
Health Services	2,012	2,238	226	111.2
Housing/Utilities/Prop. Tax	16,337	24,232	7,895	148.3
Income+Payroll Taxes	12,615	11,222	-1,393	89.0
Miscellaneous	8,563	8,563	0	100.0
Total Cost of Living	60,000	69,417	9,417	115.7

Note: Figures are based on a single income, four person family with gross annual earnings of $60,000, owning an 1,800 square-foot home, and driving two automobiles worth $22,000 30,000 miles per year.
Source: ERI's Relocation Assessor software database, quarterly effective date 4/1/2000

Cost of Living: Renter

Cost Element	U.S. ($)	City ($)	Differential ($)	Percent of U.S. Average
Consumables	10,486	12,067	1,581	115.1
Transportation	2,107	2,335	228	110.8
Health Services	1,632	1,826	194	111.9
Rent/Utilities/Insurance	9,299	13,565	4,266	145.9
Income+Payroll Taxes	8,607	8,031	-576	93.3
Miscellaneous	7,869	7,869	0	100.0
Total Cost of Living	40,000	45,693	5,693	114.2

Note: Figures are based on a single income, three person family with gross annual earnings of $40,000, renting a 1,000 square-foot home, and driving one automobile worth $8,000 12,000 miles per year.
Source: ERI's Relocation Assessor software database, quarterly effective date 4/1/2000

HOUSING

Median Home Prices and Housing Affordability

Area	Median Price[2] 4th Qtr. 1999 ($)	HOI[3] 4th Qtr. 1999	Affordability Rank[4]
MSA[1]	140,000	68.8	101
U.S.	139,000	63.8	–

Note: (1) Metropolitan Statistical Area - see Appendix A for areas included; (2) U.S. figures calculated from the sales of 687,516 new and existing homes in 192 markets; (3) Housing Opportunity Index - percent of homes sold that were within the reach of the median income household at the prevailing mortgage interest rate; (4) Rank is from 1-192 with 1 being most affordable
Source: National Association of Home Builders, Housing Opportunity Index, 4th Quarter 1999

Estimated Home Price

Area	Price ($)
City	167,333
U.S.	135,855

Note: Figures are based on an 1,800 square-foot home
Source: ERI's Relocation Assessor software database, quarterly effective date 4/1/2000

Estimated Rent

Area	Rent ($/month)
City	959
U.S.	651

Note: Figures are based on a 1,000 square-foot home
Source: ERI's Relocation Assessor software database, quarterly effective date 4/1/2000

Median Home Price Projection

It is projected that the median home price in the metropolitan area will increase from $141,825 in 1999 to $211,032 in 2010, an increase of 48.8%
Kiplinger's Personal Finance Magazine, January 2000

RESIDENTIAL UTILITIES

Average Residential Utility Costs

Area	All Electric ($/mth)	Part Electric ($/mth)	Other Energy ($/mth)	Phone ($/mth)
City	n/a	n/a	n/a	n/a
U.S.	99.25	55.47	43.48	20.29

Note: n/a not available
Source: ACCRA, Cost of Living Index, 3rd Quarter 1999

HEALTH CARE

Average Health Care Costs

Area	Hospital ($/day)	Doctor ($/visit)	Dentist ($/visit)
City	n/a	n/a	n/a
U.S.	440.96	53.83	68.42

Note: n/a not available
Source: ACCRA, Cost of Living Index, 3rd Quarter 1999

Distribution of Office-Based Physicians

Area	Family/Gen. Practitioners	Specialists Medical	Specialists Surgical	Specialists Other
MSA[1]	39	317	213	212

Note: Data as of 12/31/97; (1) Metropolitan Statistical Area - see Appendix A for areas included
Source: American Medical Assn., Physician Characteristics & Distribution in the U.S., 1999

Hospitals

Trenton has 2 general medical and surgical hospitals, 1 psychiatric.
AHA Guide to the Healthcare Field, 1999-2000

EDUCATION

Public School District Statistics

District Name	Num. Sch.	Enroll.	Classroom Teachers	Pupils per Teacher	Minority Pupils (%)	Current Exp.[1] ($/pupil)
Chesterfield Twp	1	255	21	12.1	n/a	n/a
Mercer Co Special Service	4	900	92	9.8	n/a	n/a
Mercer Co. Voc-Tech	3	366	30	12.2	n/a	n/a
Trenton City	23	12,396	910	13.6	n/a	n/a

Note: Data covers the 1997-1998 school year unless otherwise noted; (1) Data covers fiscal year 1996; SD = School District; ISD = Independent School District; n/a not available
Source: National Center for Education Statistics, Common Core of Data Public Education Agency Universe 1997-98; National Center for Education Statistics, Characteristics of the 100 Largest Public Elementary and Secondary School Districts in the United States: 1997-98, July 1999

Educational Quality

School District	Education Quotient[1]	Graduate Outcome[2]	Community Index[3]	Resource Index[4]
Trenton City	81	51	55	145

Note: Over 1,000 secondary school districts were rated in terms of educational quality. The scores range from a low of 50 to a high of 150; (1) Combination of the Graduate Outcome, Community and Resource indexes weighted to reflect the greater importance of the Graduate Outcome and Resource Index; (2) Based on graduation rates and college board scores (SAT/ACT); (3) Based on the surrounding community's level of affluence and adult education; (4) Based on teacher salaries, per-pupil expenditures and student-teacher ratios.
Source: Expansion Management, Ratings Issue, 1999

Educational Attainment by Race

Area	High School Graduate (%)					Bachelor's Degree (%)				
	Total	White	Black	Other	Hisp.[2]	Total	White	Black	Other	Hisp.[2]
City	58.2	60.9	58.2	38.3	33.9	10.5	13.5	7.8	7.1	3.8
MSA[1]	77.1	80.6	62.8	69.2	47.1	29.5	32.8	11.1	39.7	12.4
U.S.	75.2	77.9	63.1	60.4	49.8	20.3	21.5	11.4	19.4	9.2

Note: Figures shown cover persons 25 years old and over; (1) Metropolitan Statistical Area - see Appendix A for areas included; (2) people of Hispanic origin can be of any race
Source: 1990 Census of Population and Housing, Summary Tape File 3C

School Enrollment by Type

Area	Preprimary				Elementary/High School			
	Public		Private		Public		Private	
	Enrollment	%	Enrollment	%	Enrollment	%	Enrollment	%
City	932	53.9	796	46.1	12,114	78.8	3,250	21.2
MSA[1]	3,337	47.0	3,766	53.0	39,672	82.4	8,483	17.6
U.S.	2,679,029	59.5	1,824,256	40.5	38,379,689	90.2	4,187,099	9.8

Note: Figures shown cover persons 3 years old and over;
(1) Metropolitan Statistical Area - see Appendix A for areas included
Source: 1990 Census of Population and Housing, Summary Tape File 3C

School Enrollment by Race

Area	Preprimary (%)				Elementary/High School (%)			
	White	Black	Other	Hisp.[1]	White	Black	Other	Hisp.[1]
City	34.4	56.3	9.3	10.8	26.0	61.6	12.4	18.7
MSA[2]	76.5	17.5	6.0	5.6	64.4	25.9	9.7	9.1
U.S.	80.4	12.5	7.1	7.8	74.1	15.6	10.3	12.5

Note: Figures shown cover persons 3 years old and over; (1) people of Hispanic origin can be of any race; (2) Metropolitan Statistical Area - see Appendix A for areas included
Source: 1990 Census of Population and Housing, Summary Tape File 3C

Higher Education

Two-Year Colleges		Four-Year Colleges		Medical Schools	Law Schools	Voc/ Tech
Public	Private	Public	Private			
1	0	1	0	0	0	9

Source: College Blue Book, Occupational Education, 1999; Medical School Admission Requirements, 1999-2000; Peterson's Guide to Two-Year Colleges, 2000; Peterson's Guide to Four-Year Colleges, 1999; Barron's Guide to Law Schools, 1999

MAJOR EMPLOYERS

Major Employers

Building Maintenance Systems
Clark Group (trucking)
Demag Delaval Turbomachinery Corp.
Hibbert Co. (direct mail advertising)
Robert Wood Johnson University Hospital

Capital Health Systems
Congoleum Corp.
General Motors Corp.
Holzman Jewelers
Roper Scientific (optical equipment)

Note: Companies listed are located in the city
Source: D&B Business Rankings, 1999; Ward's Business Directory, 1999; America's Corporate Families, 1999

PUBLIC SAFETY

Crime Rate

Area	All Crimes	Violent Crimes				Property Crimes		
		Murder	Forcible Rape	Robbery	Aggrav. Assault	Burglary	Larceny -Theft	Motor Vehicle Theft
City	6,931.9	17.4	67.5	622.2	607.1	1,359.6	3,090.3	1,167.7
Suburbs[1]	2,904.0	0.0	15.0	74.7	82.4	484.3	1,940.8	306.9
MSA[2]	3,946.1	4.5	28.6	216.4	218.2	710.8	2,238.2	529.6
U.S.	4,615.5	6.3	34.4	165.2	360.5	862.0	2,728.1	459.0

Note: Crime rate is the number of crimes per 100,000 population; (1) Defined as all areas within the Metropolitan Statistical Area but located outside the central city; (2) Metropolitan Statistical Area - see Appendix A for areas included
Source: FBI Uniform Crime Reports, 1998

RECREATION

Culture and Recreation

Museums	Symphony Orchestras	Opera Companies	Dance Companies	Professional Theatres	Zoos	Pro Sports Teams
4	1	0	0	1	0	0

Source: Musical America, International Directory of the Performing Arts, 1999; Official Museum Directory, 2000; Stern's Performing Arts Directory, 1997; USA Today Four Sport Stadium Guide, 1997; Career Opportunities in Theatre and the Performing Arts, 1999

Library System

The Trenton Public Library has four branches, holdings of 375,000 volumes, and a budget of $2,781,731 (1996-1997).
American Library Directory, 1999-2000

MEDIA

Newspapers

Name	Type	Freq.	Distribution	Circulation
The Nubian News	Black	1x/mo	Local	7,000
The Times	General	7x/wk	Area	85,047
The Trentonian	General	7x/wk	Area	76,930

Note: Includes newspapers with circulations of 200 or more located in the city;
Source: Burrelle's Media Directory, 1999 Edition

Television Stations

Name	Ch.	Affiliation	Type	Owner
WNJS	23	PBS	Public	New Jersey Public Broadcasting Authority
WNJN	50	PBS	Public	New Jersey Public Broadcasting Authority
WNJT	52	n/a	Public	New Jersey Public Broadcasting Authority
WNJB	58	n/a	Public	New Jersey Public Broadcasting Authority

Note: Stations included broadcast in the Trenton metro area; n/a not available
Source: Burrelle's Media Directory, 1999 Edition

AM Radio Stations

Call Letters	Freq. (kHz)	Target Audience	Station Format	Music Format
WBUD	1260	General	M	Adult Contemporary/MOR
WIMG	1300	Black	M/N/S/T	Christian/Gospel/Urban Contemporary
WHWH	1350	General	M/N/S/T	Adult Standards

Note: Stations included broadcast in the Trenton metro area
Target Audience: A=Asian; B=Black; C=Christian; E=Ethnic; F=French; G=General; H=Hispanic; M=Men; N=Native American; R=Religious; S=Senior Citizen; W=Women; Y=Young Adult; Z=Children
Station Format: E=Educational; M=Music; N=News; S=Sports; T=Talk
Music Format: AOR=Album Oriented Rock; MOR=Middle-of-the-Road
Source: Burrelle's Media Directory, 1999 Edition

FM Radio Stations

Call Letters	Freq. (mHz)	Target Audience	Station Format	Music Format
WNJS	88.1	General	M/N/S	n/a
WNJT	88.1	General	M/N/S/T	Jazz
WNJP	88.5	General	M/N/S	n/a
WWFM	89.1	General	M/N	Classical
WNJB	89.3	General	N	n/a
WNJN	89.7	General	M/N/S	n/a
WWNJ	91.1	General	M/N	Classical
WTSR	91.3	General	E/M/N/S/T	Adult Contemporary/Alternative/Christian/Classic Rock/Jazz/Modern Rock/Oldies/Rhythm & Blues
WPST	97.5	General	M/N/S	Top 40
WKXW	101.5	General	M/N/S/T	Oldies
WPRB	103.3	General	M/N/S	Alternative/Classical/Jazz
WRRC	107.7	General	M	Alternative/AOR/Urban Contemporary
WWPH	107.9	General	M/N/S	Adult Contemporary/AOR/Classic Rock/Latin/Oldies/Rhythm & Blues

Note: Stations included broadcast in the Trenton metro area; n/a not available
Station Format: E=Educational; M=Music; N=News; S=Sports; T=Talk
Target Audience: A=Asian; B=Black; C=Christian; E=Ethnic; F=French; G=General; H=Hispanic; M=Men; N=Native American; R=Religious; S=Senior Citizen; W=Women; Y=Young Adult; Z=Children
Music Format: AOR=Album Oriented Rock; MOR=Middle-of-the-Road
Source: Burrelle's Media Directory, 1999 Edition

WEATHER

Temperature/Precipitation/Humidity

	Jan	Feb	Mar	Apr	May	Jun	Jul	Aug	Sep	Oct	Nov	Dec	Yr.
Max. High Temp. (°F)	56	56	73	81	92	96	102	97	95	78	73	57	102
Avg. High Temp. (°F)	27	28	38	51	63	74	79	78	69	58	45	31	53
Avg. Temp. (°F)	18	19	30	42	54	64	69	68	60	49	38	24	44
Avg. Low Temp. (°F)	10	11	22	34	45	55	60	59	51	41	31	17	36
Min. Low Temp. (°F)	-25	-26	-20	9	26	34	42	38	29	19	-3	-23	-26
Avg. Precip. (in.)	2.8	2.3	2.7	2.2	3.3	2.4	2.5	2.1	2.5	2.7	3.1	3.1	31.7
Avg. Snowfall (in.)	16.1	14.2	9.6	2.8	0	0	0	0	0	0	6.1	11.3	60.1
Avg. Rel. Hum. (%)	85	86	77	74	73	73	73	74	77	81	83	83	78

Source: National Climatic Data Center, International Station Meteorological Climate Summary, 3/95

Weather Conditions

Temperature			Precipitation		
0°F & below	32°F & below	90°F & above	0.1 inch or more precip.	1.5 inch or more snow/ice	Thunder-storms
15	144	3	82	13	20

Note: Figures are average number of days per year
Source: National Climatic Data Center, International Station Meteorological Climate Summary, 3/95

AIR & WATER QUALITY

Maximum Pollutant Concentrations

	Particulate Matter (ug/m³)	Carbon Monoxide (ppm)	Sulfur Dioxide (ppm)	Nitrogen Dioxide (ppm)	Ozone (ppm)	Lead (ug/m³)
MSA[1] Level	59	n/a	n/a	0.017	0.13	n/a
NAAQS[2]	150	9	0.140	0.053	0.12	1.50
Met NAAQS	Yes	n/a	n/a	Yes	No	n/a

Note: (1) Metropolitan Statistical Area - see Appendix A for areas included; (2) National Ambient Air Quality Standards; ppm = parts per million; ug/m³ = micrograms per cubic meter; n/a not available
Source: EPA, National Air Quality and Emissions Trends Report, 1997

Pollutant Standards Index

Data not available.
EPA, National Air Quality and Emissions Trends Report, 1997

Drinking Water

Water System Name	Pop. Served	Primary Water Source Type	Number of Violations in 1998-99	Type of Violation/ Contaminants
Trenton Water Dept.	225,000	Surface	None	None

Note: Data as of January 19, 2000
Source: EPA, Office of Ground Water and Drinking Water, Safe Drinking Water Information System

Trenton tap water is alkaline, soft, and fluoridated.
Editor & Publisher Market Guide, 2000

West Palm Beach, Florida

Background

West Palm Beach is located on the southeast Florida coast, about 70 miles north of Miami, on Florida's coastal sand ridge. The city is on Lake Worth and the Intracoastal Waterway.

West Palm Beach is the county seat and largest community in Palm Beach County. It is part of the metropolitan area known as the "Palm Beaches," including Palm Beach, North Palm Beach and other nearby communities. It is also on the northern edge of Florida's Gold Coast, and is a popular tourist area, in addition to other economic activity.

West Palm Beach was founded by Henry Flagler, founder of Standard Oil, in 1893 and incorporated in 1894. The city originated as a commercial center to compliment the resort area of Palm Beach, which is across the Intracoastal Waterway. It grew to become the region's largest city. In the 1980s and 1990s public works projects have made new land available for development. In addition to tourism, which is the region's major industry, other economic sectors include government, technology, wholesale and retail trades, agriculture, health care, manufacturing, education, business and professional services and the Port of West Palm Beach.

The Kravis Center for the Performing Arts and Coral Sky Amphitheater are multi-purpose events facilities. Arts facilities and organizations in the area also include The Armory Arts Center, Norton Museum of Art, Ballet Florida, Palm Beach Philharmonic, Palm Beach Opera, and others.

Beaches and water activities are prevalent. There are numerous local parks in West Palm Beach and surrounding areas, including Boynton Beach, Lake Worth Beach and Riviera Beach. Clematis Street in downtown West Palm Beach has been renovated as an attractive living, shopping and entertainment center. The city has 13 historic districts and neighborhoods. Area museums include the Historical Museum of West Palm Beach, South Florida Science Museum and the Palm Beach Maritime Museum, which is housed in a 1936 Coast Guard station. Palm Beach Zoo at Dreher Park is also a popular attraction.

West Palm Beach is governed by a Mayor and City Commission.

General Rankings and Evaluative Comments

■ West Palm Beach was ranked #48 out of 354 metropolitan areas in *Places Rated Almanac*. Criteria: cost of living, climate, crime, transportation, job outlook, education, the arts, health care, and recreation. *Places Rated Almanac, Millennium Edition, 2000*

■ West Palm Beach was selected by *Yahoo! Internet Life* as one of "America's Most Wired Cities & Towns." The city ranked #45 out of 50. Criteria: home and work net use, domain density, hosts per capita, directory density, and content quality. *Yahoo! Internet Life, March 1999*

■ Cognetics studied 273 metro areas in the United States, ranking them by entrepreneurial activity. West Palm Beach was ranked #24 out of 134 smaller metro areas. Criteria: Significant Starts (firms started in the last 10 years that still employ at least 5 people) and Young Growers (percent of firms 10 years old or less that grew significantly during the last 4 years). *Cognetics, "Entrepreneurial Hot Spots: The Best Places in America to Start and Grow a Company," 1999*

■ West Palm Beach was included among *Entrepreneur* magazine's listing of the "20 Best Cities for Small Business." It was ranked #1 among large metro areas and #1 among southern metro areas. Criteria: entrepreneurial activity, small-business growth, economic growth, and risk of failure. *Entrepreneur, October 1999*

■ Reliastar Financial Corporation ranked the 125 largest metropolitan areas according to the general financial security of residents. West Palm Beach was ranked #80 out of 125 with a score of -0.3 (the percentage a metropolitan area is above or below the metropolitan norm; a metro area with a score of 10.6 is 10.6% above the metro average). Criteria: Earnings and Wealth Potential (household income, education, net assets, cost of living); Safety Net (health insurance, retirement savings, life insurance, income support programs); Personal Threats (unemployment rate, low-income households, crime rate); Community Economic Vitality (cost of community services, job quality, job creation, housing costs). *Reliastar Financial Corporation, "The Best Cities to Earn and Save Money: A Ranking of the Largest 125 U.S. Cities," 2000 Edition*

Business Environment

STATE ECONOMY

State Economic Profile

"Florida's economy has been among the nation's strongest in recent years. Job growth has outpaced the nation by a considerable amount since 1992.

While Florida has been able to avoid any significant fallout from the Asian crisis, the weakening of economies in Latin American will dampen both tourism and international trade. 1998 saw the decline in Latin tourism more than offset by domestic visitors. Domestic tourism is projected to soften as U.S. growth cools, offering no offset against the expected decline in Latin tourism. Weaker tourism and trade with Latin American will slow growth in the near future; Florida will still outpace the nation in job growth as Gross State Product growth (GSP) slows.

Over half of Florida's 230,000 new jobs created in 1998 were in the services sector, which grew at 5.2%, more than offsetting a minor decline in manufacturing employment. Much of this growth is taking place in the finance and business services sector.

In spite of strong home sales and a slowing construction market, Florida's price appreciation continued to lag the nation. Although residential permits per 1,000 residents stands at 5.1, well above the national average, this number is only slightly up from 1997 and is poised to decline in the near future.

Growth in Florida, while strong throughout, has been hottest in the Naples, Ft. Myers and Orlando areas. Construction and employment in the construction industry has begun to slow in South Florida. Projected employment and housing gains will be concentrated in Northern and Central Florida. Growing diversification of the economy into financial and business services promises a strong outlook for the years ahead." *National Association of Realtors, Economic Profiles: The Fifty States and the District of Columbia, http://nar.realtor.com/databank/profiles.htm*

EXPORTS

Total Export Sales

Area	1995 ($000)	1996 ($000)	1997 ($000)	1998 ($000)	% Chg. 1995-98	% Chg. 1997-98
MSA[1]	897,955	955,846	1,156,049	958,964	6.8	-17.0
U.S.	583,030,524	622,827,063	687,597,999	680,474,251	16.7	-1.0

Note: (1) Metropolitan Statistical Area - see Appendix A for areas included
Source: U.S. Department of Commerce, International Trade Association, Metropolitan Area Exports: An Export Performance Report on Over 250 U.S. Cities, November 10, 1999

CITY FINANCES

City Government Finances

Component	1995 ($million)	1995 (per capita $)
Revenue	91.5	1,212
Expenditure	106.3	1,408
Debt Outstanding	115.1	1,525

Source: 1999 County and City Extra, Annual Metro, City, and County Data Book

City Government Revenue by Source

Source	1995 ($million)	1995 (per capita $)
Intergovernmental	13.1	173
Taxes	52.9	701
Property	33.5	445
Sales and Gross Receipts	16.0	213

Source: 1999 County and City Extra, Annual Metro, City, and County Data Book

City Government Expenditures by Function

Function	1995 ($million)	1995 (per capita $)	1995 (%)
Public Welfare	0.0	0	0.0
Highways	7.0	92	6.6
Parking Facilities	2.8	38	2.7
Education	0.0	0	0.0
Health and Hospitals	2.4	32	2.3
Police Protection	20.4	270	19.2
Sewerage and Sanitation	6.6	88	6.3
Parks and Recreation	10.4	138	9.8
Housing and Community Development	3.6	47	3.4
Interest on Debt	6.2	83	5.9

Source: 1999 County and City Extra, Annual Metro, City, and County Data Book

Municipal Bond Ratings

Area	Moody's
City	A1

Source: Mergent Bond Record, 2/2000

POPULATION

Population Growth

Area	1980 Census	1990 Census	1999 Estimate	2004 Projection	Population Growth (%) 1990-1999	Population Growth (%) 1999-2004
City	63,305	67,643	82,463	89,880	21.9	9.0
MSA[1]	576,863	863,518	1,038,254	1,126,375	20.2	8.5
U.S.	226,545,805	248,765,170	272,212,864	283,625,312	9.4	4.2

Note: (1) Metropolitan Statistical Area - see Appendix A for areas included
Source: 1990 Census of Population and Housing, Summary Tape File 3C; Claritas, Inc.

Number of Households and Average Household Size

Area	1980 Census	1990 Census	1999 Estimate	2004 Projection	1999 Average Household Size
City	27,086	28,774	35,469	39,198	2.32
MSA[1]	234,336	366,131	435,894	476,734	2.38
U.S.	80,389,592	91,993,582	102,048,200	107,302,392	2.67

Note: (1) Metropolitan Statistical Area - see Appendix A for areas included
Source: 1990 Census of Population and Housing, Summary Tape File 3C; Claritas, Inc.

Race/Ethnicity of City Population

Race/Ethnicity	1990 Census Population	1990 Census %	1999 Estimate Population	1999 Estimate %	% Change 1990-1999
White, Non-Hispanic	36,023	53.3	34,728	42.1	-3.6
Black, Non-Hispanic	21,365	31.6	31,315	38.0	46.6
Asian, Non-Hispanic	783	1.2	906	1.1	15.7
Other, Non-Hispanic	272	0.4	222	0.3	-18.4
Hispanic	9,200	13.6	15,292	18.5	66.2

Source: 1990 Census of Population and Housing, Summary Tape File 3C; Claritas, Inc.

Race/Ethnicity of Metropolitan Statistical Area Population

Race/Ethnicity	1990 Census		1999 Estimate		% Change 1990-1999
	Population	%	Population	%	
White, Non-Hispanic	684,945	79.3	758,874	73.1	10.8
Black, Non-Hispanic	103,047	11.9	146,884	14.1	42.5
Asian, Non-Hispanic	8,697	1.0	15,891	1.5	82.7
Other, Non-Hispanic	1,801	0.2	2,347	0.2	30.3
Hispanic	65,028	7.5	114,258	11.0	75.7

Note: See Appendix A for areas included in the Metropolitan Statistical Area
Source: 1990 Census of Population and Housing, Summary Tape File 3C; Claritas, Inc.

Ancestry

Area	German	Irish	English	Italian	U.S.	French	Polish	Dutch
City	13.0	10.6	10.6	5.3	4.2	3.1	2.6	1.5
MSA[1]	18.1	14.0	13.1	9.0	4.3	3.8	5.1	1.9
U.S.	23.3	15.6	13.1	5.9	5.3	4.2	3.8	2.5

Note: Figures are percentages and include persons that reported multiple ancestry (eg. if a person reported being Irish and Italian, they were included in both columns); (1) Metropolitan Statistical Area - see Appendix A for areas included
Source: 1990 Census of Population and Housing, Summary Tape File 3C

Median Age

Area	1990 Census	1999 Estimate
City	35.1	37.8
MSA[1]	39.8	42.4
U.S.	32.9	35.7

Note: (1) Metropolitan Statistical Area - see Appendix A for areas included
Source: 1990 Census of Population and Housing, Summary Tape File 3C; Claritas, Inc.

Male/Female Population

Area	Number of Males		Number of Females		Males per 100 Females	
	1990	1999	1990	1999	1990	1999
City	32,399	39,588	35,244	42,875	91.9	92.3
MSA[1]	415,137	499,041	448,381	539,213	92.6	92.5
U.S.	121,172,379	132,803,736	127,537,494	139,409,136	95.0	95.3

Note: (1) Metropolitan Statistical Area - see Appendix A for areas included
Source: 1990 Census of Population, General Population Characteristics; Claritas, Inc.

INCOME

Per Capita/Median/Average Income

Area	Per Capita ($)			Median Household ($)			Average Household ($)		
	1989	1999	% Chg.	1989	1999	% Chg.	1989	1999	% Chg.
City	15,712	24,298	54.6	26,504	40,081	51.2	36,212	56,041	54.8
MSA[1]	19,937	31,212	56.6	32,524	48,716	49.8	46,662	74,136	58.9
U.S.	14,420	21,350	48.1	30,056	40,525	34.8	38,453	56,184	46.1

Note: (1) Metropolitan Statistical Area - see Appendix A for areas included; 1989 data is from the 1990 Census; 1999 data is estimated by Claritas, Inc.
Source: 1990 Census of Population, General Population Characteristics; Claritas, Inc.

Household Income Distribution

Area	Percent of Households Earning								
	Under $5,000	$5,000 -14,999	$15,000 -24,999	$25,000 -34,999	$35,000 -49,999	$50,000 -74,999	$75,000 -99,000	$100,000 -149,999	$150,000 and up
City	4.6	13.2	13.1	13.5	17.0	19.1	8.7	6.2	4.6
MSA[1]	2.7	9.4	11.8	11.6	15.6	20.3	10.9	8.7	9.0
U.S.	3.9	13.3	13.8	12.6	16.2	19.4	9.7	6.6	4.6

Note: Data as of 1999; (1) Metropolitan Statistical Area - see Appendix A for areas included
Source: Claritas, Inc.

Effective Buying Income

Area	Per Capita ($)	Median Household ($)	Average Household ($)
City	19,099	32,626	45,100
MSA[1]	24,887	41,050	58,930
U.S.	17,496	36,603	47,036

Note: Data as of 1/1/2000; (1) Metropolitan Statistical Area - see Appendix A for areas included
Source: Standard Rate & Data Service, Newspaper Advertising Source, March 2000

Effective Household Buying Income Distribution

Area	% of Households Earning						
	$10,000 -$19,999	$20,000 -$34,999	$35,000 -$49,999	$50,000 -$74,999	$75,000 -$99,000	$100,000 -$124,999	$125,000 and up
City	15.9	23.6	17.4	16.4	6.9	2.2	3.6
MSA[1]	13.2	20.7	17.4	19.7	9.6	4.2	6.6
U.S.	15.0	21.6	17.6	19.6	8.4	3.0	3.3

Note: Data as of 1/1/2000; (1) Metropolitan Statistical Area - see Appendix A for areas included
Source: Standard Rate & Data Service, Newspaper Advertising Source, March 2000

Poverty Rates by Age

Area	People of All Ages	People Under 18 Years Old	Related Children Age 5-17 in Families in Poverty
City	20.2	n/a	n/a
County	11.9	19.5	16.7
U.S.	13.8	20.8	18.7

Note: Figures show the percent of people living below the poverty line in 1995. The average poverty threshold was $15,569 for a family of four in 1995; n/a not available
Source: Bureau of the Census, Small Area Income and Poverty Estimates Program; U.S. Department of Housing and Urban Development

EMPLOYMENT

Labor Force and Employment

Area	Civilian Labor Force			Workers Employed		
	Dec. 1998	Dec. 1999	% Chg.	Dec. 1998	Dec. 1999	% Chg.
City	46,206	47,381	2.5	43,509	45,033	3.5
MSA[1]	527,750	542,227	2.7	503,405	521,030	3.5
U.S.	138,297,000	139,941,000	1.2	132,732,000	134,696,000	1.5

Note: Data is not seasonally adjusted and covers workers 16 years of age and older;
(1) Metropolitan Statistical Area - see Appendix A for areas included
Source: Bureau of Labor Statistics, http://stats.bls.gov

Unemployment Rate

Area	1999											
	Jan.	Feb.	Mar.	Apr.	May	Jun.	Jul.	Aug.	Sep.	Oct.	Nov.	Dec.
City	6.8	6.2	5.9	6.1	6.1	6.6	6.9	7.1	7.2	6.6	6.0	5.0
MSA[1]	5.4	4.9	4.7	4.8	4.8	5.2	5.5	5.6	5.7	5.2	4.8	3.9
U.S.	4.8	4.7	4.4	4.1	4.0	4.5	4.5	4.2	4.1	3.8	3.8	3.7

Note: Data is not seasonally adjusted and covers workers 16 years of age and older; all figures are percentages; (1) Metropolitan Statistical Area - see Appendix A for areas included
Source: Bureau of Labor Statistics, http://stats.bls.gov

Employment by Industry

Sector	MSA[1]		U.S.
	Number of Employees	Percent of Total	Percent of Total
Services	198,000	40.3	30.2
Retail Trade	101,300	20.6	18.1
Government	56,200	11.4	15.8
Manufacturing	33,600	6.8	14.1
Finance/Insurance/Real Estate	34,200	7.0	5.9
Wholesale Trade	24,200	4.9	5.4
Transportation/Public Utilities	16,800	3.4	5.3
Construction	27,600	5.6	4.8
Mining	n/a	n/a	0.4

Note: Figures cover non-farm employment as of 12/99 and are not seasonally adjusted; (1) Metropolitan Statistical Area - see Appendix A for areas included; n/a not available
Source: Bureau of Labor Statistics, http://stats.bls.gov

Employment by Occupation

Occupation Category	City (%)	MSA[1] (%)	U.S. (%)
White Collar	55.0	62.0	58.1
Executive/Admin./Management	11.1	13.7	12.3
Professional	14.8	14.2	14.1
Technical & Related Support	2.8	3.5	3.7
Sales	12.6	15.5	11.8
Administrative Support/Clerical	13.8	15.0	16.3
Blue Collar	22.2	19.7	26.2
Precision Production/Craft/Repair	10.1	11.2	11.3
Machine Operators/Assem./Insp.	4.1	2.4	6.8
Transportation/Material Movers	3.9	3.2	4.1
Cleaners/Helpers/Laborers	4.0	3.0	3.9
Services	19.6	14.9	13.2
Farming/Forestry/Fishing	3.3	3.4	2.5

Note: Figures cover workers 16 years of age and older; (1) Metropolitan Statistical Area - see Appendix A for areas included
Source: 1990 Census of Population and Housing, Summary Tape File 3C

Occupational Employment Projections: 1996 - 2006

Occupations Expected to Have the Largest Job Growth (ranked by numerical growth)	Fast-Growing Occupations[1] (ranked by percent growth)
1. Cashiers	1. Systems analysts
2. Salespersons, retail	2. Physical therapy assistants and aides
3. General managers & top executives	3. Desktop publishers
4. Registered nurses	4. Home health aides
5. Waiters & waitresses	5. Computer engineers
6. Marketing & sales, supervisors	6. Medical assistants
7. Janitors/cleaners/maids, ex. priv. hshld.	7. Physical therapists
8. General office clerks	8. Paralegals
9. Food preparation workers	9. Emergency medical technicians
10. Hand packers & packagers	10. Occupational therapists

Note: Projections cover Florida; (1) Excludes occupations with total job growth less than 300
Source: U.S. Department of Labor, Employment and Training Administration, America's Labor Market Information System (ALMIS)

Average Wages

Occupation	$/Hr.	Occupation	$/Hr.
Accountants and Auditors	18.90	Maids and Housekeepers	7.50
Assemblers and Fabricators	9.46	Maintenance Repairers	11.08
Automotive Mechanics	15.41	Marketing/Advertising/PR Managers	24.18
Bookkeepers	11.77	Nurses, Licensed Practical	14.49
Carpenters	12.68	Nurses, Registered	21.20
Cashiers	7.31	Nursing Aides/Orderlies/Attendants	8.16
Clerks, General Office	9.96	Physicians and Surgeons	50.88
Clerks, Shipping/Receiving/Traffic	11.93	Receptionists/Information Clerks	9.45
Computer Programmers	29.78	Sales Reps., Exc. Scientific/Retail	17.84
Computer Support Specialists	21.48	Sales Reps., Scientific, Exc. Retail	24.72
Cooks, Restaurant	9.43	Salespersons, Retail	9.86
Electricians	14.63	Secretaries, Except Legal/Medical	11.53
Financial Managers	27.32	Stock Clerks, Sales Floor	7.85
First-Line Supervisors/Mgrs., Sales	17.52	Systems Analysts	28.69
Food Preparation Workers	7.38	Teacher Aides	9.71
General Managers/Top Executives	28.59	Teachers, Elementary School	16.86
Guards	8.13	Teachers, Secondary School	18.59
Hand Packers	6.62	Telemarketers	9.65
Janitors and Cleaners	7.22	Truck Drivers, Heavy/Tractor-Trailer	12.13
Laborers, Landscaping	8.20	Truck Drivers, Light	9.65
Lawyers	37.51	Waiters and Waitresses	6.23

Note: Wage data is for 1998 and covers the Metropolitan Statistical Area (see Appendix A for areas included). Hourly wages for elementary and secondary school teachers were calculated by the editors from annual wage data assuming a 40 hour work week; Dashes indicate that data was not available.
Source: Bureau of Labor Statistics, 1998 Metropolitan Area Occupational Employment and Wage Estimates

TAXES

Major State and Local Tax Rates

State Corporate Income (%)	State Personal Income (%)	Residential Property (%)	Sales & Use		State Gasoline (cents/ gallon)	State Cigarette (cents/ pack)
			State (%)	Local (%)		
5.5[a]	None	1.84	6.0	None	13.3[b]	33.9

Note: Personal/corporate income, sales, gasoline and cigarette tax rates as of January 2000. Property tax rates as of April 2000; (a) 3.3% Alternative Minimum Tax. An exemption of $5,000 is allowed; (b) Rate is comprised of 4 cents excise and 9.3 cents motor carrier tax. Local taxes vary from 5.5 cents to 17 cents. Plus a 2.07 cent per gallon pollution tax
Source: Federation of Tax Administrators, www.taxadmin.org; ERI's Relocation Assessor software database, quarterly effective date 4/1/2000

Total Taxes Per Capita and as a Percent of Income

Area	Per Capita Income ($)	Per Capita Taxes ($)			Percent of Income (%)		
		Total	Federal	State/Local	Total	Federal	State/Local
Florida	28,322	10,333	7,257	3,077	36.5	25.6	10.9
U.S.	28,878	10,298	7,026	3,273	35.7	24.3	11.3

Note: Figures are for 1999
Source: Tax Foundation, www.taxfoundation.org

COMMERCIAL UTILITIES

Typical Monthly Electric Bills

Area	Commercial Service ($/month)		Industrial Service ($/month)	
	12 kW demand 1,500 kWh	100 kW demand 30,000 kWh	1,000 kW demand 400,000 kWh	20,000 kW demand 10,000,000 kWh
City	118	1,993	23,247	387,510
U.S.	150	2,174	23,995	508,569

Note: Based on rates in effect January 1, 1999
Source: Edison Electric Institute, Typical Residential, Commercial and Industrial Bills, Winter 1999

TRANSPORTATION

Transportation Statistics

Average minutes to work (1990)	18.7
Interstate highways	I-95; FL TPKE; US-1; US-441
Bus lines	
In-city (1998)	Palm Tran, 122 buses
Inter-city (1999)	2
Passenger air service	
Airport	Palm Beach International
Airlines (1999)	22
Enplaned passengers (1998)	2,934,447
Amtrak service	Yes
Motor freight carriers (1999)	33
Major waterways/ports	Port of Palm Beach

Source: FAA DOT/TSC CY1998 ACAIS Database; National Transit Database, 1998; Editor & Publisher Market Guide, 2000; Amtrak National Time Table, Fall 1999/Winter 2000; 1990 Census of Population and Housing, STF 3C; Jane's Urban Transport Systems 1999-2000

Means of Transportation to Work

Area	Car/Truck/Van		Public Transportation			Bicycle	Walked	Other Means	Worked at Home
	Drove Alone	Car-pooled	Bus	Subway	Railroad				
City	74.8	14.6	2.1	0.0	0.3	1.0	2.8	2.7	1.6
MSA[1]	79.4	12.8	0.9	0.0	0.2	0.6	2.0	1.5	2.7
U.S.	73.2	13.4	3.0	1.5	0.5	0.4	3.9	1.2	3.0

Note: Figures shown are percentages and only include workers 16 years of age and older;
(1) Metropolitan Statistical Area - see Appendix A for areas included
Source: 1990 Census of Population and Housing, Summary Tape File 3C

BUSINESSES

Major Business Headquarters

Company Name	1999 Rankings	
	Fortune 500	Forbes 500
Oxbow	-	456

Note: Companies listed are located in the city; dashes indicate no ranking
Fortune 500: Companies that produce a 10-K are ranked 1 to 500 based on 1999 revenue
Forbes 500: Private companies are ranked 1 to 500 based on 1998 revenue
Source: Forbes, December 13, 1999; Fortune, April 17, 2000

HOTELS & MOTELS

Hotels/Motels

Area	Hotels/Motels	Rooms	Luxury-Level Hotels/Motels		Average Minimum Rates ($)		
			♦♦♦♦	♦♦♦♦♦	♦♦	♦♦♦	♦♦♦♦
City	12	1,139	0	0	n/a	n/a	n/a
Airport	9	1,613	0	0	n/a	n/a	n/a
Suburbs	50	5,729	3	0	n/a	n/a	n/a
Total	71	8,481	3	0	n/a	n/a	n/a

Note: n/a not available; classifications range from one diamond (budget properties with basic amenities) to five diamond (luxury properties).
Source: OAG Business Travel Planner, Winter 1999-2000

Estimated Daily Food and Lodging Costs

Area	Food/Other ($/day)	Average Hotel Cost ($/day)
City	46	103
U.S.	30	55

Source: ERI's Relocation Assessor software database, quarterly effective date 4/1/2000

CONVENTION CENTERS

Convention Centers and Event Sites

Name	Guest Rooms	Meeting Space (sq. ft.)	Capacity (Theatre Style)
Best Western Palm Beach Lakes	157	n/a	0
Burt Reynolds Theater	n/a	n/a	2,500
Courtyard by Marriott	149	n/a	0
Helen Wilkes Hotel	150	n/a	0
Holiday Inn - Palm Beach Int'l. Airport	199	n/a	0
Knights Inn	115	n/a	0
Kravis Center for the Performing Arts	n/a	n/a	2,409
Omni West Palm Beach Hotel	220	11,000	600
Palm Beach Airport Hilton	247	10,000	0
Radisson Suite Inn Palm Beach Airport	175	2,500	100
Sheraton West Palm Beach Hotel	349	18,000	1,000
South Florida Fairgrounds	n/a	n/a	0
West Palm Beach Auditorium & Stadium	n/a	n/a	6,500

Note: n/a not available
Source: EventSource.com, 3/15/2000

Living Environment

COST OF LIVING

Cost of Living: Homeowner

Cost Element	U.S. ($)	City ($)	Differential ($)	Percent of U.S. Average
Consumables	14,516	15,209	693	104.8
Transportation	5,957	6,150	193	103.2
Health Services	2,012	2,185	173	108.6
Housing/Utilities/Prop. Tax	16,337	20,200	3,863	123.6
Income+Payroll Taxes	12,615	10,327	-2,288	81.9
Miscellaneous	8,563	8,563	0	100.0
Total Cost of Living	60,000	62,634	2,634	104.4

Note: Figures are based on a single income, four person family with gross annual earnings of $60,000, owning an 1,800 square-foot home, and driving two automobiles worth $22,000 30,000 miles per year.
Source: ERI's Relocation Assessor software database, quarterly effective date 4/1/2000

Cost of Living: Renter

Cost Element	U.S. ($)	City ($)	Differential ($)	Percent of U.S. Average
Consumables	10,486	10,928	442	104.2
Transportation	2,107	2,164	57	102.7
Health Services	1,632	1,764	132	108.1
Rent/Utilities/Insurance	9,299	13,808	4,509	148.5
Income+Payroll Taxes	8,607	7,183	-1,424	83.5
Miscellaneous	7,869	7,869	0	100.0
Total Cost of Living	40,000	43,716	3,716	109.3

Note: Figures are based on a single income, three person family with gross annual earnings of $40,000, renting a 1,000 square-foot home, and driving one automobile worth $8,000 12,000 miles per year.
Source: ERI's Relocation Assessor software database, quarterly effective date 4/1/2000

HOUSING

Median Home Prices and Housing Affordability

Area	Median Price[2] 4th Qtr. 1999 ($)	HOI[3] 4th Qtr. 1999	Affordability Rank[4]
MSA[1]	123,000	73.8	74
U.S.	139,000	63.8	–

Note: (1) Metropolitan Statistical Area - see Appendix A for areas included; (2) U.S. figures calculated from the sales of 687,516 new and existing homes in 192 markets; (3) Housing Opportunity Index - percent of homes sold that were within the reach of the median income household at the prevailing mortgage interest rate; (4) Rank is from 1-192 with 1 being most affordable
Source: National Association of Home Builders, Housing Opportunity Index, 4th Quarter 1999

Estimated Home Price

Area	Price ($)
City	161,319
U.S.	135,855

Note: Figures are based on an 1,800 square-foot home
Source: ERI's Relocation Assessor software database, quarterly effective date 4/1/2000

Estimated Rent

Area	Rent ($/month)
City	1,011
U.S.	651

Note: Figures are based on a 1,000 square-foot home
Source: ERI's Relocation Assessor software database, quarterly effective date 4/1/2000

RESIDENTIAL UTILITIES

Average Residential Utility Costs

Area	All Electric ($/mth)	Part Electric ($/mth)	Other Energy ($/mth)	Phone ($/mth)
City	117.93	–	–	15.28
U.S.	100.70	55.17	43.26	20.03

Source: ACCRA, Cost of Living Index, 2nd Quarter 1999

HEALTH CARE

Average Health Care Costs

Area	Hospital ($/day)	Doctor ($/visit)	Dentist ($/visit)
City	386.00	60.60	71.80
U.S.	430.24	53.28	67.76

Note: Hospital—based on a semi-private room; Doctor—based on a general practitioner's routine exam of an established patient; Dentist—based on adult teeth cleaning and periodic oral exam.
Source: ACCRA, Cost of Living Index, 2nd Quarter 1999

Distribution of Office-Based Physicians

Area	Family/Gen. Practitioners	Specialists		
		Medical	Surgical	Other
MSA[1]	191	861	633	498

Note: Data as of 12/31/97; (1) Metropolitan Statistical Area - see Appendix A for areas included
Source: American Medical Assn., Physician Characteristics & Distribution in the U.S., 1999

Hospitals

West Palm Beach has 5 general medical and surgical hospitals, 1 psychiatric, 1 other specialty.
AHA Guide to the Healthcare Field, 1999-2000

EDUCATION

Public School District Statistics

District Name	Num. Sch.	Enroll.	Classroom Teachers	Pupils per Teacher	Minority Pupils (%)	Current Exp.[1] ($/pupil)
Palm Beach County Sch Dist	161	142,724	7,692	18.6	47.1	5,476

Note: Data covers the 1997-1998 school year unless otherwise noted; (1) Data covers fiscal year 1996; SD = School District; ISD = Independent School District; n/a not available
Source: National Center for Education Statistics, Common Core of Data Public Education Agency Universe 1997-98; National Center for Education Statistics, Characteristics of the 100 Largest Public Elementary and Secondary School Districts in the United States: 1997-98, July 1999

Educational Quality

School District	Education Quotient[1]	Graduate Outcome[2]	Community Index[3]	Resource Index[4]
Palm Beach Co. School Dist.	98	88	134	112

Note: Over 1,000 secondary school districts were rated in terms of educational quality. The scores range from a low of 50 to a high of 150; (1) Combination of the Graduate Outcome, Community and Resource indexes weighted to reflect the greater importance of the Graduate Outcome and Resource Index; (2) Based on graduation rates and college board scores (SAT/ACT); (3) Based on the surrounding community's level of affluence and adult education; (4) Based on teacher salaries, per-pupil expenditures and student-teacher ratios.
Source: Expansion Management, Ratings Issue, 1999

Educational Attainment by Race

Area	High School Graduate (%)					Bachelor's Degree (%)				
	Total	White	Black	Other	Hisp.[2]	Total	White	Black	Other	Hisp.[2]
City	71.7	79.1	55.6	50.0	50.4	20.4	24.5	11.3	11.3	10.9
MSA[1]	78.8	82.3	49.6	60.9	53.8	22.1	23.5	9.1	21.1	13.8
U.S.	75.2	77.9	63.1	60.4	49.8	20.3	21.5	11.4	19.4	9.2

Note: Figures shown cover persons 25 years old and over; (1) Metropolitan Statistical Area - see Appendix A for areas included; (2) people of Hispanic origin can be of any race
Source: 1990 Census of Population and Housing, Summary Tape File 3C

School Enrollment by Type

Area	Preprimary				Elementary/High School			
	Public		Private		Public		Private	
	Enrollment	%	Enrollment	%	Enrollment	%	Enrollment	%
City	445	43.8	571	56.2	7,615	88.2	1,019	11.8
MSA[1]	6,622	44.2	8,373	55.8	93,415	86.5	14,561	13.5
U.S.	2,679,029	59.5	1,824,256	40.5	38,379,689	90.2	4,187,099	9.8

Note: Figures shown cover persons 3 years old and over;
(1) Metropolitan Statistical Area - see Appendix A for areas included
Source: 1990 Census of Population and Housing, Summary Tape File 3C

School Enrollment by Race

Area	Preprimary (%)				Elementary/High School (%)			
	White	Black	Other	Hisp.[1]	White	Black	Other	Hisp.[1]
City	40.0	56.7	3.3	5.9	41.1	54.7	4.3	15.8
MSA[2]	78.8	18.5	2.6	7.2	72.4	23.4	4.2	11.4
U.S.	80.4	12.5	7.1	7.8	74.1	15.6	10.3	12.5

Note: Figures shown cover persons 3 years old and over; (1) people of Hispanic origin can be of any race; (2) Metropolitan Statistical Area - see Appendix A for areas included
Source: 1990 Census of Population and Housing, Summary Tape File 3C

Higher Education

Two-Year Colleges		Four-Year Colleges		Medical Schools	Law Schools	Voc/ Tech
Public	Private	Public	Private			
0	3	0	3	0	0	7

Source: College Blue Book, Occupational Education, 1999; Medical School Admission Requirements, 1999-2000; Peterson's Guide to Two-Year Colleges, 2000; Peterson's Guide to Four-Year Colleges, 1999; Barron's Guide to Law Schools, 1999

MAJOR EMPLOYERS

Major Employers

Ameripath
Columbia Hospital
Florida Power & Light
Ocwen Federal Bank
St. Mary's Hospital

China Peregrine Food Corp.
Contessa International Cruise Line
Good Samaritan Hospital
Palm Beach Hotel Group
Wellington Regional Medical Center

Note: Companies listed are located in the city
Source: D&B Business Rankings, 1999; Ward's Business Directory, 1999; America's Corporate Families, 1999

PUBLIC SAFETY

Crime Rate

Area	All Crimes	Violent Crimes				Property Crimes		
		Murder	Forcible Rape	Robbery	Aggrav. Assault	Burglary	Larceny -Theft	Motor Vehicle Theft
City	15,511.6	24.2	78.8	873.5	925.6	2,537.0	8,719.6	2,352.9
Suburbs[1]	7,738.0	5.6	49.9	235.4	595.4	1,611.8	4,390.0	850.0
MSA[2]	8,356.9	7.0	52.2	286.2	621.7	1,685.5	4,734.7	969.7
U.S.	4,615.5	6.3	34.4	165.2	360.5	862.0	2,728.1	459.0

Note: Crime rate is the number of crimes per 100,000 population; (1) Defined as all areas within the Metropolitan Statistical Area but located outside the central city; (2) Metropolitan Statistical Area - see Appendix A for areas included
Source: FBI Uniform Crime Reports, 1998

RECREATION

Culture and Recreation

Museums	Symphony Orchestras	Opera Companies	Dance Companies	Professional Theatres	Zoos	Pro Sports Teams
2	0	1	1	1	1	0

Source: Musical America, International Directory of the Performing Arts, 1999; Official Museum Directory, 2000; Stern's Performing Arts Directory, 1997; USA Today Four Sport Stadium Guide, 1997; Career Opportunities in Theatre and the Performing Arts, 1999

Library System

The Palm Beach County Library System has 14 branches, holdings of 1,008,263 volumes, and a budget of $19,661,150 (1997-1998).
American Library Directory, 1999-2000

MEDIA

Newspapers

Name	Type	Freq.	Distribution	Circulation
El Latino	Hispanic	1x/wk	Local	56,000
Florida Pennysaver	General	1x/wk	Local	360,000
Florida Photo News	Black	1x/wk	Local	3,500
The Palm Beach Post	General	7x/wk	Area	173,000

Note: Includes newspapers with circulations of 200 or more located in the city;
Source: Burrelle's Media Directory, 1999 Edition

Television Stations

Name	Ch.	Affiliation	Type	Owner
WPTV	n/a	NBCT	Commercial	Scripps Howard Broadcasting
WPEC	12	CBST	Commercial	Freedom Communications Inc.
WPBF	25	ABCT	Commercial	Hearst Corporation
WFLX	29	FBC	Commercial	Raycom Media Inc.
WTVX	34	UPN/WB	Commercial	Straight Line Communications Inc.
WXEL	42	PBS	Public	Barry Telecommunications Inc.
WHDT	55	n/a	Commercial	n/a
WFGC	61	n/a	Commercial	Christian Television of Palm Beach County
WPXP	67	n/a	Commercial	Paxson Communications Corporation

Note: Stations included broadcast in the West Palm Beach metro area; n/a not available
Source: Burrelle's Media Directory, 1999 Edition

AM Radio Stations

Call Letters	Freq. (kHz)	Target Audience	Station Format	Music Format
WLVJ	640	H/R	M/N/S	Christian
WSBR	740	General	T	n/a
WSWN	900	General	M	Christian/Urban Contemporary
WWNN	980	General	T	n/a
WJNO	1040	General	N/T	n/a
WJNA	1230	General	M	Adult Standards
WBZT	1290	General	N/S/T	n/a
WPBR	1340	General	N/T	n/a
WFTL	1400	General	T	n/a
WDBF	1420	General	M/N/S	Oldies
WPOM	1600	Black	M/N/S	Rhythm & Blues
WOWL	1610	G/H	M/N/S	n/a

Note: Stations included broadcast in the West Palm Beach metro area; n/a not available
Target Audience: A=Asian; B=Black; C=Christian; E=Ethnic; F=French; G=General; H=Hispanic; M=Men; N=Native American; R=Religious; S=Senior Citizen; W=Women; Y=Young Adult; Z=Children
Station Format: E=Educational; M=Music; N=News; S=Sports; T=Talk
Source: Burrelle's Media Directory, 1999 Edition

FM Radio Stations

Call Letters	Freq. (mHz)	Target Audience	Station Format	Music Format
WAYF	88.1	G/R/W	M	Christian
WRMB	89.3	General	M/N/S	Christian
WXEL	90.7	General	E/M/N	Classical/Jazz
WRLX	92.1	General	M	Easy Listening
WBGF	93.5	General	M/N/S	Country
WLDI	95.5	General	M/N/T	Top 40
WILD	95.5	General	M	Modern Rock
WRMF	97.9	General	M	Adult Contemporary
WKGR	98.7	General	M	Classic Rock
WMBX	102.3	General	M	Adult Contemporary
WPBZ	103.1	General	M/N/S	Alternative
WEAT	104.3	G/W	M	Adult Contemporary
WTPX	105.5	n/a	n/a	n/a
WIRK	107.9	General	M	Country

Note: Stations included broadcast in the West Palm Beach metro area; n/a not available
Station Format: E=Educational; M=Music; N=News; S=Sports; T=Talk
Target Audience: A=Asian; B=Black; C=Christian; E=Ethnic; F=French; G=General; H=Hispanic; M=Men; N=Native American; R=Religious; S=Senior Citizen; W=Women; Y=Young Adult; Z=Children
Source: Burrelle's Media Directory, 1999 Edition

WEATHER

Temperature/Precipitation/Humidity

	Jan	Feb	Mar	Apr	May	Jun	Jul	Aug	Sep	Oct	Nov	Dec	Yr.
Max. High Temp. (°F)	87	90	94	99	96	98	99	98	96	95	90	88	99
Avg. High Temp. (°F)	75	76	79	82	86	89	90	91	89	85	80	76	83
Avg. Temp. (°F)	66	67	70	74	78	81	83	83	82	78	72	68	75
Avg. Low Temp. (°F)	57	58	61	65	70	73	75	75	74	71	64	59	67
Min. Low Temp. (°F)	27	32	30	43	54	61	68	65	67	46	36	28	27
Avg. Precip. (in.)	2.7	2.6	3.3	3.3	5.7	7.5	6.2	6.3	9.0	7.0	3.9	2.5	60.0
Avg. Snowfall (in.)	Tr	0	0	0	0	0	0	0	0	0	0	0	Tr
Avg. Rel. Hum. 7am (%)	84	84	82	79	80	84	84	86	87	84	83	83	83
Avg. Rel. Hum. 4pm (%)	60	59	58	58	63	69	67	68	70	66	63	61	64

Note: Tr = Trace amounts (less than 0.05 inches of rain or less than 0.5 inches of snow)
Source: National Climatic Data Center, International Station Meteorological Climate Summary, 3/95

Weather Conditions

	Temperature			Precipitation		
	32°F & below	45°F & below	90°F & above	0.01 inch or more precip.	1.5 inch or more snow/ice	Thunder-storms
	1	13	76	133	0	79

Note: Figures are average number of days per year
Source: National Climatic Data Center, International Station Meteorological Climate Summary, 3/95

AIR & WATER QUALITY

Maximum Pollutant Concentrations

	Particulate Matter (ug/m³)	Carbon Monoxide (ppm)	Sulfur Dioxide (ppm)	Nitrogen Dioxide (ppm)	Ozone (ppm)	Lead (ug/m³)
MSA[1] Level	39	4	0.013	0.012	0.09	0.00
NAAQS[2]	150	9	0.140	0.053	0.12	1.50
Met NAAQS	Yes	Yes	Yes	Yes	Yes	Yes

Note: (1) Metropolitan Statistical Area - see Appendix A for areas included; (2) National Ambient Air Quality Standards; ppm = parts per million; ug/m³ = micrograms per cubic meter; n/a not available
Source: EPA, National Air Quality and Emissions Trends Report, 1997

Pollutant Standards Index

In the West Palm Beach MSA (see Appendix A for areas included), the Pollutant Standards Index (PSI) exceeded 100 on 0 days in 1997. A PSI value greater than 100 indicates that air quality would have been in the unhealthful range on that day.
EPA, National Air Quality and Emissions Trends Report, 1997

Drinking Water

Water System Name	Pop. Served	Primary Water Source Type	Number of Violations in 1998-99	Type of Violation/ Contaminants
City of West Palm Beach	87,769	Surface	None	None

Note: Data as of January 19, 2000
Source: EPA, Office of Ground Water and Drinking Water, Safe Drinking Water Information System

West Palm Beach tap water is neutral and soft.
Editor & Publisher Market Guide, 2000

Wilmington, Delaware

Background

Wilmington, Delaware is situated in the northern section of the state, 26 miles southwest of Philadelphia, Pennsylvania, at the junction of the Delaware and Christina Rivers and Brandywynne Creek. The city is the largest in Delaware, and the seat of New Castle county. Wilmington lies on the fall line that separates coastal plain from hilly areas.

Wilmington is Delaware's industrial, financial and commercial center, as well as the state's main port. The chemical industry is most prominent to the city's economy. Other important economic segments include the manufacture of transportation equipment, vulcanized fiber, glazed leathers, dyed cotton, rubber hoses, tanning extract, cork and floor products, ships and malleable iron. Other industries include automobile assembly, oil refining, yacht, barge and shipbuilding, copper smelting and meat-packing.

Peter Minuet landed on the site along with Swedish colonists in 1638. In 1655 Peter Stuyvesant, the governor of the then New Netherland (now New York) annexed the settlement thus ending Swedish rule. In 1731 it was renamed Willington after Thomas Willing, a prominent settler. In 1739 it became Wilmington in honor of Spencer Compton, Earl of Wilmington and was incorporated as a borough. In 1823, it became a city.

Despite its reputation for being historically conservative, Wilmington has a fine collection of extant buildings in popular styles from the Revolution through late 20th Century. Many examples of Federal, Queen Anne and American Four Square buildings can be found in the city, with fewer additional styles, including Second Empire, Italian Villa, Greek Revival, Georgian and Art Deco. Today, the City has formed 10 Historic Districts to protect its architectural heritage.

Among the city's historic sites and museums are the Fort Christina Monument, marking the site of the original settlement, Old Swedes Church, Old Town Hall Museum with exhibits about Delaware's history, Hagley Museum, occupying the original DuPont gunpowder mill complex, and the Delaware Art Museum, noted for its collections of Pre-Raphaelite English art and American art. The Winterthur Museum, which is Henry Francis du Pont's collection of early American interior architecture, furniture and accessories, is nearby.

The city's institutions of higher learning include Goldey-Beacom College and Widener University School of Law.

The Wilmington City Council is the city's legislative body.Its 13-member City Council includes the Council President and 12 Council Members.

General Rankings and Evaluative Comments

- Wilmington was ranked #155 out of 354 metropolitan areas in *Places Rated Almanac*. Criteria: cost of living, climate, crime, transportation, job outlook, education, the arts, health care, and recreation. *Places Rated Almanac, Millennium Edition, 2000*

- *Ladies Home Journal* ranked America's 200 largest cities based on the qualities women care about most. Wilmington ranked #78 out of 200. Criteria: low crime rate, well-paying jobs, quality health and child care, good public schools, the presence of women in government, size of the gender wage gap, number of sexual-harassment and discrimination complaints filed, unemployment and divorce rates, commute times, population density, number of houses of worship, parks and cultural offerings, number of women's health specialists, how well women cared for themselves, complexion kindness index based on UV radiation levels, odds of finding affordable fashions, rental rates for romance movies, champagne sales, and other matters of the heart. *Ladies Home Journal, November 1998*

- Cognetics studied 273 metro areas in the United States, ranking them by entrepreneurial activity. Wilmington was ranked #54 out of 134 smaller metro areas. Criteria: Significant Starts (firms started in the last 10 years that still employ at least 5 people) and Young Growers (percent of firms 10 years old or less that grew significantly during the last 4 years). *Cognetics, "Entrepreneurial Hot Spots: The Best Places in America to Start and Grow a Company," 1999*

- Wilmington was included among *Entrepreneur* magazine's listing of the "20 Best Cities for Small Business." It was ranked #1 among mid-sized metro areas. Criteria: entrepreneurial activity, small-business growth, economic growth, and risk of failure. *Entrepreneur, October 1999*

- Reliastar Financial Corporation ranked the 125 largest metropolitan areas according to the general financial security of residents. Wilmington was ranked #11 out of 125 with a score of 13.5 (the percentage a metropolitan area is above or below the metropolitan norm; a metro area with a score of 10.6 is 10.6% above the metro average). Criteria: Earnings and Wealth Potential (household income, education, net assets, cost of living); Safety Net (health insurance, retirement savings, life insurance, income support programs); Personal Threats (unemployment rate, low-income households, crime rate); Community Economic Vitality (cost of community services, job quality, job creation, housing costs). *Reliastar Financial Corporation, "The Best Cities to Earn and Save Money: A Ranking of the Largest 125 U.S. Cities," 2000 Edition*

Business Environment

STATE ECONOMY

State Economic Profile

"Since the beginning of 1995 Delaware has witnessed an impressive expansion. While the US added new jobs at a rate of 2.0% in 1998, Delaware's job growth was 3.2%. As long as the nation continues to grow at a healthy pace, so will Deleware. In the near term employment and job growth will likely slow slightly, but still outpace the national rate. A boom in construction, while adding to jobs and home sales, has restrained price appreciation.

The services, retail and construction sectors have largely driven Deleware's recent job expansion. Construction, which showed a 5.3% employment growth in 1998, is poised for a slowdown. Services will continue adding jobs, especially in the financial sector. Manufacturing displayed positive employment growth in 1998; however, possible restructuring in the pharmaceuticals and chemicals sector could result in some job losses in the near future. With unemployment currently at 3.8%, however, a few layoffs will not dampen job growth to a significant degree.

Home sales and new construction have been robust over the previous year. While losing some of the "typical buyer" population, Deleware still continues to attract new residents at a healthy pace. Building activity will slow slightly from 1998's high levels.

Retail trade employment is expanding strongly. Over 2,000 new jobs have been created since last year. Robust household growth in previously undeveloped areas is spawning the usual expansion of retailers such as Home Depot. Longer term prospects for the industry remain favorable. Strong population trends and healthy personal income growth will continue to bolster retail sales.

Delaware's primary long-term advantage is its business friendly environment and low cost structure in a high cost region. Even with its rapid pace of expansion, Deleware is unlikely to experience a labor shortage, because its proximity to sluggish Pennsylvania and Maryland metro areas provides the state with a pool of excess labor. Despite the risks facing the credit card industry, migration of households and firms from neighboring states will continue to buoy the economy, keeping it an above-average performer relative to the Northeast. Deleware will be an average performer relative to the US over the long term." *National Association of Realtors, Economic Profiles: The Fifty States and the District of Columbia, http://nar.realtor.com/databank/profiles.htm*

EXPORTS

Total Export Sales

Area	1995 ($000)	1996 ($000)	1997 ($000)	1998 ($000)	% Chg. 1995-98	% Chg. 1997-98
MSA[1]	4,361,106	4,551,096	5,140,642	5,027,356	15.3	-2.2
U.S.	583,030,524	622,827,063	687,597,999	680,474,251	16.7	-1.0

Note: (1) Metropolitan Statistical Area - see Appendix A for areas included
Source: U.S. Department of Commerce, International Trade Association, Metropolitan Area Exports: An Export Performance Report on Over 250 U.S. Cities, November 10, 1999

CITY FINANCES

City Government Finances

Component	1995 ($million)	1995 (per capita $)
Revenue	115.5	1,586
Expenditure	122.2	1,678
Debt Outstanding	253.1	3,477

Source: 1999 County and City Extra, Annual Metro, City, and County Data Book

City Government Revenue by Source

Source	1995 ($million)	1995 (per capita $)
Intergovernmental	14.4	197
Taxes	53.2	730
Property	17.9	247
Sales and Gross Receipts	1.6	23

Source: 1999 County and City Extra, Annual Metro, City, and County Data Book

City Government Expenditures by Function

Function	1995 ($million)	1995 (per capita $)	1995 (%)
Public Welfare	0.0	0	0.0
Highways	2.9	40	2.4
Parking Facilities	1.8	25	1.5
Education	0.0	0	0.0
Health and Hospitals	0.0	0	0.0
Police Protection	21.0	288	17.2
Sewerage and Sanitation	27.4	377	22.5
Parks and Recreation	5.7	78	4.7
Housing and Community Development	6.7	92	5.5
Interest on Debt	11.1	152	9.1

Source: 1999 County and City Extra, Annual Metro, City, and County Data Book

Municipal Bond Ratings

Area	Moody's
City	A2

Source: Mergent Bond Record, 2/2000

POPULATION

Population Growth

Area	1980 Census	1990 Census	1999 Estimate	2004 Projection	Population Growth (%) 1990-1999	Population Growth (%) 1999-2004
City	70,195	71,529	73,332	73,853	2.5	0.7
MSA[1]	523,221	578,587	569,635	590,903	-1.5	3.7
U.S.	226,545,805	248,765,170	272,212,864	283,625,312	9.4	4.2

Note: (1) Metropolitan Statistical Area - see Appendix A for areas included
Source: 1990 Census of Population and Housing, Summary Tape File 3C; Claritas, Inc.

Number of Households and Average Household Size

Area	1980 Census	1990 Census	1999 Estimate	2004 Projection	1999 Average Household Size
City	26,903	28,585	30,702	31,606	2.39
MSA[1]	158,308	212,751	217,093	229,078	2.62
U.S.	80,389,592	91,993,582	102,048,200	107,302,392	2.67

Note: (1) Metropolitan Statistical Area - see Appendix A for areas included
Source: 1990 Census of Population and Housing, Summary Tape File 3C; Claritas, Inc.

Race/Ethnicity of City Population

Race/Ethnicity	1990 Census Population	1990 Census %	1999 Estimate Population	1999 Estimate %	% Change 1990-1999
White, Non-Hispanic	29,404	41.1	25,123	34.3	-14.6
Black, Non-Hispanic	36,802	51.5	40,261	54.9	9.4
Asian, Non-Hispanic	332	0.5	382	0.5	15.1
Other, Non-Hispanic	182	0.3	242	0.3	33.0
Hispanic	4,809	6.7	7,324	10.0	52.3

Source: 1990 Census of Population and Housing, Summary Tape File 3C; Claritas, Inc.

Race/Ethnicity of Metropolitan Statistical Area Population

Race/Ethnicity	1990 Census		1999 Estimate		% Change 1990-1999
	Population	%	Population	%	
White, Non-Hispanic	472,517	81.7	440,174	77.3	-6.8
Black, Non-Hispanic	84,315	14.6	95,491	16.8	13.3
Asian, Non-Hispanic	7,258	1.3	11,904	2.1	64.0
Other, Non-Hispanic	1,553	0.3	1,319	0.2	-15.1
Hispanic	12,944	2.2	20,747	3.6	60.3

Note: See Appendix A for areas included in the Metropolitan Statistical Area
Source: 1990 Census of Population and Housing, Summary Tape File 3C; Claritas, Inc.

Ancestry

Area	German	Irish	English	Italian	U.S.	French	Polish	Dutch
City	8.1	12.0	7.3	8.2	2.0	1.3	5.2	0.6
MSA[1]	22.8	22.6	17.8	11.1	3.4	3.0	6.5	2.4
U.S.	23.3	15.6	13.1	5.9	5.3	4.2	3.8	2.5

Note: Figures are percentages and include persons that reported multiple ancestry (eg. if a person reported being Irish and Italian, they were included in both columns); (1) Metropolitan Statistical Area - see Appendix A for areas included
Source: 1990 Census of Population and Housing, Summary Tape File 3C

Median Age

Area	1990 Census	1999 Estimate
City	32.6	35.8
MSA[1]	32.7	35.6
U.S.	32.9	35.7

Note: (1) Metropolitan Statistical Area - see Appendix A for areas included
Source: 1990 Census of Population and Housing, Summary Tape File 3C; Claritas, Inc.

Male/Female Population

Area	Number of Males		Number of Females		Males per 100 Females	
	1990	1999	1990	1999	1990	1999
City	33,174	34,203	38,355	39,129	86.5	87.4
MSA[1]	280,877	276,620	297,710	293,015	94.3	94.4
U.S.	121,172,379	132,803,736	127,537,494	139,409,136	95.0	95.3

Note: (1) Metropolitan Statistical Area - see Appendix A for areas included
Source: 1990 Census of Population, General Population Characteristics; Claritas, Inc.

INCOME

Per Capita/Median/Average Income

Area	Per Capita ($)			Median Household ($)			Average Household ($)		
	1989	1999	% Chg.	1989	1999	% Chg.	1989	1999	% Chg.
City	14,256	22,193	55.7	26,389	36,982	40.1	35,059	51,633	47.3
MSA[1]	16,664	25,675	54.1	37,553	52,421	39.6	44,721	65,979	47.5
U.S.	14,420	21,350	48.1	30,056	40,525	34.8	38,453	56,184	46.1

Note: (1) Metropolitan Statistical Area - see Appendix A for areas included; 1989 data is from the 1990 Census; 1999 data is estimated by Claritas, Inc.
Source: 1990 Census of Population, General Population Characteristics; Claritas, Inc.

Household Income Distribution

Area	Percent of Households Earning								
	Under $5,000	$5,000 -14,999	$15,000 -24,999	$25,000 -34,999	$35,000 -49,999	$50,000 -74,999	$75,000 -99,000	$100,000 -149,999	$150,000 and up
City	5.3	16.4	14.2	11.9	14.5	18.9	9.0	5.9	3.8
MSA[1]	2.3	8.5	10.0	10.5	15.9	23.6	13.4	10.3	5.4
U.S.	3.9	13.3	13.8	12.6	16.2	19.4	9.7	6.6	4.6

Note: Data as of 1999; (1) Metropolitan Statistical Area - see Appendix A for areas included
Source: Claritas, Inc.

Effective Buying Income

Area	Per Capita ($)	Median Household ($)	Average Household ($)
City	17,020	32,092	42,056
MSA[1]	20,733	46,694	55,037
U.S.	17,496	36,603	47,036

Note: Data as of 1/1/2000; (1) Metropolitan Statistical Area - see Appendix A for areas included
Source: Standard Rate & Data Service, Newspaper Advertising Source, March 2000

Effective Household Buying Income Distribution

Area	% of Households Earning						
	$10,000 -$19,999	$20,000 -$34,999	$35,000 -$49,999	$50,000 -$74,999	$75,000 -$99,000	$100,000 -$124,999	$125,000 and up
City	16.9	21.6	17.0	16.9	6.8	2.3	3.1
MSA[1]	10.4	18.3	18.7	25.3	12.4	4.5	3.8
U.S.	15.0	21.6	17.6	19.6	8.4	3.0	3.3

Note: Data as of 1/1/2000; (1) Metropolitan Statistical Area - see Appendix A for areas included
Source: Standard Rate & Data Service, Newspaper Advertising Source, March 2000

Poverty Rates by Age

Area	People of All Ages	People Under 18 Years Old	Related Children Age 5-17 in Families in Poverty
City	22.7	n/a	n/a
County	8.7	12.8	11.6
U.S.	13.8	20.8	18.7

Note: Figures show the percent of people living below the poverty line in 1995. The average poverty threshold was $15,569 for a family of four in 1995; n/a not available
Source: Bureau of the Census, Small Area Income and Poverty Estimates Program; U.S. Department of Housing and Urban Development

EMPLOYMENT

Labor Force and Employment

Area	Civilian Labor Force			Workers Employed		
	Dec. 1998	Dec. 1999	% Chg.	Dec. 1998	Dec. 1999	% Chg.
City	34,406	34,038	-1.1	33,029	32,792	-0.7
MSA[1]	300,292	299,646	-0.2	292,396	291,352	-0.4
U.S.	138,297,000	139,941,000	1.2	132,732,000	134,696,000	1.5

Note: Data is not seasonally adjusted and covers workers 16 years of age and older; (1) Metropolitan Statistical Area - see Appendix A for areas included
Source: Bureau of Labor Statistics, http://stats.bls.gov

Unemployment Rate

Area	1999											
	Jan.	Feb.	Mar.	Apr.	May	Jun.	Jul.	Aug.	Sep.	Oct.	Nov.	Dec.
City	4.7	4.8	4.4	4.0	4.5	5.5	4.5	4.3	4.6	4.5	3.7	3.7
MSA[1]	3.6	3.6	3.2	2.8	2.8	3.7	4.1	3.2	2.9	3.0	2.8	2.8
U.S.	4.8	4.7	4.4	4.1	4.0	4.5	4.5	4.2	4.1	3.8	3.8	3.7

Note: Data is not seasonally adjusted and covers workers 16 years of age and older; all figures are percentages; (1) Metropolitan Statistical Area - see Appendix A for areas included
Source: Bureau of Labor Statistics, http://stats.bls.gov

Employment by Industry

Sector	MSA[1]		U.S.
	Number of Employees	Percent of Total	Percent of Total
Services	96,400	29.4	30.2
Retail Trade	55,900	17.0	18.1
Government	41,400	12.6	15.8
Manufacturing	45,400	13.8	14.1
Finance/Insurance/Real Estate	43,700	13.3	5.9
Wholesale Trade	12,800	3.9	5.4
Transportation/Public Utilities	14,500	4.4	5.3
Construction	17,900	5.5	4.8
Mining	200	0.1	0.4

Note: Figures cover non-farm employment as of 12/99 and are not seasonally adjusted;
(1) Metropolitan Statistical Area - see Appendix A for areas included
Source: Bureau of Labor Statistics, http://stats.bls.gov

Employment by Occupation

Occupation Category	City (%)	MSA[1] (%)	U.S. (%)
White Collar	57.8	62.1	58.1
Executive/Admin./Management	12.1	12.6	12.3
Professional	13.5	14.7	14.1
Technical & Related Support	3.7	4.8	3.7
Sales	8.4	10.6	11.8
Administrative Support/Clerical	20.0	19.4	16.3
Blue Collar	20.9	24.5	26.2
Precision Production/Craft/Repair	7.8	11.6	11.3
Machine Operators/Assem./Insp.	5.2	5.5	6.8
Transportation/Material Movers	3.3	3.9	4.1
Cleaners/Helpers/Laborers	4.5	3.5	3.9
Services	20.4	12.1	13.2
Farming/Forestry/Fishing	0.9	1.4	2.5

Note: Figures cover workers 16 years of age and older;
(1) Metropolitan Statistical Area - see Appendix A for areas included
Source: 1990 Census of Population and Housing, Summary Tape File 3C

Occupational Employment Projections: 1996 - 2006

Occupations Expected to Have the Largest Job Growth (ranked by numerical growth)	Fast-Growing Occupations[1] (ranked by percent growth)
1. Salespersons, retail	1. Paralegals
2. Adjustment clerks	2. Medical assistants
3. Bill and account collectors	3. Dental hygienists
4. General managers & top executives	4. Home health aides
5. Janitors/cleaners/maids, ex. priv. hshld.	5. Loan officers & counselors
6. Clerical supervisors	6. Bill and account collectors
7. Cashiers	7. Child care workers, private household
8. Guards	8. Adjustment clerks
9. Child care workers, private household	9. Securities, financial services sales
10. Registered nurses	10. Secretaries, medical

Note: Projections cover Delaware; (1) Excludes occupations with total job growth less than 300
Source: U.S. Department of Labor, Employment and Training Administration, America's Labor Market Information System (ALMIS)

Average Wages

Occupation	$/Hr.	Occupation	$/Hr.
Accountants and Auditors	19.89	Maids and Housekeepers	7.30
Assemblers and Fabricators	-	Maintenance Repairers	14.17
Automotive Mechanics	14.98	Marketing/Advertising/PR Managers	32.86
Bookkeepers	11.91	Nurses, Licensed Practical	15.79
Carpenters	14.89	Nurses, Registered	20.69
Cashiers	7.46	Nursing Aides/Orderlies/Attendants	8.58
Clerks, General Office	10.56	Physicians and Surgeons	40.69
Clerks, Shipping/Receiving/Traffic	12.21	Receptionists/Information Clerks	9.92
Computer Programmers	26.80	Sales Reps., Exc. Scientific/Retail	15.52
Computer Support Specialists	21.23	Sales Reps., Scientific, Exc. Retail	22.21
Cooks, Restaurant	9.42	Salespersons, Retail	9.07
Electricians	19.45	Secretaries, Except Legal/Medical	14.09
Financial Managers	29.29	Stock Clerks, Sales Floor	8.50
First-Line Supervisors/Mgrs., Sales	17.71	Systems Analysts	26.13
Food Preparation Workers	7.68	Teacher Aides	7.87
General Managers/Top Executives	30.31	Teachers, Elementary School	-
Guards	8.64	Teachers, Secondary School	22.05
Hand Packers	6.93	Telemarketers	-
Janitors and Cleaners	8.26	Truck Drivers, Heavy/Tractor-Trailer	14.25
Laborers, Landscaping	8.92	Truck Drivers, Light	11.54
Lawyers	37.84	Waiters and Waitresses	6.22

Note: Wage data is for 1998 and covers the Metropolitan Statistical Area (see Appendix A for areas included). Hourly wages for elementary and secondary school teachers were calculated by the editors from annual wage data assuming a 40 hour work week; Dashes indicate that data was not available.
Source: Bureau of Labor Statistics, 1998 Metropolitan Area Occupational Employment and Wage Estimates

TAXES

Major State and Local Tax Rates

State Corporate Income (%)	State Personal Income (%)	Residential Property (%)	Sales & Use		State Gasoline (cents/ gallon)	State Cigarette (cents/ pack)
			State (%)	Local (%)		
8.7	2.2 - 5.95	0.72	None	None	23.0[a]	24.0

Note: Personal/corporate income, sales, gasoline and cigarette tax rates as of January 2000. Property tax rates as of April 2000; (a) Plus 0.5% GRT. A portion of the rate is adjustable based on maintenance costs, sales volume, or cost of fuel to state government
Source: Federation of Tax Administrators, www.taxadmin.org; ERI's Relocation Assessor software database, quarterly effective date 4/1/2000

Total Taxes Per Capita and as a Percent of Income

Area	Per Capita Income ($)	Per Capita Taxes ($)			Percent of Income (%)		
		Total	Federal	State/Local	Total	Federal	State/Local
Delaware	32,215	10,798	7,610	3,188	33.5	23.6	9.9
U.S.	28,878	10,298	7,026	3,273	35.7	24.3	11.3

Note: Figures are for 1999
Source: Tax Foundation, www.taxfoundation.org

COMMERCIAL UTILITIES

Typical Monthly Electric Bills

Area	Commercial Service ($/month)		Industrial Service ($/month)	
	12 kW demand 1,500 kWh	100 kW demand 30,000 kWh	1,000 kW demand 400,000 kWh	20,000 kW demand 10,000,000 kWh
City	n/a	n/a	n/a	n/a
U.S.	150	2,174	23,995	508,569

Note: Based on rates in effect January 1, 1999; n/a not available
Source: Edison Electric Institute, Typical Residential, Commercial and Industrial Bills, Winter 1999

TRANSPORTATION

Transportation Statistics

Average minutes to work (1990)	18.1
Interstate highways	I-95; I-495; I-295; US-202
Bus lines	
In-city (1998)	Delaware Transit Corporation, 143 buses
Inter-city (1999)	4
Passenger air service	
Airport	New Castle County
Airlines (1999)	n/a
Enplaned passengers (1998)	5,738
Amtrak service	Yes
Motor freight carriers (1999)	n/a
Major waterways/ports	Port of Wilmington

Source: FAA DOT/TSC CY1998 ACAIS Database; National Transit Database, 1998; Editor &
Publisher Market Guide, 2000; Amtrak National Time Table, Fall 1999/Winter 2000; 1990 Census of
Population and Housing, STF 3C; Jane's Urban Transport Systems 1999-2000

Means of Transportation to Work

Area	Car/Truck/Van		Public Transportation			Bicycle	Walked	Other Means	Worked at Home
	Drove Alone	Car-pooled	Bus	Subway	Railroad				
City	59.7	14.7	8.7	0.1	0.6	0.4	12.3	1.4	2.2
MSA[1]	77.3	12.9	2.3	0.0	0.3	0.4	3.9	0.9	2.0
U.S.	73.2	13.4	3.0	1.5	0.5	0.4	3.9	1.2	3.0

Note: Figures shown are percentages and only include workers 16 years of age and older;
(1) Metropolitan Statistical Area - see Appendix A for areas included
Source: 1990 Census of Population and Housing, Summary Tape File 3C

BUSINESSES

Major Business Headquarters

Company Name	1999 Rankings	
	Fortune 500	Forbes 500
Conectiv	431	-
E.I. Du Pont de Nemours	42	-
Hercules	472	-
MBNA	265	-

Note: Companies listed are located in the city; dashes indicate no ranking
Fortune 500: Companies that produce a 10-K are ranked 1 to 500 based on 1999 revenue
Forbes 500: Private companies are ranked 1 to 500 based on 1998 revenue
Source: Forbes, December 13, 1999; Fortune, April 17, 2000

HOTELS & MOTELS

Hotels/Motels

Area	Hotels/Motels	Rooms	Luxury-Level Hotels/Motels		Average Minimum Rates ($)		
			♦♦♦♦	♦♦♦♦♦	♦♦	♦♦♦	♦♦♦♦
City	11	1,448	1	0	n/a	n/a	n/a
Suburbs	38	3,221	0	0	n/a	n/a	n/a
Total	49	4,669	1	0	n/a	n/a	n/a

Note: n/a not available; classifications range from one diamond (budget properties with basic amenities) to five diamond (luxury properties).
Source: OAG Business Travel Planner, Winter 1999-2000

Estimated Daily Food and Lodging Costs

Area	Food/Other ($/day)	Average Hotel Cost ($/day)
City	34	99
U.S.	30	55

Source: ERI's Relocation Assessor software database, quarterly effective date 4/1/2000

CONVENTION CENTERS

Convention Centers and Event Sites

Name	Guest Rooms	Meeting Space (sq. ft.)	Capacity (Theatre Style)
Hotel Du Pont	217	30,000	500
Radisson Hotel	154	10,000	900
Sheraton Suites	228	5,668	300

Source: EventSource.com, 3/15/2000

Living Environment

COST OF LIVING

Cost of Living: Homeowner

Cost Element	U.S. ($)	City ($)	Differential ($)	Percent of U.S. Average
Consumables	14,516	16,238	1,722	111.9
Transportation	5,957	5,687	-270	95.5
Health Services	2,012	2,170	158	107.9
Housing/Utilities/Prop. Tax	16,337	28,128	11,791	172.2
Income+Payroll Taxes	12,615	11,715	-900	92.9
Miscellaneous	8,563	8,563	0	100.0
Total Cost of Living	60,000	72,501	12,501	120.8

Note: Figures are based on a single income, four person family with gross annual earnings of $60,000, owning an 1,800 square-foot home, and driving two automobiles worth $22,000 30,000 miles per year.
Source: ERI's Relocation Assessor software database, quarterly effective date 4/1/2000

Cost of Living: Renter

Cost Element	U.S. ($)	City ($)	Differential ($)	Percent of U.S. Average
Consumables	10,486	11,765	1,279	112.2
Transportation	2,107	2,017	-90	95.7
Health Services	1,632	1,766	134	108.2
Rent/Utilities/Insurance	9,299	12,215	2,916	131.4
Income+Payroll Taxes	8,607	9,079	472	105.5
Miscellaneous	7,869	7,869	0	100.0
Total Cost of Living	40,000	44,711	4,711	111.8

Note: Figures are based on a single income, three person family with gross annual earnings of $40,000, renting a 1,000 square-foot home, and driving one automobile worth $8,000 12,000 miles per year.
Source: ERI's Relocation Assessor software database, quarterly effective date 4/1/2000

HOUSING

Median Home Prices and Housing Affordability

Area	Median Price[2] 4th Qtr. 1999 ($)	HOI[3] 4th Qtr. 1999	Affordability Rank[4]
MSA[1]	131,000	86.0	8
U.S.	139,000	63.8	–

Note: (1) Metropolitan Statistical Area - see Appendix A for areas included; (2) U.S. figures calculated from the sales of 687,516 new and existing homes in 192 markets; (3) Housing Opportunity Index - percent of homes sold that were within the reach of the median income household at the prevailing mortgage interest rate; (4) Rank is from 1-192 with 1 being most affordable
Source: National Association of Home Builders, Housing Opportunity Index, 4th Quarter 1999

Estimated Home Price

Area	Price ($)
City	262,889
U.S.	135,855

Note: Figures are based on an 1,800 square-foot home
Source: ERI's Relocation Assessor software database, quarterly effective date 4/1/2000

Estimated Rent

Area	Rent ($/month)
City	863
U.S.	651

Note: Figures are based on a 1,000 square-foot home
Source: ERI's Relocation Assessor software database, quarterly effective date 4/1/2000

Median Home Price Projection

It is projected that the median home price in the metropolitan area will increase from $127,793 in 1999 to $212,332 in 2010, an increase of 66.2%
Kiplinger's Personal Finance Magazine, January 2000

RESIDENTIAL UTILITIES

Average Residential Utility Costs

Area	All Electric ($/mth)	Part Electric ($/mth)	Other Energy ($/mth)	Phone ($/mth)
City	137.98	–	–	16.62
U.S.	99.25	55.47	43.48	20.29

Source: ACCRA, Cost of Living Index, 3rd Quarter 1999

HEALTH CARE

Average Health Care Costs

Area	Hospital ($/day)	Doctor ($/visit)	Dentist ($/visit)
City	458.00	48.25	63.25
U.S.	440.96	53.83	68.42

Note: Hospital—based on a semi-private room; Doctor—based on a general practitioner's routine exam of an established patient; Dentist—based on adult teeth cleaning and periodic oral exam.
Source: ACCRA, Cost of Living Index, 3rd Quarter 1999

Distribution of Office-Based Physicians

Area	Family/Gen. Practitioners	Specialists		
		Medical	Surgical	Other
MSA[1]	122	292	230	254

Note: Data as of 12/31/97; (1) Metropolitan Statistical Area - see Appendix A for areas included
Source: American Medical Assn., Physician Characteristics & Distribution in the U.S., 1999

Hospitals

Wilmington has 2 general medical and surgical hospitals, 1 children's general.
AHA Guide to the Healthcare Field, 1999-2000

EDUCATION

Public School District Statistics

District Name	Num. Sch.	Enroll.	Classroom Teachers	Pupils per Teacher	Minority Pupils (%)	Current Exp.[1] ($/pupil)
Charter School of Wilmington	1	396	21	18.9	n/a	n/a
East Side Charter School	1	78	5	15.6	n/a	n/a
New Castle County Voc/Tech SD	4	3,458	246	14.1	n/a	n/a
Red Clay Consolidated Sch Dist	26	15,710	904	17.4	45.5	6,971

Note: Data covers the 1997-1998 school year unless otherwise noted; (1) Data covers fiscal year 1996; SD = School District; ISD = Independent School District; n/a not available
Source: National Center for Education Statistics, Common Core of Data Public Education Agency Universe 1997-98; National Center for Education Statistics, Characteristics of the 100 Largest Public Elementary and Secondary School Districts in the United States: 1997-98, July 1999

Educational Quality

School District	Education Quotient[1]	Graduate Outcome[2]	Community Index[3]	Resource Index[4]
Red Clay Consol. School Dist.	95	87	60	117

Note: Over 1,000 secondary school districts were rated in terms of educational quality. The scores range from a low of 50 to a high of 150; (1) Combination of the Graduate Outcome, Community and Resource indexes weighted to reflect the greater importance of the Graduate Outcome and Resource Index; (2) Based on graduation rates and college board scores (SAT/ACT); (3) Based on the surrounding community's level of affluence and adult education; (4) Based on teacher salaries, per-pupil expenditures and student-teacher ratios.
Source: Expansion Management, Ratings Issue, 1999

Educational Attainment by Race

Area	High School Graduate (%)					Bachelor's Degree (%)				
	Total	White	Black	Other	Hisp.[2]	Total	White	Black	Other	Hisp.[2]
City	67.7	76.8	60.0	41.6	41.5	18.9	30.7	7.1	6.0	7.4
MSA[1]	78.7	80.8	66.4	71.1	59.0	22.1	23.4	11.2	36.8	15.8
U.S.	75.2	77.9	63.1	60.4	49.8	20.3	21.5	11.4	19.4	9.2

Note: Figures shown cover persons 25 years old and over; (1) Metropolitan Statistical Area - see Appendix A for areas included; (2) people of Hispanic origin can be of any race
Source: 1990 Census of Population and Housing, Summary Tape File 3C

School Enrollment by Type

Area	Preprimary				Elementary/High School			
	Public		Private		Public		Private	
	Enrollment	%	Enrollment	%	Enrollment	%	Enrollment	%
City	605	58.6	428	41.4	10,494	85.9	1,727	14.1
MSA[1]	5,461	48.7	5,744	51.3	77,163	81.5	17,527	18.5
U.S.	2,679,029	59.5	1,824,256	40.5	38,379,689	90.2	4,187,099	9.8

Note: Figures shown cover persons 3 years old and over;
(1) Metropolitan Statistical Area - see Appendix A for areas included
Source: 1990 Census of Population and Housing, Summary Tape File 3C

School Enrollment by Race

Area	Preprimary (%)				Elementary/High School (%)			
	White	Black	Other	Hisp.[1]	White	Black	Other	Hisp.[1]
City	41.2	52.9	5.9	6.0	23.5	67.4	9.2	11.5
MSA[2]	84.2	12.8	3.0	1.9	77.1	19.5	3.5	3.5
U.S.	80.4	12.5	7.1	7.8	74.1	15.6	10.3	12.5

Note: Figures shown cover persons 3 years old and over; (1) people of Hispanic origin can be of any race; (2) Metropolitan Statistical Area - see Appendix A for areas included
Source: 1990 Census of Population and Housing, Summary Tape File 3C

Higher Education

Two-Year Colleges		Four-Year Colleges		Medical Schools	Law Schools	Voc/ Tech
Public	Private	Public	Private			
1	1	0	1	0	1	10

Source: College Blue Book, Occupational Education, 1999; Medical School Admission Requirements, 1999-2000; Peterson's Guide to Two-Year Colleges, 2000; Peterson's Guide to Four-Year Colleges, 1999; Barron's Guide to Law Schools, 1999

MAJOR EMPLOYERS

Major Employers

Chase Manhattan	Christiana Care Health Services
Delaware Racing Association	Dupont
Dupont Dow Elastomers	Dupont Pharmaceutical
First Bank USA	MBNA Corp.
St. Francis Hospital	Zeneca Holdings (chemicals)

Note: Companies listed are located in the city
Source: D&B Business Rankings, 1999; Ward's Business Directory, 1999; America's Corporate Families, 1999

PUBLIC SAFETY

Crime Rate

Area	All Crimes	Violent Crimes				Property Crimes		
		Murder	Forcible Rape	Robbery	Aggrav. Assault	Burglary	Larceny -Theft	Motor Vehicle Theft
City	n/a	n/a	n/a	n/a	n/a	n/a	n/a	n/a
Suburbs[1]	n/a	n/a	n/a	n/a	n/a	n/a	n/a	n/a
MSA[2]	n/a	n/a	n/a	n/a	n/a	n/a	n/a	n/a
U.S.	4,615.5	6.3	34.4	165.2	360.5	862.0	2,728.1	459.0

Note: Crime rate is the number of crimes per 100,000 population; (1) Defined as all areas within the Metropolitan Statistical Area but located outside the central city; (2) Metropolitan Statistical Area - see Appendix A for areas included; n/a not available
Source: FBI Uniform Crime Reports, 1998

RECREATION

Culture and Recreation

Museums	Symphony Orchestras	Opera Companies	Dance Companies	Professional Theatres	Zoos	Pro Sports Teams
6	1	1	0	1	1	0

Source: Musical America, International Directory of the Performing Arts, 1999; Official Museum Directory, 2000; Stern's Performing Arts Directory, 1997; USA Today Four Sport Stadium Guide, 1997; Career Opportunities in Theatre and the Performing Arts, 1999

Library System

The Wilmington Institute Library has three branches, holdings of 308,147 volumes, and a budget of $2,103,791 (1997-1998).
American Library Directory, 1999-2000

MEDIA

Newspapers

Name	Type	Freq.	Distribution	Circulation

No newspapers listed.
Note: Includes newspapers with circulations of 200 or more located in the city;
Source: Burrelle's Media Directory, 1999 Edition

Television Stations

Name	Ch.	Affiliation	Type	Owner

No stations listed.
Note: Stations included broadcast in the Wilmington metro area; n/a not available
Source: Burrelle's Media Directory, 1999 Edition

AM Radio Stations

Call Letters	Freq. (kHz)	Target Audience	Station Format	Music Format
WDEL	1150	General	N/T	n/a
WNRK	1260	G/M/W	M/N/S	Latin/Oldies
WJBR	1290	General	M/N/S	Oldies
WILM	1450	General	N/T	n/a

Note: Stations included broadcast in the Wilmington metro area; n/a not available
Target Audience: A=Asian; B=Black; C=Christian; E=Ethnic; F=French; G=General; H=Hispanic; M=Men; N=Native American; R=Religious; S=Senior Citizen; W=Women; Y=Young Adult; Z=Children
Station Format: E=Educational; M=Music; N=News; S=Sports; T=Talk
Source: Burrelle's Media Directory, 1999 Edition

FM Radio Stations

Call Letters	Freq. (mHz)	Target Audience	Station Format	Music Format
WVUD	91.3	General	M/N/T	n/a
WSTW	93.7	General	M	Adult Contemporary
WRDX	94.7	General	M	AOR
WJBR	99.5	General	M/N/S/T	Adult Contemporary
WJKS	101.7	Religious	M/N/S	Adult Contemporary/Classic Rock/Rhythm & Blues

Note: Stations included broadcast in the Wilmington metro area; n/a not available
Station Format: E=Educational; M=Music; N=News; S=Sports; T=Talk
Target Audience: A=Asian; B=Black; C=Christian; E=Ethnic; F=French; G=General; H=Hispanic; M=Men; N=Native American; R=Religious; S=Senior Citizen; W=Women; Y=Young Adult; Z=Children
Music Format: AOR=Album Oriented Rock; MOR=Middle-of-the-Road
Source: Burrelle's Media Directory, 1999 Edition

WEATHER

Temperature/Precipitation/Humidity

	Jan	Feb	Mar	Apr	May	Jun	Jul	Aug	Sep	Oct	Nov	Dec	Yr.
Max. High Temp. (°F)	75	78	86	94	95	99	102	101	100	91	85	74	102
Avg. High Temp. (°F)	40	43	51	63	73	82	86	84	77	67	55	44	64
Avg. Temp. (°F)	32	34	42	53	63	72	77	75	68	57	46	36	55
Avg. Low Temp. (°F)	23	25	33	42	52	61	67	65	58	46	37	27	45
Min. Low Temp. (°F)	-14	-6	2	18	30	41	48	43	36	24	14	-7	-14
Avg. Precip. (in.)	3.0	2.9	3.7	3.3	3.7	3.5	4.2	3.8	3.6	2.8	3.3	3.5	41.4
Avg. Snowfall (in.)	7	6	3	Tr	Tr	0	0	0	0	Tr	1	3	20
Avg. Rel. Hum. 7am (%)	75	74	74	73	76	78	80	83	85	84	80	77	78
Avg. Rel. Hum. 4pm (%)	60	56	51	50	53	54	55	57	56	55	58	61	56

Note: Tr = Trace amounts (less than 0.05 inches of rain or less than 0.5 inches of snow)
Source: National Climatic Data Center, International Station Meteorological Climate Summary, 3/95

Weather Conditions

Temperature			Precipitation		
10°F & below	32°F & below	90°F & above	0.01 inch or more precip.	1.5 inch or more snow/ice	Thunder-storms
6	100	20	116	5	29

Note: Figures are average number of days per year
Source: National Climatic Data Center, International Station Meteorological Climate Summary, 3/95

AIR & WATER QUALITY

Maximum Pollutant Concentrations

	Particulate Matter (ug/m³)	Carbon Monoxide (ppm)	Sulfur Dioxide (ppm)	Nitrogen Dioxide (ppm)	Ozone (ppm)	Lead (ug/m³)
MSA[1] Level	68	5	0.057	0.018	0.15	n/a
NAAQS[2]	150	9	0.140	0.053	0.12	1.50
Met NAAQS	Yes	Yes	Yes	Yes	No	n/a

Note: (1) Metropolitan Statistical Area - see Appendix A for areas included; (2) National Ambient Air Quality Standards; ppm = parts per million; ug/m³ = micrograms per cubic meter; n/a not available
Source: EPA, National Air Quality and Emissions Trends Report, 1997

Pollutant Standards Index

In the Wilmington MSA (see Appendix A for areas included), the Pollutant Standards Index (PSI) exceeded 100 on 21 days in 1997. A PSI value greater than 100 indicates that air quality would have been in the unhealthful range on that day.
EPA, National Air Quality and Emissions Trends Report, 1997

Drinking Water

Water System Name	Pop. Served	Primary Water Source Type	Number of Violations in 1998-99	Type of Violation/ Contaminants
Wilmington Water Dept.	140,000	Surface	None	None

Note: Data as of January 19, 2000
Source: EPA, Office of Ground Water and Drinking Water, Safe Drinking Water Information System

Wilmington tap water is neutral, soft, and fluoridated.
Editor & Publisher Market Guide, 2000

Youngstown, Ohio

Background

Youngstown, Ohio is located in the northeast section of the state near the border of Pennsylvania, about 65 miles southeast of Cleveland. It is in the Mahoning Valley and the capital of Mahoning County.

The Youngstown metropolitan area includes Warren and other communities nearby. Youngstown and the Mahoning Valley have traditionally been a center for heavy industry, particularly iron and steel production.

John Young, the city's namesake, purchased a large tract at the present site of Youngstown in 1797 and a settlement was established. An iron furnace was set up by Daniel and James Heaton in the early 19th Century to process the ores from the region. The presence of limestone and coal, and the development of canals and railroads stimulated industrial development. In the late 19th Century, steel production began in Youngstown. The Mahoning Valley soon became one of the nation's leading steel producing regions. Other industries included coal and the manufacture of other products, including a General Motors automobile plant in nearby Lordstown. These industries attracted workers from a variety of ethnic backgrounds.

In the late 1970s, the area's steel industry experienced severe decline, largely due to competition from imports, which caused widespread plant closures, high unemployment and economic and social problems. The remaining steel producers recovered somewhat with new technology and other practices, although the industry's employment levels and economic role never reached its earlier heights. The economy diversified, and continues to be a manufacturing center for electrical and electronic equipment, metal fabrication and a variety of other products. Industry Week magazine rated the Mahoning Valley in 1998 as number 12 out of 315 metropolitan areas as a "World Class Community" for manufacturing.

Youngstown and nearby communities have undertaken economic development efforts, including an expansion of the Youngstown Warren Regional Airport as an air cargo hub, and development of a connected industrial park. Other significant sectors include health care, distribution and transport, retailing and services. There has also been shift towards smaller enterprises.

Schools of higher education in the Youngstown area include Youngstown State University, Kent State University Trumbull Campus in Warren and ETI Technical College in Niles.

The Youngstown Park and Recreation Commission maintains 49 parks and recreation facilities. A prominent area park is the Mill Creek Metropolitan Park District, which covers 2,530 acres and includes 21 miles of scenic drives and 15 miles of foot trails, with gardens and natural areas, golf courses and other facilities.

The Butler Institute of American Art is a well-known museum established by industrialist Joseph Butler Jr. in 1919. The Arms Museum is the headquarters of the Mahoning Valley Historical Society. The Youngstown Historical Center of Industry and Labor displays the region's industrial heritage.

Venues for events include the Youngstown Symphony Center and Edward Powers Auditorium built in 1929, and the Henry H. Stambaugh Auditorium built in 1926. The Youngstown Playhouse features performances by the Youngstown Players. Other performing arts organizations include the Youngstown Symphony, Oakland Center for the Arts and Ballet Western Reserve, among others.

The Air Force Reserve Command's 910th Airlift Wing is based at Youngstown Air Reserve Station.

General Rankings and Evaluative Comments

- Youngstown was ranked #187 out of 354 metropolitan areas in *Places Rated Almanac*. Criteria: cost of living, climate, crime, transportation, job outlook, education, the arts, health care, and recreation. *Places Rated Almanac, Millennium Edition, 2000*

- Cognetics studied 273 metro areas in the United States, ranking them by entrepreneurial activity. Youngstown was ranked #104 out of 134 smaller metro areas. Criteria: Significant Starts (firms started in the last 10 years that still employ at least 5 people) and Young Growers (percent of firms 10 years old or less that grew significantly during the last 4 years). *Cognetics, "Entrepreneurial Hot Spots: The Best Places in America to Start and Grow a Company," 1999*

- Reliastar Financial Corporation ranked the 125 largest metropolitan areas according to the general financial security of residents. Youngstown was ranked #75 out of 125 with a score of 1.6 (the percentage a metropolitan area is above or below the metropolitan norm; a metro area with a score of 10.6 is 10.6% above the metro average). Criteria: Earnings and Wealth Potential (household income, education, net assets, cost of living); Safety Net (health insurance, retirement savings, life insurance, income support programs); Personal Threats (unemployment rate, low-income households, crime rate); Community Economic Vitality (cost of community services, job quality, job creation, housing costs). *Reliastar Financial Corporation, "The Best Cities to Earn and Save Money: A Ranking of the Largest 125 U.S. Cities," 2000 Edition*

Business Environment

STATE ECONOMY

State Economic Profile

"Ohio's expansion has started to decelerate. Ohio is expected to lag the nation in growth for some time. The slowdown in employment growth is concentrated in the manufacturing sector and outside of Ohio's larger metro areas. Ohio's weak demographic trends will constrain job growth and the housing market.

Ohio manufacturing shed about 7,000 jobs in 1998. A large share of these losses were in the Cleveland and Columbus areas, while Cincinnati managed to add a small number of manufacturing jobs. Job growth in the services sectors, particularly business, financial and health services, has helped to offset a slowdown in manufacturing in these urban areas. Bank merger and acquisition activity has resulted in jobs being shifted from rural and smaller areas to the larger metropolitan areas.

While Ohio's rural areas have suffered from a declining employment base, economic activity has also been shifting from the northern part of the state toward the middle and south. Last year's employment growth for Cincinnati was 2.5%, compared to only 1.6% for Columbus and 1.6% for Cleveland. Population growth has followed a similar pattern, although the state as a whole is among one of the weakest in the nation, losing a considerable number of younger households.

Ohio's housing market had a strong 1998, with sales up 8.6% and single family permits up 3.2%. Price appreciation was just below the nation and will likely remain modest given the increase in construction. Both construction and sales should contract in 2000. Prices are likely to rise the most in Cincinnati, where construction has been modest and job growth strongest."
National Association of Realtors, Economic Profiles: The Fifty States and the District of Columbia, http://nar.realtor.com/databank/profiles.htm

EXPORTS

Total Export Sales

Area	1995 ($000)	1996 ($000)	1997 ($000)	1998 ($000)	% Chg. 1995-98	% Chg. 1997-98
MSA[1]	225,932	223,130	322,969	296,555	31.3	-8.2
U.S.	583,030,524	622,827,063	687,597,999	680,474,251	16.7	-1.0

Note: (1) Metropolitan Statistical Area - see Appendix A for areas included
Source: U.S. Department of Commerce, International Trade Association, Metropolitan Area Exports: An Export Performance Report on Over 250 U.S. Cities, November 10, 1999

CITY FINANCES

City Government Finances

Component	1995 ($million)	1995 (per capita $)
Revenue	61.3	668
Expenditure	64.4	702
Debt Outstanding	33.3	363

Source: 1999 County and City Extra, Annual Metro, City, and County Data Book

City Government Revenue by Source

Source	1995 ($million)	1995 (per capita $)
Intergovernmental	16.4	178
Taxes	30.8	336
Property	1.9	21
Sales and Gross Receipts	0.4	5

Source: 1999 County and City Extra, Annual Metro, City, and County Data Book

City Government Expenditures by Function

Function	1995 ($million)	1995 (per capita $)	1995 (%)
Public Welfare	0.0	0	0.0
Highways	6.1	66	9.5
Parking Facilities	<0.1	<1	0.1
Education	0.0	0	0.0
Health and Hospitals	1.6	17	2.5
Police Protection	12.6	137	19.6
Sewerage and Sanitation	12.4	135	19.3
Parks and Recreation	2.1	23	3.4
Housing and Community Development	8.2	89	12.8
Interest on Debt	1.6	18	2.6

Source: 1999 County and City Extra, Annual Metro, City, and County Data Book

Municipal Bond Ratings

Area	Moody's
City	Aaa (1998)

Source: Mergent Bond Record, 2/2000

POPULATION

Population Growth

Area	1980 Census	1990 Census	1999 Estimate	2004 Projection	Population Growth (%) 1990-1999	Population Growth (%) 1999-2004
City	115,435	95,732	82,842	78,004	-13.5	-5.8
MSA[1]	644,922	492,619	589,432	589,286	19.7	0.0
U.S.	226,545,805	248,765,170	272,212,864	283,625,312	9.4	4.2

Note: (1) Metropolitan Statistical Area - see Appendix A for areas included
Source: 1990 Census of Population and Housing, Summary Tape File 3C; Claritas, Inc.

Number of Households and Average Household Size

Area	1980 Census	1990 Census	1999 Estimate	2004 Projection	1999 Average Household Size
City	42,001	36,919	33,434	32,102	2.48
MSA[1]	226,663	186,902	232,552	236,940	2.53
U.S.	80,389,592	91,993,582	102,048,200	107,302,392	2.67

Note: (1) Metropolitan Statistical Area - see Appendix A for areas included
Source: 1990 Census of Population and Housing, Summary Tape File 3C; Claritas, Inc.

Race/Ethnicity of City Population

Race/Ethnicity	1990 Census Population	1990 Census %	1999 Estimate Population	1999 Estimate %	% Change 1990-1999
White, Non-Hispanic	55,402	57.9	41,505	50.1	-25.1
Black, Non-Hispanic	36,081	37.7	36,553	44.1	1.3
Asian, Non-Hispanic	297	0.3	251	0.3	-15.5
Other, Non-Hispanic	356	0.4	271	0.3	-23.9
Hispanic	3,596	3.8	4,262	5.1	18.5

Source: 1990 Census of Population and Housing, Summary Tape File 3C; Claritas, Inc.

Race/Ethnicity of Metropolitan Statistical Area Population

Race/Ethnicity	1990 Census		1999 Estimate		% Change 1990-1999
	Population	%	Population	%	
White, Non-Hispanic	428,360	87.0	515,023	87.4	20.2
Black, Non-Hispanic	54,279	11.0	60,451	10.3	11.4
Asian, Non-Hispanic	1,896	0.4	2,799	0.5	47.6
Other, Non-Hispanic	1,327	0.3	1,464	0.2	10.3
Hispanic	6,757	1.4	9,695	1.6	43.5

Note: See Appendix A for areas included in the Metropolitan Statistical Area
Source: 1990 Census of Population and Housing, Summary Tape File 3C; Claritas, Inc.

Ancestry

Area	German	Irish	English	Italian	U.S.	French	Polish	Dutch
City	14.6	11.7	5.6	13.8	1.5	1.2	3.8	1.1
MSA[1]	27.9	17.2	12.2	16.7	3.1	2.1	4.9	2.5
U.S.	23.3	15.6	13.1	5.9	5.3	4.2	3.8	2.5

Note: Figures are percentages and include persons that reported multiple ancestry (eg. if a person reported being Irish and Italian, they were included in both columns); (1) Metropolitan Statistical Area - see Appendix A for areas included
Source: 1990 Census of Population and Housing, Summary Tape File 3C

Median Age

Area	1990 Census	1999 Estimate
City	34.6	36.3
MSA[1]	35.9	38.4
U.S.	32.9	35.7

Note: (1) Metropolitan Statistical Area - see Appendix A for areas included
Source: 1990 Census of Population and Housing, Summary Tape File 3C; Claritas, Inc.

Male/Female Population

Area	Number of Males		Number of Females		Males per 100 Females	
	1990	1999	1990	1999	1990	1999
City	44,307	38,545	51,425	44,297	86.2	87.0
MSA[1]	234,143	281,010	258,476	308,422	90.6	91.1
U.S.	121,172,379	132,803,736	127,537,494	139,409,136	95.0	95.3

Note: (1) Metropolitan Statistical Area - see Appendix A for areas included
Source: 1990 Census of Population, General Population Characteristics; Claritas, Inc.

INCOME

Per Capita/Median/Average Income

Area	Per Capita ($)			Median Household ($)			Average Household ($)		
	1989	1999	% Chg.	1989	1999	% Chg.	1989	1999	% Chg.
City	8,544	11,971	40.1	17,060	21,178	24.1	21,815	28,930	32.6
MSA[1]	12,237	17,517	43.1	25,939	32,708	26.1	31,934	43,853	37.3
U.S.	14,420	21,350	48.1	30,056	40,525	34.8	38,453	56,184	46.1

Note: (1) Metropolitan Statistical Area - see Appendix A for areas included; 1989 data is from the 1990 Census; 1999 data is estimated by Claritas, Inc.
Source: 1990 Census of Population, General Population Characteristics; Claritas, Inc.

Household Income Distribution

Area		Percent of Households Earning							
	Under $5,000	$5,000 -14,999	$15,000 -24,999	$25,000 -34,999	$35,000 -49,999	$50,000 -74,999	$75,000 -99,000	$100,000 -149,999	$150,000 and up
City	10.8	26.6	18.9	14.2	14.1	11.0	2.7	1.2	0.4
MSA[1]	5.1	16.6	16.4	14.5	17.5	18.2	6.8	3.3	1.6
U.S.	3.9	13.3	13.8	12.6	16.2	19.4	9.7	6.6	4.6

Note: Data as of 1999; (1) Metropolitan Statistical Area - see Appendix A for areas included
Source: Claritas, Inc.

Effective Buying Income

Area	Per Capita ($)	Median Household ($)	Average Household ($)
City	10,857	21,166	27,676
MSA[1]	15,061	31,396	38,692
U.S.	17,496	36,603	47,036

Note: Data as of 1/1/2000; (1) Metropolitan Statistical Area - see Appendix A for areas included
Source: Standard Rate & Data Service, Newspaper Advertising Source, March 2000

Effective Household Buying Income Distribution

Area	% of Households Earning						
	$10,000 -$19,999	$20,000 -$34,999	$35,000 -$49,999	$50,000 -$74,999	$75,000 -$99,000	$100,000 -$124,999	$125,000 and up
City	23.2	23.3	14.4	10.5	2.6	0.7	0.4
MSA[1]	17.3	24.1	18.1	17.8	5.8	1.5	1.4
U.S.	15.0	21.6	17.6	19.6	8.4	3.0	3.3

Note: Data as of 1/1/2000; (1) Metropolitan Statistical Area - see Appendix A for areas included
Source: Standard Rate & Data Service, Newspaper Advertising Source, March 2000

Poverty Rates by Age

Area	People of All Ages	People Under 18 Years Old	Related Children Age 5-17 in Families in Poverty
City	29.6	n/a	n/a
County	15.3	25.1	21.6
U.S.	13.8	20.8	18.7

Note: Figures show the percent of people living below the poverty line in 1995. The average poverty threshold was $15,569 for a family of four in 1995; n/a not available
Source: Bureau of the Census, Small Area Income and Poverty Estimates Program; U.S. Department of Housing and Urban Development

EMPLOYMENT

Labor Force and Employment

Area	Civilian Labor Force			Workers Employed		
	Dec. 1998	Dec. 1999	% Chg.	Dec. 1998	Dec. 1999	% Chg.
City	35,721	35,580	-0.4	32,249	32,450	0.6
MSA[1]	288,430	288,052	-0.1	272,623	274,322	0.6
U.S.	138,297,000	139,941,000	1.2	132,732,000	134,696,000	1.5

Note: Data is not seasonally adjusted and covers workers 16 years of age and older; (1) Metropolitan Statistical Area - see Appendix A for areas included
Source: Bureau of Labor Statistics, http://stats.bls.gov

Unemployment Rate

Area	1999											
	Jan.	Feb.	Mar.	Apr.	May	Jun.	Jul.	Aug.	Sep.	Oct.	Nov.	Dec.
City	11.5	10.9	10.1	9.6	8.7	9.5	10.1	8.9	9.2	8.7	9.1	8.8
MSA[1]	6.5	6.1	5.6	5.4	4.7	5.4	6.2	5.1	5.4	4.8	4.9	4.8
U.S.	4.8	4.7	4.4	4.1	4.0	4.5	4.5	4.2	4.1	3.8	3.8	3.7

Note: Data is not seasonally adjusted and covers workers 16 years of age and older; all figures are percentages; (1) Metropolitan Statistical Area - see Appendix A for areas included
Source: Bureau of Labor Statistics, http://stats.bls.gov

Employment by Industry

Sector	MSA[1]		U.S.
	Number of Employees	Percent of Total	Percent of Total
Services	68,900	27.4	30.2
Retail Trade	53,400	21.2	18.1
Government	32,700	13.0	15.8
Manufacturing	54,000	21.5	14.1
Finance/Insurance/Real Estate	9,600	3.8	5.9
Wholesale Trade	11,400	4.5	5.4
Transportation/Public Utilities	10,200	4.1	5.3
Construction	11,000	4.4	4.8
Mining	400	0.2	0.4

Note: Figures cover non-farm employment as of 12/99 and are not seasonally adjusted;
(1) Metropolitan Statistical Area - see Appendix A for areas included
Source: Bureau of Labor Statistics, http://stats.bls.gov

Employment by Occupation

Occupation Category	City (%)	MSA[1] (%)	U.S. (%)
White Collar	46.8	50.7	58.1
Executive/Admin./Management	6.9	8.9	12.3
Professional	10.5	12.1	14.1
Technical & Related Support	3.5	3.3	3.7
Sales	10.7	11.8	11.8
Administrative Support/Clerical	15.3	14.6	16.3
Blue Collar	32.0	34.3	26.2
Precision Production/Craft/Repair	10.4	12.7	11.3
Machine Operators/Assem./Insp.	11.0	11.5	6.8
Transportation/Material Movers	4.9	5.1	4.1
Cleaners/Helpers/Laborers	5.8	5.1	3.9
Services	20.5	13.7	13.2
Farming/Forestry/Fishing	0.7	1.2	2.5

Note: Figures cover workers 16 years of age and older;
(1) Metropolitan Statistical Area - see Appendix A for areas included
Source: 1990 Census of Population and Housing, Summary Tape File 3C

Occupational Employment Projections: 1996 - 2006

Occupations Expected to Have the Largest Job Growth (ranked by numerical growth)	Fast-Growing Occupations[1] (ranked by percent growth)
1. Cashiers	1. Systems analysts
2. Salespersons, retail	2. Occupational therapy assistants
3. Systems analysts	3. Desktop publishers
4. General managers & top executives	4. Paralegals
5. Truck drivers, light	5. Physical therapy assistants and aides
6. Registered nurses	6. Medical assistants
7. Food preparation workers	7. Personal and home care aides
8. Nursing aides/orderlies/attendants	8. Home health aides
9. Home health aides	9. Physical therapists
10. Marketing & sales, supervisors	10. Occupational therapists

Note: Projections cover Ohio; (1) Excludes occupations with total job growth less than 300
Source: U.S. Department of Labor, Employment and Training Administration, America's Labor Market Information System (ALMIS)

Average Wages

Occupation	$/Hr.	Occupation	$/Hr.
Accountants and Auditors	17.86	Maids and Housekeepers	7.33
Assemblers and Fabricators	13.23	Maintenance Repairers	11.47
Automotive Mechanics	11.06	Marketing/Advertising/PR Managers	24.07
Bookkeepers	10.20	Nurses, Licensed Practical	13.26
Carpenters	16.64	Nurses, Registered	19.88
Cashiers	6.36	Nursing Aides/Orderlies/Attendants	7.56
Clerks, General Office	8.63	Physicians and Surgeons	45.99
Clerks, Shipping/Receiving/Traffic	12.32	Receptionists/Information Clerks	8.19
Computer Programmers	18.15	Sales Reps., Exc. Scientific/Retail	16.53
Computer Support Specialists	19.53	Sales Reps., Scientific, Exc. Retail	19.60
Cooks, Restaurant	6.77	Salespersons, Retail	7.73
Electricians	18.95	Secretaries, Except Legal/Medical	9.40
Financial Managers	23.81	Stock Clerks, Sales Floor	7.01
First-Line Supervisors/Mgrs., Sales	14.83	Systems Analysts	22.67
Food Preparation Workers	6.76	Teacher Aides	7.36
General Managers/Top Executives	25.39	Teachers, Elementary School	17.20
Guards	8.43	Teachers, Secondary School	19.12
Hand Packers	8.08	Telemarketers	9.26
Janitors and Cleaners	7.40	Truck Drivers, Heavy/Tractor-Trailer	14.55
Laborers, Landscaping	8.16	Truck Drivers, Light	10.22
Lawyers	33.46	Waiters and Waitresses	5.78

Note: Wage data is for 1998 and covers the Metropolitan Statistical Area (see Appendix A for areas included). Hourly wages for elementary and secondary school teachers were calculated by the editors from annual wage data assuming a 40 hour work week; Dashes indicate that data was not available.
Source: Bureau of Labor Statistics, 1998 Metropolitan Area Occupational Employment and Wage Estimates

TAXES

Major State and Local Tax Rates

State Corporate Income (%)	State Personal Income (%)	Residential Property (%)	Sales & Use		State Gasoline (cents/gallon)	State Cigarette (cents/pack)
			State (%)	Local (%)		
5.1 - 8.5[a]	0.716 - 7.228[b]	1.89	5.0	0.5	22.0[c]	24.0

Note: Personal/corporate income, sales, gasoline and cigarette tax rates as of January 2000. Property tax rates as of April 2000; (b) Plus and additional $20 per exemption tax credit; (a) Or 4.0 mils times the value of the taxpayer's issued and outstanding share of stock ($150K max). An additional litter tax is imposed equal to 0.11% on the first $50,000 of taxable income, 0.22% on income over $50,000; or 0.14 mills on net worth; (c) Plus 3 cents commercial tax
Source: Federation of Tax Administrators, www.taxadmin.org; ERI's Relocation Assessor software database, quarterly effective date 4/1/2000

Total Taxes Per Capita and as a Percent of Income

Area	Per Capita Income ($)	Per Capita Taxes ($)			Percent of Income (%)		
		Total	Federal	State/Local	Total	Federal	State/Local
Ohio	27,439	9,709	6,544	3,165	35.4	23.8	11.5
U.S.	28,878	10,298	7,026	3,273	35.7	24.3	11.3

Note: Figures are for 1999
Source: Tax Foundation, www.taxfoundation.org

COMMERCIAL UTILITIES

Typical Monthly Electric Bills

Area	Commercial Service ($/month)		Industrial Service ($/month)	
	12 kW demand 1,500 kWh	100 kW demand 30,000 kWh	1,000 kW demand 400,000 kWh	20,000 kW demand 10,000,000 kWh
City	256	3,202	32,614	455,832
U.S.	150	2,174	23,995	508,569

Note: Based on rates in effect January 1, 1999
Source: Edison Electric Institute, Typical Residential, Commercial and Industrial Bills, Winter 1999

TRANSPORTATION

Transportation Statistics

Average minutes to work (1990)	17.5
Interstate highways	I-76; I-80; I-680; US-62; US-422
Bus lines	
In-city (1998)	Western Reserve Transit Authority, 31 buses
Inter-city (1999)	3
Passenger air service	
Airport	Youngstown-Warren Regional
Airlines (1999)	4
Enplaned passengers (1998)	45,060
Amtrak service	Yes
Motor freight carriers (1999)	98
Major waterways/ports	None

Source: FAA DOT/TSC CY1998 ACAIS Database; National Transit Database, 1998; Editor & Publisher Market Guide, 2000; Amtrak National Time Table, Fall 1999/Winter 2000; 1990 Census of Population and Housing, STF 3C; Jane's Urban Transport Systems 1999-2000

Means of Transportation to Work

Area	Car/Truck/Van		Public Transportation			Bicycle	Walked	Other Means	Worked at Home
	Drove Alone	Car-pooled	Bus	Subway	Railroad				
City	79.9	12.1	2.4	0.0	0.0	0.1	3.1	1.1	1.3
MSA[1]	85.3	9.6	0.6	0.0	0.0	0.1	2.0	0.6	1.8
U.S.	73.2	13.4	3.0	1.5	0.5	0.4	3.9	1.2	3.0

Note: Figures shown are percentages and only include workers 16 years of age and older;
(1) Metropolitan Statistical Area - see Appendix A for areas included
Source: 1990 Census of Population and Housing, Summary Tape File 3C

BUSINESSES

Major Business Headquarters

Company Name	1999 Rankings	
	Fortune 500	Forbes 500
No companies listed	-	-

Note: Companies listed are located in the city; dashes indicate no ranking
Fortune 500: Companies that produce a 10-K are ranked 1 to 500 based on 1999 revenue
Forbes 500: Private companies are ranked 1 to 500 based on 1998 revenue
Source: Forbes, December 13, 1999; Fortune, April 17, 2000

HOTELS & MOTELS

Hotels/Motels

Area	Hotels/ Motels	Rooms	Luxury-Level Hotels/Motels		Average Minimum Rates ($)		
			♦♦♦♦	♦♦♦♦♦	♦♦	♦♦♦	♦♦♦♦
City	9	746	0	0	n/a	n/a	n/a

Note: n/a not available; classifications range from one diamond (budget properties with basic amenities) to five diamond (luxury properties).
Source: OAG Business Travel Planner, Winter 1999-2000

Estimated Daily Food and Lodging Costs

Area	Food/Other ($/day)	Average Hotel Cost ($/day)
City	30	55
U.S.	30	55

Source: ERI's Relocation Assessor software database, quarterly effective date 4/1/2000

CONVENTION CENTERS

Convention Centers and Event Sites

Name	Guest Rooms	Meeting Space (sq. ft.)	Capacity (Theatre Style)
Edward W. Powers Auditorium	n/a	n/a	2,351

Note: n/a not available
Source: EventSource.com, 3/15/2000

Living Environment

COST OF LIVING

Cost of Living: Homeowner

Cost Element	U.S. ($)	City ($)	Differential ($)	Percent of U.S. Average
Consumables	14,516	14,270	-246	98.3
Transportation	5,957	5,745	-212	96.4
Health Services	2,012	1,818	-194	90.4
Housing/Utilities/Prop. Tax	16,337	15,493	-844	94.8
Income+Payroll Taxes	12,615	13,117	502	104.0
Miscellaneous	8,563	8,563	0	100.0
Total Cost of Living	60,000	59,006	-994	98.3

Note: Figures are based on a single income, four person family with gross annual earnings of $60,000, owning an 1,800 square-foot home, and driving two automobiles worth $22,000 30,000 miles per year.
Source: ERI's Relocation Assessor software database, quarterly effective date 4/1/2000

Cost of Living: Renter

Cost Element	U.S. ($)	City ($)	Differential ($)	Percent of U.S. Average
Consumables	10,486	10,424	-62	99.4
Transportation	2,107	2,056	-51	97.6
Health Services	1,632	1,491	-141	91.4
Rent/Utilities/Insurance	9,299	8,638	-661	92.9
Income+Payroll Taxes	8,607	8,575	-32	99.6
Miscellaneous	7,869	7,869	0	100.0
Total Cost of Living	40,000	39,053	-947	97.6

Note: Figures are based on a single income, three person family with gross annual earnings of $40,000, renting a 1,000 square-foot home, and driving one automobile worth $8,000 12,000 miles per year.
Source: ERI's Relocation Assessor software database, quarterly effective date 4/1/2000

HOUSING

Median Home Prices and Housing Affordability

Area	Median Price[2] 4th Qtr. 1999 ($)	HOI[3] 4th Qtr. 1999	Affordability Rank[4]
MSA[1]	80,000	79.7	26
U.S.	139,000	63.8	–

Note: (1) Metropolitan Statistical Area - see Appendix A for areas included; (2) U.S. figures calculated from the sales of 687,516 new and existing homes in 192 markets; (3) Housing Opportunity Index - percent of homes sold that were within the reach of the median income household at the prevailing mortgage interest rate; (4) Rank is from 1-192 with 1 being most affordable
Source: National Association of Home Builders, Housing Opportunity Index, 4th Quarter 1999

Estimated Home Price

Area	Price ($)
City	117,106
U.S.	135,855

Note: Figures are based on an 1,800 square-foot home
Source: ERI's Relocation Assessor software database, quarterly effective date 4/1/2000

Estimated Rent

Area	Rent ($/month)
City	591
U.S.	651

Note: Figures are based on a 1,000 square-foot home
Source: ERI's Relocation Assessor software database, quarterly effective date 4/1/2000

Median Home Price Projection

It is projected that the median home price in the metropolitan area will increase from $75,827 in 1999 to $101,329 in 2010, an increase of 33.6%
Kiplinger's Personal Finance Magazine, January 2000

RESIDENTIAL UTILITIES

Average Residential Utility Costs

Area	All Electric ($/mth)	Part Electric ($/mth)	Other Energy ($/mth)	Phone ($/mth)
MSA[1]	–	75.56	45.33	21.75
U.S.	99.25	55.47	43.48	20.29

Note: (1) Metropolitan Statistical Area - see Appendix A for areas included
Source: ACCRA, Cost of Living Index, 3rd Quarter 1999

HEALTH CARE

Average Health Care Costs

Area	Hospital ($/day)	Doctor ($/visit)	Dentist ($/visit)
MSA[1]	349.00	45.20	59.00
U.S.	440.96	53.83	68.42

Note: Hospital—based on a semi-private room; Doctor—based on a general practitioner's routine exam of an established patient; Dentist—based on adult teeth cleaning and periodic oral exam; (1) Metropolitan Statistical Area - see Appendix A for areas included
Source: ACCRA, Cost of Living Index, 3rd Quarter 1999

Distribution of Office-Based Physicians

Area	Family/Gen. Practitioners	Specialists		
		Medical	Surgical	Other
MSA[1]	74	279	204	173

Note: Data as of 12/31/97; (1) Metropolitan Statistical Area - see Appendix A for areas included
Source: American Medical Assn., Physician Characteristics & Distribution in the U.S., 1999

Hospitals

Youngstown has 3 general medical and surgical hospitals, 1 psychiatric.
AHA Guide to the Healthcare Field, 1999-2000

EDUCATION

Public School District Statistics

District Name	Num. Sch.	Enroll.	Classroom Teachers	Pupils per Teacher	Minority Pupils (%)	Current Exp.[1] ($/pupil)
Austintown Local SD	8	5,175	250	20.7	n/a	n/a
Boardman Local SD	7	5,179	266	19.5	n/a	n/a
Liberty Local SD	4	1,909	106	18.0	n/a	n/a
Youngstown City SD	27	12,571	730	17.2	n/a	n/a

Note: Data covers the 1997-1998 school year unless otherwise noted; (1) Data covers fiscal year 1996; SD = School District; ISD = Independent School District; n/a not available
Source: National Center for Education Statistics, Common Core of Data Public Education Agency Universe 1997-98; National Center for Education Statistics, Characteristics of the 100 Largest Public Elementary and Secondary School Districts in the United States: 1997-98, July 1999

Educational Quality

School District	Education Quotient[1]	Graduate Outcome[2]	Community Index[3]	Resource Index[4]
Youngstown City School Dist.	78	69	57	100
Boardman Local School Dist.	97	94	95	137

Note: Over 1,000 secondary school districts were rated in terms of educational quality. The scores range from a low of 50 to a high of 150; (1) Combination of the Graduate Outcome, Community and Resource indexes weighted to reflect the greater importance of the Graduate Outcome and Resource Index; (2) Based on graduation rates and college board scores (SAT/ACT); (3) Based on the surrounding community's level of affluence and adult education; (4) Based on teacher salaries, per-pupil expenditures and student-teacher ratios.
Source: Expansion Management, Ratings Issue, 1999

Educational Attainment by Race

Area	High School Graduate (%)					Bachelor's Degree (%)				
	Total	White	Black	Other	Hisp.[2]	Total	White	Black	Other	Hisp.[2]
City	65.6	68.6	60.5	51.3	53.3	8.3	10.2	4.6	6.2	6.4
MSA[1]	74.9	76.3	62.4	65.8	63.0	12.8	13.4	5.8	20.3	8.8
U.S.	75.2	77.9	63.1	60.4	49.8	20.3	21.5	11.4	19.4	9.2

Note: Figures shown cover persons 25 years old and over; (1) Metropolitan Statistical Area - see Appendix A for areas included; (2) people of Hispanic origin can be of any race
Source: 1990 Census of Population and Housing, Summary Tape File 3C

School Enrollment by Type

Area	Preprimary				Elementary/High School			
	Public		Private		Public		Private	
	Enrollment	%	Enrollment	%	Enrollment	%	Enrollment	%
City	1,009	63.0	592	37.0	14,525	83.2	2,932	16.8
MSA[1]	5,194	59.3	3,562	40.7	74,978	88.8	9,458	11.2
U.S.	2,679,029	59.5	1,824,256	40.5	38,379,689	90.2	4,187,099	9.8

Note: Figures shown cover persons 3 years old and over;
(1) Metropolitan Statistical Area - see Appendix A for areas included
Source: 1990 Census of Population and Housing, Summary Tape File 3C

School Enrollment by Race

Area	Preprimary (%)				Elementary/High School (%)			
	White	Black	Other	Hisp.[1]	White	Black	Other	Hisp.[1]
City	55.7	41.8	2.5	6.2	43.7	52.8	3.5	5.7
MSA[2]	86.3	11.4	2.3	2.1	82.2	15.9	1.8	2.0
U.S.	80.4	12.5	7.1	7.8	74.1	15.6	10.3	12.5

Note: Figures shown cover persons 3 years old and over; (1) people of Hispanic origin can be of any race; (2) Metropolitan Statistical Area - see Appendix A for areas included
Source: 1990 Census of Population and Housing, Summary Tape File 3C

Higher Education

Two-Year Colleges		Four-Year Colleges		Medical Schools	Law Schools	Voc/ Tech
Public	Private	Public	Private			
1	1	1	0	0	0	5

Source: College Blue Book, Occupational Education, 1999; Medical School Admission Requirements, 1999-2000; Peterson's Guide to Two-Year Colleges, 2000; Peterson's Guide to Four-Year Colleges, 1999; Barron's Guide to Law Schools, 1999

MAJOR EMPLOYERS

Major Employers

American Paper Products
Cafaro Co. (real estate)
Edward J. DeBartolo Corp. (real estate)
Humility of Mary Health System

Bliss Manufacturing (automotive stampings)
Cold Metal Products
Forum Health
St. Elizabeth Hospital Medical Center

Note: Companies listed are located in the city
Source: D&B Business Rankings, 1999; Ward's Business Directory, 1999; America's Corporate Families, 1999

PUBLIC SAFETY

Crime Rate

Area	All Crimes	Violent Crimes				Property Crimes		
		Murder	Forcible Rape	Robbery	Aggrav. Assault	Burglary	Larceny -Theft	Motor Vehicle Theft
City	7,925.0	52.9	56.4	476.5	697.4	2,533.1	3,136.1	972.5
Suburbs[1]	n/a	n/a	n/a	n/a	n/a	n/a	n/a	n/a
MSA[2]	n/a	n/a	n/a	n/a	n/a	n/a	n/a	n/a
U.S.	4,615.5	6.3	34.4	165.2	360.5	862.0	2,728.1	459.0

Note: Crime rate is the number of crimes per 100,000 population; (1) Defined as all areas within the Metropolitan Statistical Area but located outside the central city; (2) Metropolitan Statistical Area - see Appendix A for areas included; n/a not available
Source: FBI Uniform Crime Reports, 1998

RECREATION

Culture and Recreation

Museums	Symphony Orchestras	Opera Companies	Dance Companies	Professional Theatres	Zoos	Pro Sports Teams
2	1	0	0	0	0	0

Source: Musical America, International Directory of the Performing Arts, 1999; Official Museum Directory, 2000; Stern's Performing Arts Directory, 1997; USA Today Four Sport Stadium Guide, 1997; Career Opportunities in Theatre and the Performing Arts, 1999

Library System

The Reuben McMillan Free Library has 18 branches and holdings of 687,493 volumes.
American Library Directory, 1999-2000

MEDIA

Newspapers

Name	Type	Freq.	Distribution	Circulation
Daily Legal News	n/a	5x/wk	Local	750
The Vindicator	General	7x/wk	Area	90,000

Note: Includes newspapers with circulations of 200 or more located in the city; n/a not available
Source: Burrelle's Media Directory, 1999 Edition

Television Stations

Name	Ch.	Affiliation	Type	Owner
WFMJ	21	NBCT	Commercial	Betty H. Jagnow
WKBN	27	CBST	Commercial	Gocom Communications
WYTV	33	ABCT	Commercial	Benedek Broadcasting Corporation

Note: Stations included broadcast in the Youngstown metro area; n/a not available
Source: Burrelle's Media Directory, 1999 Edition

AM Radio Stations

Call Letters	Freq. (kHz)	Target Audience	Station Format	Music Format
WKBN	570	General	N/T	n/a
WBBW	1240	General	S	n/a
WASN	1330	General	T	n/a
WRTK	1390	General	M/N/S/T	Adult Standards/Big Band
WRBP	1440	n/a	n/a	n/a
WGFT	1500	General	M/N/T	Christian
WNIO	1540	General	M/N	Big Band

Note: Stations included broadcast in the Youngstown metro area; n/a not available
Target Audience: A=Asian; B=Black; C=Christian; E=Ethnic; F=French; G=General; H=Hispanic; M=Men; N=Native American; R=Religious; S=Senior Citizen; W=Women; Y=Young Adult; Z=Children
Station Format: E=Educational; M=Music; N=News; S=Sports; T=Talk
Source: Burrelle's Media Directory, 1999 Edition

FM Radio Stations

Call Letters	Freq. (mHz)	Target Audience	Station Format	Music Format
WYSU	88.5	General	M/N/S	Classical/Jazz
WKTL	90.7	General	E/M/N/S	Adult Contemporary/Classic Rock
WYTN	91.7	n/a	M	Christian
WBBG	93.3	General	M	Oldies
WKBN	98.9	General	M	Easy Listening
WHOT	101.1	General	M/N/T	Top 40
WBTJ	101.9	B/G/H	M/N	Jazz/Latin/Oldies/Rhythm & Blues/Urban Contemp.
WYFM	102.9	General	M	Classic Rock
WNCD	106.1	General	M/S	AOR

Note: Stations included broadcast in the Youngstown metro area; n/a not available
Station Format: E=Educational; M=Music; N=News; S=Sports; T=Talk
Target Audience: A=Asian; B=Black; C=Christian; E=Ethnic; F=French; G=General; H=Hispanic;
M=Men; N=Native American; R=Religious; S=Senior Citizen; W=Women; Y=Young Adult; Z=Children
Music Format: AOR=Album Oriented Rock; MOR=Middle-of-the-Road
Source: Burrelle's Media Directory, 1999 Edition

WEATHER

Temperature/Precipitation/Humidity

	Jan	Feb	Mar	Apr	May	Jun	Jul	Aug	Sep	Oct	Nov	Dec	Yr.
Max. High Temp. (°F)	71	67	82	88	92	99	100	97	99	87	80	76	100
Avg. High Temp. (°F)	32	35	45	58	69	78	82	80	73	62	48	36	58
Avg. Temp. (°F)	25	27	36	48	58	67	71	69	63	52	41	30	49
Avg. Low Temp. (°F)	17	19	27	37	46	55	59	58	51	42	33	23	39
Min. Low Temp. (°F)	-20	-14	-10	11	24	30	42	32	29	20	1	-12	-20
Avg. Precip. (in.)	2.6	2.3	3.2	3.4	3.5	3.9	4.1	3.3	3.3	2.6	3.1	2.8	38.1
Avg. Snowfall (in.)	13	11	11	3	Tr	0	0	0	Tr	1	6	13	57
Avg. Rel. Hum. 7am (%)	80	80	79	77	79	82	85	88	89	85	81	82	82
Avg. Rel. Hum. 4pm (%)	70	66	61	54	53	55	54	56	57	57	66	72	60

Note: Tr = Trace amounts (less than 0.05 inches of rain or less than 0.5 inches of snow)
Source: National Climatic Data Center, International Station Meteorological Climate Summary, 3/95

Weather Conditions

Temperature			Precipitation		
5°F & below	32°F & below	90°F & above	0.01 inch or more precip.	1.5 inch or more snow/ice	Thunder-storms
13	134	7	158	12	33

Note: Figures are average number of days per year
Source: National Climatic Data Center, International Station Meteorological Climate Summary, 3/95

AIR & WATER QUALITY

Maximum Pollutant Concentrations

	Particulate Matter (ug/m³)	Carbon Monoxide (ppm)	Sulfur Dioxide (ppm)	Nitrogen Dioxide (ppm)	Ozone (ppm)	Lead (ug/m³)
MSA[1] Level	61	n/a	0.048	0.016	0.11	0.04
NAAQS[2]	150	9	0.140	0.053	0.12	1.50
Met NAAQS	Yes	n/a	Yes	Yes	Yes	Yes

Note: (1) Metropolitan Statistical Area - see Appendix A for areas included; (2) National Ambient Air Quality Standards; ppm = parts per million; ug/m³ = micrograms per cubic meter; n/a not available
Source: EPA, National Air Quality and Emissions Trends Report, 1997

Pollutant Standards Index

In the Youngstown MSA (see Appendix A for areas included), the Pollutant Standards Index (PSI) exceeded 100 on 10 days in 1997. A PSI value greater than 100 indicates that air quality would have been in the unhealthful range on that day.
EPA, National Air Quality and Emissions Trends Report, 1997

Drinking Water

Water System Name *	Pop. Served	Primary Water Source Type	Number of Violations in 1998-99	Type of Violation/ Contaminants
City of Youngstown	175,000	Purchased surface	None	None

Note: Data as of January 19, 2000
Source: EPA, Office of Ground Water and Drinking Water, Safe Drinking Water Information System

Youngstown tap water is alkaline, soft, and fluoridated.
Editor & Publisher Market Guide, 2000

Appendix A

Metropolitan Statistical Areas

Albany-Schenectady-Troy, NY

Includes Albany, Greene, Montgomery, Rensselaer, Saratoga and Schenectady Counties (prior to 6/30/93)

Includes Albany, Montgomery, Rensselaer, Saratoga, Schenectady and Schoharie Counties (as of 6/30/93)

Appleton-Oshkosh-Neenah, WI

Includes Calumet, Outagamie and Winnebago Counties

Asheville, NC

Includes Buncombe County (prior to 6/30/93)

Includes Buncombe and Madison Counties (as of 6/30/93)

Augusta-Aiken, GA-SC

Includes Columbia, McDuffie and Richmond Counties, GA; Aiken County, SC (prior to 6/30/93)

Includes Columbia, McDuffie and Richmond Counties, GA; Aiken and Edgefield Counties, SC (as of 6/30/93)

Bangor, ME

Includes parts of Penobscot and Waldo Counties

**Bellevue, WA
(Seattle-Bellevue-Everett)**

Includes King and Snohomish Counties (prior to 6/30/93)

Includes Island, King and Snohomish Counties (as of 6/30/93)

Bellingham, WA

Includes Whatcom County

Biloxi-Gulfport-Pascagoula, MS

Includes Hancock and Harrison Counties (prior to 6/30/93)

Includes Hancock, Harrison and Jackson Counties (as of 6/30/93)

Bloomington-Normal, IL

Includes McLean County

Boulder-Longmont, CO

Includes Boulder County

Bryan-College Station, TX

Includes Brazos County

Burlington, VT

Includes parts of Chittenden, Franklin and Grand Isle Counties

Canton-Massillon, OH

Includes Carroll and Stark Counties

Champaign-Urbana, IL

Includes Champaign County

**Chapel Hill, NC
(Raleigh-Durham-Chapel Hill)**

Includes Durham, Franklin, Orange and Wake Counties (prior to 6/30/93)

Includes Chatham, Durham, Franklin, Johnston, Orange and Wake Counties (as of 6/30/93)

Charleston-North Charleston, SC

Includes Berkeley, Charleston and Dorchester Counties

Charleston, WV

Includes Kanawha and Putnam Counties

Charlottesville, VA

Includes Charlottesville city and Albemarle, Fluvanna and Greene Counties

Columbia, MO

Includes Boone County

Davenport-Moline-Rock Island, IA-IL

Includes Scott County, IA; Henry and Rock Island Counties, IL

Daytona Beach, FL

Includes Volusia County (prior to 6/30/93)

Includes Flagler and Volusia Counties (as of 6/30/93)

Duluth-Superior, MN-WI

Includes St. Louis County, MN and Douglas County, WI

Eau Claire, WI

Includes Chippewa and Eau Claire Counties

Fargo-Moorhead, ND-MN

Includes Cass County, ND and Clay County, MN

Fayetteville-Springdale-Rogers, AR

Includes Washington County (prior to 6/30/93)

Includes Benton and Washington Counties (as of 6/30/93)

Fort Myers-Cape Coral, FL

Includes Lee County

Gainesville, FL

Includes Alachua and Bradford Counties (prior to 6/30/93)

Includes Alachua County (as of 6/30/93)

Greenville-Spartanburg-Anderson, SC

Includes Greenville, Pickens and Spartanburg Counties (prior to 6/30/93)

Includes Anderson, Cherokee, Greenville, Pickens and Spartanburg Counties (as of 6/30/93)

Harrisburg-Lebanon-Carlisle, PA

Includes Cumberland, Dauphin, Lebanon and Perry Counties

Hattiesburg, MS[1]

Includes Forrest and Lamar County

Hickory-Morgantown-Lenoir, NC

Includes Alexander, Burke and Catawba Counties (prior to 6/30/93)

Includes Alexander, Burke, Caldwell and Catawba Counties (as of 6/30/93)

Huntington-Ashland, WV-KY-OH

Includes Cabel and Wayne Counties, WV; Boyd, Carter and Greenup Counties, KY; Lawrence County, OH

Iowa City, IA

Includes Johnson County

Johnson City-Kingsport-Bristol, TN-VA

Includes Carter, Hawkins, Sullivan, Unicoi and Washington Counties, TN; Bristol city, Scott and Washington Counties, VA

Kalamazoo-Battle Creek, MI

Includes Kalamazoo County (prior to 6/30/93)

Includes Calhoun, Kalamazoo and Van Buren Counties (as of 6/30/93)

La Crosse, WI-MN

Includes La Crosse County (prior to 6/30/93)

Includes La Crosse County, WI and Houston County, MN (as of 6/30/93)

Lafayette, IN

Includes Tippecanoe County (prior to 6/30/93)

Includes Clinton and Tippecanoe Counties (as of 6/30/93)

Lancaster, PA

Includes Lancaster County

Melbourne-Titusville-Palm Bay, FL

Includes Brevard County

Missoula, MT[2]

Includes Missoula County

Napa, CA (Vallejo-Fairfield-Napa)

Includes Napa and Solano Counties

Ogden, UT (Salt Lake City-Ogden)

Includes Davis, Salt Lake and Weber Counties

Olympia, WA

Includes Thurston County

Pensacola, FL

Includes Escambia and Santa Rosa Counties

Portland, ME

Includes parts of Cumberland and York Counties

Provo-Orem, UT

Includes Utah County

Roanoke, VA

Includes Roanoke and Salem Cities; Botetourt and Roanoke Counties

Rochester, MN

Includes Olmsted County

Saginaw-Bay City-Midland, MI

Includes Bay, Midland and Saginaw Counties

St. Cloud, MN

Includes Benton, Sherburne and Stearns Counties (prior to 6/30/93)

Includes Benton and Stearns Counties (as of 6/30/93)

San Luis Obispo-Atascadero-Paso Robles, CA[3]

Includes San Luis Obispo County

Santa Barbara-Santa Maria-Lompoc, CA

Includes Santa Barbara County

Santa Fe, NM

Includes Los Alamos and Sante Fe Counties

Sarasota-Bradenton, FL

Includes Sarasota County (prior to 6/30/93)

Includes Manatee and Sarasota Counties (as of 6/30/93)

Scranton–Wilkes-Barre–Hazelton, PA

Includes Columbia, Lackawanna, Luzerne, Monroe and Wyoming Counties (prior to 6/30/93)

Includes Columbia, Lackawanna, Luzerne and Wyoming Counties (as of 6/30/93)

South Bend, IN

Includes St. Joseph County

Trenton, NJ

Includes Mercer County

West Palm Beach-Boca Raton, FL

Includes Palm Beach County

Wilmington-Newark, DE-MD

Includes New Castle County, DE and Cecil County, MD

Youngstown-Warren, OH

Includes Mahoning and Trumbull Counties (prior to 6/30/93)

Includes Columbiana, Mahoning and Trumbull Counties (as of 6/30/93)

Notes: (1) Officially designated as a Metropolitan Statistical Area on June 30, 1994; (2) Officially designated as a Metropolitan Statistical Area on June 30, 1998; (3) Officially designated as a Metropolitan Statistical Area on June 30, 1993

Appendix B

Chambers of Commerce and Economic Development Organizations

Albany, NY

Albany-Colonie Regional
Chamber of Commerce
107 Washington Avenue
Albany, NY 12210
Phone: 518-431-1400
Fax: 519-434-1339
Web: www.acchamber.org

Appleton, WI

Fox Cities Chamber of Commerce
227 South Walnut Street
P.O. Box 1855
Appleton, WI 54913
Phone: 920-734-7101
Fax: 920-734-7161
Web: www.foxcitieschamber.com

Asheville, NC

Asheville Chamber of Commerce
P.O. Box 1010
Asheville, NC 28801
Phone: 828-258-6101
Fax: 828-251-0926
Web: www.ashevillechamber.org

Augusta, GA

Augusta Chamber of Commerce
P.O. Box 1837
Augusta, GA 30003-1837
Phone: 706-821-1300
Fax: 706-821-1330

Bangor, ME

Bangor Region Chamber of Commerce
519 Main Street
Bangor, ME 04401
Phone: 207-947-0307
Web: www.bangorregion.com

Bellevue, WA

Bellevue Chamber of Commerce
10500 Northeast 8th Street
Suite 212
Bellevue, WA 98004
Phone: 425-454-2464
Web: www.bellevuechamber.org

Bellingham, WA

Bellingham/Whatcom
Chamber of Commerce
1801 Roeder Avenue, Suite 140
Bellingham, WA 98227
Phone: 360-734-1330
Fax: 360-734-1332
Web: www.bellingham.com

Biloxi, MS

Coast Chamber of Commerce
1401 20th Avenue
Gulfport, MS 39501
Phone: 228-863-2942
Fax: 228-563-3080

Bloomington, IL

Bloomington-Normal Area
Economic Development Council
210 South East Street
Bloomington, IL 61702-1586
Phone: 309-827-3940
Fax: 309-827-3940
Web: www.blmnmlilchmbr.com

Boulder, CO

Boulder Development Commission
P.O. Box 73
Boulder, CO 80306
Phone: 303-442-1044
Fax: 303-938-8837
Web: www.chamber.boulder.co.us

Bryan, TX

Bryan-College Station
Chamber of Commerce
4001 East 29th Street, #175
Bryan, TX 77805
Phone: 409-260-5200
Fax: 409-260-5208

Burlington, VT

Lake Champlain Chamber of Commerce
60 Main Street
Burlington, VT 05401
Phone: 802-863-3489
Fax: 802-863-1538
Web: www.vermont.org

Canton, OH

Canton Area Chamber of Commerce
229 Welles Avenue NW
Canton, OH 44703
Phone: 330-456-7253
Fax: 330-452-7786

Champaign, IL

Champaign Co. Chamber of Commerce
1817 South Neil Street
Champaign, IL 61820
Phone: 217-359-1791
Fax: 217-359-1809

Chapel Hill, NC

Chapel Hill-Carrboro
Chamber of Commerce
104 South Estes Drive
Chapel Hill, NC 27514
Phone: 919-967-7075
Fax: 919-967-7074
Web: www.herald-sun.com

Charleston, SC

Charleston Chamber of Commerce
P.O. Box 975
Charleston, SC 29472-0975
Phone: 843-577-2510
Fax: 843-723-4853
Web: www.charlestonchamber.net

Charleston, WV

The Charleston Regional
Chamber of Commerce
106 Capitol Street, Suite 100
Charleston, WV 25301-2610
Phone: 304-345-0770
Web: www.charleychamber.org

Charlottesville, VA

Charlottesville and Albemarle County
Chamber of Commerce
5th and East Market Street
P.O. Box 1564
Charlottesville, VA 22902
Phone: 804-295-3141
Fax: 804-295-3144
Web: www.cvillechamber.org

Columbia, MO

Columbia Missouri
Chamber of Commerce
300 South Providence Road
P.O. Box 1016
Columbia, MO 65205
Phone: 573-874-1132
Fax: 573-443-3986
Web: www.chamber.columbia.mo.us

Davenport, IA

The Davenport Area
Chamber of Commerce
102 South Harrison Street
Davenport, IA 52801
Phone: 319-322-1706
Fax: 319-322-7804

Daytona Beach, FL

Volusia County Business
Development Corporation
1901 Mason Avenue #107
Daytona Beach, FL 32117
Phone: 904-274-3800
Fax: 904-255-0981
Web: www.florida business.org

Duluth, MN

Duluth Area Chamber of Commerce
118 E. Superior Street
Duluth, MN 55802
Phone: 218-722-5501
Fax: 218-722-3223
Web: www.duluthchamber.com

Eau Claire, WI

The Greater Eau Claire Area
Chamber of Commerce
3625 Gateway Drive, Suite B
Eau Claire, WI 54701
Phone: 715-834-1204
Fax: 715-834-1956
Web: www.eauclairechamber.org

Fargo, ND

Fargo Chamber of Commerce
321 North Fourth Street
P.O. Box 2443
Fargo, ND 58108
Phone: 218-233-1100
Fax: 218-233-1200
Web: www.fmchamber.com

Fayetteville, AR

Fayetteville Chamber of Commerce
123 West Mountain Street
P.O. Box 4216
Fayetteville, AR 72702
Phone: 501-521-1710
Fax: 501-521-1791
Web: www.fayettevillear.com

Fort Myers, FL

Greater Fort Myers
Chamber of Commerce
P.O. Box 9289
Fort Myers, FL 33902
Phone: 941-332-3624
Fax: 941-332-7276
Web: www.fortmyers.org

Gainesville, FL

Gainesville Area
Chamber of Commerce
P.O. Box 1187
300 East University Avenue
Gainesville, FL 32602
Phone: 352-334-7100
Fax: 352-334-7141
Web: www.gainesvillechamber.com

Greenville, SC

The Greater Greenville
Chamber of Commerce
24 Cleveland Street
Greenville, SC 29601
Phone: 864-242-1050
Fax: 864-242-1054
Web: www.greatergreenville.com

Harrisburg, PA

The Greater Harrisburg
Chamber of Commerce
One Commerce Street
Harrisburg, PA 17101-1902
Phone: 717-255-3252
Fax: 717-255-3298
Web: www.HBGRegionalChamber.org

Hattiesburg, MS

Hattiesburg Chamber of Commerce
1 Convention Center Plaza
Hattiesburg, MS 39401
Phone: 601-545-3300
Fax: 601-545-3304

Hickory, NC

Catawba County
Chamber of Commerce
1055 Southgate Corporate Park SW
Hickory, NC 28602
Phone: 828-328-6111
Fax: 828-328-1175
Web: www.catwabachamber.org

Huntington, WV

Huntington Chamber of Commerce
720 Fourth Avenue
Huntington, WV 25701
Phone: 304-525-5131
Fax: 304-525-5138

Iowa City, IA

Iowa City Area Chamber of Commerce
325 East Washington Street
P.O. Box 2358
Iowa City, IA 52244-2358
Phone: 319-337-9637
Fax: 319-338-9958
Web: www.icarea.com

Johnson City, TN

Johnson City/Jonesborough,
Washington County
Economic Development Board
P.O. Box 599
Johnson City, TN 37605
Phone: 423-461-8000
Fax: 423-461-8047
Web: www.johnsoncitypn.com

Kalamazoo, MI

Kalamazoo County
Chamber of Commerce
128 North Kalamazoo Mall
P.O. Box 51169
Kalamazoo, MI 49005-1169
Phone: 616-381-4000
Fax: 616-343-0430
Web: www.kazoochamber.com

La Crosse, WI

Greater La Crosse Area
Chamber of Commerce
712 Main Street
P.O. Box 219
La Crosse, WI 54602
Phone: 608-784-4880
Fax: 608-784-4919
Web: www.centuryinter.net/lacrosse

Lafayette, IN

Greater Lafayette
Chamber of Commerce
122 N. Third Street #100
P.O. Box 348
Lafayette, IN 47902
Phone: 765-742-4041
Fax: 765-742-6276
Web: www.lafayettechamber.com

Lancaster, PA

The Lancaster Chamber of
Commerce and Industry
100 South Queen Street
P.O. Box 1558
Lancaster, PA 17608-1558
Phone: 717-397-3531
Fax: 717-293-3159
Web: www.lcci.com

Melbourne, FL

Melbourne-Palm Bay Area
Chamber of Commerce
1005 East Strawbridge Avenue
Melbourne, FL 32901-4782
Phone: 407-724-5400
Fax: 407-725-2093
Web: www.melpb-chamber.org

Missoula, MT

Missoula Chamber of Commerce
P.O. Box 7557
Missoula, MT 59807
Phone: 406-543-6623

Napa, CA

Napa Chamber of Commerce
1556 First Street
Napa, CA 94559
Phone: 707-226-7455
Fax: 707-226-1171
Web: www.napachamber.org

Ogden, UT

Ogden-Weber Chamber of Commerce
2393 Washington Boulevard
Ogden, UT 84401
Phone: 801-621-8300
Fax: 801-621-8304

Olympia, WA

Olympia/Thurston County
Chamber of Commerce
1000 Plum Street
P.O. Box 1427
Olympia, WA 98507
Phone: 360-943-1600
Fax: 360-943-5811
Web: www.awb.org

Pensacola, FL

Pensacola Area Chamber of Commerce
117 West Garden Street
P.O. Box 550
Pensacola, FL 32593-0550
Phone: 850-438-4081
Fax: 850-438-6369
Web: www.pensacolachamber.com

Portland, ME

Greater Portland Chamber of Commerce
145 Middle Street
Portland, ME 04101
Phone: 207-772-2811
Fax: 207-772-1179
Web: www.portlandregion.com

Provo, UT

Provo-Orem Chamber of Commerce
51 S. University Avenue
Suite 215
Provo, UT 84601
Phone: 801-379-2555
Fax: 801-379-2557
Web: www.thechamber.org

Roanoke, VA

Roanoke Regional
Chamber of Commerce
212 South Jefferson Street
Roanoke, VA 24011-1702
Phone: 540-983-0700
Fax: 540-983-0723
Web: www.roanokechamber.org

Rochester, MN

Rochester Area Chamber of Commerce
220 South Broadway, #100
Rochester, MN 55904
Phone: 507-288-1122
Fax: 507-288-8960

Saginaw, MI

Saginaw Chamber of Commerce
901 S. Washington Avenue
Saginaw, MI 48601
Phone: 517-752-7161
Fax: 517-752-9055
Web: www.saginawchamber.org

Saint Cloud, MN

St. Cloud Chamber of Commerce
30 Sixth Avenue South
Saint Cloud, MN 56302
Phone: 320-251-2940
Fax: 320-251-4170

San Luis Obispo, CA

San Luis Obispo
Chamber of Commerce
1039 Chorro Street
San Luis Obispo, CA 93401
Phone: 805-781-2777
Fax: 805-543-1255
Web: www.slochamber.org

Santa Barbara, CA

Santa Barbara County
Chamber of Commerce
P.O. Box 299
Santa Barbara, CA 93102
Phone: 805-965-3023
Fax: 805-966-5954
Web: www.sbchamber.org

Sante Fe, NM

Sante Fe County
Chamber of Commerce
P.O. Box 1928
510 North Guadaloupe Street
Sante Fe, NM 87504
Phone: 505-983-7317
Web: www.santefechamber.com

Sarasota, FL

The Greater Sarasota
Chamber of Commerce
1819 Main Street, Suite 240
Sarasota, FL 34236
Phone: 941-955-8187
Fax: 941-955-8185
Web: www.sarasotachamber.org

Scranton, PA

The Greater Scranton
Chamber of Commerce
222 Mulberry Street
P.O. Box 431
Scranton, PA 18501-0431
Phone: 570-342-7711
Fax: 570-347-6262
Web: www.scrantonchamber.com

South Bend, IN

South Bend Chamber of Commerce
P.O. Box 1677
South Bend, IN 46634-1677
Phone: 219-234-0051
Fax: 219-289-0358

Trenton, NJ

New Jersey Business
and Industry Association
102 West State Street
Trenton, NJ 08608-1102
Phone: 609-393-7707
Web: www.njbia.org/main.html

West Palm Beach, FL

Chamber of Commerce
of the Palm Beaches
401 North Flagler Drive
West Palm Beach, FL 33401
Phone: 561-833-3711
Fax: 561-833-5582
Web: www.palmbeaches.com

Wilmington, DE

New Castle County
Chamber of Commerce
P.O. Box 11247
Wilmington, DE 19850
Phone: 302-655-7221
Fax: 302-654-0691
Web: www.dscc.com

Youngstown, OH

Youngstown-Warren Regional
Chamber of Commerce
1200 Stambaw Building
Youngstown, OH 44503
Phone: 330-744-2131
Fax: 330-746-0330

Appendix C

State Departments of Labor and Employment

Arkansas

Arkansas Department of
Employment Security
P.O. Box 2981
Little Rock, AR 72203-2981
Phone: 501-682-2033
Fax: 501-682-3223
Web: www.state.ar.us/esd

California

State of California
Employment Development Department
800 Capital Mall
Sacramento, CA 94280
Phone: 916-227-0300
Web: www.calmis.cahwnet.gov

Colorado

Colorado Department of Labor
Labor Market Information
1515 Arapahoe Street
Denver, CO 80202
Phone: 303-572-2241
Web: lmi.cdle.state.co.us

Delaware

Delaware Department of Labor
Labor Market Information Department
4425 Market Street
Wilmington, DE 19802
Phone: 302-761-8069
Fax: 302-761-6598
Web: www.oomli.net

Florida

Florida Department of State and
Employment Security
Bureau of Labor Market Information
Hartman Building, Suite 200
2012 Capitol Circle, SE
Tallahassee, FL 32399-2151
Phone: 850-488-1048
Fax: 850-414-6210
Web: lmi.floridajobs.org

Georgia

Georgia Department of Labor
Commissioner's Office
148 International Boulevard, NE
Atlanta, GA 30303-1751
Phone: 404-656-3011
Fax: 404-656-2683
Web: www.dol.state.ga.us

Illinois

Illinois Department of Security
Economic Information Division
401 South State Street
Chicago, IL 60605
Phone: 312-793-5280
Fax: 312-798-2192
Web: lmi.ides.state.il.us

Indiana

Indiana Department of
Workforce Development
Labor Market Information Division
10 North Senate Avenue
Indianapolis, IN 46204
Phone: 317-232-8525
Fax: 317-232-8480
Web: www.dwd.state.in.us

Iowa

Iowa Workforce Development
1000 East Grand Avenue
Des Moines, IA 50319-0209
Phone: 515-532-3671
Web: www.state.ia.us/iwd/ris/lmi

Maine

Maine Department of Labor
Bureau of Labor Market Information
20 Union Street
Augusta, ME 04330
Phone: 207-287-3168
Fax: 207-287-2947
Web: janus.state.me.us/labor/lmis

Michigan

Michigan Employment
Security Division
7310 Woodward Avenue
Detroit, MI 48202
Phone: 800-638-3994
Web: www.michlmi.org

Minnesota

Minnesota Department of
Economic Security
390 North Robert Street
Saint Paul, MN 55101
Phone: 651-296-0298
Fax: 651-296-2919
Web: www.des.state.mn.us/lmi

Mississippi

Mississippi Department of Labor
Market Labor Information
P.O. Box 1699
Jackson, MS 39215
Phone: 601-961-7424
Fax: 601-961-7448
Web: www.mesc.state.ms.us

Missouri

Missouri Department of Labor and
Industrial Relations
Division of Employment Security
P.O. Box 59
Jefferson City, MO 65104
Phone: 573-751-9691
Fax: 573-751-4945
Web: www.works.state.mo.us/lmi

Montana

Montana Department of
Labor and Industry
P.O. Box 1728
Helena, MT 59624-1728
Phone: 406-444-9091
Web: dli.state.mt.us

New Jersey

New Jersey Department of Labor
Labor Planning and Analysis
Box 388
Trenton, NJ 08625-0388
Phone: 609-292-9896
Web: www.state.nj.us/labor

New Mexico

New Mexico Department of Labor
Labor and Industrial Division
501 Mountain Road
Albuquerque, NM 87102
Phone: 505-841-8983
Fax: 505-841-9317
Web: www3.state.nm.us/dol

New York

New York State Department of Labor
Division of Research and Statistics
State Campus Building 12, Room 488
Albany, NY 12214-0721
Phone: 518-474-4785
Fax: 518-473-7533
Web: www.labor.state.ny.us/html

North Carolina

Employment Security Commission
Labor Market Information Division
P.O. Box 25903
Raleigh, NC 27611-5903
Phone: 919-733-9300
Fax: 919-733-1209
Web: www.esc.state.nc.us

North Dakota

North Dakota Department of Labor
600 E. Boulevard Avenue
Department 406
Bismark, ND 58505-0340
Phone: 701-328-2660
Fax: 701-328-2031
Web: www.state.nd.us/labor

Ohio

Ohio Bureau of Employment Services
Labor Market Information Division
145 South Front Street
P.O. Box 1618
Columbus, OH 43216-1618
Phone: 614-466-2100
Fax: 614-752-9621
Web: lmi.state.oh.us

Pennsylvania

Pennsylvania Department of
Labor and Industry
Employment Security Building
7th and Forester Street
Room 615
Harrisburg, PA 17121-0001
Phone: 717-787-5279
Fax: 717-772-0344
Web: www.lmi.state.pa.us

South Carolina

South Carolina Department of Labor
Employment Security Commission
631 Hampton Street
Columbia, SC 29202
Phone: 803-737-2660
Fax: 803-737-2838
Web: www.sces.org

Tennessee

Tennessee Department of
Employment Security
Research and Statistics Division
500 James Robertson Parkway
Nashville, TN 37245
Phone: 615-741-2116
Fax: 615-532-9434
Web: www.state.tn.us/labor-wfd

Texas

Texas Employment Commission
Economic Research and Analysis
101 East 15th Street
Austin, TX 78778-0001
Phone: 512-463-2222
Fax: 512-463-7885
Web: www.twc.state.tx.us

Utah

Utah Department of
Workplace Services
Labor Market Information Division
140 East 300 South
P.O. Box 45249
Salt Lake City, UT 84145-0249
Phone: 801-526-9675
Fax: 801-526-9238
Web: www.dws.state.ut.us

Vermont

Vermont Department of Labor
Labor Market Information
P.O. Box 488
Montpelier, VT 05601
Phone: 802-951-6278
Web: www.det.state.vt.us/lmi

Virginia

Virginia Employment Commission
Economic Information Services
703 East Main Street
P.O. Box 1358
Richmond, VA 23211
Phone: 804-662-9596
Fax: 804-662-9571
Web: www.vec.state.va.us/lbrmkt

Washington

Washington Employment
Security Division
P.O. Box 9046
Olympia, WA 98507-9046
Phone: 360-902-9500
Fax: 360-902-9264
Web: www.wa.gov/esd/lmea

West Virginia

West Virginia
Bureau of Employment Programs
112 California Avenue
Charleston, WV 25305-0112
Phone: 304-558-2630
Web: www.state.wv.us/bep/lmi

Wisconsin

Wisconsin Department of
Industry, Labor, and Human Relations
Bureau of Workforce Information
P.O. Box 7944
Madison, WI 53791
Phone: 608-266-9850
Fax: 608-266-1784
Web: www.dwd.state.wi.us/dwelmi